THE ULTIMATE ATLANTA SCHOOL GUIDE

The decision tool for all parents who care
about their children's education.
In-depth comparisons of metro Atlanta public schools,
plus vital information about local private schools.

David A. Milliron
Computer-Assisted Reporting Editor

The Atlanta Journal Constitution
ajc.com

Fourth Edition
Copyright © 2002 by The Atlanta Journal-Constitution
All Rights Reserved

TABLE OF CONTENTS

Is Your School Passing or Failing?

Introduction by Patti Ghezzi 4

Keys to Interpreting The Ultimate Guide

How to read and use the elementary school listings 7
How to read and use the middle school listings 8
How to read and use the high school listings 9
Understanding test scores and school performance 11
The Atlanta Journal-Constitution's Star Rating System 15

Metro Atlanta School Rankings

Georgia Criterion-Referenced Competency Tests 496
- Fourth-grade rankings 497
- Sixth-grade rankings 500
- Eighth-grade rankings 503

Georgia High School Graduation Tests 506
- Eleventh-grade rankings 507

The SAT college entrance exam 512
- High school rankings 513

Private School Listings

Metro Atlanta private schools 516

Index

Private schools 569
Public schools 578

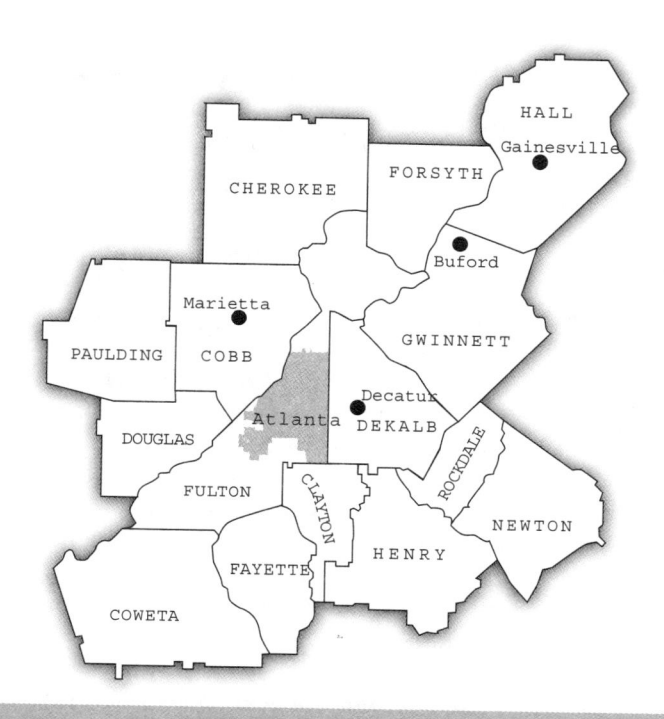

Metro Atlanta's Public School Systems

Cherokee County Schools 75
Clayton County Schools 94
Cobb County Schools 124
  • Marietta City Schools 452
Coweta County Schools 181
DeKalb County Schools 204
  • Decatur City Schools 197
Douglas County Schools 274
Fayette County Schools 291
Forsyth County Schools 307
Fulton County Schools 320
  • Atlanta City Schools 16
Gwinnett County Schools 368
  • Buford City Schools 70
Hall County Schools 418
  • Gainesville City Schools 363
Henry County Schools 436
Newton County Schools 459
Paulding County Schools 470
Rockdale County Schools 484

Is your school passing or failing?

By Patti Ghezzi

Test scores once gave parents an idea of how their children's reading and math skills compared with the skills of other kids.

Today, scores on standardized tests are used for so much more.

Principals and teachers analyze scores to figure out which teaching methods they should adopt. School districts use test data to measure how well their teachers are teaching.

And politicians and parents use test scores to gauge whether a school is good or bad.

Starting in 2004, the stakes will get higher.

The state, as part of Georgia's "A-Plus Education Reform Act of 2000," will start handing out grades and cash awards to schools that do well. Schools that get failing grades may face state takeover or other sanctions.

The push for accountability has brought more tests, including state curriculum tests, writing tests and — coming soon — standardized exams at the end of each high school course. And Georgia third-, fifth- and eighth-graders still take a standardized test that compares students nationally: the Stanford 9.

It's enough to stir a backlash among some parents who think their kids are spending more time taking tests than learning how to calculate fractions.

Making an independent assessment

At The Atlanta Journal-Constitution, we realize that so many tests can make it complicated to figure out whether a school is doing a good job. And no matter how many tests kids take, test scores alone will never provide a complete picture.

The Ultimate Atlanta School Guide provides objective information — including test scores — to assess how well a school does what it's supposed to do. Our guide is fundamentally different from report cards issued by the state in that we present a wealth of data in a way that is easy to understand, and we offer additional analysis not found anywhere else. Our guide gives you what we strive to offer our readers of The Atlanta Journal-Constitution every day —

Patti Ghezzi covers education trends and issues for The Atlanta Journal-Constitution. She earned her journalism degree from the University of Massachusetts at Amherst and previously taught English at a public high school in Japan. She won a national award from the Points of Light Foundation for her volunteer work at an Atlanta elementary school.

a credible, independent source of useful information.

Beyond test scores, we tell you which foreign languages are taught at each high school. We tell you how parent-friendly each school is, based on our own surveys. This book is not meant to pressure or promote schools, but to serve as a jumping-off point.

This guide is also for taxpayers, voters, real estate agents — anyone interested in local schools. Schools are the largest single investment of tax dollars. You pay the bills, and you can use this book to decide whether your money is being well spent. This is a resource for getting involved, even if you do not have children in the public schools. These schools, after all, belong to you.

Finding the right school

No citizen, however, will ever be as acutely interested in schools as a parent of a school-age child. Some parents choose to pay for their kids to attend private schools, more than 100 of which are represented in this book. Or, they may choose to teach their children at home.

There was a time when parents moving to a new community bought a house they loved and sent their kids to the neighborhood public school. Now, it's often the other way around. Choose a school, then find a house.

More often, parents are seeking out a school that has what they want, whether it's a diverse student body or a focus on preparing kids for top colleges. These days, with metro Atlanta's increasingly multicultural population, it's possible to find both. Check out Duluth High School in Gwinnett County or Wheeler High School in Cobb County.

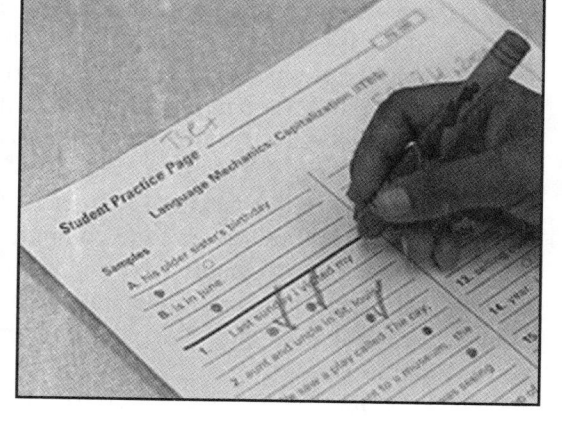

Some parents may want a smaller school, one that does not have a lot of trailers, and those are increasingly harder to find in metro Atlanta. The Decatur and Buford school districts are among a few that still have schools with fewer than 1,000 students.

This guide is intended to give newcomers a factual foundation for their search, a reality check to measure against what friends, real estate agents and school officials say.

In some cases, parents may have a choice in which public school they enroll their children. New state and federal laws are breaking new ground in public school choice.

In Georgia, a few tax-funded charter schools operate independently from the public school district. These schools offer parents more input into their children's education, although quality and independence from the local district vary widely. Neighborhood Charter School, opening in Atlanta in fall of 2002, was founded by parents who chose the curriculum and even renovated an old school to house their children. Kingsley Charter School in DeKalb County requires parents to volunteer and children to wear uniforms, yet the curriculum is similar to other DeKalb schools.

New laws also give parents some flexibility in transferring their children to a different public school if the state deems their neighborhood school as failing, if the distance to the school is too far or if the school has too many trailer classrooms. Districts are still figuring out how to comply with the laws and offer parents this kind of choice.

Walking the hallways

This book is not a substitute for actually visiting a school.

By walking the hallways, you can find out whether an elementary school manages to operate smoothly with 1,300 students. You can inspect the bathrooms and look for parent volunteers in the classrooms. You can find out whether the school has a playground and separate rooms for art and music classes.

You would learn that Grayson Elementary School in Gwinnett County has a special program that merges art and computers. If you visited Chattahoochee High School in Fulton County, you might be surprised to see cooking and sewing classes amid the traditional college prep courses. At Sequoyah High School in Cherokee County, the popular drama program might be just what you're looking for.

Checking out the cafeteria, the classrooms and the school office is how you get a sense of the school. Does the principal set a tone that is warm, friendly and conducive to learning? Or are teachers tense and defensive? As you walk through the hallways, do teachers hold their heads high, smile and say, "Hello?" Or do they walk briskly, with their heads down?

The information in this guide, combined with visits to schools that meet your criteria, will give you a wealth of information to make the best decision possible.

Keys to interpreting Elementary Schools

Percent of students by race. The "other" category includes Asian, Pacific Islander, Hispanic, American Indian, Alaskan Native and multi-racial.

"Thumbs Up" signifies school is one of the state's Top 20 public elementary schools as selected by the Georgia Public Policy Foundation, Spring 2002 — http://www.gppf.org

"Thumbs Down" signifies school has been designated a "low performer" for the past five school years (1996-97 to 2000-01) based on The Atlanta Journal-Constitution's star rating system (see pages 11-15).

Number of students enrolled in the state-funded "English to Speakers of Other Languages" program.

Number of students who have difficulty speaking, reading, writing or understanding the English language.

The student-teacher ratio. This is not the class size, but shows how much attention a student might get.

Total suspensions imposed in 2000-01 and percent served in school. Although schools are required to report all offenses and disciplinary actions to the state Department of Education, reporting is very inconsistent.

Violence offenses: Includes fighting, battery, sexual battery, etc.

Drug offenses: Includes alcohol, drugs, narcotics, etc.

Other offenses: Includes disorderly conduct, theft, weapons, tobacco, vandalism, etc.

Average Metro Atlanta Elementary School
How does your school compare?

Enrollment:	668
White / black / other:	44.7% / 42.1% / 13.2%
Not native English-speaking:	30 / 4.3%
Limited English proficiency:	60 / 9.3%
Student absenteeism:	4.4%
Students per teacher:	14.5
Parent friendliness:	①❷❸④⑤❻
Teachers with advanced degrees:	45.9%
Average years' teaching experience:	11.5
Students in gifted program:	44 / 6.5%
Students in remedial education:	19.9%
Students held back a grade:	2.5%
Total suspensions, pct. in-school:	48 / 28.5%
Offenses: violence: 14, drugs: 14, other: 44	
Eligible students, free or reduced lunch: 45.1%	
Before / after school program:	No / Yes

A black circle with a white number indicates the school offers:
❶ Special homework hotline service
❷ Parent-teacher meetings during school
❸ Parent-teacher meetings before or after school
❹ Parent-teacher meetings at parents' workplace
❺ Parent-teacher meetings at students' home
❻ Teachers allowed to contact parents by phone during school

Percent of students on federally subsidized lunches, an indicator of the poverty or wealth of the student body.

Georgia Criterion-Referenced Competency Tests - Grade 4
Pct. of students at each level

	Exceeds	Meets	Does not meet
Read	24.9%	40.4%	34.7%
Math	35.3%	51.1%	13.6%
Lang	24.3%	57.7%	18.0%

Does the school provide structured services to students prior to (or after) regular school hours?

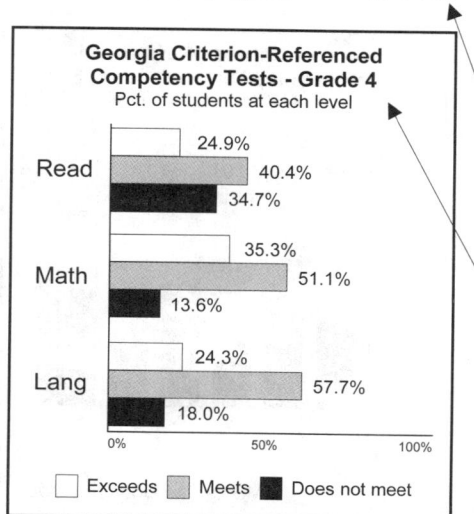

CRCT Tests taken:
Read: Reading
Math: Mathematics
Lang: English/ language arts
See pages 496-505

The Atlanta Journal-Constitution / Page 7

The Ultimate Atlanta School Guide

Keys to interpreting Middle Schools

The Ultimate Atlanta School Guide was compiled using publicly available data from the Georgia and U.S. departments of education, the Board of Regents of the University System of Georgia, the U.S. Bureau of the Census, the University of Georgia and from independent surveys of public and private schools throughout metro Atlanta.

👍 "Thumbs Up" signifies school is one of the state's Top 20 public middle schools as selected by the Georgia Public Policy Foundation, Spring 2002 — http://www.gppf.org

👎 "Thumbs Down" signifies school has been designated a "low performer" for the past five school years (1996-97 to 2000-01) based on The Atlanta Journal-Constitution's star rating system (see pages 11-15).

Average Metro Atlanta Middle School

How does your school compare?

Enrollment:	1,071
White / black / other:	50.5% / 39.0% / 10.5%
Not native English-speaking:	33 / 3.0%
Student absenteeism:	5.6%
Students per teacher:	16.1
Parent friendliness:	❶❷❸④⑤❻
Teachers with advanced degrees:	48.0%
Average years' teaching experience:	11.1
Students in gifted program:	155 / 14.0%
Students held back a grade:	2.3%
Total suspensions and expulsions:	509
Suspensions only, pct. in-school:	55.0%
Offenses:	violence: 120, drugs: 4, other: 444
Eligible students, free or reduced lunch:	37.6%
Number of dropouts:	5 / 0.4%
Pct. 8th-graders w/ basic computer skills:	92.5%

Percent of school year students were absent. Based on a 180-day school year, 5.6% equates to each student being absent 10.08 days in metro Atlanta's middle schools during the 2000-01 school year.

Percent of teachers with a master's degree or better.

Average years of service as an educator.

Gifted students receive special and/or special ancillary services to achieve at levels commensurate with their identified abilities.

Number of dropouts, which includes those leaving school due to marriage, expulsion, pregnancy, incarceration, etc.

Criterion-Referenced Competency Tests

Exceeds: Performance exceeds standards set by Georgia educators. Student performance was stronger than what a typical grade-level student is expected to do at the end of the school year.

Meets: Performance met the standard set by Georgia educators. Student performance was typical of what educators expect from a grade-level student at the end of the school year.

Does not meet: Performance did not meet the standard set by Georgia educators. Student performance was not as strong as educators expect from a grade-level student at the end of the school year; additional assistance and review most likely are needed.

Georgia Criterion-Referenced Competency Tests - Grade 6, 8

Pct. of students at each level

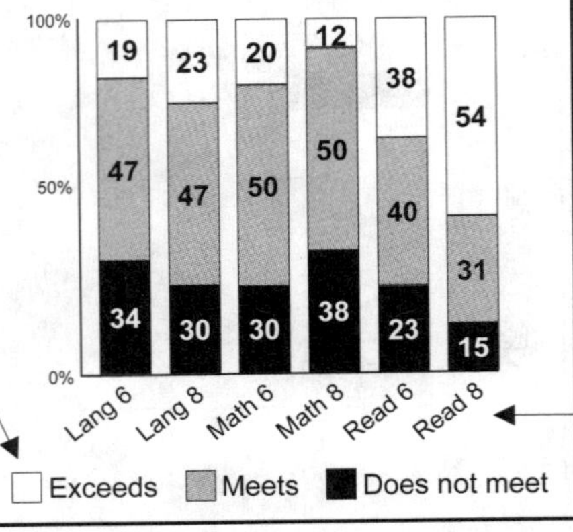
100%
50%
0%
19
47
34
23
47
30
20
50
30
12
50
38
38
40
23
54
31
15
Lang 6
Lang 8
Math 6
Math 8
Read 6
Read 8
Exceeds
Meets
Does not meet

CRCT Tests taken:

Read: Reading

Math: Mathematics

Lang: English/ language arts

See pages 496-505

Keys to interpreting High Schools

2000-2001 Graduates:

College prep/vocational diplomas: Percent of graduates who completed a program of study of 21 Carnegie units in the college preparatory program and vocational education.

College prep endorsement: Percent who completed a program of study of 21 Carnegie units in the college preparatory program.

Vocational endorsement: Percent who completed a program of study of 21 Carnegie units of which four must be in vocational education.

General high school diplomas: Percent who completed a program of study of 21 Carnegie units.

Special education diplomas: Percent of students who did not complete the requirements for a high school diploma but who did complete their Individualized Education Program (IEP) requirements.

Certificates of attendance: Percent who met the state's attendance requirements and who completed a program of study of 21 Carnegie units but did not meet the minimum standardized assessment criteria for a diploma.

Average Metro Atlanta High School
How does your school compare?

Enrollment:	1,614
White / black / other:	51.3% / 39.1% / 9.6%
Not native English-speaking:	40 / 2.7%
Limited English proficiency:	90 / 6.2%
Student absenteeism:	7.2%
Students per teacher:	17.2
Parent friendliness:	①❷❸④⑤❻
Students in gifted program:	172 / 10.1%
Students in remedial education:	5.6%
High school completion rate:	74.0%
Students held back a grade:	8.6%
Number of dropouts:	74 / 4.6%
Students in alternative programs:	29 / 2.0%
Students in special education:	146 / 9.0%
Eligible students, free or reduced lunch:	24.7%
Total suspensions and expulsions:	607
Suspensions only, pct. in-school:	604 / 45.9%
Drugs/alcohol-related offenses:	10
Violence-related offenses:	62
Firearms-related offenses:	5
Vandalism-related offenses:	5
Theft-related offenses:	6
All other disciplinary offenses:	547
Teachers with advanced degrees:	54.4%
Average years' teaching experience:	12.6

2000-2001 high school graduates:	285
College prep/vocational diplomas:	13.4%
College prep endorsement diplomas:	61.6%
Vocational endorsement diplomas:	15.4%
General high school diplomas:	1.1%
Special education diplomas:	3.9%
Certificates of attendance (no diploma):	4.6%

Of the 2000-2001 graduates, 60.8% were eligible for the HOPE scholarship.

Of the 1999-2000 graduates, 115 attended a Georgia public college or university. Of those, 19.8% met the school's minimum academic requirements.

Percent of students enrolled in the state's Remedial Education program that is designed to assist students in grades 4-5 and 9-12 as they work to improve their reading, math and writing skills.

Percent of students who entered the 9th grade during the 1997-98 school year and who graduated within four years.

Percent of students enrolled in an Alternative Program, designed for students who require a modified or altered educational environment.

Percent of graduates eligible to receive "Helping Outstanding Pupils Educationally" scholarships by maintaining a "B" average or better throughout their high school careers.

Number of graduates who attended a public Georgia college or university (data for five or fewer students are not reported for confidentiality reasons). Those not meeting minimum academic requirements are required to enroll in non-credit learning support courses.

The Atlanta Journal-Constitution / Page 9

The Ultimate Atlanta School Guide

Keys to interpreting High Schools

"Thumbs Up" signifies school is one of the state's Top 20 public high schools as selected by the Georgia Public Policy Foundation, Spring 2002. Go online to http://www.gppf.org

"Thumbs Down" signifies school has been designated a "low performer" for the past five school years (1996-97 to 2000-01) based on The Atlanta Journal-Constitution's star rating system (see pages 11-15).

Students must pass the Georgia High School Graduation Test prior to being eligible to receive a high school diploma. Students have their first chance to pass the test in the 11th grade. The chart at the right reflects the percent of 11th graders who passed the test on their first try. See pages 506-511.

Georgia statewide averages (2000-01)
Writing.......................92%
Social Studies 80%
Science......................68%
Mathematics 91%
English language arts...............94%

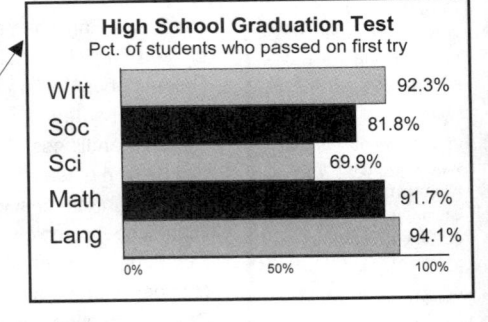

High School Graduation Test
Pct. of students who passed on first try

Writ	92.3%
Soc	81.8%
Sci	69.9%
Math	91.7%
Lang	94.1%

Georgia High School classification for interscholastic sports and activities. The GHSA (see http://www.ghsa.net) sets the standards of eligibility to be met by its member high schools for participation in interscholastic contests, and rules controlling the participation among schools. Interscholastic sports codes:

BB = basketball	RI = riflery
BS = baseball	SB = softball
CC = cross country	SO = soccer
CL = cheerleading	SW = swimming
FB = football	TE = tennis
GO = golf	TF = track & field
GY = gymnastics	VB = volleyball
LC = lacrosse	WR = wrestling

GHSA classification: 5-AAAA
Interscholastic sports offered:
BS, BB, CL, CC, FB, GO, SO, SB, SW, TE, TF, VB, WR

Advanced Placement (AP) Exams
Students tested: 110
Tests taken: 191
Pct. of test scores 3 or higher (1—5 scale): 41.9%

Languages other than English taught:
French, German, Latin, Spanish

The Advanced Placement (AP) Program is sponsored by The College Board in cooperation with secondary schools and colleges and universities. Students who receive a score of three or better can generally receive college credit for the equivalent course at a college or university that give credit for AP exams. See http://apcentral.collegeboard.com

The SAT is designed to test a student's verbal and mathematical skills. Most colleges and universities require a student's SAT scores as a basis for screening prospective students. SAT scores range from 200 to 800 points in each of the verbal and math portions of the test, for a composite score of up to 1,600 points. See pages 512-515.

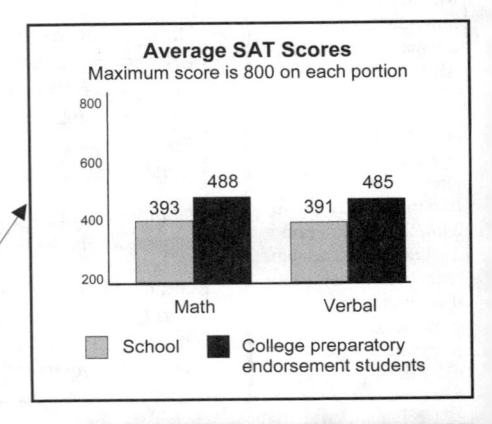

Average SAT Scores
Maximum score is 800 on each portion

	Math	Verbal
School	393	391
College preparatory endorsement students	488	485

Understanding Test Scores and School Performance

By Stephen Cramer, Ph.D.

How can you tell whether a school is doing a good job teaching its students what they need to know? Your answer to that question depends a lot on how you define "good." We deal with two kinds of test scores in this book: as-reported unadjusted test scores, and scores conditioned on socioeconomic status.

1. **Unadjusted test scores — a measure of student performance. Check a school's test-score chart for this measure.**

If the standardized test scores of the students in the school are high, it's hard to argue that the school isn't doing a good job. For example, if you check the test-score chart on a school and it shows that third-grade performance on the reading comprehension portion of the Stanford Achievement Test (SAT-9) is 4.9, that means those third-graders there are reading at nearly a fifth-grade level. High test scores on a valid and reliable test indicate that students are learning. We're pretty safe in saying that students in schools with high scores know and can do more than students in schools with lower scores.

But what are the causes behind high and low scores? Research by the Georgia Department of Education and the University of Georgia shows that the socioeconomic status of the students attending the school has a lot to do with the school's overall performance on standardized tests. This is not to say poorer students can't learn, only that socioeconomic status is related to conditions that can make learning easier or more difficult. For example, as income and education of parents goes up, the number of books present in the household goes up. More important, parents with higher incomes usually have a higher level of education and value education

Stephen Cramer is on the faculty of the College of Education at The University of Georgia, where he teaches research methods, tests and measurements, and cognitive psychology. He designed many statistical models used by the Georgia Department of Education for test score reporting and used parallel models to assign the star ratings for this book.

more. This does not mean we should lower expectations for poorer students. We need to communicate to each teacher and student the expectation that he or she always should do his or her best to teach and learn. However, 15 years of data make it possible to predict which schools are likely to perform at higher levels than others, and these are the schools whose student bodies have higher socioeconomic status. Which brings us to...

2. Adjusting for socioeconomic status — a measure of instructional quality. Check a school's AJC star rating for this measure.

The AJC rating in The Ultimate Atlanta School Guide is a measure of how well a school's students perform on tests, after taking into consideration the socioeconomic composition of the student body. In short, do the students score above or below the level predicted for school with a similar demographic mix of students? If the scores are higher, that's an indication that the quality of instruction in the school is high. If it's lower, that's an indication that something in the school is preventing students from performing as well as their peers in similar schools.

The actual level of performance and predicted performance are independent of each other. That is, regardless of how high or low a school scores on tests, it may be doing better or worse than its socioeconomic status would predict. A school in an affluent area that scores above its prediction is clearly doing a good job in both senses. However, even a low-scoring school might be considered to be doing a very good job of educating its students if those students score higher than predicted. And an affluent school where scores are lower than predicted could mean that instruction at the school is not as strong as at other affluent schools.

What do test scores tell you?

So, a school with high or higher-than-predicted scores is a good place to send my children, right? Well, maybe. Remember that more goes on in schools than purely academic learning. School is where children go to learn to get along with people and to become productive adults. Standardized tests don't measure that. Nor do they measure, except indirectly, skills learned in foreign language, art, music, drama, vocational and physical education classes.

Even if we think only about the academic areas, standardized tests still will not tell a complete story. The test scores used to evaluate elementary and middle schools in this book are from the Georgia Criterion-Referenced Competency Tests (CRCT) given in grades 4, 6, and 8. The CRCT's content coverage is based on the Georgia Quality Core Curriculum, the material that every student is supposed to be taught, so it is a good test to use for looking at school accountability. However, the CRCT was not fully implemented in 2001, so the only scores we have are Reading, Language Arts and Mathematics. These are important subjects, no doubt, but we also know that science and social studies are important as well. Still, the CRCT provides a good basis for comparing schools.

Except for Gwinnett County public schools. Gwinnett County (excluding Buford City Schools) has its own testing program, the Gateway Assessments, given in grades four, seven and 10. These tests incorporate both multiple choice and performance (i.e., the student has to write about something) assessments, and hold students to quite a high standard. Since Gwinnett's elementary schools did not take the CRCT in 2000-2001, the stars awarded to those schools are based on reading, language and math scores from the Stanford Achievement Test (SAT-9), the norm-referenced test given statewide.

For high schools, the scores reported here are based on the Georgia High School Graduation Tests (GHSGT) in English/Language Arts, Mathematics, Science, Social Studies and Writing, which are also very closely aligned after the student curriculum. They have to be, of course, because students must pass each of these tests (English, Mathematics, Social Studies and Writing) to receive a high school diploma. Students have four more opportunities to take and pass the test if they do not pass every content area; however, the school's score is based on first-time scores. Students who have not passed all four sections of the test by the time their class graduates may come back up to four times a year to try to pass it and obtain their diploma, and many do.

The CRCT and the GHSGT are criterion-referenced tests (CRT) based on the Georgia Quality Core Curriculum and written for the most part by Georgia teachers. Other Georgia teachers compared these tests and the Quality Core Curriculum and decided on the criterion score that students must achieve to meet or exceed state standards for grade-level achievement (CRCT) or to pass (GHSGT). It does not matter how other students perform (i.e., no norm-referencing or "grading on the curve"); each student must meet the criterion in each content area.

How did The Atlanta Journal-Constitution get from the standardized test scores to its star rating?

The star ratings reflect only test scores, which are the best measure of learning available to us. Remember though, that other characteristics may be more important to users of this guide.

Even after we focus on scores, we have to ask "which scores?" The CRCT has different tests. Individual students get a score for each, which helps us see that Jimmy is good in math but weak in language arts. For the school's score, though, having three scores is too complex, especially considering that a school may have scores in two different grades. So, to simplify things, the scores used for the star ratings reflect the average of a lot of scores.

To combine the scores, we performed a statistical manipulation called standardization to put the fourth-, sixth-, and eighth-grade scores into the same range. Then we averaged all of the scores together.

For the high schools, we averaged all five GHSGT content area (English, Math, Science, Social Studies, and Writing) scores. These school scores represent the average of all the students in the school, except those classified as Limited English Proficient or Special Education. These students take the test like everyone else, but their scores do not contribute to the school's average.

Starting in 1986, and over the ensuing years, the Georgia Department of Education and the University of Georgia have carried out research aimed at identifying the factors that predict schools' test score performance. Starting out with a list of more than 30 student, school and community variables, they have settled on four:

1. Percent of students eligible for federally subsidized free lunch
2. Percent of students eligible for federally subsidized reduced-price lunch
3. School size
4. The wealth of the system, in terms of its property tax base

These variables explain 40 to 70 percent of the differences between schools. The same statistical model used by the Georgia Department of Education was applied to calculate this guide's star ratings. Specifically, using a technique called multiple regression, the school score is correlated with the demographic predictors. The regression analysis yields a prediction equation. Plug in the individual school's demographic values, and you get its predicted score.

Notice the logic of this: Schools vary in their scores. We have explained much of this variance by looking at the demographic information. The remainder we attribute to other factors, among them, the quality of instruction in the school.

That's just mathematics. We still have to decide how much better than predicted is "good" and how much worse than predicted is "bad." Borrowing again from the Georgia Department of Education, we used a statistic called the standard error of prediction (SEP). State educators used the SEP to report performance on the Curriculum Based Assessments in the early 1990s.

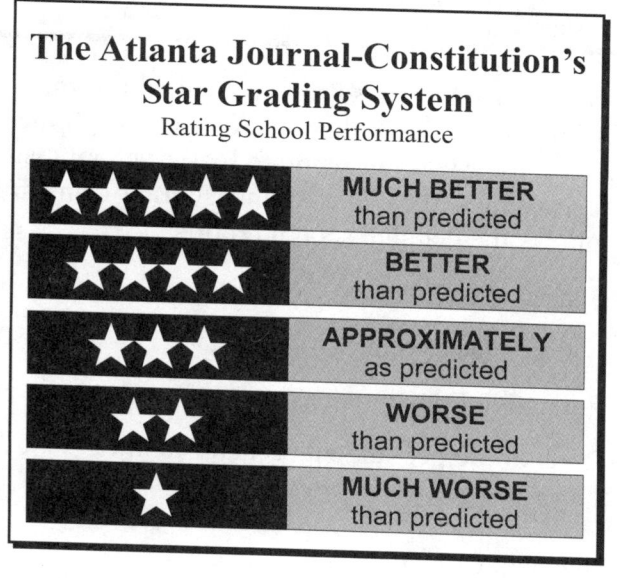

The Atlanta Journal-Constitution's Star Grading System
Rating School Performance

★★★★★	MUCH BETTER than predicted
★★★★	BETTER than predicted
★★★	APPROXIMATELY as predicted
★★	WORSE than predicted
★	MUCH WORSE than predicted

In a similar method, we made judgment that a school whose score is within plus or minus one SEP of its predicted score is doing about average, and we awarded it three stars (no grade inflation in this guide). A school that scores at least one SEP above its prediction earns four stars; two SEP's above earns five stars. Conversely, more than one SEP below prediction brings a school to two stars, and more than two SEP's below prediction awards the school only a single star.

Granted, that's an arbitrary standard, and it weights all content areas equally. Your own standards may be different, and we encourage you to look deeper into the details of the scores of your community's schools. AJC ratings serve as an overview to show that some schools are doing better than you would predict, others worse. We assume this is due, at least in part, to the quality of instruction.

Journalist and humorist Finley Peter Dunne once said the purpose of journalism is to comfort the afflicted and afflict the comfortable. We don't intend to afflict anyone, but if an inner-city or rural school with a poor population is exceeding its predictions, we want to point it out. By the same token, if a school with a wealthy suburban population is not meeting its predictions, it may need a wake-up call.

Atlanta City Public Schools

210 Pryor St SW, Atlanta, GA 30303
Phone: 404-827-8075 · Fax: 404-827-8320
http://www.atlanta.k12.ga.us

The following pages provide detailed information on every school in the Atlanta City school district. An asterisk (*) means the value of the data was zero or was not reported by the school district. A complete list of schools ranked by The Atlanta Journal-Constitution's star rating system follows the detailed school reports.

District enrollment:	57,370
White / black / other:	6.5% / 89.4% / 4.0%
Not native English-speaking:	1,085 / 1.9%
Expenditure per student (general fund):	$8,219
Students per teacher:	14.7
Teachers with advanced degrees:	47.8%
Average years, teaching experience:	12.9
Average teacher salary:	$44,800.78
Students in gifted program:	3,349 / 5.8%
Students held back a grade:	3,594 / 6.3%
Eligible students, free or reduced lunch:	44,521 / 76.5%
Number of dropouts (grades 9-12):	2,940 / 17.7%
High school completion rate:	53.6%
Graduates, pct. eligible for HOPE scholarships:	2,074 / 50.7%
Average combined SAT score (maximum 1,600):	878
Pct. of 11th-graders passing the Georgia High School Graduation Tests on first try:	50%
Percent of children 5 to 17 years of age living in poverty (2000 Census estimate):	38.3%

Adamsville Elementary School

286 Wilson Mill Rd SW, Atlanta, GA 30331
404-699-4500 · Grades K - 5

Enrollment:	342
White / black / other:	0.0% / 99.1% / 0.9%
Not native English-speaking:	1 / 0.3%
Limited English proficiency:	2 / 0.6%
Student absenteeism:	4.4%
Students per teacher:	10.8
Parent friendliness:	① ❷ ❸ ④ ❺ ❻
Teachers with advanced degrees:	52.9%
Average years' teaching experience:	17.5
Students in gifted program:	7 / 2.0%
Students in remedial education:	40.3%
Students held back a grade:	9.9%
Total suspensions, pct. in-school:	16 / 0.0%
Offenses:	violence: 4, drugs: *, other: 12
Eligible students, free or reduced lunch:	95.9%
Before / after school program:	Yes / No

Students at this school generally go on to:
Usher Middle

AJC GRADE: ★★★

Georgia Criterion-Referenced Competency Tests - Grade 4
Pct. of students at each level

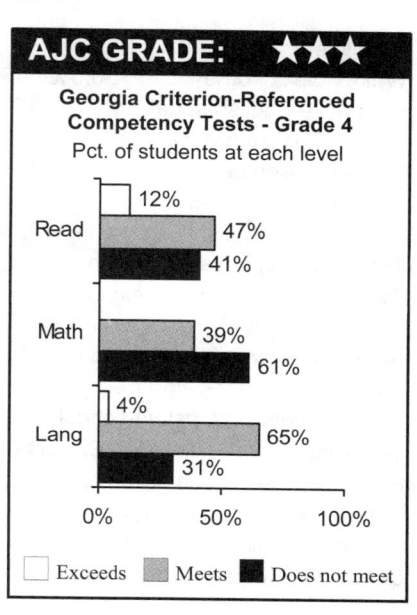

Read: Exceeds 12%, Meets 47%, Does not meet 41%
Math: Exceeds —, Meets 39%, Does not meet 61%
Lang: Exceeds 4%, Meets 65%, Does not meet 31%

Anderson Park School

2050 Tiger Flowers Dr NW, Atlanta, GA 30314
404-792-5914 · Grades K - 5

Enrollment:	397
White / black / other:	0.3% / 99.5% / 0.3%
Not native English-speaking:	1 / 0.3%
Limited English proficiency:	1 / 0.3%
Student absenteeism:	6.7%
Students per teacher:	13.1
Parent friendliness:	① ❷ ❸ ④ ❺ ❻
Teachers with advanced degrees:	32.4%
Average years' teaching experience:	13.1
Students in gifted program:	3 / 0.8%
Students in remedial education:	43.0%
Students held back a grade:	5.3%
Total suspensions, pct. in-school:	45 / 0.0%
Offenses:	violence: 43, drugs: *, other: 11
Eligible students, free or reduced lunch:	86.7%
Before / after school program:	No / Yes

Students at this school generally go on to:
Turner Middle

AJC GRADE: ★★

Georgia Criterion-Referenced Competency Tests - Grade 4
Pct. of students at each level

Read: Exceeds 14%, Meets 42%, Does not meet 44%
Math: Exceeds 3%, Meets 38%, Does not meet 59%
Lang: Exceeds 5%, Meets 53%, Does not meet 42%

The Atlanta Journal-Constitution / Page 17

Atlanta City Elementary Schools

Arkwright Elementary School

1261 Lockwood Dr SW, Atlanta, GA 30311
404-752-0746 · Grades K - 5

Enrollment:	283
White / black / other:	3.5% / 95.4% / 1.1%
Not native English-speaking:	1 / 0.4%
Limited English proficiency:	1 / 0.4%
Student absenteeism:	3.6%
Students per teacher:	13.2
Parent friendliness:	①❷❸❹❺❻
Teachers with advanced degrees:	52.0%
Average years' teaching experience:	16.3
Students in gifted program:	2 / 0.7%
Students in remedial education:	36.3%
Students held back a grade:	7.1%
Total suspensions, pct. in-school:	3 / 33.3%
Offenses:	violence: 3, drugs: *, other: 6
Eligible students, free or reduced lunch:	96.8%
Before / after school program:	No / Yes

Students at this school generally go on to:
Sylvan Hills Middle

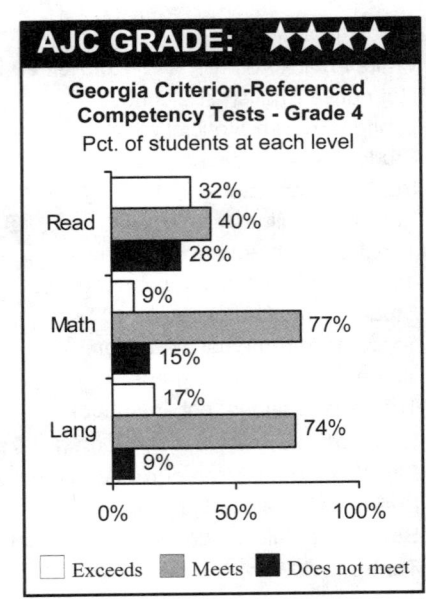

AJC GRADE: ★★★★

Georgia Criterion-Referenced Competency Tests - Grade 4
Pct. of students at each level

Read: Exceeds 38%, Meets 40%, Does not meet 21%
Math: Exceeds 14%, Meets 48%, Does not meet 38%
Lang: Exceeds 14%, Meets 71%, Does not meet 14%

Beecher Hills Elementary School

2257 Bolling Brook Dr SW, Atlanta, GA 30311
404-752-0785 · Grades K - 5

Enrollment:	277
White / black / other:	0.4% / 99.3% / 0.4%
Not native English-speaking:	*
Limited English proficiency:	*
Student absenteeism:	3.3%
Students per teacher:	11.9
Parent friendliness:	❶❷❸❹❺❻
Teachers with advanced degrees:	55.6%
Average years' teaching experience:	10.9
Students in gifted program:	*
Students in remedial education:	37.0%
Students held back a grade:	15.5%
Total suspensions, pct. in-school:	*
Offenses:	violence: *, drugs: *, other: *
Eligible students, free or reduced lunch:	87.2%
Before / after school program:	No / Yes

Students at this school generally go on to:
Brown, Young Middle

AJC GRADE: ★★★★

Georgia Criterion-Referenced Competency Tests - Grade 4
Pct. of students at each level

Read: Exceeds 32%, Meets 40%, Does not meet 28%
Math: Exceeds 9%, Meets 77%, Does not meet 15%
Lang: Exceeds 17%, Meets 74%, Does not meet 9%

Atlanta City Elementary Schools

Benteen Elementary School

200 Cassanova St SE, Atlanta, GA 30315
404-624-2000 · Grades K - 5

Enrollment:	474
White / black / other:	4.2% / 62.0% / 33.8%
Not native English-speaking:	60 / 12.7%
Limited English proficiency:	68 / 14.3%
Student absenteeism:	4.3%
Students per teacher:	12.2
Parent friendliness:	❶ ❷ ❸ ④ ❺ ❻
Teachers with advanced degrees:	42.9%
Average years' teaching experience:	9.5
Students in gifted program:	*
Students in remedial education:	36.5%
Students held back a grade:	5.5%
Total suspensions, pct. in-school:	30 / 0.0%
Offenses:	violence: 26, drugs: *, other: 4
Eligible students, free or reduced lunch:	75.3%
Before / after school program:	No / Yes
Students at this school generally go on to:	
King Middle	

AJC GRADE: ★★

Georgia Criterion-Referenced Competency Tests - Grade 4
Pct. of students at each level

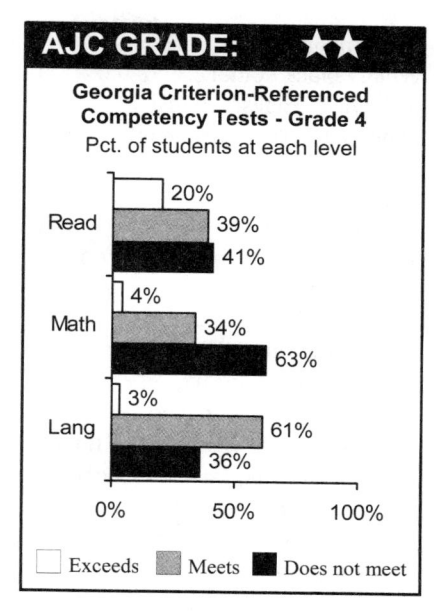

Read: Exceeds 20%, Meets 39%, Does not meet 41%
Math: Exceeds 4%, Meets 34%, Does not meet 63%
Lang: Exceeds 3%, Meets 61%, Does not meet 36%

Bethune Elementary School

220 Northside Dr NW, Atlanta, GA 30314
404-330-4641 · Grades K - 5

Enrollment:	573
White / black / other:	0.5% / 99.3% / 0.2%
Not native English-speaking:	*
Limited English proficiency:	*
Student absenteeism:	4.0%
Students per teacher:	11.9
Parent friendliness:	① ❷ ❸ ④ ❺ ❻
Teachers with advanced degrees:	47.2%
Average years' teaching experience:	12.7
Students in gifted program:	13 / 2.3%
Students in remedial education:	11.2%
Students held back a grade:	5.2%
Total suspensions, pct. in-school:	9 / 88.9%
Offenses:	violence: 5, drugs: *, other: 4
Eligible students, free or reduced lunch:	96.9%
Before / after school program:	No / Yes
Students at this school generally go on to:	
Kennedy Middle	

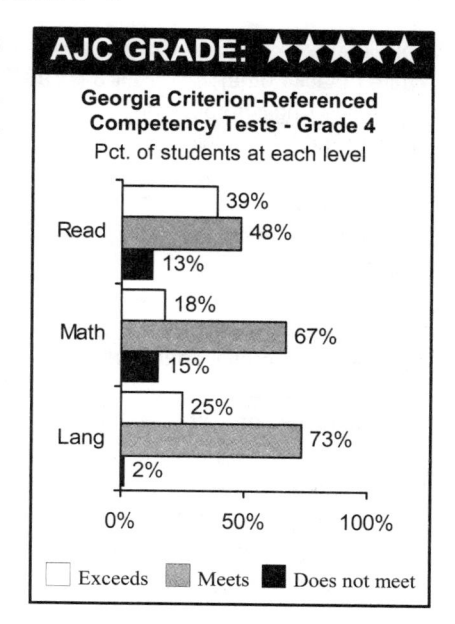

AJC GRADE: ★★★★★

Georgia Criterion-Referenced Competency Tests - Grade 4
Pct. of students at each level

Read: Exceeds 39%, Meets 48%, Does not meet 13%
Math: Exceeds 18%, Meets 67%, Does not meet 15%
Lang: Exceeds 25%, Meets 73%, Does not meet 2%

Blalock Elementary School

1445 Maynard Rd NW, Atlanta, GA 30331
404-699-4504 · Grades K - 5

Enrollment:	520
White / black / other:	0.0% / 100.0% / 0.0%
Not native English-speaking:	*
Limited English proficiency:	3 / 0.6%
Student absenteeism:	6.0%
Students per teacher:	13.3
Parent friendliness:	①❷❸④❺❻
Teachers with advanced degrees:	47.6%
Average years' teaching experience:	10.7
Students in gifted program:	2 / 0.4%
Students in remedial education:	29.1%
Students held back a grade:	9.0%
Total suspensions, pct. in-school:	36 / 25.0%
Offenses:	violence: 25, drugs: *, other: 28
Eligible students, free or reduced lunch:	95.6%
Before / after school program:	No / No
Students at this school generally go on to:	
Usher Middle	

AJC GRADE: ★★★

Georgia Criterion-Referenced Competency Tests - Grade 4
Pct. of students at each level

- Read: Exceeds 13%, Meets 39%, Does not meet 48%
- Math: Exceeds 2%, Meets 32%, Does not meet 66%
- Lang: Exceeds 3%, Meets 61%, Does not meet 36%

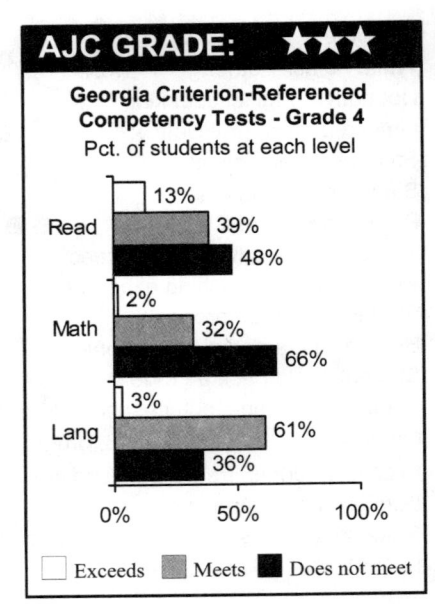

Boyd Elementary School

1891 Johnson Rd NW, Atlanta, GA 30318
404-792-5909 · Grades K - 5

Enrollment:	308
White / black / other:	1.3% / 98.7% / 0.0%
Not native English-speaking:	*
Limited English proficiency:	*
Student absenteeism:	7.2%
Students per teacher:	9.9
Parent friendliness:	①❷❸④⑤❻
Teachers with advanced degrees:	51.5%
Average years' teaching experience:	12.7
Students in gifted program:	*
Students in remedial education:	25.0%
Students held back a grade:	7.5%
Total suspensions, pct. in-school:	*
Offenses:	violence: 3, drugs: *, other: 6
Eligible students, free or reduced lunch:	99.7%
Before / after school program:	No / No
Students at this school generally go on to:	
West Fulton Middle	

AJC GRADE: ★★★

Georgia Criterion-Referenced Competency Tests - Grade 4
Pct. of students at each level

- Read: Exceeds 19%, Meets 50%, Does not meet 31%
- Math: Exceeds *, Meets 52%, Does not meet 48%
- Lang: Exceeds 12%, Meets 67%, Does not meet 21%

Atlanta City Elementary Schools

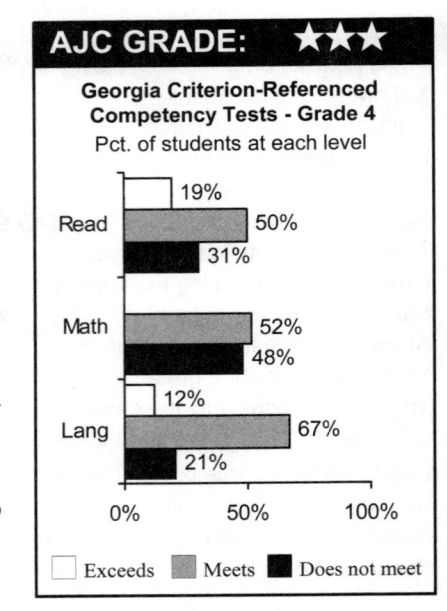

Brandon Elementary School
2741 Howell Mill Rd NW, Atlanta, GA 30327
404-350-2153 · Grades K - 5

Enrollment:	528
White / black / other:	85.8% / 12.5% / 1.7%
Not native English-speaking:	*
Limited English proficiency:	*
Student absenteeism:	3.6%
Students per teacher:	15.9
Parent friendliness:	① ❷ ❸ ④ ⑤ ❻
Teachers with advanced degrees:	63.2%
Average years' teaching experience:	14.1
Students in gifted program:	145 / 27.5%
Students in remedial education:	2.5%
Students held back a grade:	0.4%
Total suspensions, pct. in-school:	2 / 0.0%
Offenses:	violence: *, drugs: *, other: 2
Eligible students, free or reduced lunch:	4.2%
Before / after school program:	No / No
Students at this school generally go on to:	
Sutton Middle	

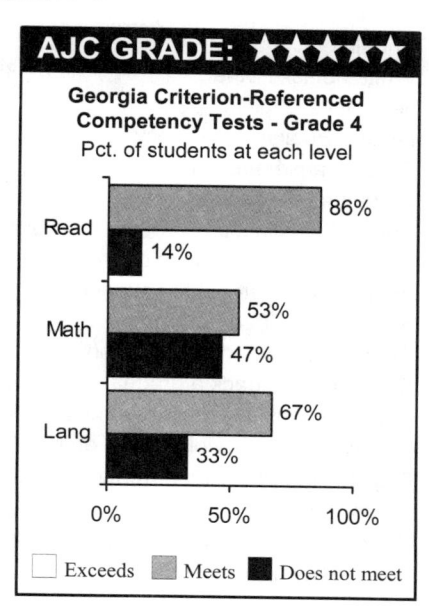

AJC GRADE: ★★★★★

Georgia Criterion-Referenced Competency Tests - Grade 4
Pct. of students at each level

- Read: 86% Meets, 14% Does not meet
- Math: 53% Meets, 47% Does not meet
- Lang: 67% Meets, 33% Does not meet

☐ Exceeds ▒ Meets ■ Does not meet

Burgess Elementary School
480 Clifton St SE, Atlanta, GA 30316
404-371-4850 · Grades K - 5

Enrollment:	319
White / black / other:	0.3% / 99.7% / 0.0%
Not native English-speaking:	*
Limited English proficiency:	*
Student absenteeism:	3.4%
Students per teacher:	11.1
Parent friendliness:	❶ ❷ ❸ ④ ❺ ❻
Teachers with advanced degrees:	53.1%
Average years' teaching experience:	12.0
Students in gifted program:	8 / 2.5%
Students in remedial education:	29.3%
Students held back a grade:	6.9%
Total suspensions, pct. in-school:	17 / 0.0%
Offenses:	violence: 8, drugs: *, other: 9
Eligible students, free or reduced lunch:	90.6%
Before / after school program:	No / Yes
Students at this school generally go on to:	
Coan Middle	

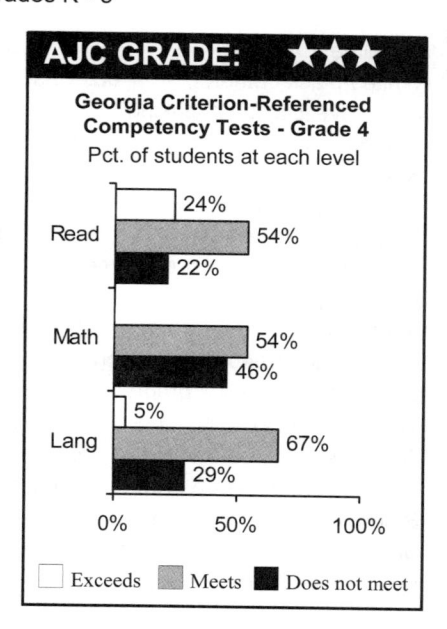

AJC GRADE: ★★★

Georgia Criterion-Referenced Competency Tests - Grade 4
Pct. of students at each level

- Read: 24% Exceeds, 54% Meets, 22% Does not meet
- Math: 54% Meets, 46% Does not meet
- Lang: 5% Exceeds, 67% Meets, 29% Does not meet

☐ Exceeds ▒ Meets ■ Does not meet

The Atlanta Journal-Constitution / Page 21

Atlanta City Elementary Schools

Capitol View Elementary School

1442 Metropolitan Pkwy SW, Atlanta, GA 30310
404-752-0759 · Grades K - 5

Enrollment:	401
White / black / other:	1.7% / 87.8% / 10.5%
Not native English-speaking:	36 / 9.0%
Limited English proficiency:	36 / 9.0%
Student absenteeism:	4.7%
Students per teacher:	14.0
Parent friendliness:	❶ ❷ ❸ ④ ⑤ ❻
Teachers with advanced degrees:	34.4%
Average years' teaching experience:	9.3
Students in gifted program:	9 / 2.2%
Students in remedial education:	14.3%
Students held back a grade:	7.0%
Total suspensions, pct. in-school:	17 / 0.0%
Offenses:	violence: 2, drugs: *, other: 15
Eligible students, free or reduced lunch:	94.8%
Before / after school program:	No / Yes
Students at this school generally go on to:	
Price, Sylvan Hills Middle	

AJC GRADE: ★★★★

Georgia Criterion-Referenced Competency Tests - Grade 4
Pct. of students at each level

Read: Exceeds 38%, Meets 43%, Does not meet 19%
Math: Exceeds 8%, Meets 62%, Does not meet 30%
Lang: Exceeds 11%, Meets 67%, Does not meet 22%

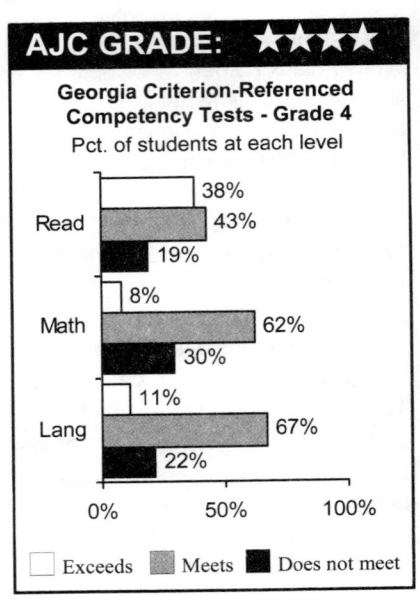

Cascade Elementary School

2326 Venetian Dr SW, Atlanta, GA 30311
404-752-0769 · Grades K - 5

Enrollment:	428
White / black / other:	0.2% / 99.8% / 0.0%
Not native English-speaking:	*
Limited English proficiency:	1 / 0.2%
Student absenteeism:	3.6%
Students per teacher:	15.1
Parent friendliness:	① ❷ ❸ ④ ❺ ❻
Teachers with advanced degrees:	48.5%
Average years' teaching experience:	13.2
Students in gifted program:	9 / 2.1%
Students in remedial education:	15.6%
Students held back a grade:	3.7%
Total suspensions, pct. in-school:	4 / 0.0%
Offenses:	violence: *, drugs: *, other: 4
Eligible students, free or reduced lunch:	99.3%
Before / after school program:	No / Yes
Students at this school generally go on to:	
Sylvan Hills, Young Middle	

AJC GRADE: ★★★★★

Georgia Criterion-Referenced Competency Tests - Grade 4
Pct. of students at each level

Read: Exceeds 33%, Meets 50%, Does not meet 17%
Math: Exceeds 13%, Meets 64%, Does not meet 23%
Lang: Exceeds 29%, Meets 63%, Does not meet 9%

Atlanta City Elementary Schools

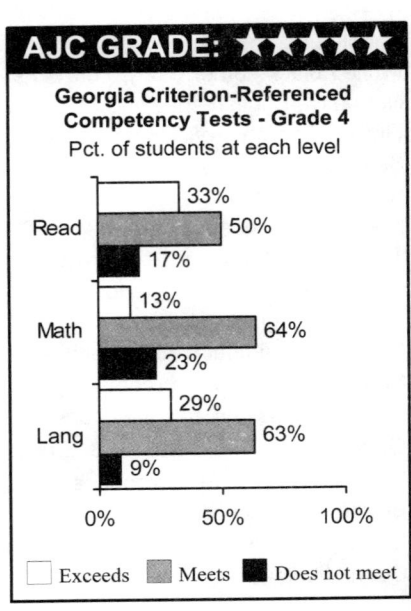

Centennial Place Elementary School

531 Luckie St NW, Atlanta, GA 30313
404-853-4022 · Grades K - 5

Enrollment:	555
White / black / other:	1.4% / 91.7% / 6.8%
Not native English-speaking:	11 / 2.0%
Limited English proficiency:	14 / 2.5%
Student absenteeism:	3.0%
Students per teacher:	12.8
Parent friendliness:	① ❷ ❸ ④ ⑤ ❻
Teachers with advanced degrees:	55.6%
Average years' teaching experience:	8.7
Students in gifted program:	57 / 10.3%
Students in remedial education:	21.2%
Students held back a grade:	5.4%
Total suspensions, pct. in-school:	1 / 0.0%
Offenses:	violence: *, drugs: *, other: 1
Eligible students, free or reduced lunch:	74.2%
Before / after school program:	No / No
Students at this school generally go on to:	Inman Middle

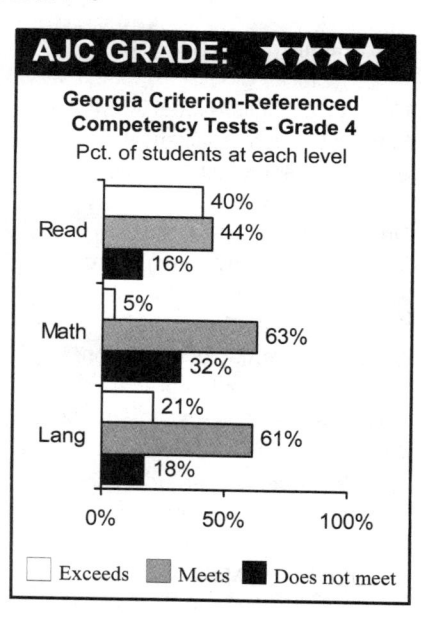

AJC GRADE: ★★★★

Georgia Criterion-Referenced Competency Tests - Grade 4
Pct. of students at each level

- Read: 40% Exceeds / 44% Meets / 16% Does not meet
- Math: 5% Exceeds / 63% Meets / 32% Does not meet
- Lang: 21% Exceeds / 61% Meets / 18% Does not meet

Charles R. Drew Charter School

301 E Lake Blvd SE, Atlanta, GA 30317
404-687-0001 · Grades K - 7

Enrollment:	240
White / black / other:	0.4% / 99.2% / 0.4%
Not native English-speaking:	*
Limited English proficiency:	*
Student absenteeism:	4.0%
Students per teacher:	*
Parent friendliness:	① ❷ ❸ ④ ❺ ❻
Teachers with advanced degrees:	*
Average years' teaching experience:	*
Students in gifted program:	*
Students in remedial education:	*
Students held back a grade:	1.3%
Total suspensions, pct. in-school:	51 / 0.0%
Offenses:	violence: 53, drugs: *, other: 62
Eligible students, free or reduced lunch:	71.7%
Before / after school program:	Yes / Yes
Students at this school generally go on to:	Several Atlanta City high schools

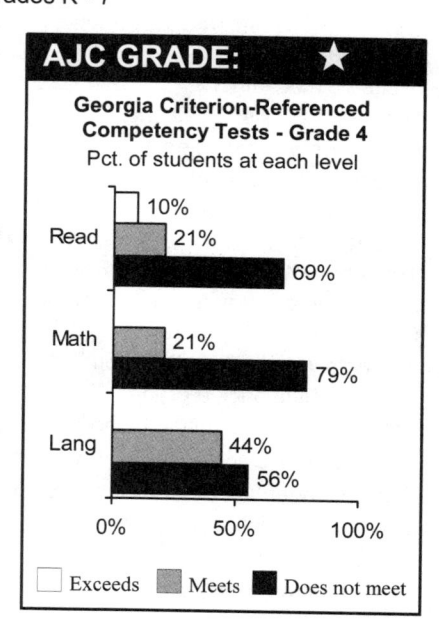

AJC GRADE: ★

Georgia Criterion-Referenced Competency Tests - Grade 4
Pct. of students at each level

- Read: 10% Exceeds / 21% Meets / 69% Does not meet
- Math: — Exceeds / 21% Meets / 79% Does not meet
- Lang: — Exceeds / 44% Meets / 56% Does not meet

Atlanta City Elementary Schools

Cleveland Avenue Elementary School

2672 Old Hapeville Rd SW, Atlanta, GA 30315
404-669-2717 · Grades K - 5

Enrollment:	742
White / black / other:	0.1% / 96.8% / 3.1%
Not native English-speaking:	16 / 2.2%
Limited English proficiency:	22 / 3.0%
Student absenteeism:	4.1%
Students per teacher:	15.5
Parent friendliness:	①②❸④❺❻
Teachers with advanced degrees:	37.3%
Average years' teaching experience:	15.0
Students in gifted program:	22 / 3.0%
Students in remedial education:	26.5%
Students held back a grade:	5.8%
Total suspensions, pct. in-school:	*
Offenses: violence: *, drugs: *, other: *	
Eligible students, free or reduced lunch:	95.3%
Before / after school program:	No / Yes
Students at this school generally go on to: Crawford Long Middle	

AJC GRADE: ★★★★

Georgia Criterion-Referenced Competency Tests - Grade 4
Pct. of students at each level

- Read: Exceeds 27%, Meets 48%, Does not meet 25%
- Math: Exceeds 10%, Meets 41%, Does not meet 49%
- Lang: Exceeds 16%, Meets 58%, Does not meet 26%

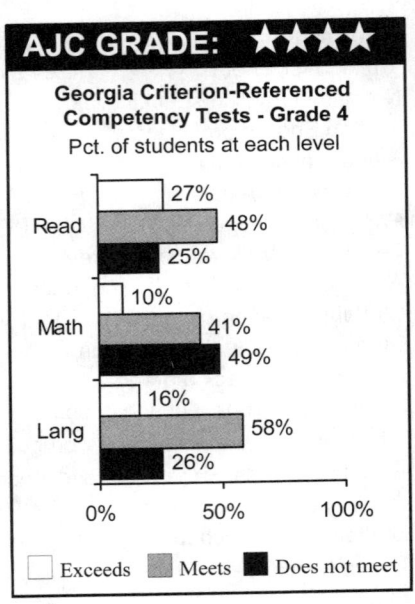

Collier Heights Elementary School

3050 Collier Dr NW, Atlanta, GA 30318
404-699-4507 · Grades K - 5

Enrollment:	543
White / black / other:	0.4% / 99.6% / 0.0%
Not native English-speaking:	*
Limited English proficiency:	*
Student absenteeism:	4.8%
Students per teacher:	15.4
Parent friendliness:	①❷❸④❺❻
Teachers with advanced degrees:	36.8%
Average years' teaching experience:	12.8
Students in gifted program:	12 / 2.2%
Students in remedial education:	26.8%
Students held back a grade:	6.3%
Total suspensions, pct. in-school:	55 / 0.0%
Offenses: violence: 32, drugs: *, other: 23	
Eligible students, free or reduced lunch:	63.5%
Before / after school program:	No / Yes
Students at this school generally go on to: Usher Middle	

AJC GRADE: ★★★

Georgia Criterion-Referenced Competency Tests - Grade 4
Pct. of students at each level

- Read: Exceeds 22%, Meets 53%, Does not meet 24%
- Math: Exceeds 5%, Meets 56%, Does not meet 38%
- Lang: Exceeds 11%, Meets 68%, Does not meet 22%

The Atlanta Journal-Constitution / Page 24

Atlanta City Elementary Schools

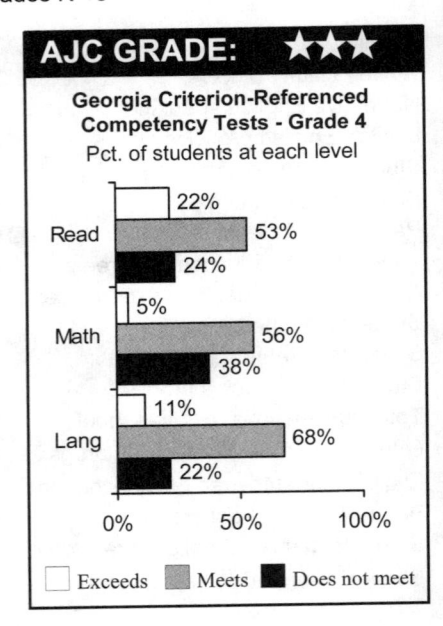

Connally Elementary School

1654 S Alvarado Ter SW, Atlanta, GA 30311
404-752-0762 · Grades K - 5

Enrollment:	672
White / black / other:	0.0% / 99.1% / 0.9%
Not native English-speaking:	*
Limited English proficiency:	*
Student absenteeism:	5.3%
Students per teacher:	13.4
Parent friendliness:	①❷❸④⑤❻
Teachers with advanced degrees:	41.5%
Average years' teaching experience:	11.5
Students in gifted program:	1 / 0.1%
Students in remedial education:	19.6%
Students held back a grade:	4.6%
Total suspensions, pct. in-school:	2 / 0.0%
Offenses:	violence: 1, drugs: * , other: 1
Eligible students, free or reduced lunch:	91.8%
Before / after school program:	Yes / Yes

Students at this school generally go on to:
Brown Middle

AJC GRADE: ★★

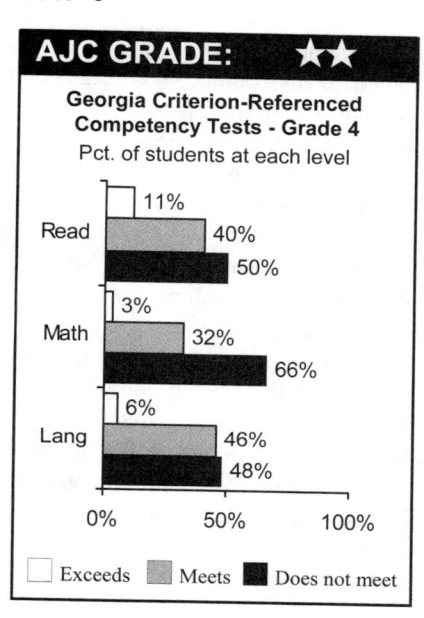

Georgia Criterion-Referenced Competency Tests - Grade 4
Pct. of students at each level

- Read: Exceeds 11%, Meets 40%, Does not meet 50%
- Math: Exceeds 3%, Meets 32%, Does not meet 66%
- Lang: Exceeds 6%, Meets 46%, Does not meet 48%

☐ Exceeds ▨ Meets ■ Does not meet

Continental Colony Elementary School

3181 Hogan Rd SW, Atlanta, GA 30331
404-346-2512 · Grades K - 5

Enrollment:	587
White / black / other:	0.0% / 99.5% / 0.5%
Not native English-speaking:	*
Limited English proficiency:	*
Student absenteeism:	4.0%
Students per teacher:	13.6
Parent friendliness:	①②❸④❺❻
Teachers with advanced degrees:	44.4%
Average years' teaching experience:	14.4
Students in gifted program:	59 / 10.1%
Students in remedial education:	21.0%
Students held back a grade:	0.7%
Total suspensions, pct. in-school:	11 / 0.0%
Offenses:	violence: 9, drugs: * , other: 17
Eligible students, free or reduced lunch:	72.4%
Before / after school program:	Yes / Yes

Students at this school generally go on to:
Bunche Middle

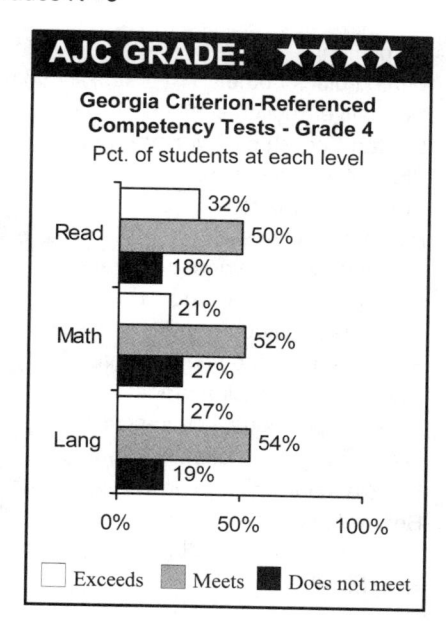

AJC GRADE: ★★★★

Georgia Criterion-Referenced Competency Tests - Grade 4
Pct. of students at each level

- Read: Exceeds 32%, Meets 50%, Does not meet 18%
- Math: Exceeds 21%, Meets 52%, Does not meet 27%
- Lang: Exceeds 27%, Meets 54%, Does not meet 19%

☐ Exceeds ▨ Meets ■ Does not meet

Atlanta City Elementary Schools

Cook Elementary School

211 Memorial Dr SE, Atlanta, GA 30312
404-330-4104 · Grades K - 5

Enrollment:	558
White / black / other:	0.2% / 99.8% / 0.0%
Not native English-speaking:	1 / 0.2%
Limited English proficiency:	1 / 0.2%
Student absenteeism:	5.5%
Students per teacher:	15.0
Parent friendliness:	①❷❸❹❺❻
Teachers with advanced degrees:	45.0%
Average years' teaching experience:	11.1
Students in gifted program:	*
Students in remedial education:	30.2%
Students held back a grade:	13.4%
Total suspensions, pct. in-school:	15 / 0.0%
Offenses:	violence: 24, drugs: *, other: 20
Eligible students, free or reduced lunch:	99.8%
Before / after school program:	Yes / Yes

Students at this school generally go on to:
King, Walden Middle

AJC GRADE: ★★★

Georgia Criterion-Referenced Competency Tests - Grade 4
Pct. of students at each level

Read: Exceeds 17%, Meets 37%, Does not meet 47%
Math: Exceeds 3%, Meets 46%, Does not meet 51%
Lang: Exceeds 9%, Meets 57%, Does not meet 34%

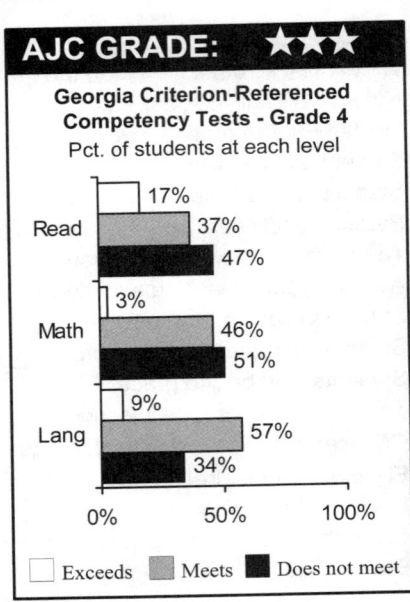

D.H. Stanton Elementary School

970 Martin St SE, Atlanta, GA 30315
404-624-2084 · Grades K - 5

Enrollment:	547
White / black / other:	0.9% / 98.0% / 1.1%
Not native English-speaking:	*
Limited English proficiency:	5 / 0.9%
Student absenteeism:	5.2%
Students per teacher:	12.7
Parent friendliness:	①❷❸④❺❻
Teachers with advanced degrees:	51.1%
Average years' teaching experience:	11.3
Students in gifted program:	*
Students in remedial education:	35.2%
Students held back a grade:	0.7%
Total suspensions, pct. in-school:	113 / 4.4%
Offenses:	violence: 42, drugs: *, other: 86
Eligible students, free or reduced lunch:	100.0%
Before / after school program:	Yes / Yes

Students at this school generally go on to:
King Middle

AJC GRADE: ★★

Georgia Criterion-Referenced Competency Tests - Grade 4
Pct. of students at each level

Read: Exceeds 9%, Meets 36%, Does not meet 55%
Math: Exceeds 1%, Meets 26%, Does not meet 73%
Lang: Exceeds 5%, Meets 44%, Does not meet 51%

Atlanta City Elementary Schools

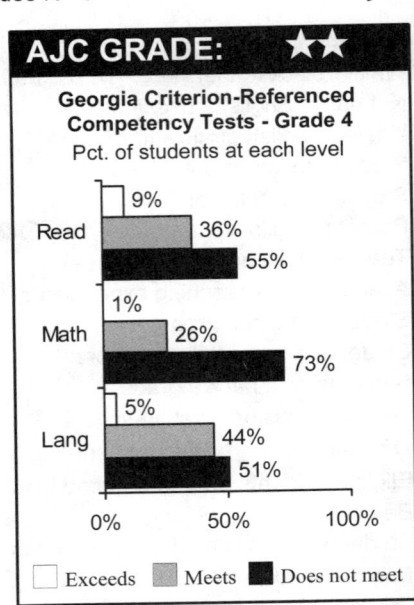

Dobbs Elementary School

1965 Lewis Rd SE, Atlanta, GA 30315
404-624-2010 · Grades K - 5

Enrollment:	309
White / black / other:	0.6% / 99.4% / 0.0%
Not native English-speaking:	*
Limited English proficiency:	*
Student absenteeism:	4.7%
Students per teacher:	13.2
Parent friendliness:	①❷❸④⑤❻
Teachers with advanced degrees:	42.3%
Average years' teaching experience:	10.8
Students in gifted program:	3 / 1.0%
Students in remedial education:	20.8%
Students held back a grade:	13.9%
Total suspensions, pct. in-school:	1 / 0.0%
Offenses:	violence: * , drugs: * , other: 1
Eligible students, free or reduced lunch:	100.0%
Before / after school program:	No / No
Students at this school generally go on to:	
Price Middle	

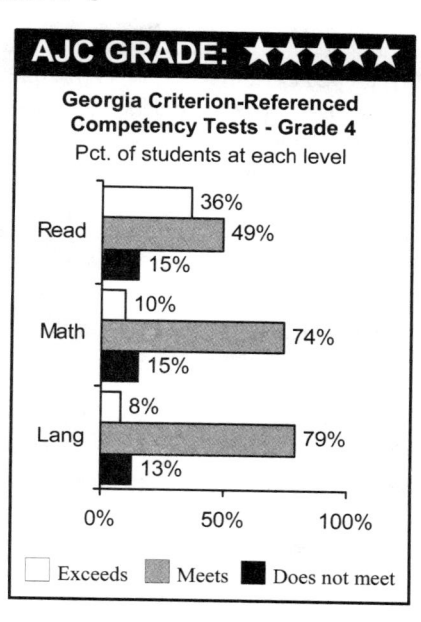

AJC GRADE: ★★★★★

Georgia Criterion-Referenced Competency Tests - Grade 4
Pct. of students at each level

- Read: Exceeds 36%, Meets 49%, Does not meet 15%
- Math: Exceeds 10%, Meets 74%, Does not meet 15%
- Lang: Exceeds 8%, Meets 79%, Does not meet 13%

Dunbar Elementary School

403 Richardson St SW, Atlanta, GA 30312
404-330-4150 · Grades K - 5

Enrollment:	516
White / black / other:	1.2% / 97.7% / 1.2%
Not native English-speaking:	1 / 0.2%
Limited English proficiency:	1 / 0.2%
Student absenteeism:	4.9%
Students per teacher:	14.0
Parent friendliness:	①❷❸④❺❻
Teachers with advanced degrees:	35.9%
Average years' teaching experience:	12.6
Students in gifted program:	2 / 0.4%
Students in remedial education:	45.6%
Students held back a grade:	2.5%
Total suspensions, pct. in-school:	17 / 0.0%
Offenses:	violence: 17, drugs: * , other: *
Eligible students, free or reduced lunch:	92.1%
Before / after school program:	Yes / Yes
Students at this school generally go on to:	
Parks Middle	

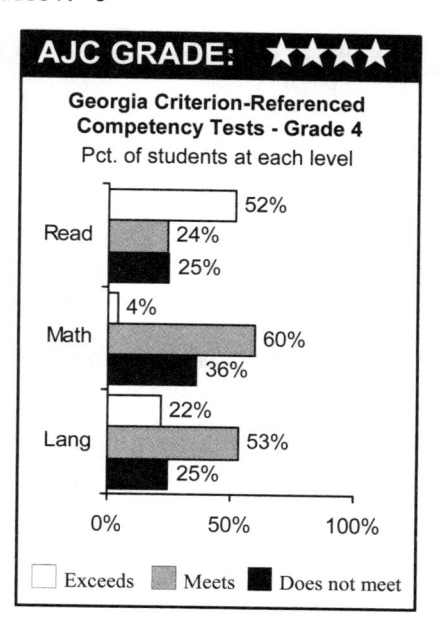

AJC GRADE: ★★★★

Georgia Criterion-Referenced Competency Tests - Grade 4
Pct. of students at each level

- Read: Exceeds 52%, Meets 24%, Does not meet 25%
- Math: Exceeds 4%, Meets 60%, Does not meet 36%
- Lang: Exceeds 22%, Meets 53%, Does not meet 25%

Atlanta City Elementary Schools

East Lake Elementary School

145 4th Ave SE, Atlanta, GA 30317
404-371-7145 · Grades K - 5

Enrollment:	274
White / black / other:	1.1% / 98.5% / 0.4%
Not native English-speaking:	*
Limited English proficiency:	2 / 0.7%
Student absenteeism:	4.5%
Students per teacher:	9.6
Parent friendliness:	①❷❸④❺❻
Teachers with advanced degrees:	45.2%
Average years' teaching experience:	18.7
Students in gifted program:	4 / 1.5%
Students in remedial education:	36.3%
Students held back a grade:	5.8%
Total suspensions, pct. in-school:	31 / 0.0%
Offenses:	violence: 32, drugs: *, other: 3
Eligible students, free or reduced lunch:	88.8%
Before / after school program:	No / Yes

Students at this school generally go on to:
Coan Middle

AJC GRADE: ★★★

Georgia Criterion-Referenced Competency Tests - Grade 4
Pct. of students at each level

- Read: Exceeds 24%, Meets 50%, Does not meet 26%
- Math: Exceeds *, Meets 58%, Does not meet 42%
- Lang: Exceeds 16%, Meets 55%, Does not meet 29%

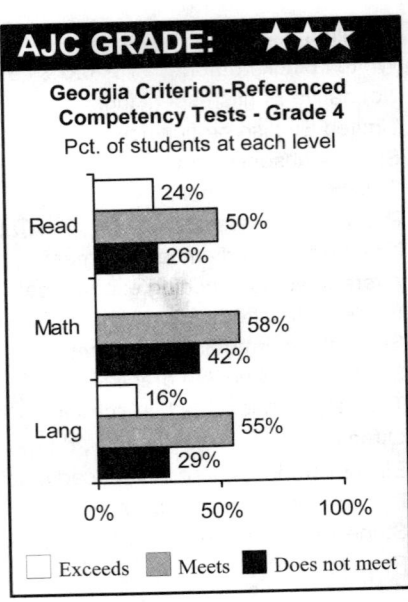

F.L. Stanton Elementary School

1625 Martin Luther King Jr Dr NW, Atlanta, GA 30314
404-752-0701 · Grades K - 5

Enrollment:	325
White / black / other:	0.3% / 99.4% / 0.3%
Not native English-speaking:	*
Limited English proficiency:	*
Student absenteeism:	4.1%
Students per teacher:	14.4
Parent friendliness:	①❷❸④❺❻
Teachers with advanced degrees:	42.3%
Average years' teaching experience:	15.1
Students in gifted program:	*
Students in remedial education:	18.5%
Students held back a grade:	5.2%
Total suspensions, pct. in-school:	8 / 0.0%
Offenses:	violence: 5, drugs: *, other: 3
Eligible students, free or reduced lunch:	99.7%
Before / after school program:	No / Yes

Students at this school generally go on to:
Turner Middle

AJC GRADE: ★★★★★

Georgia Criterion-Referenced Competency Tests - Grade 4
Pct. of students at each level

- Read: Exceeds 49%, Meets 30%, Does not meet 21%
- Math: Exceeds 6%, Meets 60%, Does not meet 34%
- Lang: Exceeds 15%, Meets 64%, Does not meet 21%

Atlanta City Elementary Schools

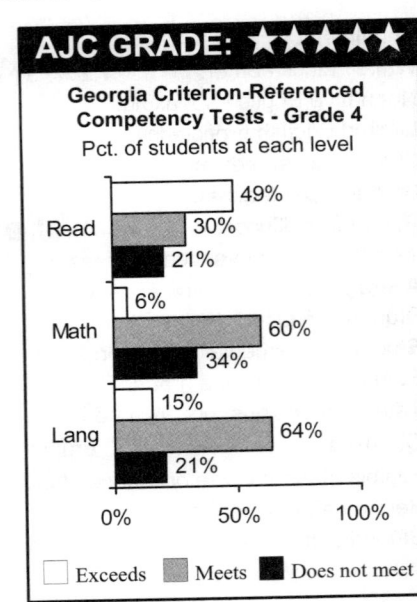

Fain Elementary School

101 Hemphill School Rd NW, Atlanta, GA 30331
404-699-4596 · Grades K - 5

Enrollment:	430
White / black / other:	0.2% / 94.4% / 5.3%
Not native English-speaking:	18 / 4.2%
Limited English proficiency:	20 / 4.7%
Student absenteeism:	3.6%
Students per teacher:	11.3
Parent friendliness:	① ❷ ❸ ④ ❺ ❻
Teachers with advanced degrees:	55.0%
Average years' teaching experience:	15.7
Students in gifted program:	12 / 2.8%
Students in remedial education:	27.0%
Students held back a grade:	9.1%
Total suspensions, pct. in-school:	25 / 0.0%
Offenses: violence: 10, drugs: *, other: 15	
Eligible students, free or reduced lunch:	98.1%
Before / after school program:	Yes / Yes

Students at this school generally go on to:
Usher Middle

AJC GRADE: ★★★

Georgia Criterion-Referenced Competency Tests - Grade 4
Pct. of students at each level

- Read: Exceeds 13%, Meets 53%, Does not meet 35%
- Math: Exceeds 9%, Meets 56%, Does not meet 35%
- Lang: Exceeds 15%, Meets 55%, Does not meet 31%

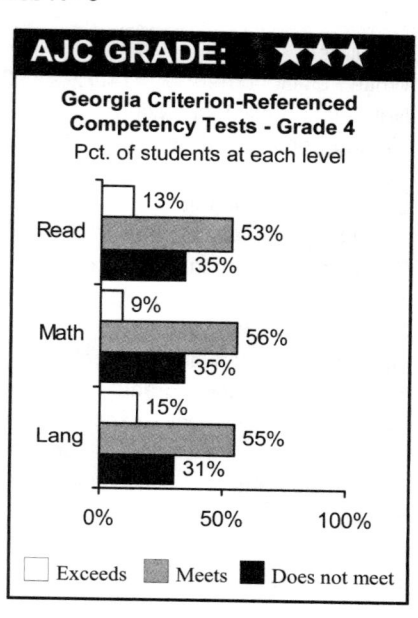

Fickett Elementary School

3935 Rux Rd SW, Atlanta, GA 30331
404-346-2516 · Grades K - 5

Enrollment:	745
White / black / other:	0.5% / 99.1% / 0.4%
Not native English-speaking:	*
Limited English proficiency:	*
Student absenteeism:	3.6%
Students per teacher:	13.5
Parent friendliness:	① ❷ ❸ ④ ⑤ ❻
Teachers with advanced degrees:	44.8%
Average years' teaching experience:	12.9
Students in gifted program:	50 / 6.7%
Students in remedial education:	18.8%
Students held back a grade:	3.0%
Total suspensions, pct. in-school:	73 / 0.0%
Offenses: violence: 58, drugs: *, other: 15	
Eligible students, free or reduced lunch:	90.6%
Before / after school program:	Yes / Yes

Students at this school generally go on to:
Bunche Middle

AJC GRADE: ★★★

Georgia Criterion-Referenced Competency Tests - Grade 4
Pct. of students at each level

- Read: Exceeds 17%, Meets 56%, Does not meet 26%
- Math: Exceeds 6%, Meets 47%, Does not meet 47%
- Lang: Exceeds 9%, Meets 74%, Does not meet 16%

Atlanta City Elementary Schools

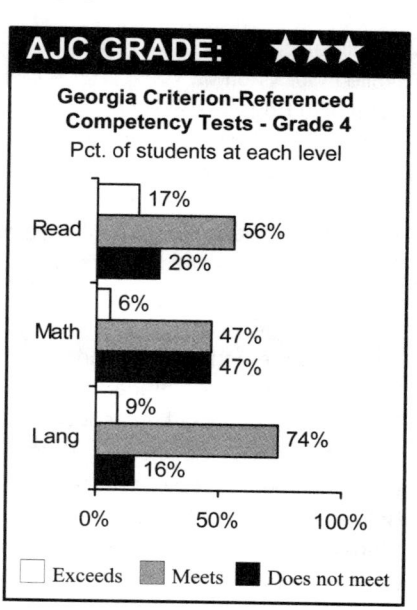

Garden Hills Elementary School

285 Sheridan Dr NE, Atlanta, GA 30305
404-842-3103 · Grades K - 5

Enrollment:	449
White / black / other:	14.9% / 23.2% / 61.9%
Not native English-speaking:	204 / 45.4%
Limited English proficiency:	233 / 51.9%
Student absenteeism:	4.9%
Students per teacher:	12.2
Parent friendliness:	①②❸④⑤❻
Teachers with advanced degrees:	53.8%
Average years' teaching experience:	13.0
Students in gifted program:	68 / 15.1%
Students in remedial education:	29.0%
Students held back a grade:	6.5%
Total suspensions, pct. in-school:	1 / 0.0%
Offenses:	violence: * , drugs: * , other: 1
Eligible students, free or reduced lunch:	73.4%
Before / after school program:	No / No

Students at this school generally go on to:
Sutton Middle

AJC GRADE: ★★★

Georgia Criterion-Referenced Competency Tests - Grade 4
Pct. of students at each level

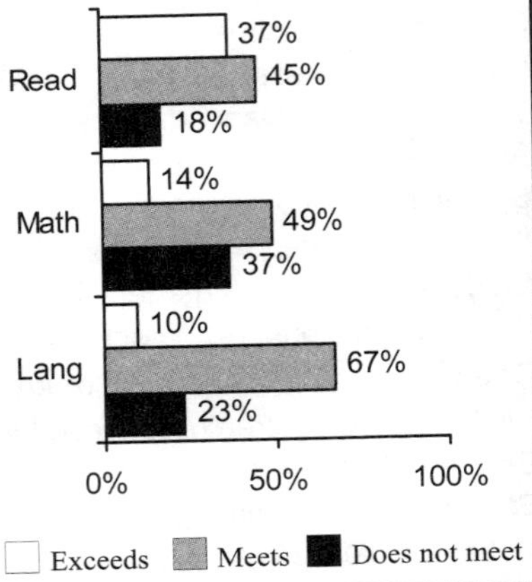

Read
37%
45%
18%
Math
14%
49%
37%
Lang
10%
67%
23%
0%
50%
100%
Exceeds
Meets
Does not meet

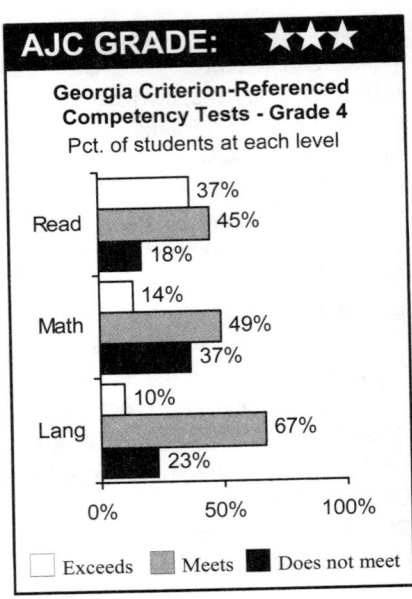

Gideons Elementary School

897 Welch St SW, Atlanta, GA 30310
404-752-0782 · Grades K - 5

Enrollment:	630
White / black / other:	1.1% / 94.3% / 4.6%
Not native English-speaking:	20 / 3.2%
Limited English proficiency:	25 / 4.0%
Student absenteeism:	4.4%
Students per teacher:	16.0
Parent friendliness:	①❷❸④⑤❻
Teachers with advanced degrees:	53.7%
Average years' teaching experience:	12.2
Students in gifted program:	1 / 0.2%
Students in remedial education:	15.6%
Students held back a grade:	1.7%
Total suspensions, pct. in-school:	*
Offenses:	violence: * , drugs: * , other: *
Eligible students, free or reduced lunch:	87.9%
Before / after school program:	Yes / Yes

Students at this school generally go on to:
Parks Middle

AJC GRADE: ★★★

Georgia Criterion-Referenced Competency Tests - Grade 4
Pct. of students at each level

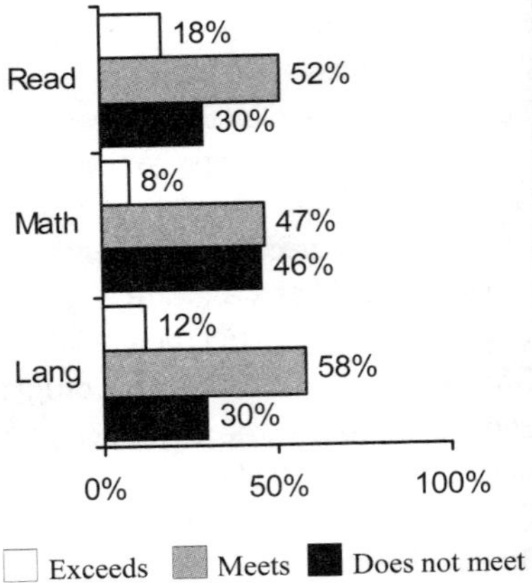

Read
18%
52%
30%
Math
8%
47%
46%
Lang
12%
58%
30%
0%
50%
100%
Exceeds
Meets
Does not meet

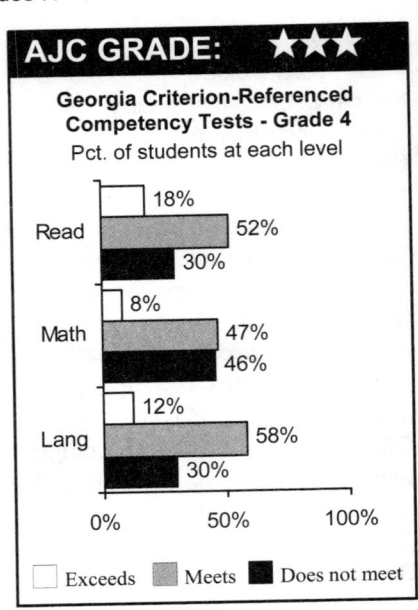

Grove Park Elementary School

20 Evelyn Way NW, Atlanta, GA 30318
404-792-5558 · Grades K - 5

Enrollment:	494
White / black / other:	0.0% / 99.6% / 0.4%
Not native English-speaking:	1 / 0.2%
Limited English proficiency:	1 / 0.2%
Student absenteeism:	3.7%
Students per teacher:	18.8
Parent friendliness:	① ❷ ❸ ④ ❺ ❻
Teachers with advanced degrees:	27.6%
Average years' teaching experience:	11.1
Students in gifted program:	4 / 0.8%
Students in remedial education:	25.6%
Students held back a grade:	9.7%
Total suspensions, pct. in-school:	18 / 55.6%
Offenses:	violence: 24, drugs: *, other: *
Eligible students, free or reduced lunch:	94.9%
Before / after school program:	No / Yes

Students at this school generally go on to:
West Fulton Middle

AJC GRADE: ★

Georgia Criterion-Referenced Competency Tests - Grade 4
Pct. of students at each level

- Read: Exceeds 5%, Meets 34%, Does not meet 61%
- Math: Exceeds —, Meets 21%, Does not meet 79%
- Lang: Exceeds 2%, Meets 37%, Does not meet 61%

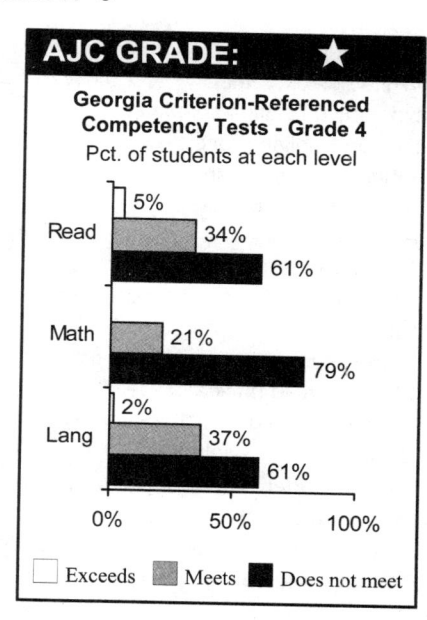

Heritage Academy

370 Blair Villa Dr SE, Atlanta, GA 30354
404-362-5052 · Grades K - 5

Enrollment:	423
White / black / other:	0.7% / 96.9% / 2.4%
Not native English-speaking:	*
Limited English proficiency:	7 / 1.7%
Student absenteeism:	5.5%
Students per teacher:	14.7
Parent friendliness:	① ❷ ❸ ④ ❺ ❻
Teachers with advanced degrees:	41.9%
Average years' teaching experience:	16.1
Students in gifted program:	*
Students in remedial education:	19.3%
Students held back a grade:	7.3%
Total suspensions, pct. in-school:	43 / 0.0%
Offenses:	violence: 20, drugs: 1, other: 80
Eligible students, free or reduced lunch:	91.3%
Before / after school program:	Yes / Yes

Students at this school generally go on to:
Crawford Long Middle

AJC GRADE: ★★

Georgia Criterion-Referenced Competency Tests - Grade 4
Pct. of students at each level

- Read: Exceeds 13%, Meets 43%, Does not meet 43%
- Math: Exceeds 3%, Meets 29%, Does not meet 68%
- Lang: Exceeds 6%, Meets 41%, Does not meet 53%

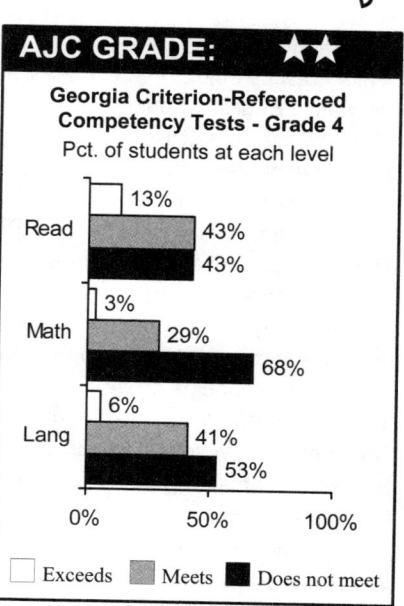

Herndon Elementary School

187 Wesley Ave NE, Atlanta, GA 30307
404-330-4127 · Grades K - 5

Enrollment:	498
White / black / other:	0.8% / 99.2% / 0.0%
Not native English-speaking:	*
Limited English proficiency:	*
Student absenteeism:	7.3%
Students per teacher:	12.7
Parent friendliness:	①❷❸❹❺❻
Teachers with advanced degrees:	42.9%
Average years' teaching experience:	12.3
Students in gifted program:	3 / 0.6%
Students in remedial education:	22.0%
Students held back a grade:	10.6%
Total suspensions, pct. in-school:	67 / 0.0%
Offenses:	violence: 32, drugs: *, other: 35
Eligible students, free or reduced lunch:	93.5%
Before / after school program:	No / Yes
Students at this school generally go on to:	
Kennedy Middle	

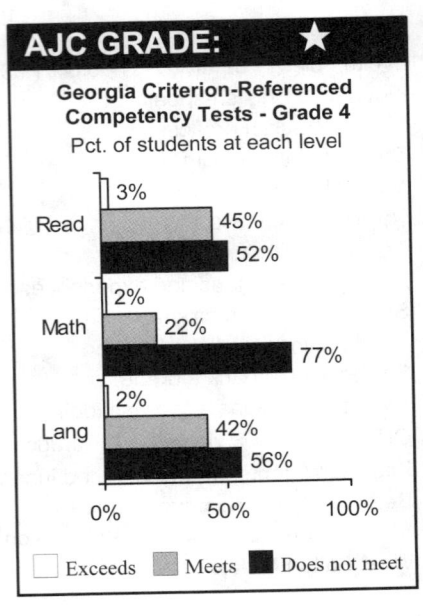

AJC GRADE: ★

Georgia Criterion-Referenced Competency Tests - Grade 4
Pct. of students at each level

- Read: Exceeds 3%, Meets 45%, Does not meet 52%
- Math: Exceeds 2%, Meets 22%, Does not meet 77%
- Lang: Exceeds 2%, Meets 42%, Does not meet 56%

Hill Elementary School

386 Pine St NE, Atlanta, GA 30308
404-853-4011 · Grades K - 5

Enrollment:	526
White / black / other:	0.2% / 99.6% / 0.2%
Not native English-speaking:	*
Limited English proficiency:	*
Student absenteeism:	4.6%
Students per teacher:	12.7
Parent friendliness:	①❷❸④❺❻
Teachers with advanced degrees:	37.8%
Average years' teaching experience:	8.6
Students in gifted program:	9 / 1.7%
Students in remedial education:	29.0%
Students held back a grade:	12.7%
Total suspensions, pct. in-school:	386 / 96.6%
Offenses:	violence: 53, drugs: *, other: 335
Eligible students, free or reduced lunch:	88.2%
Before / after school program:	Yes / Yes
Students at this school generally go on to:	
Walden Middle	

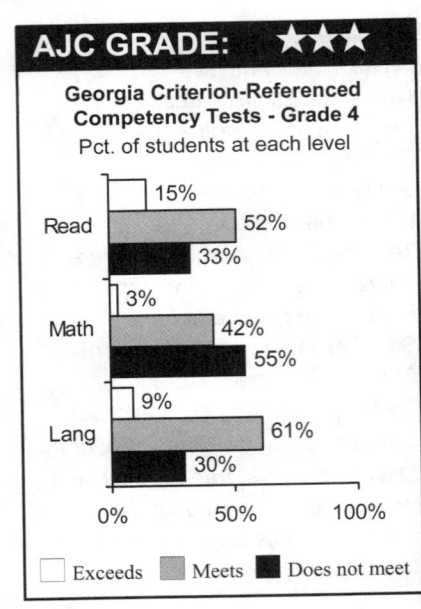

AJC GRADE: ★★★

Georgia Criterion-Referenced Competency Tests - Grade 4
Pct. of students at each level

- Read: Exceeds 15%, Meets 52%, Does not meet 33%
- Math: Exceeds 3%, Meets 42%, Does not meet 55%
- Lang: Exceeds 9%, Meets 61%, Does not meet 30%

The Atlanta Journal-Constitution / Page 32 — Atlanta City Elementary Schools

Hope Elementary School

1255 Capitol Ave SW, Atlanta, GA 30315
404-330-4131 · Grades K - 5

Enrollment: 288
White / black / other: 1.0% / 92.4% / 6.6%
Not native English-speaking: 18 / 6.3%
Limited English proficiency: 21 / 7.3%
Student absenteeism: 5.7%
Students per teacher: 9.5
Parent friendliness: ① ❷ ❸ ④ ❺ ❻
Teachers with advanced degrees: 45.5%
Average years' teaching experience: 12.1
Students in gifted program: 5 / 1.7%
Students in remedial education: 27.1%
Students held back a grade: 5.9%
Total suspensions, pct. in-school: 59 / 0.0%
Offenses: violence: 57, drugs: *, other: 2
Eligible students, free or reduced lunch: 90.6%
Before / after school program: Yes / Yes
Students at this school generally go on to:
Inman Middle

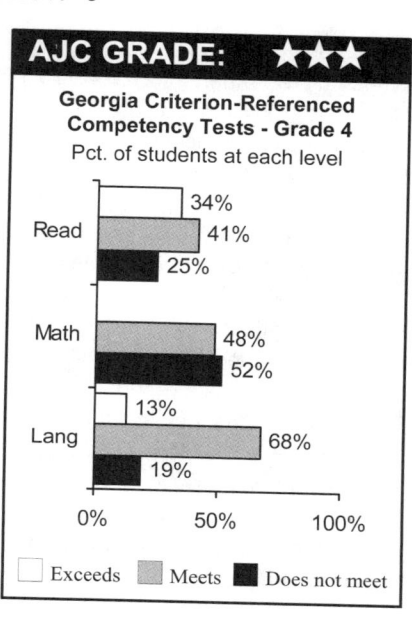

AJC GRADE: ★★★

Georgia Criterion-Referenced Competency Tests - Grade 4
Pct. of students at each level

Read: 34% / 41% / 25%
Math: — / 48% / 52%
Lang: 13% / 68% / 19%

☐ Exceeds ▨ Meets ■ Does not meet

Humphries Elementary School

3029 Humphries Dr SE, Atlanta, GA 30354
404-326-5054 · Grades K - 5

Enrollment: 619
White / black / other: 0.2% / 98.1% / 1.8%
Not native English-speaking: *
Limited English proficiency: *
Student absenteeism: 4.0%
Students per teacher: 14.9
Parent friendliness: ① ❷ ❸ ④ ❺ ❻
Teachers with advanced degrees: 40.0%
Average years' teaching experience: 10.2
Students in gifted program: 18 / 2.9%
Students in remedial education: 27.6%
Students held back a grade: 4.5%
Total suspensions, pct. in-school: *
Offenses: violence: *, drugs: *, other: *
Eligible students, free or reduced lunch: 80.5%
Before / after school program: Yes / Yes
Students at this school generally go on to:
Crawford Long Middle

AJC GRADE: ★★★

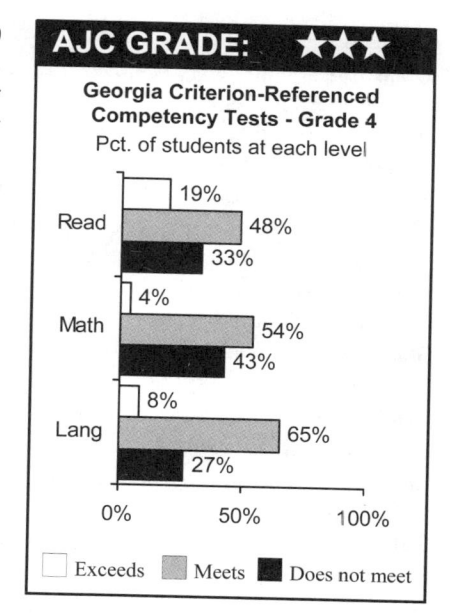

Georgia Criterion-Referenced Competency Tests - Grade 4
Pct. of students at each level

Read: 19% / 48% / 33%
Math: 4% / 54% / 43%
Lang: 8% / 65% / 27%

☐ Exceeds ▨ Meets ■ Does not meet

Atlanta City Elementary Schools

Hutchinson Elementary School

650 Cleveland Ave SW, Atlanta, GA 30315
404-669-2254 · Grades K - 5

Enrollment:	588
White / black / other:	1.7% / 75.2% / 23.1%
Not native English-speaking:	99 / 16.8%
Limited English proficiency:	117 / 19.9%
Student absenteeism:	4.3%
Students per teacher:	13.5
Parent friendliness:	① ❷ ❸ ④ ❺ ❻
Teachers with advanced degrees:	45.7%
Average years' teaching experience:	10.5
Students in gifted program:	4 / 0.7%
Students in remedial education:	15.1%
Students held back a grade:	3.6%
Total suspensions, pct. in-school:	*
Offenses: violence: *, drugs: *, other: *	
Eligible students, free or reduced lunch:	89.6%
Before / after school program:	Yes / Yes
Students at this school generally go on to: Crawford Long Middle	

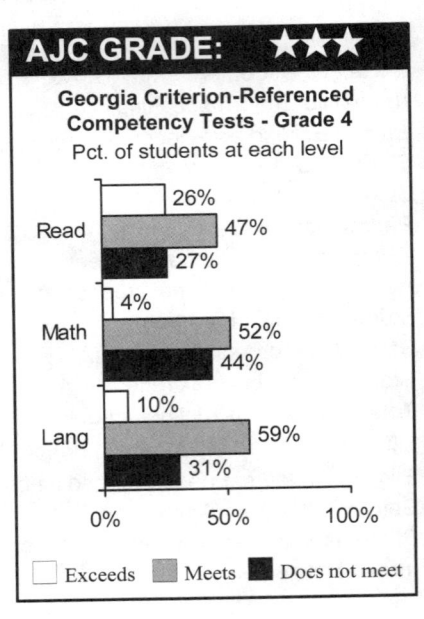

AJC GRADE: ★★★

Georgia Criterion-Referenced Competency Tests - Grade 4
Pct. of students at each level

Read: 26% / 47% / 27%
Math: 4% / 52% / 44%
Lang: 10% / 59% / 31%

☐ Exceeds ▨ Meets ■ Does not meet

Jackson Elementary School

1325 Mount Paran Rd NW, Atlanta, GA 30327
404-842-3100 · Grades K - 5

Enrollment:	573
White / black / other:	74.5% / 14.5% / 11.0%
Not native English-speaking:	27 / 4.7%
Limited English proficiency:	29 / 5.1%
Student absenteeism:	4.3%
Students per teacher:	13.9
Parent friendliness:	① ❷ ❸ ④ ❺ ❻
Teachers with advanced degrees:	35.6%
Average years' teaching experience:	10.4
Students in gifted program:	142 / 24.8%
Students in remedial education:	4.2%
Students held back a grade:	1.0%
Total suspensions, pct. in-school:	*
Offenses: violence: *, drugs: *, other: *	
Eligible students, free or reduced lunch:	25.5%
Before / after school program:	No / Yes
Students at this school generally go on to: Sutton Middle	

AJC GRADE: ★★★★★

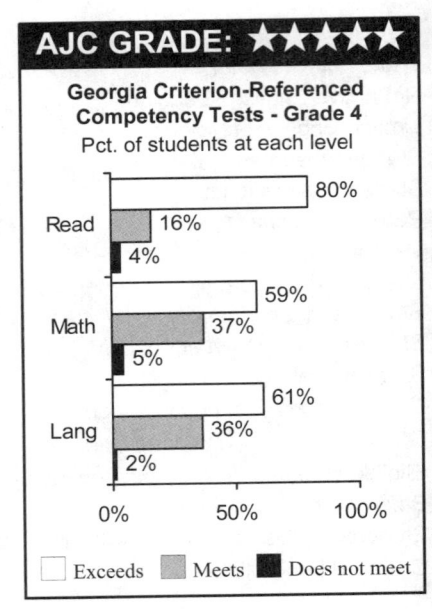

Georgia Criterion-Referenced Competency Tests - Grade 4
Pct. of students at each level

Read: 80% / 16% / 4%
Math: 59% / 37% / 5%
Lang: 61% / 36% / 2%

☐ Exceeds ▨ Meets ■ Does not meet

Atlanta City Elementary Schools

Jones Elementary School

1040 Fair St SW, Atlanta, GA 30314
404-752-0777 · Grades K - 5

Enrollment:	331
White / black / other:	0.0% / 99.4% / 0.6%
Not native English-speaking:	*
Limited English proficiency:	*
Student absenteeism:	3.6%
Students per teacher:	9.8
Parent friendliness:	① ❷ ❸ ④ ❺ ❻
Teachers with advanced degrees:	45.9%
Average years' teaching experience:	12.7
Students in gifted program:	5 / 1.5%
Students in remedial education:	27.6%
Students held back a grade:	9.1%
Total suspensions, pct. in-school:	*
Offenses:	violence: *, drugs: *, other: *
Eligible students, free or reduced lunch:	93.4%
Before / after school program:	No / Yes

Students at this school generally go on to:
Kennedy Middle

AJC GRADE: ★★★★

Georgia Criterion-Referenced Competency Tests - Grade 4
Pct. of students at each level

Read: Exceeds 30%, Meets 53%, Does not meet 18%
Math: Exceeds 3%, Meets 85%, Does not meet 13%
Lang: Exceeds 10%, Meets 80%, Does not meet 10%

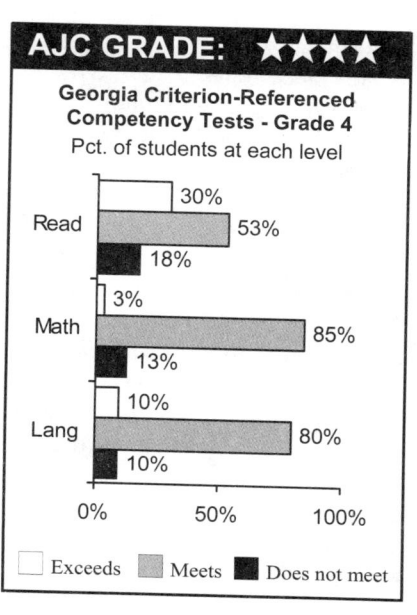

Kimberly Elementary School

3090 McMurray Dr SW, Atlanta, GA 30311
404-346-2519 · Grades K - 5

Enrollment:	634
White / black / other:	0.3% / 98.9% / 0.8%
Not native English-speaking:	*
Limited English proficiency:	*
Student absenteeism:	5.4%
Students per teacher:	13.4
Parent friendliness:	① ❷ ❸ ④ ❺ ❻
Teachers with advanced degrees:	46.9%
Average years' teaching experience:	15.9
Students in gifted program:	4 / 0.6%
Students in remedial education:	15.4%
Students held back a grade:	3.8%
Total suspensions, pct. in-school:	68 / 4.4%
Offenses:	violence: 35, drugs: *, other: 49
Eligible students, free or reduced lunch:	86.7%
Before / after school program:	Yes / Yes

Students at this school generally go on to:
Bunche Middle

AJC GRADE: ★★★

Georgia Criterion-Referenced Competency Tests - Grade 4
Pct. of students at each level

Read: Exceeds 21%, Meets 49%, Does not meet 30%
Math: Exceeds 5%, Meets 45%, Does not meet 50%
Lang: Exceeds 12%, Meets 62%, Does not meet 26%

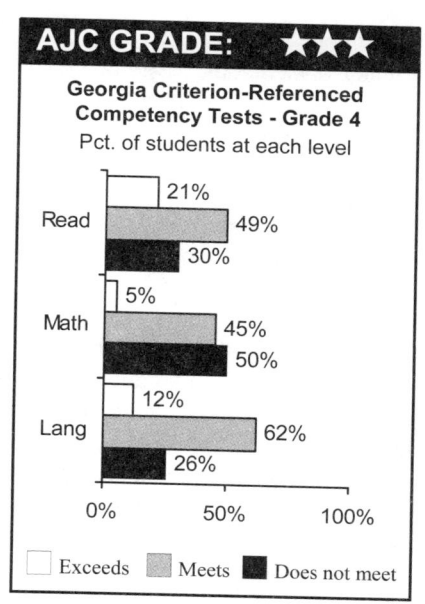

Lakewood Elementary School

335 Sawtell Ave SE, Atlanta, GA 30315
404-624-2026 · Grades K - 5

Enrollment:	328
White / black / other:	3.4% / 92.1% / 4.6%
Not native English-speaking:	5 / 1.5%
Limited English proficiency:	5 / 1.5%
Student absenteeism:	4.8%
Students per teacher:	12.7
Parent friendliness:	① ❷ ❸ ④ ⑤ ❻
Teachers with advanced degrees:	48.3%
Average years' teaching experience:	16.9
Students in gifted program:	4 / 1.2%
Students in remedial education:	*
Students held back a grade:	8.8%
Total suspensions, pct. in-school:	11 / 0.0%
Offenses:	violence: 45, drugs: *, other: 96
Eligible students, free or reduced lunch:	100.0%
Before / after school program:	No / Yes
Students at this school generally go on to:	Price Middle

AJC GRADE: ★★★

Georgia Criterion-Referenced Competency Tests - Grade 4
Pct. of students at each level

Read: 20% / 39% / 41%
Math: 6% / 37% / 58%
Lang: 11% / 44% / 44%

☐ Exceeds ▨ Meets ■ Does not meet

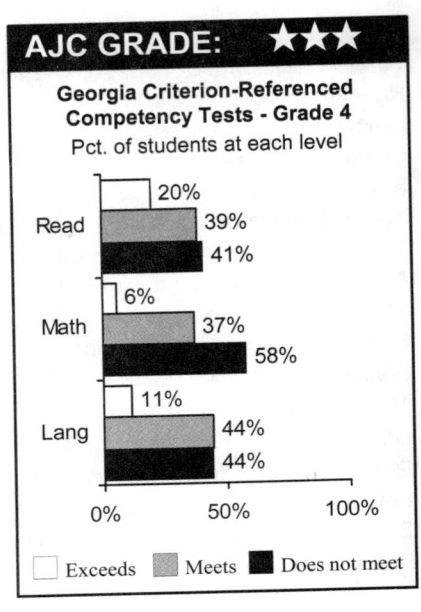

Lin Elementary School

586 Candler Park Dr NE, Atlanta, GA 30307
404-371-7158 · Grades K - 5

Enrollment:	430
White / black / other:	42.3% / 53.3% / 4.4%
Not native English-speaking:	12 / 2.8%
Limited English proficiency:	14 / 3.3%
Student absenteeism:	3.8%
Students per teacher:	13.3
Parent friendliness:	① ❷ ❸ ④ ⑤ ❻
Teachers with advanced degrees:	51.4%
Average years' teaching experience:	12.5
Students in gifted program:	60 / 14.0%
Students in remedial education:	24.5%
Students held back a grade:	2.1%
Total suspensions, pct. in-school:	7 / 0.0%
Offenses:	violence: 5, drugs: *, other: 6
Eligible students, free or reduced lunch:	61.6%
Before / after school program:	Yes / Yes
Students at this school generally go on to:	Inman Middle

AJC GRADE: ★★★★

Georgia Criterion-Referenced Competency Tests - Grade 4
Pct. of students at each level

Read: 47% / 32% / 22%
Math: 18% / 48% / 33%
Lang: 37% / 42% / 20%

☐ Exceeds ▨ Meets ■ Does not meet

Atlanta City Elementary Schools

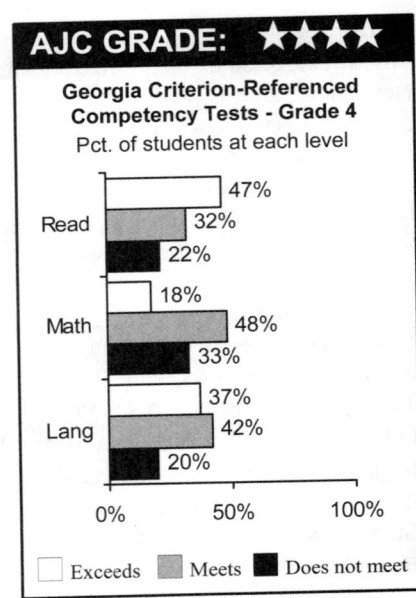

McGill Elementary School

760 Martin St SE, Atlanta, GA 30315
404-330-4157 · Grades K - 5

Enrollment:	283
White / black / other:	1.1% / 85.9% / 13.1%
Not native English-speaking:	17 / 6.0%
Limited English proficiency:	17 / 6.0%
Student absenteeism:	3.3%
Students per teacher:	13.5
Parent friendliness:	①❷❸④❺❻
Teachers with advanced degrees:	41.7%
Average years' teaching experience:	10.1
Students in gifted program:	7 / 2.5%
Students in remedial education:	49.5%
Students held back a grade:	4.9%
Total suspensions, pct. in-school:	9 / 22.2%
Offenses:	violence: 2, drugs: *, other: 11
Eligible students, free or reduced lunch:	90.7%
Before / after school program:	Yes / Yes

Students at this school generally go on to:
King Middle

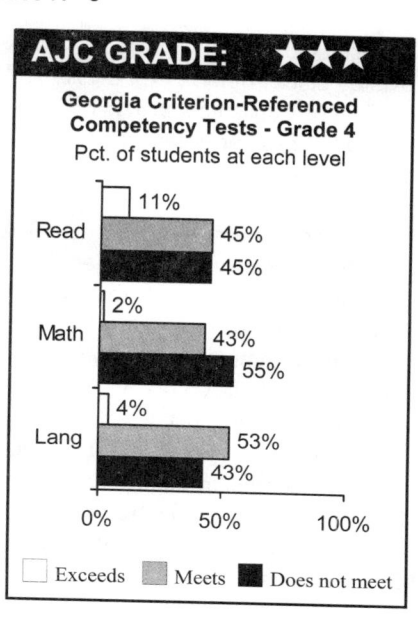

AJC GRADE: ★★★

Georgia Criterion-Referenced Competency Tests - Grade 4
Pct. of students at each level

- Read — Exceeds: 11%, Meets: 45%, Does not meet: 45%
- Math — Exceeds: 2%, Meets: 43%, Does not meet: 55%
- Lang — Exceeds: 4%, Meets: 53%, Does not meet: 43%

Miles Elementary School

2250 Perry Blvd NW, Atlanta, GA 30318
404-792-5774 · Grades K - 5

Enrollment:	451
White / black / other:	0.2% / 99.6% / 0.2%
Not native English-speaking:	*
Limited English proficiency:	*
Student absenteeism:	4.1%
Students per teacher:	12.8
Parent friendliness:	❶❷❸④❺❻
Teachers with advanced degrees:	34.2%
Average years' teaching experience:	10.1
Students in gifted program:	28 / 6.2%
Students in remedial education:	12.9%
Students held back a grade:	6.9%
Total suspensions, pct. in-school:	30 / 0.0%
Offenses:	violence: 7, drugs: *, other: 23
Eligible students, free or reduced lunch:	86.3%
Before / after school program:	No / Yes

Students at this school generally go on to:
Usher Middle

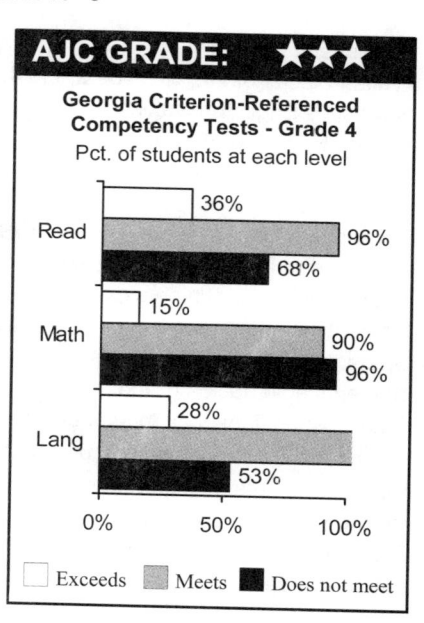

AJC GRADE: ★★★

Georgia Criterion-Referenced Competency Tests - Grade 4
Pct. of students at each level

- Read — Exceeds: 36%, Meets: 96%, Does not meet: 68%
- Math — Exceeds: 15%, Meets: 90%, Does not meet: 96%
- Lang — Exceeds: 28%, Meets: 53%, Does not meet: (not shown)

Atlanta City Elementary Schools

Mitchell Elementary School

2845 Margaret Mitchell Dr NW, Atlanta, GA 30327
404-350-2156 · Grades K - 5

Enrollment:	425
White / black / other:	6.1% / 79.3% / 14.6%
Not native English-speaking:	27 / 6.4%
Limited English proficiency:	44 / 10.4%
Student absenteeism:	4.4%
Students per teacher:	13.3
Parent friendliness:	①❷❸❹❺❻
Teachers with advanced degrees:	34.3%
Average years' teaching experience:	10.0
Students in gifted program:	8 / 1.9%
Students in remedial education:	30.0%
Students held back a grade:	4.5%
Total suspensions, pct. in-school:	25 / 0.0%
Offenses:	violence: 20, drugs: *, other: 5
Eligible students, free or reduced lunch:	86.2%
Before / after school program:	No / Yes
Students at this school generally go on to:	Sutton Middle

AJC GRADE: ★★★

Georgia Criterion-Referenced Competency Tests - Grade 4
Pct. of students at each level

- Read: Exceeds 16%, Meets 50%, Does not meet 34%
- Math: Exceeds 8%, Meets 25%, Does not meet 67%
- Lang: Exceeds 8%, Meets 53%, Does not meet 39%

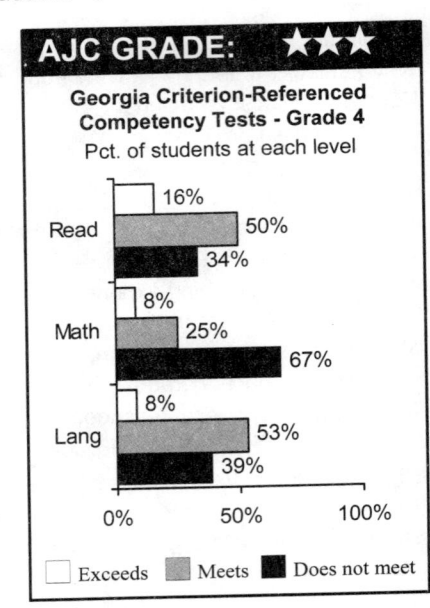

Morningside Elementary School

1053 E Rock Springs Rd NE, Atlanta, GA 30306
404-853-4024 · Grades K - 5

Enrollment:	746
White / black / other:	69.2% / 24.4% / 6.4%
Not native English-speaking:	9 / 1.2%
Limited English proficiency:	10 / 1.3%
Student absenteeism:	3.9%
Students per teacher:	14.6
Parent friendliness:	①❷❸④❺❻
Teachers with advanced degrees:	50.0%
Average years' teaching experience:	14.1
Students in gifted program:	233 / 31.2%
Students in remedial education:	5.3%
Students held back a grade:	2.4%
Total suspensions, pct. in-school:	24 / 0.0%
Offenses:	violence: 9, drugs: *, other: 22
Eligible students, free or reduced lunch:	17.8%
Before / after school program:	No / Yes
Students at this school generally go on to:	Inman Middle

AJC GRADE: ★★★★★

Georgia Criterion-Referenced Competency Tests - Grade 4
Pct. of students at each level

- Read: Exceeds 75%, Meets 22%, Does not meet 3%
- Math: Exceeds 43%, Meets 48%, Does not meet 9%
- Lang: Exceeds 54%, Meets 42%, Does not meet 4%

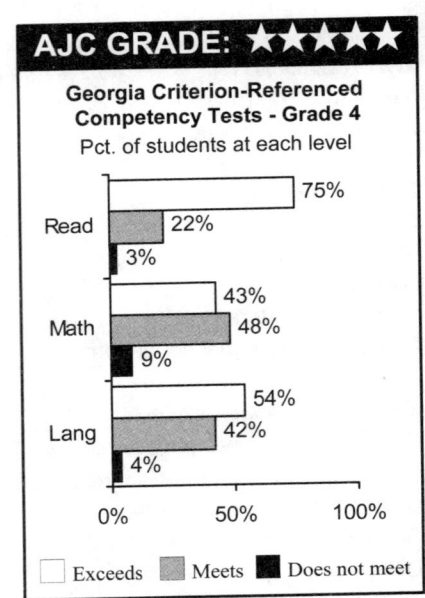

Oglethorpe Elementary School

601 Beckwith St SW, Atlanta, GA 30314
404-330-4170 · Grades K - 5

Enrollment:	376
White / black / other:	0.3% / 98.4% / 1.3%
Not native English-speaking:	*
Limited English proficiency:	*
Student absenteeism:	4.3%
Students per teacher:	15.2
Parent friendliness:	①❷❸④❺❻
Teachers with advanced degrees:	48.1%
Average years' teaching experience:	11.9
Students in gifted program:	11 / 2.9%
Students in remedial education:	16.9%
Students held back a grade:	8.5%
Total suspensions, pct. in-school:	53 / 0.0%
Offenses:	violence: 21, drugs: *, other: 32
Eligible students, free or reduced lunch:	86.7%
Before / after school program:	No / Yes

Students at this school generally go on to:
Brown, Inman, Kennedy, Young Middle

AJC GRADE: ★★★

Georgia Criterion-Referenced Competency Tests - Grade 4
Pct. of students at each level

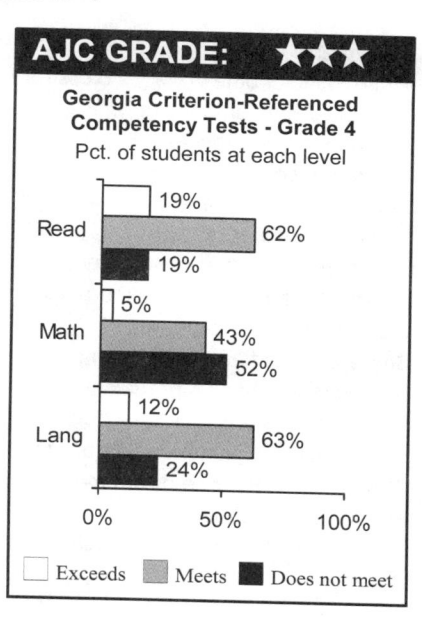

- Read: Exceeds 19%, Meets 62%, Does not meet 19%
- Math: Exceeds 5%, Meets 43%, Does not meet 52%
- Lang: Exceeds 12%, Meets 63%, Does not meet 24%

Perkerson Elementary School

2040 Brewer Blvd SW, Atlanta, GA 30310
404-756-3990 · Grades K - 5

Enrollment:	573
White / black / other:	2.1% / 94.4% / 3.5%
Not native English-speaking:	5 / 0.9%
Limited English proficiency:	10 / 1.7%
Student absenteeism:	5.2%
Students per teacher:	13.6
Parent friendliness:	①❷❸④❺❻
Teachers with advanced degrees:	43.5%
Average years' teaching experience:	9.3
Students in gifted program:	16 / 2.8%
Students in remedial education:	23.0%
Students held back a grade:	9.8%
Total suspensions, pct. in-school:	35 / 2.9%
Offenses:	violence: 18, drugs: *, other: 25
Eligible students, free or reduced lunch:	77.3%
Before / after school program:	No / Yes

Students at this school generally go on to:
Sylvan Hills Middle

AJC GRADE: ★★

Georgia Criterion-Referenced Competency Tests - Grade 4
Pct. of students at each level

- Read: Exceeds 16%, Meets 40%, Does not meet 44%
- Math: Exceeds 2%, Meets 35%, Does not meet 63%
- Lang: Exceeds 6%, Meets 53%, Does not meet 42%

Atlanta City Elementary Schools

Peterson Elementary School

1757 Mary Dell Dr SE, Atlanta, GA 30316
404-244-4312 · Grades K - 5

Enrollment:	248
White / black / other:	0.0% / 99.2% / 0.8%
Not native English-speaking:	*
Limited English proficiency:	1 / 0.4%
Student absenteeism:	3.9%
Students per teacher:	9.6
Parent friendliness:	① ② ❸ ④ ⑤ ❻
Teachers with advanced degrees:	36.7%
Average years' teaching experience:	14.4
Students in gifted program:	5 / 2.0%
Students in remedial education:	43.0%
Students held back a grade:	6.9%
Total suspensions, pct. in-school:	39 / 2.6%
Offenses:	violence: 36, drugs: *, other: 13
Eligible students, free or reduced lunch:	96.8%
Before / after school program:	No / Yes
Students at this school generally go on to:	
Coan Middle	

AJC GRADE: ★★★

Georgia Criterion-Referenced Competency Tests - Grade 4
Pct. of students at each level

Read: Exceeds 24%, Meets 50%, Does not meet 26%
Math: Exceeds 8%, Meets 53%, Does not meet 39%
Lang: Exceeds 11%, Meets 63%, Does not meet 26%

☐ Exceeds ▨ Meets ■ Does not meet

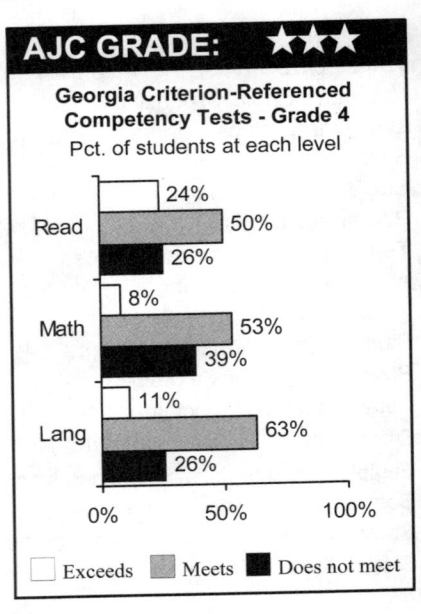

Peyton Forest Elementary School

301 Peyton Rd SW, Atlanta, GA 30311
404-699-4529 · Grades K - 5

Enrollment:	594
White / black / other:	0.3% / 96.8% / 2.9%
Not native English-speaking:	*
Limited English proficiency:	18 / 3.0%
Student absenteeism:	4.0%
Students per teacher:	12.4
Parent friendliness:	① ❷ ❸ ④ ⑤ ❻
Teachers with advanced degrees:	45.1%
Average years' teaching experience:	13.7
Students in gifted program:	51 / 8.6%
Students in remedial education:	22.6%
Students held back a grade:	3.2%
Total suspensions, pct. in-school:	9 / 0.0%
Offenses:	violence: 7, drugs: *, other: 11
Eligible students, free or reduced lunch:	69.0%
Before / after school program:	Yes / Yes
Students at this school generally go on to:	
Young Middle	

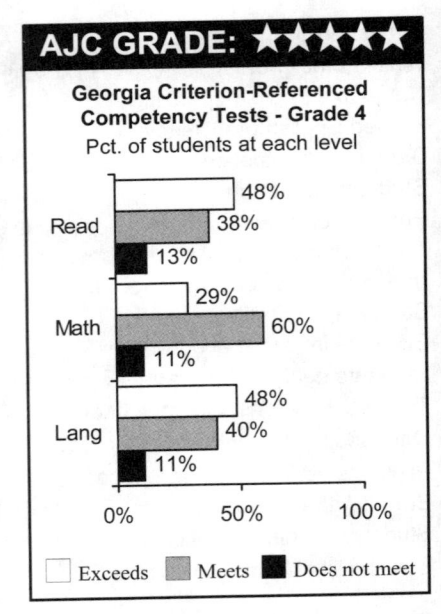

AJC GRADE: ★★★★★

Georgia Criterion-Referenced Competency Tests - Grade 4
Pct. of students at each level

Read: Exceeds 48%, Meets 38%, Does not meet 13%
Math: Exceeds 29%, Meets 60%, Does not meet 11%
Lang: Exceeds 48%, Meets 40%, Does not meet 11%

☐ Exceeds ▨ Meets ■ Does not meet

The Atlanta Journal-Constitution / Page 40

Atlanta City Elementary Schools

Pitts Elementary School

2250 Perry Blvd NW, Atlanta, GA 30318
404-792-5900 · Grades K - 5

Enrollment:	287
White / black / other:	2.8% / 92.3% / 4.9%
Not native English-speaking:	1 / 0.3%
Limited English proficiency:	9 / 3.1%
Student absenteeism:	4.4%
Students per teacher:	11.2
Parent friendliness:	① ❷ ❸ ④ ⑤ ❻
Teachers with advanced degrees:	39.3%
Average years' teaching experience:	6.6
Students in gifted program:	3 / 1.0%
Students in remedial education:	*
Students held back a grade:	5.6%
Total suspensions, pct. in-school:	26 / 0.0%
Offenses: violence: 26, drugs: *, other: 7	
Eligible students, free or reduced lunch:	96.5%
Before / after school program:	Yes / Yes

Students at this school generally go on to:
Sutton, West Fulton Middle

AJC GRADE: ★★★

Georgia Criterion-Referenced Competency Tests - Grade 4
Pct. of students at each level

- Read: Exceeds 36%, Meets 96%, Does not meet 68%
- Math: Exceeds 15%, Meets 90%, Does not meet 96%
- Lang: Exceeds 28%, Meets —, Does not meet 53%

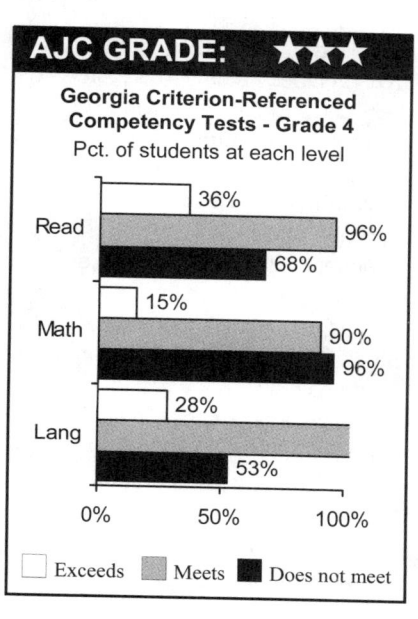

Ragsdale Elementary School

1114 Avon Ave SW, Atlanta, GA 30310
404-752-0719 · Grades K - 5

Enrollment:	401
White / black / other:	0.2% / 99.3% / 0.5%
Not native English-speaking:	*
Limited English proficiency:	*
Student absenteeism:	5.0%
Students per teacher:	14.6
Parent friendliness:	① ❷ ❸ ④ ❺ ❻
Teachers with advanced degrees:	40.0%
Average years' teaching experience:	12.8
Students in gifted program:	8 / 2.0%
Students in remedial education:	33.1%
Students held back a grade:	2.7%
Total suspensions, pct. in-school:	6 / 50.0%
Offenses: violence: 15, drugs: *, other: 17	
Eligible students, free or reduced lunch:	82.3%
Before / after school program:	Yes / Yes

Students at this school generally go on to:
Brown, Sylvan Hills Middle

AJC GRADE: ★★

Georgia Criterion-Referenced Competency Tests - Grade 4
Pct. of students at each level

- Read: Exceeds 10%, Meets 44%, Does not meet 45%
- Math: Exceeds 1%, Meets 26%, Does not meet 73%
- Lang: Exceeds 8%, Meets 39%, Does not meet 53%

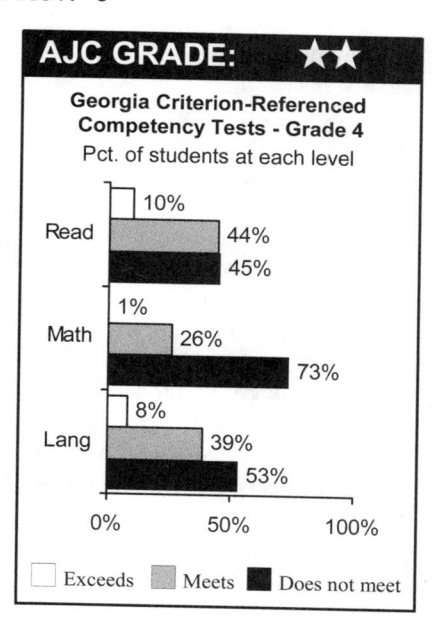

Rivers Elementary School

8 Peachtree Battle Ave NW, Atlanta, GA 30305
404-350-2150 · Grades K - 5

Enrollment:	359
White / black / other:	30.6% / 39.3% / 30.1%
Not native English-speaking:	57 / 15.9%
Limited English proficiency:	70 / 19.5%
Student absenteeism:	4.8%
Students per teacher:	10.2
Parent friendliness:	①❷❸❹❺❻
Teachers with advanced degrees:	48.7%
Average years' teaching experience:	15.1
Students in gifted program:	46 / 12.8%
Students in remedial education:	17.4%
Students held back a grade:	3.9%
Total suspensions, pct. in-school:	12 / 0.0%
Offenses:	violence: 4, drugs: *, other: 8
Eligible students, free or reduced lunch:	44.7%
Before / after school program:	No / No
Students at this school generally go on to:	
Sutton Middle	

AJC GRADE: ★★★

Georgia Criterion-Referenced Competency Tests - Grade 4
Pct. of students at each level

Read: 47% Exceeds / 35% Meets / 18% Does not meet
Math: 15% / 58% / 27%
Lang: 28% / 58% / 13%

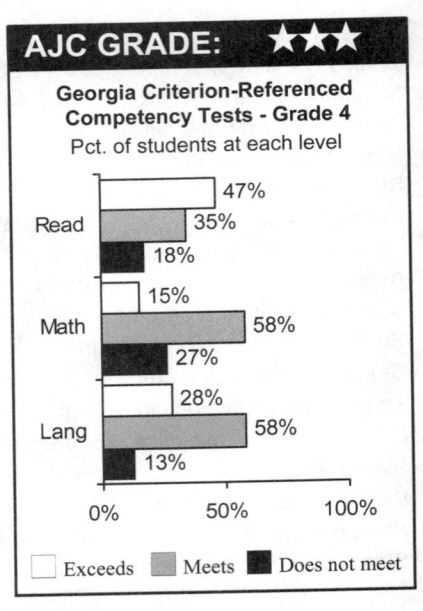

Rusk Elementary School

433 Peeples St SW, Atlanta, GA 30310
404-752-0717 · Grades K - 5

Enrollment:	413
White / black / other:	0.2% / 97.8% / 1.9%
Not native English-speaking:	*
Limited English proficiency:	2 / 0.5%
Student absenteeism:	5.2%
Students per teacher:	12.2
Parent friendliness:	①②❸❹❺❻
Teachers with advanced degrees:	42.9%
Average years' teaching experience:	14.3
Students in gifted program:	6 / 1.5%
Students in remedial education:	36.4%
Students held back a grade:	2.4%
Total suspensions, pct. in-school:	2 / 0.0%
Offenses:	violence: 1, drugs: *, other: 2
Eligible students, free or reduced lunch:	91.8%
Before / after school program:	Yes / Yes
Students at this school generally go on to:	
Brown, Turner Middle	

AJC GRADE: ★★

Georgia Criterion-Referenced Competency Tests - Grade 4
Pct. of students at each level

Read: 12% Exceeds / 38% Meets / 50% Does not meet
Math: 2% / 40% / 58%
Lang: 8% / 53% / 39%

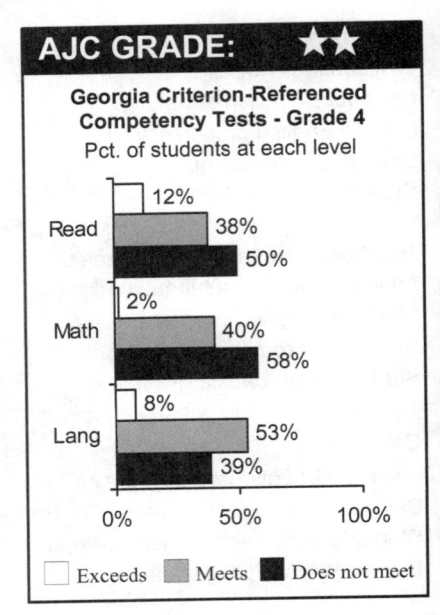

Scott Elementary School

1752 Hollywood Rd NW, Atlanta, GA 30318
404-792-5941 · Grades K - 5

Enrollment:	531
White / black / other:	0.0% / 97.7% / 2.3%
Not native English-speaking:	2 / 0.4%
Limited English proficiency:	2 / 0.4%
Student absenteeism:	7.3%
Students per teacher:	14.3
Parent friendliness:	①❷❸❹❺❻
Teachers with advanced degrees:	42.5%
Average years' teaching experience:	11.7
Students in gifted program:	5 / 0.9%
Students in remedial education:	33.3%
Students held back a grade:	5.1%
Total suspensions, pct. in-school:	35 / 2.9%
Offenses:	violence: 12, drugs: *, other: 23
Eligible students, free or reduced lunch:	83.8%
Before / after school program:	Yes / Yes

Students at this school generally go on to:
West Fulton Middle

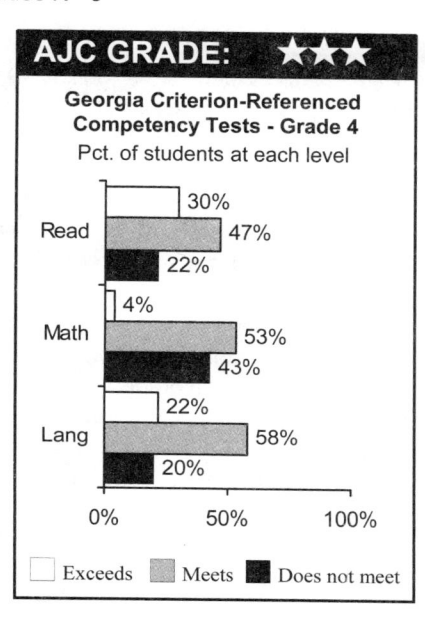

AJC GRADE: ★★★

Georgia Criterion-Referenced Competency Tests - Grade 4
Pct. of students at each level

Read: Exceeds 30%, Meets 47%, Does not meet 22%
Math: Exceeds 4%, Meets 53%, Does not meet 43%
Lang: Exceeds 22%, Meets 58%, Does not meet 20%

Slater Elementary School

1320 Pryor Rd SW, Atlanta, GA 30315
404-624-2097 · Grades K - 5

Enrollment:	405
White / black / other:	0.2% / 98.8% / 1.0%
Not native English-speaking:	*
Limited English proficiency:	3 / 0.7%
Student absenteeism:	6.1%
Students per teacher:	11.0
Parent friendliness:	①❷❸❹❺❻
Teachers with advanced degrees:	53.7%
Average years' teaching experience:	16.8
Students in gifted program:	1 / 0.2%
Students in remedial education:	42.8%
Students held back a grade:	5.9%
Total suspensions, pct. in-school:	337 / 37.4%
Offenses:	violence: 208, drugs: *, other: 455
Eligible students, free or reduced lunch:	96.3%
Before / after school program:	No / Yes

Students at this school generally go on to:
Price Middle

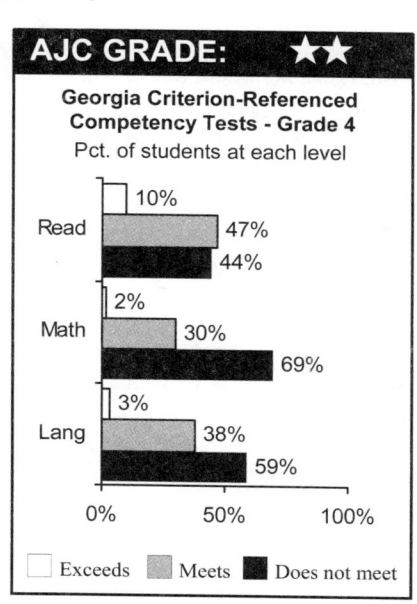

AJC GRADE: ★★

Georgia Criterion-Referenced Competency Tests - Grade 4
Pct. of students at each level

Read: Exceeds 10%, Meets 47%, Does not meet 44%
Math: Exceeds 2%, Meets 30%, Does not meet 69%
Lang: Exceeds 3%, Meets 38%, Does not meet 59%

Smith Elementary School 👍

370 Old Ivy Rd NE, Atlanta, GA 30342
404-842-3120 · Grades K - 5

Enrollment:	602
White / black / other:	83.2% / 9.6% / 7.1%
Not native English-speaking:	*
Limited English proficiency:	8 / 1.3%
Student absenteeism:	3.1%
Students per teacher:	14.5
Parent friendliness:	①❷❸④⑤❻
Teachers with advanced degrees:	45.7%
Average years' teaching experience:	9.2
Students in gifted program:	145 / 24.1%
Students in remedial education:	6.8%
Students held back a grade:	1.2%
Total suspensions, pct. in-school:	5 / 0.0%
Offenses:	violence: 1, drugs: * , other: 6
Eligible students, free or reduced lunch:	3.7%
Before / after school program:	No / Yes

Students at this school generally go on to:
Sutton Middle

AJC GRADE: ★★★★

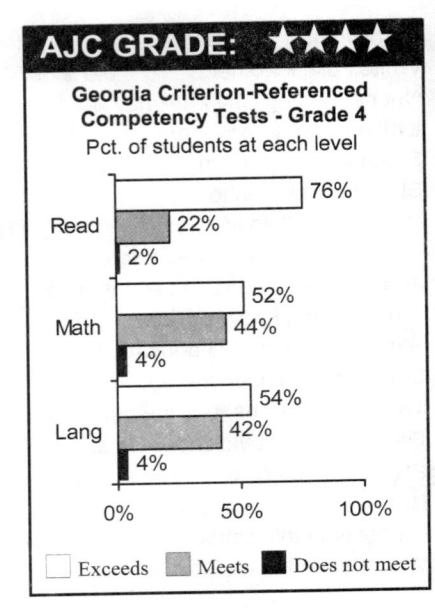

Georgia Criterion-Referenced Competency Tests - Grade 4
Pct. of students at each level

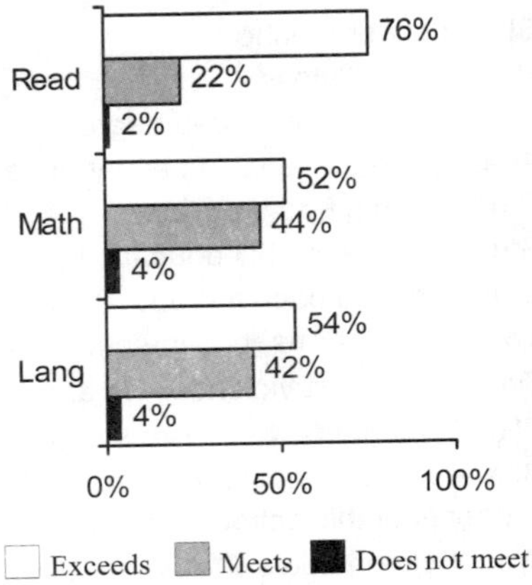
Read
76%
22%
2%
Math
52%
44%
4%
Lang
54%
42%
4%
0%
50%
100%
Exceeds
Meets
Does not meet

Thomasville Heights Elementary School

1820 Henry Thomas Dr SE, Atlanta, GA 30315
404-624-2077 · Grades K - 5

Enrollment:	606
White / black / other:	0.0% / 99.8% / 0.2%
Not native English-speaking:	2 / 0.3%
Limited English proficiency:	3 / 0.5%
Student absenteeism:	3.6%
Students per teacher:	13.7
Parent friendliness:	①❷❸❹❺❻
Teachers with advanced degrees:	39.1%
Average years' teaching experience:	14.1
Students in gifted program:	2 / 0.3%
Students in remedial education:	32.5%
Students held back a grade:	8.4%
Total suspensions, pct. in-school:	37 / 0.0%
Offenses:	violence: 26, drugs: * , other: 11
Eligible students, free or reduced lunch:	92.4%
Before / after school program:	Yes / Yes

Students at this school generally go on to:
L.J. Price Middle

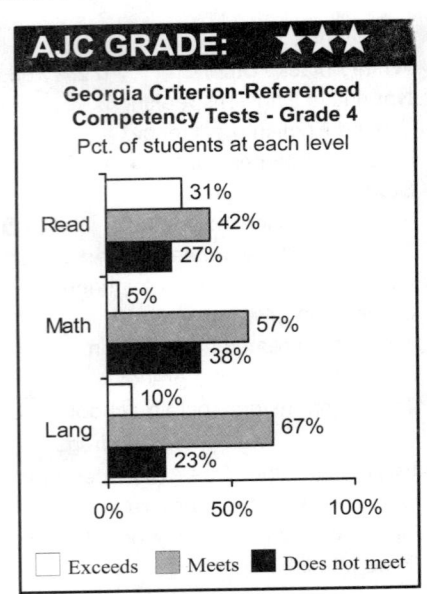

AJC GRADE: ★★★

Georgia Criterion-Referenced Competency Tests - Grade 4
Pct. of students at each level

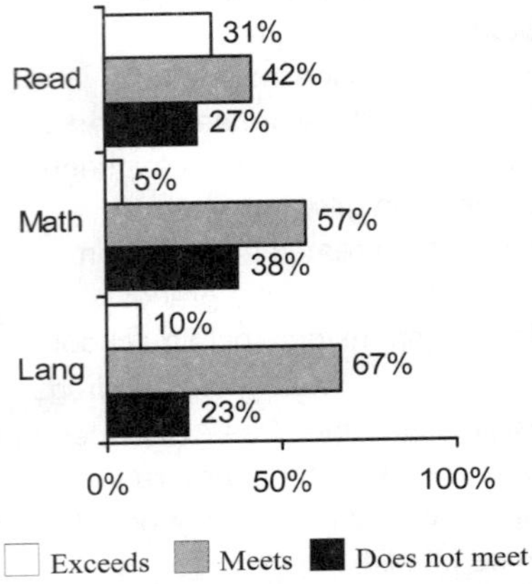
Read
31%
42%
27%
Math
5%
57%
38%
Lang
10%
67%
23%
0%
50%
100%
Exceeds
Meets
Does not meet

Toomer Elementary School

65 Rogers St NE, Atlanta, GA 30317
404-371-4876 · Grades K - 5

Enrollment:	385
White / black / other:	0.0% / 98.7% / 1.3%
Not native English-speaking:	*
Limited English proficiency:	6 / 1.6%
Student absenteeism:	4.2%
Students per teacher:	12.9
Parent friendliness:	① ❷ ❸ ❹ ❺ ❻
Teachers with advanced degrees:	65.6%
Average years' teaching experience:	14.2
Students in gifted program:	2 / 0.5%
Students in remedial education:	43.4%
Students held back a grade:	6.5%
Total suspensions, pct. in-school:	*
Offenses: violence: *, drugs: *, other: *	
Eligible students, free or reduced lunch:	99.8%
Before / after school program:	No / Yes

Students at this school generally go on to:
Coan Middle

AJC GRADE: ★★★

Georgia Criterion-Referenced Competency Tests - Grade 4
Pct. of students at each level

- Read: Exceeds 14%, Meets 41%, Does not meet 45%
- Math: Exceeds 2%, Meets 44%, Does not meet 55%
- Lang: Exceeds 6%, Meets 48%, Does not meet 45%

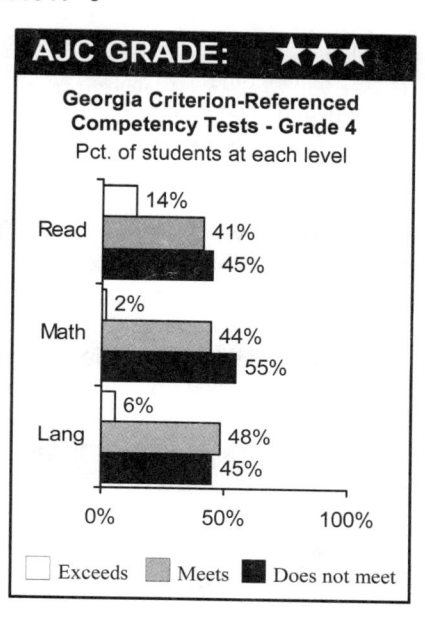

Towns Elementary School

760 Bolton Rd NW, Atlanta, GA 30331
404-699-4560 · Grades K - 5

Enrollment:	530
White / black / other:	0.2% / 97.4% / 2.5%
Not native English-speaking:	15 / 2.8%
Limited English proficiency:	20 / 3.8%
Student absenteeism:	4.9%
Students per teacher:	14.0
Parent friendliness:	① ❷ ❸ ❹ ❺ ❻
Teachers with advanced degrees:	50.0%
Average years' teaching experience:	10.4
Students in gifted program:	2 / 0.4%
Students in remedial education:	25.9%
Students held back a grade:	5.5%
Total suspensions, pct. in-school:	89 / 0.0%
Offenses: violence: 54, drugs: *, other: 35	
Eligible students, free or reduced lunch:	97.6%
Before / after school program:	No / Yes

Students at this school generally go on to:
Usher Middle

AJC GRADE: ★★★

Georgia Criterion-Referenced Competency Tests - Grade 4
Pct. of students at each level

- Read: Exceeds 15%, Meets 37%, Does not meet 48%
- Math: Exceeds 1%, Meets 44%, Does not meet 55%
- Lang: Exceeds 4%, Meets 61%, Does not meet 35%

Atlanta City Elementary Schools

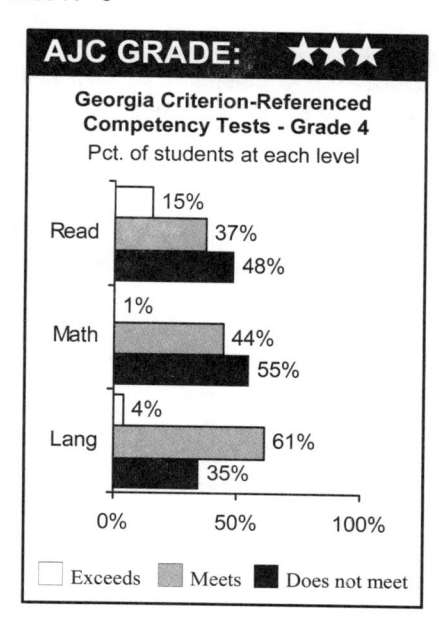

Venetian Hills Elementary School

1910 Venetian Dr SW, Atlanta, GA 30311
404-752-0736 · Grades K - 5

Enrollment:	497
White / black / other:	0.4% / 99.0% / 0.6%
Not native English-speaking:	*
Limited English proficiency:	4 / 0.8%
Student absenteeism:	3.5%
Students per teacher:	15.0
Parent friendliness:	① ❷ ❸ ❹ ❺ ❻
Teachers with advanced degrees:	51.4%
Average years' teaching experience:	9.6
Students in gifted program:	13 / 2.6%
Students in remedial education:	24.2%
Students held back a grade:	8.7%
Total suspensions, pct. in-school:	6 / 100.0%
Offenses: violence: 21, drugs: *, other: 22	
Eligible students, free or reduced lunch:	77.5%
Before / after school program:	No / Yes
Students at this school generally go on to: Sylvan Hills Middle	

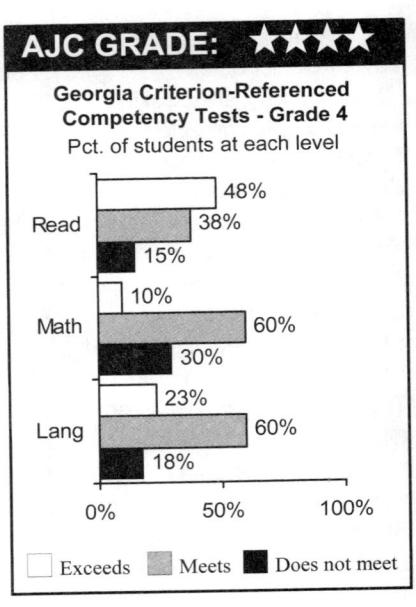

AJC GRADE: ★★★★

Georgia Criterion-Referenced Competency Tests - Grade 4
Pct. of students at each level

- Read: Exceeds 48%, Meets 38%, Does not meet 15%
- Math: Exceeds 10%, Meets 60%, Does not meet 30%
- Lang: Exceeds 23%, Meets 60%, Does not meet 18%

Waters Elementary School

660 McWilliams Rd SE, Atlanta, GA 30315
404-624-2034 · Grades K - 5

Enrollment:	555
White / black / other:	1.3% / 94.6% / 4.1%
Not native English-speaking:	10 / 1.8%
Limited English proficiency:	16 / 2.9%
Student absenteeism:	6.9%
Students per teacher:	12.7
Parent friendliness:	① ❷ ❸ ❹ ❺ ❻
Teachers with advanced degrees:	46.8%
Average years' teaching experience:	14.4
Students in gifted program:	3 / 0.5%
Students in remedial education:	33.3%
Students held back a grade:	6.1%
Total suspensions, pct. in-school:	1 / 0.0%
Offenses: violence: *, drugs: *, other: 1	
Eligible students, free or reduced lunch:	97.7%
Before / after school program:	Yes / Yes
Students at this school generally go on to: Price Middle	

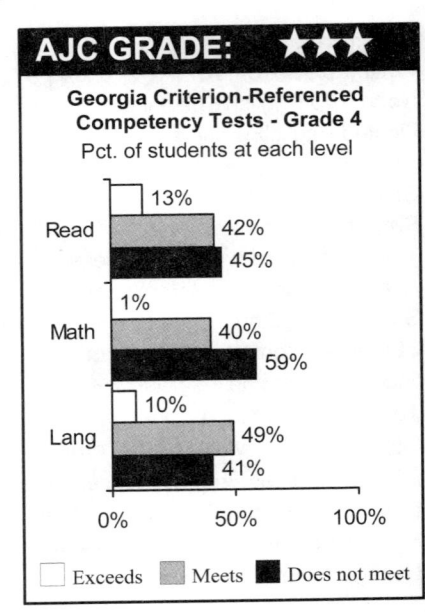

AJC GRADE: ★★★

Georgia Criterion-Referenced Competency Tests - Grade 4
Pct. of students at each level

- Read: Exceeds 13%, Meets 42%, Does not meet 45%
- Math: Exceeds 1%, Meets 40%, Does not meet 59%
- Lang: Exceeds 10%, Meets 49%, Does not meet 41%

West Manor Elementary School

570 Lynhurst Dr SW, Atlanta, GA 30311
404-699-4550 · Grades K - 5

Enrollment:	256
White / black / other:	0.0% / 100.0% / 0.0%
Not native English-speaking:	*
Limited English proficiency:	*
Student absenteeism:	3.0%
Students per teacher:	14.5
Parent friendliness:	①❷❸④⑤❻
Teachers with advanced degrees:	47.6%
Average years' teaching experience:	13.0
Students in gifted program:	37 / 14.5%
Students in remedial education:	31.8%
Students held back a grade:	2.0%
Total suspensions, pct. in-school:	3 / 0.0%
Offenses:	violence: * , drugs: * , other: 3
Eligible students, free or reduced lunch:	96.1%
Before / after school program:	No / Yes

Students at this school generally go on to:
Young Middle

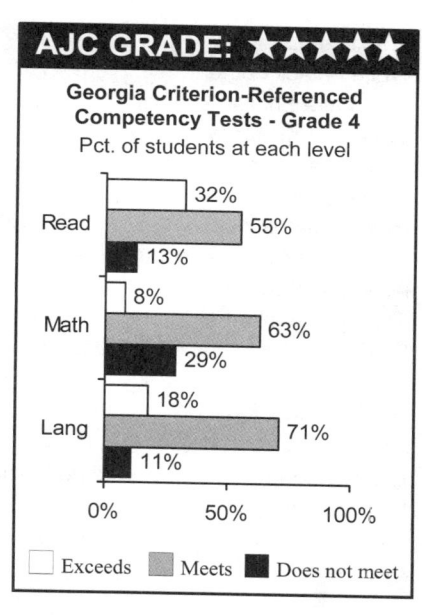

AJC GRADE: ★★★★★

Georgia Criterion-Referenced Competency Tests - Grade 4

Pct. of students at each level

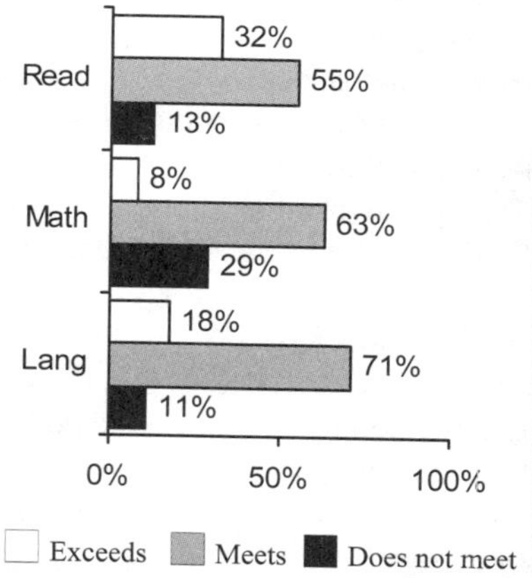
Read
32%
55%
13%
Math
8%
63%
29%
Lang
18%
71%
11%
0%
50%
100%
Exceeds
Meets
Does not meet

White Elementary School

1890 Detroit Ave NW, Atlanta, GA 30314
404-792-5956 · Grades K - 5

Enrollment:	419
White / black / other:	0.2% / 99.8% / 0.0%
Not native English-speaking:	*
Limited English proficiency:	4 / 1.0%
Student absenteeism:	6.0%
Students per teacher:	15.1
Parent friendliness:	①❷❸④❺❻
Teachers with advanced degrees:	23.3%
Average years' teaching experience:	10.9
Students in gifted program:	*
Students in remedial education:	34.1%
Students held back a grade:	7.2%
Total suspensions, pct. in-school:	1 / 0.0%
Offenses:	violence: * , drugs: * , other: 1
Eligible students, free or reduced lunch:	84.0%
Before / after school program:	Yes / Yes

Students at this school generally go on to:
Turner Middle

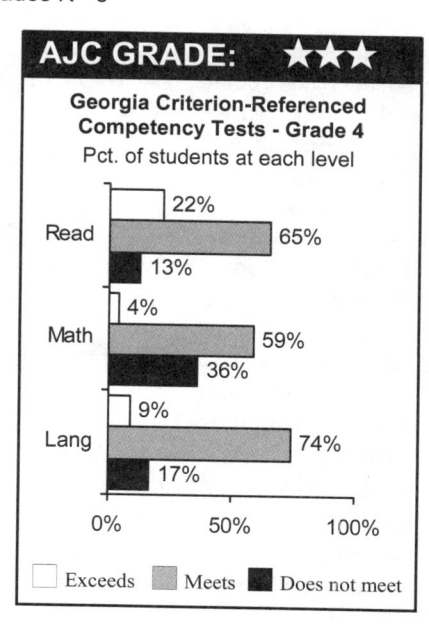

AJC GRADE: ★★★

Georgia Criterion-Referenced Competency Tests - Grade 4

Pct. of students at each level

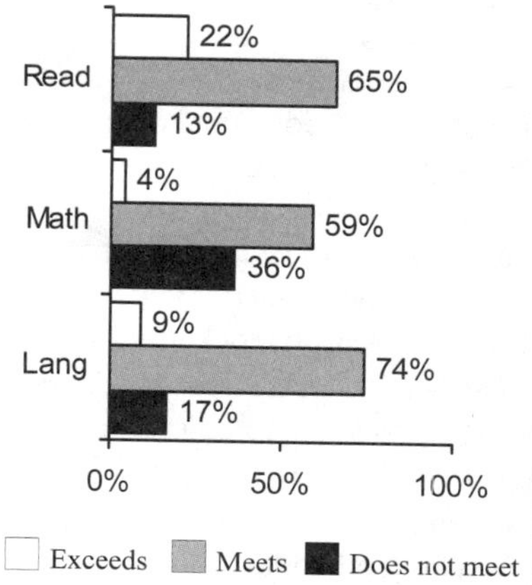
Read
22%
65%
13%
Math
4%
59%
36%
Lang
9%
74%
17%
0%
50%
100%
Exceeds
Meets
Does not meet

Whiteford Elementary School

35 Whitefoord Ave SE, Atlanta, GA 30317
404-330-4179 · Grades K - 5

Enrollment:	570
White / black / other:	0.0% / 99.6% / 0.4%
Not native English-speaking:	*
Limited English proficiency:	1 / 0.2%
Student absenteeism:	3.6%
Students per teacher:	14.1
Parent friendliness:	① ❷ ❸ ④ ⑤ ❻
Teachers with advanced degrees:	34.9%
Average years' teaching experience:	10.6
Students in gifted program:	3 / 0.5%
Students in remedial education:	22.6%
Students held back a grade:	6.7%
Total suspensions, pct. in-school:	19 / 0.0%
Offenses:	violence: 9, drugs: *, other: 10
Eligible students, free or reduced lunch:	98.4%
Before / after school program:	No / Yes
Students at this school generally go on to:	
Coan Middle	

AJC GRADE: ★★★★

Georgia Criterion-Referenced Competency Tests - Grade 4
Pct. of students at each level

Read: Exceeds 18%, Meets 59%, Does not meet 22%
Math: Exceeds 5%, Meets 54%, Does not meet 41%
Lang: Exceeds 18%, Meets 67%, Does not meet 14%

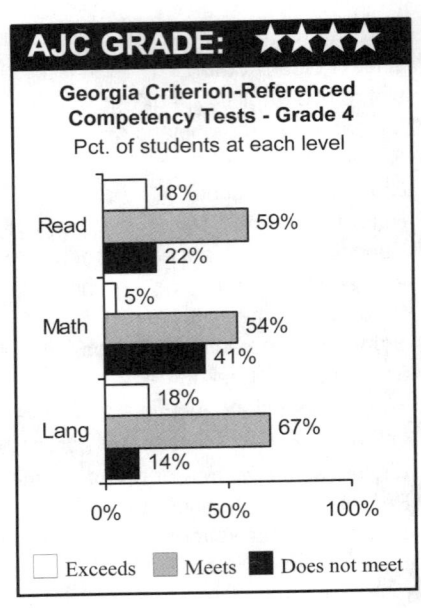

Williams Elementary School

1065 Wilkes Cir NW, Atlanta, GA 30318
404-792-5959 · Grades K - 5

Enrollment:	618
White / black / other:	0.5% / 99.4% / 0.2%
Not native English-speaking:	*
Limited English proficiency:	1 / 0.2%
Student absenteeism:	6.7%
Students per teacher:	15.0
Parent friendliness:	① ❷ ❸ ④ ❺ ❻
Teachers with advanced degrees:	44.2%
Average years' teaching experience:	12.0
Students in gifted program:	4 / 0.6%
Students in remedial education:	23.6%
Students held back a grade:	3.9%
Total suspensions, pct. in-school:	129 / 34.9%
Offenses:	violence: 25, drugs: *, other: 104
Eligible students, free or reduced lunch:	99.7%
Before / after school program:	No / No
Students at this school generally go on to:	
West Fulton Middle	

AJC GRADE: ★★

Georgia Criterion-Referenced Competency Tests - Grade 4
Pct. of students at each level

Read: Exceeds 4%, Meets 41%, Does not meet 54%
Math: Exceeds 0%, Meets 33%, Does not meet 67%
Lang: Exceeds 1%, Meets 53%, Does not meet 45%

Atlanta City Elementary Schools

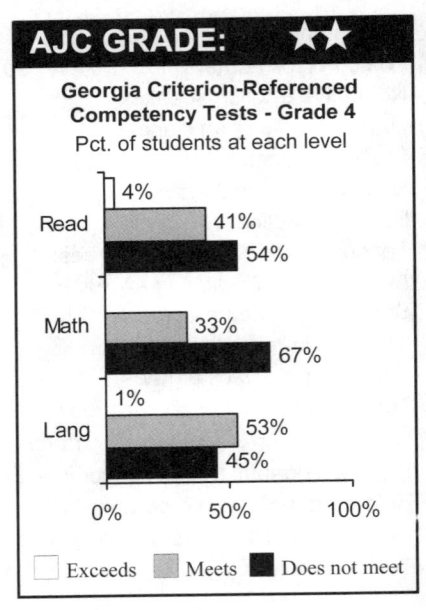

Woodson Elementary School

1605 Bankhead Ave NW, Atlanta, GA 30318
404-792-5963 · Grades K - 5

Enrollment: 532
White / black / other: 0.6% / 99.4% / 0.0%
Not native English-speaking: *
Limited English proficiency: 1 / 0.2%
Student absenteeism: 5.9%
Students per teacher: 16.1
Parent friendliness: ① ❷ ❸ ④ ❺ ❻
Teachers with advanced degrees: 41.7%
Average years' teaching experience: 13.1
Students in gifted program: 5 / 0.9%
Students in remedial education: 1.8%
Students held back a grade: 65.0%
Total suspensions, pct. in-school: 58 / 0.0%
Offenses: violence: 37, drugs: * , other: 43
Eligible students, free or reduced lunch: 92.4%
Before / after school program: No / Yes
Students at this school generally go on to:
West Fulton Middle

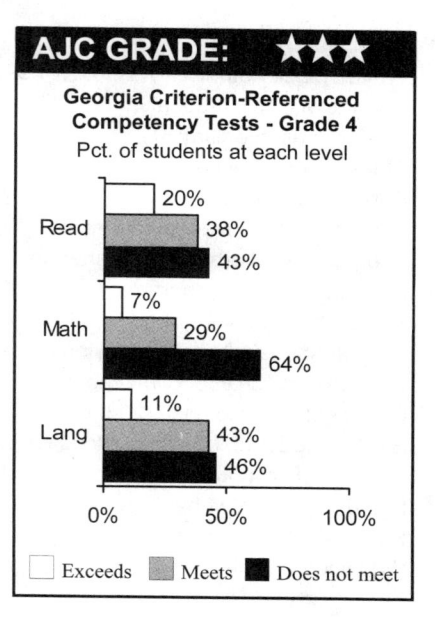

AJC GRADE: ★★★

Georgia Criterion-Referenced Competency Tests - Grade 4
Pct. of students at each level

Level	Exceeds	Meets	Does not meet
Read	20%	38%	43%
Math	7%	29%	64%
Lang	11%	43%	46%

Brown Middle School

765 Peeples St SW, Atlanta, GA 30310
404-756-6414 · Grades 6 - 8

Enrollment:	818
White / black / other:	0.0% / 99.4% / 0.6%
Not native English-speaking:	*
Student absenteeism:	4.6%
Students per teacher:	17.6
Parent friendliness:	❶❷❸④❺❻
Teachers with advanced degrees:	53.2%
Average years' teaching experience:	9.4
Students in gifted program:	156 / 19.1%
Students held back a grade:	2.0%
Total suspensions and expulsions:	192
Suspensions only, pct. in-school:	192 / 4.7%
Offenses: violence: 204, drugs: *, other: 10	
Eligible students, free or reduced lunch:	75.6%
Number of dropouts:	*
Pct. 8th-graders w/ basic computer skills:	98.0%
Students at this school generally go on to: Washington High	

AJC GRADE: ★★★

Georgia Criterion-Referenced Competency Tests - Grades 6, 8
Pct. of students at each level

	Lang 6	Math 6	Read 6
Exceeds	10	6	27
Meets	52	55	45
Does not meet	38	39	27

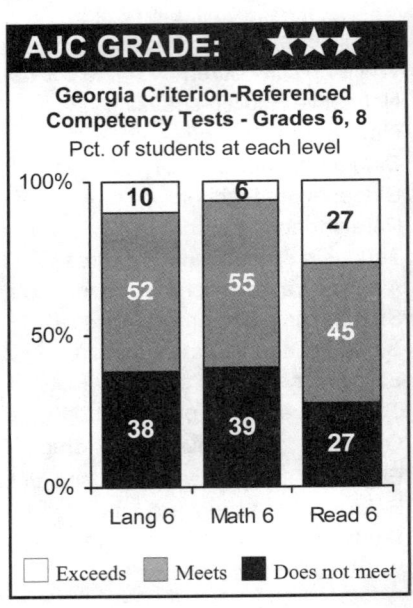

Bunche Middle School

1925 Niskey Lake Rd SW, Atlanta, GA 30331
404-346-2503 · Grades 6 - 8

Enrollment:	849
White / black / other:	0.4% / 99.4% / 0.2%
Not native English-speaking:	1 / 0.1%
Student absenteeism:	7.5%
Students per teacher:	16.2
Parent friendliness:	❶❷❸④❺❻
Teachers with advanced degrees:	58.5%
Average years' teaching experience:	10.9
Students in gifted program:	50 / 5.9%
Students held back a grade:	0.8%
Total suspensions and expulsions:	493
Suspensions only, pct. in-school:	493 / 7.9%
Offenses: violence: 120, drugs: *, other: 379	
Eligible students, free or reduced lunch:	75.1%
Number of dropouts:	2 / 0.2%
Pct. 8th-graders w/ basic computer skills:	100.0%
Students at this school generally go on to: Therrell High	

AJC GRADE: ★★★

Georgia Criterion-Referenced Competency Tests - Grades 6, 8
Pct. of students at each level

	Lang 6	Lang 8	Math 6	Math 8	Read 6	Read 8
Exceeds	8	15	15	6	20	45
Meets	41	49	56	43	50	37
Does not meet	50	37	29	51	29	18

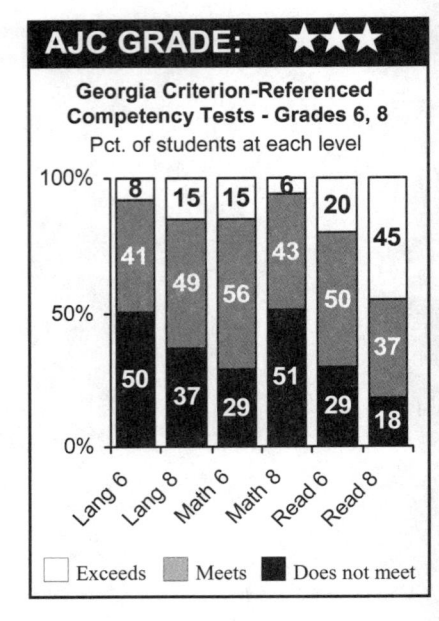

Coan Middle School

1550 Hosea L Williams Dr NE, Atlanta, GA 30317
404-371-4854 · Grades 6 - 8

Enrollment:	755
White / black / other:	0.4% / 99.5% / 0.1%
Not native English-speaking:	*
Student absenteeism:	7.5%
Students per teacher:	16.2
Parent friendliness:	❶❷❸④⑤❻
Teachers with advanced degrees:	42.9%
Average years' teaching experience:	12.5
Students in gifted program:	19 / 2.5%
Students held back a grade:	1.7%
Total suspensions and expulsions:	579
Suspensions only, pct. in-school:	577 / 38.5%
Offenses: violence: 241, drugs: 2, other: 346	
Eligible students, free or reduced lunch:	93.0%
Number of dropouts:	1 / 0.1%
Pct. 8th-graders w/ basic computer skills:	100.0%
Students at this school generally go on to: Crim High	

AJC GRADE: ★★★

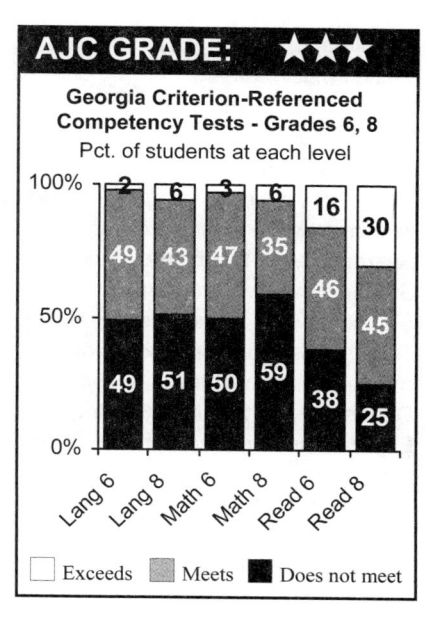

Georgia Criterion-Referenced Competency Tests - Grades 6, 8
Pct. of students at each level

	Lang 6	Lang 8	Math 6	Math 8	Read 6	Read 8
Exceeds	2	6	3	6	16	30
Meets	49	43	47	35	46	45
Does not meet	49	51	50	59	38	25

Inman Middle School

774 Virginia Ave NE, Atlanta, GA 30306
404-853-4017 · Grades 6 - 8

Enrollment:	696
White / black / other:	40.4% / 55.6% / 4.0%
Not native English-speaking:	*
Student absenteeism:	3.6%
Students per teacher:	15.3
Parent friendliness:	①❷❸④❺❻
Teachers with advanced degrees:	51.1%
Average years' teaching experience:	11.5
Students in gifted program:	253 / 36.4%
Students held back a grade:	1.9%
Total suspensions and expulsions:	516
Suspensions only, pct. in-school:	515 / 85.2%
Offenses: violence: 63, drugs: 1, other: 454	
Eligible students, free or reduced lunch:	58.6%
Number of dropouts:	*
Pct. 8th-graders w/ basic computer skills:	*
Students at this school generally go on to: Grady High	

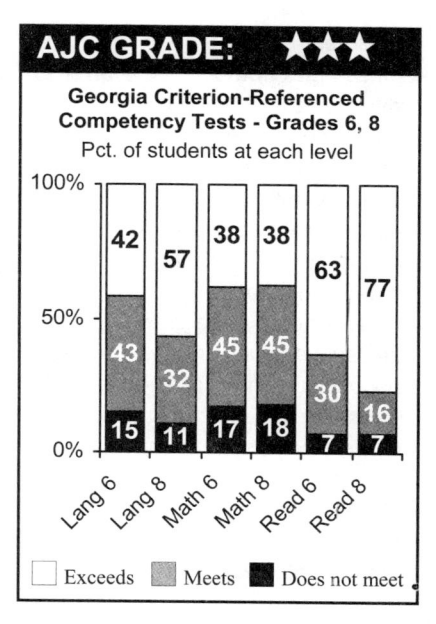

AJC GRADE: ★★★

Georgia Criterion-Referenced Competency Tests - Grades 6, 8
Pct. of students at each level

	Lang 6	Lang 8	Math 6	Math 8	Read 6	Read 8
Exceeds	42	57	38	38	63	77
Meets	43	32	45	45	30	16
Does not meet	15	11	17	18	7	7

Atlanta City Middle Schools

Kennedy Middle School

225 James P Brawley Dr NW, Atlanta, GA 30314
404-330-4140 · Grades 6 - 8

Enrollment:	720
White / black / other:	0.3% / 99.4% / 0.3%
Not native English-speaking:	*
Student absenteeism:	8.9%
Students per teacher:	18.0
Parent friendliness:	❶❷❸④❺❻
Teachers with advanced degrees:	52.4%
Average years' teaching experience:	14.8
Students in gifted program:	15 / 2.1%
Students held back a grade:	7.2%
Total suspensions and expulsions:	541
Suspensions only, pct. in-school:	539 / 10.9%
Offenses: violence: 67, drugs: *, other: 483	
Eligible students, free or reduced lunch:	75.5%
Number of dropouts:	17 / 1.8%
Pct. 8th-graders w/ basic computer skills:	93.0%
Students at this school generally go on to:	
Washington High	

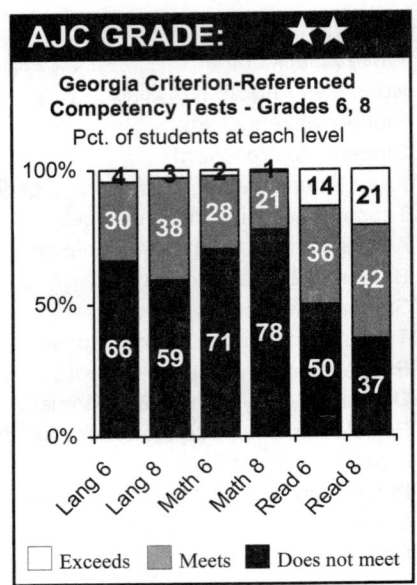

AJC GRADE: ★★

Georgia Criterion-Referenced Competency Tests - Grades 6, 8
Pct. of students at each level

	Lang 6	Lang 8	Math 6	Math 8	Read 6	Read 8
Exceeds	4	3	2	1	14	21
Meets	30	38	28	21	36	42
Does not meet	66	59	71	78	50	37

Long Middle School

3200 Latona Dr SW, Atlanta, GA 30354
404-669-2257 · Grades 6 - 8

Enrollment:	898
White / black / other:	2.7% / 91.0% / 6.3%
Not native English-speaking:	34 / 3.8%
Student absenteeism:	9.6%
Students per teacher:	19.3
Parent friendliness:	❶❷❸④❺❻
Teachers with advanced degrees:	43.8%
Average years' teaching experience:	12.9
Students in gifted program:	24 / 2.7%
Students held back a grade:	2.2%
Total suspensions and expulsions:	1,682
Suspensions only, pct. in-school:	1,677 / 33.1%
Offenses: violence: 692, drugs: 18, other: 1,407	
Eligible students, free or reduced lunch:	86.6%
Number of dropouts:	1 / 0.1%
Pct. 8th-graders w/ basic computer skills:	100.0%
Students at this school generally go on to:	
South Atlanta High	

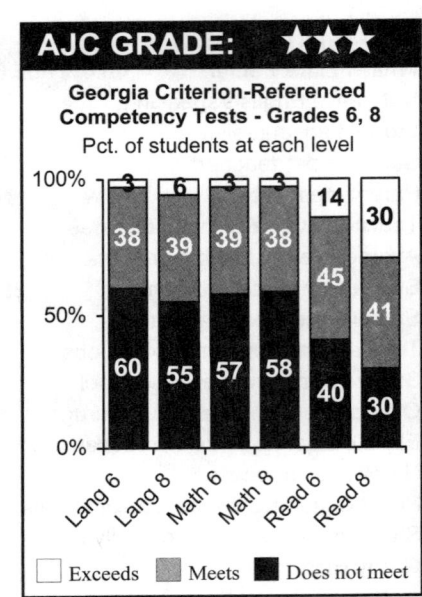

AJC GRADE: ★★★

Georgia Criterion-Referenced Competency Tests - Grades 6, 8
Pct. of students at each level

	Lang 6	Lang 8	Math 6	Math 8	Read 6	Read 8
Exceeds	3	6	3	3	14	30
Meets	38	39	39	38	45	41
Does not meet	60	55	57	58	40	30

Atlanta City Middle Schools

Martin Luther King Jr. Middle School

1820 Mary Dell Dr SE, Atlanta, GA 30316
404-330-4149 · Grades 6 - 8

Enrollment:	826
White / black / other:	2.8% / 85.5% / 11.7%
Not native English-speaking:	14 / 1.7%
Student absenteeism:	8.7%
Students per teacher:	16.0
Parent friendliness:	❶❷❸④❺❻
Teachers with advanced degrees:	58.9%
Average years' teaching experience:	15.3
Students in gifted program:	21 / 2.5%
Students held back a grade:	2.8%
Total suspensions and expulsions:	423
Suspensions only, pct. in-school:	418 / 53.6%
Offenses:	violence: 93, drugs: 2, other: 340
Eligible students, free or reduced lunch:	86.8%
Number of dropouts:	*
Pct. 8th-graders w/ basic computer skills:	100.0%

Students at this school generally go on to:
Southside High

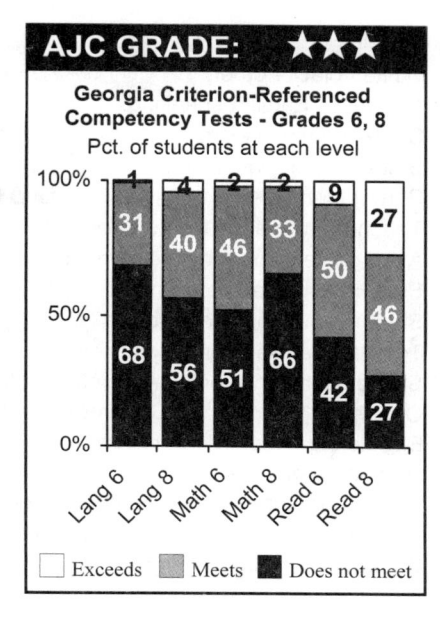

AJC GRADE: ★★★

Georgia Criterion-Referenced Competency Tests - Grades 6, 8
Pct. of students at each level

	Lang 6	Lang 8	Math 6	Math 8	Read 6	Read 8
Exceeds	1	4	2	2	9	27
Meets	31	40	46	33	50	46
Does not meet	68	56	51	66	42	27

Parks Middle School

1090 Windsor St SW, Atlanta, GA 30310
404-752-0742 · Grades 6 - 8

Enrollment:	595
White / black / other:	0.7% / 94.6% / 4.7%
Not native English-speaking:	5 / 0.8%
Student absenteeism:	9.2%
Students per teacher:	18.0
Parent friendliness:	❶❷❸④❺❻
Teachers with advanced degrees:	48.6%
Average years' teaching experience:	9.3
Students in gifted program:	11 / 1.8%
Students held back a grade:	0.8%
Total suspensions and expulsions:	11
Suspensions only, pct. in-school:	11 / 0.0%
Offenses:	violence: 10, drugs: 2, other: 10
Eligible students, free or reduced lunch:	93.8%
Number of dropouts:	3 / 0.4%
Pct. 8th-graders w/ basic computer skills:	100.0%

Students at this school generally go on to:
Carver, Washington High

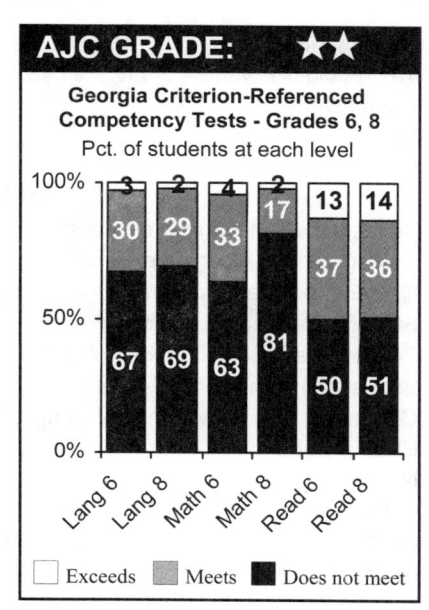

AJC GRADE: ★★

Georgia Criterion-Referenced Competency Tests - Grades 6, 8
Pct. of students at each level

	Lang 6	Lang 8	Math 6	Math 8	Read 6	Read 8
Exceeds	3	2	4	2	13	14
Meets	30	29	33	17	37	36
Does not meet	67	69	63	81	50	51

Atlanta City Middle Schools

Price Middle School

1670 Benjamin Weldon Bickers Dr SE, Atlanta, GA 30315
404-624-2028 · Grades 6 - 8

Enrollment:	890
White / black / other:	1.5% / 95.7% / 2.8%
Not native English-speaking:	17 / 1.9%
Student absenteeism:	13.4%
Students per teacher:	19.8
Parent friendliness:	❶❷❸④❺❻
Teachers with advanced degrees:	38.3%
Average years' teaching experience:	10.9
Students in gifted program:	12 / 1.3%
Students held back a grade:	2.1%
Total suspensions and expulsions:	577
Suspensions only, pct. in-school:	554 / 0.2%
Offenses: violence: 162, drugs: 14, other: 476	
Eligible students, free or reduced lunch:	80.8%
Number of dropouts:	6 / 0.5%
Pct. 8th-graders w/ basic computer skills:	99.0%
Students at this school generally go on to: Carver, South Atlanta High	

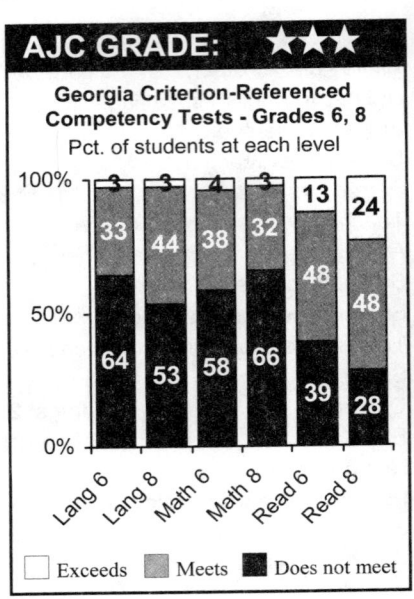

AJC GRADE: ★★★

Georgia Criterion-Referenced Competency Tests - Grades 6, 8
Pct. of students at each level

	Lang 6	Lang 8	Math 6	Math 8	Read 6	Read 8
Exceeds	3	3	4	3	13	24
Meets	33	44	38	32	48	48
Does not meet	64	53	58	66	39	28

Sutton Middle School

4360 Powers Ferry Rd NW, Atlanta, GA 30327
404-256-6920 · Grades 6 - 8

Enrollment:	796
White / black / other:	32.7% / 48.1% / 19.2%
Not native English-speaking:	77 / 9.7%
Student absenteeism:	5.3%
Students per teacher:	13.8
Parent friendliness:	❶❷❸④❺❻
Teachers with advanced degrees:	51.7%
Average years' teaching experience:	14.3
Students in gifted program:	167 / 21.0%
Students held back a grade:	0.5%
Total suspensions and expulsions:	3
Suspensions only, pct. in-school:	2 / 0.0%
Offenses: violence: 2, drugs: 1, other: *	
Eligible students, free or reduced lunch:	42.8%
Number of dropouts:	1 / 0.1%
Pct. 8th-graders w/ basic computer skills:	100.0%
Students at this school generally go on to: North Atlanta High	

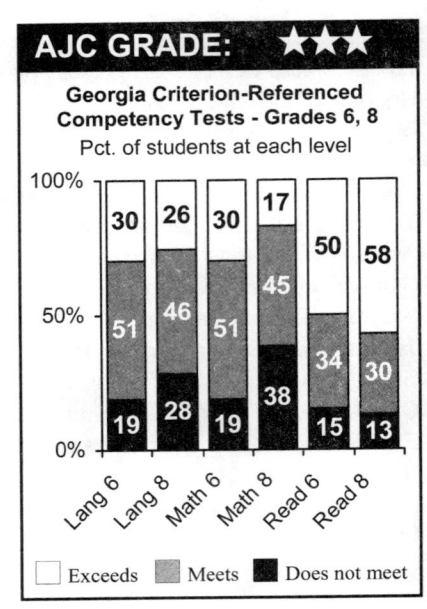

AJC GRADE: ★★★

Georgia Criterion-Referenced Competency Tests - Grades 6, 8
Pct. of students at each level

	Lang 6	Lang 8	Math 6	Math 8	Read 6	Read 8
Exceeds	30	26	30	17	50	58
Meets	51	46	51	45	34	30
Does not meet	19	28	19	38	15	13

Sylvan Hills Middle School

1461 Sylvan Rd SW, Atlanta, GA 30310
404-752-0711 · Grades 6 - 8

Enrollment:	739
White / black / other:	0.7% / 97.4% / 1.9%
Not native English-speaking:	6 / 0.8%
Student absenteeism:	8.3%
Students per teacher:	15.0
Parent friendliness:	❶❷❸④❺❻
Teachers with advanced degrees:	41.2%
Average years' teaching experience:	9.6
Students in gifted program:	30 / 4.1%
Students held back a grade:	0.8%
Total suspensions and expulsions:	348
Suspensions only, pct. in-school:	344 / 37.5%
Offenses: violence: 95, drugs: *, other: 261	
Eligible students, free or reduced lunch:	90.5%
Number of dropouts:	4 / 0.5%
Pct. 8th-graders w/ basic computer skills:	100.0%

Students at this school generally go on to:
Washington High

AJC GRADE: ★★★

Georgia Criterion-Referenced Competency Tests - Grades 6, 8
Pct. of students at each level

	Lang 6	Lang 8	Math 6	Math 8	Read 6	Read 8
Exceeds	1	5	3	1	10	29
Meets	34	39	30	34	48	41
Does not meet	64	56	67	65	43	30

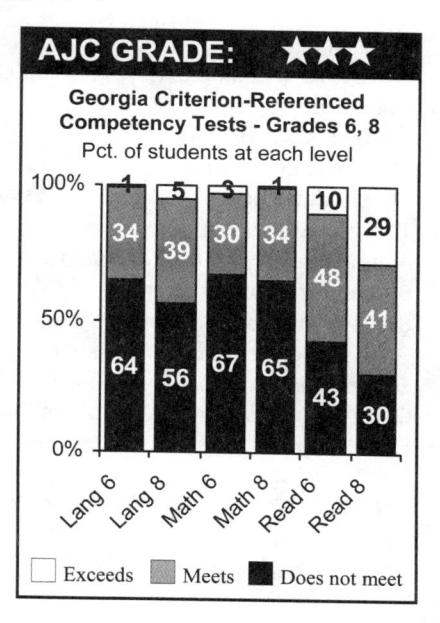

Turner Middle School

98 Anderson Ave NW, Atlanta, GA 30314
404-792-5539 · Grades 6 - 8

Enrollment:	646
White / black / other:	0.0% / 99.5% / 0.5%
Not native English-speaking:	2 / 0.3%
Student absenteeism:	9.4%
Students per teacher:	15.0
Parent friendliness:	❶❷③④❺❻
Teachers with advanced degrees:	46.7%
Average years' teaching experience:	15.9
Students in gifted program:	9 / 1.4%
Students held back a grade:	3.9%
Total suspensions and expulsions:	334
Suspensions only, pct. in-school:	333 / 61.6%
Offenses: violence: 124, drugs: 1, other: 219	
Eligible students, free or reduced lunch:	82.2%
Number of dropouts:	*
Pct. 8th-graders w/ basic computer skills:	100.0%

Students at this school generally go on to:
Douglass, Washington High

AJC GRADE: ★★

Georgia Criterion-Referenced Competency Tests - Grades 6, 8
Pct. of students at each level

	Lang 6	Lang 8	Math 6	Math 8	Read 6	Read 8
Exceeds	2	3	2	2	10	26
Meets	28	33	33	29	47	43
Does not meet	70	64	65	69	43	31

Atlanta City Middle Schools

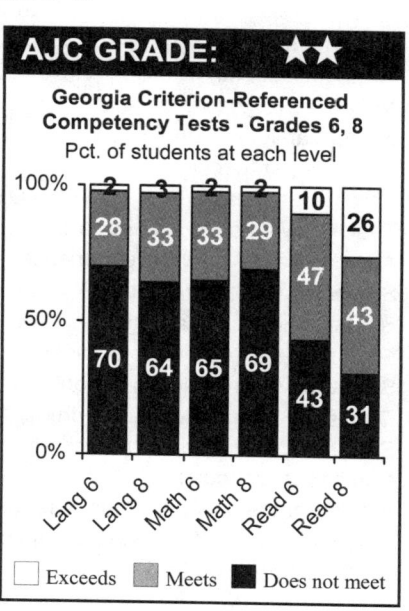

Usher Middle School

631 Harwell Rd NW, Atlanta, GA 30318
404-699-4794 · Grades 6 - 8

Enrollment:	1,026
White / black / other:	0.1% / 99.2% / 0.7%
Not native English-speaking:	3 / 0.3%
Student absenteeism:	7.5%
Students per teacher:	17.0
Parent friendliness:	❶❷❸④⑤❻
Teachers with advanced degrees:	46.8%
Average years' teaching experience:	13.2
Students in gifted program:	69 / 6.7%
Students held back a grade:	3.5%
Total suspensions and expulsions:	754
Suspensions only, pct. in-school:	754 / 41.0%
Offenses:	violence: 240, drugs: 4, other: 696
Eligible students, free or reduced lunch:	79.6%
Number of dropouts:	1 / 0.1%
Pct. 8th-graders w/ basic computer skills:	80.0%
Students at this school generally go on to:	Douglass High

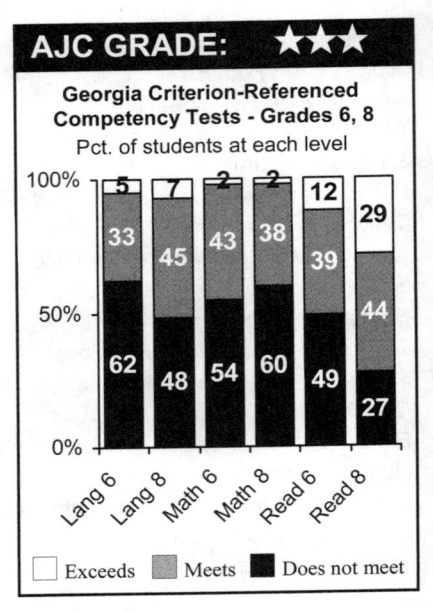

AJC GRADE: ★★★

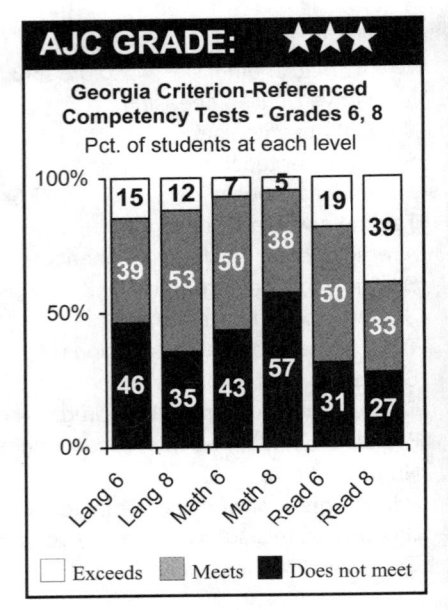

Georgia Criterion-Referenced Competency Tests - Grades 6, 8
Pct. of students at each level

	Lang 6	Lang 8	Math 6	Math 8	Read 6	Read 8
Exceeds	5	7	2	2	12	29
Meets	33	45	43	38	39	44
Does not meet	62	48	54	60	49	27

Walden Middle School

320 Irwin St NE, Atlanta, GA 30312
404-330-4173 · Grades 6 - 8

Enrollment:	389
White / black / other:	0.5% / 98.5% / 1.0%
Not native English-speaking:	6 / 1.5%
Student absenteeism:	7.1%
Students per teacher:	12.9
Parent friendliness:	❶❷❸④⑤❻
Teachers with advanced degrees:	33.3%
Average years' teaching experience:	10.0
Students in gifted program:	15 / 3.9%
Students held back a grade:	0.3%
Total suspensions and expulsions:	338
Suspensions only, pct. in-school:	338 / 19.8%
Offenses:	violence: 90, drugs: 1, other: 309
Eligible students, free or reduced lunch:	90.0%
Number of dropouts:	*
Pct. 8th-graders w/ basic computer skills:	100.0%
Students at this school generally go on to:	Grady, Southside High

AJC GRADE: ★★★

Georgia Criterion-Referenced Competency Tests - Grades 6, 8
Pct. of students at each level

	Lang 6	Lang 8	Math 6	Math 8	Read 6	Read 8
Exceeds	15	12	7	5	19	39
Meets	39	53	50	38	50	33
Does not meet	46	35	43	57	31	27

West Fulton Middle School

1890 Bankhead Ave NW, Atlanta, GA 30318
404-792-5944 · Grades 6 - 8

Enrollment:	971
White / black / other:	0.3% / 99.5% / 0.2%
Not native English-speaking:	*
Student absenteeism:	11.2%
Students per teacher:	17.8
Parent friendliness:	❶❷❸④❺❻
Teachers with advanced degrees:	52.7%
Average years' teaching experience:	12.8
Students in gifted program:	23 / 2.4%
Students held back a grade:	1.2%
Total suspensions and expulsions:	34
Suspensions only, pct. in-school:	33 / 0.0%
Offenses: violence: 12, drugs: *, other: 24	
Eligible students, free or reduced lunch:	92.3%
Number of dropouts:	19 / 1.7%
Pct. 8th-graders w/ basic computer skills:	98.0%

Students at this school generally go on to:
Douglass, North Atlanta, Washington High

AJC GRADE: ★★★

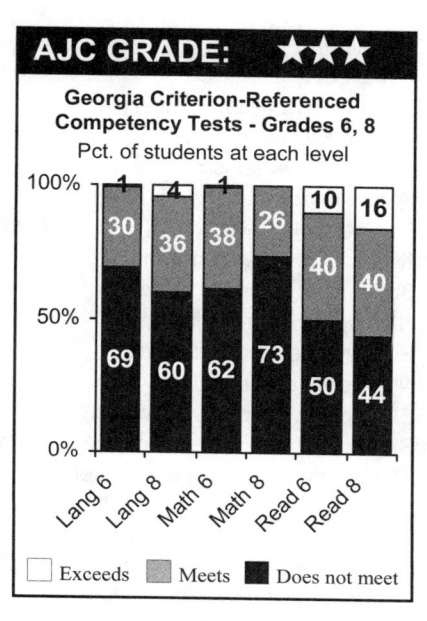

Georgia Criterion-Referenced Competency Tests - Grades 6, 8
Pct. of students at each level

	Lang 6	Lang 8	Math 6	Math 8	Read 6	Read 8
Exceeds	1	4	1		10	16
Meets	30	36	38	26	40	40
Does not meet	69	60	62	73	50	44

Young Middle School

3116 Benjamin E Mays Dr SW, Atlanta, GA 30311
404-699-4533 · Grades 6 - 8

Enrollment:	1,113
White / black / other:	0.0% / 99.3% / 0.7%
Not native English-speaking:	*
Student absenteeism:	5.0%
Students per teacher:	17.8
Parent friendliness:	❶❷❸④❺❻
Teachers with advanced degrees:	49.2%
Average years' teaching experience:	9.2
Students in gifted program:	102 / 9.2%
Students held back a grade:	0.3%
Total suspensions and expulsions:	982
Suspensions only, pct. in-school:	980 / 56.7%
Offenses: violence: 249, drugs: *, other: 738	
Eligible students, free or reduced lunch:	72.8%
Number of dropouts:	*
Pct. 8th-graders w/ basic computer skills:	100.0%

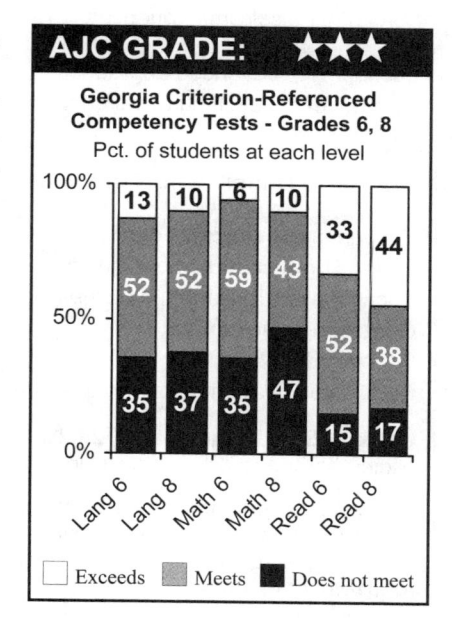

Students at this school generally go on to:
Douglass, Mays High

AJC GRADE: ★★★

Georgia Criterion-Referenced Competency Tests - Grades 6, 8
Pct. of students at each level

	Lang 6	Lang 8	Math 6	Math 8	Read 6	Read 8
Exceeds	13	10	6	10	33	44
Meets	52	52	59	43	52	38
Does not meet	35	37	35	47	15	17

Atlanta City Middle Schools

Carver High School

1275 Capitol Ave SW, Atlanta, GA 30315
404-330-4108 · Grades 9 - 12

Enrollment:	589
White / black / other:	0.5% / 98.3% / 1.2%
Not native English-speaking:	*
Limited English proficiency:	*
Student absenteeism:	19.1%
Students per teacher:	13.7
Parent friendliness:	❶❷❸④⑤❻
Students in gifted program:	5 / 0.8%
Students in remedial education:	39.7%
High school completion rate:	28.2%
Students held back a grade:	14.3%
Number of dropouts:	199 / 25.1%
Students in alternative programs:	116 / 19.7%
Students in special education:	71 / 12.1%
Eligible students, free or reduced lunch:	75.8%
Total suspensions and expulsions:	358
Suspensions only, pct. in-school:	349 / 0.3%
Drugs/alcohol-related offenses:	6
Violence-related offenses:	46
Firearms-related offenses:	4
Vandalism-related offenses:	1
Theft-related offenses:	2
All other disciplinary offenses:	321
Teachers with advanced degrees:	64.4%
Average years' teaching experience:	17.9

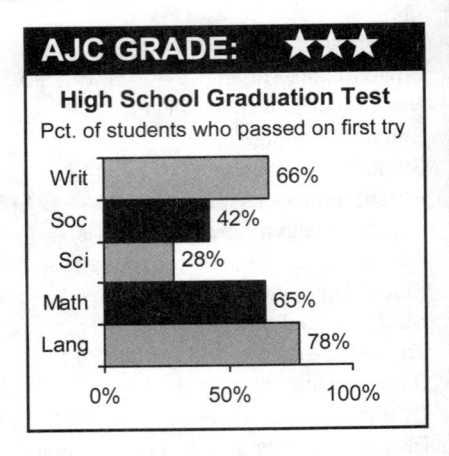

AJC GRADE: ★★★

High School Graduation Test
Pct. of students who passed on first try
- Writ: 66%
- Soc: 42%
- Sci: 28%
- Math: 65%
- Lang: 78%

GHSA classification:	5-AA
Interscholastic sports offered:	
BB, BS, CC, CL, FB, TF	
Advanced Placement (AP) Exams	
Students tested:	7
Tests taken:	7
Pct. of test scores 3 or higher (1 - 5 scale):	14.3%

Languages other than English taught:
French, Spanish

2000-2001 high school graduates: 48

College prep/vocational diplomas:	22.9%
College prep endorsement diplomas:	33.3%
Vocational endorsement diplomas:	16.7%
General high school diplomas:	0.0%
Special education diplomas:	18.8%
Certificates of attendance (no diploma):	8.3%

Of the 2000-2001 graduates, 29.2% were eligible for the HOPE scholarship.

Of the 1999-2000 graduates, 8 attended a Georgia public college or university. Of those, 12% met the school's minimum academic requirements.

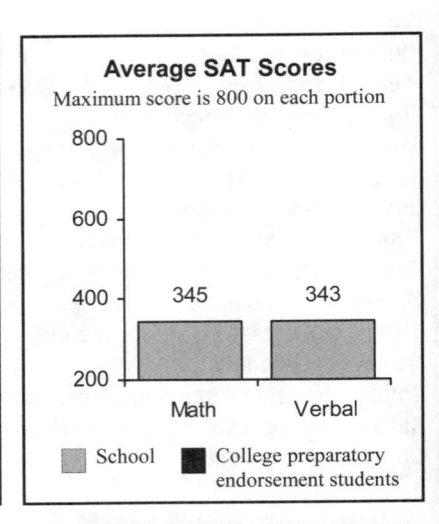

Average SAT Scores
Maximum score is 800 on each portion
- Math: 345
- Verbal: 343

School / College preparatory endorsement students

The Atlanta Journal-Constitution / Page 58

Atlanta City High Schools

Crim High School

256 Clifton St SE, Atlanta, GA 30317
404-371-4881 · Grades 9 - 12

Enrollment:	648
White / black / other:	0.2% / 99.5% / 0.3%
Not native English-speaking:	*
Limited English proficiency:	*
Student absenteeism:	15.8%
Students per teacher:	14.6
Parent friendliness:	❶❷❸④❺❻
Students in gifted program:	13 / 2.0%
Students in remedial education:	24.1%
High school completion rate:	44.4%
Students held back a grade:	12.0%
Number of dropouts:	120 / 15.8%
Students in alternative programs:	15 / 2.3%
Students in special education:	61 / 9.4%
Eligible students, free or reduced lunch:	84.6%
Total suspensions and expulsions:	679
Suspensions only, pct. in-school:	677 / 0.1%
Drugs/alcohol-related offenses:	11
Violence-related offenses:	83
Firearms-related offenses:	7
Vandalism-related offenses:	9
Theft-related offenses:	2
All other disciplinary offenses:	575
Teachers with advanced degrees:	60.0%
Average years' teaching experience:	18.0

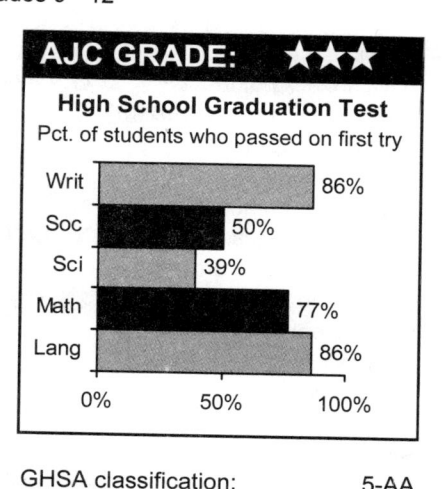

AJC GRADE: ★★★

High School Graduation Test
Pct. of students who passed on first try

- Writ: 86%
- Soc: 50%
- Sci: 39%
- Math: 77%
- Lang: 86%

GHSA classification: 5-AA
Interscholastic sports offered:
BB, BS, CC, CL, FB, SB, SO, TF, VB

Advanced Placement (AP) Exams
- Students tested: 69
- Tests taken: 100
- Pct. of test scores 3 or higher (1 - 5 scale): *

Languages other than English taught:
French, German, Spanish

2000-2001 high school graduates: 84

College prep/vocational diplomas:	29.8%
College prep endorsement diplomas:	41.7%
Vocational endorsement diplomas:	9.5%
General high school diplomas:	0.0%
Special education diplomas:	11.9%
Certificates of attendance (no diploma):	7.1%

Of the 2000-2001 graduates, 47.6% were eligible for the HOPE scholarship.

Of the 1999-2000 graduates, 10 attended a Georgia public college or university. Of those, 50% met the school's minimum academic requirements.

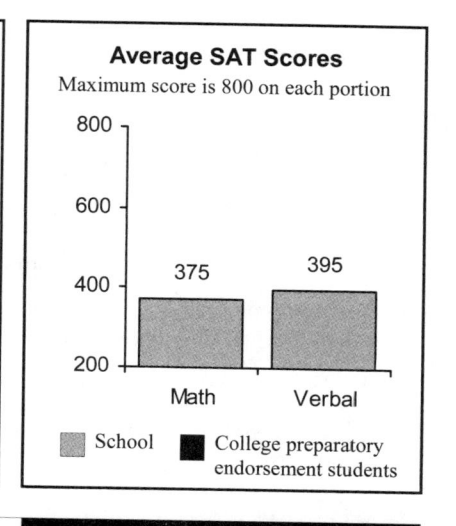

Average SAT Scores
Maximum score is 800 on each portion

- Math: 375
- Verbal: 395

School / College preparatory endorsement students

Atlanta City High Schools

Douglass High School

225 Hamilton E Holmes Dr NW, Atlanta, GA 30318
404-792-5925 · Grades 9 - 12

Enrollment:	2,083
White / black / other:	0.1% / 99.3% / 0.5%
Not native English-speaking:	1 / 0.0%
Limited English proficiency:	3 / 0.1%
Student absenteeism:	9.1%
Students per teacher:	20.0
Parent friendliness:	❶❷❸❹❺❻
Students in gifted program:	257 / 12.3%
Students in remedial education:	13.3%
High school completion rate:	69.1%
Students held back a grade:	6.0%
Number of dropouts:	213 / 9.1%
Students in alternative programs:	23 / 1.1%
Students in special education:	106 / 5.1%
Eligible students, free or reduced lunch:	53.6%

Total suspensions and expulsions:	78
Suspensions only, pct. in-school:	78 / 0.0%
Drugs/alcohol-related offenses:	7
Violence-related offenses:	41
Firearms-related offenses:	3
Vandalism-related offenses:	2
Theft-related offenses:	1
All other disciplinary offenses:	38
Teachers with advanced degrees:	64.5%
Average years' teaching experience:	15.7

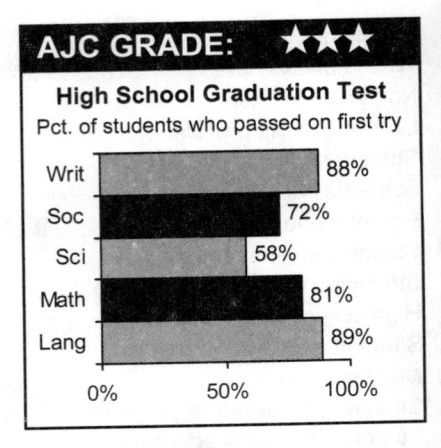

AJC GRADE: ★★★

High School Graduation Test
Pct. of students who passed on first try

- Writ: 88%
- Soc: 72%
- Sci: 58%
- Math: 81%
- Lang: 89%

GHSA classification:	7-AAAAA
Interscholastic sports offered:	BB, BS, CC, FB, GO, RI, SB, SO, TE, TF

Advanced Placement (AP) Exams

Students tested:	133
Tests taken:	246
Pct. of test scores 3 or higher (1 - 5 scale):	2.0%

Languages other than English taught: French, Spanish

2000-2001 high school graduates: 371

College prep/vocational diplomas:	28.6%
College prep endorsement diplomas:	58.8%
Vocational endorsement diplomas:	1.3%
General high school diplomas:	0.3%
Special education diplomas:	4.9%
Certificates of attendance (no diploma):	6.2%

Of the 2000-2001 graduates, 56.1% were eligible for the HOPE scholarship.

Of the 1999-2000 graduates, 82 attended a Georgia public college or university. Of those, 62% met the school's minimum academic requirements.

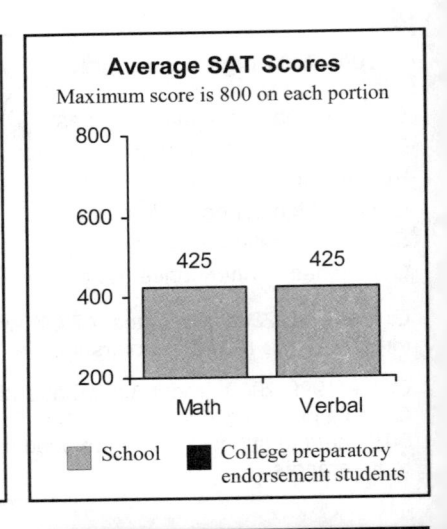

Average SAT Scores
Maximum score is 800 on each portion

- Math — School: 425
- Verbal — School: 425

Legend: School / College preparatory endorsement students

Grady High School

929 Charles Allen Dr NE, Atlanta, GA 30309
404-853-4000 · Grades 9 - 12

Enrollment:	806
White / black / other:	30.1% / 65.8% / 4.1%
Not native English-speaking:	13 / 1.6%
Limited English proficiency:	16 / 2.0%
Student absenteeism:	7.2%
Students per teacher:	15.3
Parent friendliness:	❶❷❸④⑤❻
Students in gifted program:	187 / 23.2%
Students in remedial education:	6.6%
High school completion rate:	59.0%
Students held back a grade:	6.0%
Number of dropouts:	69 / 7.7%
Students in alternative programs:	23 / 2.9%
Students in special education:	58 / 7.2%
Eligible students, free or reduced lunch:	47.6%
Total suspensions and expulsions:	3
Suspensions only, pct. in-school:	1 / 0.0%
Drugs/alcohol-related offenses:	2
Violence-related offenses:	3
Firearms-related offenses:	*
Vandalism-related offenses:	*
Theft-related offenses:	*
All other disciplinary offenses:	*
Teachers with advanced degrees:	59.3%
Average years' teaching experience:	13.5

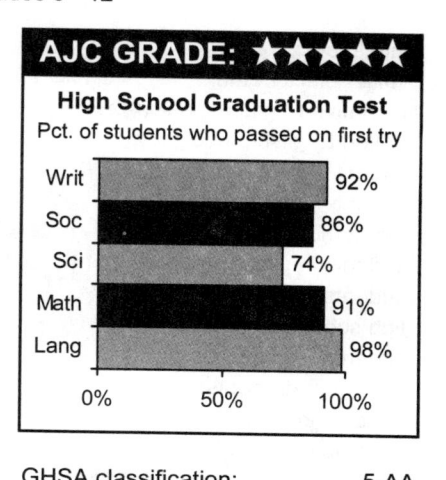

AJC GRADE: ★★★★★

High School Graduation Test
Pct. of students who passed on first try

- Writ: 92%
- Soc: 86%
- Sci: 74%
- Math: 91%
- Lang: 98%

GHSA classification:	5-AA

Interscholastic sports offered:
BB, BS, CC, CL, FB, SB, SO, TE, TF

Advanced Placement (AP) Exams
Students tested:	81
Tests taken:	155
Pct. of test scores 3 or higher (1 - 5 scale):	60.0%

Languages other than English taught:
French, Latin, Spanish

2000-2001 high school graduates: 128

College prep/vocational diplomas:	3.1%
College prep endorsement diplomas:	78.1%
Vocational endorsement diplomas:	11.7%
General high school diplomas:	0.0%
Special education diplomas:	1.6%
Certificates of attendance (no diploma):	5.5%

Of the 2000-2001 graduates, 65.6% were eligible for the HOPE scholarship.

Of the 1999-2000 graduates, 29 attended a Georgia public college or university. Of those, 82% met the school's minimum academic requirements.

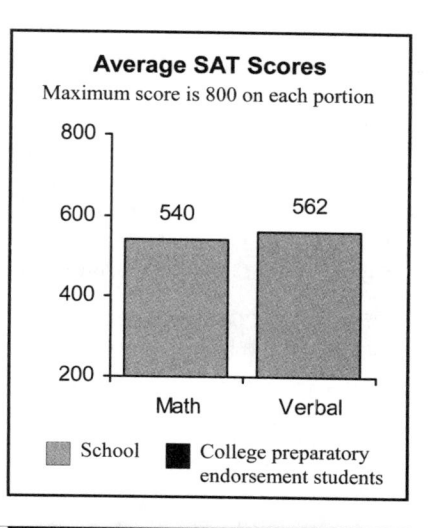

Average SAT Scores
Maximum score is 800 on each portion

- Math: 540
- Verbal: 562

School / College preparatory endorsement students

Atlanta City High Schools

Mays High School

3450 Benjamin E Mays Dr SW, Atlanta, GA 30331
404-699-4537 · Grades 9 - 12

Enrollment:	1,386
White / black / other:	0.1% / 99.1% / 0.7%
Not native English-speaking:	9 / 0.6%
Limited English proficiency:	9 / 0.6%
Student absenteeism:	7.3%
Students per teacher:	18.5
Parent friendliness:	❶ ② ❸ ④ ❺ ❻
Students in gifted program:	181 / 13.1%
Students in remedial education:	12.2%
High school completion rate:	78.1%
Students held back a grade:	3.5%
Number of dropouts:	91 / 6.1%
Students in alternative programs:	35 / 2.5%
Students in special education:	65 / 4.7%
Eligible students, free or reduced lunch:	47.8%
Total suspensions and expulsions:	8
Suspensions only, pct. in-school:	6 / 0.0%
Drugs/alcohol-related offenses:	*
Violence-related offenses:	4
Firearms-related offenses:	4
Vandalism-related offenses:	1
Theft-related offenses:	1
All other disciplinary offenses:	3
Teachers with advanced degrees:	59.7%
Average years' teaching experience:	16.8

AJC GRADE: ★★★

High School Graduation Test
Pct. of students who passed on first try

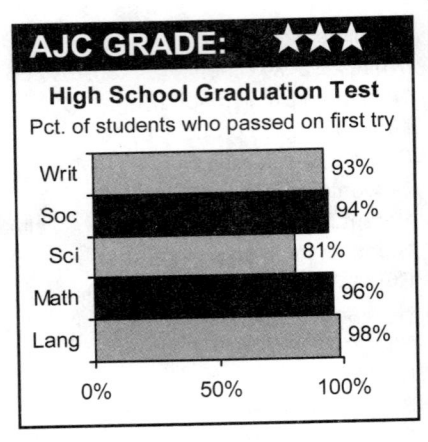

- Writ: 93%
- Soc: 94%
- Sci: 81%
- Math: 96%
- Lang: 98%

GHSA classification: 5-AAAA
Interscholastic sports offered:
  BB, BS, CC, FB, TE, TF

Advanced Placement (AP) Exams
  Students tested: 90
  Tests taken: 142
  Pct. of test scores 3 or
  higher (1 - 5 scale): 12.0%

Languages other than English taught:
  French, Latin, Spanish

2000-2001 high school graduates:	292
College prep/vocational diplomas:	36.0%
College prep endorsement diplomas:	56.8%
Vocational endorsement diplomas:	4.8%
General high school diplomas:	0.0%
Special education diplomas:	2.4%
Certificates of attendance (no diploma):	0.0%

Of the 2000-2001 graduates, 59.9% were eligible for the HOPE scholarship.

Of the 1999-2000 graduates, 106 attended a Georgia public college or university. Of those, 66% met the school's minimum academic requirements.

Average SAT Scores
Maximum score is 800 on each portion

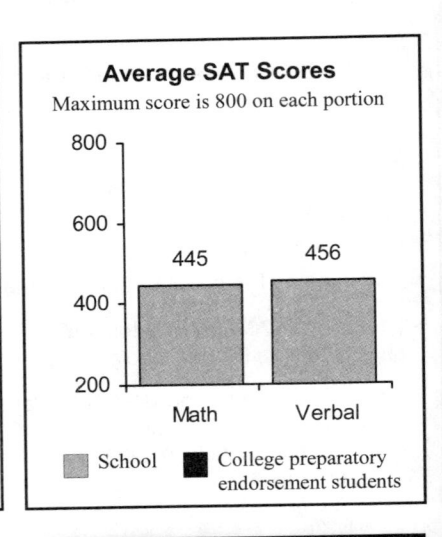

- Math: 445
- Verbal: 456

School / College preparatory endorsement students

Atlanta City High Schools

North Atlanta High School

2875 Northside Dr NW, Atlanta, GA 30305
404-351-0895 · Grades 9 - 12

Enrollment:	1,408
White / black / other:	20.2% / 68.8% / 11.0%
Not native English-speaking:	68 / 4.8%
Limited English proficiency:	68 / 4.8%
Student absenteeism:	8.8%
Students per teacher:	16.9
Parent friendliness:	❶❷❸④❺⑥
Students in gifted program:	191 / 13.6%
Students in remedial education:	10.5%
High school completion rate:	71.8%
Students held back a grade:	5.7%
Number of dropouts:	102 / 6.3%
Students in alternative programs:	28 / 2.0%
Students in special education:	64 / 4.5%
Eligible students, free or reduced lunch:	45.7%
Total suspensions and expulsions:	211
Suspensions only, pct. in-school:	211 / 0.0%
Drugs/alcohol-related offenses:	11
Violence-related offenses:	55
Firearms-related offenses:	*
Vandalism-related offenses:	*
Theft-related offenses:	3
All other disciplinary offenses:	146
Teachers with advanced degrees:	58.8%
Average years' teaching experience:	15.1

AJC GRADE: ★★★★

High School Graduation Test
Pct. of students who passed on first try

- Writ: 92%
- Soc: 85%
- Sci: 74%
- Math: 93%
- Lang: 95%

GHSA classification: 5-AAAA
Interscholastic sports offered:
BB, BS, CC, CL, FB, GO, RI, SB, SO, TE, WR

Advanced Placement (AP) Exams
- Students tested: 136
- Tests taken: 218
- Pct. of test scores 3 or higher (1 - 5 scale): 24.8%

Languages other than English taught:
Arabic, Chinese, French, Latin, Spanish

2000-2001 high school graduates: 305

College prep/vocational diplomas:	0.7%
College prep endorsement diplomas:	94.1%
Vocational endorsement diplomas:	2.6%
General high school diplomas:	0.0%
Special education diplomas:	2.6%
Certificates of attendance (no diploma):	0.0%

Of the 2000-2001 graduates, 66.2% were eligible for the HOPE scholarship.

Of the 1999-2000 graduates, 57 attended a Georgia public college or university. Of those, 78% met the school's minimum academic requirements.

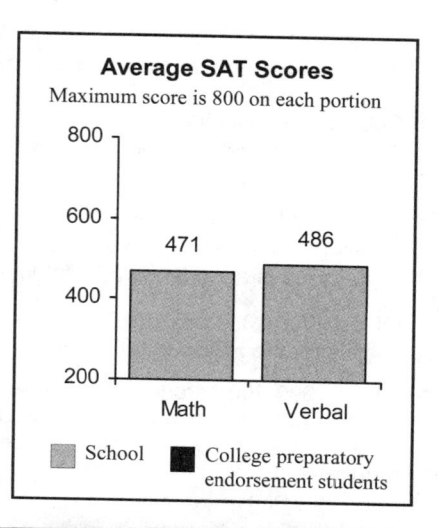

Average SAT Scores
Maximum score is 800 on each portion

- Math: 471
- Verbal: 486

School / College preparatory endorsement students

Atlanta City High Schools

South Atlanta High School

800 Hutchens Rd SE, Atlanta, GA 30354
404-362-5057 · Grades 9 - 12

Enrollment:	1,332
White / black / other:	1.7% / 91.7% / 6.6%
Not native English-speaking:	64 / 4.8%
Limited English proficiency:	74 / 5.6%
Student absenteeism:	9.8%
Students per teacher:	17.9
Parent friendliness:	❶❷❸④⑤❻
Students in gifted program:	16 / 1.2%
Students in remedial education:	8.9%
High school completion rate:	57.2%
Students held back a grade:	8.5%
Number of dropouts:	290 / 17.8%
Students in alternative programs:	13 / 1.0%
Students in special education:	193 / 14.5%
Eligible students, free or reduced lunch:	74.8%
Total suspensions and expulsions:	42
Suspensions only, pct. in-school:	40 / 0.0%
Drugs/alcohol-related offenses:	1
Violence-related offenses:	16
Firearms-related offenses:	1
Vandalism-related offenses:	*
Theft-related offenses:	*
All other disciplinary offenses:	27
Teachers with advanced degrees:	52.0%
Average years' teaching experience:	18.0

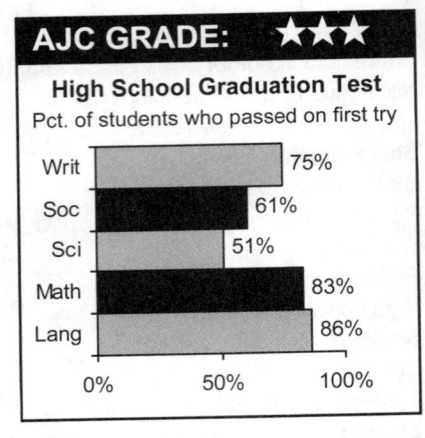

AJC GRADE: ★★★

High School Graduation Test
Pct. of students who passed on first try

- Writ: 75%
- Soc: 61%
- Sci: 51%
- Math: 83%
- Lang: 86%

GHSA classification:	5-AAAA
Interscholastic sports offered:	
BB, BS, CC, CL, FB, GO, RI, SB, SO, TE, TF, VB	

Advanced Placement (AP) Exams

Students tested:	37
Tests taken:	47
Pct. of test scores 3 or higher (1 - 5 scale):	2.1%

Languages other than English taught:
French, Spanish

2000-2001 high school graduates: 198

College prep/vocational diplomas:	17.7%
College prep endorsement diplomas:	37.4%
Vocational endorsement diplomas:	27.8%
General high school diplomas:	1.0%
Special education diplomas:	8.1%
Certificates of attendance (no diploma):	8.1%

Of the 2000-2001 graduates, 38.4% were eligible for the HOPE scholarship.

Of the 1999-2000 graduates, 34 attended a Georgia public college or university. Of those, 58% met the school's minimum academic requirements.

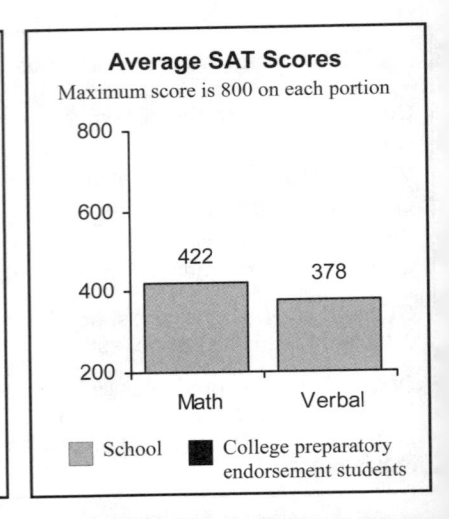

Average SAT Scores
Maximum score is 800 on each portion

- Math: 422
- Verbal: 378

School / College preparatory endorsement students

Atlanta City High Schools

Southside High School

801 Glenwood Ave SE, Atlanta, GA 30316
404-624-2064 · Grades 9 - 12

Enrollment:	1,067
White / black / other:	1.5% / 91.6% / 6.9%
Not native English-speaking:	24 / 2.2%
Limited English proficiency:	30 / 2.8%
Student absenteeism:	10.7%
Students per teacher:	15.4
Parent friendliness:	❶❷❸④❺❻
Students in gifted program:	34 / 3.2%
Students in remedial education:	6.5%
High school completion rate:	61.8%
Students held back a grade:	11.2%
Number of dropouts:	155 / 12.5%
Students in alternative programs:	42 / 3.9%
Students in special education:	114 / 10.7%
Eligible students, free or reduced lunch:	73.0%
Total suspensions and expulsions:	201
Suspensions only, pct. in-school:	201 / 0.0%
Drugs/alcohol-related offenses:	7
Violence-related offenses:	95
Firearms-related offenses:	4
Vandalism-related offenses:	2
Theft-related offenses:	*
All other disciplinary offenses:	106
Teachers with advanced degrees:	62.0%
Average years' teaching experience:	16.8

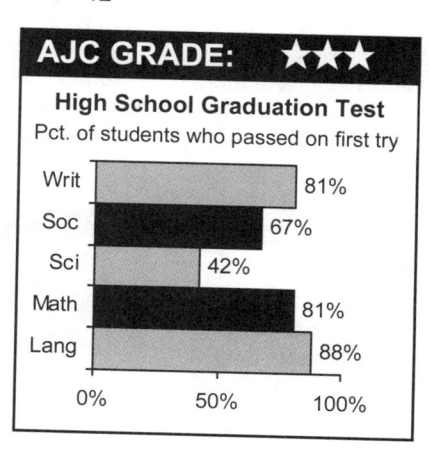

AJC GRADE: ★★★

High School Graduation Test
Pct. of students who passed on first try

- Writ: 81%
- Soc: 67%
- Sci: 42%
- Math: 81%
- Lang: 88%

GHSA classification:	5-AAA
Interscholastic sports offered:	
BB, BS, FB, SO, TE, TF	

Advanced Placement (AP) Exams

Students tested:	63
Tests taken:	90
Pct. of test scores 3 or higher (1 - 5 scale):	3.3%

Languages other than English taught:
French, Spanish

2000-2001 high school graduates: 160

College prep/vocational diplomas:	13.8%
College prep endorsement diplomas:	41.3%
Vocational endorsement diplomas:	25.0%
General high school diplomas:	0.0%
Special education diplomas:	9.4%
Certificates of attendance (no diploma):	10.6%

Of the 2000-2001 graduates, 36.9% were eligible for the HOPE scholarship.

Of the 1999-2000 graduates, 26 attended a Georgia public college or university. Of those, 46% met the school's minimum academic requirements.

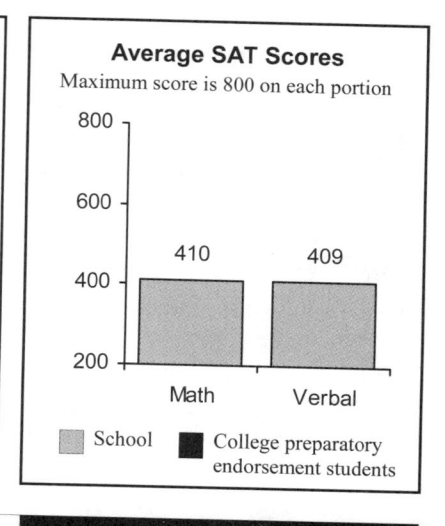

Average SAT Scores
Maximum score is 800 on each portion

- Math: 410
- Verbal: 409

☐ School ■ College preparatory endorsement students

Atlanta City High Schools

Therrell High School

3099 Panther Trl SW, Atlanta, GA 30311
404-346-2523 · Grades 9 - 12

Enrollment:	1,057
White / black / other:	0.2% / 99.1% / 0.7%
Not native English-speaking:	1 / 0.1%
Limited English proficiency:	1 / 0.1%
Student absenteeism:	15.9%
Students per teacher:	16.8
Parent friendliness:	❶❷❸④⑤❻
Students in gifted program:	18 / 1.7%
Students in remedial education:	8.8%
High school completion rate:	46.0%
Students held back a grade:	21.4%
Number of dropouts:	267 / 20.0%
Students in alternative programs:	190 / 18.0%
Students in special education:	89 / 8.4%
Eligible students, free or reduced lunch:	75.9%
Total suspensions and expulsions:	173
Suspensions only, pct. in-school:	164 / 0.0%
Drugs/alcohol-related offenses:	10
Violence-related offenses:	35
Firearms-related offenses:	4
Vandalism-related offenses:	1
Theft-related offenses:	2
All other disciplinary offenses:	135
Teachers with advanced degrees:	50.0%
Average years' teaching experience:	13.3

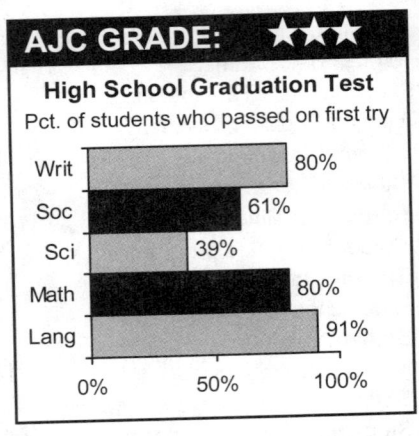

AJC GRADE: ★★★

High School Graduation Test
Pct. of students who passed on first try

- Writ: 80%
- Soc: 61%
- Sci: 39%
- Math: 80%
- Lang: 91%

GHSA classification:	5-AAA

Interscholastic sports offered:
BB, BS, CC, CL, FB, GO, RI, SB, SO, TE, TF, VB

Advanced Placement (AP) Exams
Students tested:	30
Tests taken:	34
Pct. of test scores 3 or higher (1 - 5 scale):	*

Languages other than English taught:
French, Spanish

2000-2001 high school graduates: 186

College prep/vocational diplomas:	15.6%
College prep endorsement diplomas:	46.8%
Vocational endorsement diplomas:	22.0%
General high school diplomas:	0.0%
Special education diplomas:	10.8%
Certificates of attendance (no diploma):	4.8%

Of the 2000-2001 graduates, 31.7% were eligible for the HOPE scholarship.

Of the 1999-2000 graduates, 28 attended a Georgia public college or university. Of those, 42% met the school's minimum academic requirements.

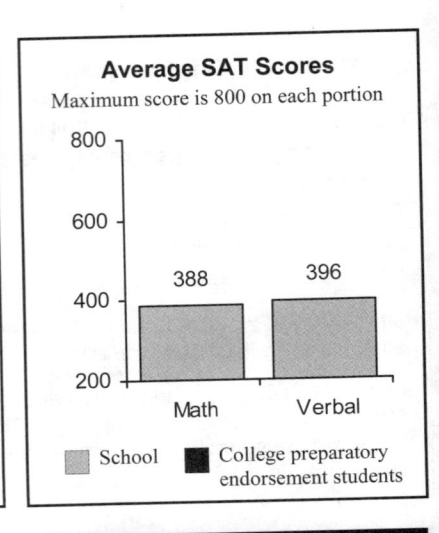

Average SAT Scores
Maximum score is 800 on each portion

- Math: 388
- Verbal: 396

School / College preparatory endorsement students

Atlanta City High Schools

Washington High School

45 Whitehouse Dr SW, Atlanta, GA 30314
404-752-0728 · Grades 9 - 12

Enrollment:	1,411
White / black / other:	0.1% / 98.4% / 1.6%
Not native English-speaking:	*
Limited English proficiency:	11 / 0.8%
Student absenteeism:	9.0%
Students per teacher:	16.8
Parent friendliness:	❶❷❸❹❺❻
Students in gifted program:	37 / 2.6%
Students in remedial education:	11.0%
High school completion rate:	62.0%
Students held back a grade:	8.8%
Number of dropouts:	119 / 7.2%
Students in alternative programs:	25 / 1.8%
Students in special education:	151 / 10.7%
Eligible students, free or reduced lunch:	61.5%
Total suspensions and expulsions:	27
Suspensions only, pct. in-school:	11 / 0.0%
Drugs/alcohol-related offenses:	2
Violence-related offenses:	34
Firearms-related offenses:	2
Vandalism-related offenses:	*
Theft-related offenses:	*
All other disciplinary offenses:	*
Teachers with advanced degrees:	48.8%
Average years' teaching experience:	13.0

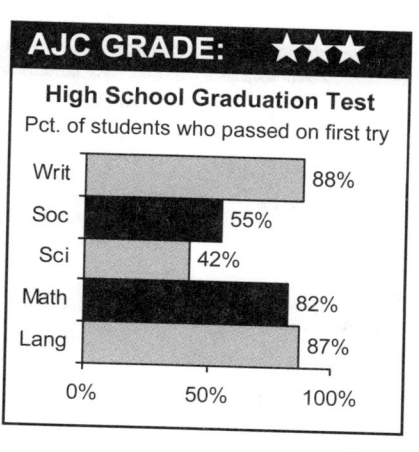

AJC GRADE: ★★★

High School Graduation Test
Pct. of students who passed on first try
- Writ: 88%
- Soc: 55%
- Sci: 42%
- Math: 82%
- Lang: 87%

GHSA classification: 5-AAAA
Interscholastic sports offered:
BB, BS, FB, RI, SB, SO, TF

Advanced Placement (AP) Exams
- Students tested: 33
- Tests taken: 49
- Pct. of test scores 3 or higher (1 - 5 scale): *

Languages other than English taught:
French, Spanish

2000-2001 high school graduates: 163

College prep/vocational diplomas:	24.5%
College prep endorsement diplomas:	38.7%
Vocational endorsement diplomas:	14.1%
General high school diplomas:	0.0%
Special education diplomas:	6.7%
Certificates of attendance (no diploma):	16.0%

Of the 2000-2001 graduates, 50.9% were eligible for the HOPE scholarship.

Of the 1999-2000 graduates, 39 attended a Georgia public college or university. Of those, 33% met the school's minimum academic requirements.

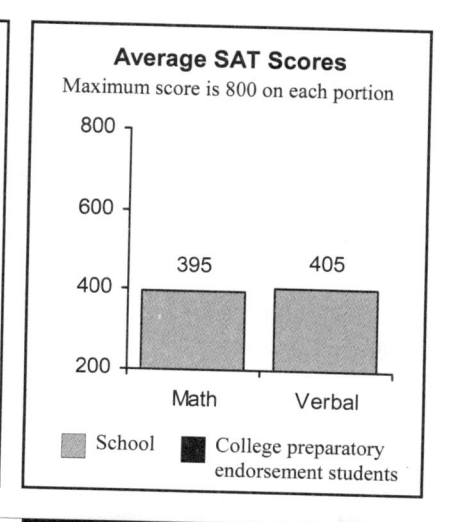

Average SAT Scores
Maximum score is 800 on each portion
- Math: 395
- Verbal: 405

School ■ College preparatory endorsement students

The Atlanta Journal-Constitution / Page 67

Atlanta City High Schools

AJC ranking of Atlanta City Schools

ELEMENTARY SCHOOLS

AJC Star Grade: ★★★★★

- Bethune Elementary
- Brandon Elementary
- Cascade Elementary
- Dobbs Elementary
- F.L. Stanton Elementary
- Jackson Elementary
- Morningside Elementary
- Peyton Forest Elementary
- West Manor Elementary

AJC Star Grade: ★★★★

- Arkwright Elementary
- Beecher Hills Elementary
- Capitol View Elementary
- Centennial Place Elementary
- Cleveland Avenue Elementary
- Continental Colony Elementary
- Dunbar Elementary
- Jones Elementary
- Lin Elementary
- Smith Elementary
- Venetian Hills Elementary
- Whitefoord Elementary

AJC Star Grade: ★★★

- Adamsville Elementary
- Blalock Elementary
- Boyd Elementary
- Burgess Elementary
- Collier Heights Elementary
- Cook Elementary
- East Lake Elementary
- Fain Elementary
- Fickett Elementary
- Garden Hills Elementary
- Gideons Elementary
- Hill Elementary
- Hope Elementary
- Humphries Elementary
- Hutchinson Elementary
- Kimberly Elementary
- Lakewood Elementary
- McGill Elementary
- Miles Elementary
- Mitchell Elementary
- Oglethorpe Elementary
- Peterson Elementary
- Pitts Elementary
- Rivers Elementary
- Scott Elementary
- Thomasville Heights Elementary
- Toomer Elementary
- Towns Elementary
- Waters Elementary
- White Elementary
- Woodson Elementary

AJC Star Grade: ★★

- Anderson Park
- Benteen Elementary
- Connally Elementary
- D.H. Stanton Elementary
- Heritage Academy
- Perkerson Elementary
- Ragsdale Elementary
- Rusk Elementary
- Slater Elementary
- Williams Elementary

Atlanta City Public Schools

AJC ranking of Atlanta City Schools

AJC Star Grade: ★

Charles R. Drew Charter
Grove Park Elementary
Herndon Elementary

AJC Star Grade: ★★★

Carver High
Crim High
Douglass High
Mays High
South Atlanta High
Southside High
Therrell High
Washington High

MIDDLE SCHOOLS

AJC Star Grade: ★★★

Brown Middle
Bunche Middle
Coan Middle
Inman Middle
Long Middle
Martin Luther King Jr. Middle
Price Middle
Sutton Middle
Sylvan Hills Middle
Usher Middle
Walden Middle
West Fulton Middle
Young Middle

AJC Star Grade: ★★

Kennedy Middle
Parks Middle
Turner Middle

HIGH SCHOOLS

AJC Star Grade: ★★★★★

Grady High

AJC Star Grade: ★★★★

North Atlanta High

The Atlanta Journal-Constitution / Page 69

Atlanta City Public Schools

Buford City Public Schools

70 Wiley Dr, Buford, GA 30518
Phone: 770-945-5035 · Fax: 770-945-4629
http://www.bufordcityschools.org

The following pages provide detailed information on every school in the Buford City school district. An asterisk (*) means the value of the data was zero or was not reported by the school district. A complete list of schools ranked by The Atlanta Journal-Constitution's star rating system follows the detailed school reports.

District enrollment:	2,145
White / black / other:	63.2% / 16.6% / 20.2%
Not native English-speaking:	175 / 8.2%
Expenditure per student (general fund):	$7,555
Students per teacher:	14.0
Teachers with advanced degrees:	56.5%
Average years, teaching experience:	13.6
Average teacher salary:	$46,288.71
Students in gifted program:	168 / 7.8%
Students held back a grade:	68 / 3.2%
Eligible students, free or reduced lunch:	863 / 40.1%
Number of dropouts (grades 9-12):	26 / 4.2%
High school completion rate:	76.1%
Graduates, pct. eligible for HOPE scholarships:	86 / 72.1%
Average combined SAT score (maximum 1,600):	994
Pct. of 11th-graders passing the Georgia High School Graduation Tests on first try:	76%
Percent of children 5 to 17 years of age living in poverty (2000 Census estimate):	8.0%

Buford Academy

2705 Sawnee Ave, Buford, GA 30518
678-482-6960 · Grades 3 - 5

Enrollment:	549
White / black / other:	61.4% / 17.5% / 21.1%
Not native English-speaking:	34 / 6.2%
Limited English proficiency:	46 / 8.4%
Student absenteeism:	4.6%
Students per teacher:	14.1
Parent friendliness:	① ❷ ❸ ④ ❺ ❻
Teachers with advanced degrees:	43.6%
Average years' teaching experience:	10.5
Students in gifted program:	43 / 7.8%
Students in remedial education:	13.1%
Students held back a grade:	0.5%
Total suspensions, pct. in-school:	82 / 65.9%
Offenses:	violence: 57, drugs: 2, other: 25
Eligible students, free or reduced lunch:	47.7%
Before / after school program:	Yes / Yes

Students at this school generally go on to:
Buford Middle

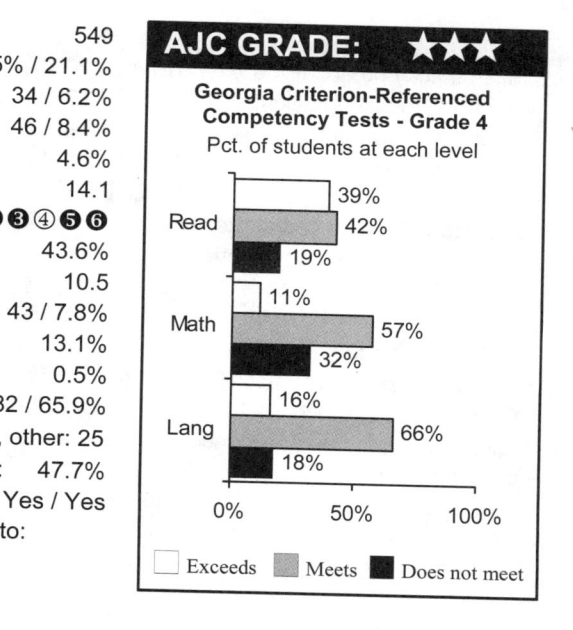

AJC GRADE: ★★★

Georgia Criterion-Referenced Competency Tests - Grade 4
Pct. of students at each level

Read: Exceeds 39%, Meets 42%, Does not meet 19%
Math: Exceeds 11%, Meets 57%, Does not meet 32%
Lang: Exceeds 16%, Meets 66%, Does not meet 18%

☐ Exceeds ▨ Meets ■ Does not meet

Buford City Elementary Schools

Buford Middle School

2200 Buford Hwy, Buford, GA 30518
770-945-2094 · Grades 6 - 8

Enrollment:	541
White / black / other:	63.0% / 16.3% / 20.7%
Not native English-speaking:	41 / 7.6%
Student absenteeism:	6.7%
Students per teacher:	13.2
Parent friendliness:	① ❷ ❸ ❹ ❺ ❻
Teachers with advanced degrees:	61.0%
Average years' teaching experience:	14.3
Students in gifted program:	77 / 14.2%
Students held back a grade:	3.9%
Total suspensions and expulsions:	168
Suspensions only, pct. in-school:	167 / 51.5%
Offenses:	violence: 127, drugs: 5, other: 120
Eligible students, free or reduced lunch:	42.1%
Number of dropouts:	*
Pct. 8th-graders w/ basic computer skills:	100.0%
Students at this school generally go on to:	
Buford High	

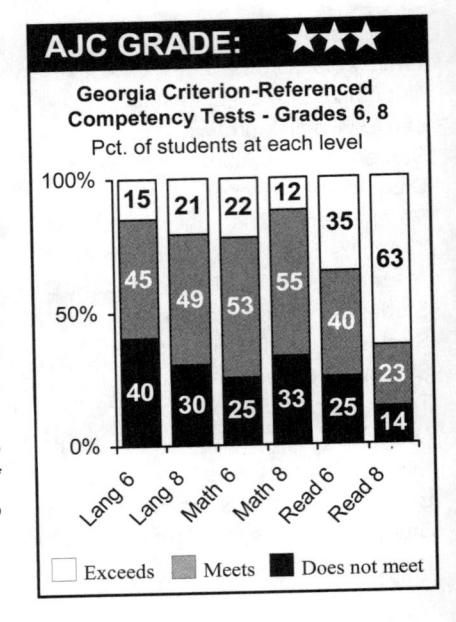

AJC GRADE: ★★★

Georgia Criterion-Referenced Competency Tests - Grades 6, 8
Pct. of students at each level

	Lang 6	Lang 8	Math 6	Math 8	Read 6	Read 8
Exceeds	15	21	22	12	35	63
Meets	45	49	53	55	40	23
Does not meet	40	30	25	33	25	14

Buford City Middle Schools

Buford High School

2750 Sawnee Ave, Buford, GA 30518
770-945-6768 · Grades 9 - 12

Enrollment:	553
White / black / other:	70.3% / 18.3% / 11.4%
Not native English-speaking:	23 / 4.2%
Limited English proficiency:	25 / 4.5%
Student absenteeism:	6.9%
Students per teacher:	15.1
Parent friendliness:	① ❷ ❸ ❹ ❺ ❻
Students in gifted program:	36 / 6.5%
Students in remedial education:	2.7%
High school completion rate:	76.1%
Students held back a grade:	5.8%
Number of dropouts:	26 / 4.2%
Students in alternative programs:	*
Students in special education:	59 / 10.7%
Eligible students, free or reduced lunch:	22.1%
Total suspensions and expulsions:	185
Suspensions only, pct. in-school:	185 / 69.7%
Drugs/alcohol-related offenses:	1
Violence-related offenses:	23
Firearms-related offenses:	2
Vandalism-related offenses:	*
Theft-related offenses:	2
All other disciplinary offenses:	192
Teachers with advanced degrees:	63.2%
Average years' teaching experience:	15.2

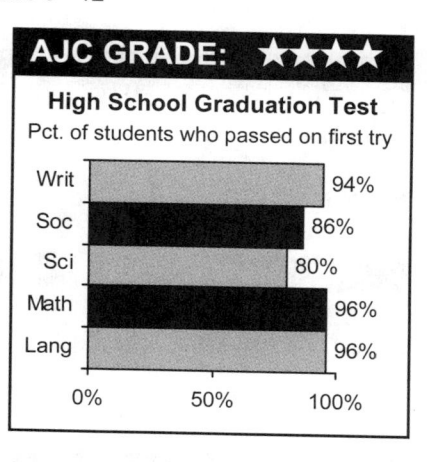

AJC GRADE: ★★★★

High School Graduation Test
Pct. of students who passed on first try

- Writ: 94%
- Soc: 86%
- Sci: 80%
- Math: 96%
- Lang: 96%

GHSA classification: 8-AA
Interscholastic sports offered:
BB, BS, CC, CL, FB, GO, SB, TE, TF, WR

Advanced Placement (AP) Exams
Students tested: 26
Tests taken: 27
Pct. of test scores 3 or higher (1 - 5 scale): 33.3%

Languages other than English taught:
French, Spanish

2000-2001 high school graduates: 86

College prep/vocational diplomas:	51.2%
College prep endorsement diplomas:	30.2%
Vocational endorsement diplomas:	18.6%
General high school diplomas:	0.0%
Special education diplomas:	0.0%
Certificates of attendance (no diploma):	0.0%

Of the 2000-2001 graduates, 72.1% were eligible for the HOPE scholarship.

Of the 1999-2000 graduates, 37 attended a Georgia public college or university. Of those, 78% met the school's minimum academic requirements.

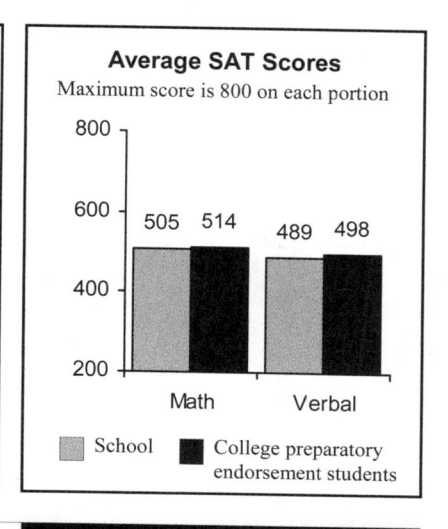

Average SAT Scores
Maximum score is 800 on each portion

- Math — School: 505, College preparatory endorsement students: 514
- Verbal — School: 489, College preparatory endorsement students: 498

Buford City High Schools

AJC ranking of Buford City Schools

ELEMENTARY SCHOOLS

AJC Star Grade: ★★★

Buford Academy

MIDDLE SCHOOLS

AJC Star Grade: ★★★

Buford Middle

HIGH SCHOOLS

AJC Star Grade: ★★★★

Buford High

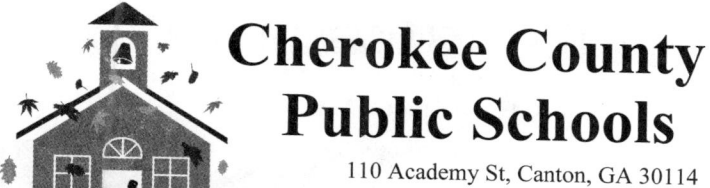

Cherokee County Public Schools

110 Academy St, Canton, GA 30114
Phone: 770-479-1871 · Fax: 770-479-7758
http://www.cherokee.k12.ga.us

The following pages provide detailed information on every school in the Cherokee County school district. An asterisk (*) means the value of the data was zero or was not reported by the school district. A complete list of schools ranked by The Atlanta Journal-Constitution's star rating system follows the detailed school reports.

District enrollment:	25,821
White / black / other:	90.3% / 3.3% / 6.4%
Not native English-speaking:	393 / 1.5%
Expenditure per student (general fund):	$6,482
Students per teacher:	15.8
Teachers with advanced degrees:	46.2%
Average years, teaching experience:	11.5
Average teacher salary:	$43,560.31
Students in gifted program:	2,143 / 8.3%
Students held back a grade:	597 / 2.3%
Eligible students, free or reduced lunch:	3,855 / 14.8%
Number of dropouts (grades 9-12):	343 / 4.5%
High school completion rate:	81.5%
Graduates, pct. eligible for HOPE scholarships:	1,229 / 66.0%
Average combined SAT score (maximum 1,600):	1,048
Pct. of 11th-graders passing the Georgia High School Graduation Tests on first try:	77%
Percent of children 5 to 17 years of age living in poverty (2000 Census estimate):	5.2%

Arnold Mill Elementary School

710 Arnold Mill Rd, Woodstock, GA 30188
770-592-3510 · Grades K - 6

Enrollment:	928
White / black / other:	90.3% / 1.9% / 7.8%
Not native English-speaking:	4 / 0.4%
Limited English proficiency:	13 / 1.4%
Student absenteeism:	4.8%
Students per teacher:	16.2
Parent friendliness:	① ❷ ❸ ④ ⑤ ❻
Teachers with advanced degrees:	48.3%
Average years' teaching experience:	12.1
Students in gifted program:	87 / 9.4%
Students in remedial education:	10.6%
Students held back a grade:	2.0%
Total suspensions, pct. in-school:	1 / 0.0%
Offenses:	violence: 2, drugs: *, other: *
Eligible students, free or reduced lunch:	12.4%
Before / after school program:	Yes / Yes

Students at this school generally go on to:
Dean Rusk Middle

AJC GRADE: ★★★

Georgia Criterion-Referenced Competency Tests - Grade 4
Pct. of students at each level

- Read: Exceeds 54%, Meets 38%, Does not meet 8%
- Math: Exceeds 18%, Meets 64%, Does not meet 18%
- Lang: Exceeds 27%, Meets 58%, Does not meet 14%

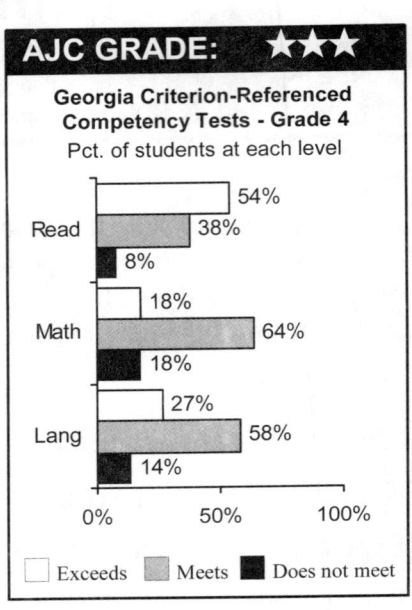

Ball Ground Elementary School

480 Old Canton Rd, Ball Ground, GA 30107
770-735-3366 · Grades K - 6

Enrollment:	387
White / black / other:	99.2% / 0.3% / 0.5%
Not native English-speaking:	1 / 0.3%
Limited English proficiency:	1 / 0.3%
Student absenteeism:	4.4%
Students per teacher:	16.3
Parent friendliness:	❶ ❷ ❸ ④ ⑤ ❻
Teachers with advanced degrees:	64.0%
Average years' teaching experience:	12.2
Students in gifted program:	13 / 3.4%
Students in remedial education:	14.3%
Students held back a grade:	2.6%
Total suspensions, pct. in-school:	5 / 80.0%
Offenses:	violence: 4, drugs: *, other: 1
Eligible students, free or reduced lunch:	24.3%
Before / after school program:	Yes / Yes

Students at this school generally go on to:
Teasley Middle

AJC GRADE: ★★★

Georgia Criterion-Referenced Competency Tests - Grade 4
Pct. of students at each level

- Read: Exceeds 31%, Meets 56%, Does not meet 13%
- Math: Exceeds 5%, Meets 66%, Does not meet 30%
- Lang: Exceeds 22%, Meets 66%, Does not meet 13%

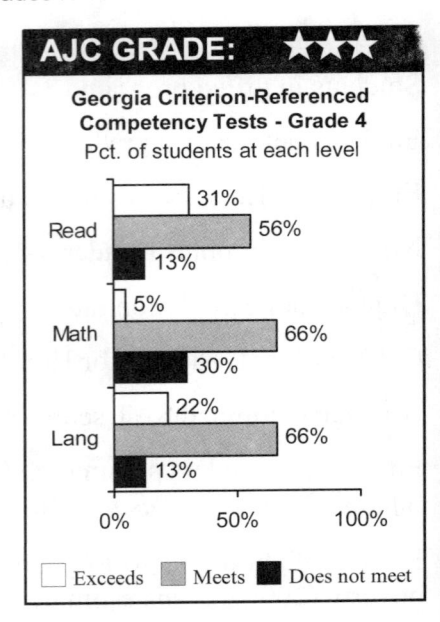

Bascomb Elementary School

1335 Wyngate Pkwy, Woodstock, GA 30189
770-592-1091 · Grades K - 4

Enrollment:	1,266
White / black / other:	94.9% / 1.9% / 3.2%
Not native English-speaking:	*
Limited English proficiency:	2 / 0.2%
Student absenteeism:	3.8%
Students per teacher:	18.0
Parent friendliness:	① ❷ ❸ ④ ⑤ ❻
Teachers with advanced degrees:	43.1%
Average years' teaching experience:	10.5
Students in gifted program:	61 / 4.8%
Students in remedial education:	5.2%
Students held back a grade:	0.6%
Total suspensions, pct. in-school:	5 / 60.0%
Offenses:	violence: 5, drugs: *, other: *
Eligible students, free or reduced lunch:	1.2%
Before / after school program:	Yes / Yes

Students at this school generally go on to:
Chapman Intermediate School

AJC GRADE: ★★★

Georgia Criterion-Referenced Competency Tests - Grade 4
Pct. of students at each level

- Read: Exceeds 60%, Meets 33%, Does not meet 7%
- Math: Exceeds 28%, Meets 59%, Does not meet 13%
- Lang: Exceeds 36%, Meets 56%, Does not meet 8%

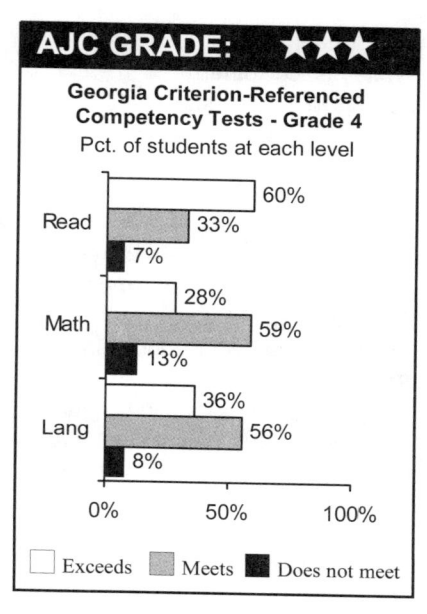

Buffington Elementary School

4568 Cumming Hwy, Canton, GA 30114
770-479-3679 · Grades K - 4

Enrollment:	172
White / black / other:	93.0% / 1.7% / 5.2%
Not native English-speaking:	*
Limited English proficiency:	1 / 0.6%
Student absenteeism:	5.2%
Students per teacher:	12.3
Parent friendliness:	① ❷ ❸ ④ ⑤ ❻
Teachers with advanced degrees:	50.0%
Average years' teaching experience:	10.1
Students in gifted program:	5 / 2.9%
Students in remedial education:	10.3%
Students held back a grade:	5.8%
Total suspensions, pct. in-school:	1 / 0.0%
Offenses:	violence: *, drugs: *, other: 1
Eligible students, free or reduced lunch:	20.9%
Before / after school program:	Yes / Yes

Students at this school generally go on to:
Macedonia Elementary

AJC GRADE: ★★★

Georgia Criterion-Referenced Competency Tests - Grade 4
Pct. of students at each level

- Read: Exceeds 59%, Meets 30%, Does not meet 11%
- Math: Exceeds 16%, Meets 72%, Does not meet 12%
- Lang: Exceeds 27%, Meets 65%, Does not meet 8%

Cherokee County Elementary Schools

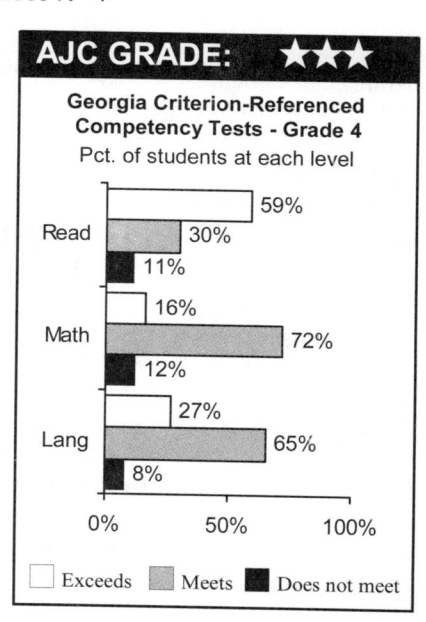

Canton Elementary School

712 Marietta Hwy, Canton, GA 30114
770-479-3221 · Grades K - 6

Enrollment:	507
White / black / other:	74.2% / 8.7% / 17.2%
Not native English-speaking:	32 / 6.3%
Limited English proficiency:	45 / 8.9%
Student absenteeism:	6.2%
Students per teacher:	12.5
Parent friendliness:	① ❷ ❸ ④ ⑤ ❻
Teachers with advanced degrees:	46.3%
Average years' teaching experience:	11.9
Students in gifted program:	12 / 2.4%
Students in remedial education:	26.5%
Students held back a grade:	5.1%
Total suspensions, pct. in-school:	21 / 81.0%
Offenses:	violence: 26, drugs: *, other: 7
Eligible students, free or reduced lunch:	43.8%
Before / after school program:	Yes / No
Students at this school generally go on to:	
Teasley Middle	

AJC GRADE: ★★★

Georgia Criterion-Referenced Competency Tests - Grade 4
Pct. of students at each level

Read: Exceeds 38%, Meets 42%, Does not meet 20%
Math: Exceeds 6%, Meets 59%, Does not meet 35%
Lang: Exceeds 8%, Meets 63%, Does not meet 29%

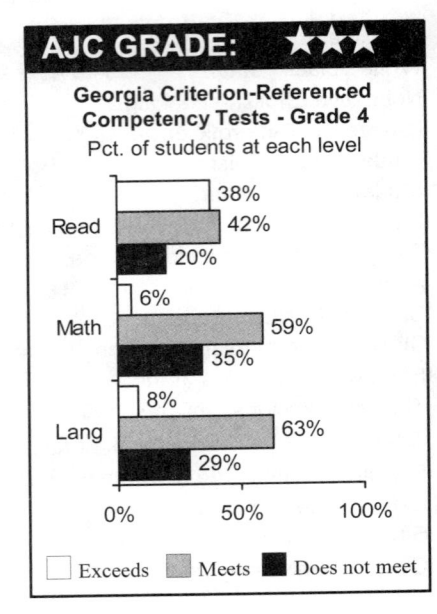

Carmel Elementary School

2275 Bascomb Carmel Rd, Woodstock, GA 30189
770-926-1237 · Grades K - 6

Enrollment:	1,484
White / black / other:	84.8% / 5.6% / 9.6%
Not native English-speaking:	25 / 1.7%
Limited English proficiency:	43 / 2.9%
Student absenteeism:	5.0%
Students per teacher:	18.6
Parent friendliness:	❶ ❷ ❸ ④ ⑤ ❻
Teachers with advanced degrees:	33.3%
Average years' teaching experience:	11.1
Students in gifted program:	42 / 2.8%
Students in remedial education:	12.1%
Students held back a grade:	0.9%
Total suspensions, pct. in-school:	15 / 60.0%
Offenses:	violence: 9, drugs: *, other: 10
Eligible students, free or reduced lunch:	17.8%
Before / after school program:	Yes / Yes
Students at this school generally go on to:	
Woodstock Middle	

AJC GRADE: ★★★

Georgia Criterion-Referenced Competency Tests - Grade 4
Pct. of students at each level

Read: Exceeds 36%, Meets 38%, Does not meet 26%
Math: Exceeds 8%, Meets 56%, Does not meet 36%
Lang: Exceeds 18%, Meets 58%, Does not meet 24%

Cherokee County Elementary Schools

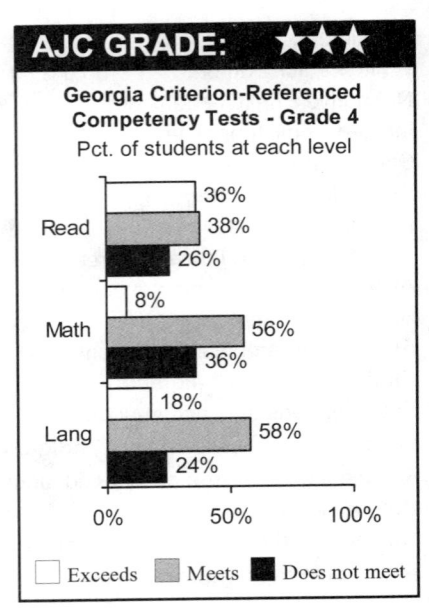

Clayton Elementary School

221 Upper Burris Rd, Canton, GA 30114
770-479-2550 · Grades K - 6

Enrollment: 358
White / black / other: 99.4% / 0.3% / 0.3%
Not native English-speaking: 1 / 0.3%
Limited English proficiency: 3 / 0.8%
Student absenteeism: 5.2%
Students per teacher: 14.8
Parent friendliness: ① ❷ ❸ ④ ⑤ ❻
Teachers with advanced degrees: 52.0%
Average years' teaching experience: 11.4
Students in gifted program: 9 / 2.5%
Students in remedial education: 16.7%
Students held back a grade: 1.4%
Total suspensions, pct. in-school: 13 / 76.9%
Offenses: violence: 8, drugs: *, other: 11
Eligible students, free or reduced lunch: 21.2%
Before / after school program: Yes / Yes
Students at this school generally go on to:
Teasley Middle

AJC GRADE: ★★

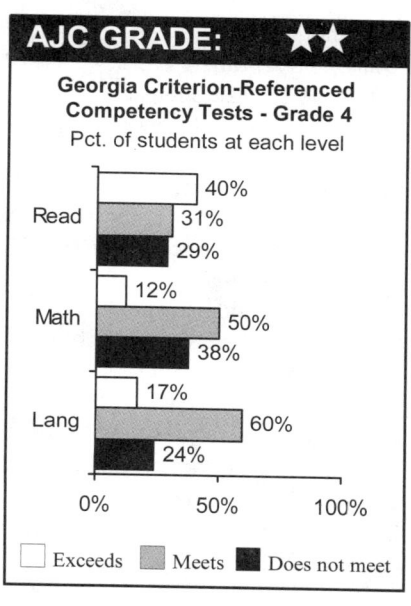

Georgia Criterion-Referenced Competency Tests - Grade 4
Pct. of students at each level

Read: Exceeds 40%, Meets 31%, Does not meet 29%
Math: Exceeds 12%, Meets 50%, Does not meet 38%
Lang: Exceeds 17%, Meets 60%, Does not meet 24%

Florine Dial Johnston Elementary School

2031 E Cherokee Dr, Woodstock, GA 30188
770-928-2910 · Grades K - 5

Enrollment: 871
White / black / other: 89.1% / 2.8% / 8.2%
Not native English-speaking: 16 / 1.8%
Limited English proficiency: 17 / 2.0%
Student absenteeism: 5.3%
Students per teacher: 16.2
Parent friendliness: ① ❷ ❸ ④ ❺ ❻
Teachers with advanced degrees: 45.5%
Average years' teaching experience: 12.0
Students in gifted program: 10 / 1.1%
Students in remedial education: 14.4%
Students held back a grade: 0.7%
Total suspensions, pct. in-school: 30 / 90.0%
Offenses: violence: 43, drugs: 1, other: 24
Eligible students, free or reduced lunch: 18.7%
Before / after school program: Yes / Yes
Students at this school generally go on to:
Dean Rusk, Woodstock Middle

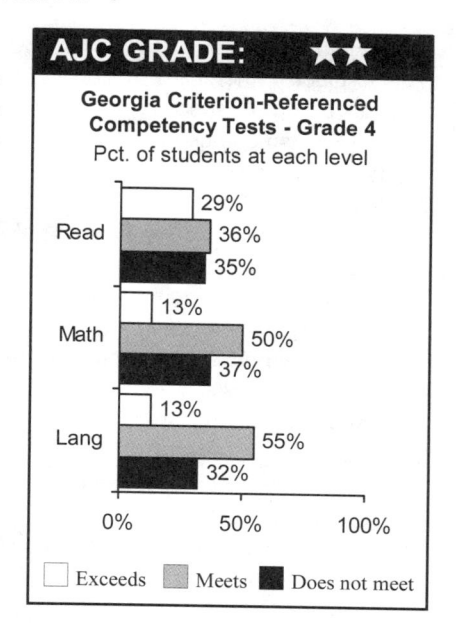

AJC GRADE: ★★

Georgia Criterion-Referenced Competency Tests - Grade 4
Pct. of students at each level

Read: Exceeds 29%, Meets 36%, Does not meet 35%
Math: Exceeds 13%, Meets 50%, Does not meet 37%
Lang: Exceeds 13%, Meets 55%, Does not meet 32%

Cherokee County Elementary Schools

Free Home Elementary School

12525 Cumming Hwy, Canton, GA 30115
770-887-5738 · Grades K - 4

Enrollment:	276
White / black / other:	96.4% / 1.4% / 2.2%
Not native English-speaking:	1 / 0.4%
Limited English proficiency:	1 / 0.4%
Student absenteeism:	4.7%
Students per teacher:	13.0
Parent friendliness:	① ❷ ❸ ④ ⑤ ❻
Teachers with advanced degrees:	59.1%
Average years' teaching experience:	14.4
Students in gifted program:	9 / 3.3%
Students in remedial education:	9.3%
Students held back a grade:	*
Total suspensions, pct. in-school:	*
Offenses:	violence: *, drugs: *, other: *
Eligible students, free or reduced lunch:	13.4%
Before / after school program:	Yes / Yes
Students at this school generally go to:	
Macedonia Elementary	

AJC GRADE: ★★

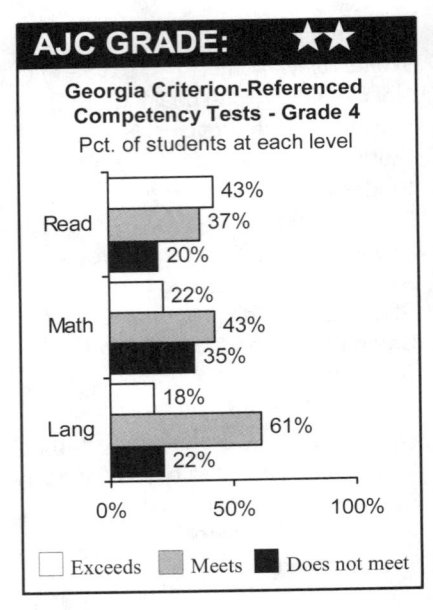

Georgia Criterion-Referenced Competency Tests - Grade 4
Pct. of students at each level

Read: Exceeds 43%, Meets 37%, Does not meet 20%
Math: Exceeds 22%, Meets 43%, Does not meet 35%
Lang: Exceeds 18%, Meets 61%, Does not meet 22%

Hickory Flat Elementary School

2755 E Cherokee Dr, Canton, GA 30115
770-345-6841 · Grades K - 6

Enrollment:	1,016
White / black / other:	93.5% / 1.2% / 5.3%
Not native English-speaking:	21 / 2.1%
Limited English proficiency:	28 / 2.8%
Student absenteeism:	4.4%
Students per teacher:	17.6
Parent friendliness:	❶ ❷ ❸ ④ ⑤ ❻
Teachers with advanced degrees:	44.3%
Average years' teaching experience:	13.0
Students in gifted program:	82 / 8.1%
Students in remedial education:	15.5%
Students held back a grade:	1.0%
Total suspensions, pct. in-school:	7 / 71.4%
Offenses:	violence: 5, drugs: *, other: 4
Eligible students, free or reduced lunch:	11.4%
Before / after school program:	Yes / Yes
Students at this school generally go to:	
Dean Rusk Middle	

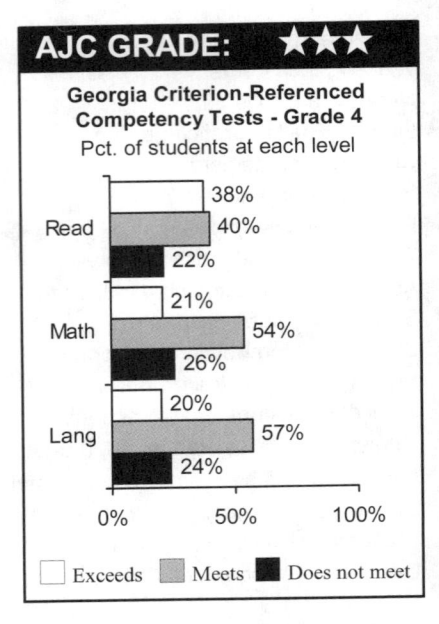

AJC GRADE: ★★★

Georgia Criterion-Referenced Competency Tests - Grade 4
Pct. of students at each level

Read: Exceeds 38%, Meets 40%, Does not meet 22%
Math: Exceeds 21%, Meets 54%, Does not meet 26%
Lang: Exceeds 20%, Meets 57%, Does not meet 24%

The Atlanta Journal-Constitution / Page 80

Cherokee County Elementary Schools

Holly Springs Elementary School

1965 Hickory Rd, Canton, GA 30115
770-345-5035 · Grades K - 6

Enrollment:	869
White / black / other:	88.7% / 3.0% / 8.3%
Not native English-speaking:	25 / 2.9%
Limited English proficiency:	32 / 3.7%
Student absenteeism:	5.1%
Students per teacher:	18.2
Parent friendliness:	❶ ❷ ❸ ④ ⑤ ❻
Teachers with advanced degrees:	43.8%
Average years' teaching experience:	13.6
Students in gifted program:	25 / 2.9%
Students in remedial education:	14.2%
Students held back a grade:	1.6%
Total suspensions, pct. in-school:	11 / 81.8%
Offenses:	violence: 7, drugs: *, other: 4
Eligible students, free or reduced lunch:	18.8%
Before / after school program:	Yes / Yes
Students at this school generally go on to:	
Teasley Middle	

AJC GRADE: ★★

Georgia Criterion-Referenced Competency Tests - Grade 4
Pct. of students at each level

Read: Exceeds 23%, Meets 44%, Does not meet 33%
Math: Exceeds 7%, Meets 39%, Does not meet 54%
Lang: Exceeds 11%, Meets 49%, Does not meet 40%

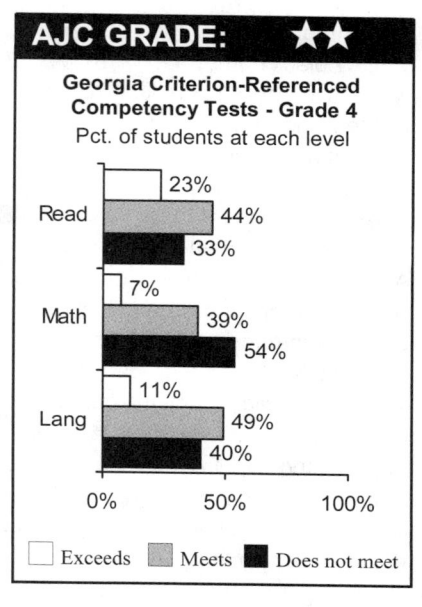

Kleven Boston Elementary School

105 Othello Dr, Woodstock, GA 30189
770-924-6260 · Grades K - 4

Enrollment:	809
White / black / other:	85.2% / 3.8% / 11.0%
Not native English-speaking:	21 / 2.6%
Limited English proficiency:	30 / 3.7%
Student absenteeism:	4.9%
Students per teacher:	14.6
Parent friendliness:	① ❷ ❸ ❹ ❺ ❻
Teachers with advanced degrees:	32.1%
Average years' teaching experience:	9.0
Students in gifted program:	58 / 7.2%
Students in remedial education:	21.2%
Students held back a grade:	1.4%
Total suspensions, pct. in-school:	5 / 40.0%
Offenses:	violence: 1, drugs: *, other: 6
Eligible students, free or reduced lunch:	22.5%
Before / after school program:	Yes / Yes
Students at this school generally go on to:	
Chapman Intermediate School	

AJC GRADE: ★★★

Georgia Criterion-Referenced Competency Tests - Grade 4
Pct. of students at each level

Read: Exceeds 44%, Meets 39%, Does not meet 17%
Math: Exceeds 13%, Meets 61%, Does not meet 26%
Lang: Exceeds 25%, Meets 59%, Does not meet 16%

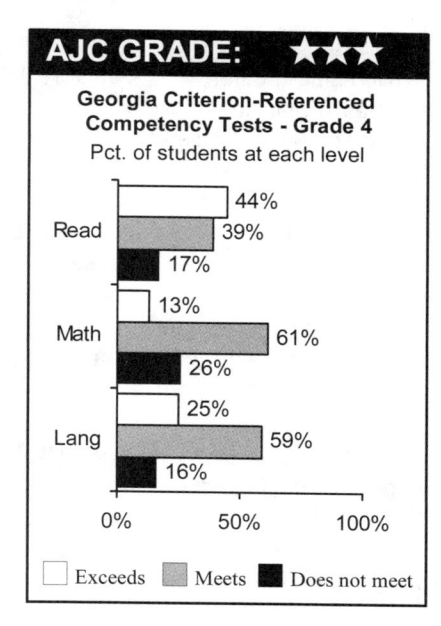

Little River Elementary School

3170 Trickum Rd, Woodstock, GA 30188
770-926-7566 · Grades K - 6

Enrollment:	692
White / black / other:	87.0% / 3.5% / 9.5%
Not native English-speaking:	11 / 1.6%
Limited English proficiency:	25 / 3.6%
Student absenteeism:	4.6%
Students per teacher:	15.6
Parent friendliness:	① ❷ ❸ ❹ ❺ ❻
Teachers with advanced degrees:	34.8%
Average years' teaching experience:	11.4
Students in gifted program:	33 / 4.8%
Students in remedial education:	11.3%
Students held back a grade:	*
Total suspensions, pct. in-school:	1 / 0.0%
Offenses:	violence: *, drugs: 1, other: *
Eligible students, free or reduced lunch:	15.5%
Before / after school program:	Yes / Yes

Students at this school generally go on to:
Woodstock Middle

AJC GRADE: ★★★

Georgia Criterion-Referenced Competency Tests - Grade 4
Pct. of students at each level

- Read: Exceeds 42%, Meets 44%, Does not meet 13%
- Math: Exceeds 15%, Meets 67%, Does not meet 18%
- Lang: Exceeds 11%, Meets 78%, Does not meet 11%

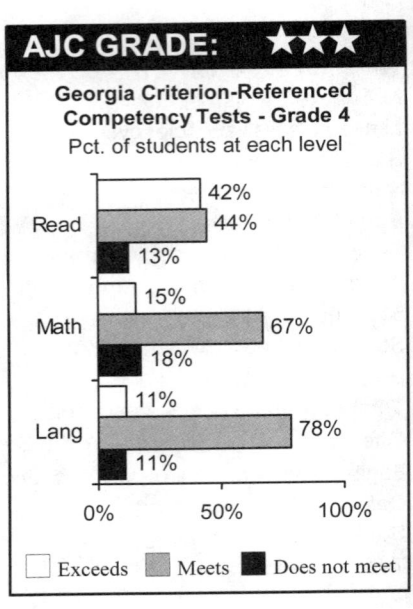

Macedonia Elementary School

10370 E Cherokee Dr, Canton, GA 30115
770-479-3429 · Grades K - 6

Enrollment:	552
White / black / other:	97.5% / 0.9% / 1.6%
Not native English-speaking:	2 / 0.4%
Limited English proficiency:	4 / 0.7%
Student absenteeism:	4.7%
Students per teacher:	17.2
Parent friendliness:	① ❷ ❸ ④ ⑤ ❻
Teachers with advanced degrees:	54.5%
Average years' teaching experience:	13.7
Students in gifted program:	20 / 3.6%
Students in remedial education:	13.1%
Students held back a grade:	1.8%
Total suspensions, pct. in-school:	29 / 65.5%
Offenses:	violence: 18, drugs: *, other: 13
Eligible students, free or reduced lunch:	11.8%
Before / after school program:	Yes / Yes

Students at this school generally go on to:
Dean Rusk, Teasley Middle

AJC GRADE: ★★★

Georgia Criterion-Referenced Competency Tests - Grade 4
Pct. of students at each level

- Read: Exceeds 52%, Meets 33%, Does not meet 15%
- Math: Exceeds 33%, Meets 44%, Does not meet 22%
- Lang: Exceeds 31%, Meets 56%, Does not meet 13%

Cherokee County Elementary Schools

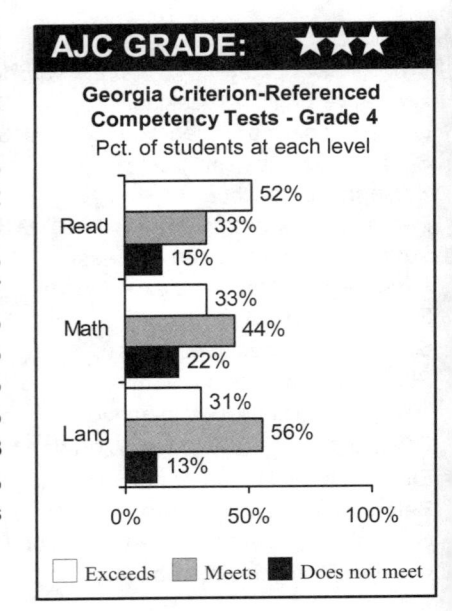

Moore Elementary School

1375 Puckett Rd, Waleska, GA 30183
770-479-3798 · Grades K - 6

Enrollment:	438
White / black / other:	97.3% / 0.5% / 2.3%
Not native English-speaking:	4 / 0.9%
Limited English proficiency:	9 / 2.1%
Student absenteeism:	5.7%
Students per teacher:	13.0
Parent friendliness:	① ❷ ❸ ❹ ❺ ❻
Teachers with advanced degrees:	45.7%
Average years' teaching experience:	9.9
Students in gifted program:	12 / 2.7%
Students in remedial education:	14.8%
Students held back a grade:	1.8%
Total suspensions, pct. in-school:	3 / 33.3%
Offenses:	violence: 1, drugs: *, other: 3
Eligible students, free or reduced lunch:	28.5%
Before / after school program:	Yes / Yes

Students at this school generally go on to:
Teasley Middle

AJC GRADE: ★★★

Georgia Criterion-Referenced Competency Tests - Grade 4
Pct. of students at each level

- Read: Exceeds 29%, Meets 44%, Does not meet 27%
- Math: Exceeds 11%, Meets 60%, Does not meet 29%
- Lang: Exceeds 22%, Meets 44%, Does not meet 35%

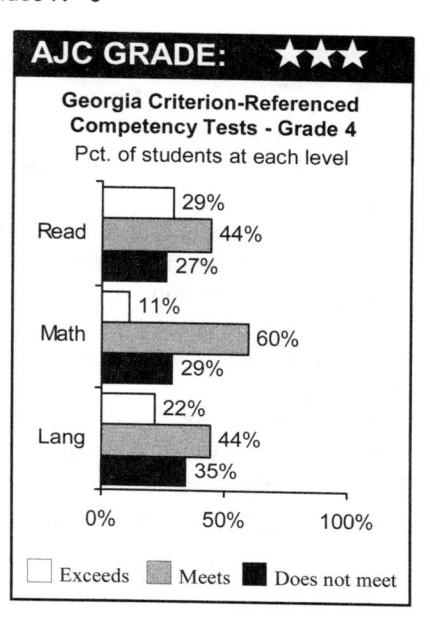

Mountain Road Elementary School

615 Mountain Rd, Woodstock, GA 30188
770-664-9708 · Grades K - 6

Enrollment:	526
White / black / other:	96.8% / 0.8% / 2.5%
Not native English-speaking:	2 / 0.4%
Limited English proficiency:	4 / 0.8%
Student absenteeism:	4.0%
Students per teacher:	13.1
Parent friendliness:	① ❷ ❸ ❹ ❺ ❻
Teachers with advanced degrees:	51.2%
Average years' teaching experience:	13.2
Students in gifted program:	43 / 8.2%
Students in remedial education:	8.3%
Students held back a grade:	0.6%
Total suspensions, pct. in-school:	9 / 44.4%
Offenses:	violence: 7, drugs: *, other: 3
Eligible students, free or reduced lunch:	5.3%
Before / after school program:	Yes / Yes

Students at this school generally go on to:
Dean Rusk Middle

AJC GRADE: ★★★

Georgia Criterion-Referenced Competency Tests - Grade 4
Pct. of students at each level

- Read: Exceeds 45%, Meets 34%, Does not meet 21%
- Math: Exceeds 20%, Meets 55%, Does not meet 25%
- Lang: Exceeds 25%, Meets 58%, Does not meet 18%

Cherokee County Elementary Schools

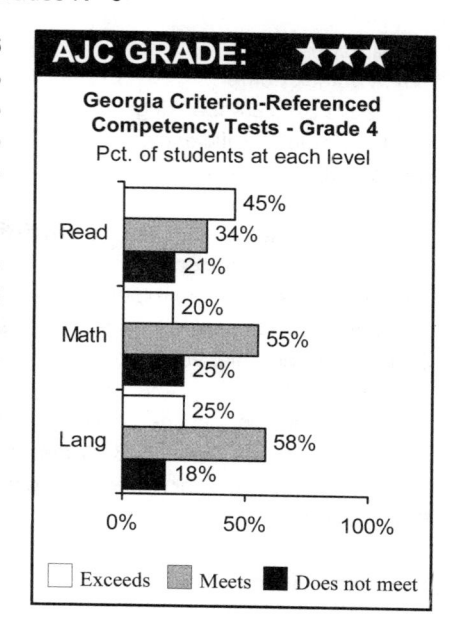

Oak Grove Elementary School

6118 Woodstock Rd, Acworth, GA 30102
770-974-6682 · Grades K - 4

Enrollment:	643
White / black / other:	86.0% / 3.6% / 10.4%
Not native English-speaking:	26 / 4.0%
Limited English proficiency:	35 / 5.4%
Student absenteeism:	4.8%
Students per teacher:	16.2
Parent friendliness:	① ❷ ❸ ④ ⑤ ❻
Teachers with advanced degrees:	45.0%
Average years' teaching experience:	13.6
Students in gifted program:	15 / 2.3%
Students in remedial education:	14.8%
Students held back a grade:	3.3%
Total suspensions, pct. in-school:	*
Offenses:	violence: *, drugs: *, other: *
Eligible students, free or reduced lunch:	21.9%
Before / after school program:	Yes / Yes

Students at this school generally go on to:
Chapman Intermediate School

AJC GRADE: ★★★

Georgia Criterion-Referenced Competency Tests - Grade 4
Pct. of students at each level

- Read: Exceeds 39%, Meets 46%, Does not meet 15%
- Math: Exceeds 14%, Meets 57%, Does not meet 29%
- Lang: Exceeds 19%, Meets 62%, Does not meet 19%

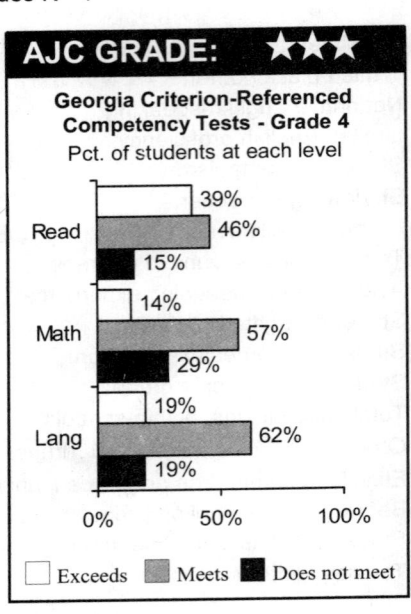

Sixes Elementary School

20 Ridge Rd, Canton, GA 30114
770-345-3070 · Grades K - 6

Enrollment:	1,172
White / black / other:	93.9% / 1.8% / 4.4%
Not native English-speaking:	12 / 1.0%
Limited English proficiency:	21 / 1.8%
Student absenteeism:	4.5%
Students per teacher:	16.4
Parent friendliness:	① ❷ ❸ ④ ❺ ❻
Teachers with advanced degrees:	32.9%
Average years' teaching experience:	9.4
Students in gifted program:	29 / 2.5%
Students in remedial education:	5.6%
Students held back a grade:	0.4%
Total suspensions, pct. in-school:	7 / 100.0%
Offenses:	violence: 6, drugs: *, other: 5
Eligible students, free or reduced lunch:	12.2%
Before / after school program:	Yes / Yes

Students at this school generally go on to:
Woodstock Middle

AJC GRADE: ★★★

Georgia Criterion-Referenced Competency Tests - Grade 4
Pct. of students at each level

- Read: Exceeds 42%, Meets 45%, Does not meet 13%
- Math: Exceeds 16%, Meets 55%, Does not meet 29%
- Lang: Exceeds 20%, Meets 68%, Does not meet 12%

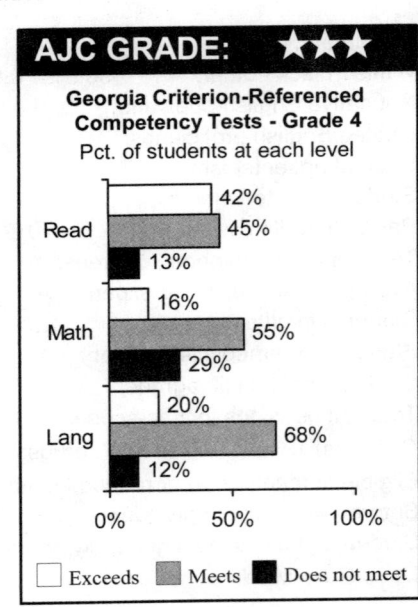

Tippens Elementary School

8 Glenwood St, Canton, GA 30114
770-479-2645 · Grades K - 6

Enrollment:	261
White / black / other:	36.0% / 24.5% / 39.5%
Not native English-speaking:	63 / 24.1%
Limited English proficiency:	67 / 25.7%
Student absenteeism:	5.1%
Students per teacher:	12.3
Parent friendliness:	① ❷ ❸ ④ ⑤ ❻
Teachers with advanced degrees:	45.5%
Average years' teaching experience:	10.7
Students in gifted program:	2 / 0.8%
Students in remedial education:	34.8%
Students held back a grade:	6.1%
Total suspensions, pct. in-school:	11 / 45.5%
Offenses:	violence: 9, drugs: *, other: 2
Eligible students, free or reduced lunch:	83.5%
Before / after school program:	Yes / No
Students at this school generally go on to:	
Teasley Middle	

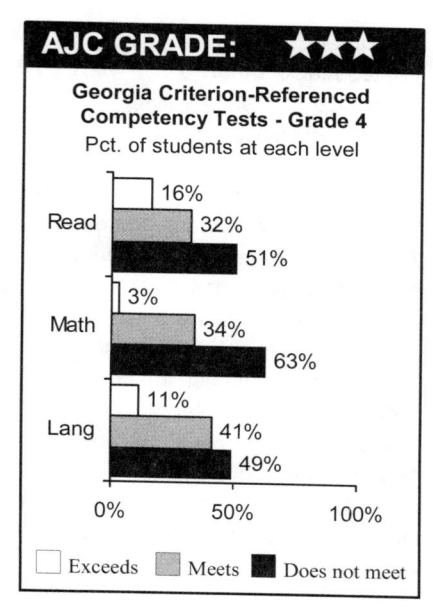

AJC GRADE: ★★★

Georgia Criterion-Referenced Competency Tests - Grade 4
Pct. of students at each level

Read: Exceeds 16%, Meets 32%, Does not meet 51%
Math: Exceeds 3%, Meets 34%, Does not meet 63%
Lang: Exceeds 11%, Meets 41%, Does not meet 49%

Woodstock Elementary School

8371 Main St, Woodstock, GA 30188
770-926-6969 · Grades K - 6

Enrollment:	559
White / black / other:	75.7% / 9.7% / 14.7%
Not native English-speaking:	*
Limited English proficiency:	55 / 9.8%
Student absenteeism:	5.0%
Students per teacher:	14.7
Parent friendliness:	① ❷ ❸ ④ ❺ ❻
Teachers with advanced degrees:	40.0%
Average years' teaching experience:	10.8
Students in gifted program:	12 / 2.1%
Students in remedial education:	15.3%
Students held back a grade:	2.9%
Total suspensions, pct. in-school:	*
Offenses:	violence: 6, drugs: *, other: 2
Eligible students, free or reduced lunch:	40.1%
Before / after school program:	Yes / Yes
Students at this school generally go on to:	
Woodstock Middle	

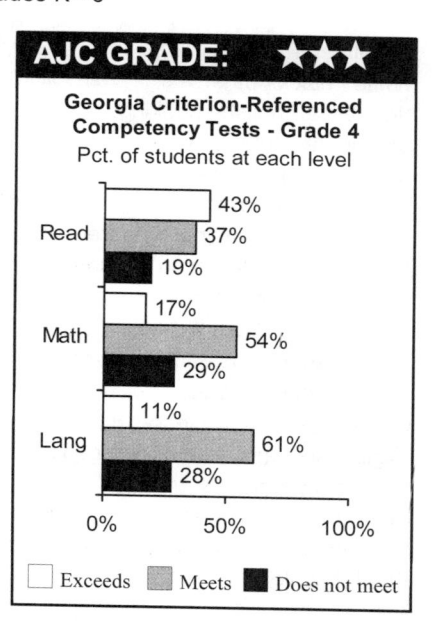

AJC GRADE: ★★★

Georgia Criterion-Referenced Competency Tests - Grade 4
Pct. of students at each level

Read: Exceeds 43%, Meets 37%, Does not meet 19%
Math: Exceeds 17%, Meets 54%, Does not meet 29%
Lang: Exceeds 11%, Meets 61%, Does not meet 28%

Cherokee County Elementary Schools

Booth Middle School

6550 Putnam Ford Dr, Woodstock, GA 30189
770-926-5707 · Grades 7 - 8

Enrollment:	975
White / black / other:	92.1% / 3.3% / 4.6%
Not native English-speaking:	12 / 1.2%
Student absenteeism:	5.5%
Students per teacher:	14.9
Parent friendliness:	❶❷❸④❺❻
Teachers with advanced degrees:	52.9%
Average years' teaching experience:	11.1
Students in gifted program:	164 / 16.8%
Students held back a grade:	1.0%
Total suspensions and expulsions:	101
Suspensions only, pct. in-school:	101 / 62.4%
Offenses:	violence: 53, drugs: 7, other: 64
Eligible students, free or reduced lunch:	12.0%
Number of dropouts:	4 / 0.4%
Pct. 8th-graders w/ basic computer skills:	100.0%

Students at this school generally go to:
Etowah High

AJC GRADE: ★★★

Georgia Criterion-Referenced Competency Tests - Grades 6, 8
Pct. of students at each level

	Lang 8	Math 8	Read 8
Exceeds	28	13	63
Meets	52	56	29
Does not meet	19	31	8

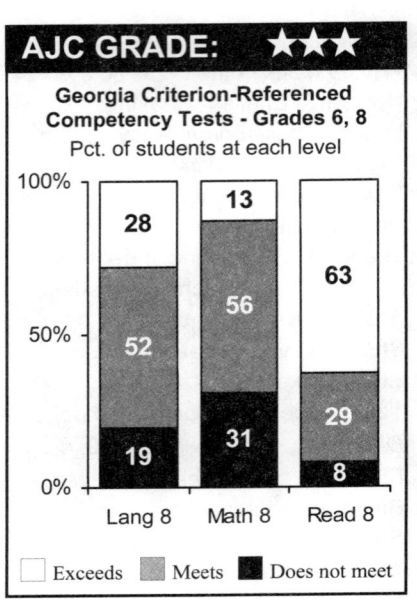

Chapman Intermediate School

6500 Putnam Ford Dr, Woodstock, GA 30189
770-926-6424 · Grades 5 - 6

Enrollment:	1,139
White / black / other:	91.7% / 3.2% / 5.2%
Not native English-speaking:	8 / 0.7%
Student absenteeism:	5.1%
Students per teacher:	19.1
Parent friendliness:	❶❷❸④⑤❻
Teachers with advanced degrees:	44.3%
Average years' teaching experience:	9.4
Students in gifted program:	192 / 16.9%
Students held back a grade:	0.1%
Total suspensions and expulsions:	95
Suspensions only, pct. in-school:	95 / 71.6%
Offenses:	violence: 88, drugs: 2, other: 26
Eligible students, free or reduced lunch:	13.7%
Number of dropouts:	1 / 0.2%
Pct. 8th-graders w/ basic computer skills:	*

Students at this school generally go to:
Booth Middle

AJC GRADE: ★★★

Georgia Criterion-Referenced Competency Tests - Grades 6, 8
Pct. of students at each level

	Lang 6	Math 6	Read 6
Exceeds	30	26	46
Meets	50	56	41
Does not meet	20	19	13

Cherokee County Middle Schools

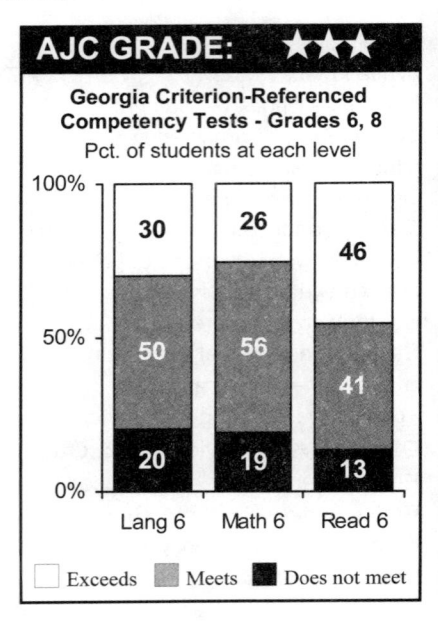

Dean Rusk Middle School

4695 Hickory Rd, Canton, GA 30115
770-345-2832 · Grades 7 - 8

Enrollment:	939
White / black / other:	95.3% / 1.4% / 3.3%
Not native English-speaking:	2 / 0.2%
Student absenteeism:	5.8%
Students per teacher:	16.4
Parent friendliness:	❶❷❸④⑤❻
Teachers with advanced degrees:	50.0%
Average years' teaching experience:	13.1
Students in gifted program:	192 / 20.4%
Students held back a grade:	0.3%
Total suspensions and expulsions:	83
Suspensions only, pct. in-school:	83 / 88.0%
Offenses: violence: 60, drugs: *, other: 27	
Eligible students, free or reduced lunch:	7.5%
Number of dropouts:	2 / 0.2%
Pct. 8th-graders w/ basic computer skills:	100.0%

Students at this school generally go on to:
Sequoyah High

AJC GRADE: ★★★

Georgia Criterion-Referenced Competency Tests - Grades 6, 8
Pct. of students at each level

	Lang 8	Math 8	Read 8
Exceeds	39	19	70
Meets	48	61	22
Does not meet	13	20	7

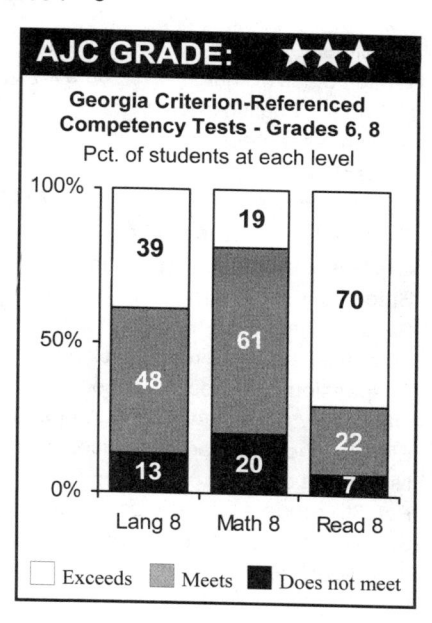

Marie Archer Teasley Middle School

8871 Knox Bridge Hwy, Canton, GA 30114
770-479-7077 · Grades 7 - 8

Enrollment:	1,035
White / black / other:	90.3% / 3.4% / 6.3%
Not native English-speaking:	22 / 2.1%
Student absenteeism:	6.9%
Students per teacher:	14.0
Parent friendliness:	❶❷❸④⑤❻
Teachers with advanced degrees:	50.0%
Average years' teaching experience:	12.2
Students in gifted program:	99 / 9.6%
Students held back a grade:	4.2%
Total suspensions and expulsions:	141
Suspensions only, pct. in-school:	141 / 70.9%
Offenses: violence: 102, drugs: 4, other: 70	
Eligible students, free or reduced lunch:	25.8%
Number of dropouts:	2 / 0.2%
Pct. 8th-graders w/ basic computer skills:	100.0%

Students at this school generally go on to:
Cherokee High

AJC GRADE: ★★★

Georgia Criterion-Referenced Competency Tests - Grades 6, 8
Pct. of students at each level

	Lang 8	Math 8	Read 8
Exceeds	26	8	57
Meets	49	58	28
Does not meet	26	34	15

Cherokee County Middle Schools

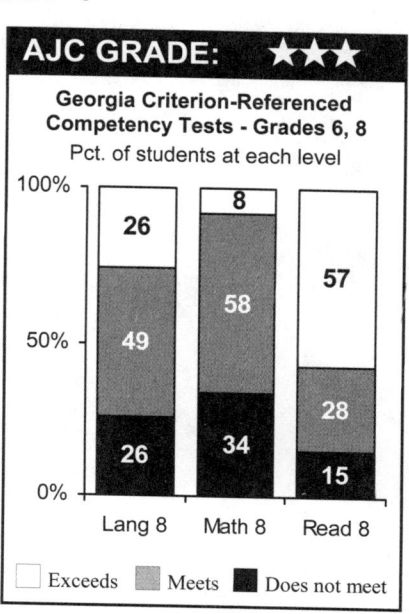

Woodstock Middle School

2000 Towne Lake Hills South Dr, Woodstock, GA 30189
770-592-3516 · Grades 7 - 8

Enrollment:	1,120
White / black / other:	88.3% / 5.4% / 6.3%
Not native English-speaking:	23 / 2.1%
Student absenteeism:	5.5%
Students per teacher:	14.5
Parent friendliness:	❶❷❸④❺❻
Teachers with advanced degrees:	49.4%
Average years' teaching experience:	10.4
Students in gifted program:	157 / 14.0%
Students held back a grade:	0.1%
Total suspensions and expulsions:	194
Suspensions only, pct. in-school:	194 / 85.1%
Offenses: violence: 106, drugs: 3, other: 122	
Eligible students, free or reduced lunch:	15.7%
Number of dropouts:	4 / 0.3%
Pct. 8th-graders w/ basic computer skills:	99.2%
Students at this school generally go on to: Woodstock High	

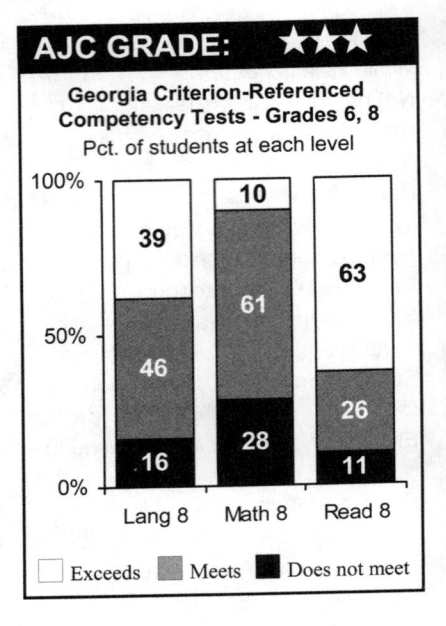

AJC GRADE: ★★★

Georgia Criterion-Referenced Competency Tests - Grades 6, 8
Pct. of students at each level

	Lang 8	Math 8	Read 8
Exceeds	39	10	63
Meets	46	61	26
Does not meet	16	28	11

Cherokee County Middle Schools

Cherokee High School

930 Marietta Hwy, Canton, GA 30114
770-479-4112 · Grades 9 - 12

Enrollment:	1,623
White / black / other:	91.4% / 3.7% / 4.9%
Not native English-speaking:	24 / 1.5%
Limited English proficiency:	31 / 1.9%
Student absenteeism:	6.2%
Students per teacher:	15.4
Parent friendliness:	① ❷ ❸ ④ ⑤ ❻
Students in gifted program:	140 / 8.6%
Students in remedial education:	4.6%
High school completion rate:	71.3%
Students held back a grade:	11.6%
Number of dropouts:	117 / 6.6%
Students in alternative programs:	50 / 3.1%
Students in special education:	228 / 14.0%
Eligible students, free or reduced lunch:	10.5%
Total suspensions and expulsions:	116
Suspensions only, pct. in-school:	116 / 82.8%
Drugs/alcohol-related offenses:	5
Violence-related offenses:	69
Firearms-related offenses:	8
Vandalism-related offenses:	14
Theft-related offenses:	3
All other disciplinary offenses:	105
Teachers with advanced degrees:	51.4%
Average years' teaching experience:	12.2

AJC GRADE: ★★★

High School Graduation Test
Pct. of students who passed on first try

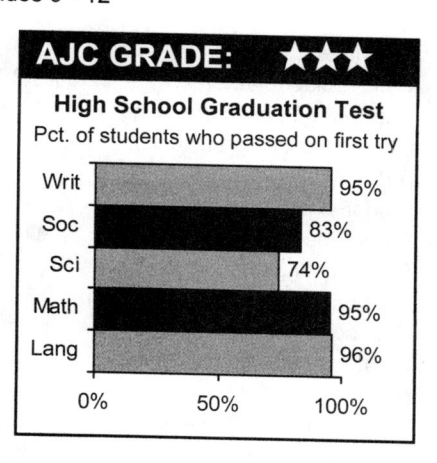

- Writ: 95%
- Soc: 83%
- Sci: 74%
- Math: 95%
- Lang: 96%

GHSA classification: 6-AAAAA
Interscholastic sports offered:
BB, BS, CC, CL, FB, GO, SB, SO, SW, TE, TF, VB, WR

Advanced Placement (AP) Exams
Students tested: 65
Tests taken: 91
Pct. of test scores 3 or higher (1 - 5 scale): 54.9%

Languages other than English taught:
French, Latin, Spanish

2000-2001 high school graduates: 236

College prep/vocational diplomas:	3.0%
College prep endorsement diplomas:	59.3%
Vocational endorsement diplomas:	36.0%
General high school diplomas:	0.0%
Special education diplomas:	1.7%
Certificates of attendance (no diploma):	0.0%

Of the 2000-2001 graduates, 68.2% were eligible for the HOPE scholarship.

Of the 1999-2000 graduates, 92 attended a Georgia public college or university. Of those, 90% met the school's minimum academic requirements.

Average SAT Scores
Maximum score is 800 on each portion

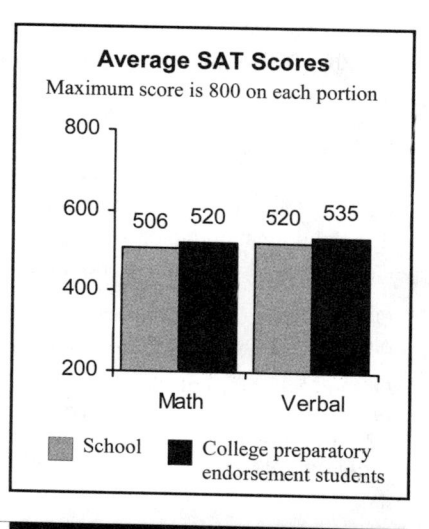

- Math: School 506, College preparatory endorsement students 520
- Verbal: School 520, College preparatory endorsement students 535

The Atlanta Journal-Constitution / Page 89

Cherokee County High Schools

Etowah High School

6565 Putnam Ford Dr, Woodstock, GA 30189
770-926-4411 · Grades 9 - 12

Enrollment:	1,549
White / black / other:	92.3% / 3.2% / 4.6%
Not native English-speaking:	5 / 0.3%
Limited English proficiency:	14 / 0.9%
Student absenteeism:	5.7%
Students per teacher:	16.6
Parent friendliness:	❶❷❸④⑤❻
Students in gifted program:	195 / 12.6%
Students in remedial education:	3.4%
High school completion rate:	87.4%
Students held back a grade:	2.4%
Number of dropouts:	50 / 2.8%
Students in alternative programs:	24 / 1.5%
Students in special education:	167 / 10.8%
Eligible students, free or reduced lunch:	3.1%
Total suspensions and expulsions:	115
Suspensions only, pct. in-school:	115 / 79.1%
Drugs/alcohol-related offenses:	7
Violence-related offenses:	38
Firearms-related offenses:	4
Vandalism-related offenses:	11
Theft-related offenses:	6
All other disciplinary offenses:	65
Teachers with advanced degrees:	52.2%
Average years' teaching experience:	13.5

AJC GRADE: ★★★

High School Graduation Test
Pct. of students who passed on first try

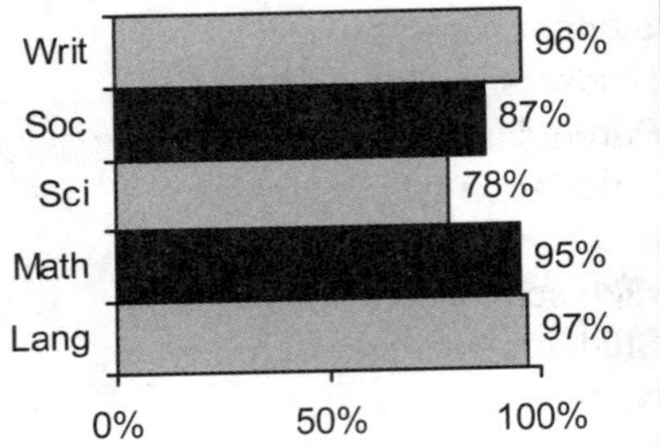

- Writ: 96%
- Soc: 87%
- Sci: 78%
- Math: 95%
- Lang: 97%

GHSA classification:	6-AAAAA

Interscholastic sports offered:
BB, BS, CC, FB, GO, SB, SW, TE, TF, VB, WR

Advanced Placement (AP) Exams
Students tested:	87
Tests taken:	175
Pct. of test scores 3 or higher (1 - 5 scale):	45.7%

Languages other than English taught:
French, Spanish

2000-2001 high school graduates: 257

College prep/vocational diplomas:	3.1%
College prep endorsement diplomas:	69.6%
Vocational endorsement diplomas:	26.1%
General high school diplomas:	0.0%
Special education diplomas:	1.2%
Certificates of attendance (no diploma):	0.0%

Of the 2000-2001 graduates, 71.6% were eligible for the HOPE scholarship.

Of the 1999-2000 graduates, 121 attended a Georgia public college or university. Of those, 92% met the school's minimum academic requirements.

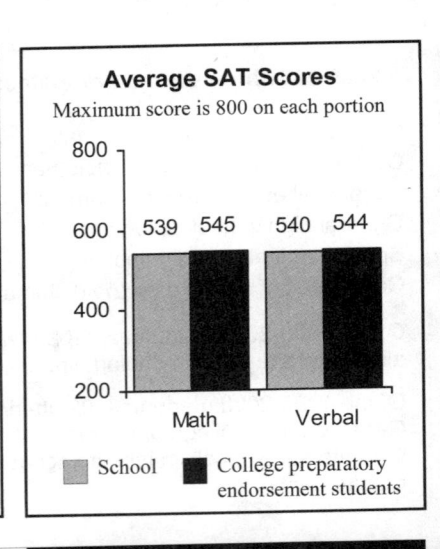

Average SAT Scores
Maximum score is 800 on each portion

- Math — School: 539, College preparatory endorsement students: 545
- Verbal — School: 540, College preparatory endorsement students: 544

Cherokee County High Schools

Sequoyah High School

4485 Hickory Rd, Canton, GA 30115
770-345-1474 · Grades 9 - 12

Enrollment:	1,586
White / black / other:	95.9% / 1.2% / 2.9%
Not native English-speaking:	10 / 0.6%
Limited English proficiency:	21 / 1.3%
Student absenteeism:	5.4%
Students per teacher:	16.4
Parent friendliness:	① ❷ ❸ ④ ❺ ❻
Students in gifted program:	233 / 14.7%
Students in remedial education:	5.7%
High school completion rate:	91.0%
Students held back a grade:	0.4%
Number of dropouts:	38 / 2.2%
Students in alternative programs:	22 / 1.4%
Students in special education:	110 / 6.9%
Eligible students, free or reduced lunch:	3.5%
Total suspensions and expulsions:	82
Suspensions only, pct. in-school:	82 / 97.6%
Drugs/alcohol-related offenses:	11
Violence-related offenses:	29
Firearms-related offenses:	3
Vandalism-related offenses:	10
Theft-related offenses:	2
All other disciplinary offenses:	75
Teachers with advanced degrees:	63.9%
Average years' teaching experience:	12.8

AJC GRADE: ★★★

High School Graduation Test
Pct. of students who passed on first try

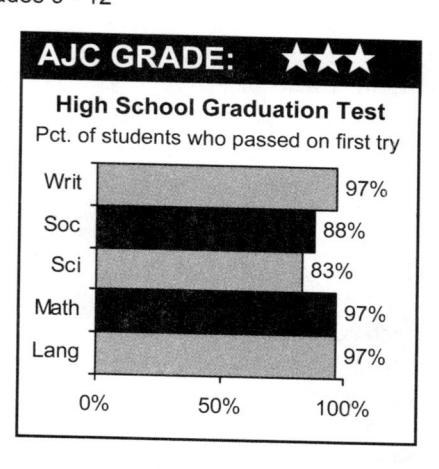

- Writ: 97%
- Soc: 88%
- Sci: 83%
- Math: 97%
- Lang: 97%

GHSA classification:	6-AAAAA

Interscholastic sports offered:
BB, BS, CC, CL, FB, GO, SB, SO, SW, TE, TF, VB, WR

Advanced Placement (AP) Exams
Students tested:	130
Tests taken:	274
Pct. of test scores 3 or higher (1 - 5 scale):	65.3%

Languages other than English taught:
French, Latin, Spanish

2000-2001 high school graduates: 284

College prep/vocational diplomas:	2.1%
College prep endorsement diplomas:	76.4%
Vocational endorsement diplomas:	20.4%
General high school diplomas:	0.0%
Special education diplomas:	1.1%
Certificates of attendance (no diploma):	0.0%

Of the 2000-2001 graduates, 79.2% were eligible for the HOPE scholarship.

Of the 1999-2000 graduates, 129 attended a Georgia public college or university. Of those, 94% met the school's minimum academic requirements.

Average SAT Scores
Maximum score is 800 on each portion

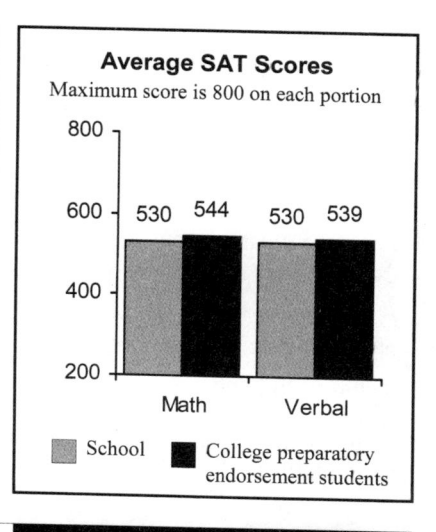

- Math: School 530, College preparatory endorsement students 544
- Verbal: School 530, College preparatory endorsement students 539

Cherokee County High Schools

Woodstock High School

2010 Towne Lake Hills South Dr, Woodstock, GA 30189
770-592-3500 · Grades 9 - 12

Enrollment:	1,936
White / black / other:	89.7% / 3.9% / 6.4%
Not native English-speaking:	20 / 1.0%
Limited English proficiency:	34 / 1.8%
Student absenteeism:	7.2%
Students per teacher:	16.5
Parent friendliness:	❶❷❸④⑤❻
Students in gifted program:	192 / 9.9%
Students in remedial education:	3.2%
High school completion rate:	85.8%
Students held back a grade:	2.6%
Number of dropouts:	76 / 3.5%
Students in alternative programs:	32 / 1.7%
Students in special education:	208 / 10.7%
Eligible students, free or reduced lunch:	8.3%
Total suspensions and expulsions:	103
Suspensions only, pct. in-school:	103 / 77.7%
Drugs/alcohol-related offenses:	6
Violence-related offenses:	42
Firearms-related offenses:	5
Vandalism-related offenses:	11
Theft-related offenses:	10
All other disciplinary offenses:	90
Teachers with advanced degrees:	37.6%
Average years' teaching experience:	9.4

AJC GRADE: ★★★

High School Graduation Test
Pct. of students who passed on first try

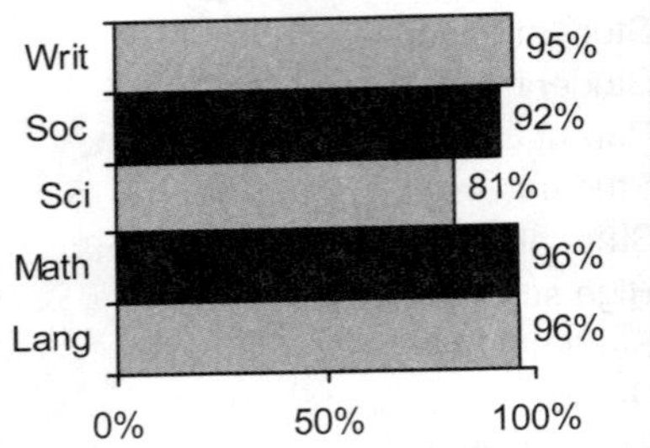

- Writ: 95%
- Soc: 92%
- Sci: 81%
- Math: 96%
- Lang: 96%

GHSA classification: 6-AAAAA
Interscholastic sports offered:
BB, BS, CC, CL, FB, GO, SB, SO, SW, TE, TF, VB, WR

Advanced Placement (AP) Exams
- Students tested: 80
- Tests taken: 125
- Pct. of test scores 3 or higher (1 - 5 scale): 56.8%

Languages other than English taught:
French, Latin, Spanish

2000-2001 high school graduates: 343

College prep/vocational diplomas:	0.9%
College prep endorsement diplomas:	66.8%
Vocational endorsement diplomas:	30.9%
General high school diplomas:	0.0%
Special education diplomas:	1.5%
Certificates of attendance (no diploma):	0.0%

Of the 2000-2001 graduates, 69.1% were eligible for the HOPE scholarship.

Of the 1999-2000 graduates, 66 attended a Georgia public college or university. Of those, 92% met the school's minimum academic requirements.

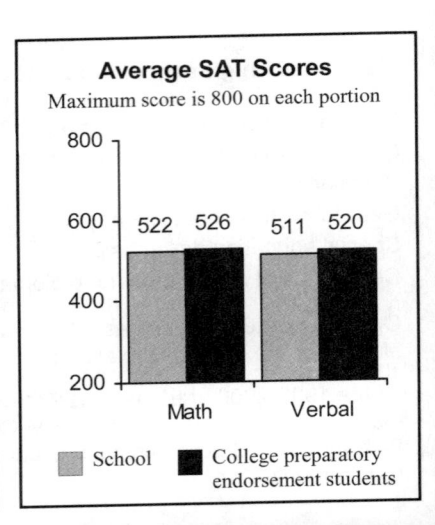

Average SAT Scores
Maximum score is 800 on each portion

- Math: School 522, College preparatory endorsement students 526
- Verbal: School 511, College preparatory endorsement students 520

Cherokee County High Schools

AJC ranking of Cherokee County Schools

ELEMENTARY SCHOOLS

AJC Star Grade: ★★★

- Arnold Mill Elementary
- Ball Ground Elementary
- Bascomb Elementary
- Buffington Elementary
- Canton Elementary
- Carmel Elementary
- Hickory Flat Elementary
- Kleven Boston Elementary
- Little River Elementary
- Macedonia Elementary
- Moore Elementary
- Mountain Road Elementary
- Oak Grove Elementary
- Sixes Elementary
- Tippens Elementary
- Woodstock Elementary

AJC Star Grade: ★★

- Clayton Elementary
- Florine Dial Johnston Elementary
- Free Home Elementary
- Holly Springs Elementary

MIDDLE SCHOOLS

AJC Star Grade: ★★★

- Booth Middle
- Chapman Intermediate
- Dean Rusk Middle
- Marie Archer Teasley Middle
- Woodstock Middle

HIGH SCHOOLS

AJC Star Grade: ★★★

- Cherokee High
- Etowah High
- Sequoyah High
- Woodstock High

Cherokee County Public Schools

Clayton County Public Schools

120 Smith St, Jonesboro, GA 30236
Phone: 770-473-2700 · Fax: 770-473-2706
http://www.clayton.k12.ga.us

The following pages provide detailed information on every school in the Clayton County school district. An asterisk (*) means the value of the data was zero or was not reported by the school district. A complete list of schools ranked by The Atlanta Journal-Constitution's star rating system follows the detailed school reports.

District enrollment:	46,281
White / black / other:	21.6% / 64.9% / 13.5%
Not native English-speaking:	1,486 / 3.2%
Expenditure per student (general fund):	$5,415
Students per teacher:	17.0
Teachers with advanced degrees:	45.5%
Average years, teaching experience:	12.2
Average teacher salary:	$42,634.03
Students in gifted program:	2,215 / 4.8%
Students held back a grade:	2,405 / 5.2%
Eligible students, free or reduced lunch:	25,836 / 55.1%
Number of dropouts (grades 9-12):	1,108 / 8.1%
High school completion rate:	62.1%
Graduates, pct. eligible for HOPE scholarships:	1,933 / 55.5%
Average combined SAT score (maximum 1,600):	940
Pct. of 11th-graders passing the Georgia High School Graduation Tests on first try:	59%
Percent of children 5 to 17 years of age living in poverty (2000 Census estimate):	12.5%

Anderson Elementary School

4199 Old Rock Cut Rd, Conley, GA 30288
404-362-3820 · Grades K - 5

Enrollment:	419
White / black / other:	23.6% / 63.7% / 12.6%
Not native English-speaking:	9 / 2.1%
Limited English proficiency:	10 / 2.4%
Student absenteeism:	4.2%
Students per teacher:	14.4
Parent friendliness:	❶❷❸④⑤❻
Teachers with advanced degrees:	48.5%
Average years' teaching experience:	12.7
Students in gifted program:	7 / 1.7%
Students in remedial education:	34.8%
Students held back a grade:	3.8%
Total suspensions, pct. in-school:	86 / 18.6%
Offenses: violence: *, drugs: *, other:	86
Eligible students, free or reduced lunch:	79.7%
Before / after school program:	No / Yes

Students at this school generally go on to:
Adamson, Babb, Forest Park Middle

AJC GRADE: ★★★

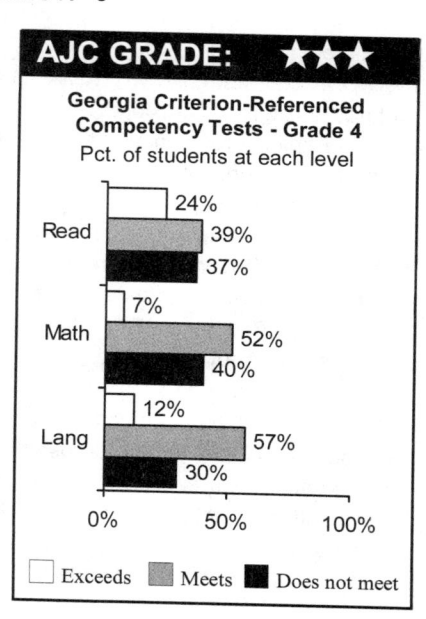

Georgia Criterion-Referenced Competency Tests - Grade 4
Pct. of students at each level

- Read: Exceeds 24%, Meets 39%, Does not meet 37%
- Math: Exceeds 7%, Meets 52%, Does not meet 40%
- Lang: Exceeds 12%, Meets 57%, Does not meet 30%

Arnold Elementary School

216 Stockbridge Rd, Jonesboro, GA 30236
770-473-2800 · Grades K - 5

Enrollment:	473
White / black / other:	51.0% / 40.6% / 8.5%
Not native English-speaking:	8 / 1.7%
Limited English proficiency:	8 / 1.7%
Student absenteeism:	3.9%
Students per teacher:	15.3
Parent friendliness:	❶❷❸④❺❻
Teachers with advanced degrees:	52.9%
Average years' teaching experience:	15.3
Students in gifted program:	48 / 10.1%
Students in remedial education:	21.2%
Students held back a grade:	1.7%
Total suspensions, pct. in-school:	65 / 90.8%
Offenses: violence: 7, drugs: *, other:	79
Eligible students, free or reduced lunch:	31.7%
Before / after school program:	Yes / Yes

Students at this school generally go on to:
Jonesboro, Roberts Middle

AJC GRADE: ★★

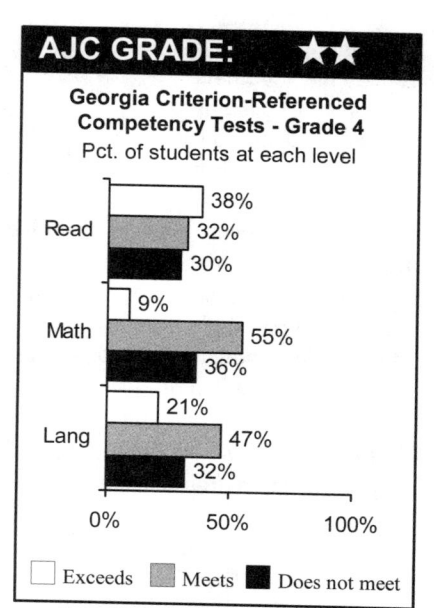

Georgia Criterion-Referenced Competency Tests - Grade 4
Pct. of students at each level

- Read: Exceeds 38%, Meets 32%, Does not meet 30%
- Math: Exceeds 9%, Meets 55%, Does not meet 36%
- Lang: Exceeds 21%, Meets 47%, Does not meet 32%

Clayton County Elementary Schools

Brown Elementary School

9771 Poston Rd, Jonesboro, GA 30238
770-473-2785 · Grades K - 5

Enrollment:	902
White / black / other:	17.5% / 73.4% / 9.1%
Not native English-speaking:	7 / 0.8%
Limited English proficiency:	15 / 1.7%
Student absenteeism:	4.4%
Students per teacher:	17.3
Parent friendliness:	①❷❸④⑤❻
Teachers with advanced degrees:	47.3%
Average years' teaching experience:	13.5
Students in gifted program:	35 / 3.9%
Students in remedial education:	32.0%
Students held back a grade:	2.1%
Total suspensions, pct. in-school:	641 / 79.7%
Offenses:	violence: 119, drugs: *, other: 615
Eligible students, free or reduced lunch:	55.0%
Before / after school program:	Yes / Yes

Students at this school generally go on to:
Mundy's Mill, Pointe South Middle

AJC GRADE: ★★★

Georgia Criterion-Referenced Competency Tests - Grade 4
Pct. of students at each level

- Read: Exceeds 15%, Meets 53%, Does not meet 31%
- Math: Exceeds 3%, Meets 48%, Does not meet 49%
- Lang: Exceeds 6%, Meets 67%, Does not meet 27%

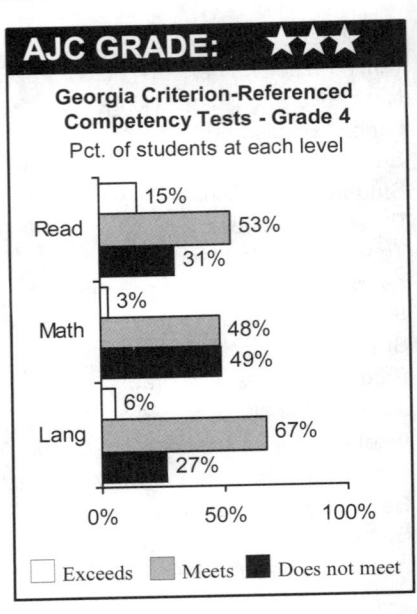

Church Street Elementary School

7013 Church St, Riverdale, GA 30274
770-994-4000 · Grades K - 5

Enrollment:	1,058
White / black / other:	5.4% / 79.2% / 15.4%
Not native English-speaking:	56 / 5.3%
Limited English proficiency:	62 / 5.9%
Student absenteeism:	4.3%
Students per teacher:	19.2
Parent friendliness:	❶❷❸④❺❻
Teachers with advanced degrees:	38.6%
Average years' teaching experience:	9.9
Students in gifted program:	46 / 4.3%
Students in remedial education:	33.4%
Students held back a grade:	1.5%
Total suspensions, pct. in-school:	109 / 16.5%
Offenses:	violence: 34, drugs: *, other: 83
Eligible students, free or reduced lunch:	67.6%
Before / after school program:	Yes / Yes

Students at this school generally go on to:
Kendrick, North Clayton, Riverdale Middle

AJC GRADE: ★★★

Georgia Criterion-Referenced Competency Tests - Grade 4
Pct. of students at each level

- Read: Exceeds 17%, Meets 42%, Does not meet 41%
- Math: Exceeds 3%, Meets 43%, Does not meet 53%
- Lang: Exceeds 8%, Meets 58%, Does not meet 34%

Clayton County Elementary Schools

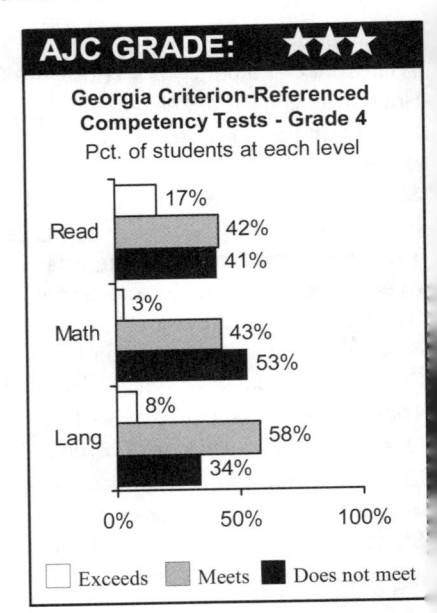

East Clayton Elementary School

2750 Ellenwood Rd, Ellenwood, GA 30294
404-362-3885 · Grades K - 5

Enrollment:	814
White / black / other:	22.9% / 64.4% / 12.8%
Not native English-speaking:	26 / 3.2%
Limited English proficiency:	32 / 3.9%
Student absenteeism:	4.2%
Students per teacher:	17.5
Parent friendliness:	❶❷❸④⑤❻
Teachers with advanced degrees:	28.6%
Average years' teaching experience:	11.8
Students in gifted program:	49 / 6.0%
Students in remedial education:	32.8%
Students held back a grade:	0.9%
Total suspensions, pct. in-school:	179 / 59.8%
Offenses:	violence: 33, drugs: 1, other: 337
Eligible students, free or reduced lunch:	53.5%
Before / after school program:	Yes / Yes

Students at this school generally go on to:
Adamson, Morrow Middle

AJC GRADE: ★★★

Georgia Criterion-Referenced Competency Tests - Grade 4
Pct. of students at each level

- Read: Exceeds 24%, Meets 44%, Does not meet 32%
- Math: Exceeds 5%, Meets 47%, Does not meet 48%
- Lang: Exceeds 13%, Meets 61%, Does not meet 26%

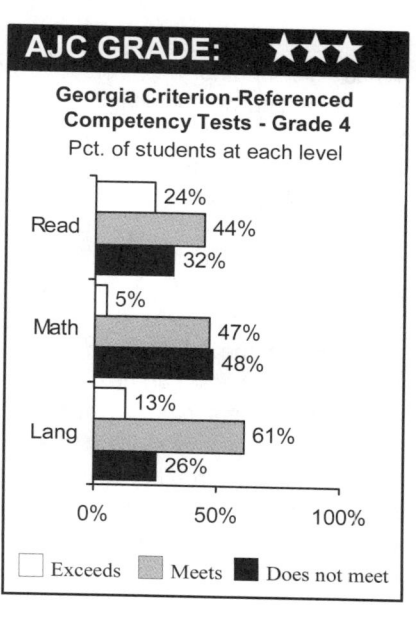

Edmonds Elementary School

4495 Simpson Rd, Forest Park, GA 30297
404-362-3830 · Grades K - 5

Enrollment:	454
White / black / other:	19.6% / 50.7% / 29.7%
Not native English-speaking:	44 / 9.7%
Limited English proficiency:	60 / 13.2%
Student absenteeism:	5.3%
Students per teacher:	13.5
Parent friendliness:	❶❷❸④⑤❻
Teachers with advanced degrees:	47.2%
Average years' teaching experience:	11.7
Students in gifted program:	11 / 2.4%
Students in remedial education:	34.7%
Students held back a grade:	4.2%
Total suspensions, pct. in-school:	97 / 84.5%
Offenses:	violence: 8, drugs: *, other: 123
Eligible students, free or reduced lunch:	82.6%
Before / after school program:	No / Yes

Students at this school generally go on to:
Forest Park Middle

AJC GRADE: ★★★

Georgia Criterion-Referenced Competency Tests - Grade 4
Pct. of students at each level

- Read: Exceeds 22%, Meets 46%, Does not meet 32%
- Math: Exceeds 7%, Meets 51%, Does not meet 42%
- Lang: Exceeds 8%, Meets 64%, Does not meet 27%

Clayton County Elementary Schools

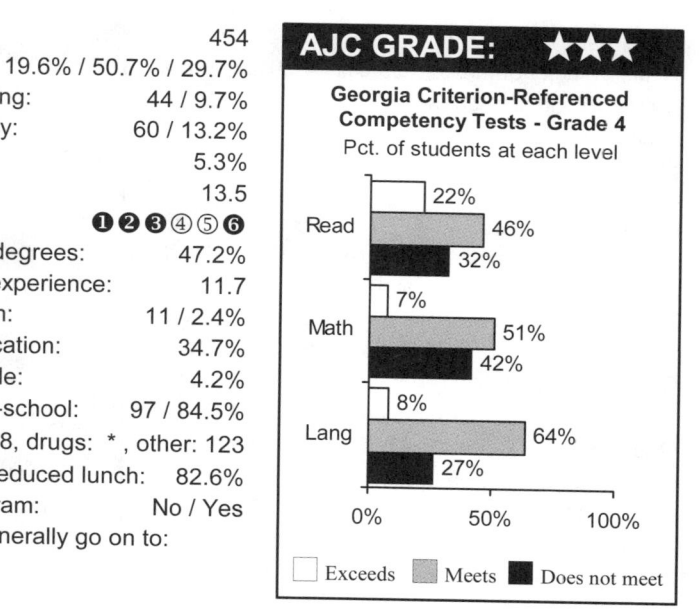

Fountain Elementary School

5215 West St, Forest Park, GA 30297
404-362-3875 · Grades K - 5

Enrollment:	830
White / black / other:	5.5% / 68.4% / 26.0%
Not native English-speaking:	98 / 11.8%
Limited English proficiency:	107 / 12.9%
Student absenteeism:	6.8%
Students per teacher:	18.1
Parent friendliness:	❶❷❸④❺❻
Teachers with advanced degrees:	47.9%
Average years' teaching experience:	10.4
Students in gifted program:	10 / 1.2%
Students in remedial education:	31.8%
Students held back a grade:	1.0%
Total suspensions, pct. in-school:	145 / 23.4%
Offenses: violence: 20, drugs: *, other: 158	
Eligible students, free or reduced lunch:	81.2%
Before / after school program:	No / Yes
Students at this school generally go on to:	
Babb Middle	

AJC GRADE: ★★★

Georgia Criterion-Referenced Competency Tests - Grade 4
Pct. of students at each level

Read: Exceeds 12%, Meets 48%, Does not meet 41%
Math: Exceeds 0%, Meets 43%, Does not meet 57%
Lang: Exceeds 6%, Meets 49%, Does not meet 45%

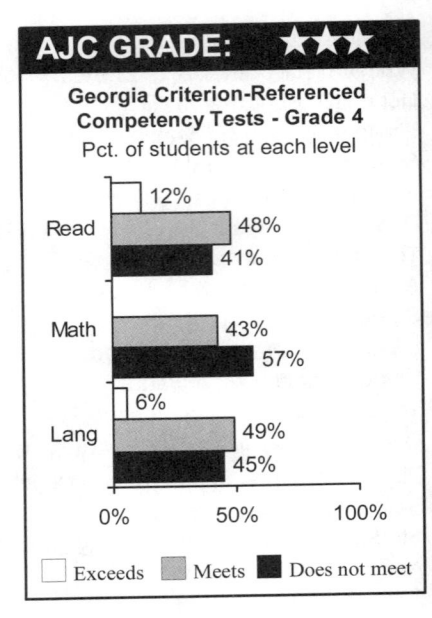

Hawthorne Elementary School

10750 English Rd, Hampton, GA 30228
770-472-7669 · Grades K - 5

Enrollment:	828
White / black / other:	39.5% / 49.9% / 10.6%
Not native English-speaking:	17 / 2.1%
Limited English proficiency:	23 / 2.8%
Student absenteeism:	5.0%
Students per teacher:	15.5
Parent friendliness:	❶❷❸④⑤❻
Teachers with advanced degrees:	49.1%
Average years' teaching experience:	12.8
Students in gifted program:	50 / 6.0%
Students in remedial education:	23.9%
Students held back a grade:	5.3%
Total suspensions, pct. in-school:	234 / 83.3%
Offenses: violence: 22, drugs: *, other: 320	
Eligible students, free or reduced lunch:	45.6%
Before / after school program:	Yes / Yes
Students at this school generally go on to:	
Lovejoy, Mundy's Mill Middle	

AJC GRADE: ★★★

Georgia Criterion-Referenced Competency Tests - Grade 4
Pct. of students at each level

Read: Exceeds 24%, Meets 47%, Does not meet 29%
Math: Exceeds 11%, Meets 59%, Does not meet 30%
Lang: Exceeds 15%, Meets 65%, Does not meet 20%

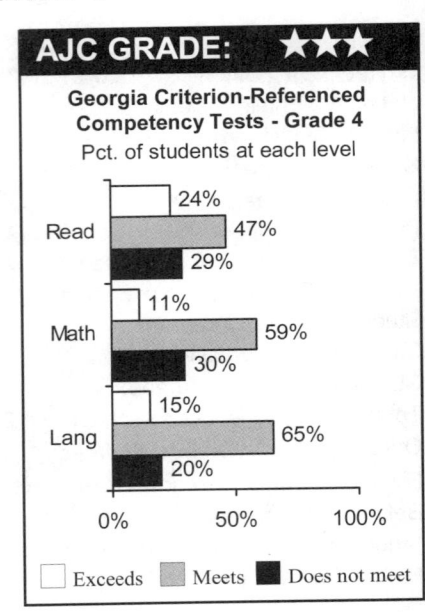

Haynie Elementary School

1169 Morrow Rd, Morrow, GA 30260
770-968-2905 · Grades K - 5

Enrollment:	1,053
White / black / other:	19.9% / 57.8% / 22.2%
Not native English-speaking:	84 / 8.0%
Limited English proficiency:	114 / 10.8%
Student absenteeism:	5.2%
Students per teacher:	16.4
Parent friendliness:	❶❷❸❹❺❻
Teachers with advanced degrees:	43.1%
Average years' teaching experience:	11.7
Students in gifted program:	26 / 2.5%
Students in remedial education:	34.1%
Students held back a grade:	3.0%
Total suspensions, pct. in-school:	399 / 78.7%
Offenses:	violence: 56, drugs: *, other: 389
Eligible students, free or reduced lunch:	73.6%
Before / after school program:	No / Yes

Students at this school generally go on to:
Babb, Kendrick Middle

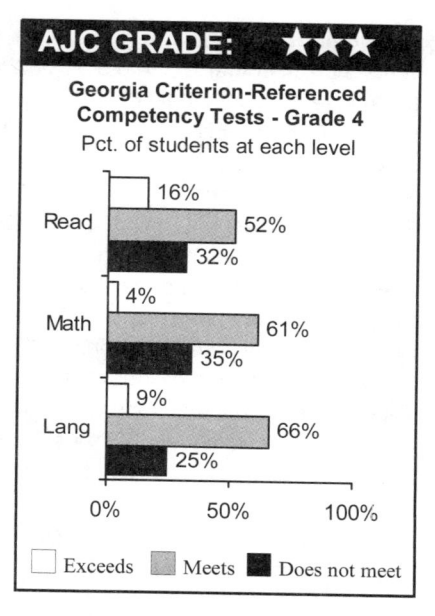

AJC GRADE: ★★★

Georgia Criterion-Referenced Competency Tests - Grade 4
Pct. of students at each level

- Read: Exceeds 16%, Meets 52%, Does not meet 32%
- Math: Exceeds 4%, Meets 61%, Does not meet 35%
- Lang: Exceeds 9%, Meets 66%, Does not meet 25%

Hendrix Drive Elementary School

4475 Hendrix Dr, Forest Park, GA 30297
404-362-3835 · Grades K - 5

Enrollment:	414
White / black / other:	17.9% / 46.9% / 35.3%
Not native English-speaking:	56 / 13.5%
Limited English proficiency:	70 / 16.9%
Student absenteeism:	5.6%
Students per teacher:	14.1
Parent friendliness:	❶❷❸④❺❻
Teachers with advanced degrees:	43.8%
Average years' teaching experience:	13.2
Students in gifted program:	10 / 2.4%
Students in remedial education:	34.9%
Students held back a grade:	4.6%
Total suspensions, pct. in-school:	26 / 38.5%
Offenses:	violence: 9, drugs: *, other: 30
Eligible students, free or reduced lunch:	81.7%
Before / after school program:	No / Yes

Students at this school generally go on to:
Babb, Forest Park, North Clayton Middle

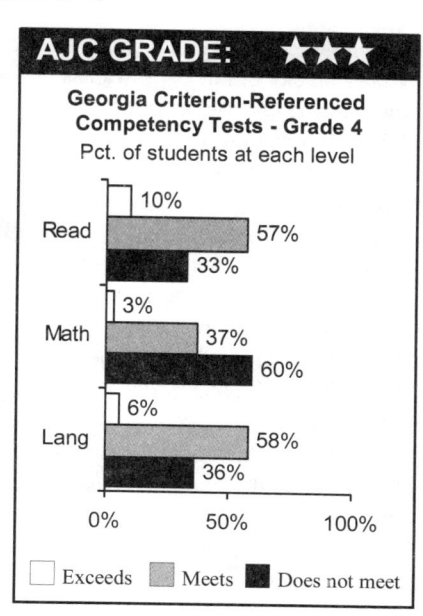

AJC GRADE: ★★★

Georgia Criterion-Referenced Competency Tests - Grade 4
Pct. of students at each level

- Read: Exceeds 10%, Meets 57%, Does not meet 33%
- Math: Exceeds 3%, Meets 37%, Does not meet 60%
- Lang: Exceeds 6%, Meets 58%, Does not meet 36%

Clayton County Elementary Schools

Huie Elementary School

1260 Rockcut Rd, Forest Park, GA 30297
404-362-3825 · Grades K - 5

Enrollment:	689
White / black / other:	8.9% / 65.2% / 26.0%
Not native English-speaking:	45 / 6.5%
Limited English proficiency:	72 / 10.4%
Student absenteeism:	4.9%
Students per teacher:	15.4
Parent friendliness:	①❷❸④❺❻
Teachers with advanced degrees:	33.3%
Average years' teaching experience:	11.8
Students in gifted program:	7 / 1.0%
Students in remedial education:	30.1%
Students held back a grade:	6.4%
Total suspensions, pct. in-school:	456 / 77.0%
Offenses:	violence: 63, drugs: *, other: 446
Eligible students, free or reduced lunch:	88.6%
Before / after school program:	No / Yes

Students at this school generally go on to:
Forest Park Middle

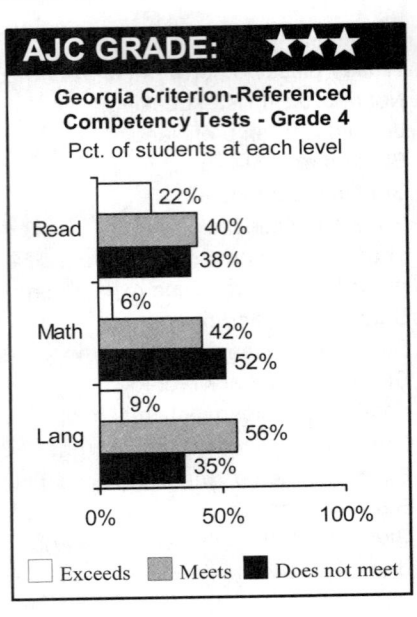

AJC GRADE: ★★★

Georgia Criterion-Referenced Competency Tests - Grade 4
Pct. of students at each level

- Read: Exceeds 22%, Meets 40%, Does not meet 38%
- Math: Exceeds 6%, Meets 42%, Does not meet 52%
- Lang: Exceeds 9%, Meets 56%, Does not meet 35%

Kemp Elementary School

10990 Folsom Rd, Hampton, GA 30228
770-473-2870 · Grades K - 5

Enrollment:	919
White / black / other:	45.7% / 44.4% / 9.9%
Not native English-speaking:	5 / 0.5%
Limited English proficiency:	7 / 0.8%
Student absenteeism:	4.8%
Students per teacher:	16.4
Parent friendliness:	❶❷❸④⑤❻
Teachers with advanced degrees:	48.2%
Average years' teaching experience:	12.6
Students in gifted program:	63 / 6.9%
Students in remedial education:	23.7%
Students held back a grade:	1.6%
Total suspensions, pct. in-school:	208 / 54.3%
Offenses:	violence: 68, drugs: *, other: 214
Eligible students, free or reduced lunch:	31.4%
Before / after school program:	Yes / Yes

Students at this school generally go on to:
Lovejoy Middle

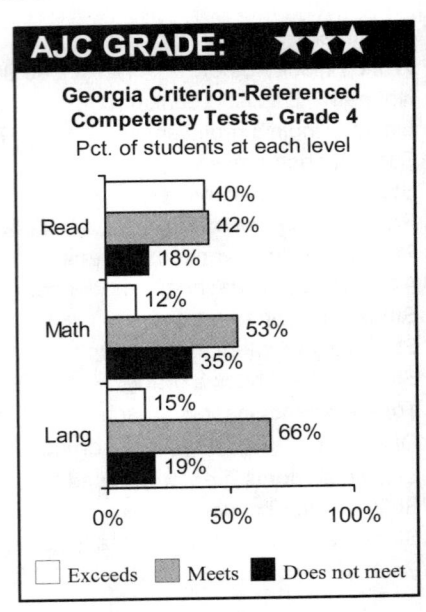

AJC GRADE: ★★★

Georgia Criterion-Referenced Competency Tests - Grade 4
Pct. of students at each level

- Read: Exceeds 40%, Meets 42%, Does not meet 18%
- Math: Exceeds 12%, Meets 53%, Does not meet 35%
- Lang: Exceeds 15%, Meets 66%, Does not meet 19%

Clayton County Elementary Schools

Kilpatrick Elementary School

7534 Tara Rd, Jonesboro, GA 30236
770-473-2790 · Grades K - 5

Enrollment:	825
White / black / other:	22.3% / 61.8% / 15.9%
Not native English-speaking:	34 / 4.1%
Limited English proficiency:	51 / 6.2%
Student absenteeism:	5.1%
Students per teacher:	17.0
Parent friendliness:	❶❷❸④⑤❻
Teachers with advanced degrees:	62.7%
Average years' teaching experience:	15.4
Students in gifted program:	24 / 2.9%
Students in remedial education:	33.0%
Students held back a grade:	1.2%
Total suspensions, pct. in-school:	305 / 75.4%
Offenses:	violence: 21, drugs: *, other: 348
Eligible students, free or reduced lunch:	63.3%
Before / after school program:	Yes / Yes

Students at this school generally go on to:
Jonesboro, Kendrick, Morrow Middle

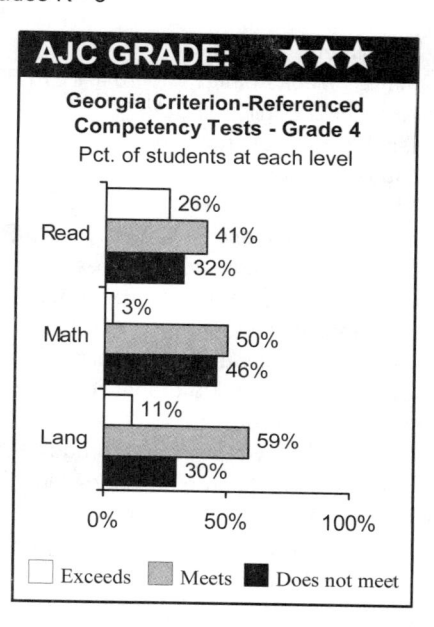

AJC GRADE: ★★★

Georgia Criterion-Referenced Competency Tests - Grade 4
Pct. of students at each level

- Read: Exceeds 26%, Meets 41%, Does not meet 32%
- Math: Exceeds 3%, Meets 50%, Does not meet 46%
- Lang: Exceeds 11%, Meets 59%, Does not meet 30%

Lake City Elementary School

5354 Phillips Dr, Lake City, GA 30260
404-362-3855 · Grades K - 5

Enrollment:	538
White / black / other:	27.9% / 49.1% / 23.0%
Not native English-speaking:	32 / 5.9%
Limited English proficiency:	53 / 9.9%
Student absenteeism:	5.0%
Students per teacher:	15.7
Parent friendliness:	①❷❸④⑤⑥
Teachers with advanced degrees:	42.1%
Average years' teaching experience:	13.4
Students in gifted program:	16 / 3.0%
Students in remedial education:	33.0%
Students held back a grade:	4.1%
Total suspensions, pct. in-school:	91 / 89.0%
Offenses:	violence: 16, drugs: *, other: 79
Eligible students, free or reduced lunch:	76.0%
Before / after school program:	No / Yes

Students at this school generally go on to:
Babb Middle

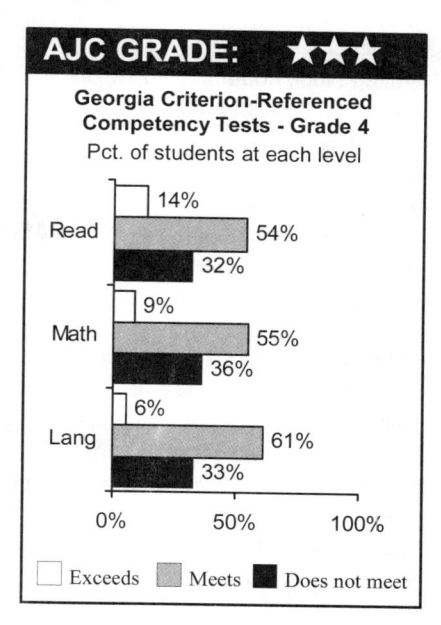

AJC GRADE: ★★★

Georgia Criterion-Referenced Competency Tests - Grade 4
Pct. of students at each level

- Read: Exceeds 14%, Meets 54%, Does not meet 32%
- Math: Exceeds 9%, Meets 55%, Does not meet 36%
- Lang: Exceeds 6%, Meets 61%, Does not meet 33%

Clayton County Elementary Schools

Lake Ridge Elementary School

7900 Lake Ridge Cir, Riverdale, GA 30296
770-907-5170 · Grades K - 5

Enrollment:	1,160
White / black / other:	10.4% / 71.6% / 17.9%
Not native English-speaking:	58 / 5.0%
Limited English proficiency:	72 / 6.2%
Student absenteeism:	6.1%
Students per teacher:	21.5
Parent friendliness:	①❷❸④⑤❻
Teachers with advanced degrees:	46.3%
Average years' teaching experience:	8.6
Students in gifted program:	16 / 1.4%
Students in remedial education:	34.5%
Students held back a grade:	2.8%
Total suspensions, pct. in-school:	715 / 79.9%
Offenses:	violence: 161, drugs: *, other: 620
Eligible students, free or reduced lunch:	62.5%
Before / after school program:	Yes / Yes
Students at this school generally go on to:	
Kendrick Middle	

AJC GRADE: ★★★

Georgia Criterion-Referenced Competency Tests - Grade 4
Pct. of students at each level

Read: Exceeds 26%, Meets 45%, Does not meet 29%
Math: Exceeds 3%, Meets 51%, Does not meet 45%
Lang: Exceeds 9%, Meets 59%, Does not meet 33%

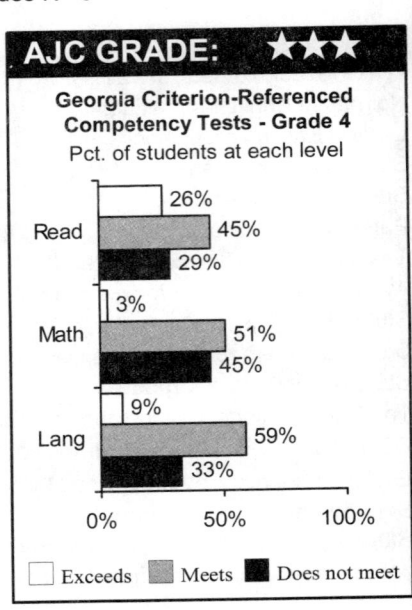

Lee Street Elementary School

178 Lee St, Jonesboro, GA 30236
770-473-2815 · Grades K - 5

Enrollment:	701
White / black / other:	27.5% / 50.8% / 21.7%
Not native English-speaking:	47 / 6.7%
Limited English proficiency:	59 / 8.4%
Student absenteeism:	6.2%
Students per teacher:	15.0
Parent friendliness:	❶❷❸④⑤❻
Teachers with advanced degrees:	40.8%
Average years' teaching experience:	11.3
Students in gifted program:	18 / 2.6%
Students in remedial education:	33.2%
Students held back a grade:	2.4%
Total suspensions, pct. in-school:	332 / 84.3%
Offenses:	violence: 17, drugs: *, other: 352
Eligible students, free or reduced lunch:	82.8%
Before / after school program:	No / Yes
Students at this school generally go on to:	
Jonesboro, Mundy's Mill Middle	

AJC GRADE: ★★★

Georgia Criterion-Referenced Competency Tests - Grade 4
Pct. of students at each level

Read: Exceeds 24%, Meets 47%, Does not meet 29%
Math: Exceeds 6%, Meets 50%, Does not meet 44%
Lang: Exceeds 9%, Meets 59%, Does not meet 31%

Clayton County Elementary Schools

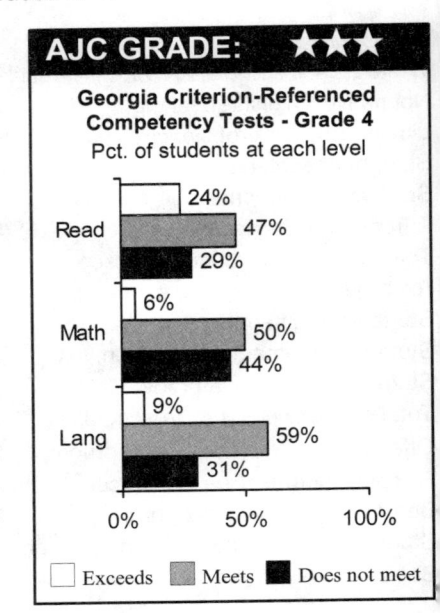

McGarrah Elementary School

2201 Lake Harbin Rd, Morrow, GA 30260
770-968-2910 · Grades K - 5

Enrollment:	983
White / black / other:	23.2% / 60.2% / 16.6%
Not native English-speaking:	50 / 5.1%
Limited English proficiency:	67 / 6.8%
Student absenteeism:	4.3%
Students per teacher:	17.1
Parent friendliness:	❶❷❸④❺❻
Teachers with advanced degrees:	47.5%
Average years' teaching experience:	12.5
Students in gifted program:	55 / 5.6%
Students in remedial education:	33.6%
Students held back a grade:	3.9%
Total suspensions, pct. in-school:	154 / 56.5%
Offenses: violence: 143, drugs: *, other: 97	
Eligible students, free or reduced lunch:	61.1%
Before / after school program:	No / Yes

Students at this school generally go on to:
Adamson, Morrow Middle

AJC GRADE: ★★★

Georgia Criterion-Referenced Competency Tests - Grade 4
Pct. of students at each level

- Read: Exceeds 30%, Meets 46%, Does not meet 24%
- Math: Exceeds 5%, Meets 49%, Does not meet 46%
- Lang: Exceeds 12%, Meets 62%, Does not meet 25%

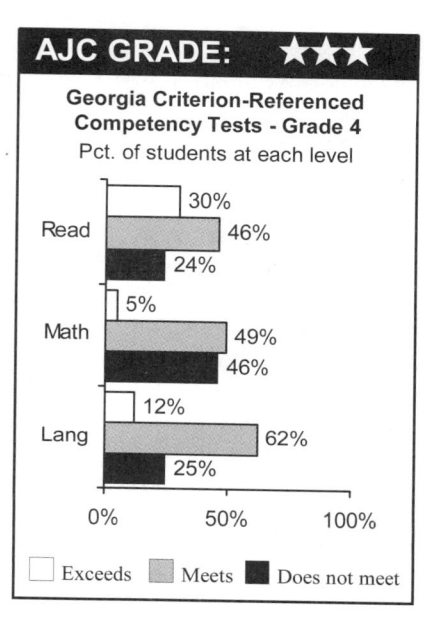

Morrow Elementary School

6115 Reynolds Rd, Morrow, GA 30260
770-968-2900 · Grades K - 5

Enrollment:	622
White / black / other:	17.4% / 59.8% / 22.8%
Not native English-speaking:	27 / 4.3%
Limited English proficiency:	35 / 5.6%
Student absenteeism:	4.7%
Students per teacher:	15.7
Parent friendliness:	①❷❸④⑤❻
Teachers with advanced degrees:	44.2%
Average years' teaching experience:	10.9
Students in gifted program:	43 / 6.9%
Students in remedial education:	30.1%
Students held back a grade:	2.4%
Total suspensions, pct. in-school:	251 / 80.9%
Offenses: violence: 4, drugs: *, other: 281	
Eligible students, free or reduced lunch:	71.9%
Before / after school program:	Yes / Yes

Students at this school generally go on to:
Morrow Middle

AJC GRADE: ★★★★

Georgia Criterion-Referenced Competency Tests - Grade 4
Pct. of students at each level

- Read: Exceeds 43%, Meets 35%, Does not meet 22%
- Math: Exceeds 21%, Meets 48%, Does not meet 32%
- Lang: Exceeds 16%, Meets 64%, Does not meet 20%

Clayton County Elementary Schools

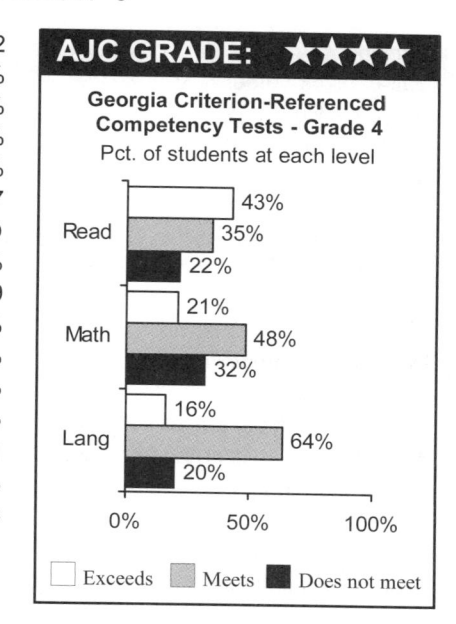

Mount Zion Elementary School

2984 Mount Zion Rd, Jonesboro, GA 30236
770-968-2935 · Grades K - 5

Enrollment:	922
White / black / other:	24.7% / 62.4% / 12.9%
Not native English-speaking:	36 / 3.9%
Limited English proficiency:	42 / 4.6%
Student absenteeism:	4.3%
Students per teacher:	17.6
Parent friendliness:	① ❷ ❸ ④ ⑤ ❻
Teachers with advanced degrees:	45.5%
Average years' teaching experience:	13.0
Students in gifted program:	40 / 4.3%
Students in remedial education:	24.5%
Students held back a grade:	5.1%
Total suspensions, pct. in-school:	239 / 50.2%
Offenses:	violence: 10, drugs: 1, other: 348
Eligible students, free or reduced lunch:	51.0%
Before / after school program:	No / Yes

Students at this school generally go on to:
Adamson, Roberts Middle

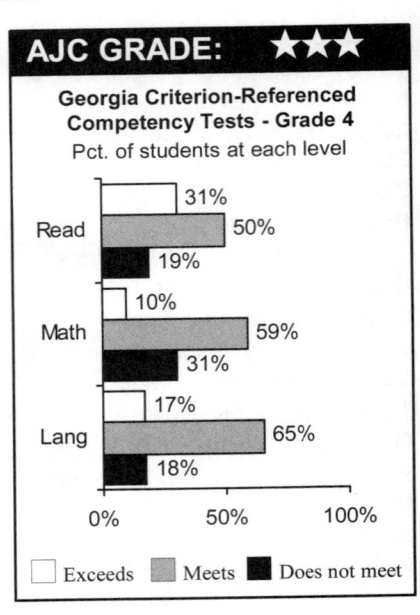

AJC GRADE: ★★★

Georgia Criterion-Referenced Competency Tests - Grade 4
Pct. of students at each level

- Read: Exceeds 31%, Meets 50%, Does not meet 19%
- Math: Exceeds 10%, Meets 59%, Does not meet 31%
- Lang: Exceeds 17%, Meets 65%, Does not meet 18%

☐ Exceeds ▨ Meets ■ Does not meet

Northcutt Elementary School

5451 W Fayetteville Rd, College Park, GA 30349
770-994-4020 · Grades K - 5

Enrollment:	528
White / black / other:	0.6% / 96.4% / 3.0%
Not native English-speaking:	20 / 3.8%
Limited English proficiency:	20 / 3.8%
Student absenteeism:	5.8%
Students per teacher:	15.1
Parent friendliness:	❶ ❷ ❸ ④ ❺ ❻
Teachers with advanced degrees:	29.7%
Average years' teaching experience:	10.8
Students in gifted program:	9 / 1.7%
Students in remedial education:	32.3%
Students held back a grade:	4.0%
Total suspensions, pct. in-school:	31 / 74.2%
Offenses:	violence: 28, drugs: *, other: 16
Eligible students, free or reduced lunch:	82.7%
Before / after school program:	No / Yes

Students at this school generally go on to:
North Clayton Middle

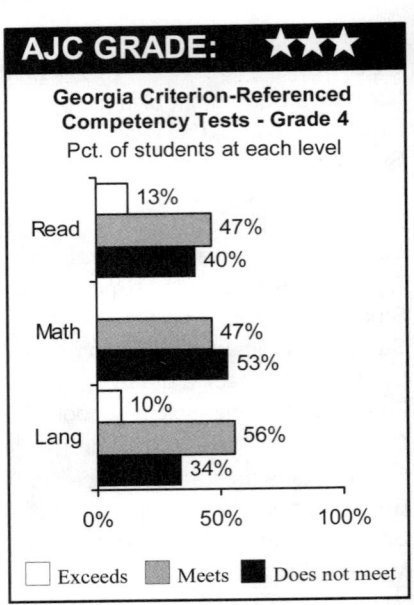

AJC GRADE: ★★★

Georgia Criterion-Referenced Competency Tests - Grade 4
Pct. of students at each level

- Read: Exceeds 13%, Meets 47%, Does not meet 40%
- Math: Exceeds *, Meets 47%, Does not meet 53%
- Lang: Exceeds 10%, Meets 56%, Does not meet 34%

☐ Exceeds ▨ Meets ■ Does not meet

Clayton County Elementary Schools

Oliver Elementary School

1725 Cheryl Leigh Dr, Riverdale, GA 30296
770-994-4010 · Grades K - 5

Enrollment:	879
White / black / other:	1.3% / 93.2% / 5.6%
Not native English-speaking:	8 / 0.9%
Limited English proficiency:	12 / 1.4%
Student absenteeism:	4.0%
Students per teacher:	18.2
Parent friendliness:	① ❷ ❸ ④ ❺ ❻
Teachers with advanced degrees:	44.9%
Average years' teaching experience:	7.6
Students in gifted program:	21 / 2.4%
Students in remedial education:	33.2%
Students held back a grade:	2.3%
Total suspensions, pct. in-school:	74 / 2.7%
Offenses:	violence: 58, drugs: *, other: 50
Eligible students, free or reduced lunch:	55.3%
Before / after school program:	Yes / Yes
Students at this school generally go on to:	
North Clayton, Riverdale Middle	

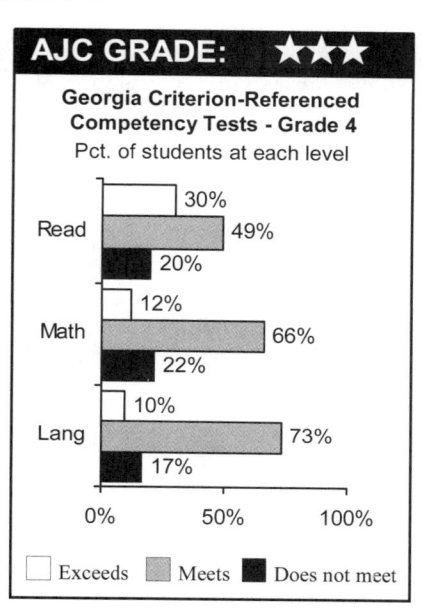

AJC GRADE: ★★★

Georgia Criterion-Referenced Competency Tests - Grade 4
Pct. of students at each level

Read: Exceeds 30%, Meets 49%, Does not meet 20%
Math: Exceeds 12%, Meets 66%, Does not meet 22%
Lang: Exceeds 10%, Meets 73%, Does not meet 17%

Pointe South Elementary School

631 Flint River Rd SW, Riverdale, GA 30274
770-473-2900 · Grades K - 5

Enrollment:	839
White / black / other:	8.0% / 85.8% / 6.2%
Not native English-speaking:	7 / 0.8%
Limited English proficiency:	11 / 1.3%
Student absenteeism:	4.4%
Students per teacher:	17.1
Parent friendliness:	❶ ❷ ❸ ④ ❺ ❻
Teachers with advanced degrees:	38.8%
Average years' teaching experience:	12.3
Students in gifted program:	20 / 2.4%
Students in remedial education:	34.3%
Students held back a grade:	3.3%
Total suspensions, pct. in-school:	285 / 50.5%
Offenses:	violence: 61, drugs: *, other: 267
Eligible students, free or reduced lunch:	64.5%
Before / after school program:	Yes / Yes
Students at this school generally go on to:	
Pointe South Middle	

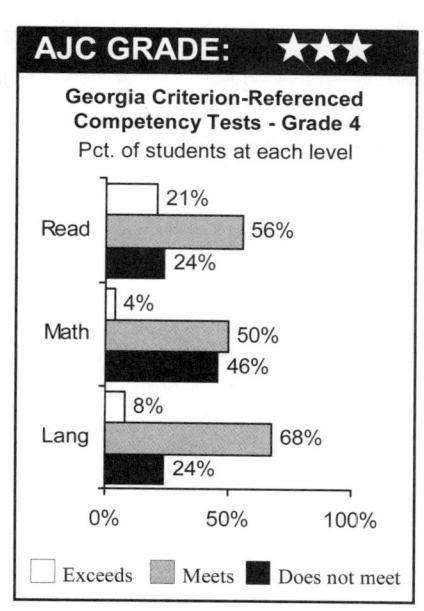

AJC GRADE: ★★★

Georgia Criterion-Referenced Competency Tests - Grade 4
Pct. of students at each level

Read: Exceeds 21%, Meets 56%, Does not meet 24%
Math: Exceeds 4%, Meets 50%, Does not meet 46%
Lang: Exceeds 8%, Meets 68%, Does not meet 24%

Clayton County Elementary Schools

Riverdale Elementary School

6630 Camp St, Riverdale, GA 30274
770-994-4015 · Grades K - 5

Enrollment:	762
White / black / other:	9.7% / 71.7% / 18.6%
Not native English-speaking:	41 / 5.4%
Limited English proficiency:	45 / 5.9%
Student absenteeism:	4.6%
Students per teacher:	16.1
Parent friendliness:	① ❷ ❸ ❹ ❺ ❻
Teachers with advanced degrees:	50.0%
Average years' teaching experience:	15.2
Students in gifted program:	28 / 3.7%
Students in remedial education:	31.8%
Students held back a grade:	1.4%
Total suspensions, pct. in-school:	212 / 50.9%
Offenses: violence: 10, drugs: *, other: 252	
Eligible students, free or reduced lunch:	76.3%
Before / after school program:	No / Yes
Students at this school generally go on to:	
Riverdale Middle	

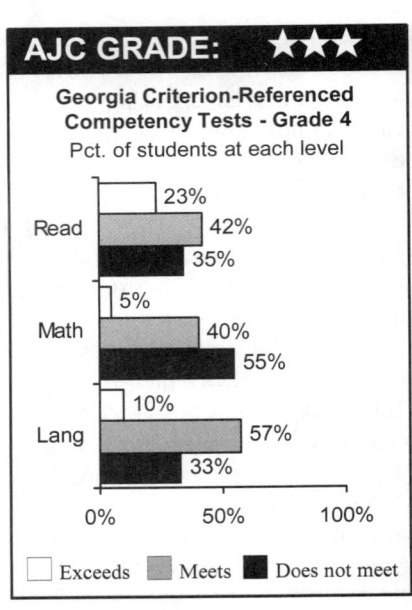

AJC GRADE: ★★★

Georgia Criterion-Referenced Competency Tests - Grade 4
Pct. of students at each level

Read: 23% Exceeds / 42% Meets / 35% Does not meet
Math: 5% Exceeds / 40% Meets / 55% Does not meet
Lang: 10% Exceeds / 57% Meets / 33% Does not meet

River's Edge Elementary School

205 Northbridge Rd, Fayetteville, GA 30215
770-460-2340 · Grades K - 5

Enrollment:	778
White / black / other:	28.9% / 62.2% / 8.9%
Not native English-speaking:	5 / 0.6%
Limited English proficiency:	6 / 0.8%
Student absenteeism:	4.2%
Students per teacher:	16.1
Parent friendliness:	❶ ❷ ❸ ④ ⑤ ❻
Teachers with advanced degrees:	58.0%
Average years' teaching experience:	15.9
Students in gifted program:	51 / 6.6%
Students in remedial education:	24.5%
Students held back a grade:	1.2%
Total suspensions, pct. in-school:	65 / 53.8%
Offenses: violence: 8, drugs: *, other: 88	
Eligible students, free or reduced lunch:	32.1%
Before / after school program:	Yes / Yes
Students at this school generally go on to:	
Lovejoy, Mundy's Mill, Pointe South Middle	

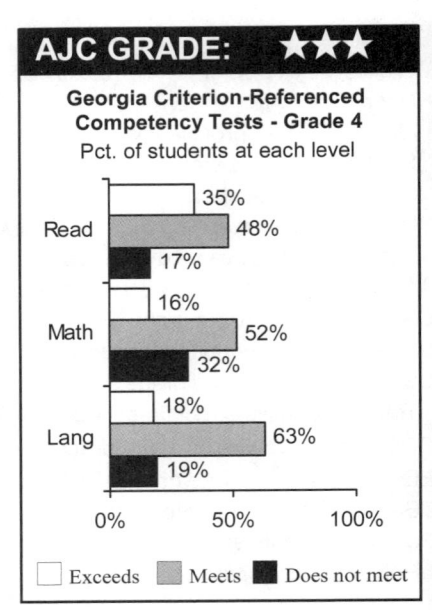

AJC GRADE: ★★★

Georgia Criterion-Referenced Competency Tests - Grade 4
Pct. of students at each level

Read: 35% Exceeds / 48% Meets / 17% Does not meet
Math: 16% Exceeds / 52% Meets / 32% Does not meet
Lang: 18% Exceeds / 63% Meets / 19% Does not meet

Clayton County Elementary Schools

Smith Elementary School

6340 Highway 42, Rex, GA 30273
770-960-5750 · Grades K - 5

Enrollment:	892
White / black / other:	36.1% / 52.2% / 11.7%
Not native English-speaking:	23 / 2.6%
Limited English proficiency:	31 / 3.5%
Student absenteeism:	4.4%
Students per teacher:	18.2
Parent friendliness:	❶❷❸④❺❻
Teachers with advanced degrees:	42.9%
Average years' teaching experience:	14.6
Students in gifted program:	47 / 5.3%
Students in remedial education:	23.7%
Students held back a grade:	3.0%
Total suspensions, pct. in-school:	51 / 37.3%
Offenses:	violence: 13, drugs: * , other: 59
Eligible students, free or reduced lunch:	45.6%
Before / after school program:	No / Yes

Students at this school generally go on to:
Adamson, Morrow, Roberts Middle

AJC GRADE: ★★★

Georgia Criterion-Referenced Competency Tests - Grade 4
Pct. of students at each level

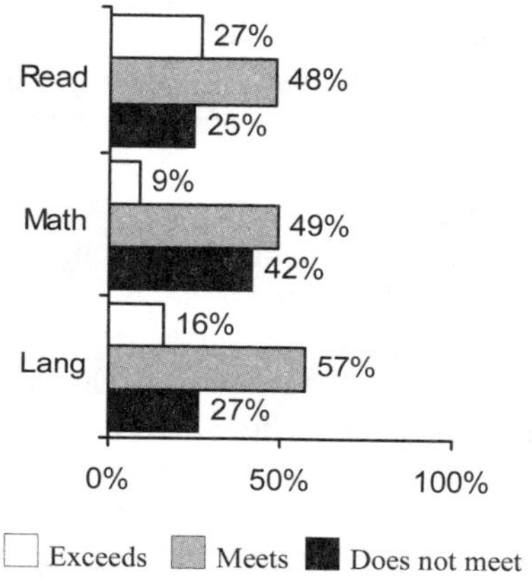

Read
27%
48%
25%
Math
9%
49%
42%
Lang
16%
57%
27%
0%
50%
100%
Exceeds
Meets
Does not meet

Suder Elementary School

1400 Lake Jodeco Rd, Jonesboro, GA 30236
770-473-2820 · Grades K - 5

Enrollment:	736
White / black / other:	44.2% / 46.2% / 9.6%
Not native English-speaking:	3 / 0.4%
Limited English proficiency:	5 / 0.7%
Student absenteeism:	5.0%
Students per teacher:	14.7
Parent friendliness:	①❷❸④⑤❻
Teachers with advanced degrees:	45.1%
Average years' teaching experience:	14.5
Students in gifted program:	33 / 4.5%
Students in remedial education:	23.3%
Students held back a grade:	1.6%
Total suspensions, pct. in-school:	316 / 88.9%
Offenses:	violence: 9, drugs: * , other: 346
Eligible students, free or reduced lunch:	44.3%
Before / after school program:	Yes / Yes

Students at this school generally go on to:
Mundy's Mill, Roberts Middle

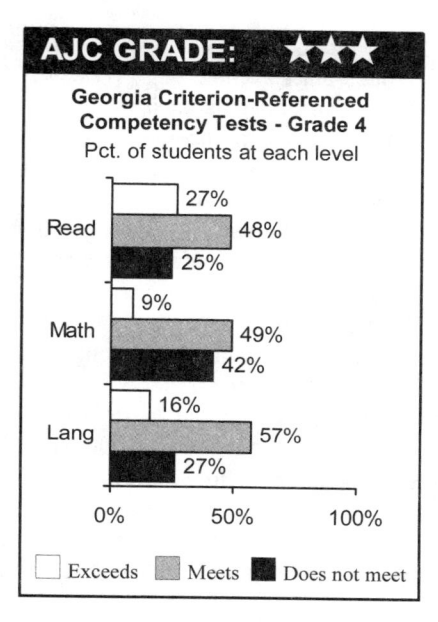

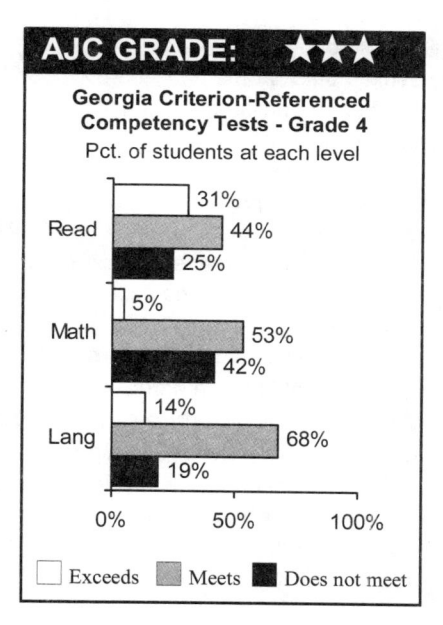

AJC GRADE: ★★★

Georgia Criterion-Referenced Competency Tests - Grade 4
Pct. of students at each level

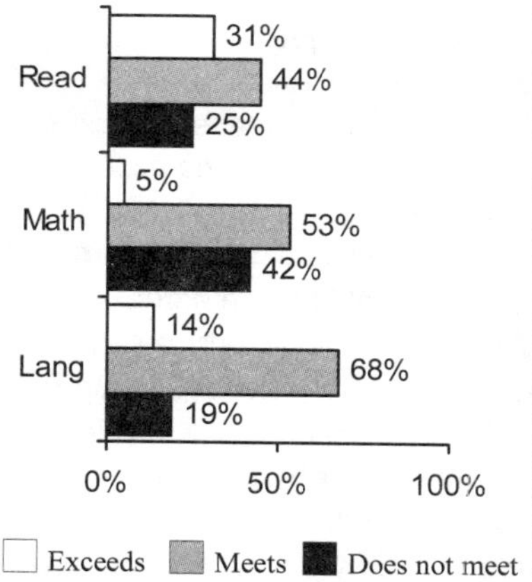

Read
31%
44%
25%
Math
5%
53%
42%
Lang
14%
68%
19%
0%
50%
100%
Exceeds
Meets
Does not meet

Swint Elementary School

500 Highway 138 W, Jonesboro, GA 30238
770-473-2780 · Grades K - 5

Enrollment:	922
White / black / other:	17.5% / 72.7% / 9.9%
Not native English-speaking:	15 / 1.6%
Limited English proficiency:	26 / 2.8%
Student absenteeism:	4.9%
Students per teacher:	18.0
Parent friendliness:	① ❷ ❸ ④ ❺ ❻
Teachers with advanced degrees:	42.3%
Average years' teaching experience:	12.8
Students in gifted program:	20 / 2.2%
Students in remedial education:	32.6%
Students held back a grade:	4.0%
Total suspensions, pct. in-school:	263 / 85.2%
Offenses: violence: 54, drugs: *, other: 252	
Eligible students, free or reduced lunch:	61.2%
Before / after school program:	Yes / Yes

Students at this school generally go on to:
Jonesboro, Kendrick, Pointe South Middle

AJC GRADE: ★★★

Georgia Criterion-Referenced Competency Tests - Grade 4
Pct. of students at each level

Read: Exceeds 24%, Meets 45%, Does not meet 31%
Math: Exceeds 2%, Meets 50%, Does not meet 48%
Lang: Exceeds 14%, Meets 56%, Does not meet 30%

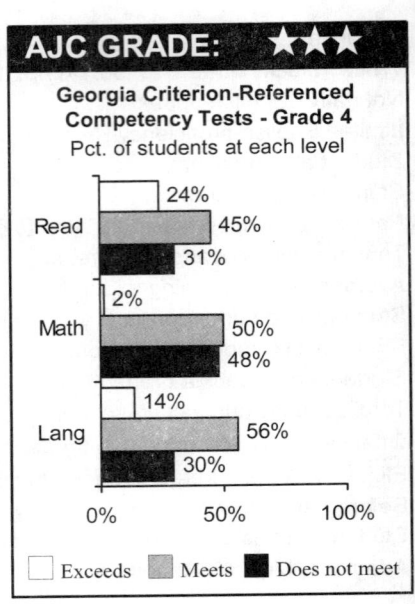

Tara Elementary School

937 Mount Zion Rd, Morrow, GA 30260
770-968-2915 · Grades K - 5

Enrollment:	938
White / black / other:	13.8% / 68.2% / 18.0%
Not native English-speaking:	44 / 4.7%
Limited English proficiency:	65 / 6.9%
Student absenteeism:	5.1%
Students per teacher:	15.7
Parent friendliness:	❶ ❷ ❸ ④ ❺ ❻
Teachers with advanced degrees:	37.1%
Average years' teaching experience:	10.3
Students in gifted program:	9 / 1.0%
Students in remedial education:	31.9%
Students held back a grade:	0.3%
Total suspensions, pct. in-school:	270 / 55.2%
Offenses: violence: 67, drugs: *, other: 229	
Eligible students, free or reduced lunch:	74.5%
Before / after school program:	Yes / Yes

Students at this school generally go on to:
Jonesboro, Kendrick, Morrow Middle

AJC GRADE: ★★

Georgia Criterion-Referenced Competency Tests - Grade 4
Pct. of students at each level

Read: Exceeds 19%, Meets 36%, Does not meet 46%
Math: Exceeds 4%, Meets 37%, Does not meet 59%
Lang: Exceeds 9%, Meets 43%, Does not meet 48%

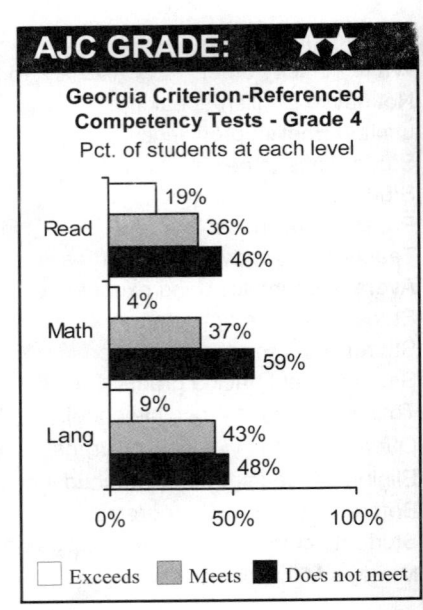

West Clayton Elementary School

5580 Riverdale Rd, College Park, GA 30349
770-994-4005 · Grades K - 5

Enrollment:	972
White / black / other:	0.9% / 88.0% / 11.1%
Not native English-speaking:	24 / 2.5%
Limited English proficiency:	25 / 2.6%
Student absenteeism:	5.1%
Students per teacher:	20.3
Parent friendliness:	❶❷❸④❺❻
Teachers with advanced degrees:	30.6%
Average years' teaching experience:	9.9
Students in gifted program:	13 / 1.3%
Students in remedial education:	31.4%
Students held back a grade:	8.3%
Total suspensions, pct. in-school:	183 / 65.6%
Offenses:	violence: 46, drugs: *, other: 144
Eligible students, free or reduced lunch:	79.2%
Before / after school program:	Yes / Yes
Students at this school generally go on to:	
North Clayton Middle	

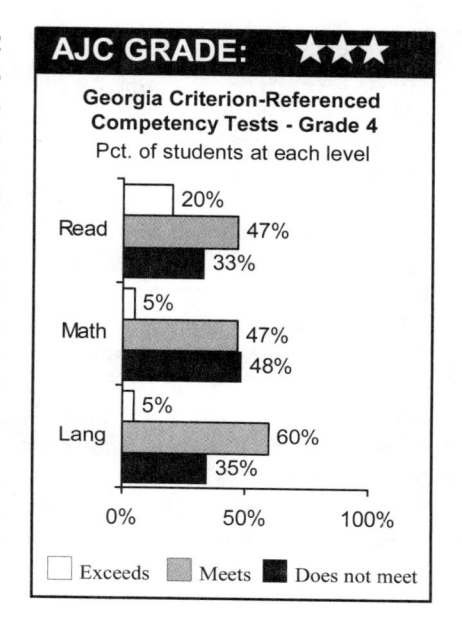

AJC GRADE: ★★★

Georgia Criterion-Referenced Competency Tests - Grade 4
Pct. of students at each level

Read: Exceeds 20%, Meets 47%, Does not meet 33%
Math: Exceeds 5%, Meets 47%, Does not meet 48%
Lang: Exceeds 5%, Meets 60%, Does not meet 35%

Clayton County Elementary Schools

Adamson Middle School

3187 Rex Rd, Rex, GA 30273
770-968-2925 · Grades 6 - 8

Enrollment:	963
White / black / other:	26.2% / 64.9% / 8.9%
Not native English-speaking:	19 / 2.0%
Student absenteeism:	4.5%
Students per teacher:	18.0
Parent friendliness:	❶❷❸④⑤❻
Teachers with advanced degrees:	48.3%
Average years' teaching experience:	12.1
Students in gifted program:	98 / 10.2%
Students held back a grade:	2.5%
Total suspensions and expulsions:	305
Suspensions only, pct. in-school:	305 / 35.7%
Offenses:	violence: 72, drugs: 3, other: 271
Eligible students, free or reduced lunch:	48.7%
Number of dropouts:	3 / 0.3%
Pct. 8th-graders w/ basic computer skills:	95.0%

Students at this school generally go on to:
Morrow, Mount Zion High

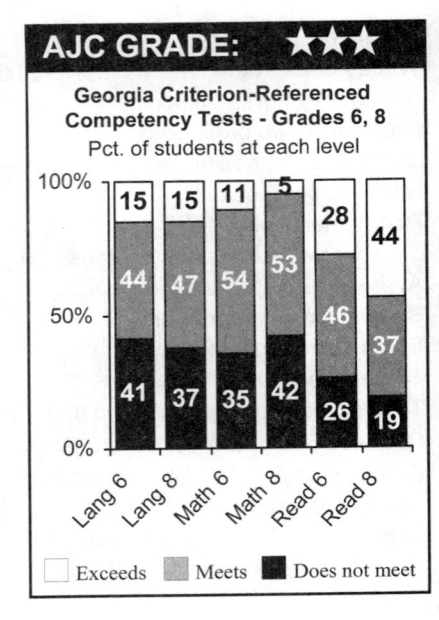

AJC GRADE: ★★★

Georgia Criterion-Referenced Competency Tests - Grades 6, 8
Pct. of students at each level

	Lang 6	Lang 8	Math 6	Math 8	Read 6	Read 8
Exceeds	15	15	11	5	28	44
Meets	44	47	54	53	46	37
Does not meet	41	37	35	42	26	19

Babb Middle School

5500 Reynolds Rd, Forest Park, GA 30297
404-362-3880 · Grades 6 - 8

Enrollment:	985
White / black / other:	18.8% / 59.6% / 21.6%
Not native English-speaking:	65 / 6.6%
Student absenteeism:	7.1%
Students per teacher:	17.6
Parent friendliness:	❶❷❸④❺❻
Teachers with advanced degrees:	35.6%
Average years' teaching experience:	10.9
Students in gifted program:	42 / 4.3%
Students held back a grade:	3.0%
Total suspensions and expulsions:	1,237
Suspensions only, pct. in-school:	1,237 / 50.7%
Offenses:	violence: 94, drugs: 6, other: 1,349
Eligible students, free or reduced lunch:	77.3%
Number of dropouts:	2 / 0.2%
Pct. 8th-graders w/ basic computer skills:	100.0%

Students at this school generally go on to:
Forest Park, North Clayton High

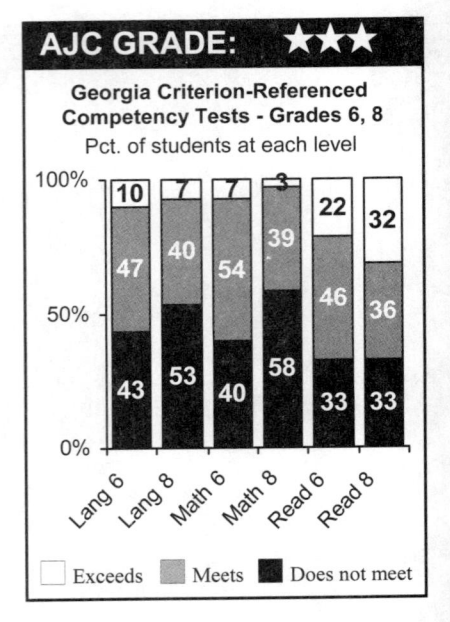

AJC GRADE: ★★★

Georgia Criterion-Referenced Competency Tests - Grades 6, 8
Pct. of students at each level

	Lang 6	Lang 8	Math 6	Math 8	Read 6	Read 8
Exceeds	10	7	7	3	22	32
Meets	47	40	54	39	46	36
Does not meet	43	53	40	58	33	33

Clayton County Middle Schools

Forest Park Middle School

930 Finley Dr, Forest Park, GA 30297
404-362-3840 · Grades 6 - 8

Enrollment:	780
White / black / other:	18.5% / 64.1% / 17.4%
Not native English-speaking:	23 / 2.9%
Student absenteeism:	8.1%
Students per teacher:	16.3
Parent friendliness:	❶❷❸④⑤❻
Teachers with advanced degrees:	42.3%
Average years' teaching experience:	9.3
Students in gifted program:	20 / 2.6%
Students held back a grade:	4.0%
Total suspensions and expulsions:	653
Suspensions only, pct. in-school:	653 / 9.8%
Offenses:	violence: 74, drugs: 1, other: 621
Eligible students, free or reduced lunch:	79.7%
Number of dropouts:	2 / 0.2%
Pct. 8th-graders w/ basic computer skills:	94.3%

Students at this school generally go on to:
Forest Park High

AJC GRADE: ★★★

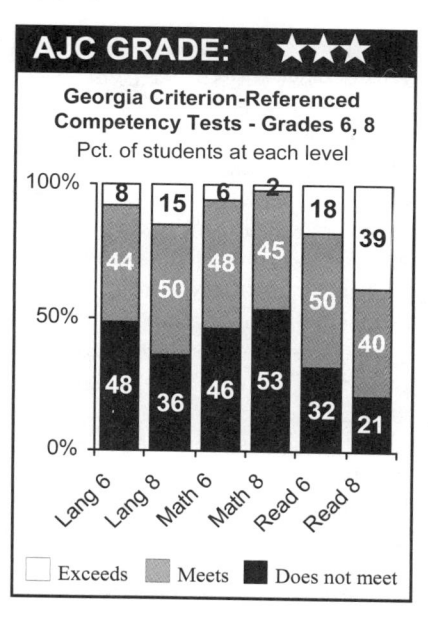

Georgia Criterion-Referenced Competency Tests - Grades 6, 8
Pct. of students at each level

	Lang 6	Lang 8	Math 6	Math 8	Read 6	Read 8
Exceeds	8	15	6	2	18	39
Meets	44	50	48	45	50	40
Does not meet	48	36	46	53	32	21

Jonesboro Middle School

137 Spring St, Jonesboro, GA 30236
770-473-2805 · Grades 6 - 8

Enrollment:	558
White / black / other:	30.1% / 55.2% / 14.7%
Not native English-speaking:	24 / 4.3%
Student absenteeism:	6.7%
Students per teacher:	14.1
Parent friendliness:	❶❷❸④⑤❻
Teachers with advanced degrees:	50.0%
Average years' teaching experience:	11.5
Students in gifted program:	28 / 5.0%
Students held back a grade:	1.8%
Total suspensions and expulsions:	733
Suspensions only, pct. in-school:	733 / 61.9%
Offenses:	violence: 58, drugs: 1, other: 692
Eligible students, free or reduced lunch:	65.2%
Number of dropouts:	2 / 0.3%
Pct. 8th-graders w/ basic computer skills:	100.0%

Students at this school generally go on to:
Jonesboro, Mount Zion High

AJC GRADE: ★★★

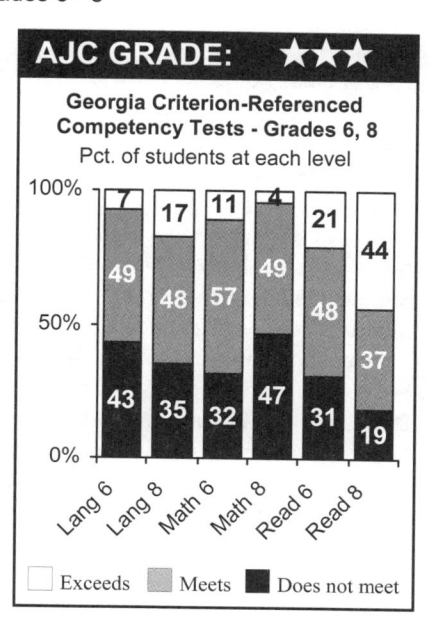

Georgia Criterion-Referenced Competency Tests - Grades 6, 8
Pct. of students at each level

	Lang 6	Lang 8	Math 6	Math 8	Read 6	Read 8
Exceeds	7	17	11	4	21	44
Meets	49	48	57	49	48	37
Does not meet	43	35	32	47	31	19

Clayton County Middle Schools

Kendrick Middle School

7971 Kendrick Rd, Jonesboro, GA 30238
770-472-8400 · Grades 6 - 8

Enrollment:	1,149
White / black / other:	10.0% / 79.3% / 10.7%
Not native English-speaking:	35 / 3.0%
Student absenteeism:	6.6%
Students per teacher:	18.7
Parent friendliness:	❶❷❸④⑤❻
Teachers with advanced degrees:	37.5%
Average years' teaching experience:	9.0
Students in gifted program:	46 / 4.0%
Students held back a grade:	2.3%
Total suspensions and expulsions:	365
Suspensions only, pct. in-school:	365 / 41.6%
Offenses:	violence: 119, drugs: 3, other: 357
Eligible students, free or reduced lunch:	66.0%
Number of dropouts:	8 / 0.6%
Pct. 8th-graders w/ basic computer skills:	100.0%

Students at this school generally go on to:
Mount Zion, Riverdale High

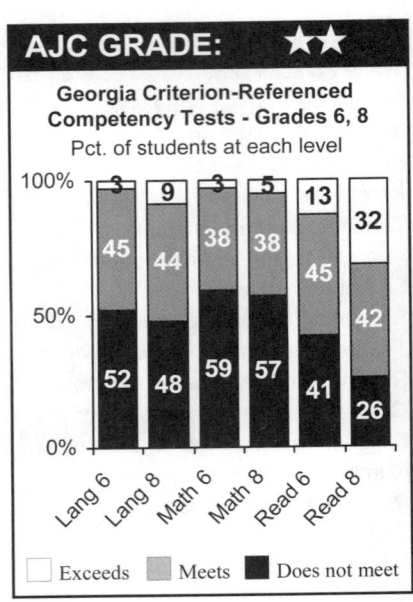

AJC GRADE: ★★

Georgia Criterion-Referenced Competency Tests - Grades 6, 8
Pct. of students at each level

	Lang 6	Lang 8	Math 6	Math 8	Read 6	Read 8
Exceeds	3	9	3	5	13	32
Meets	45	44	38	38	45	42
Does not meet	52	48	59	57	41	26

Lovejoy Middle School

1588 Lovejoy Rd, Hampton, GA 30228
770-473-2933 · Grades 6 - 8

Enrollment:	934
White / black / other:	49.3% / 43.0% / 7.7%
Not native English-speaking:	7 / 0.7%
Student absenteeism:	4.9%
Students per teacher:	17.2
Parent friendliness:	①❷❸④❺❻
Teachers with advanced degrees:	69.1%
Average years' teaching experience:	14.9
Students in gifted program:	127 / 13.6%
Students held back a grade:	1.1%
Total suspensions and expulsions:	579
Suspensions only, pct. in-school:	579 / 73.6%
Offenses:	violence: 59, drugs: *, other: 649
Eligible students, free or reduced lunch:	26.8%
Number of dropouts:	1 / 0.1%
Pct. 8th-graders w/ basic computer skills:	90.0%

Students at this school generally go on to:
Lovejoy, Mundy's Mill High

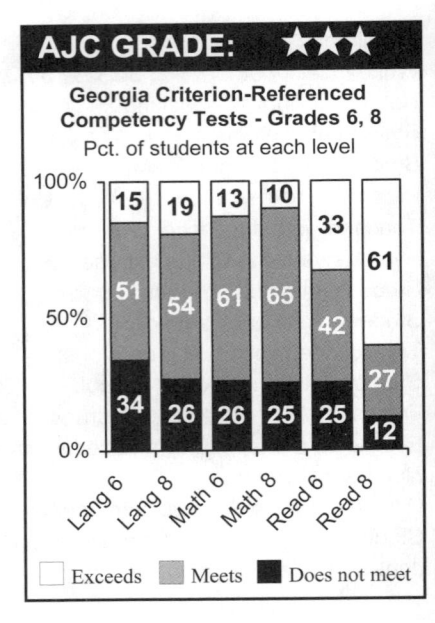

AJC GRADE: ★★★

Georgia Criterion-Referenced Competency Tests - Grades 6, 8
Pct. of students at each level

	Lang 6	Lang 8	Math 6	Math 8	Read 6	Read 8
Exceeds	15	19	13	10	33	61
Meets	51	54	61	65	42	27
Does not meet	34	26	26	25	25	12

Clayton County Middle Schools

Morrow Middle School

5968 Maddox Rd, Morrow, GA 30260
404-362-3860 · Grades 6 - 8

Enrollment:	1,042
White / black / other:	18.8% / 65.1% / 16.1%
Not native English-speaking:	42 / 4.0%
Student absenteeism:	6.6%
Students per teacher:	17.1
Parent friendliness:	❶❷❸④⑤❻
Teachers with advanced degrees:	33.9%
Average years' teaching experience:	9.6
Students in gifted program:	48 / 4.6%
Students held back a grade:	3.8%
Total suspensions and expulsions:	1,538
Suspensions only, pct. in-school:	1,538 / 61.5%
Offenses: violence: 163, drugs: 1, other:	1,503
Eligible students, free or reduced lunch:	67.0%
Number of dropouts:	2 / 0.2%
Pct. 8th-graders w/ basic computer skills:	100.0%

Students at this school generally go on to:
Morrow, Mount Zion High

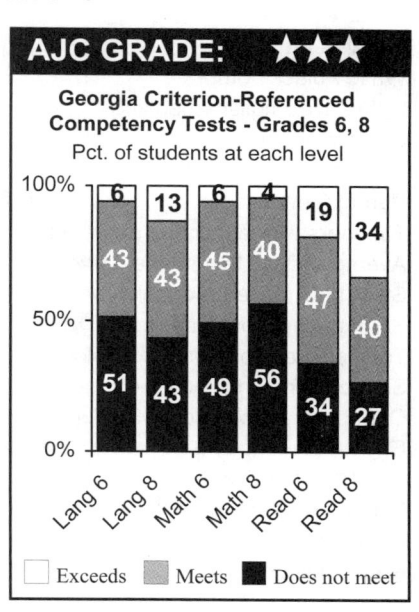

AJC GRADE: ★★★

Georgia Criterion-Referenced Competency Tests - Grades 6, 8
Pct. of students at each level

	Lang 6	Lang 8	Math 6	Math 8	Read 6	Read 8
Exceeds	6	13	6	4	19	34
Meets	43	43	45	40	47	40
Does not meet	51	43	49	56	34	27

Mundy's Mill Middle School

1251 Mundys Mill Rd, Jonesboro, GA 30238
770-473-2880 · Grades 6 - 8

Enrollment:	822
White / black / other:	26.3% / 66.7% / 7.1%
Not native English-speaking:	11 / 1.3%
Student absenteeism:	4.4%
Students per teacher:	14.9
Parent friendliness:	❶❷❸④⑤❻
Teachers with advanced degrees:	49.1%
Average years' teaching experience:	15.5
Students in gifted program:	83 / 10.1%
Students held back a grade:	1.6%
Total suspensions and expulsions:	326
Suspensions only, pct. in-school:	326 / 36.5%
Offenses: violence: 70, drugs: 2, other:	355
Eligible students, free or reduced lunch:	40.5%
Number of dropouts:	*
Pct. 8th-graders w/ basic computer skills:	95.0%

Students at this school generally go on to:
Jonesboro, Lovejoy High

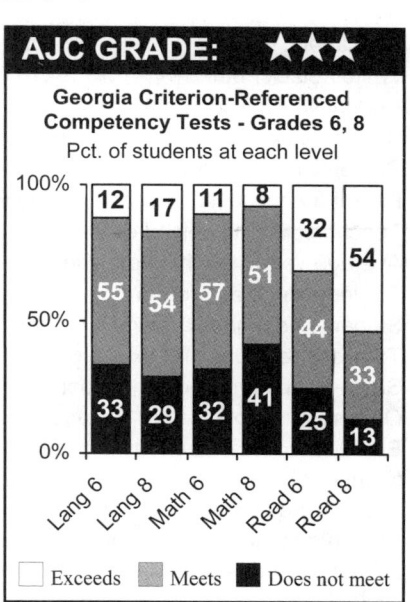

AJC GRADE: ★★★

Georgia Criterion-Referenced Competency Tests - Grades 6, 8
Pct. of students at each level

	Lang 6	Lang 8	Math 6	Math 8	Read 6	Read 8
Exceeds	12	17	11	8	32	54
Meets	55	54	57	51	44	33
Does not meet	33	29	32	41	25	13

Clayton County Middle Schools

North Clayton Middle School

5517 W Fayetteville Rd, College Park, GA 30349
770-994-4025 · Grades 6 - 8

Enrollment:	976
White / black / other:	2.7% / 88.2% / 9.1%
Not native English-speaking:	18 / 1.8%
Student absenteeism:	6.5%
Students per teacher:	18.2
Parent friendliness:	❶❷❸④❺❻
Teachers with advanced degrees:	49.1%
Average years' teaching experience:	11.7
Students in gifted program:	22 / 2.3%
Students held back a grade:	3.2%
Total suspensions and expulsions:	1,540
Suspensions only, pct. in-school:	1,540 / 55.4%
Offenses: violence: 209, drugs: 2, other: 1,449	
Eligible students, free or reduced lunch:	66.5%
Number of dropouts:	2 / 0.2%
Pct. 8th-graders w/ basic computer skills:	92.4%

Students at this school generally go on to:
North Clayton High

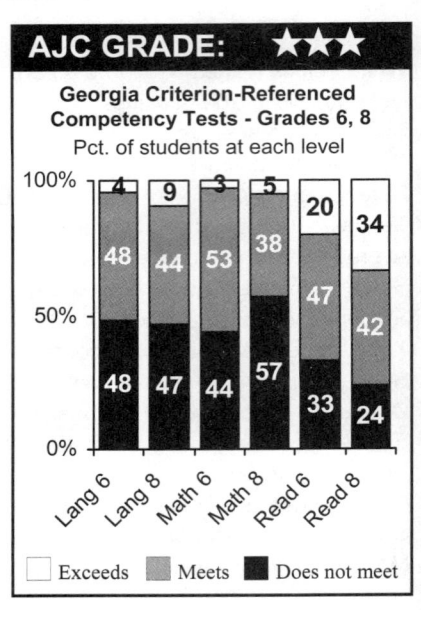

AJC GRADE: ★★★

Georgia Criterion-Referenced Competency Tests - Grades 6, 8
Pct. of students at each level

	Lang 6	Lang 8	Math 6	Math 8	Read 6	Read 8
Exceeds	4	9	3	5	20	34
Meets	48	44	53	38	47	42
Does not meet	48	47	44	57	33	24

Pointe South Middle School

626 Flint River Rd, Jonesboro, GA 30238
770-473-2890 · Grades 6 - 8

Enrollment:	1,055
White / black / other:	13.7% / 79.5% / 6.7%
Not native English-speaking:	11 / 1.0%
Student absenteeism:	7.2%
Students per teacher:	20.2
Parent friendliness:	❶❷❸④⑤❻
Teachers with advanced degrees:	53.7%
Average years' teaching experience:	11.9
Students in gifted program:	36 / 3.4%
Students held back a grade:	2.2%
Total suspensions and expulsions:	2,498
Suspensions only, pct. in-school:	2,498 / 57.2%
Offenses: violence: 291, drugs: 1, other: 2,256	
Eligible students, free or reduced lunch:	63.6%
Number of dropouts:	6 / 0.5%
Pct. 8th-graders w/ basic computer skills:	93.2%

Students at this school generally go on to:
Jonesboro, Lovejoy, Mundy's Mill, Riverdale High

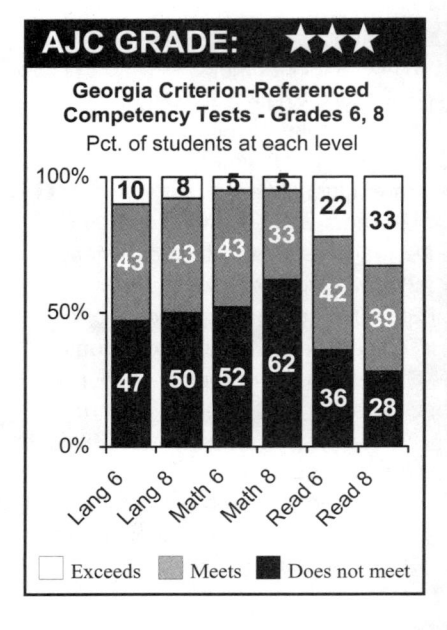

AJC GRADE: ★★★

Georgia Criterion-Referenced Competency Tests - Grades 6, 8
Pct. of students at each level

	Lang 6	Lang 8	Math 6	Math 8	Read 6	Read 8
Exceeds	10	8	5	5	22	33
Meets	43	43	43	33	42	39
Does not meet	47	50	52	62	36	28

Clayton County Middle Schools

Riverdale Middle School

400 Roberts Dr, Riverdale, GA 30274
770-994-4045 · Grades 6 - 8

Enrollment:	1,055
White / black / other:	7.2% / 81.3% / 11.5%
Not native English-speaking:	30 / 2.8%
Student absenteeism:	6.7%
Students per teacher:	20.4
Parent friendliness:	❶❷❸④⑤❻
Teachers with advanced degrees:	35.8%
Average years' teaching experience:	8.8
Students in gifted program:	60 / 5.7%
Students held back a grade:	4.7%
Total suspensions and expulsions:	1,894
Suspensions only, pct. in-school:	1,894 / 69.1%
Offenses: violence: 238, drugs: 3, other: 1,773	
Eligible students, free or reduced lunch:	65.1%
Number of dropouts:	3 / 0.2%
Pct. 8th-graders w/ basic computer skills:	93.7%

Students at this school generally go on to:
Mount Zion, North Clayton, Riverdale High

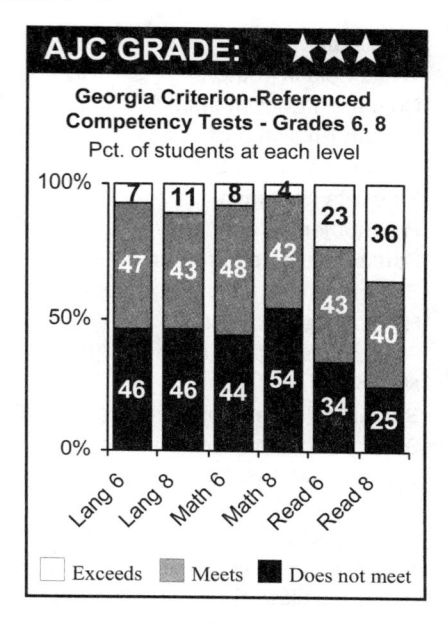

AJC GRADE: ★★★

Georgia Criterion-Referenced Competency Tests - Grades 6, 8
Pct. of students at each level

	Lang 6	Lang 8	Math 6	Math 8	Read 6	Read 8
Exceeds	7	11	8	4	23	36
Meets	47	43	48	42	43	40
Does not meet	46	46	44	54	34	25

Roberts Middle School

1905 Walt Stephens Rd, Jonesboro, GA 30236
678-479-0100 · Grades 6 - 8

Enrollment:	975
White / black / other:	42.9% / 47.8% / 9.3%
Not native English-speaking:	7 / 0.7%
Student absenteeism:	5.1%
Students per teacher:	16.9
Parent friendliness:	❶❷❸④⑤❻
Teachers with advanced degrees:	48.3%
Average years' teaching experience:	13.8
Students in gifted program:	123 / 12.6%
Students held back a grade:	1.7%
Total suspensions and expulsions:	356
Suspensions only, pct. in-school:	356 / 52.5%
Offenses: violence: 66, drugs: *, other: 325	
Eligible students, free or reduced lunch:	30.7%
Number of dropouts:	1 / 0.1%
Pct. 8th-graders w/ basic computer skills:	100.0%

Students at this school generally go on to:
Jonesboro, Mount Zion High

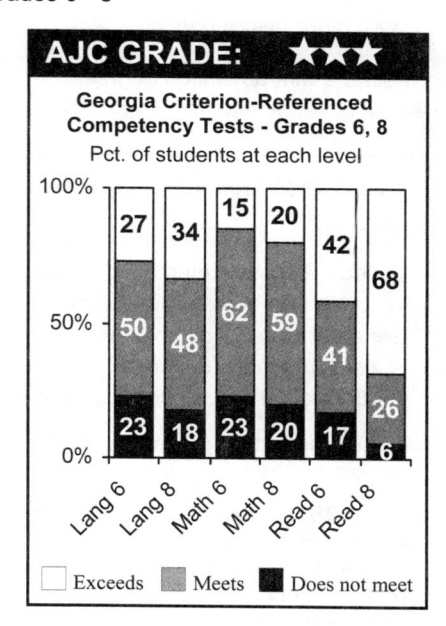

AJC GRADE: ★★★

Georgia Criterion-Referenced Competency Tests - Grades 6, 8
Pct. of students at each level

	Lang 6	Lang 8	Math 6	Math 8	Read 6	Read 8
Exceeds	27	34	15	20	42	68
Meets	50	48	62	59	41	26
Does not meet	23	18	23	20	17	6

Clayton County Middle Schools

Forest Park High School

5452 Phillips Dr, Forest Park, GA 30297
404-362-3890 · Grades 9 - 12

Enrollment:	1,591
White / black / other:	23.3% / 56.3% / 20.5%
Not native English-speaking:	74 / 4.7%
Limited English proficiency:	115 / 7.2%
Student absenteeism:	11.9%
Students per teacher:	17.6
Parent friendliness:	❶❷❸④⑤❻
Students in gifted program:	60 / 3.8%
Students in remedial education:	13.6%
High school completion rate:	46.2%
Students held back a grade:	13.0%
Number of dropouts:	167 / 9.2%
Students in alternative programs:	251 / 15.8%
Students in special education:	135 / 8.5%
Eligible students, free or reduced lunch:	53.2%
Total suspensions and expulsions:	2,393
Suspensions only, pct. in-school:	2,393 / 49.6%
Drugs/alcohol-related offenses:	6
Violence-related offenses:	44
Firearms-related offenses:	13
Vandalism-related offenses:	1
Theft-related offenses:	9
All other disciplinary offenses:	2,357
Teachers with advanced degrees:	52.1%
Average years' teaching experience:	12.9

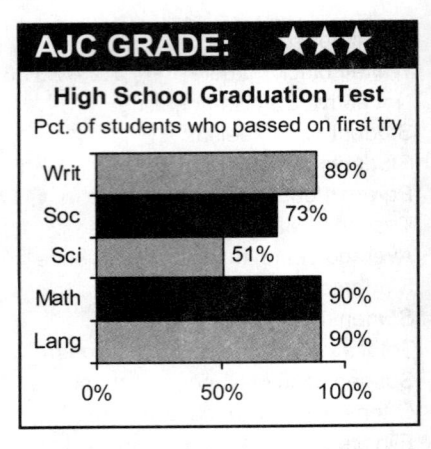

AJC GRADE: ★★★

High School Graduation Test
Pct. of students who passed on first try

- Writ: 89%
- Soc: 73%
- Sci: 51%
- Math: 90%
- Lang: 90%

GHSA classification:	4-AAAA
Interscholastic sports offered:	
BB, BS, CC, CL, FB, GO, SB, SO, SW, TE, TF, VB, WR	
Advanced Placement (AP) Exams	
Students tested:	39
Tests taken:	55
Pct. of test scores 3 or higher (1 - 5 scale):	16.4%
Languages other than English taught:	
French, Spanish	

2000-2001 high school graduates:	**246**
College prep/vocational diplomas:	41.9%
College prep endorsement diplomas:	11.4%
Vocational endorsement diplomas:	29.7%
General high school diplomas:	0.0%
Special education diplomas:	4.5%
Certificates of attendance (no diploma):	12.6%

Of the 2000-2001 graduates, 42.7% were eligible for the HOPE scholarship.

Of the 1999-2000 graduates, 74 attended a Georgia public college or university. Of those, 82% met the school's minimum academic requirements.

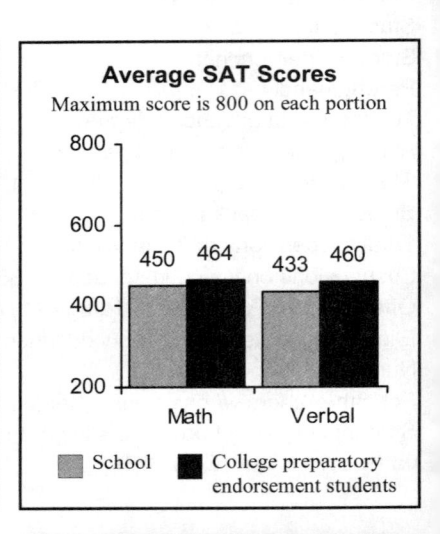

Average SAT Scores
Maximum score is 800 on each portion

- Math — School: 450, College preparatory endorsement students: 464
- Verbal — School: 433, College preparatory endorsement students: 460

The Atlanta Journal-Constitution / Page 116

Clayton County High Schools

Jonesboro High School

7728 Mount Zion Blvd, Jonesboro, GA 30236
770-473-2855 · Grades 9 - 12

Enrollment:	1,735
White / black / other:	48.4% / 43.0% / 8.6%
Not native English-speaking:	27 / 1.6%
Limited English proficiency:	46 / 2.7%
Student absenteeism:	8.3%
Students per teacher:	19.9
Parent friendliness:	❶❷❸④⑤❻
Students in gifted program:	153 / 8.8%
Students in remedial education:	8.0%
High school completion rate:	67.3%
Students held back a grade:	11.2%
Number of dropouts:	144 / 7.5%
Students in alternative programs:	226 / 13.0%
Students in special education:	141 / 8.1%
Eligible students, free or reduced lunch:	26.1%

Total suspensions and expulsions:	1,249
Suspensions only, pct. in-school:	1,249 / 54.9%
Drugs/alcohol-related offenses:	20
Violence-related offenses:	64
Firearms-related offenses:	6
Vandalism-related offenses:	8
Theft-related offenses:	17
All other disciplinary offenses:	1,179

Teachers with advanced degrees:	49.5%
Average years' teaching experience:	15.2

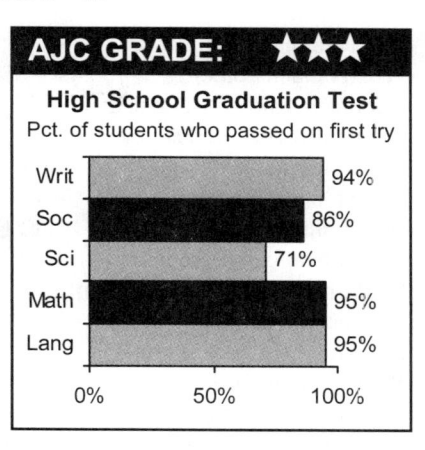

AJC GRADE: ★★★

High School Graduation Test
Pct. of students who passed on first try

- Writ: 94%
- Soc: 86%
- Sci: 71%
- Math: 95%
- Lang: 95%

GHSA classification: 2-AAAAA
Interscholastic sports offered:
BB, BS, CC, CL, FB, GO, SB, SO, SW, TE, TF, VB, WR

Advanced Placement (AP) Exams
Students tested:	117
Tests taken:	179
Pct. of test scores 3 or higher (1 - 5 scale):	43.0%

Languages other than English taught:
French, Latin, Spanish

2000-2001 high school graduates: 297

College prep/vocational diplomas:	16.5%
College prep endorsement diplomas:	67.7%
Vocational endorsement diplomas:	11.1%
General high school diplomas:	0.0%
Special education diplomas:	2.7%
Certificates of attendance (no diploma):	2.0%

Of the 2000-2001 graduates, 69.7% were eligible for the HOPE scholarship.

Of the 1999-2000 graduates, 130 attended a Georgia public college or university. Of those, 88% met the school's minimum academic requirements.

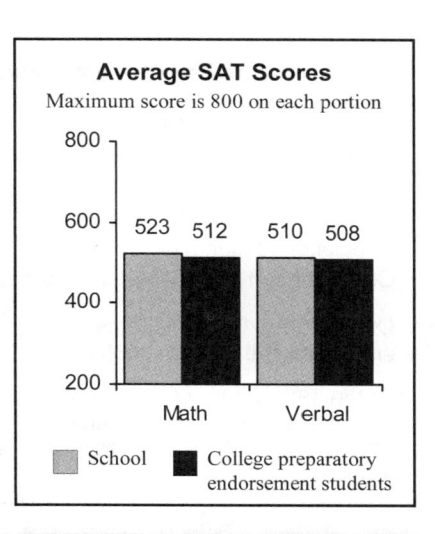

Average SAT Scores
Maximum score is 800 on each portion

	Math	Verbal
School	523	510
College preparatory endorsement students	512	508

Clayton County High Schools

Lovejoy High School

1587 McDonough Rd, Hampton, GA 30228
770-473-2920 · Grades 9 - 12

Enrollment:	2,342
White / black / other:	35.4% / 55.9% / 8.7%
Not native English-speaking:	12 / 0.5%
Limited English proficiency:	19 / 0.8%
Student absenteeism:	7.1%
Students per teacher:	19.8
Parent friendliness:	❶❷❸④❺❻
Students in gifted program:	176 / 7.5%
Students in remedial education:	7.7%
High school completion rate:	70.8%
Students held back a grade:	9.4%
Number of dropouts:	229 / 8.8%
Students in alternative programs:	278 / 11.9%
Students in special education:	270 / 11.5%
Eligible students, free or reduced lunch:	27.9%
Total suspensions and expulsions:	1,251
Suspensions only, pct. in-school:	1,251 / 65.4%
Drugs/alcohol-related offenses:	16
Violence-related offenses:	88
Firearms-related offenses:	2
Vandalism-related offenses:	24
Theft-related offenses:	24
All other disciplinary offenses:	1,186
Teachers with advanced degrees:	55.5%
Average years' teaching experience:	14.6

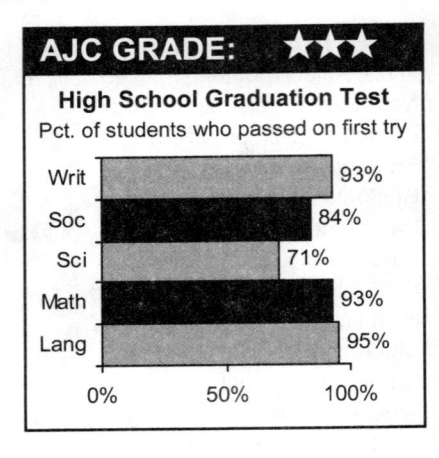

AJC GRADE: ★★★

High School Graduation Test
Pct. of students who passed on first try

Writ	93%
Soc	84%
Sci	71%
Math	93%
Lang	95%

GHSA classification: 4-AAAAA
Interscholastic sports offered:
BB, BS, CC, FB, GO, SB, SO, SW, TE, TF, WR

Advanced Placement (AP) Exams
Students tested:	92
Tests taken:	122
Pct. of test scores 3 or higher (1 - 5 scale):	45.1%

Languages other than English taught:
French, German, Spanish

2000-2001 high school graduates: 397

College prep/vocational diplomas:	8.8%
College prep endorsement diplomas:	64.5%
Vocational endorsement diplomas:	16.9%
General high school diplomas:	0.0%
Special education diplomas:	4.5%
Certificates of attendance (no diploma):	5.3%

Of the 2000-2001 graduates, 58.7% were eligible for the HOPE scholarship.

Of the 1999-2000 graduates, 143 attended a Georgia public college or university. Of those, 86% met the school's minimum academic requirements.

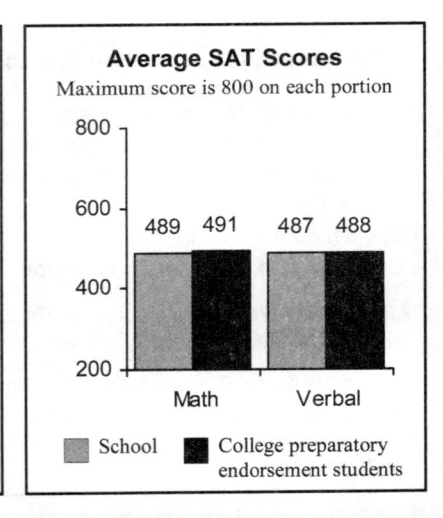

Average SAT Scores
Maximum score is 800 on each portion

	Math	Verbal
School	489	487
College preparatory endorsement students	491	488

Clayton County High Schools

Morrow High School

2299 Old Rex Morrow Rd, Morrow, GA 30260
404-362-3865 · Grades 9 - 12

Enrollment:	1,785
White / black / other:	25.4% / 59.4% / 15.2%
Not native English-speaking:	57 / 3.2%
Limited English proficiency:	68 / 3.8%
Student absenteeism:	9.1%
Students per teacher:	20.2
Parent friendliness:	① ❷ ❸ ④ ⑤ ❻
Students in gifted program:	108 / 6.1%
Students in remedial education:	9.2%
High school completion rate:	69.5%
Students held back a grade:	11.7%
Number of dropouts:	92 / 4.6%
Students in alternative programs:	186 / 10.4%
Students in special education:	154 / 8.6%
Eligible students, free or reduced lunch:	35.1%
Total suspensions and expulsions:	1,744
Suspensions only, pct. in-school:	1,744 / 62.5%
Drugs/alcohol-related offenses:	13
Violence-related offenses:	69
Firearms-related offenses:	8
Vandalism-related offenses:	8
Theft-related offenses:	7
All other disciplinary offenses:	1,678
Teachers with advanced degrees:	47.3%
Average years' teaching experience:	13.2

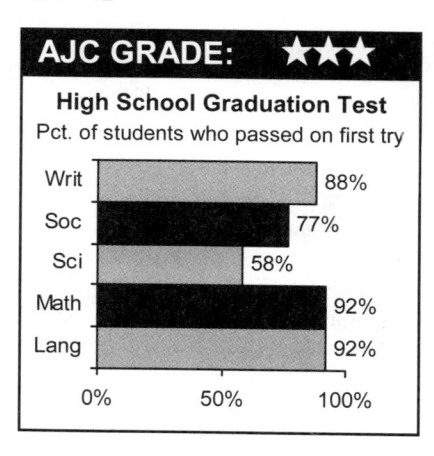

AJC GRADE: ★★★

High School Graduation Test
Pct. of students who passed on first try

Writ	88%
Soc	77%
Sci	58%
Math	92%
Lang	92%

GHSA classification:	2-AAAAA

Interscholastic sports offered:
BB, BS, CC, FB, GO, SB, SO, SW, TE, TF, WR

Advanced Placement (AP) Exams
Students tested:	77
Tests taken:	119
Pct. of test scores 3 or higher (1 - 5 scale):	43.7%

Languages other than English taught:
French, German, Latin, Spanish

2000-2001 high school graduates: 282

College prep/vocational diplomas:	12.4%
College prep endorsement diplomas:	58.9%
Vocational endorsement diplomas:	15.2%
General high school diplomas:	0.0%
Special education diplomas:	6.7%
Certificates of attendance (no diploma):	6.7%

Of the 2000-2001 graduates, 49.6% were eligible for the HOPE scholarship.

Of the 1999-2000 graduates, 99 attended a Georgia public college or university. Of those, 85% met the school's minimum academic requirements.

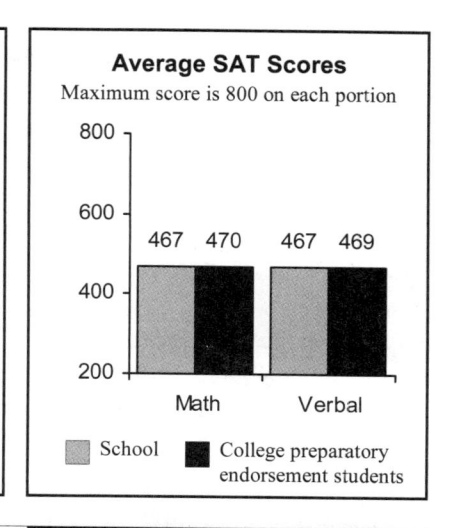

Average SAT Scores
Maximum score is 800 on each portion

	Math		Verbal	
	467	470	467	469

School / College preparatory endorsement students

Clayton County High Schools

Mount Zion High School

2535 Mount Zion Pkwy, Jonesboro, GA 30236
770-473-2940 · Grades 9 - 12

Enrollment:	1,738
White / black / other:	24.3% / 63.2% / 12.5%
Not native English-speaking:	38 / 2.2%
Limited English proficiency:	50 / 2.9%
Student absenteeism:	9.7%
Students per teacher:	18.0
Parent friendliness:	❶❷❸④⑤❻
Students in gifted program:	82 / 4.7%
Students in remedial education:	7.0%
High school completion rate:	61.0%
Students held back a grade:	11.8%
Number of dropouts:	188 / 9.4%
Students in alternative programs:	147 / 8.5%
Students in special education:	238 / 13.7%
Eligible students, free or reduced lunch:	35.5%
Total suspensions and expulsions:	1,195
Suspensions only, pct. in-school:	1,195 / 47.4%
Drugs/alcohol-related offenses:	13
Violence-related offenses:	86
Firearms-related offenses:	12
Vandalism-related offenses:	11
Theft-related offenses:	12
All other disciplinary offenses:	1,084
Teachers with advanced degrees:	50.5%
Average years' teaching experience:	13.1

AJC GRADE: ★★★

High School Graduation Test
Pct. of students who passed on first try

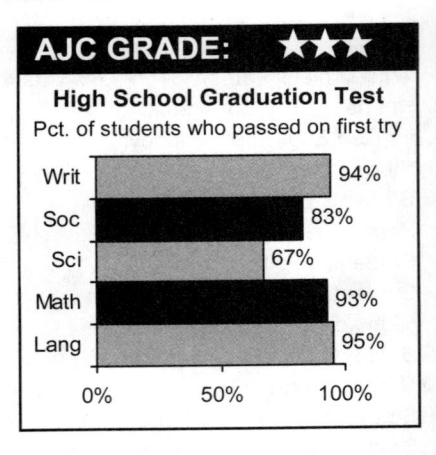

- Writ: 94%
- Soc: 83%
- Sci: 67%
- Math: 93%
- Lang: 95%

GHSA classification: 2-AAAAA
Interscholastic sports offered:
BB, BS, CL, FB, GO, SB, SO, SW, TE, TF, VB

Advanced Placement (AP) Exams
Students tested:	75
Tests taken:	110
Pct. of test scores 3 or higher (1 - 5 scale):	29.1%

Languages other than English taught:
French, Latin, Spanish

2000-2001 high school graduates: 271

College prep/vocational diplomas:	17.0%
College prep endorsement diplomas:	53.5%
Vocational endorsement diplomas:	14.4%
General high school diplomas:	0.4%
Special education diplomas:	7.4%
Certificates of attendance (no diploma):	7.4%

Of the 2000-2001 graduates, 53.5% were eligible for the HOPE scholarship.

Of the 1999-2000 graduates, 102 attended a Georgia public college or university. Of those, 89% met the school's minimum academic requirements.

Average SAT Scores
Maximum score is 800 on each portion

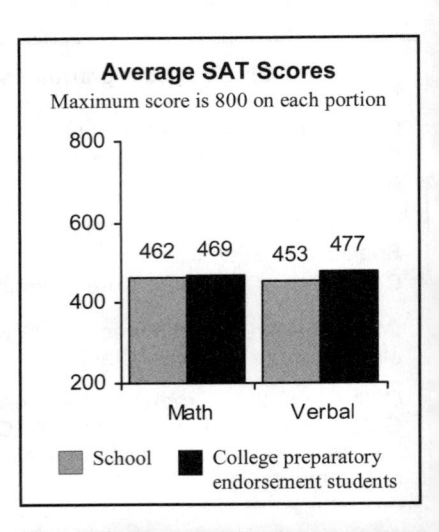

- Math: School 462, College preparatory endorsement students 469
- Verbal: School 453, College preparatory endorsement students 477

Clayton County High Schools

North Clayton High School

1525 Norman Dr, College Park, GA 30349
770-994-4035 · Grades 9 - 12

Enrollment:	1,327
White / black / other:	1.4% / 89.5% / 9.1%
Not native English-speaking:	26 / 2.0%
Limited English proficiency:	28 / 2.1%
Student absenteeism:	12.2%
Students per teacher:	18.0
Parent friendliness:	❶❷❸④⑤❻
Students in gifted program:	36 / 2.7%
Students in remedial education:	10.4%
High school completion rate:	69.9%
Students held back a grade:	13.0%
Number of dropouts:	119 / 7.8%
Students in alternative programs:	194 / 14.6%
Students in special education:	74 / 5.6%
Eligible students, free or reduced lunch:	42.4%

Total suspensions and expulsions:	2,161
Suspensions only, pct. in-school:	2,161 / 49.1%
Drugs/alcohol-related offenses:	10
Violence-related offenses:	84
Firearms-related offenses:	5
Vandalism-related offenses:	5
Theft-related offenses:	20
All other disciplinary offenses:	2,073

Teachers with advanced degrees:	43.4%
Average years' teaching experience:	13.5

AJC GRADE: ★★

High School Graduation Test
Pct. of students who passed on first try

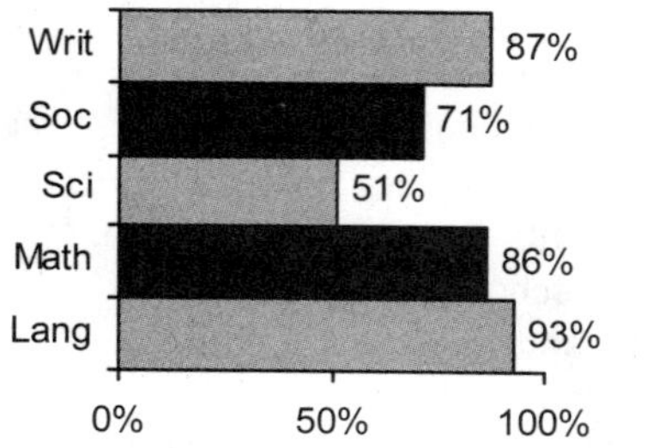

- Writ: 87%
- Soc: 71%
- Sci: 51%
- Math: 86%
- Lang: 93%

GHSA classification: 4-AAAA
Interscholastic sports offered:
BB, BS, CC, FB, GO, SB, SO, SW, TE, TF, WR

Advanced Placement (AP) Exams

Students tested:	49
Tests taken:	74
Pct. of test scores 3 or higher (1 - 5 scale):	8.1%

Languages other than English taught:
French, Latin, Spanish

2000-2001 high school graduates: 195

College prep/vocational diplomas:	17.4%
College prep endorsement diplomas:	55.9%
Vocational endorsement diplomas:	14.9%
General high school diplomas:	0.0%
Special education diplomas:	1.5%
Certificates of attendance (no diploma):	10.3%

Of the 2000-2001 graduates, 53.8% were eligible for the HOPE scholarship.

Of the 1999-2000 graduates, 62 attended a Georgia public college or university. Of those, 66% met the school's minimum academic requirements.

Average SAT Scores
Maximum score is 800 on each portion

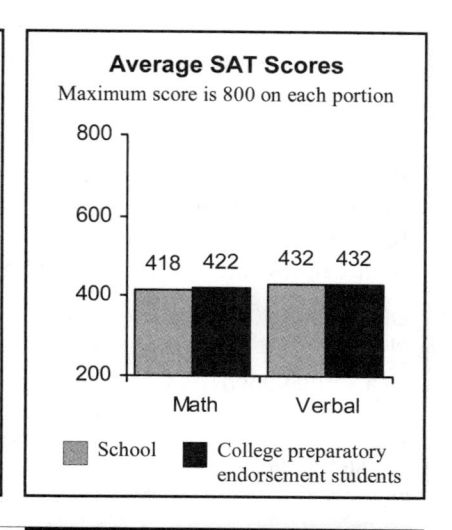

- Math — School: 418, College preparatory endorsement students: 422
- Verbal — School: 432, College preparatory endorsement students: 432

Clayton County High Schools

Riverdale High School

160 Roberts Dr, Riverdale, GA 30274
770-473-2905 · Grades 9 - 12

Enrollment:	1,619
White / black / other:	9.1% / 78.8% / 12.2%
Not native English-speaking:	31 / 1.9%
Limited English proficiency:	58 / 3.6%
Student absenteeism:	12.8%
Students per teacher:	20.5
Parent friendliness:	❶❷❸④❺❻
Students in gifted program:	42 / 2.6%
Students in remedial education:	10.3%
High school completion rate:	54.2%
Students held back a grade:	13.3%
Number of dropouts:	169 / 9.0%
Students in alternative programs:	170 / 10.5%
Students in special education:	136 / 8.4%
Eligible students, free or reduced lunch:	42.1%
Total suspensions and expulsions:	1,432
Suspensions only, pct. in-school:	1,432 / 56.8%
Drugs/alcohol-related offenses:	10
Violence-related offenses:	81
Firearms-related offenses:	5
Vandalism-related offenses:	7
Theft-related offenses:	14
All other disciplinary offenses:	1,345
Teachers with advanced degrees:	38.8%
Average years' teaching experience:	11.1

AJC GRADE: ★★

High School Graduation Test
Pct. of students who passed on first try

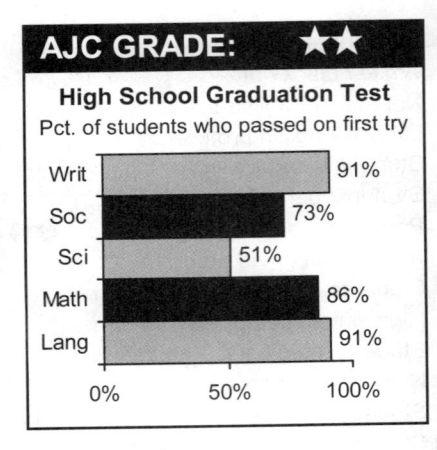

Writ	91%
Soc	73%
Sci	51%
Math	86%
Lang	91%

GHSA classification:	4-AAAAA

Interscholastic sports offered:
BB, BS, CC, FB, GO, SB, SO, SW, TE, TF, WR

Advanced Placement (AP) Exams
Students tested:	45
Tests taken:	62
Pct. of test scores 3 or higher (1 - 5 scale):	22.6%

Languages other than English taught:
French, Latin, Spanish

2000-2001 high school graduates: 245

College prep/vocational diplomas:	6.5%
College prep endorsement diplomas:	63.3%
Vocational endorsement diplomas:	15.1%
General high school diplomas:	0.0%
Special education diplomas:	6.1%
Certificates of attendance (no diploma):	9.0%

Of the 2000-2001 graduates, 55.9% were eligible for the HOPE scholarship.

Of the 1999-2000 graduates, 75 attended a Georgia public college or university. Of those, 72% met the school's minimum academic requirements.

Average SAT Scores
Maximum score is 800 on each portion

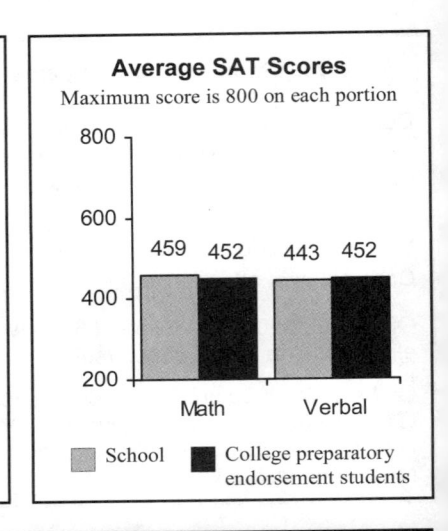

	Math	Verbal
School	459	443
College preparatory endorsement students	452	452

Clayton County High Schools

AJC ranking of Clayton County Schools

ELEMENTARY SCHOOLS

AJC Star Grade: ★★★★

Morrow Elementary

AJC Star Grade: ★★★

Anderson Elementary
Brown Elementary
Church Street Elementary
East Clayton Elementary
Edmonds Elementary
Fountain Elementary
Hawthorne Elementary
Haynie Elementary
Hendrix Drive Elementary
Huie Elementary
Kemp Elementary
Kilpatrick Elementary
Lake City Elementary
Lake Ridge Elementary
Lee Street Elementary
McGarrah Elementary
Mount Zion Elementary
Northcutt Elementary
Oliver Elementary
Pointe South Elementary
Riverdale Elementary
River's Edge Elementary
Smith Elementary
Suder Elementary
Swint Elementary
West Clayton Elementary

AJC Star Grade: ★★

Arnold Elementary

Tara Elementary

MIDDLE SCHOOLS

AJC Star Grade: ★★★

Adamson Middle
Babb Middle
Forest Park Middle
Jonesboro Middle
Lovejoy Middle
Morrow Middle
Mundy's Mill Middle
North Clayton Middle
Pointe South Middle
Riverdale Middle
Roberts Middle

AJC Star Grade: ★★

Kendrick Middle

HIGH SCHOOLS

AJC Star Grade: ★★★

Forest Park High
Jonesboro High
Lovejoy High
Morrow High
Mount Zion High

AJC Star Grade: ★★

North Clayton High
Riverdale High

Clayton County Public Schools

Cobb County Public Schools

514 Glover St SE, Marietta, GA 30060
Phone: 770-426-3300 · Fax: 770-528-6620
http://www.cobb.k12.ga.us

The following pages provide detailed information on every school in the Cobb County school district. An asterisk (*) means the value of the data was zero or was not reported by the school district. A complete list of schools ranked by The Atlanta Journal-Constitution's star rating system follows the detailed school reports.

District enrollment:	95,300
White / black / other:	63.8% / 23.4% / 12.8%
Not native English-speaking:	2,883 / 3.0%
Expenditure per student (general fund):	$6,013
Students per teacher:	14.9
Teachers with advanced degrees:	43.2%
Average years, teaching experience:	11.7
Average teacher salary:	$43,078.55
Students in gifted program:	9,430 / 9.9%
Students held back a grade:	2,438 / 2.6%
Eligible students, free or reduced lunch:	18,796 / 19.6%
Number of dropouts (grades 9-12):	1,039 / 3.5%
High school completion rate:	83.8%
Graduates, pct. eligible for HOPE scholarships:	5,541 / 69.7%
Average combined SAT score (maximum 1,600):	1,045
Pct. of 11th-graders passing the Georgia High School Graduation Tests on first try:	76%
Percent of children 5 to 17 years of age living in poverty (2000 Census estimate):	6.7%

Acworth Elementary School

4220 Cantrell Rd NW, Acworth, GA 30101
770-975-4281 · Grades K - 5

Enrollment:	558
White / black / other:	70.1% / 15.4% / 14.5%
Not native English-speaking:	*
Limited English proficiency:	45 / 8.1%
Student absenteeism:	5.7%
Students per teacher:	14.1
Parent friendliness:	❶ ❷ ❸ ④ ⑤ ❻
Teachers with advanced degrees:	31.0%
Average years' teaching experience:	13.6
Students in gifted program:	5 / 0.9%
Students in remedial education:	20.7%
Students held back a grade:	1.1%
Total suspensions, pct. in-school:	29 / 0.0%
Offenses:	violence: 11, drugs: 5, other: 17
Eligible students, free or reduced lunch:	35.5%
Before / after school program:	No / Yes

Students at this school generally go on to:
Awtrey Middle

AJC GRADE: ★★

Georgia Criterion-Referenced Competency Tests - Grade 4
Pct. of students at each level

Read: Exceeds 20%, Meets 48%, Does not meet 31%
Math: Exceeds 6%, Meets 44%, Does not meet 50%
Lang: Exceeds 10%, Meets 53%, Does not meet 37%

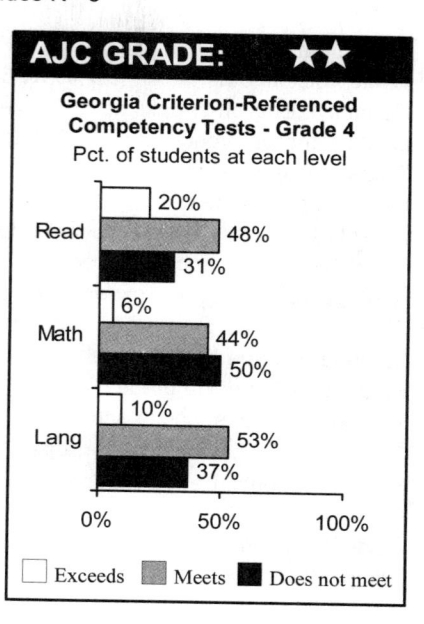

Addison Elementary School

3055 Ebenezer Rd, Marietta, GA 30066
770-509-6000 · Grades K - 5

Enrollment:	611
White / black / other:	76.8% / 11.1% / 12.1%
Not native English-speaking:	*
Limited English proficiency:	21 / 3.4%
Student absenteeism:	4.5%
Students per teacher:	12.9
Parent friendliness:	① ❷ ❸ ④ ❺ ❻
Teachers with advanced degrees:	49.0%
Average years' teaching experience:	14.5
Students in gifted program:	93 / 15.2%
Students in remedial education:	26.9%
Students held back a grade:	0.8%
Total suspensions, pct. in-school:	11 / 0.0%
Offenses:	violence: 7, drugs: *, other: 5
Eligible students, free or reduced lunch:	12.6%
Before / after school program:	No / Yes

Students at this school generally go on to:
Daniell, Simpson Middle

AJC GRADE: ★★★

Georgia Criterion-Referenced Competency Tests - Grade 4
Pct. of students at each level

Read: Exceeds 44%, Meets 44%, Does not meet 12%
Math: Exceeds 17%, Meets 61%, Does not meet 22%
Lang: Exceeds 22%, Meets 67%, Does not meet 12%

Cobb County Elementary Schools

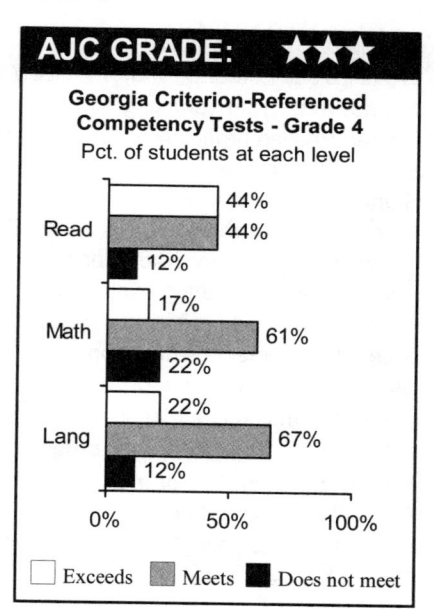

Argyle Elementary School

2420 Spring Dr SE, Smyrna, GA 30080
770-319-3700 · Grades K - 5

Enrollment:	710
White / black / other:	9.4% / 51.5% / 39.0%
Not native English-speaking:	118 / 16.6%
Limited English proficiency:	297 / 41.8%
Student absenteeism:	5.7%
Students per teacher:	13.7
Parent friendliness:	① ❷ ❸ ④ ⑤ ❻
Teachers with advanced degrees:	48.1%
Average years' teaching experience:	10.9
Students in gifted program:	3 / 0.4%
Students in remedial education:	33.3%
Students held back a grade:	2.7%
Total suspensions, pct. in-school:	22 / 4.5%
Offenses:	violence: 2, drugs: *, other: 20
Eligible students, free or reduced lunch:	66.9%
Before / after school program:	No / Yes
Students at this school generally go on to:	
Campbell Middle	

AJC GRADE: ★★★

Georgia Criterion-Referenced Competency Tests - Grade 4
Pct. of students at each level

Read: 16% / 51% / 33%
Math: 1% / 49% / 49%
Lang: 2% / 61% / 37%

☐ Exceeds ▨ Meets ■ Does not meet

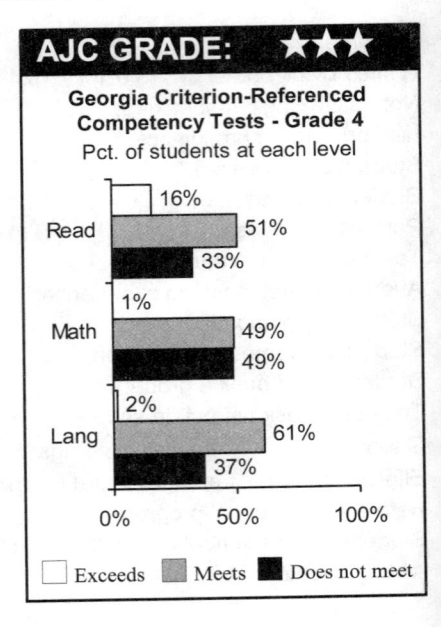

Austell Elementary School

5243 Meadows Rd, Powder Springs, GA 30127
770-732-5600 · Grades K - 5

Enrollment:	449
White / black / other:	53.7% / 30.7% / 15.6%
Not native English-speaking:	35 / 7.8%
Limited English proficiency:	55 / 12.2%
Student absenteeism:	5.9%
Students per teacher:	12.1
Parent friendliness:	① ❷ ❸ ④ ❺ ❻
Teachers with advanced degrees:	26.3%
Average years' teaching experience:	10.0
Students in gifted program:	11 / 2.4%
Students in remedial education:	35.3%
Students held back a grade:	2.4%
Total suspensions, pct. in-school:	22 / 0.0%
Offenses:	violence: 11, drugs: *, other: 12
Eligible students, free or reduced lunch:	53.5%
Before / after school program:	Yes / Yes
Students at this school generally go on to:	
Garrett Middle	

AJC GRADE: ★★★

Georgia Criterion-Referenced Competency Tests - Grade 4
Pct. of students at each level

Read: 25% / 39% / 36%
Math: 12% / 40% / 48%
Lang: 13% / 52% / 35%

☐ Exceeds ▨ Meets ■ Does not meet

Cobb County Elementary Schools

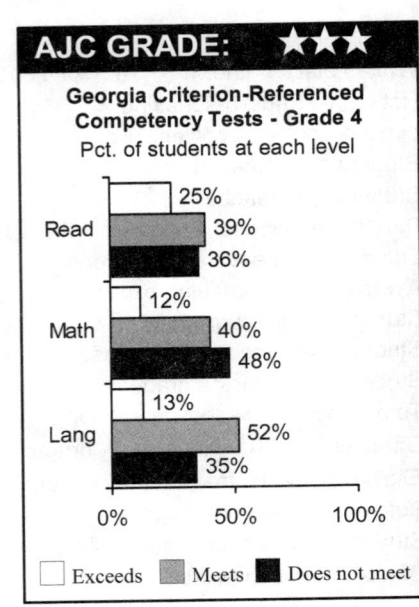

Baker Elementary School

2361 Baker Rd NW, Acworth, GA 30101
770-975-4286 · Grades K - 5

Enrollment:	1,339
White / black / other:	66.8% / 19.4% / 13.7%
Not native English-speaking:	*
Limited English proficiency:	17 / 1.3%
Student absenteeism:	5.0%
Students per teacher:	16.5
Parent friendliness:	❶❷❸④⑤❻
Teachers with advanced degrees:	36.1%
Average years' teaching experience:	12.4
Students in gifted program:	61 / 4.6%
Students in remedial education:	3.0%
Students held back a grade:	0.8%
Total suspensions, pct. in-school:	47 / 0.0%
Offenses:	violence: 21, drugs: *, other: 26
Eligible students, free or reduced lunch:	10.3%
Before / after school program:	No / Yes
Students at this school generally go on to:	
Awtrey, Palmer Middle	

AJC GRADE: ★★★

Georgia Criterion-Referenced Competency Tests - Grade 4
Pct. of students at each level

Read: Exceeds 48%, Meets 39%, Does not meet 13%
Math: Exceeds 18%, Meets 64%, Does not meet 18%
Lang: Exceeds 21%, Meets 67%, Does not meet 12%

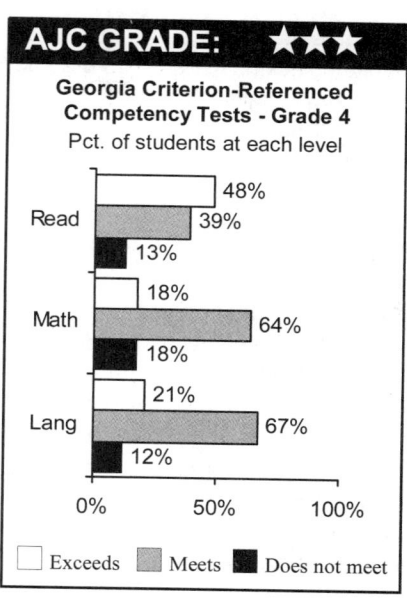

Bells Ferry Elementary School

2600 Bells Ferry Rd, Marietta, GA 30066
770-528-6540 · Grades K - 5

Enrollment:	413
White / black / other:	66.8% / 17.7% / 15.5%
Not native English-speaking:	*
Limited English proficiency:	40 / 9.7%
Student absenteeism:	4.9%
Students per teacher:	12.5
Parent friendliness:	❶❷❸④⑤❻
Teachers with advanced degrees:	54.3%
Average years' teaching experience:	13.5
Students in gifted program:	20 / 4.8%
Students in remedial education:	6.4%
Students held back a grade:	2.2%
Total suspensions, pct. in-school:	28 / 0.0%
Offenses:	violence: *, drugs: *, other: 28
Eligible students, free or reduced lunch:	15.7%
Before / after school program:	No / Yes
Students at this school generally go on to:	
Daniell Middle	

AJC GRADE: ★★★

Georgia Criterion-Referenced Competency Tests - Grade 4
Pct. of students at each level

Read: Exceeds 42%, Meets 49%, Does not meet 8%
Math: Exceeds 13%, Meets 61%, Does not meet 27%
Lang: Exceeds 15%, Meets 72%, Does not meet 13%

Cobb County Elementary Schools

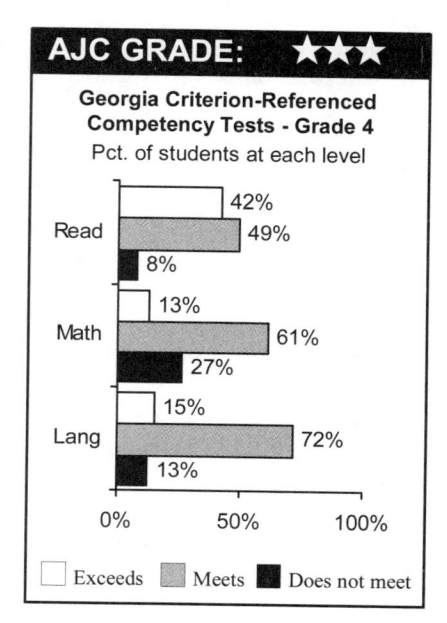

Belmont Hills Elementary School

605 Glendale Pl SE, Smyrna, GA 30080
770-319-3707 · Grades K - 5

Enrollment:	430
White / black / other:	15.6% / 35.6% / 48.8%
Not native English-speaking:	101 / 23.5%
Limited English proficiency:	266 / 61.9%
Student absenteeism:	5.8%
Students per teacher:	10.9
Parent friendliness:	① ❷ ❸ ④ ⑤ ❻
Teachers with advanced degrees:	45.0%
Average years' teaching experience:	10.6
Students in gifted program:	3 / 0.7%
Students in remedial education:	34.9%
Students held back a grade:	0.7%
Total suspensions, pct. in-school:	37 / 24.3%
Offenses:	violence: 6, drugs: 2, other: 30
Eligible students, free or reduced lunch:	79.4%
Before / after school program:	No / Yes
Students at this school generally go on to:	
Campbell, Griffin Middle	

AJC GRADE: ★★★

Georgia Criterion-Referenced Competency Tests - Grade 4
Pct. of students at each level

Read: 18% Exceeds, 41% Meets, 41% Does not meet
Math: 3% Exceeds, 42% Meets, 55% Does not meet
Lang: 8% Exceeds, 47% Meets, 45% Does not meet

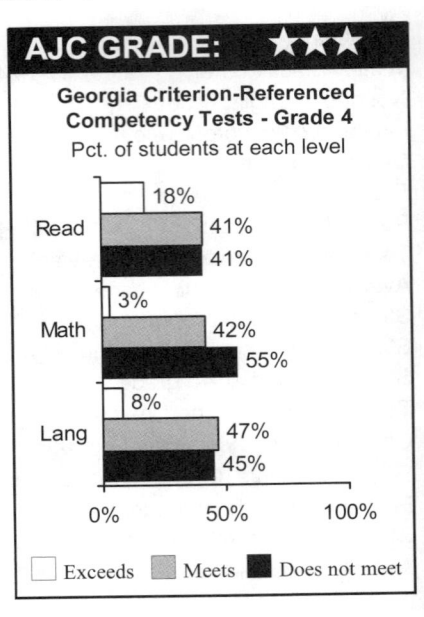

Big Shanty Elementary School

1600 Ben King Rd NW, Kennesaw, GA 30144
770-528-6546 · Grades K - 5

Enrollment:	679
White / black / other:	76.1% / 11.0% / 12.8%
Not native English-speaking:	*
Limited English proficiency:	11 / 1.6%
Student absenteeism:	4.2%
Students per teacher:	14.4
Parent friendliness:	① ② ❸ ④ ⑤ ❻
Teachers with advanced degrees:	38.8%
Average years' teaching experience:	16.2
Students in gifted program:	28 / 4.1%
Students in remedial education:	8.9%
Students held back a grade:	0.3%
Total suspensions, pct. in-school:	15 / 0.0%
Offenses:	violence: 6, drugs: *, other: 9
Eligible students, free or reduced lunch:	14.5%
Before / after school program:	No / Yes
Students at this school generally go on to:	
Palmer Middle	

AJC GRADE: ★★★

Georgia Criterion-Referenced Competency Tests - Grade 4
Pct. of students at each level

Read: 50% Exceeds, 34% Meets, 16% Does not meet
Math: 15% Exceeds, 59% Meets, 26% Does not meet
Lang: 22% Exceeds, 61% Meets, 17% Does not meet

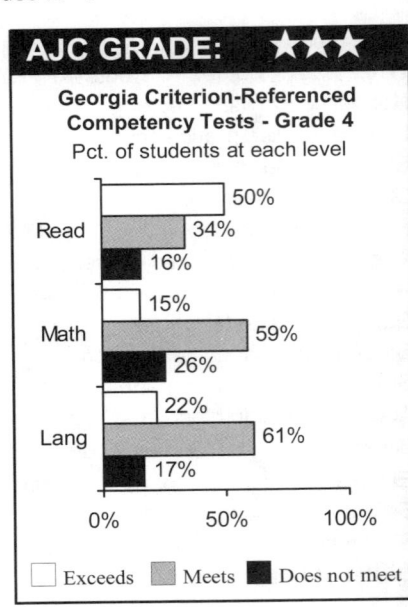

Birney Elementary School

775 Smyrna Powder Springs Rd, Marietta, GA 30060
770-319-3714 · Grades K - 5

Enrollment:	797
White / black / other:	28.9% / 51.8% / 19.3%
Not native English-speaking:	46 / 5.8%
Limited English proficiency:	146 / 18.3%
Student absenteeism:	4.6%
Students per teacher:	12.5
Parent friendliness:	❶❷❸❹❺❻
Teachers with advanced degrees:	32.8%
Average years' teaching experience:	8.6
Students in gifted program:	9 / 1.1%
Students in remedial education:	28.2%
Students held back a grade:	3.1%
Total suspensions, pct. in-school:	65 / 0.0%
Offenses:	violence: 21, drugs: *, other: 44
Eligible students, free or reduced lunch:	47.2%
Before / after school program:	Yes / Yes

Students at this school generally go on to:
Floyd, Smitha Middle

AJC GRADE: ★★

Georgia Criterion-Referenced Competency Tests - Grade 4
Pct. of students at each level

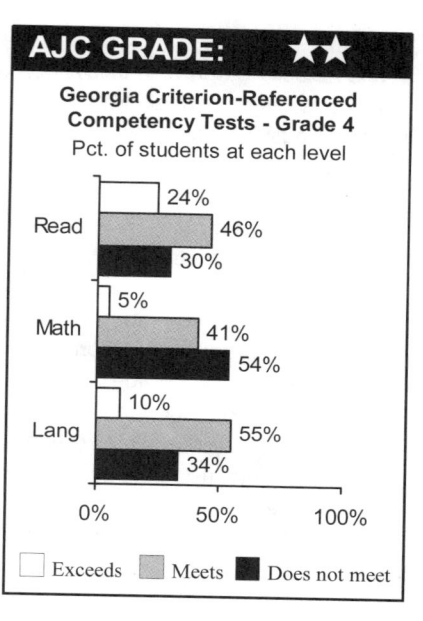

Read: Exceeds 24%, Meets 46%, Does not meet 30%
Math: Exceeds 5%, Meets 41%, Does not meet 54%
Lang: Exceeds 10%, Meets 55%, Does not meet 34%

Blackwell Elementary School

3470 Canton Rd, Marietta, GA 30066
770-591-6800 · Grades K - 5

Enrollment:	838
White / black / other:	72.3% / 10.9% / 16.8%
Not native English-speaking:	23 / 2.7%
Limited English proficiency:	43 / 5.1%
Student absenteeism:	4.4%
Students per teacher:	13.7
Parent friendliness:	①❷❸④⑤❻
Teachers with advanced degrees:	39.1%
Average years' teaching experience:	12.4
Students in gifted program:	47 / 5.6%
Students in remedial education:	16.9%
Students held back a grade:	1.0%
Total suspensions, pct. in-school:	9 / 0.0%
Offenses:	violence: 3, drugs: 1, other: 13
Eligible students, free or reduced lunch:	17.3%
Before / after school program:	No / Yes

Students at this school generally go on to:
Daniell, McCleskey Middle

AJC GRADE: ★★★

Georgia Criterion-Referenced Competency Tests - Grade 4
Pct. of students at each level

Read: Exceeds 43%, Meets 36%, Does not meet 20%
Math: Exceeds 16%, Meets 60%, Does not meet 24%
Lang: Exceeds 13%, Meets 66%, Does not meet 21%

Cobb County Elementary Schools

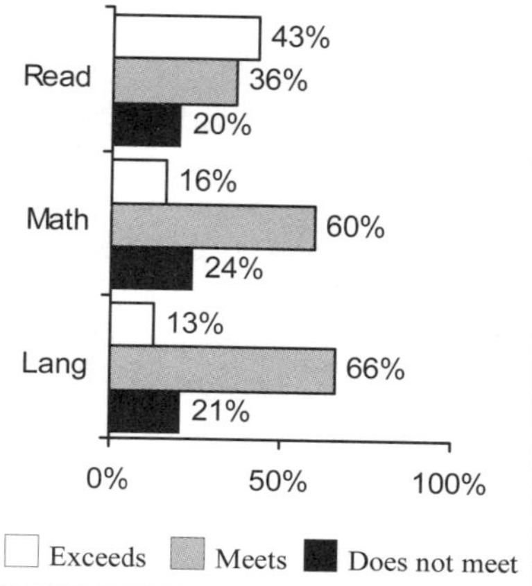

Brown Elementary School

3265 Brown Rd SE, Smyrna, GA 30080
770-319-3719 · Grades K - 5

Enrollment:	264
White / black / other:	37.9% / 33.3% / 28.8%
Not native English-speaking:	26 / 9.8%
Limited English proficiency:	77 / 29.2%
Student absenteeism:	5.5%
Students per teacher:	9.8
Parent friendliness:	① ❷ ❸ ④ ⑤ ❻
Teachers with advanced degrees:	44.8%
Average years' teaching experience:	11.5
Students in gifted program:	2 / 0.8%
Students in remedial education:	27.1%
Students held back a grade:	2.7%
Total suspensions, pct. in-school:	71 / 66.2%
Offenses: violence: *, drugs: *, other:	81
Eligible students, free or reduced lunch:	67.2%
Before / after school program:	No / Yes
Students at this school generally go on to:	
Campbell Middle	

AJC GRADE: ★★

Georgia Criterion-Referenced Competency Tests - Grade 4
Pct. of students at each level

- Read: Exceeds 15%, Meets 37%, Does not meet 49%
- Math: Exceeds 5%, Meets 45%, Does not meet 50%
- Lang: Exceeds 2%, Meets 46%, Does not meet 51%

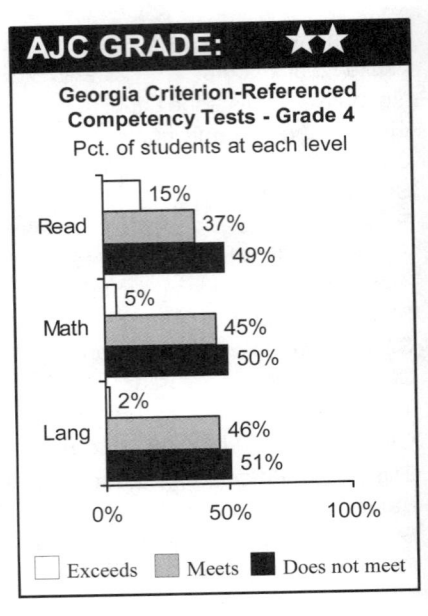

Brumby Elementary School

1306 Powers Ferry Rd SE, Marietta, GA 30067
770-916-2200 · Grades K - 5

👎

Enrollment:	844
White / black / other:	11.7% / 54.9% / 33.4%
Not native English-speaking:	187 / 22.2%
Limited English proficiency:	315 / 37.3%
Student absenteeism:	5.2%
Students per teacher:	12.0
Parent friendliness:	① ❷ ❸ ④ ⑤ ❻
Teachers with advanced degrees:	39.7%
Average years' teaching experience:	9.4
Students in gifted program:	14 / 1.7%
Students in remedial education:	26.5%
Students held back a grade:	3.1%
Total suspensions, pct. in-school:	*
Offenses: violence: *, drugs: *, other:	*
Eligible students, free or reduced lunch:	49.8%
Before / after school program:	No / Yes
Students at this school generally go on to:	
East Cobb Middle	

AJC GRADE: ★★

Georgia Criterion-Referenced Competency Tests - Grade 4
Pct. of students at each level

- Read: Exceeds 21%, Meets 43%, Does not meet 37%
- Math: Exceeds 6%, Meets 41%, Does not meet 53%
- Lang: Exceeds 7%, Meets 58%, Does not meet 35%

Cobb County Elementary Schools

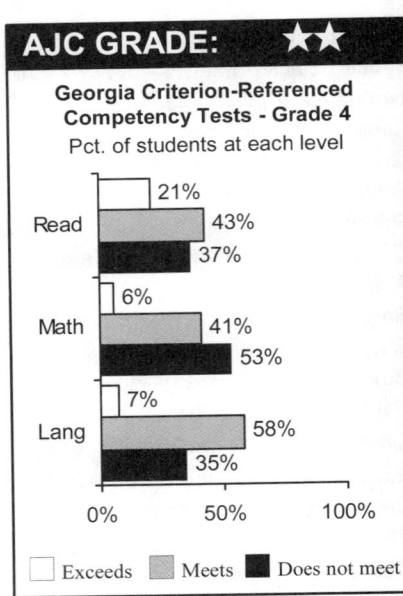

Bryant Elementary School

6800 Factory Shoals Rd SW, Mableton, GA 30126
770-732-5697 · Grades K - 5

Enrollment:	1,077
White / black / other:	8.4% / 73.4% / 18.2%
Not native English-speaking:	52 / 4.8%
Limited English proficiency:	178 / 16.5%
Student absenteeism:	5.4%
Students per teacher:	14.3
Parent friendliness:	①❷❸④⑤❻
Teachers with advanced degrees:	39.5%
Average years' teaching experience:	8.0
Students in gifted program:	15 / 1.4%
Students in remedial education:	36.2%
Students held back a grade:	0.4%
Total suspensions, pct. in-school:	337 / 0.0%
Offenses: violence: 120, drugs: *, other: 217	
Eligible students, free or reduced lunch:	62.2%
Before / after school program:	Yes / Yes

Students at this school generally go on to:
Garrett, Lindley Middle

AJC GRADE: ★★★

Georgia Criterion-Referenced Competency Tests - Grade 4
Pct. of students at each level

Read: 23% Exceeds / 38% Meets / 38% Does not meet
Math: 8% Exceeds / 41% Meets / 51% Does not meet
Lang: 12% Exceeds / 53% Meets / 35% Does not meet

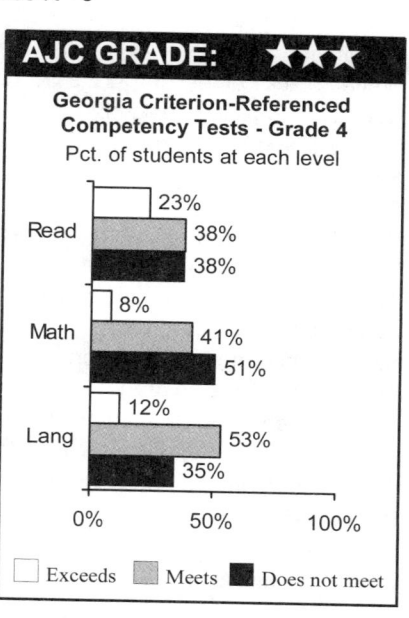

Chalker Elementary School

325 N Booth Rd NW, Kennesaw, GA 30144
770-591-6911 · Grades K - 5

Enrollment:	1,036
White / black / other:	72.1% / 12.9% / 15.0%
Not native English-speaking:	*
Limited English proficiency:	59 / 5.7%
Student absenteeism:	4.2%
Students per teacher:	17.1
Parent friendliness:	①❷❸④⑤❻
Teachers with advanced degrees:	27.9%
Average years' teaching experience:	7.7
Students in gifted program:	39 / 3.8%
Students in remedial education:	17.0%
Students held back a grade:	0.5%
Total suspensions, pct. in-school:	1 / 0.0%
Offenses: violence: *, drugs: *, other: 1	
Eligible students, free or reduced lunch:	11.8%
Before / after school program:	No / Yes

Students at this school generally go on to:
Daniell, Palmer Middle

AJC GRADE: ★★★

Georgia Criterion-Referenced Competency Tests - Grade 4
Pct. of students at each level

Read: 52% Exceeds / 33% Meets / 16% Does not meet
Math: 23% Exceeds / 54% Meets / 24% Does not meet
Lang: 31% Exceeds / 56% Meets / 13% Does not meet

Cobb County Elementary Schools

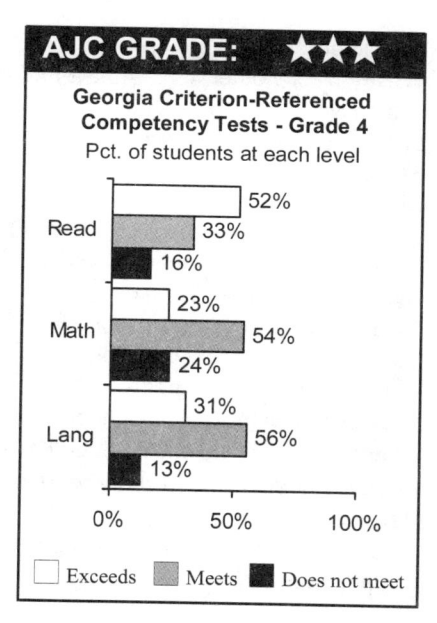

Cheatham Hill Elementary School

1350 John Ward Rd SW, Marietta, GA 30064
770-528-6781 · Grades K - 5

Enrollment:	1,105
White / black / other:	72.2% / 18.7% / 9.0%
Not native English-speaking:	*
Limited English proficiency:	29 / 2.6%
Student absenteeism:	4.1%
Students per teacher:	15.2
Parent friendliness:	❶❷❸④⑤❻
Teachers with advanced degrees:	38.2%
Average years' teaching experience:	10.3
Students in gifted program:	59 / 5.3%
Students in remedial education:	11.3%
Students held back a grade:	1.5%
Total suspensions, pct. in-school:	22 / 9.1%
Offenses:	violence: 13, drugs: *, other: 9
Eligible students, free or reduced lunch:	11.3%
Before / after school program:	No / Yes
Students at this school generally go on to:	
Pine Mountain, Smitha Middle	

AJC GRADE: ★★★

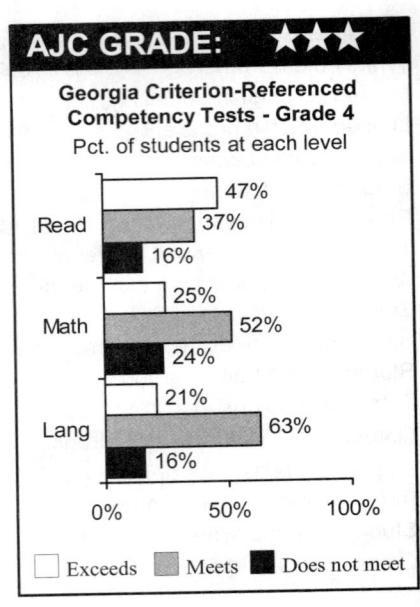

Georgia Criterion-Referenced Competency Tests - Grade 4
Pct. of students at each level

Read: 47% / 37% / 16%
Math: 25% / 52% / 24%
Lang: 21% / 63% / 16%

Exceeds | Meets | Does not meet

Clarkdale Elementary School

4455 Wesley Dr, Austell, GA 30106
770-732-5607 · Grades K - 5

Enrollment:	479
White / black / other:	43.2% / 47.8% / 9.0%
Not native English-speaking:	*
Limited English proficiency:	29 / 6.1%
Student absenteeism:	4.9%
Students per teacher:	14.0
Parent friendliness:	①❷❸④⑤❻
Teachers with advanced degrees:	37.8%
Average years' teaching experience:	11.2
Students in gifted program:	5 / 1.0%
Students in remedial education:	21.1%
Students held back a grade:	2.5%
Total suspensions, pct. in-school:	19 / 5.3%
Offenses:	violence: 13, drugs: *, other: 8
Eligible students, free or reduced lunch:	34.2%
Before / after school program:	No / Yes
Students at this school generally go on to:	
Cooper, Garrett Middle	

AJC GRADE: ★★

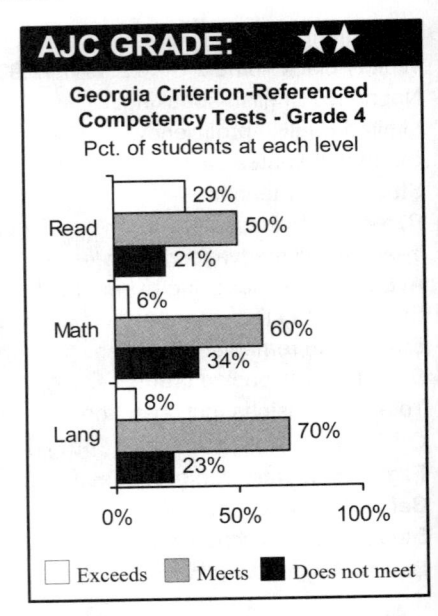

Georgia Criterion-Referenced Competency Tests - Grade 4
Pct. of students at each level

Read: 29% / 50% / 21%
Math: 6% / 60% / 34%
Lang: 8% / 70% / 23%

Exceeds | Meets | Does not meet

Clay Elementary School

730 Boggs Rd SW, Mableton, GA 30126
770-732-5614 · Grades K - 5

Enrollment:	546
White / black / other:	16.7% / 45.1% / 38.3%
Not native English-speaking:	89 / 16.3%
Limited English proficiency:	211 / 38.6%
Student absenteeism:	5.8%
Students per teacher:	10.3
Parent friendliness:	① ❷ ❸ ❹ ❺ ❻
Teachers with advanced degrees:	31.5%
Average years' teaching experience:	5.8
Students in gifted program:	2 / 0.4%
Students in remedial education:	35.2%
Students held back a grade:	1.3%
Total suspensions, pct. in-school:	16 / 0.0%
Offenses:	violence: 7, drugs: *, other: 9
Eligible students, free or reduced lunch:	77.1%
Before / after school program:	No / Yes

Students at this school generally go on to:
Lindley Middle

AJC GRADE: ★★★

Georgia Criterion-Referenced Competency Tests - Grade 4
Pct. of students at each level

- Read: Exceeds 22%, Meets 47%, Does not meet 31%
- Math: Exceeds 7%, Meets 47%, Does not meet 46%
- Lang: Exceeds 9%, Meets 54%, Does not meet 37%

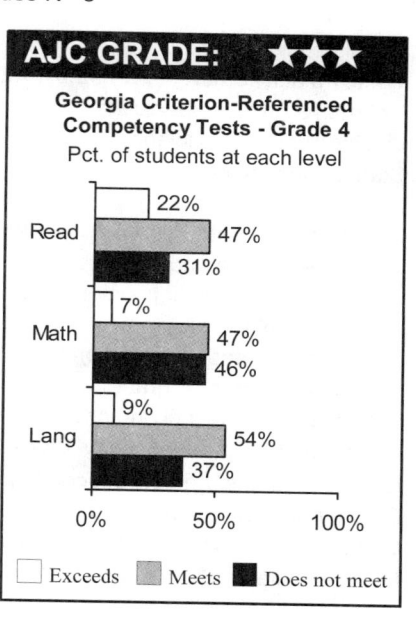

Compton Elementary School

3450 New Macland Rd, Powder Springs, GA 30127
770-439-4716 · Grades K - 5

Enrollment:	894
White / black / other:	36.8% / 54.7% / 8.5%
Not native English-speaking:	19 / 2.1%
Limited English proficiency:	48 / 5.4%
Student absenteeism:	4.4%
Students per teacher:	15.1
Parent friendliness:	❶ ❷ ❸ ❹ ❺ ❻
Teachers with advanced degrees:	21.7%
Average years' teaching experience:	8.8
Students in gifted program:	24 / 2.7%
Students in remedial education:	25.1%
Students held back a grade:	1.1%
Total suspensions, pct. in-school:	86 / 0.0%
Offenses:	violence: 21, drugs: 2, other: 63
Eligible students, free or reduced lunch:	44.3%
Before / after school program:	Yes / Yes

Students at this school generally go on to:
Tapp Middle

AJC GRADE: ★★★

Georgia Criterion-Referenced Competency Tests - Grade 4
Pct. of students at each level

- Read: Exceeds 31%, Meets 38%, Does not meet 31%
- Math: Exceeds 12%, Meets 42%, Does not meet 46%
- Lang: Exceeds 13%, Meets 52%, Does not meet 35%

Cobb County Elementary Schools

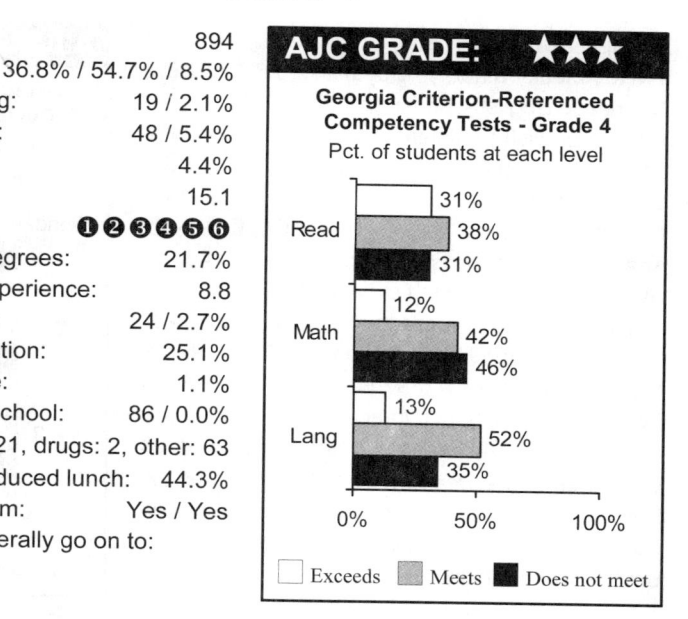

Davis Elementary School

2433 Jamerson Rd, Marietta, GA 30066
770-591-6807 · Grades K - 5

Enrollment:	627
White / black / other:	92.0% / 2.2% / 5.7%
Not native English-speaking:	*
Limited English proficiency:	12 / 1.9%
Student absenteeism:	3.8%
Students per teacher:	14.6
Parent friendliness:	① ❷ ❸ ④ ⑤ ❻
Teachers with advanced degrees:	59.1%
Average years' teaching experience:	17.3
Students in gifted program:	70 / 11.2%
Students in remedial education:	0.8%
Students held back a grade:	1.3%
Total suspensions, pct. in-school:	1 / 0.0%
Offenses:	violence: *, drugs: *, other: 1
Eligible students, free or reduced lunch:	1.9%
Before / after school program:	No / Yes

Students at this school generally go to:
Mabry Middle

AJC GRADE: ★★★

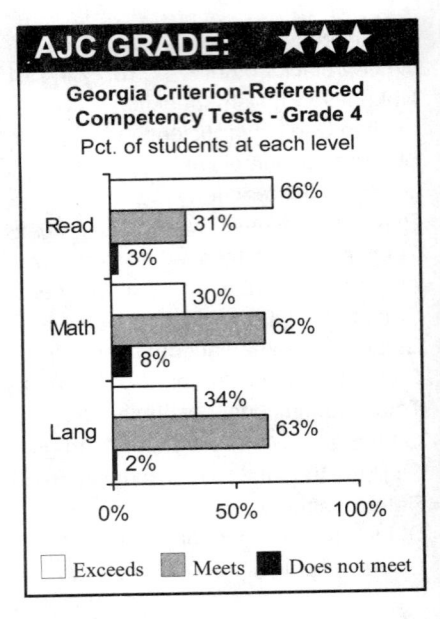

Georgia Criterion-Referenced Competency Tests - Grade 4
Pct. of students at each level

- Read: Exceeds 66%, Meets 31%, Does not meet 3%
- Math: Exceeds 30%, Meets 62%, Does not meet 8%
- Lang: Exceeds 34%, Meets 63%, Does not meet 2%

Dowell Elementary School

2121 W Sandtown Rd SW, Marietta, GA 30064
770-528-6554 · Grades K - 5

Enrollment:	876
White / black / other:	58.3% / 29.8% / 11.9%
Not native English-speaking:	*
Limited English proficiency:	28 / 3.2%
Student absenteeism:	4.5%
Students per teacher:	14.1
Parent friendliness:	① ❷ ❸ ④ ⑤ ❻
Teachers with advanced degrees:	46.0%
Average years' teaching experience:	13.9
Students in gifted program:	28 / 3.2%
Students in remedial education:	18.5%
Students held back a grade:	0.5%
Total suspensions, pct. in-school:	16 / 0.0%
Offenses:	violence: 2, drugs: *, other: 28
Eligible students, free or reduced lunch:	18.3%
Before / after school program:	No / Yes

Students at this school generally go to:
Smitha, Tapp Middle

AJC GRADE: ★★★

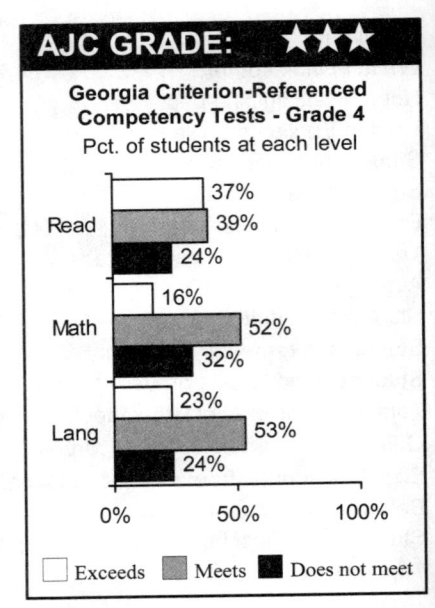

Georgia Criterion-Referenced Competency Tests - Grade 4
Pct. of students at each level

- Read: Exceeds 37%, Meets 39%, Does not meet 24%
- Math: Exceeds 16%, Meets 52%, Does not meet 32%
- Lang: Exceeds 23%, Meets 53%, Does not meet 24%

Cobb County Elementary Schools

Due West Elementary School

3900 Due West Rd NW, Marietta, GA 30064
770-528-6563 · Grades K - 5

Enrollment:	517
White / black / other:	92.8% / 2.1% / 5.0%
Not native English-speaking:	*
Limited English proficiency:	9 / 1.7%
Student absenteeism:	4.0%
Students per teacher:	16.2
Parent friendliness:	① ❷ ❸ ❹ ❺ ❻
Teachers with advanced degrees:	41.2%
Average years' teaching experience:	16.3
Students in gifted program:	31 / 6.0%
Students in remedial education:	5.7%
Students held back a grade:	0.4%
Total suspensions, pct. in-school:	2 / 0.0%
Offenses: violence: 1, drugs: *, other: 1	
Eligible students, free or reduced lunch:	3.1%
Before / after school program:	No / Yes

Students at this school generally go on to:
Lost Mountain Middle

AJC GRADE: ★★★

Georgia Criterion-Referenced Competency Tests - Grade 4
Pct. of students at each level

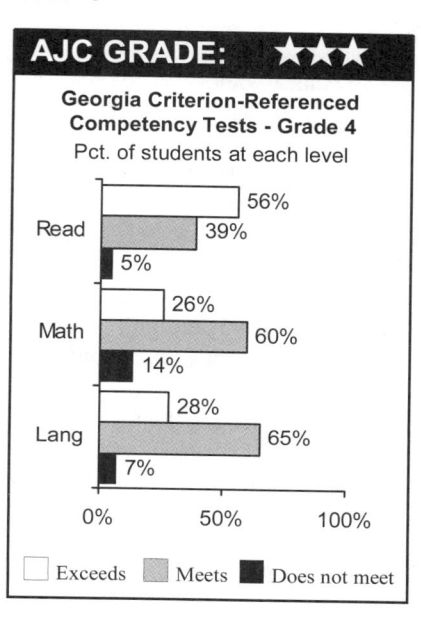

- Read: Exceeds 56%, Meets 39%, Does not meet 5%
- Math: Exceeds 26%, Meets 60%, Does not meet 14%
- Lang: Exceeds 28%, Meets 65%, Does not meet 7%

East Side Elementary School

3850 Roswell Rd, Marietta, GA 30062
770-509-6031 · Grades K - 5

Enrollment:	757
White / black / other:	78.2% / 4.1% / 17.7%
Not native English-speaking:	18 / 2.4%
Limited English proficiency:	96 / 12.7%
Student absenteeism:	3.3%
Students per teacher:	14.6
Parent friendliness:	① ❷ ❸ ④ ⑤ ❻
Teachers with advanced degrees:	30.2%
Average years' teaching experience:	12.4
Students in gifted program:	83 / 11.0%
Students in remedial education:	10.2%
Students held back a grade:	0.5%
Total suspensions, pct. in-school:	11 / 27.3%
Offenses: violence: 5, drugs: *, other: 6	
Eligible students, free or reduced lunch:	1.4%
Before / after school program:	No / Yes

Students at this school generally go on to:
Dickerson, Dodgen Middle

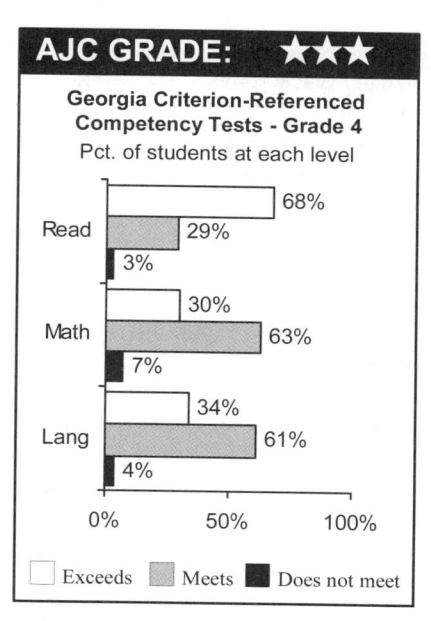

AJC GRADE: ★★★

Georgia Criterion-Referenced Competency Tests - Grade 4
Pct. of students at each level

- Read: Exceeds 68%, Meets 29%, Does not meet 3%
- Math: Exceeds 30%, Meets 63%, Does not meet 7%
- Lang: Exceeds 34%, Meets 61%, Does not meet 4%

Cobb County Elementary Schools

Eastvalley Elementary School

2570 Lower Roswell Rd, Marietta, GA 30068
770-509-6039 · Grades K - 5

Enrollment:	518
White / black / other:	61.6% / 23.9% / 14.5%
Not native English-speaking:	*
Limited English proficiency:	54 / 10.4%
Student absenteeism:	4.3%
Students per teacher:	14.7
Parent friendliness:	①❷❸④⑤❻
Teachers with advanced degrees:	60.5%
Average years' teaching experience:	13.0
Students in gifted program:	42 / 8.1%
Students in remedial education:	7.8%
Students held back a grade:	1.0%
Total suspensions, pct. in-school:	6 / 100.0%
Offenses:	violence: * , drugs: * , other: 6
Eligible students, free or reduced lunch:	9.5%
Before / after school program:	No / Yes
Students at this school generally go on to:	
East Cobb Middle	

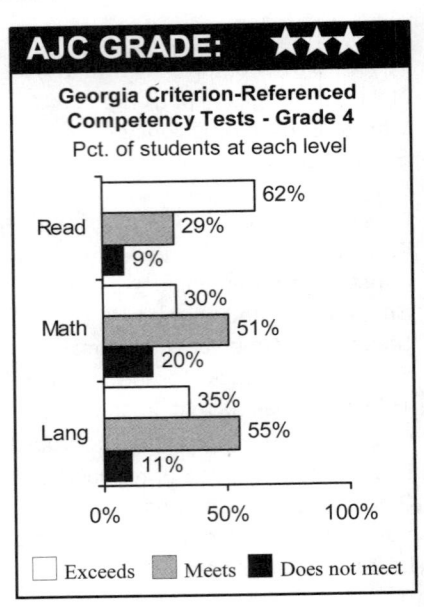

AJC GRADE: ★★★

Georgia Criterion-Referenced Competency Tests - Grade 4
Pct. of students at each level

Read: Exceeds 62%, Meets 29%, Does not meet 9%
Math: Exceeds 30%, Meets 51%, Does not meet 20%
Lang: Exceeds 35%, Meets 55%, Does not meet 11%

Fair Oaks Elementary School

407 Barber Rd SE, Marietta, GA 30060
770-528-6570 · Grades K - 5

Enrollment:	582
White / black / other:	19.1% / 27.7% / 53.3%
Not native English-speaking:	171 / 29.4%
Limited English proficiency:	373 / 64.1%
Student absenteeism:	6.5%
Students per teacher:	10.4
Parent friendliness:	①❷❸④❺❻
Teachers with advanced degrees:	38.6%
Average years' teaching experience:	10.8
Students in gifted program:	2 / 0.3%
Students in remedial education:	35.5%
Students held back a grade:	3.1%
Total suspensions, pct. in-school:	39 / 0.0%
Offenses:	violence: 12, drugs: 1, other: 26
Eligible students, free or reduced lunch:	77.9%
Before / after school program:	No / Yes
Students at this school generally go on to:	
Griffin Middle	

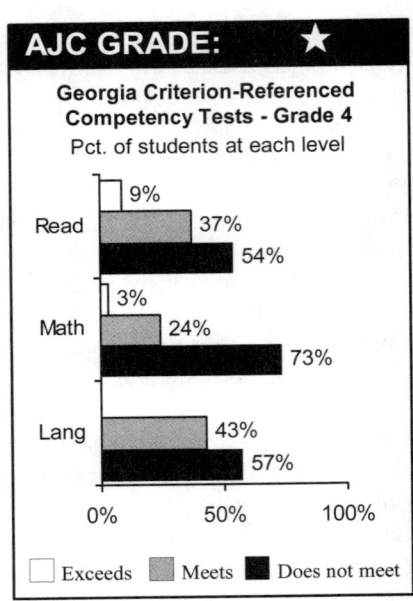

AJC GRADE: ★

Georgia Criterion-Referenced Competency Tests - Grade 4
Pct. of students at each level

Read: Exceeds 9%, Meets 37%, Does not meet 54%
Math: Exceeds 3%, Meets 24%, Does not meet 73%
Lang: Exceeds 43%, Meets 57%

Cobb County Elementary Schools

Ford Elementary School

1345 Mars Hill Rd NW, Acworth, GA 30101
770-528-6493 · Grades K - 5

Enrollment:	802
White / black / other:	94.6% / 2.5% / 2.9%
Not native English-speaking:	*
Limited English proficiency:	1 / 0.1%
Student absenteeism:	3.5%
Students per teacher:	16.5
Parent friendliness:	①❷❸④⑤❻
Teachers with advanced degrees:	36.0%
Average years' teaching experience:	11.8
Students in gifted program:	119 / 14.8%
Students in remedial education:	5.8%
Students held back a grade:	0.4%
Total suspensions, pct. in-school:	4 / 100.0%
Offenses:	violence: * , drugs: * , other: 7
Eligible students, free or reduced lunch:	1.2%
Before / after school program:	No / Yes

Students at this school generally go on to:
Durham Middle

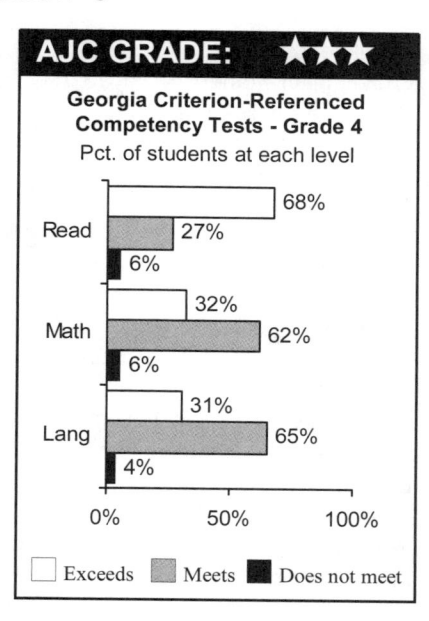

AJC GRADE: ★★★

Georgia Criterion-Referenced Competency Tests - Grade 4
Pct. of students at each level

Read: 68% / 27% / 6%
Math: 32% / 62% / 6%
Lang: 31% / 65% / 4%

☐ Exceeds ▨ Meets ■ Does not meet

Frey Elementary School

2865 Mars Hill Rd NW, Acworth, GA 30101
770-975-4167 · Grades K - 5

Enrollment:	1,278
White / black / other:	84.1% / 7.6% / 8.3%
Not native English-speaking:	*
Limited English proficiency:	22 / 1.7%
Student absenteeism:	4.5%
Students per teacher:	15.8
Parent friendliness:	①❷❸④⑤❻
Teachers with advanced degrees:	34.9%
Average years' teaching experience:	9.8
Students in gifted program:	60 / 4.7%
Students in remedial education:	21.1%
Students held back a grade:	0.6%
Total suspensions, pct. in-school:	9 / 11.1%
Offenses:	violence: 6, drugs: * , other: 6
Eligible students, free or reduced lunch:	8.9%
Before / after school program:	No / Yes

Students at this school generally go on to:
Awtrey, Durham Middle

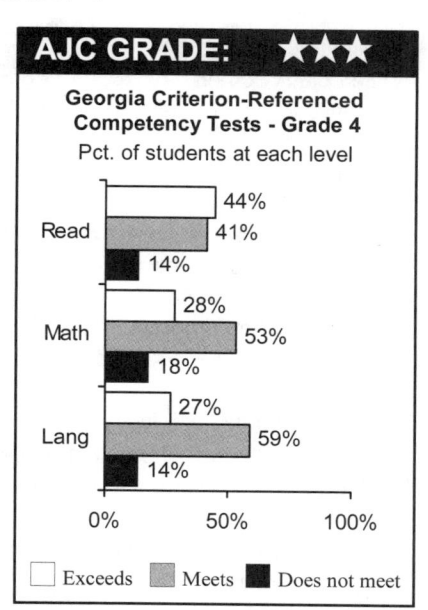

AJC GRADE: ★★★

Georgia Criterion-Referenced Competency Tests - Grade 4
Pct. of students at each level

Read: 44% / 41% / 14%
Math: 28% / 53% / 18%
Lang: 27% / 59% / 14%

☐ Exceeds ▨ Meets ■ Does not meet

Garrison Mill Elementary School

4111 Wesley Chapel Rd, Marietta, GA 30062
770-640-4801 · Grades K - 5

Enrollment:	610
White / black / other:	90.0% / 4.8% / 5.2%
Not native English-speaking:	*
Limited English proficiency:	12 / 2.0%
Student absenteeism:	4.1%
Students per teacher:	13.7
Parent friendliness:	①❷❸④⑤❻
Teachers with advanced degrees:	56.5%
Average years' teaching experience:	14.9
Students in gifted program:	60 / 9.8%
Students in remedial education:	9.7%
Students held back a grade:	1.8%
Total suspensions, pct. in-school:	17 / 76.5%
Offenses:	violence: 13, drugs: 1, other: 3
Eligible students, free or reduced lunch:	3.1%
Before / after school program:	No / Yes

Students at this school generally go on to:
Mabry Middle

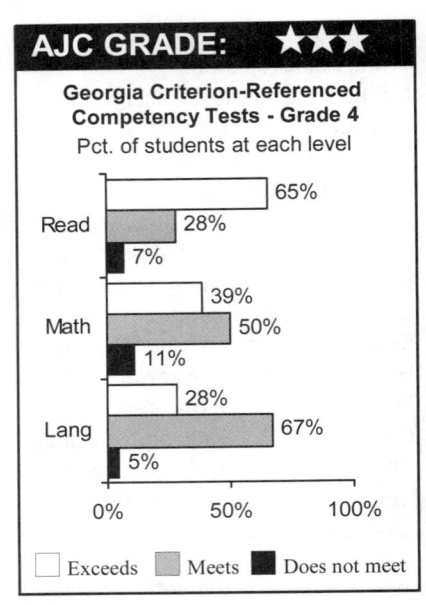

AJC GRADE: ★★★

Georgia Criterion-Referenced Competency Tests - Grade 4
Pct. of students at each level

Read: Exceeds 65%, Meets 28%, Does not meet 7%
Math: Exceeds 39%, Meets 50%, Does not meet 11%
Lang: Exceeds 28%, Meets 67%, Does not meet 5%

Green Acres Elementary School

2000 Gober Ave SE, Smyrna, GA 30080
770-319-3873 · Grades K - 5

Enrollment:	841
White / black / other:	16.5% / 46.5% / 37.0%
Not native English-speaking:	192 / 22.8%
Limited English proficiency:	318 / 37.8%
Student absenteeism:	4.8%
Students per teacher:	12.2
Parent friendliness:	①②❸④❺❻
Teachers with advanced degrees:	35.2%
Average years' teaching experience:	8.2
Students in gifted program:	12 / 1.4%
Students in remedial education:	32.3%
Students held back a grade:	1.5%
Total suspensions, pct. in-school:	6 / 0.0%
Offenses:	violence: 3, drugs: *, other: 3
Eligible students, free or reduced lunch:	69.8%
Before / after school program:	No / Yes

Students at this school generally go on to:
Campbell, Griffin Middle

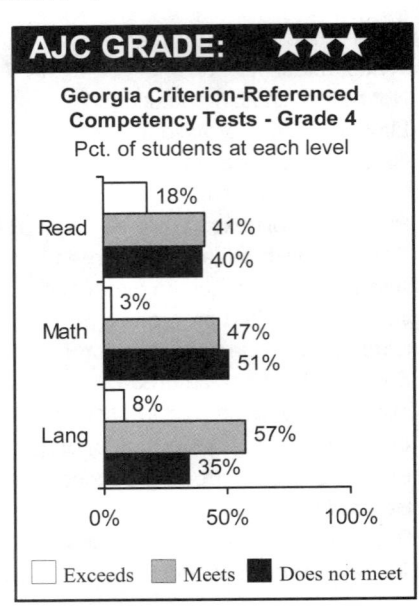

AJC GRADE: ★★★

Georgia Criterion-Referenced Competency Tests - Grade 4
Pct. of students at each level

Read: Exceeds 18%, Meets 41%, Does not meet 40%
Math: Exceeds 3%, Meets 47%, Does not meet 51%
Lang: Exceeds 8%, Meets 57%, Does not meet 35%

Cobb County Elementary Schools

Harmony Leland Elementary School

5891 Dodgen Rd SW, Mableton, GA 30126
770-732-5635 · Grades K - 5

Enrollment:	448
White / black / other:	31.7% / 57.1% / 11.2%
Not native English-speaking:	*
Limited English proficiency:	20 / 4.5%
Student absenteeism:	4.8%
Students per teacher:	11.4
Parent friendliness:	①❷❸④⑤❻
Teachers with advanced degrees:	30.0%
Average years' teaching experience:	6.3
Students in gifted program:	9 / 2.0%
Students in remedial education:	34.8%
Students held back a grade:	0.2%
Total suspensions, pct. in-school:	94 / 50.0%
Offenses:	violence: 13, drugs: *, other: 83
Eligible students, free or reduced lunch:	56.0%
Before / after school program:	No / Yes
Students at this school generally go on to: Lindley Middle	

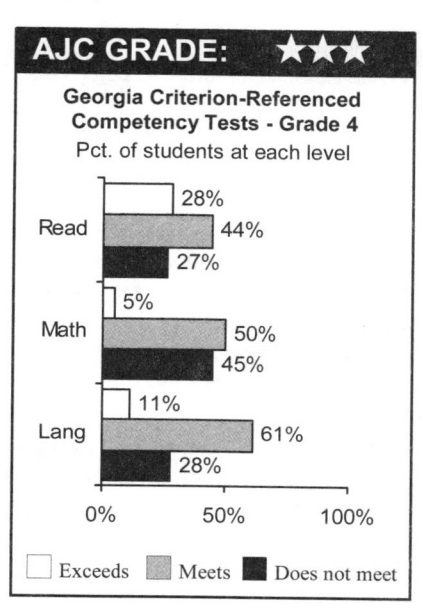

AJC GRADE: ★★★

Georgia Criterion-Referenced Competency Tests - Grade 4
Pct. of students at each level

- Read: 28% / 44% / 27%
- Math: 5% / 50% / 45%
- Lang: 11% / 61% / 28%

□ Exceeds ▨ Meets ■ Does not meet

Hayes Elementary School

1501 Kennesaw Due West Rd NW, Kennesaw, GA 30152
770-528-6450 · Grades K - 5

Enrollment:	1,093
White / black / other:	75.7% / 8.1% / 16.2%
Not native English-speaking:	46 / 4.2%
Limited English proficiency:	129 / 11.8%
Student absenteeism:	4.9%
Students per teacher:	16.1
Parent friendliness:	❶❷❸④⑤❻
Teachers with advanced degrees:	46.5%
Average years' teaching experience:	10.7
Students in gifted program:	59 / 5.4%
Students in remedial education:	12.2%
Students held back a grade:	1.0%
Total suspensions, pct. in-school:	38 / 0.0%
Offenses:	violence: 13, drugs: *, other: 26
Eligible students, free or reduced lunch:	19.4%
Before / after school program:	Yes / Yes
Students at this school generally go on to: Pine Mountain Middle	

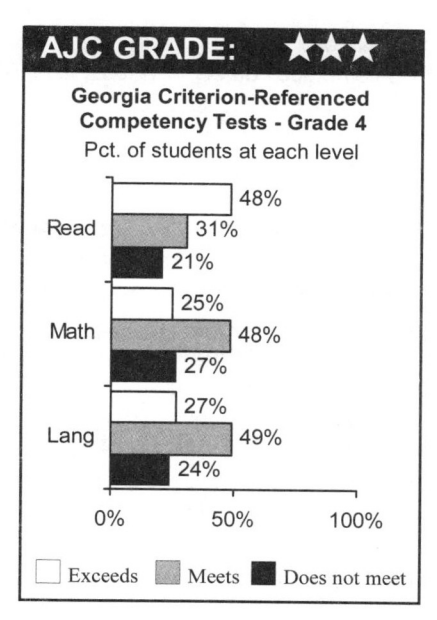

AJC GRADE: ★★★

Georgia Criterion-Referenced Competency Tests - Grade 4
Pct. of students at each level

- Read: 48% / 31% / 21%
- Math: 25% / 48% / 27%
- Lang: 27% / 49% / 24%

□ Exceeds ▨ Meets ■ Does not meet

Cobb County Elementary Schools

Hollydale Elementary School

2901 Bay Berry Dr SW, Marietta, GA 30008
770-528-6577 · Grades K - 5

Enrollment:	799
White / black / other:	29.5% / 52.2% / 18.3%
Not native English-speaking:	31 / 3.9%
Limited English proficiency:	83 / 10.4%
Student absenteeism:	4.3%
Students per teacher:	13.8
Parent friendliness:	❶❷❸④❺❻
Teachers with advanced degrees:	38.7%
Average years' teaching experience:	11.1
Students in gifted program:	18 / 2.3%
Students in remedial education:	23.5%
Students held back a grade:	0.5%
Total suspensions, pct. in-school:	42 / 4.8%
Offenses:	violence: 10, drugs: 1, other: 31
Eligible students, free or reduced lunch:	30.3%
Before / after school program:	Yes / Yes
Students at this school generally go on to:	
Smitha Middle	

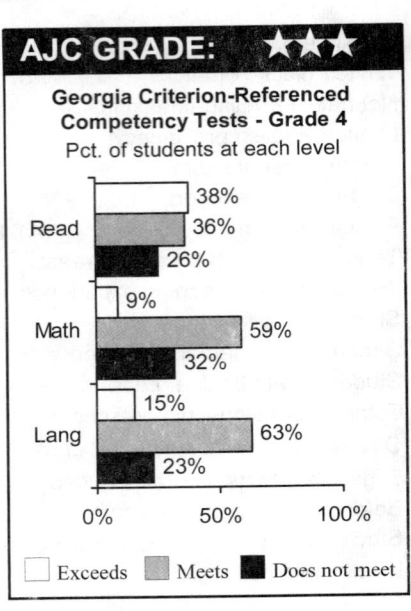

AJC GRADE: ★★★

Georgia Criterion-Referenced Competency Tests - Grade 4
Pct. of students at each level

- Read: Exceeds 38%, Meets 36%, Does not meet 26%
- Math: Exceeds 9%, Meets 59%, Does not meet 32%
- Lang: Exceeds 15%, Meets 63%, Does not meet 23%

Keheley Elementary School

1985 Kemp Rd, Marietta, GA 30066
770-591-6813 · Grades K - 5

Enrollment:	618
White / black / other:	80.1% / 9.5% / 10.4%
Not native English-speaking:	*
Limited English proficiency:	12 / 1.9%
Student absenteeism:	4.0%
Students per teacher:	14.9
Parent friendliness:	❶❷❸④⑤❻
Teachers with advanced degrees:	36.4%
Average years' teaching experience:	13.5
Students in gifted program:	53 / 8.6%
Students in remedial education:	9.1%
Students held back a grade:	1.3%
Total suspensions, pct. in-school:	11 / 27.3%
Offenses:	violence: 4, drugs: *, other: 7
Eligible students, free or reduced lunch:	8.7%
Before / after school program:	No / Yes
Students at this school generally go on to:	
McCleskey Middle	

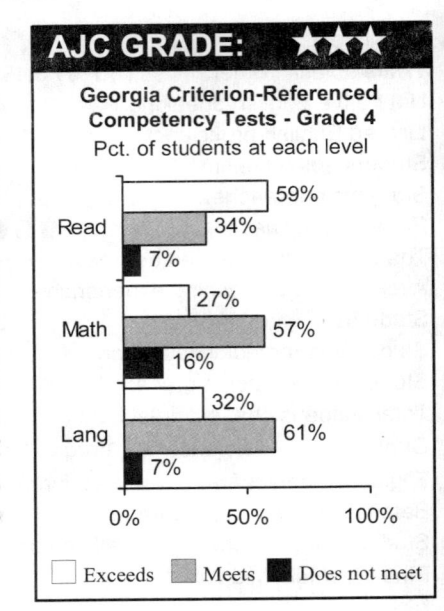

AJC GRADE: ★★★

Georgia Criterion-Referenced Competency Tests - Grade 4
Pct. of students at each level

- Read: Exceeds 59%, Meets 34%, Does not meet 7%
- Math: Exceeds 27%, Meets 57%, Does not meet 16%
- Lang: Exceeds 32%, Meets 61%, Does not meet 7%

Cobb County Elementary Schools

Kennesaw Elementary School

3155 Jiles Rd NW, Kennesaw, GA 30144
770-528-6584 · Grades K - 5

Enrollment:	1,248
White / black / other:	76.4% / 12.8% / 10.8%
Not native English-speaking:	32 / 2.6%
Limited English proficiency:	88 / 7.1%
Student absenteeism:	4.6%
Students per teacher:	16.5
Parent friendliness:	① ❷ ❸ ❹ ❺ ❻
Teachers with advanced degrees:	36.4%
Average years' teaching experience:	10.0
Students in gifted program:	63 / 5.0%
Students in remedial education:	10.3%
Students held back a grade:	1.2%
Total suspensions, pct. in-school:	25 / 32.0%
Offenses:	violence: 8, drugs: *, other: 38
Eligible students, free or reduced lunch:	10.8%
Before / after school program:	No / Yes

Students at this school generally go on to:
Awtrey Middle

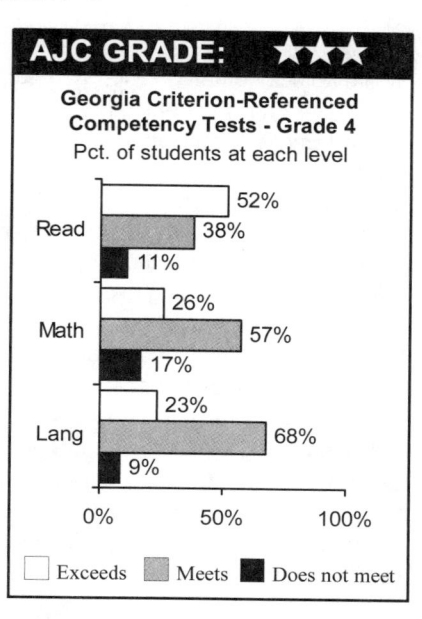

AJC GRADE: ★★★

Georgia Criterion-Referenced Competency Tests - Grade 4
Pct. of students at each level

Read: 52% Exceeds / 38% Meets / 11% Does not meet
Math: 26% Exceeds / 57% Meets / 17% Does not meet
Lang: 23% Exceeds / 68% Meets / 9% Does not meet

Kincaid Elementary School

1410 Kincaid Rd, Marietta, GA 30066
770-509-6047 · Grades K - 5

Enrollment:	648
White / black / other:	76.1% / 12.8% / 11.1%
Not native English-speaking:	*
Limited English proficiency:	19 / 2.9%
Student absenteeism:	4.5%
Students per teacher:	13.4
Parent friendliness:	① ❷ ❸ ❹ ❺ ❻
Teachers with advanced degrees:	49.0%
Average years' teaching experience:	16.3
Students in gifted program:	68 / 10.5%
Students in remedial education:	6.7%
Students held back a grade:	0.5%
Total suspensions, pct. in-school:	37 / 10.8%
Offenses:	violence: 11, drugs: *, other: 28
Eligible students, free or reduced lunch:	10.6%
Before / after school program:	No / Yes

Students at this school generally go on to:
Daniell, Dodgen, Simpson Middle

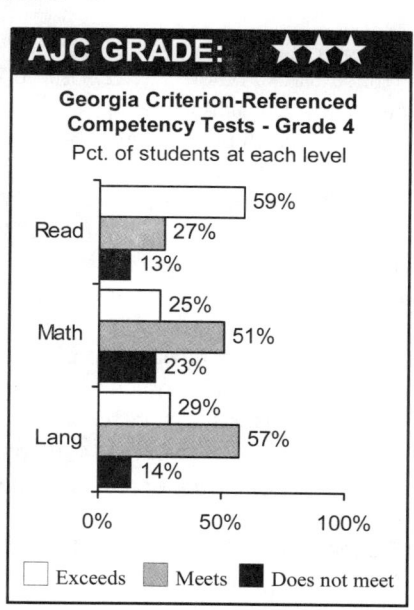

AJC GRADE: ★★★

Georgia Criterion-Referenced Competency Tests - Grade 4
Pct. of students at each level

Read: 59% Exceeds / 27% Meets / 13% Does not meet
Math: 25% Exceeds / 51% Meets / 23% Does not meet
Lang: 29% Exceeds / 57% Meets / 14% Does not meet

Cobb County Elementary Schools

King Springs Elementary School

1041 Reed Rd SE, Smyrna, GA 30082
770-319-3757 · Grades K - 5

Enrollment:	629
White / black / other:	42.3% / 45.3% / 12.4%
Not native English-speaking:	17 / 2.7%
Limited English proficiency:	38 / 6.0%
Student absenteeism:	4.2%
Students per teacher:	14.3
Parent friendliness:	①②③④❺❻
Teachers with advanced degrees:	29.8%
Average years' teaching experience:	10.2
Students in gifted program:	33 / 5.2%
Students in remedial education:	16.4%
Students held back a grade:	1.3%
Total suspensions, pct. in-school:	20 / 0.0%
Offenses:	violence: 10, drugs: *, other: 11
Eligible students, free or reduced lunch:	28.9%
Before / after school program:	No / Yes
Students at this school generally go on to:	Griffin Middle

AJC GRADE: ★★

Georgia Criterion-Referenced Competency Tests - Grade 4
Pct. of students at each level

Read: Exceeds 29%, Meets 44%, Does not meet 28%
Math: Exceeds 12%, Meets 47%, Does not meet 40%
Lang: Exceeds 15%, Meets 58%, Does not meet 27%

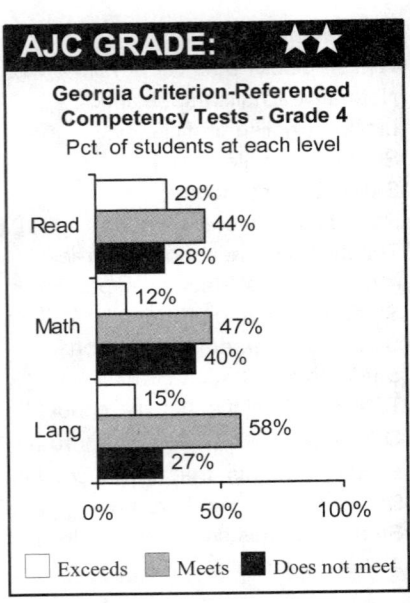

LaBelle Elementary School

230 Cresson Dr SW, Marietta, GA 30060
770-319-3764 · Grades K - 5

Enrollment:	397
White / black / other:	22.9% / 30.2% / 46.9%
Not native English-speaking:	107 / 27.0%
Limited English proficiency:	205 / 51.6%
Student absenteeism:	5.3%
Students per teacher:	11.7
Parent friendliness:	①❷❸❹❺❻
Teachers with advanced degrees:	36.1%
Average years' teaching experience:	9.6
Students in gifted program:	11 / 2.8%
Students in remedial education:	37.4%
Students held back a grade:	2.0%
Total suspensions, pct. in-school:	20 / 0.0%
Offenses:	violence: 14, drugs: 1, other: 6
Eligible students, free or reduced lunch:	72.0%
Before / after school program:	Yes / Yes
Students at this school generally go on to:	Griffin Middle

AJC GRADE: ★★★

Georgia Criterion-Referenced Competency Tests - Grade 4
Pct. of students at each level

Read: Exceeds 20%, Meets 43%, Does not meet 36%
Math: Exceeds 6%, Meets 48%, Does not meet 45%
Lang: Exceeds 7%, Meets 49%, Does not meet 44%

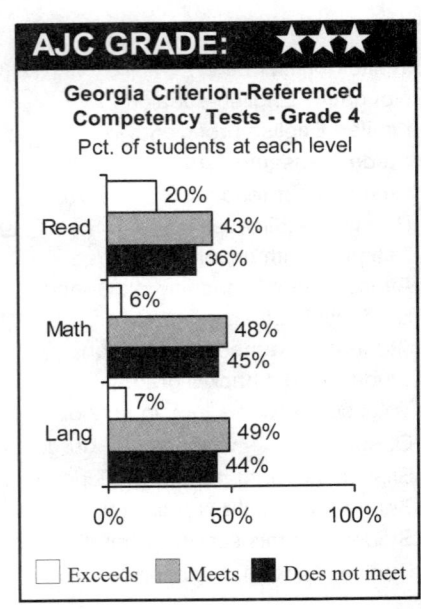

Lewis Elementary School

4179 Jim Owens Rd NW, Kennesaw, GA 30152
770-975-4293 · Grades K - 5

Enrollment:	923
White / black / other:	86.6% / 7.5% / 6.0%
Not native English-speaking:	*
Limited English proficiency:	10 / 1.1%
Student absenteeism:	4.4%
Students per teacher:	15.1
Parent friendliness:	❶❷❸④❺❻
Teachers with advanced degrees:	48.4%
Average years' teaching experience:	13.0
Students in gifted program:	30 / 3.3%
Students in remedial education:	13.0%
Students held back a grade:	1.0%
Total suspensions, pct. in-school:	5 / 40.0%
Offenses:	violence: * , drugs: * , other: 5
Eligible students, free or reduced lunch:	6.1%
Before / after school program:	No / Yes

Students at this school generally go on to:
Durham Middle

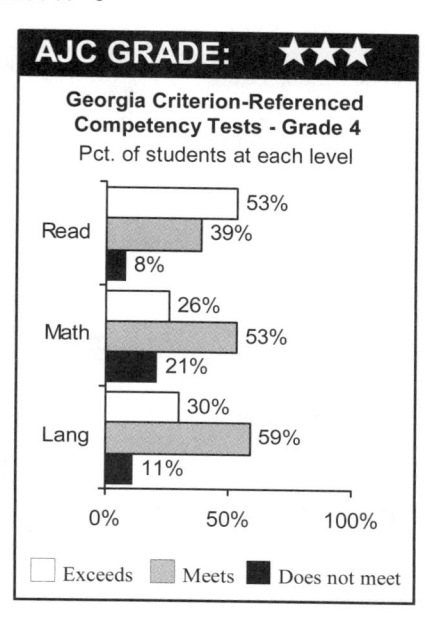

AJC GRADE: ★★★

Georgia Criterion-Referenced Competency Tests - Grade 4
Pct. of students at each level

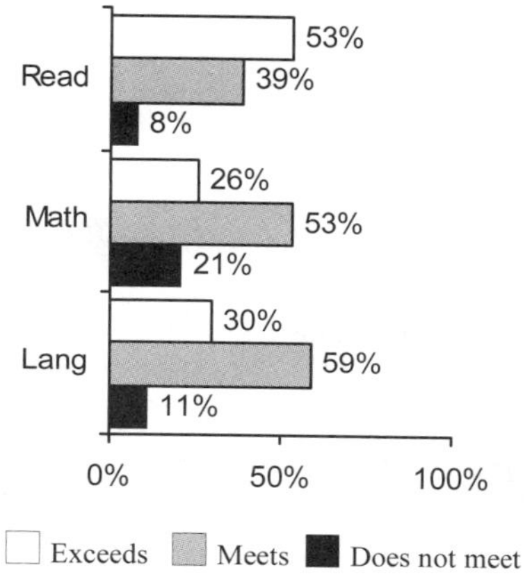
Read
53%
39%
8%
Math
26%
53%
21%
Lang
30%
59%
11%
0%
50%
100%
Exceeds
Meets
Does not meet

Mableton Elementary School

5220 Church St SW, Mableton, GA 30126
770-732-5651 · Grades K - 5

Enrollment:	434
White / black / other:	62.0% / 25.1% / 12.9%
Not native English-speaking:	*
Limited English proficiency:	9 / 2.1%
Student absenteeism:	5.9%
Students per teacher:	12.4
Parent friendliness:	①❷❸④⑤❻
Teachers with advanced degrees:	46.2%
Average years' teaching experience:	15.0
Students in gifted program:	20 / 4.6%
Students in remedial education:	23.1%
Students held back a grade:	2.1%
Total suspensions, pct. in-school:	18 / 50.0%
Offenses:	violence: 5, drugs: 2, other: 11
Eligible students, free or reduced lunch:	34.4%
Before / after school program:	No / Yes

Students at this school generally go on to:
Floyd Middle

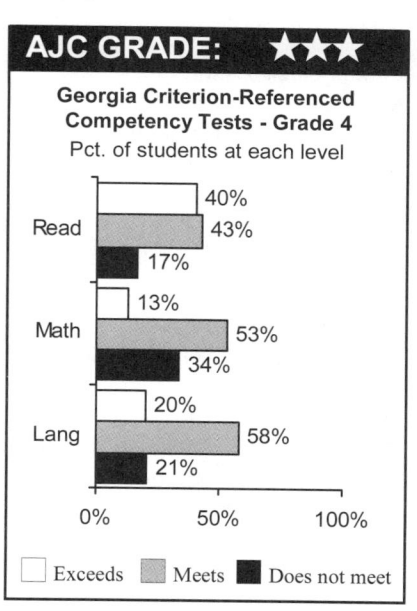

AJC GRADE: ★★★

Georgia Criterion-Referenced Competency Tests - Grade 4
Pct. of students at each level

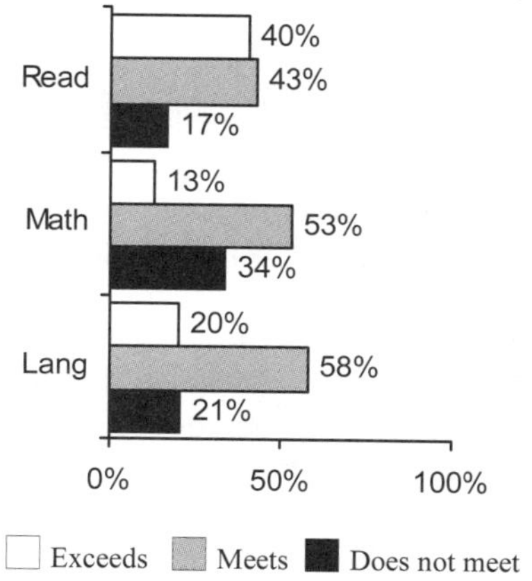
Read
40%
43%
17%
Math
13%
53%
34%
Lang
20%
58%
21%
0%
50%
100%
Exceeds
Meets
Does not meet

Milford Elementary School

2390 Austell Rd SW, Marietta, GA 30008
770-319-3771 · Grades K - 5

Enrollment:	466
White / black / other:	21.5% / 39.3% / 39.3%
Not native English-speaking:	116 / 24.9%
Limited English proficiency:	198 / 42.5%
Student absenteeism:	5.6%
Students per teacher:	10.1
Parent friendliness:	① ❷ ❸ ④ ❺ ❻
Teachers with advanced degrees:	46.8%
Average years' teaching experience:	11.6
Students in gifted program:	3 / 0.6%
Students in remedial education:	33.6%
Students held back a grade:	2.1%
Total suspensions, pct. in-school:	54 / 0.0%
Offenses:	violence: 18, drugs: 1, other: 46
Eligible students, free or reduced lunch:	46.6%
Before / after school program:	Yes / Yes
Students at this school generally go on to: Smitha Middle	

AJC GRADE: ★★

Georgia Criterion-Referenced Competency Tests - Grade 4
Pct. of students at each level

Read: Exceeds 24%, Meets 41%, Does not meet 35%
Math: Exceeds 9%, Meets 56%, Does not meet 36%
Lang: Exceeds 9%, Meets 62%, Does not meet 29%

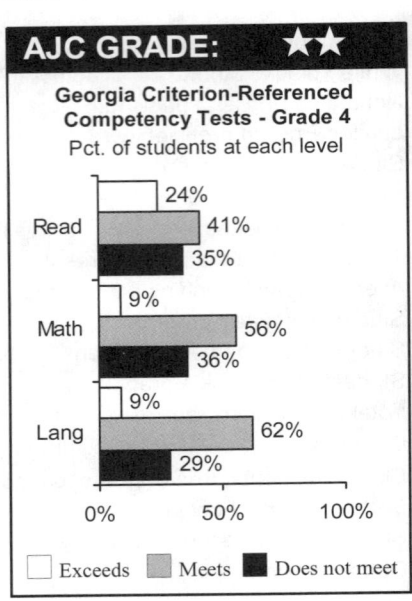

Mount Bethel Elementary School

1210 Johnson Ferry Rd, Marietta, GA 30068
770-509-6063 · Grades K - 5

Enrollment:	1,129
White / black / other:	90.2% / 2.0% / 7.8%
Not native English-speaking:	*
Limited English proficiency:	10 / 0.9%
Student absenteeism:	3.4%
Students per teacher:	16.9
Parent friendliness:	① ❷ ❸ ④ ⑤ ❻
Teachers with advanced degrees:	47.8%
Average years' teaching experience:	15.9
Students in gifted program:	142 / 12.6%
Students in remedial education:	6.0%
Students held back a grade:	0.1%
Total suspensions, pct. in-school:	1 / 0.0%
Offenses:	violence: 1, drugs: *, other: *
Eligible students, free or reduced lunch:	0.3%
Before / after school program:	No / Yes
Students at this school generally go on to: Dickerson Middle	

AJC GRADE: ★★★★

Georgia Criterion-Referenced Competency Tests - Grade 4
Pct. of students at each level

Read: Exceeds 69%, Meets 28%, Does not meet 2%
Math: Exceeds 33%, Meets 60%, Does not meet 6%
Lang: Exceeds 45%, Meets 51%, Does not meet 4%

Cobb County Elementary Schools

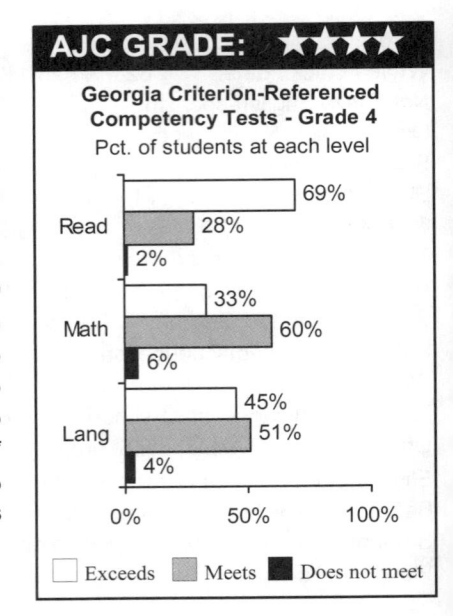

Mountain View Elementary School

3448 Sandy Plains Rd, Marietta, GA 30066
770-509-6055 · Grades K - 5

Enrollment:	800
White / black / other:	81.9% / 7.5% / 10.6%
Not native English-speaking:	*
Limited English proficiency:	27 / 3.4%
Student absenteeism:	3.8%
Students per teacher:	15.0
Parent friendliness:	❶❷❸④⑤❻
Teachers with advanced degrees:	36.4%
Average years' teaching experience:	11.4
Students in gifted program:	67 / 8.4%
Students in remedial education:	6.8%
Students held back a grade:	0.4%
Total suspensions, pct. in-school:	*
Offenses: violence: *, drugs: *, other: *	
Eligible students, free or reduced lunch:	4.7%
Before / after school program:	No / Yes

Students at this school generally go on to:
Hightower Trail, Simpson Middle

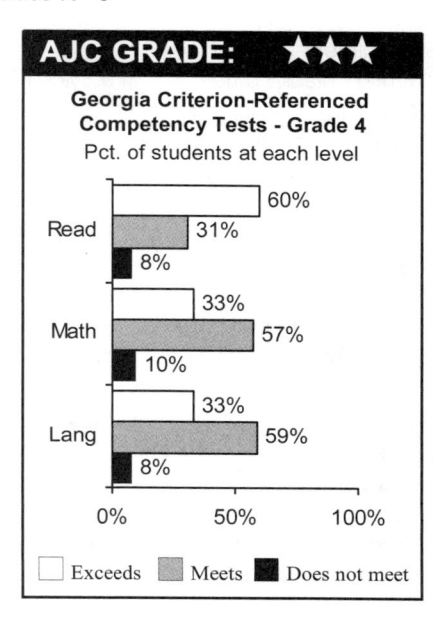

AJC GRADE: ★★★

Georgia Criterion-Referenced Competency Tests - Grade 4
Pct. of students at each level

Read: Exceeds 60%, Meets 31%, Does not meet 8%
Math: Exceeds 33%, Meets 57%, Does not meet 10%
Lang: Exceeds 33%, Meets 59%, Does not meet 8%

Murdock Elementary School

2320 Murdock Rd, Marietta, GA 30062
770-509-6069 · Grades K - 5

Enrollment:	819
White / black / other:	84.0% / 5.7% / 10.3%
Not native English-speaking:	*
Limited English proficiency:	16 / 2.0%
Student absenteeism:	3.7%
Students per teacher:	14.0
Parent friendliness:	①❷❸❹❺❻
Teachers with advanced degrees:	51.6%
Average years' teaching experience:	16.2
Students in gifted program:	88 / 10.7%
Students in remedial education:	16.7%
Students held back a grade:	0.7%
Total suspensions, pct. in-school:	7 / 0.0%
Offenses: violence: *, drugs: *, other: 8	
Eligible students, free or reduced lunch:	3.5%
Before / after school program:	No / Yes

Students at this school generally go on to:
Dodgen, Hightower Trail Middle

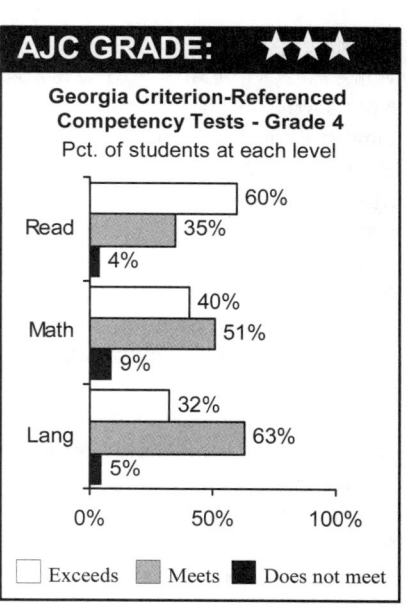

AJC GRADE: ★★★

Georgia Criterion-Referenced Competency Tests - Grade 4
Pct. of students at each level

Read: Exceeds 60%, Meets 35%, Does not meet 4%
Math: Exceeds 40%, Meets 51%, Does not meet 9%
Lang: Exceeds 32%, Meets 63%, Does not meet 5%

Nicholson Elementary School

1599 Shallowford Rd, Marietta, GA 30066
770-591-6849 · Grades K - 5

Enrollment:	627
White / black / other:	79.6% / 9.6% / 10.8%
Not native English-speaking:	*
Limited English proficiency:	46 / 7.3%
Student absenteeism:	4.3%
Students per teacher:	13.8
Parent friendliness:	①❷❸④⑤❻
Teachers with advanced degrees:	40.4%
Average years' teaching experience:	13.8
Students in gifted program:	36 / 5.7%
Students in remedial education:	16.1%
Students held back a grade:	2.9%
Total suspensions, pct. in-school:	10 / 0.0%
Offenses:	violence: 6, drugs: 1, other: 3
Eligible students, free or reduced lunch:	15.0%
Before / after school program:	No / Yes

Students at this school generally go on to:
McCleskey Middle

AJC GRADE: ★★★

Georgia Criterion-Referenced Competency Tests - Grade 4
Pct. of students at each level

Read: 33% Exceeds / 51% Meets / 16% Does not meet
Math: 17% Exceeds / 62% Meets / 20% Does not meet
Lang: 23% Exceeds / 67% Meets / 10% Does not meet

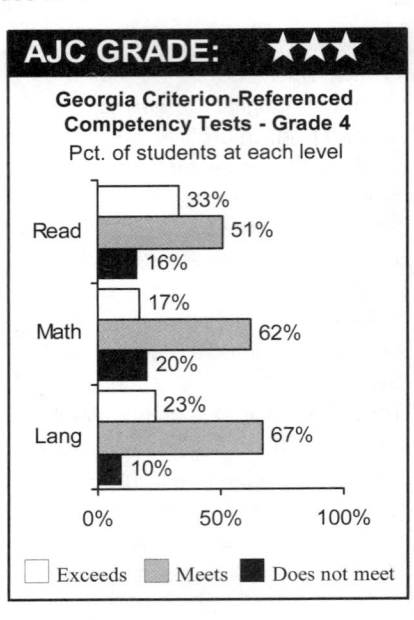

Nickajack Elementary School

4555 Mavell Rd SE, Smyrna, GA 30082
770-319-3966 · Grades K - 5

Enrollment:	593
White / black / other:	32.2% / 54.1% / 13.7%
Not native English-speaking:	*
Limited English proficiency:	7 / 1.2%
Student absenteeism:	5.3%
Students per teacher:	13.0
Parent friendliness:	①❷❸④⑤❻
Teachers with advanced degrees:	42.9%
Average years' teaching experience:	10.1
Students in gifted program:	20 / 3.4%
Students in remedial education:	25.3%
Students held back a grade:	3.2%
Total suspensions, pct. in-school:	109 / 71.6%
Offenses:	violence: 5, drugs: 1, other: 107
Eligible students, free or reduced lunch:	32.8%
Before / after school program:	Yes / Yes

Students at this school generally go on to:
Campbell, Griffin Middle

AJC GRADE: ★★

Georgia Criterion-Referenced Competency Tests - Grade 4
Pct. of students at each level

Read: 27% Exceeds / 44% Meets / 29% Does not meet
Math: 6% Exceeds / 48% Meets / 46% Does not meet
Lang: 14% Exceeds / 54% Meets / 31% Does not meet

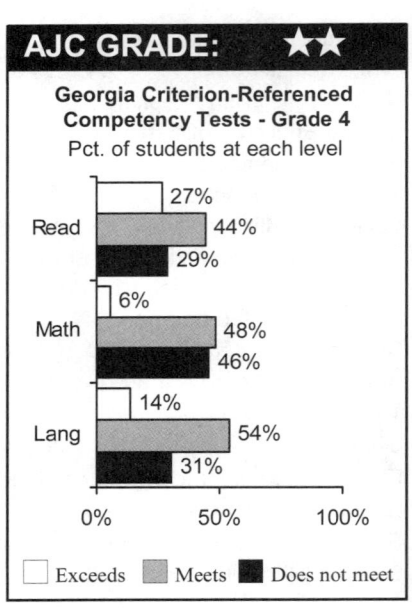

Norton Park Elementary School

3041 Gray Rd SE, Smyrna, GA 30082
770-319-3784 · Grades K - 5

Enrollment:	692
White / black / other:	16.6% / 54.9% / 28.5%
Not native English-speaking:	95 / 13.7%
Limited English proficiency:	195 / 28.2%
Student absenteeism:	5.6%
Students per teacher:	13.2
Parent friendliness:	①❷❸④❺❻
Teachers with advanced degrees:	37.0%
Average years' teaching experience:	9.5
Students in gifted program:	4 / 0.6%
Students in remedial education:	33.0%
Students held back a grade:	2.3%
Total suspensions, pct. in-school:	12 / 0.0%
Offenses:	violence: 3, drugs: * , other: 9
Eligible students, free or reduced lunch:	68.0%
Before / after school program:	Yes / Yes

Students at this school generally go on to:
Floyd, Griffin Middle

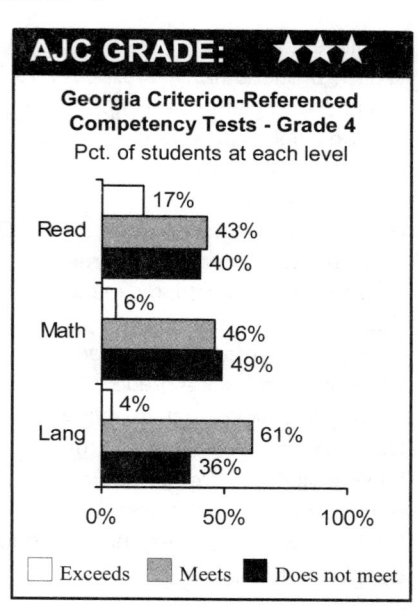

AJC GRADE: ★★★

Georgia Criterion-Referenced Competency Tests - Grade 4
Pct. of students at each level

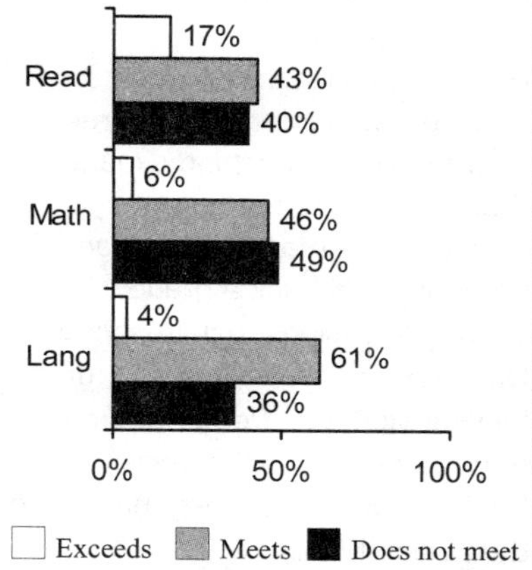
Read
17%
43%
40%
Math
6%
46%
49%
Lang
4%
61%
36%
0%
50%
100%
Exceeds
Meets
Does not meet

Powder Springs Elementary School

4570 Grady Grier Dr, Powder Springs, GA 30127
770-439-4722 · Grades K - 5

Enrollment:	1,007
White / black / other:	56.2% / 35.7% / 8.1%
Not native English-speaking:	*
Limited English proficiency:	7 / 0.7%
Student absenteeism:	4.2%
Students per teacher:	15.2
Parent friendliness:	❶❷❸④⑤❻
Teachers with advanced degrees:	37.7%
Average years' teaching experience:	12.4
Students in gifted program:	21 / 2.1%
Students in remedial education:	11.3%
Students held back a grade:	1.5%
Total suspensions, pct. in-school:	66 / 0.0%
Offenses:	violence: 22, drugs: 2, other: 42
Eligible students, free or reduced lunch:	22.9%
Before / after school program:	Yes / Yes

Students at this school generally go on to:
Cooper Middle

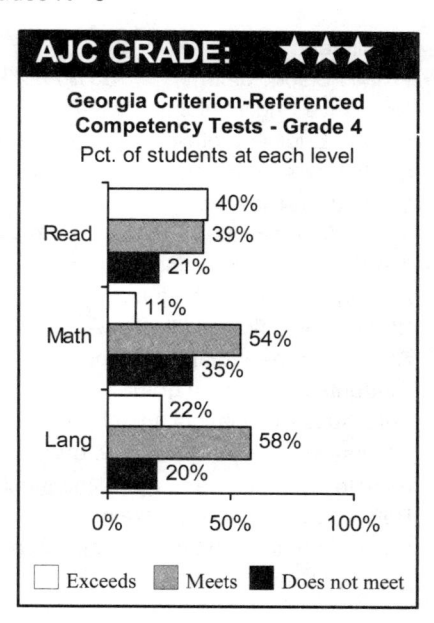

AJC GRADE: ★★★

Georgia Criterion-Referenced Competency Tests - Grade 4
Pct. of students at each level

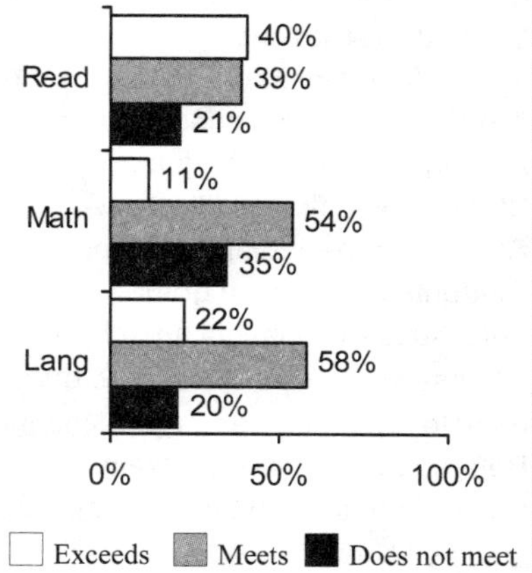
Read
40%
39%
21%
Math
11%
54%
35%
Lang
22%
58%
20%
0%
50%
100%
Exceeds
Meets
Does not meet

Powers Ferry Elementary School

403 Powers Ferry Rd SE, Marietta, GA 30067
770-509-6088 · Grades K - 5

Enrollment:	444
White / black / other:	21.6% / 45.9% / 32.4%
Not native English-speaking:	81 / 18.2%
Limited English proficiency:	123 / 27.7%
Student absenteeism:	6.0%
Students per teacher:	13.1
Parent friendliness:	①❷❸④⑤❻
Teachers with advanced degrees:	34.3%
Average years' teaching experience:	12.1
Students in gifted program:	10 / 2.3%
Students in remedial education:	34.2%
Students held back a grade:	0.9%
Total suspensions, pct. in-school:	20 / 0.0%
Offenses:	violence: 1, drugs: *, other: 19
Eligible students, free or reduced lunch:	58.3%
Before / after school program:	No / Yes
Students at this school generally go on to:	
East Cobb Middle	

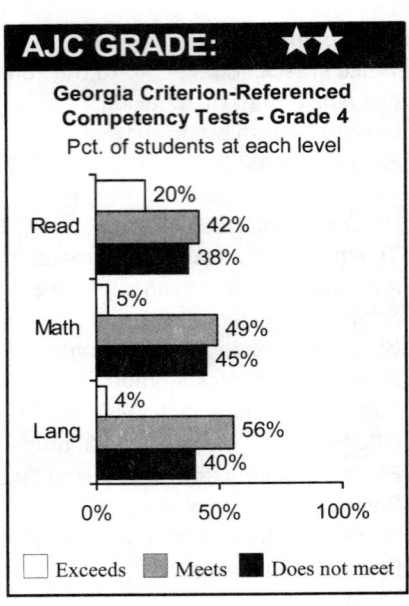

AJC GRADE: ★★

Georgia Criterion-Referenced Competency Tests - Grade 4
Pct. of students at each level

Read: 20% Exceeds / 42% Meets / 38% Does not meet
Math: 5% Exceeds / 49% Meets / 45% Does not meet
Lang: 4% Exceeds / 56% Meets / 40% Does not meet

Riverside Elementary School

285 S Gordon Rd SW, Mableton, GA 30126
770-732-5668 · Grades K - 5

Enrollment:	706
White / black / other:	1.3% / 86.3% / 12.5%
Not native English-speaking:	40 / 5.7%
Limited English proficiency:	73 / 10.3%
Student absenteeism:	5.4%
Students per teacher:	14.7
Parent friendliness:	❶❷❸❹❺❻
Teachers with advanced degrees:	34.7%
Average years' teaching experience:	7.9
Students in gifted program:	8 / 1.1%
Students in remedial education:	26.0%
Students held back a grade:	5.0%
Total suspensions, pct. in-school:	54 / 0.0%
Offenses:	violence: 9, drugs: 1, other: 45
Eligible students, free or reduced lunch:	69.9%
Before / after school program:	Yes / Yes
Students at this school generally go on to:	
Lindley Middle	

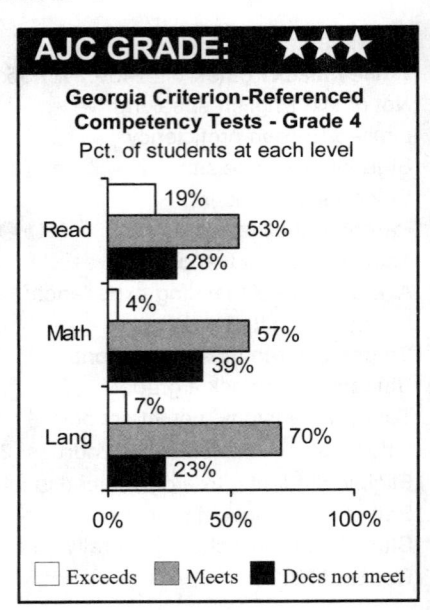

AJC GRADE: ★★★

Georgia Criterion-Referenced Competency Tests - Grade 4
Pct. of students at each level

Read: 19% Exceeds / 53% Meets / 28% Does not meet
Math: 4% Exceeds / 57% Meets / 39% Does not meet
Lang: 7% Exceeds / 70% Meets / 23% Does not meet

Rocky Mount Elementary School

2400 Rocky Mountain Rd NE, Marietta, GA 30066
770-591-6857 · Grades K - 5

Enrollment:	636
White / black / other:	85.5% / 4.9% / 9.6%
Not native English-speaking:	*
Limited English proficiency:	21 / 3.3%
Student absenteeism:	3.6%
Students per teacher:	14.6
Parent friendliness:	①❷❸④❺❻
Teachers with advanced degrees:	66.7%
Average years' teaching experience:	16.6
Students in gifted program:	38 / 6.0%
Students in remedial education:	6.4%
Students held back a grade:	1.6%
Total suspensions, pct. in-school:	12 / 0.0%
Offenses:	violence: 10, drugs: *, other: 2
Eligible students, free or reduced lunch:	5.5%
Before / after school program:	No / Yes

Students at this school generally go on to:
Mabry, Simpson Middle

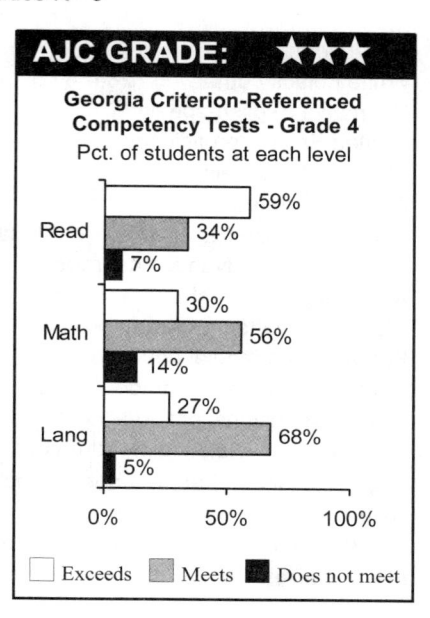

AJC GRADE: ★★★

Georgia Criterion-Referenced Competency Tests - Grade 4
Pct. of students at each level

Read: Exceeds 59%, Meets 34%, Does not meet 7%
Math: Exceeds 30%, Meets 56%, Does not meet 14%
Lang: Exceeds 27%, Meets 68%, Does not meet 5%

Russell Elementary School

3920 S Hurt Rd SW, Smyrna, GA 30082
770-319-3910 · Grades K - 5

Enrollment:	631
White / black / other:	42.9% / 37.9% / 19.2%
Not native English-speaking:	30 / 4.8%
Limited English proficiency:	56 / 8.9%
Student absenteeism:	3.9%
Students per teacher:	14.3
Parent friendliness:	①❷❸④❺❻
Teachers with advanced degrees:	41.3%
Average years' teaching experience:	12.2
Students in gifted program:	31 / 4.9%
Students in remedial education:	18.3%
Students held back a grade:	0.3%
Total suspensions, pct. in-school:	19 / 0.0%
Offenses:	violence: 7, drugs: *, other: 21
Eligible students, free or reduced lunch:	29.3%
Before / after school program:	No / Yes

Students at this school generally go on to:
Floyd Middle

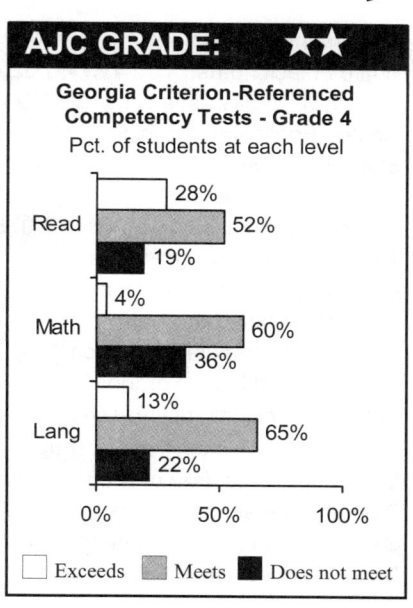

AJC GRADE: ★★

Georgia Criterion-Referenced Competency Tests - Grade 4
Pct. of students at each level

Read: Exceeds 28%, Meets 52%, Does not meet 19%
Math: Exceeds 4%, Meets 60%, Does not meet 36%
Lang: Exceeds 13%, Meets 65%, Does not meet 22%

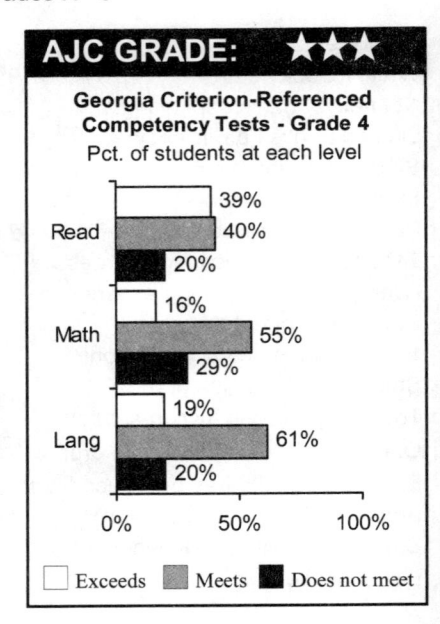

Sanders Elementary School

1550 Anderson Mill Rd, Austell, GA 30106
770-732-5751 · Grades K - 5

Enrollment:	906
White / black / other:	28.4% / 59.4% / 12.3%
Not native English-speaking:	28 / 3.1%
Limited English proficiency:	65 / 7.2%
Student absenteeism:	4.8%
Students per teacher:	13.8
Parent friendliness:	① ❷ ❸ ④ ⑤ ❻
Teachers with advanced degrees:	24.2%
Average years' teaching experience:	6.5
Students in gifted program:	11 / 1.2%
Students in remedial education:	32.2%
Students held back a grade:	1.2%
Total suspensions, pct. in-school:	77 / 0.0%
Offenses:	violence: 31, drugs: *, other: 110
Eligible students, free or reduced lunch:	45.1%
Before / after school program:	No / Yes

Students at this school generally go on to:
Floyd, Garrett Middle

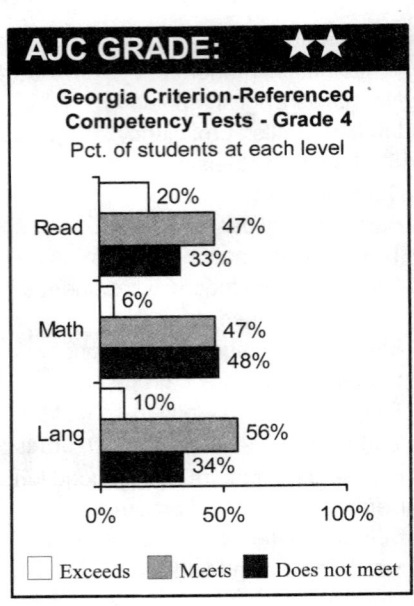

AJC GRADE: ★★

Georgia Criterion-Referenced Competency Tests - Grade 4
Pct. of students at each level

Read: Exceeds 20%, Meets 47%, Does not meet 33%
Math: Exceeds 6%, Meets 47%, Does not meet 48%
Lang: Exceeds 10%, Meets 56%, Does not meet 34%

Sedalia Park Elementary School

2230 Lower Roswell Rd, Marietta, GA 30068
770-509-6095 · Grades K - 5

Enrollment:	719
White / black / other:	42.7% / 32.4% / 24.9%
Not native English-speaking:	90 / 12.5%
Limited English proficiency:	172 / 23.9%
Student absenteeism:	4.6%
Students per teacher:	12.7
Parent friendliness:	① ❷ ❸ ④ ⑤ ❻
Teachers with advanced degrees:	45.0%
Average years' teaching experience:	13.4
Students in gifted program:	28 / 3.9%
Students in remedial education:	17.3%
Students held back a grade:	2.5%
Total suspensions, pct. in-school:	39 / 0.0%
Offenses:	violence: *, drugs: *, other: 56
Eligible students, free or reduced lunch:	30.3%
Before / after school program:	No / Yes

Students at this school generally go on to:
Daniell, East Cobb Middle

AJC GRADE: ★★★

Georgia Criterion-Referenced Competency Tests - Grade 4
Pct. of students at each level

Read: Exceeds 39%, Meets 40%, Does not meet 20%
Math: Exceeds 16%, Meets 55%, Does not meet 29%
Lang: Exceeds 19%, Meets 61%, Does not meet 20%

Cobb County Elementary Schools

Shallowford Falls Elementary School

3500 Lassiter Rd, Marietta, GA 30062
770-640-4815 · Grades K - 5

Enrollment:	721
White / black / other:	86.7% / 3.6% / 9.7%
Not native English-speaking:	*
Limited English proficiency:	42 / 5.8%
Student absenteeism:	3.7%
Students per teacher:	15.8
Parent friendliness:	❶❷❸④⑤❻
Teachers with advanced degrees:	52.2%
Average years' teaching experience:	14.8
Students in gifted program:	65 / 9.0%
Students in remedial education:	5.9%
Students held back a grade:	0.4%
Total suspensions, pct. in-school:	*
Offenses:	violence: * , drugs: * , other: 1
Eligible students, free or reduced lunch:	2.1%
Before / after school program:	No / Yes

Students at this school generally go on to:
Hightower Trail, Simpson Middle

AJC GRADE: ★★★★

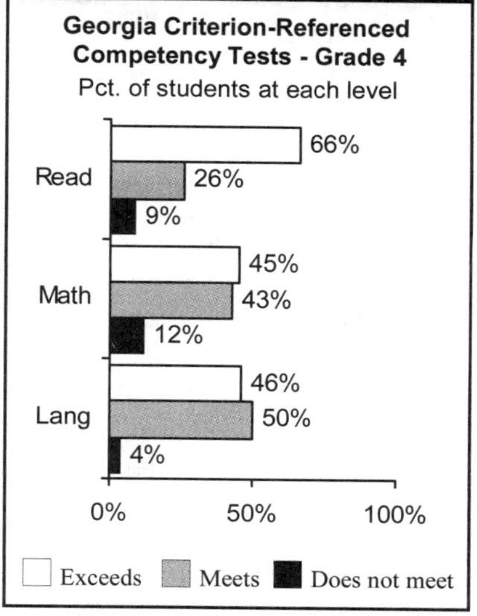
Georgia Criterion-Referenced
Competency Tests - Grade 4
Pct. of students at each level
Read
66%
26%
9%
Math
45%
43%
12%
Lang
46%
50%
4%
0%
50%
100%
Exceeds
Meets
Does not meet

Sky View Elementary School

5805 Dunn Rd SW, Mableton, GA 30126
770-732-5675 · Grades K - 5

Enrollment:	415
White / black / other:	51.1% / 30.8% / 18.1%
Not native English-speaking:	*
Limited English proficiency:	22 / 5.3%
Student absenteeism:	5.4%
Students per teacher:	11.0
Parent friendliness:	①❷❸④❺❻
Teachers with advanced degrees:	38.5%
Average years' teaching experience:	7.5
Students in gifted program:	8 / 1.9%
Students in remedial education:	34.0%
Students held back a grade:	0.2%
Total suspensions, pct. in-school:	41 / 0.0%
Offenses:	violence: 14, drugs: 1, other: 26
Eligible students, free or reduced lunch:	56.4%
Before / after school program:	No / Yes

Students at this school generally go on to:
Garrett Middle

AJC GRADE: ★★★

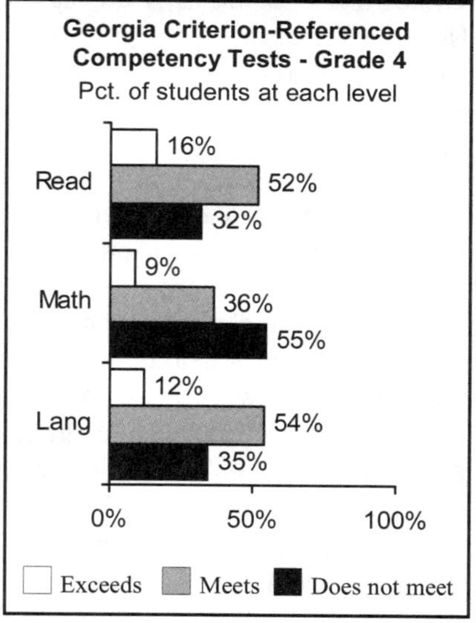
Georgia Criterion-Referenced
Competency Tests - Grade 4
Pct. of students at each level
Read
16%
52%
32%
Math
9%
36%
55%
Lang
12%
54%
35%
0%
50%
100%
Exceeds
Meets
Does not meet

Sope Creek Elementary School

3320 Paper Mill Rd SE, Marietta, GA 30067
770-916-2300 · Grades K - 5

Enrollment:	1,075
White / black / other:	84.0% / 2.8% / 13.2%
Not native English-speaking:	24 / 2.2%
Limited English proficiency:	72 / 6.7%
Student absenteeism:	3.3%
Students per teacher:	15.7
Parent friendliness:	① ❷ ❸ ④ ⑤ ❻
Teachers with advanced degrees:	41.4%
Average years' teaching experience:	13.3
Students in gifted program:	148 / 13.8%
Students in remedial education:	7.8%
Students held back a grade:	1.0%
Total suspensions, pct. in-school:	*
Offenses:	violence: *, drugs: *, other: *
Eligible students, free or reduced lunch:	1.0%
Before / after school program:	No / Yes
Students at this school generally go on to:	
Dickerson, East Cobb Middle	

AJC GRADE: ★★★★

Georgia Criterion-Referenced Competency Tests - Grade 4
Pct. of students at each level

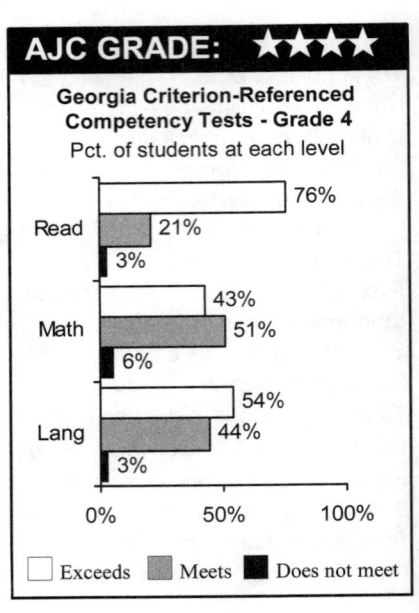

Read: 76% / 21% / 3%
Math: 43% / 51% / 6%
Lang: 54% / 44% / 3%

☐ Exceeds ▨ Meets ■ Does not meet

Still Elementary School

870 Casteel Rd, Powder Springs, GA 30127
770-528-6591 · Grades K - 5

Enrollment:	805
White / black / other:	83.4% / 10.7% / 6.0%
Not native English-speaking:	*
Limited English proficiency:	14 / 1.7%
Student absenteeism:	3.7%
Students per teacher:	16.3
Parent friendliness:	① ❷ ❸ ④ ⑤ ❻
Teachers with advanced degrees:	42.0%
Average years' teaching experience:	13.6
Students in gifted program:	66 / 8.2%
Students in remedial education:	5.9%
Students held back a grade:	1.0%
Total suspensions, pct. in-school:	8 / 25.0%
Offenses:	violence: 2, drugs: *, other: 6
Eligible students, free or reduced lunch:	7.7%
Before / after school program:	No / Yes
Students at this school generally go on to:	
Lost Mountain, Pine Mountain, Tapp Middle	

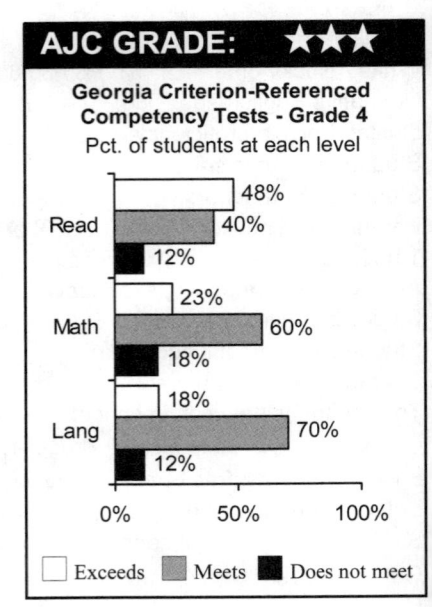

AJC GRADE: ★★★

Georgia Criterion-Referenced Competency Tests - Grade 4
Pct. of students at each level

Read: 48% / 40% / 12%
Math: 23% / 60% / 18%
Lang: 18% / 70% / 12%

☐ Exceeds ▨ Meets ■ Does not meet

Cobb County Elementary Schools

Teasley Elementary School

3640 Spring Hill Rd SE, Smyrna, GA 30080
770-319-3917 · Grades K - 5

Enrollment:	377
White / black / other:	60.7% / 28.1% / 11.1%
Not native English-speaking:	16 / 4.2%
Limited English proficiency:	50 / 13.3%
Student absenteeism:	4.3%
Students per teacher:	13.7
Parent friendliness:	①❷❸④❺❻
Teachers with advanced degrees:	48.3%
Average years' teaching experience:	11.1
Students in gifted program:	43 / 11.4%
Students in remedial education:	12.3%
Students held back a grade:	1.1%
Total suspensions, pct. in-school:	4 / 0.0%
Offenses:	violence: 1, drugs: * , other: 3
Eligible students, free or reduced lunch:	20.1%
Before / after school program:	No / Yes

Students at this school generally go on to:
Campbell Middle

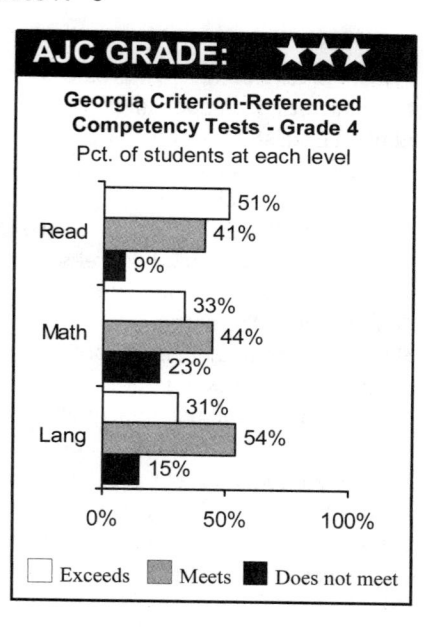

AJC GRADE: ★★★

Georgia Criterion-Referenced Competency Tests - Grade 4
Pct. of students at each level

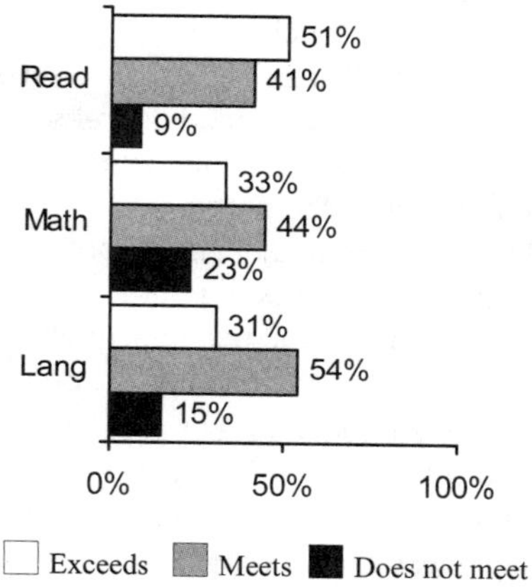

Read
51%
41%
9%
Math
33%
44%
23%
Lang
31%
54%
15%
0%
50%
100%
Exceeds
Meets
Does not meet

Timber Ridge Elementary School

5000 Timber Ridge Rd, Marietta, GA 30068
770-640-4808 · Grades K - 5

Enrollment:	579
White / black / other:	90.2% / 1.4% / 8.5%
Not native English-speaking:	*
Limited English proficiency:	19 / 3.3%
Student absenteeism:	3.6%
Students per teacher:	13.9
Parent friendliness:	①❷❸④⑤❻
Teachers with advanced degrees:	59.1%
Average years' teaching experience:	15.6
Students in gifted program:	52 / 9.0%
Students in remedial education:	3.0%
Students held back a grade:	1.7%
Total suspensions, pct. in-school:	*
Offenses:	violence: * , drugs: * , other: *
Eligible students, free or reduced lunch:	0.5%
Before / after school program:	No / Yes

Students at this school generally go on to:
Dickerson, Dodgen Middle

AJC GRADE: ★★★

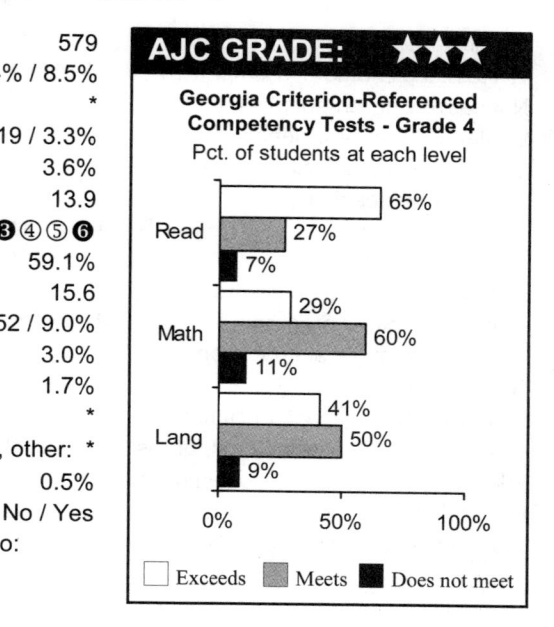

Georgia Criterion-Referenced Competency Tests - Grade 4
Pct. of students at each level

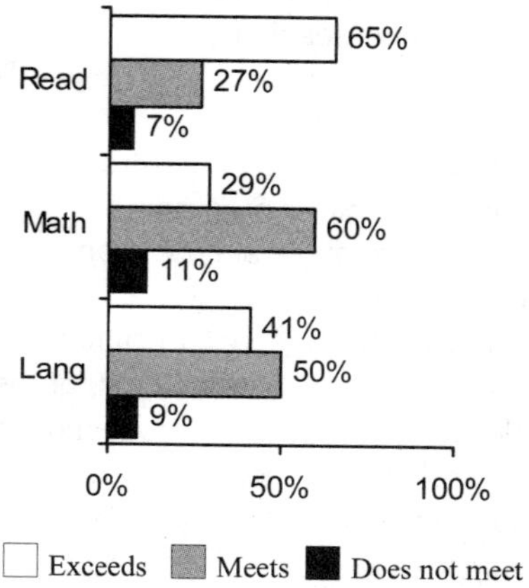

Read
65%
27%
7%
Math
29%
60%
11%
Lang
41%
50%
9%
0%
50%
100%
Exceeds
Meets
Does not meet

Tritt Elementary School

4435 Post Oak Tritt Rd, Marietta, GA 30062
770-640-4822 · Grades K - 5

Enrollment:	892
White / black / other:	92.3% / 3.5% / 4.3%
Not native English-speaking:	*
Limited English proficiency:	19 / 2.1%
Student absenteeism:	3.7%
Students per teacher:	16.5
Parent friendliness:	① ❷ ❸ ④ ⑤ ❻
Teachers with advanced degrees:	52.7%
Average years' teaching experience:	15.1
Students in gifted program:	177 / 19.8%
Students in remedial education:	3.5%
Students held back a grade:	0.6%
Total suspensions, pct. in-school:	*
Offenses:	violence: *, drugs: *, other: *
Eligible students, free or reduced lunch:	1.9%
Before / after school program:	No / Yes
Students at this school generally go on to:	
Hightower Trail Middle	

AJC GRADE: ★★★★

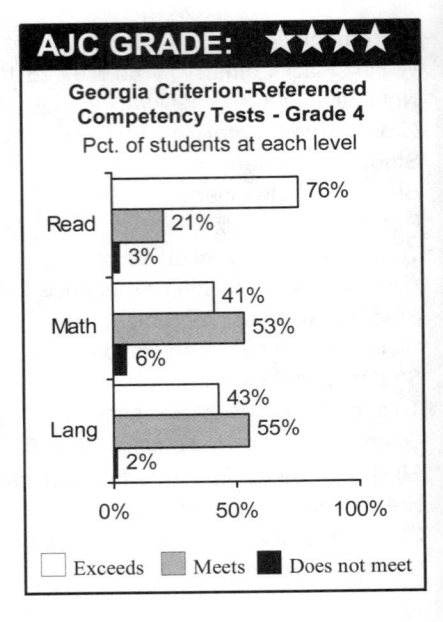

Georgia Criterion-Referenced Competency Tests - Grade 4
Pct. of students at each level

Read: Exceeds 76%, Meets 21%, Does not meet 3%
Math: Exceeds 41%, Meets 53%, Does not meet 6%
Lang: Exceeds 43%, Meets 55%, Does not meet 2%

Varner Elementary School

4761 Gaydon Rd, Powder Springs, GA 30127
770-439-4712 · Grades K - 5

Enrollment:	1,192
White / black / other:	81.5% / 13.0% / 5.5%
Not native English-speaking:	*
Limited English proficiency:	5 / 0.4%
Student absenteeism:	3.9%
Students per teacher:	17.5
Parent friendliness:	① ❷ ❸ ④ ⑤ ❻
Teachers with advanced degrees:	38.2%
Average years' teaching experience:	10.8
Students in gifted program:	47 / 3.9%
Students in remedial education:	14.0%
Students held back a grade:	0.8%
Total suspensions, pct. in-school:	15 / 13.3%
Offenses:	violence: 7, drugs: *, other: 8
Eligible students, free or reduced lunch:	9.2%
Before / after school program:	No / Yes
Students at this school generally go on to:	
Tapp Middle	

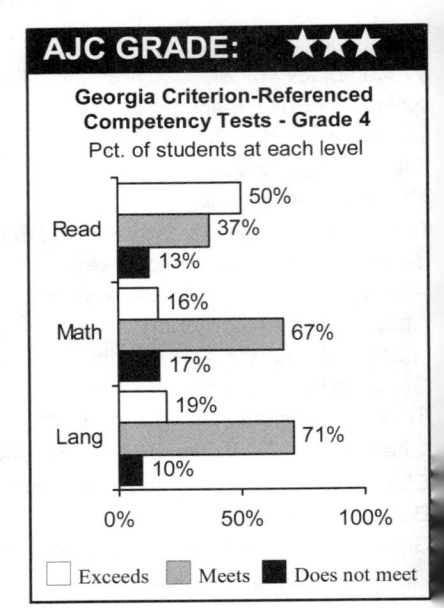

AJC GRADE: ★★★

Georgia Criterion-Referenced Competency Tests - Grade 4
Pct. of students at each level

Read: Exceeds 50%, Meets 37%, Does not meet 13%
Math: Exceeds 16%, Meets 67%, Does not meet 17%
Lang: Exceeds 19%, Meets 71%, Does not meet 10%

Cobb County Elementary Schools

Vaughan Elementary School

5950 Nichols Rd, Powder Springs, GA 30127
770-528-4230 · Grades K - 5

Enrollment:	986
White / black / other:	93.2% / 3.5% / 3.2%
Not native English-speaking:	*
Limited English proficiency:	3 / 0.3%
Student absenteeism:	4.0%
Students per teacher:	17.1
Parent friendliness:	① ❷ ❸ ④ ❺ ❻
Teachers with advanced degrees:	40.0%
Average years' teaching experience:	10.0
Students in gifted program:	83 / 8.4%
Students in remedial education:	14.2%
Students held back a grade:	0.6%
Total suspensions, pct. in-school:	11 / 90.9%
Offenses:	violence: 4, drugs: *, other: 7
Eligible students, free or reduced lunch:	1.8%
Before / after school program:	No / Yes

Students at this school generally go on to:
Lost Mountain Middle

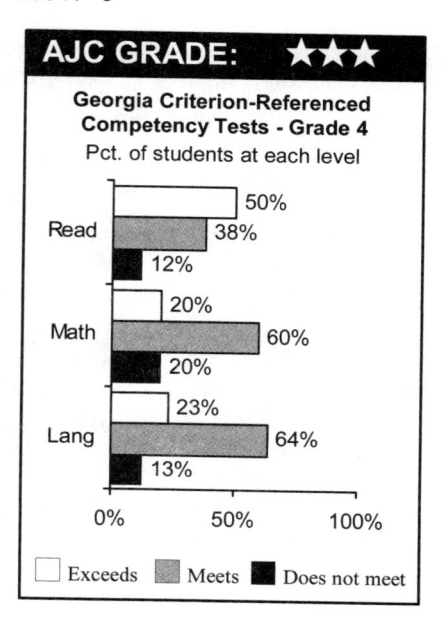

AJC GRADE: ★★★

Georgia Criterion-Referenced Competency Tests - Grade 4
Pct. of students at each level

Read: Exceeds 50%, Meets 38%, Does not meet 12%
Math: Exceeds 20%, Meets 60%, Does not meet 20%
Lang: Exceeds 23%, Meets 64%, Does not meet 13%

Cobb County Elementary Schools

Awtrey Middle School

3601 Nowlin Rd NW, Kennesaw, GA 30144
770-975-4272 · Grades 6 - 8

Enrollment:	1,796
White / black / other:	72.9% / 16.0% / 11.0%
Not native English-speaking:	25 / 1.4%
Student absenteeism:	5.9%
Students per teacher:	16.7
Parent friendliness:	❶❷❸④❺❻
Teachers with advanced degrees:	41.8%
Average years' teaching experience:	9.6
Students in gifted program:	250 / 13.9%
Students held back a grade:	1.2%
Total suspensions and expulsions:	955
Suspensions only, pct. in-school:	955 / 74.9%
Offenses: violence: 145, drugs: 16, other: 972	
Eligible students, free or reduced lunch:	14.7%
Number of dropouts:	*
Pct. 8th-graders w/ basic computer skills:	100.0%

Students at this school generally go on to:
North Cobb High

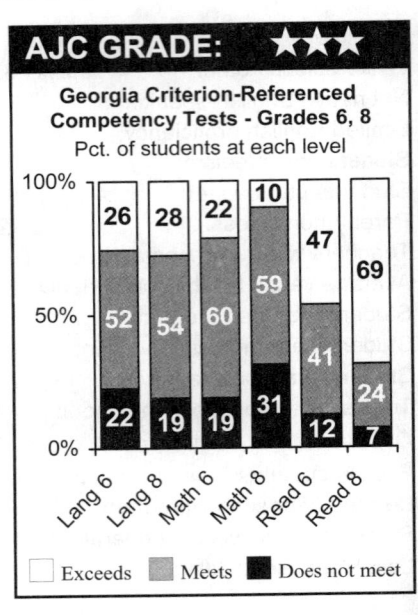

AJC GRADE: ★★★

Georgia Criterion-Referenced Competency Tests - Grades 6, 8
Pct. of students at each level

	Lang 6	Lang 8	Math 6	Math 8	Read 6	Read 8
Exceeds	26	28	22	10	47	69
Meets	52	54	60	59	41	24
Does not meet	22	19	19	31	12	7

Campbell Middle School

3295 Atlanta Rd SE, Smyrna, GA 30080
770-319-3776 · Grades 6 - 8

Enrollment:	1,160
White / black / other:	28.3% / 47.0% / 24.7%
Not native English-speaking:	111 / 9.6%
Student absenteeism:	7.4%
Students per teacher:	13.9
Parent friendliness:	❶❷❸④❺❻
Teachers with advanced degrees:	35.7%
Average years' teaching experience:	9.8
Students in gifted program:	55 / 4.7%
Students held back a grade:	3.7%
Total suspensions and expulsions:	5
Suspensions only, pct. in-school:	5 / 0.0%
Offenses: violence: 1, drugs: *, other: 4	
Eligible students, free or reduced lunch:	61.3%
Number of dropouts:	*
Pct. 8th-graders w/ basic computer skills:	100.0%

Students at this school generally go on to:
Campbell, Osborne High

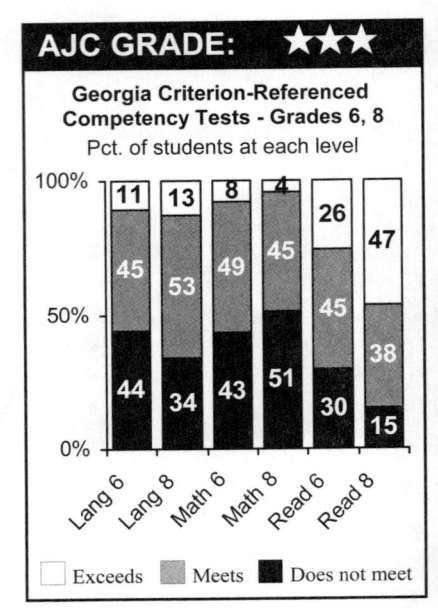

AJC GRADE: ★★★

Georgia Criterion-Referenced Competency Tests - Grades 6, 8
Pct. of students at each level

	Lang 6	Lang 8	Math 6	Math 8	Read 6	Read 8
Exceeds	11	13	8	4	26	47
Meets	45	53	49	45	45	38
Does not meet	44	34	43	51	30	15

Cobb County Middle Schools

Daniell Middle School

2900 Scott Rd, Marietta, GA 30066
770-528-6520 · Grades 6 - 8

Enrollment:	1,304
White / black / other:	68.3% / 17.0% / 14.6%
Not native English-speaking:	40 / 3.1%
Student absenteeism:	5.2%
Students per teacher:	15.4
Parent friendliness:	❶❷❸④⑤❻
Teachers with advanced degrees:	36.8%
Average years' teaching experience:	13.3
Students in gifted program:	207 / 15.9%
Students held back a grade:	1.6%
Total suspensions and expulsions:	867
Suspensions only, pct. in-school:	867 / 77.7%
Offenses:	violence: 132, drugs: 9, other: 777
Eligible students, free or reduced lunch:	13.6%
Number of dropouts:	1 / 0.1%
Pct. 8th-graders w/ basic computer skills:	100.0%

Students at this school generally go on to:
Sprayberry High

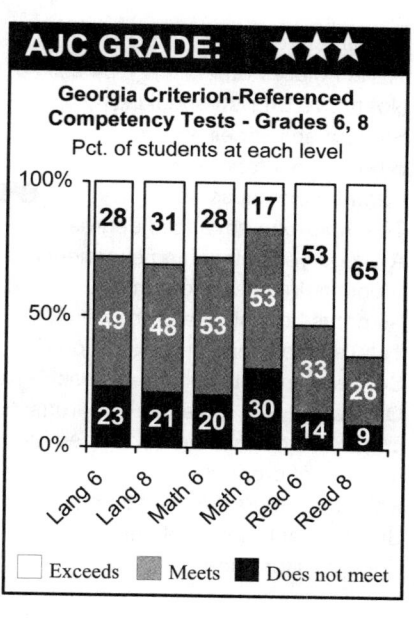

AJC GRADE: ★★★

Georgia Criterion-Referenced Competency Tests - Grades 6, 8
Pct. of students at each level

	Lang 6	Lang 8	Math 6	Math 8	Read 6	Read 8
Exceeds	28	31	28	17	53	65
Meets	49	48	53	53	33	26
Does not meet	23	21	20	30	14	9

Dickerson Middle School

855 Woodlawn Dr NE, Marietta, GA 30068
770-509-6007 · Grades 6 - 8

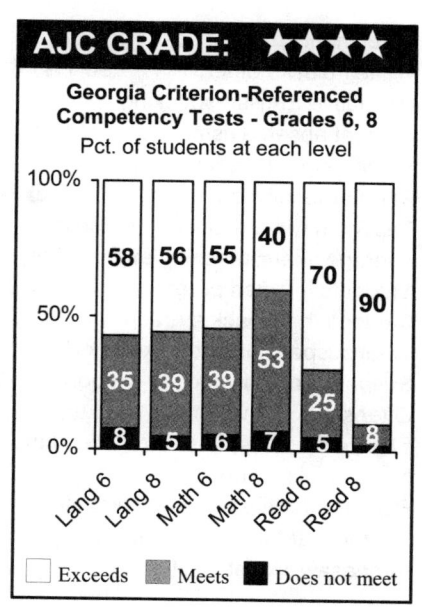

Enrollment:	1,467
White / black / other:	86.0% / 2.0% / 12.0%
Not native English-speaking:	27 / 1.8%
Student absenteeism:	3.9%
Students per teacher:	16.2
Parent friendliness:	❶❷❸④⑤❻
Teachers with advanced degrees:	41.8%
Average years' teaching experience:	12.9
Students in gifted program:	535 / 36.5%
Students held back a grade:	0.3%
Total suspensions and expulsions:	419
Suspensions only, pct. in-school:	419 / 90.5%
Offenses:	violence: 13, drugs: 1, other: 454
Eligible students, free or reduced lunch:	0.6%
Number of dropouts:	*
Pct. 8th-graders w/ basic computer skills:	100.0%

Students at this school generally go on to:
Walton High

AJC GRADE: ★★★★

Georgia Criterion-Referenced Competency Tests - Grades 6, 8
Pct. of students at each level

	Lang 6	Lang 8	Math 6	Math 8	Read 6	Read 8
Exceeds	58	56	55	40	70	90
Meets	35	39	39	53	25	
Does not meet	8	5	6	7	5	2

Cobb County Middle Schools

Dodgen Middle School

1725 Bill Murdock Rd, Marietta, GA 30062
770-509-6017 · Grades 6 - 8

Enrollment:	779
White / black / other:	84.9% / 5.1% / 10.0%
Not native English-speaking:	10 / 1.3%
Student absenteeism:	4.2%
Students per teacher:	14.7
Parent friendliness:	❶❷❸④⑤❻
Teachers with advanced degrees:	50.9%
Average years' teaching experience:	14.3
Students in gifted program:	269 / 34.5%
Students held back a grade:	0.3%
Total suspensions and expulsions:	230
Suspensions only, pct. in-school:	230 / 80.4%
Offenses: violence: 24, drugs: 3, other: 249	
Eligible students, free or reduced lunch:	2.2%
Number of dropouts:	*
Pct. 8th-graders w/ basic computer skills:	100.0%

Students at this school generally go on to:
Pope, Walton High

AJC GRADE: ★★★★

Georgia Criterion-Referenced Competency Tests - Grades 6, 8
Pct. of students at each level

	Lang 6	Lang 8	Math 6	Math 8	Read 6	Read 8
Exceeds	53	45	55	25	77	84
Meets	42	48	43	60	20	13
Does not meet	5	7	2	15	3	3

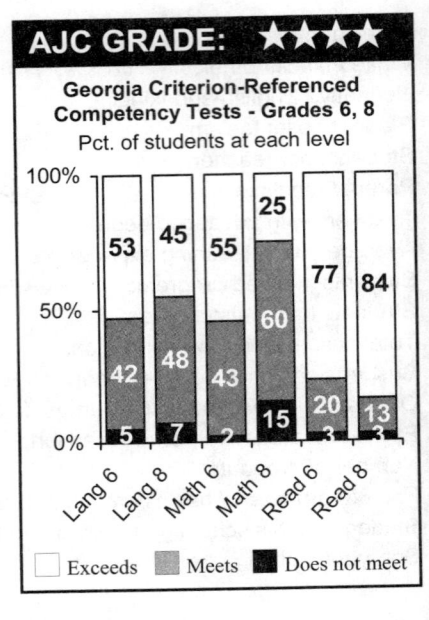

Durham Middle School

2891 Mars Hill Rd NW, Acworth, GA 30101
770-975-4204 · Grades 6 - 8

Enrollment:	1,351
White / black / other:	90.1% / 5.8% / 4.1%
Not native English-speaking:	*
Student absenteeism:	4.2%
Students per teacher:	15.6
Parent friendliness:	❶❷❸④⑤❻
Teachers with advanced degrees:	37.9%
Average years' teaching experience:	10.0
Students in gifted program:	249 / 18.4%
Students held back a grade:	1.2%
Total suspensions and expulsions:	224
Suspensions only, pct. in-school:	224 / 89.3%
Offenses: violence: 14, drugs: *, other: 274	
Eligible students, free or reduced lunch:	5.7%
Number of dropouts:	1 / 0.1%
Pct. 8th-graders w/ basic computer skills:	100.0%

Students at this school generally go on to:
Kennesaw Mountain High

AJC GRADE: ★★★

Georgia Criterion-Referenced Competency Tests - Grades 6, 8
Pct. of students at each level

	Lang 6	Lang 8	Math 6	Math 8	Read 6	Read 8
Exceeds	35	43	28	24	60	78
Meets	51	45	58	60	33	17
Does not meet	14	12	13	16	8	5

Cobb County Middle Schools

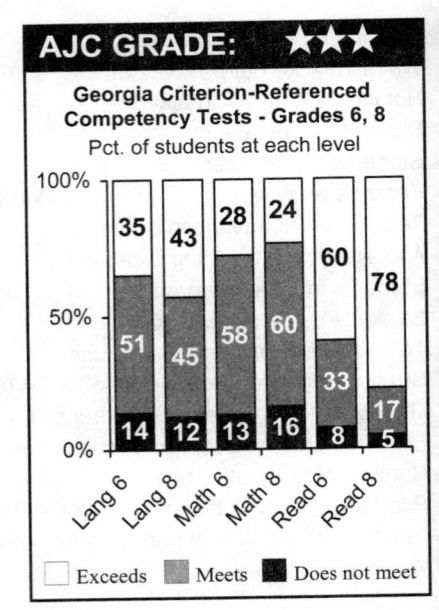

East Cobb Middle School

380 Holt Rd NE, Marietta, GA 30068
770-509-6023 · Grades 6 - 8

Enrollment:	1,322
White / black / other:	44.9% / 35.0% / 20.0%
Not native English-speaking:	112 / 8.5%
Student absenteeism:	6.4%
Students per teacher:	14.3
Parent friendliness:	❶❷❸④❺❻
Teachers with advanced degrees:	31.2%
Average years' teaching experience:	11.2
Students in gifted program:	196 / 14.8%
Students held back a grade:	2.9%
Total suspensions and expulsions:	2
Suspensions only, pct. in-school:	2 / 0.0%
Offenses: violence: *, drugs: *, other:	2
Eligible students, free or reduced lunch:	25.9%
Number of dropouts:	4 / 0.3%
Pct. 8th-graders w/ basic computer skills:	100.0%

Students at this school generally go on to:
Wheeler High

AJC GRADE: ★★★

Georgia Criterion-Referenced Competency Tests - Grades 6, 8
Pct. of students at each level

	Lang 6	Lang 8	Math 6	Math 8	Read 6	Read 8
Exceeds	19	29	25	14		55
Meets	48	45	40	45	39	32
Does not meet	34	25	35	41	28	13

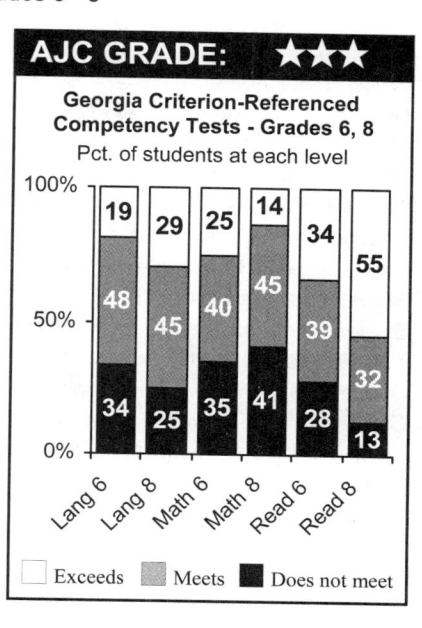

Floyd Middle School

4803 Floyd Rd SW, Mableton, GA 30126
770-732-5619 · Grades 6 - 8

Enrollment:	1,029
White / black / other:	44.4% / 42.6% / 13.0%
Not native English-speaking:	29 / 2.8%
Student absenteeism:	6.9%
Students per teacher:	15.4
Parent friendliness:	❶❷❸❹⑤❻
Teachers with advanced degrees:	38.2%
Average years' teaching experience:	9.3
Students in gifted program:	76 / 7.4%
Students held back a grade:	5.5%
Total suspensions and expulsions:	2
Suspensions only, pct. in-school:	2 / 0.0%
Offenses: violence: *, drugs: *, other:	2
Eligible students, free or reduced lunch:	39.6%
Number of dropouts:	1 / 0.1%
Pct. 8th-graders w/ basic computer skills:	100.0%

Students at this school generally go on to:
Osborne, South Cobb High

AJC GRADE: ★★★

Georgia Criterion-Referenced Competency Tests - Grades 6, 8
Pct. of students at each level

	Lang 6	Lang 8	Math 6	Math 8	Read 6	Read 8
Exceeds	10	17	10	5	29	57
Meets	47	54	52	48	44	32
Does not meet	43	28	38	47	27	11

Cobb County Middle Schools

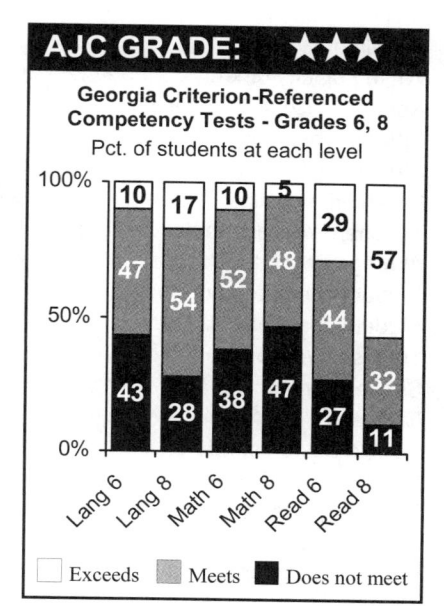

Garrett Middle School

5235 Austell Powder Springs Rd, Austell, GA 30106
770-732-5628 · Grades 6 - 8

Enrollment:	1,103
White / black / other:	44.1% / 45.1% / 10.9%
Not native English-speaking:	34 / 3.1%
Student absenteeism:	7.6%
Students per teacher:	14.4
Parent friendliness:	❶❷❸④⑤❻
Teachers with advanced degrees:	35.9%
Average years' teaching experience:	7.5
Students in gifted program:	52 / 4.7%
Students held back a grade:	3.2%
Total suspensions and expulsions:	6
Suspensions only, pct. in-school:	6 / 0.0%
Offenses: violence: 1, drugs: * , other: 5	
Eligible students, free or reduced lunch:	48.6%
Number of dropouts:	*
Pct. 8th-graders w/ basic computer skills:	100.0%
Students at this school generally go on to: Pebblebrook, South Cobb High	

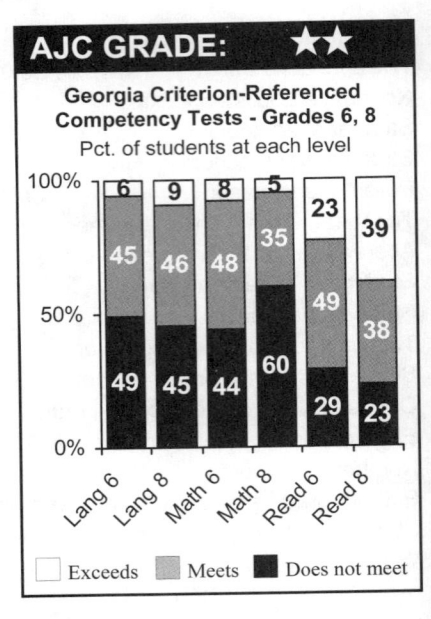

AJC GRADE: ★★

Georgia Criterion-Referenced Competency Tests - Grades 6, 8
Pct. of students at each level

	Lang 6	Lang 8	Math 6	Math 8	Read 6	Read 8
Exceeds	6	9	8	5	23	39
Meets	45	46	48	35	49	38
Does not meet	49	45	44	60	29	23

Griffin Middle School

4010 King Springs Rd SE, Smyrna, GA 30082
770-319-3744 · Grades 6 - 8

Enrollment:	952
White / black / other:	35.8% / 38.9% / 25.3%
Not native English-speaking:	78 / 8.2%
Student absenteeism:	6.7%
Students per teacher:	16.0
Parent friendliness:	❶❷❸④❺❻
Teachers with advanced degrees:	47.5%
Average years' teaching experience:	8.7
Students in gifted program:	64 / 6.7%
Students held back a grade:	1.1%
Total suspensions and expulsions:	1
Suspensions only, pct. in-school:	1 / 0.0%
Offenses: violence: 1, drugs: * , other: *	
Eligible students, free or reduced lunch:	49.1%
Number of dropouts:	6 / 0.5%
Pct. 8th-graders w/ basic computer skills:	100.0%
Students at this school generally go on to: Campbell, Osborne High	

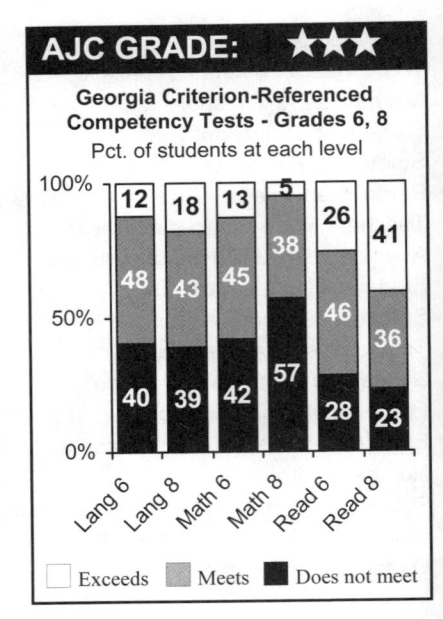

AJC GRADE: ★★★

Georgia Criterion-Referenced Competency Tests - Grades 6, 8
Pct. of students at each level

	Lang 6	Lang 8	Math 6	Math 8	Read 6	Read 8
Exceeds	12	18	13	5	26	41
Meets	48	43	45	38	46	36
Does not meet	40	39	42	57	28	23

Cobb County Middle Schools

Hightower Trail Middle School

3905 Post Oak Tritt Rd, Marietta, GA 30062
770-509-6201 · Grades 6 - 8

Enrollment:	1,047
White / black / other:	89.0% / 3.9% / 7.1%
Not native English-speaking:	6 / 0.6%
Student absenteeism:	4.3%
Students per teacher:	15.0
Parent friendliness:	❶❷❸④⑤❻
Teachers with advanced degrees:	46.5%
Average years' teaching experience:	11.9
Students in gifted program:	354 / 33.8%
Students held back a grade:	0.9%
Total suspensions and expulsions:	323
Suspensions only, pct. in-school:	323 / 82.7%
Offenses: violence: 29, drugs: 2, other: 343	
Eligible students, free or reduced lunch:	1.8%
Number of dropouts:	*
Pct. 8th-graders w/ basic computer skills:	100.0%
Students at this school generally go on to: Pope High	

AJC GRADE: ★★★★

Georgia Criterion-Referenced Competency Tests - Grades 6, 8
Pct. of students at each level

	Lang 6	Lang 8	Math 6	Math 8	Read 6	Read 8
Exceeds	51	59	58	33	74	83
Meets	43	34	36	57	23	15
Does not meet	6	6	6	10	3	2

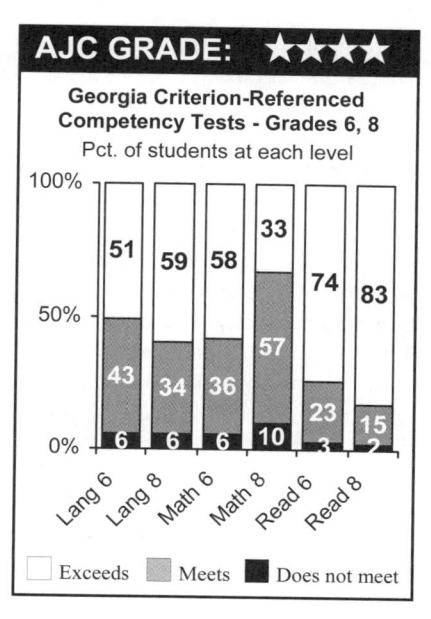

Lindley Middle School

50 Veterans Memorial Hwy SE, Mableton, GA 30126
770-732-5642 · Grades 6 - 8

Enrollment:	1,266
White / black / other:	14.9% / 71.4% / 13.7%
Not native English-speaking:	40 / 3.2%
Student absenteeism:	7.5%
Students per teacher:	16.9
Parent friendliness:	❶❷❸④❺❻
Teachers with advanced degrees:	26.7%
Average years' teaching experience:	7.8
Students in gifted program:	34 / 2.7%
Students held back a grade:	1.9%
Total suspensions and expulsions:	1
Suspensions only, pct. in-school:	1 / 0.0%
Offenses: violence: 1, drugs: *, other: *	
Eligible students, free or reduced lunch:	66.7%
Number of dropouts:	*
Pct. 8th-graders w/ basic computer skills:	90.0%
Students at this school generally go on to: Pebblebrook High	

AJC GRADE: ★★★

Georgia Criterion-Referenced Competency Tests - Grades 6, 8
Pct. of students at each level

	Lang 6	Lang 8	Math 6	Math 8	Read 6	Read 8
Exceeds	8	8	5	1	21	31
Meets	47	48	46	32	48	47
Does not meet	45	45	50	68	31	22

Cobb County Middle Schools

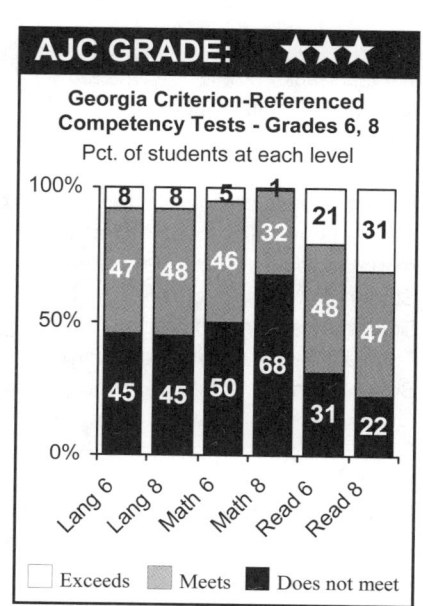

Lost Mountain Middle School

700 Old Mountain Rd NW, Kennesaw, GA 30152
770-528-6627 · Grades 6 - 8

Enrollment:	1,259
White / black / other:	93.1% / 4.4% / 2.5%
Not native English-speaking:	*
Student absenteeism:	3.9%
Students per teacher:	16.4
Parent friendliness:	❶❷❸④⑤❻
Teachers with advanced degrees:	44.9%
Average years' teaching experience:	11.0
Students in gifted program:	282 / 22.4%
Students held back a grade:	0.9%
Total suspensions and expulsions:	2
Suspensions only, pct. in-school:	2 / 0.0%
Offenses: violence: 1, drugs: *, other: 1	
Eligible students, free or reduced lunch:	2.3%
Number of dropouts:	*
Pct. 8th-graders w/ basic computer skills:	90.0%
Students at this school generally go on to: Harrison, McEachern High	

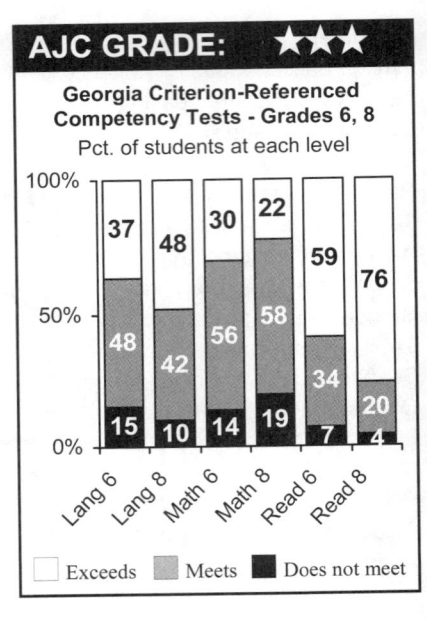

AJC GRADE: ★★★

Georgia Criterion-Referenced Competency Tests - Grades 6, 8
Pct. of students at each level

	Lang 6	Lang 8	Math 6	Math 8	Read 6	Read 8
Exceeds	37		30	22		
		48			59	76
Meets	48	42	56	58	34	20
Does not meet	15	10	14	19	7	4

Mabry Middle School

2700 Jims Rd NE, Marietta, GA 30066
770-591-6833 · Grades 6 - 8

Enrollment:	1,017
White / black / other:	92.3% / 3.5% / 4.1%
Not native English-speaking:	*
Student absenteeism:	4.4%
Students per teacher:	15.0
Parent friendliness:	❶❷❸④⑤❻
Teachers with advanced degrees:	33.3%
Average years' teaching experience:	11.6
Students in gifted program:	289 / 28.4%
Students held back a grade:	0.2%
Total suspensions and expulsions:	233
Suspensions only, pct. in-school:	233 / 80.3%
Offenses: violence: 13, drugs: 2, other: 265	
Eligible students, free or reduced lunch:	1.8%
Number of dropouts:	*
Pct. 8th-graders w/ basic computer skills:	100.0%
Students at this school generally go on to: Lassiter High	

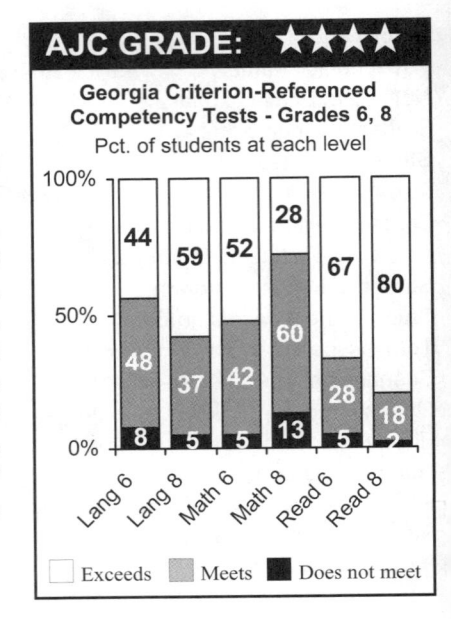

AJC GRADE: ★★★★

Georgia Criterion-Referenced Competency Tests - Grades 6, 8
Pct. of students at each level

	Lang 6	Lang 8	Math 6	Math 8	Read 6	Read 8
Exceeds	44	59	52	28	67	80
Meets	48	37	42	60	28	18
Does not meet	8	5	5	13	5	2

The Atlanta Journal-Constitution

Cobb County Middle Schools

McCleskey Middle School

4080 Maybreeze Rd, Marietta, GA 30066
770-591-6841 · Grades 6 - 8

Enrollment:	1,049
White / black / other:	79.6% / 10.3% / 10.1%
Not native English-speaking:	13 / 1.2%
Student absenteeism:	4.8%
Students per teacher:	15.7
Parent friendliness:	❶❷❸④❺❻
Teachers with advanced degrees:	51.4%
Average years' teaching experience:	14.0
Students in gifted program:	199 / 19.0%
Students held back a grade:	2.4%
Total suspensions and expulsions:	534
Suspensions only, pct. in-school:	534 / 79.2%
Offenses:	violence: 14, drugs: 2, other: 556
Eligible students, free or reduced lunch:	10.2%
Number of dropouts:	5 / 0.4%
Pct. 8th-graders w/ basic computer skills:	100.0%

Students at this school generally go on to:
Kell, Sprayberry High

AJC GRADE: ★★★

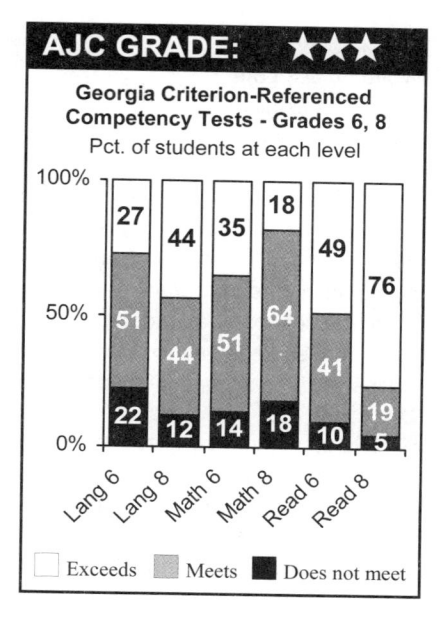

Georgia Criterion-Referenced Competency Tests - Grades 6, 8
Pct. of students at each level

	Lang 6	Lang 8	Math 6	Math 8	Read 6	Read 8
Exceeds	27		35	18		76
		44			49	
Meets	51	44	51	64	41	19
Does not meet	22	12	14	18	10	5

Pine Mountain Middle School

2720 Pine Mountain Cir NW, Kennesaw, GA 30152
770-528-6529 · Grades 6 - 8

Enrollment:	1,077
White / black / other:	82.1% / 9.9% / 8.0%
Not native English-speaking:	20 / 1.9%
Student absenteeism:	4.5%
Students per teacher:	14.7
Parent friendliness:	❶❷❸④⑤❻
Teachers with advanced degrees:	44.6%
Average years' teaching experience:	12.8
Students in gifted program:	202 / 18.8%
Students held back a grade:	1.3%
Total suspensions and expulsions:	515
Suspensions only, pct. in-school:	515 / 89.1%
Offenses:	violence: 3, drugs: 1, other: 617
Eligible students, free or reduced lunch:	10.6%
Number of dropouts:	*
Pct. 8th-graders w/ basic computer skills:	100.0%

Students at this school generally go on to:
Kennesaw Mountain High

AJC GRADE: ★★★

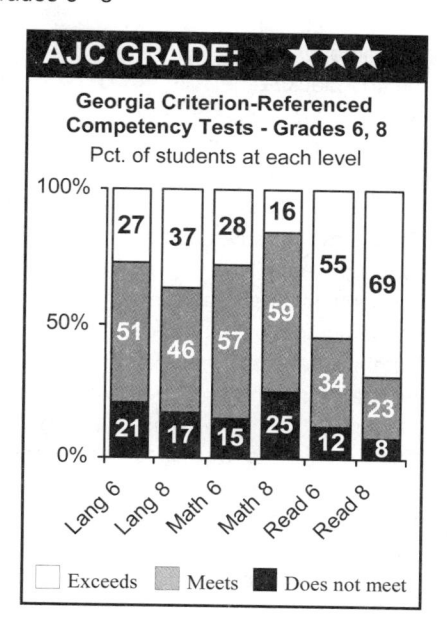

Georgia Criterion-Referenced Competency Tests - Grades 6, 8
Pct. of students at each level

	Lang 6	Lang 8	Math 6	Math 8	Read 6	Read 8
Exceeds	27	37	28	16		69
				59	55	
Meets	51	46	57		34	23
Does not meet	21	17	15	25	12	8

Cobb County Middle Schools

Simpson Middle School

3340 Trickum Rd NE, Marietta, GA 30066
770-509-6103 · Grades 6 - 8

Enrollment:	921
White / black / other:	81.0% / 8.9% / 10.1%
Not native English-speaking:	*
Student absenteeism:	4.1%
Students per teacher:	14.6
Parent friendliness:	❶❷❸④⑤❻
Teachers with advanced degrees:	46.2%
Average years' teaching experience:	14.1
Students in gifted program:	254 / 27.6%
Students held back a grade:	0.5%
Total suspensions and expulsions:	4
Suspensions only, pct. in-school:	4 / 25.0%
Offenses:	violence: *, drugs: *, other: 4
Eligible students, free or reduced lunch:	3.9%
Number of dropouts:	*
Pct. 8th-graders w/ basic computer skills:	100.0%
Students at this school generally go on to:	
Lassiter, Sprayberry High	

AJC GRADE: ★★★★

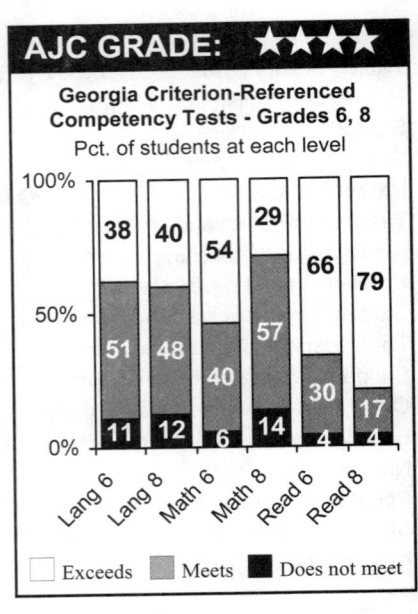

Georgia Criterion-Referenced Competency Tests - Grades 6, 8
Pct. of students at each level

	Lang 6	Lang 8	Math 6	Math 8	Read 6	Read 8
Exceeds	38	40	54	29	66	79
Meets	51	48	40	57	30	17
Does not meet	11	12	6	14	4	4

Smitha Middle School

2025 Powder Springs Rd SW, Marietta, GA 30064
770-528-6460 · Grades 6 - 8

Enrollment:	1,352
White / black / other:	47.5% / 38.5% / 14.1%
Not native English-speaking:	36 / 2.7%
Student absenteeism:	5.7%
Students per teacher:	13.7
Parent friendliness:	❶❷❸④⑤❻
Teachers with advanced degrees:	41.2%
Average years' teaching experience:	8.9
Students in gifted program:	133 / 9.8%
Students held back a grade:	1.3%
Total suspensions and expulsions:	11
Suspensions only, pct. in-school:	11 / 0.0%
Offenses:	violence: 4, drugs: *, other: 7
Eligible students, free or reduced lunch:	28.0%
Number of dropouts:	6 / 0.4%
Pct. 8th-graders w/ basic computer skills:	100.0%
Students at this school generally go on to:	
McEachern, Osborne High	

AJC GRADE: ★★★

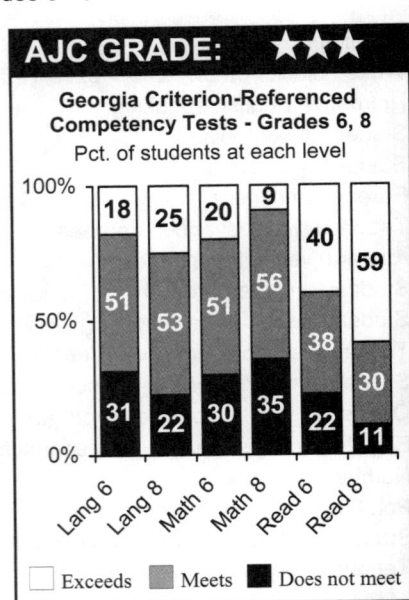

Georgia Criterion-Referenced Competency Tests - Grades 6, 8
Pct. of students at each level

	Lang 6	Lang 8	Math 6	Math 8	Read 6	Read 8
Exceeds	18	25	20	9	40	59
Meets	51	53	51	56	38	30
Does not meet	31	22	30	35	22	11

Cobb County Middle Schools

Tapp Middle School

3900 Macedonia Rd, Powder Springs, GA 30127
770-439-4730 · Grades 6 - 8

Enrollment:	1,636
White / black / other:	57.8% / 36.4% / 5.7%
Not native English-speaking:	13 / 0.8%
Student absenteeism:	5.4%
Students per teacher:	16.4
Parent friendliness:	❶❷❸❹❺❻
Teachers with advanced degrees:	37.6%
Average years' teaching experience:	10.1
Students in gifted program:	167 / 10.2%
Students held back a grade:	2.6%
Total suspensions and expulsions:	4
Suspensions only, pct. in-school:	4 / 0.0%
Offenses: violence: *, drugs: *, other: 4	
Eligible students, free or reduced lunch:	23.7%
Number of dropouts:	3 / 0.2%
Pct. 8th-graders w/ basic computer skills:	100.0%

Students at this school generally go on to:
McEachern High

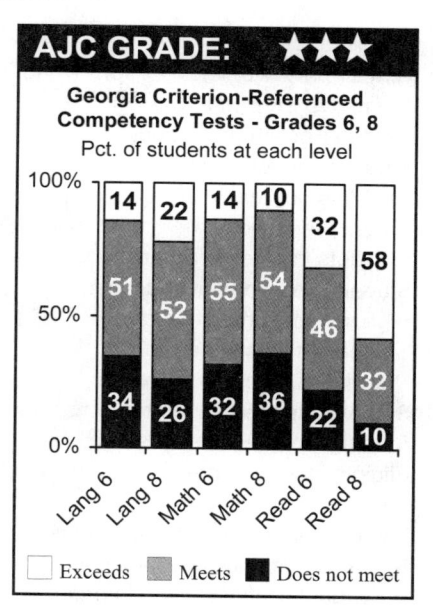

AJC GRADE: ★★★

Georgia Criterion-Referenced Competency Tests - Grades 6, 8
Pct. of students at each level

	Lang 6	Lang 8	Math 6	Math 8	Read 6	Read 8
Exceeds	14	22	14	10	32	58
Meets	51	52	55	54	46	32
Does not meet	34	26	32	36	22	10

Cobb County Middle Schools

Campbell High School

5265 Ward St SE, Smyrna, GA 30080
770-319-3726 · Grades 9 - 12

Enrollment:	2,074
White / black / other:	36.7% / 43.8% / 19.5%
Not native English-speaking:	118 / 5.7%
Limited English proficiency:	309 / 14.9%
Student absenteeism:	10.3%
Students per teacher:	16.5
Parent friendliness:	①**❷❸**④**❺❻**
Students in gifted program:	267 / 12.9%
Students in remedial education:	21.0%
High school completion rate:	75.1%
Students held back a grade:	9.7%
Number of dropouts:	80 / 3.4%
Students in alternative programs:	8 / 0.4%
Students in special education:	182 / 8.8%
Eligible students, free or reduced lunch:	24.0%

Total suspensions and expulsions:	13
Suspensions only, pct. in-school:	13 / 0.0%
Drugs/alcohol-related offenses:	*
Violence-related offenses:	2
Firearms-related offenses:	*
Vandalism-related offenses:	*
Theft-related offenses:	*
All other disciplinary offenses:	11
Teachers with advanced degrees:	50.0%
Average years' teaching experience:	10.7

AJC GRADE: ★★★

High School Graduation Test
Pct. of students who passed on first try

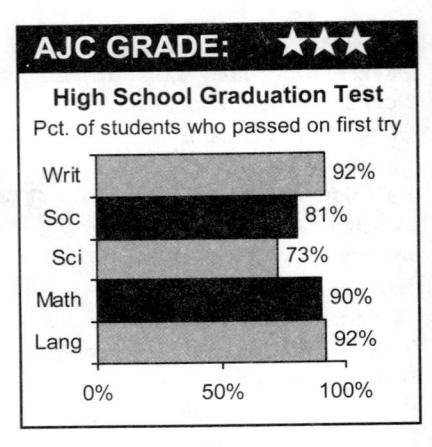

- Writ: 92%
- Soc: 81%
- Sci: 73%
- Math: 90%
- Lang: 92%

GHSA classification:	5-AAAAA

Interscholastic sports offered:
BB, BS, CC, CL, FB, GO, RI, SB, SO, SW, TE, TF, VB

Advanced Placement (AP) Exams
Students tested:	84
Tests taken:	144
Pct. of test scores 3 or higher (1 - 5 scale):	66.7%

Languages other than English taught:
French, German, Japanese, Spanish

2000-2001 high school graduates: 374

College prep/vocational diplomas:	27.5%
College prep endorsement diplomas:	51.3%
Vocational endorsement diplomas:	6.1%
General high school diplomas:	0.0%
Special education diplomas:	5.3%
Certificates of attendance (no diploma):	9.6%

Of the 2000-2001 graduates, 69.8% were eligible for the HOPE scholarship.

Of the 1999-2000 graduates, 99 attended a Georgia public college or university. Of those, 87% met the school's minimum academic requirements.

Average SAT Scores
Maximum score is 800 on each portion

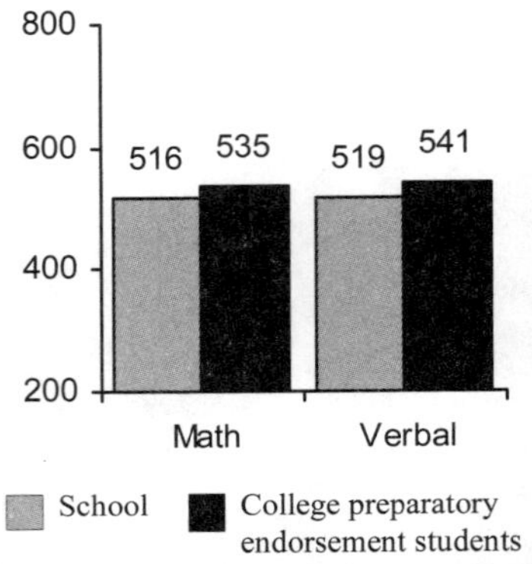

- Math: School 516, College preparatory endorsement students 535
- Verbal: School 519, College preparatory endorsement students 541

Harrison High School

4500 Due West Rd NW, Kennesaw, GA 30152
770-528-6638 · Grades 9 - 12

Enrollment:	2,282
White / black / other:	92.3% / 4.3% / 3.3%
Not native English-speaking:	4 / 0.2%
Limited English proficiency:	12 / 0.5%
Student absenteeism:	4.3%
Students per teacher:	17.7
Parent friendliness:	❶❷❸④⑤❻
Students in gifted program:	132 / 5.8%
Students in remedial education:	2.2%
High school completion rate:	94.1%
Students held back a grade:	1.3%
Number of dropouts:	21 / 0.9%
Students in alternative programs:	2 / 0.1%
Students in special education:	177 / 7.8%
Eligible students, free or reduced lunch:	1.0%

Total suspensions and expulsions:	562
Suspensions only, pct. in-school:	562 / 85.8%
Drugs/alcohol-related offenses:	19
Violence-related offenses:	20
Firearms-related offenses:	13
Vandalism-related offenses:	2
Theft-related offenses:	7
All other disciplinary offenses:	543

Teachers with advanced degrees:	50.4%
Average years' teaching experience:	13.8

AJC GRADE: ★★★

High School Graduation Test

Pct. of students who passed on first try

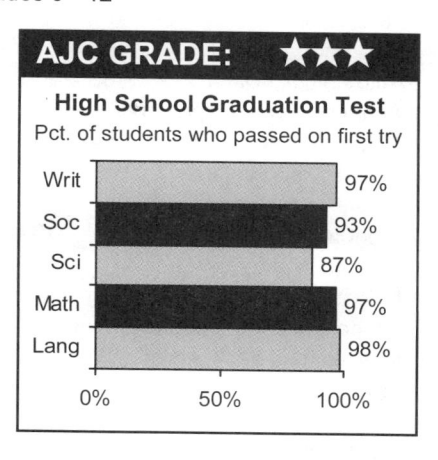

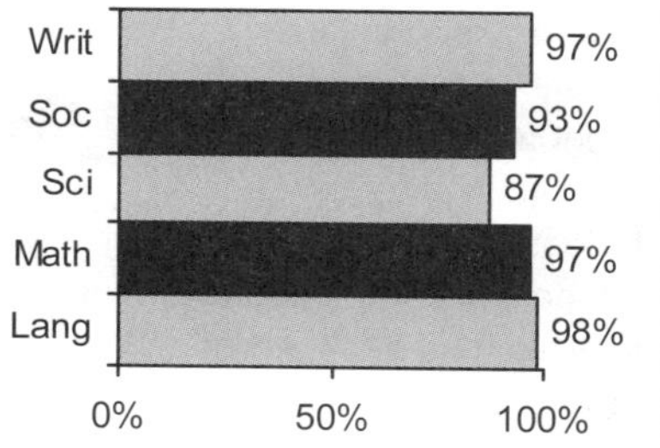
Writ
97%
Soc
93%
Sci
87%
Math
97%
Lang
98%
0%
50%
100%

GHSA classification:	5-AAAAA

Interscholastic sports offered:
BB, BS, CC, CL, FB, GO, LC, RI, SB, SO, SW, TE, TF, VB

Advanced Placement (AP) Exams

Students tested:	142
Tests taken:	272
Pct. of test scores 3 or higher (1 - 5 scale):	79.8%

Languages other than English taught:
French, German, Latin, Spanish

2000-2001 high school graduates: 704

College prep/vocational diplomas:	22.4%
College prep endorsement diplomas:	65.9%
Vocational endorsement diplomas:	9.8%
General high school diplomas:	0.0%
Special education diplomas:	1.0%
Certificates of attendance (no diploma):	0.9%

Of the 2000-2001 graduates, 72.9% were eligible for the HOPE scholarship.

Of the 1999-2000 graduates, 371 attended a Georgia public college or university. Of those, 95% met the school's minimum academic requirements.

Average SAT Scores

Maximum score is 800 on each portion

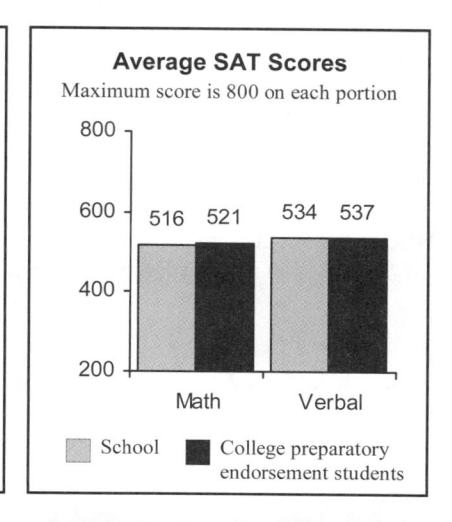

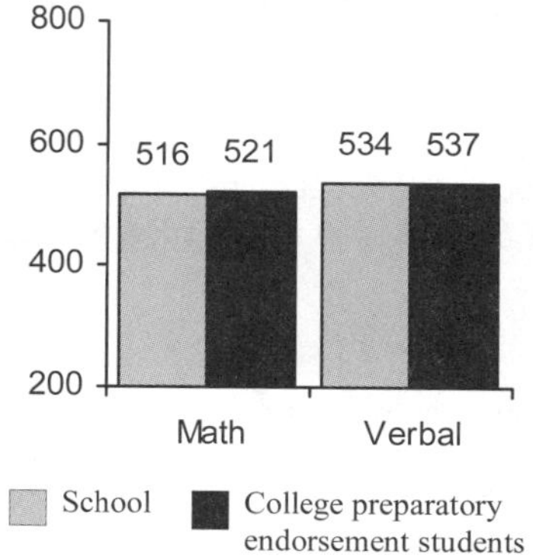
800
600
400
200
516
521
534
537
Math
Verbal
School
College preparatory endorsement students

Kennesaw Mountain High School

1898 Kennesaw Due West Rd NW, Kennesaw, GA 30152
770-528-6920 · Grades 9 - 12

Enrollment:	1,250
White / black / other:	83.1% / 9.2% / 7.7%
Not native English-speaking:	10 / 0.8%
Limited English proficiency:	39 / 3.1%
Student absenteeism:	5.1%
Students per teacher:	15.3
Parent friendliness:	❶❷❸④⑤❻
Students in gifted program:	112 / 9.0%
Students in remedial education:	2.5%
High school completion rate:	*
Students held back a grade:	0.4%
Number of dropouts:	28 / 2.0%
Students in alternative programs:	1 / 0.1%
Students in special education:	144 / 11.5%
Eligible students, free or reduced lunch:	5.8%

Total suspensions and expulsions:	2
Suspensions only, pct. in-school:	2 / 0.0%
Drugs/alcohol-related offenses:	*
Violence-related offenses:	*
Firearms-related offenses:	*
Vandalism-related offenses:	*
Theft-related offenses:	1
All other disciplinary offenses:	1

Teachers with advanced degrees:	50.6%
Average years' teaching experience:	11.2

AJC GRADE: ★★★

High School Graduation Test
Pct. of students who passed on first try

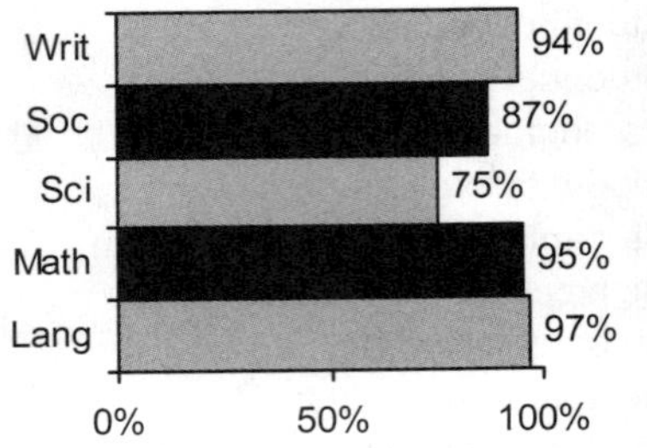
Writ
94%
Soc
87%
Sci
75%
Math
95%
Lang
97%
0%
50%
100%

GHSA classification:	5-AAAAA

Interscholastic sports offered:
BB, BS, CC, CL, GO, SB, SB, SO, SW, TF, VB, WR

Advanced Placement (AP) Exams

Students tested:	*
Tests taken:	*
Pct. of test scores 3 or higher (1 - 5 scale):	*

Languages other than English taught:
French, German, Japanese, Latin, Spanish

2000-2001 high school graduates: None

College prep/vocational diplomas:	0.0%
College prep endorsement diplomas:	0.0%
Vocational endorsement diplomas:	0.0%
General high school diplomas:	0.0%
Special education diplomas:	0.0%
Certificates of attendance (no diploma):	0.0%

Kennesaw Mountain High School is a new school and therefore some data was not available for this report.

Average SAT Scores
Maximum score is 800 on each portion

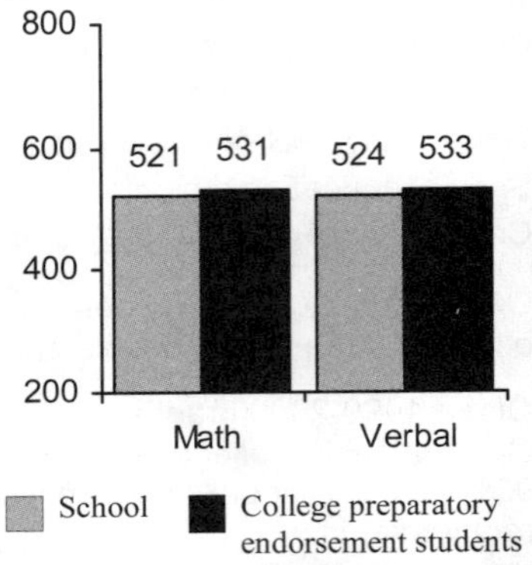
800
600
400
200
521
531
524
533
Math
Verbal
School
College preparatory endorsement students

Lassiter High School

2601 Shallowford Rd, Marietta, GA 30066
770-591-6819 · Grades 9 - 12

👍

Enrollment:	2,887
White / black / other:	88.1% / 5.5% / 6.4%
Not native English-speaking:	8 / 0.3%
Limited English proficiency:	32 / 1.1%
Student absenteeism:	4.7%
Students per teacher:	17.1
Parent friendliness:	①❷❸④⑤❻
Students in gifted program:	666 / 23.1%
Students in remedial education:	4.3%
High school completion rate:	92.6%
Students held back a grade:	2.9%
Number of dropouts:	41 / 1.4%
Students in alternative programs:	2 / 0.1%
Students in special education:	292 / 10.1%
Eligible students, free or reduced lunch:	1.4%

Total suspensions and expulsions:	2
Suspensions only, pct. in-school:	2 / 0.0%
Drugs/alcohol-related offenses:	*
Violence-related offenses:	*
Firearms-related offenses:	1
Vandalism-related offenses:	*
Theft-related offenses:	*
All other disciplinary offenses:	1

Teachers with advanced degrees:	47.7%
Average years' teaching experience:	13.1

AJC GRADE: ★★★

High School Graduation Test

Pct. of students who passed on first try

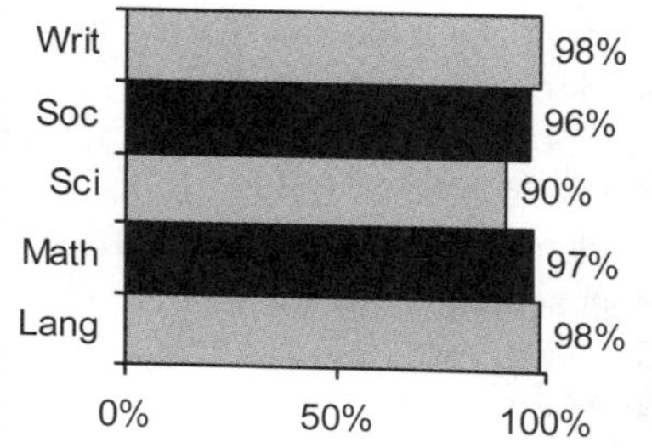
Writ
98%
Soc
96%
Sci
90%
Math
97%
Lang
98%
0%
50%
100%

GHSA classification:	6-AAAAA

Interscholastic sports offered:
BB, BS, CC, CL, FB, GO, GY, LC, SB, SO, SW, TE, TF, VB, WR

Advanced Placement (AP) Exams

Students tested:	250
Tests taken:	468
Pct. of test scores 3 or higher (1 - 5 scale):	76.7%

Languages other than English taught:
French, German, Italian, Latin, Spanish

2000-2001 high school graduates: 639

College prep/vocational diplomas:	3.9%
College prep endorsement diplomas:	91.2%
Vocational endorsement diplomas:	3.8%
General high school diplomas:	0.0%
Special education diplomas:	0.3%
Certificates of attendance (no diploma):	0.8%

Of the 2000-2001 graduates, 86.5% were eligible for the HOPE scholarship.

Of the 1999-2000 graduates, 317 attended a Georgia public college or university. Of those, 94% met the school's minimum academic requirements.

Average SAT Scores

Maximum score is 800 on each portion

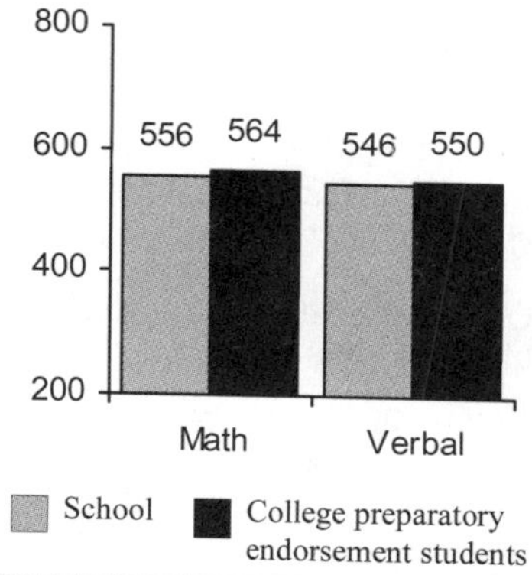
800
600
400
200
556
564
546
550
Math
Verbal
School
College preparatory endorsement students

McEachern High School

2400 New Macland Rd, Powder Springs, GA 30127
770-439-4700 · Grades 9 - 12

Enrollment:	2,862
White / black / other:	68.3% / 26.6% / 5.1%
Not native English-speaking:	11 / 0.4%
Limited English proficiency:	34 / 1.2%
Student absenteeism:	7.1%
Students per teacher:	18.4
Parent friendliness:	❶❷❸❹⑤❻
Students in gifted program:	155 / 5.4%
Students in remedial education:	8.9%
High school completion rate:	90.4%
Students held back a grade:	5.2%
Number of dropouts:	88 / 2.9%
Students in alternative programs:	3 / 0.1%
Students in special education:	299 / 10.4%
Eligible students, free or reduced lunch:	10.8%
Total suspensions and expulsions:	3
Suspensions only, pct. in-school:	3 / 0.0%
Drugs/alcohol-related offenses:	*
Violence-related offenses:	*
Firearms-related offenses:	*
Vandalism-related offenses:	*
Theft-related offenses:	*
All other disciplinary offenses:	3
Teachers with advanced degrees:	41.7%
Average years' teaching experience:	12.1

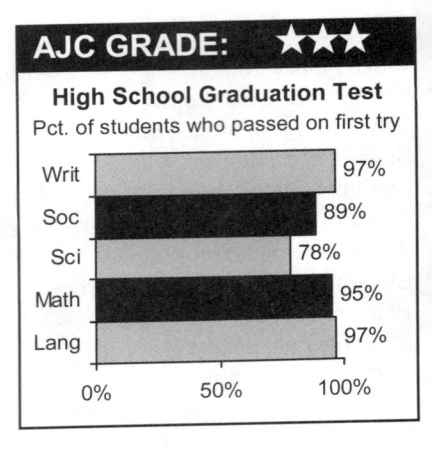

AJC GRADE: ★★★

High School Graduation Test
Pct. of students who passed on first try

- Writ: 97%
- Soc: 89%
- Sci: 78%
- Math: 95%
- Lang: 97%

GHSA classification: 5-AAAAA
Interscholastic sports offered:
BB, BS, CC, CL, FB, GO, RI, SB, SO, SW, TE, TF, VB, WR

Advanced Placement (AP) Exams
- Students tested: 83
- Tests taken: 154
- Pct. of test scores 3 or higher (1 - 5 scale): 64.3%

Languages other than English taught:
French, German, Spanish

2000-2001 high school graduates: 492

College prep/vocational diplomas:	4.7%
College prep endorsement diplomas:	72.8%
Vocational endorsement diplomas:	14.8%
General high school diplomas:	0.0%
Special education diplomas:	4.5%
Certificates of attendance (no diploma):	3.3%

Of the 2000-2001 graduates, 63.0% were eligible for the HOPE scholarship.

Of the 1999-2000 graduates, 240 attended a Georgia public college or university. Of those, 92% met the school's minimum academic requirements.

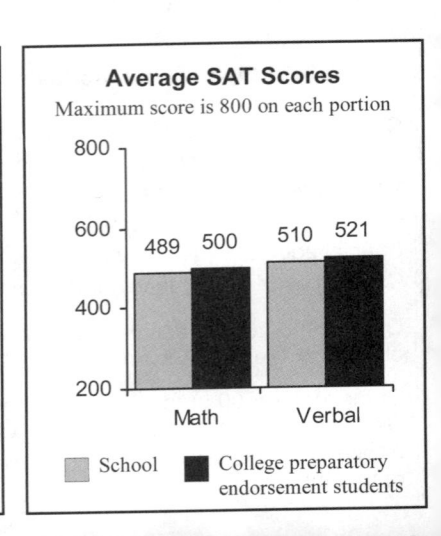

Average SAT Scores
Maximum score is 800 on each portion

- Math: School 489, College preparatory endorsement students 500
- Verbal: School 510, College preparatory endorsement students 521

The Atlanta Journal-Constitution / Page 170

Cobb County High Schools

North Cobb High School

3400 Hwy 293 N, Kennesaw, GA 30144
770-975-4261 · Grades 9 - 12

Enrollment:	2,542
White / black / other:	74.4% / 14.8% / 10.8%
Not native English-speaking:	36 / 1.4%
Limited English proficiency:	172 / 6.8%
Student absenteeism:	7.3%
Students per teacher:	18.5
Parent friendliness:	❶❷❸④⑤❻
Students in gifted program:	123 / 4.8%
Students in remedial education:	4.2%
High school completion rate:	86.5%
Students held back a grade:	6.3%
Number of dropouts:	99 / 3.5%
Students in alternative programs:	3 / 0.1%
Students in special education:	260 / 10.2%
Eligible students, free or reduced lunch:	5.6%

Total suspensions and expulsions:	1
Suspensions only, pct. in-school:	1 / 0.0%
Drugs/alcohol-related offenses:	*
Violence-related offenses:	1
Firearms-related offenses:	*
Vandalism-related offenses:	*
Theft-related offenses:	*
All other disciplinary offenses:	*

Teachers with advanced degrees:	50.3%
Average years' teaching experience:	12.8

2000-2001 high school graduates: 534

College prep/vocational diplomas:	21.3%
College prep endorsement diplomas:	65.2%
Vocational endorsement diplomas:	9.0%
General high school diplomas:	0.0%
Special education diplomas:	2.2%
Certificates of attendance (no diploma):	2.2%

Of the 2000-2001 graduates, 64.8% were eligible for the HOPE scholarship.

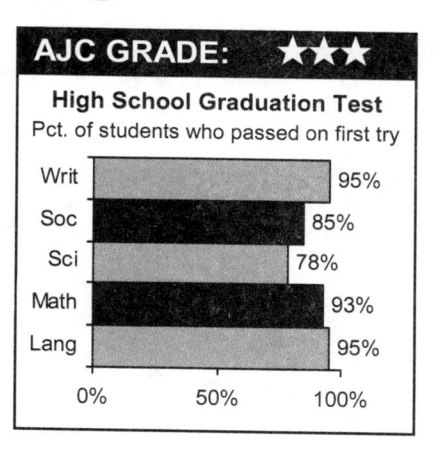

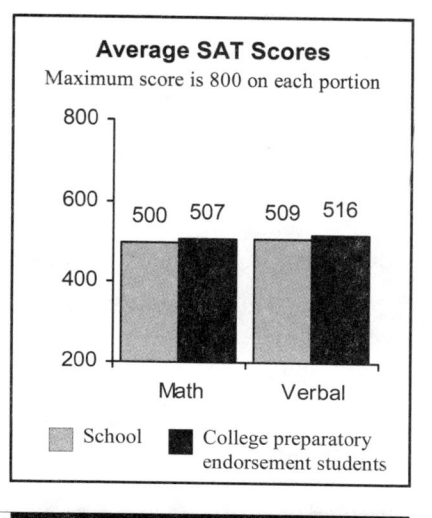

Of the 1999-2000 graduates, 264 attended a Georgia public college or university. Of those, 87% met the school's minimum academic requirements.

AJC GRADE: ★★★

High School Graduation Test

Pct. of students who passed on first try

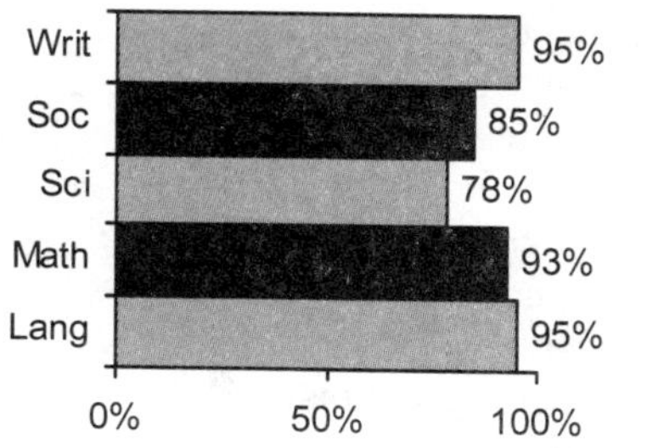
Writ
95%
Soc
85%
Sci
78%
Math
93%
Lang
95%
0%
50%
100%

GHSA classification:	5-AAAAA

Interscholastic sports offered:
BB, BS, CC, CL, FB, GO, RI, SB, SO, SW, TE, TF, VB, WR

Advanced Placement (AP) Exams

Students tested:	140
Tests taken:	234
Pct. of test scores 3 or higher (1 - 5 scale):	78.6%

Languages other than English taught:
French, German, Japanese, Latin, Spanish

Average SAT Scores

Maximum score is 800 on each portion

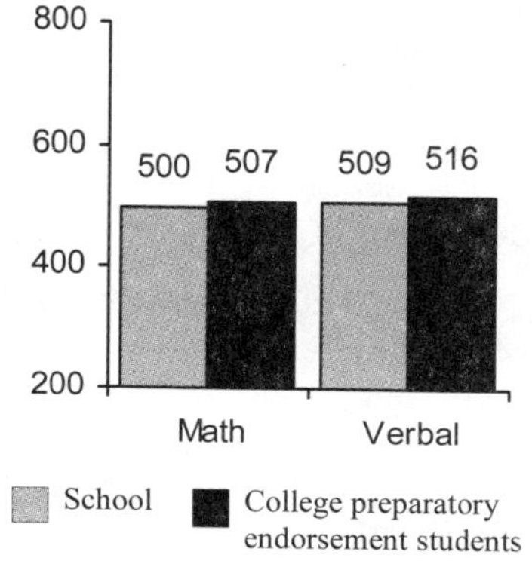
800
600
400
200
500
507
509
516
Math
Verbal
School
College preparatory endorsement students

Osborne High School

2451 Favor Rd SW, Marietta, GA 30060
770-319-3791 · Grades 9 - 12

👎

Enrollment:	1,734
White / black / other:	36.5% / 45.4% / 18.1%
Not native English-speaking:	58 / 3.3%
Limited English proficiency:	296 / 17.1%
Student absenteeism:	12.3%
Students per teacher:	16.4
Parent friendliness:	①❷❸④⑤❻
Students in gifted program:	14 / 0.8%
Students in remedial education:	17.0%
High school completion rate:	74.8%
Students held back a grade:	5.4%
Number of dropouts:	120 / 5.9%
Students in alternative programs:	2 / 0.1%
Students in special education:	224 / 12.9%
Eligible students, free or reduced lunch:	24.5%

Total suspensions and expulsions:	14
Suspensions only, pct. in-school:	14 / 0.0%
Drugs/alcohol-related offenses:	1
Violence-related offenses:	2
Firearms-related offenses:	*
Vandalism-related offenses:	1
Theft-related offenses:	*
All other disciplinary offenses:	10

Teachers with advanced degrees:	41.8%
Average years' teaching experience:	10.3

AJC GRADE: ★★

High School Graduation Test

Pct. of students who passed on first try

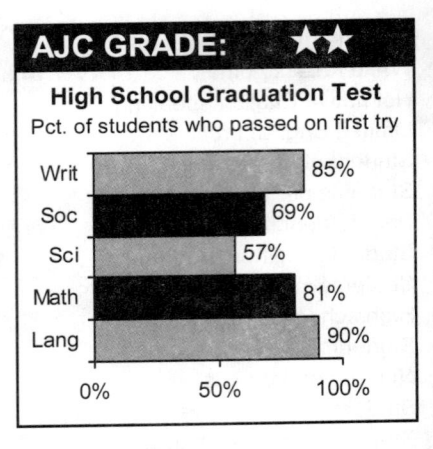

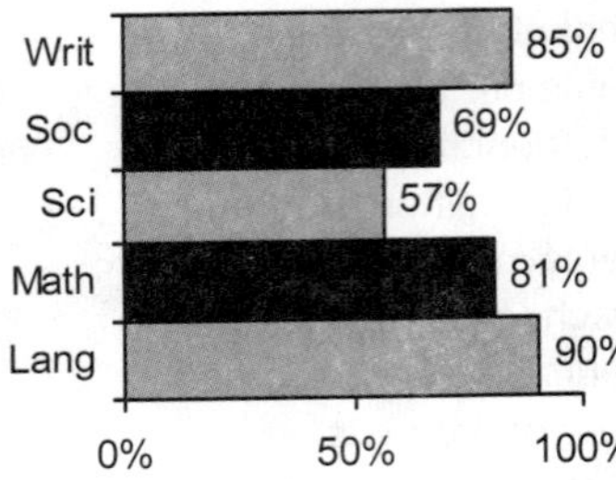
Writ
85%
Soc
69%
Sci
57%
Math
81%
Lang
90%
0%
50%
100%

GHSA classification:	5-AAAAA

Interscholastic sports offered:
BB, BS, CC, CL, FB, GO, SB, SO, TE, TF, VB, WR

Advanced Placement (AP) Exams

Students tested:	88
Tests taken:	119
Pct. of test scores 3 or higher (1 - 5 scale):	26.1%

Languages other than English taught:
French, German, Latin, Spanish

2000-2001 high school graduates: 297

College prep/vocational diplomas:	43.8%
College prep endorsement diplomas:	25.3%
Vocational endorsement diplomas:	16.2%
General high school diplomas:	0.0%
Special education diplomas:	2.4%
Certificates of attendance (no diploma):	12.5%

Of the 2000-2001 graduates, 55.9% were eligible for the HOPE scholarship.

Of the 1999-2000 graduates, 77 attended a Georgia public college or university. Of those, 93% met the school's minimum academic requirements.

Average SAT Scores

Maximum score is 800 on each portion

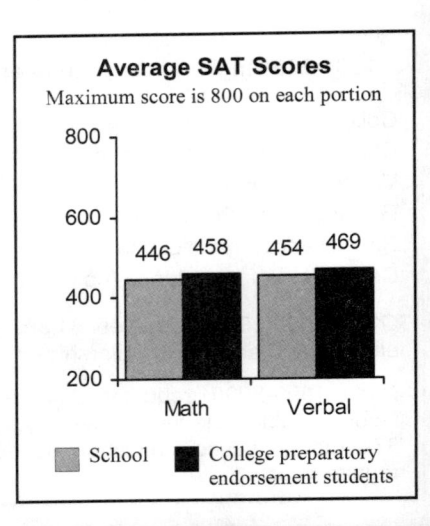

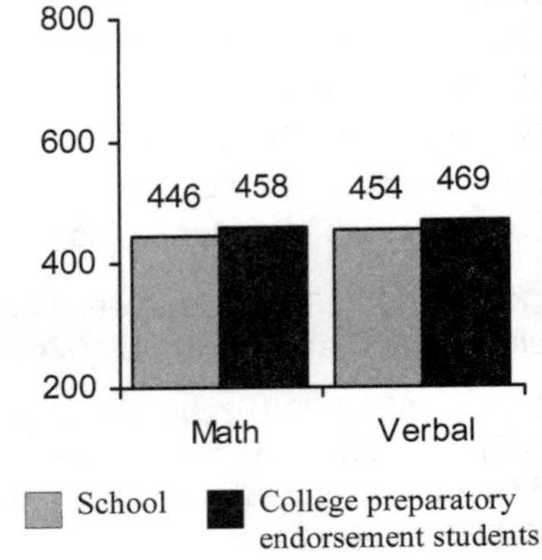
800
600
400
200
446
458
454
469
Math
Verbal
School
College preparatory endorsement students

Pebblebrook High School

991 Old Alabama Rd SW, Mableton, GA 30126
770-732-5658 · Grades 9 - 12

Enrollment:	1,496
White / black / other:	28.3% / 61.0% / 10.7%
Not native English-speaking:	24 / 1.6%
Limited English proficiency:	103 / 6.9%
Student absenteeism:	9.9%
Students per teacher:	14.8
Parent friendliness:	❶❷❸❹❺❻
Students in gifted program:	29 / 1.9%
Students in remedial education:	17.1%
High school completion rate:	76.7%
Students held back a grade:	10.3%
Number of dropouts:	77 / 4.5%
Students in alternative programs:	6 / 0.4%
Students in special education:	169 / 11.3%
Eligible students, free or reduced lunch:	26.2%
Total suspensions and expulsions:	7
Suspensions only, pct. in-school:	7 / 0.0%
Drugs/alcohol-related offenses:	*
Violence-related offenses:	3
Firearms-related offenses:	*
Vandalism-related offenses:	*
Theft-related offenses:	*
All other disciplinary offenses:	4
Teachers with advanced degrees:	46.7%
Average years' teaching experience:	9.2

AJC GRADE: ★★

High School Graduation Test
Pct. of students who passed on first try

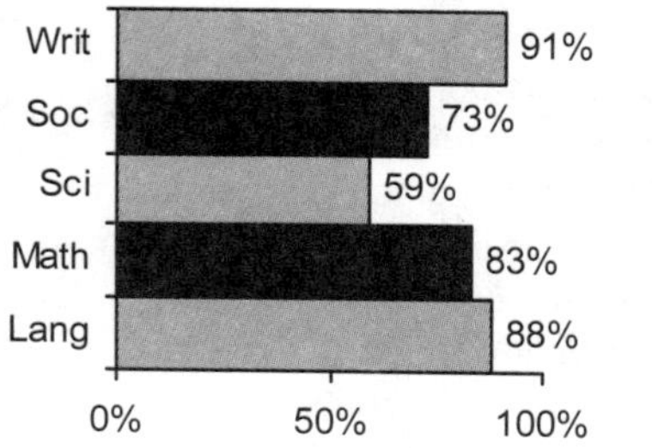

- Writ: 91%
- Soc: 73%
- Sci: 59%
- Math: 83%
- Lang: 88%

GHSA classification: 4-AAAA
Interscholastic sports offered:
BB, BS, CC, CL, FB, GO, SB, SO, TE, TF, VB, WR

Advanced Placement (AP) Exams
- Students tested: 18
- Tests taken: 23
- Pct. of test scores 3 or higher (1 - 5 scale): 39.1%

Languages other than English taught:
French, German, Spanish

2000-2001 high school graduates: 280

College prep/vocational diplomas:	32.9%
College prep endorsement diplomas:	41.8%
Vocational endorsement diplomas:	10.7%
General high school diplomas:	0.0%
Special education diplomas:	4.6%
Certificates of attendance (no diploma):	10.0%

Of the 2000-2001 graduates, 53.9% were eligible for the HOPE scholarship.

Of the 1999-2000 graduates, 60 attended a Georgia public college or university. Of those, 81% met the school's minimum academic requirements.

Average SAT Scores
Maximum score is 800 on each portion

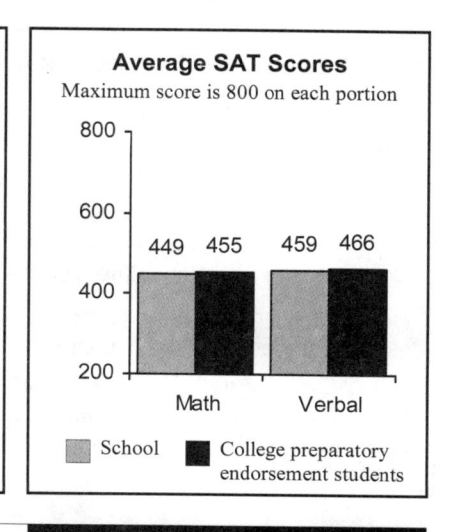

- Math: School 449, College preparatory endorsement students 455
- Verbal: School 459, College preparatory endorsement students 466

Cobb County High Schools

Pope High School

3001 Hembree Rd NE, Marietta, GA 30062
770-509-6077 · Grades 9 - 12

👍

Enrollment:	2,091
White / black / other:	87.6% / 5.6% / 6.8%
Not native English-speaking:	5 / 0.2%
Limited English proficiency:	35 / 1.7%
Student absenteeism:	4.6%
Students per teacher:	17.1
Parent friendliness:	①❷❸④⑤❻
Students in gifted program:	432 / 20.7%
Students in remedial education:	2.6%
High school completion rate:	93.2%
Students held back a grade:	0.9%
Number of dropouts:	22 / 1.0%
Students in alternative programs:	*
Students in special education:	227 / 10.9%
Eligible students, free or reduced lunch:	0.6%

Total suspensions and expulsions:	4
Suspensions only, pct. in-school:	4 / 0.0%
Drugs/alcohol-related offenses:	*
Violence-related offenses:	2
Firearms-related offenses:	*
Vandalism-related offenses:	*
Theft-related offenses:	*
All other disciplinary offenses:	2

Teachers with advanced degrees:	51.2%
Average years' teaching experience:	14.1

AJC GRADE: ★★★

High School Graduation Test

Pct. of students who passed on first try

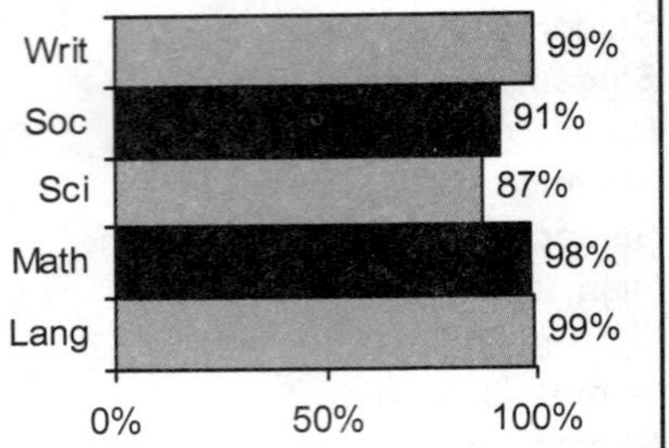

Writ
99%
Soc
91%
Sci
87%
Math
98%
Lang
99%
0%
50%
100%

GHSA classification:	6-AAAAA

Interscholastic sports offered:
BB, BS, CC, CL, FB, GO, LC, SB, SO, SW, TF, VB, WR

Advanced Placement (AP) Exams

Students tested:	102
Tests taken:	204
Pct. of test scores 3 or higher (1 - 5 scale):	84.8%

Languages other than English taught:
French, German, Japanese, Latin, Spanish

2000-2001 high school graduates: 479

College prep/vocational diplomas:	2.7%
College prep endorsement diplomas:	91.4%
Vocational endorsement diplomas:	4.4%
General high school diplomas:	0.0%
Special education diplomas:	0.6%
Certificates of attendance (no diploma):	0.8%

Of the 2000-2001 graduates, 81.2% were eligible for the HOPE scholarship.

Of the 1999-2000 graduates, 251 attended a Georgia public college or university. Of those, 93% met the school's minimum academic requirements.

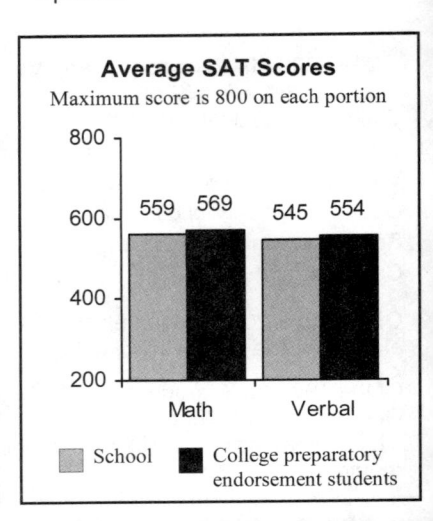

Average SAT Scores

Maximum score is 800 on each portion

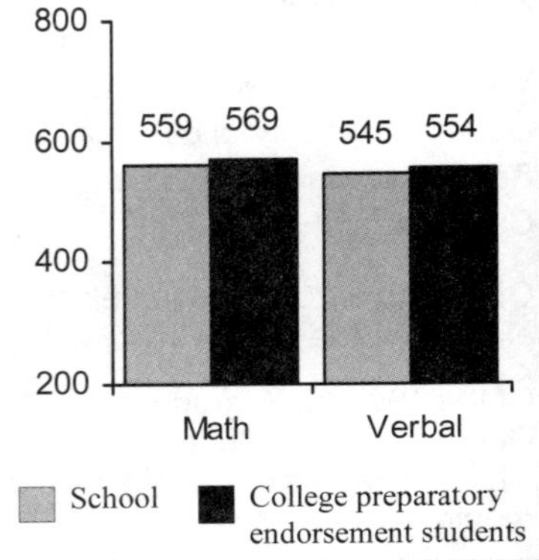

800
600
400
200
559
569
545
554
Math
Verbal
School
College preparatory endorsement students

South Cobb High School

1920 Clay Rd, Austell, GA 30106
770-732-5682 · Grades 9 - 12

Enrollment:	1,700
White / black / other:	53.0% / 37.6% / 9.4%
Not native English-speaking:	21 / 1.2%
Limited English proficiency:	100 / 5.9%
Student absenteeism:	8.5%
Students per teacher:	16.6
Parent friendliness:	① ② **❸** ④ ⑤ **❻**
Students in gifted program:	59 / 3.5%
Students in remedial education:	19.4%
High school completion rate:	79.9%
Students held back a grade:	6.8%
Number of dropouts:	61 / 3.2%
Students in alternative programs:	4 / 0.2%
Students in special education:	216 / 12.7%
Eligible students, free or reduced lunch:	22.0%
Total suspensions and expulsions:	3
Suspensions only, pct. in-school:	3 / 0.0%
Drugs/alcohol-related offenses:	*
Violence-related offenses:	2
Firearms-related offenses:	*
Vandalism-related offenses:	*
Theft-related offenses:	1
All other disciplinary offenses:	*
Teachers with advanced degrees:	45.3%
Average years' teaching experience:	11.2

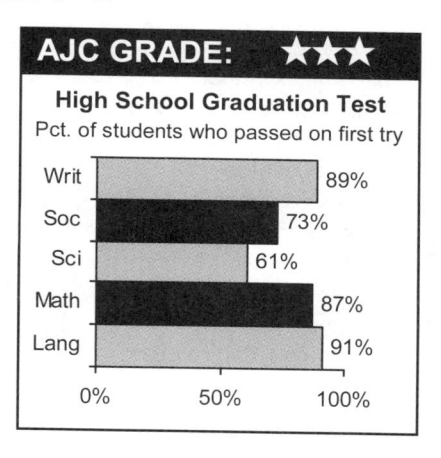

AJC GRADE: ★★★

High School Graduation Test
Pct. of students who passed on first try

- Writ: 89%
- Soc: 73%
- Sci: 61%
- Math: 87%
- Lang: 91%

GHSA classification: 5-AAAAA
Interscholastic sports offered:
BB, BS, CC, CL, FB, GO, RI, SB, SO, SW, TE, TF, VB, WR

Advanced Placement (AP) Exams
- Students tested: 45
- Tests taken: 51
- Pct. of test scores 3 or higher (1 - 5 scale): 45.1%

Languages other than English taught:
French, German, Spanish

2000-2001 high school graduates: 333

College prep/vocational diplomas:	41.4%
College prep endorsement diplomas:	21.6%
Vocational endorsement diplomas:	23.4%
General high school diplomas:	0.0%
Special education diplomas:	5.1%
Certificates of attendance (no diploma):	8.4%

Of the 2000-2001 graduates, 55.0% were eligible for the HOPE scholarship.

Of the 1999-2000 graduates, 101 attended a Georgia public college or university. Of those, 88% met the school's minimum academic requirements.

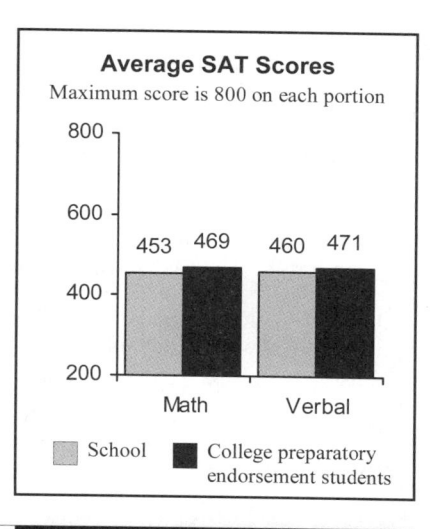

Average SAT Scores
Maximum score is 800 on each portion

- Math: School 453, College preparatory endorsement students 469
- Verbal: School 460, College preparatory endorsement students 471

Cobb County High Schools

Sprayberry High School

2525 Sandy Plains Rd, Marietta, GA 30066
770-509-6111 · Grades 9 - 12

Enrollment:	2,149
White / black / other:	75.3% / 12.4% / 12.3%
Not native English-speaking:	27 / 1.3%
Limited English proficiency:	65 / 3.0%
Student absenteeism:	7.5%
Students per teacher:	16.2
Parent friendliness:	①❷❸④⑤❻
Students in gifted program:	346 / 16.1%
Students in remedial education:	8.5%
High school completion rate:	84.6%
Students held back a grade:	8.7%
Number of dropouts:	64 / 2.8%
Students in alternative programs:	1 / 0.0%
Students in special education:	256 / 11.9%
Eligible students, free or reduced lunch:	6.3%

Total suspensions and expulsions:	7
Suspensions only, pct. in-school:	7 / 0.0%
Drugs/alcohol-related offenses:	*
Violence-related offenses:	2
Firearms-related offenses:	*
Vandalism-related offenses:	*
Theft-related offenses:	1
All other disciplinary offenses:	4

Teachers with advanced degrees:	54.7%
Average years' teaching experience:	14.0

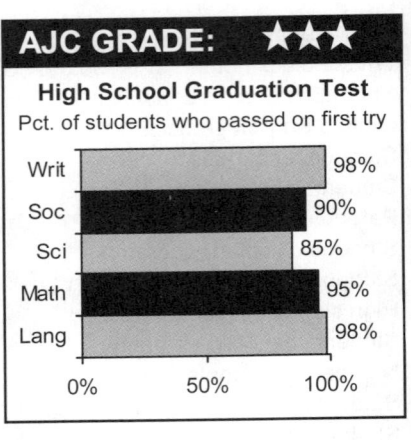

AJC GRADE: ★★★

High School Graduation Test

Pct. of students who passed on first try

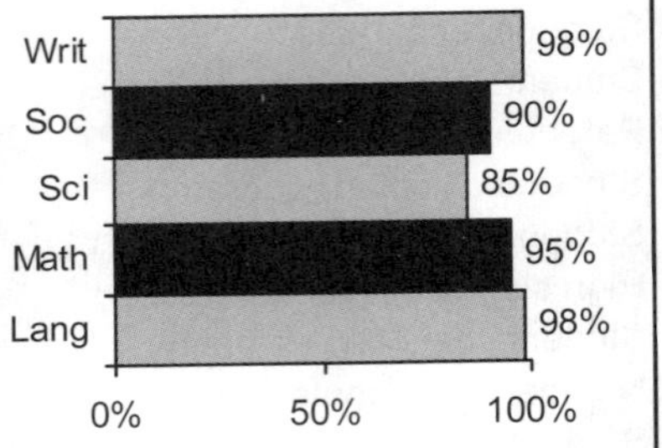

Writ
98%
Soc
90%
Sci
85%
Math
95%
Lang
98%
0%
50%
100%

GHSA classification:	5-AAAAA

Interscholastic sports offered:
BB, BS, CC, CL, FB, GO, GY, LC, SB, SO, SW, TE, TF, VB, WR

Advanced Placement (AP) Exams

Students tested:	133
Tests taken:	283
Pct. of test scores 3 or higher (1 - 5 scale):	64.3%

Languages other than English taught:
French, German, Latin, Spanish

2000-2001 high school graduates: 416

College prep/vocational diplomas:	2.9%
College prep endorsement diplomas:	86.1%
Vocational endorsement diplomas:	8.2%
General high school diplomas:	0.0%
Special education diplomas:	2.4%
Certificates of attendance (no diploma):	0.5%

Of the 2000-2001 graduates, 68.0% were eligible for the HOPE scholarship.

Of the 1999-2000 graduates, 234 attended a Georgia public college or university. Of those, 94% met the school's minimum academic requirements.

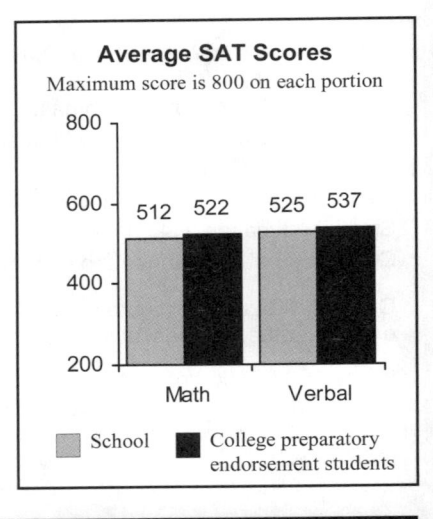

Average SAT Scores

Maximum score is 800 on each portion

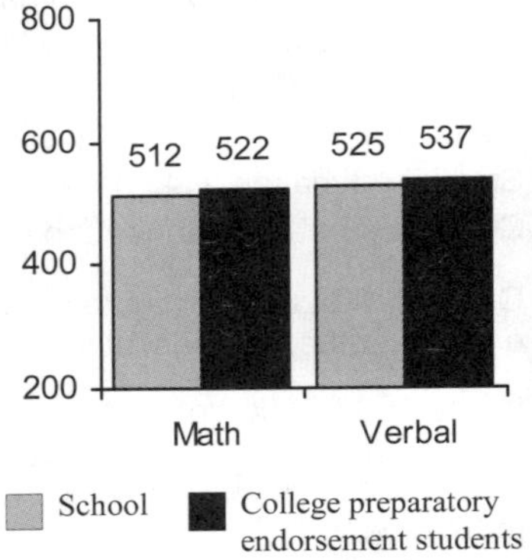

800
600
400
200
512
522
525
537
Math
Verbal
School
College preparatory endorsement students

Walton High School

1590 Bill Murdock Rd, Marietta, GA 30062
770-509-6125 · Grades 9 - 12

Enrollment:	2,344
White / black / other:	86.8% / 3.5% / 9.7%
Not native English-speaking:	27 / 1.2%
Limited English proficiency:	67 / 2.9%
Student absenteeism:	4.1%
Students per teacher:	17.8
Parent friendliness:	①❷❸④⑤❻
Students in gifted program:	462 / 19.7%
Students in remedial education:	1.2%
High school completion rate:	95.8%
Students held back a grade:	1.3%
Number of dropouts:	15 / 0.6%
Students in alternative programs:	*
Students in special education:	244 / 10.4%
Eligible students, free or reduced lunch:	0.3%
Total suspensions and expulsions:	2
Suspensions only, pct. in-school:	2 / 0.0%
Drugs/alcohol-related offenses:	*
Violence-related offenses:	2
Firearms-related offenses:	*
Vandalism-related offenses:	*
Theft-related offenses:	*
All other disciplinary offenses:	*
Teachers with advanced degrees:	60.4%
Average years' teaching experience:	14.6

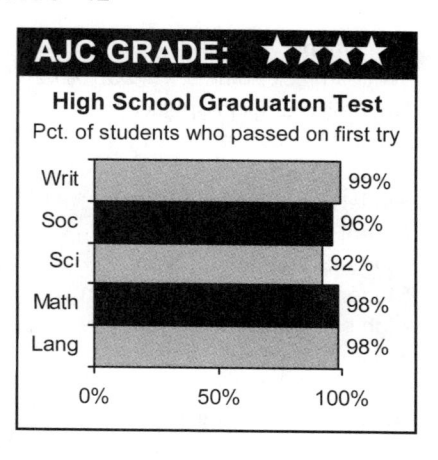

AJC GRADE: ★★★★

High School Graduation Test
Pct. of students who passed on first try

- Writ: 99%
- Soc: 96%
- Sci: 92%
- Math: 98%
- Lang: 98%

GHSA classification:	5-AAAAA

Interscholastic sports offered:
BB, BS, CC, CL, FB, GO, GY, LC, SB, SO, SW, TE, TF, VB, WR

Advanced Placement (AP) Exams
Students tested:	329
Tests taken:	846
Pct. of test scores 3 or higher (1 - 5 scale):	66.1%

Languages other than English taught:
French, Latin, Spanish

2000-2001 high school graduates: 524

College prep/vocational diplomas:	7.3%
College prep endorsement diplomas:	89.1%
Vocational endorsement diplomas:	3.4%
General high school diplomas:	0.0%
Special education diplomas:	0.0%
Certificates of attendance (no diploma):	0.2%

Of the 2000-2001 graduates, 81.5% were eligible for the HOPE scholarship.

Of the 1999-2000 graduates, 237 attended a Georgia public college or university. Of those, 97% met the school's minimum academic requirements.

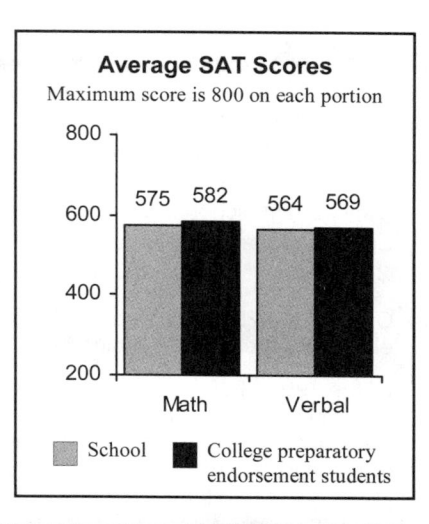

Average SAT Scores
Maximum score is 800 on each portion

- Math: School 575, College preparatory endorsement students 582
- Verbal: School 564, College preparatory endorsement students 569

The Atlanta Journal-Constitution / Page 177

Cobb County High Schools

Wheeler High School

375 Holt Rd NE, Marietta, GA 30068
770-509-6138 · Grades 9 - 12

Enrollment:	1,807
White / black / other:	53.7% / 28.0% / 18.3%
Not native English-speaking:	110 / 6.1%
Limited English proficiency:	234 / 12.9%
Student absenteeism:	6.1%
Students per teacher:	15.8
Parent friendliness:	① ❷ ❸ ④ ⑤ ❻
Students in gifted program:	259 / 14.3%
Students in remedial education:	2.4%
High school completion rate:	86.6%
Students held back a grade:	8.1%
Number of dropouts:	81 / 4.0%
Students in alternative programs:	4 / 0.2%
Students in special education:	146 / 8.1%
Eligible students, free or reduced lunch:	10.0%
Total suspensions and expulsions:	1
Suspensions only, pct. in-school:	1 / 0.0%
Drugs/alcohol-related offenses:	*
Violence-related offenses:	*
Firearms-related offenses:	*
Vandalism-related offenses:	*
Theft-related offenses:	*
All other disciplinary offenses:	1
Teachers with advanced degrees:	50.0%
Average years' teaching experience:	11.9

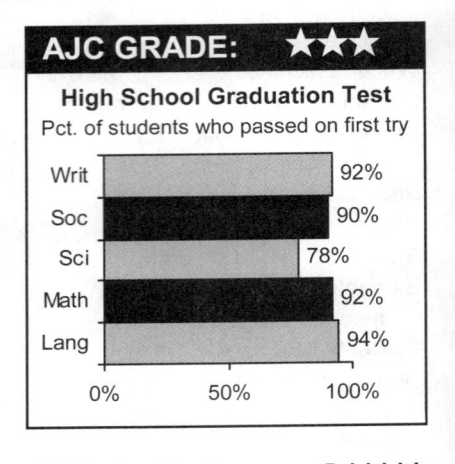

AJC GRADE: ★★★

High School Graduation Test
Pct. of students who passed on first try

- Writ: 92%
- Soc: 90%
- Sci: 78%
- Math: 92%
- Lang: 94%

GHSA classification: 5-AAAAA
Interscholastic sports offered:
BB, BS, CC, CL, FB, GO, SB, SO, SW, TE, TF, VB, WR

Advanced Placement (AP) Exams
- Students tested: 120
- Tests taken: 227
- Pct. of test scores 3 or higher (1 - 5 scale): 68.7%

Languages other than English taught:
French, German, Latin, Spanish

2000-2001 high school graduates: 317

College prep/vocational diplomas:	38.2%
College prep endorsement diplomas:	53.3%
Vocational endorsement diplomas:	3.8%
General high school diplomas:	0.0%
Special education diplomas:	1.6%
Certificates of attendance (no diploma):	3.2%

Of the 2000-2001 graduates, 77.6% were eligible for the HOPE scholarship.

Of the 1999-2000 graduates, 130 attended a Georgia public college or university. Of those, 93% met the school's minimum academic requirements.

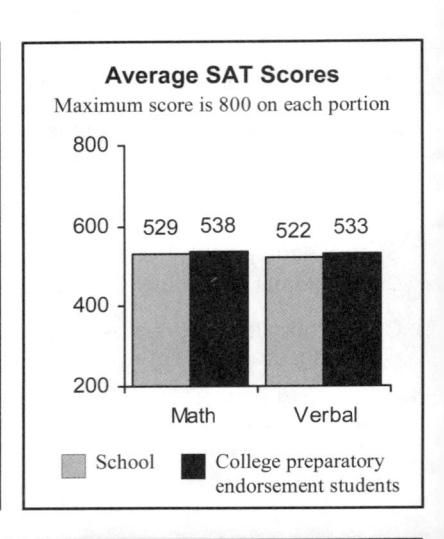

Average SAT Scores
Maximum score is 800 on each portion

- Math — School: 529, College preparatory endorsement students: 538
- Verbal — School: 522, College preparatory endorsement students: 533

Cobb County High Schools

AJC ranking of Cobb County Schools

ELEMENTARY SCHOOLS

AJC Star Grade: ★★★★

Mount Bethel Elementary
Shallowford Falls Elementary
Sope Creek Elementary
Tritt Elementary

AJC Star Grade: ★★★

Addison Elementary
Argyle Elementary
Austell Elementary
Baker Elementary
Bells Ferry Elementary
Belmont Hills Elementary
Big Shanty Elementary
Blackwell Elementary
Bryant Elementary
Chalker Elementary
Cheatham Hill Elementary
Clay Elementary
Compton Elementary
Davis Elementary
Dowell Elementary
Due West Elementary
East Side Elementary
Eastvalley Elementary
Ford Elementary
Frey Elementary
Garrison Mill Elementary
Green Acres Elementary
Harmony Leland Elementary
Hayes Elementary
Hollydale Elementary
Keheley Elementary
Kennesaw Elementary
Kincaid Elementary
LaBelle Elementary
Lewis Elementary
Mableton Elementary
Mountain View Elementary
Murdock Elementary
Nicholson Elementary
Norton Park Elementary
Powder Springs Elementary
Riverside Elementary
Rocky Mount Elementary
Sedalia Park Elementary
Sky View Elementary
Still Elementary
Teasley Elementary
Timber Ridge Elementary
Varner Elementary
Vaughan Elementary

AJC Star Grade: ★★

Acworth Elementary
Birney Elementary
Brown Elementary
Brumby Elementary
Clarkdale Elementary
King Springs Elementary
Milford Elementary
Nickajack Elementary
Powers Ferry Elementary
Russell Elementary
Sanders Elementary

AJC Star Grade: ★

Fair Oaks Elementary

AJC ranking of Cobb County Schools

MIDDLE SCHOOLS

AJC Star Grade: ★★★★

Dickerson Middle
Dodgen Middle
Hightower Trail Middle
Mabry Middle
Simpson Middle

AJC Star Grade: ★★★

Awtrey Middle
Campbell Middle
Daniell Middle
Durham Middle
East Cobb Middle
Floyd Middle
Griffin Middle
Lindley Middle
Lost Mountain Middle
McCleskey Middle
Pine Mountain Middle
Smitha Middle
Tapp Middle

AJC Star Grade: ★★

Garrett Middle

HIGH SCHOOLS

AJC Star Grade: ★★★★

Walton High

AJC Star Grade: ★★★

Campbell High
Harrison High
Kennesaw Mountain High
Lassiter High
McEachern High
North Cobb High
Pope High
South Cobb High
Sprayberry High
Wheeler High

AJC Star Grade: ★★

Osborne High
Pebblebrook High

Cobb County Public Schools

Coweta County Public Schools

237 Jackson St, Newnan, GA 30263
Phone: 770-254-2801 · Fax: 770-254-2807
http://www.coweta.k12.ga.us

The following pages provide detailed information on every school in the Coweta County school district. An asterisk (*) means the value of the data was zero or was not reported by the school district. A complete list of schools ranked by The Atlanta Journal-Constitution's star rating system follows the detailed school reports.

District enrollment:	16,295
White / black / other:	72.3% / 24.4% / 3.2%
Not native English-speaking:	89 / 0.5%
Expenditure per student (general fund):	$5,856
Students per teacher:	15.3
Teachers with advanced degrees:	48.2%
Average years, teaching experience:	11.2
Average teacher salary:	$41,715.82
Students in gifted program:	1,305 / 8.0%
Students held back a grade:	536 / 3.3%
Eligible students, free or reduced lunch:	4,649 / 27.7%
Number of dropouts (grades 9-12):	151 / 3.1%
High school completion rate:	66.9%
Graduates, pct. eligible for HOPE scholarships:	732 / 60.8%
Average combined SAT score (maximum 1,600):	995
Pct. of 11th-graders passing the Georgia High School Graduation Tests on first try:	68%
Percent of children 5 to 17 years of age living in poverty (2000 Census estimate):	9.4%

Arbor Springs Elementary School

4840 Highway 29 N, Newnan, GA 30265
770-463-5903 · Grades K - 5

Enrollment:	520
White / black / other:	81.0% / 13.3% / 5.8%
Not native English-speaking:	*
Limited English proficiency:	22 / 4.2%
Student absenteeism:	4.6%
Students per teacher:	16.5
Parent friendliness:	❶②③④⑤⑥
Teachers with advanced degrees:	50.0%
Average years' teaching experience:	7.3
Students in gifted program:	32 / 6.2%
Students in remedial education:	8.3%
Students held back a grade:	4.4%
Total suspensions, pct. in-school:	*
Offenses: violence: *, drugs: *, other:	*
Eligible students, free or reduced lunch:	34.0%
Before / after school program:	No / Yes

Students at this school generally go on to:
Madras Middle

AJC GRADE: ★★★

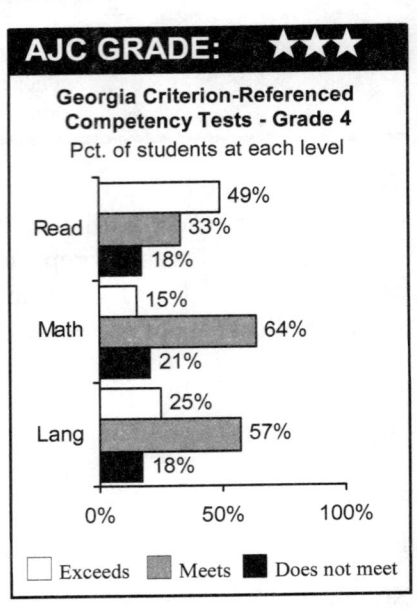

Georgia Criterion-Referenced Competency Tests - Grade 4
Pct. of students at each level

Read: Exceeds 49%, Meets 33%, Does not meet 18%
Math: Exceeds 15%, Meets 64%, Does not meet 21%
Lang: Exceeds 25%, Meets 57%, Does not meet 18%

Arnco-Sargent Elementary School

2449 Highway 16 W, Newnan, GA 30263
770-254-2830 · Grades K - 5

Enrollment:	435
White / black / other:	87.8% / 9.7% / 2.5%
Not native English-speaking:	*
Limited English proficiency:	3 / 0.7%
Student absenteeism:	4.9%
Students per teacher:	13.8
Parent friendliness:	❶❷❸④❺❻
Teachers with advanced degrees:	46.9%
Average years' teaching experience:	13.7
Students in gifted program:	29 / 6.7%
Students in remedial education:	25.2%
Students held back a grade:	1.4%
Total suspensions, pct. in-school:	1 / 0.0%
Offenses: violence: *, drugs: *, other:	1
Eligible students, free or reduced lunch:	41.4%
Before / after school program:	No / Yes

Students at this school generally go on to:
Evans Middle

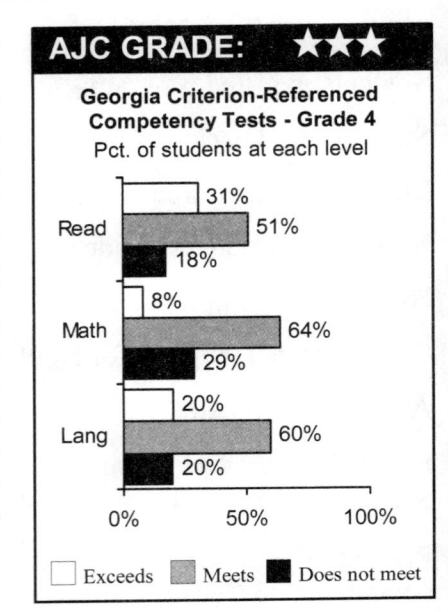

AJC GRADE: ★★★

Georgia Criterion-Referenced Competency Tests - Grade 4
Pct. of students at each level

Read: Exceeds 31%, Meets 51%, Does not meet 18%
Math: Exceeds 8%, Meets 64%, Does not meet 29%
Lang: Exceeds 20%, Meets 60%, Does not meet 20%

Coweta County Elementary Schools

Atkinson Elementary School

14 Nimmons St, Newnan, GA 30263
770-254-2835 · Grades K - 5

Enrollment:	398
White / black / other:	53.8% / 42.5% / 3.8%
Not native English-speaking:	*
Limited English proficiency:	1 / 0.3%
Student absenteeism:	3.9%
Students per teacher:	13.0
Parent friendliness:	❶❷❸④❺❻
Teachers with advanced degrees:	46.9%
Average years' teaching experience:	8.8
Students in gifted program:	35 / 8.8%
Students in remedial education:	26.4%
Students held back a grade:	2.8%
Total suspensions, pct. in-school:	6 / 33.3%
Offenses: violence: 3, drugs: *, other: 7	
Eligible students, free or reduced lunch:	53.0%
Before / after school program:	No / Yes
Students at this school generally go on to: Smokey Road Middle	

AJC GRADE: ★★★

Georgia Criterion-Referenced Competency Tests - Grade 4
Pct. of students at each level

Read: 27% Exceeds, 46% Meets, 27% Does not meet
Math: 15% Exceeds, 49% Meets, 36% Does not meet
Lang: 17% Exceeds, 54% Meets, 29% Does not meet

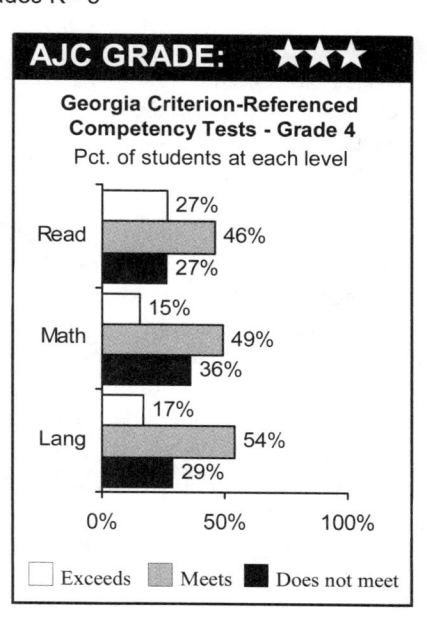

Canongate Elementary School

200 Petes Rd, Sharpsburg, GA 30277
770-463-8010 · Grades K - 5

Enrollment:	573
White / black / other:	89.2% / 6.3% / 4.5%
Not native English-speaking:	*
Limited English proficiency:	2 / 0.3%
Student absenteeism:	3.6%
Students per teacher:	16.4
Parent friendliness:	❶❷❸④❺❻
Teachers with advanced degrees:	54.3%
Average years' teaching experience:	10.4
Students in gifted program:	48 / 8.4%
Students in remedial education:	15.3%
Students held back a grade:	1.9%
Total suspensions, pct. in-school:	2 / 0.0%
Offenses: violence: 1, drugs: *, other: 1	
Eligible students, free or reduced lunch:	6.6%
Before / after school program:	Yes / Yes
Students at this school generally go on to: Madras Middle	

AJC GRADE: ★★★

Georgia Criterion-Referenced Competency Tests - Grade 4
Pct. of students at each level

Read: 47% Exceeds, 46% Meets, 8% Does not meet
Math: 10% Exceeds, 71% Meets, 20% Does not meet
Lang: 28% Exceeds, 67% Meets, 4% Does not meet

The Atlanta Journal-Constitution / Page 183

Coweta County Elementary Schools

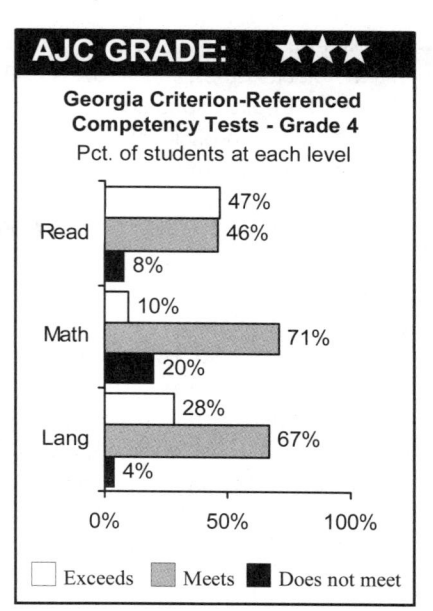

Eastside Elementary School

👎

1225 Eastside School Rd, Senoia, GA 30276
770-599-6621 · Grades K - 5

Enrollment:	632
White / black / other:	74.2% / 23.6% / 2.2%
Not native English-speaking:	*
Limited English proficiency:	2 / 0.3%
Student absenteeism:	4.8%
Students per teacher:	14.5
Parent friendliness:	❶❷❸④⑤❻
Teachers with advanced degrees:	34.1%
Average years' teaching experience:	9.7
Students in gifted program:	15 / 2.4%
Students in remedial education:	25.3%
Students held back a grade:	4.7%
Total suspensions, pct. in-school:	26 / 61.5%
Offenses:	violence: 20, drugs: * , other: 11
Eligible students, free or reduced lunch:	34.5%
Before / after school program:	Yes / Yes

Students at this school generally go on to:
East Coweta Middle

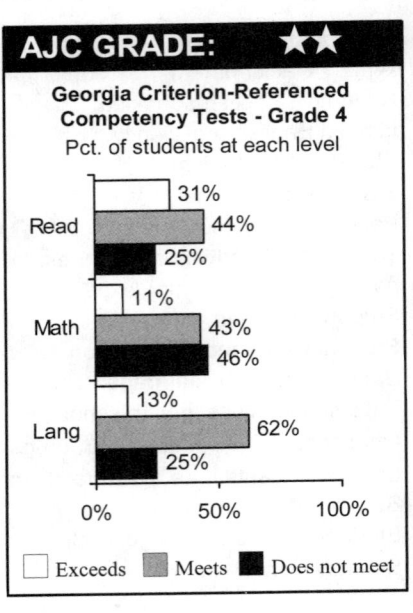

AJC GRADE: ★★

Georgia Criterion-Referenced Competency Tests - Grade 4
Pct. of students at each level

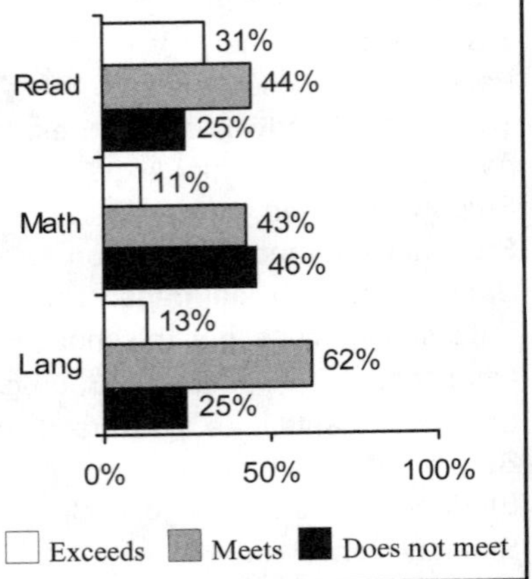
Read
31%
44%
25%
Math
11%
43%
46%
Lang
13%
62%
25%
0%
50%
100%
Exceeds
Meets
Does not meet

Elm Street Elementary School

46 Elm St, Newnan, GA 30263
770-254-2865 · Grades K - 5

Enrollment:	429
White / black / other:	66.2% / 30.3% / 3.5%
Not native English-speaking:	*
Limited English proficiency:	15 / 3.5%
Student absenteeism:	4.0%
Students per teacher:	12.8
Parent friendliness:	❶❷❸④❺❻
Teachers with advanced degrees:	44.1%
Average years' teaching experience:	15.7
Students in gifted program:	22 / 5.1%
Students in remedial education:	18.0%
Students held back a grade:	1.2%
Total suspensions, pct. in-school:	5 / 60.0%
Offenses:	violence: * , drugs: * , other: 9
Eligible students, free or reduced lunch:	34.9%
Before / after school program:	Yes / Yes

Students at this school generally go on to:
O.P. Evans Middle

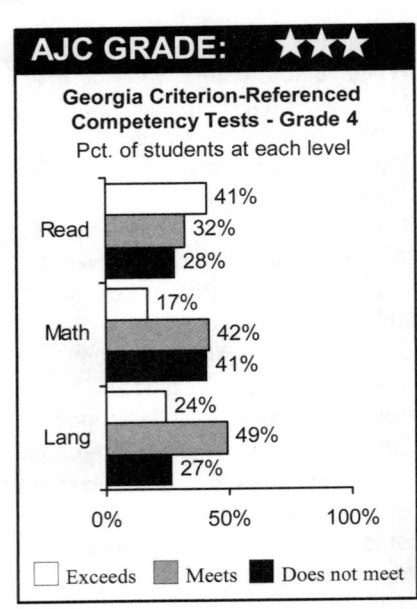

AJC GRADE: ★★★

Georgia Criterion-Referenced Competency Tests - Grade 4
Pct. of students at each level

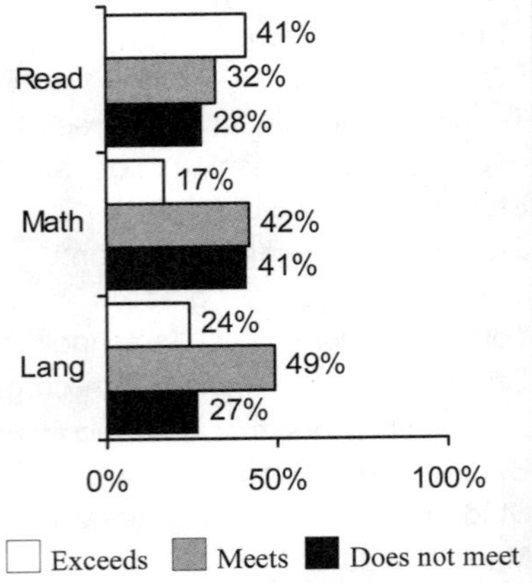
Read
41%
32%
28%
Math
17%
42%
41%
Lang
24%
49%
27%
0%
50%
100%
Exceeds
Meets
Does not meet

Jefferson Parkway Elementary School

154 Millard Farmer Ind Blvd, Newnan, GA 30263
770-254-2771 · Grades K - 5

Enrollment:	377
White / black / other:	47.2% / 42.7% / 10.1%
Not native English-speaking:	32 / 8.5%
Limited English proficiency:	60 / 15.9%
Student absenteeism:	5.6%
Students per teacher:	9.2
Parent friendliness:	① ❷ ❸ ④ ❺ ❻
Teachers with advanced degrees:	50.0%
Average years' teaching experience:	9.2
Students in gifted program:	3 / 0.8%
Students in remedial education:	28.3%
Students held back a grade:	1.1%
Total suspensions, pct. in-school:	*
Offenses: violence: *, drugs: *, other: *	
Eligible students, free or reduced lunch:	52.9%
Before / after school program:	No / Yes

Students at this school generally go on to:
Arnall, O.P. Evans, Smokey Road Middle

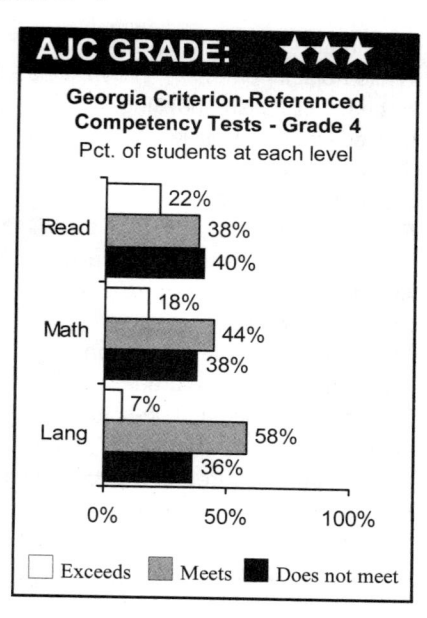

AJC GRADE: ★★★

Georgia Criterion-Referenced Competency Tests - Grade 4
Pct. of students at each level

- Read: Exceeds 22%, Meets 38%, Does not meet 40%
- Math: Exceeds 18%, Meets 44%, Does not meet 38%
- Lang: Exceeds 7%, Meets 58%, Does not meet 36%

Moreland Elementary School

145 Railroad St, Moreland, GA 30259
770-254-2875 · Grades K - 5

Enrollment:	570
White / black / other:	85.4% / 13.9% / 0.7%
Not native English-speaking:	*
Limited English proficiency:	3 / 0.5%
Student absenteeism:	4.1%
Students per teacher:	16.8
Parent friendliness:	❶ ❷ ❸ ④ ⑤ ❻
Teachers with advanced degrees:	38.2%
Average years' teaching experience:	13.8
Students in gifted program:	34 / 6.0%
Students in remedial education:	12.6%
Students held back a grade:	3.9%
Total suspensions, pct. in-school:	11 / 90.9%
Offenses: violence: 19, drugs: *, other: 5	
Eligible students, free or reduced lunch:	31.7%
Before / after school program:	No / Yes

Students at this school generally go on to:
Smokey Road Middle

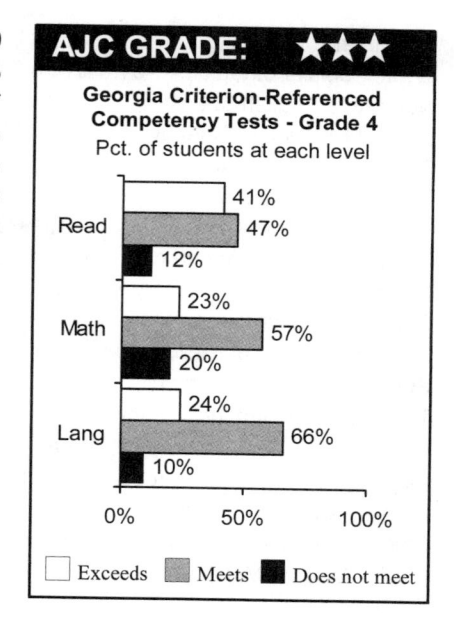

AJC GRADE: ★★★

Georgia Criterion-Referenced Competency Tests - Grade 4
Pct. of students at each level

- Read: Exceeds 41%, Meets 47%, Does not meet 12%
- Math: Exceeds 23%, Meets 57%, Does not meet 20%
- Lang: Exceeds 24%, Meets 66%, Does not meet 10%

Coweta County Elementary Schools

Newnan Crossing Elementary School

1267 Lower Fayetteville Rd, Newnan, GA 30265
770-254-2872 · Grades K - 5

Enrollment:	682
White / black / other:	56.7% / 39.1% / 4.1%
Not native English-speaking:	*
Limited English proficiency:	5 / 0.7%
Student absenteeism:	4.6%
Students per teacher:	12.4
Parent friendliness:	❶❷❸④❺❻
Teachers with advanced degrees:	42.9%
Average years' teaching experience:	8.7
Students in gifted program:	54 / 7.9%
Students in remedial education:	16.6%
Students held back a grade:	1.0%
Total suspensions, pct. in-school:	41 / 61.0%
Offenses:	violence: 57, drugs: * , other: 1
Eligible students, free or reduced lunch:	42.2%
Before / after school program:	Yes / Yes

Students at this school generally go on to:
Arnall, East Coweta Middle

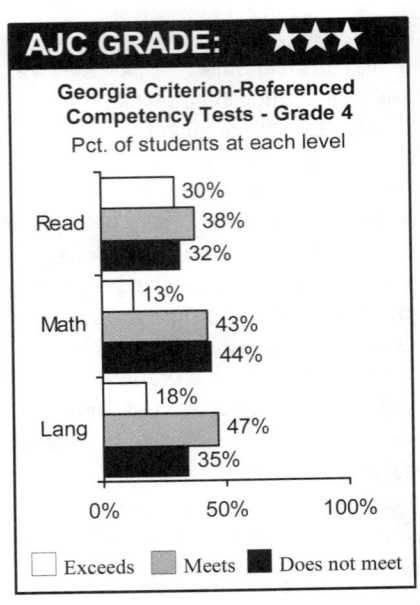

AJC GRADE: ★★★

Georgia Criterion-Referenced Competency Tests - Grade 4
Pct. of students at each level

Read: Exceeds 30%, Meets 38%, Does not meet 32%
Math: Exceeds 13%, Meets 43%, Does not meet 44%
Lang: Exceeds 18%, Meets 47%, Does not meet 35%

Northside Elementary School

720 Country Club Rd, Newnan, GA 30263
770-254-2890 · Grades K - 5

Enrollment:	405
White / black / other:	61.0% / 30.6% / 8.4%
Not native English-speaking:	26 / 6.4%
Limited English proficiency:	46 / 11.4%
Student absenteeism:	4.1%
Students per teacher:	14.2
Parent friendliness:	❶❷❸④❺❻
Teachers with advanced degrees:	55.2%
Average years' teaching experience:	11.4
Students in gifted program:	36 / 8.9%
Students in remedial education:	8.6%
Students held back a grade:	2.5%
Total suspensions, pct. in-school:	2 / 50.0%
Offenses:	violence: 2, drugs: * , other: *
Eligible students, free or reduced lunch:	32.5%
Before / after school program:	Yes / Yes

Students at this school generally go on to:
Evans, Madras Middle

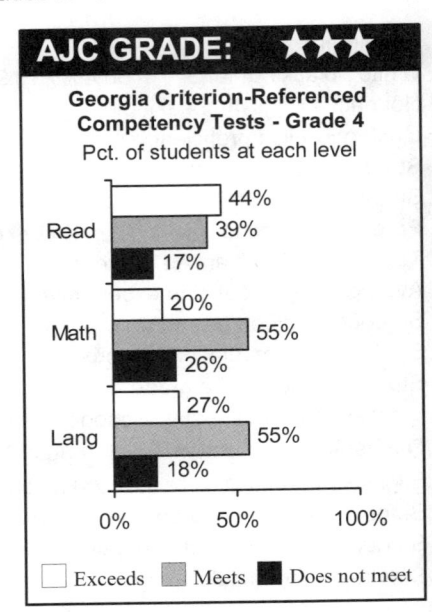

AJC GRADE: ★★★

Georgia Criterion-Referenced Competency Tests - Grade 4
Pct. of students at each level

Read: Exceeds 44%, Meets 39%, Does not meet 17%
Math: Exceeds 20%, Meets 55%, Does not meet 26%
Lang: Exceeds 27%, Meets 55%, Does not meet 18%

Coweta County Elementary Schools

Poplar Road Elementary School

2925 Poplar Rd, Sharpsburg, GA 30277
770-254-2740 · Grades K - 5

Enrollment:	731
White / black / other:	68.5% / 27.8% / 3.7%
Not native English-speaking:	*
Limited English proficiency:	11 / 1.5%
Student absenteeism:	4.9%
Students per teacher:	13.8
Parent friendliness:	❶❷❸④❺❻
Teachers with advanced degrees:	43.4%
Average years' teaching experience:	7.9
Students in gifted program:	34 / 4.7%
Students in remedial education:	12.8%
Students held back a grade:	2.9%
Total suspensions, pct. in-school:	44 / 97.7%
Offenses: violence: 58, drugs: *, other: 10	
Eligible students, free or reduced lunch:	34.6%
Before / after school program:	No / Yes
Students at this school generally go on to: Arnall, East Coweta Middle	

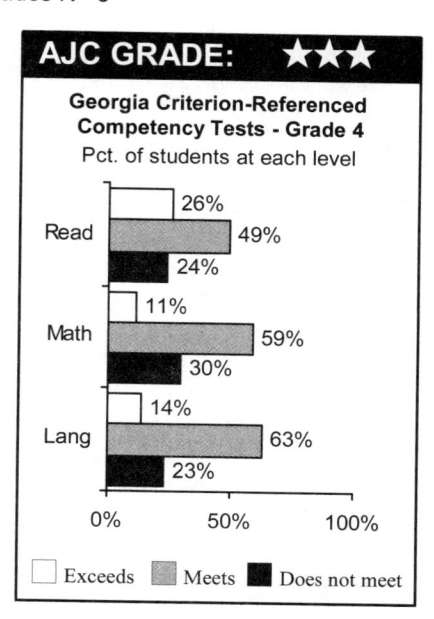

AJC GRADE: ★★★

Georgia Criterion-Referenced Competency Tests - Grade 4
Pct. of students at each level

- Read: Exceeds 26%, Meets 49%, Does not meet 24%
- Math: Exceeds 11%, Meets 59%, Does not meet 30%
- Lang: Exceeds 14%, Meets 63%, Does not meet 23%

Ruth Hill Elementary School

57 Sunset Ln, Newnan, GA 30263
770-254-2895 · Grades K - 5

Enrollment:	413
White / black / other:	21.8% / 76.5% / 1.7%
Not native English-speaking:	*
Limited English proficiency:	3 / 0.7%
Student absenteeism:	3.3%
Students per teacher:	12.7
Parent friendliness:	①❷❸④❺❻
Teachers with advanced degrees:	51.5%
Average years' teaching experience:	11.1
Students in gifted program:	15 / 3.6%
Students in remedial education:	31.3%
Students held back a grade:	4.4%
Total suspensions, pct. in-school:	*
Offenses: violence: *, drugs: *, other: *	
Eligible students, free or reduced lunch:	74.1%
Before / after school program:	No / Yes
Students at this school generally go on to: O.P. Evans, Smokey Road Middle	

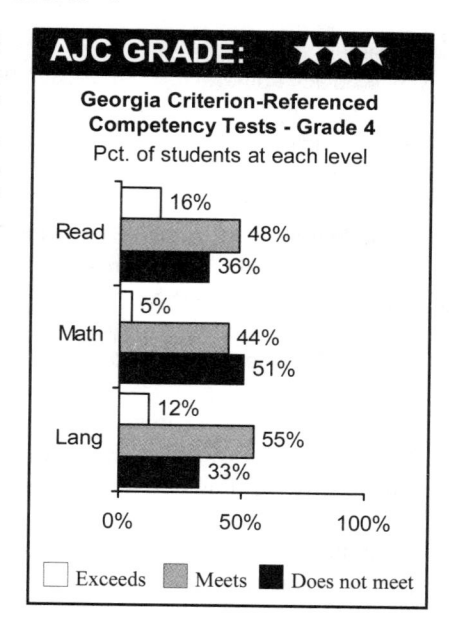

AJC GRADE: ★★★

Georgia Criterion-Referenced Competency Tests - Grade 4
Pct. of students at each level

- Read: Exceeds 16%, Meets 48%, Does not meet 36%
- Math: Exceeds 5%, Meets 44%, Does not meet 51%
- Lang: Exceeds 12%, Meets 55%, Does not meet 33%

Coweta County Elementary Schools

Thomas Crossroads Elementary School

3530 Highway 34 E, Sharpsburg, GA 30277
770-254-2751 · Grades K - 5

Enrollment:	689
White / black / other:	89.7% / 7.7% / 2.6%
Not native English-speaking:	*
Limited English proficiency:	4 / 0.6%
Student absenteeism:	3.6%
Students per teacher:	17.4
Parent friendliness:	①②❸④⑤❻
Teachers with advanced degrees:	47.5%
Average years' teaching experience:	13.5
Students in gifted program:	46 / 6.7%
Students in remedial education:	8.2%
Students held back a grade:	4.9%
Total suspensions, pct. in-school:	*
Offenses:	violence: * , drugs: * , other: *
Eligible students, free or reduced lunch:	6.2%
Before / after school program:	No / Yes

Students at this school generally go on to:
Arnall, East Coweta, Madras Middle

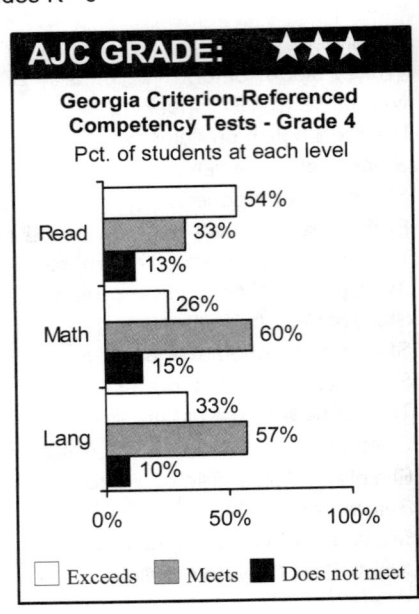

AJC GRADE: ★★★

Georgia Criterion-Referenced Competency Tests - Grade 4
Pct. of students at each level

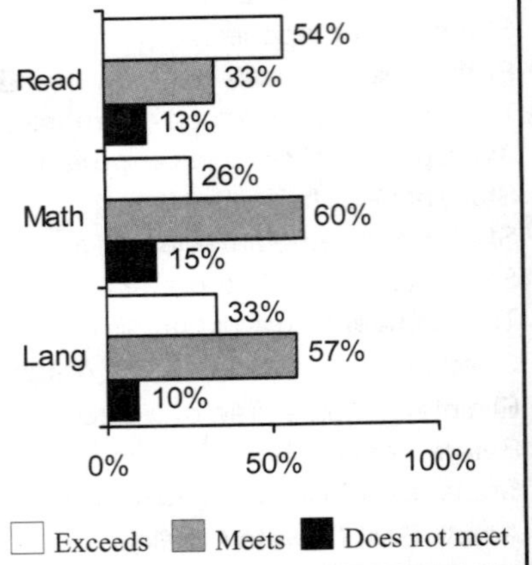
Read
54%
33%
13%
Math
26%
60%
15%
Lang
33%
57%
10%
0%
50%
100%
Exceeds
Meets
Does not meet

Western Elementary School

1730 Welcome Rd, Newnan, GA 30263
770-254-2790 · Grades K - 5

Enrollment:	446
White / black / other:	86.8% / 11.0% / 2.2%
Not native English-speaking:	*
Limited English proficiency:	4 / 0.9%
Student absenteeism:	4.7%
Students per teacher:	13.5
Parent friendliness:	❶❷❸④⑤❻
Teachers with advanced degrees:	45.5%
Average years' teaching experience:	11.0
Students in gifted program:	24 / 5.4%
Students in remedial education:	16.6%
Students held back a grade:	3.4%
Total suspensions, pct. in-school:	7 / 42.9%
Offenses:	violence: 1, drugs: 1, other: 13
Eligible students, free or reduced lunch:	29.9%
Before / after school program:	Yes / Yes

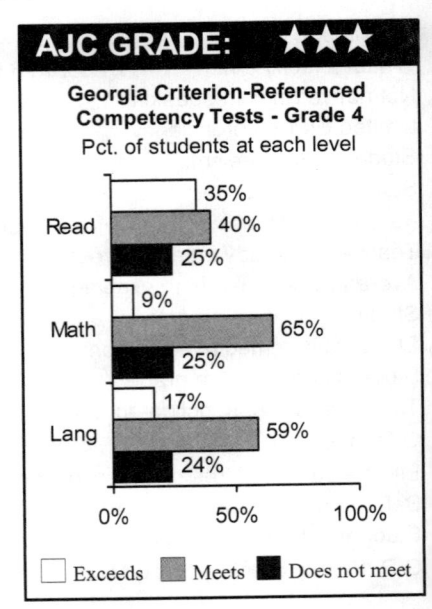

Students at this school generally go on to:
Smokey Road Middle

AJC GRADE: ★★★

Georgia Criterion-Referenced Competency Tests - Grade 4
Pct. of students at each level

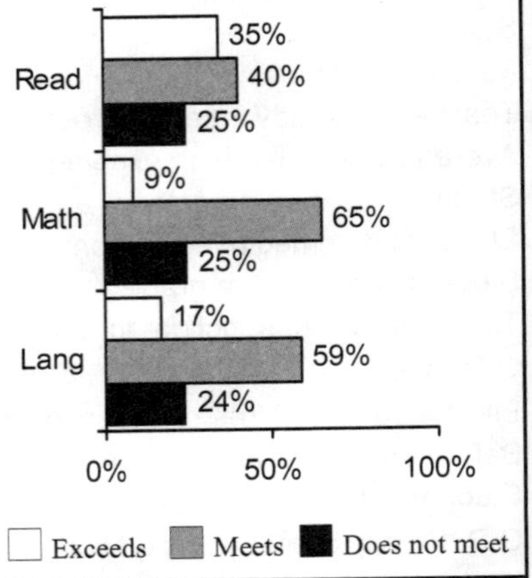
Read
35%
40%
25%
Math
9%
65%
25%
Lang
17%
59%
24%
0%
50%
100%
Exceeds
Meets
Does not meet

White Oak Elementary School

770 Lora Smith Rd, Newnan, GA 30265
770-254-2860 · Grades K - 5

Enrollment: 770
White / black / other: 81.2% / 14.2% / 4.7%
Not native English-speaking: *
Limited English proficiency: 1 / 0.1%
Student absenteeism: 3.5%
Students per teacher: 15.7
Parent friendliness: ❶❷❸❹❺❻
Teachers with advanced degrees: 61.2%
Average years' teaching experience: 13.4
Students in gifted program: 78 / 10.1%
Students in remedial education: 8.9%
Students held back a grade: 2.1%
Total suspensions, pct. in-school: 8 / 0.0%
Offenses: violence: 4, drugs: *, other: 5
Eligible students, free or reduced lunch: 14.5%
Before / after school program: No / Yes
Students at this school generally go on to:
Arnall, East Coweta Middle

AJC GRADE: ★★★

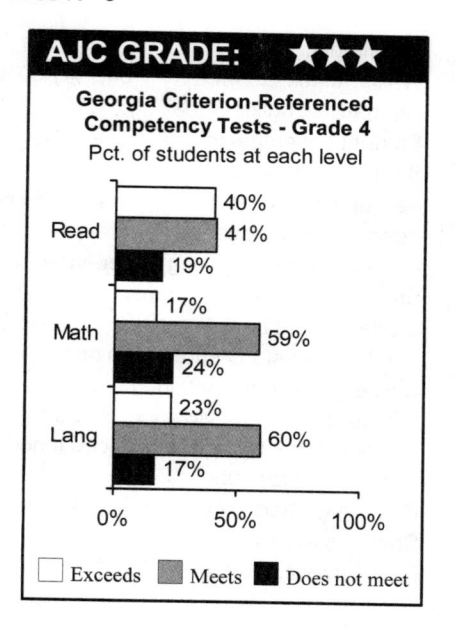

Georgia Criterion-Referenced Competency Tests - Grade 4
Pct. of students at each level

Read: 40% / 41% / 19%
Math: 17% / 59% / 24%
Lang: 23% / 60% / 17%

☐ Exceeds ▨ Meets ■ Does not meet

Coweta County Elementary Schools

Arnall Middle School

700 Lora Smith Rd, Newnan, GA 30265
770-254-2765 · Grades 6 - 8

Enrollment:	883
White / black / other:	64.7% / 30.4% / 5.0%
Not native English-speaking:	19 / 2.2%
Student absenteeism:	5.1%
Students per teacher:	16.7
Parent friendliness:	❶❷❸④⑤❻
Teachers with advanced degrees:	60.4%
Average years' teaching experience:	11.7
Students in gifted program:	114 / 12.9%
Students held back a grade:	1.8%
Total suspensions and expulsions:	5
Suspensions only, pct. in-school:	5 / 40.0%
Offenses:	violence: 6, drugs: * , other: 1
Eligible students, free or reduced lunch:	28.8%
Number of dropouts:	8 / 0.8%
Pct. 8th-graders w/ basic computer skills:	85.0%

Students at this school generally go on to:
East Coweta, Northgate High

AJC GRADE: ★★★

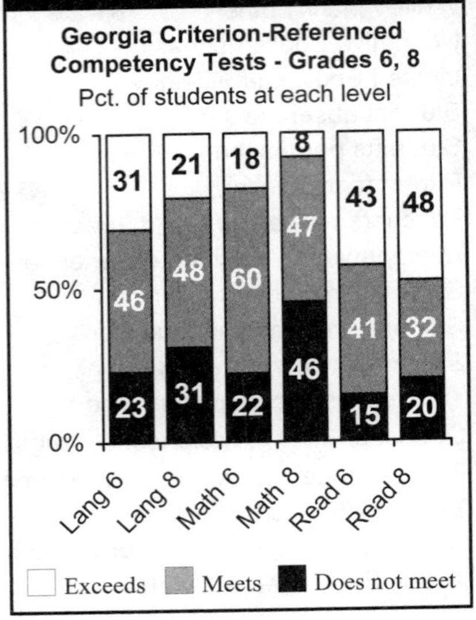
Georgia Criterion-Referenced
Competency Tests - Grades 6, 8
Pct. of students at each level
100%
50%
0%
31
46
23
21
48
31
18
60
22
8
47
46
43
41
15
48
32
20
Lang 6
Lang 8
Math 6
Math 8
Read 6
Read 8
Exceeds
Meets
Does not meet

East Coweta Middle School

6291 Highway 16, Senoia, GA 30276
770-599-6607 · Grades 6 - 8

Enrollment:	797
White / black / other:	78.2% / 18.7% / 3.1%
Not native English-speaking:	*
Student absenteeism:	4.7%
Students per teacher:	17.1
Parent friendliness:	❶❷❸④❺❻
Teachers with advanced degrees:	44.7%
Average years' teaching experience:	9.8
Students in gifted program:	88 / 11.0%
Students held back a grade:	0.5%
Total suspensions and expulsions:	*
Suspensions only, pct. in-school:	*
Offenses:	violence: * , drugs: * , other: *
Eligible students, free or reduced lunch:	24.1%
Number of dropouts:	2 / 0.2%
Pct. 8th-graders w/ basic computer skills:	96.0%

Students at this school generally go on to:
East Coweta High

AJC GRADE: ★★★

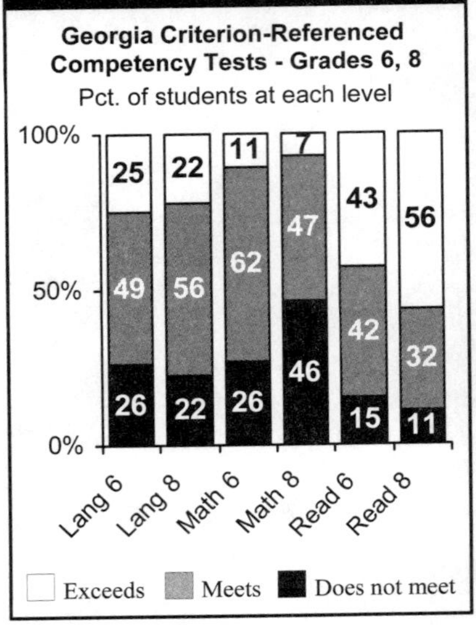
Georgia Criterion-Referenced
Competency Tests - Grades 6, 8
Pct. of students at each level
100%
50%
0%
25
49
26
22
56
22
11
62
26
7
47
46
43
42
15
56
32
11
Lang 6
Lang 8
Math 6
Math 8
Read 6
Read 8
Exceeds
Meets
Does not meet

Evans Middle School

1 Evans Dr, Newnan, GA 30263
770-254-2780 · Grades 6 - 8

Enrollment:	717
White / black / other:	66.1% / 31.9% / 2.0%
Not native English-speaking:	*
Student absenteeism:	5.6%
Students per teacher:	14.8
Parent friendliness:	❶❷❸④⑤❻
Teachers with advanced degrees:	61.2%
Average years' teaching experience:	13.1
Students in gifted program:	92 / 12.8%
Students held back a grade:	3.5%
Total suspensions and expulsions:	2
Suspensions only, pct. in-school:	2 / 0.0%
Offenses: violence: 3, drugs: *, other: 3	
Eligible students, free or reduced lunch:	39.9%
Number of dropouts:	11 / 1.4%
Pct. 8th-graders w/ basic computer skills:	84.8%

Students at this school generally go on to:
Newnan, Northgate High

AJC GRADE: ★★★

Georgia Criterion-Referenced Competency Tests - Grades 6, 8
Pct. of students at each level

	Lang 6	Lang 8	Math 6	Math 8	Read 6	Read 8
Exceeds	21	30	14	13	43	54
Meets	48	43	56	50	35	26
Does not meet	30	28	30	36	23	20

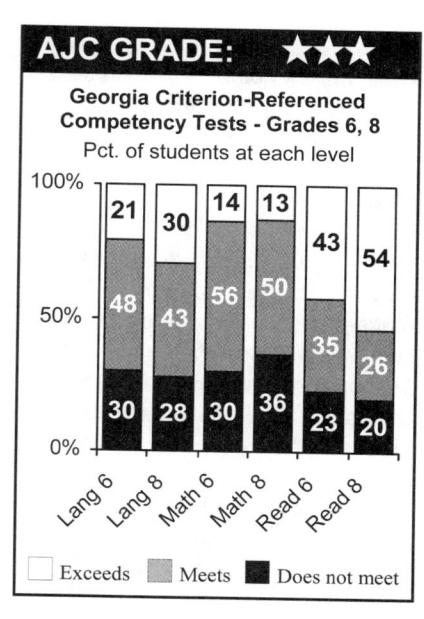

Madras Middle School

240 Edgeworth Rd, Newnan, GA 30263
770-254-2744 · Grades 6 - 8

Enrollment:	724
White / black / other:	85.8% / 10.9% / 3.3%
Not native English-speaking:	*
Student absenteeism:	4.6%
Students per teacher:	17.7
Parent friendliness:	❶❷❸④⑤❻
Teachers with advanced degrees:	47.6%
Average years' teaching experience:	10.5
Students in gifted program:	94 / 13.0%
Students held back a grade:	1.0%
Total suspensions and expulsions:	16
Suspensions only, pct. in-school:	16 / 12.5%
Offenses: violence: 4, drugs: 7, other: 5	
Eligible students, free or reduced lunch:	17.3%
Number of dropouts:	*
Pct. 8th-graders w/ basic computer skills:	92.0%

Students at this school generally go on to:
Northgate High

AJC GRADE: ★★★

Georgia Criterion-Referenced Competency Tests - Grades 6, 8
Pct. of students at each level

	Lang 6	Lang 8	Math 6	Math 8	Read 6	Read 8
Exceeds	26	35	28	14	52	59
Meets	53	46	53	53	35	29
Does not meet	21	19	19	34	13	12

Coweta County Middle Schools

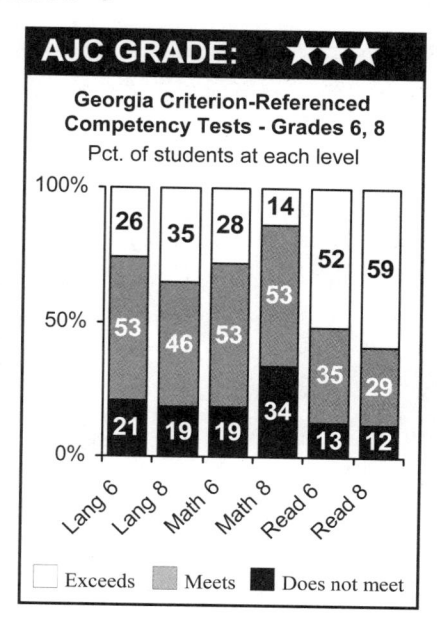

Smokey Road Middle School

965 Smokey Rd, Newnan, GA 30263
770-254-2840 · Grades 6 - 8

Enrollment:	792
White / black / other:	66.9% / 31.3% / 1.8%
Not native English-speaking:	*
Student absenteeism:	5.9%
Students per teacher:	15.3
Parent friendliness:	❶❷❸④❺❻
Teachers with advanced degrees:	30.8%
Average years' teaching experience:	10.9
Students in gifted program:	53 / 6.7%
Students held back a grade:	2.8%
Total suspensions and expulsions:	56
Suspensions only, pct. in-school:	56 / 32.1%
Offenses:	violence: 29, drugs: 6, other: 27
Eligible students, free or reduced lunch:	38.4%
Number of dropouts:	4 / 0.4%
Pct. 8th-graders w/ basic computer skills:	80.0%

Students at this school generally go on to:
East Coweta, Newnan High

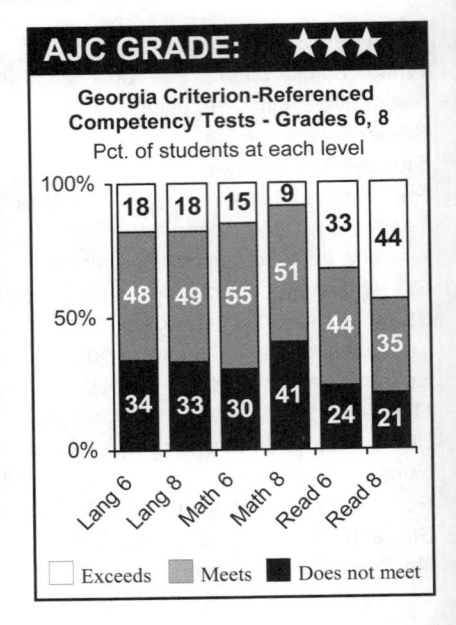

AJC GRADE: ★★★

Georgia Criterion-Referenced Competency Tests - Grades 6, 8
Pct. of students at each level

	Lang 6	Lang 8	Math 6	Math 8	Read 6	Read 8
Exceeds	18	18	15	9	33	44
Meets	48	49	55	51	44	35
Does not meet	34	33	30	41	24	21

East Coweta High School

400 Highway 154, Sharpsburg, GA 30277
770-254-2850 · Grades 9 - 12

Enrollment:	1,660
White / black / other:	69.2% / 27.0% / 3.7%
Not native English-speaking:	12 / 0.7%
Limited English proficiency:	24 / 1.4%
Student absenteeism:	6.9%
Students per teacher:	17.8
Parent friendliness:	① ❷ ❸ ④ ❺ ❻
Students in gifted program:	105 / 6.3%
Students in remedial education:	0.5%
High school completion rate:	62.1%
Students held back a grade:	5.0%
Number of dropouts:	55 / 2.9%
Students in alternative programs:	30 / 1.8%
Students in special education:	211 / 12.7%
Eligible students, free or reduced lunch:	18.9%
Total suspensions and expulsions:	72
Suspensions only, pct. in-school:	72 / 19.4%
Drugs/alcohol-related offenses:	5
Violence-related offenses:	43
Firearms-related offenses:	4
Vandalism-related offenses:	7
Theft-related offenses:	2
All other disciplinary offenses:	22
Teachers with advanced degrees:	41.5%
Average years' teaching experience:	10.1

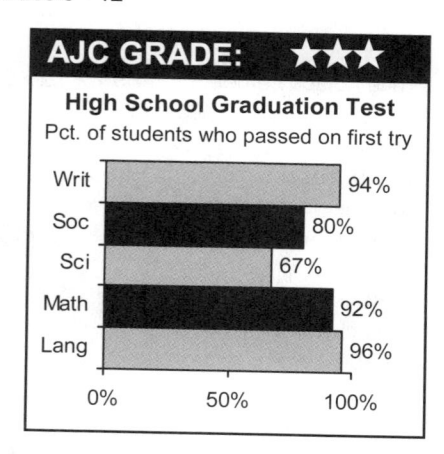

AJC GRADE: ★★★

High School Graduation Test
Pct. of students who passed on first try

- Writ: 94%
- Soc: 80%
- Sci: 67%
- Math: 92%
- Lang: 96%

GHSA classification: 4-AAAAA
Interscholastic sports offered:
BB, BS, CC, CL, FB, GO, RI, SB, SO, TE, TF, VB, WR

Advanced Placement (AP) Exams
Students tested: 86
Tests taken: 123
Pct. of test scores 3 or higher (1 - 5 scale): 43.9%

Languages other than English taught:
French, German, Spanish

2000-2001 high school graduates:	**260**
College prep/vocational diplomas:	31.5%
College prep endorsement diplomas:	35.8%
Vocational endorsement diplomas:	26.5%
General high school diplomas:	1.5%
Special education diplomas:	4.2%
Certificates of attendance (no diploma):	0.4%

Of the 2000-2001 graduates, 55.0% were eligible for the HOPE scholarship.

Of the 1999-2000 graduates, 114 attended a Georgia public college or university. Of those, 83% met the school's minimum academic requirements.

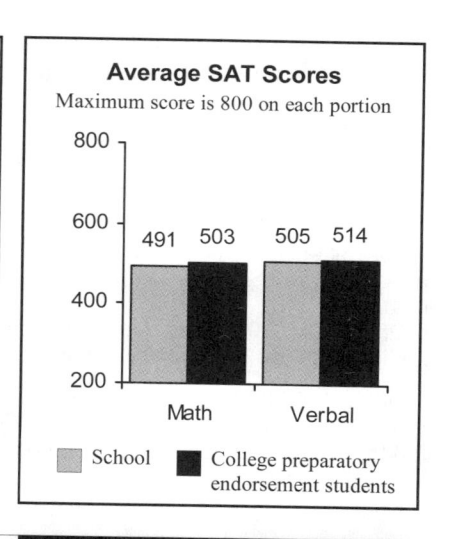

Average SAT Scores
Maximum score is 800 on each portion

- Math: School 491, College preparatory endorsement students 503
- Verbal: School 505, College preparatory endorsement students 514

Coweta County High Schools

Newnan High School

190 LaGrange St, Newnan, GA 30263
770-254-2880 · Grades 9 - 12

Enrollment:	1,623
White / black / other:	69.7% / 29.5% / 0.8%
Not native English-speaking:	*
Limited English proficiency:	3 / 0.2%
Student absenteeism:	7.8%
Students per teacher:	20.2
Parent friendliness:	① ❷ ③ ④ ⑤ ❻
Students in gifted program:	159 / 9.8%
Students in remedial education:	6.2%
High school completion rate:	62.0%
Students held back a grade:	8.6%
Number of dropouts:	74 / 4.2%
Students in alternative programs:	36 / 2.2%
Students in special education:	187 / 11.5%
Eligible students, free or reduced lunch:	18.5%
Total suspensions and expulsions:	20
Suspensions only, pct. in-school:	18 / 5.6%
Drugs/alcohol-related offenses:	3
Violence-related offenses:	8
Firearms-related offenses:	3
Vandalism-related offenses:	*
Theft-related offenses:	3
All other disciplinary offenses:	4
Teachers with advanced degrees:	58.5%
Average years' teaching experience:	14.2

AJC GRADE: ★★★

High School Graduation Test
Pct. of students who passed on first try

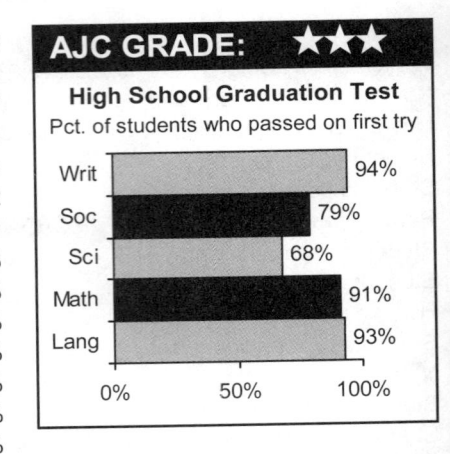

- Writ: 94%
- Soc: 79%
- Sci: 68%
- Math: 91%
- Lang: 93%

GHSA classification: 4-AAAAA
Interscholastic sports offered:
BB, BS, CC, CL, FB, GO, SB, SO, TE, TF, VB, WR

Advanced Placement (AP) Exams
- Students tested: 80
- Tests taken: 104
- Pct. of test scores 3 or higher (1 - 5 scale): 63.5%

Languages other than English taught:
French, German, Spanish

2000-2001 high school graduates: 279

College prep/vocational diplomas:	2.2%
College prep endorsement diplomas:	68.5%
Vocational endorsement diplomas:	16.8%
General high school diplomas:	7.9%
Special education diplomas:	2.9%
Certificates of attendance (no diploma):	1.8%

Of the 2000-2001 graduates, 59.5% were eligible for the HOPE scholarship.

Of the 1999-2000 graduates, 99 attended a Georgia public college or university. Of those, 84% met the school's minimum academic requirements.

Average SAT Scores
Maximum score is 800 on each portion

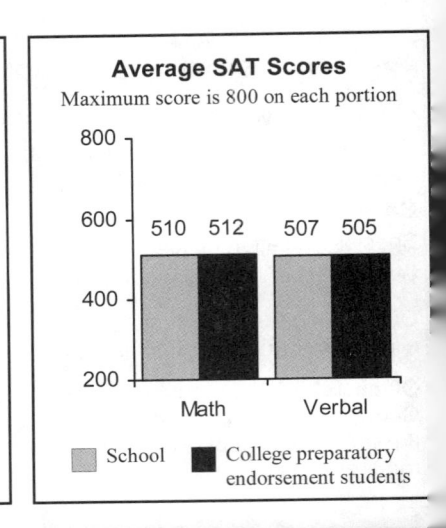

- Math: School 510, College preparatory endorsement students 512
- Verbal: School 507, College preparatory endorsement students 505

Coweta County High Schools

Northgate High School

3220 Fischer Rd, Newnan, GA 30265
770-463-5585 · Grades 9 - 12

👍

Enrollment:	1,029
White / black / other:	86.2% / 12.0% / 1.8%
Not native English-speaking:	*
Limited English proficiency:	3 / 0.3%
Student absenteeism:	6.4%
Students per teacher:	19.1
Parent friendliness:	①❷❸④❺❻
Students in gifted program:	95 / 9.2%
Students in remedial education:	2.4%
High school completion rate:	85.8%
Students held back a grade:	0.6%
Number of dropouts:	22 / 1.9%
Students in alternative programs:	5 / 0.5%
Students in special education:	93 / 9.0%
Eligible students, free or reduced lunch:	8.8%

Total suspensions and expulsions:	34
Suspensions only, pct. in-school:	34 / 44.1%
Drugs/alcohol-related offenses:	6
Violence-related offenses:	10
Firearms-related offenses:	3
Vandalism-related offenses:	3
Theft-related offenses:	2
All other disciplinary offenses:	11

Teachers with advanced degrees:	46.4%
Average years' teaching experience:	8.8

AJC GRADE: ★★★

High School Graduation Test
Pct. of students who passed on first try

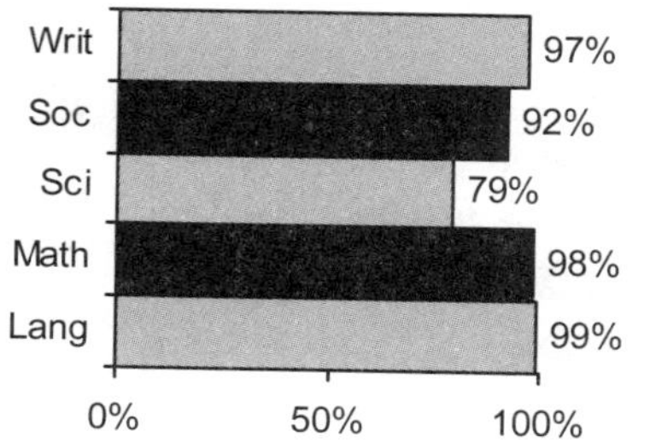
Writ
97%
Soc
92%
Sci
79%
Math
98%
Lang
99%
0%
50%
100%

GHSA classification:	4-AAAA

Interscholastic sports offered:
BB, BS, CC, CL, FB, GO, SB, SO, TE, TF, VB, WR

Advanced Placement (AP) Exams

Students tested:	43
Tests taken:	49
Pct. of test scores 3 or higher (1 - 5 scale):	63.3%

Languages other than English taught:
French, German, Latin, Spanish

2000-2001 high school graduates: 193

College prep/vocational diplomas:	20.2%
College prep endorsement diplomas:	63.2%
Vocational endorsement diplomas:	11.4%
General high school diplomas:	4.7%
Special education diplomas:	0.5%
Certificates of attendance (no diploma):	0.0%

Of the 2000-2001 graduates, 70.5% were eligible for the HOPE scholarship.

Of the 1999-2000 graduates, 46 attended a Georgia public college or university. Of those, 95% met the school's minimum academic requirements.

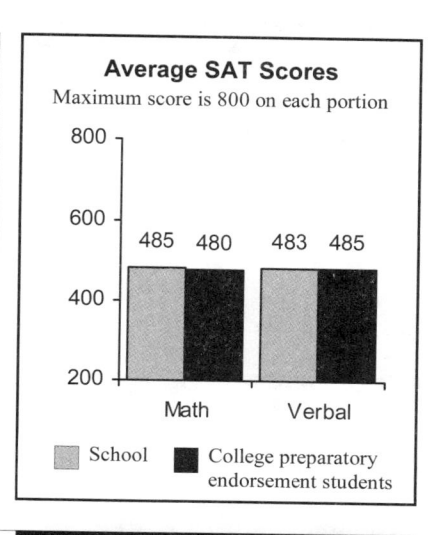

Average SAT Scores
Maximum score is 800 on each portion

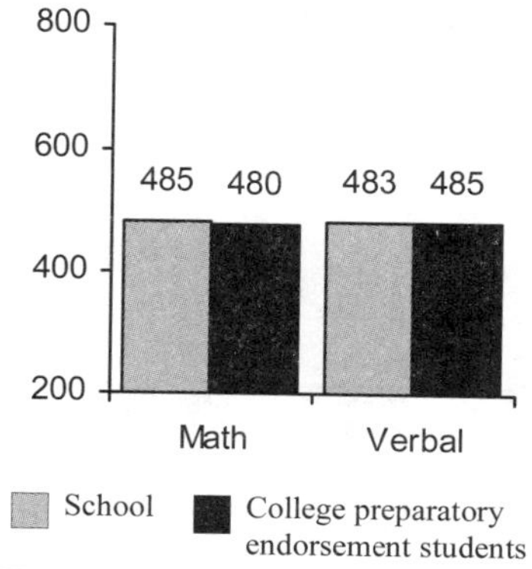
800
600
400
200
485
480
483
485
Math
Verbal
School
College preparatory endorsement students

AJC ranking of Coweta County Schools

ELEMENTARY SCHOOLS

AJC Star Grade: ★★★

Arbor Springs Elementary
Arnco-Sargent Elementary
Atkinson Elementary
Canongate Elementary
Elm Street Elementary
Jefferson Parkway Elementary
Moreland Elementary
Newnan Crossing Elementary
Northside Elementary
Poplar Road Elementary
Ruth Hill Elementary
Thomas Crossroads Elementary
Western Elementary
White Oak Elementary

AJC Star Grade: ★★

Eastside Elementary

MIDDLE SCHOOLS

AJC Star Grade: ★★★

Arnall Middle
East Coweta Middle
Evans Middle
Madras Middle
Smokey Road Middle

HIGH SCHOOLS

AJC Star Grade: ★★★

East Coweta High
Newnan High
Northgate High

Decatur City Public Schools

320 N McDonough St, Decatur, GA 30030
Phone: 404-370-4400 · Fax: 404-370-4413
http://www.decatur-city.k12.ga.us

The following pages provide detailed information on every school in the Decatur City school district. An asterisk (*) means the value of the data was zero or was not reported by the school district. A complete list of schools ranked by The Atlanta Journal-Constitution's star rating system follows the detailed school reports.

District enrollment:	2,502
White / black / other:	42.8% / 53.2% / 4.0%
Not native English-speaking:	31 / 1.2%
Expenditure per student (general fund):	$9,046
Students per teacher:	11.8
Teachers with advanced degrees:	70.6%
Average years, teaching experience:	11.6
Average teacher salary:	$43,838.88
Students in gifted program:	479 / 19.1%
Students held back a grade:	175 / 7.0%
Eligible students, free or reduced lunch:	1,003 / 37.7%
Number of dropouts (grades 9-12):	32 / 3.2%
High school completion rate:	76.6%
Graduates, pct. eligible for HOPE scholarships:	121 / 63.6%
Average combined SAT score (maximum 1,600):	1,072
Pct. of 11th-graders passing the Georgia High School Graduation Tests on first try:	68%
Percent of children 5 to 17 years of age living in poverty (2000 Census estimate):	16.0%

Clairemont Elementary School

155 Erie Ave, Decatur, GA 30030
404-370-4450 · Grades K - 5

Enrollment:	235
White / black / other:	60.0% / 36.6% / 3.4%
Not native English-speaking:	2 / 0.9%
Limited English proficiency:	2 / 0.9%
Student absenteeism:	3.5%
Students per teacher:	13.6
Parent friendliness:	① ❷ ❸ ④ ❺ ❻
Teachers with advanced degrees:	66.7%
Average years' teaching experience:	8.8
Students in gifted program:	44 / 18.7%
Students in remedial education:	20.5%
Students held back a grade:	6.8%
Total suspensions, pct. in-school:	14 / 71.4%
Offenses:	violence: *, drugs: *, other: 18
Eligible students, free or reduced lunch:	35.3%
Before / after school program:	No / Yes

Students at this school generally go on to:
Renfroe Middle

AJC GRADE: ★★★

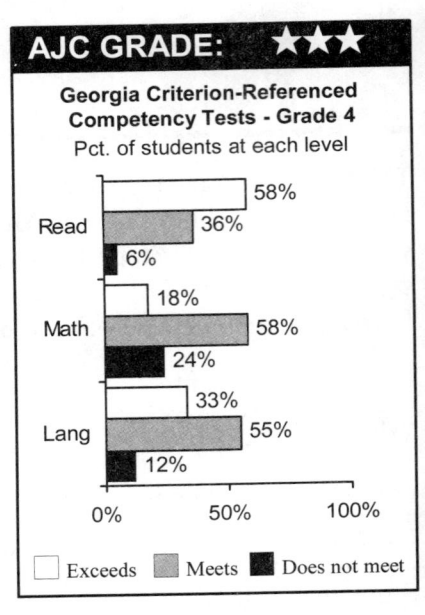

Georgia Criterion-Referenced Competency Tests - Grade 4
Pct. of students at each level

- Read: Exceeds 58%, Meets 36%, Does not meet 6%
- Math: Exceeds 18%, Meets 58%, Does not meet 24%
- Lang: Exceeds 33%, Meets 55%, Does not meet 12%

College Heights Elementary School

917 S McDonough St, Decatur, GA 30030
404-370-4455 · Grades K - 5

Enrollment:	152
White / black / other:	7.2% / 90.8% / 2.0%
Not native English-speaking:	*
Limited English proficiency:	*
Student absenteeism:	4.0%
Students per teacher:	9.0
Parent friendliness:	① ❷ ❸ ④ ❺ ❻
Teachers with advanced degrees:	42.9%
Average years' teaching experience:	9.0
Students in gifted program:	2 / 1.3%
Students in remedial education:	25.5%
Students held back a grade:	3.9%
Total suspensions, pct. in-school:	1 / 0.0%
Offenses:	violence: *, drugs: *, other: 1
Eligible students, free or reduced lunch:	50.5%
Before / after school program:	No / Yes

Students at this school generally go on to:
Renfroe Middle

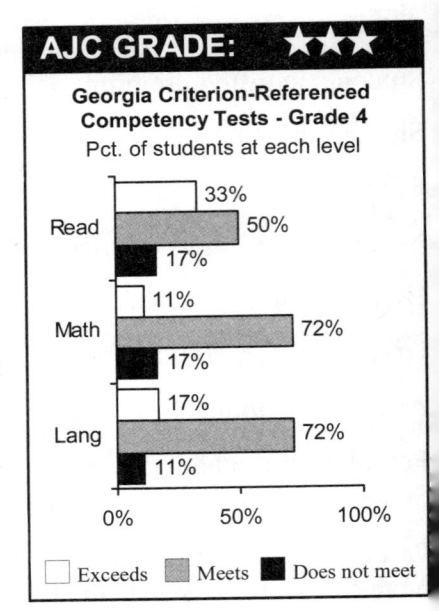

AJC GRADE: ★★★

Georgia Criterion-Referenced Competency Tests - Grade 4
Pct. of students at each level

- Read: Exceeds 33%, Meets 50%, Does not meet 17%
- Math: Exceeds 11%, Meets 72%, Does not meet 17%
- Lang: Exceeds 17%, Meets 72%, Does not meet 11%

Decatur City Elementary Schools

Glennwood Elementary School

440 E Ponce de Leon Ave, Decatur, GA 30030
404-370-4435 · Grades K - 5

Enrollment:	161
White / black / other:	36.0% / 60.2% / 3.7%
Not native English-speaking:	10 / 6.2%
Limited English proficiency:	10 / 6.2%
Student absenteeism:	4.5%
Students per teacher:	9.5
Parent friendliness:	❶❷❸❹❺❻
Teachers with advanced degrees:	38.1%
Average years' teaching experience:	7.5
Students in gifted program:	18 / 11.2%
Students in remedial education:	30.8%
Students held back a grade:	3.1%
Total suspensions, pct. in-school:	19 / 52.6%
Offenses:	violence: 9, drugs: *, other: 11
Eligible students, free or reduced lunch:	50.5%
Before / after school program:	No / Yes

Students at this school generally go on to:
Renfroe Middle

AJC GRADE: ★

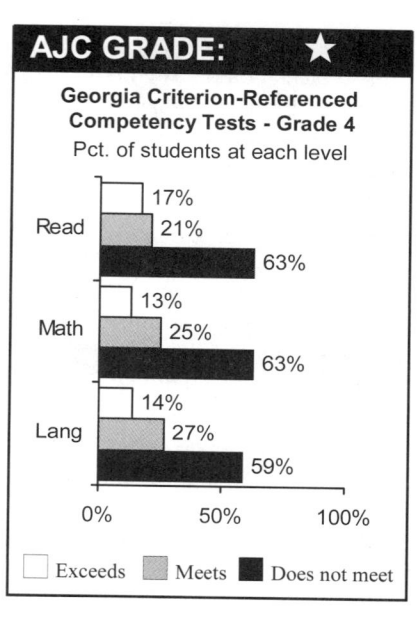

Georgia Criterion-Referenced Competency Tests - Grade 4
Pct. of students at each level

Read: 17% Exceeds / 21% Meets / 63% Does not meet
Math: 13% Exceeds / 25% Meets / 63% Does not meet
Lang: 14% Exceeds / 27% Meets / 59% Does not meet

Oakhurst Elementary School

175 Mead Rd, Decatur, GA 30030
404-370-4470 · Grades K - 5

Enrollment:	139
White / black / other:	1.4% / 97.1% / 1.4%
Not native English-speaking:	*
Limited English proficiency:	*
Student absenteeism:	5.2%
Students per teacher:	9.0
Parent friendliness:	①❷❸❹❺❻
Teachers with advanced degrees:	57.9%
Average years' teaching experience:	12.9
Students in gifted program:	1 / 0.7%
Students in remedial education:	42.4%
Students held back a grade:	10.8%
Total suspensions, pct. in-school:	1 / 0.0%
Offenses:	violence: *, drugs: *, other: 1
Eligible students, free or reduced lunch:	68.9%
Before / after school program:	Yes / Yes

Students at this school generally go on to:
Renfroe Middle

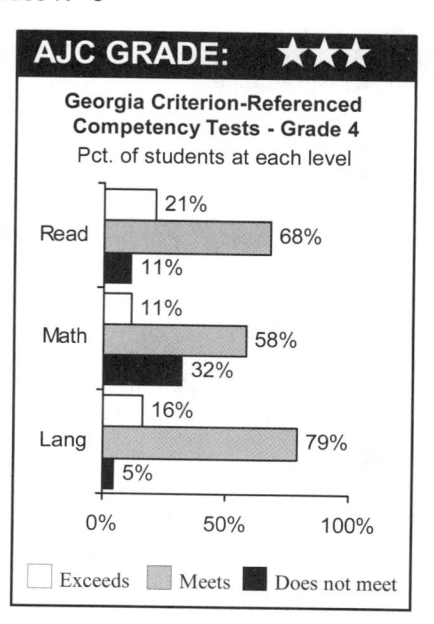

AJC GRADE: ★★★

Georgia Criterion-Referenced Competency Tests - Grade 4
Pct. of students at each level

Read: 21% Exceeds / 68% Meets / 11% Does not meet
Math: 11% Exceeds / 58% Meets / 32% Does not meet
Lang: 16% Exceeds / 79% Meets / 5% Does not meet

Decatur City Elementary Schools

Westchester Elementary School

758 Scott Blvd, Decatur, GA 30030
404-370-4480 · Grades K - 5

Enrollment:	233
White / black / other:	66.5% / 23.2% / 10.3%
Not native English-speaking:	2 / 0.9%
Limited English proficiency:	2 / 0.9%
Student absenteeism:	2.7%
Students per teacher:	14.1
Parent friendliness:	①❷❸④❺❻
Teachers with advanced degrees:	65.0%
Average years' teaching experience:	10.8
Students in gifted program:	37 / 15.9%
Students in remedial education:	20.2%
Students held back a grade:	3.4%
Total suspensions, pct. in-school:	17 / 70.6%
Offenses:	violence: 9, drugs: *, other: 8
Eligible students, free or reduced lunch:	22.3%
Before / after school program:	No / Yes
Students at this school generally go on to: Renfroe Middle	

AJC GRADE: ★★★

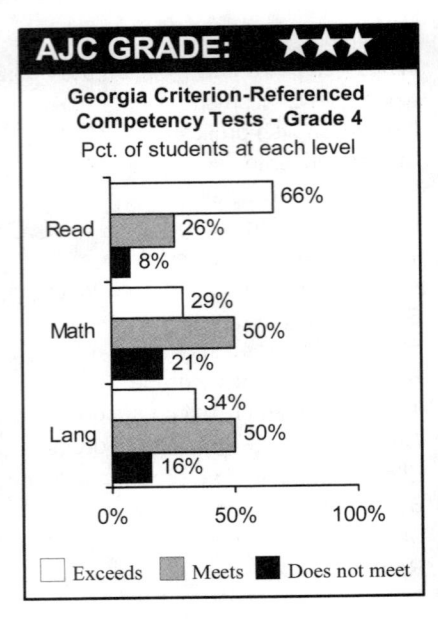

Georgia Criterion-Referenced Competency Tests - Grade 4
Pct. of students at each level

Read: 66% / 26% / 8%
Math: 29% / 50% / 21%
Lang: 34% / 50% / 16%

☐ Exceeds ▨ Meets ■ Does not meet

Winnona Park Elementary School

510 Avery St, Decatur, GA 30030
404-370-4490 · Grades K - 5

Enrollment:	222
White / black / other:	64.4% / 29.3% / 6.3%
Not native English-speaking:	*
Limited English proficiency:	2 / 0.9%
Student absenteeism:	4.5%
Students per teacher:	12.5
Parent friendliness:	①❷❸④❺❻
Teachers with advanced degrees:	54.5%
Average years' teaching experience:	11.0
Students in gifted program:	60 / 27.0%
Students in remedial education:	8.5%
Students held back a grade:	3.2%
Total suspensions, pct. in-school:	3 / 33.3%
Offenses:	violence: 1, drugs: *, other: 2
Eligible students, free or reduced lunch:	17.1%
Before / after school program:	No / Yes
Students at this school generally go on to: Renfroe Middle	

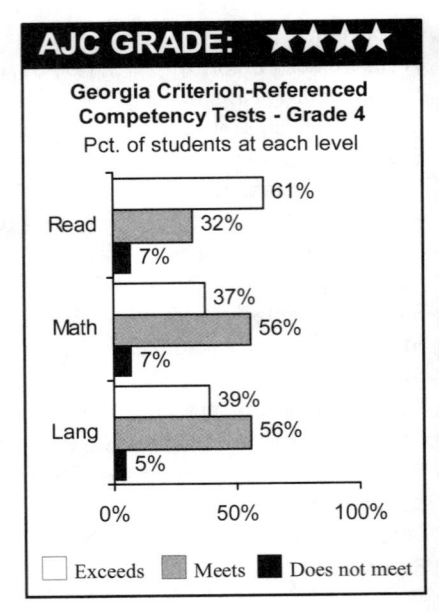

AJC GRADE: ★★★★

Georgia Criterion-Referenced Competency Tests - Grade 4
Pct. of students at each level

Read: 61% / 32% / 7%
Math: 37% / 56% / 7%
Lang: 39% / 56% / 5%

☐ Exceeds ▨ Meets ■ Does not meet

The Atlanta Journal-Constitution / Page 200

Decatur City Elementary Schools

Renfroe Middle School

220 W College Ave, Decatur, GA 30030
404-370-4440 · Grades 6 - 8

Enrollment:	564
White / black / other:	44.5% / 52.8% / 2.7%
Not native English-speaking:	7 / 1.2%
Student absenteeism:	5.1%
Students per teacher:	11.9
Parent friendliness:	① ❷ ❸ ④ ❺ ❻
Teachers with advanced degrees:	83.3%
Average years' teaching experience:	12.0
Students in gifted program:	159 / 28.2%
Students held back a grade:	2.5%
Total suspensions and expulsions:	317
Suspensions only, pct. in-school:	317 / 77.3%
Offenses: violence: 26, drugs: 2, other: 289	
Eligible students, free or reduced lunch:	37.2%
Number of dropouts:	*
Pct. 8th-graders w/ basic computer skills:	100.0%

Students at this school generally go on to:
Decatur High

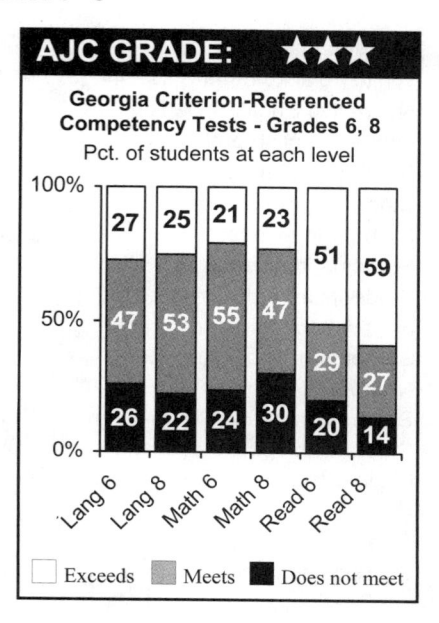

AJC GRADE: ★★★

Georgia Criterion-Referenced Competency Tests - Grades 6, 8
Pct. of students at each level

	Lang 6	Lang 8	Math 6	Math 8	Read 6	Read 8
Exceeds	27	25	21	23	51	59
Meets	47	53	55	47	29	27
Does not meet	26	22	24	30	20	14

Decatur City Middle Schools

Decatur High School

310 N McDonough St, Decatur, GA 30030
404-370-4420 · Grades 9 - 12

Enrollment:	692
White / black / other:	44.7% / 51.6% / 3.8%
Not native English-speaking:	10 / 1.4%
Limited English proficiency:	10 / 1.4%
Student absenteeism:	11.9%
Students per teacher:	14.3
Parent friendliness:	❶❷❸④❺❻
Students in gifted program:	157 / 22.7%
Students in remedial education:	4.3%
High school completion rate:	76.6%
Students held back a grade:	12.4%
Number of dropouts:	32 / 3.2%
Students in alternative programs:	28 / 4.0%
Students in special education:	69 / 10.0%
Eligible students, free or reduced lunch:	26.4%
Total suspensions and expulsions:	544
Suspensions only, pct. in-school:	542 / 66.4%
Drugs/alcohol-related offenses:	8
Violence-related offenses:	15
Firearms-related offenses:	3
Vandalism-related offenses:	*
Theft-related offenses:	2
All other disciplinary offenses:	516
Teachers with advanced degrees:	84.3%
Average years' teaching experience:	13.5

AJC GRADE: ★★★★

High School Graduation Test
Pct. of students who passed on first try

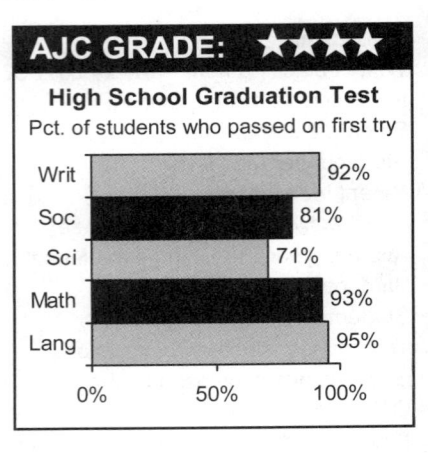

- Writ: 92%
- Soc: 81%
- Sci: 71%
- Math: 93%
- Lang: 95%

GHSA classification: 5-AA
Interscholastic sports offered:
BB, BS, CC, CL, FB, GO, RI, SB, SO, SW, TE, TF, VB, WR

Advanced Placement (AP) Exams
Students tested: 75
Tests taken: 138
Pct. of test scores 3 or higher (1 - 5 scale): 64.5%

Languages other than English taught:
French, German, Latin, Spanish

2000-2001 high school graduates: 121

College prep/vocational diplomas:	19.8%
College prep endorsement diplomas:	73.6%
Vocational endorsement diplomas:	6.6%
General high school diplomas:	0.0%
Special education diplomas:	0.0%
Certificates of attendance (no diploma):	0.0%

Of the 2000-2001 graduates, 63.6% were eligible for the HOPE scholarship.

Of the 1999-2000 graduates, 47 attended a Georgia public college or university. Of those, 87% met the school's minimum academic requirements.

Average SAT Scores
Maximum score is 800 on each portion

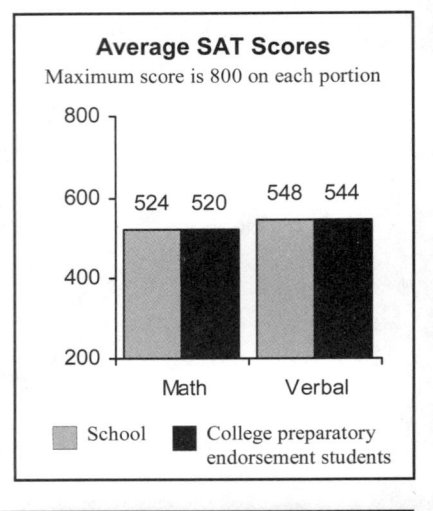

- Math — School: 524, College preparatory endorsement students: 520
- Verbal — School: 548, College preparatory endorsement students: 544

The Atlanta Journal-Constitution / Page 202

Decatur City High Schools

AJC ranking of Decatur City Schools

ELEMENTARY SCHOOLS

AJC Star Grade: ★★★★

Winnona Park Elementary

AJC Star Grade: ★★★

Clairemont Elementary
College Heights Elementary
Oakhurst Elementary
Westchester Elementary

AJC Star Grade: ★

Glennwood Elementary

MIDDLE SCHOOLS

AJC Star Grade: ★★★

Renfroe Middle

HIGH SCHOOLS

AJC Star Grade: ★★★★

Decatur High

DeKalb County Public Schools

3770 N Decatur Rd, Decatur, GA 30032
Phone: 404-297-1200 · Fax: 404-297-1254
http://www.dekalb.k12.ga.us

The following pages provide detailed information on every school in the DeKalb County school district. An asterisk (*) means the value of the data was zero or was not reported by the school district. A complete list of schools ranked by The Atlanta Journal-Constitution's star rating system follows the detailed school reports.

District enrollment:	93,543
White / black / other:	11.3% / 76.7% / 12.0%
Not native English-speaking:	3,910 / 4.2%
Expenditure per student (general fund):	$6,622
Students per teacher:	15.9
Teachers with advanced degrees:	47.3%
Average years, teaching experience:	11.0
Average teacher salary:	$43,614.26
Students in gifted program:	7,867 / 8.4%
Students held back a grade:	4,788 / 5.1%
Eligible students, free or reduced lunch:	52,699 / 54.9%
Number of dropouts (grades 9-12):	1,891 / 6.4%
High school completion rate:	73.5%
Graduates, pct. eligible for HOPE scholarships:	4,591 / 55.3%
Average combined SAT score (maximum 1,600):	953
Pct. of 11th-graders passing the Georgia High School Graduation Tests on first try:	62%
Percent of children 5 to 17 years of age living in poverty (2000 Census estimate):	13.7%

Allgood Elementary School

659 Allgood Rd, Stone Mountain, GA 30083
678-676-5102 · Grades K - 5

Enrollment:	607
White / black / other:	1.2% / 90.1% / 8.7%
Not native English-speaking:	25 / 4.1%
Limited English proficiency:	66 / 10.9%
Student absenteeism:	4.1%
Students per teacher:	15.8
Parent friendliness:	❶❷❸④❺❻
Teachers with advanced degrees:	56.1%
Average years' teaching experience:	11.3
Students in gifted program:	26 / 4.3%
Students in remedial education:	19.1%
Students held back a grade:	1.3%
Total suspensions, pct. in-school:	140 / 59.3%
Offenses:	violence: 38, drugs: *, other: 112
Eligible students, free or reduced lunch:	56.6%
Before / after school program:	Yes / Yes

Students at this school generally go on to:
Freedom Middle

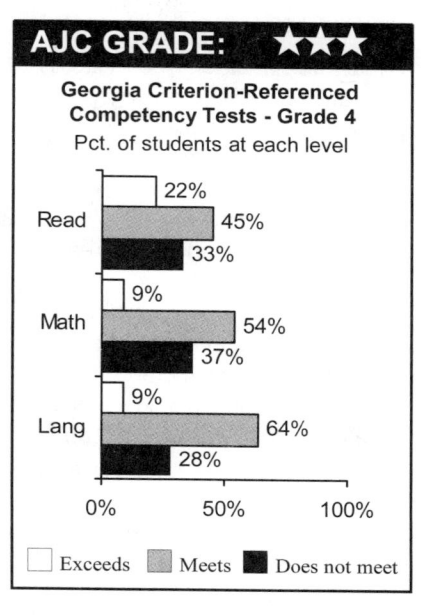

AJC GRADE: ★★★

Georgia Criterion-Referenced Competency Tests - Grade 4
Pct. of students at each level

- Read: Exceeds 22%, Meets 45%, Does not meet 33%
- Math: Exceeds 9%, Meets 54%, Does not meet 37%
- Lang: Exceeds 9%, Meets 64%, Does not meet 28%

Ashford Park Elementary School

2968 Cravenridge Dr NE, Atlanta, GA 30319
678-676-6702 · Grades K - 6

Enrollment:	369
White / black / other:	31.2% / 40.7% / 28.2%
Not native English-speaking:	21 / 5.7%
Limited English proficiency:	109 / 29.5%
Student absenteeism:	5.1%
Students per teacher:	12.7
Parent friendliness:	①❷❸④⑤❻
Teachers with advanced degrees:	60.0%
Average years' teaching experience:	12.1
Students in gifted program:	52 / 14.1%
Students in remedial education:	29.5%
Students held back a grade:	*
Total suspensions, pct. in-school:	1 / 0.0%
Offenses:	violence: 1, drugs: *, other: *
Eligible students, free or reduced lunch:	60.6%
Before / after school program:	Yes / Yes

Students at this school generally go on to:
Chamblee Middle

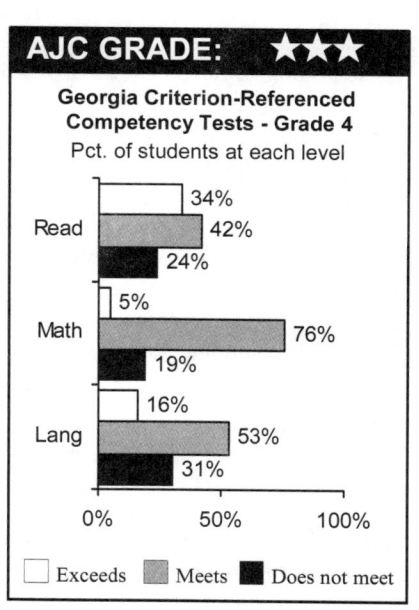

AJC GRADE: ★★★

Georgia Criterion-Referenced Competency Tests - Grade 4
Pct. of students at each level

- Read: Exceeds 34%, Meets 42%, Does not meet 24%
- Math: Exceeds 5%, Meets 76%, Does not meet 19%
- Lang: Exceeds 16%, Meets 53%, Does not meet 31%

DeKalb County Elementary Schools

Atherton Elementary School

1674 Atherton Dr, Decatur, GA 30035
404-284-6662 · Grades K - 7

Enrollment:	820
White / black / other:	2.3% / 91.7% / 6.0%
Not native English-speaking:	13 / 1.6%
Limited English proficiency:	48 / 5.9%
Student absenteeism:	4.7%
Students per teacher:	16.0
Parent friendliness:	① ❷ ❸ ❹ ⑤ ❻
Teachers with advanced degrees:	38.2%
Average years' teaching experience:	10.6
Students in gifted program:	67 / 8.2%
Students in remedial education:	29.4%
Students held back a grade:	0.7%
Total suspensions, pct. in-school:	38 / 42.1%
Offenses: violence: 20, drugs: *, other: 24	
Eligible students, free or reduced lunch:	80.4%
Before / after school program:	No / Yes

Students at this school generally go on to:
Bethune Middle

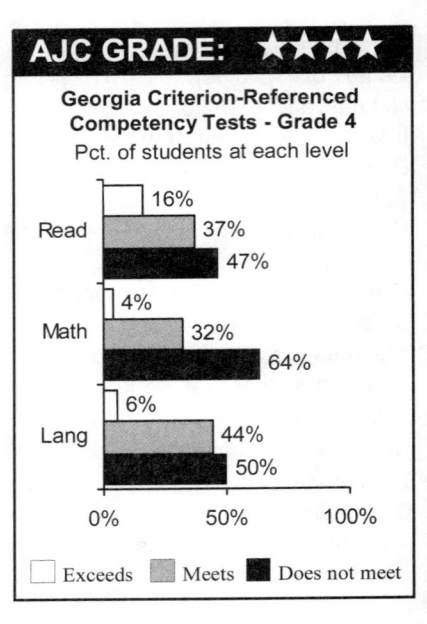

AJC GRADE: ★★★★

Georgia Criterion-Referenced Competency Tests - Grade 4
Pct. of students at each level

Read: 16% Exceeds / 37% Meets / 47% Does not meet
Math: 4% Exceeds / 32% Meets / 64% Does not meet
Lang: 6% Exceeds / 44% Meets / 50% Does not meet

Austin Elementary School

5435 Roberts Dr, Dunwoody, GA 30338
770-393-0038 · Grades K - 5

Enrollment:	471
White / black / other:	75.2% / 15.9% / 8.9%
Not native English-speaking:	3 / 0.6%
Limited English proficiency:	45 / 9.6%
Student absenteeism:	2.9%
Students per teacher:	13.0
Parent friendliness:	① ❷ ❸ ④ ⑤ ❻
Teachers with advanced degrees:	62.2%
Average years' teaching experience:	12.4
Students in gifted program:	169 / 35.9%
Students in remedial education:	3.5%
Students held back a grade:	0.4%
Total suspensions, pct. in-school:	5 / 60.0%
Offenses: violence: *, drugs: *, other: 7	
Eligible students, free or reduced lunch:	4.7%
Before / after school program:	No / Yes

Students at this school generally go on to:
Peachtree Charter Middle

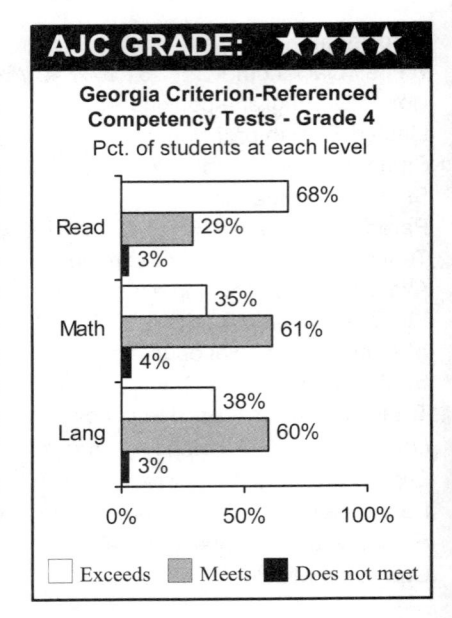

AJC GRADE: ★★★★

Georgia Criterion-Referenced Competency Tests - Grade 4
Pct. of students at each level

Read: 68% Exceeds / 29% Meets / 3% Does not meet
Math: 35% Exceeds / 61% Meets / 4% Does not meet
Lang: 38% Exceeds / 60% Meets / 3% Does not meet

Avondale Elementary School

10 Lakeshore Dr, Avondale Estates, GA 30002
678-676-5202 · Grades K - 7

Enrollment:	658
White / black / other:	11.1% / 83.9% / 5.0%
Not native English-speaking:	70 / 10.6%
Limited English proficiency:	186 / 28.3%
Student absenteeism:	5.5%
Students per teacher:	13.2
Parent friendliness:	① ❷ ❸ ❹ ❺ ❻
Teachers with advanced degrees:	42.0%
Average years' teaching experience:	8.3
Students in gifted program:	34 / 5.2%
Students in remedial education:	30.2%
Students held back a grade:	0.6%
Total suspensions, pct. in-school:	39 / 7.7%
Offenses: violence: 14, drugs: * , other: 32	
Eligible students, free or reduced lunch:	82.9%
Before / after school program:	Yes / Yes

Students at this school generally go on to:
Avondale Middle

AJC GRADE: ★★★★

Georgia Criterion-Referenced Competency Tests - Grade 4
Pct. of students at each level

- Read: Exceeds 24%, Meets 46%, Does not meet 30%
- Math: Exceeds 5%, Meets 46%, Does not meet 49%
- Lang: Exceeds 10%, Meets 57%, Does not meet 33%

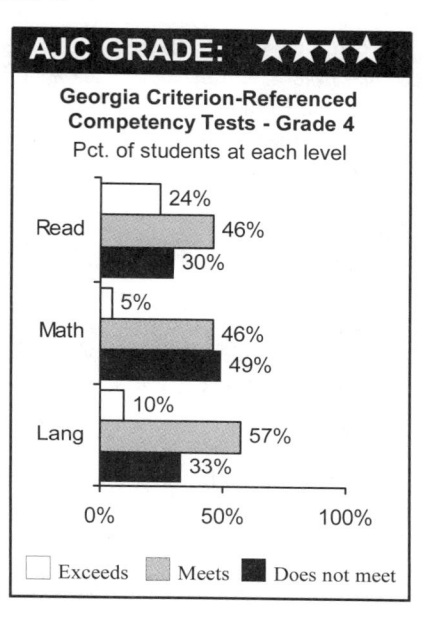

Bob Mathis Elementary School

3505 Boring Rd, Decatur, GA 30034
404-243-6215 · Grades K - 5

Enrollment:	367
White / black / other:	0.0% / 99.5% / 0.5%
Not native English-speaking:	*
Limited English proficiency:	11 / 3.0%
Student absenteeism:	3.4%
Students per teacher:	14.0
Parent friendliness:	① ❷ ❸ ④ ❺ ❻
Teachers with advanced degrees:	34.5%
Average years' teaching experience:	10.1
Students in gifted program:	23 / 6.3%
Students in remedial education:	42.2%
Students held back a grade:	0.5%
Total suspensions, pct. in-school:	4 / 50.0%
Offenses: violence: 4, drugs: * , other: 2	
Eligible students, free or reduced lunch:	65.6%
Before / after school program:	No / Yes

Students at this school generally go on to:
Cedar Grove, Chapel Hill, Columbia Middle

AJC GRADE: ★★★

Georgia Criterion-Referenced Competency Tests - Grade 4
Pct. of students at each level

- Read: Exceeds 30%, Meets 45%, Does not meet 25%
- Math: Exceeds 7%, Meets 60%, Does not meet 33%
- Lang: Exceeds 26%, Meets 47%, Does not meet 27%

DeKalb County Elementary Schools

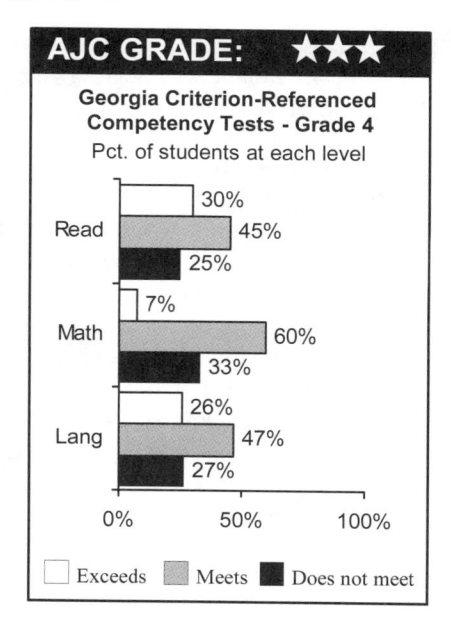

Bouie Elementary School

5100 Rock Springs Rd, Lithonia, GA 30038
678-670-8202 · Grades K - 6

Enrollment:	946
White / black / other:	0.1% / 98.6% / 1.3%
Not native English-speaking:	*
Limited English proficiency:	7 / 0.7%
Student absenteeism:	3.2%
Students per teacher:	16.8
Parent friendliness:	❶ ❷ ❸ ④ ⑤ ❻
Teachers with advanced degrees:	36.8%
Average years' teaching experience:	8.4
Students in gifted program:	104 / 11.0%
Students in remedial education:	37.3%
Students held back a grade:	0.3%
Total suspensions, pct. in-school:	115 / 73.9%
Offenses:	violence: 59, drugs: *, other: 59
Eligible students, free or reduced lunch:	41.8%
Before / after school program:	Yes / Yes

Students at this school generally go on to:
Chapel Hill, Miller Grove, Salem Middle

AJC GRADE: ★★★

Georgia Criterion-Referenced Competency Tests - Grade 4
Pct. of students at each level

- Read: Exceeds 31%, Meets 45%, Does not meet 24%
- Math: Exceeds 12%, Meets 53%, Does not meet 35%
- Lang: Exceeds 20%, Meets 58%, Does not meet 22%

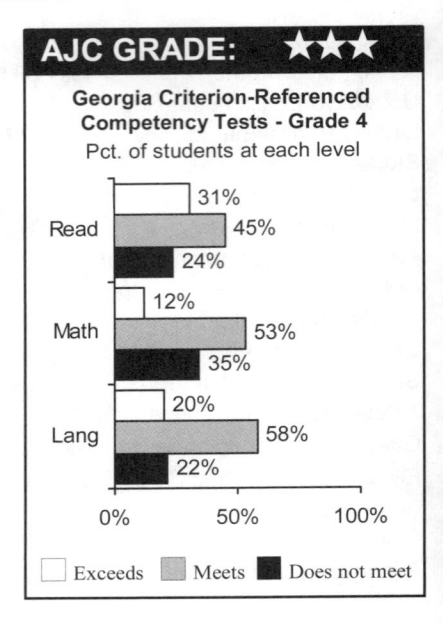

Briar Vista Elementary School

1131 Briar Vista Ter NE, Atlanta, GA 30324
404-634-0972 · Grades K - 5

Enrollment:	289
White / black / other:	30.1% / 40.5% / 29.4%
Not native English-speaking:	6 / 2.1%
Limited English proficiency:	85 / 29.4%
Student absenteeism:	5.9%
Students per teacher:	11.8
Parent friendliness:	① ❷ ❸ ④ ❺ ❻
Teachers with advanced degrees:	38.5%
Average years' teaching experience:	11.2
Students in gifted program:	23 / 8.0%
Students in remedial education:	24.5%
Students held back a grade:	*
Total suspensions, pct. in-school:	10 / 0.0%
Offenses:	violence: 7, drugs: *, other: 12
Eligible students, free or reduced lunch:	45.1%
Before / after school program:	Yes / Yes

Students at this school generally go on to:
Shamrock Middle

AJC GRADE: ★★★

Georgia Criterion-Referenced Competency Tests - Grade 4
Pct. of students at each level

- Read: Exceeds 34%, Meets 47%, Does not meet 19%
- Math: Exceeds *, Meets 63%, Does not meet 37%
- Lang: Exceeds 15%, Meets 64%, Does not meet 21%

DeKalb County Elementary Schools

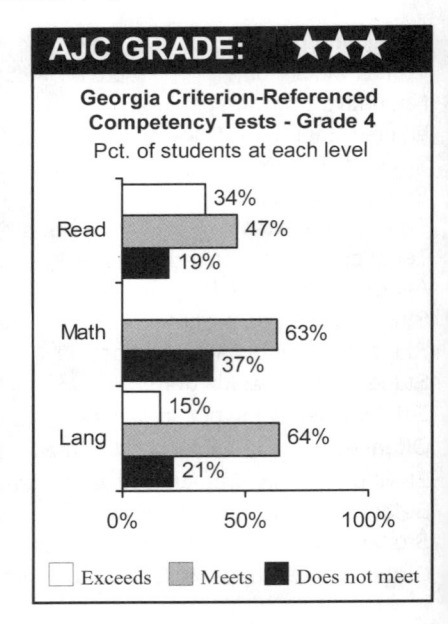

Briarlake Elementary School

3590 LaVista Rd, Decatur, GA 30033
404-325-4088 · Grades K - 5

Enrollment:	314
White / black / other:	58.9% / 24.5% / 16.6%
Not native English-speaking:	5 / 1.6%
Limited English proficiency:	43 / 13.7%
Student absenteeism:	3.4%
Students per teacher:	11.2
Parent friendliness:	① ❷ ❸ ④ ⑤ ❻
Teachers with advanced degrees:	50.0%
Average years' teaching experience:	13.9
Students in gifted program:	85 / 27.1%
Students in remedial education:	12.1%
Students held back a grade:	2.2%
Total suspensions, pct. in-school:	7 / 100.0%
Offenses:	violence: 1, drugs: * , other: 6
Eligible students, free or reduced lunch:	16.5%
Before / after school program:	No / Yes

Students at this school generally go on to:
Shamrock Middle

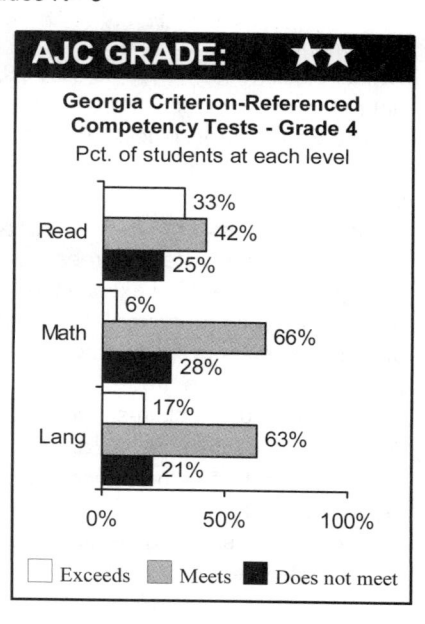

AJC GRADE: ★★

Georgia Criterion-Referenced Competency Tests - Grade 4
Pct. of students at each level

Read: 33% / 42% / 25%
Math: 6% / 66% / 28%
Lang: 17% / 63% / 21%

☐ Exceeds ▨ Meets ■ Does not meet

Brockett Elementary School

1855 Brockett Rd, Tucker, GA 30084
770-938-4343 · Grades K - 6

Enrollment:	417
White / black / other:	31.2% / 42.4% / 26.4%
Not native English-speaking:	6 / 1.4%
Limited English proficiency:	100 / 24.0%
Student absenteeism:	4.3%
Students per teacher:	13.2
Parent friendliness:	① ❷ ❸ ④ ⑤ ❻
Teachers with advanced degrees:	60.6%
Average years' teaching experience:	15.3
Students in gifted program:	54 / 12.9%
Students in remedial education:	20.8%
Students held back a grade:	1.7%
Total suspensions, pct. in-school:	65 / 56.9%
Offenses:	violence: 32, drugs: * , other: 44
Eligible students, free or reduced lunch:	53.2%
Before / after school program:	Yes / Yes

Students at this school generally go on to:
Henderson Middle

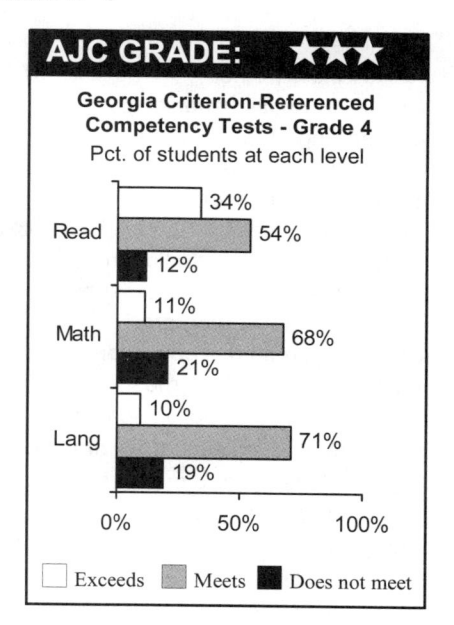

AJC GRADE: ★★★

Georgia Criterion-Referenced Competency Tests - Grade 4
Pct. of students at each level

Read: 34% / 54% / 12%
Math: 11% / 68% / 21%
Lang: 10% / 71% / 19%

☐ Exceeds ▨ Meets ■ Does not meet

Browns Mill Elementary School

4863 Browns Mill Rd, Lithonia, GA 30038
678-676-8302 · Grades K - 6

Enrollment:	853
White / black / other:	0.8% / 95.7% / 3.5%
Not native English-speaking:	*
Limited English proficiency:	23 / 2.7%
Student absenteeism:	3.5%
Students per teacher:	17.3
Parent friendliness:	① ❷ ❸ ④ ❺ ❻
Teachers with advanced degrees:	42.0%
Average years' teaching experience:	9.8
Students in gifted program:	150 / 17.6%
Students in remedial education:	18.0%
Students held back a grade:	0.5%
Total suspensions, pct. in-school:	84 / 0.0%
Offenses:	violence: 40, drugs: *, other: 46
Eligible students, free or reduced lunch:	43.7%
Before / after school program:	Yes / Yes

Students at this school generally go on to:
Chapel Hill, Salem Middle

AJC GRADE: ★★★★★

Georgia Criterion-Referenced Competency Tests - Grade 4
Pct. of students at each level

Read: Exceeds 49%, Meets 33%, Does not meet 18%
Math: Exceeds 21%, Meets 48%, Does not meet 32%
Lang: Exceeds 26%, Meets 54%, Does not meet 20%

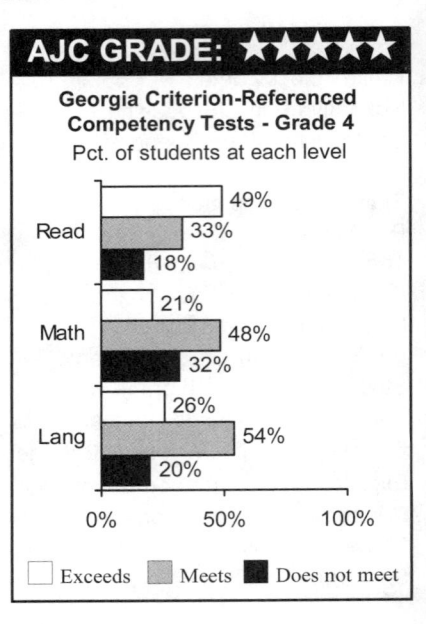

Canby Lane Elementary School

4150 Green Hawk Trl, Decatur, GA 30035
404-284-1069 · Grades K - 5

Enrollment:	851
White / black / other:	0.4% / 97.3% / 2.4%
Not native English-speaking:	*
Limited English proficiency:	21 / 2.5%
Student absenteeism:	4.3%
Students per teacher:	19.5
Parent friendliness:	① ❷ ❸ ④ ❺ ❻
Teachers with advanced degrees:	48.9%
Average years' teaching experience:	10.4
Students in gifted program:	53 / 6.2%
Students in remedial education:	18.6%
Students held back a grade:	0.9%
Total suspensions, pct. in-school:	27 / 25.9%
Offenses:	violence: 14, drugs: *, other: 14
Eligible students, free or reduced lunch:	73.9%
Before / after school program:	Yes / Yes

Students at this school generally go on to:
Bethune Middle

AJC GRADE: ★★★

Georgia Criterion-Referenced Competency Tests - Grade 4
Pct. of students at each level

Read: Exceeds 16%, Meets 46%, Does not meet 38%
Math: Exceeds 2%, Meets 46%, Does not meet 53%
Lang: Exceeds 8%, Meets 57%, Does not meet 35%

DeKalb County Elementary Schools

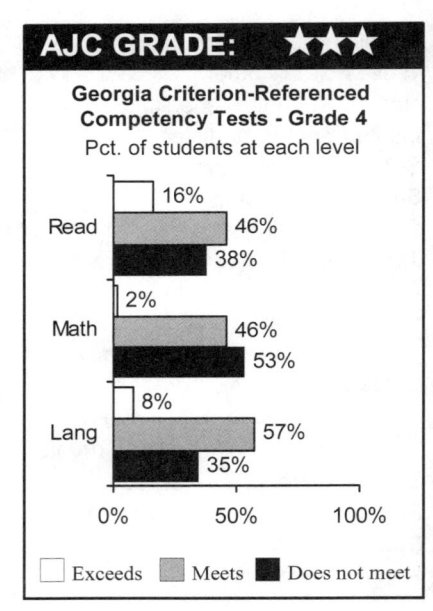

Cary Reynolds Elementary School

3498 Pine St, Atlanta, GA 30340
678-676-6802 · Grades K - 5

Enrollment:	820
White / black / other:	7.2% / 14.9% / 77.9%
Not native English-speaking:	349 / 42.6%
Limited English proficiency:	770 / 93.9%
Student absenteeism:	5.8%
Students per teacher:	13.6
Parent friendliness:	❶❷❸④⑤❻
Teachers with advanced degrees:	49.2%
Average years' teaching experience:	12.3
Students in gifted program:	30 / 3.7%
Students in remedial education:	36.9%
Students held back a grade:	0.6%
Total suspensions, pct. in-school:	42 / 50.0%
Offenses:	violence: 24, drugs: * , other: 18
Eligible students, free or reduced lunch:	93.3%
Before / after school program:	Yes / No

Students at this school generally go on to:
Sequoyah Middle

AJC GRADE: ★★

Georgia Criterion-Referenced Competency Tests - Grade 4
Pct. of students at each level

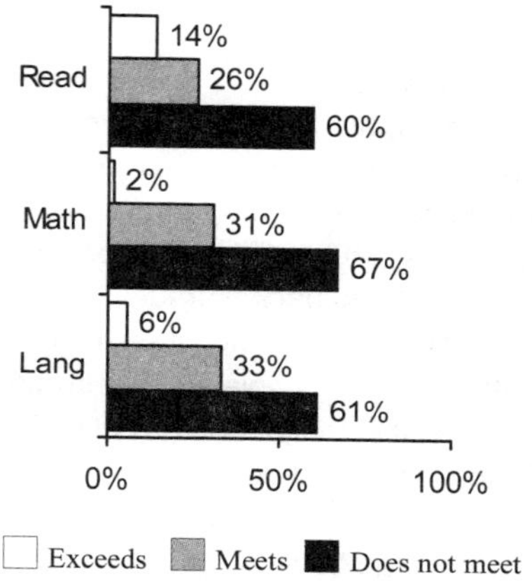

Read
14%
26%
60%
Math
2%
31%
67%
Lang
6%
33%
61%
0%
50%
100%
Exceeds
Meets
Does not meet

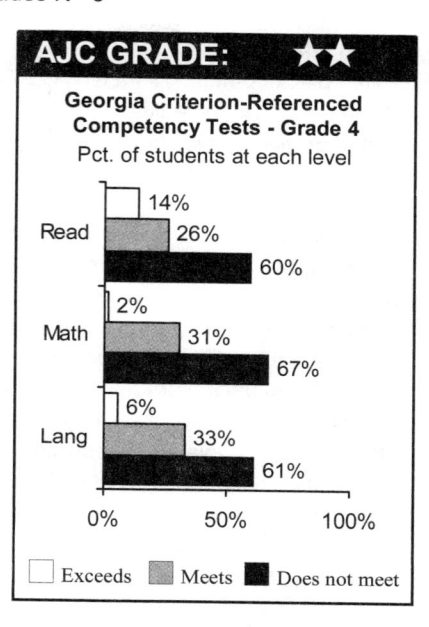

Cedar Grove Elementary School

2330 River Rd, Ellenwood, GA 30294
404-241-2742 · Grades K - 5

Enrollment:	986
White / black / other:	0.2% / 97.7% / 2.1%
Not native English-speaking:	2 / 0.2%
Limited English proficiency:	29 / 2.9%
Student absenteeism:	4.5%
Students per teacher:	18.6
Parent friendliness:	❶❷❸④⑤❻
Teachers with advanced degrees:	33.9%
Average years' teaching experience:	9.2
Students in gifted program:	49 / 5.0%
Students in remedial education:	22.0%
Students held back a grade:	1.3%
Total suspensions, pct. in-school:	33 / 6.1%
Offenses:	violence: 15, drugs: * , other: 31
Eligible students, free or reduced lunch:	66.9%
Before / after school program:	No / Yes

Students at this school generally go on to:
Cedar Grove Middle

AJC GRADE: ★★

Georgia Criterion-Referenced Competency Tests - Grade 4
Pct. of students at each level

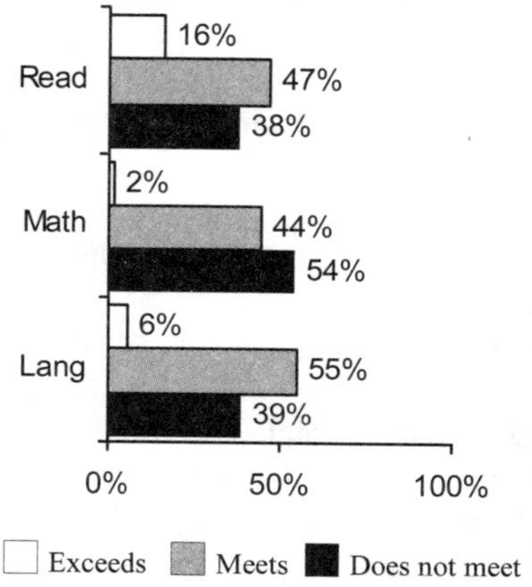

Read
16%
47%
38%
Math
2%
44%
54%
Lang
6%
55%
39%
0%
50%
100%
Exceeds
Meets
Does not meet

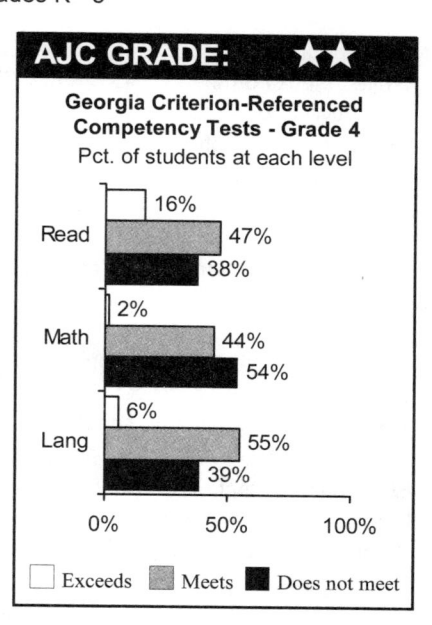

Chapel Hill Elementary School

3536 Radcliffe Blvd, Decatur, GA 30034
770-981-3110 · Grades K - 5

Enrollment:	682
White / black / other:	0.3% / 97.5% / 2.2%
Not native English-speaking:	1 / 0.1%
Limited English proficiency:	23 / 3.4%
Student absenteeism:	4.8%
Students per teacher:	16.4
Parent friendliness:	① ❷ ❸ ④ ⑤ ❻
Teachers with advanced degrees:	37.8%
Average years' teaching experience:	12.0
Students in gifted program:	67 / 9.8%
Students in remedial education:	28.0%
Students held back a grade:	1.0%
Total suspensions, pct. in-school:	51 / 21.6%
Offenses:	violence: 24, drugs: *, other: 30
Eligible students, free or reduced lunch:	64.1%
Before / after school program:	No / Yes

Students at this school generally go on to:
Chapel Hill Middle

AJC GRADE: ★★

Georgia Criterion-Referenced Competency Tests - Grade 4
Pct. of students at each level

Read: Exceeds 12%, Meets 43%, Does not meet 45%
Math: Exceeds 4%, Meets 31%, Does not meet 66%
Lang: Exceeds 5%, Meets 55%, Does not meet 40%

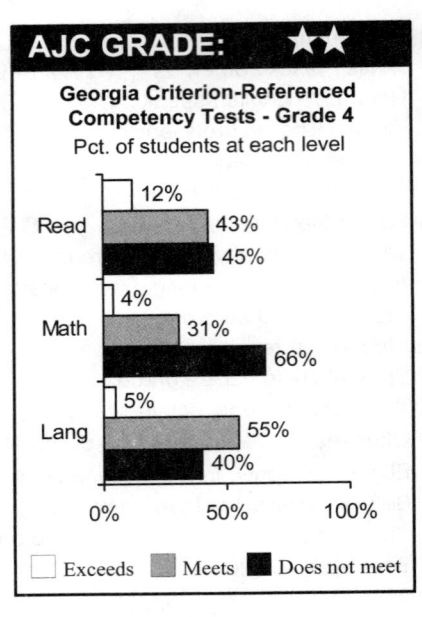

Chesnut Charter Elementary School

4576 N Peachtree Rd, Atlanta, GA 30338
678-676-7102 · Grades K - 5

Enrollment:	477
White / black / other:	43.8% / 27.7% / 28.5%
Not native English-speaking:	62 / 13.0%
Limited English proficiency:	149 / 31.2%
Student absenteeism:	4.0%
Students per teacher:	15.5
Parent friendliness:	① ❷ ❸ ④ ⑤ ❻
Teachers with advanced degrees:	38.7%
Average years' teaching experience:	11.7
Students in gifted program:	69 / 14.5%
Students in remedial education:	15.4%
Students held back a grade:	0.8%
Total suspensions, pct. in-school:	*
Offenses:	violence: *, drugs: *, other: *
Eligible students, free or reduced lunch:	22.8%
Before / after school program:	No / Yes

Students at this school generally go on to:
Peachtree Charter Middle

AJC GRADE: ★★★

Georgia Criterion-Referenced Competency Tests - Grade 4
Pct. of students at each level

Read: Exceeds 46%, Meets 30%, Does not meet 24%
Math: Exceeds 23%, Meets 48%, Does not meet 29%
Lang: Exceeds 22%, Meets 61%, Does not meet 16%

The Atlanta Journal-Constitution / Page 212

DeKalb County Elementary Schools

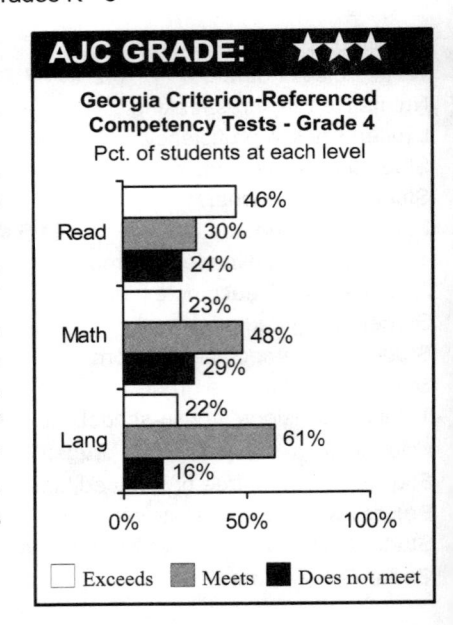

Clifton Elementary School

3132 Clifton Church Rd SE, Atlanta, GA 30316
404-241-1601 · Grades K - 7

Enrollment:	619
White / black / other:	0.6% / 96.9% / 2.4%
Not native English-speaking:	*
Limited English proficiency:	21 / 3.4%
Student absenteeism:	4.1%
Students per teacher:	14.9
Parent friendliness:	❶ ② ❸ ④ ⑤ ❻
Teachers with advanced degrees:	53.5%
Average years' teaching experience:	9.0
Students in gifted program:	42 / 6.8%
Students in remedial education:	20.9%
Students held back a grade:	0.6%
Total suspensions, pct. in-school:	157 / 67.5%
Offenses:	violence: 47, drugs: *, other: 113
Eligible students, free or reduced lunch:	69.6%
Before / after school program:	No / No

Students at this school generally go on to:
Cedar Grove, Columbia Middle

AJC GRADE: ★★★

Georgia Criterion-Referenced Competency Tests - Grade 4
Pct. of students at each level

- Read: Exceeds 24%, Meets 44%, Does not meet 32%
- Math: Exceeds 8%, Meets 50%, Does not meet 42%
- Lang: Exceeds 16%, Meets 53%, Does not meet 31%

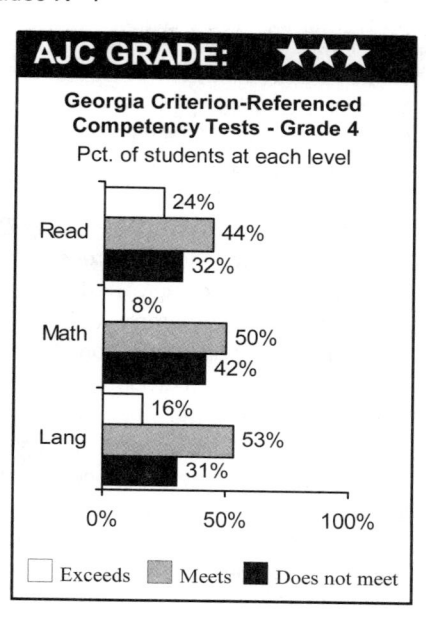

Columbia Elementary School

3230 Columbia Woods Dr, Decatur, GA 30032
404-284-5881 · Grades K - 7

Enrollment:	599
White / black / other:	0.0% / 98.2% / 1.8%
Not native English-speaking:	*
Limited English proficiency:	23 / 3.8%
Student absenteeism:	5.1%
Students per teacher:	16.6
Parent friendliness:	① ❷ ❸ ④ ⑤ ❻
Teachers with advanced degrees:	44.7%
Average years' teaching experience:	9.2
Students in gifted program:	28 / 4.7%
Students in remedial education:	32.4%
Students held back a grade:	0.2%
Total suspensions, pct. in-school:	62 / 40.3%
Offenses:	violence: 23, drugs: *, other: 42
Eligible students, free or reduced lunch:	85.1%
Before / after school program:	No / Yes

Students at this school generally go on to:
Columbia Middle

AJC GRADE: ★★★

Georgia Criterion-Referenced Competency Tests - Grade 4
Pct. of students at each level

- Read: Exceeds 15%, Meets 40%, Does not meet 45%
- Math: Exceeds 1%, Meets 45%, Does not meet 54%
- Lang: Exceeds 2%, Meets 64%, Does not meet 34%

DeKalb County Elementary Schools

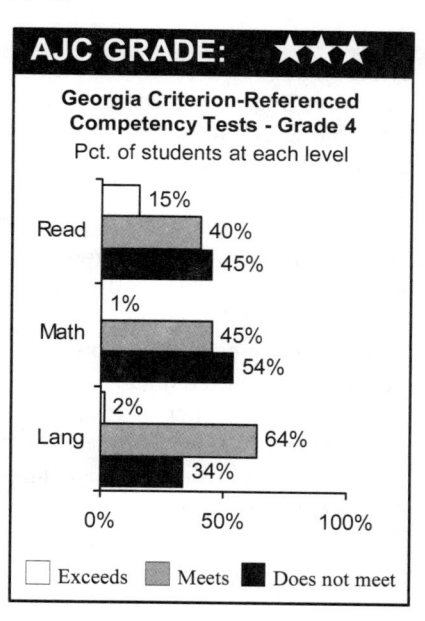

Dresden Elementary School

2449 Dresden Dr, Chamblee, GA 30341
678-676-7202 · Grades K - 5

Enrollment:	744
White / black / other:	3.0% / 15.2% / 81.9%
Not native English-speaking:	218 / 29.3%
Limited English proficiency:	660 / 88.7%
Student absenteeism:	4.5%
Students per teacher:	14.6
Parent friendliness:	❶❷❸④❺❻
Teachers with advanced degrees:	55.8%
Average years' teaching experience:	12.1
Students in gifted program:	35 / 4.7%
Students in remedial education:	33.3%
Students held back a grade:	4.0%
Total suspensions, pct. in-school:	*
Offenses:	violence: *, drugs: *, other: *
Eligible students, free or reduced lunch:	89.0%
Before / after school program:	No / Yes
Students at this school generally go on to:	
Sequoyah Middle	

AJC GRADE: ★★

Georgia Criterion-Referenced Competency Tests - Grade 4
Pct. of students at each level

- Read: Exceeds 14%, Meets 31%, Does not meet 55%
- Math: Exceeds 5%, Meets 36%, Does not meet 59%
- Lang: Exceeds 3%, Meets 46%, Does not meet 51%

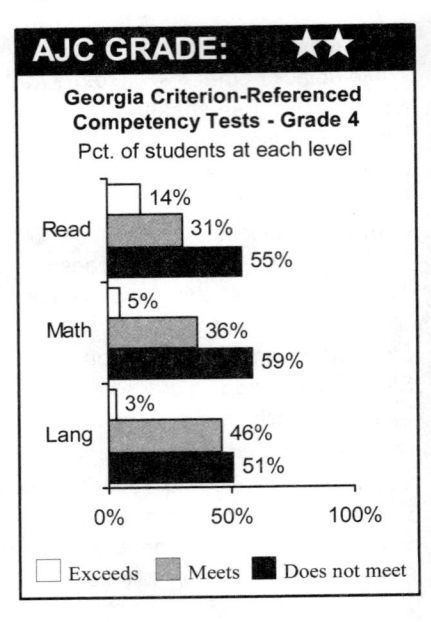

Dunaire Elementary School

651 S Indian Creek Dr, Stone Mountain, GA 30083
678-676-5502 · Grades K - 5

Enrollment:	645
White / black / other:	1.9% / 89.9% / 8.2%
Not native English-speaking:	9 / 1.4%
Limited English proficiency:	104 / 16.1%
Student absenteeism:	5.7%
Students per teacher:	15.7
Parent friendliness:	①❷❸④⑤⑥
Teachers with advanced degrees:	32.6%
Average years' teaching experience:	10.0
Students in gifted program:	20 / 3.1%
Students in remedial education:	30.5%
Students held back a grade:	1.6%
Total suspensions, pct. in-school:	62 / 53.2%
Offenses:	violence: 30, drugs: *, other: 32
Eligible students, free or reduced lunch:	73.5%
Before / after school program:	Yes / Yes
Students at this school generally go on to:	
Freedom Middle	

AJC GRADE: ★★★

Georgia Criterion-Referenced Competency Tests - Grade 4
Pct. of students at each level

- Read: Exceeds 28%, Meets 40%, Does not meet 32%
- Math: Exceeds 3%, Meets 63%, Does not meet 34%
- Lang: Exceeds 13%, Meets 59%, Does not meet 28%

DeKalb County Elementary Schools

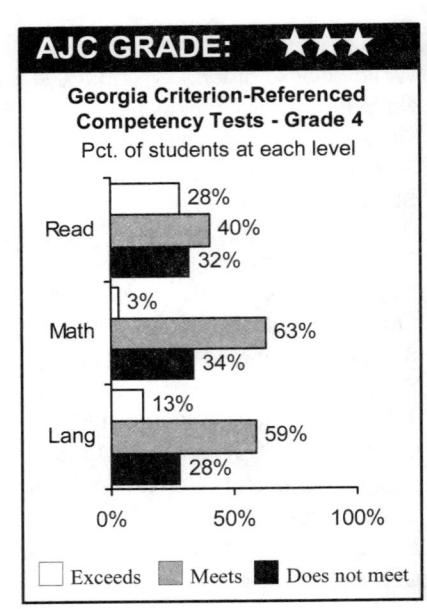

Eldridge Miller Elementary School

919 Martin Rd, Stone Mountain, GA 30088
678-676-3302 · Grades K - 5

Enrollment:	732
White / black / other:	1.4% / 94.3% / 4.4%
Not native English-speaking:	7 / 1.0%
Limited English proficiency:	32 / 4.4%
Student absenteeism:	4.8%
Students per teacher:	17.5
Parent friendliness:	① ❷ ❸ ④ ⑤ ❻
Teachers with advanced degrees:	52.3%
Average years' teaching experience:	11.4
Students in gifted program:	61 / 8.3%
Students in remedial education:	24.1%
Students held back a grade:	1.8%
Total suspensions, pct. in-school:	84 / 41.7%
Offenses:	violence: 47, drugs: *, other: 39
Eligible students, free or reduced lunch:	63.9%
Before / after school program:	Yes / Yes
Students at this school generally go on to:	
Miller Grove Middle	

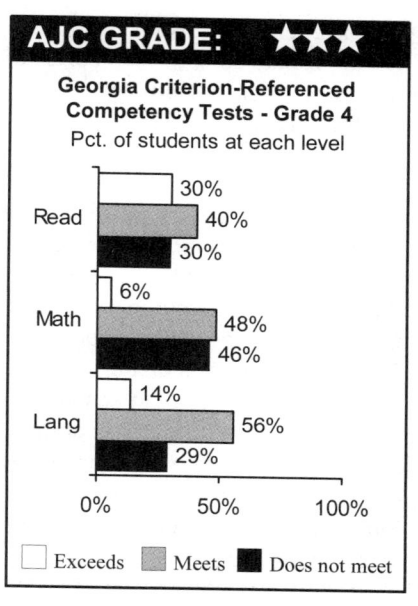

AJC GRADE: ★★★

Georgia Criterion-Referenced Competency Tests - Grade 4
Pct. of students at each level

- Read: Exceeds 30%, Meets 40%, Does not meet 30%
- Math: Exceeds 6%, Meets 48%, Does not meet 46%
- Lang: Exceeds 14%, Meets 56%, Does not meet 29%

Evansdale Elementary School

2914 Evans Woods Dr, Atlanta, GA 30340
770-939-1270 · Grades K - 6

Enrollment:	503
White / black / other:	42.7% / 33.2% / 24.1%
Not native English-speaking:	16 / 3.2%
Limited English proficiency:	70 / 13.9%
Student absenteeism:	3.9%
Students per teacher:	12.9
Parent friendliness:	① ❷ ❸ ④ ❺ ❻
Teachers with advanced degrees:	58.1%
Average years' teaching experience:	13.2
Students in gifted program:	104 / 20.7%
Students in remedial education:	7.0%
Students held back a grade:	1.2%
Total suspensions, pct. in-school:	*
Offenses:	violence: *, drugs: *, other: *
Eligible students, free or reduced lunch:	22.8%
Before / after school program:	Yes / No
Students at this school generally go on to:	
Henderson Middle	

AJC GRADE: ★★★

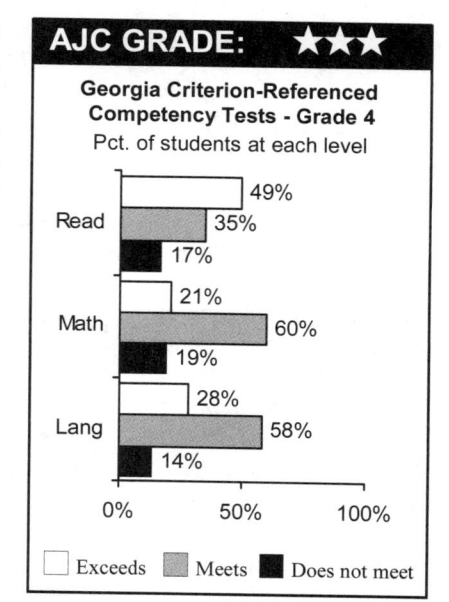

Georgia Criterion-Referenced Competency Tests - Grade 4
Pct. of students at each level

- Read: Exceeds 49%, Meets 35%, Does not meet 17%
- Math: Exceeds 21%, Meets 60%, Does not meet 19%
- Lang: Exceeds 28%, Meets 58%, Does not meet 14%

DeKalb County Elementary Schools

Fairington Elementary School

5505 Philip Bradley Dr, Lithonia, GA 30038
770-981-1610 · Grades K - 5

Enrollment:	907
White / black / other:	0.2% / 97.2% / 2.5%
Not native English-speaking:	*
Limited English proficiency:	53 / 5.8%
Student absenteeism:	5.0%
Students per teacher:	18.8
Parent friendliness:	①❷❸❹❺❻
Teachers with advanced degrees:	32.0%
Average years' teaching experience:	7.5
Students in gifted program:	22 / 2.4%
Students in remedial education:	15.8%
Students held back a grade:	0.2%
Total suspensions, pct. in-school:	26 / 23.1%
Offenses:	violence: 9, drugs: *, other: 21
Eligible students, free or reduced lunch:	69.2%
Before / after school program:	Yes / Yes
Students at this school generally go on to: Miller Grove Middle	

AJC GRADE: ★★

Georgia Criterion-Referenced Competency Tests - Grade 4
Pct. of students at each level

Read: Exceeds 10%, Meets 46%, Does not meet 44%
Math: Exceeds 1%, Meets 50%, Does not meet 49%
Lang: Exceeds 3%, Meets 59%, Does not meet 38%

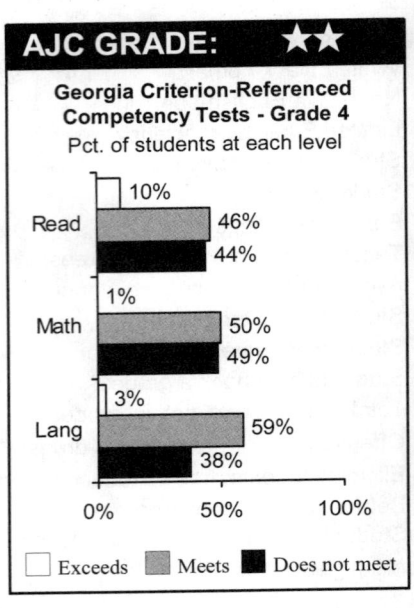

Fernbank Elementary School

157 Heaton Park Dr NE, Atlanta, GA 30307
404-378-1623 · Grades K - 5

Enrollment:	487
White / black / other:	66.5% / 20.7% / 12.7%
Not native English-speaking:	10 / 2.1%
Limited English proficiency:	57 / 11.7%
Student absenteeism:	3.3%
Students per teacher:	14.2
Parent friendliness:	❶❷❸④⑤⑥
Teachers with advanced degrees:	54.1%
Average years' teaching experience:	12.1
Students in gifted program:	95 / 19.5%
Students in remedial education:	8.3%
Students held back a grade:	0.2%
Total suspensions, pct. in-school:	*
Offenses:	violence: *, drugs: *, other: *
Eligible students, free or reduced lunch:	9.5%
Before / after school program:	No / Yes
Students at this school generally go on to: Shamrock Middle	

AJC GRADE: ★★★

Georgia Criterion-Referenced Competency Tests - Grade 4
Pct. of students at each level

Read: Exceeds 63%, Meets 31%, Does not meet 6%
Math: Exceeds 19%, Meets 68%, Does not meet 13%
Lang: Exceeds 32%, Meets 58%, Does not meet 10%

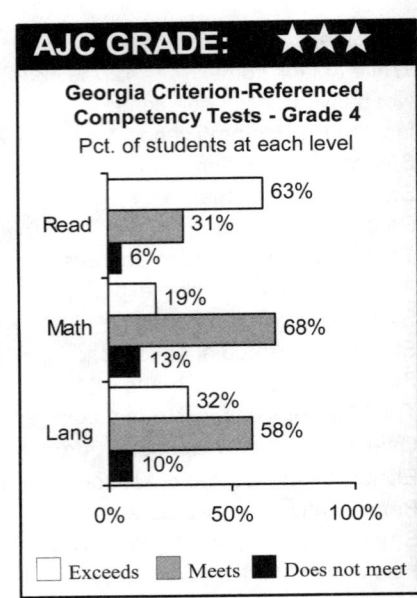

Flat Shoals Elementary School

3226 Flat Shoals Rd, Decatur, GA 30034
404-241-6832 · Grades K - 5

Enrollment:	495
White / black / other:	0.2% / 98.6% / 1.2%
Not native English-speaking:	*
Limited English proficiency:	61 / 12.3%
Student absenteeism:	4.9%
Students per teacher:	14.0
Parent friendliness:	① ❷ ❸ ④ ❺ ❻
Teachers with advanced degrees:	41.7%
Average years' teaching experience:	13.3
Students in gifted program:	15 / 3.0%
Students in remedial education:	36.8%
Students held back a grade:	1.6%
Total suspensions, pct. in-school:	37 / 0.0%
Offenses: violence: 14, drugs: *, other: 23	
Eligible students, free or reduced lunch:	82.3%
Before / after school program:	No / Yes
Students at this school generally go on to:	
Cedar Grove, Chapel Hill, McNair Middle	

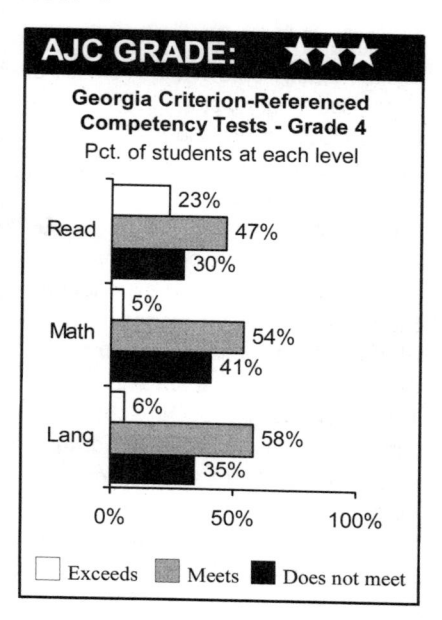

AJC GRADE: ★★★

Georgia Criterion-Referenced Competency Tests - Grade 4
Pct. of students at each level

Read — Exceeds: 23%, Meets: 47%, Does not meet: 30%
Math — Exceeds: 5%, Meets: 54%, Does not meet: 41%
Lang — Exceeds: 6%, Meets: 58%, Does not meet: 35%

Forrest Hills Elementary School

923 Forrest Blvd, Decatur, GA 30030
404-289-9361 · Grades K - 5

Enrollment:	357
White / black / other:	6.2% / 86.0% / 7.8%
Not native English-speaking:	5 / 1.4%
Limited English proficiency:	96 / 26.9%
Student absenteeism:	5.2%
Students per teacher:	12.8
Parent friendliness:	① ❷ ❸ ④ ❺ ❻
Teachers with advanced degrees:	55.2%
Average years' teaching experience:	10.6
Students in gifted program:	23 / 6.4%
Students in remedial education:	39.3%
Students held back a grade:	1.4%
Total suspensions, pct. in-school:	73 / 26.0%
Offenses: violence: 38, drugs: *, other: 36	
Eligible students, free or reduced lunch:	90.7%
Before / after school program:	Yes / Yes
Students at this school generally go on to:	
Avondale Middle	

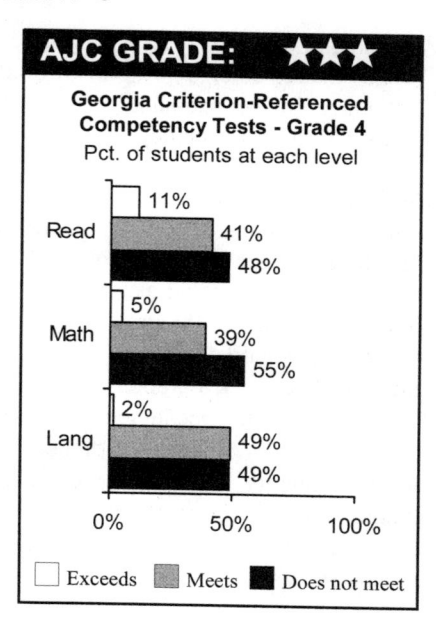

AJC GRADE: ★★★

Georgia Criterion-Referenced Competency Tests - Grade 4
Pct. of students at each level

Read — Exceeds: 11%, Meets: 41%, Does not meet: 48%
Math — Exceeds: 5%, Meets: 39%, Does not meet: 55%
Lang — Exceeds: 2%, Meets: 49%, Does not meet: 49%

DeKalb County Elementary Schools

Glen Haven Elementary School

1402 Austin Dr, Decatur, GA 30032
404-289-0121 · Grades K - 7

Enrollment:	754
White / black / other:	0.4% / 92.3% / 7.3%
Not native English-speaking:	5 / 0.7%
Limited English proficiency:	58 / 7.7%
Student absenteeism:	6.0%
Students per teacher:	17.2
Parent friendliness:	❶❷❸④❺❻
Teachers with advanced degrees:	51.1%
Average years' teaching experience:	9.5
Students in gifted program:	23 / 3.1%
Students in remedial education:	24.2%
Students held back a grade:	0.3%
Total suspensions, pct. in-school:	103 / 31.1%
Offenses:	violence: 47, drugs: *, other: 60
Eligible students, free or reduced lunch:	82.6%
Before / after school program:	No / Yes
Students at this school generally go on to:	Bethune Middle

AJC GRADE: ★★★★

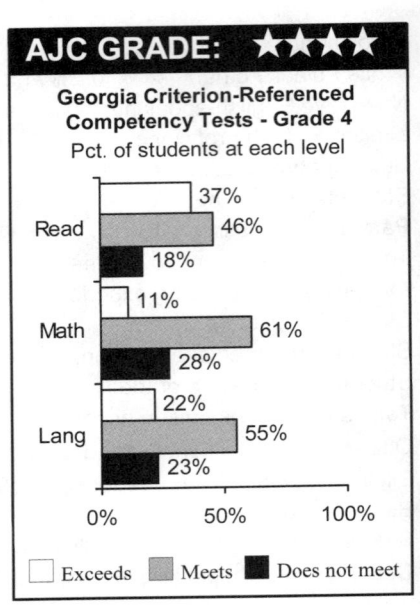

Georgia Criterion-Referenced Competency Tests - Grade 4
Pct. of students at each level

Read: 37% / 46% / 18%
Math: 11% / 61% / 28%
Lang: 22% / 55% / 23%

☐ Exceeds ▨ Meets ■ Does not meet

Gresham Park Elementary School

1848 Vicki Ln SE, Atlanta, GA 30316
404-241-7353 · Grades K - 6

Enrollment:	484
White / black / other:	0.6% / 98.8% / 0.6%
Not native English-speaking:	*
Limited English proficiency:	8 / 1.7%
Student absenteeism:	4.9%
Students per teacher:	13.1
Parent friendliness:	①❷❸④❺❻
Teachers with advanced degrees:	41.0%
Average years' teaching experience:	11.8
Students in gifted program:	25 / 5.2%
Students in remedial education:	35.8%
Students held back a grade:	0.6%
Total suspensions, pct. in-school:	28 / 67.9%
Offenses:	violence: 7, drugs: *, other: 21
Eligible students, free or reduced lunch:	91.1%
Before / after school program:	Yes / Yes
Students at this school generally go on to:	McNair Middle

AJC GRADE: ★★★

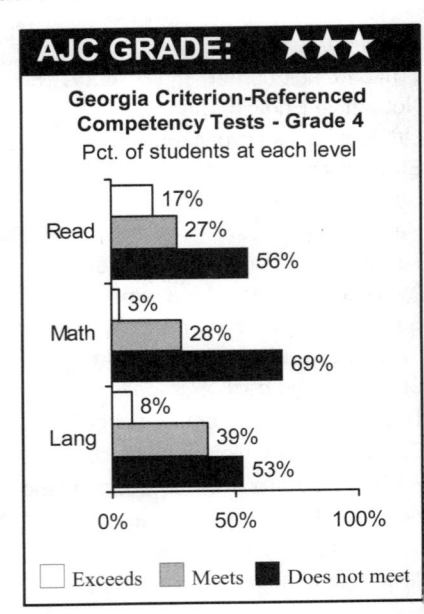

Georgia Criterion-Referenced Competency Tests - Grade 4
Pct. of students at each level

Read: 17% / 27% / 56%
Math: 3% / 28% / 69%
Lang: 8% / 39% / 53%

☐ Exceeds ▨ Meets ■ Does not meet

DeKalb County Elementary Schools

Hambrick Elementary School

1101 Hambrick Rd, Stone Mountain, GA 30083
678-676-5602 · Grades K - 6

Enrollment:	779
White / black / other:	3.9% / 86.3% / 9.9%
Not native English-speaking:	41 / 5.3%
Limited English proficiency:	102 / 13.1%
Student absenteeism:	4.7%
Students per teacher:	17.7
Parent friendliness:	①❷❸④❺❻
Teachers with advanced degrees:	34.8%
Average years' teaching experience:	8.8
Students in gifted program:	48 / 6.2%
Students in remedial education:	22.3%
Students held back a grade:	0.5%
Total suspensions, pct. in-school:	46 / 2.2%
Offenses:	violence: 31, drugs: 4, other: 15
Eligible students, free or reduced lunch:	74.7%
Before / after school program:	Yes / Yes

Students at this school generally go on to:
Stone Mountain Middle

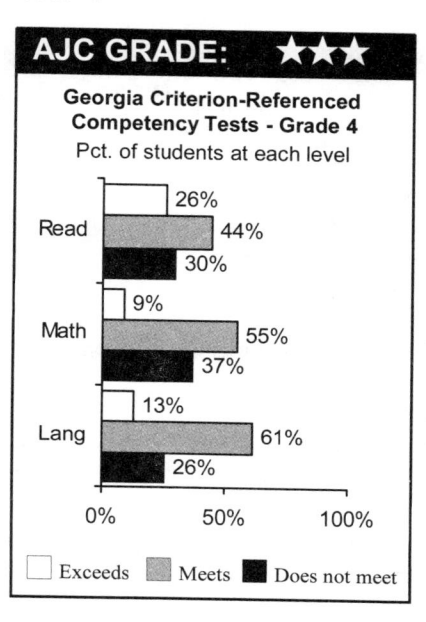

AJC GRADE: ★★★

Georgia Criterion-Referenced Competency Tests - Grade 4
Pct. of students at each level

- Read: Exceeds 26%, Meets 44%, Does not meet 30%
- Math: Exceeds 9%, Meets 55%, Does not meet 37%
- Lang: Exceeds 13%, Meets 61%, Does not meet 26%

Hawthorne Elementary School

2535 Caladium Dr NE, Atlanta, GA 30345
770-938-4122 · Grades K - 6

Enrollment:	319
White / black / other:	27.6% / 31.7% / 40.8%
Not native English-speaking:	63 / 19.7%
Limited English proficiency:	173 / 54.2%
Student absenteeism:	5.7%
Students per teacher:	9.9
Parent friendliness:	❶❷❸④❺❻
Teachers with advanced degrees:	47.1%
Average years' teaching experience:	9.2
Students in gifted program:	38 / 11.9%
Students in remedial education:	25.9%
Students held back a grade:	2.2%
Total suspensions, pct. in-school:	2 / 0.0%
Offenses:	violence: 1, drugs: *, other: 1
Eligible students, free or reduced lunch:	65.9%
Before / after school program:	Yes / Yes

Students at this school generally go on to:
Henderson Middle

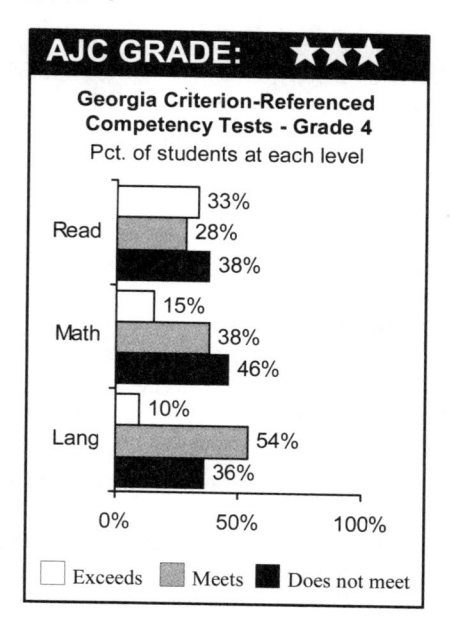

AJC GRADE: ★★★

Georgia Criterion-Referenced Competency Tests - Grade 4
Pct. of students at each level

- Read: Exceeds 33%, Meets 28%, Does not meet 38%
- Math: Exceeds 15%, Meets 38%, Does not meet 46%
- Lang: Exceeds 10%, Meets 54%, Does not meet 36%

DeKalb County Elementary Schools

Henderson Mill Elementary School

2408 Henderson Mill Rd NE, Atlanta, GA 30345
770-938-5271 · Grades K - 6

Enrollment:	501
White / black / other:	41.7% / 26.9% / 31.3%
Not native English-speaking:	26 / 5.2%
Limited English proficiency:	157 / 31.3%
Student absenteeism:	4.0%
Students per teacher:	14.1
Parent friendliness:	①❷❸❹❺❻
Teachers with advanced degrees:	60.5%
Average years' teaching experience:	16.1
Students in gifted program:	116 / 23.2%
Students in remedial education:	27.7%
Students held back a grade:	2.4%
Total suspensions, pct. in-school:	1 / 0.0%
Offenses:	violence: * , drugs: * , other: 1
Eligible students, free or reduced lunch:	31.9%
Before / after school program:	Yes / Yes
Students at this school generally go on to:	
Henderson Middle	

AJC GRADE: ★★★

Georgia Criterion-Referenced Competency Tests - Grade 4
Pct. of students at each level

Read: Exceeds 46%, Meets 39%, Does not meet 15%
Math: Exceeds 16%, Meets 59%, Does not meet 24%
Lang: Exceeds 30%, Meets 59%, Does not meet 11%

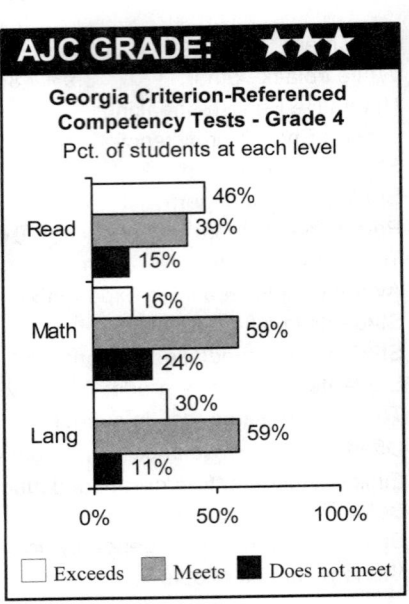

Hightower Elementary School

4236 Tilly Mill Rd, Atlanta, GA 30360
770-457-6241 · Grades K - 5

Enrollment:	420
White / black / other:	8.1% / 33.3% / 58.6%
Not native English-speaking:	107 / 25.5%
Limited English proficiency:	292 / 69.5%
Student absenteeism:	5.0%
Students per teacher:	12.9
Parent friendliness:	❶❷❸❹⑤❻
Teachers with advanced degrees:	52.9%
Average years' teaching experience:	13.7
Students in gifted program:	8 / 1.9%
Students in remedial education:	35.4%
Students held back a grade:	0.5%
Total suspensions, pct. in-school:	4 / 75.0%
Offenses:	violence: * , drugs: * , other: 4
Eligible students, free or reduced lunch:	83.1%
Before / after school program:	No / Yes
Students at this school generally go on to:	
Peachtree Charter Middle	

AJC GRADE: ★★★

Georgia Criterion-Referenced Competency Tests - Grade 4
Pct. of students at each level

Read: Exceeds 14%, Meets 48%, Does not meet 38%
Math: Exceeds 2%, Meets 50%, Does not meet 48%
Lang: Exceeds 2%, Meets 56%, Does not meet 43%

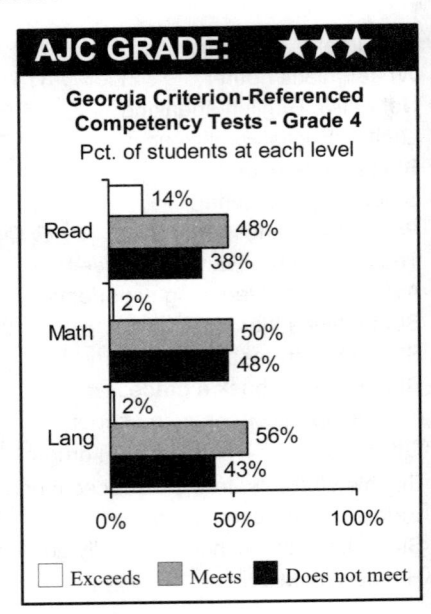

Hooper Alexander Elementary School

3414 Memorial Dr, Decatur, GA 30032
404-289-1933 · Grades K - 7

Enrollment:	351
White / black / other:	0.9% / 92.6% / 6.6%
Not native English-speaking:	7 / 2.0%
Limited English proficiency:	21 / 6.0%
Student absenteeism:	3.0%
Students per teacher:	10.4
Parent friendliness:	① ❷ ❸ ④ ⑤ ❻
Teachers with advanced degrees:	55.6%
Average years' teaching experience:	14.1
Students in gifted program:	26 / 7.4%
Students in remedial education:	36.5%
Students held back a grade:	0.6%
Total suspensions, pct. in-school:	133 / 62.4%
Offenses:	violence: 32, drugs: *, other: 114
Eligible students, free or reduced lunch:	86.9%
Before / after school program:	Yes / Yes

Students at this school generally go on to:
Avondale Middle

AJC GRADE: ★★★

Georgia Criterion-Referenced Competency Tests - Grade 4
Pct. of students at each level

- Read — Exceeds: 15%, Meets: 46%, Does not meet: 39%
- Math — Exceeds: 1%, Meets: 35%, Does not meet: 65%
- Lang — Exceeds: 4%, Meets: 56%, Does not meet: 40%

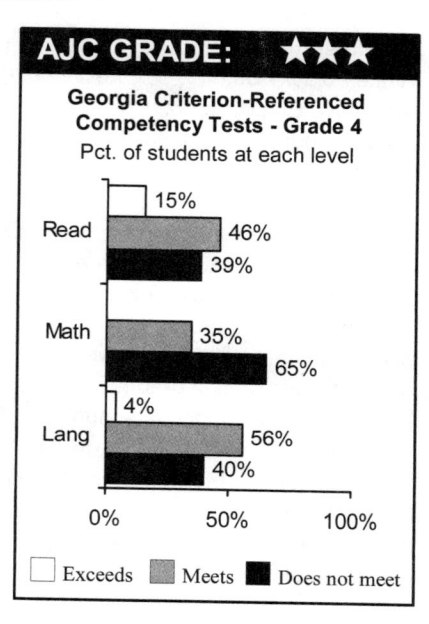

Huntley Hills Elementary School

2112 Seaman Cir, Atlanta, GA 30341
678-676-7402 · Grades K - 6

Enrollment:	265
White / black / other:	25.7% / 52.1% / 22.3%
Not native English-speaking:	13 / 4.9%
Limited English proficiency:	63 / 23.8%
Student absenteeism:	6.5%
Students per teacher:	10.2
Parent friendliness:	① ❷ ❸ ④ ⑤ ❻
Teachers with advanced degrees:	55.2%
Average years' teaching experience:	14.9
Students in gifted program:	53 / 20.0%
Students in remedial education:	18.2%
Students held back a grade:	3.0%
Total suspensions, pct. in-school:	1 / 0.0%
Offenses:	violence: *, drugs: *, other: 1
Eligible students, free or reduced lunch:	55.1%
Before / after school program:	No / Yes

Students at this school generally go on to:
Chamblee Middle

AJC GRADE: ★★★★

Georgia Criterion-Referenced Competency Tests - Grade 4
Pct. of students at each level

- Read — Exceeds: 50%, Meets: 35%, Does not meet: 15%
- Math — Exceeds: 24%, Meets: 59%, Does not meet: 18%
- Lang — Exceeds: 50%, Meets: 35%, Does not meet: 15%

DeKalb County Elementary Schools

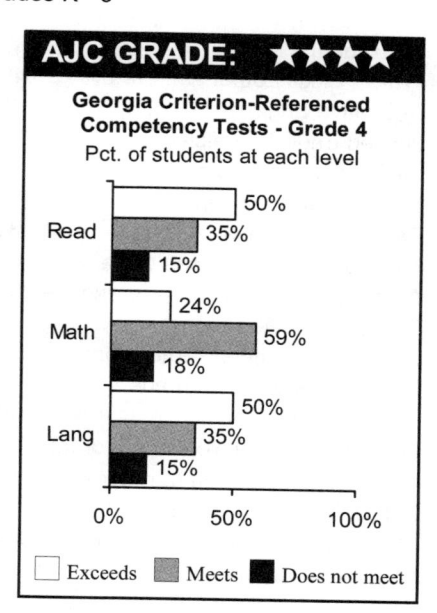

Idlewood Elementary School

1484 Idlewood Rd, Tucker, GA 30084
770-939-2996 · Grades K - 5

Enrollment:	799
White / black / other:	4.8% / 80.1% / 15.1%
Not native English-speaking:	75 / 9.4%
Limited English proficiency:	211 / 26.4%
Student absenteeism:	5.2%
Students per teacher:	16.1
Parent friendliness:	①❷❸④⑤⑥
Teachers with advanced degrees:	38.5%
Average years' teaching experience:	9.2
Students in gifted program:	22 / 2.8%
Students in remedial education:	20.7%
Students held back a grade:	4.3%
Total suspensions, pct. in-school:	81 / 70.4%
Offenses:	violence: 34, drugs: * , other: 52
Eligible students, free or reduced lunch:	89.2%
Before / after school program:	No / No

Students at this school generally go on to:
Henderson Middle

AJC GRADE: ★★★★

Georgia Criterion-Referenced Competency Tests - Grade 4
Pct. of students at each level

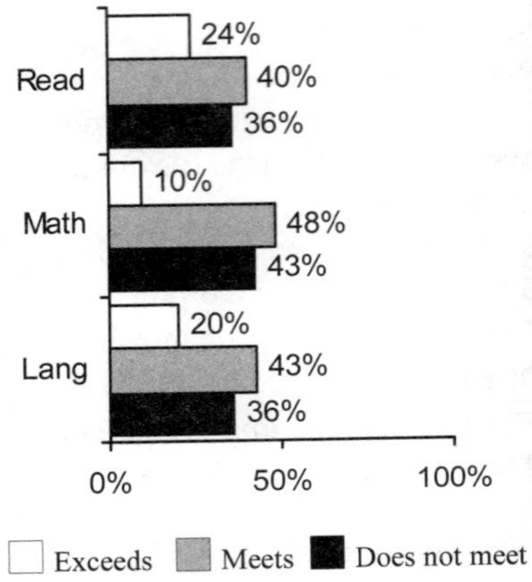
Read
24%
40%
36%
Math
10%
48%
43%
Lang
20%
43%
36%
0%
50%
100%
Exceeds
Meets
Does not meet

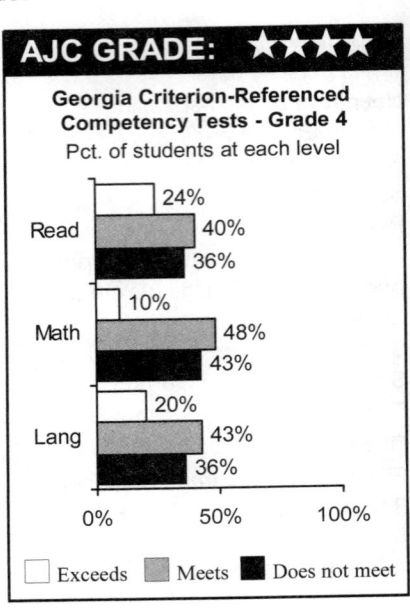

Indian Creek Elementary School

724 N Indian Creek Dr, Clarkston, GA 30021
678-676-5702 · Grades K - 5

Enrollment:	737
White / black / other:	18.6% / 57.4% / 24.0%
Not native English-speaking:	159 / 21.6%
Limited English proficiency:	604 / 82.0%
Student absenteeism:	4.2%
Students per teacher:	15.0
Parent friendliness:	①❷❸④❺❻
Teachers with advanced degrees:	36.0%
Average years' teaching experience:	11.4
Students in gifted program:	16 / 2.2%
Students in remedial education:	38.3%
Students held back a grade:	0.3%
Total suspensions, pct. in-school:	82 / 70.7%
Offenses:	violence: 30, drugs: * , other: 52
Eligible students, free or reduced lunch:	92.0%
Before / after school program:	Yes / Yes

Students at this school generally go on to:
Freedom Middle

AJC GRADE: ★

Georgia Criterion-Referenced Competency Tests - Grade 4
Pct. of students at each level

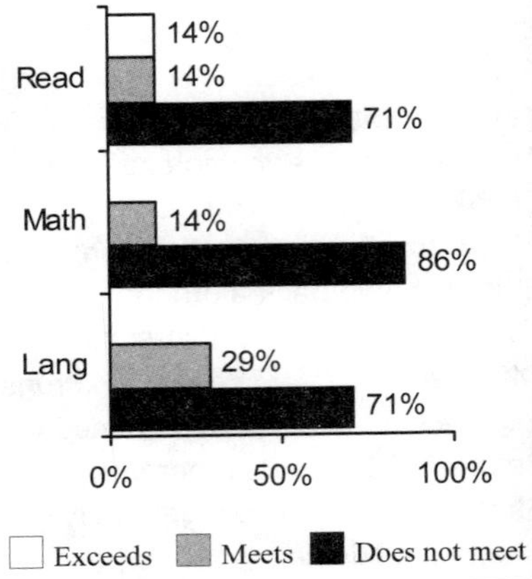
Read
14%
14%
71%
Math
14%
86%
Lang
29%
71%
0%
50%
100%
Exceeds
Meets
Does not meet

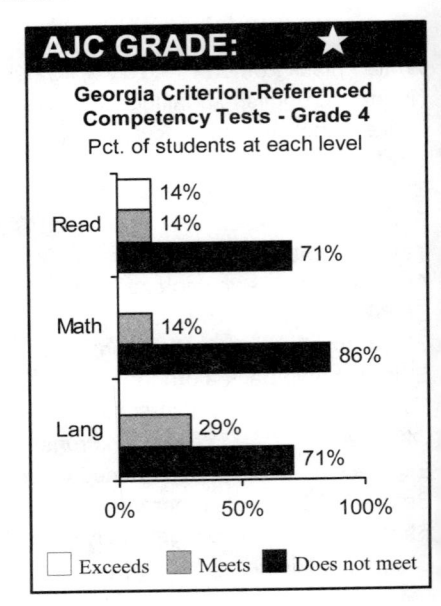

Jolly Elementary School

1070 Otello Ave, Clarkston, GA 30021
678-676-5802 · Grades K - 5

Enrollment:	493
White / black / other:	3.0% / 78.9% / 18.1%
Not native English-speaking:	36 / 7.3%
Limited English proficiency:	195 / 39.6%
Student absenteeism:	5.0%
Students per teacher:	12.6
Parent friendliness:	①❷❸④⑤❻
Teachers with advanced degrees:	67.5%
Average years' teaching experience:	13.5
Students in gifted program:	55 / 11.2%
Students in remedial education:	30.1%
Students held back a grade:	1.2%
Total suspensions, pct. in-school:	65 / 29.2%
Offenses:	violence: 36, drugs: * , other: 31
Eligible students, free or reduced lunch:	80.8%
Before / after school program:	Yes / Yes

Students at this school generally go on to:
Freedom Middle

AJC GRADE: ★★★

Georgia Criterion-Referenced Competency Tests - Grade 4
Pct. of students at each level

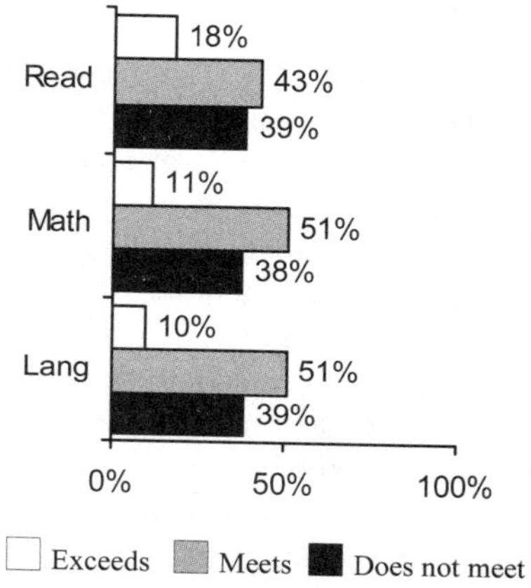
Read
18%
43%
39%
Math
11%
51%
38%
Lang
10%
51%
39%
0%
50%
100%
Exceeds
Meets
Does not meet

Kelley Lake Elementary School

2590 Kelly Lake Rd, Decatur, GA 30032
404-241-5642 · Grades K - 6

Enrollment:	500
White / black / other:	0.0% / 98.2% / 1.8%
Not native English-speaking:	4 / 0.8%
Limited English proficiency:	24 / 4.8%
Student absenteeism:	5.8%
Students per teacher:	12.8
Parent friendliness:	①❷❸④⑤❻
Teachers with advanced degrees:	31.7%
Average years' teaching experience:	9.4
Students in gifted program:	15 / 3.0%
Students in remedial education:	50.7%
Students held back a grade:	0.6%
Total suspensions, pct. in-school:	*
Offenses:	violence: * , drugs: * , other: *
Eligible students, free or reduced lunch:	94.2%
Before / after school program:	No / Yes

Students at this school generally go on to:
Columbia Middle

AJC GRADE: ★★★

Georgia Criterion-Referenced Competency Tests - Grade 4
Pct. of students at each level

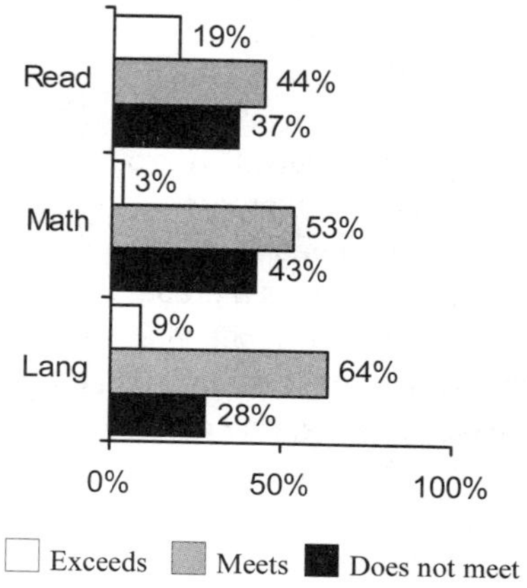
Read
19%
44%
37%
Math
3%
53%
43%
Lang
9%
64%
28%
0%
50%
100%
Exceeds
Meets
Does not meet

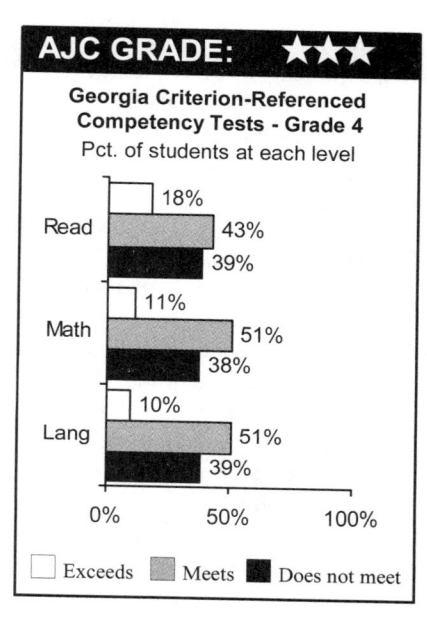

Kingsley Charter Elementary School

2051 Brendon Dr, Dunwoody, GA 30338
770-394-5779 · Grades K - 5

Enrollment:	356
White / black / other:	36.5% / 49.7% / 13.8%
Not native English-speaking:	7 / 2.0%
Limited English proficiency:	52 / 14.6%
Student absenteeism:	4.1%
Students per teacher:	15.4
Parent friendliness:	①❷❸④❺❻
Teachers with advanced degrees:	45.8%
Average years' teaching experience:	13.3
Students in gifted program:	51 / 14.3%
Students in remedial education:	22.8%
Students held back a grade:	1.7%
Total suspensions, pct. in-school:	11 / 54.5%
Offenses:	violence: 12, drugs: *, other: 5
Eligible students, free or reduced lunch:	30.3%
Before / after school program:	Yes / Yes

Students at this school generally go on to:
Peachtree Charter Middle

AJC GRADE: ★★★

Georgia Criterion-Referenced Competency Tests - Grade 4
Pct. of students at each level

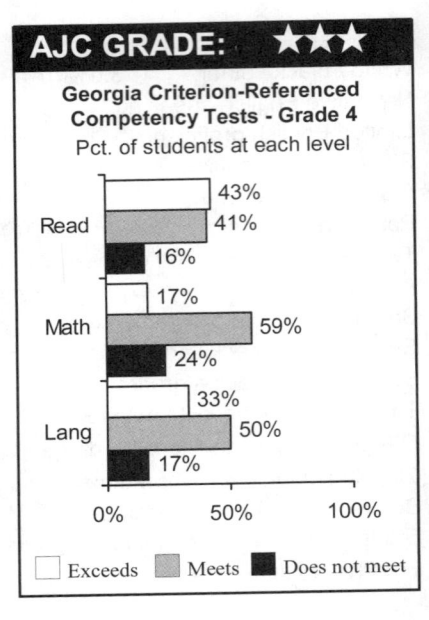

Read: Exceeds 43%, Meets 41%, Does not meet 16%
Math: Exceeds 17%, Meets 59%, Does not meet 24%
Lang: Exceeds 33%, Meets 50%, Does not meet 17%

Kittredge Magnet School for High Achievers

2383 N Druid Hills Rd NE, Atlanta, GA 30329
404-636-7509 · Grades 4 - 6

Enrollment:	411
White / black / other:	62.0% / 26.3% / 11.7%
Not native English-speaking:	*
Limited English proficiency:	22 / 5.4%
Student absenteeism:	2.7%
Students per teacher:	15.5
Parent friendliness:	❶❷❸④❺❻
Teachers with advanced degrees:	60.7%
Average years' teaching experience:	15.0
Students in gifted program:	332 / 80.8%
Students in remedial education:	*
Students held back a grade:	*
Total suspensions, pct. in-school:	*
Offenses:	violence: *, drugs: *, other: *
Eligible students, free or reduced lunch:	4.1%
Before / after school program:	No / No

Students at this school generally go on to:
Chamblee Middle

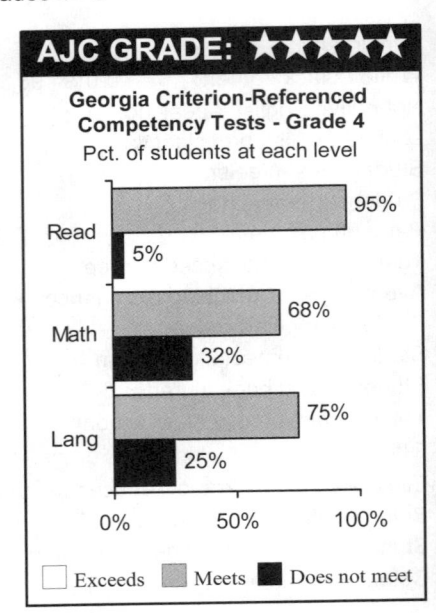

AJC GRADE: ★★★★★

Georgia Criterion-Referenced Competency Tests - Grade 4
Pct. of students at each level

Read: Exceeds 95%, Meets 5%
Math: Exceeds 68%, Meets 32%
Lang: Exceeds 75%, Meets 25%

DeKalb County Elementary Schools

Knollwood Elementary School

3039 Santa Monica Dr, Decatur, GA 30032
404-289-2966 · Grades K - 5

Enrollment:	440
White / black / other:	0.7% / 97.0% / 2.3%
Not native English-speaking:	*
Limited English proficiency:	18 / 4.1%
Student absenteeism:	5.8%
Students per teacher:	13.1
Parent friendliness:	❶❷❸④❺❻
Teachers with advanced degrees:	41.2%
Average years' teaching experience:	11.3
Students in gifted program:	40 / 9.1%
Students in remedial education:	36.6%
Students held back a grade:	1.6%
Total suspensions, pct. in-school:	139 / 61.2%
Offenses:	violence: 32, drugs: *, other: 109
Eligible students, free or reduced lunch:	96.8%
Before / after school program:	Yes / Yes

Students at this school generally go on to:
Avondale Middle

AJC GRADE: ★★★

Georgia Criterion-Referenced Competency Tests - Grade 4
Pct. of students at each level

- Read: Exceeds 17%, Meets 45%, Does not meet 38%
- Math: Exceeds 0%, Meets 39%, Does not meet 61%
- Lang: Exceeds 6%, Meets 51%, Does not meet 43%

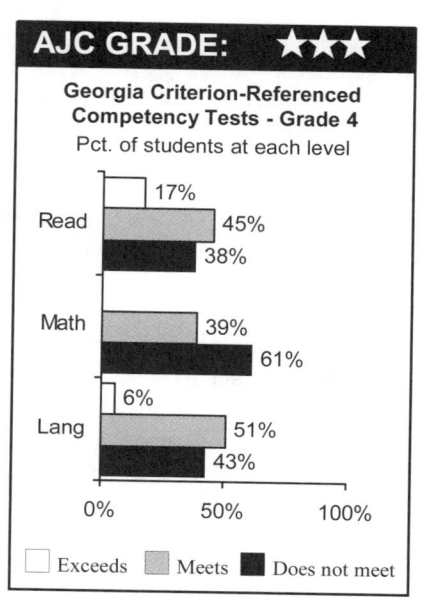

Laurel Ridge Elementary School

1215 Balsam Dr, Decatur, GA 30033
404-636-7212 · Grades K - 5

Enrollment:	323
White / black / other:	35.0% / 48.6% / 16.4%
Not native English-speaking:	7 / 2.2%
Limited English proficiency:	54 / 16.7%
Student absenteeism:	4.9%
Students per teacher:	10.9
Parent friendliness:	①❷❸④⑤❻
Teachers with advanced degrees:	51.5%
Average years' teaching experience:	15.8
Students in gifted program:	17 / 5.3%
Students in remedial education:	6.0%
Students held back a grade:	*
Total suspensions, pct. in-school:	*
Offenses:	violence: *, drugs: *, other: *
Eligible students, free or reduced lunch:	40.5%
Before / after school program:	No / Yes

Students at this school generally go on to:
Shamrock Middle

AJC GRADE: ★★★

Georgia Criterion-Referenced Competency Tests - Grade 4
Pct. of students at each level

- Read: Exceeds 32%, Meets 48%, Does not meet 20%
- Math: Exceeds 12%, Meets 60%, Does not meet 28%
- Lang: Exceeds 16%, Meets 62%, Does not meet 22%

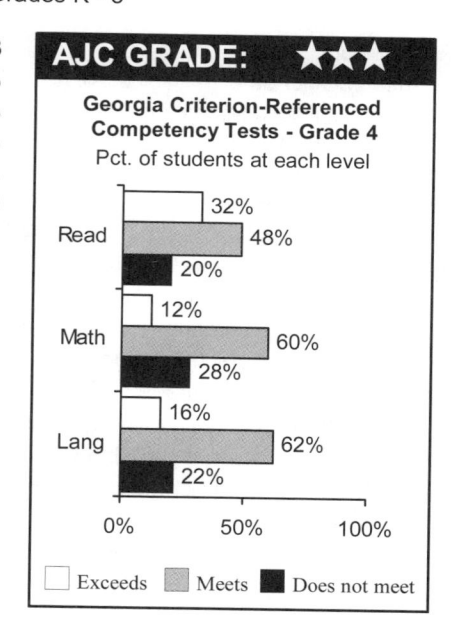

Livsey Elementary School

4137 Livsey Rd, Tucker, GA 30084
770-934-8283 · Grades K - 6

Enrollment:	291
White / black / other:	67.0% / 17.5% / 15.5%
Not native English-speaking:	4 / 1.4%
Limited English proficiency:	30 / 10.3%
Student absenteeism:	3.3%
Students per teacher:	13.0
Parent friendliness:	❶❷❸④❺❻
Teachers with advanced degrees:	54.2%
Average years' teaching experience:	14.8
Students in gifted program:	59 / 20.3%
Students in remedial education:	8.5%
Students held back a grade:	1.0%
Total suspensions, pct. in-school:	9 / 66.7%
Offenses:	violence: 8, drugs: *, other: 4
Eligible students, free or reduced lunch:	8.5%
Before / after school program:	No / Yes

Students at this school generally go on to:
Henderson Middle

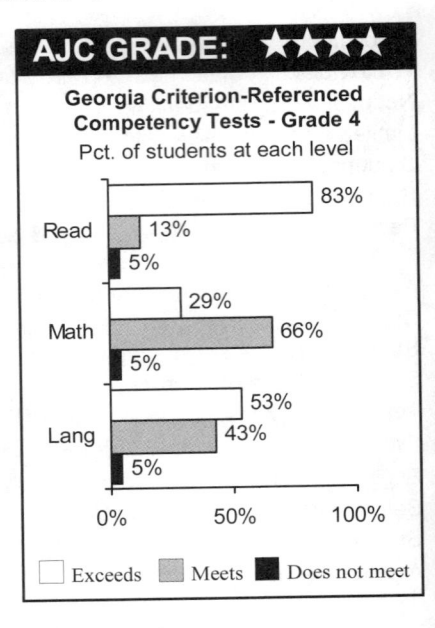

AJC GRADE: ★★★★

Georgia Criterion-Referenced Competency Tests - Grade 4
Pct. of students at each level

Read: 83% / 13% / 5%
Math: 29% / 66% / 5%
Lang: 53% / 43% / 5%

☐ Exceeds ▨ Meets ■ Does not meet

Marbut Elementary School

5776 Marbut Rd, Lithonia, GA 30058
678-676-8802 · Grades K - 6

Enrollment:	1,002
White / black / other:	0.5% / 97.3% / 2.2%
Not native English-speaking:	*
Limited English proficiency:	4 / 0.4%
Student absenteeism:	2.2%
Students per teacher:	16.7
Parent friendliness:	❶❷❸④⑤❻
Teachers with advanced degrees:	39.7%
Average years' teaching experience:	9.0
Students in gifted program:	161 / 16.1%
Students in remedial education:	28.0%
Students held back a grade:	0.1%
Total suspensions, pct. in-school:	206 / 71.8%
Offenses:	violence: 35, drugs: *, other: 173
Eligible students, free or reduced lunch:	38.6%
Before / after school program:	No / No

Students at this school generally go on to:
Miller Grove, Salem, Stephenson Middle

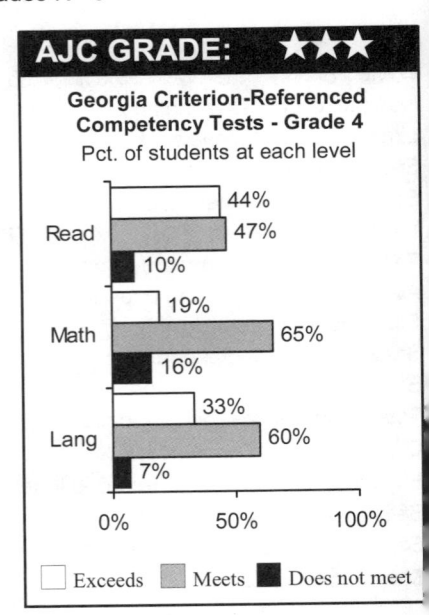

AJC GRADE: ★★★

Georgia Criterion-Referenced Competency Tests - Grade 4
Pct. of students at each level

Read: 44% / 47% / 10%
Math: 19% / 65% / 16%
Lang: 33% / 60% / 7%

☐ Exceeds ▨ Meets ■ Does not meet

McLendon Elementary School

3169 Hollywood Dr, Decatur, GA 30033
678-676-5902 · Grades K - 5

Enrollment:	616
White / black / other:	16.4% / 68.2% / 15.4%
Not native English-speaking:	101 / 16.4%
Limited English proficiency:	223 / 36.2%
Student absenteeism:	5.1%
Students per teacher:	15.2
Parent friendliness:	❶❷❸❹❺❻
Teachers with advanced degrees:	36.6%
Average years' teaching experience:	10.1
Students in gifted program:	6 / 1.0%
Students in remedial education:	26.4%
Students held back a grade:	3.2%
Total suspensions, pct. in-school:	45 / 2.2%
Offenses:	violence: 27, drugs: *, other: 18
Eligible students, free or reduced lunch:	84.7%
Before / after school program:	No / No

Students at this school generally go on to:
Shamrock Middle

AJC GRADE: ★★

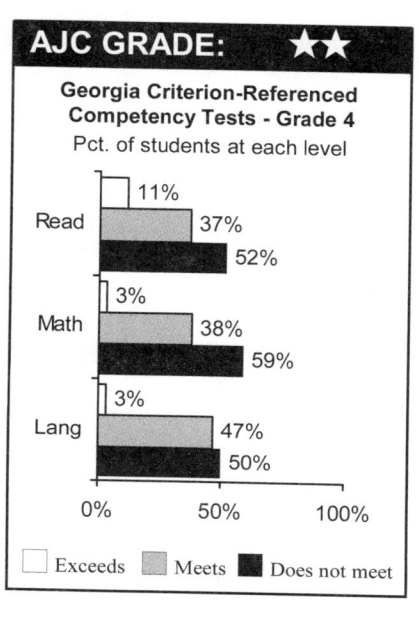

Georgia Criterion-Referenced Competency Tests - Grade 4
Pct. of students at each level

Read: Exceeds 11%, Meets 37%, Does not meet 52%
Math: Exceeds 3%, Meets 38%, Does not meet 59%
Lang: Exceeds 3%, Meets 47%, Does not meet 50%

Meadowview Elementary School

1879 Wee Kirk Rd SE, Atlanta, GA 30316
404-241-1066 · Grades K - 5

Enrollment:	444
White / black / other:	3.8% / 91.4% / 4.7%
Not native English-speaking:	*
Limited English proficiency:	54 / 12.2%
Student absenteeism:	4.4%
Students per teacher:	12.3
Parent friendliness:	①❷❸④⑤❻
Teachers with advanced degrees:	47.2%
Average years' teaching experience:	11.6
Students in gifted program:	43 / 9.7%
Students in remedial education:	43.6%
Students held back a grade:	2.0%
Total suspensions, pct. in-school:	20 / 0.0%
Offenses:	violence: 4, drugs: *, other: 17
Eligible students, free or reduced lunch:	92.6%
Before / after school program:	Yes / Yes

Students at this school generally go on to:
McNair Middle

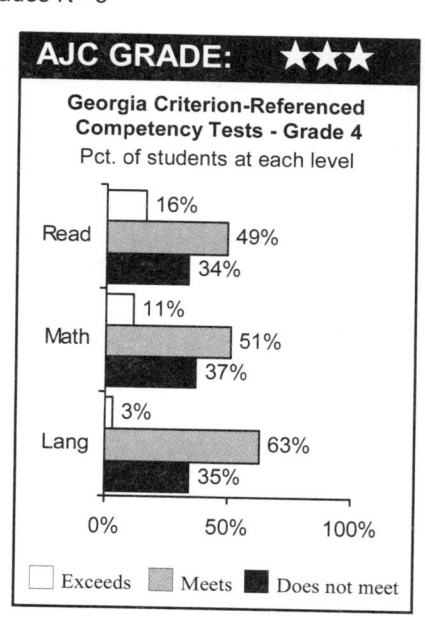

AJC GRADE: ★★★

Georgia Criterion-Referenced Competency Tests - Grade 4
Pct. of students at each level

Read: Exceeds 16%, Meets 49%, Does not meet 34%
Math: Exceeds 11%, Meets 51%, Does not meet 37%
Lang: Exceeds 3%, Meets 63%, Does not meet 35%

The Atlanta Journal-Constitution / Page 227

DeKalb County Elementary Schools

Medlock Elementary School

2418 Wood Trail Ln, Decatur, GA 30033
404-634-8458 · Grades K - 5

Enrollment:	281
White / black / other:	27.0% / 52.3% / 20.6%
Not native English-speaking:	19 / 6.8%
Limited English proficiency:	52 / 18.5%
Student absenteeism:	6.0%
Students per teacher:	9.7
Parent friendliness:	① ❷ ❸ ④ ❺ ❻
Teachers with advanced degrees:	46.9%
Average years' teaching experience:	12.1
Students in gifted program:	19 / 6.8%
Students in remedial education:	36.4%
Students held back a grade:	2.5%
Total suspensions, pct. in-school:	16 / 6.3%
Offenses:	violence: 7, drugs: *, other: 9
Eligible students, free or reduced lunch:	66.7%
Before / after school program:	Yes / Yes
Students at this school generally go on to:	
Shamrock Middle	

AJC GRADE: ★★★★

Georgia Criterion-Referenced Competency Tests - Grade 4
Pct. of students at each level

Read: 43% Exceeds / 33% Meets / 24% Does not meet
Math: 18% Exceeds / 59% Meets / 22% Does not meet
Lang: 22% Exceeds / 59% Meets / 18% Does not meet

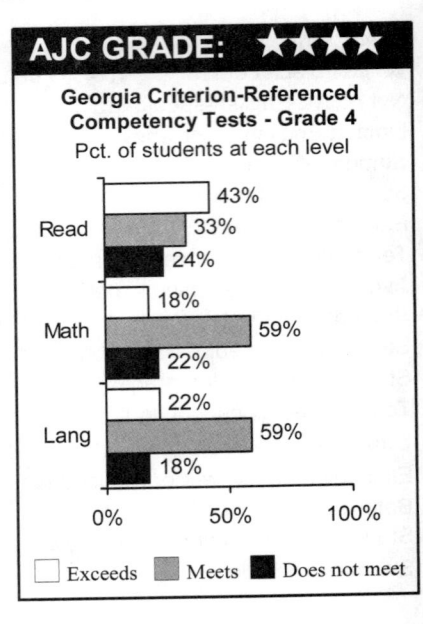

Midvale Elementary School

3836 Midvale Rd, Tucker, GA 30084
770-938-5938 · Grades K - 6

Enrollment:	444
White / black / other:	34.7% / 49.8% / 15.5%
Not native English-speaking:	6 / 1.4%
Limited English proficiency:	62 / 14.0%
Student absenteeism:	3.4%
Students per teacher:	15.0
Parent friendliness:	❶ ② ❸ ④ ⑤ ❻
Teachers with advanced degrees:	53.1%
Average years' teaching experience:	14.1
Students in gifted program:	55 / 12.4%
Students in remedial education:	17.4%
Students held back a grade:	2.0%
Total suspensions, pct. in-school:	50 / 62.0%
Offenses:	violence: 23, drugs: *, other: 27
Eligible students, free or reduced lunch:	46.6%
Before / after school program:	No / Yes
Students at this school generally go on to:	
Henderson Middle	

AJC GRADE: ★★★

Georgia Criterion-Referenced Competency Tests - Grade 4
Pct. of students at each level

Read: 50% Exceeds / 38% Meets / 12% Does not meet
Math: 25% Exceeds / 61% Meets / 14% Does not meet
Lang: 27% Exceeds / 63% Meets / 10% Does not meet

DeKalb County Elementary Schools

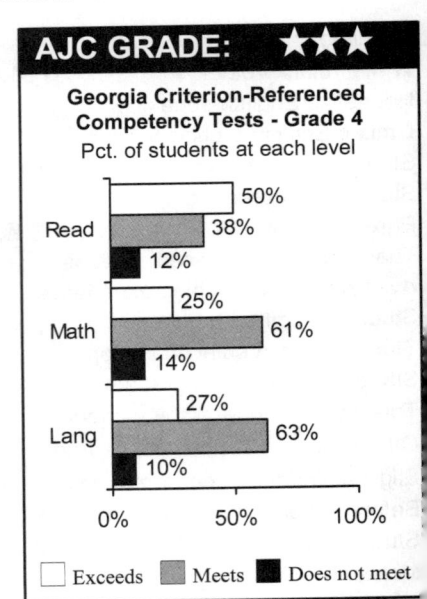

Montclair Elementary School

1680 Clairmont Pl NE, Atlanta, GA 30329
404-634-4282 · Grades K - 5

Enrollment: 541
White / black / other: 7.4% / 37.9% / 54.7%
Not native English-speaking: 56 / 10.4%
Limited English proficiency: 377 / 69.7%
Student absenteeism: 6.0%
Students per teacher: 16.6
Parent friendliness: ① ❷ ❸ ④ ⑤ ❻
Teachers with advanced degrees: 42.4%
Average years' teaching experience: 9.8
Students in gifted program: 16 / 3.0%
Students in remedial education: 33.5%
Students held back a grade: 1.7%
Total suspensions, pct. in-school: *
Offenses: violence: * , drugs: * , other: *
Eligible students, free or reduced lunch: 90.0%
Before / after school program: No / Yes
Students at this school generally go on to:
Sequoyah Middle

AJC GRADE: ★★★★

Georgia Criterion-Referenced Competency Tests - Grade 4
Pct. of students at each level

Read: 28% / 43% / 29%
Math: 15% / 49% / 37%
Lang: 16% / 54% / 30%

☐ Exceeds ▨ Meets ■ Does not meet

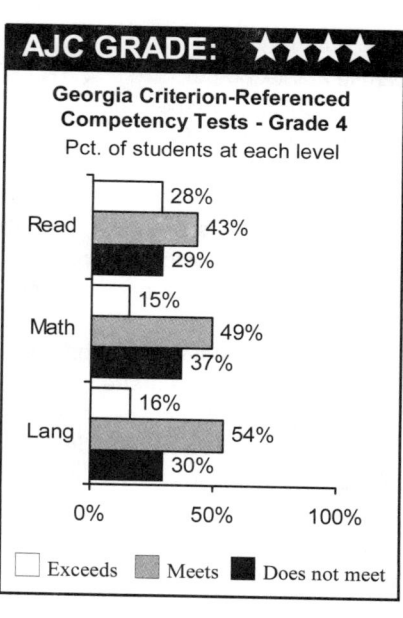

Montgomery Elementary School

3995 Ashford Dunwoody Rd NE, Atlanta, GA 30319
678-676-7502 · Grades K - 6

Enrollment: 360
White / black / other: 39.2% / 49.7% / 11.1%
Not native English-speaking: 14 / 3.9%
Limited English proficiency: 42 / 11.7%
Student absenteeism: 3.8%
Students per teacher: 11.1
Parent friendliness: ❶ ② ❸ ❹ ❺ ❻
Teachers with advanced degrees: 47.2%
Average years' teaching experience: 12.9
Students in gifted program: 55 / 15.3%
Students in remedial education: 14.4%
Students held back a grade: 1.9%
Total suspensions, pct. in-school: *
Offenses: violence: * , drugs: * , other: *
Eligible students, free or reduced lunch: 37.6%
Before / after school program: Yes / Yes
Students at this school generally go on to:
Chamblee Middle

AJC GRADE: ★★★

Georgia Criterion-Referenced Competency Tests - Grade 4
Pct. of students at each level

Read: 51% / 33% / 16%
Math: 30% / 44% / 26%
Lang: 37% / 49% / 14%

☐ Exceeds ▨ Meets ■ Does not meet

The Atlanta Journal-Constitution / Page 229

DeKalb County Elementary Schools

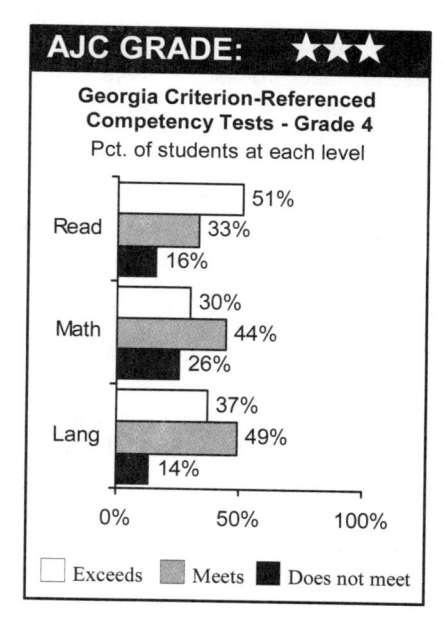

Murphey Candler Elementary School

6775 S Goddard Rd, Lithonia, GA 30038
770-987-0632 · Grades K - 6

Enrollment:	760
White / black / other:	0.5% / 97.1% / 2.4%
Not native English-speaking:	3 / 0.4%
Limited English proficiency:	24 / 3.2%
Student absenteeism:	3.5%
Students per teacher:	18.0
Parent friendliness:	①❷❸④⑤❻
Teachers with advanced degrees:	46.7%
Average years' teaching experience:	11.2
Students in gifted program:	57 / 7.5%
Students in remedial education:	22.5%
Students held back a grade:	0.8%
Total suspensions, pct. in-school:	133 / 38.3%
Offenses: violence: 49, drugs: *, other: 114	
Eligible students, free or reduced lunch:	49.6%
Before / after school program:	Yes / Yes

Students at this school generally go on to:
Salem Middle

AJC GRADE: ★★

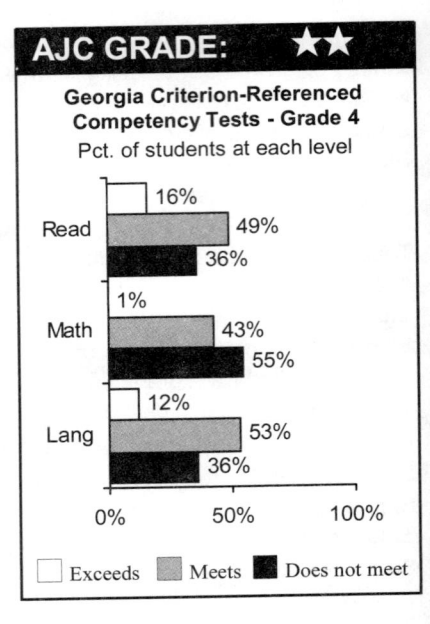

Georgia Criterion-Referenced Competency Tests - Grade 4
Pct. of students at each level

- Read: Exceeds 16%, Meets 49%, Does not meet 36%
- Math: Exceeds 1%, Meets 43%, Does not meet 55%
- Lang: Exceeds 12%, Meets 53%, Does not meet 36%

Nancy Creek Elementary School

1663 E Nancy Creek Dr NE, Atlanta, GA 30319
678-676-7602 · Grades K - 6

Enrollment:	361
White / black / other:	18.8% / 49.3% / 31.9%
Not native English-speaking:	38 / 10.5%
Limited English proficiency:	127 / 35.2%
Student absenteeism:	4.5%
Students per teacher:	13.9
Parent friendliness:	①❷❸❹❺❻
Teachers with advanced degrees:	64.3%
Average years' teaching experience:	16.2
Students in gifted program:	29 / 8.0%
Students in remedial education:	36.7%
Students held back a grade:	1.9%
Total suspensions, pct. in-school:	5 / 40.0%
Offenses: violence: 1, drugs: *, other: 4	
Eligible students, free or reduced lunch:	69.3%
Before / after school program:	Yes / Yes

Students at this school generally go on to:
Chamblee Middle

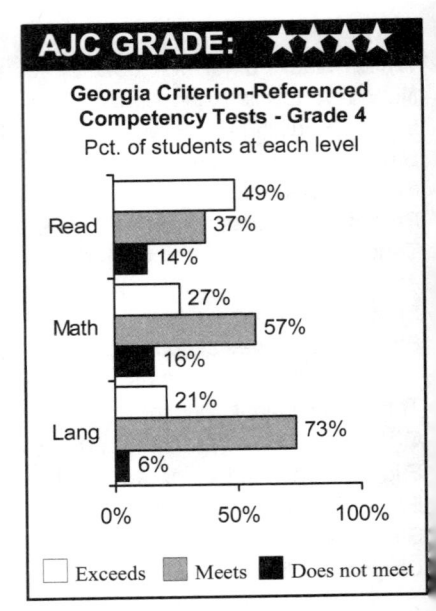

AJC GRADE: ★★★★

Georgia Criterion-Referenced Competency Tests - Grade 4
Pct. of students at each level

- Read: Exceeds 49%, Meets 37%, Does not meet 14%
- Math: Exceeds 27%, Meets 57%, Does not meet 16%
- Lang: Exceeds 21%, Meets 73%, Does not meet 6%

DeKalb County Elementary Schools

Narvie Harris Elementary School

3981 McGill Dr, Decatur, GA 30034
770-981-3254 · Grades K - 5

Enrollment:	972
White / black / other:	0.0% / 99.3% / 0.7%
Not native English-speaking:	*
Limited English proficiency:	8 / 0.8%
Student absenteeism:	2.6%
Students per teacher:	17.2
Parent friendliness:	①②❸④❺❻
Teachers with advanced degrees:	38.6%
Average years' teaching experience:	9.6
Students in gifted program:	93 / 9.6%
Students in remedial education:	30.7%
Students held back a grade:	0.5%
Total suspensions, pct. in-school:	51 / 51.0%
Offenses:	violence: 29, drugs: *, other: 33
Eligible students, free or reduced lunch:	34.1%
Before / after school program:	No / Yes

Students at this school generally go on to:
Cedar Grove, Chapel Hill Middle

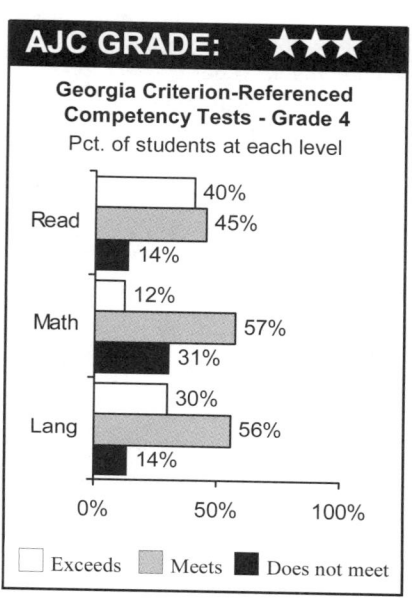

AJC GRADE: ★★★

Georgia Criterion-Referenced Competency Tests - Grade 4
Pct. of students at each level

- Read: Exceeds 40%, Meets 45%, Does not meet 14%
- Math: Exceeds 12%, Meets 57%, Does not meet 31%
- Lang: Exceeds 30%, Meets 56%, Does not meet 14%

Oak Grove Elementary School

1857 Oak Grove Rd NE, Atlanta, GA 30345
404-636-5377 · Grades K - 5

Enrollment:	469
White / black / other:	75.9% / 13.9% / 10.2%
Not native English-speaking:	3 / 0.6%
Limited English proficiency:	15 / 3.2%
Student absenteeism:	3.4%
Students per teacher:	13.6
Parent friendliness:	①❷❸④❺❻
Teachers with advanced degrees:	41.7%
Average years' teaching experience:	10.8
Students in gifted program:	130 / 27.7%
Students in remedial education:	7.6%
Students held back a grade:	0.4%
Total suspensions, pct. in-school:	6 / 66.7%
Offenses:	violence: 4, drugs: *, other: 2
Eligible students, free or reduced lunch:	8.0%
Before / after school program:	No / Yes

Students at this school generally go on to:
Shamrock Middle

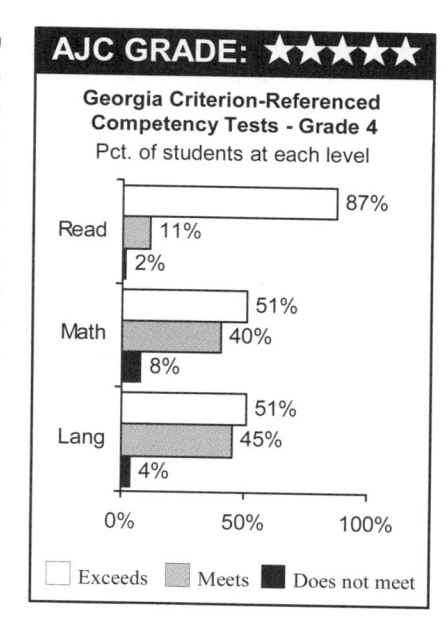

AJC GRADE: ★★★★★

Georgia Criterion-Referenced Competency Tests - Grade 4
Pct. of students at each level

- Read: Exceeds 87%, Meets 11%, Does not meet 2%
- Math: Exceeds 51%, Meets 40%, Does not meet 8%
- Lang: Exceeds 51%, Meets 45%, Does not meet 4%

The Atlanta Journal-Constitution / Page 231

DeKalb County Elementary Schools

Oakcliff Traditional Theme School

3150 Willow Oak Way, Atlanta, GA 30340
678-676-3102 · Grades K - 5

Enrollment:	639
White / black / other:	17.2% / 35.1% / 47.7%
Not native English-speaking:	52 / 8.1%
Limited English proficiency:	311 / 48.7%
Student absenteeism:	3.6%
Students per teacher:	15.1
Parent friendliness:	❶❷❸❹❺❻
Teachers with advanced degrees:	37.2%
Average years' teaching experience:	7.0
Students in gifted program:	70 / 11.0%
Students in remedial education:	27.8%
Students held back a grade:	0.3%
Total suspensions, pct. in-school:	1 / 0.0%
Offenses: violence: * , drugs: * , other:	1
Eligible students, free or reduced lunch:	64.1%
Before / after school program:	Yes / Yes

Students at this school generally go on to:
Sequoyah Middle

AJC GRADE: ★★★

Georgia Criterion-Referenced Competency Tests - Grade 4
Pct. of students at each level

Read: Exceeds 29%, Meets 49%, Does not meet 23%
Math: Exceeds 13%, Meets 57%, Does not meet 30%
Lang: Exceeds 17%, Meets 64%, Does not meet 19%

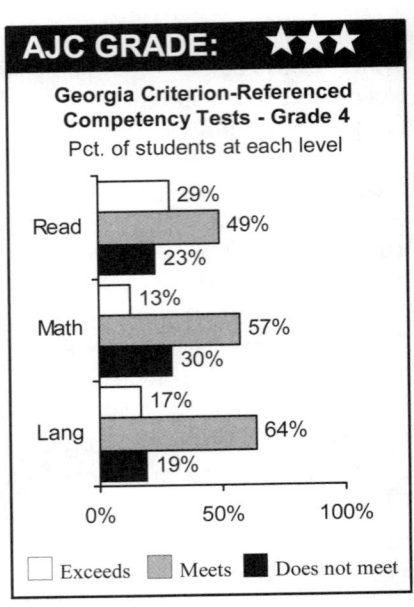

Panola Way Elementary School

2170 Panola Way Ct, Lithonia, GA 30058
770-593-0242 · Grades K - 5

Enrollment:	957
White / black / other:	0.4% / 94.9% / 4.7%
Not native English-speaking:	6 / 0.6%
Limited English proficiency:	53 / 5.5%
Student absenteeism:	4.4%
Students per teacher:	16.7
Parent friendliness:	①②❸④❺❻
Teachers with advanced degrees:	25.9%
Average years' teaching experience:	8.9
Students in gifted program:	44 / 4.6%
Students in remedial education:	54.4%
Students held back a grade:	1.5%
Total suspensions, pct. in-school:	17 / 23.5%
Offenses: violence: 10, drugs: * , other:	7
Eligible students, free or reduced lunch:	72.1%
Before / after school program:	No / Yes

Students at this school generally go on to:
Miller Grove, Salem Middle

AJC GRADE: ★★★

Georgia Criterion-Referenced Competency Tests - Grade 4
Pct. of students at each level

Read: Exceeds 22%, Meets 48%, Does not meet 30%
Math: Exceeds 5%, Meets 49%, Does not meet 46%
Lang: Exceeds 9%, Meets 62%, Does not meet 29%

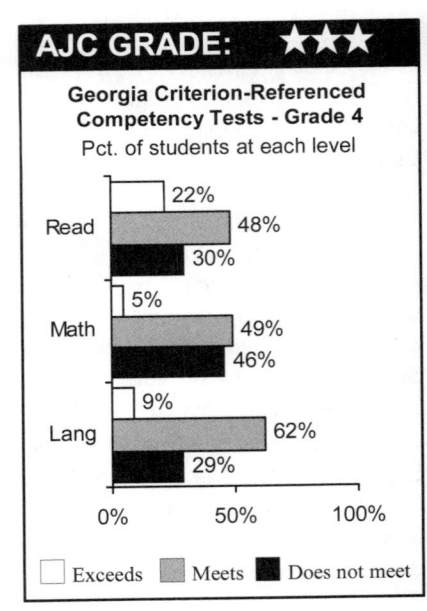

Peachcrest Elementary School

1530 Joy Ln, Decatur, GA 30032
404-284-4081 · Grades K - 7

Enrollment:	496
White / black / other:	0.8% / 90.5% / 8.7%
Not native English-speaking:	15 / 3.0%
Limited English proficiency:	54 / 10.9%
Student absenteeism:	5.6%
Students per teacher:	13.4
Parent friendliness:	①❷❸④❺❻
Teachers with advanced degrees:	30.8%
Average years' teaching experience:	13.0
Students in gifted program:	32 / 6.5%
Students in remedial education:	30.6%
Students held back a grade:	2.0%
Total suspensions, pct. in-school:	27 / 0.0%
Offenses:	violence: 11, drugs: *, other: 19
Eligible students, free or reduced lunch:	89.7%
Before / after school program:	Yes / No

Students at this school generally go on to:
Bethune Middle

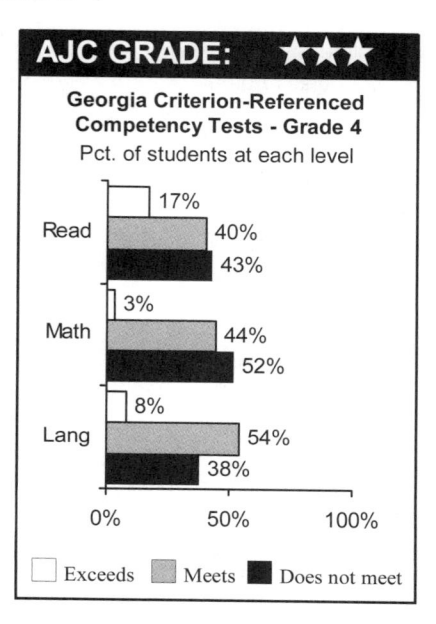

AJC GRADE: ★★★

Georgia Criterion-Referenced Competency Tests - Grade 4
Pct. of students at each level

Read: 17% Exceeds / 40% Meets / 43% Does not meet
Math: 3% Exceeds / 44% Meets / 52% Does not meet
Lang: 8% Exceeds / 54% Meets / 38% Does not meet

Pine Ridge Elementary School

750 Pine Ridge Dr, Stone Mountain, GA 30087
678-676-3402 · Grades K - 5

Enrollment:	1,150
White / black / other:	2.6% / 91.9% / 5.5%
Not native English-speaking:	*
Limited English proficiency:	52 / 4.5%
Student absenteeism:	4.2%
Students per teacher:	19.1
Parent friendliness:	❶②❸④⑤❻
Teachers with advanced degrees:	34.4%
Average years' teaching experience:	8.1
Students in gifted program:	60 / 5.2%
Students in remedial education:	8.9%
Students held back a grade:	0.3%
Total suspensions, pct. in-school:	11 / 54.5%
Offenses:	violence: 2, drugs: *, other: 10
Eligible students, free or reduced lunch:	40.7%
Before / after school program:	Yes / Yes

Students at this school generally go on to:
Stephenson Middle

AJC GRADE: ★★

Georgia Criterion-Referenced Competency Tests - Grade 4
Pct. of students at each level

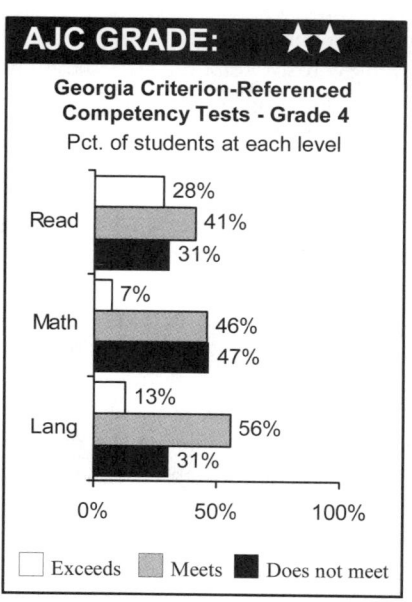

Read: 28% Exceeds / 41% Meets / 31% Does not meet
Math: 7% Exceeds / 46% Meets / 47% Does not meet
Lang: 13% Exceeds / 56% Meets / 31% Does not meet

DeKalb County Elementary Schools

Pleasantdale Elementary School

3695 Northlake Dr, Doraville, GA 30340
770-939-7115 · Grades K - 5

Enrollment:	624
White / black / other:	8.7% / 53.4% / 38.0%
Not native English-speaking:	77 / 12.3%
Limited English proficiency:	238 / 38.1%
Student absenteeism:	5.0%
Students per teacher:	16.8
Parent friendliness:	① ❷ ❸ ④ ⑤ ❻
Teachers with advanced degrees:	35.9%
Average years' teaching experience:	11.6
Students in gifted program:	40 / 6.4%
Students in remedial education:	23.7%
Students held back a grade:	2.1%
Total suspensions, pct. in-school:	47 / 76.6%
Offenses:	violence: 19, drugs: * , other: 35
Eligible students, free or reduced lunch:	72.1%
Before / after school program:	No / Yes
Students at this school generally go on to:	
Henderson Middle	

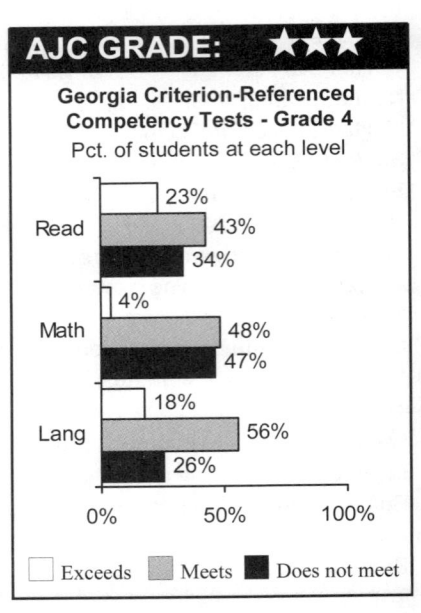

AJC GRADE: ★★★

Georgia Criterion-Referenced Competency Tests - Grade 4
Pct. of students at each level

Read: 23% Exceeds / 43% Meets / 34% Does not meet
Math: 4% Exceeds / 48% Meets / 47% Does not meet
Lang: 18% Exceeds / 56% Meets / 26% Does not meet

Rainbow Charter Elementary School

2801 Kelley Chapel Rd, Decatur, GA 30034
404-284-8109 · Grades K - 5

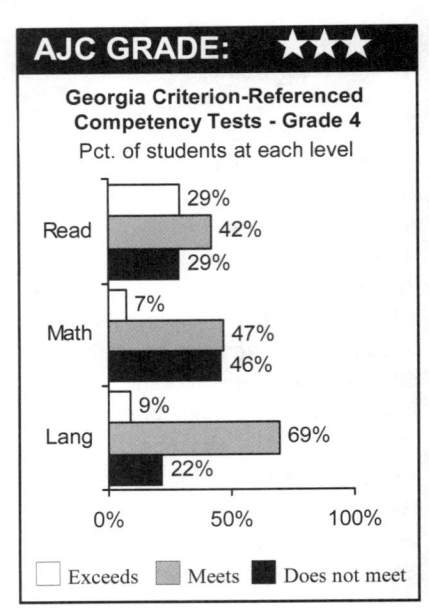

Enrollment:	619
White / black / other:	0.5% / 98.1% / 1.5%
Not native English-speaking:	*
Limited English proficiency:	32 / 5.2%
Student absenteeism:	4.3%
Students per teacher:	16.0
Parent friendliness:	① ❷ ❸ ④ ❺ ❻
Teachers with advanced degrees:	35.7%
Average years' teaching experience:	10.9
Students in gifted program:	31 / 5.0%
Students in remedial education:	32.2%
Students held back a grade:	*
Total suspensions, pct. in-school:	44 / 52.3%
Offenses:	violence: 13, drugs: * , other: 32
Eligible students, free or reduced lunch:	62.3%
Before / after school program:	No / Yes
Students at this school generally go on to:	
Chapel Hill Middle	

AJC GRADE: ★★★

Georgia Criterion-Referenced Competency Tests - Grade 4
Pct. of students at each level

Read: 29% Exceeds / 42% Meets / 29% Does not meet
Math: 7% Exceeds / 47% Meets / 46% Does not meet
Lang: 9% Exceeds / 69% Meets / 22% Does not meet

Redan Elementary School

1914 Stone Mountain-Lithonia Rd, Redan, GA 30074
678-676-3502 · Grades K - 5

Enrollment:	862
White / black / other:	0.5% / 96.2% / 3.4%
Not native English-speaking:	7 / 0.8%
Limited English proficiency:	39 / 4.5%
Student absenteeism:	4.3%
Students per teacher:	16.2
Parent friendliness:	① ❷ ❸ ④ ⑤ ❻
Teachers with advanced degrees:	40.4%
Average years' teaching experience:	10.0
Students in gifted program:	40 / 4.6%
Students in remedial education:	20.2%
Students held back a grade:	0.3%
Total suspensions, pct. in-school:	26 / 23.1%
Offenses:	violence: 16, drugs: *, other: 15
Eligible students, free or reduced lunch:	57.2%
Before / after school program:	No / Yes

Students at this school generally go on to:
Miller Grove, Salem, Stephenson Middle

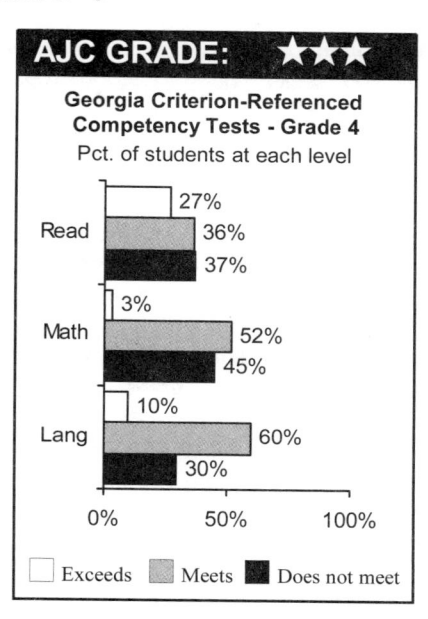

AJC GRADE: ★★★

Georgia Criterion-Referenced Competency Tests - Grade 4
Pct. of students at each level

- Read: Exceeds 27%, Meets 36%, Does not meet 37%
- Math: Exceeds 3%, Meets 52%, Does not meet 45%
- Lang: Exceeds 10%, Meets 60%, Does not meet 30%

Robert Shaw Elementary School

385 Glendale Rd, Scottdale, GA 30079
678-676-6002 · Grades K - 6

Enrollment:	531
White / black / other:	2.6% / 91.7% / 5.6%
Not native English-speaking:	2 / 0.4%
Limited English proficiency:	29 / 5.5%
Student absenteeism:	3.5%
Students per teacher:	13.0
Parent friendliness:	① ❷ ❸ ④ ⑤ ❻
Teachers with advanced degrees:	35.7%
Average years' teaching experience:	10.4
Students in gifted program:	27 / 5.1%
Students in remedial education:	22.4%
Students held back a grade:	1.7%
Total suspensions, pct. in-school:	1 / 0.0%
Offenses:	violence: 1, drugs: *, other: *
Eligible students, free or reduced lunch:	68.4%
Before / after school program:	No / Yes

Students at this school generally go on to:
Avondale, Freedom, Salem, Shamrock Middle

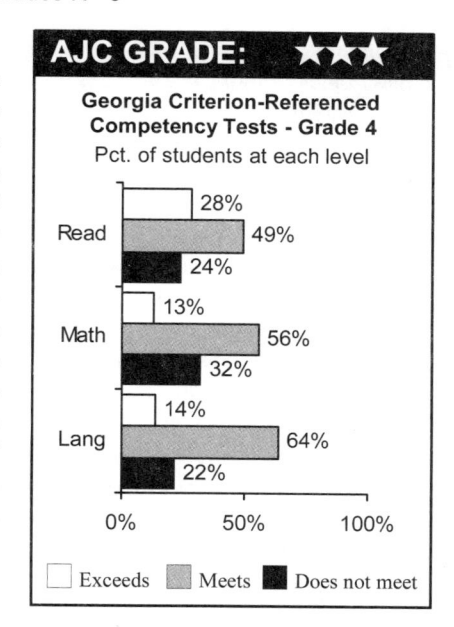

AJC GRADE: ★★★

Georgia Criterion-Referenced Competency Tests - Grade 4
Pct. of students at each level

- Read: Exceeds 28%, Meets 49%, Does not meet 24%
- Math: Exceeds 13%, Meets 56%, Does not meet 32%
- Lang: Exceeds 14%, Meets 64%, Does not meet 22%

Rock Chapel Elementary School

1130 Rock Chapel Rd, Lithonia, GA 30058
678-676-3802 · Grades K - 5

Enrollment:	983
White / black / other:	2.0% / 92.6% / 5.4%
Not native English-speaking:	1 / 0.1%
Limited English proficiency:	31 / 3.2%
Student absenteeism:	3.8%
Students per teacher:	18.9
Parent friendliness:	① ❷ ❸ ④ ❺ ❻
Teachers with advanced degrees:	42.3%
Average years' teaching experience:	11.3
Students in gifted program:	71 / 7.2%
Students in remedial education:	12.3%
Students held back a grade:	1.8%
Total suspensions, pct. in-school:	35 / 0.0%
Offenses:	violence: 25, drugs: *, other: 11
Eligible students, free or reduced lunch:	36.5%
Before / after school program:	No / Yes
Students at this school generally go on to: Salem, Stephenson Middle	

AJC GRADE: ★★

Georgia Criterion-Referenced Competency Tests - Grade 4
Pct. of students at each level

Read: Exceeds 21%, Meets 46%, Does not meet 33%
Math: Exceeds 7%, Meets 50%, Does not meet 44%
Lang: Exceeds 15%, Meets 50%, Does not meet 35%

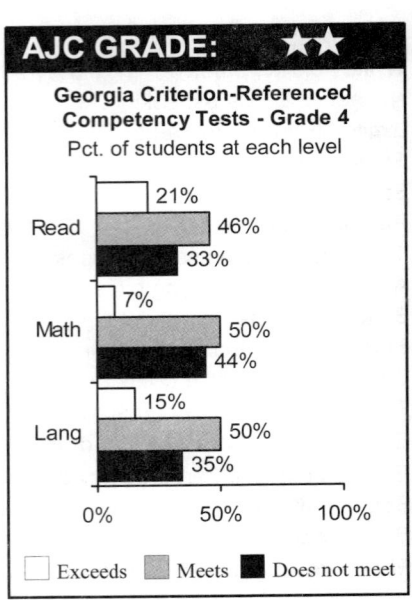

Rockbridge Elementary School

445 Halwick Way, Stone Mountain, GA 30083
678-676-6102 · Grades K - 6

Enrollment:	708
White / black / other:	2.5% / 87.9% / 9.6%
Not native English-speaking:	25 / 3.5%
Limited English proficiency:	56 / 7.9%
Student absenteeism:	4.5%
Students per teacher:	15.5
Parent friendliness:	① ❷ ❸ ④ ❺ ❻
Teachers with advanced degrees:	34.0%
Average years' teaching experience:	9.1
Students in gifted program:	39 / 5.5%
Students in remedial education:	28.8%
Students held back a grade:	1.7%
Total suspensions, pct. in-school:	*
Offenses:	violence: *, drugs: *, other: *
Eligible students, free or reduced lunch:	59.8%
Before / after school program:	Yes / Yes
Students at this school generally go on to: Stone Mountain Middle	

AJC GRADE: ★★★

Georgia Criterion-Referenced Competency Tests - Grade 4
Pct. of students at each level

Read: Exceeds 15%, Meets 42%, Does not meet 44%
Math: Exceeds 3%, Meets 47%, Does not meet 50%
Lang: Exceeds 8%, Meets 60%, Does not meet 33%

The Atlanta Journal-Constitution / Page 236

DeKalb County Elementary Schools

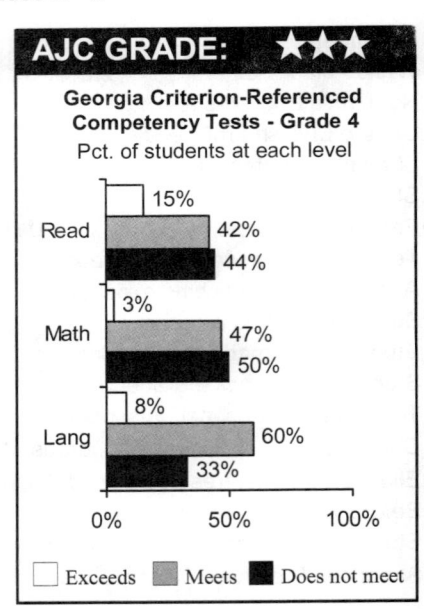

Rowland Elementary School

1317 S Indian Creek Dr, Stone Mountain, GA 30083
678-676-6202 · Grades K - 5

Enrollment:	657
White / black / other:	0.6% / 90.7% / 8.7%
Not native English-speaking:	9 / 1.4%
Limited English proficiency:	53 / 8.1%
Student absenteeism:	3.8%
Students per teacher:	14.5
Parent friendliness:	❶❷❸④⑤❻
Teachers with advanced degrees:	43.8%
Average years' teaching experience:	10.9
Students in gifted program:	46 / 7.0%
Students in remedial education:	25.4%
Students held back a grade:	0.5%
Total suspensions, pct. in-school:	42 / 33.3%
Offenses:	violence: 23, drugs: * , other: 23
Eligible students, free or reduced lunch:	72.2%
Before / after school program:	No / Yes

Students at this school generally go on to:
Bethune Middle

AJC GRADE: ★★★

Georgia Criterion-Referenced Competency Tests - Grade 4
Pct. of students at each level

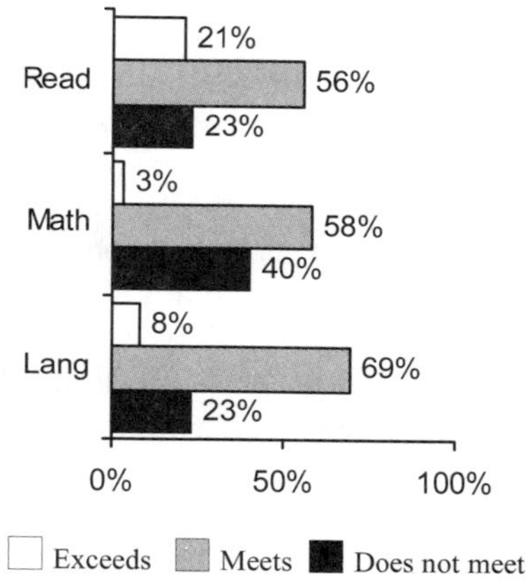
Read
21%
56%
23%
Math
3%
58%
40%
Lang
8%
69%
23%
0%
50%
100%
Exceeds
Meets
Does not meet

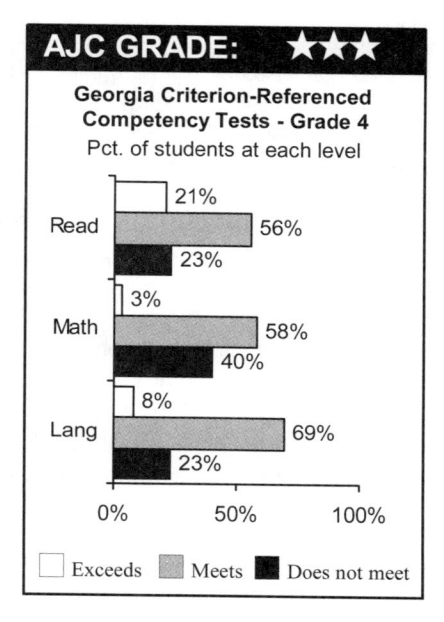

Sagamore Hills Elementary School

1865 Alderbrook Rd NE, Atlanta, GA 30345
404-636-8120 · Grades K - 5

Enrollment:	343
White / black / other:	51.0% / 30.9% / 18.1%
Not native English-speaking:	13 / 3.8%
Limited English proficiency:	41 / 12.0%
Student absenteeism:	4.3%
Students per teacher:	11.9
Parent friendliness:	①❷❸④❺❻
Teachers with advanced degrees:	45.2%
Average years' teaching experience:	12.9
Students in gifted program:	35 / 10.2%
Students in remedial education:	18.9%
Students held back a grade:	1.2%
Total suspensions, pct. in-school:	8 / 62.5%
Offenses:	violence: 3, drugs: * , other: 5
Eligible students, free or reduced lunch:	29.4%
Before / after school program:	Yes / Yes

Students at this school generally go on to:
Shamrock Middle

AJC GRADE: ★★★

Georgia Criterion-Referenced Competency Tests - Grade 4
Pct. of students at each level

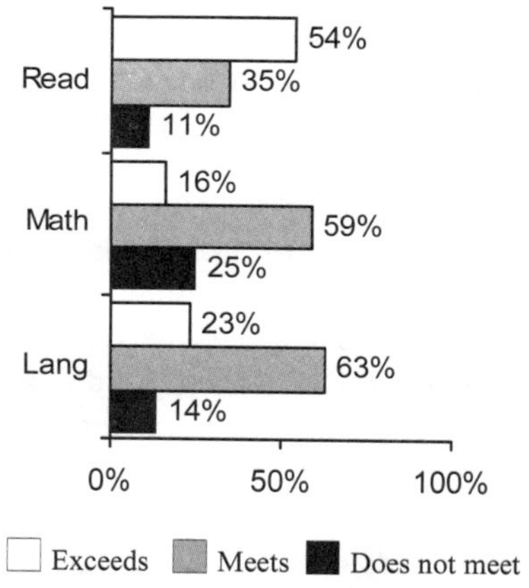
Read
54%
35%
11%
Math
16%
59%
25%
Lang
23%
63%
14%
0%
50%
100%
Exceeds
Meets
Does not meet

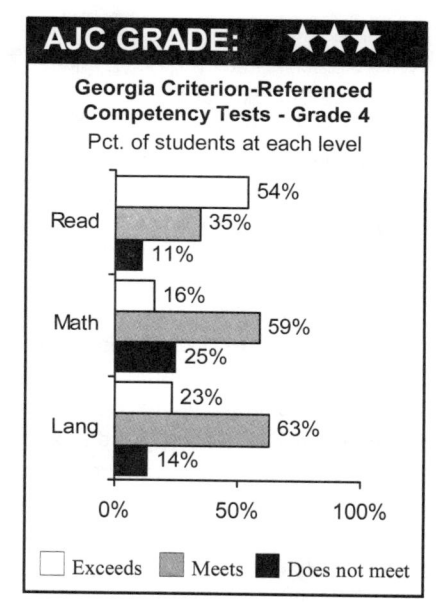

Shadow Rock Elementary School

1040 Kingsway Dr, Lithonia, GA 30058
678-676-3902 · Grades K - 6

Enrollment:	938
White / black / other:	0.5% / 94.6% / 4.9%
Not native English-speaking:	*
Limited English proficiency:	47 / 5.0%
Student absenteeism:	3.7%
Students per teacher:	18.3
Parent friendliness:	❶❷❸④⑤❻
Teachers with advanced degrees:	45.5%
Average years' teaching experience:	8.9
Students in gifted program:	71 / 7.6%
Students in remedial education:	23.8%
Students held back a grade:	0.5%
Total suspensions, pct. in-school:	153 / 63.4%
Offenses: violence: 49, drugs: *, other: 129	
Eligible students, free or reduced lunch:	53.4%
Before / after school program:	No / Yes

Students at this school generally go on to:
Miller Grove, Stephenson Middle

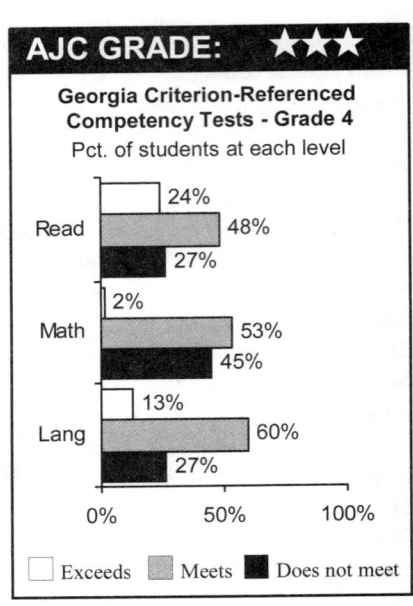

AJC GRADE: ★★★

Georgia Criterion-Referenced Competency Tests - Grade 4
Pct. of students at each level

- Read: Exceeds 24%, Meets 48%, Does not meet 27%
- Math: Exceeds 2%, Meets 53%, Does not meet 45%
- Lang: Exceeds 13%, Meets 60%, Does not meet 27%

Sky Haven Elementary School

1372 Sky Haven Rd SE, Atlanta, GA 30316
404-622-8425 · Grades K - 5

Enrollment:	643
White / black / other:	1.1% / 94.7% / 4.2%
Not native English-speaking:	6 / 0.9%
Limited English proficiency:	31 / 4.8%
Student absenteeism:	5.2%
Students per teacher:	13.6
Parent friendliness:	①❷❸④❺❻
Teachers with advanced degrees:	40.0%
Average years' teaching experience:	10.6
Students in gifted program:	33 / 5.1%
Students in remedial education:	50.2%
Students held back a grade:	0.8%
Total suspensions, pct. in-school:	98 / 37.8%
Offenses: violence: 31, drugs: *, other: 77	
Eligible students, free or reduced lunch:	96.8%
Before / after school program:	Yes / Yes

Students at this school generally go on to:
McNair Middle

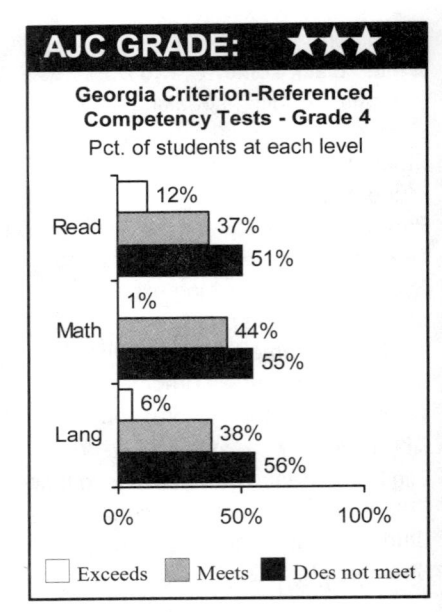

AJC GRADE: ★★★

Georgia Criterion-Referenced Competency Tests - Grade 4
Pct. of students at each level

- Read: Exceeds 12%, Meets 37%, Does not meet 51%
- Math: Exceeds 1%, Meets 44%, Does not meet 55%
- Lang: Exceeds 6%, Meets 38%, Does not meet 56%

Smoke Rise Elementary School

1991 Silver Hill Rd, Stone Mountain, GA 30087
770-939-6714 · Grades K - 6

Enrollment:	553
White / black / other:	33.1% / 49.4% / 17.5%
Not native English-speaking:	28 / 5.1%
Limited English proficiency:	74 / 13.4%
Student absenteeism:	4.2%
Students per teacher:	15.5
Parent friendliness:	① ❷ ❸ ④ ⑤ ❻
Teachers with advanced degrees:	53.8%
Average years' teaching experience:	14.8
Students in gifted program:	76 / 13.7%
Students in remedial education:	20.2%
Students held back a grade:	2.0%
Total suspensions, pct. in-school:	*
Offenses:	violence: *, drugs: *, other: *
Eligible students, free or reduced lunch:	36.5%
Before / after school program:	Yes / Yes
Students at this school generally go on to: Henderson Middle	

AJC GRADE: ★★★

Georgia Criterion-Referenced Competency Tests - Grade 4
Pct. of students at each level

- Read: Exceeds 36%, Meets 49%, Does not meet 16%
- Math: Exceeds 26%, Meets 47%, Does not meet 27%
- Lang: Exceeds 18%, Meets 61%, Does not meet 21%

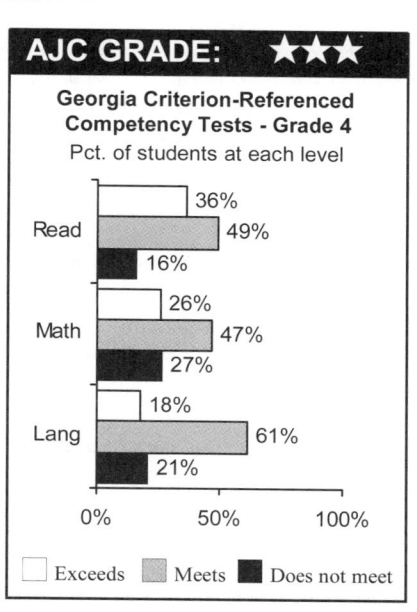

Snapfinger Elementary School

1365 Snapfinger Rd, Decatur, GA 30032
404-289-1735 · Grades K - 5

Enrollment:	1,041
White / black / other:	0.4% / 97.4% / 2.2%
Not native English-speaking:	3 / 0.3%
Limited English proficiency:	40 / 3.8%
Student absenteeism:	4.5%
Students per teacher:	17.0
Parent friendliness:	① ❷ ❸ ④ ⑤ ❻
Teachers with advanced degrees:	42.2%
Average years' teaching experience:	9.4
Students in gifted program:	85 / 8.2%
Students in remedial education:	32.7%
Students held back a grade:	0.1%
Total suspensions, pct. in-school:	51 / 43.1%
Offenses:	violence: 13, drugs: *, other: 43
Eligible students, free or reduced lunch:	75.2%
Before / after school program:	No / Yes
Students at this school generally go on to: Columbia Middle	

AJC GRADE: ★★★

Georgia Criterion-Referenced Competency Tests - Grade 4
Pct. of students at each level

- Read: Exceeds 21%, Meets 50%, Does not meet 29%
- Math: Exceeds 12%, Meets 50%, Does not meet 38%
- Lang: Exceeds 12%, Meets 57%, Does not meet 31%

DeKalb County Elementary Schools

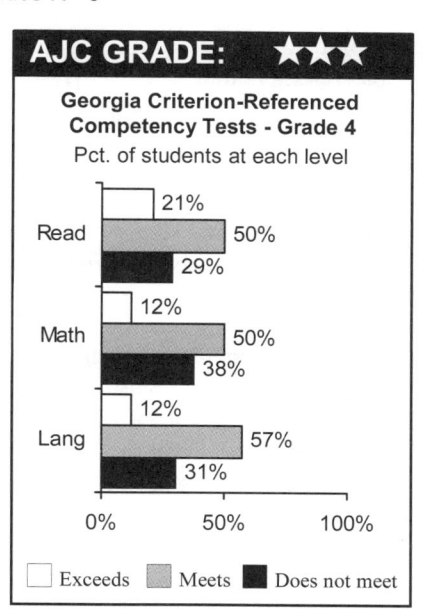

Steele Elementary School

2162 Second Ave, Decatur, GA 30032
404-377-0469 · Grades K - 6

Enrollment:	375
White / black / other:	0.5% / 98.9% / 0.5%
Not native English-speaking:	*
Limited English proficiency:	4 / 1.1%
Student absenteeism:	5.2%
Students per teacher:	12.3
Parent friendliness:	① ❷ ❸ ④ ❺ ❻
Teachers with advanced degrees:	31.3%
Average years' teaching experience:	10.8
Students in gifted program:	27 / 7.2%
Students in remedial education:	32.6%
Students held back a grade:	1.1%
Total suspensions, pct. in-school:	7 / 0.0%
Offenses:	violence: 3, drugs: *, other: 5
Eligible students, free or reduced lunch:	90.5%
Before / after school program:	Yes / Yes
Students at this school generally go on to:	
McNair Middle	

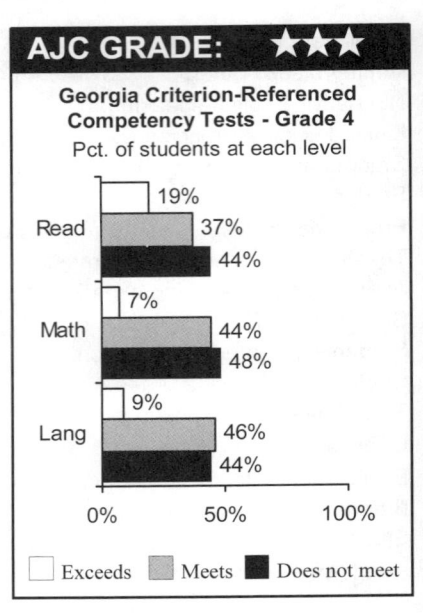

AJC GRADE: ★★★

Georgia Criterion-Referenced Competency Tests - Grade 4
Pct. of students at each level

Read: Exceeds 19%, Meets 37%, Does not meet 44%
Math: Exceeds 7%, Meets 44%, Does not meet 48%
Lang: Exceeds 9%, Meets 46%, Does not meet 44%

Stone Mill Elementary School

4900 Sheila Ln, Stone Mountain, GA 30083
678-676-4602 · Grades K - 5

Enrollment:	686
White / black / other:	5.7% / 76.2% / 18.1%
Not native English-speaking:	94 / 13.7%
Limited English proficiency:	184 / 26.8%
Student absenteeism:	5.1%
Students per teacher:	15.2
Parent friendliness:	① ❷ ❸ ④ ❺ ❻
Teachers with advanced degrees:	29.8%
Average years' teaching experience:	9.3
Students in gifted program:	8 / 1.2%
Students in remedial education:	34.8%
Students held back a grade:	2.8%
Total suspensions, pct. in-school:	12 / 58.3%
Offenses:	violence: 4, drugs: *, other: 8
Eligible students, free or reduced lunch:	84.8%
Before / after school program:	No / Yes
Students at this school generally go on to:	
Stone Mountain Middle	

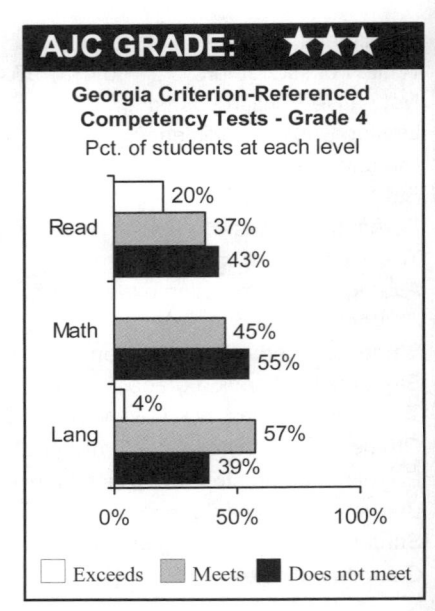

AJC GRADE: ★★★

Georgia Criterion-Referenced Competency Tests - Grade 4
Pct. of students at each level

Read: Exceeds 20%, Meets 37%, Does not meet 43%
Math: Exceeds *, Meets 45%, Does not meet 55%
Lang: Exceeds 4%, Meets 57%, Does not meet 39%

DeKalb County Elementary Schools

Stone Mountain Elementary School

6720 James B Rivers Dr, Stone Mountain, GA 30083
678-676-4702 · Grades K - 5

Enrollment:	797
White / black / other:	5.1% / 87.0% / 7.9%
Not native English-speaking:	23 / 2.9%
Limited English proficiency:	85 / 10.7%
Student absenteeism:	4.8%
Students per teacher:	18.6
Parent friendliness:	① ❷ ❸ ④ ❺ ❻
Teachers with advanced degrees:	35.6%
Average years' teaching experience:	10.2
Students in gifted program:	23 / 2.9%
Students in remedial education:	32.7%
Students held back a grade:	0.4%
Total suspensions, pct. in-school:	4 / 0.0%
Offenses:	violence: 3, drugs: *, other: 1
Eligible students, free or reduced lunch:	71.5%
Before / after school program:	Yes / Yes

Students at this school generally go on to:
Stone Mountain Middle

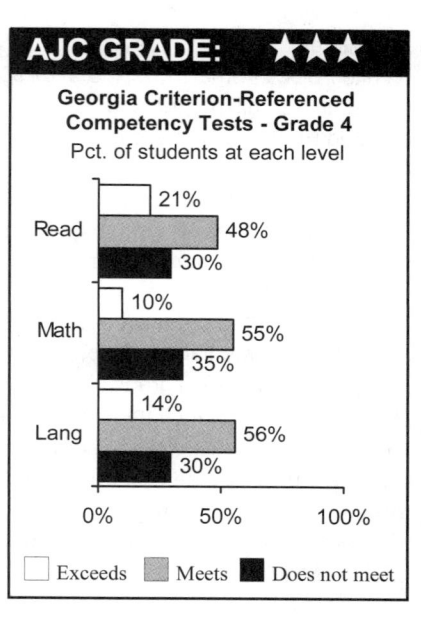

AJC GRADE: ★★★

Georgia Criterion-Referenced Competency Tests - Grade 4
Pct. of students at each level

Read: Exceeds 21%, Meets 48%, Does not meet 30%
Math: Exceeds 10%, Meets 55%, Does not meet 35%
Lang: Exceeds 14%, Meets 56%, Does not meet 30%

Stoneview Elementary School

2629 Huber St, Lithonia, GA 30058
678-676-3202 · Grades K - 5

Enrollment:	774
White / black / other:	2.6% / 89.4% / 8.0%
Not native English-speaking:	13 / 1.7%
Limited English proficiency:	54 / 7.0%
Student absenteeism:	5.4%
Students per teacher:	17.7
Parent friendliness:	① ❷ ❸ ④ ⑤ ❻
Teachers with advanced degrees:	46.7%
Average years' teaching experience:	10.3
Students in gifted program:	13 / 1.7%
Students in remedial education:	13.8%
Students held back a grade:	1.7%
Total suspensions, pct. in-school:	377 / 57.0%
Offenses:	violence: 113, drugs: *, other: 299
Eligible students, free or reduced lunch:	86.3%
Before / after school program:	Yes / Yes

Students at this school generally go on to:
Salem Middle

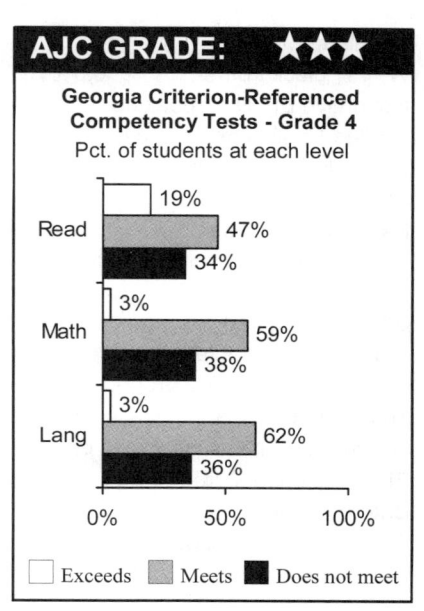

AJC GRADE: ★★★

Georgia Criterion-Referenced Competency Tests - Grade 4
Pct. of students at each level

Read: Exceeds 19%, Meets 47%, Does not meet 34%
Math: Exceeds 3%, Meets 59%, Does not meet 38%
Lang: Exceeds 3%, Meets 62%, Does not meet 36%

DeKalb County Elementary Schools

Terry Mill Elementary School

797 Fayetteville Rd SE, Atlanta, GA 30316
404-373-3463 · Grades K - 5

Enrollment:	668
White / black / other:	0.3% / 98.4% / 1.3%
Not native English-speaking:	2 / 0.3%
Limited English proficiency:	33 / 4.9%
Student absenteeism:	5.9%
Students per teacher:	15.1
Parent friendliness:	①②❸④❺❻
Teachers with advanced degrees:	35.6%
Average years' teaching experience:	8.4
Students in gifted program:	11 / 1.6%
Students in remedial education:	37.4%
Students held back a grade:	0.1%
Total suspensions, pct. in-school:	100 / 22.0%
Offenses:	violence: 53, drugs: *, other: 53
Eligible students, free or reduced lunch:	92.9%
Before / after school program:	No / Yes

Students at this school generally go on to:
McNair Middle

AJC GRADE: ★★★

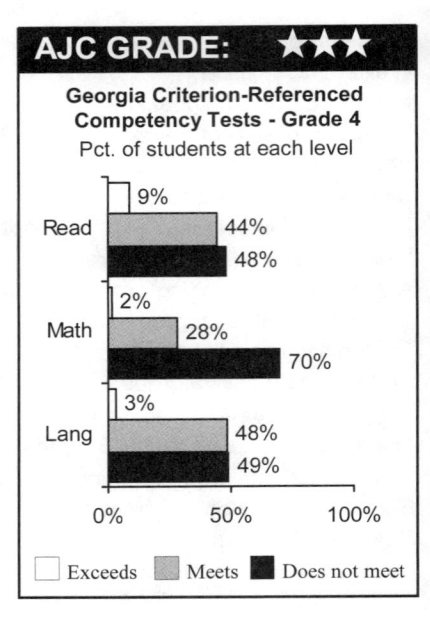

Georgia Criterion-Referenced Competency Tests - Grade 4
Pct. of students at each level

Read: Exceeds 9%, Meets 44%, Does not meet 48%
Math: Exceeds 2%, Meets 28%, Does not meet 70%
Lang: Exceeds 3%, Meets 48%, Does not meet 49%

Tilson Elementary School

2100 Bixler Cir, Decatur, GA 30032
404-241-5122 · Grades K - 6

Enrollment:	520
White / black / other:	0.0% / 99.0% / 1.0%
Not native English-speaking:	2 / 0.4%
Limited English proficiency:	12 / 2.3%
Student absenteeism:	4.8%
Students per teacher:	14.1
Parent friendliness:	①❷❸④❺❻
Teachers with advanced degrees:	43.6%
Average years' teaching experience:	9.9
Students in gifted program:	16 / 3.1%
Students in remedial education:	46.7%
Students held back a grade:	0.4%
Total suspensions, pct. in-school:	16 / 50.0%
Offenses:	violence: 6, drugs: *, other: 13
Eligible students, free or reduced lunch:	93.9%
Before / after school program:	No / Yes

Students at this school generally go on to:
McNair Middle

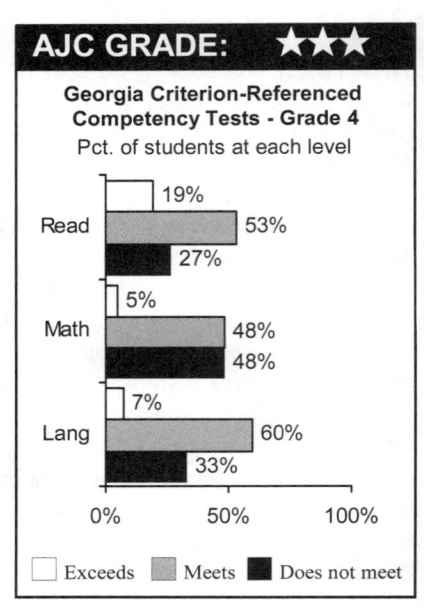

AJC GRADE: ★★★

Georgia Criterion-Referenced Competency Tests - Grade 4
Pct. of students at each level

Read: Exceeds 19%, Meets 53%, Does not meet 27%
Math: Exceeds 5%, Meets 48%, Does not meet 48%
Lang: Exceeds 7%, Meets 60%, Does not meet 33%

The Atlanta Journal-Constitution / Page 242

DeKalb County Elementary Schools

Toney Elementary School

2701 Oakland Ter, Decatur, GA 30032
404-284-1051 · Grades K - 7

Enrollment:	507
White / black / other:	0.2% / 98.6% / 1.2%
Not native English-speaking:	*
Limited English proficiency:	28 / 5.5%
Student absenteeism:	6.3%
Students per teacher:	15.0
Parent friendliness:	①❷❸④❺❻
Teachers with advanced degrees:	47.2%
Average years' teaching experience:	11.2
Students in gifted program:	25 / 4.9%
Students in remedial education:	44.8%
Students held back a grade:	0.2%
Total suspensions, pct. in-school:	34 / 55.9%
Offenses:	violence: 22, drugs: *, other: 16
Eligible students, free or reduced lunch:	94.4%
Before / after school program:	Yes / Yes

Students at this school generally go on to:
Columbia Middle

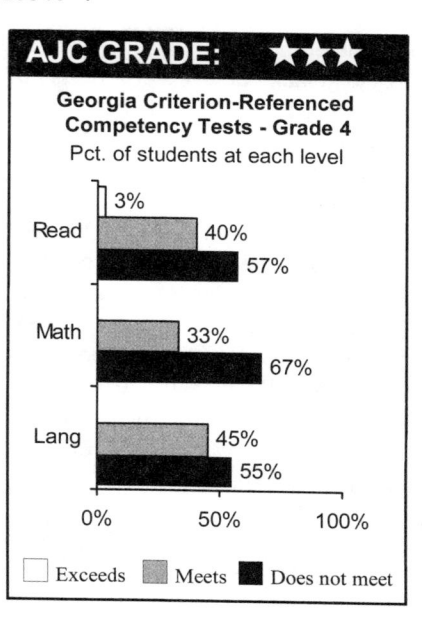

AJC GRADE: ★★★

Georgia Criterion-Referenced Competency Tests - Grade 4
Pct. of students at each level

- Read: Exceeds 3%, Meets 40%, Does not meet 57%
- Math: Exceeds *, Meets 33%, Does not meet 67%
- Lang: Exceeds *, Meets 45%, Does not meet 55%

Vanderlyn Elementary School

1877 Vanderlyn Dr, Dunwoody, GA 30338
770-394-2624 · Grades K - 5

Enrollment:	603
White / black / other:	85.9% / 4.1% / 10.0%
Not native English-speaking:	10 / 1.7%
Limited English proficiency:	42 / 7.0%
Student absenteeism:	3.4%
Students per teacher:	17.5
Parent friendliness:	①❷❸④❺❻
Teachers with advanced degrees:	54.3%
Average years' teaching experience:	14.6
Students in gifted program:	179 / 29.7%
Students in remedial education:	0.5%
Students held back a grade:	*
Total suspensions, pct. in-school:	*
Offenses:	violence: *, drugs: *, other: *
Eligible students, free or reduced lunch:	1.8%
Before / after school program:	No / Yes

Students at this school generally go on to:
Peachtree Charter Middle

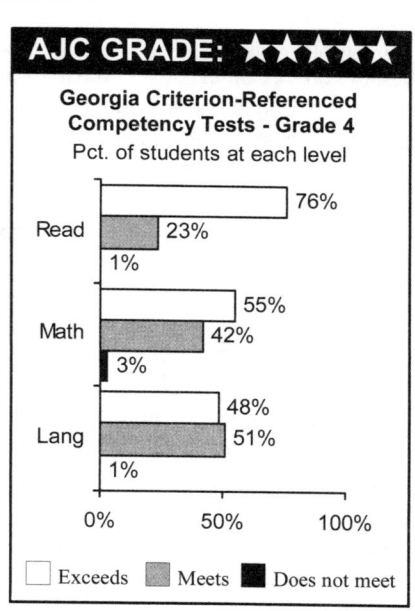

AJC GRADE: ★★★★★

Georgia Criterion-Referenced Competency Tests - Grade 4
Pct. of students at each level

- Read: Exceeds 76%, Meets 23%, Does not meet 1%
- Math: Exceeds 55%, Meets 42%, Does not meet 3%
- Lang: Exceeds 48%, Meets 51%, Does not meet 1%

The Atlanta Journal-Constitution / Page 243

DeKalb County Elementary Schools

Wadsworth Elementary School

2084 Green Forrest Dr, Decatur, GA 30032
404-289-4818 · Grades K - 5

Enrollment:	391
White / black / other:	0.5% / 97.4% / 2.0%
Not native English-speaking:	2 / 0.5%
Limited English proficiency:	29 / 7.4%
Student absenteeism:	4.1%
Students per teacher:	11.7
Parent friendliness:	①❷❸④❺❻
Teachers with advanced degrees:	44.4%
Average years' teaching experience:	12.0
Students in gifted program:	13 / 3.3%
Students in remedial education:	22.4%
Students held back a grade:	0.8%
Total suspensions, pct. in-school:	35 / 14.3%
Offenses:	violence: 18, drugs: *, other: 17
Eligible students, free or reduced lunch:	94.5%
Before / after school program:	No / Yes
Students at this school generally go to:	
Columbia Middle	

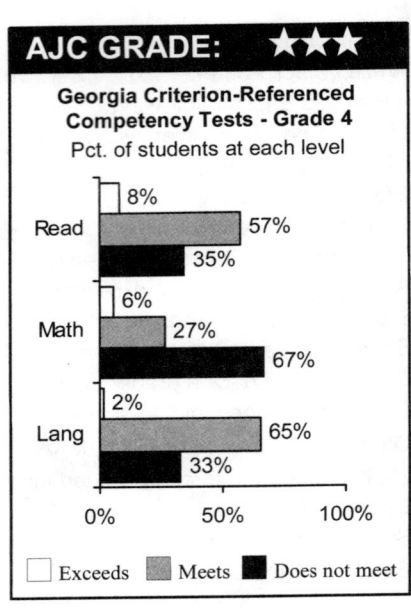

AJC GRADE: ★★★

Georgia Criterion-Referenced Competency Tests - Grade 4
Pct. of students at each level

Read: Exceeds 8%, Meets 57%, Does not meet 35%
Math: Exceeds 6%, Meets 27%, Does not meet 67%
Lang: Exceeds 2%, Meets 65%, Does not meet 33%

Woodridge Elementary School

4120 Cedar Ridge Trl, Stone Mountain, GA 30083
770-981-3980 · Grades K - 5

Enrollment:	665
White / black / other:	0.6% / 95.3% / 4.1%
Not native English-speaking:	3 / 0.5%
Limited English proficiency:	29 / 4.4%
Student absenteeism:	4.1%
Students per teacher:	16.7
Parent friendliness:	①❷❸④❺❻
Teachers with advanced degrees:	40.5%
Average years' teaching experience:	8.9
Students in gifted program:	56 / 8.4%
Students in remedial education:	36.4%
Students held back a grade:	1.1%
Total suspensions, pct. in-school:	62 / 66.1%
Offenses:	violence: 28, drugs: *, other: 42
Eligible students, free or reduced lunch:	59.5%
Before / after school program:	Yes / Yes
Students at this school generally go to:	
Miller Grove Middle	

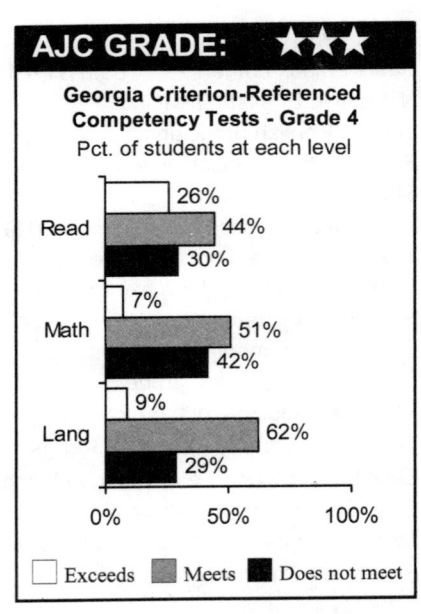

AJC GRADE: ★★★

Georgia Criterion-Referenced Competency Tests - Grade 4
Pct. of students at each level

Read: Exceeds 26%, Meets 44%, Does not meet 30%
Math: Exceeds 7%, Meets 51%, Does not meet 42%
Lang: Exceeds 9%, Meets 62%, Does not meet 29%

DeKalb County Elementary Schools

Woodward Elementary School

3034 Curtis Dr NE, Atlanta, GA 30319
404-634-5355 · Grades K - 5

Enrollment:	701
White / black / other:	3.3% / 18.5% / 78.2%
Not native English-speaking:	213 / 30.4%
Limited English proficiency:	624 / 89.0%
Student absenteeism:	5.8%
Students per teacher:	15.4
Parent friendliness:	① ❷ ❸ ④ ❺ ❻
Teachers with advanced degrees:	53.2%
Average years' teaching experience:	10.6
Students in gifted program:	17 / 2.4%
Students in remedial education:	38.5%
Students held back a grade:	1.3%
Total suspensions, pct. in-school:	44 / 11.4%
Offenses:	violence: 12, drugs: *, other: 36
Eligible students, free or reduced lunch:	81.8%
Before / after school program:	Yes / Yes

Students at this school generally go on to:
Sequoyah Middle

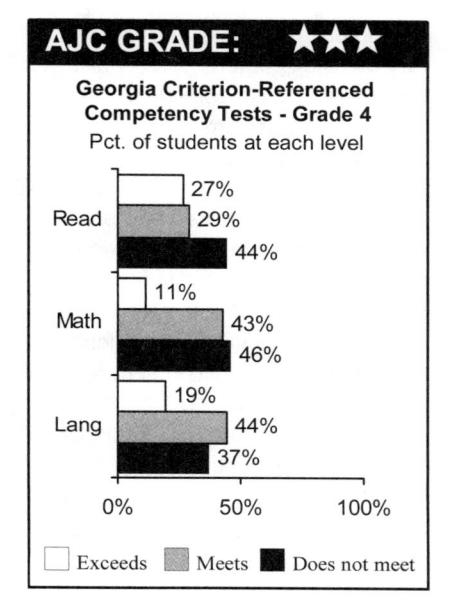

AJC GRADE: ★★★

Georgia Criterion-Referenced Competency Tests - Grade 4
Pct. of students at each level

- Read: Exceeds 27%, Meets 29%, Does not meet 44%
- Math: Exceeds 11%, Meets 43%, Does not meet 46%
- Lang: Exceeds 19%, Meets 44%, Does not meet 37%

DeKalb County Elementary Schools

Avondale Middle School

3131 Old Rockbridge Rd, Avondale Estates, GA 30002
404-508-0086 · Grades 6 - 8

Enrollment:	974
White / black / other:	6.9% / 89.7% / 3.4%
Not native English-speaking:	65 / 6.7%
Student absenteeism:	11.0%
Students per teacher:	23.3
Parent friendliness:	❶❷❸④⑤❻
Teachers with advanced degrees:	30.2%
Average years' teaching experience:	7.6
Students in gifted program:	32 / 3.3%
Students held back a grade:	2.9%
Total suspensions and expulsions:	994
Suspensions only, pct. in-school:	991 / 35.2%
Offenses:	violence: 276, drugs: 5, other: 781
Eligible students, free or reduced lunch:	80.5%
Number of dropouts:	6 / 0.5%
Pct. 8th-graders w/ basic computer skills:	99.0%

Students at this school generally go on to:
Avondale High

AJC GRADE: ★★★

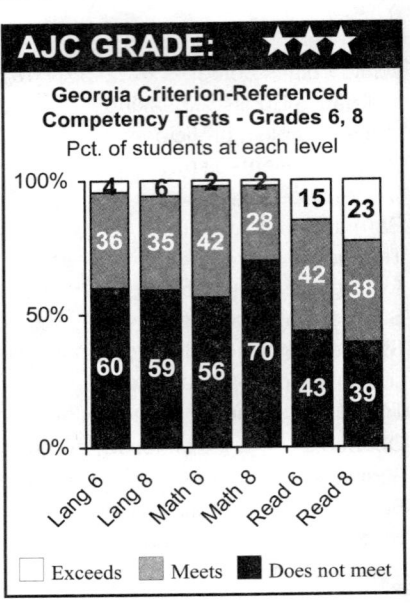

Georgia Criterion-Referenced Competency Tests - Grades 6, 8

Pct. of students at each level

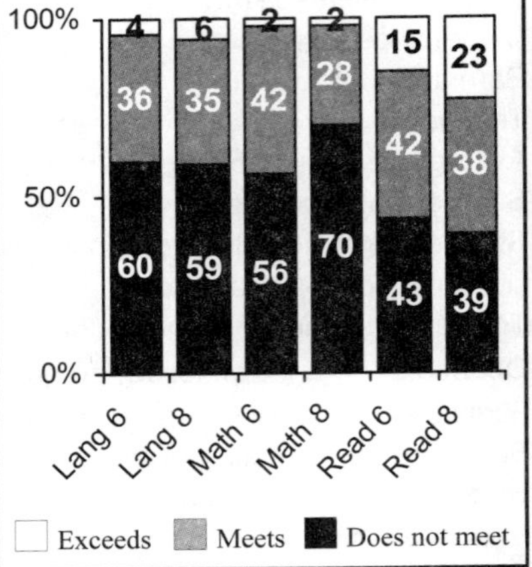
100%
50%
0%
4
6
2
2
15
23
36
35
42
28
42
38
60
59
56
70
43
39
Lang 6
Lang 8
Math 6
Math 8
Read 6
Read 8
Exceeds
Meets
Does not meet

Cedar Grove Middle School

2300 Wildcat Rd, Decatur, GA 30034
404-241-2626 · Grades 6 - 8

Enrollment:	1,390
White / black / other:	0.4% / 98.3% / 1.4%
Not native English-speaking:	5 / 0.4%
Student absenteeism:	4.8%
Students per teacher:	18.9
Parent friendliness:	①❷❸④⑤❻
Teachers with advanced degrees:	36.4%
Average years' teaching experience:	7.7
Students in gifted program:	114 / 8.2%
Students held back a grade:	2.1%
Total suspensions and expulsions:	1,594
Suspensions only, pct. in-school:	1,589 / 60.9%
Offenses:	violence: 492, drugs: 5, other: 1,163
Eligible students, free or reduced lunch:	50.2%
Number of dropouts:	6 / 0.4%
Pct. 8th-graders w/ basic computer skills:	100.0%

Students at this school generally go on to:
Cedar Grove High

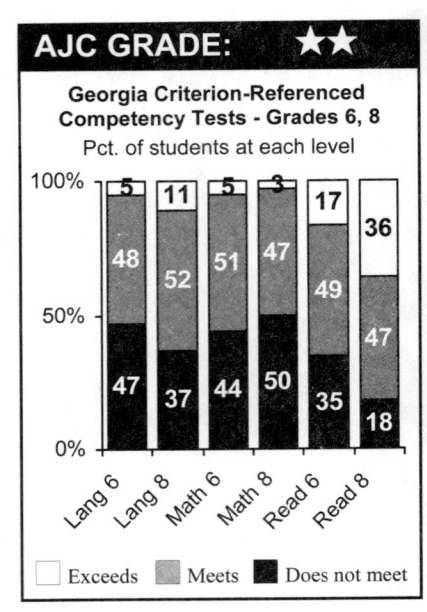

AJC GRADE: ★★

Georgia Criterion-Referenced Competency Tests - Grades 6, 8

Pct. of students at each level

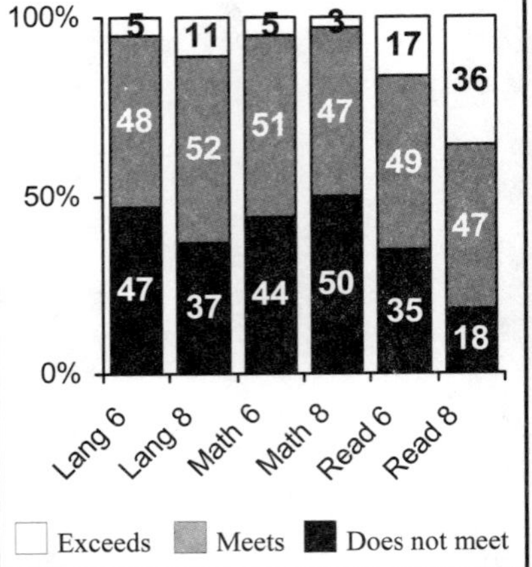
100%
50%
0%
5
11
5
3
17
36
48
52
51
47
49
47
47
37
44
50
35
18
Lang 6
Lang 8
Math 6
Math 8
Read 6
Read 8
Exceeds
Meets
Does not meet

Chamblee Middle School

4680 Chamblee-Dunwoody Rd, Atlanta, GA 30338
770-391-9916 · Grades 7 - 8

Enrollment: 668
White / black / other: 39.5% / 42.4% / 18.1%
Not native English-speaking: 30 / 4.5%
Student absenteeism: 4.8%
Students per teacher: 16.7
Parent friendliness: ❶❷❸④❺❻
Teachers with advanced degrees: 52.4%
Average years' teaching experience: 10.7
Students in gifted program: 280 / 41.9%
Students held back a grade: 1.0%
Total suspensions and expulsions: 308
Suspensions only, pct. in-school: 307 / 31.6%
Offenses: violence: 98, drugs: *, other: 218
Eligible students, free or reduced lunch: 27.4%
Number of dropouts: 11 / 1.5%
Pct. 8th-graders w/ basic computer skills: 96.0%
Students at this school generally go on to:
Chamblee High

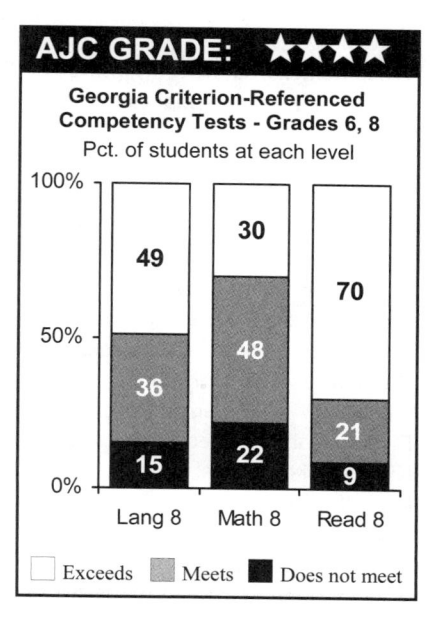

AJC GRADE: ★★★★

Georgia Criterion-Referenced Competency Tests - Grades 6, 8
Pct. of students at each level

	Lang 8	Math 8	Read 8
Exceeds	—	30	70
Meets	49	48	21
Does not meet	36 / 15	22	9

Chapel Hill Middle School

3535 Dogwood Farm Rd, Decatur, GA 30034
770-593-3109 · Grades 6 - 8

Enrollment: 1,168
White / black / other: 0.2% / 98.1% / 1.7%
Not native English-speaking: 3 / 0.3%
Student absenteeism: 7.4%
Students per teacher: 16.4
Parent friendliness: ①❷❸④⑤❻
Teachers with advanced degrees: 54.2%
Average years' teaching experience: 9.7
Students in gifted program: 78 / 6.7%
Students held back a grade: 3.6%
Total suspensions and expulsions: 1,196
Suspensions only, pct. in-school: 1,188 / 50.3%
Offenses: violence: 400, drugs: 7, other: 834
Eligible students, free or reduced lunch: 59.9%
Number of dropouts: 13 / 1.0%
Pct. 8th-graders w/ basic computer skills: 89.0%
Students at this school generally go on to:
Southwest DeKalb High

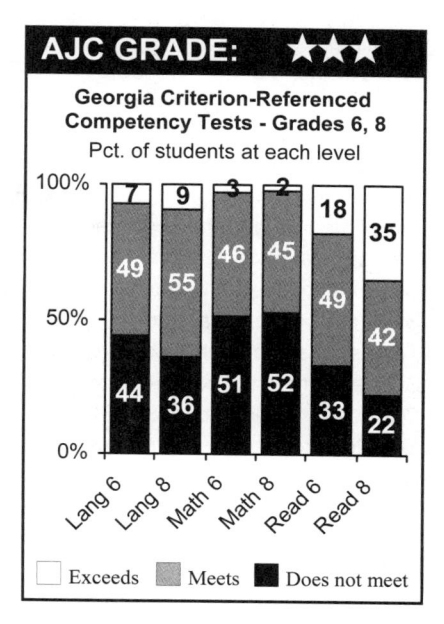

AJC GRADE: ★★★

Georgia Criterion-Referenced Competency Tests - Grades 6, 8
Pct. of students at each level

	Lang 6	Lang 8	Math 6	Math 8	Read 6	Read 8
Exceeds	7	9	3	2	18	35
Meets	49	55	46	45	49	42
Does not meet	44	36	51	52	33	22

DeKalb County Middle Schools

Freedom Middle School

505 S Hairston Rd, Stone Mountain, GA 30088
404-298-8888 · Grades 6 - 8

Enrollment:	1,320
White / black / other:	6.9% / 80.5% / 12.6%
Not native English-speaking:	158 / 12.0%
Student absenteeism:	8.0%
Students per teacher:	19.4
Parent friendliness:	①❷❸④❺❻
Teachers with advanced degrees:	35.3%
Average years' teaching experience:	8.8
Students in gifted program:	83 / 6.3%
Students held back a grade:	2.5%
Total suspensions and expulsions:	652
Suspensions only, pct. in-school:	650 / 45.4%
Offenses:	violence: 260, drugs: 6, other: 450
Eligible students, free or reduced lunch:	68.4%
Number of dropouts:	17 / 1.1%
Pct. 8th-graders w/ basic computer skills:	100.0%

Students at this school generally go on to:
Clarkston, Redan High

AJC GRADE: ★★★

Georgia Criterion-Referenced Competency Tests - Grades 6, 8
Pct. of students at each level

	Lang 6	Lang 8	Math 6	Math 8	Read 6	Read 8
Exceeds	7	9	7	4	19	30
Meets	43	41	42	38	40	40
Does not meet	51	49	51	58	41	31

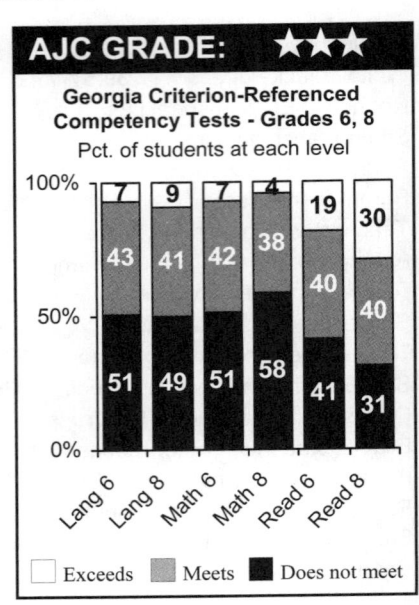

Henderson Middle School

2830 Henderson Mill Rd, Atlanta, GA 30341
770-939-3242 · Grades 6 - 8

Enrollment:	1,397
White / black / other:	28.5% / 47.7% / 23.8%
Not native English-speaking:	105 / 7.5%
Student absenteeism:	5.9%
Students per teacher:	16.4
Parent friendliness:	❶❷❸④⑤❻
Teachers with advanced degrees:	53.3%
Average years' teaching experience:	12.9
Students in gifted program:	210 / 15.0%
Students held back a grade:	1.1%
Total suspensions and expulsions:	959
Suspensions only, pct. in-school:	953 / 41.3%
Offenses:	violence: 386, drugs: 14, other: 623
Eligible students, free or reduced lunch:	49.2%
Number of dropouts:	83 / 5.1%
Pct. 8th-graders w/ basic computer skills:	95.0%

Students at this school generally go on to:
Lakeside, Tucker High

AJC GRADE: ★★★

Georgia Criterion-Referenced Competency Tests - Grades 6, 8
Pct. of students at each level

	Lang 6	Lang 8	Math 6	Math 8	Read 6	Read 8
Exceeds	4	24	3	12	15	49
Meets	34	42	46	53	33	31
Does not meet	62	34	52	35	52	19

DeKalb County Middle Schools

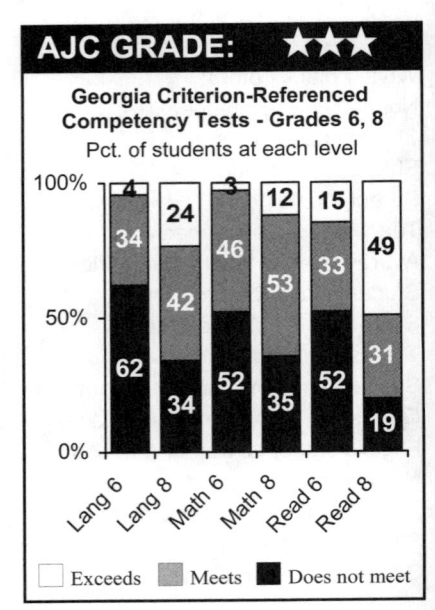

Miller Grove Middle School

2215 Miller Rd, Decatur, GA 30035
770-987-7470 · Grades 6 - 8

Enrollment:	1,444
White / black / other:	0.8% / 95.1% / 4.2%
Not native English-speaking:	2 / 0.1%
Student absenteeism:	6.3%
Students per teacher:	18.1
Parent friendliness:	① ❷ ❸ ④ ⑤ ❻
Teachers with advanced degrees:	33.3%
Average years' teaching experience:	7.8
Students in gifted program:	173 / 12.0%
Students held back a grade:	5.4%
Total suspensions and expulsions:	1,316
Suspensions only, pct. in-school:	1,307 / 46.7%
Offenses: violence: 273, drugs: 5, other: 1,088	
Eligible students, free or reduced lunch:	50.4%
Number of dropouts:	69 / 4.2%
Pct. 8th-graders w/ basic computer skills:	45.0%
Students at this school generally go on to: Redan High	

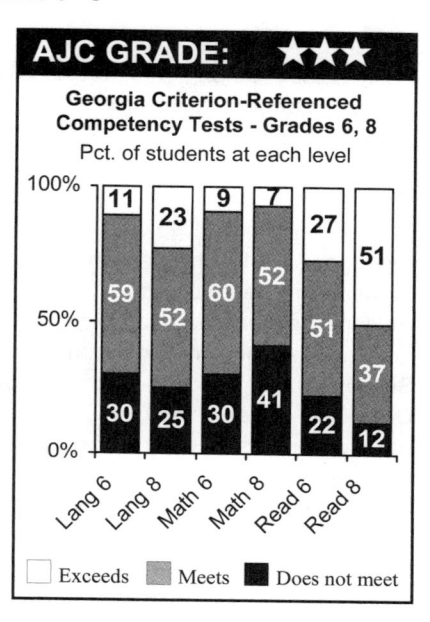

AJC GRADE: ★★★

Georgia Criterion-Referenced Competency Tests - Grades 6, 8
Pct. of students at each level

	Lang 6	Lang 8	Math 6	Math 8	Read 6	Read 8
Exceeds	11	23	9	7	27	51
Meets	59	52	60	52	51	37
Does not meet	30	25	30	41	22	12

Peachtree Charter Middle School

4664 N Peachtree Rd, Atlanta, GA 30338
678-676-7702 · Grades 6 - 8

Enrollment:	1,044
White / black / other:	39.8% / 42.0% / 18.1%
Not native English-speaking:	35 / 3.4%
Student absenteeism:	4.6%
Students per teacher:	14.4
Parent friendliness:	① ❷ ❸ ④ ⑤ ❻
Teachers with advanced degrees:	49.3%
Average years' teaching experience:	11.7
Students in gifted program:	276 / 26.4%
Students held back a grade:	1.3%
Total suspensions and expulsions:	635
Suspensions only, pct. in-school:	631 / 81.0%
Offenses: violence: 179, drugs: 5, other: 505	
Eligible students, free or reduced lunch:	31.8%
Number of dropouts:	*
Pct. 8th-graders w/ basic computer skills:	100.0%
Students at this school generally go on to: Dunwoody High	

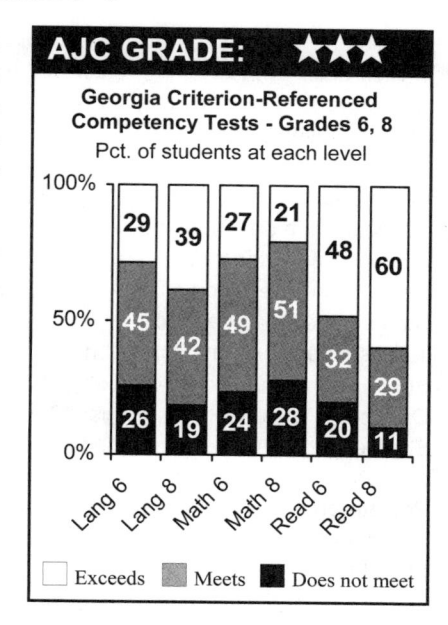

AJC GRADE: ★★★

Georgia Criterion-Referenced Competency Tests - Grades 6, 8
Pct. of students at each level

	Lang 6	Lang 8	Math 6	Math 8	Read 6	Read 8
Exceeds	29	39	27	21	48	60
Meets	45	42	49	51	32	29
Does not meet	26	19	24	28	20	11

The Atlanta Journal-Constitution / Page 249

DeKalb County Middle Schools

Ronald McNair Middle School

2190 Wallingford Dr, Decatur, GA 30032
404-241-5576 · Grades 6 - 8

Enrollment:	1,200
White / black / other:	0.3% / 98.4% / 1.3%
Not native English-speaking:	*
Student absenteeism:	10.7%
Students per teacher:	18.2
Parent friendliness:	①❷❸④❺❻
Teachers with advanced degrees:	53.7%
Average years' teaching experience:	13.0
Students in gifted program:	37 / 3.1%
Students held back a grade:	15.3%
Total suspensions and expulsions:	3,598
Suspensions only, pct. in-school:	3,576 / 31.3%
Offenses: violence: 800, drugs: 29, other: 2,903	
Eligible students, free or reduced lunch:	83.8%
Number of dropouts:	27 / 1.9%
Pct. 8th-graders w/ basic computer skills:	97.9%
Students at this school generally go on to:	
McNair High	

AJC GRADE: ★★★

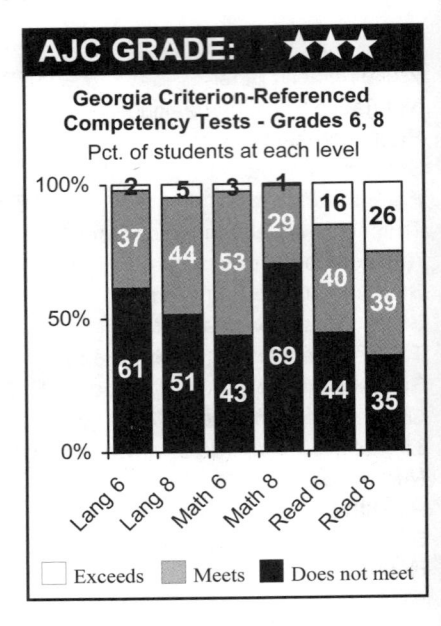

Georgia Criterion-Referenced Competency Tests - Grades 6, 8
Pct. of students at each level

	Lang 6	Lang 8	Math 6	Math 8	Read 6	Read 8
Exceeds	2	5	3	1	16	26
Meets	37	44	53	29	40	39
Does not meet	61	51	43	69	44	35

Salem Middle School

5333 Salem Rd, Lithonia, GA 30038
770-593-2007 · Grades 6 - 8

Enrollment:	1,785
White / black / other:	0.8% / 97.0% / 2.2%
Not native English-speaking:	4 / 0.2%
Student absenteeism:	6.9%
Students per teacher:	19.0
Parent friendliness:	①❷❸④❺❻
Teachers with advanced degrees:	40.6%
Average years' teaching experience:	8.7
Students in gifted program:	85 / 4.8%
Students held back a grade:	2.9%
Total suspensions and expulsions:	2,363
Suspensions only, pct. in-school:	2,345 / 43.4%
Offenses: violence: 752, drugs: 13, other: 1,766	
Eligible students, free or reduced lunch:	58.4%
Number of dropouts:	67 / 3.2%
Pct. 8th-graders w/ basic computer skills:	98.1%
Students at this school generally go on to:	
King, Lithonia High	

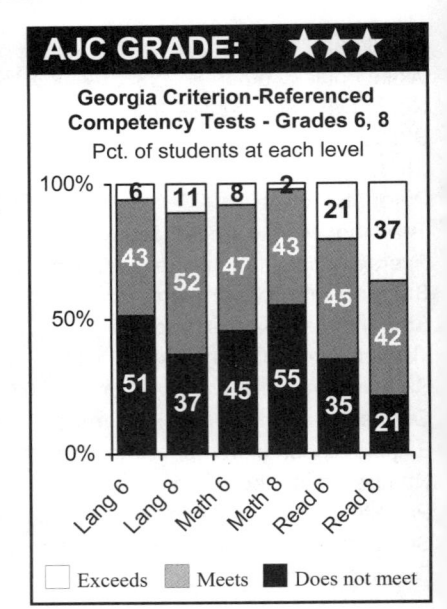

AJC GRADE: ★★★

Georgia Criterion-Referenced Competency Tests - Grades 6, 8
Pct. of students at each level

	Lang 6	Lang 8	Math 6	Math 8	Read 6	Read 8
Exceeds	6	11	8	2	21	37
Meets	43	52	47	43	45	42
Does not meet	51	37	45	55	35	21

DeKalb County Middle Schools

Sequoyah Middle School

3456 Aztec Rd, Atlanta, GA 30340
678-676-7902 · Grades 6 - 8

Enrollment:	1,052
White / black / other:	7.0% / 28.2% / 64.7%
Not native English-speaking:	282 / 26.8%
Student absenteeism:	8.1%
Students per teacher:	14.1
Parent friendliness:	① ❷ ❸ ④ ⑤ ❻
Teachers with advanced degrees:	54.7%
Average years' teaching experience:	11.3
Students in gifted program:	69 / 6.6%
Students held back a grade:	4.0%
Total suspensions and expulsions:	1,045
Suspensions only, pct. in-school:	1,038 / 51.3%
Offenses:	violence: 301, drugs: 8, other: 770
Eligible students, free or reduced lunch:	84.9%
Number of dropouts:	15 / 1.2%
Pct. 8th-graders w/ basic computer skills:	98.2%

Students at this school generally go on to:
Cross Keys High

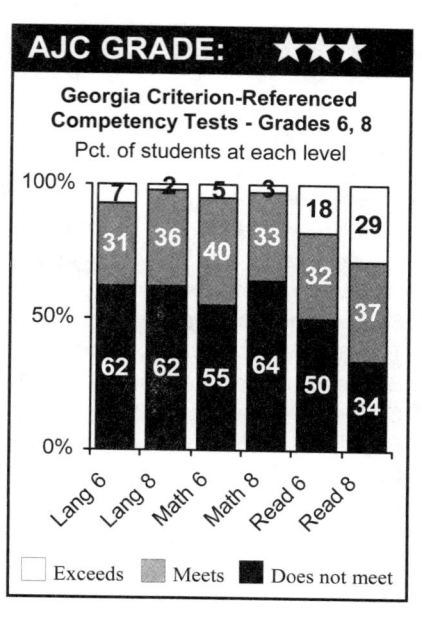

AJC GRADE: ★★★

Georgia Criterion-Referenced Competency Tests - Grades 6, 8
Pct. of students at each level

	Lang 6	Lang 8	Math 6	Math 8	Read 6	Read 8
Exceeds	7	2	5	3	18	29
Meets	31	36	40	33	32	37
Does not meet	62	62	55	64	50	34

Shamrock Middle School

3100 Mount Olive Dr, Decatur, GA 30033
404-633-9235 · Grades 6 - 8

Enrollment:	1,320
White / black / other:	40.1% / 46.6% / 13.3%
Not native English-speaking:	86 / 6.5%
Student absenteeism:	6.0%
Students per teacher:	14.7
Parent friendliness:	① ❷ ❸ ④ ⑤ ❻
Teachers with advanced degrees:	54.9%
Average years' teaching experience:	10.6
Students in gifted program:	317 / 24.0%
Students held back a grade:	0.7%
Total suspensions and expulsions:	1,180
Suspensions only, pct. in-school:	1,172 / 62.1%
Offenses:	violence: 269, drugs: 1, other: 977
Eligible students, free or reduced lunch:	41.5%
Number of dropouts:	48 / 3.2%
Pct. 8th-graders w/ basic computer skills:	27.0%

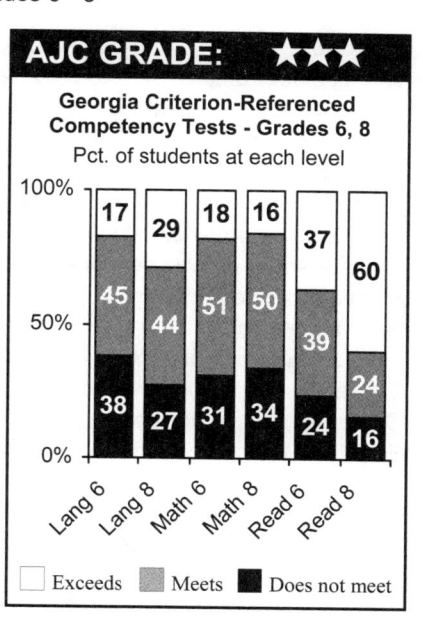

Students at this school generally go on to:
Druid Hills, Lakeside High

AJC GRADE: ★★★

Georgia Criterion-Referenced Competency Tests - Grades 6, 8
Pct. of students at each level

	Lang 6	Lang 8	Math 6	Math 8	Read 6	Read 8
Exceeds	17	29	18	16	37	60
Meets	45	44	51	50	39	24
Does not meet	38	27	31	34	24	16

DeKalb County Middle Schools

Stephenson Middle School

922 Stephenson Rd, Stone Mountain, GA 30087
678-676-4402 · Grades 6 - 8

Enrollment:	1,551
White / black / other:	1.0% / 95.6% / 3.4%
Not native English-speaking:	*
Student absenteeism:	5.2%
Students per teacher:	17.4
Parent friendliness:	①❷❸④⑤❻
Teachers with advanced degrees:	41.8%
Average years' teaching experience:	8.5
Students in gifted program:	92 / 5.9%
Students held back a grade:	9.2%
Total suspensions and expulsions:	1,599
Suspensions only, pct. in-school:	1,593 / 62.3%
Offenses:	violence: 466, drugs: 9, other: 1,179
Eligible students, free or reduced lunch:	36.7%
Number of dropouts:	21 / 1.2%
Pct. 8th-graders w/ basic computer skills:	90.0%

Students at this school generally go on to:
Stephenson High

AJC GRADE: ★★★

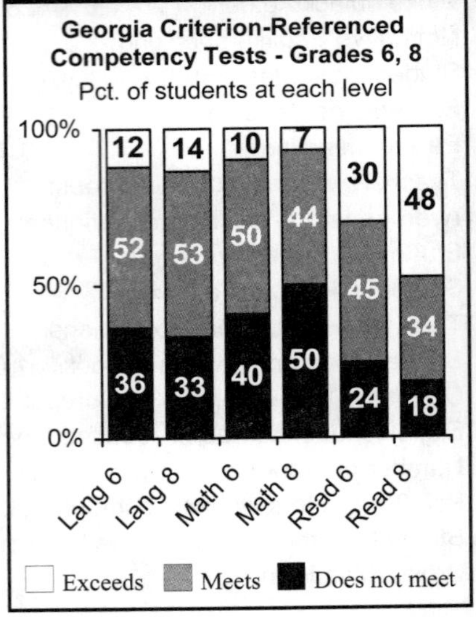
Georgia Criterion-Referenced Competency Tests - Grades 6, 8
Pct. of students at each level
100%
50%
0%
12 52 36
14 53 33
10 50 40
7 44 50
30 45 24
48 34 18
Lang 6
Lang 8
Math 6
Math 8
Read 6
Read 8
Exceeds
Meets
Does not meet

Stone Mountain Charter School

6206 Memorial Dr, Stone Mountain, GA 30083
678-676-4702 · Grades 6 - 9

Enrollment:	150
White / black / other:	6.0% / 92.0% / 2.0%
Not native English-speaking:	*
Student absenteeism:	3.6%
Students per teacher:	33.3
Parent friendliness:	①❷❸④❺❻
Teachers with advanced degrees:	80.0%
Average years' teaching experience:	0.6
Students in gifted program:	*
Students held back a grade:	*
Total suspensions and expulsions:	2
Suspensions only, pct. in-school:	2 / 0.0%
Offenses:	violence: * , drugs: * , other: 3
Eligible students, free or reduced lunch:	*
Number of dropouts:	2 / 1.3%
Pct. 8th-graders w/ basic computer skills:	100.0%

Students at this school generally go on to:
Stone Mountain, Tucker High

AJC GRADE: ★

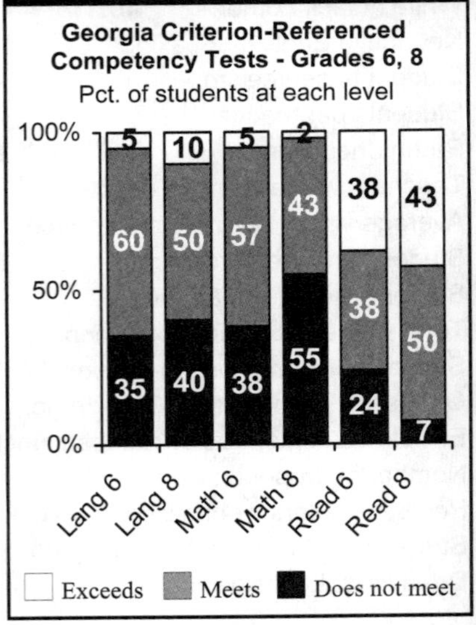
Georgia Criterion-Referenced Competency Tests - Grades 6, 8
Pct. of students at each level
100%
50%
0%
5 60 35
10 50 40
5 57 38
2 43 55
38 38 24
43 50 7
Lang 6
Lang 8
Math 6
Math 8
Read 6
Read 8
Exceeds
Meets
Does not meet

Stone Mountain Middle School

5265 Mimosa Dr, Stone Mountain, GA 30083
678-676-4802 · Grades 6 - 8

Enrollment:	1,040
White / black / other:	4.7% / 84.7% / 10.6%
Not native English-speaking:	31 / 3.0%
Student absenteeism:	7.1%
Students per teacher:	15.9
Parent friendliness:	①❷❸④⑤❻
Teachers with advanced degrees:	37.3%
Average years' teaching experience:	7.9
Students in gifted program:	43 / 4.1%
Students held back a grade:	0.6%
Total suspensions and expulsions:	1,345
Suspensions only, pct. in-school:	1,340 / 54.1%
Offenses: violence: 446, drugs: 1, other: 953	
Eligible students, free or reduced lunch:	74.0%
Number of dropouts:	24 / 1.9%
Pct. 8th-graders w/ basic computer skills:	98.1%

Students at this school generally go on to:
Stone Mountain High

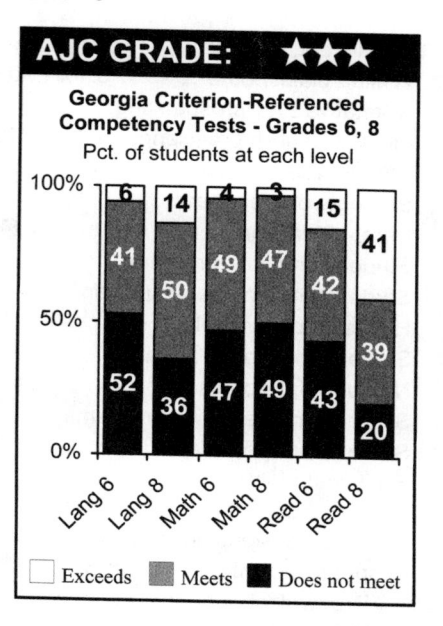

AJC GRADE: ★★★

Georgia Criterion-Referenced Competency Tests - Grades 6, 8
Pct. of students at each level

	Lang 6	Lang 8	Math 6	Math 8	Read 6	Read 8
Exceeds	6	14	4	3	15	41
Meets	41	50	49	47	42	39
Does not meet	52	36	47	49	43	20

DeKalb County Middle Schools

Avondale High School

1192 Clarendon Ave, Avondale Estates, GA 30002
404-289-6766 · Grades 9 - 12

Enrollment:	932
White / black / other:	6.1% / 90.8% / 3.1%
Not native English-speaking:	46 / 4.9%
Limited English proficiency:	160 / 17.2%
Student absenteeism:	9.0%
Students per teacher:	17.1
Parent friendliness:	① ❷ ❸ ④ ⑤ ❻
Students in gifted program:	32 / 3.4%
Students in remedial education:	0.5%
High school completion rate:	59.6%
Students held back a grade:	24.7%
Number of dropouts:	77 / 7.2%
Students in alternative programs:	8 / 0.9%
Students in special education:	71 / 7.6%
Eligible students, free or reduced lunch:	72.7%
Total suspensions and expulsions:	1,662
Suspensions only, pct. in-school:	1,653 / 59.0%
Drugs/alcohol-related offenses:	21
Violence-related offenses:	148
Firearms-related offenses:	9
Vandalism-related offenses:	10
Theft-related offenses:	12
All other disciplinary offenses:	1,471
Teachers with advanced degrees:	51.7%
Average years' teaching experience:	12.1

AJC GRADE: ★★★

High School Graduation Test
Pct. of students who passed on first try

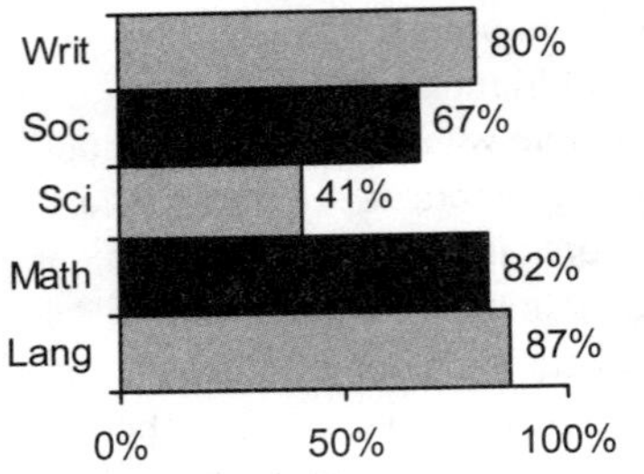

- Writ: 80%
- Soc: 67%
- Sci: 41%
- Math: 82%
- Lang: 87%

GHSA classification: 5-AAA
Interscholastic sports offered:
BB, BS, CC, CL, FB, GO, SB, SO, SW, TE, TF, WR

Advanced Placement (AP) Exams
Students tested: 51
Tests taken: 86
Pct. of test scores 3 or higher (1 - 5 scale): 10.5%

Languages other than English taught:
French, German, Spanish

2000-2001 high school graduates: 124

College prep/vocational diplomas:	13.7%
College prep endorsement diplomas:	49.2%
Vocational endorsement diplomas:	22.6%
General high school diplomas:	1.6%
Special education diplomas:	1.6%
Certificates of attendance (no diploma):	11.3%

Of the 2000-2001 graduates, 53.2% were eligible for the HOPE scholarship.

Of the 1999-2000 graduates, 31 attended a Georgia public college or university. Of those, 58% met the school's minimum academic requirements.

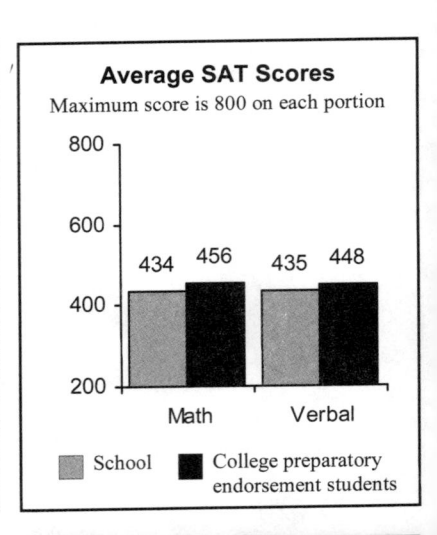

Average SAT Scores
Maximum score is 800 on each portion

- Math: School 434, College preparatory endorsement students 456
- Verbal: School 435, College preparatory endorsement students 448

The Atlanta Journal-Constitution / Page 254

DeKalb County High Schools

Cedar Grove High School

2360 River Rd, Ellenwood, GA 30294
404-243-3770 · Grades 9 - 12

Enrollment:	1,565
White / black / other:	0.2% / 98.7% / 1.1%
Not native English-speaking:	1 / 0.1%
Limited English proficiency:	33 / 2.1%
Student absenteeism:	9.6%
Students per teacher:	21.8
Parent friendliness:	❶❷③❹❺⑥
Students in gifted program:	62 / 4.0%
Students in remedial education:	1.0%
High school completion rate:	80.1%
Students held back a grade:	18.8%
Number of dropouts:	91 / 5.2%
Students in alternative programs:	18 / 1.2%
Students in special education:	74 / 4.7%
Eligible students, free or reduced lunch:	42.7%

Total suspensions and expulsions:	658
Suspensions only, pct. in-school:	650 / 68.9%
Drugs/alcohol-related offenses:	7
Violence-related offenses:	111
Firearms-related offenses:	4
Vandalism-related offenses:	7
Theft-related offenses:	6
All other disciplinary offenses:	537

Teachers with advanced degrees:	53.9%
Average years' teaching experience:	11.5

AJC GRADE: ★★★

High School Graduation Test

Pct. of students who passed on first try

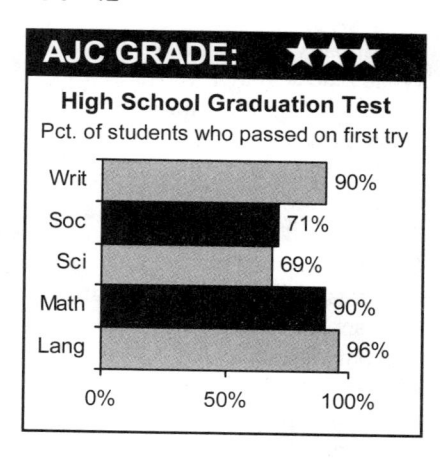

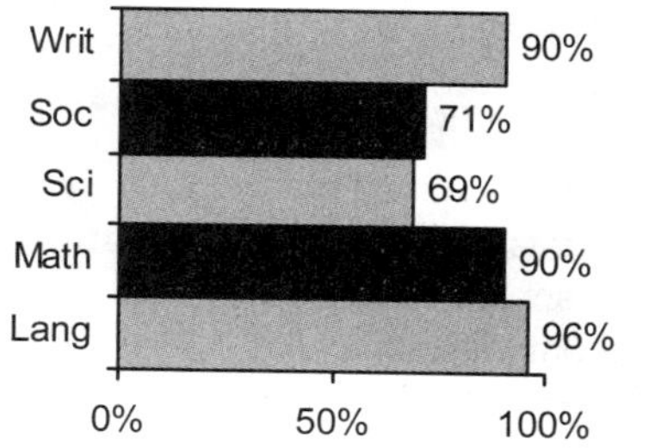
Writ 90%
Soc 71%
Sci 69%
Math 90%
Lang 96%
0%
50%
100%

GHSA classification:	7-AAAAA

Interscholastic sports offered:
BB, BS, CC, CL, FB, GO, GY, SB, SO, SW, TE, TF, VB, WR

Advanced Placement (AP) Exams

Students tested:	56
Tests taken:	110
Pct. of test scores 3 or higher (1 - 5 scale):	12.7%

Languages other than English taught:
French, German, Latin, Spanish

2000-2001 high school graduates: 237

College prep/vocational diplomas:	0.8%
College prep endorsement diplomas:	83.5%
Vocational endorsement diplomas:	6.8%
General high school diplomas:	0.0%
Special education diplomas:	1.7%
Certificates of attendance (no diploma):	7.2%

Of the 2000-2001 graduates, 56.5% were eligible for the HOPE scholarship.

Of the 1999-2000 graduates, 98 attended a Georgia public college or university. Of those, 57% met the school's minimum academic requirements.

Average SAT Scores

Maximum score is 800 on each portion

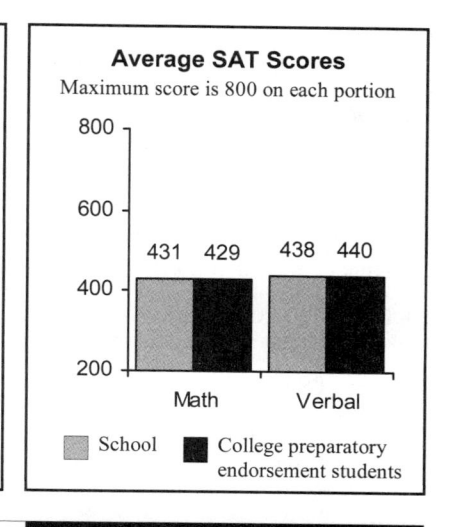

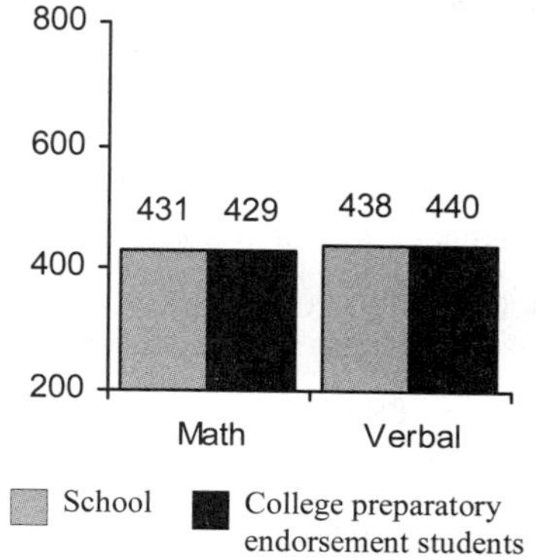
800
600
400
200
431 429
438 440
Math
Verbal
School
College preparatory endorsement students

Chamblee Charter High School

3688 Chamblee-Dunwoody Rd, Atlanta, GA 30341
678-676-6902 · Grades 9 - 12

Enrollment:	1,265
White / black / other:	35.4% / 48.9% / 15.7%
Not native English-speaking:	32 / 2.5%
Limited English proficiency:	149 / 11.8%
Student absenteeism:	6.3%
Students per teacher:	19.8
Parent friendliness:	①❷❸④⑤❻
Students in gifted program:	267 / 21.1%
Students in remedial education:	1.5%
High school completion rate:	89.9%
Students held back a grade:	5.0%
Number of dropouts:	18 / 1.3%
Students in alternative programs:	8 / 0.6%
Students in special education:	87 / 6.9%
Eligible students, free or reduced lunch:	18.0%
Total suspensions and expulsions:	1,087
Suspensions only, pct. in-school:	1,085 / 75.9%
Drugs/alcohol-related offenses:	19
Violence-related offenses:	71
Firearms-related offenses:	12
Vandalism-related offenses:	16
Theft-related offenses:	18
All other disciplinary offenses:	982
Teachers with advanced degrees:	61.2%
Average years' teaching experience:	13.7

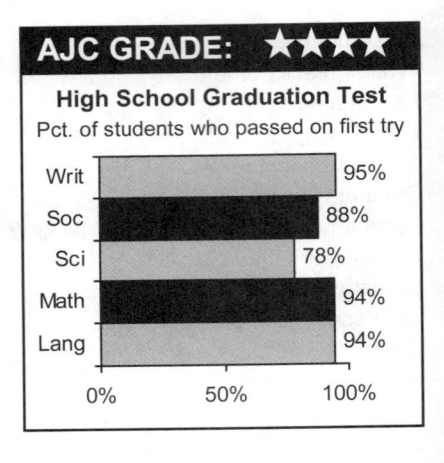

AJC GRADE: ★★★★

High School Graduation Test
Pct. of students who passed on first try

- Writ: 95%
- Soc: 88%
- Sci: 78%
- Math: 94%
- Lang: 94%

GHSA classification: 6-AAAA
Interscholastic sports offered:
BB, BS, CC, CL, FB, GO, GY, RI, SB, SO, SW, TE, TF, VB, WR

Advanced Placement (AP) Exams
Students tested:	195
Tests taken:	443
Pct. of test scores 3 or higher (1 - 5 scale):	89.2%

Languages other than English taught:
Chinese, French, German, Latin, Spanish

2000-2001 high school graduates: 240

College prep/vocational diplomas:	0.0%
College prep endorsement diplomas:	90.0%
Vocational endorsement diplomas:	3.3%
General high school diplomas:	0.0%
Special education diplomas:	4.6%
Certificates of attendance (no diploma):	2.1%

Of the 2000-2001 graduates, 78.3% were eligible for the HOPE scholarship.

Of the 1999-2000 graduates, 95 attended a Georgia public college or university. Of those, 92% met the school's minimum academic requirements.

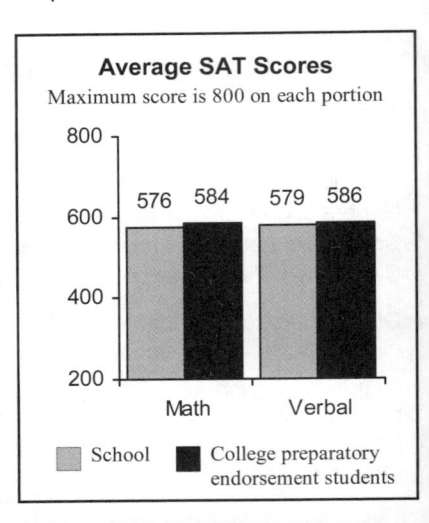

Average SAT Scores
Maximum score is 800 on each portion

- Math — School: 576, College preparatory endorsement students: 584
- Verbal — School: 579, College preparatory endorsement students: 586

The Atlanta Journal-Constitution / Page 256

DeKalb County High Schools

Clarkston High School

618 N Indian Creek Dr, Clarkston, GA 30021
678-676-5302 · Grades 9 - 12

Enrollment:	1,116
White / black / other:	6.3% / 72.0% / 21.7%
Not native English-speaking:	222 / 19.9%
Limited English proficiency:	636 / 57.0%
Student absenteeism:	9.3%
Students per teacher:	14.8
Parent friendliness:	❶❷❸④⑤❻
Students in gifted program:	3 / 0.3%
Students in remedial education:	12.1%
High school completion rate:	60.4%
Students held back a grade:	17.2%
Number of dropouts:	111 / 8.1%
Students in alternative programs:	3 / 0.3%
Students in special education:	94 / 8.4%
Eligible students, free or reduced lunch:	51.1%
Total suspensions and expulsions:	1,204
Suspensions only, pct. in-school:	1,199 / 53.5%
Drugs/alcohol-related offenses:	2
Violence-related offenses:	137
Firearms-related offenses:	2
Vandalism-related offenses:	12
Theft-related offenses:	3
All other disciplinary offenses:	1,061
Teachers with advanced degrees:	52.6%
Average years' teaching experience:	11.0

AJC GRADE: ★★★

High School Graduation Test
Pct. of students who passed on first try

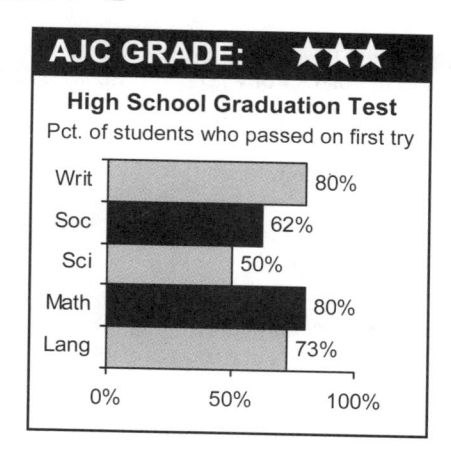

- Writ: 80%
- Soc: 62%
- Sci: 50%
- Math: 80%
- Lang: 73%

GHSA classification: 5-AAAA
Interscholastic sports offered:
BB, BS, CC, CL, FB, GO, SB, SO, SW, TE, TF, VB, WR

Advanced Placement (AP) Exams
Students tested: 36
Tests taken: 39
Pct. of test scores 3 or higher (1 - 5 scale): 7.7%

Languages other than English taught:
American Sign Language, French, German, Latin, Russian, Spanish

2000-2001 high school graduates: 139

College prep/vocational diplomas:	10.8%
College prep endorsement diplomas:	64.0%
Vocational endorsement diplomas:	8.6%
General high school diplomas:	0.0%
Special education diplomas:	6.5%
Certificates of attendance (no diploma):	10.1%

Of the 2000-2001 graduates, 60.4% were eligible for the HOPE scholarship.

Of the 1999-2000 graduates, 60 attended a Georgia public college or university. Of those, 75% met the school's minimum academic requirements.

Average SAT Scores
Maximum score is 800 on each portion

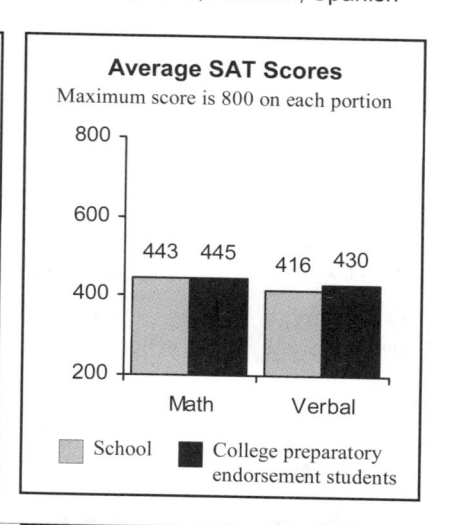

- Math — School: 443, College preparatory endorsement students: 445
- Verbal — School: 416, College preparatory endorsement students: 430

DeKalb County High Schools

Columbia High School

2106 Columbia Dr, Decatur, GA 30032
404-284-8720 · Grades 9 - 12

👎

Enrollment:	1,449
White / black / other:	1.0% / 96.2% / 2.8%
Not native English-speaking:	1 / 0.1%
Limited English proficiency:	39 / 2.7%
Student absenteeism:	8.0%
Students per teacher:	18.4
Parent friendliness:	①❷❸④⑤❻
Students in gifted program:	72 / 5.0%
Students in remedial education:	7.6%
High school completion rate:	69.2%
Students held back a grade:	13.2%
Number of dropouts:	71 / 4.5%
Students in alternative programs:	8 / 0.6%
Students in special education:	110 / 7.6%
Eligible students, free or reduced lunch:	52.8%

Total suspensions and expulsions:	1,722
Suspensions only, pct. in-school:	1,702 / 43.7%
Drugs/alcohol-related offenses:	3
Violence-related offenses:	344
Firearms-related offenses:	19
Vandalism-related offenses:	11
Theft-related offenses:	8
All other disciplinary offenses:	1,398

Teachers with advanced degrees:	55.4%
Average years' teaching experience:	12.3

2000-2001 high school graduates: 184

College prep/vocational diplomas:	3.3%
College prep endorsement diplomas:	75.5%
Vocational endorsement diplomas:	9.8%
General high school diplomas:	0.0%
Special education diplomas:	6.0%
Certificates of attendance (no diploma):	5.4%

Of the 2000-2001 graduates, 57.6% were eligible for the HOPE scholarship.

Of the 1999-2000 graduates, 75 attended a Georgia public college or university. Of those, 76% met the school's minimum academic requirements.

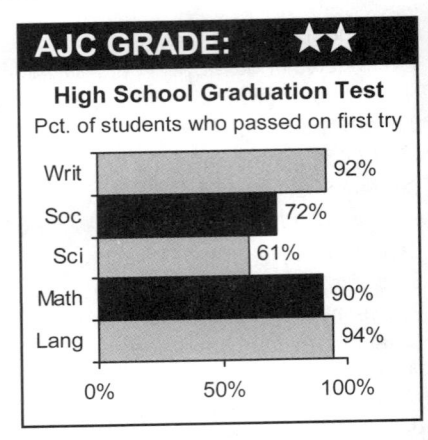

AJC GRADE: ★★

High School Graduation Test
Pct. of students who passed on first try

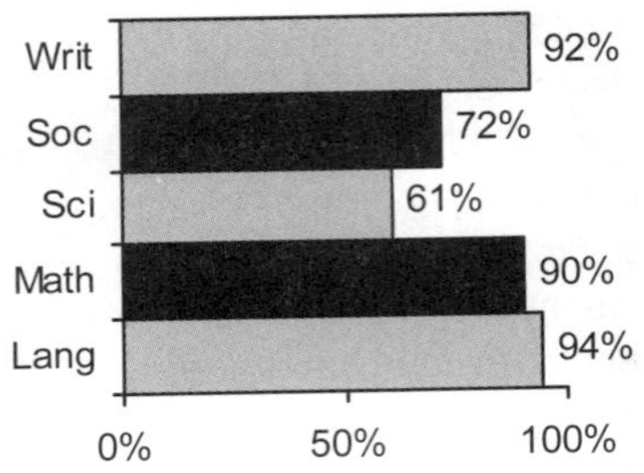
Writ
92%
Soc
72%
Sci
61%
Math
90%
Lang
94%
0%
50%
100%

GHSA classification:	5-AAAA

Interscholastic sports offered:
BB, BS, CC, CL, FB, GO, GY, SB, SO, SW, TE, TF, WR

Advanced Placement (AP) Exams

Students tested:	48
Tests taken:	64
Pct. of test scores 3 or higher (1 - 5 scale):	20.3%

Languages other than English taught:
French, German, Spanish

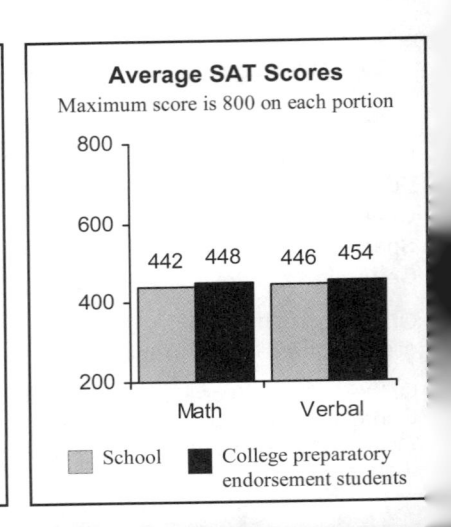

Average SAT Scores
Maximum score is 800 on each portion

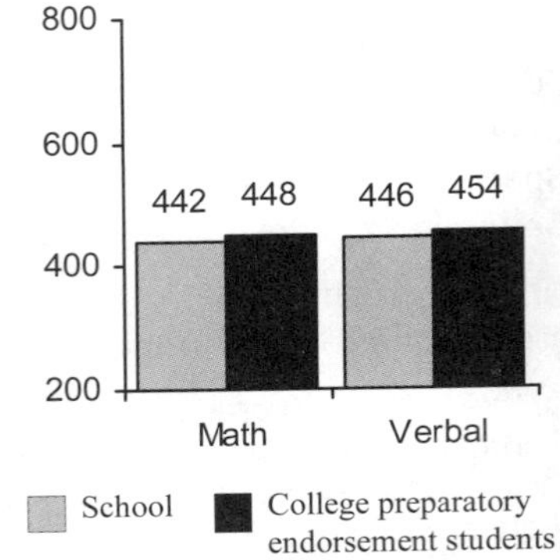
800
600
400
200
442
448
446
454
Math
Verbal
School
College preparatory endorsement students

Cross Keys High School

1626 N Druid Hills Rd NE, Atlanta, GA 30319
404-633-5141 · Grades 9 - 12

Enrollment:	1,161
White / black / other:	8.3% / 38.3% / 53.4%
Not native English-speaking:	310 / 26.7%
Limited English proficiency:	818 / 70.5%
Student absenteeism:	9.5%
Students per teacher:	16.4
Parent friendliness:	❶❷❸④❺❻
Students in gifted program:	31 / 2.7%
Students in remedial education:	1.1%
High school completion rate:	54.6%
Students held back a grade:	19.2%
Number of dropouts:	72 / 5.3%
Students in alternative programs:	7 / 0.6%
Students in special education:	52 / 4.5%
Eligible students, free or reduced lunch:	58.7%
Total suspensions and expulsions:	1,221
Suspensions only, pct. in-school:	1,209 / 81.0%
Drugs/alcohol-related offenses:	9
Violence-related offenses:	113
Firearms-related offenses:	16
Vandalism-related offenses:	3
Theft-related offenses:	9
All other disciplinary offenses:	1,090
Teachers with advanced degrees:	56.8%
Average years' teaching experience:	12.5

AJC GRADE: ★★★

High School Graduation Test
Pct. of students who passed on first try

- Writ: 75%
- Soc: 58%
- Sci: 43%
- Math: 85%
- Lang: 81%

GHSA classification:	5-AAA
Interscholastic sports offered:	
BB, BS, CC, CL, FB, GO, RI, SB, SO, SW, TE, TF, VB, WR	
Advanced Placement (AP) Exams	
Students tested:	45
Tests taken:	78
Pct. of test scores 3 or higher (1 - 5 scale):	20.5%

Languages other than English taught:
Chinese, French, German, Latin, Spanish

2000-2001 high school graduates: 137

College prep/vocational diplomas:	4.4%
College prep endorsement diplomas:	76.6%
Vocational endorsement diplomas:	4.4%
General high school diplomas:	0.0%
Special education diplomas:	2.9%
Certificates of attendance (no diploma):	11.7%

Of the 2000-2001 graduates, 58.4% were eligible for the HOPE scholarship.

Of the 1999-2000 graduates, 63 attended a Georgia public college or university. Of those, 84% met the school's minimum academic requirements.

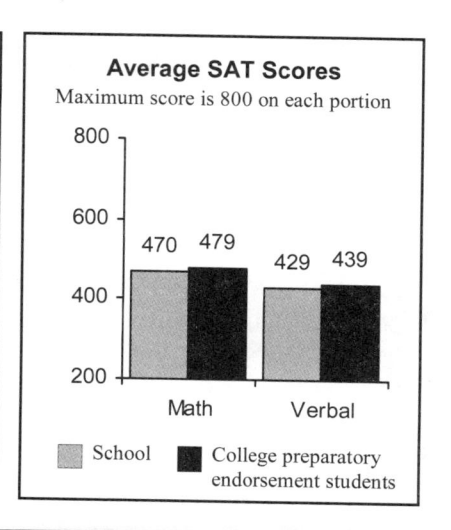

Average SAT Scores
Maximum score is 800 on each portion

- Math — School: 470, College preparatory endorsement students: 479
- Verbal — School: 429, College preparatory endorsement students: 439

DeKalb County High Schools

DeKalb School of the Arts

👍

2415 N Druid Hills Rd NE Ste B, Atlanta, GA 30329
404-248-0017 · Grades 8 - 12

Enrollment:	206
White / black / other:	27.2% / 61.2% / 11.7%
Not native English-speaking:	*
Limited English proficiency:	10 / 4.9%
Student absenteeism:	2.8%
Students per teacher:	10.0
Parent friendliness:	①❷❸④⑤❻
Students in gifted program:	61 / 29.6%
Students in remedial education:	*
High school completion rate:	*
Students held back a grade:	*
Number of dropouts:	3 / 1.4%
Students in alternative programs:	*
Students in special education:	3 / 1.5%
Eligible students, free or reduced lunch:	24.3%

Total suspensions and expulsions:	48
Suspensions only, pct. in-school:	48 / 2.1%
Drugs/alcohol-related offenses:	*
Violence-related offenses:	5
Firearms-related offenses:	3
Vandalism-related offenses:	2
Theft-related offenses:	*
All other disciplinary offenses:	38

Teachers with advanced degrees:	52.2%
Average years' teaching experience:	8.1

AJC GRADE: ★★★★

High School Graduation Test
Pct. of students who passed on first try

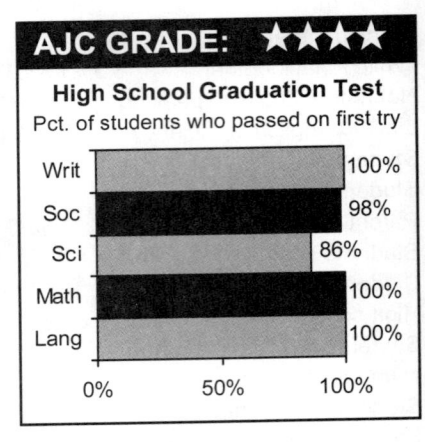

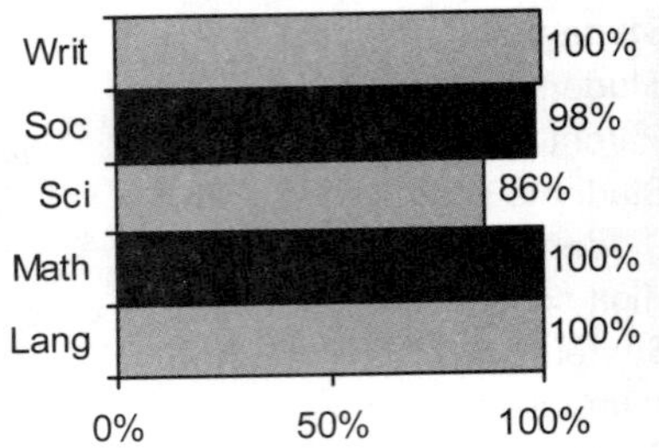
Writ
100%
Soc
98%
Sci
86%
Math
100%
Lang
100%
0%
50%
100%

GHSA classification:	5-AA
Interscholastic sports offered:	
None	

Advanced Placement (AP) Exams

Students tested:	41
Tests taken:	47
Pct. of test scores 3 or higher (1 - 5 scale):	8.5%

Languages other than English taught:
French, German, Latin, Spanish

2000-2001 high school graduates: 27

College prep/vocational diplomas:	0.0%
College prep endorsement diplomas:	92.6%
Vocational endorsement diplomas:	7.4%
General high school diplomas:	0.0%
Special education diplomas:	0.0%
Certificates of attendance (no diploma):	0.0%

Of the 2000-2001 graduates, 77.8% were eligible for the HOPE scholarship.

Of the 1999-2000 graduates, 3 attended a Georgia public college or university. Of those, 100% met the school's minimum academic requirements.

Average SAT Scores
Maximum score is 800 on each portion

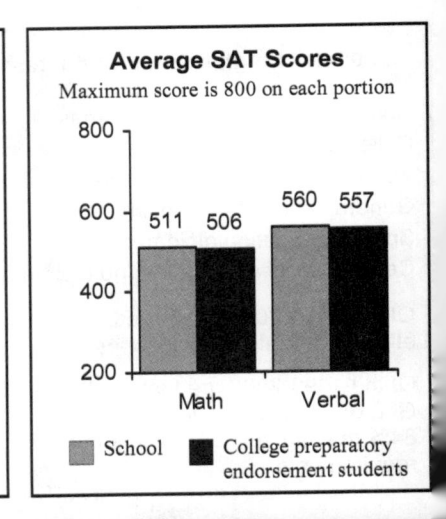

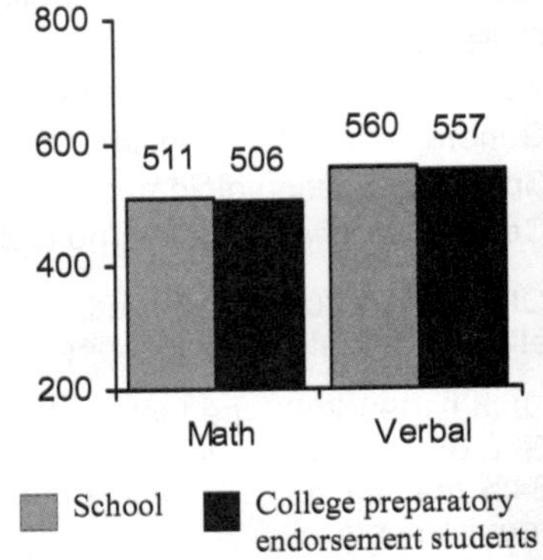
800
600
400
200
511
506
560
557
Math
Verbal
School
College preparatory endorsement students

Druid Hills Charter High School

1798 Haygood Dr NE, Atlanta, GA 30307
404-325-4755 · Grades 9 - 12

Enrollment:	1,257
White / black / other:	37.6% / 47.4% / 15.0%
Not native English-speaking:	29 / 2.3%
Limited English proficiency:	275 / 21.9%
Student absenteeism:	8.6%
Students per teacher:	20.8
Parent friendliness:	❶ ❷ ③ ④ ⑤ ❻
Students in gifted program:	188 / 15.0%
Students in remedial education:	1.0%
High school completion rate:	78.7%
Students held back a grade:	7.8%
Number of dropouts:	97 / 7.0%
Students in alternative programs:	1 / 0.1%
Students in special education:	83 / 6.6%
Eligible students, free or reduced lunch:	33.1%
Total suspensions and expulsions:	1,103
Suspensions only, pct. in-school:	1,091 / 63.3%
Drugs/alcohol-related offenses:	24
Violence-related offenses:	94
Firearms-related offenses:	23
Vandalism-related offenses:	8
Theft-related offenses:	9
All other disciplinary offenses:	980
Teachers with advanced degrees:	61.9%
Average years' teaching experience:	11.8

AJC GRADE: ★★★

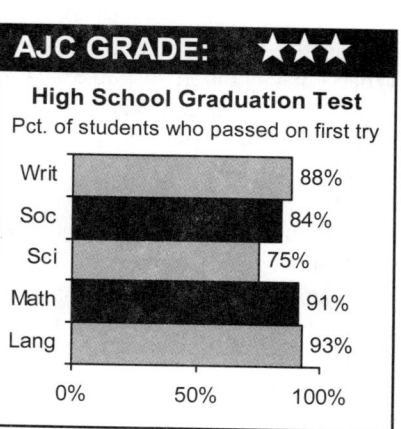

High School Graduation Test
Pct. of students who passed on first try

- Writ: 88%
- Soc: 84%
- Sci: 75%
- Math: 91%
- Lang: 93%

GHSA classification: 5-AAAA
Interscholastic sports offered:
BB, BS, CC, CL, FB, GO, SB, SO, SW, TE, TF, VB, WR

Advanced Placement (AP) Exams
Students tested:	137
Tests taken:	239
Pct. of test scores 3 or higher (1 - 5 scale):	57.7%

Languages other than English taught:
French, German, Japanese, Latin, Spanish

2000-2001 high school graduates: 203

College prep/vocational diplomas:	26.6%
College prep endorsement diplomas:	65.5%
Vocational endorsement diplomas:	3.0%
General high school diplomas:	0.0%
Special education diplomas:	1.5%
Certificates of attendance (no diploma):	3.4%

Of the 2000-2001 graduates, 70.9% were eligible for the HOPE scholarship.

Of the 1999-2000 graduates, 77 attended a Georgia public college or university. Of those, 81% met the school's minimum academic requirements.

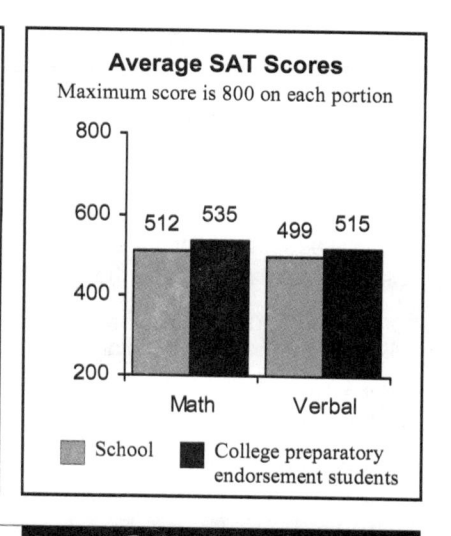

Average SAT Scores
Maximum score is 800 on each portion

- Math: School 512, College preparatory endorsement students 535
- Verbal: School 499, College preparatory endorsement students 515

DeKalb County High Schools

Dunwoody High School

5035 Vermack Rd, Atlanta, GA 30338
770-394-4442 · Grades 9 - 12

Enrollment:	1,276
White / black / other:	39.6% / 45.7% / 14.7%
Not native English-speaking:	42 / 3.3%
Limited English proficiency:	203 / 15.9%
Student absenteeism:	5.1%
Students per teacher:	17.5
Parent friendliness:	❶❷❸④⑤❻
Students in gifted program:	200 / 15.7%
Students in remedial education:	0.2%
High school completion rate:	85.8%
Students held back a grade:	8.2%
Number of dropouts:	33 / 2.3%
Students in alternative programs:	17 / 1.3%
Students in special education:	93 / 7.3%
Eligible students, free or reduced lunch:	18.7%

Total suspensions and expulsions:	1,601
Suspensions only, pct. in-school:	1,600 / 63.6%
Drugs/alcohol-related offenses:	11
Violence-related offenses:	64
Firearms-related offenses:	6
Vandalism-related offenses:	3
Theft-related offenses:	15
All other disciplinary offenses:	1,520

Teachers with advanced degrees:	64.5%
Average years' teaching experience:	12.8

AJC GRADE: ★★★

High School Graduation Test
Pct. of students who passed on first try

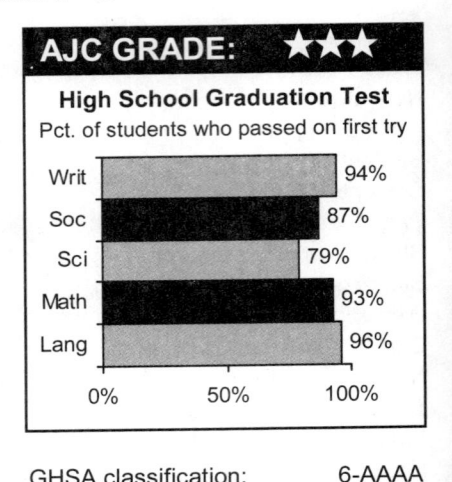

- Writ: 94%
- Soc: 87%
- Sci: 79%
- Math: 93%
- Lang: 96%

GHSA classification:	6-AAAA
Interscholastic sports offered:	
BB, BS, CC, CL, FB, GO, GY, SB, SO, SW, TE, TF, VB, WR	

Advanced Placement (AP) Exams

Students tested:	222
Tests taken:	368
Pct. of test scores 3 or higher (1 - 5 scale):	43.5%

Languages other than English taught:
French, German, Latin, Spanish

2000-2001 high school graduates: 273

College prep/vocational diplomas:	0.4%
College prep endorsement diplomas:	90.1%
Vocational endorsement diplomas:	2.9%
General high school diplomas:	0.0%
Special education diplomas:	3.3%
Certificates of attendance (no diploma):	3.3%

Of the 2000-2001 graduates, 73.6% were eligible for the HOPE scholarship.

Of the 1999-2000 graduates, 139 attended a Georgia public college or university. Of those, 88% met the school's minimum academic requirements.

Average SAT Scores
Maximum score is 800 on each portion

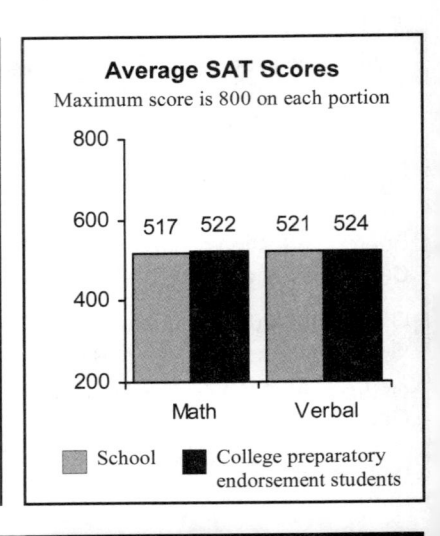

- Math: School 517, College preparatory endorsement students 522
- Verbal: School 521, College preparatory endorsement students 524

Lakeside High School

3801 Briarcliff Rd NE, Atlanta, GA 30345
404-633-2631 · Grades 9 - 12

Enrollment:	1,518
White / black / other:	47.0% / 33.6% / 19.4%
Not native English-speaking:	53 / 3.5%
Limited English proficiency:	296 / 19.5%
Student absenteeism:	5.9%
Students per teacher:	20.1
Parent friendliness:	① ❷ ❸ ④ ⑤ ❻
Students in gifted program:	219 / 14.4%
Students in remedial education:	2.0%
High school completion rate:	82.3%
Students held back a grade:	6.7%
Number of dropouts:	76 / 4.5%
Students in alternative programs:	1 / 0.1%
Students in special education:	90 / 5.9%
Eligible students, free or reduced lunch:	17.1%
Total suspensions and expulsions:	713
Suspensions only, pct. in-school:	709 / 74.8%
Drugs/alcohol-related offenses:	3
Violence-related offenses:	85
Firearms-related offenses:	9
Vandalism-related offenses:	6
Theft-related offenses:	12
All other disciplinary offenses:	608
Teachers with advanced degrees:	62.5%
Average years' teaching experience:	15.2

AJC GRADE: ★★★★

High School Graduation Test
Pct. of students who passed on first try

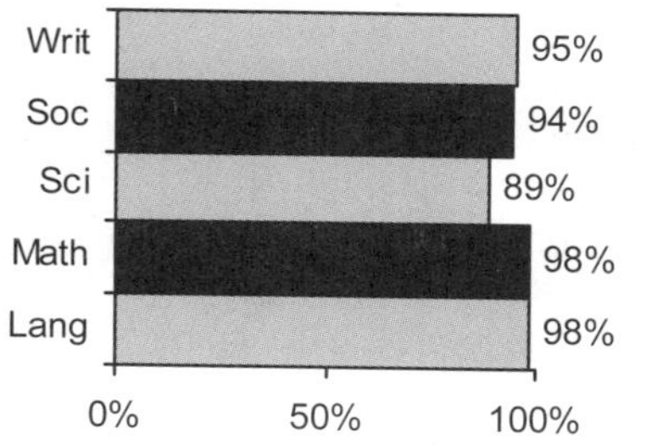

- Writ: 95%
- Soc: 94%
- Sci: 89%
- Math: 98%
- Lang: 98%

GHSA classification: 7-AAAAA
Interscholastic sports offered:
BB, BS, CC, CL, FB, GO, GY, SB, SO, SW, TE, TF, WR

Advanced Placement (AP) Exams
Students tested:	244
Tests taken:	538
Pct. of test scores 3 or higher (1 - 5 scale):	50.7%

Languages other than English taught:
French, German, Japanese, Latin, Spanish

2000-2001 high school graduates: 279

College prep/vocational diplomas:	0.7%
College prep endorsement diplomas:	92.8%
Vocational endorsement diplomas:	3.2%
General high school diplomas:	0.0%
Special education diplomas:	2.5%
Certificates of attendance (no diploma):	0.7%

Of the 2000-2001 graduates, 81.0% were eligible for the HOPE scholarship.

Of the 1999-2000 graduates, 169 attended a Georgia public college or university. Of those, 88% met the school's minimum academic requirements.

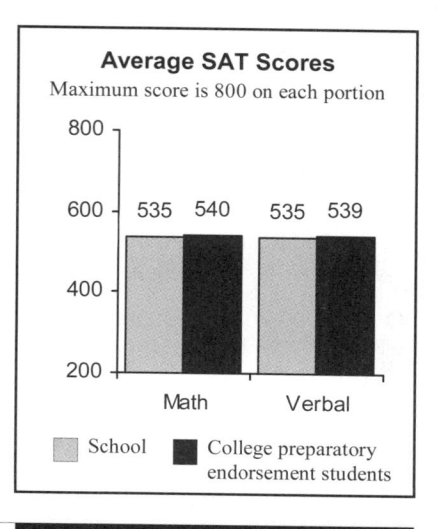

Average SAT Scores
Maximum score is 800 on each portion

- Math: School 535, College preparatory endorsement students 540
- Verbal: School 535, College preparatory endorsement students 539

DeKalb County High Schools

Lithonia High School

2451 Randall Ave, Lithonia, GA 30058
678-676-2902 · Grades 9 - 12

Enrollment:	1,948
White / black / other:	1.0% / 97.1% / 1.9%
Not native English-speaking:	2 / 0.1%
Limited English proficiency:	54 / 2.8%
Student absenteeism:	9.3%
Students per teacher:	23.3
Parent friendliness:	① ❷ ❸ ④ ❺ ❻
Students in gifted program:	63 / 3.2%
Students in remedial education:	1.6%
High school completion rate:	75.3%
Students held back a grade:	10.8%
Number of dropouts:	125 / 5.6%
Students in alternative programs:	13 / 0.7%
Students in special education:	121 / 6.2%
Eligible students, free or reduced lunch:	35.0%
Total suspensions and expulsions:	2,608
Suspensions only, pct. in-school:	2,588 / 49.3%
Drugs/alcohol-related offenses:	30
Violence-related offenses:	265
Firearms-related offenses:	7
Vandalism-related offenses:	16
Theft-related offenses:	18
All other disciplinary offenses:	2,324
Teachers with advanced degrees:	62.1%
Average years' teaching experience:	10.0

AJC GRADE: ★★

High School Graduation Test
Pct. of students who passed on first try

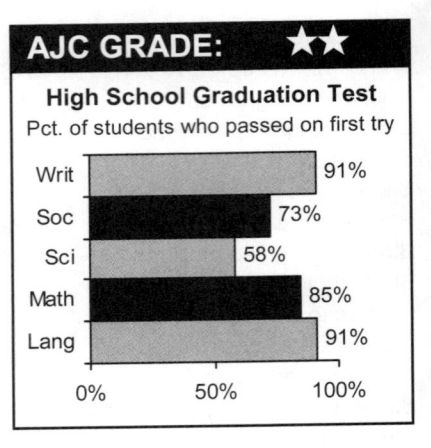

- Writ: 91%
- Soc: 73%
- Sci: 58%
- Math: 85%
- Lang: 91%

GHSA classification: 7-AAAAA
Interscholastic sports offered:
BB, BS, CC, CL, FB, GO, GY, SB, SO, SW, TE, TF, VB, WR

Advanced Placement (AP) Exams
- Students tested: 78
- Tests taken: 119
- Pct. of test scores 3 or higher (1 - 5 scale): 6.7%

Languages other than English taught:
Chinese, French, German, Latin, Spanish

2000-2001 high school graduates: 259

College prep/vocational diplomas:	1.2%
College prep endorsement diplomas:	77.6%
Vocational endorsement diplomas:	13.1%
General high school diplomas:	0.4%
Special education diplomas:	3.9%
Certificates of attendance (no diploma):	3.9%

Of the 2000-2001 graduates, 65.6% were eligible for the HOPE scholarship.

Of the 1999-2000 graduates, 94 attended a Georgia public college or university. Of those, 52% met the school's minimum academic requirements.

Average SAT Scores
Maximum score is 800 on each portion

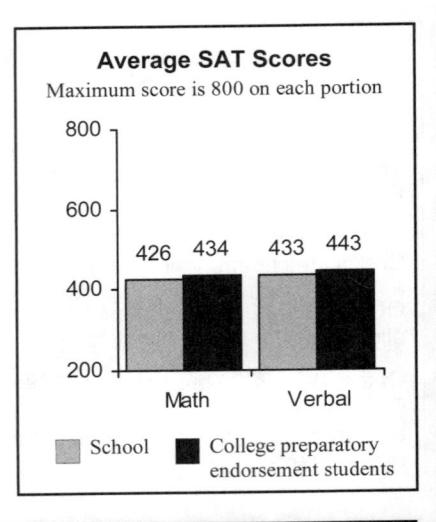

- Math: School 426, College preparatory endorsement students 434
- Verbal: School 433, College preparatory endorsement students 443

DeKalb County High Schools

Redan High School

5247 Redan Rd, Stone Mountain, GA 30088
678-676-3602 · Grades 9 - 12

Enrollment:	1,896
White / black / other:	0.6% / 95.9% / 3.5%
Non native English-speaking:	5 / 0.3%
Limited English proficiency:	69 / 3.6%
Student absenteeism:	8.7%
Students per teacher:	21.1
Parent friendliness:	①❷❸④⑤❻
Students in gifted program:	66 / 3.5%
Students in remedial education:	3.5%
High school completion rate:	77.1%
Students held back a grade:	11.8%
Number of dropouts:	103 / 4.8%
Students in alternative programs:	18 / 0.9%
Students in special education:	120 / 6.3%
Eligible students, free or reduced lunch:	28.2%

Total suspensions and expulsions:	1,302
Suspensions only, pct. in-school:	1,285 / 66.1%
Drugs/alcohol-related offenses:	21
Violence-related offenses:	124
Firearms-related offenses:	22
Vandalism-related offenses:	3
Theft-related offenses:	8
All other disciplinary offenses:	1,142

Teachers with advanced degrees:	56.4%
Average years' teaching experience:	10.9

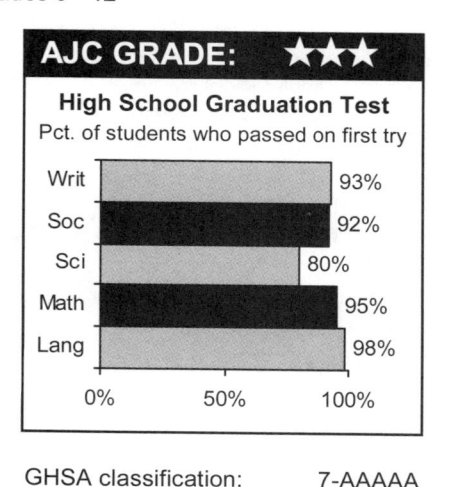

AJC GRADE: ★★★

High School Graduation Test
Pct. of students who passed on first try

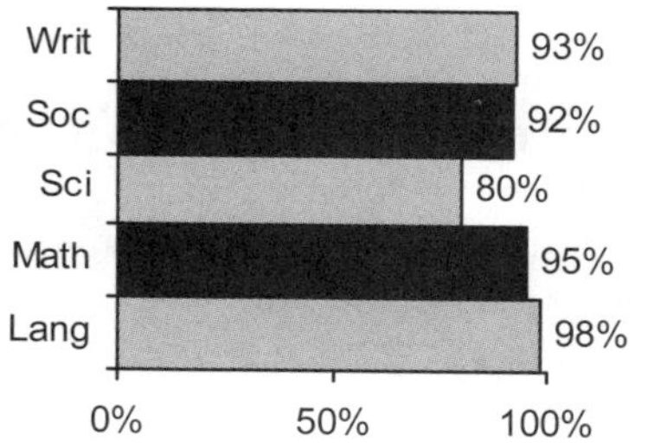
Writ
93%
Soc
92%
Sci
80%
Math
95%
Lang
98%
0%
50%
100%

GHSA classification:	7-AAAAA

Interscholastic sports offered:
BB, BS, CC, CL, FB, GY, SB, SO, SW, TE, TF, WR

Advanced Placement (AP) Exams

Students tested:	101
Tests taken:	164
Pct. of test scores 3 or higher (1 - 5 scale):	12.2%

Languages other than English taught:
French, German, Spanish

2000-2001 high school graduates: 343

College prep/vocational diplomas:	4.1%
College prep endorsement diplomas:	77.6%
Vocational endorsement diplomas:	11.7%
General high school diplomas:	0.3%
Special education diplomas:	1.2%
Certificates of attendance (no diploma):	5.2%

Of the 2000-2001 graduates, 56.6% were eligible for the HOPE scholarship.

Of the 1999-2000 graduates, 106 attended a Georgia public college or university. Of those, 67% met the school's minimum academic requirements.

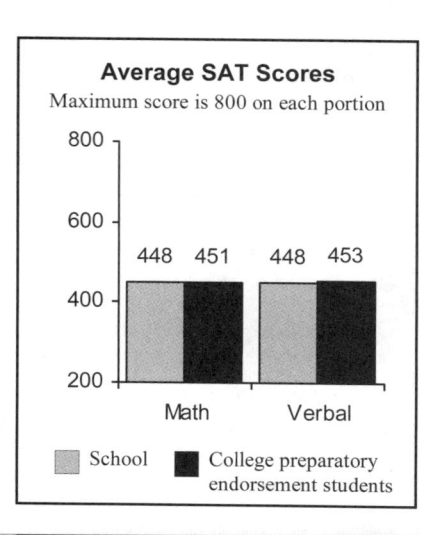

Average SAT Scores
Maximum score is 800 on each portion

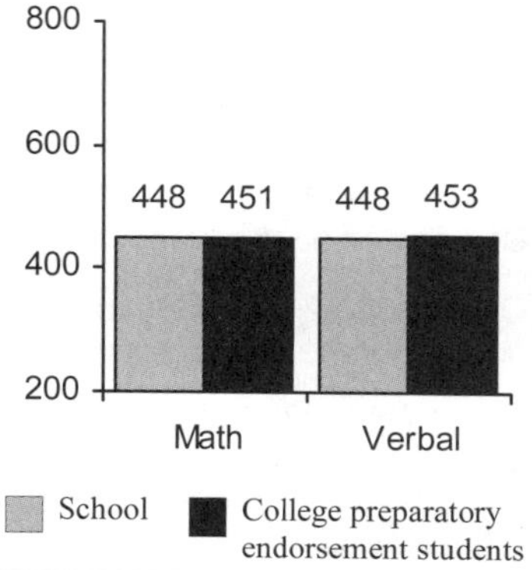
800
600
400
200
448
451
448
453
Math
Verbal
School
College preparatory endorsement students

Ronald McNair Senior High School

1804 Bouldercrest Rd SE, Atlanta, GA 30316
404-241-5000 · Grades 9 - 12

Enrollment:	1,489
White / black / other:	0.1% / 99.1% / 0.7%
Not native English-speaking:	*
Limited English proficiency:	24 / 1.6%
Student absenteeism:	12.2%
Students per teacher:	21.0
Parent friendliness:	❶❷❸④⑤❻
Students in gifted program:	13 / 0.9%
Students in remedial education:	2.7%
High school completion rate:	63.6%
Students held back a grade:	23.2%
Number of dropouts:	141 / 8.5%
Students in alternative programs:	12 / 0.8%
Students in special education:	111 / 7.5%
Eligible students, free or reduced lunch:	66.6%

Total suspensions and expulsions:	1,595
Suspensions only, pct. in-school:	1,576 / 32.1%
Drugs/alcohol-related offenses:	10
Violence-related offenses:	208
Firearms-related offenses:	17
Vandalism-related offenses:	8
Theft-related offenses:	4
All other disciplinary offenses:	1,380
Teachers with advanced degrees:	49.3%
Average years' teaching experience:	10.8

AJC GRADE: ★★★

High School Graduation Test
Pct. of students who passed on first try

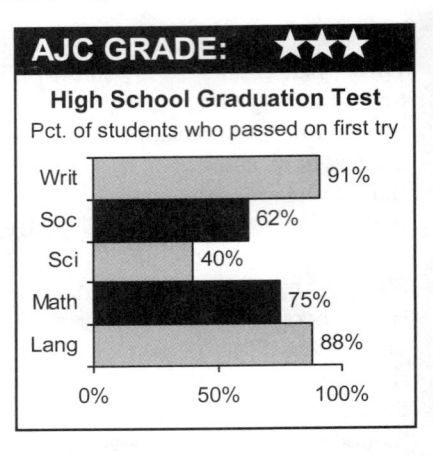

- Writ: 91%
- Soc: 62%
- Sci: 40%
- Math: 75%
- Lang: 88%

GHSA classification: 5-AAAA
Interscholastic sports offered:
  BB, BS, FB, GO, SO, SW, TE, TF, WR

Advanced Placement (AP) Exams
  Students tested: 51
  Tests taken: 80
  Pct. of test scores 3 or higher (1 - 5 scale): 1.3%

Languages other than English taught:
  French, German, Latin, Spanish

2000-2001 high school graduates: 168

College prep/vocational diplomas:	12.5%
College prep endorsement diplomas:	61.9%
Vocational endorsement diplomas:	8.3%
General high school diplomas:	0.0%
Special education diplomas:	11.3%
Certificates of attendance (no diploma):	6.0%

Of the 2000-2001 graduates, 54.2% were eligible for the HOPE scholarship.

Of the 1999-2000 graduates, 51 attended a Georgia public college or university. Of those, 70% met the school's minimum academic requirements.

Average SAT Scores
Maximum score is 800 on each portion

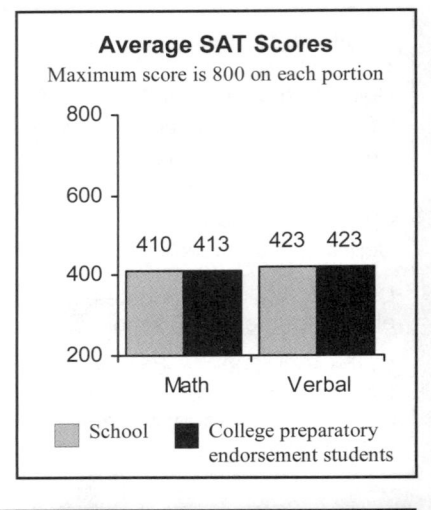

- Math: School 410, College preparatory endorsement students 413
- Verbal: School 423, College preparatory endorsement students 423

DeKalb County High Schools

Southwest DeKalb High School

2863 Kelley Chapel Rd, Decatur, GA 30034
404-288-2461 · Grades 9 - 12

Enrollment:	1,819
White / black / other:	0.9% / 97.6% / 1.5%
Not native English-speaking:	2 / 0.1%
Limited English proficiency:	46 / 2.5%
Student absenteeism:	8.0%
Students per teacher:	19.5
Parent friendliness:	❶❷❸④⑤❻
Students in gifted program:	104 / 5.7%
Students in remedial education:	3.4%
High school completion rate:	77.7%
Students held back a grade:	8.3%
Number of dropouts:	117 / 5.8%
Students in alternative programs:	15 / 0.8%
Students in special education:	123 / 6.8%
Eligible students, free or reduced lunch:	27.0%
Total suspensions and expulsions:	1,546
Suspensions only, pct. in-school:	1,534 / 62.9%
Drugs/alcohol-related offenses:	8
Violence-related offenses:	90
Firearms-related offenses:	10
Vandalism-related offenses:	8
Theft-related offenses:	19
All other disciplinary offenses:	1,438
Teachers with advanced degrees:	53.7%
Average years' teaching experience:	12.2

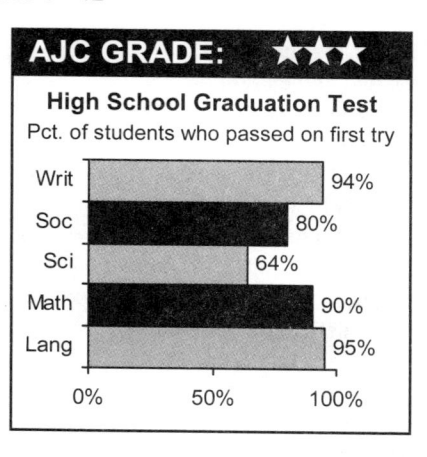

AJC GRADE: ★★★

High School Graduation Test
Pct. of students who passed on first try

- Writ: 94%
- Soc: 80%
- Sci: 64%
- Math: 90%
- Lang: 95%

GHSA classification: 7-AAAAA
Interscholastic sports offered:
BB, BS, CC, CL, FB, GO, GY, SB, SO, SW, TF, VB

Advanced Placement (AP) Exams
- Students tested: 159
- Tests taken: 281
- Pct. of test scores 3 or higher (1 - 5 scale): 29.5%

Languages other than English taught:
French, German, Latin, Spanish

2000-2001 high school graduates: 285

College prep/vocational diplomas:	0.7%
College prep endorsement diplomas:	82.8%
Vocational endorsement diplomas:	5.6%
General high school diplomas:	0.0%
Special education diplomas:	0.0%
Certificates of attendance (no diploma):	10.9%

Of the 2000-2001 graduates, 66.7% were eligible for the HOPE scholarship.

Of the 1999-2000 graduates, 111 attended a Georgia public college or university. Of those, 64% met the school's minimum academic requirements.

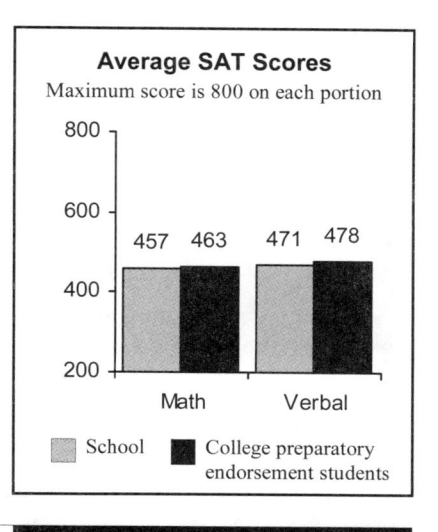

Average SAT Scores
Maximum score is 800 on each portion

- Math — School: 457, College preparatory endorsement students: 463
- Verbal — School: 471, College preparatory endorsement students: 478

DeKalb County High Schools

Stephenson High School

701 Stephenson Rd, Stone Mountain, GA 30087
678-676-4202 · Grades 9 - 12

Enrollment:	1,938
White / black / other:	1.1% / 95.8% / 3.0%
Not native English-speaking:	3 / 0.2%
Limited English proficiency:	53 / 2.7%
Student absenteeism:	7.5%
Students per teacher:	21.1
Parent friendliness:	❶❷❸④❺❻
Students in gifted program:	42 / 2.2%
Students in remedial education:	2.1%
High school completion rate:	89.4%
Students held back a grade:	13.0%
Number of dropouts:	81 / 3.8%
Students in alternative programs:	4 / 0.2%
Students in special education:	121 / 6.2%
Eligible students, free or reduced lunch:	26.9%

Total suspensions and expulsions:	1,861
Suspensions only, pct. in-school:	1,836 / 62.5%
Drugs/alcohol-related offenses:	19
Violence-related offenses:	220
Firearms-related offenses:	9
Vandalism-related offenses:	27
Theft-related offenses:	19
All other disciplinary offenses:	1,593

Teachers with advanced degrees:	47.9%
Average years' teaching experience:	10.0

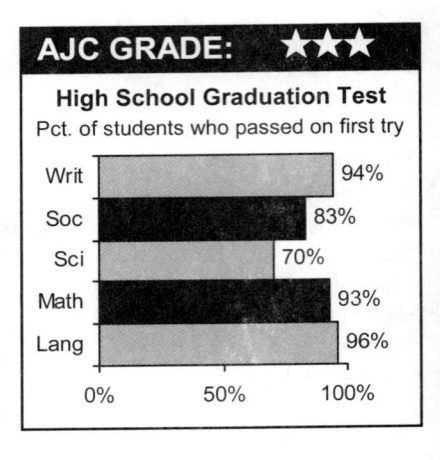

AJC GRADE: ★★★

High School Graduation Test
Pct. of students who passed on first try

- Writ: 94%
- Soc: 83%
- Sci: 70%
- Math: 93%
- Lang: 96%

GHSA classification:	7-AAAAA

Interscholastic sports offered:
BB, BS, CC, FB, GO, GY, SB, SO, TE, WR

Advanced Placement (AP) Exams	
Students tested:	125
Tests taken:	186
Pct. of test scores 3 or higher (1 - 5 scale):	40.3%

Languages other than English taught:
French, German, Latin, Spanish

2000-2001 high school graduates:	337
College prep/vocational diplomas:	12.8%
College prep endorsement diplomas:	72.4%
Vocational endorsement diplomas:	8.3%
General high school diplomas:	0.0%
Special education diplomas:	3.3%
Certificates of attendance (no diploma):	3.3%

Of the 2000-2001 graduates, 60.8% were eligible for the HOPE scholarship.

Of the 1999-2000 graduates, 137 attended a Georgia public college or university. Of those, 66% met the school's minimum academic requirements.

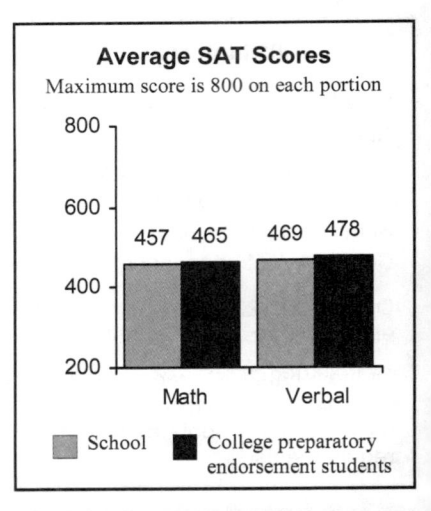

Average SAT Scores
Maximum score is 800 on each portion

	Math	Verbal
School	457	469
College preparatory endorsement students	465	478

DeKalb County High Schools

Stone Mountain High School

4555 Central Dr, Stone Mountain, GA 30083
678-676-6302 · Grades 9 - 12

Enrollment:	1,257
White / black / other:	4.9% / 84.8% / 10.3%
Not native English-speaking:	42 / 3.3%
Limited English proficiency:	203 / 16.1%
Student absenteeism:	7.0%
Students per teacher:	18.3
Parent friendliness:	❶❷❸④❺❻
Students in gifted program:	37 / 2.9%
Students in remedial education:	5.3%
High school completion rate:	55.3%
Students held back a grade:	12.0%
Number of dropouts:	117 / 7.8%
Students in alternative programs:	11 / 0.9%
Students in special education:	110 / 8.8%
Eligible students, free or reduced lunch:	57.6%
Total suspensions and expulsions:	751
Suspensions only, pct. in-school:	741 / 61.7%
Drugs/alcohol-related offenses:	7
Violence-related offenses:	111
Firearms-related offenses:	16
Vandalism-related offenses:	5
Theft-related offenses:	6
All other disciplinary offenses:	634
Teachers with advanced degrees:	59.2%
Average years' teaching experience:	11.9

AJC GRADE: ★★★

High School Graduation Test
Pct. of students who passed on first try

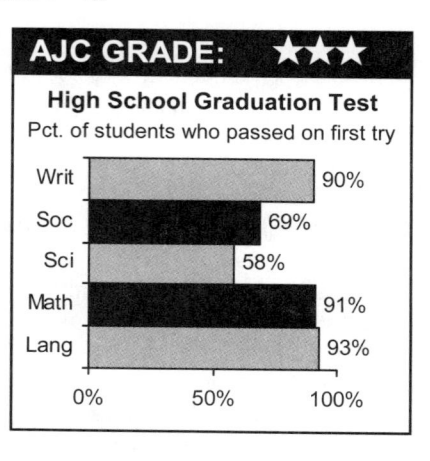

Writ	90%
Soc	69%
Sci	58%
Math	91%
Lang	93%

GHSA classification: 5-AAAA
Interscholastic sports offered:
BB, BS, CC, CL, FB, GO, SB, SO, SW, TE, TF, VB, WR

Advanced Placement (AP) Exams
Students tested:	69
Tests taken:	121
Pct. of test scores 3 or higher (1 - 5 scale):	11.6%

Languages other than English taught:
French, German, Latin, Spanish

2000-2001 high school graduates: 162

College prep/vocational diplomas:	0.0%
College prep endorsement diplomas:	81.5%
Vocational endorsement diplomas:	6.2%
General high school diplomas:	0.6%
Special education diplomas:	8.6%
Certificates of attendance (no diploma):	3.1%

Of the 2000-2001 graduates, 60.5% were eligible for the HOPE scholarship.

Of the 1999-2000 graduates, 72 attended a Georgia public college or university. Of those, 70% met the school's minimum academic requirements.

Average SAT Scores
Maximum score is 800 on each portion

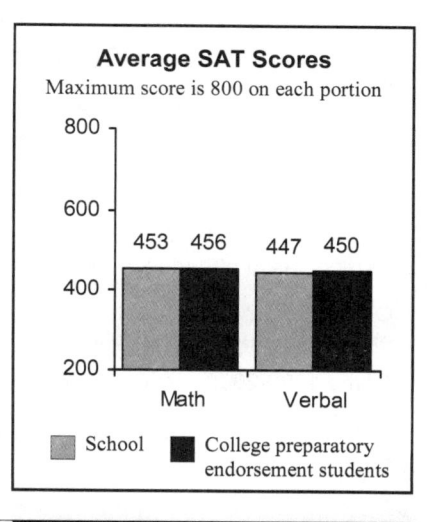

	Math	Verbal
School	453	447
College preparatory endorsement students	456	450

The Atlanta Journal-Constitution / Page 269

DeKalb County High Schools

Towers High School

3919 Brookcrest Cir, Decatur, GA 30032
404-289-7166 · Grades 9 - 12

Enrollment:	1,426
White / black / other:	0.8% / 95.7% / 3.4%
Not native English-speaking:	11 / 0.8%
Limited English proficiency:	86 / 6.0%
Student absenteeism:	10.9%
Students per teacher:	17.2
Parent friendliness:	① ❷ ❸ ④ ⑤ ❻
Students in gifted program:	50 / 3.5%
Students in remedial education:	5.9%
High school completion rate:	69.8%
Students held back a grade:	17.7%
Number of dropouts:	77 / 4.9%
Students in alternative programs:	*
Students in special education:	127 / 8.9%
Eligible students, free or reduced lunch:	48.4%

Total suspensions and expulsions:	2,020
Suspensions only, pct. in-school:	2,007 / 32.5%
Drugs/alcohol-related offenses:	10
Violence-related offenses:	351
Firearms-related offenses:	20
Vandalism-related offenses:	26
Theft-related offenses:	17
All other disciplinary offenses:	1,632

Teachers with advanced degrees:	48.3%
Average years' teaching experience:	13.0

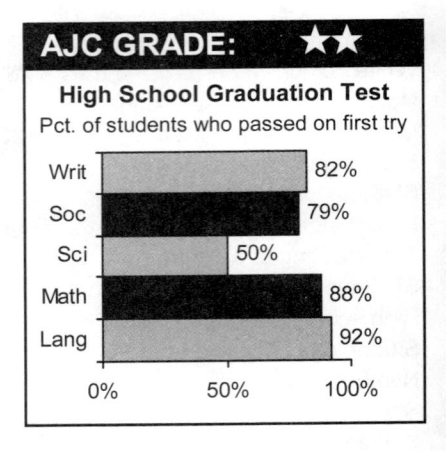

AJC GRADE: ★★

High School Graduation Test
Pct. of students who passed on first try

- Writ: 82%
- Soc: 79%
- Sci: 50%
- Math: 88%
- Lang: 92%

GHSA classification:	5-AAA

Interscholastic sports offered:
BB, BS, CC, CL, FB, GY, SB, SO, SW, TF, VB, WR

Advanced Placement (AP) Exams
Students tested:	82
Tests taken:	126
Pct. of test scores 3 or higher (1 - 5 scale):	4.0%

Languages other than English taught:
Chinese, French, German, Japanese, Latin, Spanish

2000-2001 high school graduates: 132

College prep/vocational diplomas:	1.5%
College prep endorsement diplomas:	78.0%
Vocational endorsement diplomas:	8.3%
General high school diplomas:	0.0%
Special education diplomas:	4.5%
Certificates of attendance (no diploma):	7.6%

Of the 2000-2001 graduates, 56.1% were eligible for the HOPE scholarship.

Of the 1999-2000 graduates, 42 attended a Georgia public college or university. Of those, 50% met the school's minimum academic requirements.

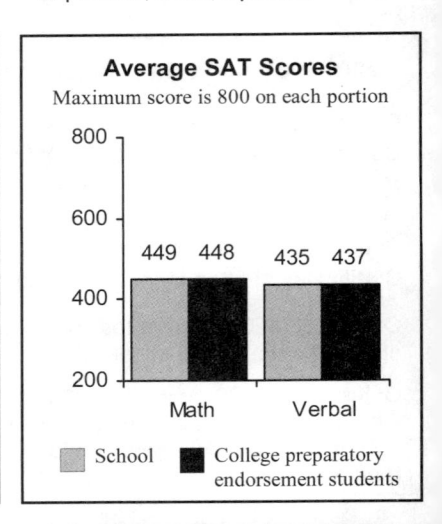

Average SAT Scores
Maximum score is 800 on each portion

- Math — School: 449, College preparatory endorsement students: 448
- Verbal — School: 435, College preparatory endorsement students: 437

DeKalb County High Schools

Tucker High School

5036 LaVista Rd, Tucker, GA 30084
770-938-4471 · Grades 9 - 12

Enrollment:	1,332
White / black / other:	32.3% / 51.8% / 15.9%
Not native English-speaking:	70 / 5.3%
Limited English proficiency:	280 / 21.0%
Student absenteeism:	6.5%
Students per teacher:	19.6
Parent friendliness:	① ❷ ❸ ④ ⑤ ❻
Students in gifted program:	103 / 7.7%
Students in remedial education:	1.3%
High school completion rate:	83.3%
Students held back a grade:	6.2%
Number of dropouts:	34 / 2.3%
Students in alternative programs:	*
Students in special education:	140 / 10.5%
Eligible students, free or reduced lunch:	28.2%
Total suspensions and expulsions:	821
Suspensions only, pct. in-school:	816 / 68.3%
Drugs/alcohol-related offenses:	18
Violence-related offenses:	119
Firearms-related offenses:	7
Vandalism-related offenses:	5
Theft-related offenses:	7
All other disciplinary offenses:	715
Teachers with advanced degrees:	62.0%
Average years' teaching experience:	14.8

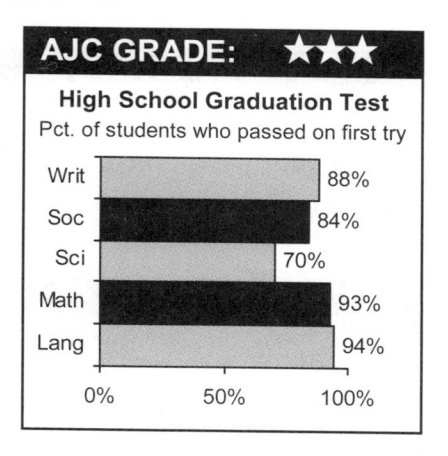

AJC GRADE: ★★★

High School Graduation Test
Pct. of students who passed on first try

- Writ: 88%
- Soc: 84%
- Sci: 70%
- Math: 93%
- Lang: 94%

GHSA classification: 5-AAAA
Interscholastic sports offered:
BB, BS, CC, CL, FB, GO, GY, SB, SO, SW, TE, TF, VB, WR

Advanced Placement (AP) Exams
- Students tested: 136
- Tests taken: 247
- Pct. of test scores 3 or higher (1 - 5 scale): 40.5%

Languages other than English taught:
French, German, Japanese, Latin, Spanish

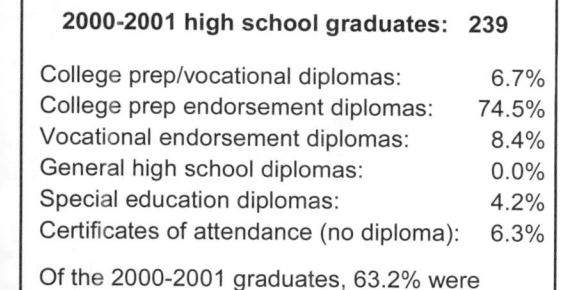

2000-2001 high school graduates: 239

College prep/vocational diplomas:	6.7%
College prep endorsement diplomas:	74.5%
Vocational endorsement diplomas:	8.4%
General high school diplomas:	0.0%
Special education diplomas:	4.2%
Certificates of attendance (no diploma):	6.3%

Of the 2000-2001 graduates, 63.2% were eligible for the HOPE scholarship.

Of the 1999-2000 graduates, 117 attended a Georgia public college or university. Of those, 79% met the school's minimum academic requirements.

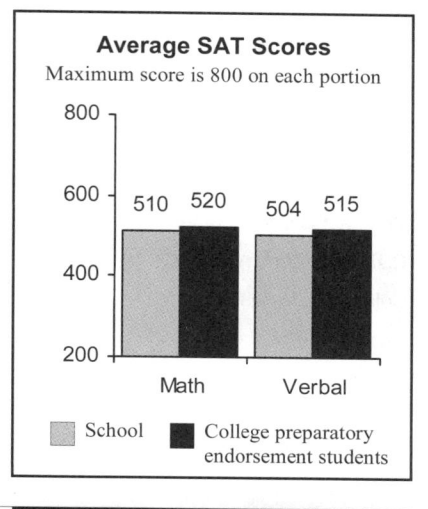

Average SAT Scores
Maximum score is 800 on each portion

- Math: School 510, College preparatory endorsement students 520
- Verbal: School 504, College preparatory endorsement students 515

DeKalb County High Schools

AJC ranking of DeKalb County Schools

ELEMENTARY SCHOOLS

AJC Star Grade: ★★★★★

Browns Mill Elementary
Kittredge Magnet for High Achievers
Oak Grove Elementary
Vanderlyn Elementary

AJC Star Grade: ★★★★

Atherton Elementary
Austin Elementary
Avondale Elementary
Glen Haven Elementary
Huntley Hills Elementary
Idlewood Elementary
Livsey Elementary
Medlock Elementary
Montclair Elementary
Nancy Creek Elementary

AJC Star Grade: ★★★

Allgood Elementary
Ashford Park Elementary
Bob Mathis Elementary
Bouie Elementary
Briar Vista Elementary
Brockett Elementary
Canby Lane Elementary
Chestnut Charter Elementary
Clifton Elementary
Columbia Elementary
Dunaire Elementary
Eldridge Miller Elementary
Evansdale Elementary
Fernbank Elementary
Flat Shoals Elementary
Forrest Hills Elementary
Gresham Park Elementary
Hambrick Elementary
Hawthorne Elementary
Henderson Mill Elementary
Hightower Elementary
Hooper Alexander Elementary
Jolly Elementary
Kelley Lake Elementary
Kingsley Charter Elementary
Knollwood Elementary
Laurel Ridge Elementary
Marbut Elementary
Meadowview Elementary
Midvale Elementary
Montgomery Elementary
Narvie Harris Elementary
Oakcliff Traditional Theme
Panola Way Elementary
Peachcrest Elementary
Pleasantdale Elementary
Rainbow Charter Elementary
Redan Elementary
Robert Shaw Elementary
Rockbridge Elementary
Rowland Elementary
Sagamore Hills Elementary
Shadow Rock Elementary
Sky Haven Elementary
Smoke Rise Elementary
Snapfinger Elementary
Steele Elementary
Stone Mill Elementary
Stone Mountain Elementary
Stoneview Elementary
Terry Mill Elementary

DeKalb County Public Schools

AJC ranking of DeKalb County Schools

Tilson Elementary
Toney Elementary
Wadsworth Elementary
Woodridge Elementary
Woodward Elementary

AJC Star Grade: ★★

Briarlake Elementary
Cary Reynolds Elementary
Cedar Grove Elementary
Chapel Hill Elementary
Dresden Elementary
Fairington Elementary
McLendon Elementary
Murphey Candler Elementary
Pine Ridge Elementary
Rock Chapel Elementary

AJC Star Grade: ★

Indian Creek Elementary

MIDDLE SCHOOLS

AJC Star Grade: ★★★★

Chamblee Middle

AJC Star Grade: ★★★

Avondale Middle
Chapel Hill Middle
Freedom Middle
Henderson Middle
Miller Grove Middle
Peachtree Charter Middle
Ronald McNair Middle
Salem Middle
Sequoyah Middle
Shamrock Middle
Stephenson Middle
Stone Mountain Middle

AJC Star Grade: ★★

Cedar Grove Middle

AJC Star Grade: ★

Stone Mountain Charter

HIGH SCHOOLS

AJC Star Grade: ★★★★

Chamblee Charter High
DeKalb of the Arts
Lakeside High

AJC Star Grade: ★★★

Avondale High
Cedar Grove High
Clarkston High
Cross Keys High
Druid Hills Charter High
Dunwoody High
Redan High
Ronald McNair Senior High
Southwest DeKalb High
Stephenson High
Stone Mountain High
Tucker High

AJC Star Grade: ★★

Columbia High
Lithonia High
Towers High

DeKalb County Public Schools

Douglas County Public Schools

9030 Ga. Hwy 5, Douglasville, GA 30134
Phone: 770-920-4000 · Fax: 770-920-4027
http://www.douglas.k12.ga.us

The following pages provide detailed information on every school in the Douglas County school district. An asterisk (*) means the value of the data was zero or was not reported by the school district. A complete list of schools ranked by The Atlanta Journal-Constitution's star rating system follows the detailed school reports.

District enrollment:	17,145
White / black / other:	69.9% / 24.1% / 6.1%
Not native English-speaking:	156 / 0.9%
Expenditure per student (general fund):	$5,853
Students per teacher:	15.4
Teachers with advanced degrees:	50.2%
Average years, teaching experience:	12.3
Average teacher salary:	$42,547.65
Students in gifted program:	1,900 / 11.1%
Students held back a grade:	422 / 2.5%
Eligible students, free or reduced lunch:	5,161 / 29.5%
Number of dropouts (grades 9-12):	266 / 4.8%
High school completion rate:	74.9%
Graduates, pct. eligible for HOPE scholarships:	909 / 55.8%
Average combined SAT score (maximum 1,600):	979
Pct. of 11th-graders passing the Georgia High School Graduation Tests on first try:	66%
Percent of children 5 to 17 years of age living in poverty (2000 Census estimate):	9.8%

Arbor Station Elementary School

9999 Parkway S, Douglasville, GA 30135
770-920-4305 · Grades K - 5

Enrollment:	508
White / black / other:	72.2% / 19.5% / 8.3%
Not native English-speaking:	5 / 1.0%
Limited English proficiency:	8 / 1.6%
Student absenteeism:	4.5%
Students per teacher:	14.2
Parent friendliness:	❶❷❸④⑤❻
Teachers with advanced degrees:	62.2%
Average years' teaching experience:	13.1
Students in gifted program:	42 / 8.3%
Students in remedial education:	14.5%
Students held back a grade:	1.8%
Total suspensions, pct. in-school:	5 / 0.0%
Offenses:	violence: 18, drugs: *, other: 4
Eligible students, free or reduced lunch:	20.4%
Before / after school program:	No / No

Students at this school generally go on to:
Chapel Hill, Yeager Middle

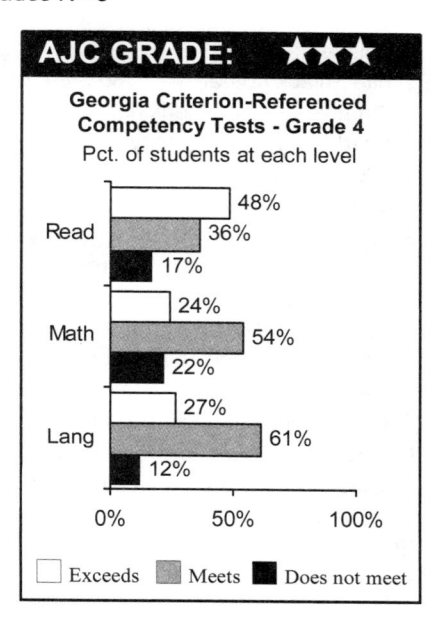

AJC GRADE: ★★★

Georgia Criterion-Referenced Competency Tests - Grade 4
Pct. of students at each level

Read: 48% / 36% / 17%
Math: 24% / 54% / 22%
Lang: 27% / 61% / 12%

☐ Exceeds ▨ Meets ■ Does not meet

Beulah Elementary School

1150 S Burnt Hickory Rd, Douglasville, GA 30134
770-920-4320 · Grades K - 5

Enrollment:	420
White / black / other:	81.7% / 10.7% / 7.6%
Not native English-speaking:	7 / 1.7%
Limited English proficiency:	15 / 3.6%
Student absenteeism:	4.4%
Students per teacher:	14.0
Parent friendliness:	①❷❸❹❺❻
Teachers with advanced degrees:	43.8%
Average years' teaching experience:	13.7
Students in gifted program:	35 / 8.3%
Students in remedial education:	23.6%
Students held back a grade:	2.1%
Total suspensions, pct. in-school:	3 / 0.0%
Offenses:	violence: *, drugs: *, other: 9
Eligible students, free or reduced lunch:	33.5%
Before / after school program:	Yes / Yes

Students at this school generally go on to:
Turner Middle

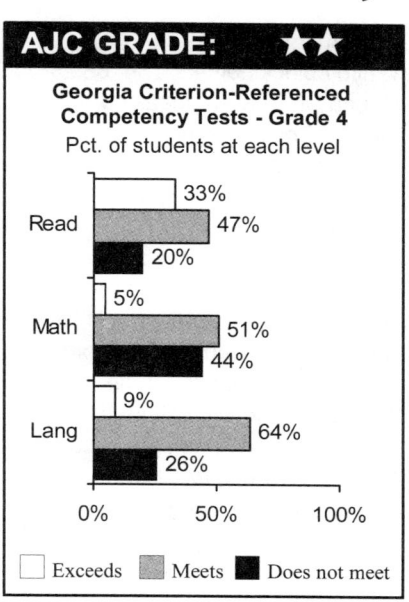

AJC GRADE: ★★

Georgia Criterion-Referenced Competency Tests - Grade 4
Pct. of students at each level

Read: 33% / 47% / 20%
Math: 5% / 51% / 44%
Lang: 9% / 64% / 26%

☐ Exceeds ▨ Meets ■ Does not meet

The Atlanta Journal-Constitution / Page 275

Douglas County Elementary Schools

Bill Arp Elementary School

4841 Highway 5, Douglasville, GA 30135
770-920-4335 · Grades K - 5

Enrollment:	456
White / black / other:	80.3% / 13.2% / 6.6%
Not native English-speaking:	*
Limited English proficiency:	1 / 0.2%
Student absenteeism:	3.8%
Students per teacher:	15.1
Parent friendliness:	❶❷❸❹❺❻
Teachers with advanced degrees:	43.8%
Average years' teaching experience:	12.8
Students in gifted program:	83 / 18.2%
Students in remedial education:	14.0%
Students held back a grade:	1.8%
Total suspensions, pct. in-school:	23 / 0.0%
Offenses:	violence: * , drugs: * , other: 27
Eligible students, free or reduced lunch:	34.6%
Before / after school program:	No / No

Students at this school generally go on to:
Fairplay Middle

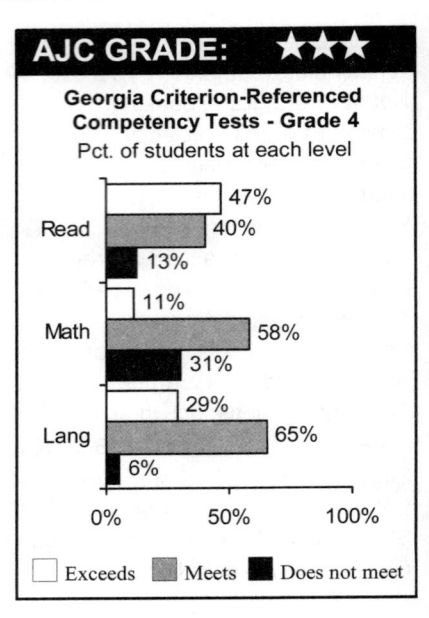

AJC GRADE: ★★★

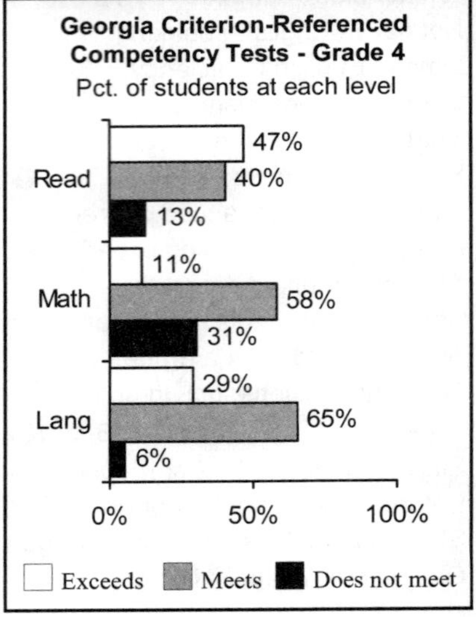
Georgia Criterion-Referenced Competency Tests - Grade 4
Pct. of students at each level
Read
47%
40%
13%
Math
11%
58%
31%
Lang
29%
65%
6%
0%
50%
100%
Exceeds
Meets
Does not meet

Bright Star Elementary School

6300 John West Rd, Douglasville, GA 30134
770-920-4120 · Grades K - 5

Enrollment:	478
White / black / other:	68.2% / 23.6% / 8.2%
Not native English-speaking:	8 / 1.7%
Limited English proficiency:	10 / 2.1%
Student absenteeism:	4.6%
Students per teacher:	14.3
Parent friendliness:	①❷❸❹❺❻
Teachers with advanced degrees:	40.0%
Average years' teaching experience:	7.9
Students in gifted program:	24 / 5.0%
Students in remedial education:	23.1%
Students held back a grade:	2.3%
Total suspensions, pct. in-school:	23 / 0.0%
Offenses:	violence: 2, drugs: * , other: 44
Eligible students, free or reduced lunch:	37.5%
Before / after school program:	Yes / Yes

Students at this school generally go on to:
Fairplay, Stewart, Yeager Middle

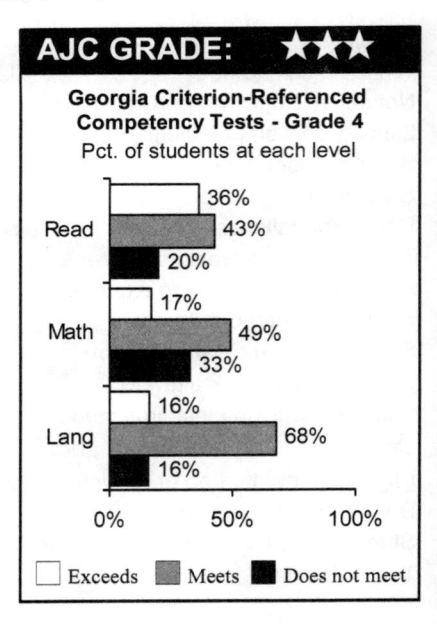

AJC GRADE: ★★★

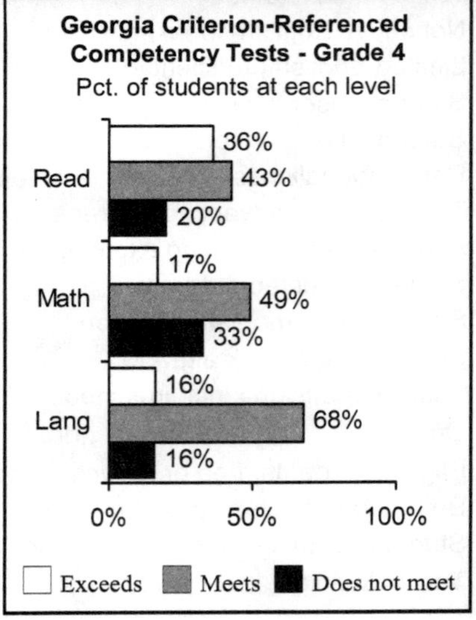
Georgia Criterion-Referenced Competency Tests - Grade 4
Pct. of students at each level
Read
36%
43%
20%
Math
17%
49%
33%
Lang
16%
68%
16%
0%
50%
100%
Exceeds
Meets
Does not meet

Burnett Elementary School

8277 Connally Dr, Douglasville, GA 30134
770-920-4350 · Grades K - 5

Enrollment:	619
White / black / other:	38.8% / 50.1% / 11.1%
Not native English-speaking:	2 / 0.3%
Limited English proficiency:	5 / 0.8%
Student absenteeism:	5.3%
Students per teacher:	12.3
Parent friendliness:	① ❷ ❸ ❹ ❺ ❻
Teachers with advanced degrees:	43.4%
Average years' teaching experience:	9.9
Students in gifted program:	30 / 4.8%
Students in remedial education:	31.7%
Students held back a grade:	1.1%
Total suspensions, pct. in-school:	193 / 35.8%
Offenses:	violence: 15, drugs: *, other: 259
Eligible students, free or reduced lunch:	68.8%
Before / after school program:	No / Yes

Students at this school generally go on to:
Chestnut Log, Stewart Middle

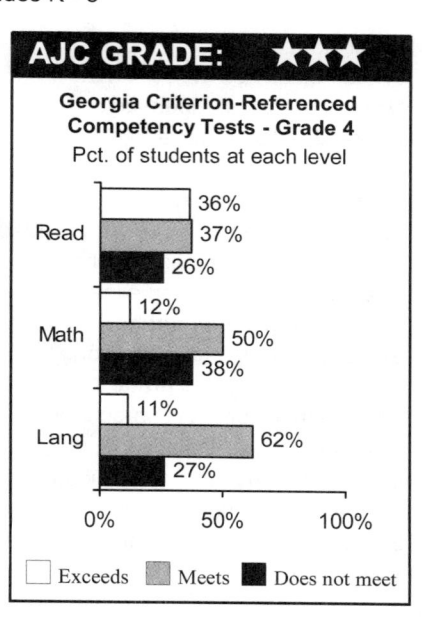

AJC GRADE: ★★★

Georgia Criterion-Referenced Competency Tests - Grade 4
Pct. of students at each level

Read: 36% Exceeds / 37% Meets / 26% Does not meet
Math: 12% Exceeds / 50% Meets / 38% Does not meet
Lang: 11% Exceeds / 62% Meets / 27% Does not meet

Chapel Hill Elementary School

3991 Chapel Hill Rd, Douglasville, GA 30135
770-920-4245 · Grades K - 5

Enrollment:	543
White / black / other:	79.9% / 16.4% / 3.7%
Not native English-speaking:	1 / 0.2%
Limited English proficiency:	4 / 0.7%
Student absenteeism:	4.0%
Students per teacher:	14.7
Parent friendliness:	① ❷ ❸ ④ ❺ ❻
Teachers with advanced degrees:	51.3%
Average years' teaching experience:	13.6
Students in gifted program:	80 / 14.7%
Students in remedial education:	12.0%
Students held back a grade:	0.4%
Total suspensions, pct. in-school:	10 / 0.0%
Offenses:	violence: 3, drugs: *, other: 17
Eligible students, free or reduced lunch:	15.3%
Before / after school program:	Yes / No

Students at this school generally go on to:
Chapel Hill, Chestnut Log Middle

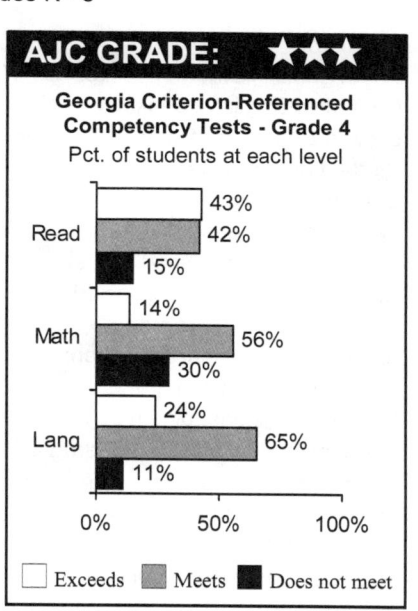

AJC GRADE: ★★★

Georgia Criterion-Referenced Competency Tests - Grade 4
Pct. of students at each level

Read: 43% Exceeds / 42% Meets / 15% Does not meet
Math: 14% Exceeds / 56% Meets / 30% Does not meet
Lang: 24% Exceeds / 65% Meets / 11% Does not meet

Douglas County Elementary Schools

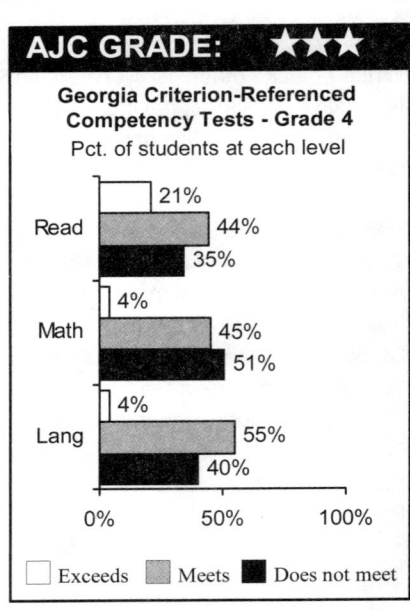

Dorsett Shoals Elementary School

5866 Dorsett Shoals Rd, Douglasville, GA 30135
770-920-4260 · Grades K - 5

Enrollment:	491
White / black / other:	79.0% / 15.1% / 5.9%
Not native English-speaking:	1 / 0.2%
Limited English proficiency:	1 / 0.2%
Student absenteeism:	4.8%
Students per teacher:	14.0
Parent friendliness:	①❷❸④⑤❻
Teachers with advanced degrees:	56.8%
Average years' teaching experience:	13.2
Students in gifted program:	48 / 9.8%
Students in remedial education:	19.4%
Students held back a grade:	0.8%
Total suspensions, pct. in-school:	8 / 0.0%
Offenses:	violence: 2, drugs: * , other: 40
Eligible students, free or reduced lunch:	22.7%
Before / after school program:	No / No

Students at this school generally go on to:
Yeager Middle

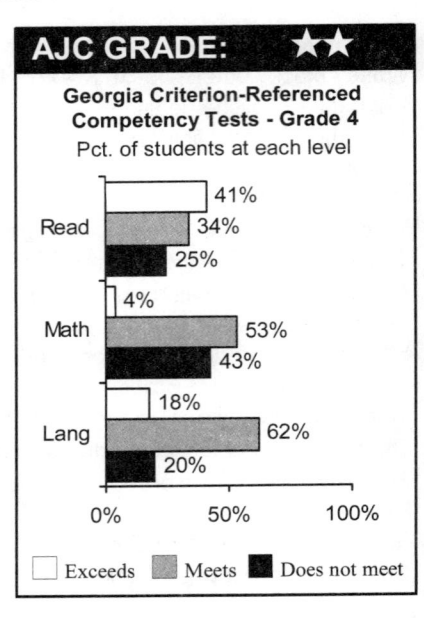

AJC GRADE: ★★

Georgia Criterion-Referenced Competency Tests - Grade 4
Pct. of students at each level

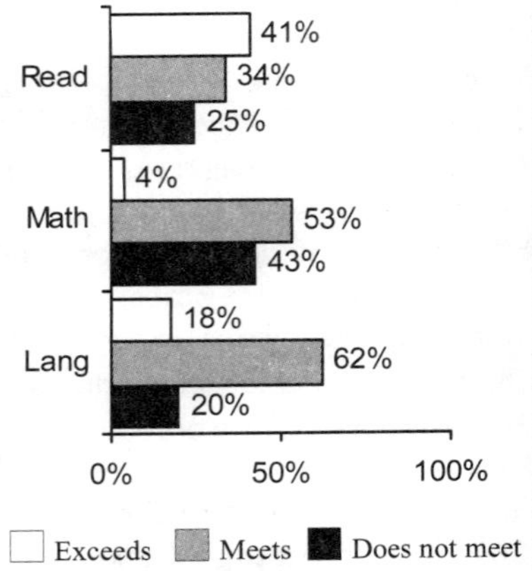
Read
41%
34%
25%
Math
4%
53%
43%
Lang
18%
62%
20%
0%
50%
100%
Exceeds
Meets
Does not meet

Eastside Elementary School

8266 Connally Dr, Douglasville, GA 30134
770-920-4275 · Grades K - 5

Enrollment:	572
White / black / other:	43.4% / 46.9% / 9.8%
Not native English-speaking:	20 / 3.5%
Limited English proficiency:	22 / 3.8%
Student absenteeism:	5.7%
Students per teacher:	12.1
Parent friendliness:	①❷❸④⑤❻
Teachers with advanced degrees:	49.0%
Average years' teaching experience:	12.3
Students in gifted program:	26 / 4.5%
Students in remedial education:	25.8%
Students held back a grade:	0.3%
Total suspensions, pct. in-school:	68 / 0.0%
Offenses:	violence: 28, drugs: * , other: 293
Eligible students, free or reduced lunch:	64.6%
Before / after school program:	Yes / Yes

Students at this school generally go on to:
Chestnut Log, Stewart Middle

AJC GRADE: ★★★

Georgia Criterion-Referenced Competency Tests - Grade 4
Pct. of students at each level

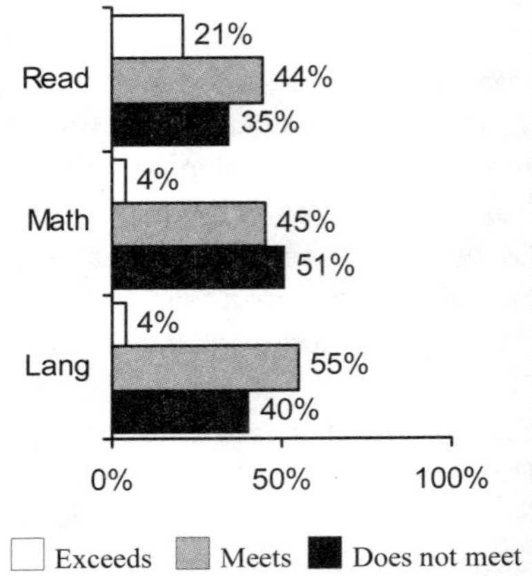
Read
21%
44%
35%
Math
4%
45%
51%
Lang
4%
55%
40%
0%
50%
100%
Exceeds
Meets
Does not meet

Factory Shoals Elementary School

3046 Fairburn Rd, Douglasville, GA 30135
770-920-4365 · Grades K - 5

Enrollment:	519
White / black / other:	70.5% / 22.4% / 7.1%
Not native English-speaking:	2 / 0.4%
Limited English proficiency:	7 / 1.3%
Student absenteeism:	4.5%
Students per teacher:	14.5
Parent friendliness:	①❷❸④❺❻
Teachers with advanced degrees:	40.5%
Average years' teaching experience:	12.6
Students in gifted program:	62 / 11.9%
Students in remedial education:	20.7%
Students held back a grade:	0.4%
Total suspensions, pct. in-school:	2 / 0.0%
Offenses:	violence: *, drugs: *, other: 6
Eligible students, free or reduced lunch:	32.8%
Before / after school program:	No / No
Students at this school generally go on to:	Chapel Hill, Chestnut Log Middle

AJC GRADE: ★★★

Georgia Criterion-Referenced Competency Tests - Grade 4
Pct. of students at each level

- Read — Exceeds: 40%, Meets: 45%, Does not meet: 15%
- Math — Exceeds: 6%, Meets: 63%, Does not meet: 31%
- Lang — Exceeds: 14%, Meets: 65%, Does not meet: 21%

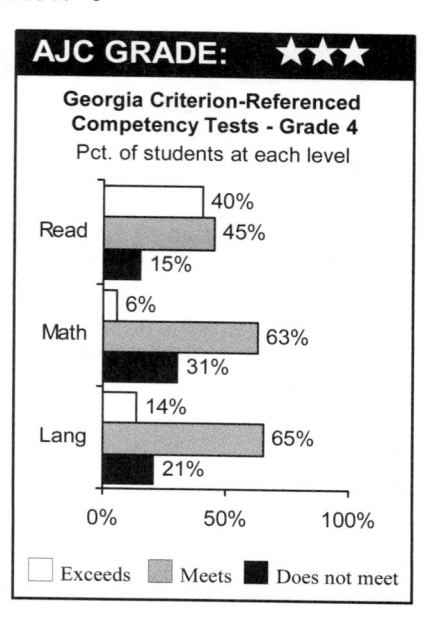

Holly Springs Elementary School

4909 W Chapel Hill Rd, Douglasville, GA 30135
770-947-7601 · Grades K - 5

Enrollment:	492
White / black / other:	69.7% / 24.0% / 6.3%
Not native English-speaking:	3 / 0.6%
Limited English proficiency:	7 / 1.4%
Student absenteeism:	3.9%
Students per teacher:	14.1
Parent friendliness:	①❷❸④❺❻
Teachers with advanced degrees:	52.6%
Average years' teaching experience:	10.4
Students in gifted program:	40 / 8.1%
Students in remedial education:	21.3%
Students held back a grade:	0.4%
Total suspensions, pct. in-school:	25 / 4.0%
Offenses:	violence: 21, drugs: *, other: 32
Eligible students, free or reduced lunch:	20.3%
Before / after school program:	No / Yes
Students at this school generally go on to:	Chapel Hill Middle

AJC GRADE: ★★★

Georgia Criterion-Referenced Competency Tests - Grade 4
Pct. of students at each level

- Read — Exceeds: 40%, Meets: 44%, Does not meet: 16%
- Math — Exceeds: 19%, Meets: 47%, Does not meet: 34%
- Lang — Exceeds: 18%, Meets: 58%, Does not meet: 24%

Douglas County Elementary Schools

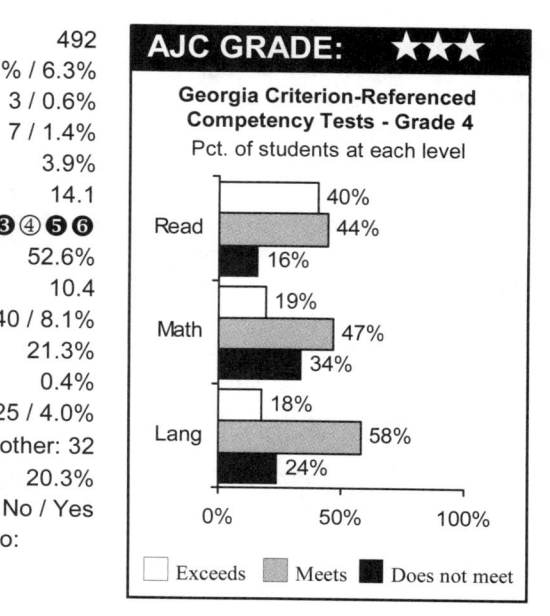

Lithia Springs Elementary School

6946 Florence Dr, Lithia Springs, GA 30122
770-732-2670 · Grades K - 5

Enrollment:	467
White / black / other:	70.2% / 21.4% / 8.4%
Not native English-speaking:	7 / 1.5%
Limited English proficiency:	8 / 1.7%
Student absenteeism:	4.2%
Students per teacher:	14.1
Parent friendliness:	① ❷ ❸ ④ ❺ ❻
Teachers with advanced degrees:	28.6%
Average years' teaching experience:	7.9
Students in gifted program:	31 / 6.6%
Students in remedial education:	22.1%
Students held back a grade:	0.9%
Total suspensions, pct. in-school:	8 / 0.0%
Offenses:	violence: 4, drugs: *, other: 89
Eligible students, free or reduced lunch:	33.5%
Before / after school program:	Yes / Yes

Students at this school generally go on to:
Turner Middle

AJC GRADE: ★★★

Georgia Criterion-Referenced Competency Tests - Grade 4
Pct. of students at each level

- Read: Exceeds 36%, Meets 40%, Does not meet 24%
- Math: Exceeds 5%, Meets 53%, Does not meet 43%
- Lang: Exceeds 9%, Meets 69%, Does not meet 22%

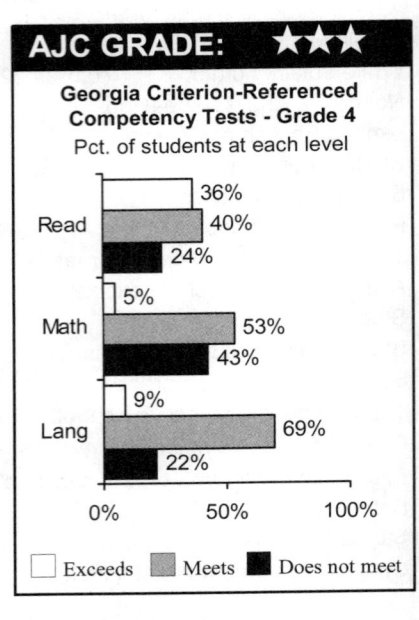

Mount Carmel Elementary School

2356 Fairburn Rd, Douglasville, GA 30135
770-920-4460 · Grades K - 5

Enrollment:	555
White / black / other:	66.1% / 24.1% / 9.7%
Not native English-speaking:	7 / 1.3%
Limited English proficiency:	8 / 1.4%
Student absenteeism:	3.9%
Students per teacher:	15.8
Parent friendliness:	① ❷ ❸ ④ ❺ ❻
Teachers with advanced degrees:	54.1%
Average years' teaching experience:	14.6
Students in gifted program:	31 / 5.6%
Students in remedial education:	14.7%
Students held back a grade:	0.9%
Total suspensions, pct. in-school:	31 / 0.0%
Offenses:	violence: 12, drugs: *, other: 62
Eligible students, free or reduced lunch:	29.2%
Before / after school program:	No / Yes

Students at this school generally go on to:
Chapel Hill, Chestnut Log, Turner Middle

AJC GRADE: ★★★

Georgia Criterion-Referenced Competency Tests - Grade 4
Pct. of students at each level

- Read: Exceeds 47%, Meets 39%, Does not meet 14%
- Math: Exceeds 20%, Meets 58%, Does not meet 22%
- Lang: Exceeds 28%, Meets 58%, Does not meet 14%

Douglas County Elementary Schools

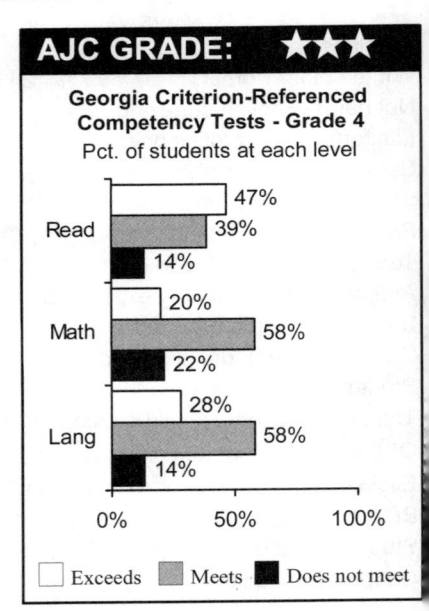

South Douglas Elementary School

8299 Highway 166, Douglasville, GA 30135
770-920-4475 · Grades K - 5

Enrollment:	471
White / black / other:	93.8% / 4.7% / 1.5%
Not native English-speaking:	*
Limited English proficiency:	*
Student absenteeism:	4.3%
Students per teacher:	14.0
Parent friendliness:	① ❷ ❸ ❹ ❺ ❻
Teachers with advanced degrees:	54.3%
Average years' teaching experience:	9.1
Students in gifted program:	57 / 12.1%
Students in remedial education:	21.7%
Students held back a grade:	1.3%
Total suspensions, pct. in-school:	1 / 0.0%
Offenses: violence: *, drugs: *, other: 6	
Eligible students, free or reduced lunch:	19.5%
Before / after school program:	Yes / Yes
Students at this school generally go on to: Fairplay Middle	

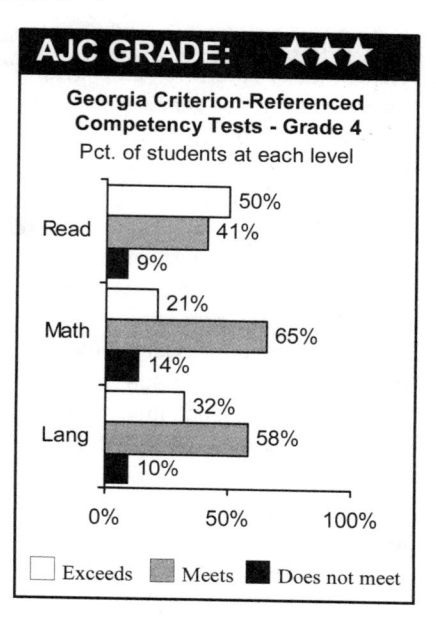

AJC GRADE: ★★★

Georgia Criterion-Referenced Competency Tests - Grade 4
Pct. of students at each level

Read — Exceeds: 50%, Meets: 41%, Does not meet: 9%
Math — Exceeds: 21%, Meets: 65%, Does not meet: 14%
Lang — Exceeds: 32%, Meets: 58%, Does not meet: 10%

Sweetwater Elementary School

2505 E County Line Rd, Lithia Springs, GA 30122
770-732-5960 · Grades K - 5

Enrollment:	565
White / black / other:	55.0% / 35.6% / 9.4%
Not native English-speaking:	15 / 2.7%
Limited English proficiency:	32 / 5.7%
Student absenteeism:	3.6%
Students per teacher:	14.3
Parent friendliness:	❶ ❷ ❸ ④ ❺ ❻
Teachers with advanced degrees:	61.9%
Average years' teaching experience:	11.5
Students in gifted program:	28 / 5.0%
Students in remedial education:	20.9%
Students held back a grade:	0.2%
Total suspensions, pct. in-school:	11 / 0.0%
Offenses: violence: 1, drugs: *, other: 27	
Eligible students, free or reduced lunch:	42.4%
Before / after school program:	Yes / Yes
Students at this school generally go on to: Chestnut Log, Turner Middle	

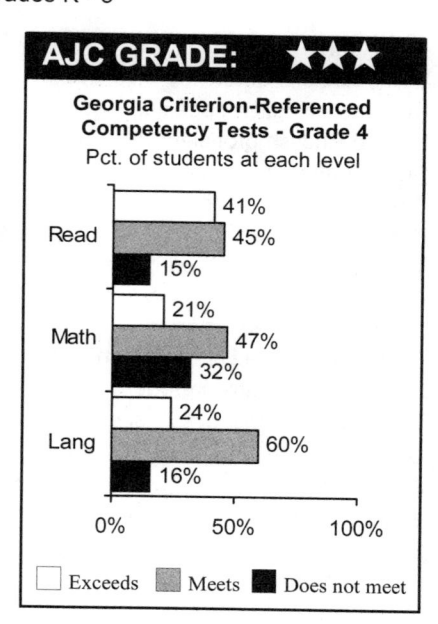

AJC GRADE: ★★★

Georgia Criterion-Referenced Competency Tests - Grade 4
Pct. of students at each level

Read — Exceeds: 41%, Meets: 45%, Does not meet: 15%
Math — Exceeds: 21%, Meets: 47%, Does not meet: 32%
Lang — Exceeds: 24%, Meets: 60%, Does not meet: 16%

Douglas County Elementary Schools

Winn Elementary School

3536 Veterans Memorial Hwy, Lithia Springs, GA 30122
770-732-2685 · Grades K - 5

Enrollment:	427
White / black / other:	52.2% / 33.7% / 14.1%
Not native English-speaking:	16 / 3.7%
Limited English proficiency:	36 / 8.4%
Student absenteeism:	5.6%
Students per teacher:	13.4
Parent friendliness:	① ❷ ❸ ④ ⑤ ❻
Teachers with advanced degrees:	48.5%
Average years' teaching experience:	13.3
Students in gifted program:	15 / 3.5%
Students in remedial education:	17.4%
Students held back a grade:	0.5%
Total suspensions, pct. in-school:	6 / 0.0%
Offenses:	violence: 3, drugs: 1, other: 110
Eligible students, free or reduced lunch:	46.0%
Before / after school program:	No / No
Students at this school generally go on to: Turner Middle	

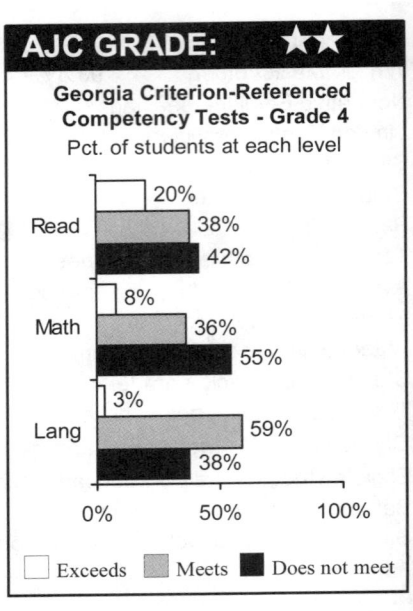

AJC GRADE: ★★

Georgia Criterion-Referenced Competency Tests - Grade 4
Pct. of students at each level

Read: Exceeds 20%, Meets 38%, Does not meet 42%
Math: Exceeds 8%, Meets 36%, Does not meet 55%
Lang: Exceeds 3%, Meets 59%, Does not meet 38%

Winston Elementary School

7465 Highway 78, Winston, GA 30187
770-920-4165 · Grades K - 5

Enrollment:	501
White / black / other:	78.2% / 18.4% / 3.4%
Not native English-speaking:	6 / 1.2%
Limited English proficiency:	8 / 1.6%
Student absenteeism:	5.0%
Students per teacher:	15.1
Parent friendliness:	① ❷ ❸ ④ ❺ ❻
Teachers with advanced degrees:	42.9%
Average years' teaching experience:	10.6
Students in gifted program:	39 / 7.8%
Students in remedial education:	24.4%
Students held back a grade:	1.2%
Total suspensions, pct. in-school:	*
Offenses:	violence: *, drugs: *, other: 4
Eligible students, free or reduced lunch:	38.9%
Before / after school program:	Yes / Yes
Students at this school generally go on to: Fairplay Middle	

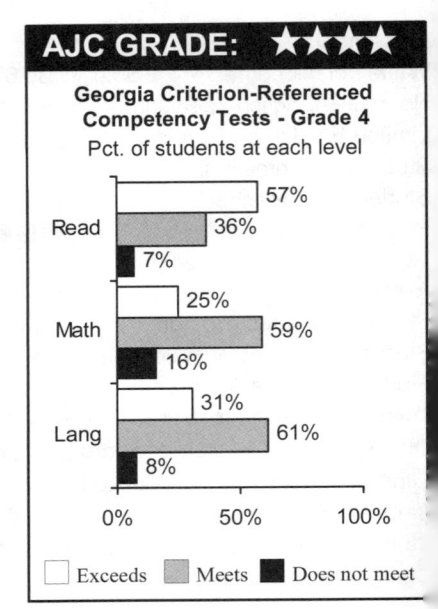

AJC GRADE: ★★★★

Georgia Criterion-Referenced Competency Tests - Grade 4
Pct. of students at each level

Read: Exceeds 57%, Meets 36%, Does not meet 7%
Math: Exceeds 25%, Meets 59%, Does not meet 16%
Lang: Exceeds 31%, Meets 61%, Does not meet 8%

Douglas County Elementary Schools

Chapel Hill Middle School

3989 Chapel Hill Rd, Douglasville, GA 30135
770-920-4230 · Grades 6 - 8

Enrollment:	950
White / black / other:	74.8% / 19.4% / 5.8%
Not native English-speaking:	11 / 1.2%
Student absenteeism:	4.3%
Students per teacher:	18.4
Parent friendliness:	① ❷ ❸ ④ ⑤ ❻
Teachers with advanced degrees:	37.7%
Average years' teaching experience:	12.5
Students in gifted program:	236 / 24.8%
Students held back a grade:	0.5%
Total suspensions and expulsions:	511
Suspensions only, pct. in-school:	511 / 91.2%
Offenses: violence: 16, drugs: *, other: 610	
Eligible students, free or reduced lunch:	12.4%
Number of dropouts:	*
Pct. 8th-graders w/ basic computer skills:	100.0%
Students at this school generally go on to: Chapel Hill, Douglas County High	

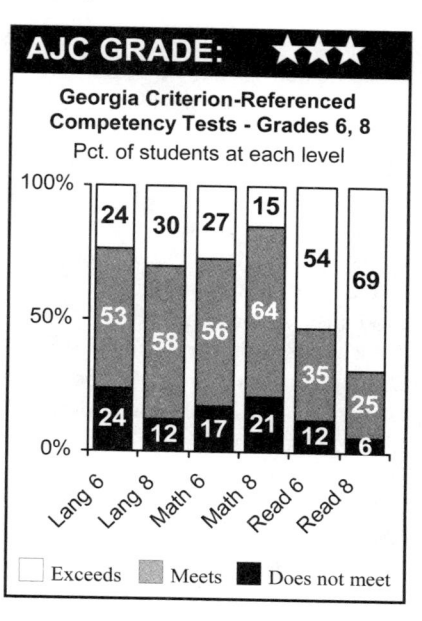

AJC GRADE: ★★★

Georgia Criterion-Referenced Competency Tests - Grades 6, 8
Pct. of students at each level

	Lang 6	Lang 8	Math 6	Math 8	Read 6	Read 8
Exceeds	24	30	27	15	54	69
Meets	53	58	56	64	35	25
Does not meet	24	12	17	21	12	6

Chestnut Log Middle School

2544 Pope Rd, Douglasville, GA 30135
770-920-4550 · Grades 6 - 8

Enrollment:	908
White / black / other:	64.1% / 31.5% / 4.4%
Not native English-speaking:	6 / 0.7%
Student absenteeism:	6.2%
Students per teacher:	18.6
Parent friendliness:	① ❷ ❸ ④ ⑤ ❻
Teachers with advanced degrees:	46.0%
Average years' teaching experience:	12.7
Students in gifted program:	150 / 16.5%
Students held back a grade:	0.3%
Total suspensions and expulsions:	1,042
Suspensions only, pct. in-school:	1,042 / 78.1%
Offenses: violence: 188, drugs: 4, other: 946	
Eligible students, free or reduced lunch:	30.3%
Number of dropouts:	2 / 0.2%
Pct. 8th-graders w/ basic computer skills:	72.0%
Students at this school generally go on to: Chapel Hill, Lithia Springs High	

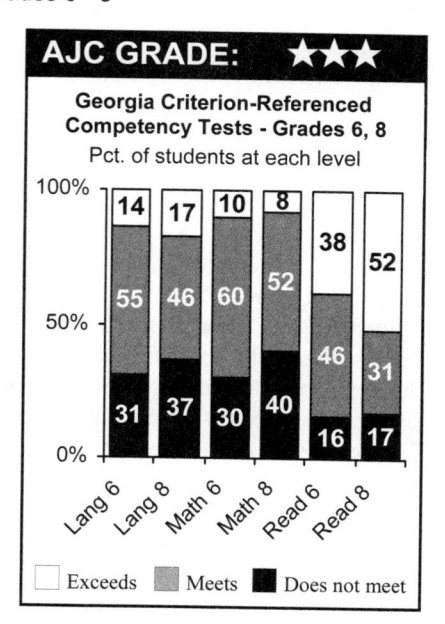

AJC GRADE: ★★★

Georgia Criterion-Referenced Competency Tests - Grades 6, 8
Pct. of students at each level

	Lang 6	Lang 8	Math 6	Math 8	Read 6	Read 8
Exceeds	14	17	10	8	38	52
Meets	55	46	60	52	46	31
Does not meet	31	37	30	40	16	17

Douglas County Middle Schools

Fairplay Middle School

8311 Highway 166, Douglasville, GA 30135
770-920-4200 · Grades 6 - 8

Enrollment:	779
White / black / other:	85.6% / 11.8% / 2.6%
Not native English-speaking:	*
Student absenteeism:	5.1%
Students per teacher:	17.8
Parent friendliness:	①❷❸④⑤❻
Teachers with advanced degrees:	37.8%
Average years' teaching experience:	10.0
Students in gifted program:	102 / 13.1%
Students held back a grade:	0.4%
Total suspensions and expulsions:	497
Suspensions only, pct. in-school:	497 / 90.1%
Offenses:	violence: 7, drugs: 4, other: 630
Eligible students, free or reduced lunch:	22.1%
Number of dropouts:	*
Pct. 8th-graders w/ basic computer skills:	97.0%

Students at this school generally go on to:
Alexander High

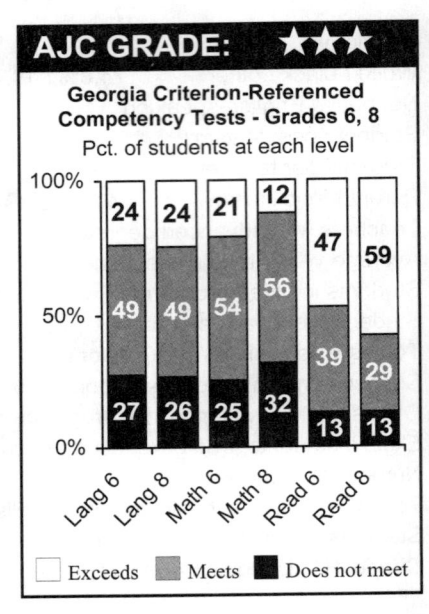

AJC GRADE: ★★★

Georgia Criterion-Referenced Competency Tests - Grades 6, 8
Pct. of students at each level

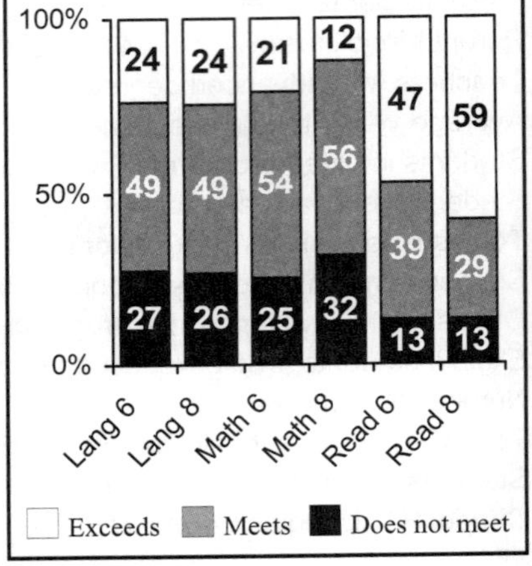
100%
50%
0%
24
24
21
12
47
59
49
49
54
56
39
29
27
26
25
32
13
13
Lang 6
Lang 8
Math 6
Math 8
Read 6
Read 8
Exceeds
Meets
Does not meet

Stewart Middle School

8138 Malone St, Douglasville, GA 30134
770-920-4215 · Grades 6 - 8

Enrollment:	723
White / black / other:	48.5% / 45.9% / 5.5%
Not native English-speaking:	7 / 1.0%
Student absenteeism:	8.9%
Students per teacher:	16.9
Parent friendliness:	❶❷❸④❺❻
Teachers with advanced degrees:	36.4%
Average years' teaching experience:	11.3
Students in gifted program:	76 / 10.5%
Students held back a grade:	1.2%
Total suspensions and expulsions:	1,299
Suspensions only, pct. in-school:	1,299 / 67.1%
Offenses:	violence: 145, drugs: 4, other: 1,452
Eligible students, free or reduced lunch:	54.8%
Number of dropouts:	*
Pct. 8th-graders w/ basic computer skills:	84.6%

Students at this school generally go on to:
Alexander, Douglas County High

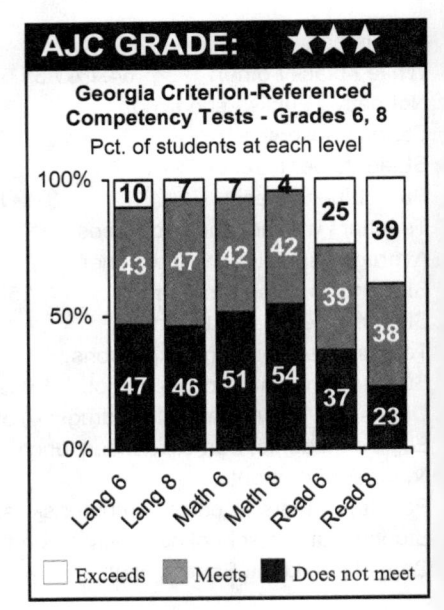

AJC GRADE: ★★★

Georgia Criterion-Referenced Competency Tests - Grades 6, 8
Pct. of students at each level

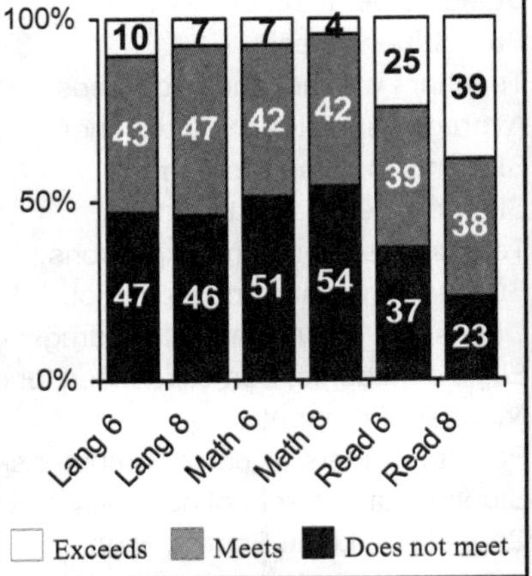
100%
50%
0%
10
7
7
4
25
39
43
47
42
42
39
38
47
46
51
54
37
23
Lang 6
Lang 8
Math 6
Math 8
Read 6
Read 8
Exceeds
Meets
Does not meet

Turner Middle School

7101 Junior High Drive, Lithia Springs, GA 30122
770-732-2655 · Grades 6 - 8

Enrollment:	712
White / black / other:	68.8% / 23.9% / 7.3%
Not native English-speaking:	15 / 2.1%
Student absenteeism:	5.9%
Students per teacher:	18.2
Parent friendliness:	① ❷ ❸ ④ ⑤ ❻
Teachers with advanced degrees:	58.5%
Average years' teaching experience:	12.5
Students in gifted program:	92 / 12.9%
Students held back a grade:	0.7%
Total suspensions and expulsions:	766
Suspensions only, pct. in-school:	766 / 88.9%
Offenses: violence: 73, drugs: 4, other: 779	
Eligible students, free or reduced lunch:	37.4%
Number of dropouts:	*
Pct. 8th-graders w/ basic computer skills:	100.0%

Students at this school generally go on to:
Lithia Springs High

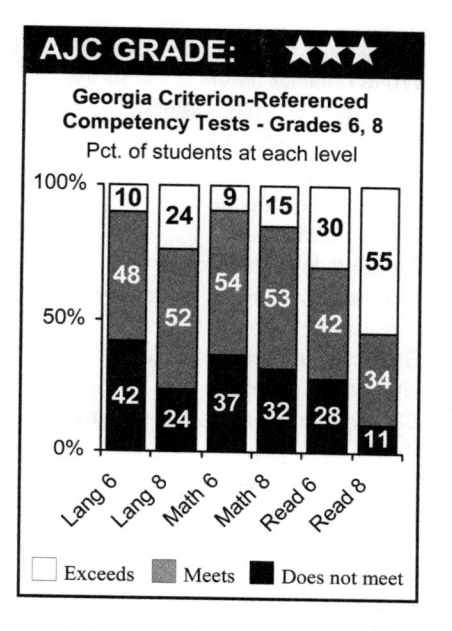

AJC GRADE: ★★★

Georgia Criterion-Referenced Competency Tests - Grades 6, 8
Pct. of students at each level

	Exceeds	Meets	Does not meet
Lang 6	10	48	42
Lang 8	24	52	24
Math 6	9	54	37
Math 8	15	53	32
Read 6	30	42	28
Read 8	55	34	11

Douglas County Middle Schools

Alexander High School

6500 Alexander Pkwy, Douglasville, GA 30135
770-920-4500 · Grades 9 - 12

Enrollment:	1,313
White / black / other:	85.9% / 11.7% / 2.4%
Not native English-speaking:	*
Limited English proficiency:	2 / 0.2%
Student absenteeism:	7.4%
Students per teacher:	17.5
Parent friendliness:	① ❷ ❸ ④ ❺ ❻
Students in gifted program:	196 / 14.9%
Students in remedial education:	2.0%
High school completion rate:	74.7%
Students held back a grade:	5.9%
Number of dropouts:	61 / 4.3%
Students in alternative programs:	61 / 4.6%
Students in special education:	172 / 13.1%
Eligible students, free or reduced lunch:	13.5%
Total suspensions and expulsions:	819
Suspensions only, pct. in-school:	819 / 88.9%
Drugs/alcohol-related offenses:	23
Violence-related offenses:	44
Firearms-related offenses:	3
Vandalism-related offenses:	8
Theft-related offenses:	3
All other disciplinary offenses:	839
Teachers with advanced degrees:	63.2%
Average years' teaching experience:	16.0

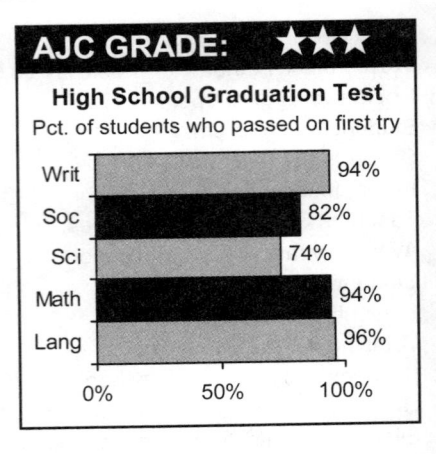

AJC GRADE: ★★★

High School Graduation Test
Pct. of students who passed on first try

- Writ: 94%
- Soc: 82%
- Sci: 74%
- Math: 94%
- Lang: 96%

GHSA classification: 4-AAAA
Interscholastic sports offered:
BB, BS, CC, CL, FB, GO, SB, SO, TE, TF, VB, WR

Advanced Placement (AP) Exams
- Students tested: 83
- Tests taken: 96
- Pct. of test scores 3 or higher (1 - 5 scale): 49.0%

Languages other than English taught:
French, Latin, Spanish

2000-2001 high school graduates: 233

College prep/vocational diplomas:	43.3%
College prep endorsement diplomas:	24.5%
Vocational endorsement diplomas:	18.9%
General high school diplomas:	0.0%
Special education diplomas:	3.9%
Certificates of attendance (no diploma):	9.4%

Of the 2000-2001 graduates, 52.8% were eligible for the HOPE scholarship.

Of the 1999-2000 graduates, 77 attended a Georgia public college or university. Of those, 87% met the school's minimum academic requirements.

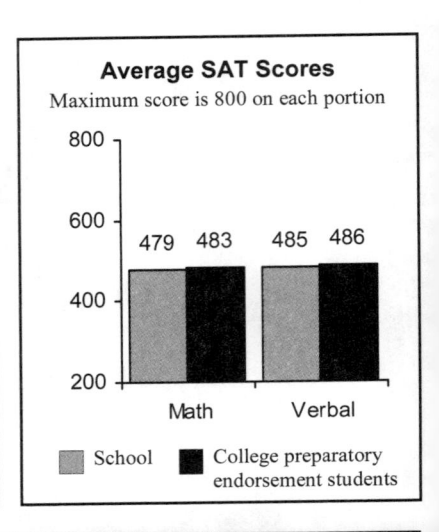

Average SAT Scores
Maximum score is 800 on each portion

- Math — School: 479, College preparatory endorsement students: 483
- Verbal — School: 485, College preparatory endorsement students: 486

The Atlanta Journal-Constitution / Page 286

Douglas County High Schools

Chapel Hill High School

4899 Chapel Hill Rd, Douglasville, GA 30135
770-947-7501 · Grades 9 - 12

Enrollment:	803
White / black / other:	83.3% / 13.1% / 3.6%
Not native English-speaking:	*
Limited English proficiency:	*
Student absenteeism:	4.4%
Students per teacher:	17.5
Parent friendliness:	① ❷ ❸ ④ ⑤ ❻
Students in gifted program:	59 / 7.3%
Students in remedial education:	4.1%
High school completion rate:	*
Students held back a grade:	2.5%
Number of dropouts:	15 / 1.7%
Students in alternative programs:	15 / 1.9%
Students in special education:	63 / 7.8%
Eligible students, free or reduced lunch:	7.8%
Total suspensions and expulsions:	500
Suspensions only, pct. in-school:	500 / 87.6%
Drugs/alcohol-related offenses:	13
Violence-related offenses:	26
Firearms-related offenses:	8
Vandalism-related offenses:	2
Theft-related offenses:	5
All other disciplinary offenses:	506
Teachers with advanced degrees:	41.3%
Average years' teaching experience:	10.0

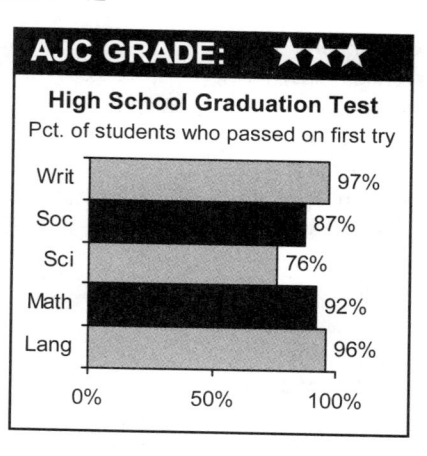

AJC GRADE: ★★★

High School Graduation Test
Pct. of students who passed on first try

- Writ: 97%
- Soc: 87%
- Sci: 76%
- Math: 92%
- Lang: 96%

GHSA classification: 4-AAAA
Interscholastic sports offered:
 None

Advanced Placement (AP) Exams
 Students tested: 62
 Tests taken: 63
 Pct. of test scores 3 or higher (1 - 5 scale): 41.3%

Languages other than English taught:
 French, Spanish

2000-2001 high school graduates:	2
College prep/vocational diplomas:	0.0%
College prep endorsement diplomas:	0.0%
Vocational endorsement diplomas:	0.0%
General high school diplomas:	0.0%
Special education diplomas:	100.0%
Certificates of attendance (no diploma):	0.0%

Chapel Hill High School is a new school and therefore some data was not available for this report.

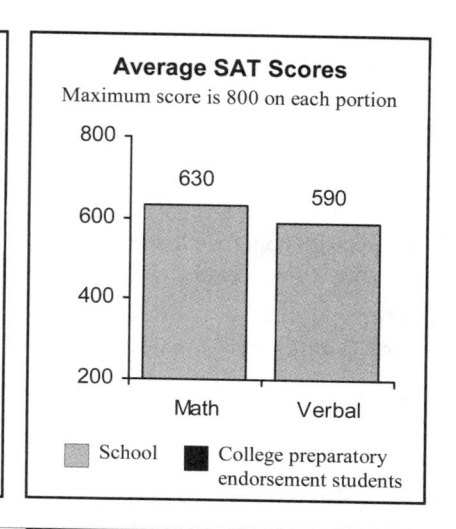

Average SAT Scores
Maximum score is 800 on each portion

- Math: 630
- Verbal: 590

School / College preparatory endorsement students

Douglas County High Schools

Douglas County High School

8705 Campbellton St, Douglasville, GA 30134
770-920-4400 · Grades 9 - 12

Enrollment:	1,408
White / black / other:	63.6% / 30.9% / 5.5%
Not native English-speaking:	17 / 1.2%
Limited English proficiency:	26 / 1.8%
Student absenteeism:	7.8%
Students per teacher:	17.4
Parent friendliness:	①❷❸❹❺❻
Students in gifted program:	199 / 14.1%
Students in remedial education:	4.3%
High school completion rate:	77.6%
Students held back a grade:	8.7%
Number of dropouts:	92 / 5.9%
Students in alternative programs:	104 / 7.4%
Students in special education:	152 / 10.8%
Eligible students, free or reduced lunch:	24.0%
Total suspensions and expulsions:	1,101
Suspensions only, pct. in-school:	1,101 / 75.4%
Drugs/alcohol-related offenses:	7
Violence-related offenses:	104
Firearms-related offenses:	5
Vandalism-related offenses:	1
Theft-related offenses:	6
All other disciplinary offenses:	1,076
Teachers with advanced degrees:	55.4%
Average years' teaching experience:	15.1

AJC GRADE: ★★★

High School Graduation Test
Pct. of students who passed on first try

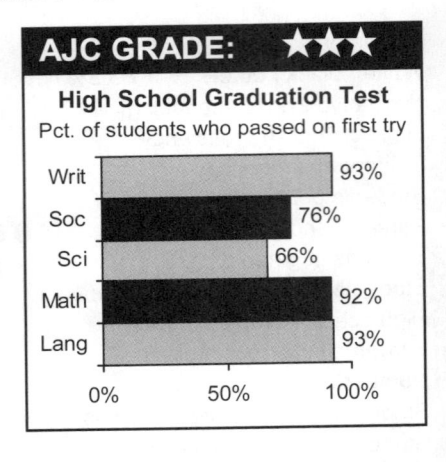

- Writ: 93%
- Soc: 76%
- Sci: 66%
- Math: 92%
- Lang: 93%

GHSA classification:	4-AAAA

Interscholastic sports offered:
BB, BS, CC, CL, FB, GO, SB, SO, TE, TF, WR

Advanced Placement (AP) Exams
Students tested:	55
Tests taken:	66
Pct. of test scores 3 or higher (1 - 5 scale):	42.4%

Languages other than English taught:
French, Russian, Spanish

2000-2001 high school graduates: 332

College prep/vocational diplomas:	38.0%
College prep endorsement diplomas:	23.5%
Vocational endorsement diplomas:	22.0%
General high school diplomas:	0.0%
Special education diplomas:	6.3%
Certificates of attendance (no diploma):	10.2%

Of the 2000-2001 graduates, 55.4% were eligible for the HOPE scholarship.

Of the 1999-2000 graduates, 103 attended a Georgia public college or university. Of those, 91% met the school's minimum academic requirements.

Average SAT Scores
Maximum score is 800 on each portion

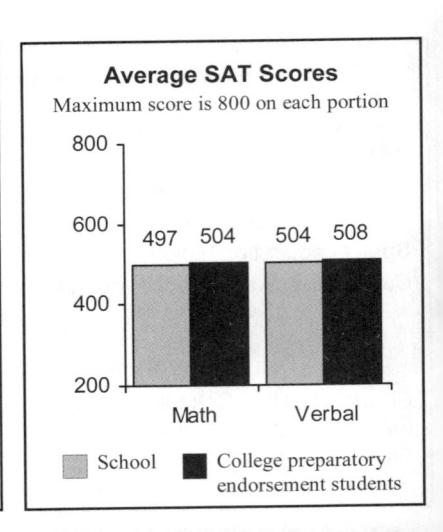

- Math: School 497, College preparatory endorsement students 504
- Verbal: School 504, College preparatory endorsement students 508

Douglas County High Schools

Lithia Springs High School

2520 E County Line Rd, Lithia Springs, GA 30122
770-732-2600 · Grades 9 - 12

👎

Enrollment:	1,465
White / black / other:	68.2% / 26.2% / 5.6%
Not native English-speaking:	*
Limited English proficiency:	10 / 0.7%
Student absenteeism:	8.6%
Students per teacher:	17.3
Parent friendliness:	①❷❸④⑤❻
Students in gifted program:	119 / 8.1%
Students in remedial education:	3.0%
High school completion rate:	73.1%
Students held back a grade:	6.7%
Number of dropouts:	98 / 6.0%
Students in alternative programs:	76 / 5.2%
Students in special education:	192 / 13.1%
Eligible students, free or reduced lunch:	22.9%

Total suspensions and expulsions:	1,211
Suspensions only, pct. in-school:	1,211 / 78.4%
Drugs/alcohol-related offenses:	9
Violence-related offenses:	36
Firearms-related offenses:	2
Vandalism-related offenses:	*
Theft-related offenses:	1
All other disciplinary offenses:	1,317

Teachers with advanced degrees:	62.4%
Average years' teaching experience:	13.8

AJC GRADE: ★★

High School Graduation Test

Pct. of students who passed on first try

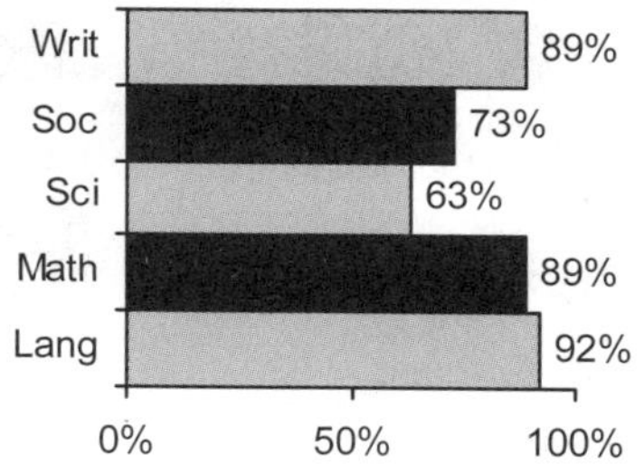
Writ
89%
Soc
73%
Sci
63%
Math
89%
Lang
92%
0%
50%
100%

GHSA classification:	4-AAAA

Interscholastic sports offered:
BB, BS, CC, CL, FB, GO, RI, SB, SO, TE, TF, WR

Advanced Placement (AP) Exams

Students tested:	119
Tests taken:	180
Pct. of test scores 3 or higher (1 - 5 scale):	24.4%

Languages other than English taught:
French, Spanish

2000-2001 high school graduates: 342

College prep/vocational diplomas:	52.0%
College prep endorsement diplomas:	15.8%
Vocational endorsement diplomas:	19.0%
General high school diplomas:	0.0%
Special education diplomas:	5.6%
Certificates of attendance (no diploma):	7.6%

Of the 2000-2001 graduates, 58.5% were eligible for the HOPE scholarship.

Of the 1999-2000 graduates, 101 attended a Georgia public college or university. Of those, 81% met the school's minimum academic requirements.

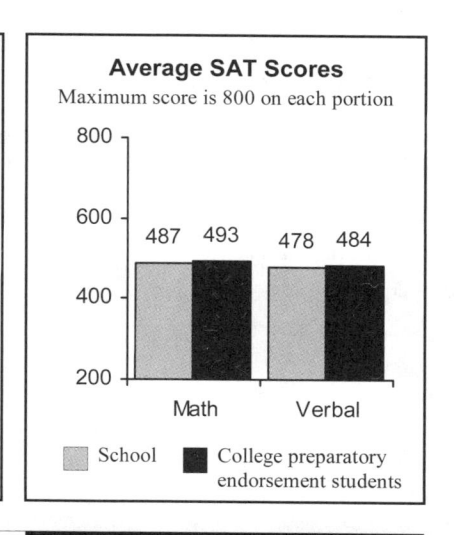

Average SAT Scores

Maximum score is 800 on each portion

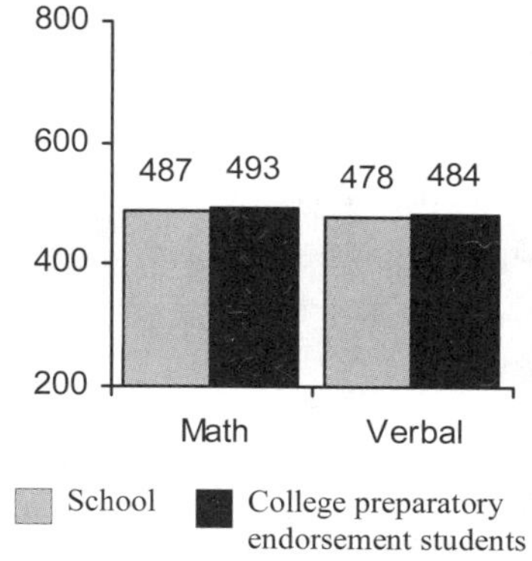
800
600
400
200
487
493
478
484
Math
Verbal
School
College preparatory endorsement students

AJC ranking of Douglas County Schools

ELEMENTARY SCHOOLS

AJC Star Grade: ★★★★

Winston Elementary

AJC Star Grade: ★★★

Arbor Station Elementary
Bill Arp Elementary
Bright Star Elementary
Burnett Elementary
Chapel Hill Elementary
Eastside Elementary
Factory Shoals Elementary
Holly Springs Elementary
Lithia Springs Elementary
Mount Carmel Elementary
South Douglas Elementary
Sweetwater Elementary

AJC Star Grade: ★★

Beulah Elementary
Dorsett Shoals Elementary
Winn Elementary

MIDDLE SCHOOLS

AJC Star Grade: ★★★

Chapel Hill Middle
Chestnut Log Middle
Fairplay Middle
Stewart Middle
Turner Middle

HIGH SCHOOLS

AJC Star Grade: ★★★

Alexander High
Chapel Hill High
Douglas County High

AJC Star Grade: ★★

Lithia Springs High

Douglas County Public Schools

Fayette County Public Schools

210 Stonewall Ave W, Fayetteville, GA 30214
Phone: 770-460-3535 · Fax: 770-460-8191
http://www.fcboe.org

The following pages provide detailed information on every school in the Fayette County school district. An asterisk (*) means the value of the data was zero or was not reported by the school district. A complete list of schools ranked by The Atlanta Journal-Constitution's star rating system follows the detailed school reports.

District enrollment:	19,456
White / black / other:	79.0% / 14.1% / 6.8%
Not native English-speaking:	244 / 1.3%
Expenditure per student (general fund):	$6,313
Students per teacher:	14.1
Teachers with advanced degrees:	54.1%
Average years, teaching experience:	12.3
Average teacher salary:	$43,147.03
Students in gifted program:	3,233 / 16.6%
Students held back a grade:	491 / 2.5%
Eligible students, free or reduced lunch:	1,355 / 6.9%
Number of dropouts (grades 9-12):	136 / 2.0%
High school completion rate:	88.5%
Graduates, pct. eligible for HOPE scholarships:	1,402 / 67.3%
Average combined SAT score (maximum 1,600):	1,068
Pct. of 11th-graders passing the Georgia High School Graduation Tests on first try:	84%
Percent of children 5 to 17 years of age living in poverty (2000 Census estimate):	2.8%

Braelinn Elementary School

975 Robinson Rd, Peachtree City, GA 30269
770-631-5410 · Grades K - 5

Enrollment:	694
White / black / other:	90.8% / 2.3% / 6.9%
Not native English-speaking:	11 / 1.6%
Limited English proficiency:	11 / 1.6%
Student absenteeism:	3.3%
Students per teacher:	15.1
Parent friendliness:	① ❷ ❸ ④ ⑤ ❻
Teachers with advanced degrees:	52.1%
Average years' teaching experience:	14.0
Students in gifted program:	91 / 13.1%
Students in remedial education:	5.2%
Students held back a grade:	0.4%
Total suspensions, pct. in-school:	*
Offenses: violence: *, drugs: *, other:	*
Eligible students, free or reduced lunch:	1.1%
Before / after school program:	No / Yes
Students at this school generally go on to:	
Rising Starr Middle	

AJC GRADE: ★★★★

Georgia Criterion-Referenced Competency Tests - Grade 4
Pct. of students at each level

Read: 69% Exceeds / 27% Meets / 4% Does not meet
Math: 46% Exceeds / 50% Meets / 4% Does not meet
Lang: 36% Exceeds / 61% Meets / 3% Does not meet

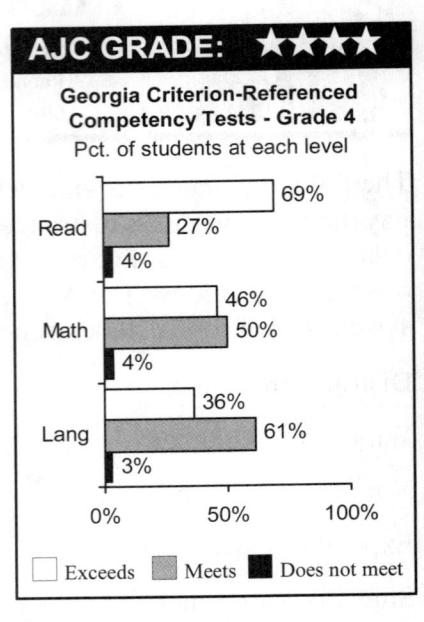

Brooks Elementary School

119 Price Rd, Brooks, GA 30205
770-719-8150 · Grades K - 5

Enrollment:	501
White / black / other:	95.8% / 2.4% / 1.8%
Not native English-speaking:	*
Limited English proficiency:	*
Student absenteeism:	4.3%
Students per teacher:	12.8
Parent friendliness:	① ❷ ❸ ④ ❺ ❻
Teachers with advanced degrees:	43.6%
Average years' teaching experience:	14.1
Students in gifted program:	58 / 11.6%
Students in remedial education:	14.0%
Students held back a grade:	4.6%
Total suspensions, pct. in-school:	12 / 75.0%
Offenses: violence: *, drugs: *, other:	13
Eligible students, free or reduced lunch:	6.6%
Before / after school program:	No / Yes
Students at this school generally go on to:	
Whitewater Middle	

AJC GRADE: ★★

Georgia Criterion-Referenced Competency Tests - Grade 4
Pct. of students at each level

Read: 38% Exceeds / 46% Meets / 15% Does not meet
Math: 18% Exceeds / 54% Meets / 29% Does not meet
Lang: 20% Exceeds / 60% Meets / 20% Does not meet

Fayette County Elementary Schools

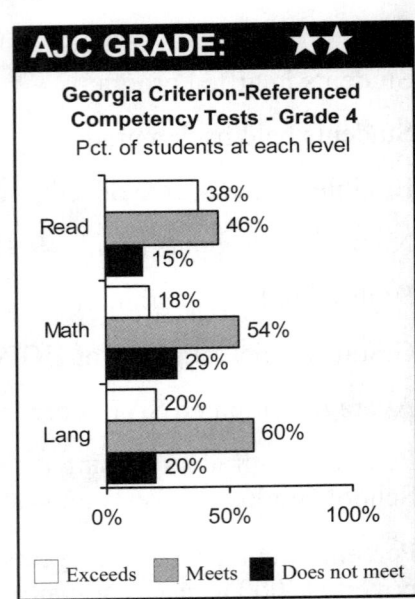

Burch Elementary School

330 Jenkins Rd, Tyrone, GA 30290
770-969-2820 · Grades K - 5

Enrollment:	620
White / black / other:	76.6% / 16.0% / 7.4%
Not native English-speaking:	13 / 2.1%
Limited English proficiency:	15 / 2.4%
Student absenteeism:	4.5%
Students per teacher:	12.7
Parent friendliness:	①❷❸④⑤❻
Teachers with advanced degrees:	55.1%
Average years' teaching experience:	13.0
Students in gifted program:	57 / 9.2%
Students in remedial education:	21.8%
Students held back a grade:	3.2%
Total suspensions, pct. in-school:	68 / 95.6%
Offenses:	violence: *, drugs: *, other: 83
Eligible students, free or reduced lunch:	21.3%
Before / after school program:	Yes / Yes

Students at this school generally go on to:
Flat Rock Middle

AJC GRADE: ★★★

Georgia Criterion-Referenced Competency Tests - Grade 4
Pct. of students at each level

- Read — Exceeds: 46%, Meets: 35%, Does not meet: 19%
- Math — Exceeds: 23%, Meets: 56%, Does not meet: 21%
- Lang — Exceeds: 17%, Meets: 66%, Does not meet: 17%

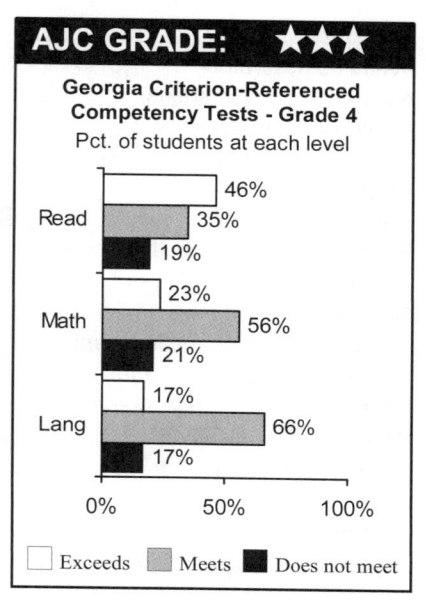

East Fayette Elementary School

245 Booker Ave, Fayetteville, GA 30215
770-460-3565 · Grades K - 5

Enrollment:	622
White / black / other:	75.6% / 12.1% / 12.4%
Not native English-speaking:	20 / 3.2%
Limited English proficiency:	35 / 5.6%
Student absenteeism:	4.2%
Students per teacher:	14.0
Parent friendliness:	❶❷❸④⑤❻
Teachers with advanced degrees:	44.4%
Average years' teaching experience:	12.4
Students in gifted program:	55 / 8.8%
Students in remedial education:	15.8%
Students held back a grade:	1.0%
Total suspensions, pct. in-school:	81 / 91.4%
Offenses:	violence: *, drugs: *, other: 92
Eligible students, free or reduced lunch:	14.7%
Before / after school program:	Yes / Yes

Students at this school generally go on to:
Fayette Middle

AJC GRADE: ★★★

Georgia Criterion-Referenced Competency Tests - Grade 4
Pct. of students at each level

- Read — Exceeds: 47%, Meets: 39%, Does not meet: 14%
- Math — Exceeds: 25%, Meets: 63%, Does not meet: 12%
- Lang — Exceeds: 28%, Meets: 60%, Does not meet: 12%

Fayette County Elementary Schools

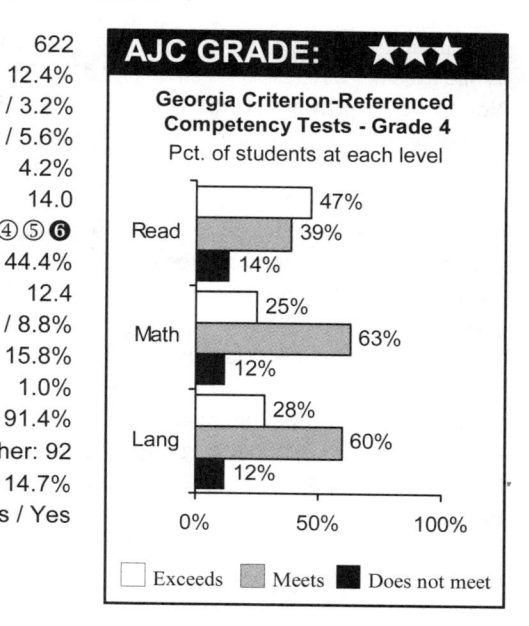

Fayetteville Intermediate School

440 Hood Ave, Fayetteville, GA 30214
770-460-3555 · Grades K - 5

Enrollment:	1,020
White / black / other:	67.5% / 24.5% / 7.9%
Not native English-speaking:	11 / 1.1%
Limited English proficiency:	30 / 2.9%
Student absenteeism:	4.2%
Students per teacher:	14.3
Parent friendliness:	① ❷ ❸ ④ ⑤ ❻
Teachers with advanced degrees:	47.2%
Average years' teaching experience:	14.3
Students in gifted program:	81 / 7.9%
Students in remedial education:	17.3%
Students held back a grade:	0.9%
Total suspensions, pct. in-school:	94 / 75.5%
Offenses:	violence: 1, drugs: *, other: 113
Eligible students, free or reduced lunch:	10.9%
Before / after school program:	No / Yes
Students at this school generally go on to:	
Fayette, Whitewater Middle	

AJC GRADE: ★★

Georgia Criterion-Referenced Competency Tests - Grade 4
Pct. of students at each level

Read: Exceeds 40%, Meets 39%, Does not meet 21%
Math: Exceeds 15%, Meets 59%, Does not meet 27%
Lang: Exceeds 21%, Meets 61%, Does not meet 18%

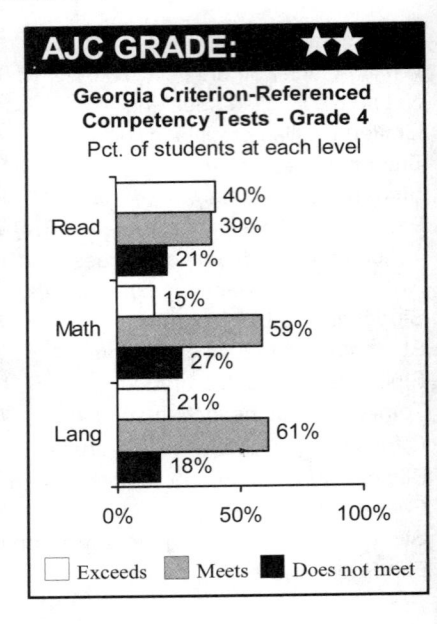

Huddleston Elementary School

200 McIntosh Trl, Peachtree City, GA 30269
770-631-3255 · Grades K - 5

Enrollment:	649
White / black / other:	84.1% / 7.1% / 8.8%
Not native English-speaking:	11 / 1.7%
Limited English proficiency:	18 / 2.8%
Student absenteeism:	4.1%
Students per teacher:	14.6
Parent friendliness:	① ❷ ❸ ④ ❺ ❻
Teachers with advanced degrees:	43.5%
Average years' teaching experience:	13.3
Students in gifted program:	36 / 5.5%
Students in remedial education:	10.0%
Students held back a grade:	1.7%
Total suspensions, pct. in-school:	37 / 97.3%
Offenses:	violence: *, drugs: *, other: 42
Eligible students, free or reduced lunch:	5.8%
Before / after school program:	No / Yes
Students at this school generally go on to:	
Booth, Rising Starr Middle	

AJC GRADE: ★★★

Georgia Criterion-Referenced Competency Tests - Grade 4
Pct. of students at each level

Read: Exceeds 54%, Meets 35%, Does not meet 11%
Math: Exceeds 24%, Meets 64%, Does not meet 12%
Lang: Exceeds 22%, Meets 68%, Does not meet 10%

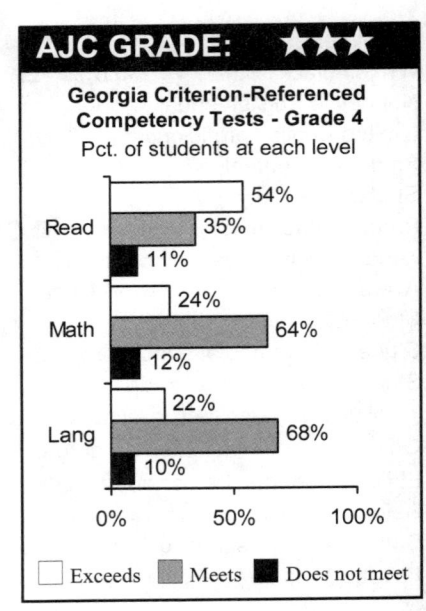

Kedron Elementary School

200 Kedron Dr, Peachtree City, GA 30269
770-486-2700 · Grades K - 5

Enrollment:	818
White / black / other:	88.6% / 3.4% / 7.9%
Not native English-speaking:	6 / 0.7%
Limited English proficiency:	8 / 1.0%
Student absenteeism:	3.6%
Students per teacher:	14.6
Parent friendliness:	①❷❸❹⑤❻
Teachers with advanced degrees:	51.8%
Average years' teaching experience:	9.6
Students in gifted program:	71 / 8.7%
Students in remedial education:	4.6%
Students held back a grade:	0.6%
Total suspensions, pct. in-school:	17 / 88.2%
Offenses:	violence: * , drugs: * , other: 19
Eligible students, free or reduced lunch:	1.6%
Before / after school program:	No / Yes

Students at this school generally go on to:
Booth, Flat Rock Middle

AJC GRADE: ★★★★

Georgia Criterion-Referenced Competency Tests - Grade 4
Pct. of students at each level

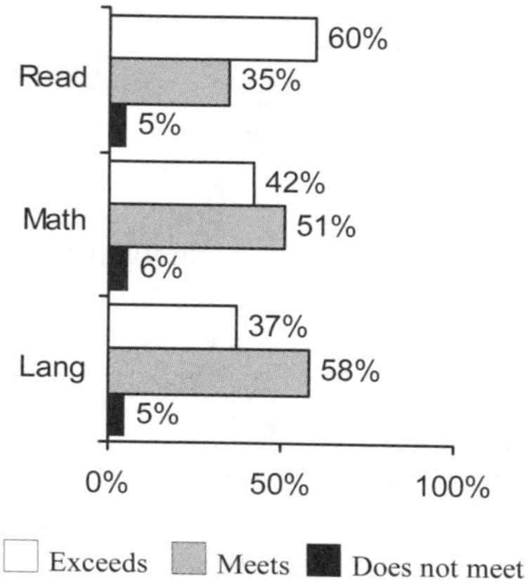
Read
60%
35%
5%
Math
42%
51%
6%
Lang
37%
58%
5%
0%
50%
100%
Exceeds
Meets
Does not meet

North Fayette Elementary School

609 Kenwood Rd, Fayetteville, GA 30214
770-460-3570 · Grades K - 5

Enrollment:	393
White / black / other:	27.7% / 65.1% / 7.1%
Not native English-speaking:	3 / 0.8%
Limited English proficiency:	4 / 1.0%
Student absenteeism:	4.1%
Students per teacher:	10.9
Parent friendliness:	①❷❸④❺❻
Teachers with advanced degrees:	52.8%
Average years' teaching experience:	12.8
Students in gifted program:	13 / 3.3%
Students in remedial education:	25.2%
Students held back a grade:	1.5%
Total suspensions, pct. in-school:	1 / 0.0%
Offenses:	violence: 4, drugs: * , other: 2
Eligible students, free or reduced lunch:	20.6%
Before / after school program:	No / Yes

Students at this school generally go on to:
Flat Rock Middle

AJC GRADE: ★★★

Georgia Criterion-Referenced Competency Tests - Grade 4
Pct. of students at each level

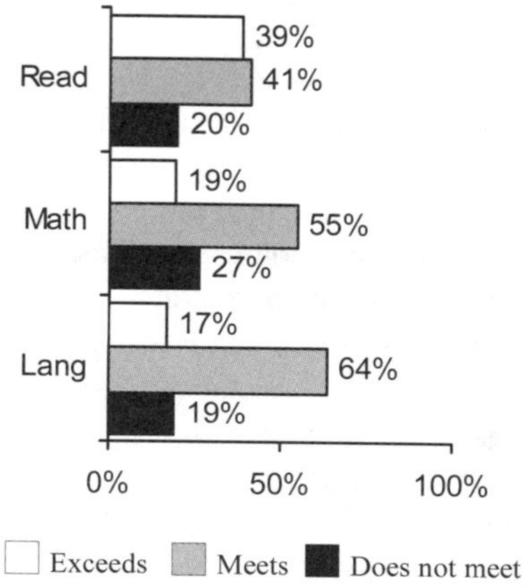
Read
39%
41%
20%
Math
19%
55%
27%
Lang
17%
64%
19%
0%
50%
100%
Exceeds
Meets
Does not meet

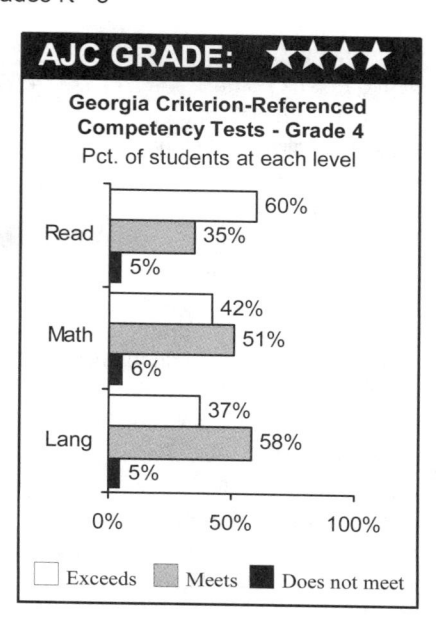

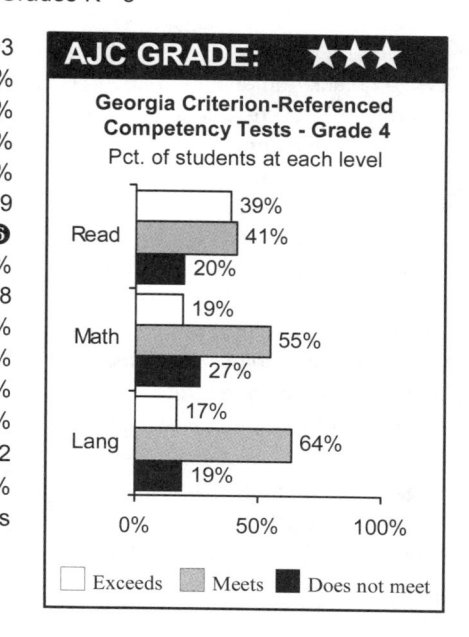

Oak Grove Elementary School

101 Crosstown Rd, Peachtree City, GA 30269
770-631-3260 · Grades K - 5

Enrollment:	627
White / black / other:	70.2% / 14.5% / 15.3%
Not native English-speaking:	43 / 6.9%
Limited English proficiency:	65 / 10.4%
Student absenteeism:	4.3%
Students per teacher:	13.6
Parent friendliness:	① ❷ ❸ ❹ ❺ ❻
Teachers with advanced degrees:	58.7%
Average years' teaching experience:	14.9
Students in gifted program:	47 / 7.5%
Students in remedial education:	17.3%
Students held back a grade:	0.3%
Total suspensions, pct. in-school:	8 / 87.5%
Offenses:	violence: 5, drugs: *, other: 5
Eligible students, free or reduced lunch:	16.9%
Before / after school program:	No / Yes
Students at this school generally go on to:	
Booth, Rising Starr Middle	

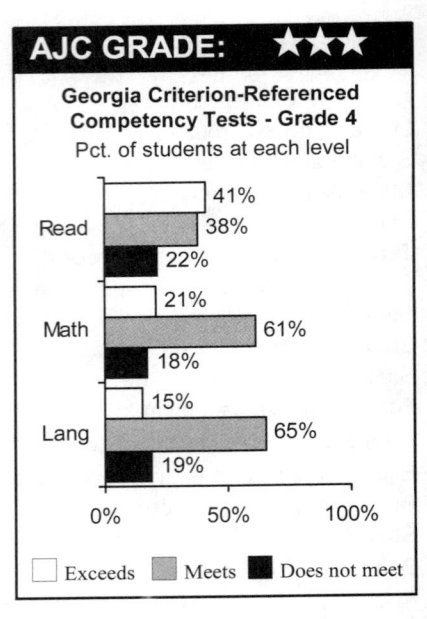

AJC GRADE: ★★★

Georgia Criterion-Referenced Competency Tests - Grade 4
Pct. of students at each level

Read: 41% / 38% / 22%
Math: 21% / 61% / 18%
Lang: 15% / 65% / 19%

☐ Exceeds ▨ Meets ■ Does not meet

Peachtree City Elementary School

201 Wisdom Rd, Peachtree City, GA 30269
770-631-3250 · Grades K - 5

Enrollment:	388
White / black / other:	67.5% / 17.5% / 14.9%
Not native English-speaking:	15 / 3.9%
Limited English proficiency:	21 / 5.4%
Student absenteeism:	4.4%
Students per teacher:	10.8
Parent friendliness:	① ❷ ❸ ❹ ❺ ❻
Teachers with advanced degrees:	54.1%
Average years' teaching experience:	12.8
Students in gifted program:	51 / 13.1%
Students in remedial education:	18.2%
Students held back a grade:	*
Total suspensions, pct. in-school:	41 / 92.7%
Offenses:	violence: 1, drugs: *, other: 45
Eligible students, free or reduced lunch:	18.8%
Before / after school program:	Yes / Yes
Students at this school generally go on to:	
Booth Middle	

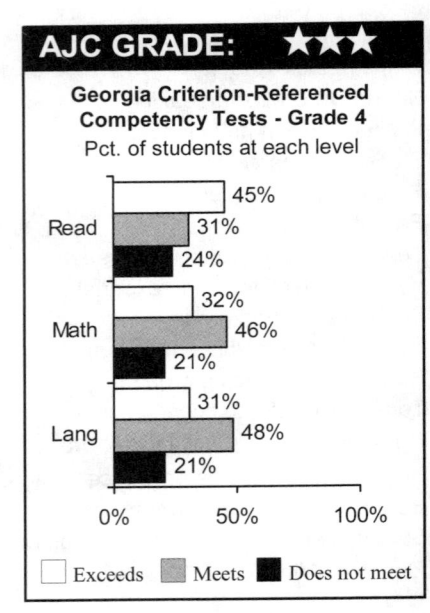

AJC GRADE: ★★★

Georgia Criterion-Referenced Competency Tests - Grade 4
Pct. of students at each level

Read: 45% / 31% / 24%
Math: 32% / 46% / 21%
Lang: 31% / 48% / 21%

☐ Exceeds ▨ Meets ■ Does not meet

The Atlanta Journal-Constitution / Page 296

Fayette County Elementary Schools

Peeples Elementary School

153 Panther Path, Fayetteville, GA 30215
770-486-2734 · Grades K - 5

Enrollment:	593
White / black / other:	90.4% / 5.4% / 4.2%
Not native English-speaking:	4 / 0.7%
Limited English proficiency:	7 / 1.2%
Student absenteeism:	3.8%
Students per teacher:	13.3
Parent friendliness:	❶❷❸④❺❻
Teachers with advanced degrees:	55.6%
Average years' teaching experience:	10.8
Students in gifted program:	58 / 9.8%
Students in remedial education:	6.3%
Students held back a grade:	0.3%
Total suspensions, pct. in-school:	3 / 66.7%
Offenses: violence: 16, drugs: *, other: 2	
Eligible students, free or reduced lunch:	1.1%
Before / after school program:	No / Yes

Students at this school generally go on to:
Rising Starr Middle

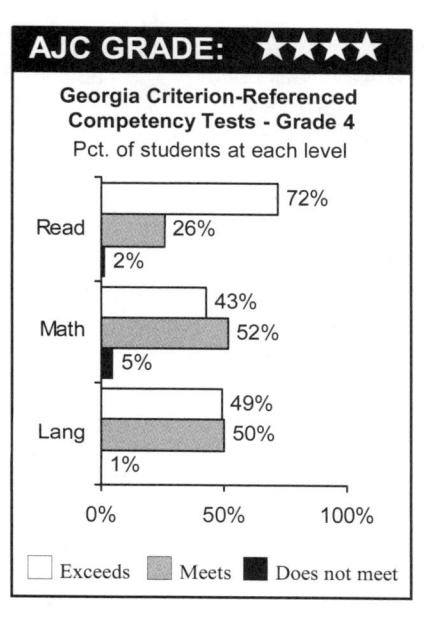

AJC GRADE: ★★★★

Georgia Criterion-Referenced Competency Tests - Grade 4
Pct. of students at each level

- Read: Exceeds 72%, Meets 26%, Does not meet 2%
- Math: Exceeds 43%, Meets 52%, Does not meet 5%
- Lang: Exceeds 49%, Meets 50%, Does not meet 1%

Spring Hill Elementary School

100 Bradford Dr, Fayetteville, GA 30214
770-460-3432 · Grades K - 5

Enrollment:	850
White / black / other:	81.5% / 12.2% / 6.2%
Not native English-speaking:	*
Limited English proficiency:	*
Student absenteeism:	3.7%
Students per teacher:	14.7
Parent friendliness:	①❷❸④❺❻
Teachers with advanced degrees:	57.6%
Average years' teaching experience:	11.7
Students in gifted program:	70 / 8.2%
Students in remedial education:	7.3%
Students held back a grade:	0.1%
Total suspensions, pct. in-school:	32 / 90.6%
Offenses: violence: 4, drugs: *, other: 30	
Eligible students, free or reduced lunch:	4.8%
Before / after school program:	No / Yes

Students at this school generally go on to:
Fayette, Whitewater Middle

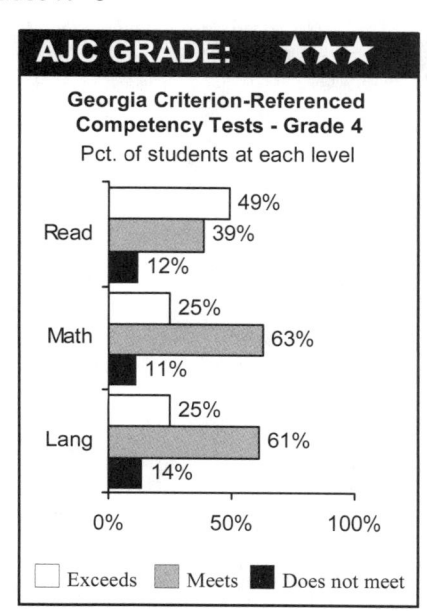

AJC GRADE: ★★★

Georgia Criterion-Referenced Competency Tests - Grade 4
Pct. of students at each level

- Read: Exceeds 49%, Meets 39%, Does not meet 12%
- Math: Exceeds 25%, Meets 63%, Does not meet 11%
- Lang: Exceeds 25%, Meets 61%, Does not meet 14%

Fayette County Elementary Schools

Tyrone Elementary School

876 Senoia Rd, Tyrone, GA 30290
770-631-3265 · Grades K - 5

Enrollment:	375
White / black / other:	92.5% / 3.5% / 4.0%
Not native English-speaking:	4 / 1.1%
Limited English proficiency:	8 / 2.1%
Student absenteeism:	4.4%
Students per teacher:	11.9
Parent friendliness:	① ❷ ❸ ④ ⑤ ❻
Teachers with advanced degrees:	34.4%
Average years' teaching experience:	11.1
Students in gifted program:	24 / 6.4%
Students in remedial education:	21.4%
Students held back a grade:	*
Total suspensions, pct. in-school:	19 / 84.2%
Offenses: violence: 2, drugs: *, other: 30	
Eligible students, free or reduced lunch:	12.1%
Before / after school program:	No / Yes

Students at this school generally go on to:
Flat Rock Middle

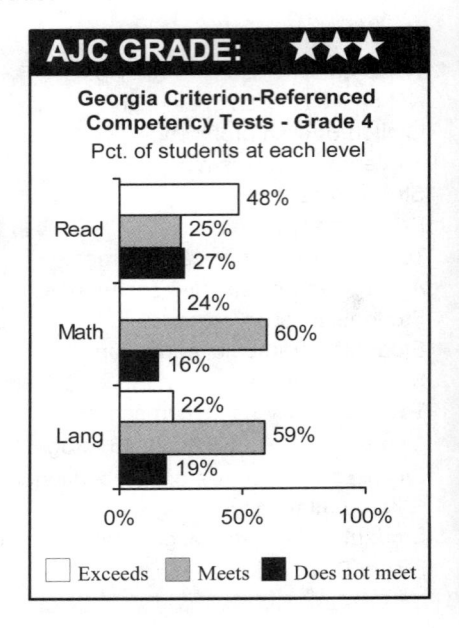

AJC GRADE: ★★★

Georgia Criterion-Referenced Competency Tests - Grade 4
Pct. of students at each level

Read: Exceeds 48%, Meets 25%, Does not meet 27%
Math: Exceeds 24%, Meets 60%, Does not meet 16%
Lang: Exceeds 22%, Meets 59%, Does not meet 19%

Fayette County Elementary Schools

Booth Middle School

250 S Peachtree Pkwy, Peachtree City, GA 30269
770-631-3240 · Grades 6 - 8

Enrollment:	1,049
White / black / other:	81.7% / 9.6% / 8.7%
Not native English-speaking:	23 / 2.2%
Student absenteeism:	3.7%
Students per teacher:	14.1
Parent friendliness:	❶❷❸④⑤❻
Teachers with advanced degrees:	49.3%
Average years' teaching experience:	11.5
Students in gifted program:	310 / 29.6%
Students held back a grade:	0.3%
Total suspensions and expulsions:	340
Suspensions only, pct. in-school:	340 / 97.1%
Offenses: violence: 25, drugs: *, other: 329	
Eligible students, free or reduced lunch:	5.4%
Number of dropouts:	2 / 0.2%
Pct. 8th-graders w/ basic computer skills:	98.0%
Students at this school generally go on to: McIntosh High	

AJC GRADE: ★★★

Georgia Criterion-Referenced Competency Tests - Grades 6, 8
Pct. of students at each level

	Lang 6	Lang 8	Math 6	Math 8	Read 6	Read 8
Exceeds	34	46	42	33	63	72
Meets	53	41	50	51	29	23
Does not meet	13	13	8	16	8	5

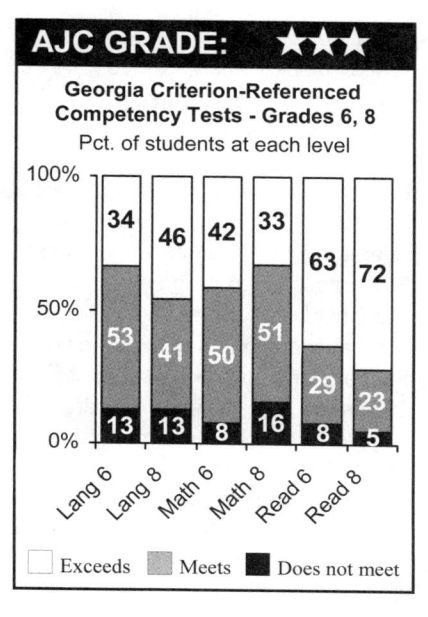

Fayette Middle School

450 Grady Ave, Fayetteville, GA 30214
770-460-3550 · Grades 6 - 8

Enrollment:	938
White / black / other:	72.5% / 21.5% / 6.0%
Not native English-speaking:	4 / 0.4%
Student absenteeism:	4.8%
Students per teacher:	13.4
Parent friendliness:	❶❷❸④⑤❻
Teachers with advanced degrees:	58.6%
Average years' teaching experience:	12.5
Students in gifted program:	176 / 18.8%
Students held back a grade:	1.3%
Total suspensions and expulsions:	378
Suspensions only, pct. in-school:	378 / 93.1%
Offenses: violence: 16, drugs: *, other: 381	
Eligible students, free or reduced lunch:	8.1%
Number of dropouts:	1 / 0.1%
Pct. 8th-graders w/ basic computer skills:	100.0%
Students at this school generally go on to: Fayette County High	

AJC GRADE: ★★★

Georgia Criterion-Referenced Competency Tests - Grades 6, 8
Pct. of students at each level

	Lang 6	Lang 8	Math 6	Math 8	Read 6	Read 8
Exceeds	22	38	34	23	45	71
Meets	55	49	52	62	43	25
Does not meet	23	13	15	15	12	4

Fayette County Middle Schools

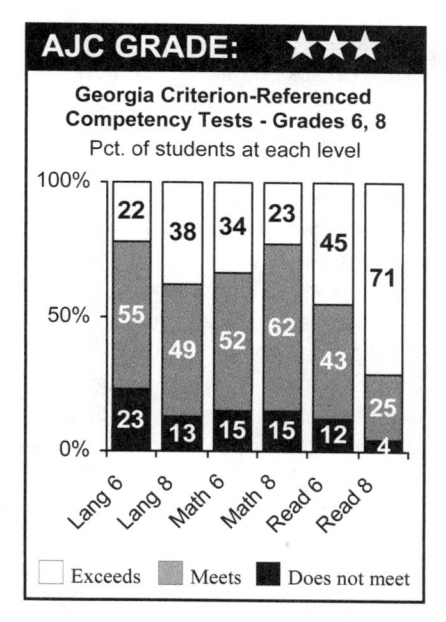

Flat Rock Middle School

325 Jenkins Rd, Tyrone, GA 30290
770-969-2830 · Grades 6 - 8

Enrollment:	929
White / black / other:	63.9% / 30.8% / 5.3%
Not native English-speaking:	4 / 0.4%
Student absenteeism:	4.6%
Students per teacher:	14.1
Parent friendliness:	❶❷❸④⑤❻
Teachers with advanced degrees:	59.1%
Average years' teaching experience:	9.6
Students in gifted program:	178 / 19.2%
Students held back a grade:	1.3%
Total suspensions and expulsions:	906
Suspensions only, pct. in-school:	906 / 85.9%
Offenses:	violence: 47, drugs: 4, other: 913
Eligible students, free or reduced lunch:	14.0%
Number of dropouts:	2 / 0.2%
Pct. 8th-graders w/ basic computer skills:	100.0%

Students at this school generally go on to:
Sandy Creek High

AJC GRADE: ★★★

Georgia Criterion-Referenced Competency Tests - Grades 6, 8
Pct. of students at each level

	Lang 6	Lang 8	Math 6	Math 8	Read 6	Read 8
Exceeds	25	27	28	18	49	64
Meets	54	52	54	59	37	26
Does not meet	21	21	18	24	13	10

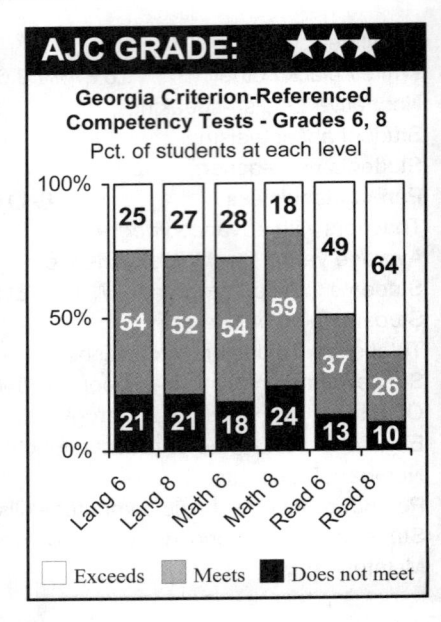

Rising Starr Middle School

183 Panther Path, Fayetteville, GA 30215
770-486-2721 · Grades 6 - 8

Enrollment:	1,112
White / black / other:	87.9% / 7.9% / 4.1%
Not native English-speaking:	14 / 1.3%
Student absenteeism:	4.0%
Students per teacher:	13.7
Parent friendliness:	❶❷❸④⑤❻
Teachers with advanced degrees:	61.0%
Average years' teaching experience:	12.0
Students in gifted program:	385 / 34.6%
Students held back a grade:	1.6%
Total suspensions and expulsions:	253
Suspensions only, pct. in-school:	253 / 91.3%
Offenses:	violence: 17, drugs: 4, other: 234
Eligible students, free or reduced lunch:	4.9%
Number of dropouts:	*
Pct. 8th-graders w/ basic computer skills:	100.0%

Students at this school generally go on to:
Starr's Mill High

AJC GRADE: ★★★★

Georgia Criterion-Referenced Competency Tests - Grades 6, 8
Pct. of students at each level

	Lang 6	Lang 8	Math 6	Math 8	Read 6	Read 8
Exceeds	39	42	52	34	64	75
Meets	51	46	41	56	30	21
Does not meet	10	12	7	11	6	4

Fayette County Middle Schools

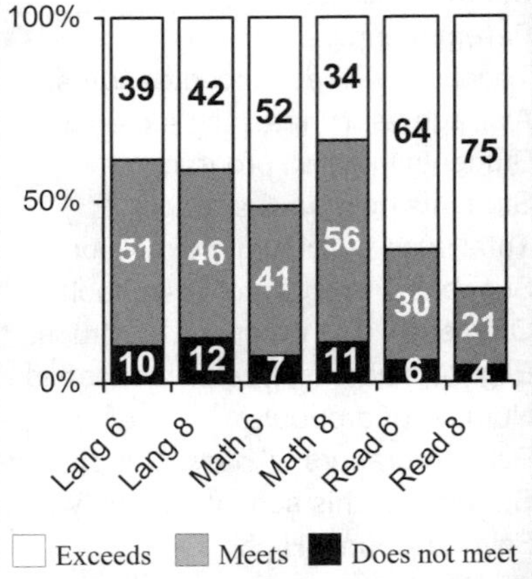

Whitewater Middle School

1533 Highway 85 S, Fayetteville, GA 30215
770-460-3450 · Grades 6 - 8

Enrollment: 903
White / black / other: 83.6% / 12.1% / 4.3%
Not native English-speaking: *
Student absenteeism: 4.2%
Students per teacher: 14.6
Parent friendliness: ❶❷❸④⑤❻
Teachers with advanced degrees: 58.1%
Average years' teaching experience: 13.5
Students in gifted program: 256 / 28.3%
Students held back a grade: 0.3%
Total suspensions and expulsions: 312
Suspensions only, pct. in-school: 312 / 87.8%
Offenses: violence: 21, drugs: 4, other: 318
Eligible students, free or reduced lunch: 5.2%
Number of dropouts: *
Pct. 8th-graders w/ basic computer skills: 82.3%
Students at this school generally go on to:
Fayette County, Starr's Mill High

AJC GRADE: ★★★

Georgia Criterion-Referenced
Competency Tests - Grades 6, 8
Pct. of students at each level

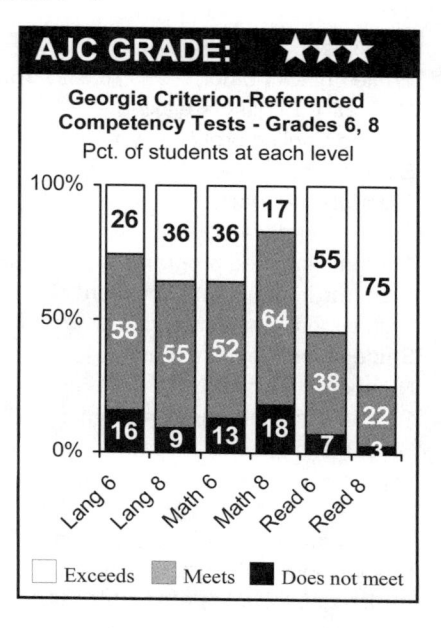

	Lang 6	Lang 8	Math 6	Math 8	Read 6	Read 8
Exceeds	26	36	36	17	55	75
Meets	58	55	52	64	38	22
Does not meet	16	9	13	18	7	3

Fayette County Middle Schools

Fayette County High School

1 Tiger Trl, Fayetteville, GA 30214
770-460-3540 · Grades 9 - 12

Enrollment:	2,042
White / black / other:	78.3% / 16.3% / 5.4%
Not native English-speaking:	10 / 0.5%
Limited English proficiency:	20 / 1.0%
Student absenteeism:	5.0%
Students per teacher:	16.7
Parent friendliness:	① ❷ ❸ ④ ⑤ ❻
Students in gifted program:	330 / 16.2%
Students in remedial education:	0.7%
High school completion rate:	92.8%
Students held back a grade:	7.5%
Number of dropouts:	29 / 1.3%
Students in alternative programs:	35 / 1.7%
Students in special education:	185 / 9.1%
Eligible students, free or reduced lunch:	2.3%
Total suspensions and expulsions:	905
Suspensions only, pct. in-school:	889 / 83.2%
Drugs/alcohol-related offenses:	16
Violence-related offenses:	64
Firearms-related offenses:	10
Vandalism-related offenses:	10
Theft-related offenses:	1
All other disciplinary offenses:	871
Teachers with advanced degrees:	56.9%
Average years' teaching experience:	14.1

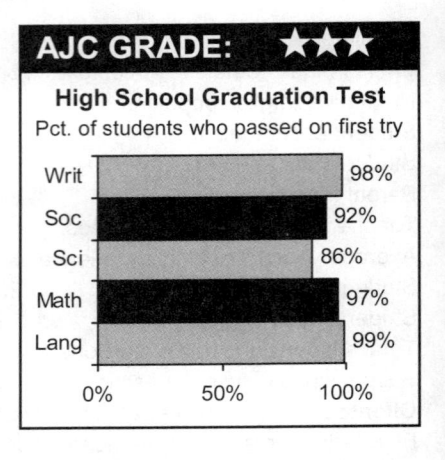

AJC GRADE: ★★★

High School Graduation Test
Pct. of students who passed on first try

- Writ: 98%
- Soc: 92%
- Sci: 86%
- Math: 97%
- Lang: 99%

GHSA classification: 4-AAAAA
Interscholastic sports offered:
BB, BS, CC, CL, FB, GO, SB, SO, SW, TE, TF

Advanced Placement (AP) Exams
Students tested: 119
Tests taken: 222
Pct. of test scores 3 or higher (1 - 5 scale): 67.6%

Languages other than English taught:
French, German, Spanish

2000-2001 high school graduates: 388

College prep/vocational diplomas:	9.0%
College prep endorsement diplomas:	71.6%
Vocational endorsement diplomas:	16.0%
General high school diplomas:	0.0%
Special education diplomas:	0.3%
Certificates of attendance (no diploma):	3.1%

Of the 2000-2001 graduates, 65.7% were eligible for the HOPE scholarship.

Of the 1999-2000 graduates, 210 attended a Georgia public college or university. Of those, 89% met the school's minimum academic requirements.

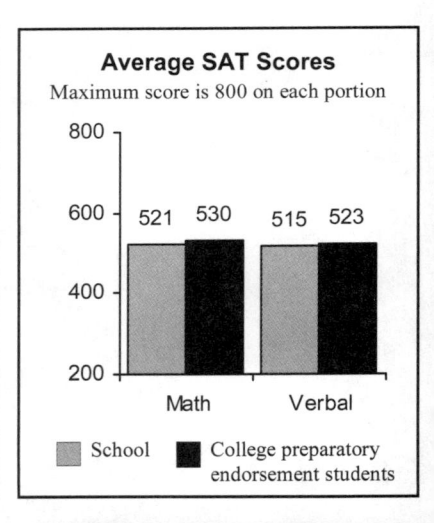

Average SAT Scores
Maximum score is 800 on each portion

- Math — School: 521, College preparatory endorsement students: 530
- Verbal — School: 515, College preparatory endorsement students: 523

The Atlanta Journal-Constitution / Page 302

Fayette County High Schools

McIntosh High School

201 Walt Banks Rd, Peachtree City, GA 30269
770-631-3232 · Grades 9 - 12

Enrollment:	1,464
White / black / other:	83.7% / 7.1% / 9.2%
Not native English-speaking:	28 / 1.9%
Limited English proficiency:	41 / 2.8%
Student absenteeism:	4.5%
Students per teacher:	14.9
Parent friendliness:	①❷❸④⑤❻
Students in gifted program:	300 / 20.5%
Students in remedial education:	0.8%
High school completion rate:	92.2%
Students held back a grade:	4.3%
Number of dropouts:	20 / 1.3%
Students in alternative programs:	8 / 0.5%
Students in special education:	118 / 8.1%
Eligible students, free or reduced lunch:	2.9%
Total suspensions and expulsions:	472
Suspensions only, pct. in-school:	471 / 71.8%
Drugs/alcohol-related offenses:	2
Violence-related offenses:	43
Firearms-related offenses:	4
Vandalism-related offenses:	5
Theft-related offenses:	8
All other disciplinary offenses:	427
Teachers with advanced degrees:	59.6%
Average years' teaching experience:	13.4

AJC GRADE: ★★★★

High School Graduation Test
Pct. of students who passed on first try

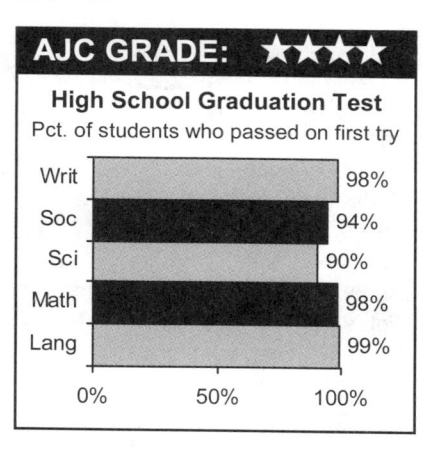

- Writ: 98%
- Soc: 94%
- Sci: 90%
- Math: 98%
- Lang: 99%

GHSA classification:	4-AAAAA

Interscholastic sports offered:
BB, BS, CC, CL, FB, GO, SB, SO, SW, TE, TF, VB, WR

Advanced Placement (AP) Exams
Students tested:	165
Tests taken:	267
Pct. of test scores 3 or higher (1 - 5 scale):	78.3%

Languages other than English taught:
French, German, Spanish

2000-2001 high school graduates: 355

College prep/vocational diplomas:	2.5%
College prep endorsement diplomas:	79.4%
Vocational endorsement diplomas:	17.5%
General high school diplomas:	0.0%
Special education diplomas:	0.6%
Certificates of attendance (no diploma):	0.0%

Of the 2000-2001 graduates, 69.3% were eligible for the HOPE scholarship.

Of the 1999-2000 graduates, 168 attended a Georgia public college or university. Of those, 93% met the school's minimum academic requirements.

Average SAT Scores
Maximum score is 800 on each portion

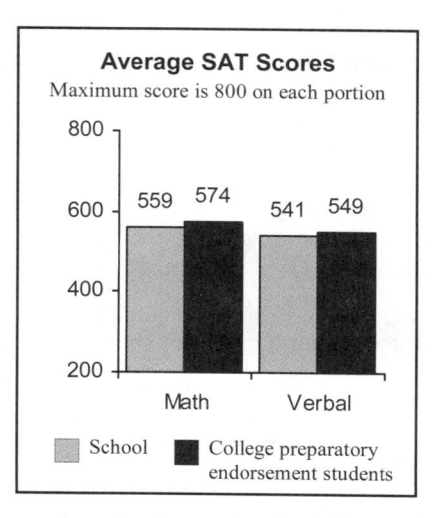

- Math — School: 559, College preparatory endorsement students: 574
- Verbal — School: 541, College preparatory endorsement students: 549

Fayette County High Schools

Sandy Creek High School

360 Jenkins Rd, Tyrone, GA 30290
770-969-2840 · Grades 9 - 12

Enrollment:	1,216
White / black / other:	68.3% / 27.6% / 4.0%
Not native English-speaking:	4 / 0.3%
Limited English proficiency:	7 / 0.6%
Student absenteeism:	4.8%
Students per teacher:	14.0
Parent friendliness:	❶❷❸④⑤❻
Students in gifted program:	197 / 16.2%
Students in remedial education:	0.9%
High school completion rate:	87.0%
Students held back a grade:	5.1%
Number of dropouts:	32 / 2.5%
Students in alternative programs:	21 / 1.7%
Students in special education:	141 / 11.6%
Eligible students, free or reduced lunch:	4.8%
Total suspensions and expulsions:	718
Suspensions only, pct. in-school:	706 / 86.0%
Drugs/alcohol-related offenses:	5
Violence-related offenses:	32
Firearms-related offenses:	2
Vandalism-related offenses:	1
Theft-related offenses:	3
All other disciplinary offenses:	712
Teachers with advanced degrees:	50.6%
Average years' teaching experience:	10.2

AJC GRADE: ★★★

High School Graduation Test
Pct. of students who passed on first try

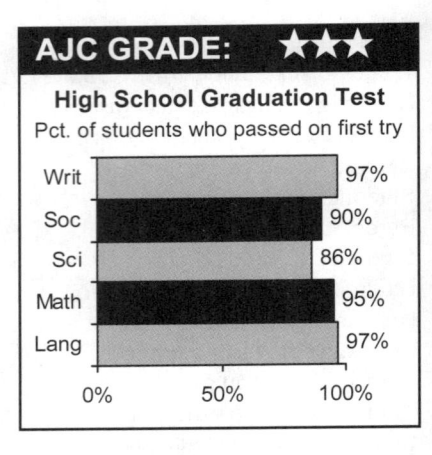

- Writ: 97%
- Soc: 90%
- Sci: 86%
- Math: 95%
- Lang: 97%

GHSA classification: 4-AAAA
Interscholastic sports offered:
BB, BS, CC, CL, FB, GO, SB, SO, SW, TE, TF, VB, WR

Advanced Placement (AP) Exams
Students tested: 138
Tests taken: 218
Pct. of test scores 3 or
higher (1 - 5 scale): 54.1%

Languages other than English taught:
French, German, Spanish

2000-2001 high school graduates: 288

College prep/vocational diplomas:	1.4%
College prep endorsement diplomas:	77.8%
Vocational endorsement diplomas:	20.1%
General high school diplomas:	0.0%
Special education diplomas:	0.7%
Certificates of attendance (no diploma):	0.0%

Of the 2000-2001 graduates, 66.0% were eligible for the HOPE scholarship.

Of the 1999-2000 graduates, 113 attended a Georgia public college or university. Of those, 90% met the school's minimum academic requirements.

Average SAT Scores
Maximum score is 800 on each portion

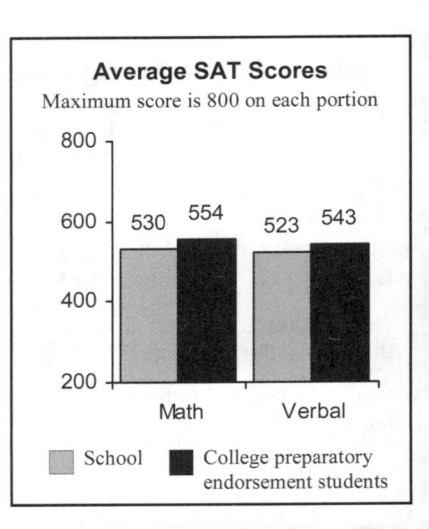

- Math: School 530, College preparatory endorsement students 554
- Verbal: School 523, College preparatory endorsement students 543

The Atlanta Journal-Constitution / Page 304

Fayette County High Schools

Starr's Mill High School

193 Panther Path, Fayetteville, GA 30215
770-486-2710 · Grades 9 - 12

Enrollment:	1,596
White / black / other:	88.2% / 6.1% / 5.8%
Not native English-speaking:	16 / 1.0%
Limited English proficiency:	16 / 1.0%
Student absenteeism:	4.4%
Students per teacher:	15.5
Parent friendliness:	①❷❸④❺❻
Students in gifted program:	389 / 24.4%
Students in remedial education:	0.6%
High school completion rate:	93.2%
Students held back a grade:	3.6%
Number of dropouts:	50 / 3.0%
Students in alternative programs:	5 / 0.3%
Students in special education:	155 / 9.7%
Eligible students, free or reduced lunch:	2.9%
Total suspensions and expulsions:	437
Suspensions only, pct. in-school:	433 / 79.4%
Drugs/alcohol-related offenses:	12
Violence-related offenses:	19
Firearms-related offenses:	1
Vandalism-related offenses:	2
Theft-related offenses:	1
All other disciplinary offenses:	426
Teachers with advanced degrees:	56.4%
Average years' teaching experience:	10.7

AJC GRADE: ★★★★

High School Graduation Test
Pct. of students who passed on first try

Subject	%
Writ	97%
Soc	93%
Sci	85%
Math	98%
Lang	98%

GHSA classification: 4-AAAAA
Interscholastic sports offered:
BB, BS, CC, CL, FB, GO, SB, SO, SW, TE, TF, VB, WR

Advanced Placement (AP) Exams
  Students tested: *
  Tests taken: *
  Pct. of test scores 3 or higher (1 - 5 scale): *

Languages other than English taught:
  French, German, Spanish

2000-2001 high school graduates: 331

College prep/vocational diplomas:	6.3%
College prep endorsement diplomas:	78.5%
Vocational endorsement diplomas:	11.8%
General high school diplomas:	0.0%
Special education diplomas:	0.0%
Certificates of attendance (no diploma):	3.3%

Of the 2000-2001 graduates, 75.5% were eligible for the HOPE scholarship.

Of the 1999-2000 graduates, 102 attended a Georgia public college or university. Of those, 97% met the school's minimum academic requirements.

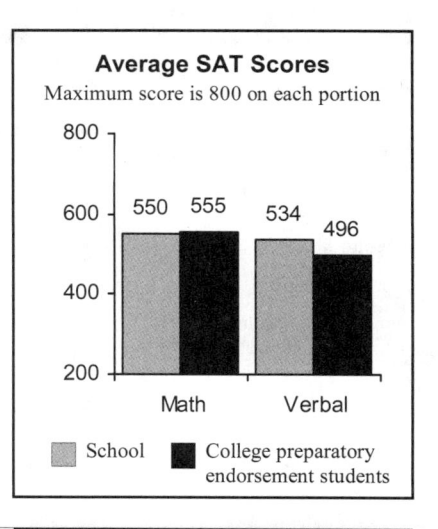

Average SAT Scores
Maximum score is 800 on each portion

	Math	Verbal
School	550	534
College preparatory endorsement students	555	496

The Atlanta Journal-Constitution / Page 305

Fayette County High Schools

AJC ranking of Fayette County Schools

ELEMENTARY SCHOOLS

AJC Star Grade: ★★★★

Braelinn Elementary
Kedron Elementary
Peeples Elementary

AJC Star Grade: ★★★

Burch Elementary
East Fayette Elementary
Huddleston Elementary
North Fayette Elementary
Oak Grove Elementary
Peachtree City Elementary
Spring Hill Elementary
Tyrone Elementary

AJC Star Grade: ★★

Brooks Elementary
Fayetteville Elementary

MIDDLE SCHOOLS

AJC Star Grade: ★★★★

Rising Starr Middle

AJC Star Grade: ★★★

Booth Middle
Fayette Middle
Flat Rock Middle
Whitewater Middle

HIGH SCHOOLS

AJC Star Grade: ★★★★

McIntosh High
Starr's Mill High

AJC Star Grade: ★★★

Fayette County High
Sandy Creek High

Forsyth County Public Schools

1120 Dahlonega Hwy, Cumming, GA 30040
Phone: 770-887-2461 · Fax: 770-781-6632
http://www.forsyth.k12.ga.us

The following pages provide detailed information on every school in the Forsyth County school district. An asterisk (*) means the value of the data was zero or was not reported by the school district. A complete list of schools ranked by The Atlanta Journal-Constitution's star rating system follows the detailed school reports.

District enrollment:	17,061
White / black / other:	93.8% / 0.4% / 5.8%
Not native English-speaking:	376 / 2.2%
Expenditure per student (general fund):	$6,370
Students per teacher:	15.4
Teachers with advanced degrees:	50.4%
Average years, teaching experience:	9.9
Average teacher salary:	$41,076.06
Students in gifted program:	2,120 / 12.4%
Students held back a grade:	423 / 2.5%
Eligible students, free or reduced lunch:	1,935 / 11.3%
Number of dropouts (grades 9-12):	207 / 4.6%
High school completion rate:	77.5%
Graduates, pct. eligible for HOPE scholarships:	667 / 63.7%
Average combined SAT score (maximum 1,600):	1,010
Pct. of 11th-graders passing the Georgia High School Graduation Tests on first try:	74%
Percent of children 5 to 17 years of age living in poverty (2000 Census estimate):	5.7%

Big Creek Elementary School

1994 Peachtree Pkwy, Cumming, GA 30041
770-887-4584 · Grades K - 5

Enrollment:	1,056
White / black / other:	92.0% / 1.5% / 6.5%
Not native English-speaking:	*
Limited English proficiency:	*
Student absenteeism:	2.9%
Students per teacher:	15.8
Parent friendliness:	❶❷❸④⑤❻
Teachers with advanced degrees:	35.8%
Average years' teaching experience:	7.9
Students in gifted program:	145 / 13.7%
Students in remedial education:	3.0%
Students held back a grade:	1.3%
Total suspensions, pct. in-school:	23 / 78.3%
Offenses:	violence: 2, drugs: * , other: 27
Eligible students, free or reduced lunch:	5.5%
Before / after school program:	No / Yes

Students at this school generally go on to:
South Forsyth Middle

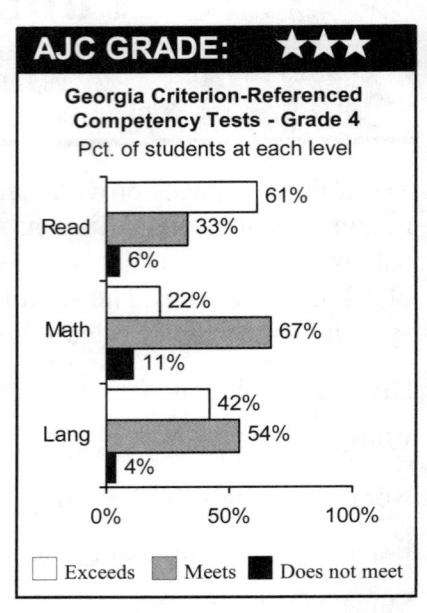

AJC GRADE: ★★★

Georgia Criterion-Referenced Competency Tests - Grade 4
Pct. of students at each level

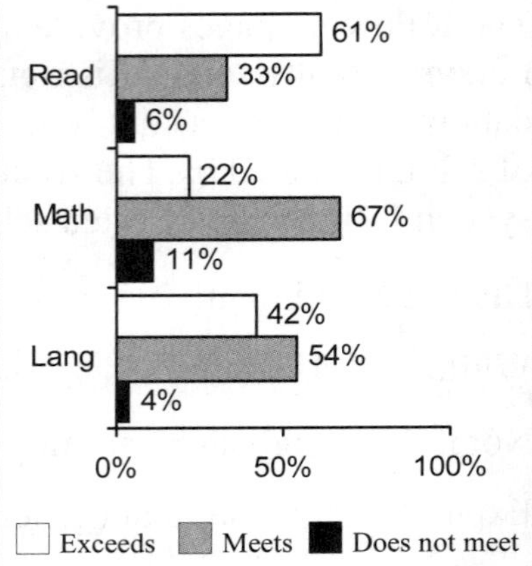
Read
61%
33%
6%
Math
22%
67%
11%
Lang
42%
54%
4%
0%
50%
100%
Exceeds
Meets
Does not meet

Chattahoochee Elementary School

2800 Holtzclaw Rd, Cumming, GA 30041
770-781-2240 · Grades K - 5

Enrollment:	728
White / black / other:	93.7% / 0.3% / 6.0%
Not native English-speaking:	38 / 5.2%
Limited English proficiency:	57 / 7.8%
Student absenteeism:	2.8%
Students per teacher:	15.0
Parent friendliness:	❶❷❸❹❺❻
Teachers with advanced degrees:	40.8%
Average years' teaching experience:	8.0
Students in gifted program:	72 / 9.9%
Students in remedial education:	12.2%
Students held back a grade:	15.4%
Total suspensions, pct. in-school:	3 / 100.0%
Offenses:	violence: * , drugs: * , other: 5
Eligible students, free or reduced lunch:	13.0%
Before / after school program:	Yes / Yes

Students at this school generally go on to:
North Forsyth, Otwell Middle

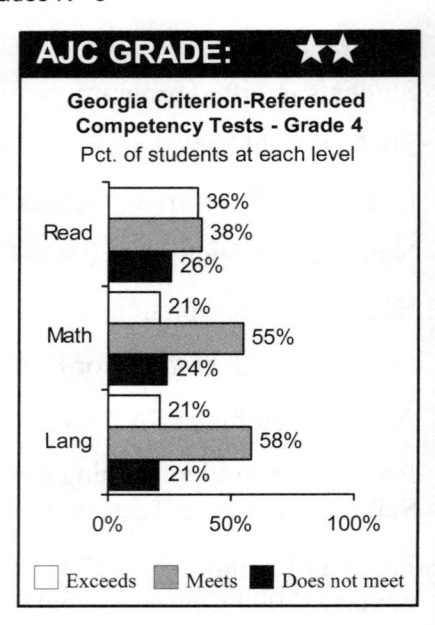

AJC GRADE: ★★

Georgia Criterion-Referenced Competency Tests - Grade 4
Pct. of students at each level

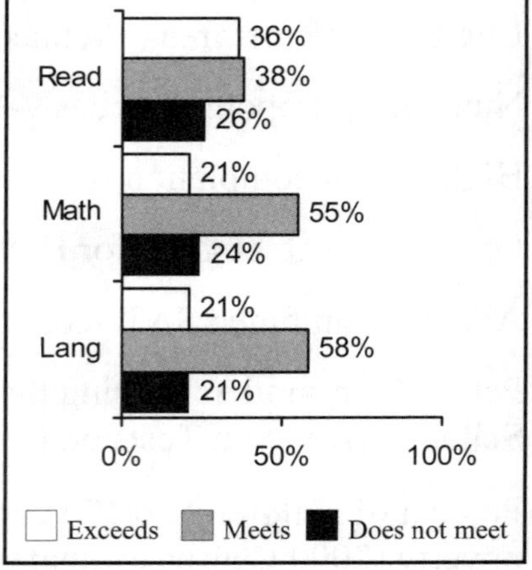
Read
36%
38%
26%
Math
21%
55%
24%
Lang
21%
58%
21%
0%
50%
100%
Exceeds
Meets
Does not meet

Chestatee Elementary School

6945 Keith Bridge Rd, Gainesville, GA 30506
770-887-2341 · Grades 3 - 5

Enrollment:	413
White / black / other:	95.6% / 0.0% / 4.4%
Not native English-speaking:	3 / 0.7%
Limited English proficiency:	6 / 1.5%
Student absenteeism:	3.4%
Students per teacher:	12.7
Parent friendliness:	❶②❸④❺❻
Teachers with advanced degrees:	54.5%
Average years' teaching experience:	10.9
Students in gifted program:	41 / 9.9%
Students in remedial education:	14.9%
Students held back a grade:	3.9%
Total suspensions, pct. in-school:	10 / 0.0%
Offenses: violence: *, drugs: *, other: 10	
Eligible students, free or reduced lunch:	*
Before / after school program:	No / Yes

Students at this school generally go on to:
North Forsyth Middle

AJC GRADE: ★

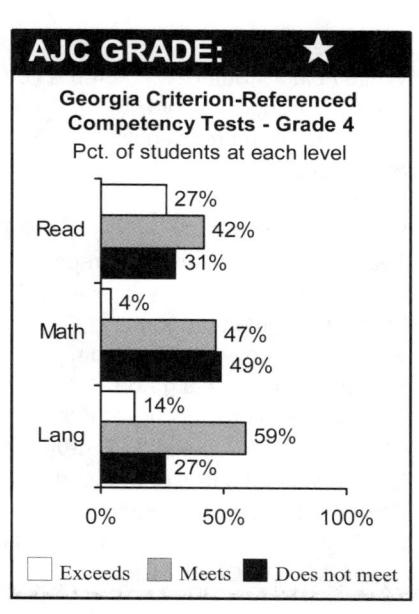

Georgia Criterion-Referenced Competency Tests - Grade 4
Pct. of students at each level

- Read: Exceeds 27%, Meets 42%, Does not meet 31%
- Math: Exceeds 4%, Meets 47%, Does not meet 49%
- Lang: Exceeds 14%, Meets 59%, Does not meet 27%

Coal Mountain Elementary School

3455 Coal Mountain Dr, Cumming, GA 30040
770-887-7705 · Grades K - 5

Enrollment:	849
White / black / other:	99.4% / 0.2% / 0.4%
Not native English-speaking:	*
Limited English proficiency:	*
Student absenteeism:	3.2%
Students per teacher:	16.6
Parent friendliness:	❶❷❸④❺❻
Teachers with advanced degrees:	62.7%
Average years' teaching experience:	11.3
Students in gifted program:	37 / 4.4%
Students in remedial education:	12.5%
Students held back a grade:	2.5%
Total suspensions, pct. in-school:	4 / 0.0%
Offenses: violence: *, drugs: *, other: 36	
Eligible students, free or reduced lunch:	9.6%
Before / after school program:	No / Yes

Students at this school generally go on to:
Liberty, North Forsyth Middle

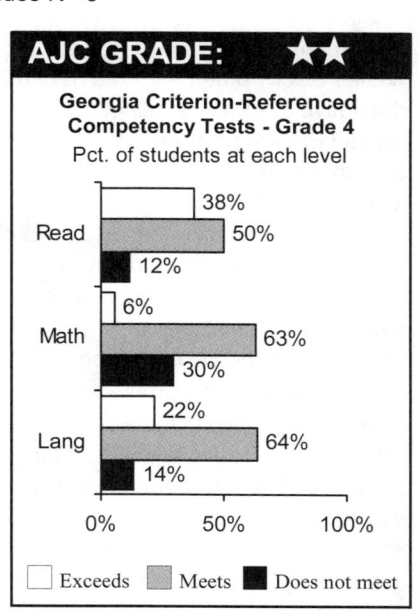

AJC GRADE: ★★

Georgia Criterion-Referenced Competency Tests - Grade 4
Pct. of students at each level

- Read: Exceeds 38%, Meets 50%, Does not meet 12%
- Math: Exceeds 6%, Meets 63%, Does not meet 30%
- Lang: Exceeds 22%, Meets 64%, Does not meet 14%

Forsyth County Elementary Schools

Cumming Elementary School

540 Dahlonega St, Cumming, GA 30040
770-887-7749 · Grades K - 5

Enrollment:	716
White / black / other:	84.9% / 0.0% / 15.1%
Not native English-speaking:	74 / 10.3%
Limited English proficiency:	90 / 12.6%
Student absenteeism:	3.4%
Students per teacher:	12.8
Parent friendliness:	❶❷❸④⑤❻
Teachers with advanced degrees:	51.8%
Average years' teaching experience:	10.5
Students in gifted program:	39 / 5.4%
Students in remedial education:	19.2%
Students held back a grade:	1.8%
Total suspensions, pct. in-school:	22 / 63.6%
Offenses:	violence: 7, drugs: * , other: 22
Eligible students, free or reduced lunch:	31.6%
Before / after school program:	No / Yes

Students at this school generally go on to:
Otwell, Vickery Creek Middle

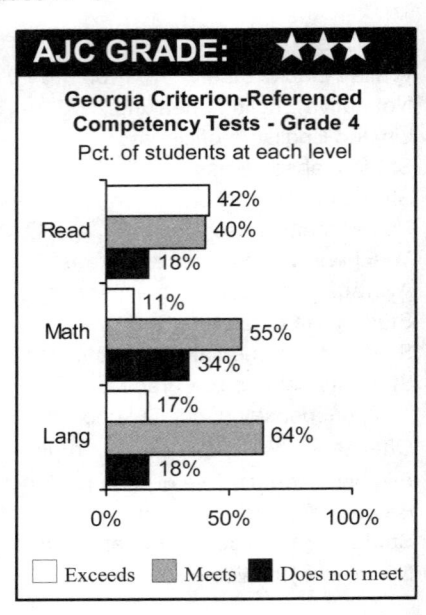

AJC GRADE: ★★★

Georgia Criterion-Referenced Competency Tests - Grade 4
Pct. of students at each level

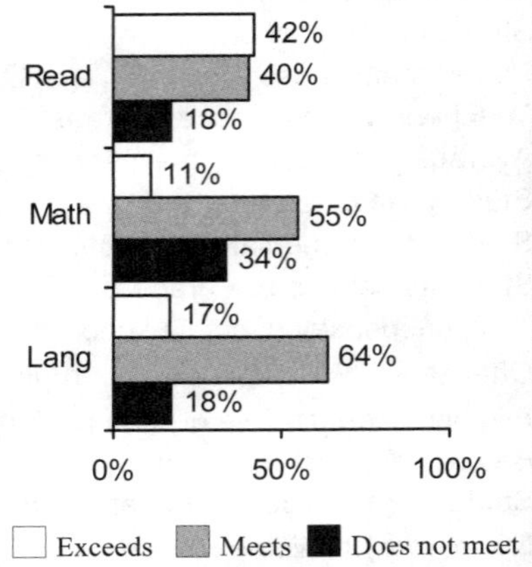
Read
42%
40%
18%
Math
11%
55%
34%
Lang
17%
64%
18%
0%
50%
100%
Exceeds
Meets
Does not meet

Daves Creek Elementary School

3740 Trammel Rd, Cumming, GA 30041
770-888-1222 · Grades K - 5

Enrollment:	891
White / black / other:	83.8% / 0.3% / 15.8%
Not native English-speaking:	59 / 6.6%
Limited English proficiency:	98 / 11.0%
Student absenteeism:	3.0%
Students per teacher:	15.4
Parent friendliness:	❶❷❸④❺❻
Teachers with advanced degrees:	44.1%
Average years' teaching experience:	8.8
Students in gifted program:	37 / 4.2%
Students in remedial education:	15.3%
Students held back a grade:	1.2%
Total suspensions, pct. in-school:	*
Offenses:	violence: * , drugs: * , other: *
Eligible students, free or reduced lunch:	16.7%
Before / after school program:	Yes / Yes

Students at this school generally go on to:
South Forsyth Middle

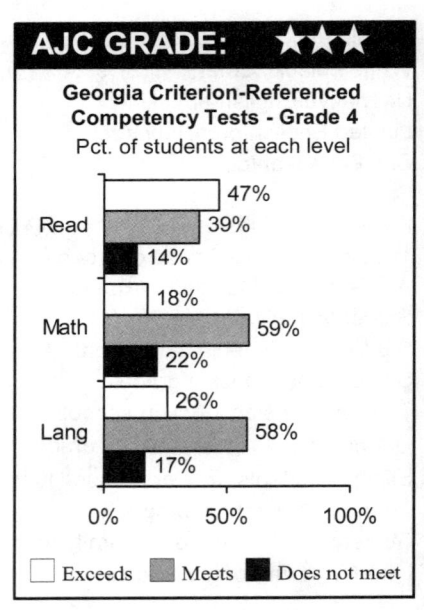

AJC GRADE: ★★★

Georgia Criterion-Referenced Competency Tests - Grade 4
Pct. of students at each level

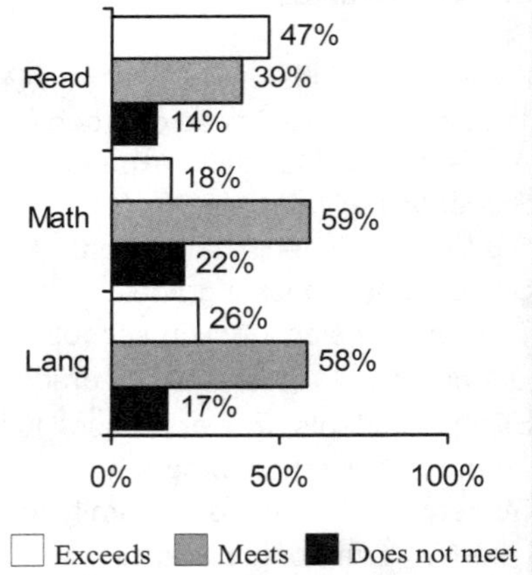
Read
47%
39%
14%
Math
18%
59%
22%
Lang
26%
58%
17%
0%
50%
100%
Exceeds
Meets
Does not meet

Mashburn Elementary School

3777 Samples Rd, Cumming, GA 30041
770-889-1630 · Grades K - 5

Enrollment:	697
White / black / other:	97.7% / 0.7% / 1.6%
Not native English-speaking:	*
Limited English proficiency:	1 / 0.1%
Student absenteeism:	3.3%
Students per teacher:	16.6
Parent friendliness:	❶❷❸❹❺❻
Teachers with advanced degrees:	31.0%
Average years' teaching experience:	5.6
Students in gifted program:	68 / 9.8%
Students in remedial education:	10.3%
Students held back a grade:	0.6%
Total suspensions, pct. in-school:	2 / 0.0%
Offenses: violence: *, drugs: *, other: 2	
Eligible students, free or reduced lunch:	4.6%
Before / after school program:	No / Yes

Students at this school generally go on to:
Otwell Middle

AJC GRADE: ★★★

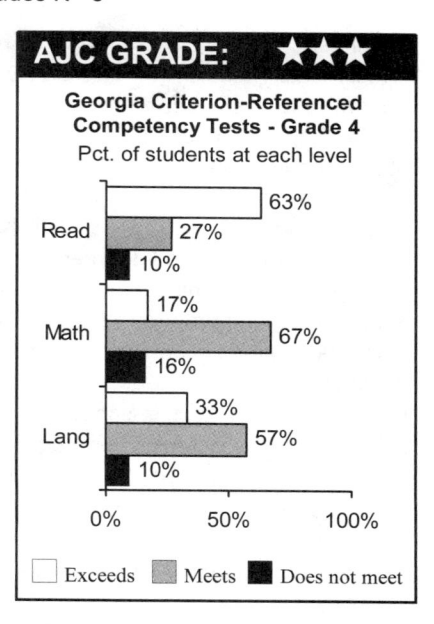

Georgia Criterion-Referenced Competency Tests - Grade 4
Pct. of students at each level

- Read: Exceeds 63%, Meets 27%, Does not meet 10%
- Math: Exceeds 17%, Meets 67%, Does not meet 16%
- Lang: Exceeds 33%, Meets 57%, Does not meet 10%

☐ Exceeds ▨ Meets ■ Does not meet

Midway Elementary School

4805 Highway 9 N, Alpharetta, GA 30004
770-475-6670 · Grades K - 5

Enrollment:	577
White / black / other:	76.1% / 0.9% / 23.1%
Not native English-speaking:	58 / 10.1%
Limited English proficiency:	101 / 17.5%
Student absenteeism:	3.0%
Students per teacher:	13.9
Parent friendliness:	❶❷❸❹❺❻
Teachers with advanced degrees:	61.9%
Average years' teaching experience:	11.6
Students in gifted program:	39 / 6.8%
Students in remedial education:	17.2%
Students held back a grade:	0.5%
Total suspensions, pct. in-school:	*
Offenses: violence: *, drugs: *, other: *	
Eligible students, free or reduced lunch:	30.5%
Before / after school program:	No / Yes

Students at this school generally go on to:
Vickery Creek Middle

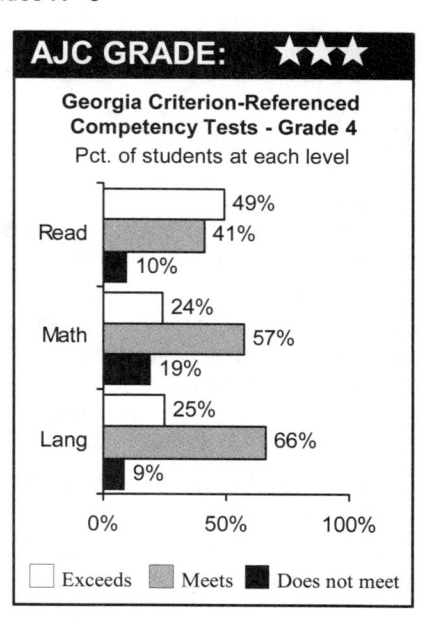

AJC GRADE: ★★★

Georgia Criterion-Referenced Competency Tests - Grade 4
Pct. of students at each level

- Read: Exceeds 49%, Meets 41%, Does not meet 10%
- Math: Exceeds 24%, Meets 57%, Does not meet 19%
- Lang: Exceeds 25%, Meets 66%, Does not meet 9%

☐ Exceeds ▨ Meets ■ Does not meet

Forsyth County Elementary Schools

Sawnee Elementary School

1616 Canton Hwy, Cumming, GA 30040
770-887-6161 · Grades 3 - 5

Enrollment:	569
White / black / other:	96.3% / 0.2% / 3.5%
Not native English-speaking:	*
Limited English proficiency:	*
Student absenteeism:	3.2%
Students per teacher:	14.4
Parent friendliness:	❶❷❸❹❺❻
Teachers with advanced degrees:	65.0%
Average years' teaching experience:	12.1
Students in gifted program:	76 / 13.4%
Students in remedial education:	17.9%
Students held back a grade:	1.1%
Total suspensions, pct. in-school:	57 / 96.5%
Offenses:	violence: 35, drugs: 1, other: 22
Eligible students, free or reduced lunch:	14.1%
Before / after school program:	No / Yes

Students at this school generally go on to:
Liberty, Vickery Creek Middle

AJC GRADE: ★★★

Georgia Criterion-Referenced Competency Tests - Grade 4
Pct. of students at each level

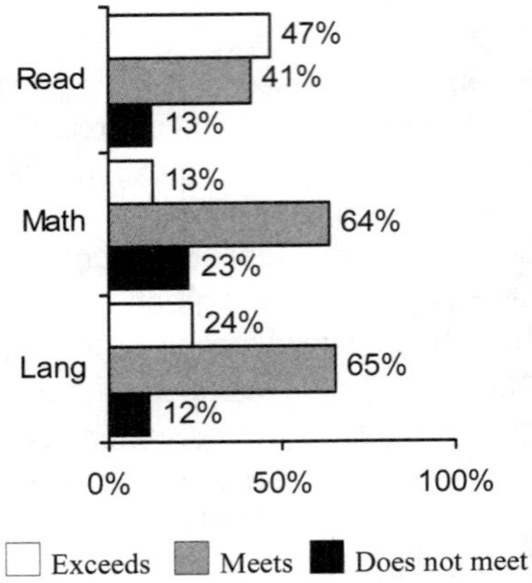
Read
47%
41%
13%
Math
13%
64%
23%
Lang
24%
65%
12%
0%
50%
100%
Exceeds
Meets
Does not meet

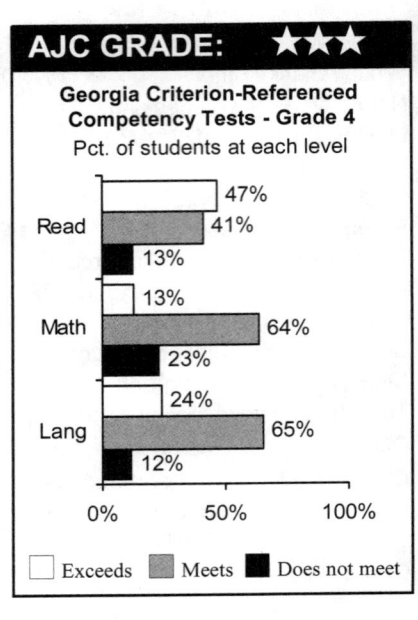

Settles Bridge Elementary School 👍

600 James Burgess Rd, Suwanee, GA 30024
770-887-1883 · Grades K - 5

Enrollment:	734
White / black / other:	98.0% / 0.0% / 2.0%
Not native English-speaking:	*
Limited English proficiency:	*
Student absenteeism:	3.0%
Students per teacher:	16.3
Parent friendliness:	❶❷❸④⑤❻
Teachers with advanced degrees:	44.4%
Average years' teaching experience:	8.1
Students in gifted program:	100 / 13.6%
Students in remedial education:	6.0%
Students held back a grade:	1.2%
Total suspensions, pct. in-school:	2 / 0.0%
Offenses:	violence: * , drugs: * , other: 14
Eligible students, free or reduced lunch:	1.9%
Before / after school program:	Yes / Yes

Students at this school generally go on to:
South Forsyth Middle

AJC GRADE: ★★★★

Georgia Criterion-Referenced Competency Tests - Grade 4
Pct. of students at each level

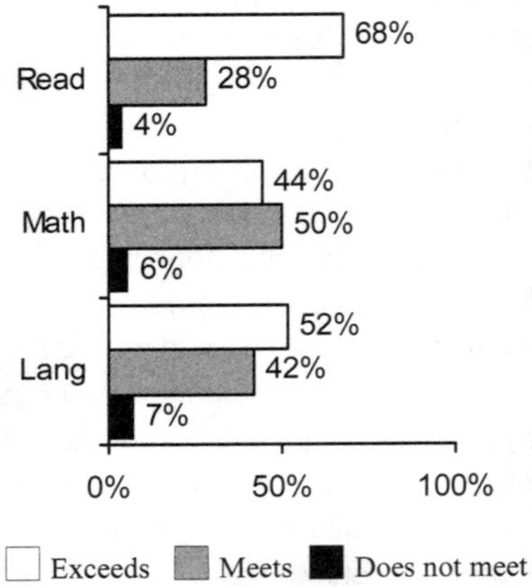
Read
68%
28%
4%
Math
44%
50%
6%
Lang
52%
42%
7%
0%
50%
100%
Exceeds
Meets
Does not meet

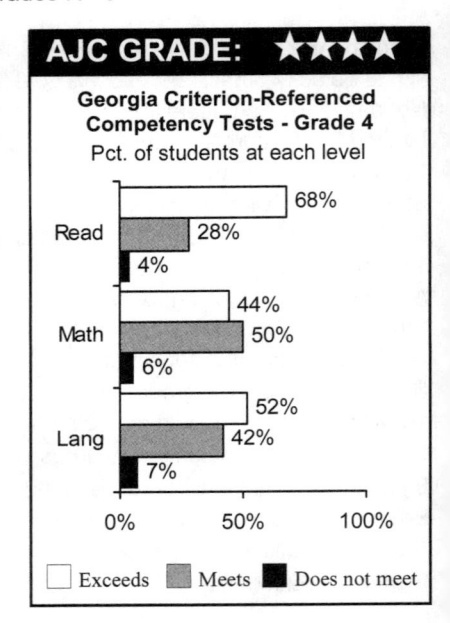

Vickery Creek Elementary School

6280 Post Rd, Cumming, GA 30040
770-346-0040 · Grades K - 5

Enrollment:	897
White / black / other:	97.9% / 0.2% / 1.9%
Not native English-speaking:	*
Limited English proficiency:	1 / 0.1%
Student absenteeism:	2.9%
Students per teacher:	14.7
Parent friendliness:	❶❷❸④❺❻
Teachers with advanced degrees:	45.9%
Average years' teaching experience:	8.3
Students in gifted program:	104 / 11.6%
Students in remedial education:	2.5%
Students held back a grade:	1.8%
Total suspensions, pct. in-school:	1 / 0.0%
Offenses:	violence: * , drugs: * , other: 2
Eligible students, free or reduced lunch:	3.8%
Before / after school program:	Yes / Yes

Students at this school generally go on to:
Vickery Creek Middle

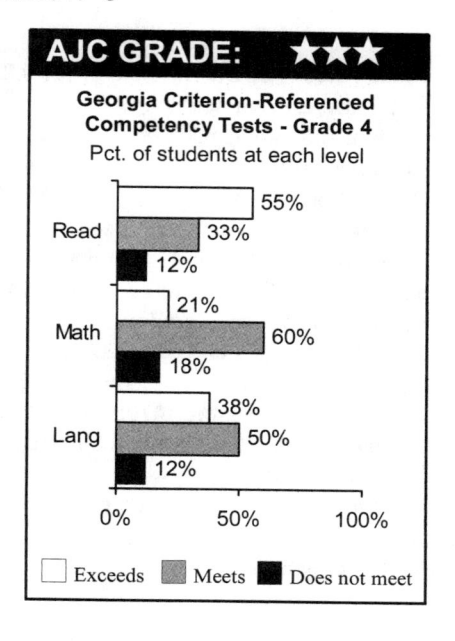

AJC GRADE: ★★★

Georgia Criterion-Referenced Competency Tests - Grade 4
Pct. of students at each level

Read: 55% Exceeds / 33% Meets / 12% Does not meet
Math: 21% Exceeds / 60% Meets / 18% Does not meet
Lang: 38% Exceeds / 50% Meets / 12% Does not meet

Forsyth County Elementary Schools

North Forsyth Middle School

3645 Coal Mountain Dr, Cumming, GA 30040
770-889-0743 · Grades 6 - 8

Enrollment:	1,139
White / black / other:	97.9% / 0.2% / 1.9%
Not native English-speaking:	*
Student absenteeism:	4.1%
Students per teacher:	16.6
Parent friendliness:	❶❷❸④⑤❻
Teachers with advanced degrees:	61.4%
Average years' teaching experience:	10.9
Students in gifted program:	145 / 12.7%
Students held back a grade:	1.4%
Total suspensions and expulsions:	632
Suspensions only, pct. in-school:	630 / 84.8%
Offenses:	violence: 147, drugs: 11, other: 555
Eligible students, free or reduced lunch:	15.5%
Number of dropouts:	*
Pct. 8th-graders w/ basic computer skills:	100.0%
Students at this school generally go on to: North Forsyth High	

AJC GRADE: ★★★

Georgia Criterion-Referenced Competency Tests - Grades 6, 8
Pct. of students at each level

	Lang 6	Lang 8	Math 6	Math 8	Read 6	Read 8
Exceeds	21	23	25	9	47	60
Meets	56	56	57	55	37	28
Does not meet	23	22	18	36	15	13

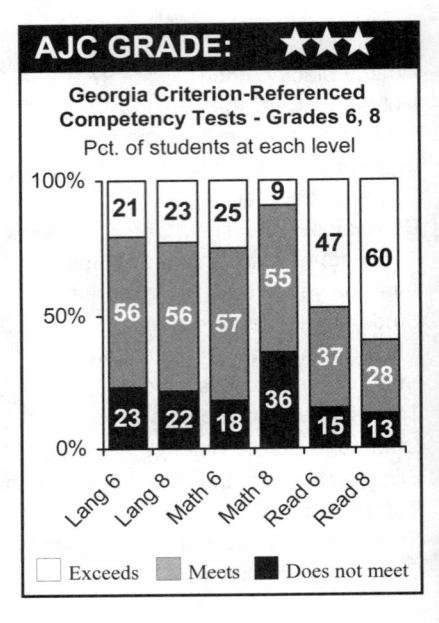

Otwell Middle School

605 Tribble Gap Rd, Cumming, GA 30040
770-887-5248 · Grades 6 - 8

Enrollment:	846
White / black / other:	92.2% / 0.0% / 7.8%
Not native English-speaking:	31 / 3.7%
Student absenteeism:	3.7%
Students per teacher:	15.7
Parent friendliness:	❶❷❸④⑤❻
Teachers with advanced degrees:	51.9%
Average years' teaching experience:	9.0
Students in gifted program:	138 / 16.3%
Students held back a grade:	1.5%
Total suspensions and expulsions:	453
Suspensions only, pct. in-school:	453 / 92.9%
Offenses:	violence: 76, drugs: 3, other: 391
Eligible students, free or reduced lunch:	15.2%
Number of dropouts:	*
Pct. 8th-graders w/ basic computer skills:	99.0%
Students at this school generally go on to: Forsyth Central High	

AJC GRADE: ★★★

Georgia Criterion-Referenced Competency Tests - Grades 6, 8
Pct. of students at each level

	Lang 6	Lang 8	Math 6	Math 8	Read 6	Read 8
Exceeds	31	31	26	11	53	64
Meets	49	47	51	53	36	26
Does not meet	20	22	23	36	10	10

Forsyth County Middle Schools

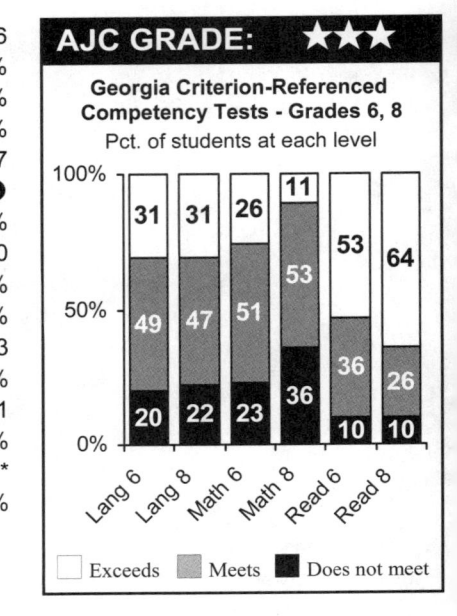

South Forsyth Middle School

2865 Old Atlanta Rd, Cumming, GA 30041
770-888-3170 · Grades 6 - 8

Enrollment:	996
White / black / other:	94.1% / 0.9% / 5.0%
Not native English-speaking:	*
Student absenteeism:	3.1%
Students per teacher:	17.2
Parent friendliness:	❶❷❸④❺❻
Teachers with advanced degrees:	50.0%
Average years' teaching experience:	8.2
Students in gifted program:	259 / 26.0%
Students held back a grade:	*
Total suspensions and expulsions:	198
Suspensions only, pct. in-school:	198 / 94.9%
Offenses:	violence: 35, drugs: 1, other: 214
Eligible students, free or reduced lunch:	5.2%
Number of dropouts:	*
Pct. 8th-graders w/ basic computer skills:	100.0%

Students at this school generally go on to:
South Forsyth High

AJC GRADE: ★★★

Georgia Criterion-Referenced Competency Tests - Grades 6, 8
Pct. of students at each level

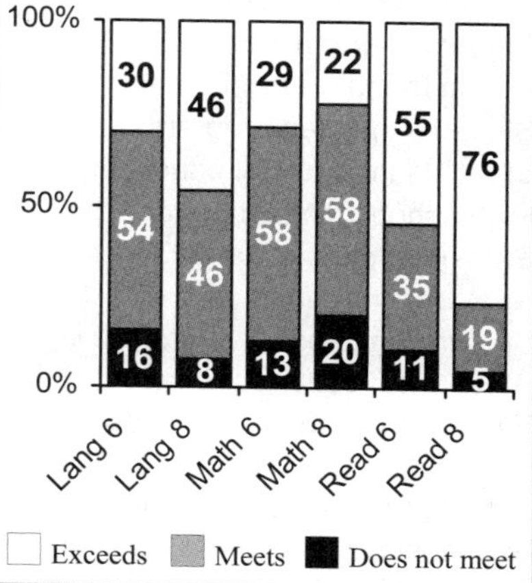
100%
50%
0%
30
54
16
46
46
8
29
58
13
22
58
20
55
35
11
76
19
5
Lang 6
Lang 8
Math 6
Math 8
Read 6
Read 8
Exceeds
Meets
Does not meet

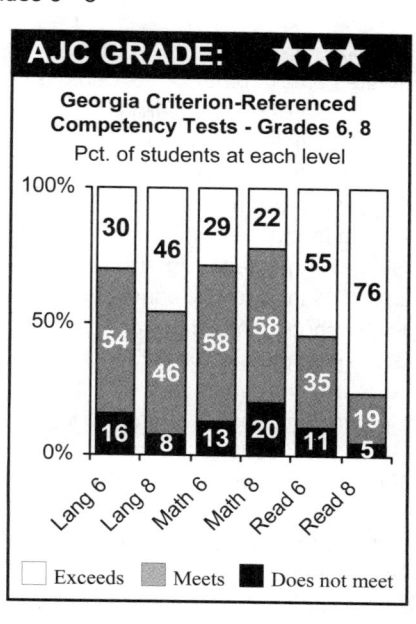

Vickery Creek Middle School

6240 Post Rd, Cumming, GA 30040
770-667-2580 · Grades 6 - 8

Enrollment:	1,039
White / black / other:	92.3% / 0.5% / 7.2%
Not native English-speaking:	33 / 3.2%
Student absenteeism:	3.6%
Students per teacher:	16.0
Parent friendliness:	❶②③④⑤⑥
Teachers with advanced degrees:	41.5%
Average years' teaching experience:	8.3
Students in gifted program:	160 / 15.4%
Students held back a grade:	1.3%
Total suspensions and expulsions:	317
Suspensions only, pct. in-school:	316 / 78.8%
Offenses:	violence: 24, drugs: 2, other: 318
Eligible students, free or reduced lunch:	12.0%
Number of dropouts:	*
Pct. 8th-graders w/ basic computer skills:	100.0%

Students at this school generally go on to:
Forsyth Central, South Forsyth High

AJC GRADE: ★★★

Georgia Criterion-Referenced Competency Tests - Grades 6, 8
Pct. of students at each level

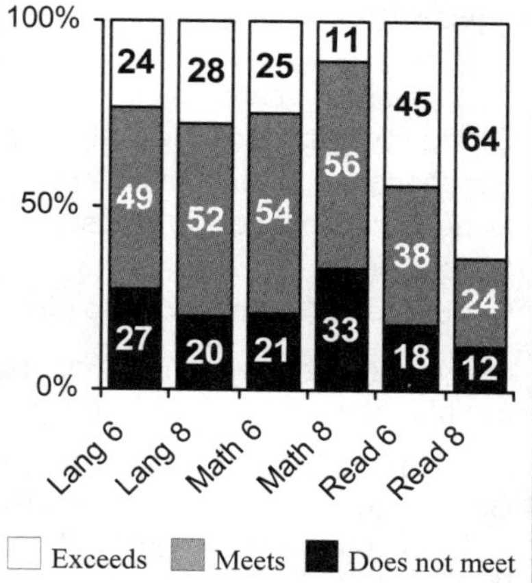
100%
50%
0%
24
49
27
28
52
20
25
54
21
11
56
33
45
38
18
64
24
12
Lang 6
Lang 8
Math 6
Math 8
Read 6
Read 8
Exceeds
Meets
Does not meet

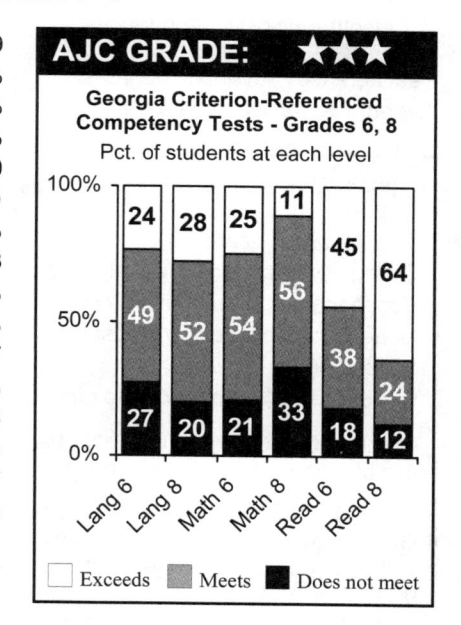

Forsyth Central High School

520 Tribble Gap Rd, Cumming, GA 30040
770-887-8151 · Grades 9 - 12

Enrollment:	1,218
White / black / other:	95.6% / 0.0% / 4.4%
Not native English-speaking:	34 / 2.8%
Limited English proficiency:	62 / 5.1%
Student absenteeism:	4.6%
Students per teacher:	16.5
Parent friendliness:	❶❷❸❹❺❻
Students in gifted program:	266 / 21.8%
Students in remedial education:	3.0%
High school completion rate:	79.6%
Students held back a grade:	7.9%
Number of dropouts:	69 / 4.9%
Students in alternative programs:	*
Students in special education:	96 / 7.9%
Eligible students, free or reduced lunch:	6.2%
Total suspensions and expulsions:	696
Suspensions only, pct. in-school:	694 / 87.0%
Drugs/alcohol-related offenses:	19
Violence-related offenses:	25
Firearms-related offenses:	1
Vandalism-related offenses:	2
Theft-related offenses:	5
All other disciplinary offenses:	661
Teachers with advanced degrees:	50.0%
Average years' teaching experience:	12.3

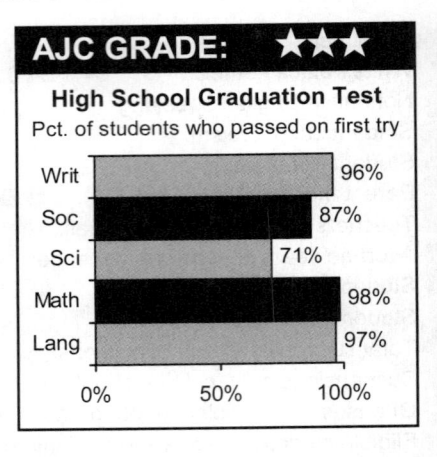

AJC GRADE: ★★★

High School Graduation Test
Pct. of students who passed on first try

- Writ: 96%
- Soc: 87%
- Sci: 71%
- Math: 98%
- Lang: 97%

GHSA classification:	6-AAAA
Interscholastic sports offered:	
BB, BS, CC, CL, FB, GO, SO, TE, TF, WR	

Advanced Placement (AP) Exams
Students tested:	85
Tests taken:	105
Pct. of test scores 3 or higher (1 - 5 scale):	32.4%

Languages other than English taught:
French, German, Latin, Spanish

2000-2001 high school graduates: 203

College prep/vocational diplomas:	39.9%
College prep endorsement diplomas:	45.8%
Vocational endorsement diplomas:	12.8%
General high school diplomas:	0.0%
Special education diplomas:	0.5%
Certificates of attendance (no diploma):	1.0%

Of the 2000-2001 graduates, 72.4% were eligible for the HOPE scholarship.

Of the 1999-2000 graduates, 83 attended a Georgia public college or university. Of those, 74% met the school's minimum academic requirements.

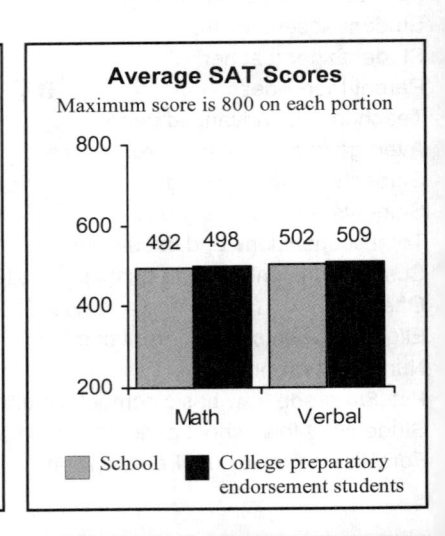

Average SAT Scores
Maximum score is 800 on each portion

- Math — School: 492, College preparatory endorsement students: 498
- Verbal — School: 502, College preparatory endorsement students: 509

Forsyth County High Schools

North Forsyth High School

3635 Coal Mountain Dr, Cumming, GA 30040
770-781-6637 · Grades 9 - 12

Enrollment:	1,286
White / black / other:	98.1% / 0.2% / 1.7%
Not native English-speaking:	*
Limited English proficiency:	*
Student absenteeism:	1.2%
Students per teacher:	15.9
Parent friendliness:	❶❷❸④⑤❻
Students in gifted program:	131 / 10.2%
Students in remedial education:	1.6%
High school completion rate:	77.0%
Students held back a grade:	0.1%
Number of dropouts:	86 / 6.0%
Students in alternative programs:	*
Students in special education:	115 / 8.9%
Eligible students, free or reduced lunch:	7.0%
Total suspensions and expulsions:	920
Suspensions only, pct. in-school:	920 / 96.4%
Drugs/alcohol-related offenses:	7
Violence-related offenses:	40
Firearms-related offenses:	2
Vandalism-related offenses:	2
Theft-related offenses:	1
All other disciplinary offenses:	926
Teachers with advanced degrees:	59.3%
Average years' teaching experience:	11.6

AJC GRADE: ★★★

High School Graduation Test
Pct. of students who passed on first try

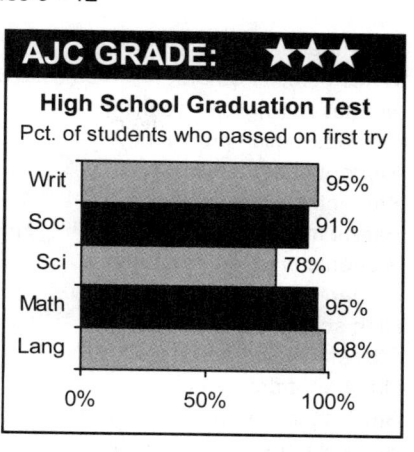

- Writ: 95%
- Soc: 91%
- Sci: 78%
- Math: 95%
- Lang: 98%

GHSA classification: 6-AAAA
Interscholastic sports offered:
  BB, BS, CC, CL, FB, GO, RI, SB,
  SO, SW, TE, TF, WR

Advanced Placement (AP) Exams
  Students tested: 55
  Tests taken: 95
  Pct. of test scores 3 or
  higher (1 - 5 scale): 45.3%

Languages other than English taught:
  French, German, Spanish

2000-2001 high school graduates: 217

College prep/vocational diplomas:	34.6%
College prep endorsement diplomas:	44.2%
Vocational endorsement diplomas:	17.5%
General high school diplomas:	0.0%
Special education diplomas:	1.8%
Certificates of attendance (no diploma):	1.8%

Of the 2000-2001 graduates, 52.5% were eligible for the HOPE scholarship.

Of the 1999-2000 graduates, 81 attended a Georgia public college or university. Of those, 91% met the school's minimum academic requirements.

Average SAT Scores
Maximum score is 800 on each portion

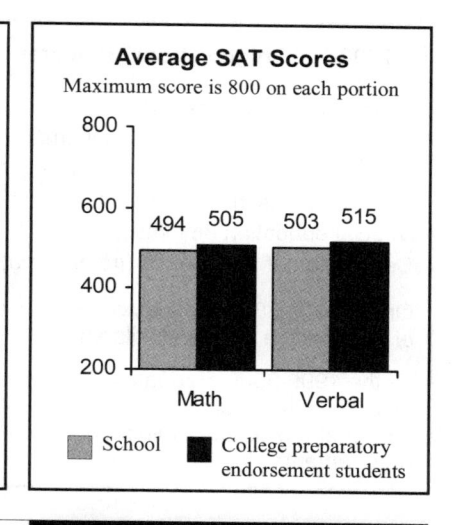

- Math: School 494, College preparatory endorsement students 505
- Verbal: School 503, College preparatory endorsement students 515

Forsyth County High Schools

South Forsyth High School

585 Peachtree Pkwy, Cumming, GA 30041
770-781-2264 · Grades 9 - 12

Enrollment:	1,434
White / black / other:	93.6% / 0.7% / 5.7%
Not native English-speaking:	23 / 1.6%
Limited English proficiency:	28 / 2.0%
Student absenteeism:	3.4%
Students per teacher:	16.0
Parent friendliness:	❶❷❸④❺❻
Students in gifted program:	218 / 15.2%
Students in remedial education:	2.2%
High school completion rate:	85.3%
Students held back a grade:	2.5%
Number of dropouts:	48 / 3.0%
Students in alternative programs:	*
Students in special education:	101 / 7.0%
Eligible students, free or reduced lunch:	3.1%
Total suspensions and expulsions:	659
Suspensions only, pct. in-school:	658 / 88.6%
Drugs/alcohol-related offenses:	18
Violence-related offenses:	37
Firearms-related offenses:	16
Vandalism-related offenses:	14
Theft-related offenses:	9
All other disciplinary offenses:	640
Teachers with advanced degrees:	47.8%
Average years' teaching experience:	10.5

AJC GRADE: ★★★

High School Graduation Test
Pct. of students who passed on first try

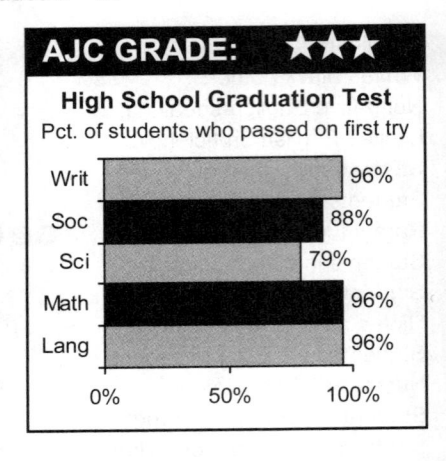

- Writ: 96%
- Soc: 88%
- Sci: 79%
- Math: 96%
- Lang: 96%

GHSA classification: 6-AAAA
Interscholastic sports offered:
BB, BS, CC, CL, FB, GO, SB, SO, TF

Advanced Placement (AP) Exams
- Students tested: 179
- Tests taken: 352
- Pct. of test scores 3 or higher (1 - 5 scale): 49.1%

Languages other than English taught:
French, German, Latin, Spanish

2000-2001 high school graduates: 243

College prep/vocational diplomas:	27.2%
College prep endorsement diplomas:	58.4%
Vocational endorsement diplomas:	12.8%
General high school diplomas:	0.0%
Special education diplomas:	0.8%
Certificates of attendance (no diploma):	0.8%

Of the 2000-2001 graduates, 67.5% were eligible for the HOPE scholarship.

Of the 1999-2000 graduates, 91 attended a Georgia public college or university. Of those, 83% met the school's minimum academic requirements.

Average SAT Scores
Maximum score is 800 on each portion

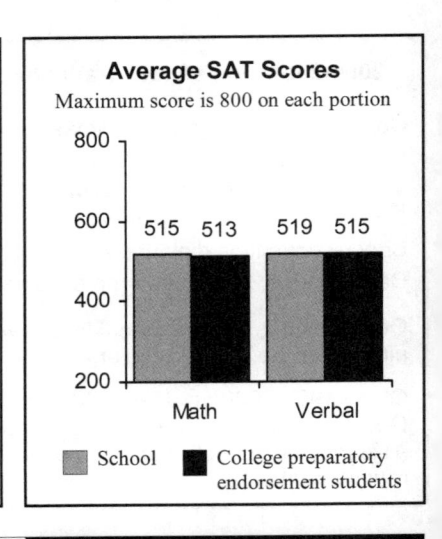

- Math: School 515, College preparatory endorsement students 513
- Verbal: School 519, College preparatory endorsement students 515

Forsyth County High Schools

AJC ranking of Forsyth County Schools

ELEMENTARY SCHOOLS

AJC Star Grade: ★★★★

Settles Bridge Elementary

AJC Star Grade: ★★★

Big Creek Elementary
Cumming Elementary
Daves Creek Elementary
Mashburn Elementary
Midway Elementary
Sawnee Elementary
Vickery Creek Elementary

AJC Star Grade: ★★

Chattahoochee Elementary
Coal Mountain Elementary

AJC Star Grade: ★

Chestatee Elementary

MIDDLE SCHOOLS

AJC Star Grade: ★★★

North Forsyth Middle
Otwell Middle
South Forsyth Middle
Vickery Creek Middle

HIGH SCHOOLS

AJC Star Grade: ★★★

Forsyth Central High
North Forsyth High
South Forsyth High

Forsyth County Public Schools

Fulton County Public Schools

786 Cleveland Ave SW, Atlanta, GA 30315
Phone: 404-768-3600 · Fax: 404-763-6853
http://www.fulton.k12.ga.us

The following pages provide detailed information on every school in the Fulton County school district. An asterisk (*) means the value of the data was zero or was not reported by the school district. A complete list of schools ranked by The Atlanta Journal-Constitution's star rating system follows the detailed school reports.

District enrollment:	66,918
White / black / other:	47.1% / 38.5% / 14.3%
Not native English-speaking:	2,668 / 4.0%
Expenditure per student (general fund):	$7,601
Students per teacher:	15.3
Teachers with advanced degrees:	46.2%
Average years, teaching experience:	10.9
Average teacher salary:	$44,912.34
Students in gifted program:	8,226 / 12.3%
Students held back a grade:	3,707 / 5.5%
Eligible students, free or reduced lunch:	21,659 / 31.6%
Number of dropouts (grades 9-12):	920 / 4.2%
High school completion rate:	83.1%
Graduates, pct. eligible for HOPE scholarships:	3,520 / 67.4%
Average combined SAT score (maximum 1,600):	1,055
Pct. of 11th-graders passing the Georgia High School Graduation Tests on first try:	77%
Percent of children 5 to 17 years of age living in poverty (2000 Census estimate):	22.0%

Abbotts Hill Elementary School

5575 Abbotts Bridge Rd, Duluth, GA 30097
770-667-2860 · Grades K - 5

Enrollment:	734
White / black / other:	75.2% / 6.4% / 18.4%
Not native English-speaking:	*
Limited English proficiency:	15 / 2.0%
Student absenteeism:	3.6%
Students per teacher:	17.3
Parent friendliness:	①②③④⑤⑥
Teachers with advanced degrees:	32.6%
Average years' teaching experience:	8.5
Students in gifted program:	52 / 7.1%
Students in remedial education:	9.1%
Students held back a grade:	1.0%
Total suspensions, pct. in-school:	4 / 25.0%
Offenses:	violence: *, drugs: *, other: 4
Eligible students, free or reduced lunch:	3.3%
Before / after school program:	No / Yes

Students at this school generally go on to:
River Trail, Webb Bridge Middle

AJC GRADE: ★★★

Georgia Criterion-Referenced Competency Tests - Grade 4
Pct. of students at each level

- Read: Exceeds 66%, Meets 24%, Does not meet 10%
- Math: Exceeds 37%, Meets 51%, Does not meet 12%
- Lang: Exceeds 35%, Meets 55%, Does not meet 10%

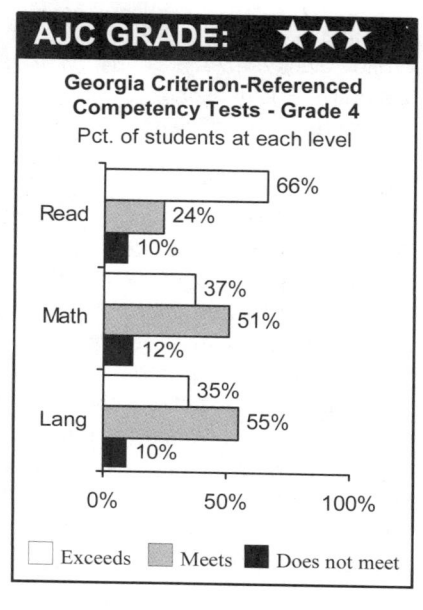

Alpharetta Elementary School

192 Mayfield Rd, Alpharetta, GA 30004
770-740-7015 · Grades K - 5

Enrollment:	1,000
White / black / other:	83.7% / 5.8% / 10.5%
Not native English-speaking:	26 / 2.6%
Limited English proficiency:	47 / 4.7%
Student absenteeism:	4.8%
Students per teacher:	13.7
Parent friendliness:	①❷❸④⑤❻
Teachers with advanced degrees:	41.8%
Average years' teaching experience:	11.3
Students in gifted program:	33 / 3.3%
Students in remedial education:	12.0%
Students held back a grade:	3.6%
Total suspensions, pct. in-school:	9 / 0.0%
Offenses:	violence: *, drugs: *, other: 10
Eligible students, free or reduced lunch:	6.0%
Before / after school program:	No / Yes

Students at this school generally go on to:
Northwestern Middle

AJC GRADE: ★★★

Georgia Criterion-Referenced Competency Tests - Grade 4
Pct. of students at each level

- Read: Exceeds 59%, Meets 32%, Does not meet 9%
- Math: Exceeds 31%, Meets 55%, Does not meet 14%
- Lang: Exceeds 32%, Meets 57%, Does not meet 12%

Fulton County Elementary Schools

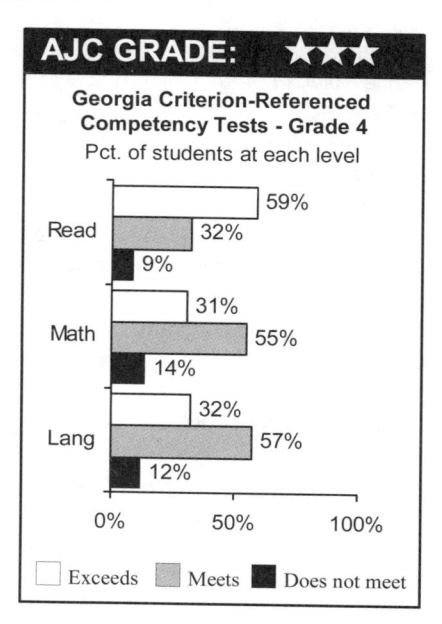

Barnwell Elementary School

9425 Barnwell Rd, Alpharetta, GA 30022
770-552-4960 · Grades K - 5

Enrollment:	942
White / black / other:	84.1% / 4.8% / 11.1%
Not native English-speaking:	*
Limited English proficiency:	6 / 0.6%
Student absenteeism:	4.7%
Students per teacher:	15.5
Parent friendliness:	❶❷❸④⑤❻
Teachers with advanced degrees:	45.5%
Average years' teaching experience:	10.8
Students in gifted program:	71 / 7.5%
Students in remedial education:	4.2%
Students held back a grade:	1.4%
Total suspensions, pct. in-school:	32 / 84.4%
Offenses:	violence: * , drugs: * , other: 41
Eligible students, free or reduced lunch:	2.8%
Before / after school program:	Yes / Yes

Students at this school generally go on to:
Haynes Bridge Middle

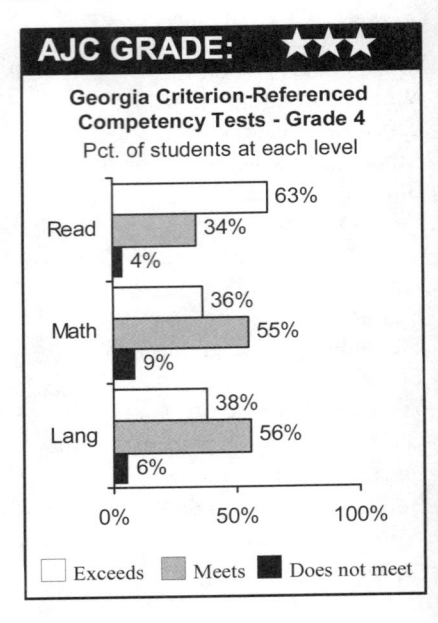

AJC GRADE: ★★★

Georgia Criterion-Referenced Competency Tests - Grade 4
Pct. of students at each level

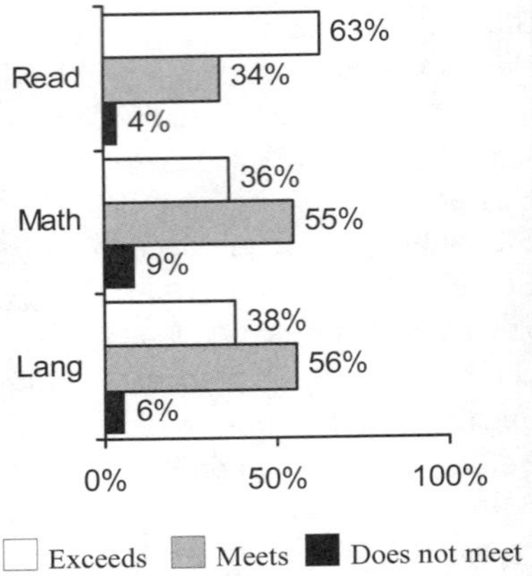
Read
63%
34%
4%
Math
36%
55%
9%
Lang
38%
56%
6%
0%
50%
100%
Exceeds
Meets
Does not meet

Bethune Elementary School

5925 Old Carriage Dr, College Park, GA 30349
770-991-7940 · Grades K - 5

Enrollment:	446
White / black / other:	0.2% / 95.3% / 4.5%
Not native English-speaking:	*
Limited English proficiency:	*
Student absenteeism:	5.2%
Students per teacher:	14.0
Parent friendliness:	❶❷❸④⑤❻
Teachers with advanced degrees:	48.5%
Average years' teaching experience:	16.3
Students in gifted program:	13 / 2.9%
Students in remedial education:	27.7%
Students held back a grade:	*
Total suspensions, pct. in-school:	93 / 0.0%
Offenses:	violence: * , drugs: * , other: 134
Eligible students, free or reduced lunch:	81.8%
Before / after school program:	No / Yes

Students at this school generally go on to:
McNair Middle

AJC GRADE: ★★★

Georgia Criterion-Referenced Competency Tests - Grade 4
Pct. of students at each level

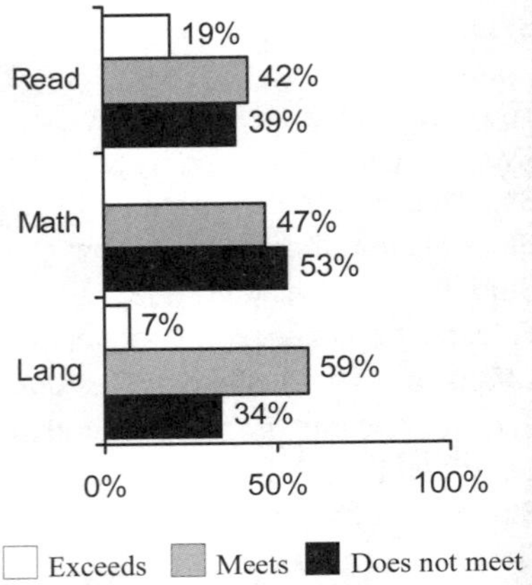
Read
19%
42%
39%
Math
47%
53%
Lang
7%
59%
34%
0%
50%
100%
Exceeds
Meets
Does not meet

Crabapple Crossing Elementary School

12775 Birmingham Hwy, Alpharetta, GA 30004
770-740-7055 · Grades K - 5

Enrollment:	714
White / black / other:	91.0% / 2.8% / 6.2%
Not native English-speaking:	*
Limited English proficiency:	8 / 1.1%
Student absenteeism:	4.3%
Students per teacher:	16.7
Parent friendliness:	❶❷❸④⑤❻
Teachers with advanced degrees:	45.7%
Average years' teaching experience:	14.1
Students in gifted program:	62 / 8.7%
Students in remedial education:	9.2%
Students held back a grade:	1.3%
Total suspensions, pct. in-school:	*
Offenses:	violence: *, drugs: *, other: 4
Eligible students, free or reduced lunch:	1.8%
Before / after school program:	No / Yes

Students at this school generally go on to:
Northwestern Middle

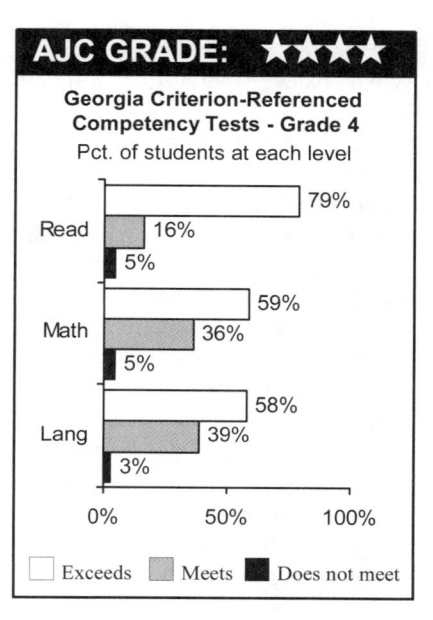

AJC GRADE: ★★★★

Georgia Criterion-Referenced Competency Tests - Grade 4
Pct. of students at each level

- Read: Exceeds 79%, Meets 16%, Does not meet 5%
- Math: Exceeds 59%, Meets 36%, Does not meet 5%
- Lang: Exceeds 58%, Meets 39%, Does not meet 3%

☐ Exceeds ▨ Meets ■ Does not meet

Dolvin Elementary School

10495 Jones Bridge Rd, Alpharetta, GA 30022
770-740-7020 · Grades K - 5

Enrollment:	646
White / black / other:	71.7% / 6.0% / 22.3%
Not native English-speaking:	54 / 8.4%
Limited English proficiency:	112 / 17.3%
Student absenteeism:	3.8%
Students per teacher:	13.9
Parent friendliness:	①❷❸④⑤❻
Teachers with advanced degrees:	48.0%
Average years' teaching experience:	10.1
Students in gifted program:	42 / 6.5%
Students in remedial education:	12.7%
Students held back a grade:	1.1%
Total suspensions, pct. in-school:	6 / 0.0%
Offenses:	violence: *, drugs: *, other: 6
Eligible students, free or reduced lunch:	6.9%
Before / after school program:	Yes / Yes

Students at this school generally go on to:
Taylor Road Middle

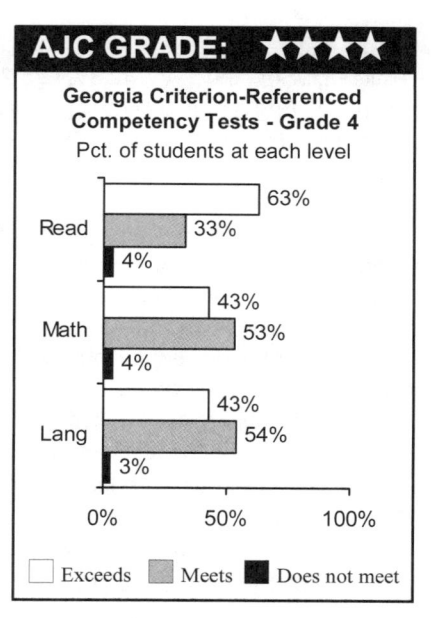

AJC GRADE: ★★★★

Georgia Criterion-Referenced Competency Tests - Grade 4
Pct. of students at each level

- Read: Exceeds 63%, Meets 33%, Does not meet 4%
- Math: Exceeds 43%, Meets 53%, Does not meet 4%
- Lang: Exceeds 43%, Meets 54%, Does not meet 3%

☐ Exceeds ▨ Meets ■ Does not meet

Fulton County Elementary Schools

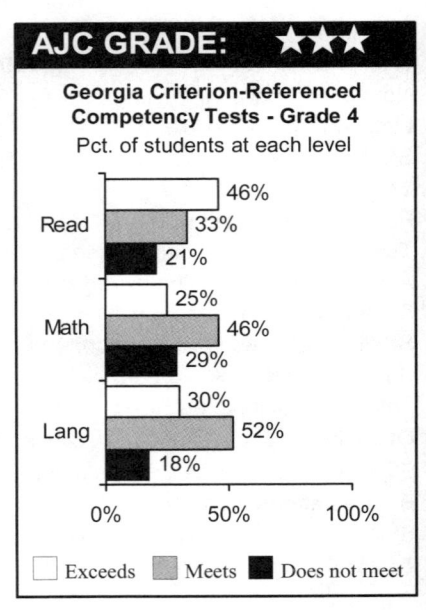

Dunwoody Springs Elementary School

8100 Roberts Dr, Atlanta, GA 30350
770-673-4060 · Grades K - 5

Enrollment:	719
White / black / other:	31.4% / 39.2% / 29.3%
Not native English-speaking:	68 / 9.5%
Limited English proficiency:	120 / 16.7%
Student absenteeism:	5.6%
Students per teacher:	16.7
Parent friendliness:	①❷❸❹❺❻
Teachers with advanced degrees:	34.8%
Average years' teaching experience:	6.2
Students in gifted program:	46 / 6.4%
Students in remedial education:	20.0%
Students held back a grade:	2.5%
Total suspensions, pct. in-school:	135 / 48.1%
Offenses: violence: *, drugs: *, other:	162
Eligible students, free or reduced lunch:	46.0%
Before / after school program:	No / Yes

Students at this school generally go on to:
Sandy Springs Middle

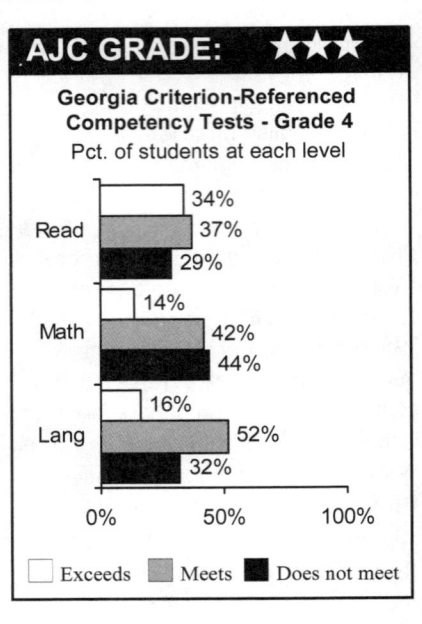

AJC GRADE: ★★★

Georgia Criterion-Referenced Competency Tests - Grade 4
Pct. of students at each level

- Read: 34% Exceeds / 37% Meets / 29% Does not meet
- Math: 14% Exceeds / 42% Meets / 44% Does not meet
- Lang: 16% Exceeds / 52% Meets / 32% Does not meet

Esther Jackson Elementary School

1400 Martin Rd, Roswell, GA 30076
770-594-5290 · Grades K - 5

Enrollment:	699
White / black / other:	42.3% / 25.2% / 32.5%
Not native English-speaking:	104 / 14.9%
Limited English proficiency:	227 / 32.5%
Student absenteeism:	5.1%
Students per teacher:	11.7
Parent friendliness:	①❷❸④❺❻
Teachers with advanced degrees:	28.4%
Average years' teaching experience:	9.8
Students in gifted program:	46 / 6.6%
Students in remedial education:	22.6%
Students held back a grade:	1.6%
Total suspensions, pct. in-school:	34 / 14.7%
Offenses: violence: *, drugs: *, other:	38
Eligible students, free or reduced lunch:	38.3%
Before / after school program:	No / Yes

Students at this school generally go on to:
Holcomb Bridge Middle

AJC GRADE: ★★★

Georgia Criterion-Referenced Competency Tests - Grade 4
Pct. of students at each level

- Read: 46% Exceeds / 33% Meets / 21% Does not meet
- Math: 25% Exceeds / 46% Meets / 29% Does not meet
- Lang: 30% Exceeds / 52% Meets / 18% Does not meet

Fulton County Elementary Schools

Findley Oaks Elementary School

5880 Findley Chase Dr, Duluth, GA 30097
770-497-3800 · Grades K - 5

Enrollment:	892
White / black / other:	78.5% / 5.7% / 15.8%
Not native English-speaking:	*
Limited English proficiency:	4 / 0.4%
Student absenteeism:	3.7%
Students per teacher:	15.7
Parent friendliness:	①❷❸❹❺❻
Teachers with advanced degrees:	29.5%
Average years' teaching experience:	11.2
Students in gifted program:	171 / 19.2%
Students in remedial education:	12.1%
Students held back a grade:	0.4%
Total suspensions, pct. in-school:	4 / 75.0%
Offenses:	violence: * , drugs: * , other: 6
Eligible students, free or reduced lunch:	1.3%
Before / after school program:	Yes / Yes
Students at this school generally go on to:	
River Trail Middle	

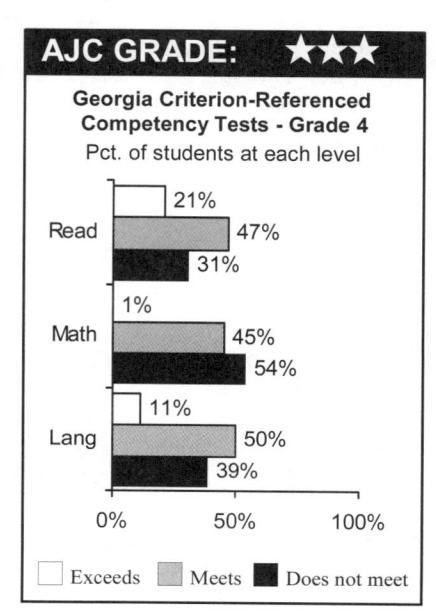

AJC GRADE: ★★★★

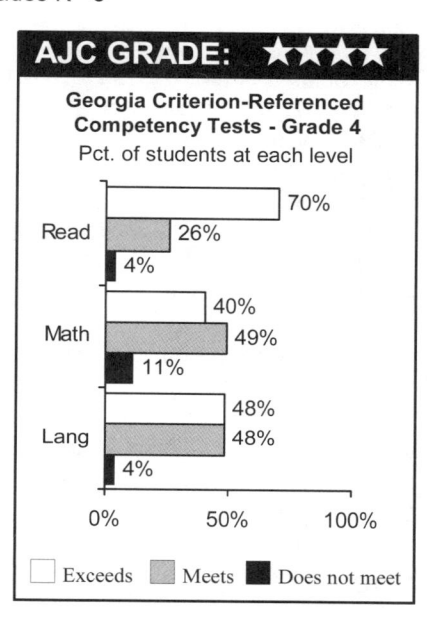

Georgia Criterion-Referenced Competency Tests - Grade 4
Pct. of students at each level

- Read: Exceeds 70%, Meets 26%, Does not meet 4%
- Math: Exceeds 40%, Meets 49%, Does not meet 11%
- Lang: Exceeds 48%, Meets 48%, Does not meet 4%

Gullatt Elementary School

6110 Dodson Rd, Union City, GA 30291
770-969-3425 · Grades K - 5

Enrollment:	514
White / black / other:	3.3% / 94.0% / 2.7%
Not native English-speaking:	*
Limited English proficiency:	*
Student absenteeism:	5.6%
Students per teacher:	13.4
Parent friendliness:	❶❷❸④❺❻
Teachers with advanced degrees:	45.0%
Average years' teaching experience:	14.8
Students in gifted program:	8 / 1.6%
Students in remedial education:	32.5%
Students held back a grade:	2.7%
Total suspensions, pct. in-school:	33 / 3.0%
Offenses:	violence: * , drugs: * , other: 38
Eligible students, free or reduced lunch:	83.4%
Before / after school program:	No / Yes
Students at this school generally go on to:	
Bear Creek Middle	

AJC GRADE: ★★★

Georgia Criterion-Referenced Competency Tests - Grade 4
Pct. of students at each level

- Read: Exceeds 21%, Meets 47%, Does not meet 31%
- Math: Exceeds 1%, Meets 45%, Does not meet 54%
- Lang: Exceeds 11%, Meets 50%, Does not meet 39%

The Atlanta Journal-Constitution / Page 327

Fulton County Elementary Schools

Hapeville Elementary School

3440 N Fulton Ave, Hapeville, GA 30354
404-669-8220 · Grades K - 5

Enrollment:	876
White / black / other:	19.2% / 44.1% / 36.8%
Not native English-speaking:	121 / 13.8%
Limited English proficiency:	193 / 22.0%
Student absenteeism:	5.8%
Students per teacher:	14.1
Parent friendliness:	① ❷ ❸ ④ ❺ ❻
Teachers with advanced degrees:	43.3%
Average years' teaching experience:	7.2
Students in gifted program:	12 / 1.4%
Students in remedial education:	32.5%
Students held back a grade:	4.6%
Total suspensions, pct. in-school:	96 / 5.2%
Offenses: violence: 1, drugs: *, other: 113	
Eligible students, free or reduced lunch:	85.2%
Before / after school program:	Yes / Yes
Students at this school generally go on to:	
Paul D. West Middle	

AJC GRADE: ★★★

Georgia Criterion-Referenced Competency Tests - Grade 4
Pct. of students at each level

Read: Exceeds 23%, Meets 36%, Does not meet 41%
Math: Exceeds 7%, Meets 56%, Does not meet 37%
Lang: Exceeds 11%, Meets 54%, Does not meet 35%

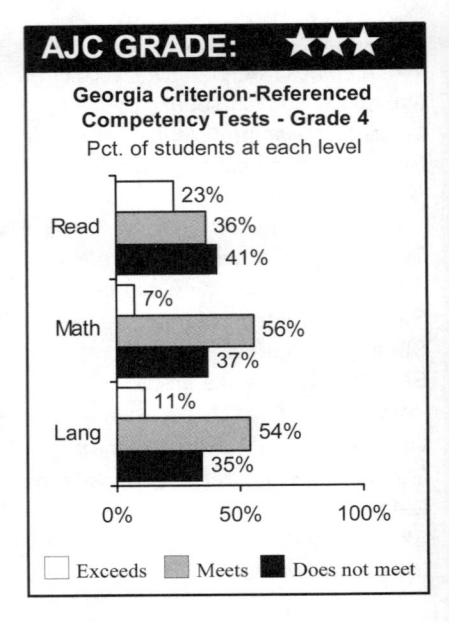

Harriet Tubman Elementary School

2861 Lakeshore Dr, College Park, GA 30337
404-669-8115 · Grades K - 5

Enrollment:	597
White / black / other:	0.3% / 92.3% / 7.4%
Not native English-speaking:	23 / 3.9%
Limited English proficiency:	37 / 6.2%
Student absenteeism:	5.6%
Students per teacher:	12.7
Parent friendliness:	① ❷ ❸ ④ ❺ ❻
Teachers with advanced degrees:	46.3%
Average years' teaching experience:	11.6
Students in gifted program:	*
Students in remedial education:	29.3%
Students held back a grade:	3.7%
Total suspensions, pct. in-school:	14 / 42.9%
Offenses: violence: *, drugs: *, other: 17	
Eligible students, free or reduced lunch:	88.8%
Before / after school program:	Yes / Yes
Students at this school generally go on to:	
Woodland Middle	

AJC GRADE: ★★★

Georgia Criterion-Referenced Competency Tests - Grade 4
Pct. of students at each level

Read: Exceeds 18%, Meets 51%, Does not meet 31%
Math: Exceeds 6%, Meets 52%, Does not meet 42%
Lang: Exceeds 5%, Meets 62%, Does not meet 33%

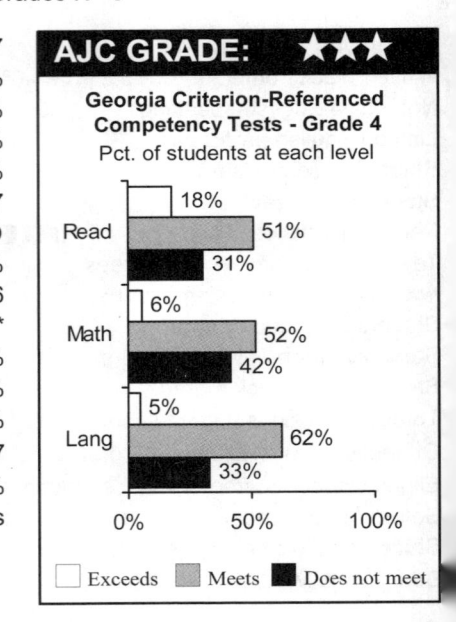

Heards Ferry Elementary School

1050 Heards Ferry Rd NW, Atlanta, GA 30328
770-933-6190 · Grades K - 5

Enrollment:	493
White / black / other:	47.1% / 15.4% / 37.5%
Not native English-speaking:	112 / 22.7%
Limited English proficiency:	205 / 41.6%
Student absenteeism:	4.4%
Students per teacher:	11.6
Parent friendliness:	❶❷❸④❺❻
Teachers with advanced degrees:	45.8%
Average years' teaching experience:	10.9
Students in gifted program:	74 / 15.0%
Students in remedial education:	21.0%
Students held back a grade:	1.4%
Total suspensions, pct. in-school:	35 / 51.4%
Offenses: violence: *, drugs: *, other:	45
Eligible students, free or reduced lunch:	40.2%
Before / after school program:	No / Yes

Students at this school generally go on to:
Ridgeview Middle

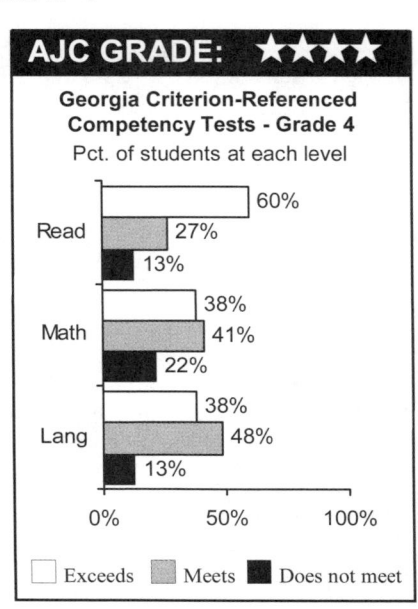

AJC GRADE: ★★★★

Georgia Criterion-Referenced Competency Tests - Grade 4
Pct. of students at each level

- Read: Exceeds 60%, Meets 27%, Does not meet 13%
- Math: Exceeds 38%, Meets 41%, Does not meet 22%
- Lang: Exceeds 38%, Meets 48%, Does not meet 13%

Heritage Elementary School

2600 Jolly Rd, College Park, GA 30349
404-669-8144 · Grades K - 5

Enrollment:	717
White / black / other:	0.4% / 96.9% / 2.6%
Not native English-speaking:	*
Limited English proficiency:	2 / 0.3%
Student absenteeism:	7.4%
Students per teacher:	19.1
Parent friendliness:	①❷❸④❺❻
Teachers with advanced degrees:	34.9%
Average years' teaching experience:	6.2
Students in gifted program:	18 / 2.5%
Students in remedial education:	29.0%
Students held back a grade:	6.1%
Total suspensions, pct. in-school:	131 / 0.0%
Offenses: violence: *, drugs: *, other:	164
Eligible students, free or reduced lunch:	94.7%
Before / after school program:	No / Yes

Students at this school generally go on to:
McNair Middle

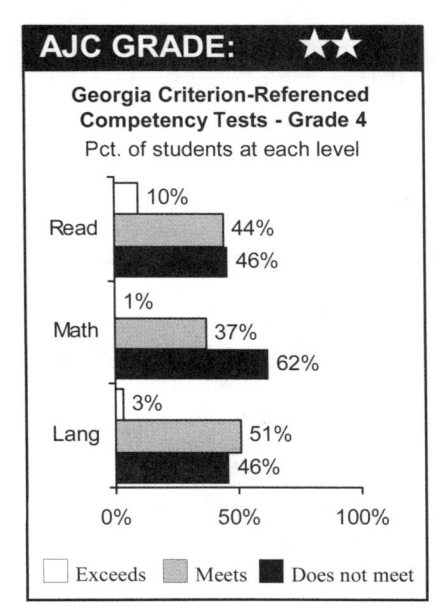

AJC GRADE: ★★

Georgia Criterion-Referenced Competency Tests - Grade 4
Pct. of students at each level

- Read: Exceeds 10%, Meets 44%, Does not meet 46%
- Math: Exceeds 1%, Meets 37%, Does not meet 62%
- Lang: Exceeds 3%, Meets 51%, Does not meet 46%

Fulton County Elementary Schools

Highpoint Elementary School

520 Greenland Rd NE, Atlanta, GA 30342
404-843-7716 · Grades K - 5

Enrollment:	525
White / black / other:	25.5% / 19.8% / 54.7%
Not native English-speaking:	169 / 32.2%
Limited English proficiency:	243 / 46.3%
Student absenteeism:	6.0%
Students per teacher:	11.4
Parent friendliness:	❶❷❸④❺❻
Teachers with advanced degrees:	44.9%
Average years' teaching experience:	14.3
Students in gifted program:	23 / 4.4%
Students in remedial education:	32.9%
Students held back a grade:	4.0%
Total suspensions, pct. in-school:	72 / 52.8%
Offenses:	violence: *, drugs: *, other: 77
Eligible students, free or reduced lunch:	64.0%
Before / after school program:	Yes / Yes
Students at this school generally go on to:	
Ridgeview Middle	

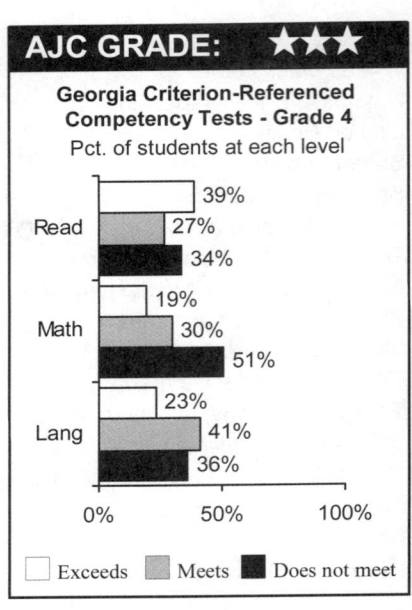

AJC GRADE: ★★★

Georgia Criterion-Referenced Competency Tests - Grade 4
Pct. of students at each level

- Read: Exceeds 39%, Meets 27%, Does not meet 34%
- Math: Exceeds 19%, Meets 30%, Does not meet 51%
- Lang: Exceeds 23%, Meets 41%, Does not meet 36%

Lake Windward Elementary School

11770 E Fox Ct, Alpharetta, GA 30005
770-740-7050 · Grades K - 5

Enrollment:	924
White / black / other:	77.1% / 7.8% / 15.2%
Not native English-speaking:	*
Limited English proficiency:	12 / 1.3%
Student absenteeism:	4.4%
Students per teacher:	16.0
Parent friendliness:	❶❷❸④❺❻
Teachers with advanced degrees:	35.9%
Average years' teaching experience:	10.6
Students in gifted program:	58 / 6.3%
Students in remedial education:	12.0%
Students held back a grade:	0.9%
Total suspensions, pct. in-school:	11 / 45.5%
Offenses:	violence: *, drugs: *, other: 11
Eligible students, free or reduced lunch:	2.7%
Before / after school program:	No / Yes
Students at this school generally go on to:	
Webb Bridge Middle	

AJC GRADE: ★★★★

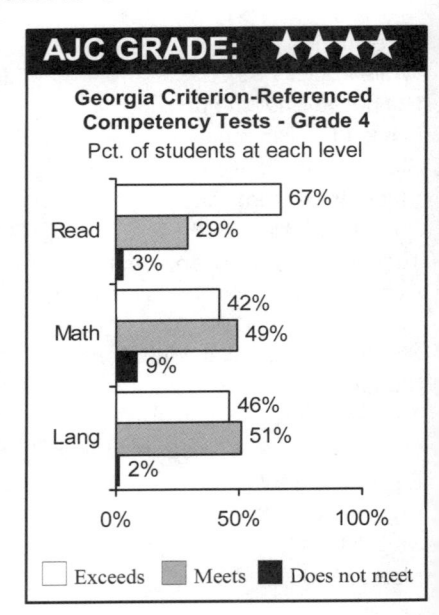

Georgia Criterion-Referenced Competency Tests - Grade 4
Pct. of students at each level

- Read: Exceeds 67%, Meets 29%, Does not meet 3%
- Math: Exceeds 42%, Meets 49%, Does not meet 9%
- Lang: Exceeds 46%, Meets 51%, Does not meet 2%

Fulton County Elementary Schools

Lewis Elementary School

6201 Connell Rd, College Park, GA 30349
770-969-3450 · Grades K - 5

Enrollment:	491
White / black / other:	0.4% / 94.7% / 4.9%
Not native English-speaking:	*
Limited English proficiency:	*
Student absenteeism:	5.2%
Students per teacher:	12.4
Parent friendliness:	① ❷ ❸ ④ ⑤ ❻
Teachers with advanced degrees:	59.5%
Average years' teaching experience:	12.0
Students in gifted program:	*
Students in remedial education:	30.7%
Students held back a grade:	1.4%
Total suspensions, pct. in-school:	108 / 11.1%
Offenses: violence: *, drugs: *, other:	110
Eligible students, free or reduced lunch:	74.4%
Before / after school program:	No / Yes

Students at this school generally go on to:
McNair Middle

AJC GRADE: ★★

Georgia Criterion-Referenced Competency Tests - Grade 4
Pct. of students at each level

- Read: 21% Exceeds / 39% Meets / 40% Does not meet
- Math: 1% Exceeds / 32% Meets / 67% Does not meet
- Lang: 9% Exceeds / 56% Meets / 35% Does not meet

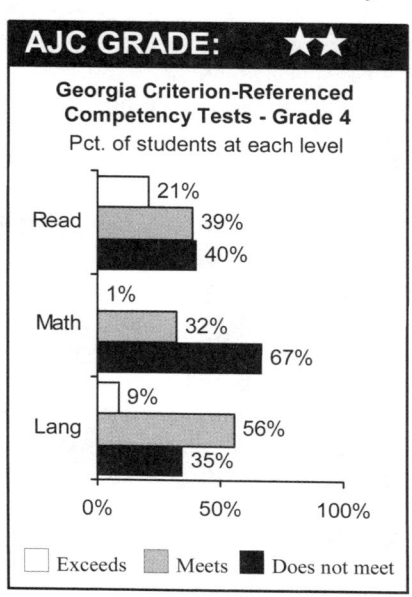

Manning Oaks Elementary School

405 Cumming St, Alpharetta, GA 30004
770-667-2912 · Grades K - 5

Enrollment:	1,060
White / black / other:	72.6% / 10.9% / 16.4%
Not native English-speaking:	*
Limited English proficiency:	11 / 1.0%
Student absenteeism:	4.8%
Students per teacher:	18.9
Parent friendliness:	❶ ❷ ❸ ④ ⑤ ❻
Teachers with advanced degrees:	26.6%
Average years' teaching experience:	7.5
Students in gifted program:	64 / 6.0%
Students in remedial education:	10.5%
Students held back a grade:	1.1%
Total suspensions, pct. in-school:	8 / 0.0%
Offenses: violence: *, drugs: *, other:	11
Eligible students, free or reduced lunch:	6.1%
Before / after school program:	No / Yes

Students at this school generally go on to:
Northwestern Middle

AJC GRADE: ★★★

Georgia Criterion-Referenced Competency Tests - Grade 4
Pct. of students at each level

- Read: 56% Exceeds / 35% Meets / 9% Does not meet
- Math: 34% Exceeds / 55% Meets / 11% Does not meet
- Lang: 37% Exceeds / 54% Meets / 9% Does not meet

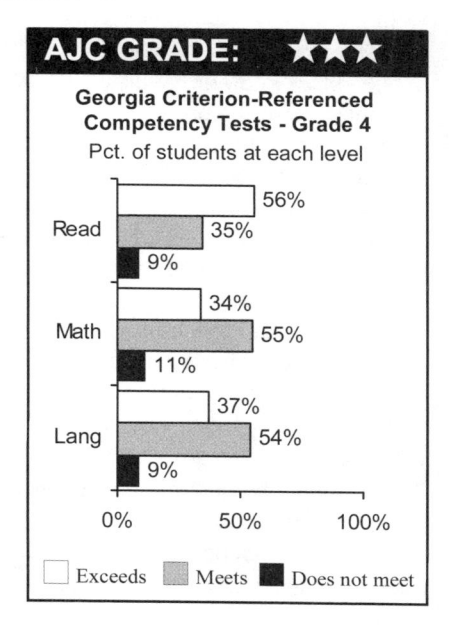

Medlock Bridge Elementary School

10215 Medlock Bridge Pkwy, Alpharetta, GA 30022
770-623-2980 · Grades K - 5

Enrollment:	793
White / black / other:	65.7% / 7.3% / 27.0%
Not native English-speaking:	32 / 4.0%
Limited English proficiency:	60 / 7.6%
Student absenteeism:	4.1%
Students per teacher:	15.6
Parent friendliness:	❶❷❸④⑤❻
Teachers with advanced degrees:	44.6%
Average years' teaching experience:	8.7
Students in gifted program:	100 / 12.6%
Students in remedial education:	13.6%
Students held back a grade:	0.6%
Total suspensions, pct. in-school:	1 / 0.0%
Offenses:	violence: *, drugs: *, other: 2
Eligible students, free or reduced lunch:	4.3%
Before / after school program:	Yes / Yes
Students at this school generally go on to:	
River Trail Middle	

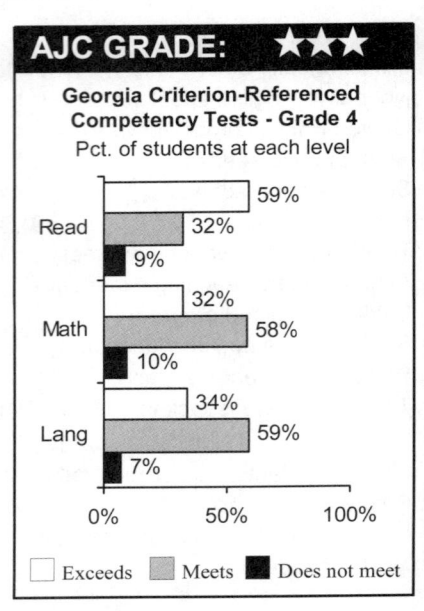

AJC GRADE: ★★★

Georgia Criterion-Referenced Competency Tests - Grade 4
Pct. of students at each level

Read: Exceeds 59%, Meets 32%, Does not meet 9%
Math: Exceeds 32%, Meets 58%, Does not meet 10%
Lang: Exceeds 34%, Meets 59%, Does not meet 7%

Mimosa Elementary School

1550 Warsaw Rd, Roswell, GA 30076
770-552-4540 · Grades K - 5

Enrollment:	670
White / black / other:	34.2% / 17.8% / 48.1%
Not native English-speaking:	166 / 24.8%
Limited English proficiency:	316 / 47.2%
Student absenteeism:	5.1%
Students per teacher:	11.1
Parent friendliness:	❶❷❸④❺❻
Teachers with advanced degrees:	57.6%
Average years' teaching experience:	10.1
Students in gifted program:	33 / 4.9%
Students in remedial education:	21.9%
Students held back a grade:	2.7%
Total suspensions, pct. in-school:	13 / 0.0%
Offenses:	violence: *, drugs: *, other: 13
Eligible students, free or reduced lunch:	54.8%
Before / after school program:	Yes / Yes
Students at this school generally go on to:	
Elkins Pointe Middle	

AJC GRADE: ★★★

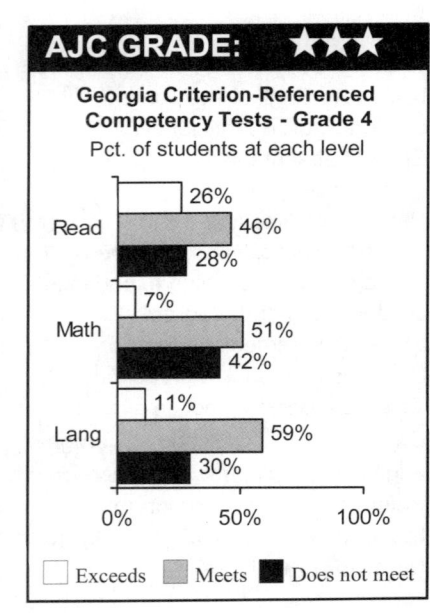

Georgia Criterion-Referenced Competency Tests - Grade 4
Pct. of students at each level

Read: Exceeds 26%, Meets 46%, Does not meet 28%
Math: Exceeds 7%, Meets 51%, Does not meet 42%
Lang: Exceeds 11%, Meets 59%, Does not meet 30%

Fulton County Elementary Schools

Mount Olive Elementary School

3353 Mount Olive Rd, East Point, GA 30344
404-669-8050 · Grades K - 5

Enrollment:	492
White / black / other:	1.0% / 95.9% / 3.0%
Not native English-speaking:	*
Limited English proficiency:	*
Student absenteeism:	5.4%
Students per teacher:	11.6
Parent friendliness:	❶❷❸④❺❻
Teachers with advanced degrees:	51.1%
Average years' teaching experience:	14.1
Students in gifted program:	10 / 2.0%
Students in remedial education:	33.7%
Students held back a grade:	3.0%
Total suspensions, pct. in-school:	102 / 2.9%
Offenses:	violence: * , drugs: * , other: 116
Eligible students, free or reduced lunch:	93.4%
Before / after school program:	Yes / Yes

Students at this school generally go on to:
Woodland Middle

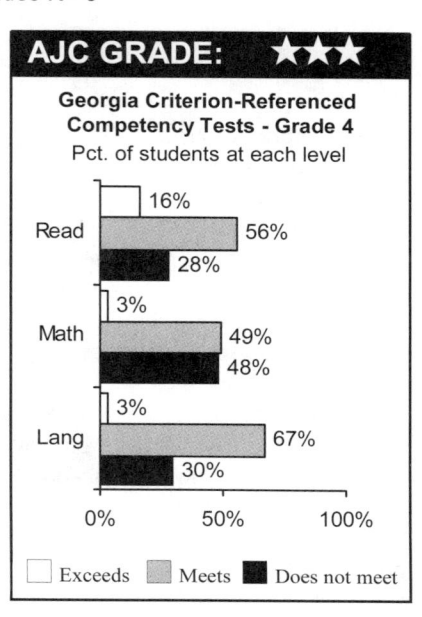

AJC GRADE: ★★★

Georgia Criterion-Referenced Competency Tests - Grade 4
Pct. of students at each level

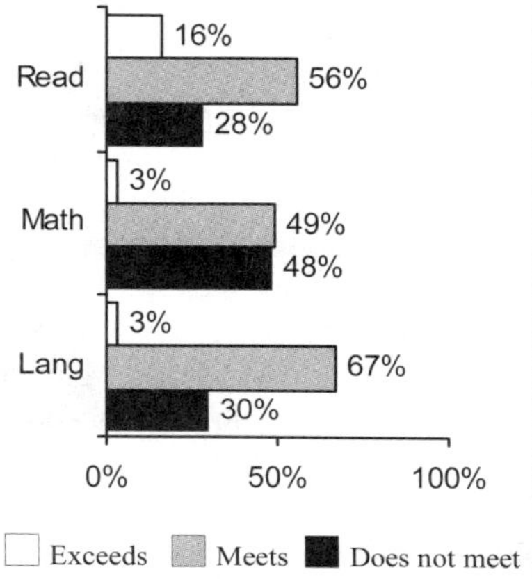

Read
16%
56%
28%
Math
3%
49%
48%
Lang
3%
67%
30%
0%
50%
100%
Exceeds
Meets
Does not meet

Mountain Park Elementary School

👍

11895 Mountain Park Rd, Roswell, GA 30075
770-552-4530 · Grades K - 5

Enrollment:	761
White / black / other:	89.2% / 5.3% / 5.5%
Not native English-speaking:	*
Limited English proficiency:	*
Student absenteeism:	4.1%
Students per teacher:	15.5
Parent friendliness:	①②❸④⑤❻
Teachers with advanced degrees:	55.4%
Average years' teaching experience:	15.1
Students in gifted program:	119 / 15.6%
Students in remedial education:	6.1%
Students held back a grade:	*
Total suspensions, pct. in-school:	3 / 33.3%
Offenses:	violence: * , drugs: * , other: 5
Eligible students, free or reduced lunch:	3.9%
Before / after school program:	No / Yes

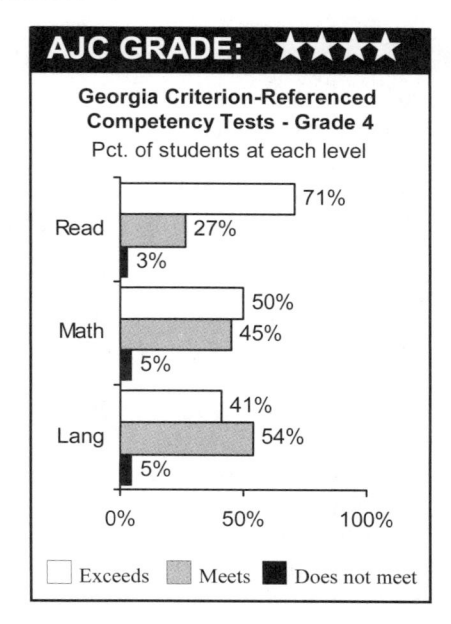

Students at this school generally go on to:
Crabapple Middle

AJC GRADE: ★★★★

Georgia Criterion-Referenced Competency Tests - Grade 4
Pct. of students at each level

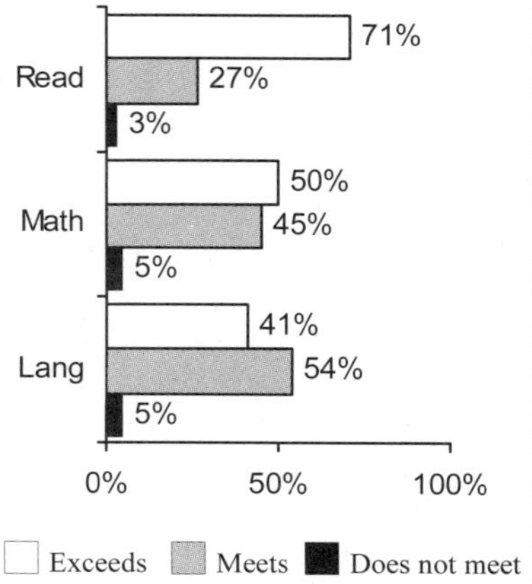

Read
71%
27%
3%
Math
50%
45%
5%
Lang
41%
54%
5%
0%
50%
100%
Exceeds
Meets
Does not meet

New Prospect Elementary School

3055 Kimball Bridge Rd, Alpharetta, GA 30022
770-667-2800 · Grades K - 5

Enrollment:	842
White / black / other:	80.3% / 6.7% / 13.1%
Not native English-speaking:	*
Limited English proficiency:	3 / 0.4%
Student absenteeism:	3.7%
Students per teacher:	16.6
Parent friendliness:	① ❷ ❸ ④ ❺ ❻
Teachers with advanced degrees:	35.7%
Average years' teaching experience:	8.5
Students in gifted program:	65 / 7.7%
Students in remedial education:	6.1%
Students held back a grade:	1.5%
Total suspensions, pct. in-school:	3 / 33.3%
Offenses: violence: *, drugs: *, other: 3	
Eligible students, free or reduced lunch:	2.0%
Before / after school program:	No / Yes

Students at this school generally go on to:
Webb Bridge Middle

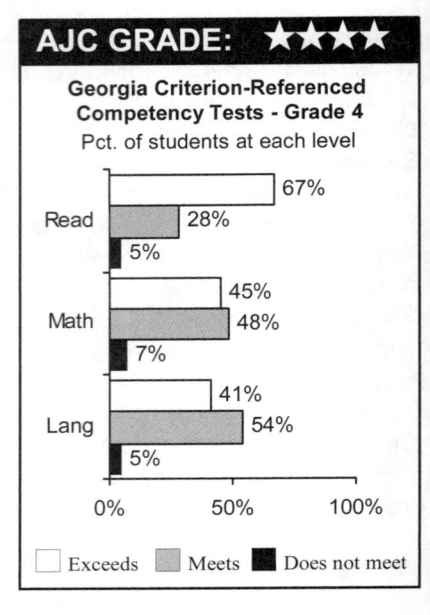

AJC GRADE: ★★★★

Georgia Criterion-Referenced Competency Tests - Grade 4
Pct. of students at each level

Read: Exceeds 67%, Meets 28%, Does not meet 5%
Math: Exceeds 45%, Meets 48%, Does not meet 7%
Lang: Exceeds 41%, Meets 54%, Does not meet 5%

Nolan Elementary School

2725 Creel Rd, College Park, GA 30349
770-991-7950 · Grades K - 5

Enrollment:	524
White / black / other:	0.4% / 95.6% / 4.0%
Not native English-speaking:	*
Limited English proficiency:	*
Student absenteeism:	4.3%
Students per teacher:	13.5
Parent friendliness:	❶ ❷ ❸ ❹ ❺ ❻
Teachers with advanced degrees:	30.2%
Average years' teaching experience:	8.5
Students in gifted program:	13 / 2.5%
Students in remedial education:	33.9%
Students held back a grade:	4.6%
Total suspensions, pct. in-school:	83 / 50.6%
Offenses: violence: *, drugs: *, other: 90	
Eligible students, free or reduced lunch:	69.0%
Before / after school program:	No / Yes

Students at this school generally go on to:
McNair Middle

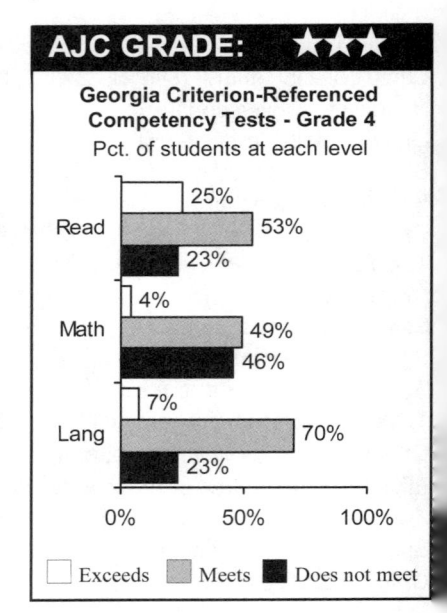

AJC GRADE: ★★★

Georgia Criterion-Referenced Competency Tests - Grade 4
Pct. of students at each level

Read: Exceeds 25%, Meets 53%, Does not meet 23%
Math: Exceeds 4%, Meets 49%, Does not meet 46%
Lang: Exceeds 7%, Meets 70%, Does not meet 23%

Northwood Elementary School

10200 Wooten Rd, Roswell, GA 30076
770-552-6390 · Grades K - 5

Enrollment:	877
White / black / other:	66.7% / 15.3% / 18.0%
Not native English-speaking:	52 / 5.9%
Limited English proficiency:	92 / 10.5%
Student absenteeism:	4.4%
Students per teacher:	16.3
Parent friendliness:	❶❷❸❹❺❻
Teachers with advanced degrees:	40.4%
Average years' teaching experience:	8.3
Students in gifted program:	60 / 6.8%
Students in remedial education:	17.1%
Students held back a grade:	1.7%
Total suspensions, pct. in-school:	24 / 8.3%
Offenses: violence: *, drugs: *, other:	41
Eligible students, free or reduced lunch:	15.2%
Before / after school program:	Yes / Yes

Students at this school generally go on to:
Haynes Bridge Middle

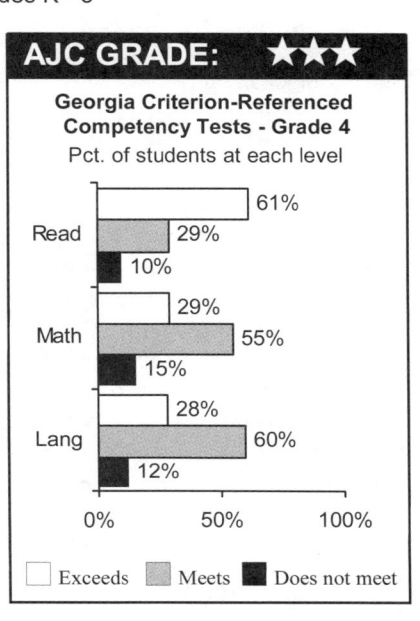

AJC GRADE: ★★★

Georgia Criterion-Referenced Competency Tests - Grade 4
Pct. of students at each level

- Read: Exceeds 61%, Meets 29%, Does not meet 10%
- Math: Exceeds 29%, Meets 55%, Does not meet 15%
- Lang: Exceeds 28%, Meets 60%, Does not meet 12%

Oak Knoll Elementary School

2626 Hogan Rd, East Point, GA 30344
404-669-8060 · Grades K - 5

Enrollment:	972
White / black / other:	1.5% / 77.4% / 21.1%
Not native English-speaking:	122 / 12.6%
Limited English proficiency:	203 / 20.9%
Student absenteeism:	4.6%
Students per teacher:	16.5
Parent friendliness:	❶❷❸④❺❻
Teachers with advanced degrees:	38.1%
Average years' teaching experience:	8.6
Students in gifted program:	*
Students in remedial education:	32.3%
Students held back a grade:	2.9%
Total suspensions, pct. in-school:	75 / 0.0%
Offenses: violence: *, drugs: *, other:	98
Eligible students, free or reduced lunch:	81.6%
Before / after school program:	No / Yes

Students at this school generally go on to:
Paul West, Woodland Middle

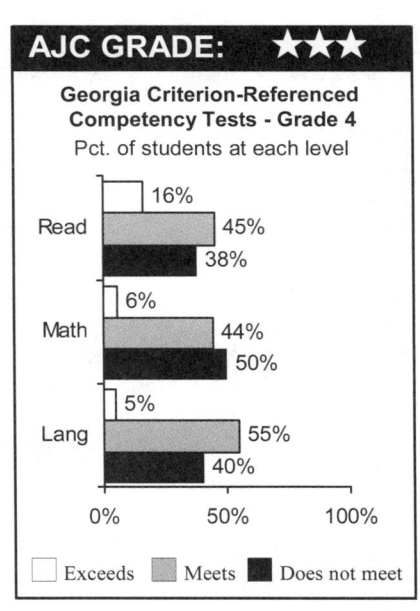

AJC GRADE: ★★★

Georgia Criterion-Referenced Competency Tests - Grade 4
Pct. of students at each level

- Read: Exceeds 16%, Meets 45%, Does not meet 38%
- Math: Exceeds 6%, Meets 44%, Does not meet 50%
- Lang: Exceeds 5%, Meets 55%, Does not meet 40%

Fulton County Elementary Schools

Ocee Elementary School

4375 Kimball Bridge Rd, Alpharetta, GA 30022
770-667-2960 · Grades K - 5

Enrollment:	832
White / black / other:	72.5% / 5.9% / 21.6%
Not native English-speaking:	33 / 4.0%
Limited English proficiency:	60 / 7.2%
Student absenteeism:	3.9%
Students per teacher:	17.7
Parent friendliness:	①❷❸④❺❻
Teachers with advanced degrees:	43.1%
Average years' teaching experience:	8.1
Students in gifted program:	66 / 7.9%
Students in remedial education:	4.6%
Students held back a grade:	1.1%
Total suspensions, pct. in-school:	12 / 91.7%
Offenses: violence: *, drugs: *, other:	13
Eligible students, free or reduced lunch:	1.4%
Before / after school program:	No / Yes

Students at this school generally go on to:
Taylor Road, Webb Bridge Middle

AJC GRADE: ★★★

Georgia Criterion-Referenced Competency Tests - Grade 4
Pct. of students at each level

Read: Exceeds 65%, Meets 28%, Does not meet 7%
Math: Exceeds 35%, Meets 55%, Does not meet 10%
Lang: Exceeds 44%, Meets 50%, Does not meet 6%

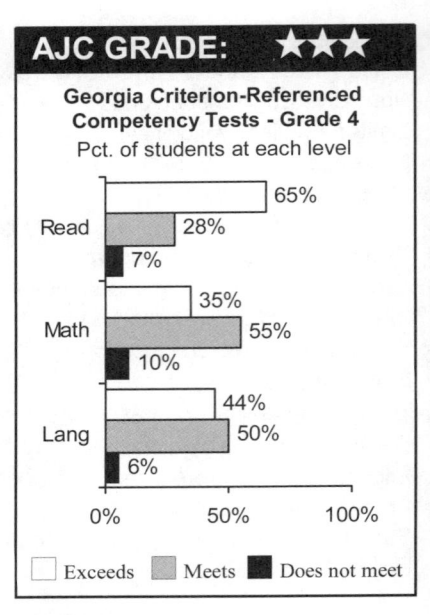

Palmetto Elementary School

505 Carlton Rd, Palmetto, GA 30268
770-463-6100 · Grades K - 5

Enrollment:	426
White / black / other:	40.6% / 49.1% / 10.3%
Not native English-speaking:	*
Limited English proficiency:	3 / 0.7%
Student absenteeism:	5.9%
Students per teacher:	15.0
Parent friendliness:	❶❷❸④❺❻
Teachers with advanced degrees:	63.3%
Average years' teaching experience:	15.9
Students in gifted program:	12 / 2.8%
Students in remedial education:	41.4%
Students held back a grade:	2.6%
Total suspensions, pct. in-school:	37 / 8.1%
Offenses: violence: *, drugs: *, other:	48
Eligible students, free or reduced lunch:	64.6%
Before / after school program:	No / Yes

Students at this school generally go on to:
Bear Creek Middle

AJC GRADE: ★★

Georgia Criterion-Referenced Competency Tests - Grade 4
Pct. of students at each level

Read: Exceeds 22%, Meets 46%, Does not meet 33%
Math: Exceeds 6%, Meets 43%, Does not meet 51%
Lang: Exceeds 8%, Meets 57%, Does not meet 35%

Fulton County Elementary Schools

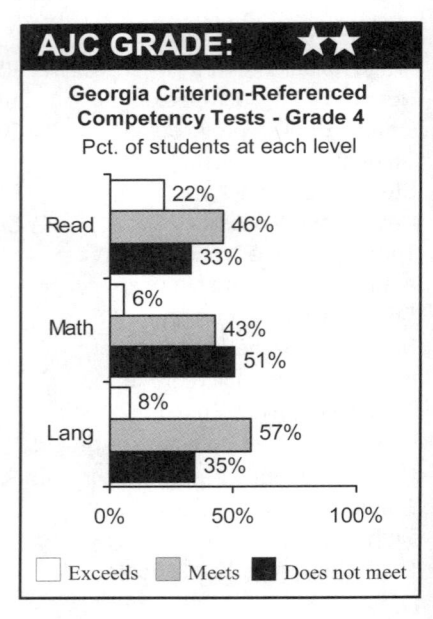

Parklane Elementary School

2809 Blount St, East Point, GA 30344
404-669-8070 · Grades K - 5

Enrollment:	763
White / black / other:	3.0% / 81.5% / 15.5%
Not native English-speaking:	71 / 9.3%
Limited English proficiency:	108 / 14.2%
Student absenteeism:	6.4%
Students per teacher:	14.2
Parent friendliness:	① ❷ ❸ ❹ ❺ ❻
Teachers with advanced degrees:	34.5%
Average years' teaching experience:	11.6
Students in gifted program:	4 / 0.5%
Students in remedial education:	32.8%
Students held back a grade:	3.3%
Total suspensions, pct. in-school:	261 / 1.5%
Offenses: violence: *, drugs: *, other: 327	
Eligible students, free or reduced lunch:	92.6%
Before / after school program:	No / No

Students at this school generally go on to:
Paul West Middle

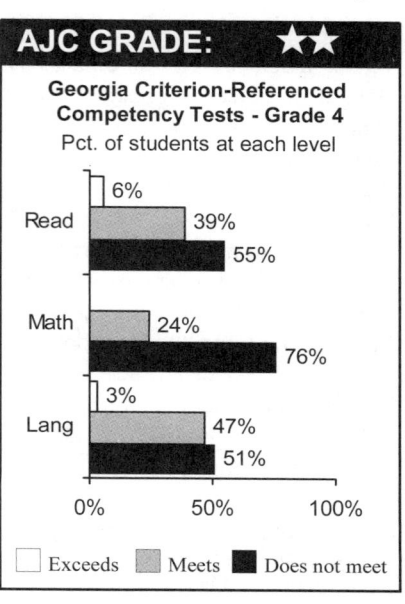

AJC GRADE: ★★

Georgia Criterion-Referenced Competency Tests - Grade 4
Pct. of students at each level

- Read: Exceeds 6%, Meets 39%, Does not meet 55%
- Math: Exceeds *, Meets 24%, Does not meet 76%
- Lang: Exceeds 3%, Meets 47%, Does not meet 51%

Randolph Elementary School

5320 Campbellton Rd SW, Atlanta, GA 30331
404-346-6520 · Grades K - 5

Enrollment:	634
White / black / other:	0.0% / 99.4% / 0.6%
Not native English-speaking:	*
Limited English proficiency:	*
Student absenteeism:	4.0%
Students per teacher:	15.7
Parent friendliness:	❶ ❷ ❸ ④ ⑤ ❻
Teachers with advanced degrees:	52.4%
Average years' teaching experience:	8.8
Students in gifted program:	25 / 3.9%
Students in remedial education:	26.0%
Students held back a grade:	1.3%
Total suspensions, pct. in-school:	49 / 0.0%
Offenses: violence: *, drugs: *, other: 138	
Eligible students, free or reduced lunch:	52.3%
Before / after school program:	Yes / Yes

Students at this school generally go on to:
Camp Creek Middle

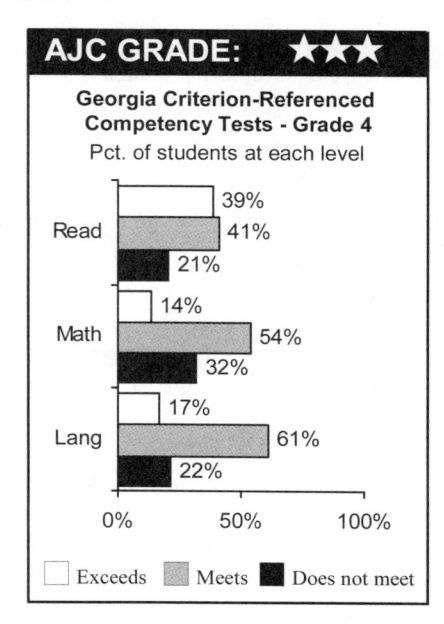

AJC GRADE: ★★★

Georgia Criterion-Referenced Competency Tests - Grade 4
Pct. of students at each level

- Read: Exceeds 39%, Meets 41%, Does not meet 21%
- Math: Exceeds 14%, Meets 54%, Does not meet 32%
- Lang: Exceeds 17%, Meets 61%, Does not meet 22%

Fulton County Elementary Schools

River Eves Elementary School

9000 Eves Rd, Roswell, GA 30076
770-552-4550 · Grades K - 5

Enrollment:	935
White / black / other:	63.2% / 17.6% / 19.1%
Not native English-speaking:	61 / 6.5%
Limited English proficiency:	122 / 13.0%
Student absenteeism:	4.1%
Students per teacher:	17.3
Parent friendliness:	❶❷❸④⑤❻
Teachers with advanced degrees:	37.3%
Average years' teaching experience:	9.4
Students in gifted program:	63 / 6.7%
Students in remedial education:	15.0%
Students held back a grade:	1.5%
Total suspensions, pct. in-school:	2 / 100.0%
Offenses: violence: *, drugs: *, other:	20
Eligible students, free or reduced lunch:	15.1%
Before / after school program:	Yes / Yes

Students at this school generally go on to:
Holcomb Bridge Middle

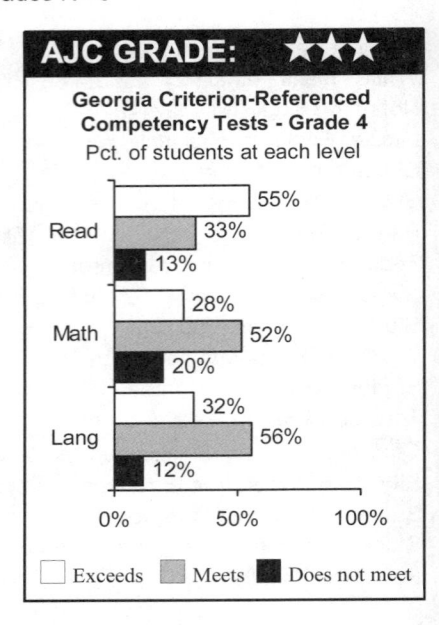

AJC GRADE: ★★★

Georgia Criterion-Referenced Competency Tests - Grade 4
Pct. of students at each level

- Read: Exceeds 55%, Meets 33%, Does not meet 13%
- Math: Exceeds 28%, Meets 52%, Does not meet 20%
- Lang: Exceeds 32%, Meets 56%, Does not meet 12%

Roswell North Elementary School

10525 Woodstock Rd, Roswell, GA 30075
770-552-6320 · Grades K - 5

Enrollment:	834
White / black / other:	62.8% / 12.9% / 24.2%
Not native English-speaking:	86 / 10.3%
Limited English proficiency:	124 / 14.9%
Student absenteeism:	4.8%
Students per teacher:	14.4
Parent friendliness:	①❷❸④⑤❻
Teachers with advanced degrees:	41.9%
Average years' teaching experience:	11.5
Students in gifted program:	31 / 3.7%
Students in remedial education:	16.2%
Students held back a grade:	1.9%
Total suspensions, pct. in-school:	23 / 65.2%
Offenses: violence: *, drugs: *, other:	49
Eligible students, free or reduced lunch:	27.5%
Before / after school program:	No / Yes

Students at this school generally go on to:
Crabapple Middle

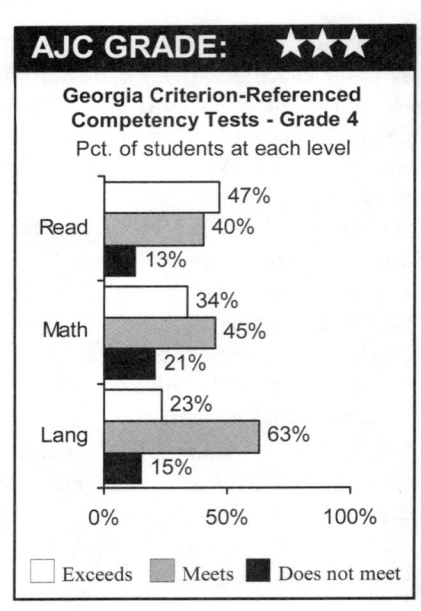

AJC GRADE: ★★★

Georgia Criterion-Referenced Competency Tests - Grade 4
Pct. of students at each level

- Read: Exceeds 47%, Meets 40%, Does not meet 13%
- Math: Exceeds 34%, Meets 45%, Does not meet 21%
- Lang: Exceeds 23%, Meets 63%, Does not meet 15%

Fulton County Elementary Schools

Seaborn Lee Elementary School

4600 Scarborough Rd, College Park, GA 30349
404-669-8025 · Grades K - 5

Enrollment:	517
White / black / other:	1.0% / 97.7% / 1.4%
Not native English-speaking:	*
Limited English proficiency:	*
Student absenteeism:	7.1%
Students per teacher:	13.8
Parent friendliness:	① ❷ ❸ ❹ ❺ ❻
Teachers with advanced degrees:	53.8%
Average years' teaching experience:	11.2
Students in gifted program:	9 / 1.7%
Students in remedial education:	29.9%
Students held back a grade:	4.6%
Total suspensions, pct. in-school:	220 / 0.0%
Offenses: violence: *, drugs: *, other:	350
Eligible students, free or reduced lunch:	89.8%
Before / after school program:	Yes / Yes

Students at this school generally go on to:
Camp Creek Middle

AJC GRADE: ★★

Georgia Criterion-Referenced Competency Tests - Grade 4
Pct. of students at each level

Read: Exceeds 14%, Meets 38%, Does not meet 49%
Math: Exceeds 3%, Meets 28%, Does not meet 70%
Lang: Exceeds 9%, Meets 38%, Does not meet 53%

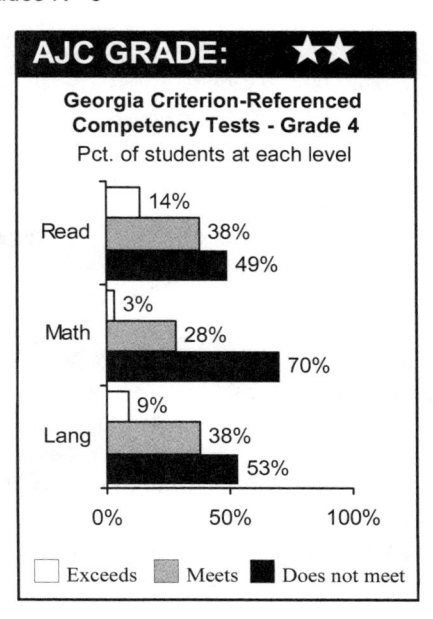

Shakerag Elementary School

10885 Rogers Cir, Duluth, GA 30097
770-497-3880 · Grades K - 5

Enrollment:	896
White / black / other:	73.9% / 4.9% / 21.2%
Not native English-speaking:	*
Limited English proficiency:	1 / 0.1%
Student absenteeism:	3.7%
Students per teacher:	17.1
Parent friendliness:	❶ ❷ ❸ ④ ⑤ ❻
Teachers with advanced degrees:	37.9%
Average years' teaching experience:	10.2
Students in gifted program:	57 / 6.4%
Students in remedial education:	14.1%
Students held back a grade:	1.0%
Total suspensions, pct. in-school:	1 / 0.0%
Offenses: violence: *, drugs: *, other:	1
Eligible students, free or reduced lunch:	1.3%
Before / after school program:	Yes / Yes

Students at this school generally go on to:
River Trail Middle

AJC GRADE: ★★★★

Georgia Criterion-Referenced Competency Tests - Grade 4
Pct. of students at each level

Read: Exceeds 65%, Meets 30%, Does not meet 5%
Math: Exceeds 40%, Meets 56%, Does not meet 5%
Lang: Exceeds 46%, Meets 49%, Does not meet 5%

The Atlanta Journal-Constitution / Page 339

Fulton County Elementary Schools

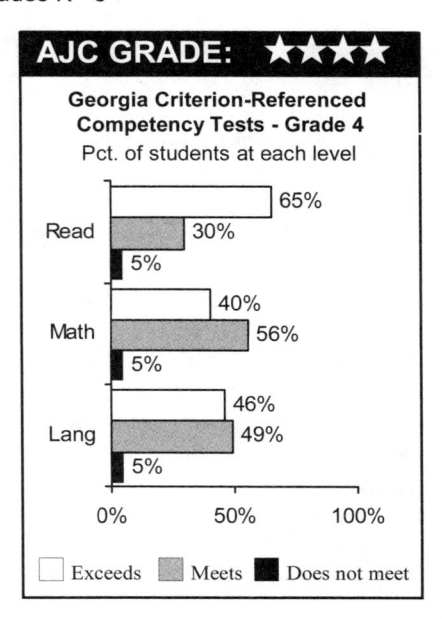

Spalding Drive Elementary School

130 W Spalding Dr NE, Atlanta, GA 30328
770-551-5880 · Grades K - 5

Enrollment:	566
White / black / other:	33.9% / 35.0% / 31.1%
Not native English-speaking:	94 / 16.6%
Limited English proficiency:	177 / 31.3%
Student absenteeism:	6.2%
Students per teacher:	13.5
Parent friendliness:	❶❷❸❹❺❻
Teachers with advanced degrees:	37.8%
Average years' teaching experience:	10.4
Students in gifted program:	29 / 5.1%
Students in remedial education:	27.3%
Students held back a grade:	1.6%
Total suspensions, pct. in-school:	55 / 14.5%
Offenses:	violence: * , drugs: * , other: 68
Eligible students, free or reduced lunch:	42.7%
Before / after school program:	Yes / Yes

Students at this school generally go on to:
Ridgeview, Sandy Springs Middle

AJC GRADE: ★★★

Georgia Criterion-Referenced Competency Tests - Grade 4
Pct. of students at each level

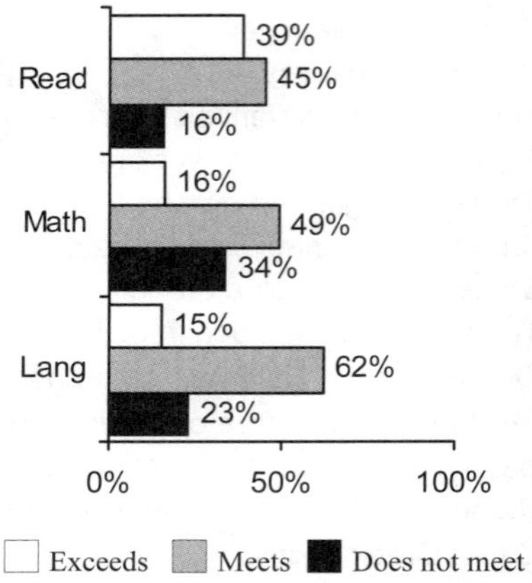

Read
39%
45%
16%
Math
16%
49%
34%
Lang
15%
62%
23%
0%
50%
100%
Exceeds
Meets
Does not meet

State Bridge Crossing Elementary School

5530 State Bridge Rd, Alpharetta, GA 30022
770-497-3850 · Grades K - 5

Enrollment:	864
White / black / other:	67.1% / 6.7% / 26.2%
Not native English-speaking:	59 / 6.8%
Limited English proficiency:	85 / 9.8%
Student absenteeism:	4.0%
Students per teacher:	15.2
Parent friendliness:	❶❷❸④⑤❻
Teachers with advanced degrees:	39.3%
Average years' teaching experience:	8.0
Students in gifted program:	62 / 7.2%
Students in remedial education:	11.8%
Students held back a grade:	0.1%
Total suspensions, pct. in-school:	21 / 4.8%
Offenses:	violence: * , drugs: * , other: 39
Eligible students, free or reduced lunch:	4.0%
Before / after school program:	No / Yes

Students at this school generally go on to:
Taylor Road Middle

AJC GRADE: ★★★

Georgia Criterion-Referenced Competency Tests - Grade 4
Pct. of students at each level

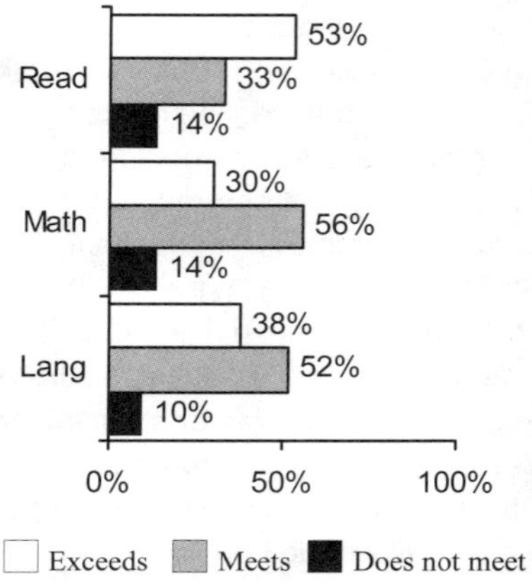

Read
53%
33%
14%
Math
30%
56%
14%
Lang
38%
52%
10%
0%
50%
100%
Exceeds
Meets
Does not meet

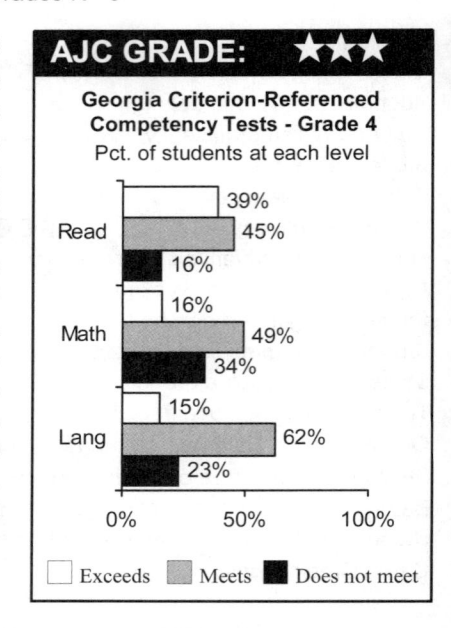

Stonewall Tell Elementary School

3310 Stonewall Tell Rd, College Park, GA 30349
770-306-3500 · Grades K - 5

Enrollment:	622
White / black / other:	2.7% / 92.9% / 4.3%
Not native English-speaking:	*
Limited English proficiency:	1 / 0.2%
Student absenteeism:	6.3%
Students per teacher:	14.5
Parent friendliness:	❶❷❸❹❺❻
Teachers with advanced degrees:	50.0%
Average years' teaching experience:	11.5
Students in gifted program:	9 / 1.4%
Students in remedial education:	26.5%
Students held back a grade:	2.6%
Total suspensions, pct. in-school:	122 / 9.8%
Offenses: violence: *, drugs: *, other:	217
Eligible students, free or reduced lunch:	78.8%
Before / after school program:	No / Yes

Students at this school generally go on to:
Camp Creek Middle

AJC GRADE: ★★★

Georgia Criterion-Referenced Competency Tests - Grade 4
Pct. of students at each level

- Read: 21% Exceeds / 37% Meets / 41% Does not meet
- Math: 2% Exceeds / 45% Meets / 54% Does not meet
- Lang: 5% Exceeds / 57% Meets / 38% Does not meet

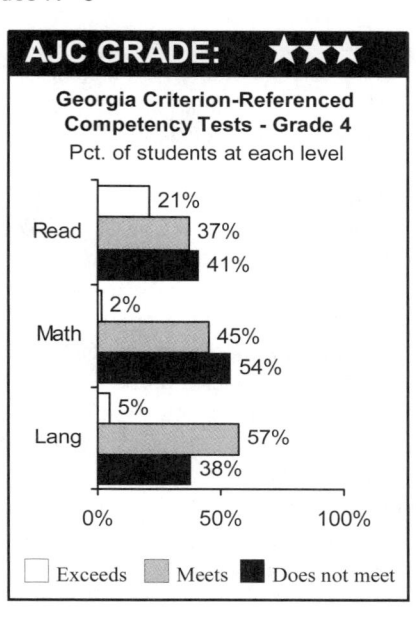

Summit Hill Elementary School

13855 Providence Rd, Alpharetta, GA 30004
770-667-2830 · Grades K - 5

Enrollment:	863
White / black / other:	93.2% / 2.0% / 4.9%
Not native English-speaking:	*
Limited English proficiency:	*
Student absenteeism:	4.0%
Students per teacher:	16.6
Parent friendliness:	①❷❸④⑤❻
Teachers with advanced degrees:	41.4%
Average years' teaching experience:	8.1
Students in gifted program:	57 / 6.6%
Students in remedial education:	7.1%
Students held back a grade:	0.8%
Total suspensions, pct. in-school:	2 / 50.0%
Offenses: violence: *, drugs: *, other:	2
Eligible students, free or reduced lunch:	0.9%
Before / after school program:	Yes / Yes

Students at this school generally go on to:
Northwestern Middle

AJC GRADE: ★★★★

Georgia Criterion-Referenced Competency Tests - Grade 4
Pct. of students at each level

- Read: 68% Exceeds / 28% Meets / 4% Does not meet
- Math: 39% Exceeds / 53% Meets / 9% Does not meet
- Lang: 42% Exceeds / 54% Meets / 4% Does not meet

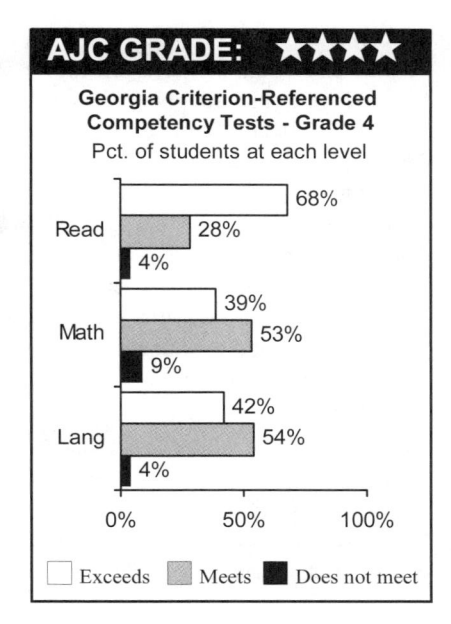

Sweet Apple Elementary School

12025 Etris Rd, Roswell, GA 30075
770-643-3310 · Grades K - 5

Enrollment:	1,180
White / black / other:	79.5% / 7.9% / 12.6%
Not native English-speaking:	32 / 2.7%
Limited English proficiency:	52 / 4.4%
Student absenteeism:	4.3%
Students per teacher:	16.5
Parent friendliness:	❶❷❸④⑤⑥
Teachers with advanced degrees:	38.2%
Average years' teaching experience:	8.2
Students in gifted program:	117 / 9.9%
Students in remedial education:	8.3%
Students held back a grade:	1.4%
Total suspensions, pct. in-school:	15 / 6.7%
Offenses: violence: *, drugs: *, other: 25	
Eligible students, free or reduced lunch:	5.1%
Before / after school program:	No / Yes
Students at this school generally go on to: Elkins Pointe Middle	

AJC GRADE: ★★★

Georgia Criterion-Referenced Competency Tests - Grade 4
Pct. of students at each level

Read: Exceeds 61%, Meets 25%, Does not meet 14%
Math: Exceeds 32%, Meets 55%, Does not meet 13%
Lang: Exceeds 32%, Meets 56%, Does not meet 13%

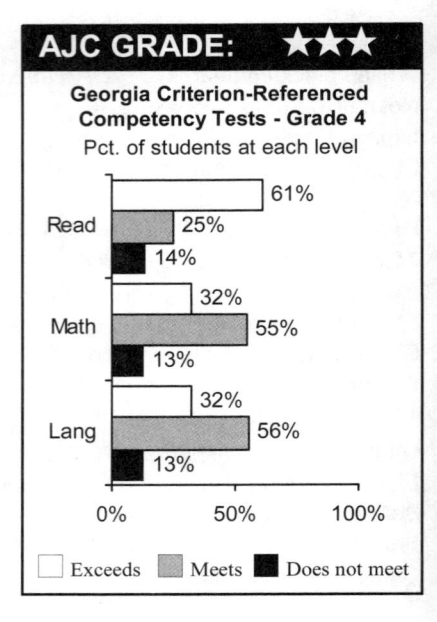

Victory Charter School

1312 Knotts Ave, East Point, GA 30344
404-753-7045 · Grades K - 7

Enrollment:	485
White / black / other:	6.8% / 91.5% / 1.6%
Not native English-speaking:	*
Limited English proficiency:	*
Student absenteeism:	5.6%
Students per teacher:	*
Parent friendliness:	①❷❸④⑤⑥
Teachers with advanced degrees:	*
Average years' teaching experience:	*
Students in gifted program:	*
Students in remedial education:	*
Students held back a grade:	1.4%
Total suspensions, pct. in-school:	*
Offenses: violence: *, drugs: *, other: *	
Eligible students, free or reduced lunch:	*
Before / after school program:	No / Yes
Students at this school generally go on to: Several Fulton County middle schools	

AJC GRADE: ★

Georgia Criterion-Referenced Competency Tests - Grade 4
Pct. of students at each level

Read: Exceeds 16%, Meets 47%, Does not meet 37%
Math: Exceeds 1%, Meets 34%, Does not meet 64%
Lang: Exceeds 5%, Meets 55%, Does not meet 40%

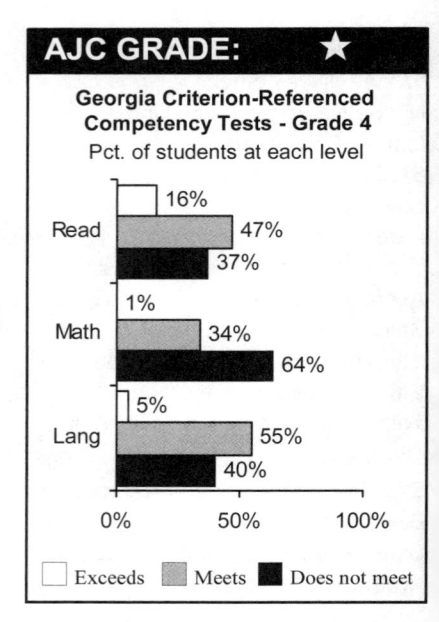

West Elementary School

7040 Rivertown Rd, Fairburn, GA 30213
770-969-3460 · Grades K - 5

Enrollment:	460
White / black / other:	33.7% / 47.8% / 18.5%
Not native English-speaking:	33 / 7.2%
Limited English proficiency:	84 / 18.3%
Student absenteeism:	5.8%
Students per teacher:	14.4
Parent friendliness:	①❷❸④❺❻
Teachers with advanced degrees:	50.0%
Average years' teaching experience:	17.1
Students in gifted program:	11 / 2.4%
Students in remedial education:	33.9%
Students held back a grade:	0.7%
Total suspensions, pct. in-school:	29 / 0.0%
Offenses: violence: *, drugs: *, other: 40	
Eligible students, free or reduced lunch:	56.6%
Before / after school program:	No / Yes

Students at this school generally go on to:
Bear Creek Middle

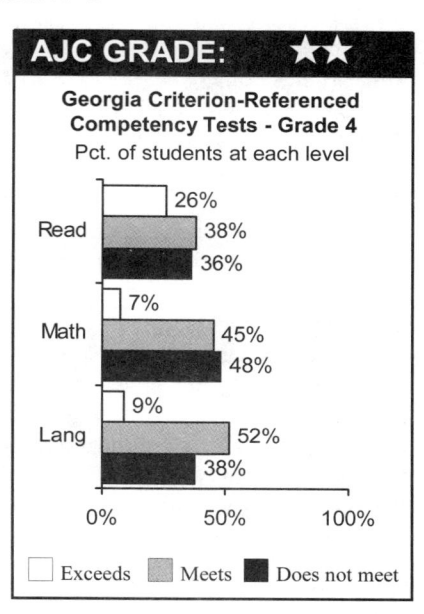

AJC GRADE: ★★

Georgia Criterion-Referenced Competency Tests - Grade 4
Pct. of students at each level

- Read: Exceeds 26%, Meets 38%, Does not meet 36%
- Math: Exceeds 7%, Meets 45%, Does not meet 48%
- Lang: Exceeds 9%, Meets 52%, Does not meet 38%

Woodland Charter Elementary School

1130 Spalding Dr, Atlanta, GA 30350
770-551-5890 · Grades K - 5

Enrollment:	539
White / black / other:	35.4% / 37.1% / 27.5%
Not native English-speaking:	50 / 9.3%
Limited English proficiency:	106 / 19.7%
Student absenteeism:	5.6%
Students per teacher:	10.8
Parent friendliness:	❶❷❸④❺❻
Teachers with advanced degrees:	48.3%
Average years' teaching experience:	10.2
Students in gifted program:	31 / 5.8%
Students in remedial education:	15.2%
Students held back a grade:	1.5%
Total suspensions, pct. in-school:	5 / 0.0%
Offenses: violence: *, drugs: *, other: 8	
Eligible students, free or reduced lunch:	28.8%
Before / after school program:	No / Yes

Students at this school generally go on to:
Sandy Springs Middle

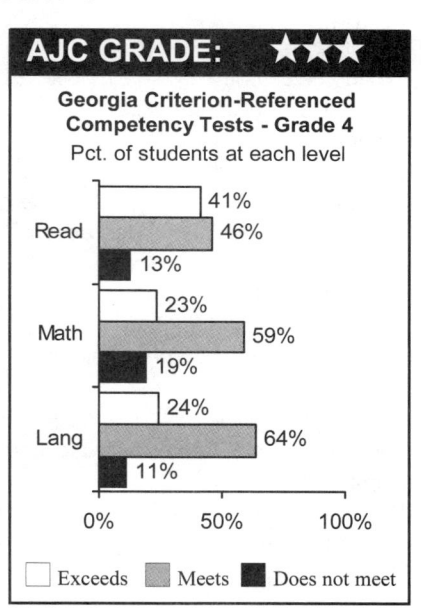

AJC GRADE: ★★★

Georgia Criterion-Referenced Competency Tests - Grade 4
Pct. of students at each level

- Read: Exceeds 41%, Meets 46%, Does not meet 13%
- Math: Exceeds 23%, Meets 59%, Does not meet 19%
- Lang: Exceeds 24%, Meets 64%, Does not meet 11%

Fulton County Elementary Schools

Bear Creek Middle School

7415 Herndon Rd, Fairburn, GA 30213
770-969-6080 · Grades 6 - 8

Enrollment:	1,173
White / black / other:	17.8% / 73.8% / 8.4%
Not native English-speaking:	13 / 1.1%
Student absenteeism:	6.0%
Students per teacher:	16.3
Parent friendliness:	❶❷❸❹❺❻
Teachers with advanced degrees:	34.2%
Average years' teaching experience:	11.9
Students in gifted program:	57 / 4.9%
Students held back a grade:	4.6%
Total suspensions and expulsions:	1,041
Suspensions only, pct. in-school:	1,040 / 66.4%
Offenses: violence: 171, drugs: 1, other: 1,008	
Eligible students, free or reduced lunch:	68.2%
Number of dropouts:	8 / 0.6%
Pct. 8th-graders w/ basic computer skills:	100.0%

Students at this school generally go on to:
Creekside High

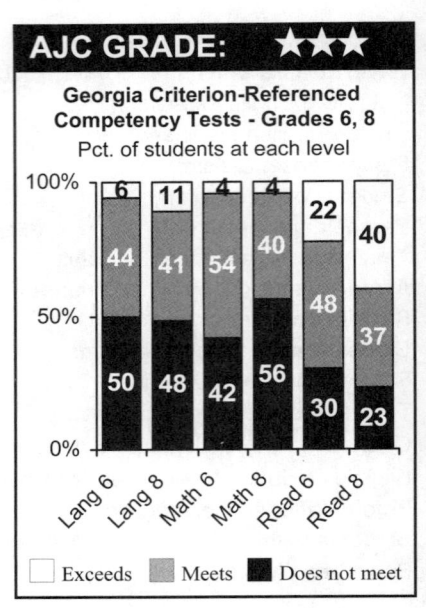

AJC GRADE: ★★★

Georgia Criterion-Referenced Competency Tests - Grades 6, 8
Pct. of students at each level

	Lang 6	Lang 8	Math 6	Math 8	Read 6	Read 8
Exceeds	6	11	4	4	22	40
Meets	44	41	54	40	48	37
Does not meet	50	48	42	56	30	23

Camp Creek Middle School

4345 Welcome All Rd SW, Atlanta, GA 30349
404-669-8030 · Grades 6 - 8

Enrollment:	1,041
White / black / other:	1.0% / 97.8% / 1.2%
Not native English-speaking:	*
Student absenteeism:	3.8%
Students per teacher:	15.0
Parent friendliness:	❶❷❸④❺❻
Teachers with advanced degrees:	41.7%
Average years' teaching experience:	9.0
Students in gifted program:	50 / 4.8%
Students held back a grade:	7.6%
Total suspensions and expulsions:	560
Suspensions only, pct. in-school:	560 / 47.1%
Offenses: violence: 203, drugs: *, other: 410	
Eligible students, free or reduced lunch:	66.3%
Number of dropouts:	23 / 1.8%
Pct. 8th-graders w/ basic computer skills:	100.0%

Students at this school generally go on to:
Westlake High

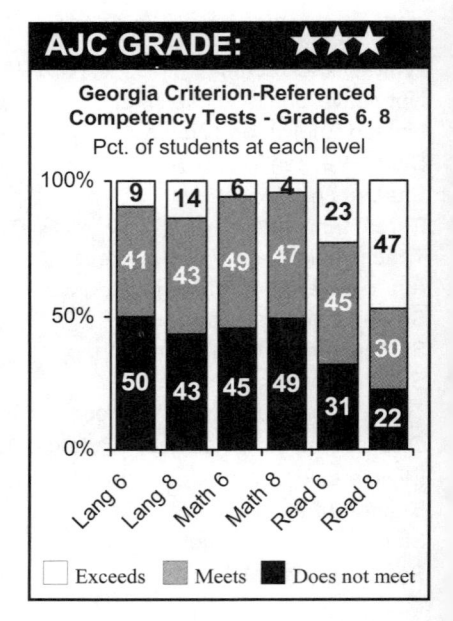

AJC GRADE: ★★★

Georgia Criterion-Referenced Competency Tests - Grades 6, 8
Pct. of students at each level

	Lang 6	Lang 8	Math 6	Math 8	Read 6	Read 8
Exceeds	9	14	6	4	23	47
Meets	41	43	49	47	45	30
Does not meet	50	43	45	49	31	22

Fulton County Middle Schools

Crabapple Middle School

10700 Crabapple Rd, Roswell, GA 30075
770-552-4520 · Grades 6 - 8

Enrollment:	1,184
White / black / other:	63.6% / 19.6% / 16.8%
Not native English-speaking:	89 / 7.5%
Student absenteeism:	4.8%
Students per teacher:	14.0
Parent friendliness:	① ❷ ❸ ④ ❺ ❻
Teachers with advanced degrees:	48.2%
Average years' teaching experience:	10.8
Students in gifted program:	376 / 31.8%
Students held back a grade:	0.8%
Total suspensions and expulsions:	383
Suspensions only, pct. in-school:	383 / 72.1%
Offenses:	violence: 82, drugs: 2, other: 394
Eligible students, free or reduced lunch:	18.4%
Number of dropouts:	*
Pct. 8th-graders w/ basic computer skills:	88.0%

Students at this school generally go on to:
Roswell High

AJC GRADE: ★★★

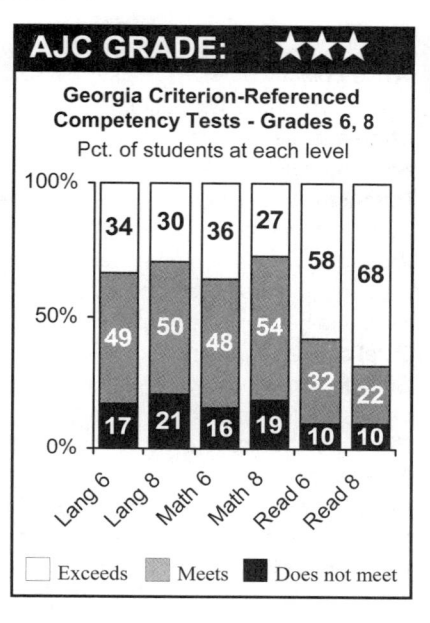

Georgia Criterion-Referenced Competency Tests - Grades 6, 8
Pct. of students at each level

	Lang 6	Lang 8	Math 6	Math 8	Read 6	Read 8
Exceeds	34	30	36	27	58	68
Meets	49	50	48	54	32	22
Does not meet	17	21	16	19	10	10

Haynes Bridge Middle School

10665 Haynes Bridge Rd, Alpharetta, GA 30022
770-740-7030 · Grades 6 - 8

Enrollment:	985
White / black / other:	75.7% / 14.7% / 9.5%
Not native English-speaking:	*
Student absenteeism:	4.5%
Students per teacher:	13.9
Parent friendliness:	① ❷ ❸ ④ ❺ ❻
Teachers with advanced degrees:	48.6%
Average years' teaching experience:	12.7
Students in gifted program:	335 / 34.0%
Students held back a grade:	0.1%
Total suspensions and expulsions:	342
Suspensions only, pct. in-school:	342 / 93.3%
Offenses:	violence: 63, drugs: *, other: 390
Eligible students, free or reduced lunch:	7.6%
Number of dropouts:	*
Pct. 8th-graders w/ basic computer skills:	100.0%

Students at this school generally go on to:
Centennial High

AJC GRADE: ★★★

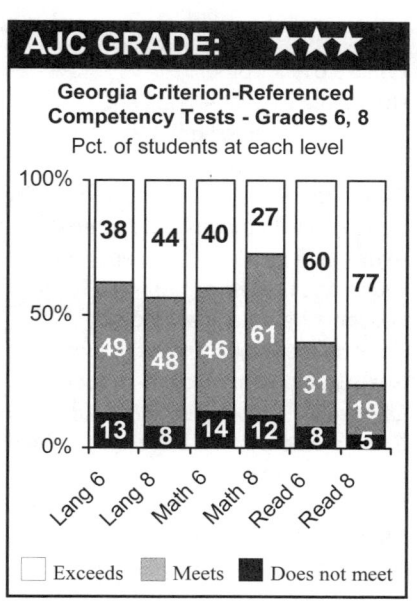

Georgia Criterion-Referenced Competency Tests - Grades 6, 8
Pct. of students at each level

	Lang 6	Lang 8	Math 6	Math 8	Read 6	Read 8
Exceeds	38	44	40	27	60	77
Meets	49	48	46	61	31	19
Does not meet	13	8	14	12	8	5

Fulton County Middle Schools

Holcomb Bridge Middle School

2700 Holcomb Bridge Rd, Alpharetta, GA 30022
770-594-5280 · Grades 6 - 8

Enrollment:	888
White / black / other:	54.5% / 23.5% / 22.0%
Not native English-speaking:	87 / 9.8%
Student absenteeism:	5.5%
Students per teacher:	13.7
Parent friendliness:	❶❷❸❹❺❻
Teachers with advanced degrees:	48.5%
Average years' teaching experience:	12.1
Students in gifted program:	209 / 23.5%
Students held back a grade:	1.5%
Total suspensions and expulsions:	697
Suspensions only, pct. in-school:	695 / 80.0%
Offenses: violence: 119, drugs: * , other: 699	
Eligible students, free or reduced lunch:	23.3%
Number of dropouts:	*
Pct. 8th-graders w/ basic computer skills: 100.0%	

Students at this school generally go on to:
Centennial High

AJC GRADE: ★★★

Georgia Criterion-Referenced Competency Tests - Grades 6, 8
Pct. of students at each level

	Lang 6	Lang 8	Math 6	Math 8	Read 6	Read 8
Exceeds	31	29	32	25		
Meets	46	52	44	50	49	70
					37	19
Does not meet	23	20	24	25	15	11

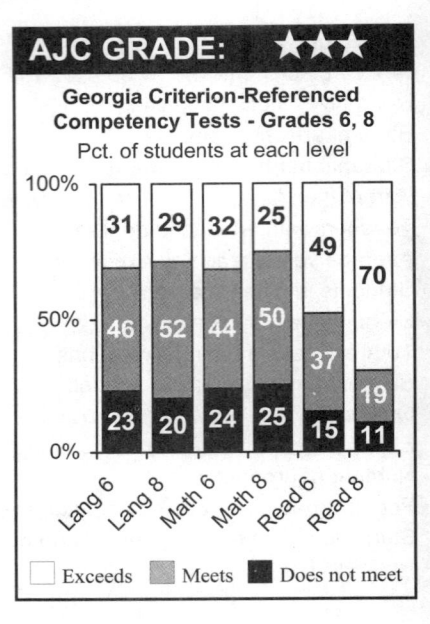

McNair Middle School

2800 Burdett Rd, College Park, GA 30349
770-991-4160 · Grades 6 - 8

Enrollment:	1,171
White / black / other:	0.3% / 98.0% / 1.7%
Not native English-speaking:	*
Student absenteeism:	4.0%
Students per teacher:	16.4
Parent friendliness:	❶❷❸④⑤❻
Teachers with advanced degrees:	51.4%
Average years' teaching experience:	10.4
Students in gifted program:	79 / 6.7%
Students held back a grade:	32.8%
Total suspensions and expulsions:	1,397
Suspensions only, pct. in-school:	1,397 / 50.8%
Offenses: violence: 288, drugs: 1, other: 1,201	
Eligible students, free or reduced lunch:	71.8%
Number of dropouts:	1 / 0.1%
Pct. 8th-graders w/ basic computer skills: 100.0%	

Students at this school generally go on to:
Banneker, Tri-Cities, Westlake High

AJC GRADE: ★★★

Georgia Criterion-Referenced Competency Tests - Grades 6, 8
Pct. of students at each level

	Lang 6	Lang 8	Math 6	Math 8	Read 6	Read 8
Exceeds	8	7	5	2	22	35
Meets	42	43	41	40	42	41
Does not meet	51	50	53	58	36	24

The Atlanta Journal-Constitution / Page 346

Fulton County Middle Schools

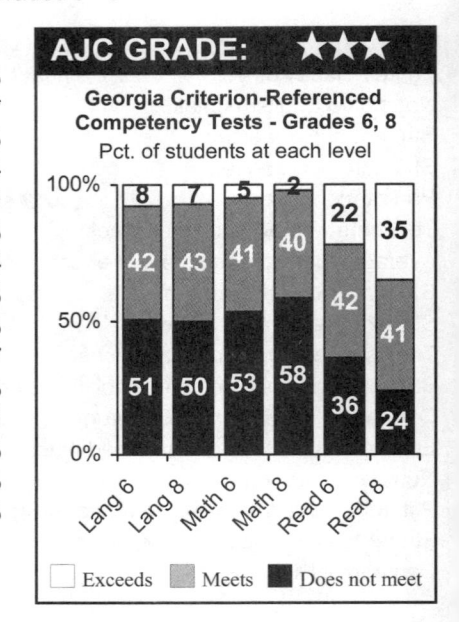

Northwestern Middle School

12805 Birmingham Hwy, Alpharetta, GA 30004
770-667-2870 · Grades 6 - 8

👍

Enrollment:	1,987
White / black / other:	86.3% / 6.3% / 7.3%
Not native English-speaking:	*
Student absenteeism:	4.8%
Students per teacher:	16.6
Parent friendliness:	①❷❸④⑤❻
Teachers with advanced degrees:	43.0%
Average years' teaching experience:	10.5
Students in gifted program:	663 / 33.4%
Students held back a grade:	1.0%
Total suspensions and expulsions:	191
Suspensions only, pct. in-school:	191 / 69.1%
Offenses:	violence: 34, drugs: 16, other: 210
Eligible students, free or reduced lunch:	2.6%
Number of dropouts:	*
Pct. 8th-graders w/ basic computer skills:	100.0%

Students at this school generally go on to:
Milton, Roswell High

AJC GRADE: ★★★

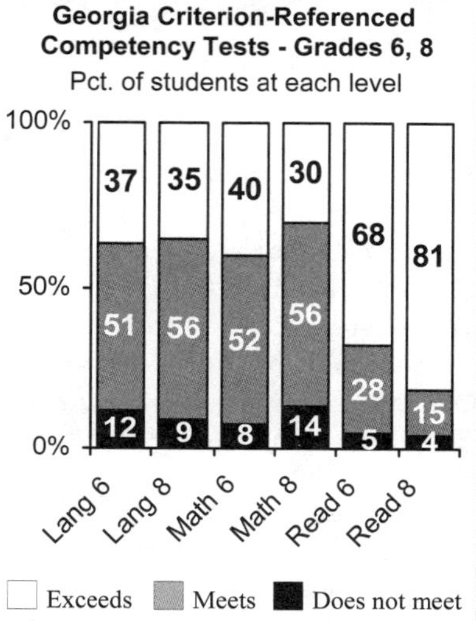
Georgia Criterion-Referenced
Competency Tests - Grades 6, 8
Pct. of students at each level
100%
50%
0%
37 35 40 30 68 81
51 56 52 56 28 15
12 9 8 14 5 4
Lang 6
Lang 8
Math 6
Math 8
Read 6
Read 8
Exceeds
Meets
Does not meet

Ridgeview Middle School

5340 Trimble Rd NE, Atlanta, GA 30342
404-843-7710 · Grades 6 - 8

Enrollment:	556
White / black / other:	46.2% / 22.1% / 31.7%
Not native English-speaking:	88 / 15.8%
Student absenteeism:	4.6%
Students per teacher:	12.0
Parent friendliness:	❶❷❸④❺❻
Teachers with advanced degrees:	51.1%
Average years' teaching experience:	12.2
Students in gifted program:	152 / 27.3%
Students held back a grade:	3.1%
Total suspensions and expulsions:	240
Suspensions only, pct. in-school:	240 / 86.7%
Offenses:	violence: 85, drugs: 4, other: 179
Eligible students, free or reduced lunch:	48.2%
Number of dropouts:	1 / 0.1%
Pct. 8th-graders w/ basic computer skills:	100.0%

Students at this school generally go on to:
Riverwood High

AJC GRADE: ★★★

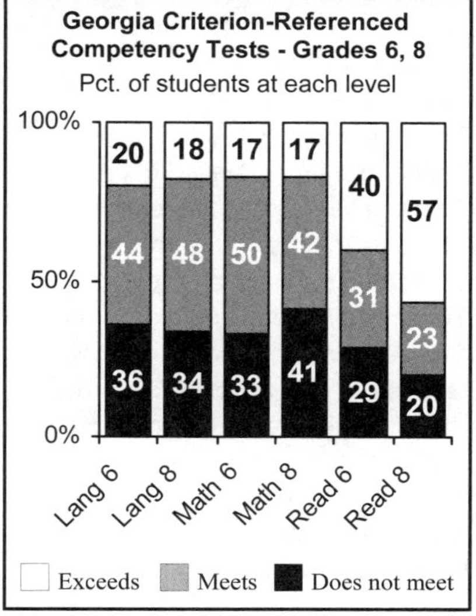
Georgia Criterion-Referenced
Competency Tests - Grades 6, 8
Pct. of students at each level
100%
50%
0%
20 18 17 17 40 57
44 48 50 42 31 23
36 34 33 41 29 20
Lang 6
Lang 8
Math 6
Math 8
Read 6
Read 8
Exceeds
Meets
Does not meet

Sandy Springs Middle School

8750 Colonel Dr, Atlanta, GA 30350
770-552-4970 · Grades 6 - 8

Enrollment:	713
White / black / other:	46.3% / 37.3% / 16.4%
Not native English-speaking:	65 / 9.1%
Student absenteeism:	6.4%
Students per teacher:	13.6
Parent friendliness:	❶ ❷ ❸ ④ ⑤ ❻
Teachers with advanced degrees:	45.3%
Average years' teaching experience:	10.9
Students in gifted program:	175 / 24.5%
Students held back a grade:	2.4%
Total suspensions and expulsions:	733
Suspensions only, pct. in-school:	733 / 70.9%
Offenses: violence: 71, drugs: * , other: 674	
Eligible students, free or reduced lunch:	31.3%
Number of dropouts:	*
Pct. 8th-graders w/ basic computer skills:	100.0%
Students at this school generally go on to:	
North Springs High	

AJC GRADE: ★★★

Georgia Criterion-Referenced Competency Tests - Grades 6, 8
Pct. of students at each level

	Lang 6	Lang 8	Math 6	Math 8	Read 6	Read 8
Exceeds	29	27	27	21	49	56
Meets	47	49	47	47	29	29
Does not meet	24	24	26	31	22	15

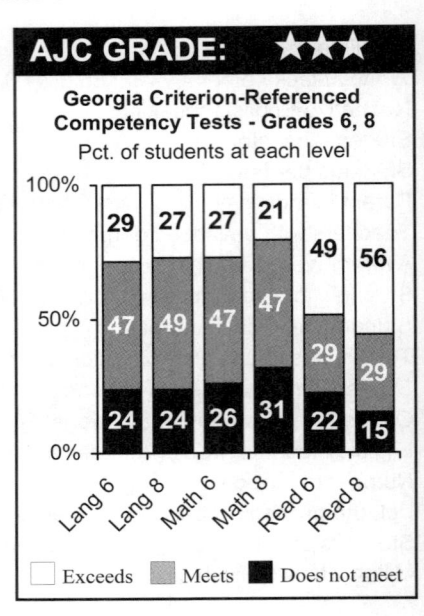

Taylor Road Middle School

5150 Taylor Rd, Alpharetta, GA 30022
770-740-7090 · Grades 6 - 8

Enrollment:	1,689
White / black / other:	69.4% / 7.9% / 22.7%
Not native English-speaking:	83 / 4.9%
Student absenteeism:	3.8%
Students per teacher:	16.2
Parent friendliness:	① ❷ ❸ ④ ⑤ ❻
Teachers with advanced degrees:	53.3%
Average years' teaching experience:	10.9
Students in gifted program:	494 / 29.2%
Students held back a grade:	0.2%
Total suspensions and expulsions:	318
Suspensions only, pct. in-school:	318 / 86.2%
Offenses: violence: 70, drugs: 10, other: 297	
Eligible students, free or reduced lunch:	3.0%
Number of dropouts:	*
Pct. 8th-graders w/ basic computer skills:	80.0%
Students at this school generally go on to:	
Chattahoochee High	

AJC GRADE: ★★★

Georgia Criterion-Referenced Competency Tests - Grades 6, 8
Pct. of students at each level

	Lang 6	Lang 8	Math 6	Math 8	Read 6	Read 8
Exceeds	39	40	44	33	62	77
Meets	50	47	48	54	33	21
Does not meet	11	13	8	13	5	2

Fulton County Middle Schools

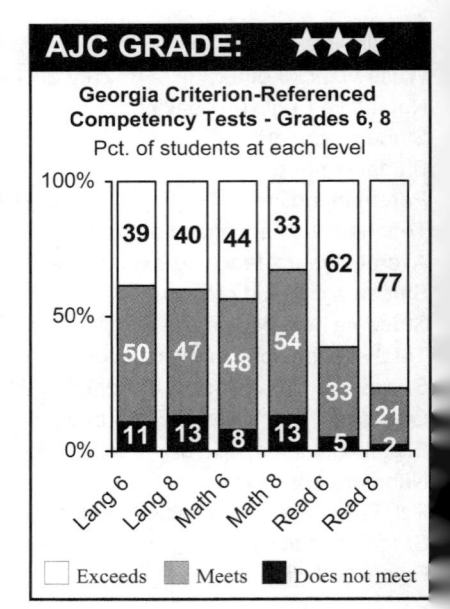

Webb Bridge Middle School

4455 Webb Bridge Rd, Alpharetta, GA 30005
770-667-2940 · Grades 6 - 8

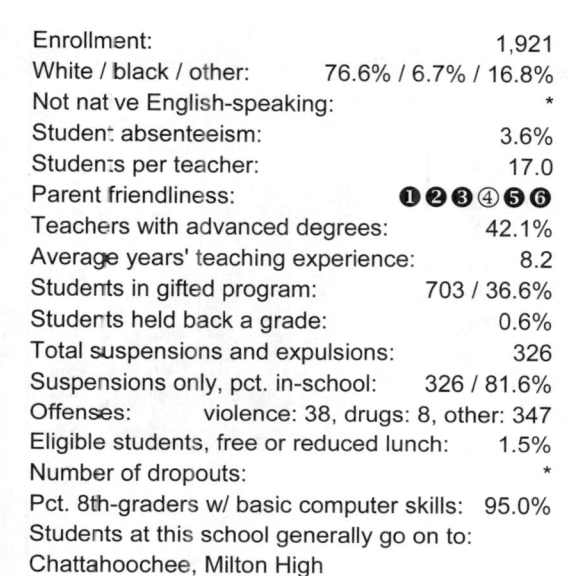

Enrollment:	1,921
White / black / other:	76.6% / 6.7% / 16.8%
Not native English-speaking:	*
Student absenteeism:	3.6%
Students per teacher:	17.0
Parent friendliness:	❶❷❸④❺❻
Teachers with advanced degrees:	42.1%
Average years' teaching experience:	8.2
Students in gifted program:	703 / 36.6%
Students held back a grade:	0.6%
Total suspensions and expulsions:	326
Suspensions only, pct. in-school:	326 / 81.6%
Offenses: violence: 38, drugs: 8, other: 347	
Eligible students, free or reduced lunch:	1.5%
Number of dropouts:	*
Pct. 8th-graders w/ basic computer skills:	95.0%

Students at this school generally go on to:
Chattahoochee, Milton High

AJC GRADE: ★★★★

Georgia Criterion-Referenced Competency Tests - Grades 6, 8
Pct. of students at each level

	Lang 6	Lang 8	Math 6	Math 8	Read 6	Read 8
Exceeds	47	46	52	39	71	84
Meets	44	48	41	54	25	14
Does not meet	9	6	7	6	5	2

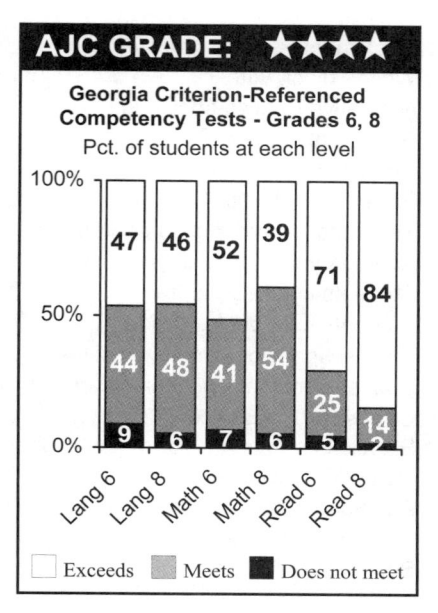

West Middle School

2376 Headland Dr, East Point, GA 30344
404-669-8130 · Grades 6 - 8

Enrollment:	923
White / black / other:	3.7% / 88.7% / 7.6%
Not native English-speaking:	*
Student absenteeism:	6.4%
Students per teacher:	15.0
Parent friendliness:	❶❷❸④❺❻
Teachers with advanced degrees:	50.0%
Average years' teaching experience:	11.5
Students in gifted program:	39 / 4.2%
Students held back a grade:	4.3%
Total suspensions and expulsions:	1,230
Suspensions only, pct. in-school:	1,230 / 56.3%
Offenses: violence: 293, drugs: *, other: 1,079	
Eligible students, free or reduced lunch:	84.7%
Number of dropouts:	*
Pct. 8th-graders w/ basic computer skills:	95.0%

Students at this school generally go on to:
Tri-Cities High

AJC GRADE: ★★★

Georgia Criterion-Referenced Competency Tests - Grades 6, 8
Pct. of students at each level

	Lang 6	Lang 8	Math 6	Math 8	Read 6	Read 8
Exceeds	6	4	4	3	17	31
Meets	44	45	43	38	46	38
Does not meet	51	51	53	58	38	31

Fulton County Middle Schools

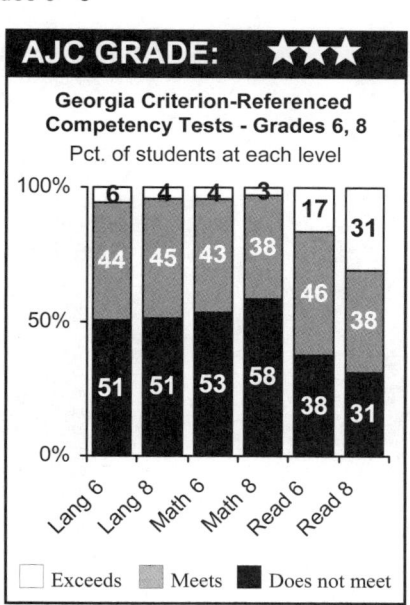

Woodland Middle School

2816 Briarwood Blvd, East Point, GA 30344
404-346-6420 · Grades 6 - 8

Enrollment:	1,205
White / black / other:	5.4% / 78.3% / 16.3%
Not native English-speaking:	79 / 6.6%
Student absenteeism:	6.5%
Students per teacher:	13.9
Parent friendliness:	①❷❸④⑤❻
Teachers with advanced degrees:	46.0%
Average years' teaching experience:	9.9
Students in gifted program:	33 / 2.7%
Students held back a grade:	3.2%
Total suspensions and expulsions:	1,446
Suspensions only, pct. in-school:	1,445 / 76.1%
Offenses:	violence: 272, drugs: 5, other: 1,296
Eligible students, free or reduced lunch:	81.5%
Number of dropouts:	4 / 0.3%
Pct. 8th-graders w/ basic computer skills:	100.0%

Students at this school generally go on to:
Banneker, Tri-Cities High

AJC GRADE: ★★★

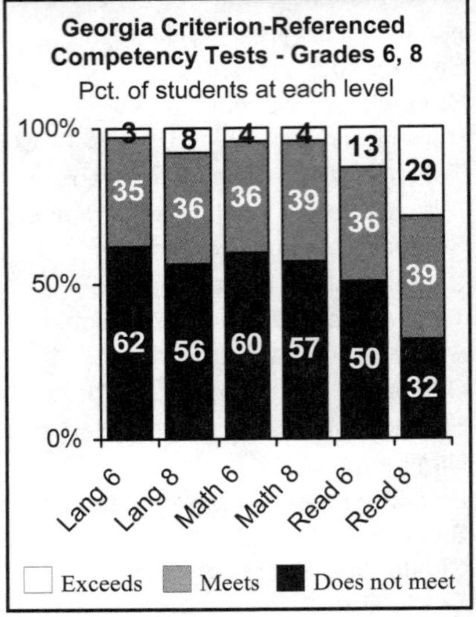
Georgia Criterion-Referenced Competency Tests - Grades 6, 8
Pct. of students at each level
100%
50%
0%
3
8
4
4
13
29
35
36
36
39
36
39
62
56
60
57
50
32
Lang 6
Lang 8
Math 6
Math 8
Read 6
Read 8
Exceeds
Meets
Does not meet

Banneker High School

5935 Feldwood Rd, College Park, GA 30349
770-969-3410 · Grades 9 - 12

Enrollment:	1,093
White / black / other:	0.8% / 97.1% / 2.1%
Not native English-speaking:	*
Limited English proficiency:	1 / 0.1%
Student absenteeism:	7.5%
Students per teacher:	14.0
Parent friendliness:	❶❷❸④⑤❻
Students in gifted program:	43 / 3.9%
Students in remedial education:	6.3%
High school completion rate:	83.7%
Students held back a grade:	21.0%
Number of dropouts:	78 / 5.5%
Students in alternative programs:	5 / 0.5%
Students in special education:	148 / 13.5%
Eligible students, free or reduced lunch:	61.5%

Total suspensions and expulsions:	1,204
Suspensions only, pct. in-school:	1,204 / 55.1%
Drugs/alcohol-related offenses:	5
Violence-related offenses:	84
Firearms-related offenses:	2
Vandalism-related offenses:	1
Theft-related offenses:	4
All other disciplinary offenses:	1,153

Teachers with advanced degrees:	57.5%
Average years' teaching experience:	14.3

AJC GRADE: ★★★

High School Graduation Test
Pct. of students who passed on first try

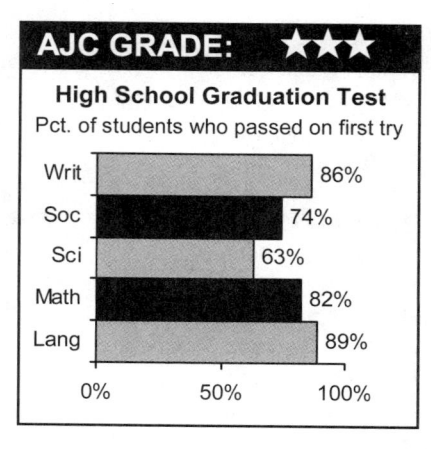

- Writ: 86%
- Soc: 74%
- Sci: 63%
- Math: 82%
- Lang: 89%

GHSA classification:	5-AAA

Interscholastic sports offered:
BB, BS, CC, CL, FB, GO, RI, SB, SO, SW, TE, TF, VB

Advanced Placement (AP) Exams
Students tested:	66
Tests taken:	72
Pct. of test scores 3 or higher (1 - 5 scale):	6.9%

Languages other than English taught:
French, Spanish

2000-2001 high school graduates: 185

College prep/vocational diplomas:	7.0%
College prep endorsement diplomas:	64.3%
Vocational endorsement diplomas:	11.4%
General high school diplomas:	0.0%
Special education diplomas:	7.6%
Certificates of attendance (no diploma):	9.7%

Of the 2000-2001 graduates, 42.7% were eligible for the HOPE scholarship.

Of the 1999-2000 graduates, 38 attended a Georgia public college or university. Of those, 55% met the school's minimum academic requirements.

Average SAT Scores
Maximum score is 800 on each portion

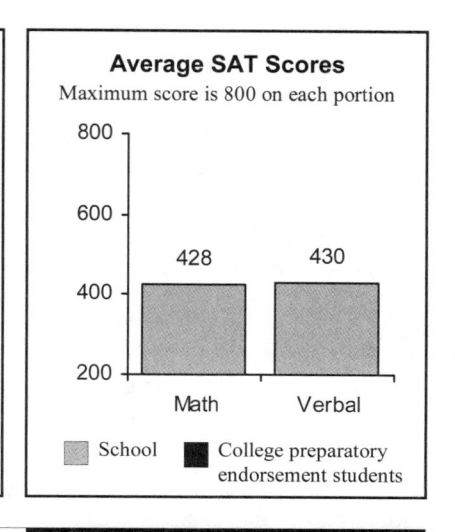

- Math: 428
- Verbal: 430

School / College preparatory endorsement students

Fulton County High Schools

Centennial High School

9310 Scott Rd, Roswell, GA 30076
770-650-4230 · Grades 9 - 12

Enrollment:	2,176
White / black / other:	73.6% / 15.6% / 10.8%
Not native English-speaking:	*
Limited English proficiency:	55 / 2.5%
Student absenteeism:	5.6%
Students per teacher:	15.3
Parent friendliness:	❶❷❸④⑤❻
Students in gifted program:	452 / 20.8%
Students in remedial education:	0.1%
High school completion rate:	97.0%
Students held back a grade:	6.0%
Number of dropouts:	22 / 0.9%
Students in alternative programs:	11 / 0.5%
Students in special education:	261 / 12.0%
Eligible students, free or reduced lunch:	4.8%
Total suspensions and expulsions:	1,336
Suspensions only, pct. in-school:	1,336 / 79.3%
Drugs/alcohol-related offenses:	28
Violence-related offenses:	67
Firearms-related offenses:	3
Vandalism-related offenses:	7
Theft-related offenses:	31
All other disciplinary offenses:	1,253
Teachers with advanced degrees:	54.5%
Average years' teaching experience:	8.0

AJC GRADE: ★★★★

High School Graduation Test
Pct. of students who passed on first try

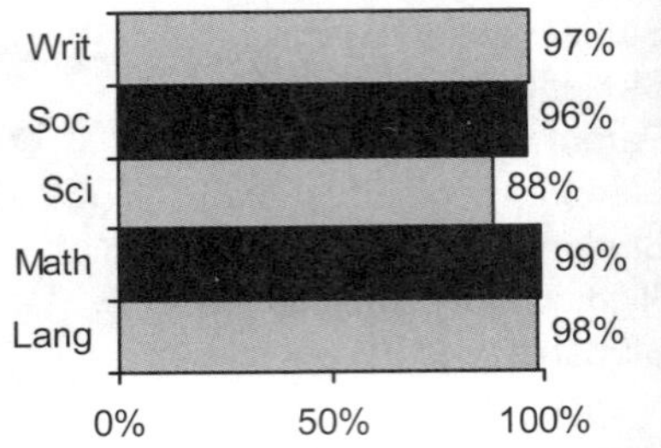

- Writ: 97%
- Soc: 96%
- Sci: 88%
- Math: 99%
- Lang: 98%

GHSA classification:	6-AAAAA

Interscholastic sports offered:
BB, BS, CC, CL, FB, GO, LC, SB, SO, SW, TE, TF, VB, WR

Advanced Placement (AP) Exams
Students tested:	256
Tests taken:	491
Pct. of test scores 3 or higher (1 - 5 scale):	89.8%

Languages other than English taught:
French, German, Latin, Spanish

2000-2001 high school graduates: 423

College prep/vocational diplomas:	4.3%
College prep endorsement diplomas:	88.2%
Vocational endorsement diplomas:	4.3%
General high school diplomas:	0.0%
Special education diplomas:	2.6%
Certificates of attendance (no diploma):	0.7%

Of the 2000-2001 graduates, 80.1% were eligible for the HOPE scholarship.

Of the 1999-2000 graduates, 177 attended a Georgia public college or university. Of those, 90% met the school's minimum academic requirements.

Average SAT Scores
Maximum score is 800 on each portion

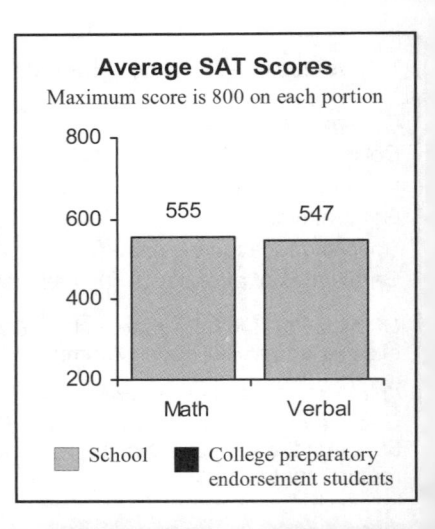

- Math: 555
- Verbal: 547

Legend: School | College preparatory endorsement students

The Atlanta Journal-Constitution / Page 352

Fulton County High Schools

Chattahoochee High School

5230 Taylor Rd, Alpharetta, GA 30022
770-521-7600 · Grades 9 - 12

Enrollment:	2,678
White / black / other:	72.3% / 7.0% / 20.7%
Not native English-speaking:	*
Limited English proficiency:	40 / 1.5%
Student absenteeism:	4.9%
Students per teacher:	18.0
Parent friendliness:	❶ ② ❸ ④ ⑤ ❻
Students in gifted program:	647 / 24.2%
Students in remedial education:	1.4%
High school completion rate:	96.9%
Students held back a grade:	2.5%
Number of dropouts:	33 / 1.1%
Students in alternative programs:	6 / 0.2%
Students in special education:	148 / 5.5%
Eligible students, free or reduced lunch:	1.0%
Total suspensions and expulsions:	695
Suspensions only, pct. in-school:	694 / 72.8%
Drugs/alcohol-related offenses:	28
Violence-related offenses:	66
Firearms-related offenses:	2
Vandalism-related offenses:	18
Theft-related offenses:	33
All other disciplinary offenses:	610
Teachers with advanced degrees:	53.6%
Average years' teaching experience:	13.2

AJC GRADE: ★★★

High School Graduation Test
Pct. of students who passed on first try

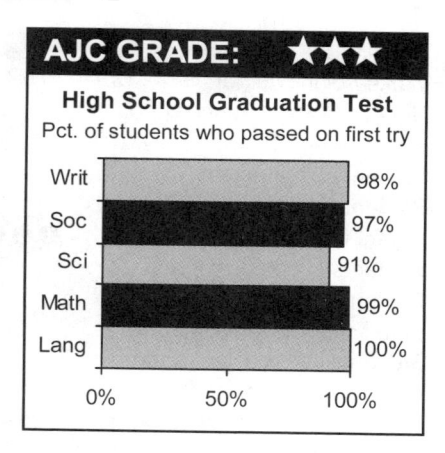

- Writ: 98%
- Soc: 97%
- Sci: 91%
- Math: 99%
- Lang: 100%

GHSA classification:	6-AAAAA

Interscholastic sports offered:
BB, BS, CC, CL, FB, GO, LC, SB, SO, SW, TE, TF, VB, WR

Advanced Placement (AP) Exams
Students tested:	367
Tests taken:	737
Pct. of test scores 3 or higher (1 - 5 scale):	86.3%

Languages other than English taught:
French, German, Latin, Spanish

2000-2001 high school graduates: 559

College prep/vocational diplomas:	1.6%
College prep endorsement diplomas:	95.2%
Vocational endorsement diplomas:	2.3%
General high school diplomas:	0.0%
Special education diplomas:	0.7%
Certificates of attendance (no diploma):	0.2%

Of the 2000-2001 graduates, 84.4% were eligible for the HOPE scholarship.

Of the 1999-2000 graduates, 266 attended a Georgia public college or university. Of those, 96% met the school's minimum academic requirements.

Average SAT Scores
Maximum score is 800 on each portion

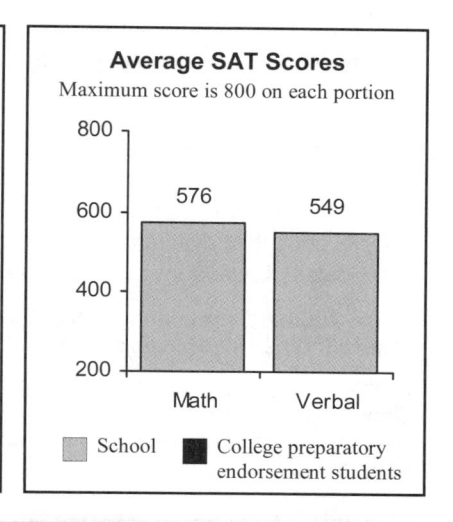

- Math: 576
- Verbal: 549

School / College preparatory endorsement students

Fulton County High Schools

Creekside High School

7405 Herndon Rd, Fairburn, GA 30213
770-306-4300 · Grades 9 - 12

Enrollment:	1,387
White / black / other:	18.7% / 75.4% / 5.8%
Not native English-speaking:	20 / 1.4%
Limited English proficiency:	26 / 1.9%
Student absenteeism:	6.2%
Students per teacher:	16.6
Parent friendliness:	❶❷❸❹❺❻
Students in gifted program:	71 / 5.1%
Students in remedial education:	9.2%
High school completion rate:	77.7%
Students held back a grade:	30.6%
Number of dropouts:	82 / 5.0%
Students in alternative programs:	13 / 0.9%
Students in special education:	135 / 9.7%
Eligible students, free or reduced lunch:	34.5%
Total suspensions and expulsions:	1,361
Suspensions only, pct. in-school:	1,361 / 54.9%
Drugs/alcohol-related offenses:	32
Violence-related offenses:	68
Firearms-related offenses:	7
Vandalism-related offenses:	3
Theft-related offenses:	14
All other disciplinary offenses:	1,277
Teachers with advanced degrees:	60.5%
Average years' teaching experience:	11.8

AJC GRADE: ★★★

High School Graduation Test
Pct. of students who passed on first try

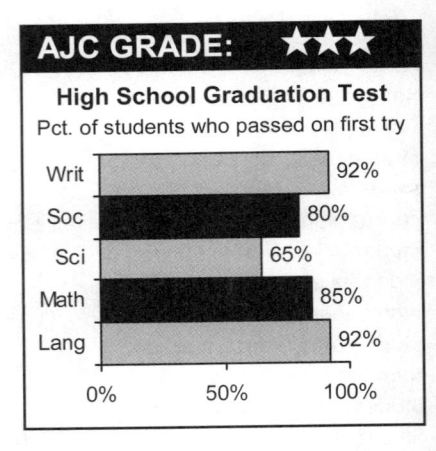

- Writ: 92%
- Soc: 80%
- Sci: 65%
- Math: 85%
- Lang: 92%

GHSA classification: 5-AAAA
Interscholastic sports offered:
BB, FB, SB, SW, TF, VB

Advanced Placement (AP) Exams
Students tested: 46
Tests taken: 68
Pct. of test scores 3 or higher (1 - 5 scale): 26.5%

Languages other than English taught:
French, Spanish

2000-2001 high school graduates: 202

College prep/vocational diplomas:	1.0%
College prep endorsement diplomas:	69.8%
Vocational endorsement diplomas:	17.3%
General high school diplomas:	0.0%
Special education diplomas:	1.5%
Certificates of attendance (no diploma):	10.4%

Of the 2000-2001 graduates, 45.0% were eligible for the HOPE scholarship.

Of the 1999-2000 graduates, 66 attended a Georgia public college or university. Of those, 71% met the school's minimum academic requirements.

Average SAT Scores
Maximum score is 800 on each portion

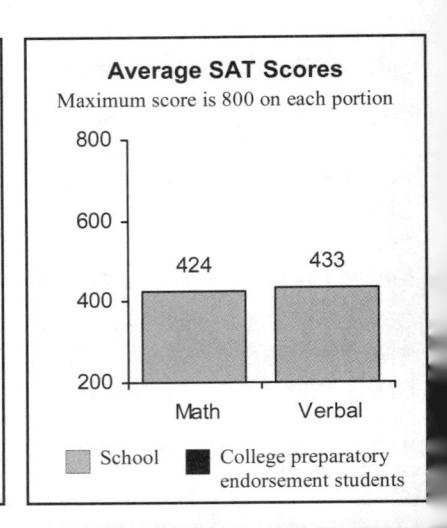

- Math: 424
- Verbal: 433

School / College preparatory endorsement students

Fulton County High Schools

Milton High School

86 School Dr, Alpharetta, GA 30004
770-740-7000 · Grades 9 - 12

Enrollment:	2,580
White / black / other:	86.0% / 6.2% / 7.8%
Not native English-speaking:	*
Limited English proficiency:	13 / 0.5%
Student absenteeism:	5.3%
Students per teacher:	16.7
Parent friendliness:	①❷❸④⑤❻
Students in gifted program:	521 / 20.2%
Students in remedial education:	0.9%
High school completion rate:	94.0%
Students held back a grade:	5.0%
Number of dropouts:	35 / 1.2%
Students in alternative programs:	10 / 0.4%
Students in special education:	212 / 8.2%
Eligible students, free or reduced lunch:	0.9%

Total suspensions and expulsions:	1,301
Suspensions only, pct. in-school:	1,301 / 75.7%
Drugs/alcohol-related offenses:	*
Violence-related offenses:	*
Firearms-related offenses:	*
Vandalism-related offenses:	*
Theft-related offenses:	*
All other disciplinary offenses:	1,341

Teachers with advanced degrees:	59.2%
Average years' teaching experience:	11.8

AJC GRADE: ★★★

High School Graduation Test
Pct. of students who passed on first try

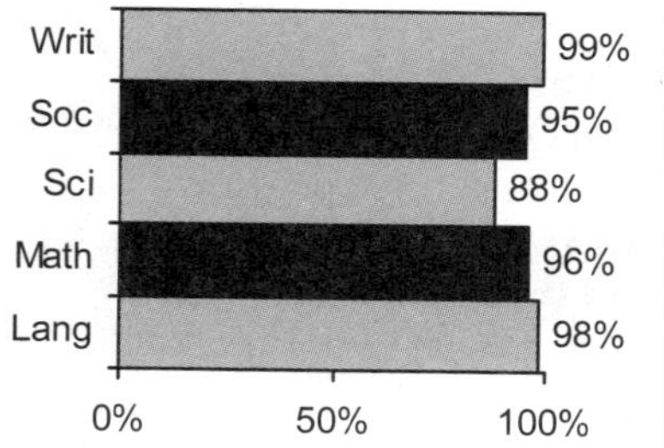
Writ
99%
Soc
95%
Sci
88%
Math
96%
Lang
98%
0%
50%
100%

GHSA classification:	6-AAAAA

Interscholastic sports offered:
BB, BS, CC, CL, FB, GO, SB, SO, SW, TE, TF, VB, WR

Advanced Placement (AP) Exams

Students tested:	363
Tests taken:	657
Pct. of test scores 3 or higher (1 - 5 scale):	77.3%

Languages other than English taught:
French, German, Latin, Spanish

2000-2001 high school graduates: 504

College prep/vocational diplomas:	2.2%
College prep endorsement diplomas:	89.3%
Vocational endorsement diplomas:	7.3%
General high school diplomas:	0.0%
Special education diplomas:	0.2%
Certificates of attendance (no diploma):	1.0%

Of the 2000-2001 graduates, 81.2% were eligible for the HOPE scholarship.

Of the 1999-2000 graduates, 207 attended a Georgia public college or university. Of those, 94% met the school's minimum academic requirements.

Average SAT Scores
Maximum score is 800 on each portion

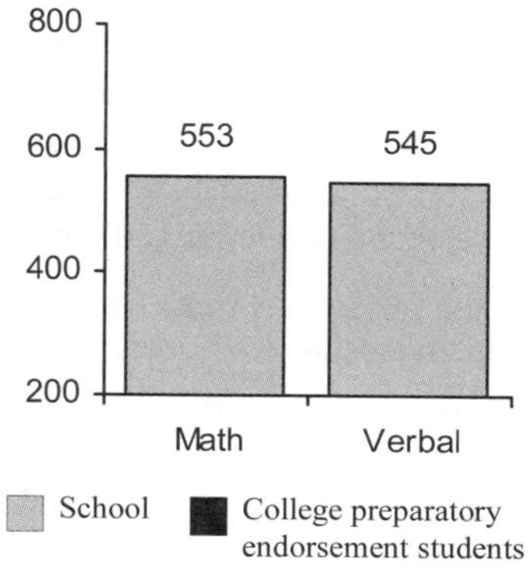
800
600
400
200
553
545
Math
Verbal
School
College preparatory endorsement students

North Springs High School

7447 Roswell Rd NE, Atlanta, GA 30328
770-551-2490 · Grades 9 - 12

Enrollment:	1,339
White / black / other:	52.7% / 36.6% / 10.7%
Not native English-speaking:	*
Limited English proficiency:	28 / 2.1%
Student absenteeism:	6.3%
Students per teacher:	16.5
Parent friendliness:	❶❷❸④⑤❻
Students in gifted program:	353 / 26.4%
Students in remedial education:	10.1%
High school completion rate:	95.7%
Students held back a grade:	4.0%
Number of dropouts:	21 / 1.4%
Students in alternative programs:	13 / 1.0%
Students in special education:	74 / 5.5%
Eligible students, free or reduced lunch:	15.4%
Total suspensions and expulsions:	745
Suspensions only, pct. in-school:	742 / 82.1%
Drugs/alcohol-related offenses:	14
Violence-related offenses:	31
Firearms-related offenses:	7
Vandalism-related offenses:	4
Theft-related offenses:	10
All other disciplinary offenses:	718
Teachers with advanced degrees:	55.4%
Average years' teaching experience:	13.1

AJC GRADE: ★★★★

High School Graduation Test
Pct. of students who passed on first try

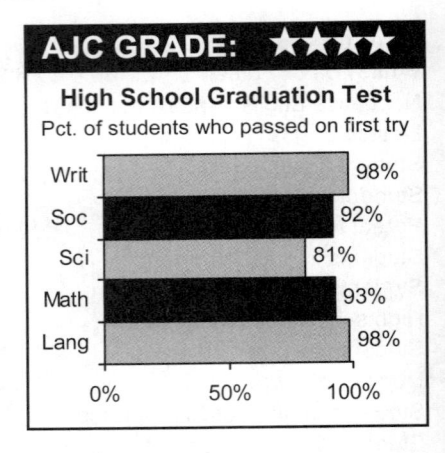

- Writ: 98%
- Soc: 92%
- Sci: 81%
- Math: 93%
- Lang: 98%

GHSA classification: 6-AAAA
Interscholastic sports offered:
BB, BS, CC, CL, FB, GO, LC, SB, SO, SW, TE, TF, VB, WR

Advanced Placement (AP) Exams
Students tested:	190
Tests taken:	363
Pct. of test scores 3 or higher (1 - 5 scale):	80.4%

Languages other than English taught:
French, German, Latin, Spanish

2000-2001 high school graduates: 244

College prep/vocational diplomas:	10.7%
College prep endorsement diplomas:	82.0%
Vocational endorsement diplomas:	5.7%
General high school diplomas:	0.0%
Special education diplomas:	0.8%
Certificates of attendance (no diploma):	0.8%

Of the 2000-2001 graduates, 74.2% were eligible for the HOPE scholarship.

Of the 1999-2000 graduates, 88 attended a Georgia public college or university. Of those, 85% met the school's minimum academic requirements.

Average SAT Scores
Maximum score is 800 on each portion

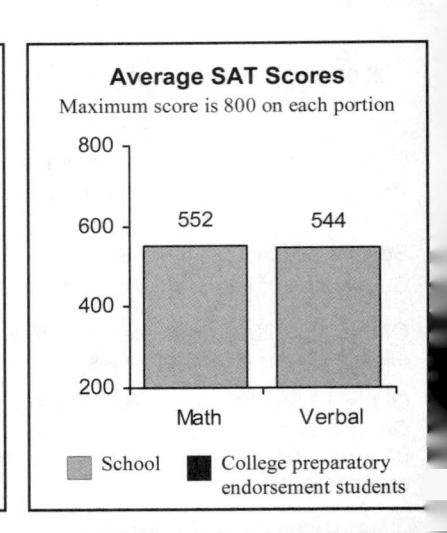

- Math: 552
- Verbal: 544

School / College preparatory endorsement students

Fulton County High Schools

Riverwood High School

5900 Heards Dr NW, Atlanta, GA 30328
404-847-1980 · Grades 9 - 12

Enrollment:	1,211
White / black / other:	48.3% / 19.7% / 32.0%
Not native English-speaking:	417 / 34.4%
Limited English proficiency:	717 / 59.2%
Student absenteeism:	8.1%
Students per teacher:	14.4
Parent friendliness:	① ❷ ❸ ④ ⑤ ❻
Students in gifted program:	169 / 14.0%
Students in remedial education:	1.6%
High school completion rate:	88.1%
Students held back a grade:	5.0%
Number of dropouts:	58 / 4.0%
Students in alternative programs:	*
Students in special education:	47 / 3.9%
Eligible students, free or reduced lunch:	23.8%
Total suspensions and expulsions:	218
Suspensions only, pct. in-school:	218 / 71.1%
Drugs/alcohol-related offenses:	3
Violence-related offenses:	15
Firearms-related offenses:	2
Vandalism-related offenses:	*
Theft-related offenses:	4
All other disciplinary offenses:	205
Teachers with advanced degrees:	52.3%
Average years' teaching experience:	10.5

AJC GRADE: ★★★★

High School Graduation Test
Pct. of students who passed on first try

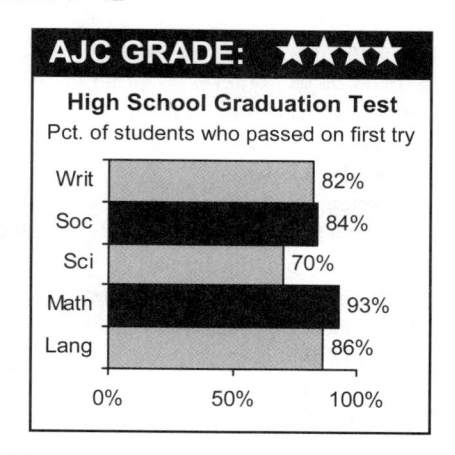

- Writ: 82%
- Soc: 84%
- Sci: 70%
- Math: 93%
- Lang: 86%

GHSA classification: 6-AAAA
Interscholastic sports offered:
BB, BS, CC, CL, FB, GO, SO, SW, TE, TF, VB, WR

Advanced Placement (AP) Exams
Students tested:	130
Tests taken:	229
Pct. of test scores 3 or higher (1 - 5 scale):	66.8%

Languages other than English taught:
Chinese, French, Hebrew, Japanese, Latin, Spanish

2000-2001 high school graduates: 207

College prep/vocational diplomas:	9.7%
College prep endorsement diplomas:	79.2%
Vocational endorsement diplomas:	3.4%
General high school diplomas:	0.0%
Special education diplomas:	0.0%
Certificates of attendance (no diploma):	7.7%

Of the 2000-2001 graduates, 82.6% were eligible for the HOPE scholarship.

Of the 1999-2000 graduates, 71 attended a Georgia public college or university. Of those, 90% met the school's minimum academic requirements.

Average SAT Scores
Maximum score is 800 on each portion

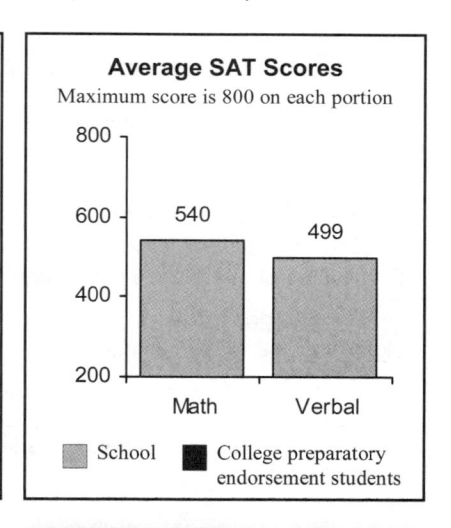

- Math: 540
- Verbal: 499

School / College preparatory endorsement students

Fulton County High Schools

Roswell High School

11595 King Rd, Roswell, GA 30075
770-552-4500 · Grades 9 - 12

Enrollment:	2,193
White / black / other:	78.1% / 12.5% / 9.3%
Not native English-speaking:	*
Limited English proficiency:	8 / 0.4%
Student absenteeism:	4.3%
Students per teacher:	15.5
Parent friendliness:	① ❷ ❸ ④ ⑤ ❻
Students in gifted program:	624 / 28.5%
Students in remedial education:	8.5%
High school completion rate:	95.8%
Students held back a grade:	3.9%
Number of dropouts:	16 / 0.7%
Students in alternative programs:	12 / 0.5%
Students in special education:	222 / 10.1%
Eligible students, free or reduced lunch:	6.1%
Total suspensions and expulsions:	681
Suspensions only, pct. in-school:	681 / 75.0%
Drugs/alcohol-related offenses:	11
Violence-related offenses:	23
Firearms-related offenses:	13
Vandalism-related offenses:	3
Theft-related offenses:	4
All other disciplinary offenses:	675
Teachers with advanced degrees:	54.7%
Average years' teaching experience:	12.6

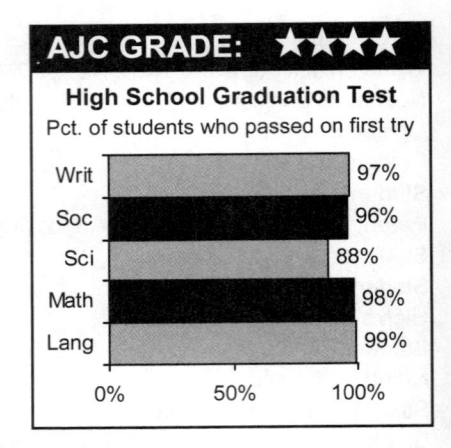

AJC GRADE: ★★★★

High School Graduation Test
Pct. of students who passed on first try

- Writ: 97%
- Soc: 96%
- Sci: 88%
- Math: 98%
- Lang: 99%

GHSA classification:	6-AAAAA

Interscholastic sports offered:
BB, BS, CC, CL, FB, GO, GY, LC, RI, SB, SO, SW, TE, TF, VB, WR

Advanced Placement (AP) Exams
Students tested:	334
Tests taken:	709
Pct. of test scores 3 or higher (1 - 5 scale):	80.0%

Languages other than English taught:
French, German, Japanese, Latin, Spanish

2000-2001 high school graduates: 456

College prep/vocational diplomas:	0.0%
College prep endorsement diplomas:	90.6%
Vocational endorsement diplomas:	5.0%
General high school diplomas:	0.0%
Special education diplomas:	3.9%
Certificates of attendance (no diploma):	0.4%

Of the 2000-2001 graduates, 77.0% were eligible for the HOPE scholarship.

Of the 1999-2000 graduates, 194 attended a Georgia public college or university. Of those, 96% met the school's minimum academic requirements.

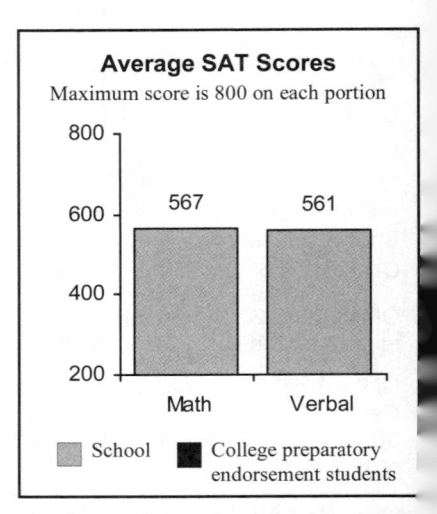

Average SAT Scores
Maximum score is 800 on each portion

- Math: 567
- Verbal: 561

School / College preparatory endorsement students

The Atlanta Journal-Constitution / Page 358

Fulton County High Schools

Tri-Cities High School

2575 Harris St, East Point, GA 30344
404-669-8200 · Grades 9 - 12

Enrollment:	2,005
White / black / other:	3.5% / 88.1% / 8.3%
Not native English-speaking:	48 / 2.4%
Limited English proficiency:	117 / 5.8%
Student absenteeism:	9.6%
Students per teacher:	16.4
Parent friendliness:	❶❷❸❹❺❻
Students in gifted program:	72 / 3.6%
Students in remedial education:	10.6%
High school completion rate:	70.4%
Students held back a grade:	27.9%
Number of dropouts:	101 / 4.4%
Students in alternative programs:	14 / 0.7%
Students in special education:	140 / 7.0%
Eligible students, free or reduced lunch:	42.4%
Total suspensions and expulsions:	901
Suspensions only, pct. in-school:	898 / 53.6%
Drugs/alcohol-related offenses:	9
Violence-related offenses:	75
Firearms-related offenses:	11
Vandalism-related offenses:	6
Theft-related offenses:	7
All other disciplinary offenses:	819
Teachers with advanced degrees:	48.4%
Average years' teaching experience:	10.4

AJC GRADE: ★★★

High School Graduation Test
Pct. of students who passed on first try

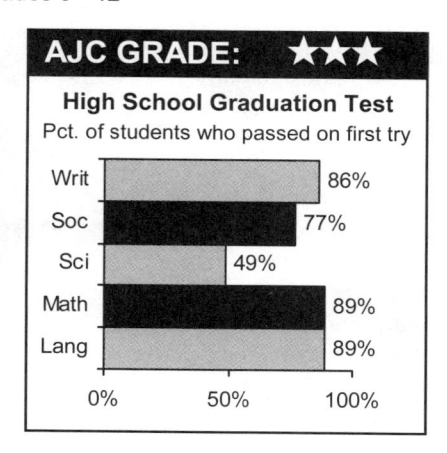

- Writ: 86%
- Soc: 77%
- Sci: 49%
- Math: 89%
- Lang: 89%

GHSA classification:	7-AAAAA

Interscholastic sports offered:
BB, BS, CC, CL, FB, GO, LC, RI, SB, SO, SW, TE, TF, VB, WR

Advanced Placement (AP) Exams
Students tested:	55
Tests taken:	76
Pct. of test scores 3 or higher (1 - 5 scale):	14.5%

Languages other than English taught:
French, Spanish

2000-2001 high school graduates: 269

College prep/vocational diplomas:	17.1%
College prep endorsement diplomas:	47.2%
Vocational endorsement diplomas:	17.5%
General high school diplomas:	0.0%
Special education diplomas:	4.5%
Certificates of attendance (no diploma):	13.8%

Of the 2000-2001 graduates, 52.0% were eligible for the HOPE scholarship.

Of the 1999-2000 graduates, 102 attended a Georgia public college or university. Of those, 65% met the school's minimum academic requirements.

Average SAT Scores
Maximum score is 800 on each portion

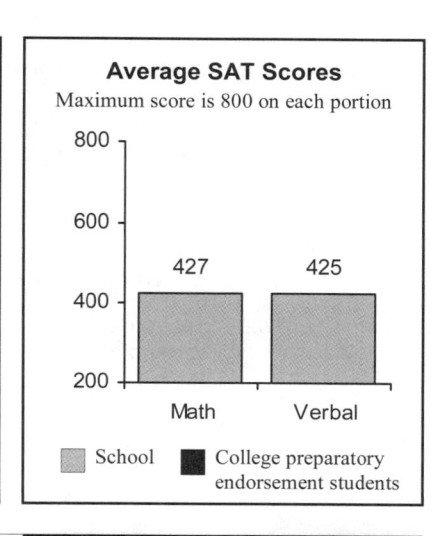

- Math: 427
- Verbal: 425

School ▪ College preparatory endorsement students

Fulton County High Schools

Westlake High School

2370 Union Rd SW, Atlanta, GA 30331
404-346-6400 · Grades 9 - 12

Enrollment:	1,289
White / black / other:	0.2% / 98.6% / 1.2%
Not native English-speaking:	*
Limited English proficiency:	*
Student absenteeism:	9.0%
Students per teacher:	16.4
Parent friendliness:	❶❷❸④❺❻
Students in gifted program:	114 / 8.8%
Students in remedial education:	4.8%
High school completion rate:	85.0%
Students held back a grade:	12.1%
Number of dropouts:	54 / 3.6%
Students in alternative programs:	*
Students in special education:	80 / 6.2%
Eligible students, free or reduced lunch:	32.6%
Total suspensions and expulsions:	1,241
Suspensions only, pct. in-school:	1,241 / 33.0%
Drugs/alcohol-related offenses:	11
Violence-related offenses:	155
Firearms-related offenses:	6
Vandalism-related offenses:	6
Theft-related offenses:	16
All other disciplinary offenses:	1,088
Teachers with advanced degrees:	58.8%
Average years' teaching experience:	12.7

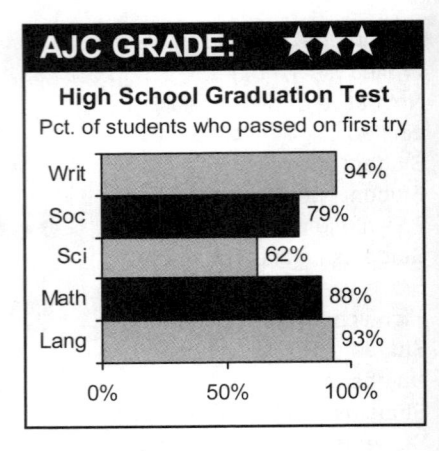

AJC GRADE: ★★★

High School Graduation Test
Pct. of students who passed on first try

- Writ: 94%
- Soc: 79%
- Sci: 62%
- Math: 88%
- Lang: 93%

GHSA classification: 5-AAAA
Interscholastic sports offered:
BB, BS, CC, CL, FB, GO, RI, SB, SO, SW, TE, TF, VB

Advanced Placement (AP) Exams
Students tested: 99
Tests taken: 147
Pct. of test scores 3 or higher (1 - 5 scale): 10.9%

Languages other than English taught:
French, German, Latin, Spanish

2000-2001 high school graduates: 210

College prep/vocational diplomas:	3.3%
College prep endorsement diplomas:	70.5%
Vocational endorsement diplomas:	18.6%
General high school diplomas:	0.0%
Special education diplomas:	2.4%
Certificates of attendance (no diploma):	5.2%

Of the 2000-2001 graduates, 51.0% were eligible for the HOPE scholarship.

Of the 1999-2000 graduates, 85 attended a Georgia public college or university. Of those, 70% met the school's minimum academic requirements.

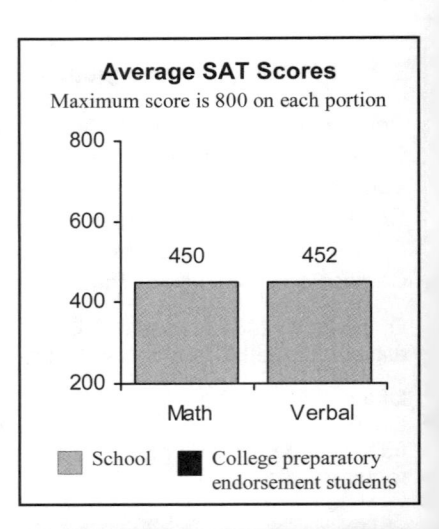

Average SAT Scores
Maximum score is 800 on each portion

- Math: 450
- Verbal: 452

School | College preparatory endorsement students

The Atlanta Journal-Constitution / Page 360

Fulton County High Schools

AJC ranking of Fulton County Schools

ELEMENTARY SCHOOLS

AJC Star Grade: ★★★★

Crabapple Crossing Elementary
Dolvin Elementary
Findley Oaks Elementary
Heards Ferry Elementary
Lake Windward Elementary
Mountain Park Elementary
New Prospect Elementary
Shakerag Elementary
Summit Hill Elementary

AJC Star Grade: ★★★

Abbotts Hill Elementary
Alpharetta Elementary
Barnwell Elementary
Bethune Elementary
Brookview Elementary
Campbell Elementary
College Park Elementary
Conley Hills Elementary
Dunwoody Springs Elementary
Esther Jackson Elementary
Gullatt Elementary
Hapeville Elementary
Harriet Tubman Elementary
Highpoint Elementary
Manning Oaks Elementary
Medlock Bridge Elementary
Mimosa Elementary
Mount Olive Elementary
Nolan Elementary
Northwood Elementary
Oak Knoll Elementary
Ocee Elementary
Randolph Elementary
River Eves Elementary
Roswell North Elementary
Spalding Drive Elementary
State Bridge Crossing Elementary
Stonewall Tell Elementary
Sweet Apple Elementary
Woodland Charter Elementary

AJC Star Grade: ★★

Heritage Elementary
Lewis Elementary
Palmetto Elementary
Parklane Elementary
Seaborn Lee Elementary
West Elementary

AJC Star Grade: ★

Victory Charter

MIDDLE SCHOOLS

AJC Star Grade: ★★★★

Webb Bridge Middle

AJC Star Grade: ★★★

Bear Creek Middle
Camp Creek Middle
Crabapple Middle
Haynes Bridge Middle
Holcomb Bridge Middle
McNair Middle
Northwestern Middle
Ridgeview Middle
Sandy Springs Middle

AJC ranking of Fulton County Schools

Taylor Road Middle
West Middle
Woodland Middle

HIGH SCHOOLS

AJC Star Grade: ★★★★

Centennial High
North Springs High
Riverwood High
Roswell High

AJC Star Grade: ★★★

Banneker High
Chattahoochee High
Creekside High
Milton High
Tri-Cities High
Westlake High

Gainesville City Public Schools

508 Oak St, Gainesville, GA 30501
Phone: 770-536-5275 · Fax: 770-287-2004
http://www.gainesville-city.k12.ga.us

The following pages provide detailed information on every school in the Gainesville City school district. An asterisk (*) means the value of the data was zero or was not reported by the school district. A complete list of schools ranked by The Atlanta Journal-Constitution's star rating system follows the detailed school reports.

District enrollment:	3,966
White / black / other:	27.7% / 26.8% / 45.5%
Not native English-speaking:	690 / 17.4%
Expenditure per student (general fund):	$7,040
Students per teacher:	14.5
Teachers with advanced degrees:	65.9%
Average years, teaching experience:	14.6
Average teacher salary:	$45,511.61
Students in gifted program:	246 / 6.2%
Students held back a grade:	297 / 7.5%
Eligible students, free or reduced lunch:	2,501 / 62.8%
Number of dropouts (grades 9-12):	69 / 5.9%
High school completion rate:	72.1%
Graduates, pct. eligible for HOPE scholarships:	176 / 57.4%
Average combined SAT score (maximum 1,600):	990
Pct. of 11th-graders passing the Georgia High School Graduation Tests on first try:	63%
Percent of children 5 to 17 years of age living in poverty (2000 Census estimate):	30.1%

Fair Street Elementary School

695 Fair St, Gainesville, GA 30501
770-536-5295 · Grades 4 - 5

Enrollment:	555
White / black / other:	22.0% / 33.0% / 45.0%
Not native English-speaking:	55 / 9.9%
Limited English proficiency:	59 / 10.6%
Student absenteeism:	3.9%
Students per teacher:	13.9
Parent friendliness:	① ❷ ❸ ❹ ❺ ❻
Teachers with advanced degrees:	72.5%
Average years' teaching experience:	15.5
Students in gifted program:	38 / 6.8%
Students in remedial education:	27.6%
Students held back a grade:	0.2%
Total suspensions, pct. in-school:	53 / 0.0%
Offenses: violence: 175, drugs: *, other: 119	
Eligible students, free or reduced lunch:	90.8%
Before / after school program:	Yes / Yes

Students at this school generally go on to:
Gainesville Middle

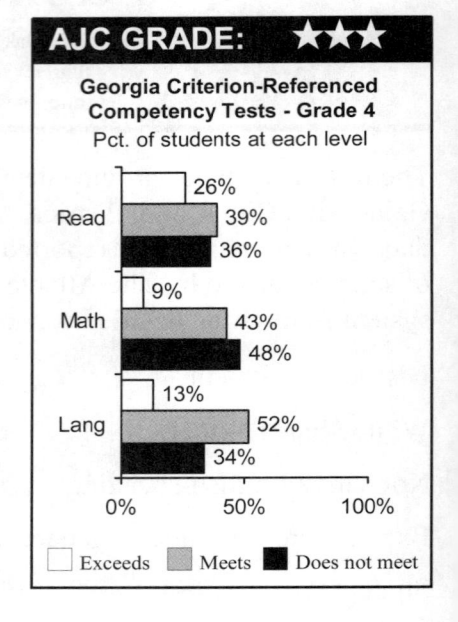

AJC GRADE: ★★★

Georgia Criterion-Referenced Competency Tests - Grade 4
Pct. of students at each level

Read: Exceeds 26%, Meets 39%, Does not meet 36%
Math: Exceeds 9%, Meets 43%, Does not meet 48%
Lang: Exceeds 13%, Meets 52%, Does not meet 34%

Gainesville City Elementary Schools

Gainesville Middle School

715 Woodsmill Rd, Gainesville, GA 30501
770-534-4237 · Grades 6 - 8

Enrollment:	875
White / black / other:	29.7% / 27.7% / 42.6%
Not native English-speaking:	136 / 15.5%
Student absenteeism:	0.2%
Students per teacher:	15.1
Parent friendliness:	① ❷ ❸ ④ ❺ ❻
Teachers with advanced degrees:	67.2%
Average years' teaching experience:	13.6
Students in gifted program:	102 / 11.7%
Students held back a grade:	2.4%
Total suspensions and expulsions:	823
Suspensions only, pct. in-school:	821 / 60.2%
Offenses: violence: 138, drugs: *, other: 738	
Eligible students, free or reduced lunch:	58.4%
Number of dropouts:	23 / 2.2%
Pct. 8th-graders w/ basic computer skills:	32.0%
Students at this school generally go on to: Gainesville High	

AJC GRADE: ★★★

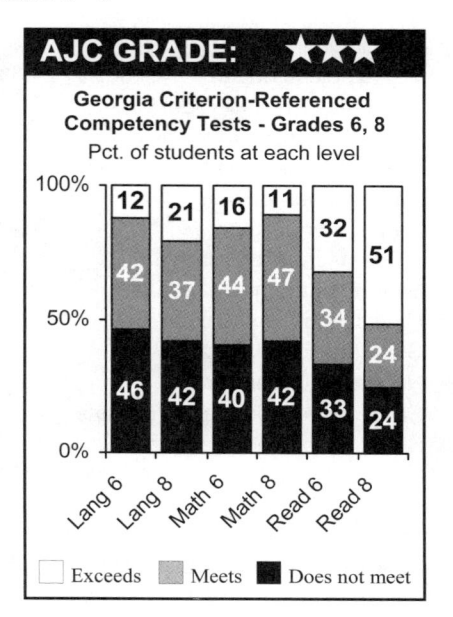

Georgia Criterion-Referenced Competency Tests - Grades 6, 8
Pct. of students at each level

	Lang 6	Lang 8	Math 6	Math 8	Read 6	Read 8
Exceeds	12	21	16	11	32	51
Meets	42	37	44	47	34	24
Does not meet	46	42	40	42	33	24

Gainesville City Middle Schools

Gainesville High School

830 Century Pl, Gainesville, GA 30501
770-536-4441 · Grades 9 - 12

Enrollment:	1,060
White / black / other:	43.0% / 24.3% / 32.6%
Not native English-speaking:	145 / 13.7%
Limited English proficiency:	216 / 20.4%
Student absenteeism:	6.1%
Students per teacher:	16.3
Parent friendliness:	❶❷❸④❺❻
Students in gifted program:	92 / 8.7%
Students in remedial education:	*
High school completion rate:	72.1%
Students held back a grade:	11.4%
Number of dropouts:	69 / 5.9%
Students in alternative programs:	5 / 0.5%
Students in special education:	71 / 6.7%
Eligible students, free or reduced lunch:	31.2%
Total suspensions and expulsions:	680
Suspensions only, pct. in-school:	679 / 82.8%
Drugs/alcohol-related offenses:	6
Violence-related offenses:	33
Firearms-related offenses:	4
Vandalism-related offenses:	11
Theft-related offenses:	3
All other disciplinary offenses:	645
Teachers with advanced degrees:	54.5%
Average years' teaching experience:	15.1

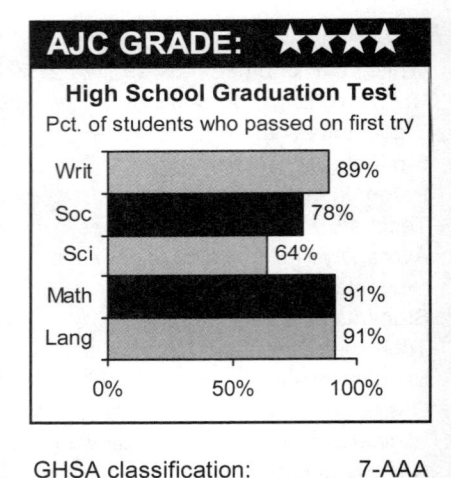

AJC GRADE: ★★★★

High School Graduation Test
Pct. of students who passed on first try

- Writ: 89%
- Soc: 78%
- Sci: 64%
- Math: 91%
- Lang: 91%

GHSA classification: 7-AAA
Interscholastic sports offered:
BB, BS, CC, FB, GO, SB, SO, SW, TE, TF, VB, WR

Advanced Placement (AP) Exams
Students tested:	78
Tests taken:	82
Pct. of test scores 3 or higher (1 - 5 scale):	56.1%

Languages other than English taught:
French, German, Spanish

2000-2001 high school graduates: 176

College prep/vocational diplomas:	19.9%
College prep endorsement diplomas:	35.8%
Vocational endorsement diplomas:	25.0%
General high school diplomas:	0.0%
Special education diplomas:	1.7%
Certificates of attendance (no diploma):	17.6%

Of the 2000-2001 graduates, 57.4% were eligible for the HOPE scholarship.

Of the 1999-2000 graduates, 73 attended a Georgia public college or university. Of those, 71% met the school's minimum academic requirements.

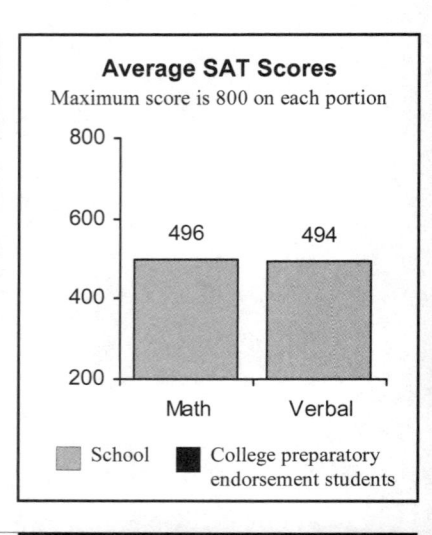

Average SAT Scores
Maximum score is 800 on each portion

- Math: 496
- Verbal: 494

School / College preparatory endorsement students

Gainesville City High Schools

AJC ranking of Gainesville City Schools

ELEMENTARY SCHOOLS

AJC Star Grade: ★★★

Fair Street Elementary

MIDDLE SCHOOLS

AJC Star Grade: ★★★

Gainesville Middle

HIGH SCHOOLS

AJC Star Grade: ★★★★

Gainesville High

Gwinnett County Public Schools

52 Gwinnett Dr, Lawrenceville, GA 30045
Phone: 770-963-8651 · Fax: 770-513-6650
http://www.gwinnett.k12.ga.us

The following pages provide detailed information on every school in the Gwinnett County school district. An asterisk (*) means the value of the data was zero or was not reported by the school district. A complete list of schools ranked by The Atlanta Journal-Constitution's star rating system follows the detailed school reports.

District enrollment:	109,603
White / black / other:	62.3% / 16.4% / 21.2%
Not native English-speaking:	7,099 / 6.5%
Expenditure per student (general fund):	$6,130
Students per teacher:	15.3
Teachers with advanced degrees:	52.1%
Average years, teaching experience:	11.7
Average teacher salary:	$43,490.85
Students in gifted program:	12,972 / 11.8%
Students held back a grade:	3,744 / 3.4%
Eligible students, free or reduced lunch:	22,874 / 20.8%
Number of dropouts (grades 9-12):	466 / 1.4%
High school completion rate:	84.8%
Graduates, pct. eligible for HOPE scholarships:	6,102 / 61.9%
Average combined SAT score (maximum 1,600):	1,046
Pct. of 11th-graders passing the Georgia High School Graduation Tests on first try:	75%
Percent of children 5 to 17 years of age living in poverty (2000 Census estimate):	5.5%

Annistown Elementary School

3150 Spain Rd, Snellville, GA 30039
770-979-2950 · Grades K - 5

Enrollment:	591
White / black / other:	48.6% / 37.9% / 13.5%
Not native English-speaking:	23 / 3.9%
Limited English proficiency:	24 / 4.1%
Student absenteeism:	2.4%
Students per teacher:	12.7
Parent friendliness:	① ❷ ❸ ④ ⑤ ❻
Teachers with advanced degrees:	59.6%
Average years' teaching experience:	14.4
Students in gifted program:	67 / 11.3%
Students in remedial education:	19.3%
Students held back a grade:	3.2%
Total suspensions, pct. in-school:	1 / 100.0%
Offenses:	violence: * , drugs: * , other: 1
Eligible students, free or reduced lunch:	31.8%
Before / after school program:	Yes / Yes

Students at this school generally go on to:
Shiloh Middle

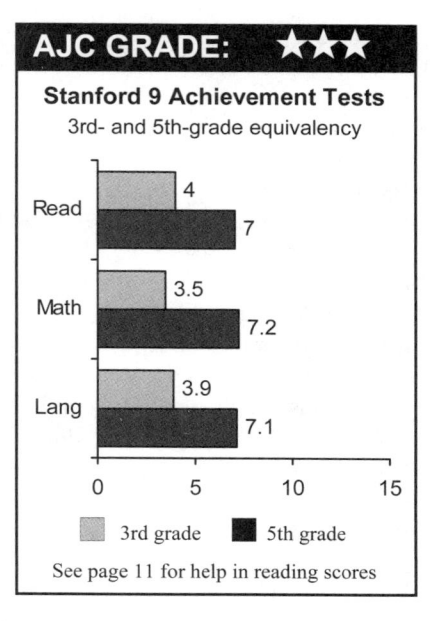

AJC GRADE: ★★★

Stanford 9 Achievement Tests
3rd- and 5th-grade equivalency

- Read: 3rd grade 4, 5th grade 7
- Math: 3rd grade 3.5, 5th grade 7.2
- Lang: 3rd grade 3.9, 5th grade 7.1

See page 11 for help in reading scores

Arcado Elementary School

5150 Arcado Rd SW, Lilburn, GA 30047
770-925-2100 · Grades K - 5

Enrollment:	822
White / black / other:	62.9% / 7.9% / 29.2%
Not native English-speaking:	61 / 7.4%
Limited English proficiency:	68 / 8.3%
Student absenteeism:	3.0%
Students per teacher:	14.3
Parent friendliness:	① ❷ ❸ ④ ⑤ ❻
Teachers with advanced degrees:	52.5%
Average years' teaching experience:	12.2
Students in gifted program:	149 / 18.1%
Students in remedial education:	10.9%
Students held back a grade:	1.3%
Total suspensions, pct. in-school:	14 / 7.1%
Offenses:	violence: 12, drugs: * , other: 6
Eligible students, free or reduced lunch:	16.9%
Before / after school program:	No / No

Students at this school generally go on to:
Trickum Middle

AJC GRADE: ★★★

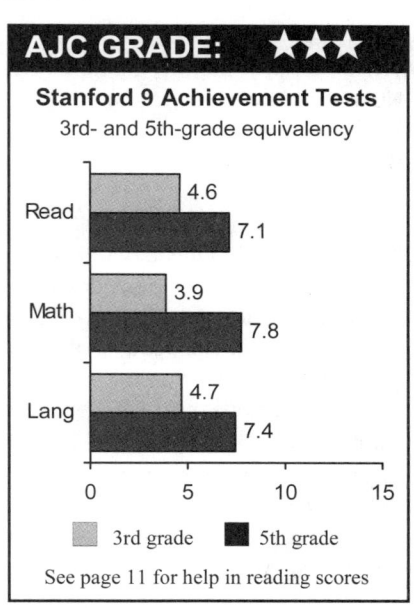

Stanford 9 Achievement Tests
3rd- and 5th-grade equivalency

- Read: 3rd grade 4.6, 5th grade 7.1
- Math: 3rd grade 3.9, 5th grade 7.8
- Lang: 3rd grade 4.7, 5th grade 7.4

See page 11 for help in reading scores

Gwinnett County Elementary Schools

Beaver Ridge Elementary School

1978 Beaver Ruin Rd, Norcross, GA 30071
770-447-6307 · Grades K - 5

Enrollment:	966
White / black / other:	19.0% / 30.5% / 50.4%
Not native English-speaking:	260 / 26.9%
Limited English proficiency:	297 / 30.7%
Student absenteeism:	3.0%
Students per teacher:	13.4
Parent friendliness:	❶❷❸④⑤❻
Teachers with advanced degrees:	39.7%
Average years' teaching experience:	9.3
Students in gifted program:	48 / 5.0%
Students in remedial education:	20.3%
Students held back a grade:	2.3%
Total suspensions, pct. in-school:	8 / 0.0%
Offenses:	violence: 12, drugs: *, other: 2
Eligible students, free or reduced lunch:	53.8%
Before / after school program:	Yes / Yes

Students at this school generally go on to:
Summerour Middle

AJC GRADE: ★★★

Stanford 9 Achievement Tests
3rd- and 5th-grade equivalency

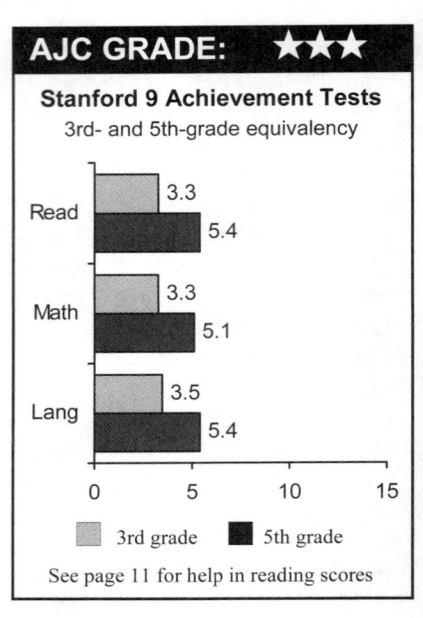

- Read: 3rd grade 3.3 / 5th grade 5.4
- Math: 3rd grade 3.3 / 5th grade 5.1
- Lang: 3rd grade 3.5 / 5th grade 5.4

See page 11 for help in reading scores

Benefield Elementary School

970 McElvaney Ln, Lawrenceville, GA 30044
770-962-3771 · Grades K - 5

Enrollment:	1,184
White / black / other:	40.5% / 25.3% / 34.2%
Not native English-speaking:	132 / 11.1%
Limited English proficiency:	152 / 12.8%
Student absenteeism:	3.3%
Students per teacher:	15.6
Parent friendliness:	①❷❸❹❺❻
Teachers with advanced degrees:	46.1%
Average years' teaching experience:	11.8
Students in gifted program:	36 / 3.0%
Students in remedial education:	10.1%
Students held back a grade:	2.2%
Total suspensions, pct. in-school:	4 / 0.0%
Offenses:	violence: 4, drugs: *, other: *
Eligible students, free or reduced lunch:	32.8%
Before / after school program:	Yes / Yes

Students at this school generally go on to:
Sweetwater Middle

AJC GRADE: ★★★

Stanford 9 Achievement Tests
3rd- and 5th-grade equivalency

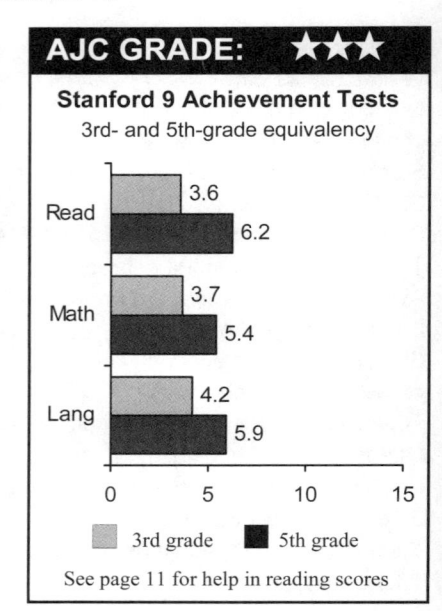

- Read: 3rd grade 3.6 / 5th grade 6.2
- Math: 3rd grade 3.7 / 5th grade 5.4
- Lang: 3rd grade 4.2 / 5th grade 5.9

See page 11 for help in reading scores

Berkeley Lake Elementary School

4300 S Berkeley Lake Rd NW, Duluth, GA 30096
770-446-0947 · Grades K - 5

Enrollment:	1,138
White / black / other:	50.1% / 8.6% / 41.3%
Not native English-speaking:	131 / 11.5%
Limited English proficiency:	131 / 11.5%
Student absenteeism:	3.0%
Students per teacher:	14.3
Parent friendliness:	①❷❸④⑤❻
Teachers with advanced degrees:	54.9%
Average years' teaching experience:	11.7
Students in gifted program:	155 / 13.6%
Students in remedial education:	4.3%
Students held back a grade:	2.4%
Total suspensions, pct. in-school:	*
Offenses:	violence: *, drugs: *, other: *
Eligible students, free or reduced lunch:	12.8%
Before / after school program:	Yes / Yes

Students at this school generally go on to:
Duluth Middle

AJC GRADE: ★★★

Stanford 9 Achievement Tests
3rd- and 5th-grade equivalency

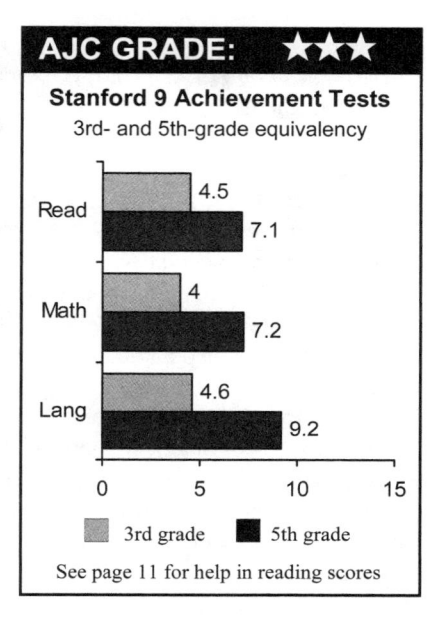

- Read: 3rd grade 4.5, 5th grade 7.1
- Math: 3rd grade 4, 5th grade 7.2
- Lang: 3rd grade 4.6, 5th grade 9.2

See page 11 for help in reading scores

Bethesda Elementary School

525 Bethesda School Rd, Lawrenceville, GA 30044
770-921-2000 · Grades K - 5

Enrollment:	1,115
White / black / other:	40.5% / 26.2% / 33.3%
Not native English-speaking:	49 / 4.4%
Limited English proficiency:	59 / 5.3%
Student absenteeism:	2.9%
Students per teacher:	14.0
Parent friendliness:	①❷❸④⑤❻
Teachers with advanced degrees:	48.8%
Average years' teaching experience:	12.7
Students in gifted program:	65 / 5.8%
Students in remedial education:	14.1%
Students held back a grade:	1.9%
Total suspensions, pct. in-school:	6 / 16.7%
Offenses:	violence: 10, drugs: *, other: 5
Eligible students, free or reduced lunch:	31.6%
Before / after school program:	Yes / Yes

Students at this school generally go on to:
Sweetwater Middle

AJC GRADE: ★★★

Stanford 9 Achievement Tests
3rd- and 5th-grade equivalency

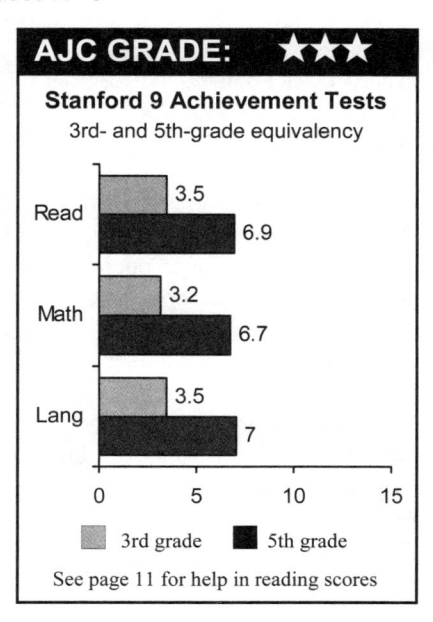

- Read: 3rd grade 3.5, 5th grade 6.9
- Math: 3rd grade 3.2, 5th grade 6.7
- Lang: 3rd grade 3.5, 5th grade 7

See page 11 for help in reading scores

Britt Elementary School

2503 Skyland Dr, Snellville, GA 30078
770-972-4500 · Grades K - 5

Enrollment:	806
White / black / other:	70.6% / 17.4% / 12.0%
Not native English-speaking:	21 / 2.6%
Limited English proficiency:	21 / 2.6%
Student absenteeism:	2.8%
Students per teacher:	15.7
Parent friendliness:	①❷❸④⑤❻
Teachers with advanced degrees:	66.0%
Average years' teaching experience:	15.6
Students in gifted program:	41 / 5.1%
Students in remedial education:	16.4%
Students held back a grade:	2.6%
Total suspensions, pct. in-school:	7 / 28.6%
Offenses:	violence: 7, drugs: *, other: *
Eligible students, free or reduced lunch:	15.9%
Before / after school program:	No / No

Students at this school generally go on to:
Snellville Middle

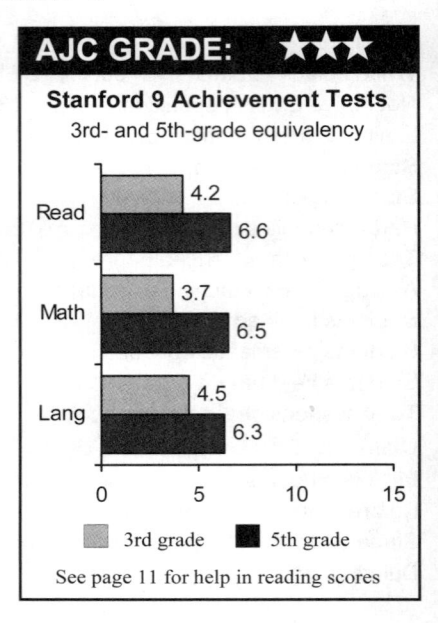

AJC GRADE: ★★★

Stanford 9 Achievement Tests
3rd- and 5th-grade equivalency

- Read: 4.2 (3rd grade) / 6.6 (5th grade)
- Math: 3.7 (3rd grade) / 6.5 (5th grade)
- Lang: 4.5 (3rd grade) / 6.3 (5th grade)

See page 11 for help in reading scores

Brookwood Elementary School

1330 Holly Brook Rd, Snellville, GA 30078
770-736-4360 · Grades K - 5

Enrollment:	993
White / black / other:	73.5% / 8.5% / 18.0%
Not native English-speaking:	26 / 2.6%
Limited English proficiency:	30 / 3.0%
Student absenteeism:	2.4%
Students per teacher:	14.1
Parent friendliness:	①❷❸④⑤❻
Teachers with advanced degrees:	52.8%
Average years' teaching experience:	13.7
Students in gifted program:	124 / 12.5%
Students in remedial education:	1.7%
Students held back a grade:	1.3%
Total suspensions, pct. in-school:	1 / 0.0%
Offenses:	violence: *, drugs: *, other: 1
Eligible students, free or reduced lunch:	8.2%
Before / after school program:	No / No

Students at this school generally go on to:
Alton C. Crews Middle

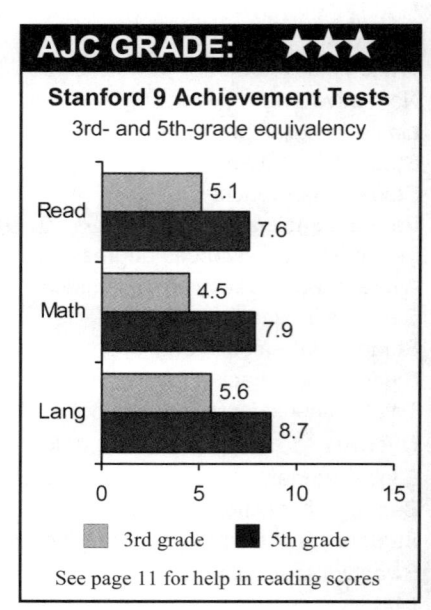

AJC GRADE: ★★★

Stanford 9 Achievement Tests
3rd- and 5th-grade equivalency

- Read: 5.1 (3rd grade) / 7.6 (5th grade)
- Math: 4.5 (3rd grade) / 7.9 (5th grade)
- Lang: 5.6 (3rd grade) / 8.7 (5th grade)

See page 11 for help in reading scores

Camp Creek Elementary School

958 Cole Dr SW, Lilburn, GA 30047
770-921-1626 · Grades K - 5

Enrollment:	846
White / black / other:	73.4% / 7.6% / 19.0%
Not native English-speaking:	19 / 2.2%
Limited English proficiency:	20 / 2.4%
Student absenteeism:	2.5%
Students per teacher:	14.9
Parent friendliness:	① ❷ ❸ ④ ⑤ ❻
Teachers with advanced degrees:	66.1%
Average years' teaching experience:	15.7
Students in gifted program:	103 / 12.2%
Students in remedial education:	19.2%
Students held back a grade:	1.3%
Total suspensions, pct. in-school:	2 / 0.0%
Offenses:	violence: 3, drugs: *, other: *
Eligible students, free or reduced lunch:	6.3%
Before / after school program:	Yes / Yes

Students at this school generally go on to:
Trickum Middle

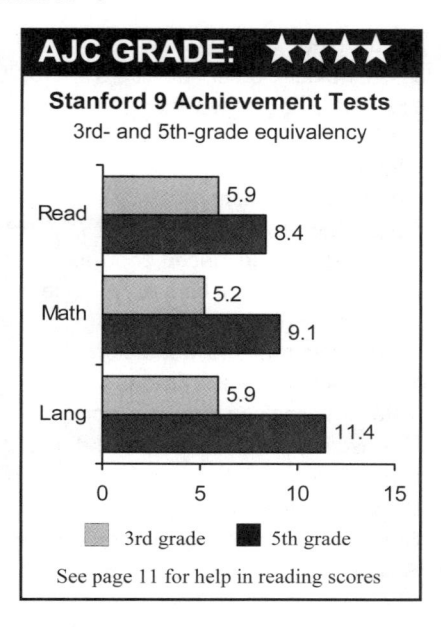

AJC GRADE: ★★★★

Stanford 9 Achievement Tests
3rd- and 5th-grade equivalency

- Read: 3rd grade 5.9, 5th grade 8.4
- Math: 3rd grade 5.2, 5th grade 9.1
- Lang: 3rd grade 5.9, 5th grade 11.4

See page 11 for help in reading scores

Cedar Hill Elementary School

3615 Sugarloaf Pkwy, Lawrenceville, GA 30044
770-962-5015 · Grades K - 5

Enrollment:	1,148
White / black / other:	57.3% / 22.0% / 20.6%
Not native English-speaking:	82 / 7.1%
Limited English proficiency:	94 / 8.2%
Student absenteeism:	3.3%
Students per teacher:	15.4
Parent friendliness:	① ❷ ❸ ④ ⑤ ❻
Teachers with advanced degrees:	52.6%
Average years' teaching experience:	11.4
Students in gifted program:	76 / 6.6%
Students in remedial education:	14.9%
Students held back a grade:	1.6%
Total suspensions, pct. in-school:	1 / 0.0%
Offenses:	violence: 1, drugs: *, other: *
Eligible students, free or reduced lunch:	25.8%
Before / after school program:	No / No

Students at this school generally go on to:
J.E. Richards Middle

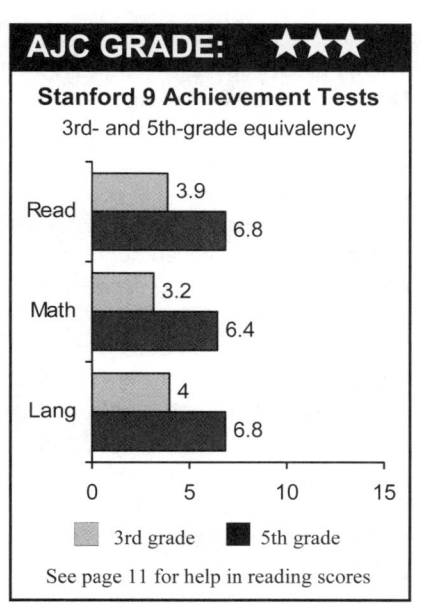

AJC GRADE: ★★★

Stanford 9 Achievement Tests
3rd- and 5th-grade equivalency

- Read: 3rd grade 3.9, 5th grade 6.8
- Math: 3rd grade 3.2, 5th grade 6.4
- Lang: 3rd grade 4, 5th grade 6.8

See page 11 for help in reading scores

The Atlanta Journal-Constitution / Page 373

Gwinnett County Elementary Schools

Centerville Elementary School

3115 Centerville Hwy, Snellville, GA 30039
770-972-2220 · Grades K - 5

Enrollment:	728
White / black / other:	66.8% / 19.2% / 14.0%
Not native English-speaking:	35 / 4.8%
Limited English proficiency:	35 / 4.8%
Student absenteeism:	3.0%
Students per teacher:	14.4
Parent friendliness:	① ❷ ❸ ④ ⑤ ❻
Teachers with advanced degrees:	54.9%
Average years' teaching experience:	13.9
Students in gifted program:	28 / 3.8%
Students in remedial education:	4.5%
Students held back a grade:	0.7%
Total suspensions, pct. in-school:	3 / 0.0%
Offenses:	violence: 1, drugs: *, other: 2
Eligible students, free or reduced lunch:	19.5%
Before / after school program:	No / No

Students at this school generally go on to:
Shiloh Middle

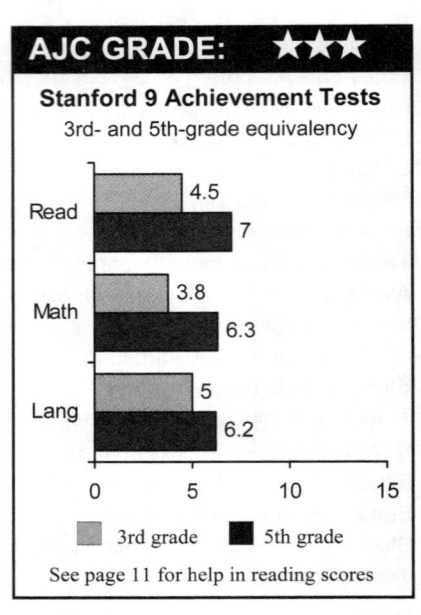

AJC GRADE: ★★★

Stanford 9 Achievement Tests
3rd- and 5th-grade equivalency

- Read: 3rd grade 4.5 / 5th grade 7
- Math: 3rd grade 3.8 / 5th grade 6.3
- Lang: 3rd grade 5 / 5th grade 6.2

See page 11 for help in reading scores

Chattahoochee Elementary School

2930 Albion Farm Rd, Duluth, GA 30097
770-497-9907 · Grades K - 5

Enrollment:	1,339
White / black / other:	55.9% / 13.1% / 31.0%
Not native English-speaking:	119 / 8.9%
Limited English proficiency:	119 / 8.9%
Student absenteeism:	2.8%
Students per teacher:	14.7
Parent friendliness:	① ❷ ❸ ④ ❺ ❻
Teachers with advanced degrees:	50.5%
Average years' teaching experience:	10.6
Students in gifted program:	126 / 9.4%
Students in remedial education:	16.8%
Students held back a grade:	1.8%
Total suspensions, pct. in-school:	2 / 0.0%
Offenses:	violence: *, drugs: *, other: 2
Eligible students, free or reduced lunch:	10.0%
Before / after school program:	No / No

Students at this school generally go on to:
Duluth Middle

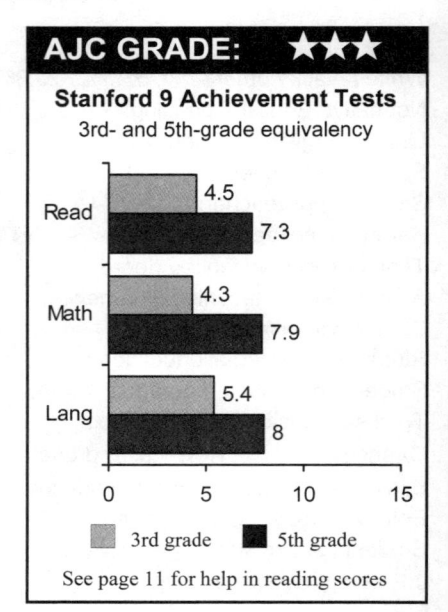

AJC GRADE: ★★★

Stanford 9 Achievement Tests
3rd- and 5th-grade equivalency

- Read: 3rd grade 4.5 / 5th grade 7.3
- Math: 3rd grade 4.3 / 5th grade 7.9
- Lang: 3rd grade 5.4 / 5th grade 8

See page 11 for help in reading scores

Gwinnett County Elementary Schools

Craig Elementary School

1075 Rocky Rd, Lawrenceville, GA 30044
770-978-5560 · Grades K - 5

Enrollment:	904
White / black / other:	87.5% / 4.0% / 8.5%
Not native English-speaking:	11 / 1.2%
Limited English proficiency:	13 / 1.4%
Student absenteeism:	2.6%
Students per teacher:	14.8
Parent friendliness:	① ❷ ❸ ④ ⑤ ❻
Teachers with advanced degrees:	55.6%
Average years' teaching experience:	12.6
Students in gifted program:	185 / 20.5%
Students in remedial education:	6.5%
Students held back a grade:	2.2%
Total suspensions, pct. in-school:	1 / 0.0%
Offenses:	violence: 1, drugs: *, other: 5
Eligible students, free or reduced lunch:	4.9%
Before / after school program:	No / Yes
Students at this school generally go to:	
Alton C. Crews Middle	

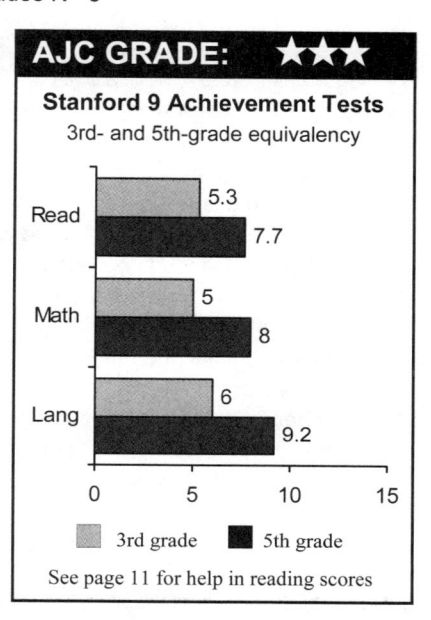

AJC GRADE: ★★★

Stanford 9 Achievement Tests
3rd- and 5th-grade equivalency

- Read: 3rd grade 5.3, 5th grade 7.7
- Math: 3rd grade 5, 5th grade 8
- Lang: 3rd grade 6, 5th grade 9.2

See page 11 for help in reading scores

Dacula Elementary School

2500 Fence Rd, Dacula, GA 30019
770-963-7174 · Grades K - 5

Enrollment:	931
White / black / other:	85.9% / 5.5% / 8.6%
Not native English-speaking:	36 / 3.9%
Limited English proficiency:	43 / 4.6%
Student absenteeism:	3.1%
Students per teacher:	15.5
Parent friendliness:	① ❷ ❸ ❹ ❺ ❻
Teachers with advanced degrees:	43.8%
Average years' teaching experience:	10.4
Students in gifted program:	156 / 16.8%
Students in remedial education:	18.1%
Students held back a grade:	1.9%
Total suspensions, pct. in-school:	*
Offenses:	violence: 1, drugs: *, other: *
Eligible students, free or reduced lunch:	9.7%
Before / after school program:	Yes / Yes
Students at this school generally go to:	
Dacula Middle	

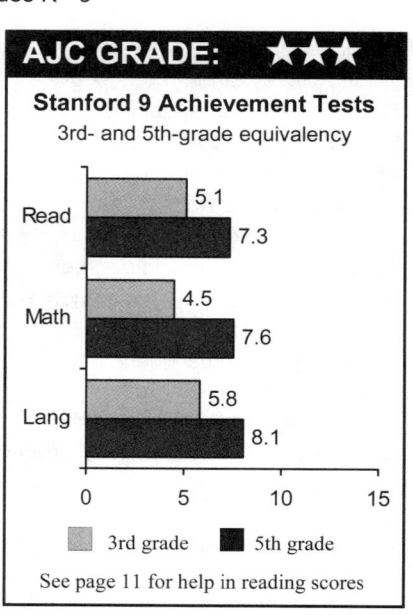

AJC GRADE: ★★★

Stanford 9 Achievement Tests
3rd- and 5th-grade equivalency

- Read: 3rd grade 5.1, 5th grade 7.3
- Math: 3rd grade 4.5, 5th grade 7.6
- Lang: 3rd grade 5.8, 5th grade 8.1

See page 11 for help in reading scores

Gwinnett County Elementary Schools

Dyer Elementary School

713 Hi Hope Rd, Lawrenceville, GA 30043
770-963-6214 · Grades K - 5

Enrollment:	631
White / black / other:	73.5% / 13.8% / 12.7%
Not native English-speaking:	20 / 3.2%
Limited English proficiency:	24 / 3.8%
Student absenteeism:	2.7%
Students per teacher:	12.7
Parent friendliness:	❶❷❸④⑤❻
Teachers with advanced degrees:	62.7%
Average years' teaching experience:	12.3
Students in gifted program:	63 / 10.0%
Students in remedial education:	6.9%
Students held back a grade:	0.8%
Total suspensions, pct. in-school:	5 / 0.0%
Offenses:	violence: 4, drugs: *, other: 2
Eligible students, free or reduced lunch:	14.1%
Before / after school program:	Yes / Yes

Students at this school generally go on to:
Creekland Middle

AJC GRADE: ★★★

Stanford 9 Achievement Tests
3rd- and 5th-grade equivalency

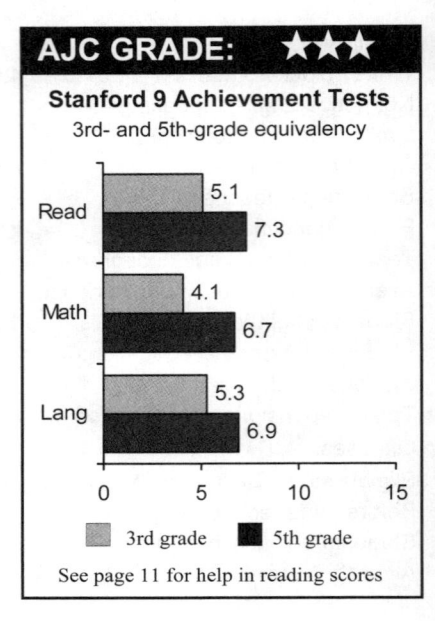

	3rd grade	5th grade
Read	5.1	7.3
Math	4.1	6.7
Lang	5.3	6.9

See page 11 for help in reading scores

Fort Daniel Elementary School

1725 Auburn Rd, Dacula, GA 30019
770-932-7400 · Grades K - 5

Enrollment:	1,235
White / black / other:	88.5% / 4.1% / 7.4%
Not native English-speaking:	18 / 1.5%
Limited English proficiency:	18 / 1.5%
Student absenteeism:	2.8%
Students per teacher:	15.7
Parent friendliness:	①❷❸④⑤❻
Teachers with advanced degrees:	65.9%
Average years' teaching experience:	11.9
Students in gifted program:	98 / 7.9%
Students in remedial education:	10.8%
Students held back a grade:	1.2%
Total suspensions, pct. in-school:	*
Offenses:	violence: 3, drugs: *, other: *
Eligible students, free or reduced lunch:	6.3%
Before / after school program:	Yes / Yes

Students at this school generally go on to:
Dacula Middle

AJC GRADE: ★★★

Stanford 9 Achievement Tests
3rd- and 5th-grade equivalency

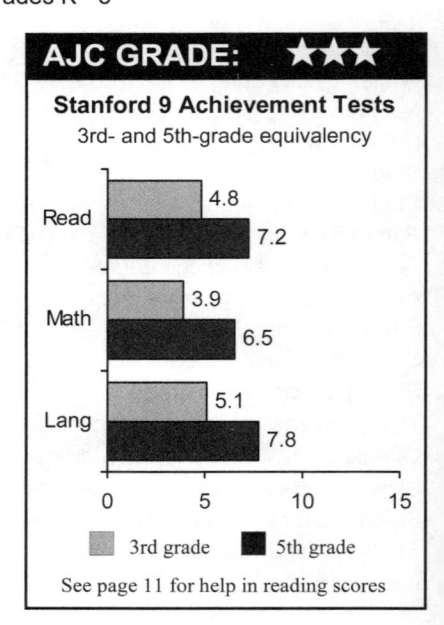

	3rd grade	5th grade
Read	4.8	7.2
Math	3.9	6.5
Lang	5.1	7.8

See page 11 for help in reading scores

Gwinnett County Elementary Schools

Freeman's Mill Elementary School

2303 Old Peachtree Rd NE, Lawrenceville, GA 30043
678-377-8955 · Grades K - 5

Enrollment:	1,006
White / black / other:	86.2% / 4.1% / 9.7%
Not native English-speaking:	22 / 2.2%
Limited English proficiency:	31 / 3.1%
Student absenteeism:	2.9%
Students per teacher:	14.4
Parent friendliness:	①②❸④❺❻
Teachers with advanced degrees:	41.7%
Average years' teaching experience:	8.6
Students in gifted program:	132 / 13.1%
Students in remedial education:	7.6%
Students held back a grade:	1.9%
Total suspensions, pct. in-school:	2 / 0.0%
Offenses:	violence: 2, drugs: * , other: *
Eligible students, free or reduced lunch:	7.9%
Before / after school program:	No / Yes

Students at this school generally go on to:
Dacula Middle

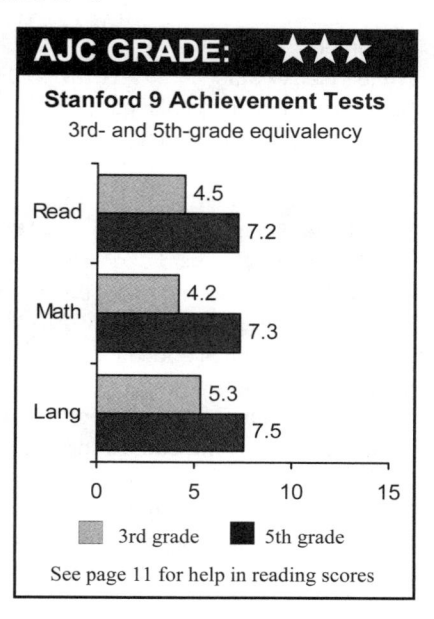

AJC GRADE: ★★★

Stanford 9 Achievement Tests
3rd- and 5th-grade equivalency

- Read: 3rd grade 4.5, 5th grade 7.2
- Math: 3rd grade 4.2, 5th grade 7.3
- Lang: 3rd grade 5.3, 5th grade 7.5

See page 11 for help in reading scores

Grayson Elementary School

460 Grayson Pkwy, Grayson, GA 30017
770-963-7189 · Grades K - 5

Enrollment:	1,306
White / black / other:	89.6% / 4.2% / 6.2%
Not native English-speaking:	9 / 0.7%
Limited English proficiency:	9 / 0.7%
Student absenteeism:	3.4%
Students per teacher:	15.9
Parent friendliness:	①❷❸④❺❻
Teachers with advanced degrees:	54.1%
Average years' teaching experience:	11.8
Students in gifted program:	107 / 8.2%
Students in remedial education:	6.0%
Students held back a grade:	3.8%
Total suspensions, pct. in-school:	1 / 0.0%
Offenses:	violence: 1, drugs: * , other: 1
Eligible students, free or reduced lunch:	8.0%
Before / after school program:	No / Yes

Students at this school generally go on to:
McConnell Middle

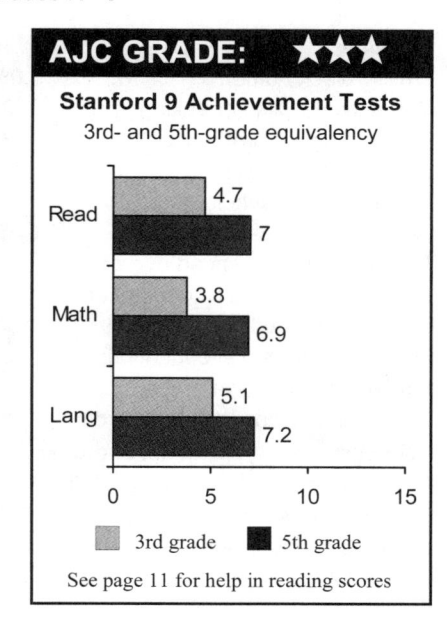

AJC GRADE: ★★★

Stanford 9 Achievement Tests
3rd- and 5th-grade equivalency

- Read: 3rd grade 4.7, 5th grade 7
- Math: 3rd grade 3.8, 5th grade 6.9
- Lang: 3rd grade 5.1, 5th grade 7.2

See page 11 for help in reading scores

Gwinnett County Elementary Schools

Gwin Oaks Elementary School

400 Gwin Oaks Dr, Lawrenceville, GA 30044
770-972-3110 · Grades K - 5

Enrollment:	1,036
White / black / other:	75.0% / 10.3% / 14.7%
Not native English-speaking:	40 / 3.9%
Limited English proficiency:	45 / 4.3%
Student absenteeism:	3.0%
Students per teacher:	15.3
Parent friendliness:	①❷❸④⑤❻
Teachers with advanced degrees:	44.9%
Average years' teaching experience:	13.4
Students in gifted program:	92 / 8.9%
Students in remedial education:	7.8%
Students held back a grade:	1.0%
Total suspensions, pct. in-school:	2 / 100.0%
Offenses:	violence: 2, drugs: * , other: *
Eligible students, free or reduced lunch:	14.0%
Before / after school program:	Yes / Yes

Students at this school generally go on to:
Five Forks Middle

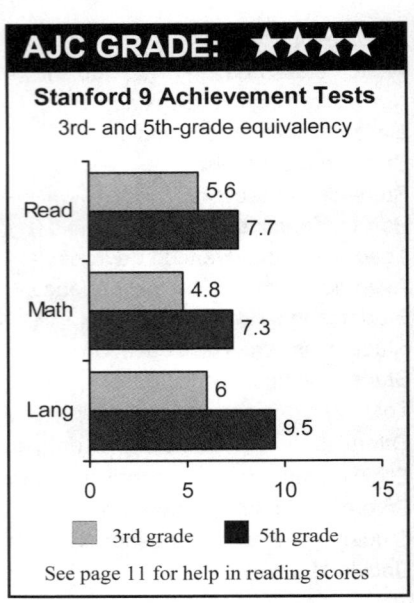

AJC GRADE: ★★★★

Stanford 9 Achievement Tests
3rd- and 5th-grade equivalency

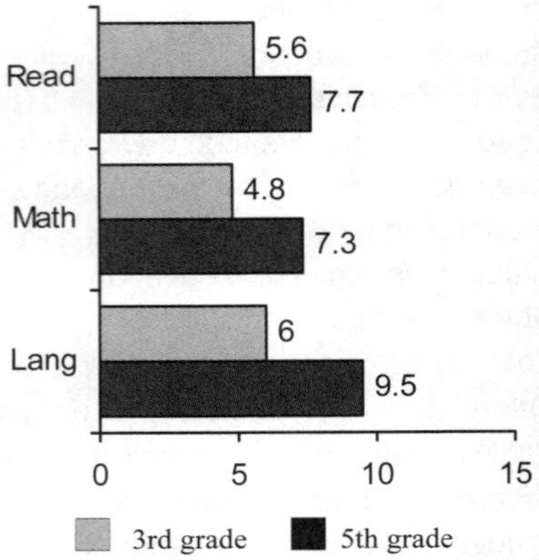

Read
5.6
7.7
Math
4.8
7.3
Lang
6
9.5
0
5
10
15
3rd grade
5th grade

See page 11 for help in reading scores

Harbins Elementary School

3550 New Hope Rd, Dacula, GA 30019
770-682-4270 · Grades K - 5

Enrollment:	989
White / black / other:	85.7% / 6.0% / 8.3%
Not native English-speaking:	30 / 3.0%
Limited English proficiency:	30 / 3.0%
Student absenteeism:	3.1%
Students per teacher:	15.0
Parent friendliness:	①❷❸④❺❻
Teachers with advanced degrees:	60.3%
Average years' teaching experience:	12.6
Students in gifted program:	75 / 7.6%
Students in remedial education:	10.0%
Students held back a grade:	1.1%
Total suspensions, pct. in-school:	2 / 50.0%
Offenses:	violence: 2, drugs: * , other: *
Eligible students, free or reduced lunch:	20.1%
Before / after school program:	Yes / Yes

Students at this school generally go on to:
Dacula Middle

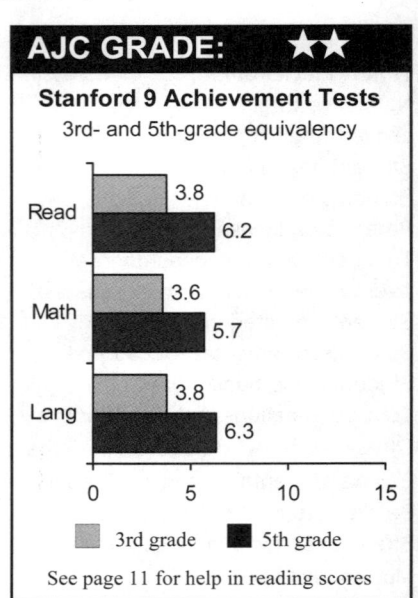

AJC GRADE: ★★

Stanford 9 Achievement Tests
3rd- and 5th-grade equivalency

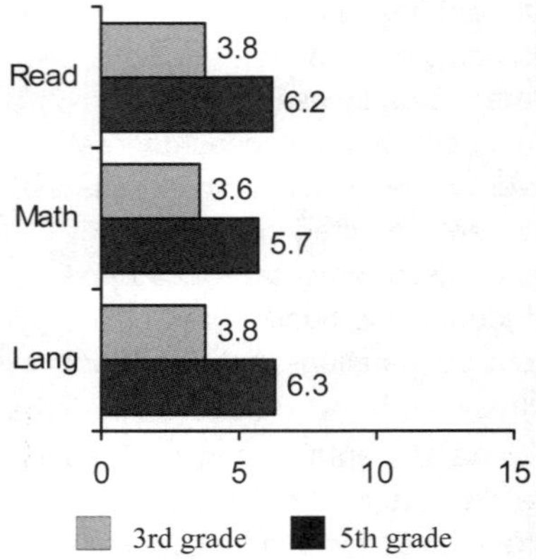

Read
3.8
6.2
Math
3.6
5.7
Lang
3.8
6.3
0
5
10
15
3rd grade
5th grade

See page 11 for help in reading scores

Harmony Elementary School

3946 S Bogan Rd, Buford, GA 30519
770-945-7272 · Grades K - 5

Enrollment:	1,010
White / black / other:	87.9% / 3.4% / 8.7%
Not native English-speaking:	27 / 2.7%
Limited English proficiency:	34 / 3.4%
Student absenteeism:	3.1%
Students per teacher:	15.8
Parent friendliness:	① ❷ ❸ ④ ⑤ ❻
Teachers with advanced degrees:	52.9%
Average years' teaching experience:	13.6
Students in gifted program:	71 / 7.0%
Students in remedial education:	3.4%
Students held back a grade:	2.8%
Total suspensions, pct. in-school:	2 / 0.0%
Offenses:	violence: 3, drugs: *, other: 3
Eligible students, free or reduced lunch:	10.4%
Before / after school program:	Yes / No

Students at this school generally go on to:
Lanier Middle

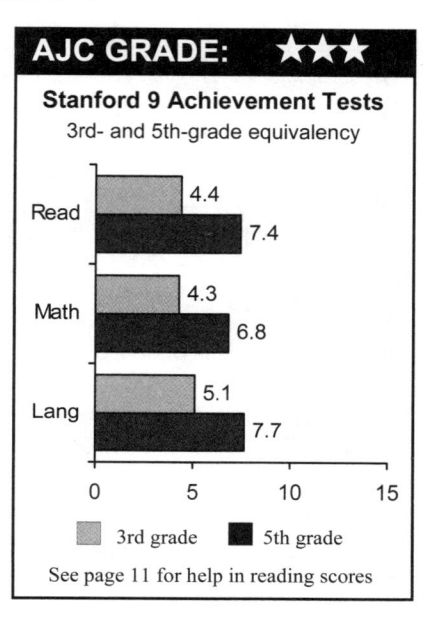

AJC GRADE: ★★★

Stanford 9 Achievement Tests
3rd- and 5th-grade equivalency

	3rd grade	5th grade
Read	4.4	7.4
Math	4.3	6.8
Lang	5.1	7.7

See page 11 for help in reading scores

Harris Elementary School

3123 Claiborne Dr, Duluth, GA 30096
770-476-2241 · Grades K - 5

Enrollment:	970
White / black / other:	43.4% / 16.3% / 40.3%
Not native English-speaking:	133 / 13.7%
Limited English proficiency:	146 / 15.1%
Student absenteeism:	3.1%
Students per teacher:	13.9
Parent friendliness:	① ❷ ❸ ④ ❺ ❻
Teachers with advanced degrees:	40.3%
Average years' teaching experience:	9.3
Students in gifted program:	136 / 14.0%
Students in remedial education:	17.3%
Students held back a grade:	4.2%
Total suspensions, pct. in-school:	9 / 11.1%
Offenses:	violence: 5, drugs: *, other: 4
Eligible students, free or reduced lunch:	29.0%
Before / after school program:	Yes / Yes

Students at this school generally go on to:
Duluth, Hull Middle

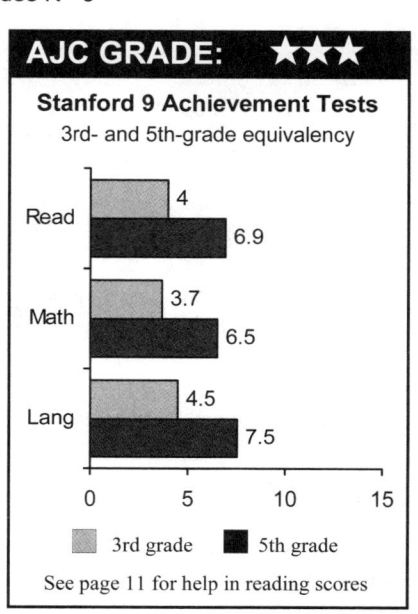

AJC GRADE: ★★★

Stanford 9 Achievement Tests
3rd- and 5th-grade equivalency

	3rd grade	5th grade
Read	4	6.9
Math	3.7	6.5
Lang	4.5	7.5

See page 11 for help in reading scores

Gwinnett County Elementary Schools

Head Elementary School

1801 Hewatt Rd SW, Lilburn, GA 30047
770-972-8050 · Grades K - 5

Enrollment:	646
White / black / other:	75.9% / 11.1% / 13.0%
Not native English-speaking:	13 / 2.0%
Limited English proficiency:	13 / 2.0%
Student absenteeism:	2.6%
Students per teacher:	14.1
Parent friendliness:	① ❷ ❸ ④ ❺ ❻
Teachers with advanced degrees:	52.1%
Average years' teaching experience:	16.0
Students in gifted program:	104 / 16.1%
Students in remedial education:	3.0%
Students held back a grade:	1.9%
Total suspensions, pct. in-school:	2 / 0.0%
Offenses:	violence: 1, drugs: *, other: 2
Eligible students, free or reduced lunch:	7.7%
Before / after school program:	No / Yes
Students at this school generally go on to:	
Five Forks Middle	

AJC GRADE: ★★★★

Stanford 9 Achievement Tests
3rd- and 5th-grade equivalency

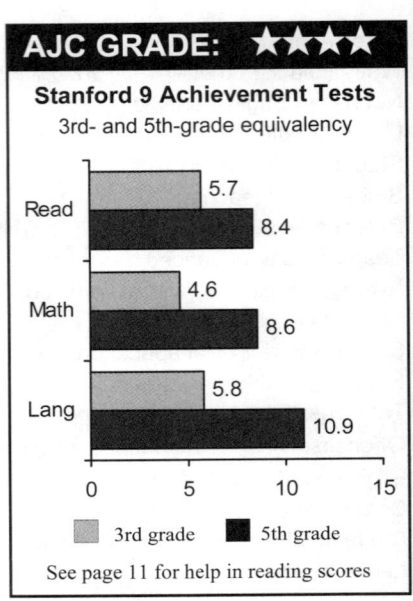

- Read: 3rd grade 5.7, 5th grade 8.4
- Math: 3rd grade 4.6, 5th grade 8.6
- Lang: 3rd grade 5.8, 5th grade 10.9

See page 11 for help in reading scores

Hopkins Elementary School

1315 Dickens Rd NW, Lilburn, GA 30047
770-564-2661 · Grades K - 5

Enrollment:	973
White / black / other:	18.3% / 32.0% / 49.7%
Not native English-speaking:	180 / 18.5%
Limited English proficiency:	180 / 18.5%
Student absenteeism:	3.5%
Students per teacher:	12.8
Parent friendliness:	① ❷ ❸ ④ ❺ ❻
Teachers with advanced degrees:	36.4%
Average years' teaching experience:	10.2
Students in gifted program:	66 / 6.8%
Students in remedial education:	5.4%
Students held back a grade:	2.1%
Total suspensions, pct. in-school:	13 / 38.5%
Offenses:	violence: 10, drugs: *, other: 4
Eligible students, free or reduced lunch:	51.8%
Before / after school program:	No / Yes
Students at this school generally go on to:	
Lilburn Middle	

AJC GRADE: ★★★

Stanford 9 Achievement Tests
3rd- and 5th-grade equivalency

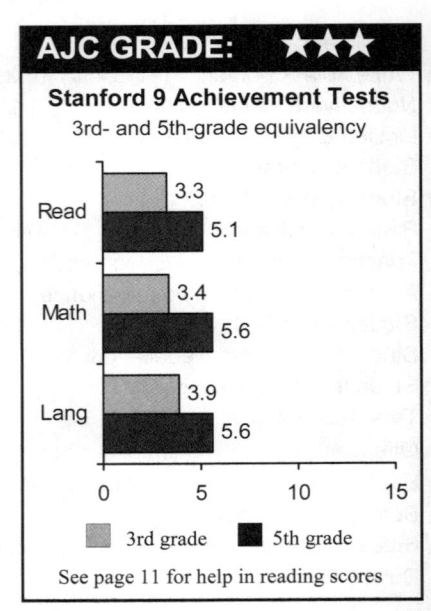

- Read: 3rd grade 3.3, 5th grade 5.1
- Math: 3rd grade 3.4, 5th grade 5.6
- Lang: 3rd grade 3.9, 5th grade 5.6

See page 11 for help in reading scores

Jackson Elementary School

1970 Sever Rd, Lawrenceville, GA 30043
770-682-4200 · Grades K - 5

Enrollment:	1,505
White / black / other:	67.1% / 12.8% / 20.1%
Not native English-speaking:	67 / 4.5%
Limited English proficiency:	85 / 5.6%
Student absenteeism:	2.5%
Students per teacher:	15.9
Parent friendliness:	① ❷ ❸ ❹ ❺ ❻
Teachers with advanced degrees:	37.5%
Average years' teaching experience:	9.5
Students in gifted program:	160 / 10.6%
Students in remedial education:	17.7%
Students held back a grade:	1.5%
Total suspensions, pct. in-school:	1 / 0.0%
Offenses: violence: *, drugs: *, other: 1	
Eligible students, free or reduced lunch:	12.5%
Before / after school program:	Yes / No

Students at this school generally go on to:
Hull Middle

AJC GRADE: ★★★

Stanford 9 Achievement Tests
3rd- and 5th-grade equivalency

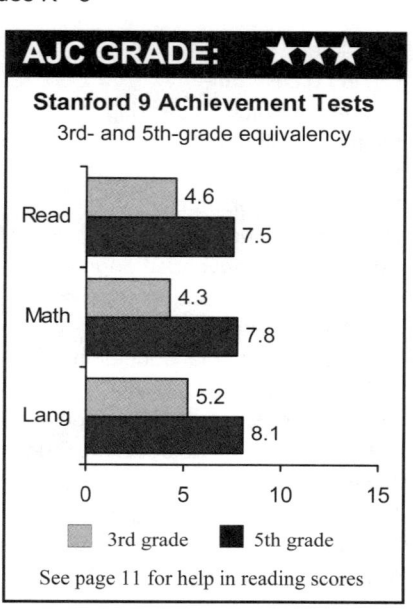

- Read: 3rd grade 4.6, 5th grade 7.5
- Math: 3rd grade 4.3, 5th grade 7.8
- Lang: 3rd grade 5.2, 5th grade 8.1

See page 11 for help in reading scores

Kanoheda Elementary School

1025 Herrington Rd, Lawrenceville, GA 30044
770-682-4221 · Grades K - 5

Enrollment:	1,419
White / black / other:	21.1% / 43.8% / 35.2%
Not native English-speaking:	207 / 14.6%
Limited English proficiency:	226 / 15.9%
Student absenteeism:	3.3%
Students per teacher:	15.0
Parent friendliness:	① ❷ ❸ ④ ❺ ❻
Teachers with advanced degrees:	30.9%
Average years' teaching experience:	8.7
Students in gifted program:	40 / 2.8%
Students in remedial education:	17.0%
Students held back a grade:	1.5%
Total suspensions, pct. in-school:	42 / 23.8%
Offenses: violence: 27, drugs: *, other: 15	
Eligible students, free or reduced lunch:	47.1%
Before / after school program:	No / No

Students at this school generally go on to:
Sweetwater Middle

AJC GRADE: ★★★

Stanford 9 Achievement Tests
3rd- and 5th-grade equivalency

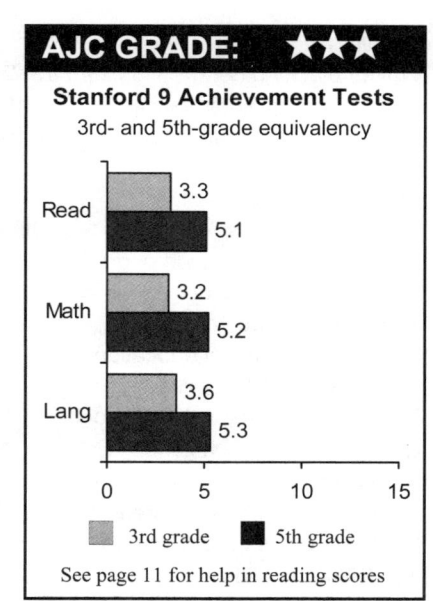

- Read: 3rd grade 3.3, 5th grade 5.1
- Math: 3rd grade 3.2, 5th grade 5.2
- Lang: 3rd grade 3.6, 5th grade 5.3

See page 11 for help in reading scores

Knight Elementary School

401 N River Dr SW, Lilburn, GA 30047
770-921-2400 · Grades K - 5

Enrollment:	529
White / black / other:	64.3% / 12.3% / 23.4%
Not native English-speaking:	22 / 4.2%
Limited English proficiency:	30 / 5.7%
Student absenteeism:	2.7%
Students per teacher:	13.8
Parent friendliness:	① ❷ ❸ ❹ ❺ ❻
Teachers with advanced degrees:	51.3%
Average years' teaching experience:	15.4
Students in gifted program:	69 / 13.0%
Students in remedial education:	21.0%
Students held back a grade:	6.0%
Total suspensions, pct. in-school:	*
Offenses:	violence: *, drugs: *, other: *
Eligible students, free or reduced lunch:	19.9%
Before / after school program:	Yes / No
Students at this school generally go on to:	
Trickum Midle Middle	

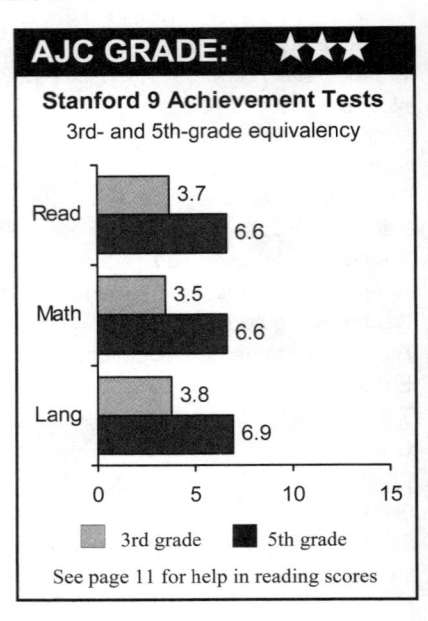

AJC GRADE: ★★★

Stanford 9 Achievement Tests
3rd- and 5th-grade equivalency

- Read: 3rd grade 3.7, 5th grade 6.6
- Math: 3rd grade 3.5, 5th grade 6.6
- Lang: 3rd grade 3.8, 5th grade 6.9

See page 11 for help in reading scores

Lawrenceville Elementary School

122 Gwinnett Dr, Lawrenceville, GA 30045
770-963-1813 · Grades K - 5

Enrollment:	1,051
White / black / other:	53.2% / 23.2% / 23.6%
Not native English-speaking:	151 / 14.4%
Limited English proficiency:	156 / 14.8%
Student absenteeism:	3.7%
Students per teacher:	14.3
Parent friendliness:	① ❷ ❸ ❹ ❺ ❻
Teachers with advanced degrees:	39.2%
Average years' teaching experience:	8.7
Students in gifted program:	70 / 6.7%
Students in remedial education:	17.3%
Students held back a grade:	3.2%
Total suspensions, pct. in-school:	6 / 0.0%
Offenses:	violence: 5, drugs: *, other: 1
Eligible students, free or reduced lunch:	19.3%
Before / after school program:	Yes / Yes
Students at this school generally go on to:	
J.E. Richards Middle	

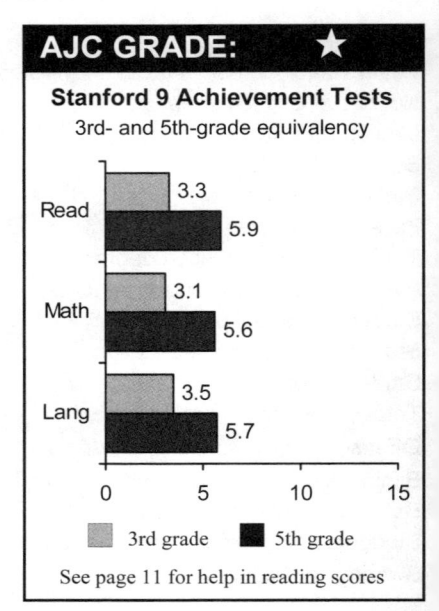

AJC GRADE: ★

Stanford 9 Achievement Tests
3rd- and 5th-grade equivalency

- Read: 3rd grade 3.3, 5th grade 5.9
- Math: 3rd grade 3.1, 5th grade 5.6
- Lang: 3rd grade 3.5, 5th grade 5.7

See page 11 for help in reading scores

Gwinnett County Elementary Schools

Lilburn Elementary School

531 Lilburn School Rd NW, Lilburn, GA 30047
770-921-7707 · Grades K - 5

Enrollment:	1,078
White / black / other:	20.1% / 26.9% / 53.0%
Not native English-speaking:	321 / 29.8%
Limited English proficiency:	335 / 31.1%
Student absenteeism:	3.4%
Students per teacher:	12.6
Parent friendliness:	① ❷ ❸ ④ ❺ ❻
Teachers with advanced degrees:	58.6%
Average years' teaching experience:	10.4
Students in gifted program:	58 / 5.4%
Students in remedial education:	37.8%
Students held back a grade:	2.7%
Total suspensions, pct. in-school:	4 / 0.0%
Offenses:	violence: 2, drugs: * , other: 3
Eligible students, free or reduced lunch:	57.2%
Before / after school program:	Yes / Yes

Students at this school generally go on to:
Lilburn Middle

AJC GRADE: ★★★

Stanford 9 Achievement Tests
3rd- and 5th-grade equivalency

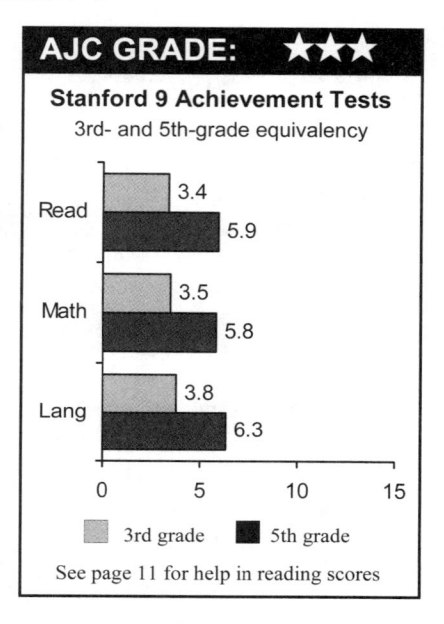

- Read: 3.4 (3rd grade) / 5.9 (5th grade)
- Math: 3.5 (3rd grade) / 5.8 (5th grade)
- Lang: 3.8 (3rd grade) / 6.3 (5th grade)

See page 11 for help in reading scores

Magill Elementary School

3900 Brushy Fork Rd, Loganville, GA 30052
770-554-1030 · Grades K - 5

Enrollment:	1,071
White / black / other:	83.9% / 8.8% / 7.3%
Not native English-speaking:	23 / 2.1%
Limited English proficiency:	24 / 2.2%
Student absenteeism:	3.2%
Students per teacher:	15.4
Parent friendliness:	① ❷ ❸ ④ ⑤ ❻
Teachers with advanced degrees:	46.6%
Average years' teaching experience:	9.7
Students in gifted program:	99 / 9.2%
Students in remedial education:	6.0%
Students held back a grade:	1.4%
Total suspensions, pct. in-school:	2 / 50.0%
Offenses:	violence: 2, drugs: * , other: 2
Eligible students, free or reduced lunch:	17.1%
Before / after school program:	Yes / Yes

Students at this school generally go on to:
Snellville Middle

AJC GRADE: ★★★

Stanford 9 Achievement Tests
3rd- and 5th-grade equivalency

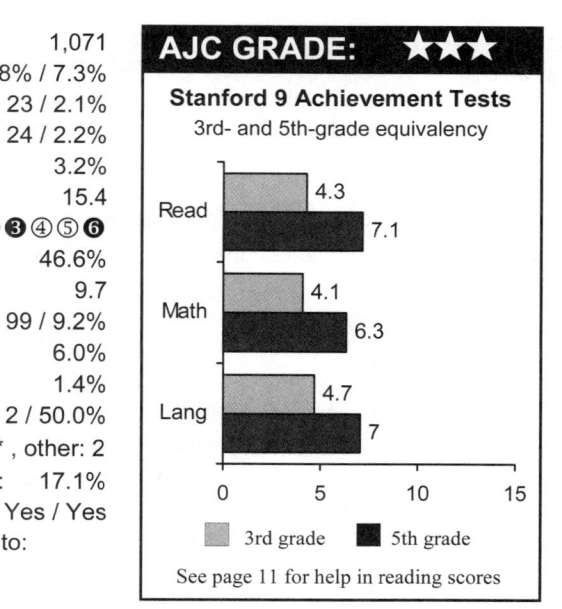

- Read: 4.3 (3rd grade) / 7.1 (5th grade)
- Math: 4.1 (3rd grade) / 6.3 (5th grade)
- Lang: 4.7 (3rd grade) / 7 (5th grade)

See page 11 for help in reading scores

Mason Elementary School

3030 Bunten Rd, Duluth, GA 30096
770-232-3370 · Grades K - 5

Enrollment:	870
White / black / other:	62.9% / 17.6% / 19.5%
Not native English-speaking:	45 / 5.2%
Limited English proficiency:	63 / 7.2%
Student absenteeism:	3.0%
Students per teacher:	12.8
Parent friendliness:	① ❷ ❸ ④ ⑤ ❻
Teachers with advanced degrees:	42.3%
Average years' teaching experience:	10.5
Students in gifted program:	156 / 17.9%
Students in remedial education:	2.0%
Students held back a grade:	2.6%
Total suspensions, pct. in-school:	2 / 0.0%
Offenses:	violence: 2, drugs: *, other: *
Eligible students, free or reduced lunch:	15.4%
Before / after school program:	Yes / No

Students at this school generally go on to:
Hull Middle

AJC GRADE: ★★★

Stanford 9 Achievement Tests
3rd- and 5th-grade equivalency

Read: 3rd grade 4.9 / 5th grade 7.3
Math: 3rd grade 4.5 / 5th grade 7.6
Lang: 3rd grade 6 / 5th grade 7.4

See page 11 for help in reading scores

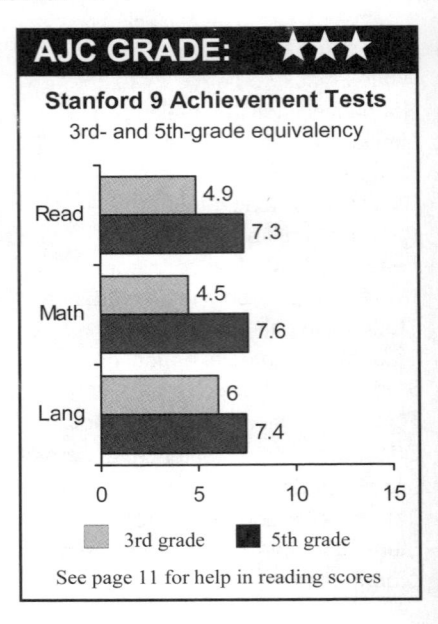

McKendree Elementary School

1600 Riverside Pkwy, Lawrenceville, GA 30043
678-377-8933 · Grades K - 5

Enrollment:	1,097
White / black / other:	64.2% / 14.4% / 21.4%
Not native English-speaking:	76 / 6.9%
Limited English proficiency:	87 / 7.9%
Student absenteeism:	2.6%
Students per teacher:	14.8
Parent friendliness:	① ❷ ❸ ④ ❺ ❻
Teachers with advanced degrees:	57.3%
Average years' teaching experience:	10.5
Students in gifted program:	79 / 7.2%
Students in remedial education:	22.6%
Students held back a grade:	2.3%
Total suspensions, pct. in-school:	*
Offenses:	violence: *, drugs: *, other: *
Eligible students, free or reduced lunch:	10.8%
Before / after school program:	No / No

Students at this school generally go on to:
Creekland Middle

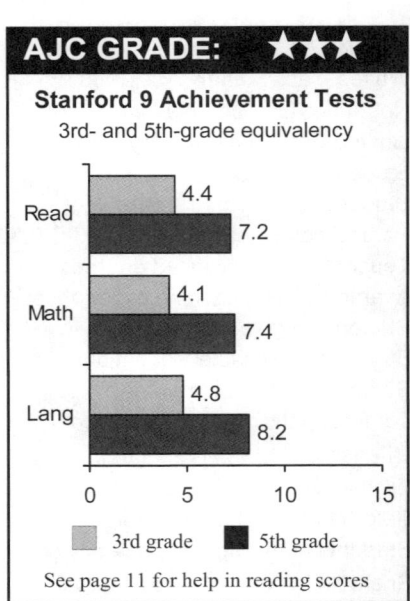

AJC GRADE: ★★★

Stanford 9 Achievement Tests
3rd- and 5th-grade equivalency

Read: 3rd grade 4.4 / 5th grade 7.2
Math: 3rd grade 4.1 / 5th grade 7.4
Lang: 3rd grade 4.8 / 5th grade 8.2

See page 11 for help in reading scores

The Atlanta Journal-Constitution / Page 384

Gwinnett County Elementary Schools

Meadowcreek Elementary School

5025 Georgia Belle Ct, Norcross, GA 30093
770-931-5701 · Grades K - 5

Enrollment:	1,294
White / black / other:	13.9% / 31.5% / 54.6%
Not native English-speaking:	304 / 23.5%
Limited English proficiency:	399 / 30.8%
Student absenteeism:	3.3%
Students per teacher:	14.1
Parent friendliness:	①❷❸④⑤❻
Teachers with advanced degrees:	36.2%
Average years' teaching experience:	8.4
Students in gifted program:	37 / 2.9%
Students in remedial education:	13.1%
Students held back a grade:	3.9%
Total suspensions, pct. in-school:	7 / 0.0%
Offenses:	violence: 5, drugs: * , other: 3
Eligible students, free or reduced lunch:	63.5%
Before / after school program:	No / No

Students at this school generally go on to:
Lilburn Middle

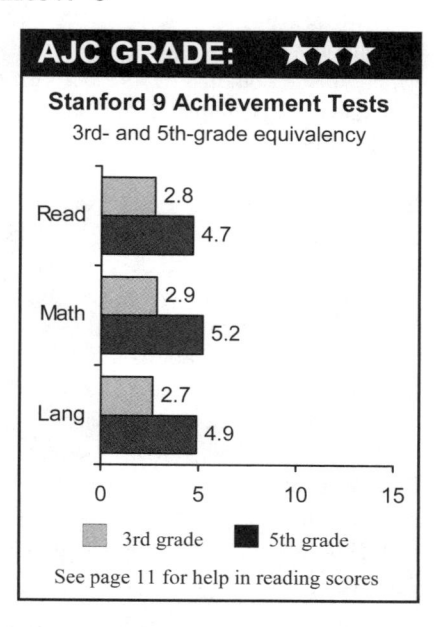

AJC GRADE: ★★★

Stanford 9 Achievement Tests

3rd- and 5th-grade equivalency

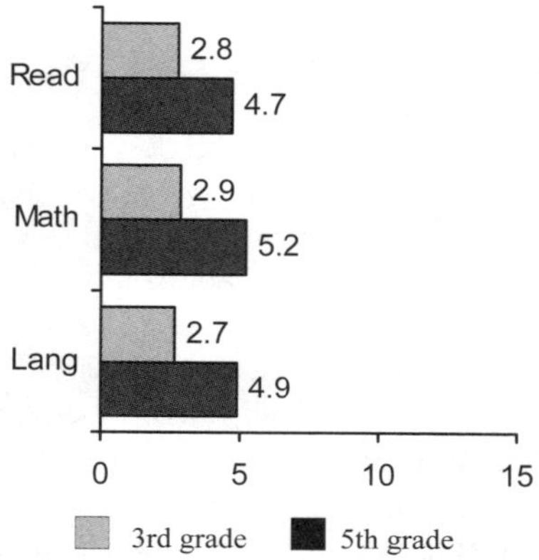
Read
2.8
4.7
Math
2.9
5.2
Lang
2.7
4.9
0
5
10
15
3rd grade
5th grade

See page 11 for help in reading scores

Minor Elementary School

4129 Shady Dr NW, Lilburn, GA 30047
770-925-9543 · Grades K - 5

Enrollment:	1,380
White / black / other:	28.6% / 30.4% / 41.0%
Not native English-speaking:	206 / 14.9%
Limited English proficiency:	240 / 17.4%
Student absenteeism:	3.7%
Students per teacher:	14.1
Parent friendliness:	①❷❸④❺❻
Teachers with advanced degrees:	44.1%
Average years' teaching experience:	10.3
Students in gifted program:	86 / 6.2%
Students in remedial education:	10.2%
Students held back a grade:	3.1%
Total suspensions, pct. in-school:	18 / 0.0%
Offenses:	violence: 20, drugs: * , other: 6
Eligible students, free or reduced lunch:	42.5%
Before / after school program:	Yes / Yes

Students at this school generally go on to:
Sweetwater Middle

AJC GRADE: ★★★

Stanford 9 Achievement Tests

3rd- and 5th-grade equivalency

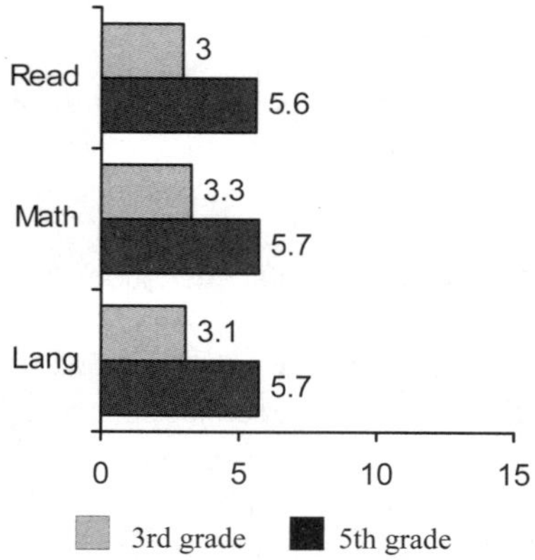
Read
3
5.6
Math
3.3
5.7
Lang
3.1
5.7
0
5
10
15
3rd grade
5th grade

See page 11 for help in reading scores

Mountain Park Elementary School

1500 Pounds Rd SW, Lilburn, GA 30047
770-921-2224 · Grades K - 5

Enrollment:	545
White / black / other:	72.5% / 8.3% / 19.3%
Not native English-speaking:	28 / 5.1%
Limited English proficiency:	28 / 5.1%
Student absenteeism:	2.6%
Students per teacher:	12.1
Parent friendliness:	①❷❸④⑤❻
Teachers with advanced degrees:	57.8%
Average years' teaching experience:	13.7
Students in gifted program:	64 / 11.7%
Students in remedial education:	4.6%
Students held back a grade:	1.3%
Total suspensions, pct. in-school:	1 / 0.0%
Offenses:	violence: * , drugs: * , other: 1
Eligible students, free or reduced lunch:	14.1%
Before / after school program:	No / No

Students at this school generally go on to:
Trickum Middle

AJC GRADE: ★★★

Stanford 9 Achievement Tests
3rd- and 5th-grade equivalency

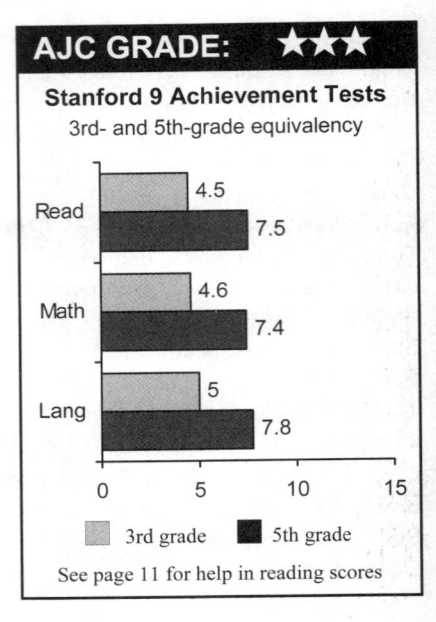

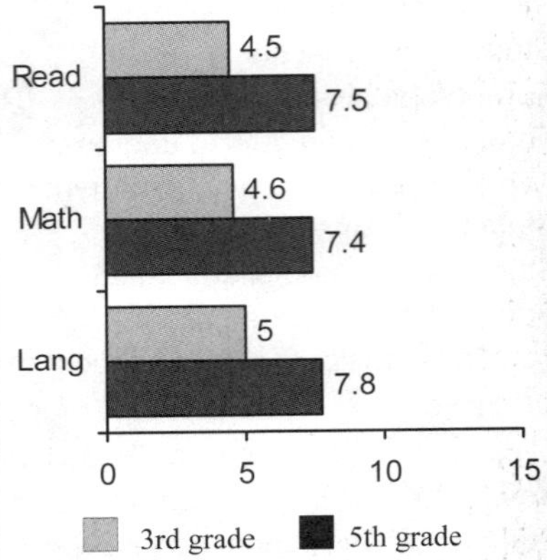
Read
4.5
7.5
Math
4.6
7.4
Lang
5
7.8
0
5
10
15
3rd grade
5th grade

See page 11 for help in reading scores

Nesbit Elementary School

6575 Cherokee Dr, Tucker, GA 30084
770-414-2740 · Grades K - 5

Enrollment:	1,128
White / black / other:	8.2% / 46.5% / 45.3%
Not native English-speaking:	251 / 22.3%
Limited English proficiency:	252 / 22.3%
Student absenteeism:	3.6%
Students per teacher:	13.8
Parent friendliness:	①❷❸④❺❻
Teachers with advanced degrees:	37.3%
Average years' teaching experience:	7.8
Students in gifted program:	41 / 3.6%
Students in remedial education:	30.1%
Students held back a grade:	3.9%
Total suspensions, pct. in-school:	33 / 27.3%
Offenses:	violence: 20, drugs: * , other: 20
Eligible students, free or reduced lunch:	67.6%
Before / after school program:	No / No

Students at this school generally go on to:
Lilburn Middle

AJC GRADE: ★★★

Stanford 9 Achievement Tests
3rd- and 5th-grade equivalency

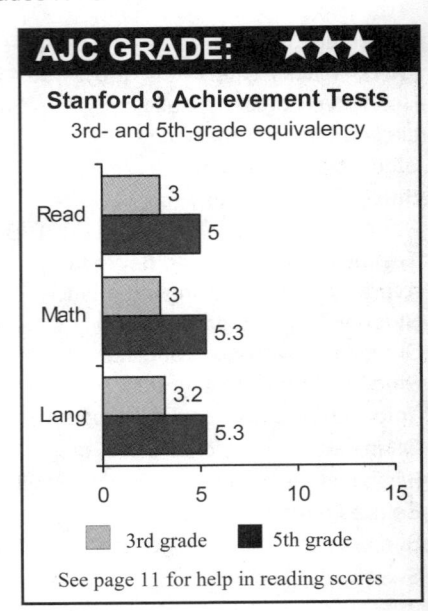

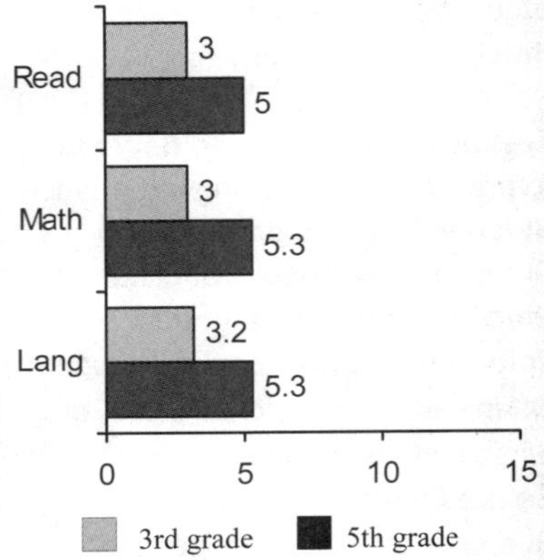
Read
3
5
Math
3
5.3
Lang
3.2
5.3
0
5
10
15
3rd grade
5th grade

See page 11 for help in reading scores

Norcross Elementary School

150 Hunt St, Norcross, GA 30071
770-448-2188 · Grades K - 5

Enrollment:	849
White / black / other:	17.0% / 29.2% / 53.8%
Not native English-speaking:	243 / 28.6%
Limited English proficiency:	261 / 30.7%
Student absenteeism:	3.4%
Students per teacher:	13.1
Parent friendliness:	① ❷ ❸ ④ ❺ ❻
Teachers with advanced degrees:	43.9%
Average years' teaching experience:	8.6
Students in gifted program:	65 / 7.7%
Students in remedial education:	34.1%
Students held back a grade:	1.4%
Total suspensions, pct. in-school:	19 / 26.3%
Offenses	violence: 27, drugs: *, other: 1
Eligible students, free or reduced lunch:	69.4%
Before / after school program:	No / Yes
Students at this school generally go on to:	
Summerour Middle	

AJC GRADE: ★★★

Stanford 9 Achievement Tests
3rd- and 5th-grade equivalency

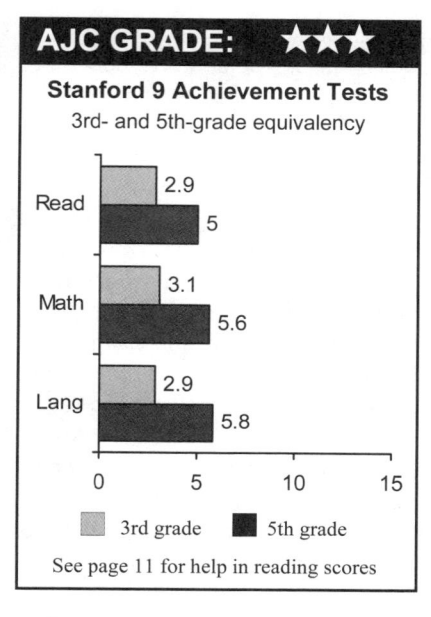

Read: 2.9 / 5
Math: 3.1 / 5.6
Lang: 2.9 / 5.8

3rd grade ▪ 5th grade

See page 11 for help in reading scores

Norton Elementary School

3050 Carson Rd, Snellville, GA 30039
770-985-1933 · Grades K - 5

Enrollment:	969
White / black / other:	75.3% / 16.7% / 7.9%
Not native English-speaking:	13 / 1.3%
Limited English proficiency:	17 / 1.8%
Student absenteeism:	2.9%
Students per teacher:	15.9
Parent friendliness:	① ❷ ❸ ④ ⑤ ❻
Teachers with advanced degrees:	54.8%
Average years' teaching experience:	15.6
Students in gifted program:	63 / 6.5%
Students in remedial education:	2.9%
Students held back a grade:	1.8%
Total suspensions, pct. in-school:	2 / 0.0%
Offenses:	violence: 8, drugs: *, other: *
Eligible students, free or reduced lunch:	16.3%
Before / after school program:	Yes / No
Students at this school generally go on to:	
Snellville Middle	

AJC GRADE: ★★★

Stanford 9 Achievement Tests
3rd- and 5th-grade equivalency

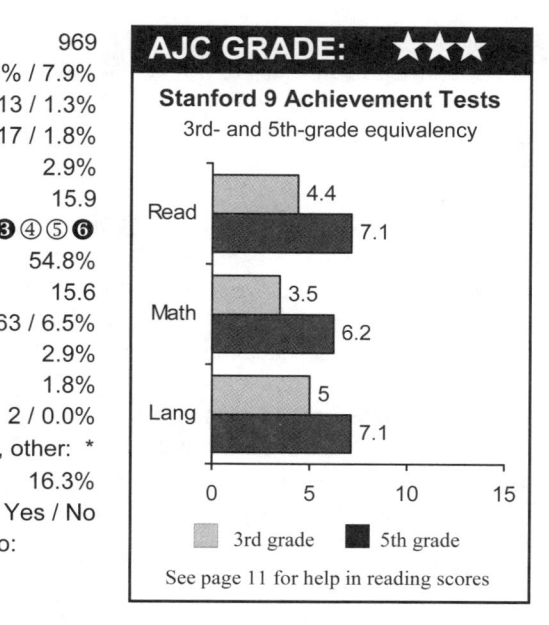

Read: 4.4 / 7.1
Math: 3.5 / 6.2
Lang: 5 / 7.1

3rd grade ▪ 5th grade

See page 11 for help in reading scores

Gwinnett County Elementary Schools

Partee Elementary School

4350 Campbell Rd, Snellville, GA 30039
770-982-6920 · Grades K - 5

Enrollment:	438
White / black / other:	66.4% / 24.2% / 9.4%
Not native English-speaking:	9 / 2.1%
Limited English proficiency:	14 / 3.2%
Student absenteeism:	3.1%
Students per teacher:	10.2
Parent friendliness:	① ❷ ❸ ❹ ❺ ❻
Teachers with advanced degrees:	56.8%
Average years' teaching experience:	11.2
Students in gifted program:	56 / 12.8%
Students in remedial education:	13.4%
Students held back a grade:	2.5%
Total suspensions, pct. in-school:	*
Offenses:	violence: *, drugs: *, other: *
Eligible students, free or reduced lunch:	18.4%
Before / after school program:	Yes / Yes

Students at this school generally go on to:
Shiloh Middle

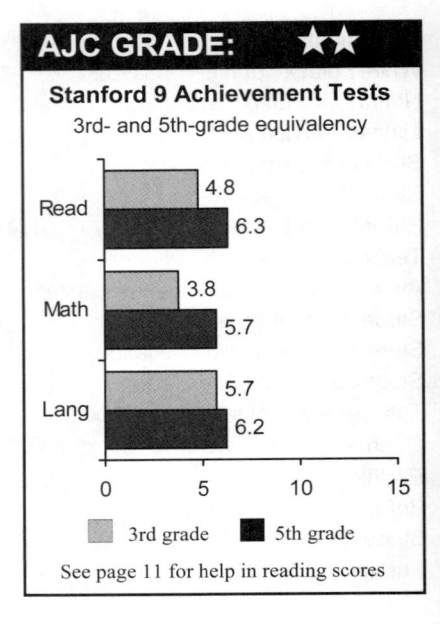

AJC GRADE: ★★

Stanford 9 Achievement Tests
3rd- and 5th-grade equivalency

Read: 3rd grade 4.8 / 5th grade 6.3
Math: 3rd grade 3.8 / 5th grade 5.7
Lang: 3rd grade 5.7 / 5th grade 6.2

See page 11 for help in reading scores

Peachtree Elementary School

5995 Crooked Creek Rd, Norcross, GA 30092
770-448-8710 · Grades K - 5

Enrollment:	1,234
White / black / other:	26.6% / 48.1% / 25.4%
Not native English-speaking:	120 / 9.7%
Limited English proficiency:	177 / 14.3%
Student absenteeism:	3.3%
Students per teacher:	14.6
Parent friendliness:	① ❷ ❸ ❹ ❺ ❻
Teachers with advanced degrees:	54.7%
Average years' teaching experience:	12.2
Students in gifted program:	134 / 10.9%
Students in remedial education:	23.3%
Students held back a grade:	2.9%
Total suspensions, pct. in-school:	26 / 0.0%
Offenses:	violence: 22, drugs: 4, other: 2
Eligible students, free or reduced lunch:	38.0%
Before / after school program:	No / Yes

Students at this school generally go on to:
Pickneyville Middle

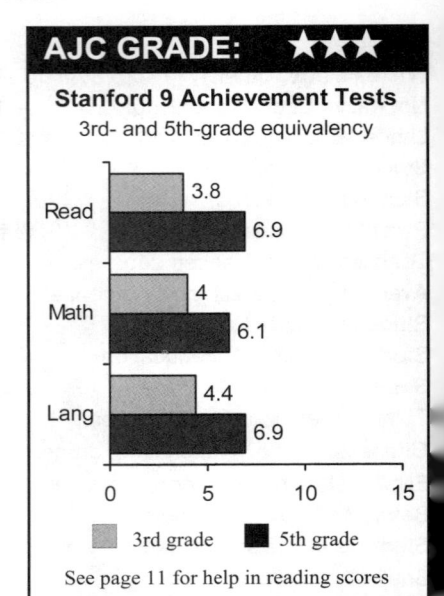

AJC GRADE: ★★★

Stanford 9 Achievement Tests
3rd- and 5th-grade equivalency

Read: 3rd grade 3.8 / 5th grade 6.9
Math: 3rd grade 4 / 5th grade 6.1
Lang: 3rd grade 4.4 / 5th grade 6.9

See page 11 for help in reading scores

Gwinnett County Elementary Schools

Pharr Elementary School

1500 North Rd, Snellville, GA 30078
770-985-0244 · Grades K - 5

Enrollment:	1,147
White / black / other:	81.6% / 9.6% / 8.8%
Not native English-speaking:	29 / 2.5%
Limited English proficiency:	29 / 2.5%
Student absenteeism:	2.8%
Students per teacher:	15.7
Parent friendliness:	① ❷ ❸ ④ ⑤ ❻
Teachers with advanced degrees:	46.6%
Average years' teaching experience:	10.8
Students in gifted program:	122 / 10.6%
Students in remedial education:	4.3%
Students held back a grade:	0.9%
Total suspensions, pct. in-school:	4 / 0.0%
Offenses:	violence: 2, drugs: *, other: 2
Eligible students, free or reduced lunch:	10.2%
Before / after school program:	No / Yes

Students at this school generally go on to:
McConnell Middle

AJC GRADE: ★★★

Stanford 9 Achievement Tests
3rd- and 5th-grade equivalency

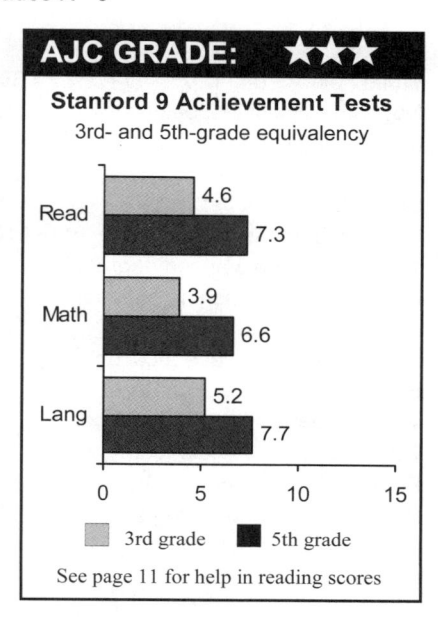

	3rd grade	5th grade
Read	4.6	7.3
Math	3.9	6.6
Lang	5.2	7.7

See page 11 for help in reading scores

Riverside Elementary School

5445 Settles Bridge Rd, Suwanee, GA 30024
678-482-1000 · Grades K - 5

Enrollment:	1,367
White / black / other:	86.5% / 4.0% / 9.5%
Not native English-speaking:	16 / 1.2%
Limited English proficiency:	24 / 1.8%
Student absenteeism:	2.9%
Students per teacher:	16.6
Parent friendliness:	① ❷ ❸ ④ ⑤ ❻
Teachers with advanced degrees:	44.6%
Average years' teaching experience:	11.0
Students in gifted program:	173 / 12.7%
Students in remedial education:	11.4%
Students held back a grade:	2.6%
Total suspensions, pct. in-school:	*
Offenses:	violence: *, drugs: *, other: *
Eligible students, free or reduced lunch:	2.6%
Before / after school program:	No / No

Students at this school generally go on to:
Lanier Middle

AJC GRADE: ★★★

Stanford 9 Achievement Tests
3rd- and 5th-grade equivalency

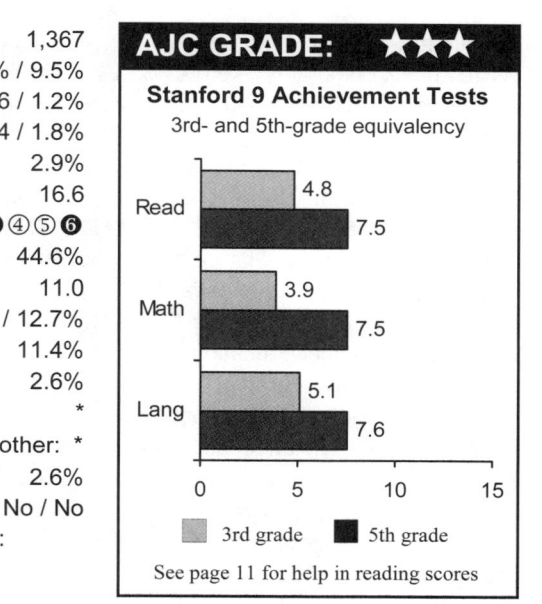

	3rd grade	5th grade
Read	4.8	7.5
Math	3.9	7.5
Lang	5.1	7.6

See page 11 for help in reading scores

Rock Springs Elementary School

888 Rock Springs Rd, Lawrenceville, GA 30043
770-932-7474 · Grades K - 5

Enrollment:	1,083
White / black / other:	77.7% / 6.8% / 15.4%
Not native English-speaking:	21 / 1.9%
Limited English proficiency:	21 / 1.9%
Student absenteeism:	2.8%
Students per teacher:	15.4
Parent friendliness:	① ❷ ❸ ④ ⑤ ❻
Teachers with advanced degrees:	43.2%
Average years' teaching experience:	9.9
Students in gifted program:	90 / 8.3%
Students in remedial education:	4.3%
Students held back a grade:	1.6%
Total suspensions, pct. in-school:	1 / 0.0%
Offenses:	violence: *, drugs: *, other: 1
Eligible students, free or reduced lunch:	8.1%
Before / after school program:	Yes / Yes
Students at this school generally go on to:	
Creekland Middle	

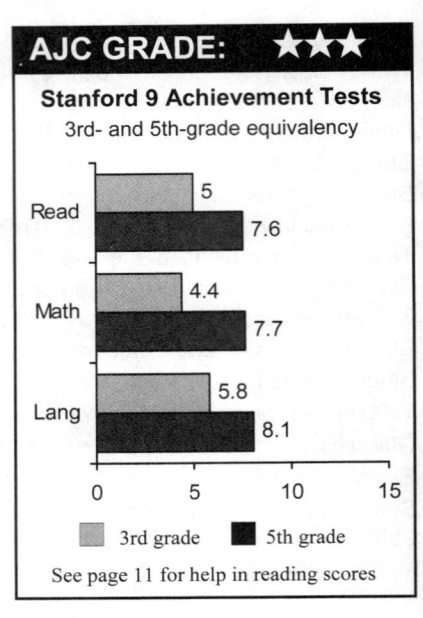

AJC GRADE: ★★★

Stanford 9 Achievement Tests
3rd- and 5th-grade equivalency

- Read: 3rd grade 5, 5th grade 7.6
- Math: 3rd grade 4.4, 5th grade 7.7
- Lang: 3rd grade 5.8, 5th grade 8.1

See page 11 for help in reading scores

Rockbridge Elementary School

6066 Rockbridge School Rd, Norcross, GA 30093
770-448-9363 · Grades K - 5

Enrollment:	911
White / black / other:	9.0% / 32.2% / 58.8%
Not native English-speaking:	326 / 35.8%
Limited English proficiency:	335 / 36.8%
Student absenteeism:	3.4%
Students per teacher:	10.7
Parent friendliness:	① ❷ ❸ ④ ❺ ❻
Teachers with advanced degrees:	38.8%
Average years' teaching experience:	10.7
Students in gifted program:	63 / 6.9%
Students in remedial education:	26.4%
Students held back a grade:	7.4%
Total suspensions, pct. in-school:	25 / 24.0%
Offenses:	violence: 23, drugs: *, other: 5
Eligible students, free or reduced lunch:	69.9%
Before / after school program:	No / No
Students at this school generally go on to:	
Lilburn Middle	

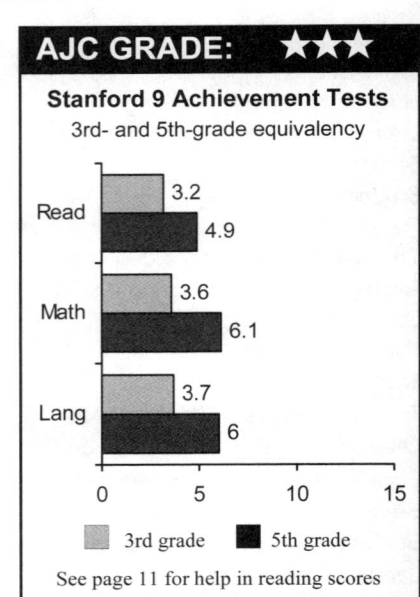

AJC GRADE: ★★★

Stanford 9 Achievement Tests
3rd- and 5th-grade equivalency

- Read: 3rd grade 3.2, 5th grade 4.9
- Math: 3rd grade 3.6, 5th grade 6.1
- Lang: 3rd grade 3.7, 5th grade 6

See page 11 for help in reading scores

Gwinnett County Elementary Schools

Shiloh Elementary School

2400 Ross Rd, Snellville, GA 30039
770-985-6883 · Grades K - 5

Enrollment:	887
White / black / other:	54.8% / 33.6% / 11.6%
Not native English-speaking:	20 / 2.3%
Limited English proficiency:	21 / 2.4%
Student absenteeism:	2.9%
Students per teacher:	15.3
Parent friendliness:	① ❷ ❸ ④ ❺ ❻
Teachers with advanced degrees:	59.3%
Average years' teaching experience:	13.2
Students in gifted program:	54 / 6.1%
Students in remedial education:	8.3%
Students held back a grade:	1.6%
Total suspensions, pct. in-school:	9 / 0.0%
Offenses:	violence: 7, drugs: *, other: 2
Eligible students, free or reduced lunch:	17.5%
Before / after school program:	No / No

Students at this school generally go on to:
Shiloh Middle

AJC GRADE: ★★★

Stanford 9 Achievement Tests
3rd- and 5th-grade equivalency

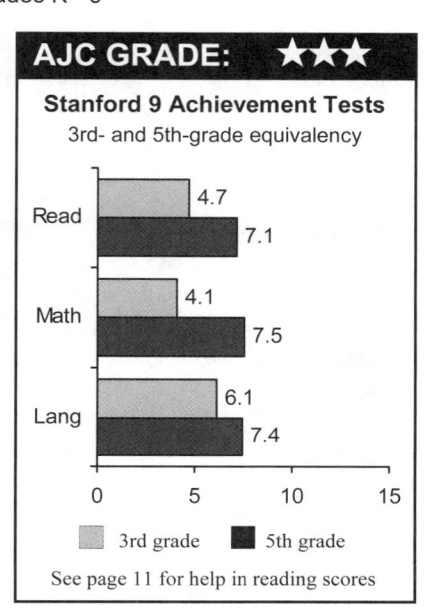

Read: 3rd grade 4.7 / 5th grade 7.1
Math: 3rd grade 4.1 / 5th grade 7.5
Lang: 3rd grade 6.1 / 5th grade 7.4

See page 11 for help in reading scores

Simonton Elementary School

275 Simonton Rd, Lawrenceville, GA 30045
770-513-6637 · Grades K - 5

Enrollment:	1,375
White / black / other:	58.3% / 18.2% / 23.5%
Not native English-speaking:	117 / 8.5%
Limited English proficiency:	132 / 9.6%
Student absenteeism:	3.4%
Students per teacher:	14.9
Parent friendliness:	① ❷ ❸ ④ ❺ ❻
Teachers with advanced degrees:	49.5%
Average years' teaching experience:	10.7
Students in gifted program:	81 / 5.9%
Students in remedial education:	17.4%
Students held back a grade:	3.1%
Total suspensions, pct. in-school:	1 / 0.0%
Offenses:	violence: 1, drugs: *, other: *
Eligible students, free or reduced lunch:	35.2%
Before / after school program:	Yes / Yes

Students at this school generally go on to:
J.E. Richards Middle

AJC GRADE: ★★★

Stanford 9 Achievement Tests
3rd- and 5th-grade equivalency

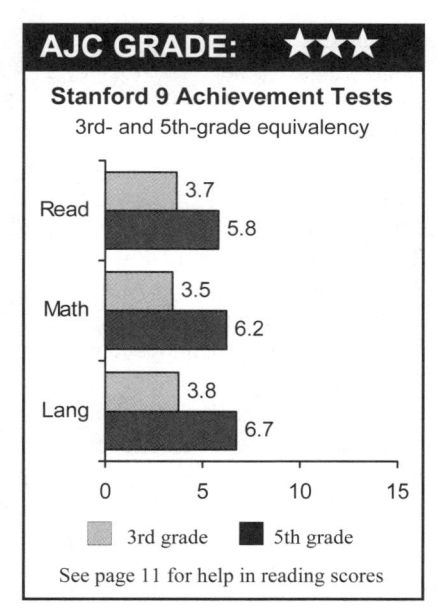

Read: 3rd grade 3.7 / 5th grade 5.8
Math: 3rd grade 3.5 / 5th grade 6.2
Lang: 3rd grade 3.8 / 5th grade 6.7

See page 11 for help in reading scores

Gwinnett County Elementary Schools

Simpson Elementary School

4525 E Jones Bridge Rd, Norcross, GA 30092
770-417-2400 · Grades K - 5

Enrollment:	1,118
White / black / other:	84.3% / 3.8% / 11.9%
Not native English-speaking:	11 / 1.0%
Limited English proficiency:	11 / 1.0%
Student absenteeism:	2.8%
Students per teacher:	14.8
Parent friendliness:	①❷❸④⑤❻
Teachers with advanced degrees:	47.4%
Average years' teaching experience:	10.9
Students in gifted program:	253 / 22.6%
Students in remedial education:	13.9%
Students held back a grade:	0.5%
Total suspensions, pct. in-school:	5 / 0.0%
Offenses:	violence: 3, drugs: * , other: 2
Eligible students, free or reduced lunch:	2.8%
Before / after school program:	No / No

Students at this school generally go on to:
Pickneyville Middle

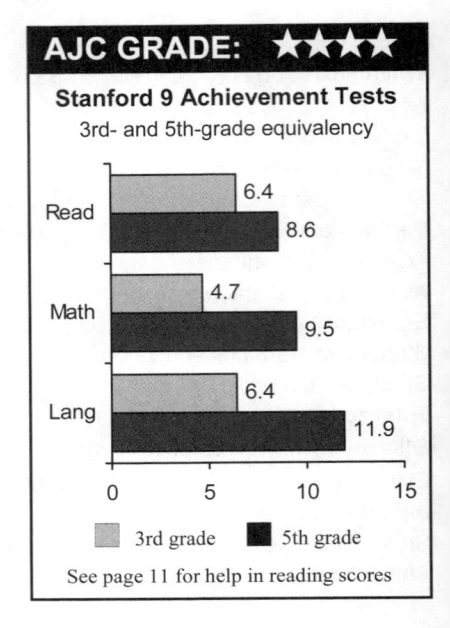

AJC GRADE: ★★★★

Stanford 9 Achievement Tests
3rd- and 5th-grade equivalency

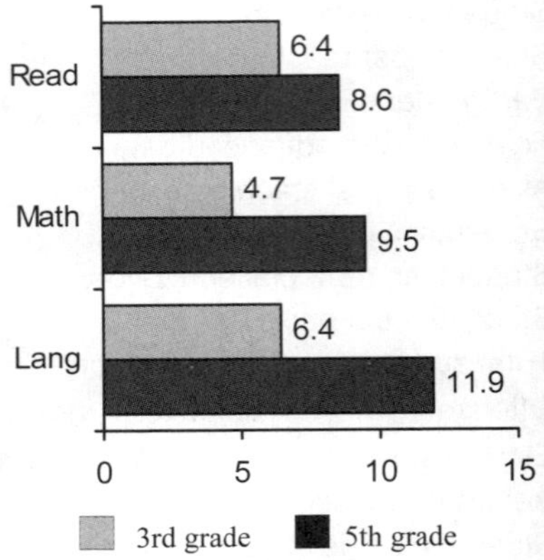
Read
6.4
8.6
Math
4.7
9.5
Lang
6.4
11.9
0
5
10
15
3rd grade
5th grade

See page 11 for help in reading scores

Stripling Elementary School

6155 Atlantic Blvd, Norcross, GA 30071
770-582-7577 · Grades K - 5

Enrollment:	898
White / black / other:	16.1% / 31.4% / 52.4%
Not native English-speaking:	255 / 28.4%
Limited English proficiency:	274 / 30.5%
Student absenteeism:	3.5%
Students per teacher:	13.0
Parent friendliness:	①②③④⑤⑥
Teachers with advanced degrees:	40.8%
Average years' teaching experience:	7.6
Students in gifted program:	20 / 2.2%
Students in remedial education:	31.0%
Students held back a grade:	4.7%
Total suspensions, pct. in-school:	29 / 0.0%
Offenses:	violence: 25, drugs: * , other: 11
Eligible students, free or reduced lunch:	67.3%
Before / after school program:	Yes / Yes

Students at this school generally go on to:
Pickneyville, Summerour Middle

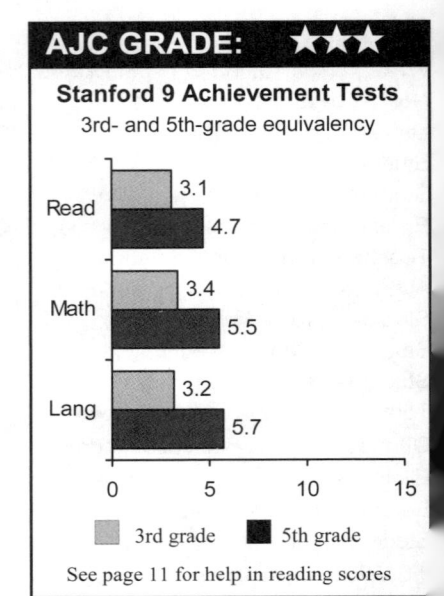

AJC GRADE: ★★★

Stanford 9 Achievement Tests
3rd- and 5th-grade equivalency

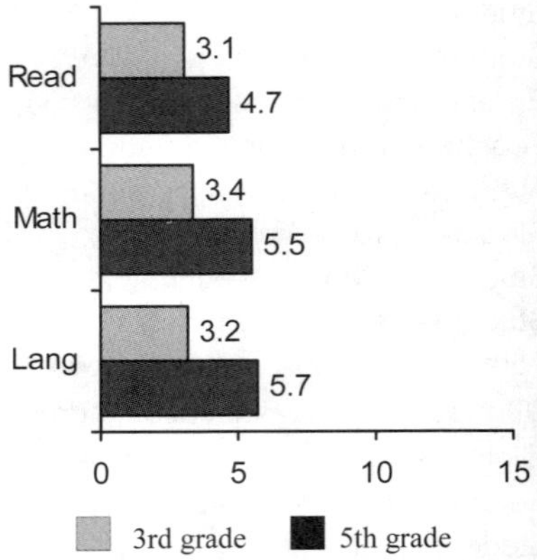
Read
3.1
4.7
Math
3.4
5.5
Lang
3.2
5.7
0
5
10
15
3rd grade
5th grade

See page 11 for help in reading scores

Sugar Hill Elementary School

939 Level Creek Rd, Buford, GA 30518
770-945-5735 · Grades K - 5

Enrollment:	1,129
White / black / other:	78.3% / 5.1% / 16.6%
Not native English-speaking:	52 / 4.6%
Limited English proficiency:	66 / 5.8%
Student absenteeism:	2.9%
Students per teacher:	14.5
Parent friendliness:	①❷❸④❺❻
Teachers with advanced degrees:	40.5%
Average years' teaching experience:	10.0
Students in gifted program:	142 / 12.6%
Students in remedial education:	16.1%
Students held back a grade:	3.5%
Total suspensions, pct. in-school:	1 / 0.0%
Offenses:	violence: 1, drugs: *, other: *
Eligible students, free or reduced lunch:	25.9%
Before / after school program:	No / Yes

Students at this school generally go on to:
Lanier Middle

AJC GRADE: ★★★

Stanford 9 Achievement Tests
3rd- and 5th-grade equivalency

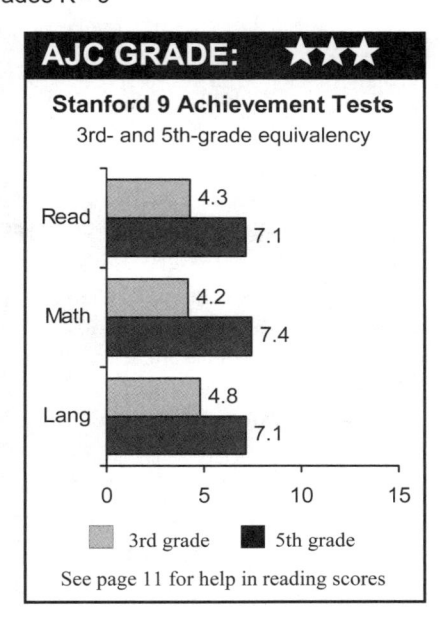

- Read: 3rd grade 4.3, 5th grade 7.1
- Math: 3rd grade 4.2, 5th grade 7.4
- Lang: 3rd grade 4.8, 5th grade 7.1

See page 11 for help in reading scores

Suwanee Elementary School

3875 Smithtown Rd, Suwanee, GA 30024
770-945-5763 · Grades K - 5

Enrollment:	1,202
White / black / other:	74.7% / 9.5% / 15.8%
Not native English-speaking:	39 / 3.2%
Limited English proficiency:	50 / 4.2%
Student absenteeism:	2.9%
Students per teacher:	15.9
Parent friendliness:	①❷❸❹❺❻
Teachers with advanced degrees:	51.3%
Average years' teaching experience:	11.6
Students in gifted program:	134 / 11.1%
Students in remedial education:	4.6%
Students held back a grade:	0.8%
Total suspensions, pct. in-school:	4 / 25.0%
Offenses:	violence: 4, drugs: *, other: 1
Eligible students, free or reduced lunch:	4.2%
Before / after school program:	Yes / Yes

Students at this school generally go on to:
Lanier Middle

AJC GRADE: ★★★

Stanford 9 Achievement Tests
3rd- and 5th-grade equivalency

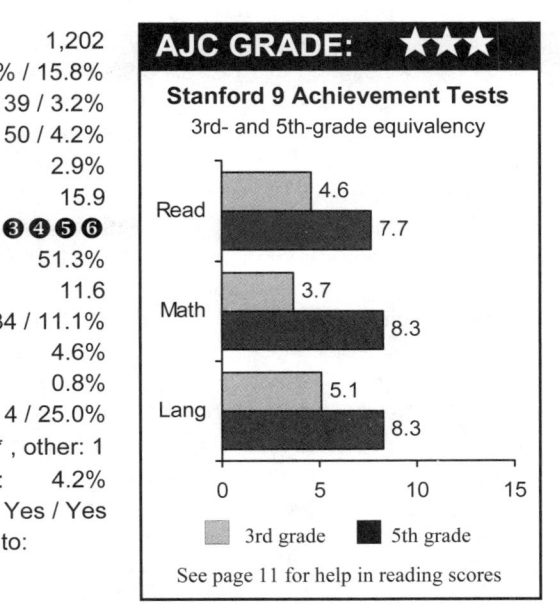

- Read: 3rd grade 4.6, 5th grade 7.7
- Math: 3rd grade 3.7, 5th grade 8.3
- Lang: 3rd grade 5.1, 5th grade 8.3

See page 11 for help in reading scores

Gwinnett County Elementary Schools

Taylor Elementary School

600 Taylor School Dr, Lawrenceville, GA 30043
770-338-4680 · Grades K - 5

Enrollment:	1,307
White / black / other:	76.4% / 9.3% / 14.3%
Not native English-speaking:	19 / 1.5%
Limited English proficiency:	23 / 1.8%
Student absenteeism:	2.8%
Students per teacher:	15.0
Parent friendliness:	①❷❸④❺❻
Teachers with advanced degrees:	49.4%
Average years' teaching experience:	8.3
Students in gifted program:	86 / 6.6%
Students in remedial education:	5.2%
Students held back a grade:	0.5%
Total suspensions, pct. in-school:	6 / 100.0%
Offenses:	violence: 1, drugs: *, other: 5
Eligible students, free or reduced lunch:	7.1%
Before / after school program:	No / No
Students at this school generally go on to:	
Creekland Middle	

AJC GRADE: ★★★

Stanford 9 Achievement Tests
3rd- and 5th-grade equivalency

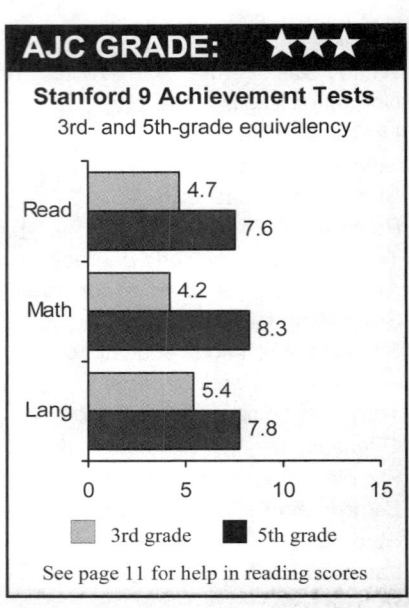

	3rd grade	5th grade
Read	4.7	7.6
Math	4.2	8.3
Lang	5.4	7.8

See page 11 for help in reading scores

Walnut Grove Elementary School

75 Taylor Rd, Suwanee, GA 30024
770-513-6892 · Grades K - 5

Enrollment:	1,063
White / black / other:	72.9% / 8.9% / 18.2%
Not native English-speaking:	44 / 4.1%
Limited English proficiency:	45 / 4.2%
Student absenteeism:	2.7%
Students per teacher:	15.0
Parent friendliness:	①❷❸④❺❻
Teachers with advanced degrees:	59.7%
Average years' teaching experience:	12.5
Students in gifted program:	104 / 9.8%
Students in remedial education:	10.4%
Students held back a grade:	3.9%
Total suspensions, pct. in-school:	4 / 100.0%
Offenses:	violence: 4, drugs: *, other: *
Eligible students, free or reduced lunch:	6.8%
Before / after school program:	No / No
Students at this school generally go on to:	
Creekland Middle	

AJC GRADE: ★★★

Stanford 9 Achievement Tests
3rd- and 5th-grade equivalency

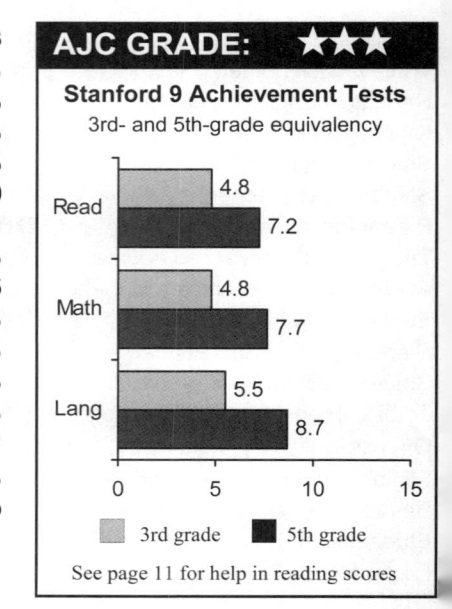

	3rd grade	5th grade
Read	4.8	7.2
Math	4.8	7.7
Lang	5.5	8.7

See page 11 for help in reading scores

Creekland Middle School

170 Russell Rd, Lawrenceville, GA 30043
770-338-4700 · Grades 6 - 8

Enrollment:	3,139
White / black / other:	72.9% / 11.3% / 15.8%
Not native English-speaking:	99 / 3.2%
Student absenteeism:	2.8%
Students per teacher:	16.4
Parent friendliness:	① ❷ ❸ ❹ ❺ ❻
Teachers with advanced degrees:	53.6%
Average years' teaching experience:	13.0
Students in gifted program:	570 / 18.2%
Students held back a grade:	1.9%
Total suspensions and expulsions:	81
Suspensions only, pct. in-school:	81 / 65.4%
Offenses:	violence: 65, drugs: 2, other: 53
Eligible students, free or reduced lunch:	9.6%
Number of dropouts:	1 / 0.0%
Pct. 8th-graders w/ basic computer skills:	94.0%

Students at this school generally go on to:
Collins Hill High

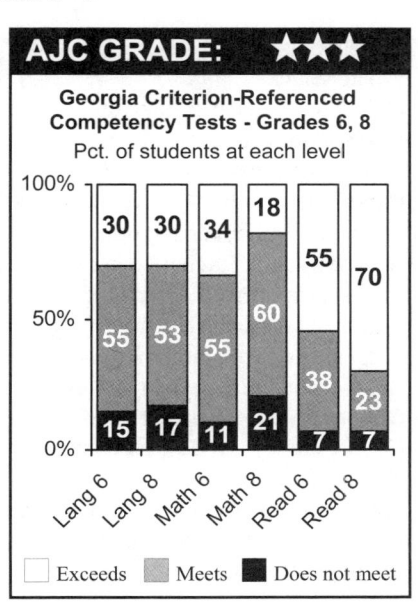

AJC GRADE: ★★★

Georgia Criterion-Referenced Competency Tests - Grades 6, 8
Pct. of students at each level

	Lang 6	Lang 8	Math 6	Math 8	Read 6	Read 8
Exceeds	30	30	34	18	55	70
Meets	55	53	55	60	38	23
Does not meet	15	17	11	21	7	7

Crews Middle School

1000 Old Snellville Hwy, Lawrenceville, GA 30044
770-982-6940 · Grades 6 - 8

Enrollment:	1,159
White / black / other:	85.3% / 4.9% / 9.7%
Not native English-speaking:	10 / 0.9%
Student absenteeism:	2.4%
Students per teacher:	15.2
Parent friendliness:	❶ ❷ ❸ ❹ ❺ ❻
Teachers with advanced degrees:	59.7%
Average years' teaching experience:	13.5
Students in gifted program:	278 / 24.0%
Students held back a grade:	0.3%
Total suspensions and expulsions:	14
Suspensions only, pct. in-school:	14 / 71.4%
Offenses:	violence: 14, drugs: *, other: 7
Eligible students, free or reduced lunch:	4.9%
Number of dropouts:	*
Pct. 8th-graders w/ basic computer skills:	100.0%

Students at this school generally go on to:
Brookwood High

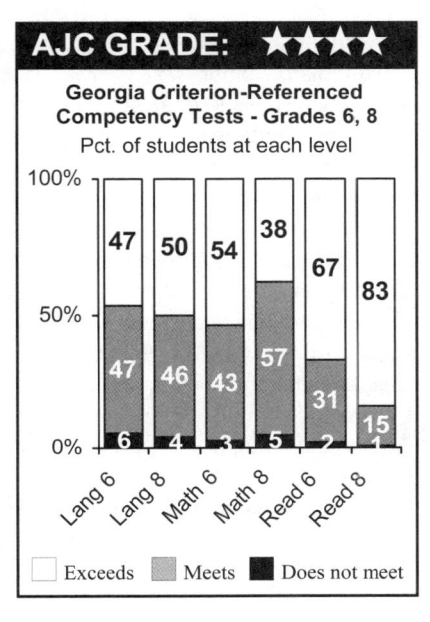

AJC GRADE: ★★★★

Georgia Criterion-Referenced Competency Tests - Grades 6, 8
Pct. of students at each level

	Lang 6	Lang 8	Math 6	Math 8	Read 6	Read 8
Exceeds	47	50	54	38	67	83
Meets	47	46	43	57	31	15
Does not meet	6	4	3	5	2	1

Gwinnett County Middle Schools

Dacula Middle School

137 Dacula Rd, Dacula, GA 30019
770-963-1110 · Grades 6 - 8

Enrollment:	1,930
White / black / other:	88.2% / 5.5% / 6.2%
Not native English-speaking:	29 / 1.5%
Student absenteeism:	3.2%
Students per teacher:	15.9
Parent friendliness:	❶❷❸④⑤❻
Teachers with advanced degrees:	51.2%
Average years' teaching experience:	11.1
Students in gifted program:	351 / 18.2%
Students held back a grade:	0.6%
Total suspensions and expulsions:	82
Suspensions only, pct. in-school:	82 / 78.0%
Offenses:	violence: 44, drugs: * , other: 41
Eligible students, free or reduced lunch:	8.9%
Number of dropouts:	*
Pct. 8th-graders w/ basic computer skills:	100.0%

Students at this school generally go on to:
Dacula High

AJC GRADE: ★★★

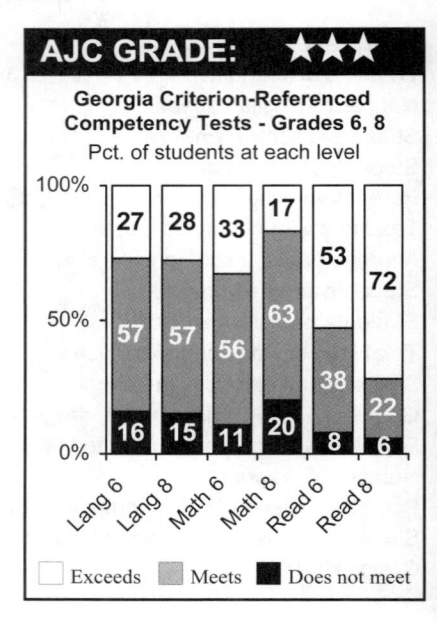

Georgia Criterion-Referenced Competency Tests - Grades 6, 8
Pct. of students at each level

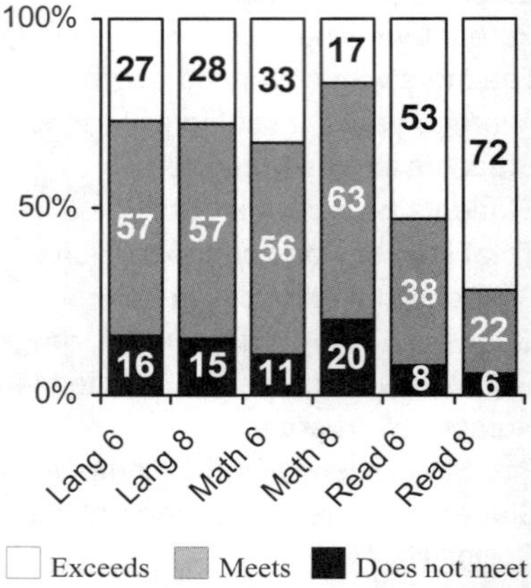
100%
50%
0%
27
28
33
17
53
72
57
57
56
63
38
22
16
15
11
20
8
6
Lang 6
Lang 8
Math 6
Math 8
Read 6
Read 8
Exceeds
Meets
Does not meet

Duluth Middle School

3057 Main St, Duluth, GA 30096
770-476-3372 · Grades 6 - 8

Enrollment:	1,129
White / black / other:	57.7% / 12.8% / 29.5%
Not native English-speaking:	77 / 6.8%
Student absenteeism:	2.9%
Students per teacher:	15.0
Parent friendliness:	❶❷❸④❺❻
Teachers with advanced degrees:	40.8%
Average years' teaching experience:	10.1
Students in gifted program:	228 / 20.2%
Students held back a grade:	1.9%
Total suspensions and expulsions:	67
Suspensions only, pct. in-school:	67 / 70.1%
Offenses:	violence: 37, drugs: 11, other: 19
Eligible students, free or reduced lunch:	12.1%
Number of dropouts:	*
Pct. 8th-graders w/ basic computer skills:	100.0%

Students at this school generally go on to:
Duluth High

AJC GRADE: ★★★

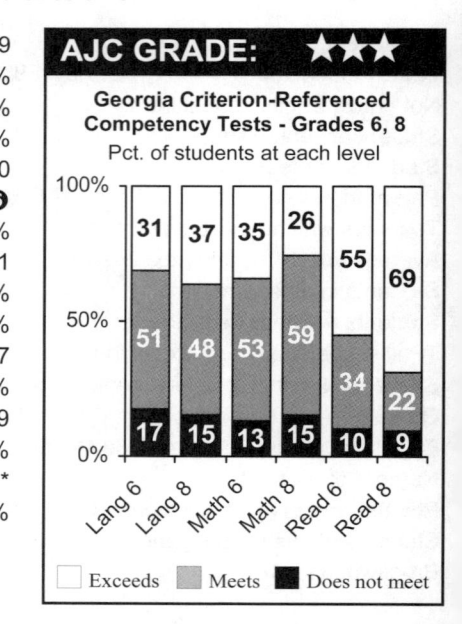

Georgia Criterion-Referenced Competency Tests - Grades 6, 8
Pct. of students at each level

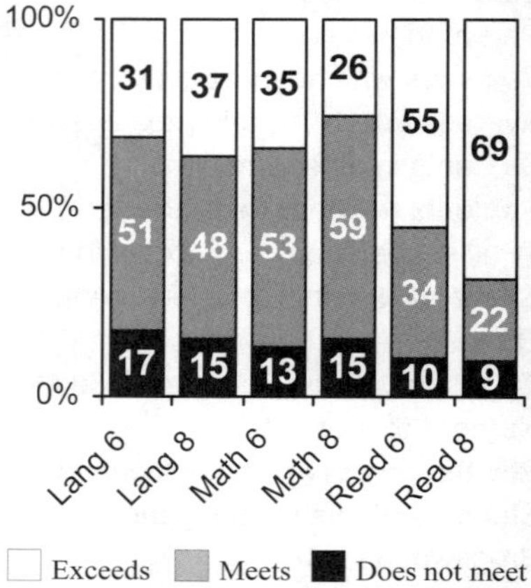
100%
50%
0%
31
37
35
26
55
69
51
48
53
59
34
22
17
15
13
15
10
9
Lang 6
Lang 8
Math 6
Math 8
Read 6
Read 8
Exceeds
Meets
Does not meet

Five Forks Middle School

3250 River Dr, Lawrenceville, GA 30044
770-972-1506 · Grades 6 - 8

Enrollment:	1,050
White / black / other:	79.6% / 9.0% / 11.3%
Not native English-speaking:	15 / 1.4%
Student absenteeism:	2.8%
Students per teacher:	14.4
Parent friendliness:	①❷❸④⑤❻
Teachers with advanced degrees:	45.3%
Average years' teaching experience:	11.9
Students in gifted program:	218 / 20.8%
Students held back a grade:	0.6%
Total suspensions and expulsions:	60
Suspensions only, pct. in-school:	58 / 44.8%
Offenses:	violence: 29, drugs: 2, other: 32
Eligible students, free or reduced lunch:	8.8%
Number of dropouts:	1 / 0.1%
Pct. 8th-graders w/ basic computer skills:	100.0%

Students at this school generally go on to:
Brookwood High

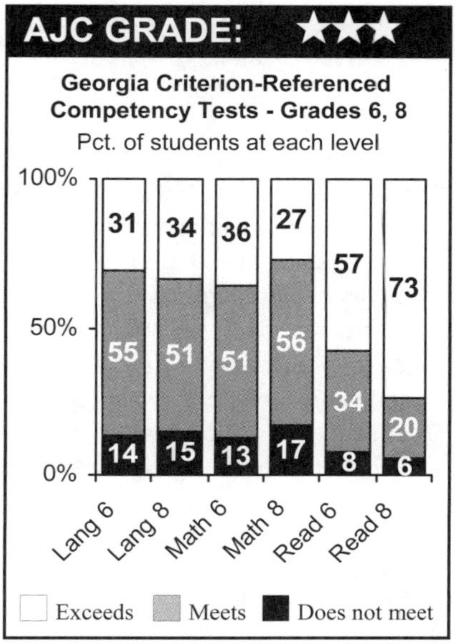
AJC GRADE: ★★★
Georgia Criterion-Referenced
Competency Tests - Grades 6, 8
Pct. of students at each level
100%
50%
0%
31
34
36
27
57
73
55
51
51
56
34
20
14
15
13
17
8
6
Lang 6
Lang 8
Math 6
Math 8
Read 6
Read 8
Exceeds
Meets
Does not meet

Hull Middle School

1950 Old Peachtree Rd, Duluth, GA 30097
770-232-3200 · Grades 6 - 8

Enrollment:	1,030
White / black / other:	60.8% / 13.4% / 25.8%
Not native English-speaking:	75 / 7.3%
Student absenteeism:	3.1%
Students per teacher:	14.5
Parent friendliness:	❶❷❸④⑤❻
Teachers with advanced degrees:	61.6%
Average years' teaching experience:	11.1
Students in gifted program:	220 / 21.4%
Students held back a grade:	1.5%
Total suspensions and expulsions:	51
Suspensions only, pct. in-school:	51 / 51.0%
Offenses:	violence: 34, drugs: * , other: 22
Eligible students, free or reduced lunch:	19.7%
Number of dropouts:	*
Pct. 8th-graders w/ basic computer skills:	26.0%

Students at this school generally go on to:
Collins Hill, Duluth High

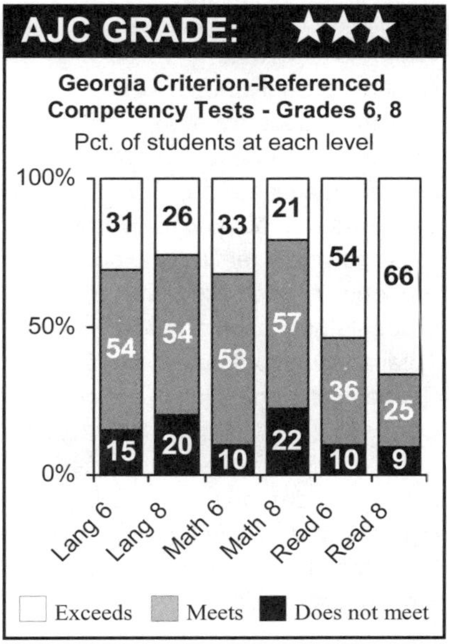
AJC GRADE: ★★★
Georgia Criterion-Referenced
Competency Tests - Grades 6, 8
Pct. of students at each level
100%
50%
0%
31
26
33
21
54
66
54
54
58
57
36
25
15
20
10
22
10
9
Lang 6
Lang 8
Math 6
Math 8
Read 6
Read 8
Exceeds
Meets
Does not meet

Lanier Middle School

918 Buford Hwy, Buford, GA 30518
770-945-8419 · Grades 6 - 8

Enrollment:	1,974
White / black / other:	80.2% / 7.4% / 12.4%
Not native English-speaking:	40 / 2.0%
Student absenteeism:	3.1%
Students per teacher:	16.1
Parent friendliness:	❶❷❸④⑤❻
Teachers with advanced degrees:	57.5%
Average years' teaching experience:	13.8
Students in gifted program:	332 / 16.8%
Students held back a grade:	0.9%
Total suspensions and expulsions:	78
Suspensions only, pct. in-school:	78 / 76.9%
Offenses:	violence: 39, drugs: 3, other: 36
Eligible students, free or reduced lunch:	9.6%
Number of dropouts:	*
Pct. 8th-graders w/ basic computer skills:	85.0%
Students at this school generally go on to:	North Gwinnett High

AJC GRADE: ★★★

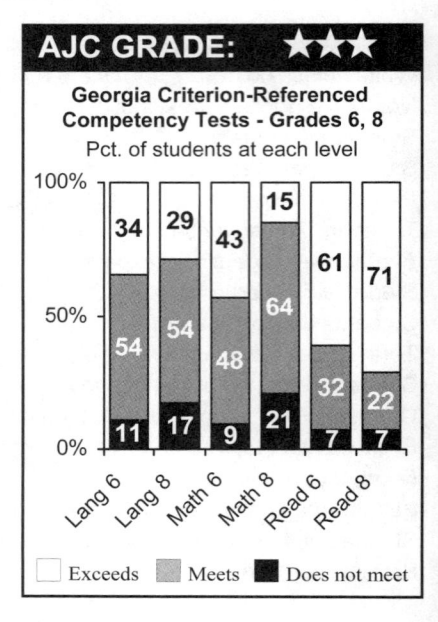

Georgia Criterion-Referenced Competency Tests - Grades 6, 8
Pct. of students at each level

	Lang 6	Lang 8	Math 6	Math 8	Read 6	Read 8
Exceeds	34	29	43	15	61	71
Meets	54	54	48	64	32	22
Does not meet	11	17	9	21	7	7

Lilburn Middle School

4994 Lawrenceville Hwy NW, Lilburn, GA 30047
770-921-1776 · Grades 6 - 8

Enrollment:	2,077
White / black / other:	17.0% / 36.8% / 46.2%
Not native English-speaking:	336 / 16.2%
Student absenteeism:	3.9%
Students per teacher:	13.9
Parent friendliness:	❶❷❸④❺❻
Teachers with advanced degrees:	42.4%
Average years' teaching experience:	8.7
Students in gifted program:	130 / 6.3%
Students held back a grade:	3.9%
Total suspensions and expulsions:	277
Suspensions only, pct. in-school:	277 / 27.8%
Offenses:	violence: 196, drugs: 10, other: 79
Eligible students, free or reduced lunch:	65.1%
Number of dropouts:	4 / 0.2%
Pct. 8th-graders w/ basic computer skills:	90.0%
Students at this school generally go on to:	Meadowcreek High

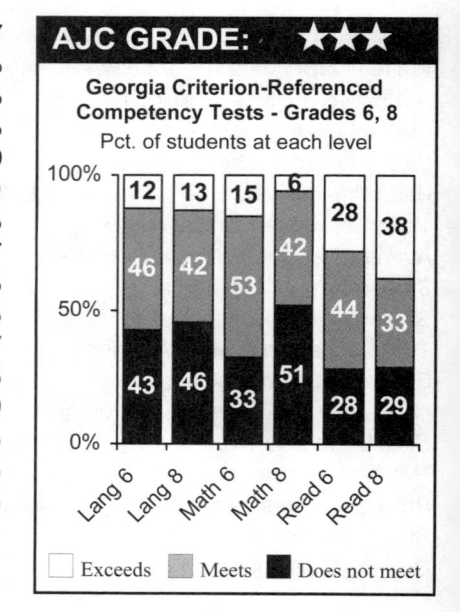

AJC GRADE: ★★★

Georgia Criterion-Referenced Competency Tests - Grades 6, 8
Pct. of students at each level

	Lang 6	Lang 8	Math 6	Math 8	Read 6	Read 8
Exceeds	12	13	15	6	28	38
Meets	46	42	53	42	44	33
Does not meet	43	46	33	51	28	29

Gwinnett County Middle Schools

McConnell Middle School

550 Ozora Rd, Loganville, GA 30052
770-554-1000 · Grades 6 - 8

Enrollment:	1,278
White / black / other:	88.9% / 5.1% / 6.0%
Not native English-speaking:	12 / 0.9%
Student absenteeism:	3.1%
Students per teacher:	16.5
Parent friendliness:	❶❷❸④❺❻
Teachers with advanced degrees:	61.5%
Average years' teaching experience:	12.1
Students in gifted program:	121 / 9.5%
Students held back a grade:	0.9%
Total suspensions and expulsions:	84
Suspensions only, pct. in-school:	84 / 64.3%
Offenses: violence: 44, drugs: *, other: 40	
Eligible students, free or reduced lunch:	8.0%
Number of dropouts:	*
Pct. 8th-graders w/ basic computer skills:	100.0%
Students at this school generally go on to: Grayson High	

AJC GRADE: ★★★

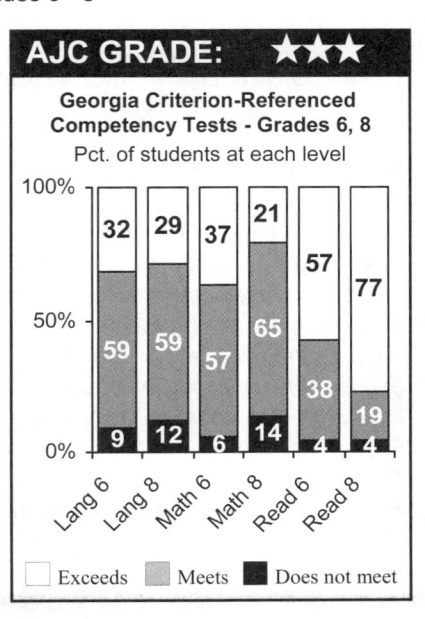

Georgia Criterion-Referenced Competency Tests - Grades 6, 8
Pct. of students at each level

	Lang 6	Lang 8	Math 6	Math 8	Read 6	Read 8
Exceeds	32	29	37	21	57	77
Meets	59	59	57	65	38	19
Does not meet	9	12	6	14	4	4

Pinckneyville Middle School

5440 W Jones Bridge Rd, Norcross, GA 30092
770-263-0860 · Grades 6 - 8

Enrollment:	1,126
White / black / other:	51.0% / 27.7% / 21.3%
Not native English-speaking:	66 / 5.9%
Student absenteeism:	3.0%
Students per teacher:	14.3
Parent friendliness:	❶❷❸④⑤❻
Teachers with advanced degrees:	54.9%
Average years' teaching experience:	12.2
Students in gifted program:	260 / 23.1%
Students held back a grade:	2.4%
Total suspensions and expulsions:	110
Suspensions only, pct. in-school:	110 / 77.3%
Offenses: violence: 58, drugs: 2, other: 64	
Eligible students, free or reduced lunch:	26.2%
Number of dropouts:	*
Pct. 8th-graders w/ basic computer skills:	100.0%
Students at this school generally go on to: Norcross High	

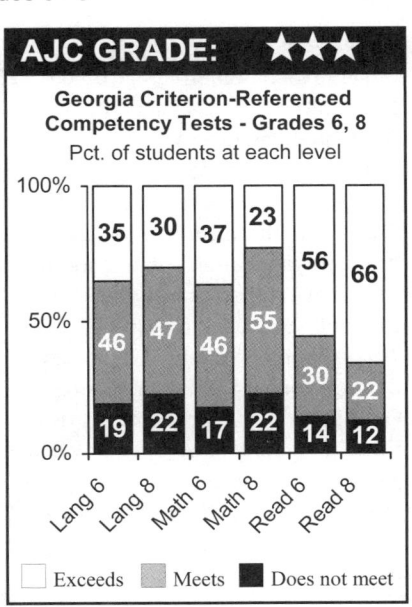

AJC GRADE: ★★★

Georgia Criterion-Referenced Competency Tests - Grades 6, 8
Pct. of students at each level

	Lang 6	Lang 8	Math 6	Math 8	Read 6	Read 8
Exceeds	35	30	37	23	56	66
Meets	46	47	46	55	30	22
Does not meet	19	22	17	22	14	12

The Atlanta Journal-Constitution / Page 399

Gwinnett County Middle Schools

Richards Middle School

3555 Sugarloaf Pkwy, Lawrenceville, GA 30044
770-995-7133 · Grades 6 - 8

Enrollment:	1,726
White / black / other:	62.2% / 20.1% / 17.7%
Not native English-speaking:	139 / 8.1%
Student absenteeism:	3.9%
Students per teacher:	15.3
Parent friendliness:	❶❷❸④❺❻
Teachers with advanced degrees:	60.0%
Average years' teaching experience:	12.2
Students in gifted program:	141 / 8.2%
Students held back a grade:	1.7%
Total suspensions and expulsions:	201
Suspensions only, pct. in-school:	201 / 49.3%
Offenses:	violence: 167, drugs: 4, other: 74
Eligible students, free or reduced lunch:	34.3%
Number of dropouts:	5 / 0.3%
Pct. 8th-graders w/ basic computer skills:	38.0%

Students at this school generally go on to:
Central Gwinnett High

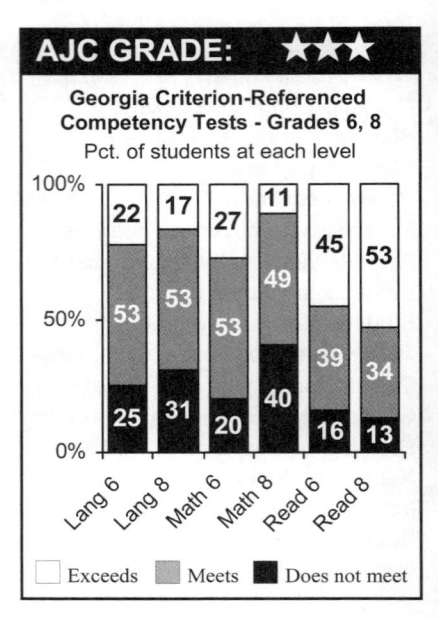

AJC GRADE: ★★★

Georgia Criterion-Referenced Competency Tests - Grades 6, 8
Pct. of students at each level

	Lang 6	Lang 8	Math 6	Math 8	Read 6	Read 8
Exceeds	22	17	27	11	45	53
Meets	53	53	53	49	39	34
Does not meet	25	31	20	40	16	13

Shiloh Middle School

4285 Shiloh Rd, Snellville, GA 30039
770-972-3224 · Grades 6 - 8

Enrollment:	1,500
White / black / other:	66.0% / 25.3% / 8.7%
Not native English-speaking:	22 / 1.5%
Student absenteeism:	3.2%
Students per teacher:	15.7
Parent friendliness:	❶❷❸④❺❻
Teachers with advanced degrees:	63.5%
Average years' teaching experience:	14.9
Students in gifted program:	248 / 16.5%
Students held back a grade:	1.4%
Total suspensions and expulsions:	69
Suspensions only, pct. in-school:	63 / 85.7%
Offenses:	violence: 42, drugs: 4, other: 28
Eligible students, free or reduced lunch:	18.3%
Number of dropouts:	*
Pct. 8th-graders w/ basic computer skills:	100.0%

Students at this school generally go on to:
Shiloh High

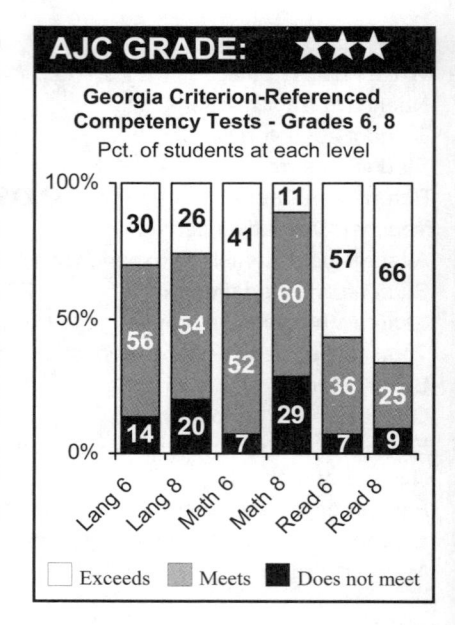

AJC GRADE: ★★★

Georgia Criterion-Referenced Competency Tests - Grades 6, 8
Pct. of students at each level

	Lang 6	Lang 8	Math 6	Math 8	Read 6	Read 8
Exceeds	30	26	41	11	57	66
Meets	56	54	52	60	36	25
Does not meet	14	20	7	29	7	9

Gwinnett County Middle Schools

Snellville Middle School

3155 Pate Rd, Snellville, GA 30078
770-972-1530 · Grades 6 - 8

Enrollment:	1,454
White / black / other:	78.1% / 14.5% / 7.4%
Not native English-speaking:	24 / 1.7%
Student absenteeism:	3.0%
Students per teacher:	16.5
Parent friendliness:	❶❷❸④❺❻
Teachers with advanced degrees:	47.8%
Average years' teaching experience:	12.7
Students in gifted program:	244 / 16.8%
Students held back a grade:	2.2%
Total suspensions and expulsions:	123
Suspensions only, pct. in-school:	123 / 49.6%
Offenses: violence: 66, drugs: 1, other: 60	
Eligible students, free or reduced lunch:	15.1%
Number of dropouts:	*
Pct. 8th-graders w/ basic computer skills:	100.0%
Students at this school generally go on to: South Gwinnett High	

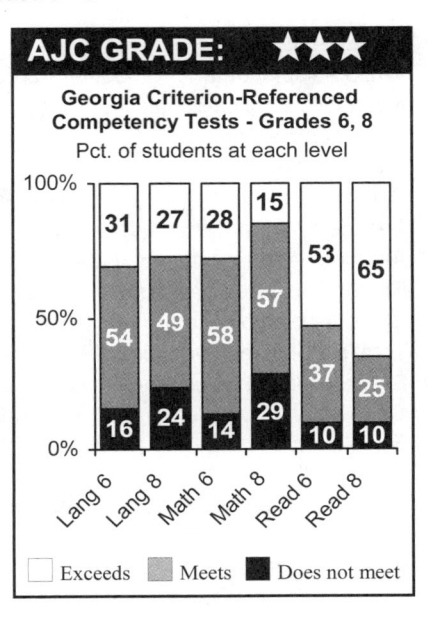

AJC GRADE: ★★★

Georgia Criterion-Referenced Competency Tests - Grades 6, 8
Pct. of students at each level

	Lang 6	Lang 8	Math 6	Math 8	Read 6	Read 8
Exceeds	31	27	28	15	53	65
Meets	54	49	58	57	37	25
Does not meet	16	24	14	29	10	10

Summerour Middle School

585 Mitchell Rd, Norcross, GA 30071
770-448-3045 · Grades 6 - 8

Enrollment:	1,093
White / black / other:	22.6% / 29.7% / 47.7%
Not native English-speaking:	170 / 15.6%
Student absenteeism:	3.6%
Students per teacher:	15.4
Parent friendliness:	❶❷❸④❺❻
Teachers with advanced degrees:	40.3%
Average years' teaching experience:	10.5
Students in gifted program:	81 / 7.4%
Students held back a grade:	4.5%
Total suspensions and expulsions:	114
Suspensions only, pct. in-school:	114 / 60.5%
Offenses: violence: 101, drugs: 2, other: 19	
Eligible students, free or reduced lunch:	69.3%
Number of dropouts:	3 / 0.2%
Pct. 8th-graders w/ basic computer skills:	52.0%
Students at this school generally go on to: Norcross High	

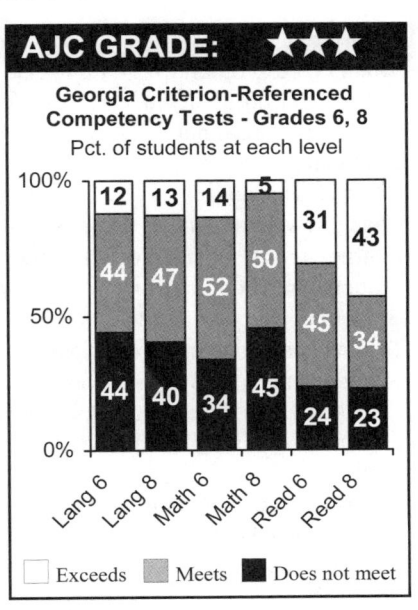

AJC GRADE: ★★★

Georgia Criterion-Referenced Competency Tests - Grades 6, 8
Pct. of students at each level

	Lang 6	Lang 8	Math 6	Math 8	Read 6	Read 8
Exceeds	12	13	14	5	31	43
Meets	44	47	52	50	45	34
Does not meet	44	40	34	45	24	23

Gwinnett County Middle Schools

Sweetwater Middle School

3500 Cruse Rd, Lawrenceville, GA 30044
770-923-4131 · Grades 6 - 8

Enrollment:	2,111
White / black / other:	36.4% / 33.3% / 30.3%
Not native English-speaking:	164 / 7.8%
Student absenteeism:	3.7%
Students per teacher:	16.6
Parent friendliness:	❶❷❸❹❺❻
Teachers with advanced degrees:	45.7%
Average years' teaching experience:	8.6
Students in gifted program:	178 / 8.4%
Students held back a grade:	0.7%
Total suspensions and expulsions:	217
Suspensions only, pct. in-school:	206 / 48.5%
Offenses:	violence: 166, drugs: 5, other: 72
Eligible students, free or reduced lunch:	40.5%
Number of dropouts:	6 / 0.3%
Pct. 8th-graders w/ basic computer skills:	100.0%

Students at this school generally go on to: Berkmar High

AJC GRADE: ★★★

Georgia Criterion-Referenced Competency Tests - Grades 6, 8
Pct. of students at each level

	Lang 6	Lang 8	Math 6	Math 8	Read 6	Read 8
Exceeds	16	20	21	11	39	54
Meets	57	49	58	56	44	29
Does not meet	27	31	21	33	17	16

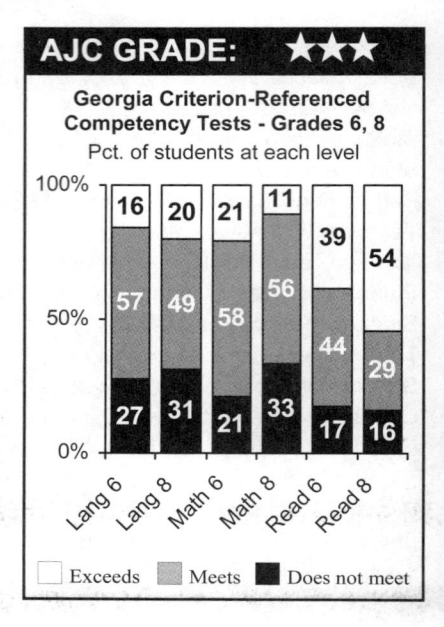

Trickum Middle School

948 Cole Dr SW, Lilburn, GA 30047
770-921-2705 · Grades 6 - 8

Enrollment:	1,697
White / black / other:	72.7% / 8.0% / 19.3%
Not native English-speaking:	46 / 2.7%
Student absenteeism:	2.6%
Students per teacher:	15.0
Parent friendliness:	①❷❸④❺❻
Teachers with advanced degrees:	65.2%
Average years' teaching experience:	14.7
Students in gifted program:	426 / 25.1%
Students held back a grade:	1.3%
Total suspensions and expulsions:	34
Suspensions only, pct. in-school:	34 / 64.7%
Offenses:	violence: 24, drugs: 4, other: 10
Eligible students, free or reduced lunch:	12.3%
Number of dropouts:	*
Pct. 8th-graders w/ basic computer skills:	98.3%

Students at this school generally go on to: Parkview High

AJC GRADE: ★★★★

Georgia Criterion-Referenced Competency Tests - Grades 6, 8
Pct. of students at each level

	Lang 6	Lang 8	Math 6	Math 8	Read 6	Read 8
Exceeds	43	41	40	26	65	73
Meets	47	46	51	61	28	21
Does not meet	10	13	9	13	7	5

Gwinnett County Middle Schools

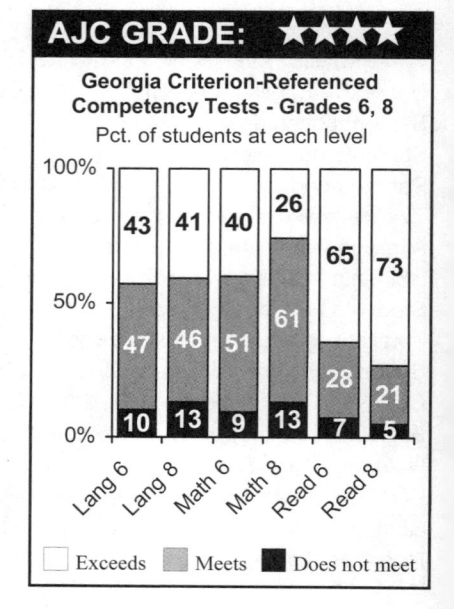

Berkmar High School

405 Pleasant Hill Rd NW, Lilburn, GA 30047
770-921-3636 · Grades 9 - 12

Enrollment:	2,598
White / black / other:	40.8% / 28.8% / 30.5%
Not native English-speaking:	166 / 6.4%
Limited English proficiency:	226 / 8.7%
Student absenteeism:	4.8%
Students per teacher:	17.4
Parent friendliness:	① ❷ ❸ ④ ❺ ❻
Students in gifted program:	311 / 12.0%
Students in remedial education:	11.7%
High school completion rate:	87.3%
Students held back a grade:	11.0%
Number of dropouts:	36 / 1.3%
Students in alternative programs:	62 / 2.4%
Students in special education:	195 / 7.5%
Eligible students, free or reduced lunch:	26.3%
Total suspensions and expulsions:	130
Suspensions only, pct. in-school:	130 / 21.5%
Drugs/alcohol-related offenses:	9
Violence-related offenses:	80
Firearms-related offenses:	4
Vandalism-related offenses:	4
Theft-related offenses:	2
All other disciplinary offenses:	36
Teachers with advanced degrees:	55.3%
Average years' teaching experience:	10.5

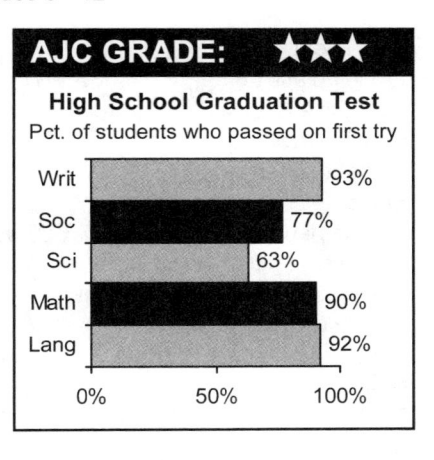

AJC GRADE: ★★★

High School Graduation Test
Pct. of students who passed on first try

- Writ: 93%
- Soc: 77%
- Sci: 63%
- Math: 90%
- Lang: 92%

GHSA classification: 8-AAAAA
Interscholastic sports offered:
BB, CC, CL, FB, GO, SB, SO, SW, TE, TF, WR

Advanced Placement (AP) Exams
Students tested: 141
Tests taken: 220
Pct. of test scores 3 or higher (1 - 5 scale): 48.2%

Languages other than English taught:
French, German, Spanish

2000-2001 high school graduates: 461

College prep/vocational diplomas:	7.4%
College prep endorsement diplomas:	64.6%
Vocational endorsement diplomas:	19.5%
General high school diplomas:	0.0%
Special education diplomas:	1.7%
Certificates of attendance (no diploma):	6.7%

Of the 2000-2001 graduates, 58.6% were eligible for the HOPE scholarship.

Of the 1999-2000 graduates, 169 attended a Georgia public college or university. Of those, 88% met the school's minimum academic requirements.

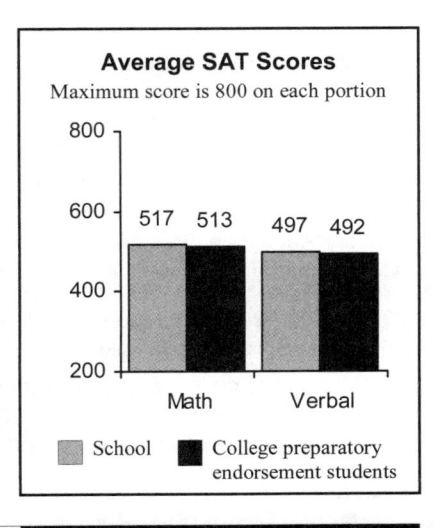

Average SAT Scores
Maximum score is 800 on each portion

- Math — School: 517, College preparatory endorsement students: 513
- Verbal — School: 497, College preparatory endorsement students: 492

Gwinnett County High Schools

Brookwood High School

1255 Dogwood Rd, Snellville, GA 30078
770-972-7642 · Grades 9 - 12

Enrollment:	2,958
White / black / other:	87.1% / 4.4% / 8.5%
Not native English-speaking:	22 / 0.7%
Limited English proficiency:	22 / 0.7%
Student absenteeism:	3.4%
Students per teacher:	18.6
Parent friendliness:	①❷❸④⑤❻
Students in gifted program:	634 / 21.4%
Students in remedial education:	0.6%
High school completion rate:	99.0%
Students held back a grade:	2.9%
Number of dropouts:	2 / 0.1%
Students in alternative programs:	2 / 0.1%
Students in special education:	246 / 8.3%
Eligible students, free or reduced lunch:	4.3%
Total suspensions and expulsions:	102
Suspensions only, pct. in-school:	102 / 33.3%
Drugs/alcohol-related offenses:	13
Violence-related offenses:	53
Firearms-related offenses:	*
Vandalism-related offenses:	4
Theft-related offenses:	*
All other disciplinary offenses:	34
Teachers with advanced degrees:	59.4%
Average years' teaching experience:	15.1

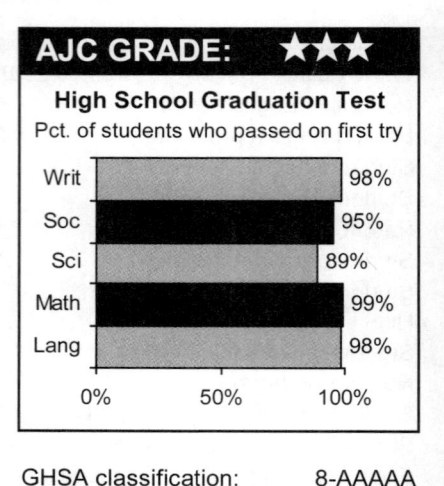

AJC GRADE: ★★★

High School Graduation Test
Pct. of students who passed on first try

- Writ: 98%
- Soc: 95%
- Sci: 89%
- Math: 99%
- Lang: 98%

GHSA classification: 8-AAAAA
Interscholastic sports offered:
BB, BS, CC, CL, FB, GO, SO, SW, TE, TF, VB, WR

Advanced Placement (AP) Exams
- Students tested: 431
- Tests taken: 764
- Pct. of test scores 3 or higher (1 - 5 scale): 78.1%

Languages other than English taught:
French, German, Latin, Spanish

2000-2001 high school graduates: 688

College prep/vocational diplomas:	0.0%
College prep endorsement diplomas:	81.8%
Vocational endorsement diplomas:	16.3%
General high school diplomas:	0.0%
Special education diplomas:	0.9%
Certificates of attendance (no diploma):	1.0%

Of the 2000-2001 graduates, 72.4% were eligible for the HOPE scholarship.

Of the 1999-2000 graduates, 323 attended a Georgia public college or university. Of those, 87% met the school's minimum academic requirements.

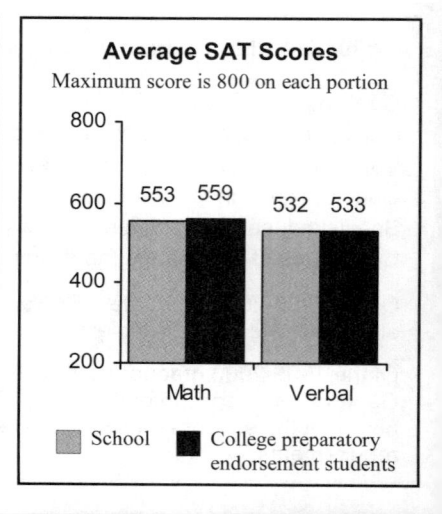

Average SAT Scores
Maximum score is 800 on each portion

- Math: School 553, College preparatory endorsement students 559
- Verbal: School 532, College preparatory endorsement students 533

The Atlanta Journal-Constitution / Page 404

Gwinnett County High Schools

Central Gwinnett High School

564 W Crogan St, Lawrenceville, GA 30045
770-963-8041 · Grades 9 - 12

Enrollment:	1,785
White / black / other:	66.9% / 18.7% / 14.3%
Not native English-speaking:	112 / 6.3%
Limited English proficiency:	130 / 7.3%
Student absenteeism:	4.2%
Students per teacher:	18.0
Parent friendliness:	① ❷ ❸ ❹ ❺ ❻
Students in gifted program:	153 / 8.6%
Students in remedial education:	1.4%
High school completion rate:	86.1%
Students held back a grade:	9.6%
Number of dropouts:	29 / 1.5%
Students in alternative programs:	14 / 0.8%
Students in special education:	174 / 9.7%
Eligible students, free or reduced lunch:	21.9%
Total suspensions and expulsions:	168
Suspensions only, pct. in-school:	168 / 48.2%
Drugs/alcohol-related offenses:	18
Violence-related offenses:	77
Firearms-related offenses:	2
Vandalism-related offenses:	5
Theft-related offenses:	1
All other disciplinary offenses:	73
Teachers with advanced degrees:	59.4%
Average years' teaching experience:	14.1

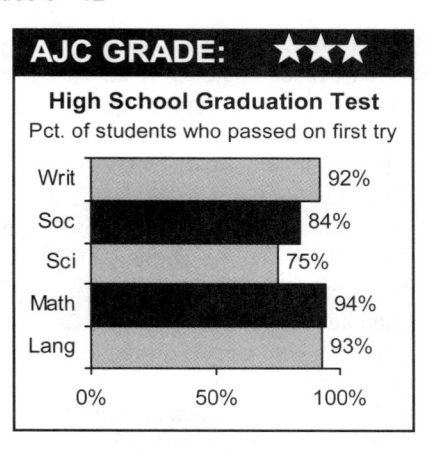

AJC GRADE: ★★★

High School Graduation Test
Pct. of students who passed on first try

- Writ: 92%
- Soc: 84%
- Sci: 75%
- Math: 94%
- Lang: 93%

GHSA classification:	8-AAAAA

Interscholastic sports offered:
BB, BS, CC, CL, FB, GO, SB, SO, SW, TE, TF, WR

Advanced Placement (AP) Exams
Students tested:	85
Tests taken:	127
Pct. of test scores 3 or higher (1 - 5 scale):	55.9%

Languages other than English taught:
French, German, Latin, Spanish

2000-2001 high school graduates: 285

College prep/vocational diplomas:	0.4%
College prep endorsement diplomas:	73.3%
Vocational endorsement diplomas:	18.2%
General high school diplomas:	0.0%
Special education diplomas:	1.1%
Certificates of attendance (no diploma):	7.0%

Of the 2000-2001 graduates, 61.4% were eligible for the HOPE scholarship.

Of the 1999-2000 graduates, 136 attended a Georgia public college or university. Of those, 83% met the school's minimum academic requirements.

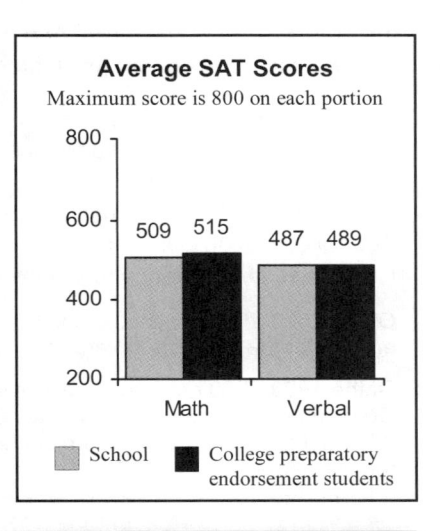

Average SAT Scores
Maximum score is 800 on each portion

- Math: School 509, College preparatory endorsement students 515
- Verbal: School 487, College preparatory endorsement students 489

Gwinnett County High Schools

Collins Hill High School

50 Taylor Rd, Suwanee, GA 30024
770-682-4100 · Grades 9 - 12

Enrollment:	3,543
White / black / other:	72.5% / 10.4% / 17.1%
Not native English-speaking:	79 / 2.2%
Limited English proficiency:	79 / 2.2%
Student absenteeism:	3.5%
Students per teacher:	18.2
Parent friendliness:	① ❷ ❸ ④ ⑤ ❻
Students in gifted program:	433 / 12.2%
Students in remedial education:	3.9%
High school completion rate:	92.8%
Students held back a grade:	5.3%
Number of dropouts:	25 / 0.7%
Students in alternative programs:	7 / 0.2%
Students in special education:	233 / 6.6%
Eligible students, free or reduced lunch:	6.6%
Total suspensions and expulsions:	173
Suspensions only, pct. in-school:	173 / 28.9%
Drugs/alcohol-related offenses:	15
Violence-related offenses:	55
Firearms-related offenses:	*
Vandalism-related offenses:	17
Theft-related offenses:	2
All other disciplinary offenses:	90
Teachers with advanced degrees:	57.4%
Average years' teaching experience:	11.4

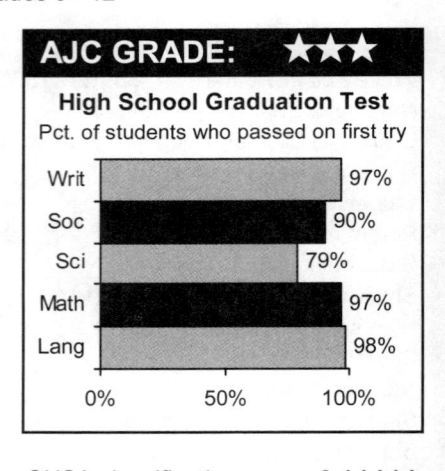

AJC GRADE: ★★★

High School Graduation Test
Pct. of students who passed on first try

- Writ: 97%
- Soc: 90%
- Sci: 79%
- Math: 97%
- Lang: 98%

GHSA classification: 8-AAAAA
Interscholastic sports offered:
BB, BS, CC, CL, FB, GO, SB, SO, SW, TE, TF, VB, WR

Advanced Placement (AP) Exams
Students tested:	253
Tests taken:	457
Pct. of test scores 3 or higher (1 - 5 scale):	72.2%

Languages other than English taught:
French, German, Latin, Spanish

2000-2001 high school graduates: 669

College prep/vocational diplomas:	1.8%
College prep endorsement diplomas:	87.9%
Vocational endorsement diplomas:	9.4%
General high school diplomas:	0.0%
Special education diplomas:	0.7%
Certificates of attendance (no diploma):	0.1%

Of the 2000-2001 graduates, 69.4% were eligible for the HOPE scholarship.

Of the 1999-2000 graduates, 363 attended a Georgia public college or university. Of those, 87% met the school's minimum academic requirements.

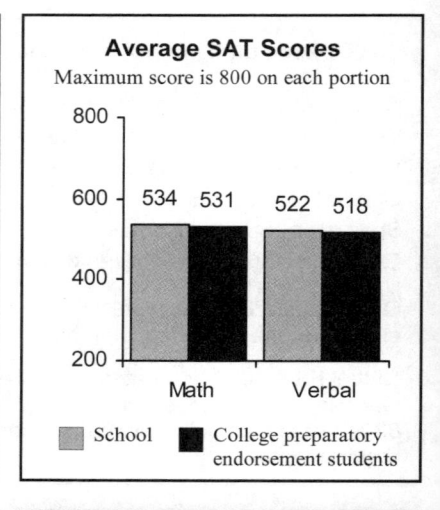

Average SAT Scores
Maximum score is 800 on each portion

- Math: School 534, College preparatory endorsement students 531
- Verbal: School 522, College preparatory endorsement students 518

The Atlanta Journal-Constitution / Page 406

Gwinnett County High Schools

Dacula High School

123 Broad St, Dacula, GA 30019
770-963-6664 · Grades 9 - 12

Enrollment:	2,035
White / black / other:	87.9% / 6.0% / 6.1%
Not native English-speaking:	29 / 1.4%
Limited English proficiency:	29 / 1.4%
Student absenteeism:	2.9%
Students per teacher:	17.4
Parent friendliness:	① ❷ ③ ④ ⑤ ❻
Students in gifted program:	326 / 16.0%
Students in remedial education:	2.8%
High school completion rate:	94.4%
Students held back a grade:	5.7%
Number of dropouts:	9 / 0.4%
Students in alternative programs:	2 / 0.1%
Students in special education:	211 / 10.4%
Eligible students, free or reduced lunch:	7.6%

Total suspensions and expulsions:	102
Suspensions only, pct. in-school:	102 / 37.3%
Drugs/alcohol-related offenses:	6
Violence-related offenses:	55
Firearms-related offenses:	3
Vandalism-related offenses:	5
Theft-related offenses:	*
All other disciplinary offenses:	33

Teachers with advanced degrees:	50.4%
Average years' teaching experience:	10.9

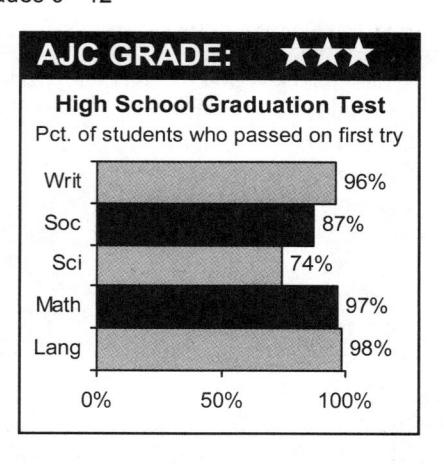

AJC GRADE: ★★★

High School Graduation Test
Pct. of students who passed on first try

- Writ: 96%
- Soc: 87%
- Sci: 74%
- Math: 97%
- Lang: 98%

GHSA classification:	8-AAAAA

Interscholastic sports offered:
BB, BS, CC, CL, FB, GO, SB, SO, SW, TE, TF, VB, WR

Advanced Placement (AP) Exams
Students tested:	158
Tests taken:	234
Pct. of test scores 3 or higher (1 - 5 scale):	39.7%

Languages other than English taught:
French, German, Latin, Spanish

2000-2001 high school graduates: 371

College prep/vocational diplomas:	2.2%
College prep endorsement diplomas:	74.9%
Vocational endorsement diplomas:	21.6%
General high school diplomas:	0.0%
Special education diplomas:	1.3%
Certificates of attendance (no diploma):	0.0%

Of the 2000-2001 graduates, 64.4% were eligible for the HOPE scholarship.

Of the 1999-2000 graduates, 170 attended a Georgia public college or university. Of those, 78% met the school's minimum academic requirements.

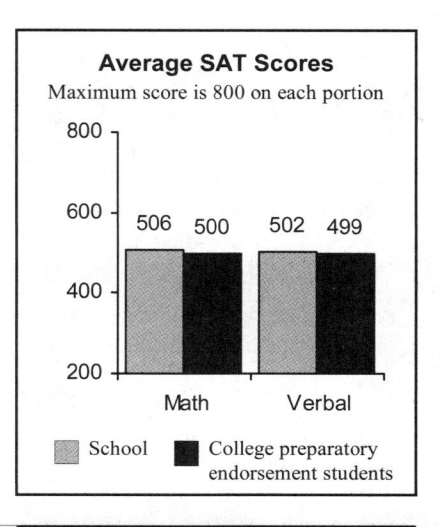

Average SAT Scores
Maximum score is 800 on each portion

- Math — School: 506, College preparatory endorsement students: 500
- Verbal — School: 502, College preparatory endorsement students: 499

The Atlanta Journal-Constitution / Page 407

Gwinnett County High Schools

Duluth High School

3737 Brock Rd, Duluth, GA 30096
770-476-5206 · Grades 9 - 12

Enrollment:	2,376
White / black / other:	61.6% / 10.5% / 27.9%
Not native English-speaking:	162 / 6.8%
Limited English proficiency:	179 / 7.5%
Student absenteeism:	3.6%
Students per teacher:	17.7
Parent friendliness:	❶❷❸④⑤❻
Students in gifted program:	255 / 10.7%
Students in remedial education:	1.5%
High school completion rate:	95.2%
Students held back a grade:	6.6%
Number of dropouts:	*
Students in alternative programs:	3 / 0.1%
Students in special education:	186 / 7.8%
Eligible students, free or reduced lunch:	9.0%
Total suspensions and expulsions:	*
Suspensions only, pct. in-school:	*
Drugs/alcohol-related offenses:	*
Violence-related offenses:	*
Firearms-related offenses:	*
Vandalism-related offenses:	*
Theft-related offenses:	*
All other disciplinary offenses:	*
Teachers with advanced degrees:	61.6%
Average years' teaching experience:	13.7

AJC GRADE: ★★★

High School Graduation Test
Pct. of students who passed on first try

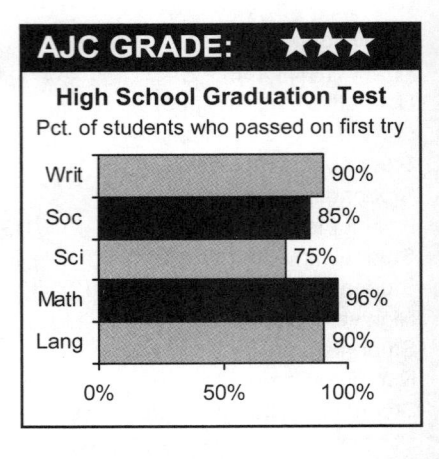

- Writ: 90%
- Soc: 85%
- Sci: 75%
- Math: 96%
- Lang: 90%

GHSA classification:	8-AAAAA

Interscholastic sports offered:
BB, CC, CL, FB, GO, SB, SO, SW, TE, TF, WR

Advanced Placement (AP) Exams
Students tested:	281
Tests taken:	491
Pct. of test scores 3 or higher (1 - 5 scale):	80.7%

Languages other than English taught:
French, German, Japanese, Latin, Spanish

2000-2001 high school graduates: 437

College prep/vocational diplomas:	1.6%
College prep endorsement diplomas:	83.5%
Vocational endorsement diplomas:	13.7%
General high school diplomas:	0.0%
Special education diplomas:	1.1%
Certificates of attendance (no diploma):	0.0%

Of the 2000-2001 graduates, 70.9% were eligible for the HOPE scholarship.

Of the 1999-2000 graduates, 236 attended a Georgia public college or university. Of those, 89% met the school's minimum academic requirements.

Average SAT Scores
Maximum score is 800 on each portion

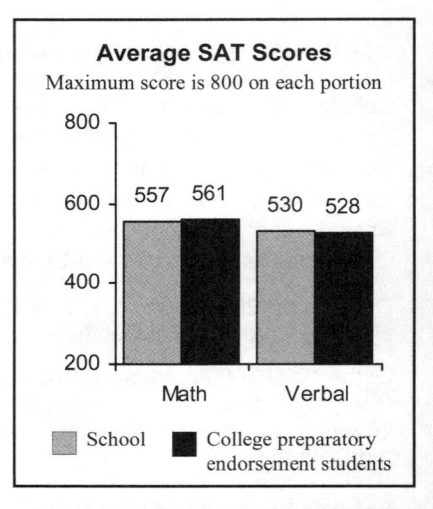

- Math: School 557, College preparatory endorsement students 561
- Verbal: School 530, College preparatory endorsement students 528

Gwinnett County High Schools

Grayson High School

50 Hope Hollow Rd, Loganville, GA 30052
770-554-1071 · Grades 9 - 12

Enrollment:	1,038
White / black / other:	85.8% / 6.5% / 7.7%
Not native English-speaking:	16 / 1.5%
Limited English proficiency:	16 / 1.5%
Student absenteeism:	4.0%
Students per teacher:	17.7
Parent friendliness:	❶❷❸④⑤❻
Students in gifted program:	24 / 2.3%
Students in remedial education:	1.4%
High school completion rate:	*
Students held back a grade:	5.8%
Number of dropouts:	7 / 0.6%
Students in alternative programs:	*
Students in special education:	73 / 7.0%
Eligible students, free or reduced lunch:	7.5%
Total suspensions and expulsions:	49
Suspensions only, pct. in-school:	49 / 8.2%
Drugs/alcohol-related offenses:	4
Violence-related offenses:	28
Firearms-related offenses:	1
Vandalism-related offenses:	4
Theft-related offenses:	*
All other disciplinary offenses:	16
Teachers with advanced degrees:	61.7%
Average years' teaching experience:	12.1

AJC GRADE: ★★★

High School Graduation Test
Pct. of students who passed on first try

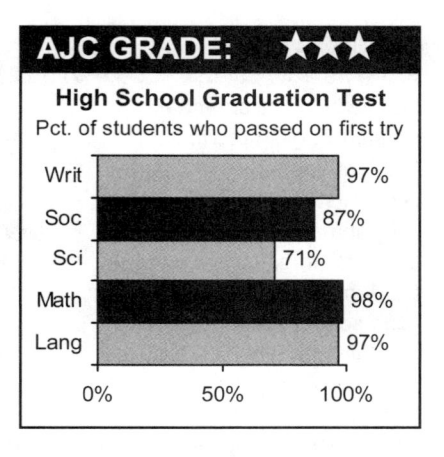

- Writ: 97%
- Soc: 87%
- Sci: 71%
- Math: 98%
- Lang: 97%

GHSA classification: 8-AAA
Interscholastic sports offered: None

Advanced Placement (AP) Exams
Students tested: *
Tests taken: *
Pct. of test scores 3 or higher (1 - 5 scale): *

Languages other than English taught:
French, Latin, Spanish

2000-2001 high school graduates: 74

College prep/vocational diplomas:	6.8%
College prep endorsement diplomas:	45.9%
Vocational endorsement diplomas:	39.2%
General high school diplomas:	0.0%
Special education diplomas:	0.0%
Certificates of attendance (no diploma):	8.1%

Of the 2000-2001 graduates, 35.1% were eligible for the HOPE scholarship.

Grayson High School is a new school and therefore some data was not available for this report.

Average SAT Scores
Maximum score is 800 on each portion

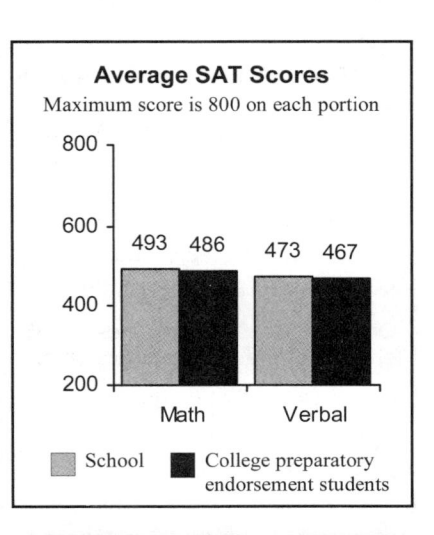

- Math — School: 493, College preparatory endorsement students: 486
- Verbal — School: 473, College preparatory endorsement students: 467

The Atlanta Journal-Constitution / Page 409

Gwinnett County High Schools

Meadowcreek High School

4455 Steve Reynolds Blvd, Norcross, GA 30093
770-381-9680 · Grades 9 - 12

Enrollment:	2,189
White / black / other:	20.9% / 33.2% / 45.9%
Not native English-speaking:	343 / 15.7%
Limited English proficiency:	343 / 15.7%
Student absenteeism:	5.6%
Students per teacher:	17.1
Parent friendliness:	①❷❸❹❺❻
Students in gifted program:	128 / 5.8%
Students in remedial education:	13.2%
High school completion rate:	73.3%
Students held back a grade:	13.1%
Number of dropouts:	34 / 1.4%
Students in alternative programs:	*
Students in special education:	158 / 7.2%
Eligible students, free or reduced lunch:	43.9%
Total suspensions and expulsions:	148
Suspensions only, pct. in-school:	148 / 13.5%
Drugs/alcohol-related offenses:	13
Violence-related offenses:	88
Firearms-related offenses:	4
Vandalism-related offenses:	8
Theft-related offenses:	2
All other disciplinary offenses:	37
Teachers with advanced degrees:	47.7%
Average years' teaching experience:	9.8

AJC GRADE: ★★

High School Graduation Test
Pct. of students who passed on first try

- Writ: 87%
- Soc: 71%
- Sci: 56%
- Math: 91%
- Lang: 88%

GHSA classification:	8-AAAAA
Interscholastic sports offered:	
BB, BS, CC, CL, FB, GO, SB, SO, SW, TE, TF, WR	
Advanced Placement (AP) Exams	
Students tested:	136
Tests taken:	265
Pct. of test scores 3 or higher (1 - 5 scale):	41.5%

Languages other than English taught:
French, German, Japanese, Latin, Spanish

2000-2001 high school graduates: 340

College prep/vocational diplomas:	1.2%
College prep endorsement diplomas:	67.9%
Vocational endorsement diplomas:	29.7%
General high school diplomas:	0.0%
Special education diplomas:	1.2%
Certificates of attendance (no diploma):	0.0%

Of the 2000-2001 graduates, 50.3% were eligible for the HOPE scholarship.

Of the 1999-2000 graduates, 178 attended a Georgia public college or university. Of those, 81% met the school's minimum academic requirements.

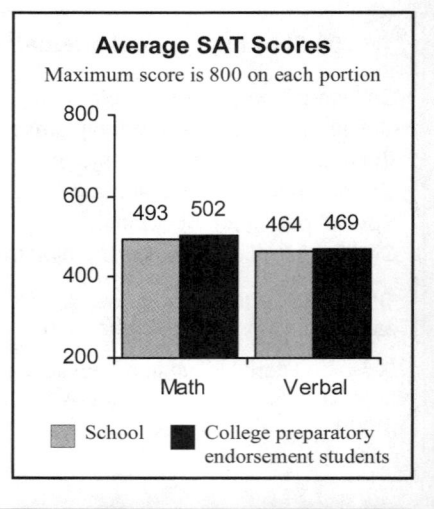

Average SAT Scores
Maximum score is 800 on each portion

	Math	Verbal
School	493	464
College preparatory endorsement students	502	469

Gwinnett County High Schools

Norcross High School

5300 Spalding Dr, Norcross, GA 30092
770-448-3674 · Grades 9 - 12

Enrollment:	2,249
White / black / other:	44.5% / 26.5% / 28.9%
Not native English-speaking:	189 / 8.4%
Limited English proficiency:	241 / 10.7%
Student absenteeism:	4.1%
Students per teacher:	16.0
Parent friendliness:	❶❷❸④⑤❻
Students in gifted program:	405 / 18.0%
Students in remedial education:	13.2%
High school completion rate:	82.5%
Students held back a grade:	10.9%
Number of dropouts:	28 / 1.2%
Students in alternative programs:	16 / 0.7%
Students in special education:	155 / 6.9%
Eligible students, free or reduced lunch:	29.6%
Total suspensions and expulsions:	106
Suspensions only, pct. in-school:	106 / 23.6%
Drugs/alcohol-related offenses:	11
Violence-related offenses:	34
Firearms-related offenses:	1
Vandalism-related offenses:	3
Theft-related offenses:	1
All other disciplinary offenses:	65
Teachers with advanced degrees:	51.4%
Average years' teaching experience:	11.9

AJC GRADE: ★★★

High School Graduation Test
Pct. of students who passed on first try

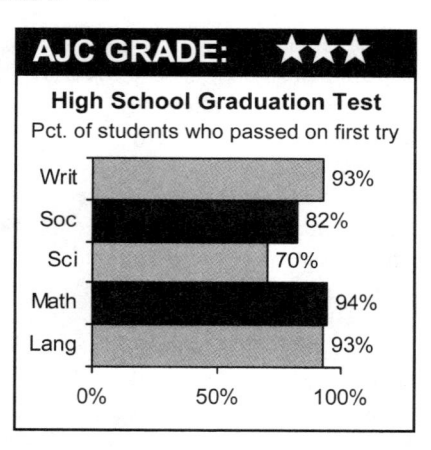

- Writ: 93%
- Soc: 82%
- Sci: 70%
- Math: 94%
- Lang: 93%

GHSA classification:	8-AAAAA

Interscholastic sports offered:
BB, CC, CL, FB, GO, SB, SO, SW, TE, TF, WR

Advanced Placement (AP) Exams
Students tested:	177
Tests taken:	348
Pct. of test scores 3 or higher (1 - 5 scale):	62.6%

Languages other than English taught:
French, German, Japanese, Latin, Spanish

2000-2001 high school graduates: 429

College prep/vocational diplomas:	0.0%
College prep endorsement diplomas:	76.5%
Vocational endorsement diplomas:	23.1%
General high school diplomas:	0.0%
Special education diplomas:	0.5%
Certificates of attendance (no diploma):	0.0%

Of the 2000-2001 graduates, 59.2% were eligible for the HOPE scholarship.

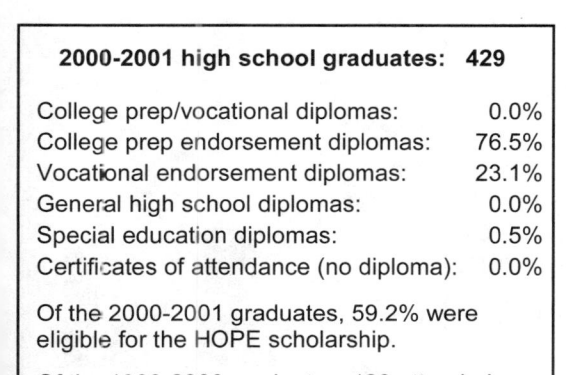

Of the 1999-2000 graduates, 180 attended a Georgia public college or university. Of those, 89% met the school's minimum academic requirements.

Average SAT Scores
Maximum score is 800 on each portion

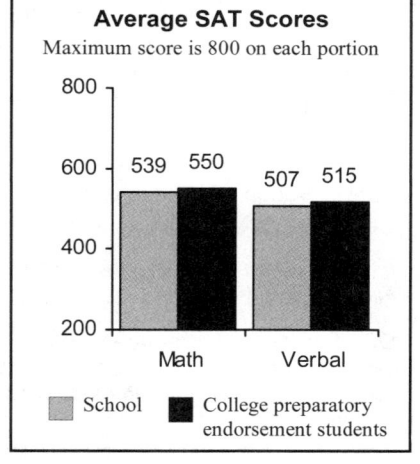

- Math: School 539, College preparatory endorsement students 550
- Verbal: School 507, College preparatory endorsement students 515

Gwinnett County High Schools

North Gwinnett High School

20 Level Creek Rd, Suwanee, GA 30024
770-945-9558 · Grades 9 - 12

Enrollment:	2,235
White / black / other:	84.7% / 5.9% / 9.4%
Not native English-speaking:	24 / 1.1%
Limited English proficiency:	24 / 1.1%
Student absenteeism:	3.4%
Students per teacher:	18.5
Parent friendliness:	①❷❸④⑤❻
Students in gifted program:	271 / 12.1%
Students in remedial education:	1.6%
High school completion rate:	90.9%
Students held back a grade:	5.5%
Number of dropouts:	10 / 0.4%
Students in alternative programs:	1 / 0.0%
Students in special education:	201 / 9.0%
Eligible students, free or reduced lunch:	6.5%
Total suspensions and expulsions:	165
Suspensions only, pct. in-school:	165 / 52.1%
Drugs/alcohol-related offenses:	24
Violence-related offenses:	47
Firearms-related offenses:	*
Vandalism-related offenses:	2
Theft-related offenses:	1
All other disciplinary offenses:	91
Teachers with advanced degrees:	59.3%
Average years' teaching experience:	11.5

AJC GRADE: ★★★

High School Graduation Test
Pct. of students who passed on first try

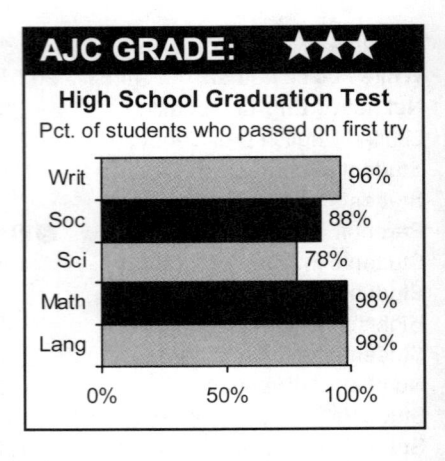

- Writ: 96%
- Soc: 88%
- Sci: 78%
- Math: 98%
- Lang: 98%

GHSA classification: 8-AAAAA
Interscholastic sports offered:
BB, BS, CC, CL, FB, GO, SB, SO, SW, TE, TF, VB, WR

Advanced Placement (AP) Exams
Students tested: 153
Tests taken: 280
Pct. of test scores 3 or higher (1 - 5 scale): 54.3%

Languages other than English taught:
French, German, Spanish

2000-2001 high school graduates: 420

College prep/vocational diplomas:	4.5%
College prep endorsement diplomas:	68.1%
Vocational endorsement diplomas:	21.4%
General high school diplomas:	0.0%
Special education diplomas:	2.9%
Certificates of attendance (no diploma):	3.1%

Of the 2000-2001 graduates, 58.3% were eligible for the HOPE scholarship.

Of the 1999-2000 graduates, 160 attended a Georgia public college or university. Of those, 83% met the school's minimum academic requirements.

Average SAT Scores
Maximum score is 800 on each portion

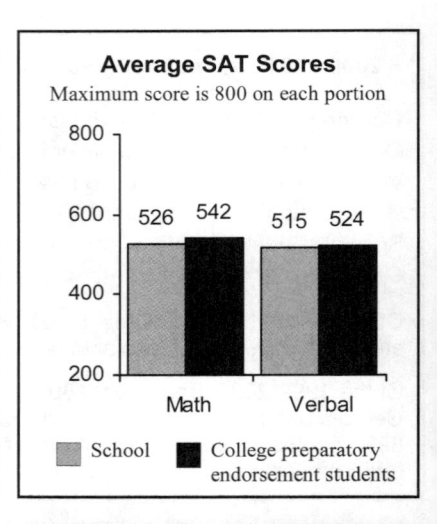

- Math — School: 526, College preparatory endorsement students: 542
- Verbal — School: 515, College preparatory endorsement students: 524

Gwinnett County High Schools

Parkview High School

998 Cole Dr SW, Lilburn, GA 30047
770-921-2874 · Grades 9 - 12

Enrollment:	2,568
White / black / other:	78.5% / 5.9% / 15.6%
Not native English-speaking:	56 / 2.2%
Limited English proficiency:	56 / 2.2%
Student absenteeism:	2.7%
Students per teacher:	17.3
Parent friendliness:	① ❷ ❸ ④ ⑤ ❻
Students in gifted program:	542 / 21.1%
Students in remedial education:	1.6%
High school completion rate:	99.1%
Students held back a grade:	3.9%
Number of dropouts:	3 / 0.1%
Students in alternative programs:	3 / 0.1%
Students in special education:	219 / 8.5%
Eligible students, free or reduced lunch:	5.2%
Total suspensions and expulsions:	122
Suspensions only, pct. in-school:	122 / 46.7%
Drugs/alcohol-related offenses:	10
Violence-related offenses:	57
Firearms-related offenses:	4
Vandalism-related offenses:	7
Theft-related offenses:	*
All other disciplinary offenses:	46
Teachers with advanced degrees:	56.3%
Average years' teaching experience:	13.9

AJC GRADE: ★★★★

High School Graduation Test
Pct. of students who passed on first try

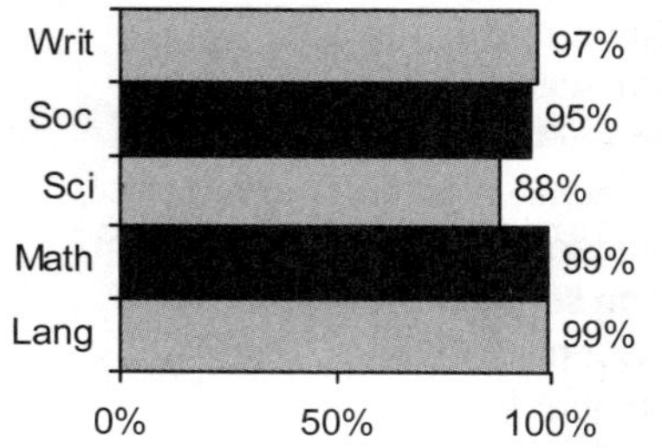

- Writ: 97%
- Soc: 95%
- Sci: 88%
- Math: 99%
- Lang: 99%

GHSA classification: 8-AAAAA
Interscholastic sports offered:
BB, BS, CC, CL, FB, GO, SB, SO, SW, TE, TF, VB, WR

Advanced Placement (AP) Exams
Students tested: 308
Tests taken: 567
Pct. of test scores 3 or higher (1 - 5 scale): 71.3%

Languages other than English taught:
French, German, Latin, Spanish

2000-2001 high school graduates: 557

College prep/vocational diplomas:	4.1%
College prep endorsement diplomas:	82.8%
Vocational endorsement diplomas:	9.9%
General high school diplomas:	0.0%
Special education diplomas:	0.9%
Certificates of attendance (no diploma):	2.3%

Of the 2000-2001 graduates, 75.4% were eligible for the HOPE scholarship.

Of the 1999-2000 graduates, 314 attended a Georgia public college or university. Of those, 91% met the school's minimum academic requirements.

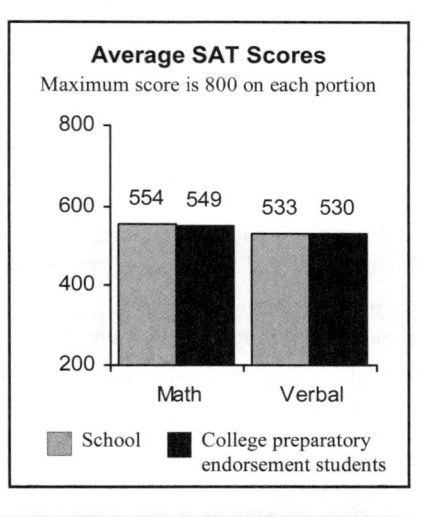

Average SAT Scores
Maximum score is 800 on each portion

- Math: School 554, College preparatory endorsement students 549
- Verbal: School 533, College preparatory endorsement students 530

Gwinnett County High Schools

Shiloh High School

4210 Shiloh Rd, Snellville, GA 30039
770-972-8471 · Grades 9 - 12

Enrollment:	2,086
White / black / other:	73.3% / 19.2% / 7.5%
Not native English-speaking:	19 / 0.9%
Limited English proficiency:	24 / 1.2%
Student absenteeism:	3.4%
Students per teacher:	17.0
Parent friendliness:	①❷❸④⑤❻
Students in gifted program:	319 / 15.3%
Students in remedial education:	1.7%
High school completion rate:	93.7%
Students held back a grade:	5.0%
Number of dropouts:	1 / 0.0%
Students in alternative programs:	7 / 0.3%
Students in special education:	178 / 8.5%
Eligible students, free or reduced lunch:	9.8%
Total suspensions and expulsions:	88
Suspensions only, pct. in-school:	87 / 28.7%
Drugs/alcohol-related offenses:	10
Violence-related offenses:	45
Firearms-related offenses:	*
Vandalism-related offenses:	5
Theft-related offenses:	*
All other disciplinary offenses:	29
Teachers with advanced degrees:	69.6%
Average years' teaching experience:	12.6

AJC GRADE: ★★★

High School Graduation Test
Pct. of students who passed on first try

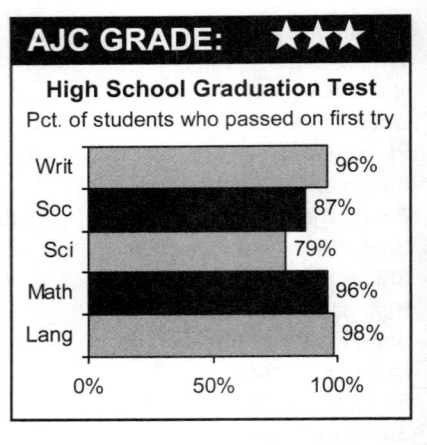

- Writ: 96%
- Soc: 87%
- Sci: 79%
- Math: 96%
- Lang: 98%

GHSA classification: 8-AAAAA
Interscholastic sports offered:
BB, BS, CC, CL, FB, GO, SB, SO, SW, TE, TF, VB, WR

Advanced Placement (AP) Exams
Students tested:	178
Tests taken:	258
Pct. of test scores 3 or higher (1 - 5 scale):	72.9%

Languages other than English taught:
French, German, Latin, Spanish

2000-2001 high school graduates: 478

College prep/vocational diplomas:	1.5%
College prep endorsement diplomas:	76.4%
Vocational endorsement diplomas:	18.6%
General high school diplomas:	0.0%
Special education diplomas:	1.3%
Certificates of attendance (no diploma):	2.3%

Of the 2000-2001 graduates, 63.8% were eligible for the HOPE scholarship.

Of the 1999-2000 graduates, 256 attended a Georgia public college or university. Of those, 88% met the school's minimum academic requirements.

Average SAT Scores
Maximum score is 800 on each portion

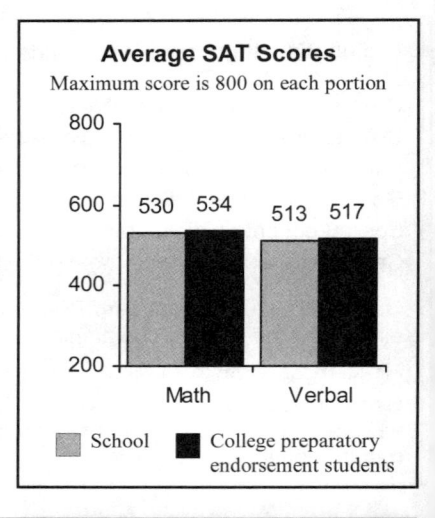

- Math: School 530, College preparatory endorsement students 534
- Verbal: School 513, College preparatory endorsement students 517

Gwinnett County High Schools

South Gwinnett High School

2288 Main St E, Snellville, GA 30078
770-972-4840 · Grades 9 - 12

👍

Enrollment:	2,092
White / black / other:	84.7% / 8.7% / 6.5%
Not native English-speaking:	26 / 1.2%
Limited English proficiency:	29 / 1.4%
Student absenteeism:	3.2%
Students per teacher:	18.5
Parent friendliness:	①❷❸④⑤❻
Students in gifted program:	242 / 11.6%
Students in remedial education:	1.2%
High school completion rate:	88.1%
Students held back a grade:	5.8%
Number of dropouts:	16 / 0.7%
Students in alternative programs:	*
Students in special education:	163 / 7.8%
Eligible students, free or reduced lunch:	7.6%

Total suspensions and expulsions:	118
Suspensions only, pct. in-school:	117 / 17.9%
Drugs/alcohol-related offenses:	16
Violence-related offenses:	61
Firearms-related offenses:	3
Vandalism-related offenses:	5
Theft-related offenses:	*
All other disciplinary offenses:	44

Teachers with advanced degrees:	56.1%
Average years' teaching experience:	14.0

AJC GRADE: ★★★

High School Graduation Test
Pct. of students who passed on first try

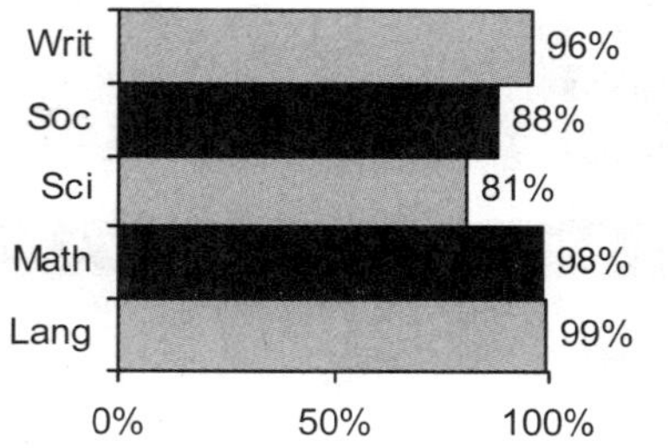

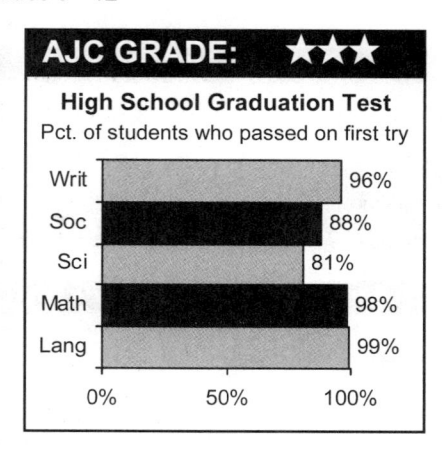

Writ
96%
Soc
88%
Sci
81%
Math
98%
Lang
99%
0%
50%
100%

GHSA classification: 8-AAAAA
Interscholastic sports offered:
BB, BS, CL, FB, SO, TE, WR

Advanced Placement (AP) Exams

Students tested:	177
Tests taken:	302
Pct. of test scores 3 or higher (1 - 5 scale):	56.6%

Languages other than English taught:
French, German, Latin, Spanish

2000-2001 high school graduates: 496

College prep/vocational diplomas:	1.0%
College prep endorsement diplomas:	73.8%
Vocational endorsement diplomas:	20.4%
General high school diplomas:	0.0%
Special education diplomas:	1.8%
Certificates of attendance (no diploma):	3.0%

Of the 2000-2001 graduates, 64.1% were eligible for the HOPE scholarship.

Of the 1999-2000 graduates, 306 attended a Georgia public college or university. Of those, 84% met the school's minimum academic requirements.

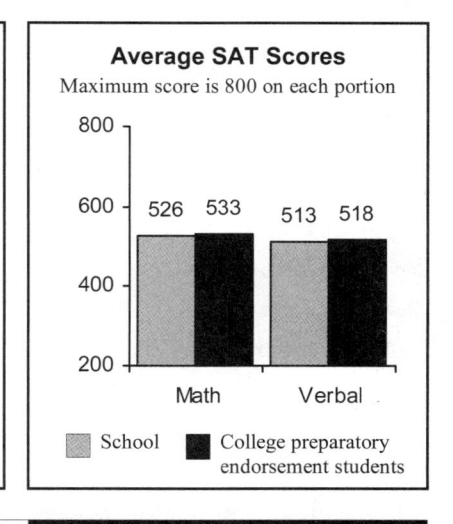

Average SAT Scores
Maximum score is 800 on each portion

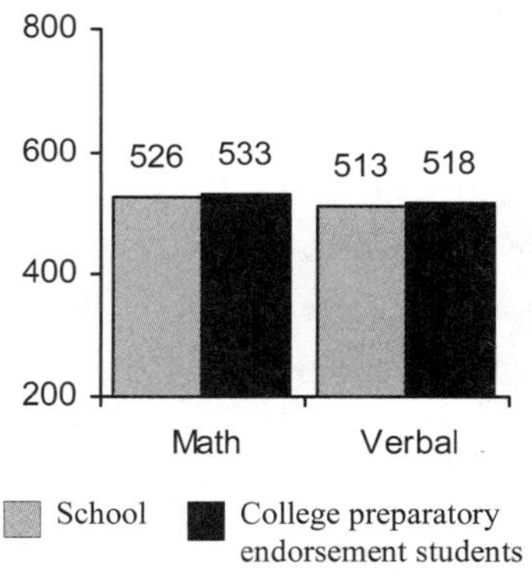

800
600
400
200
526
533
513
518
Math
Verbal
School
College preparatory endorsement students

AJC ranking of Gwinnett County Schools

ELEMENTARY SCHOOLS

AJC Star Grade: ★★★★

Camp Creek Elementary
Gwin Oaks Elementary
Head Elementary
Simpson Elementary

AJC Star Grade: ★★★

Annistown Elementary
Arcado Elementary
Beaver Ridge Elementary
Benefield Elementary
Berkeley Lake Elementary
Bethesda Elementary
Britt Elementary
Brookwood Elementary
Cedar Hill Elementary
Centerville Elementary
Chattahoochee Elementary
Craig Elementary
Dacula Elementary
Dyer Elementary
Fort Daniel Elementary
Freeman's Mill Elementary
Grayson Elementary
Harmony Elementary
Harris Elementary
Hopkins Elementary
Jackson Elementary
Kanoheda Elementary
Knight Elementary
Lilburn Elementary
Magill Elementary
Mason Elementary
McKendree Elementary
Meadowcreek Elementary
Minor Elementary
Mountain Park Elementary
Nesbit Elementary
Norcross Elementary
Norton Elementary
Peachtree Elementary
Pharr Elementary
Riverside Elementary
Rock Springs Elementary
Rockbridge Elementary
Shiloh Elementary
Simonton Elementary
Stripling Elementary
Sugar Hill Elementary
Suwanee Elementary
Taylor Elementary
Walnut Grove Elementary

AJC Star Grade: ★★

Harbins Elementary
Partee Elementary

AJC Star Grade: ★

Lawrenceville Elementary

MIDDLE SCHOOLS

AJC Star Grade: ★★★★

Crews Middle
Trickum Middle

AJC Star Grade: ★★★

Creekland Middle
Dacula Middle

Gwinnett County Public Schools

AJC ranking of Gwinnett County Schools

Duluth Middle
Five Forks Middle
Hull Middle
Lanier Middle
Lilburn Middle
McConnell Middle
Pinckneyville Middle
Richards Middle
Shiloh Middle
Snellville Middle
Summerour Middle
Sweetwater Middle

HIGH SCHOOLS

AJC Star Grade: ★★★★

Parkview High

AJC Star Grade: ★★★

Berkmar High
Brookwood High
Central Gwinnett High
Collins Hill High
Dacula High
Duluth High
Grayson High
Norcross High
North Gwinnett High
Shiloh High
South Gwinnett High

AJC Star Grade: ★★

Meadowcreek High

Gwinnett County Public Schools

Hall County Public Schools

711 Green St NW, Gainesville, GA 30501
Phone: 770-534-1080 · Fax: 770-535-7404
http://www.hallco.org

The following pages provide detailed information on every school in the Hall County school district. An asterisk (*) means the value of the data was zero or was not reported by the school district. A complete list of schools ranked by The Atlanta Journal-Constitution's star rating system follows the detailed school reports.

District enrollment:	20,238
White / black / other:	72.2% / 5.8% / 22.0%
Not native English-speaking:	1,431 / 7.1%
Expenditure per student (general fund):	$5,468
Students per teacher:	15.7
Teachers with advanced degrees:	60.7%
Average years, teaching experience:	12.5
Average teacher salary:	$42,534.35
Students in gifted program:	1,574 / 7.8%
Students held back a grade:	549 / 2.7%
Eligible students, free or reduced lunch:	6,991 / 34.4%
Number of dropouts (grades 9-12):	322 / 5.4%
High school completion rate:	75.3%
Graduates, pct. eligible for HOPE scholarships:	831 / 53.8%
Average combined SAT score (maximum 1,600):	997
Pct. of 11th-graders passing the Georgia High School Graduation Tests on first try:	64%
Percent of children 5 to 17 years of age living in poverty (2000 Census estimate):	14.8%

Chestnut Mountain Elementary School

4670 Winder Hwy, Flowery Branch, GA 30542
770-967-3121 · Grades K - 5

Enrollment:	461
White / black / other:	87.6% / 2.8% / 9.5%
Not native English-speaking:	6 / 1.3%
Limited English proficiency:	32 / 6.9%
Student absenteeism:	3.6%
Students per teacher:	14.9
Parent friendliness:	① ❷ ❸ ④ ❺ ❻
Teachers with advanced degrees:	78.8%
Average years' teaching experience:	13.2
Students in gifted program:	69 / 15.0%
Students in remedial education:	11.0%
Students held back a grade:	0.4%
Total suspensions, pct. in-school:	1 / 0.0%
Offenses:	violence: 1, drugs: *, other: *
Eligible students, free or reduced lunch:	15.9%
Before / after school program:	No / Yes

Students at this school generally go on to:
South Hall Middle

AJC GRADE: ★★

Georgia Criterion-Referenced Competency Tests - Grade 4
Pct. of students at each level

Read: 38% / 41% / 21%
Math: 12% / 59% / 29%
Lang: 18% / 58% / 24%

☐ Exceeds ▨ Meets ■ Does not meet

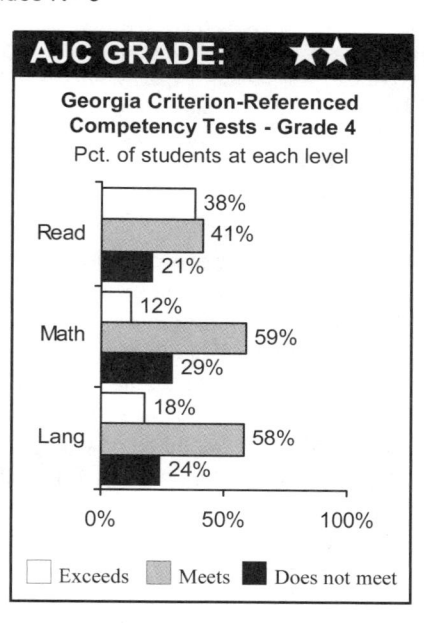

Flowery Branch Elementary School

5544 Radford Rd, Flowery Branch, GA 30542
770-967-6621 · Grades K - 5

Enrollment:	579
White / black / other:	83.9% / 5.5% / 10.5%
Not native English-speaking:	9 / 1.6%
Limited English proficiency:	49 / 8.5%
Student absenteeism:	4.3%
Students per teacher:	16.5
Parent friendliness:	① ❷ ❸ ④ ⑤ ❻
Teachers with advanced degrees:	48.6%
Average years' teaching experience:	13.9
Students in gifted program:	63 / 10.9%
Students in remedial education:	15.8%
Students held back a grade:	0.7%
Total suspensions, pct. in-school:	11 / 63.6%
Offenses:	violence: 10, drugs: *, other: 3
Eligible students, free or reduced lunch:	21.3%
Before / after school program:	Yes / Yes

Students at this school generally go on to:
West Hall Middle

AJC GRADE: ★★★

Georgia Criterion-Referenced Competency Tests - Grade 4
Pct. of students at each level

Read: 48% / 37% / 15%
Math: 23% / 57% / 20%
Lang: 27% / 60% / 13%

☐ Exceeds ▨ Meets ■ Does not meet

Hall County Elementary Schools

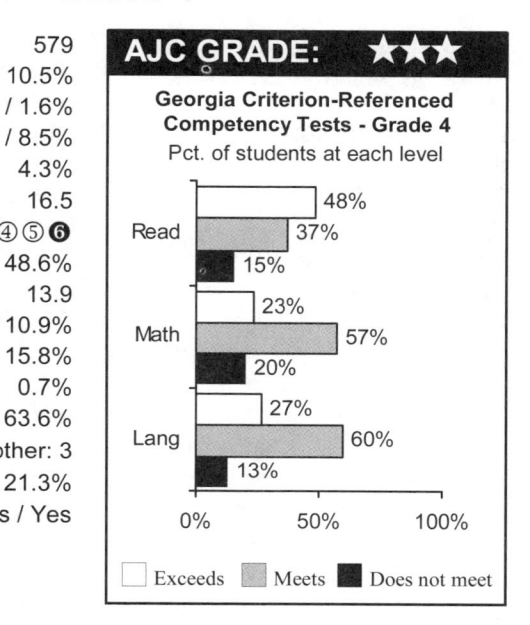

Friendship Elementary School

4450 Friendship Rd, Buford, GA 30519
770-932-1223 · Grades K - 5

Enrollment:	604
White / black / other:	86.9% / 2.3% / 10.8%
Not native English-speaking:	6 / 1.0%
Limited English proficiency:	27 / 4.5%
Student absenteeism:	4.3%
Students per teacher:	15.8
Parent friendliness:	①❷❸④⑤❻
Teachers with advanced degrees:	34.2%
Average years' teaching experience:	7.2
Students in gifted program:	44 / 7.3%
Students in remedial education:	12.6%
Students held back a grade:	0.5%
Total suspensions, pct. in-school:	*
Offenses:	violence: * , drugs: * , other: *
Eligible students, free or reduced lunch:	22.3%
Before / after school program:	No / Yes

Students at this school generally go on to:
C.W. Davis Middle

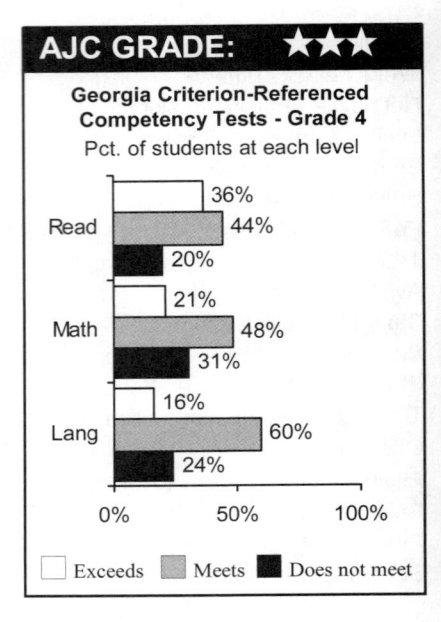

AJC GRADE: ★★★

Georgia Criterion-Referenced Competency Tests - Grade 4
Pct. of students at each level

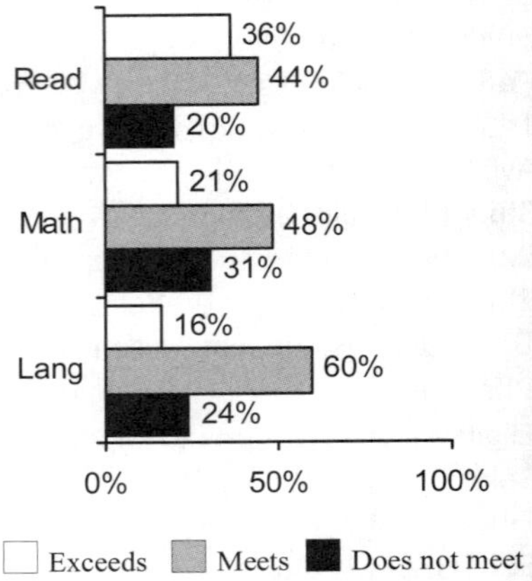
Read
36%
44%
20%
Math
21%
48%
31%
Lang
16%
60%
24%
0%
50%
100%
Exceeds
Meets
Does not meet

Jones Elementary School

50 Sixth St, Gainesville, GA 30504
770-534-3939 · Grades K - 5

Enrollment:	344
White / black / other:	34.9% / 2.0% / 63.1%
Not native English-speaking:	88 / 25.6%
Limited English proficiency:	262 / 76.2%
Student absenteeism:	4.8%
Students per teacher:	11.7
Parent friendliness:	①❷③④⑤❻
Teachers with advanced degrees:	64.5%
Average years' teaching experience:	13.4
Students in gifted program:	5 / 1.5%
Students in remedial education:	33.3%
Students held back a grade:	*
Total suspensions, pct. in-school:	20 / 0.0%
Offenses:	violence: 15, drugs: 1, other: 4
Eligible students, free or reduced lunch:	66.0%
Before / after school program:	Yes / Yes

Students at this school generally go on to:
South Hall, West Hall Middle

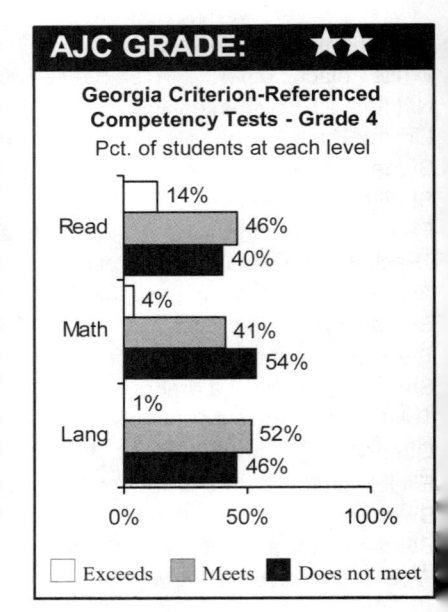

AJC GRADE: ★★

Georgia Criterion-Referenced Competency Tests - Grade 4
Pct. of students at each level

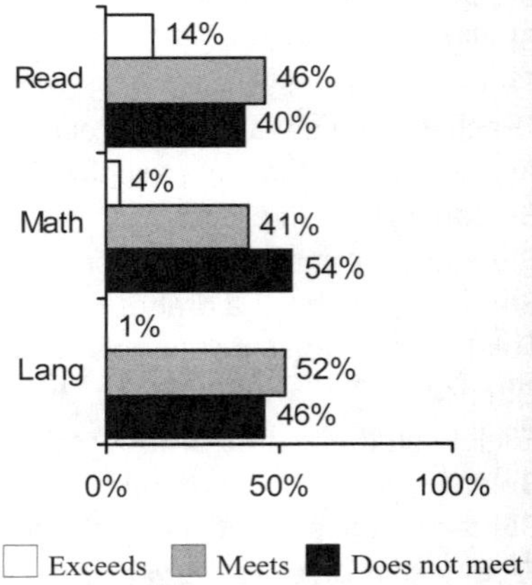
Read
14%
46%
40%
Math
4%
41%
54%
Lang
1%
52%
46%
0%
50%
100%
Exceeds
Meets
Does not meet

Lanier Elementary School

4782 Thompson Bridge Rd, Gainesville, GA 30506
770-532-8781 · Grades K - 5

Enrollment:	598
White / black / other:	89.1% / 1.2% / 9.7%
Not native English-speaking:	5 / 0.8%
Limited English proficiency:	59 / 9.9%
Student absenteeism:	4.1%
Students per teacher:	15.3
Parent friendliness:	① ❷ ❸ ④ ❺ ❻
Teachers with advanced degrees:	65.0%
Average years' teaching experience:	16.1
Students in gifted program:	86 / 14.4%
Students in remedial education:	21.2%
Students held back a grade:	0.5%
Total suspensions, pct. in-school:	24 / 58.3%
Offenses:	violence: 4, drugs: 18, other: 2
Eligible students, free or reduced lunch:	29.7%
Before / after school program:	No / Yes

Students at this school generally go on to:
Chestatee, North Hall Middle

AJC GRADE: ★★

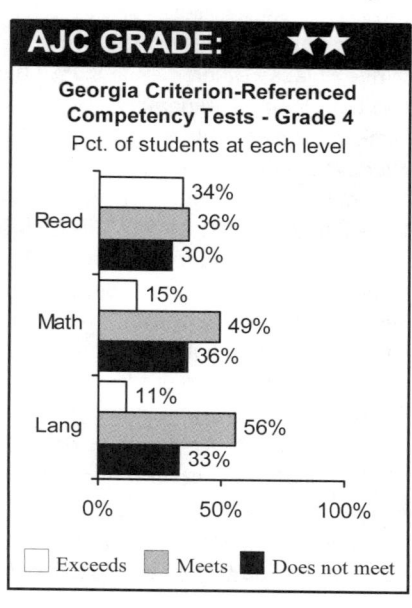

Georgia Criterion-Referenced Competency Tests - Grade 4
Pct. of students at each level

- Read: 34% / 36% / 30%
- Math: 15% / 49% / 36%
- Lang: 11% / 56% / 33%

☐ Exceeds ▨ Meets ■ Does not meet

Lula Elementary School

6130 Chattahoochee St, Lula, GA 30554
770-869-3261 · Grades K - 5

Enrollment:	418
White / black / other:	91.9% / 4.5% / 3.6%
Not native English-speaking:	2 / 0.5%
Limited English proficiency:	4 / 1.0%
Student absenteeism:	4.9%
Students per teacher:	16.0
Parent friendliness:	① ❷ ❸ ④ ⑤ ❻
Teachers with advanced degrees:	85.2%
Average years' teaching experience:	12.1
Students in gifted program:	19 / 4.5%
Students in remedial education:	*
Students held back a grade:	1.4%
Total suspensions, pct. in-school:	8 / 0.0%
Offenses:	violence: 7, drugs: * , other: 1
Eligible students, free or reduced lunch:	27.1%
Before / after school program:	No / Yes

Students at this school generally go on to:
East Hall Middle

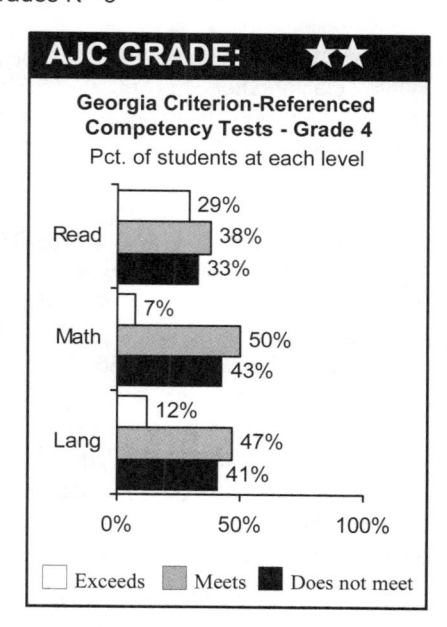

AJC GRADE: ★★

Georgia Criterion-Referenced Competency Tests - Grade 4
Pct. of students at each level

- Read: 29% / 38% / 33%
- Math: 7% / 50% / 43%
- Lang: 12% / 47% / 41%

☐ Exceeds ▨ Meets ■ Does not meet

Hall County Elementary Schools

Lyman Hall Elementary School

2150 Memorial Park Rd, Gainesville, GA 30504
770-534-7044 · Grades K - 5

Enrollment:	596
White / black / other:	6.4% / 0.5% / 93.1%
Not native English-speaking:	186 / 31.2%
Limited English proficiency:	665 / 111.6%
Student absenteeism:	4.3%
Students per teacher:	12.4
Parent friendliness:	①❷❸④❺❻
Teachers with advanced degrees:	50.0%
Average years' teaching experience:	11.5
Students in gifted program:	*
Students in remedial education:	32.5%
Students held back a grade:	4.9%
Total suspensions, pct. in-school:	*
Offenses: violence: *, drugs: *, other: *	
Eligible students, free or reduced lunch:	93.5%
Before / after school program:	Yes / Yes

Students at this school generally go on to:
Chestatee, South Hall, West Hall Middle

AJC GRADE: ★

Georgia Criterion-Referenced Competency Tests - Grade 4
Pct. of students at each level

Read: 4% Exceeds / 27% Meets / 70% Does not meet
Math: 19% Meets / 81% Does not meet
Lang: 28% Meets / 72% Does not meet

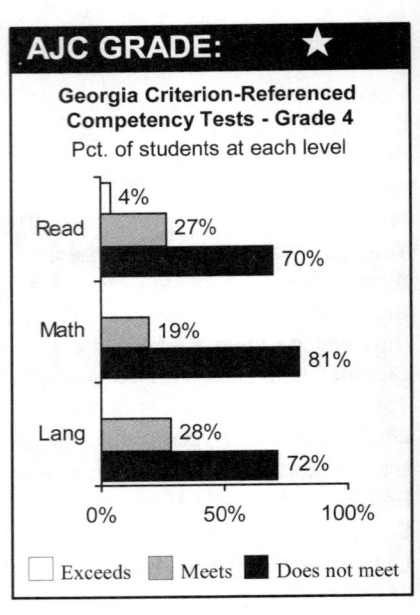

Martin Elementary School

4216 Martin Rd, Flowery Branch, GA 30542
770-965-1578 · Grades K - 5

Enrollment:	649
White / black / other:	69.2% / 8.2% / 22.7%
Not native English-speaking:	55 / 8.5%
Limited English proficiency:	147 / 22.7%
Student absenteeism:	4.6%
Students per teacher:	16.4
Parent friendliness:	①❷❸④❺❻
Teachers with advanced degrees:	47.5%
Average years' teaching experience:	8.5
Students in gifted program:	35 / 5.4%
Students in remedial education:	*
Students held back a grade:	0.9%
Total suspensions, pct. in-school:	2 / 0.0%
Offenses: violence: *, drugs: *, other: 2	
Eligible students, free or reduced lunch:	31.1%
Before / after school program:	No / Yes

Students at this school generally go on to:
C.W. Davis, South Hall Middle

AJC GRADE: ★★

Georgia Criterion-Referenced Competency Tests - Grade 4
Pct. of students at each level

Read: 30% Exceeds / 36% Meets / 34% Does not meet
Math: 9% Exceeds / 52% Meets / 39% Does not meet
Lang: 11% Exceeds / 61% Meets / 28% Does not meet

Hall County Elementary Schools

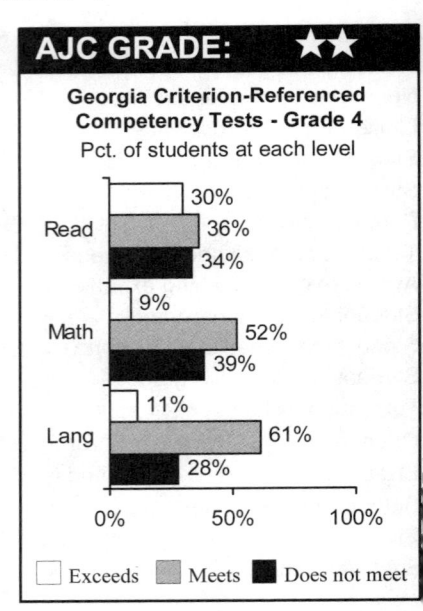

McEver Elementary School

3265 Montgomery Dr, Gainesville, GA 30504
770-534-7473 · Grades K - 5

Enrollment:	454
White / black / other:	55.5% / 1.8% / 42.7%
Not native English-speaking:	38 / 8.4%
Limited English proficiency:	230 / 50.7%
Student absenteeism:	3.3%
Students per teacher:	15.1
Parent friendliness:	① ❷ ❸ ④ ⑤ ❻
Teachers with advanced degrees:	61.3%
Average years' teaching experience:	11.0
Students in gifted program:	56 / 12.3%
Students in remedial education:	*
Students held back a grade:	0.7%
Total suspensions, pct. in-school:	25 / 96.0%
Offenses:	violence: 13, drugs: *, other: 12
Eligible students, free or reduced lunch:	44.4%
Before / after school program:	No / Yes

Students at this school generally go on to:
Chestatee, West Hall Middle

AJC GRADE: ★★★★

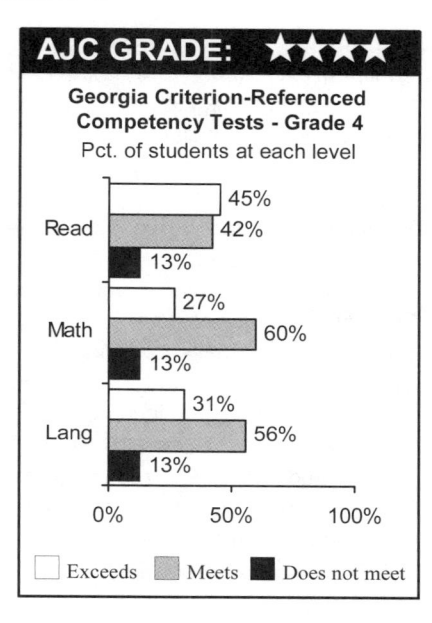

Georgia Criterion-Referenced Competency Tests - Grade 4
Pct. of students at each level

- Read: Exceeds 45%, Meets 42%, Does not meet 13%
- Math: Exceeds 27%, Meets 60%, Does not meet 13%
- Lang: Exceeds 31%, Meets 56%, Does not meet 13%

Mount Vernon Elementary School

4844 Jim Hood Rd, Gainesville, GA 30506
770-983-1760 · Grades K - 5

Enrollment:	693
White / black / other:	92.9% / 0.4% / 6.6%
Not native English-speaking:	8 / 1.2%
Limited English proficiency:	27 / 3.9%
Student absenteeism:	3.9%
Students per teacher:	16.1
Parent friendliness:	① ❷ ❸ ❹ ❺ ❻
Teachers with advanced degrees:	75.0%
Average years' teaching experience:	13.8
Students in gifted program:	107 / 15.4%
Students in remedial education:	*
Students held back a grade:	0.6%
Total suspensions, pct. in-school:	7 / 28.6%
Offenses:	violence: 1, drugs: *, other: 8
Eligible students, free or reduced lunch:	19.2%
Before / after school program:	Yes / Yes

Students at this school generally go on to:
North Hall Middle

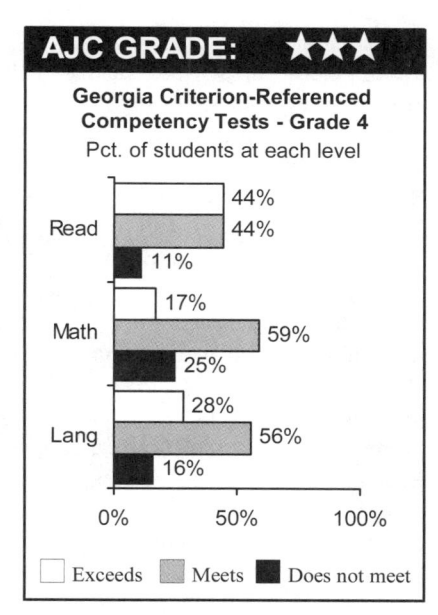

AJC GRADE: ★★★

Georgia Criterion-Referenced Competency Tests - Grade 4
Pct. of students at each level

- Read: Exceeds 44%, Meets 44%, Does not meet 11%
- Math: Exceeds 17%, Meets 59%, Does not meet 25%
- Lang: Exceeds 28%, Meets 56%, Does not meet 16%

Hall County Elementary Schools

Myers Elementary School

2676 Candler Rd, Gainesville, GA 30507
770-536-0814 · Grades K - 5

Enrollment:	693
White / black / other:	33.9% / 9.4% / 56.7%
Not native English-speaking:	163 / 23.5%
Limited English proficiency:	454 / 65.5%
Student absenteeism:	4.3%
Students per teacher:	14.7
Parent friendliness:	① ❷ ❸ ④ ❺ ❻
Teachers with advanced degrees:	54.2%
Average years' teaching experience:	10.4
Students in gifted program:	21 / 3.0%
Students in remedial education:	25.4%
Students held back a grade:	1.3%
Total suspensions, pct. in-school:	15 / 0.0%
Offenses:	violence: 6, drugs: 2, other: 11
Eligible students, free or reduced lunch:	73.9%
Before / after school program:	No / Yes

Students at this school generally go on to:
C.W. Davis, South Hall Middle

AJC GRADE: ★★★

Georgia Criterion-Referenced Competency Tests - Grade 4
Pct. of students at each level

Read — Exceeds: 19%, Meets: 41%, Does not meet: 40%
Math — Exceeds: 5%, Meets: 36%, Does not meet: 59%
Lang — Exceeds: 9%, Meets: 52%, Does not meet: 39%

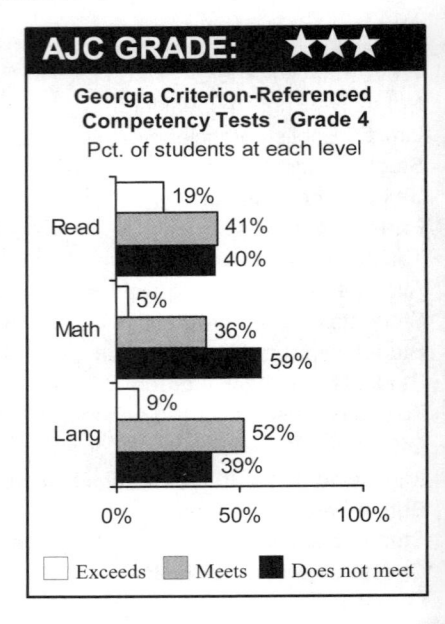

Oakwood Elementary School

4500 Allen St, Oakwood, GA 30566
770-532-1656 · Grades K - 5

Enrollment:	516
White / black / other:	69.6% / 6.0% / 24.4%
Not native English-speaking:	31 / 6.0%
Limited English proficiency:	142 / 27.5%
Student absenteeism:	4.2%
Students per teacher:	14.7
Parent friendliness:	① ② ❸ ④ ❺ ❻
Teachers with advanced degrees:	63.9%
Average years' teaching experience:	13.4
Students in gifted program:	62 / 12.0%
Students in remedial education:	14.5%
Students held back a grade:	1.7%
Total suspensions, pct. in-school:	1 / 0.0%
Offenses:	violence: *, drugs: 1, other: 2
Eligible students, free or reduced lunch:	31.0%
Before / after school program:	Yes / Yes

Students at this school generally go on to:
West Hall Middle

AJC GRADE: ★★★

Georgia Criterion-Referenced Competency Tests - Grade 4
Pct. of students at each level

Read — Exceeds: 49%, Meets: 35%, Does not meet: 15%
Math — Exceeds: 21%, Meets: 49%, Does not meet: 30%
Lang — Exceeds: 21%, Meets: 65%, Does not meet: 14%

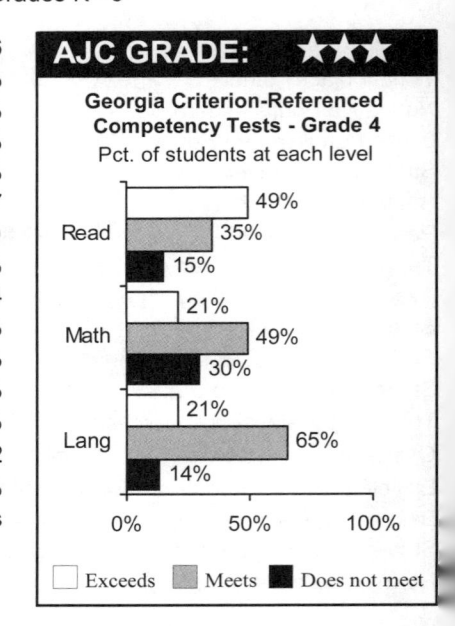

Riverbend Elementary School

1742 Cleveland Hwy, Gainesville, GA 30501
770-534-4141 · Grades K - 5

Enrollment:	467
White / black / other:	77.9% / 1.7% / 20.3%
Not native English-speaking:	45 / 9.6%
Limited English proficiency:	143 / 30.6%
Student absenteeism:	4.2%
Students per teacher:	14.8
Parent friendliness:	① ❷ ❸ ④ ⑤ ❻
Teachers with advanced degrees:	60.6%
Average years' teaching experience:	12.7
Students in gifted program:	28 / 6.0%
Students in remedial education:	16.7%
Students held back a grade:	1.5%
Total suspensions, pct. in-school:	7 / 0.0%
Offenses:	violence: 7, drugs: *, other: *
Eligible students, free or reduced lunch:	36.8%
Before / after school program:	No / Yes

Students at this school generally go on to:
Chestatee, North Hall Middle

AJC GRADE: ★★★

Georgia Criterion-Referenced Competency Tests - Grade 4
Pct. of students at each level

- Read: Exceeds 38%, Meets 34%, Does not meet 28%
- Math: Exceeds 23%, Meets 45%, Does not meet 31%
- Lang: Exceeds 15%, Meets 56%, Does not meet 29%

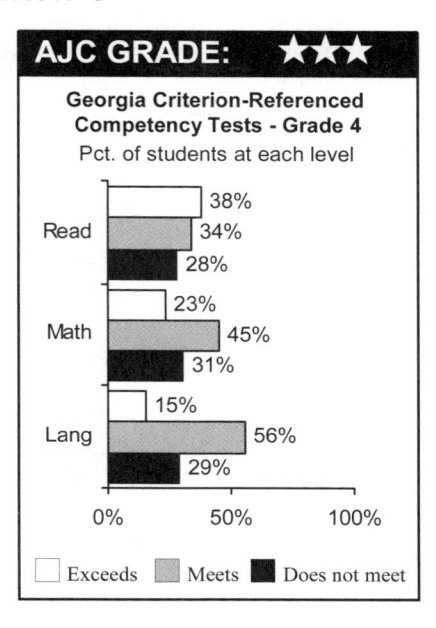

Sardis Elementary School

2805 Sardis Rd, Gainesville, GA 30506
770-532-0104 · Grades K - 5

👎

Enrollment:	615
White / black / other:	81.6% / 0.7% / 17.7%
Not native English-speaking:	38 / 6.2%
Limited English proficiency:	105 / 17.1%
Student absenteeism:	4.4%
Students per teacher:	16.0
Parent friendliness:	① ❷ ❸ ④ ❺ ❻
Teachers with advanced degrees:	75.0%
Average years' teaching experience:	13.4
Students in gifted program:	56 / 9.1%
Students in remedial education:	17.6%
Students held back a grade:	0.3%
Total suspensions, pct. in-school:	7 / 0.0%
Offenses:	violence: 5, drugs: *, other: 2
Eligible students, free or reduced lunch:	31.2%
Before / after school program:	No / Yes

Students at this school generally go on to:
Chestatee Middle

AJC GRADE: ★★

Georgia Criterion-Referenced Competency Tests - Grade 4
Pct. of students at each level

- Read: Exceeds 36%, Meets 29%, Does not meet 35%
- Math: Exceeds 17%, Meets 42%, Does not meet 41%
- Lang: Exceeds 17%, Meets 48%, Does not meet 35%

Hall County Elementary Schools

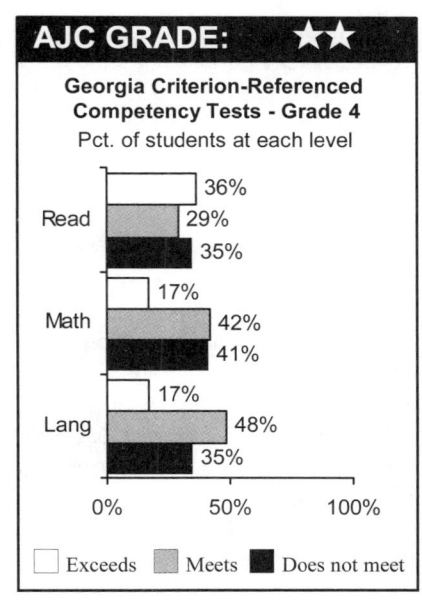

Spout Springs Elementary School

6640 Spout Springs Rd, Flowery Branch, GA 30542
770-967-4860 · Grades K - 5

Enrollment:	581
White / black / other:	80.9% / 6.5% / 12.6%
Not native English-speaking:	7 / 1.2%
Limited English proficiency:	53 / 9.1%
Student absenteeism:	3.7%
Students per teacher:	15.6
Parent friendliness:	① ❷ ❸ ④ ⑤ ❻
Teachers with advanced degrees:	59.5%
Average years' teaching experience:	12.8
Students in gifted program:	30 / 5.2%
Students in remedial education:	15.4%
Students held back a grade:	0.9%
Total suspensions, pct. in-school:	10 / 60.0%
Offenses:	violence: 2, drugs: *, other: 8
Eligible students, free or reduced lunch:	23.1%
Before / after school program:	No / Yes

Students at this school generally go on to:
C.W. Davis Middle

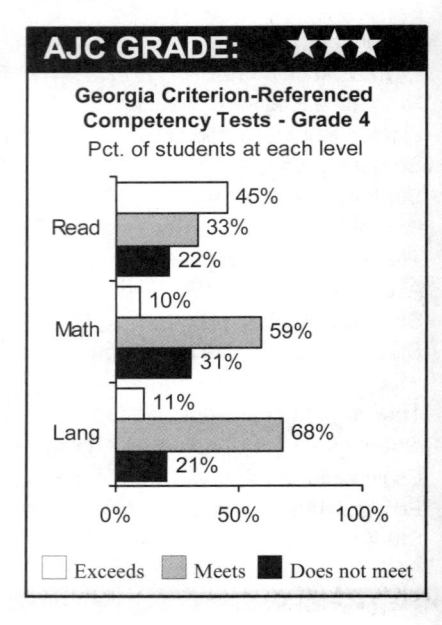

AJC GRADE: ★★★

Georgia Criterion-Referenced Competency Tests - Grade 4
Pct. of students at each level

Read: Exceeds 45%, Meets 33%, Does not meet 22%
Math: Exceeds 10%, Meets 59%, Does not meet 31%
Lang: Exceeds 11%, Meets 68%, Does not meet 21%

Tadmore Elementary School

3278 Gillsville Hwy, Gainesville, GA 30507
770-536-9929 · Grades K - 5

Enrollment:	845
White / black / other:	40.6% / 8.8% / 50.7%
Not native English-speaking:	96 / 11.4%
Limited English proficiency:	468 / 55.4%
Student absenteeism:	4.0%
Students per teacher:	15.5
Parent friendliness:	① ② ❸ ④ ⑤ ❻
Teachers with advanced degrees:	48.2%
Average years' teaching experience:	11.9
Students in gifted program:	24 / 2.8%
Students in remedial education:	24.2%
Students held back a grade:	1.1%
Total suspensions, pct. in-school:	31 / 64.5%
Offenses:	violence: 29, drugs: *, other: 2
Eligible students, free or reduced lunch:	69.2%
Before / after school program:	No / Yes

Students at this school generally go on to:
East Hall Middle

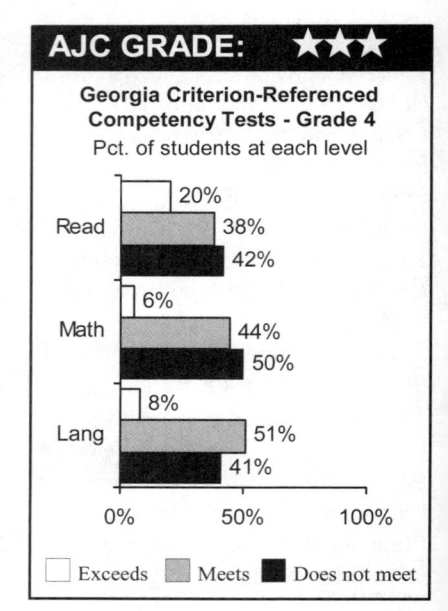

AJC GRADE: ★★★

Georgia Criterion-Referenced Competency Tests - Grade 4
Pct. of students at each level

Read: Exceeds 20%, Meets 38%, Does not meet 42%
Math: Exceeds 6%, Meets 44%, Does not meet 50%
Lang: Exceeds 8%, Meets 51%, Does not meet 41%

Hall County Elementary Schools

Wauka Mountain Elementary School

5850 Brookton Lula Rd, Gainesville, GA 30506
770-983-3221 · Grades K - 5

Enrollment:	400
White / black / other:	94.0% / 1.0% / 5.0%
Not native English-speaking:	2 / 0.5%
Limited English proficiency:	11 / 2.8%
Student absenteeism:	4.6%
Students per teacher:	14.2
Parent friendliness:	① ❷ ❸ ④ ⑤ ❻
Teachers with advanced degrees:	62.1%
Average years' teaching experience:	12.6
Students in gifted program:	58 / 14.5%
Students in remedial education:	2.2%
Students held back a grade:	*
Total suspensions, pct. in-school:	13 / 15.4%
Offenses:	violence: 9, drugs: *, other: 4
Eligible students, free or reduced lunch:	19.2%
Before / after school program:	No / Yes
Students at this school generally go on to:	
North Hall Middle	

AJC GRADE: ★★★

Georgia Criterion-Referenced Competency Tests - Grade 4
Pct. of students at each level

Read: Exceeds 51%, Meets 35%, Does not meet 14%
Math: Exceeds 14%, Meets 68%, Does not meet 17%
Lang: Exceeds 26%, Meets 63%, Does not meet 11%

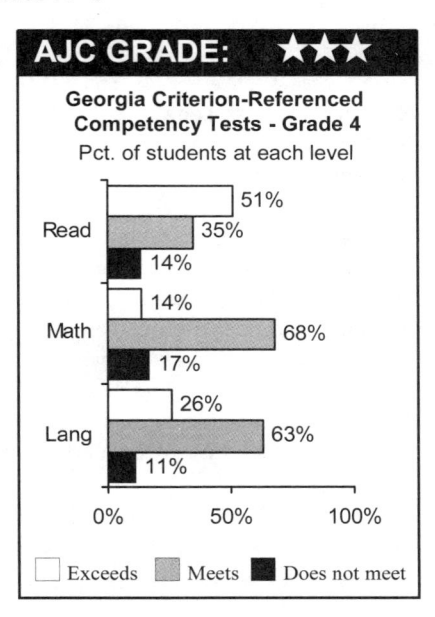

White Sulphur Elementary School

2480 Old Cornelia Hwy, Gainesville, GA 30507
770-532-0945 · Grades K - 5

Enrollment:	545
White / black / other:	51.7% / 25.9% / 22.4%
Not native English-speaking:	46 / 8.4%
Limited English proficiency:	140 / 25.7%
Student absenteeism:	4.4%
Students per teacher:	14.8
Parent friendliness:	① ❷ ❸ ④ ⑤ ❻
Teachers with advanced degrees:	56.4%
Average years' teaching experience:	13.1
Students in gifted program:	20 / 3.7%
Students in remedial education:	33.3%
Students held back a grade:	0.7%
Total suspensions, pct. in-school:	28 / 0.0%
Offenses:	violence: 15, drugs: 2, other: 11
Eligible students, free or reduced lunch:	63.2%
Before / after school program:	Yes / Yes
Students at this school generally go on to:	
East Hall Middle	

AJC GRADE: ★★★

Georgia Criterion-Referenced Competency Tests - Grade 4
Pct. of students at each level

Read: Exceeds 11%, Meets 47%, Does not meet 42%
Math: Exceeds 6%, Meets 48%, Does not meet 47%
Lang: Exceeds 4%, Meets 61%, Does not meet 35%

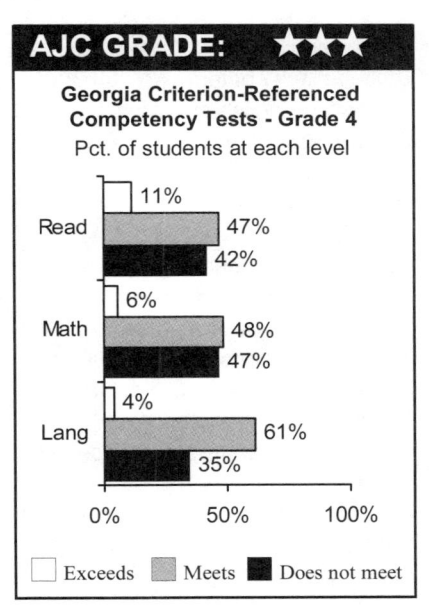

Chestatee Middle School

2740 Fran Mar Dr, Gainesville, GA 30506
770-297-6270 · Grades 6 - 8

Enrollment:	770
White / black / other:	75.3% / 0.8% / 23.9%
Not native English-speaking:	66 / 8.6%
Student absenteeism:	5.3%
Students per teacher:	14.5
Parent friendliness:	①❷❸④⑤❻
Teachers with advanced degrees:	52.8%
Average years' teaching experience:	7.5
Students in gifted program:	98 / 12.7%
Students held back a grade:	0.5%
Total suspensions and expulsions:	166
Suspensions only, pct. in-school:	166 / 42.8%
Offenses:	violence: 124, drugs: 3, other: 39
Eligible students, free or reduced lunch:	38.4%
Number of dropouts:	1 / 0.1%
Pct. 8th-graders w/ basic computer skills:	90.0%

Students at this school generally go on to:
Chestatee High

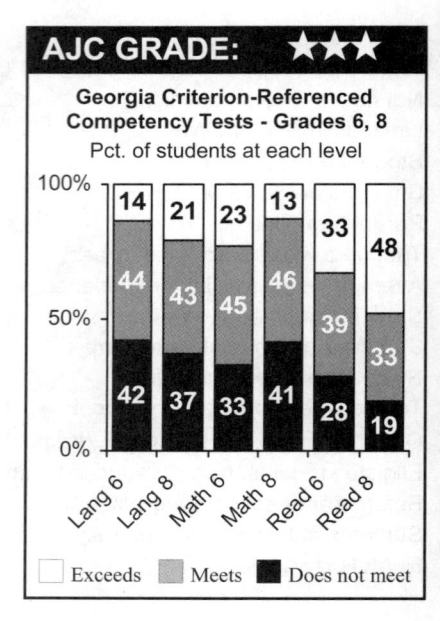

AJC GRADE: ★★★

Georgia Criterion-Referenced Competency Tests - Grades 6, 8
Pct. of students at each level

	Lang 6	Lang 8	Math 6	Math 8	Read 6	Read 8
Exceeds	14	21	23	13	33	48
Meets	44	43	45	46	39	33
Does not meet	42	37	33	41	28	19

Davis Middle School

4335 Falcon Pkwy, Flowery Branch, GA 30542
770-965-3020 · Grades 6 - 8

Enrollment:	788
White / black / other:	83.8% / 6.0% / 10.3%
Not native English-speaking:	22 / 2.8%
Student absenteeism:	5.8%
Students per teacher:	16.4
Parent friendliness:	①❷❸④⑤❻
Teachers with advanced degrees:	42.0%
Average years' teaching experience:	9.0
Students in gifted program:	93 / 11.8%
Students held back a grade:	0.9%
Total suspensions and expulsions:	123
Suspensions only, pct. in-school:	122 / 74.6%
Offenses:	violence: 71, drugs: 8, other: 44
Eligible students, free or reduced lunch:	24.1%
Number of dropouts:	1 / 0.1%
Pct. 8th-graders w/ basic computer skills:	90.0%

Students at this school generally go on to:
Flowery Branch High

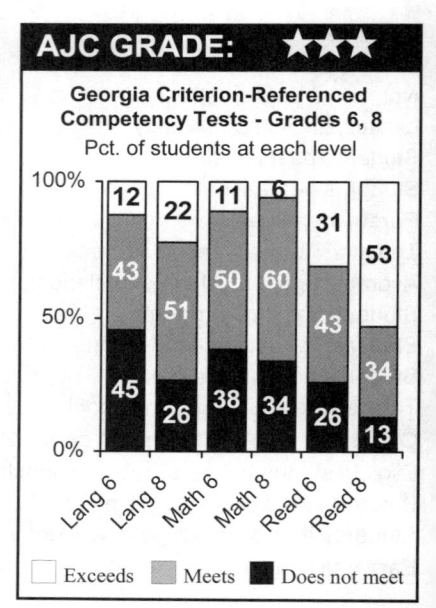

AJC GRADE: ★★★

Georgia Criterion-Referenced Competency Tests - Grades 6, 8
Pct. of students at each level

	Lang 6	Lang 8	Math 6	Math 8	Read 6	Read 8
Exceeds	12	22	11	6	31	53
Meets	43	51	50	60	43	34
Does not meet	45	26	38	34	26	13

Hall County Middle Schools

East Hall Middle School

4120 E Hall Rd, Gainesville, GA 30507
770-531-9457 · Grades 6 - 8

Enrollment:	808
White / black / other:	63.9% / 19.4% / 16.7%
Not native English-speaking:	46 / 5.7%
Student absenteeism:	5.2%
Students per teacher:	16.2
Parent friendliness:	① ❷ ❸ ④ ⑤ ❻
Teachers with advanced degrees:	48.0%
Average years' teaching experience:	10.7
Students in gifted program:	71 / 8.8%
Students held back a grade:	0.7%
Total suspensions and expulsions:	277
Suspensions only, pct. in-school:	277 / 52.7%
Offenses:	violence: 70, drugs: 10, other: 197
Eligible students, free or reduced lunch:	53.8%
Number of dropouts:	*
Pct. 8th-graders w/ basic computer skills:	100.0%

Students at this school generally go on to:
East Hall High

AJC GRADE: ★★★

Georgia Criterion-Referenced Competency Tests - Grades 6, 8
Pct. of students at each level

	Lang 6	Lang 8	Math 6	Math 8	Read 6	Read 8
Exceeds	9	17	14	2	27	40
Meets	42	38	50	32	38	33
Does not meet	49	45	36	66	35	27

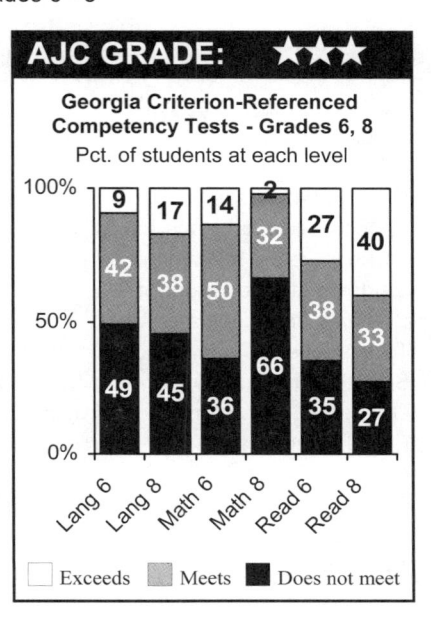

North Hall Middle School

4956 Rilla Rd, Gainesville, GA 30506
770-983-9749 · Grades 6 - 8

Enrollment:	872
White / black / other:	94.8% / 0.6% / 4.6%
Not native English-speaking:	13 / 1.5%
Student absenteeism:	4.5%
Students per teacher:	15.3
Parent friendliness:	❶ ❷ ❸ ④ ⑤ ❻
Teachers with advanced degrees:	71.9%
Average years' teaching experience:	14.0
Students in gifted program:	179 / 20.5%
Students held back a grade:	*
Total suspensions and expulsions:	108
Suspensions only, pct. in-school:	106 / 35.8%
Offenses:	violence: 65, drugs: 9, other: 35
Eligible students, free or reduced lunch:	18.6%
Number of dropouts:	2 / 0.2%
Pct. 8th-graders w/ basic computer skills:	100.0%

Students at this school generally go on to:
North Hall High

AJC GRADE: ★★★

Georgia Criterion-Referenced Competency Tests - Grades 6, 8
Pct. of students at each level

	Lang 6	Lang 8	Math 6	Math 8	Read 6	Read 8
Exceeds	22	27	29	10	49	64
Meets	56	51	54	58	39	25
Does not meet	22	22	18	31	13	10

Hall County Middle Schools

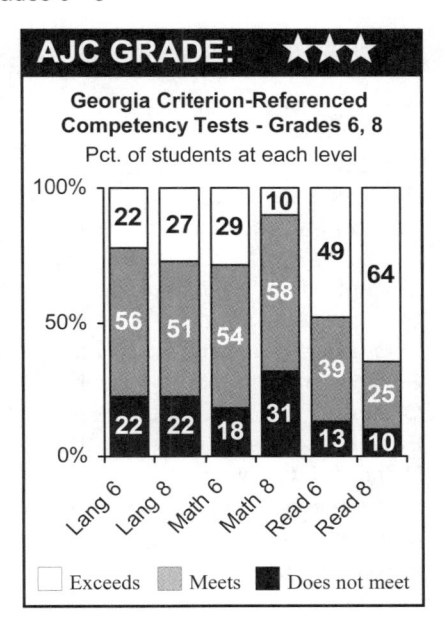

South Hall Middle School

3215 Poplar Springs Rd, Gainesville, GA 30507
770-532-4416 · Grades 6 - 8

Enrollment:	817
White / black / other:	62.7% / 6.6% / 30.7%
Not native English-speaking:	88 / 10.8%
Student absenteeism:	5.1%
Students per teacher:	15.4
Parent friendliness:	① ❷ ❸ ④ ⑤ ❻
Teachers with advanced degrees:	66.0%
Average years' teaching experience:	13.4
Students in gifted program:	75 / 9.2%
Students held back a grade:	0.9%
Total suspensions and expulsions:	182
Suspensions only, pct. in-school:	182 / 40.1%
Offenses: violence: 64, drugs: 12, other: 131	
Eligible students, free or reduced lunch:	48.6%
Number of dropouts:	1 / 0.1%
Pct. 8th-graders w/ basic computer skills: 100.0%	
Students at this school generally go on to:	
Johnson High	

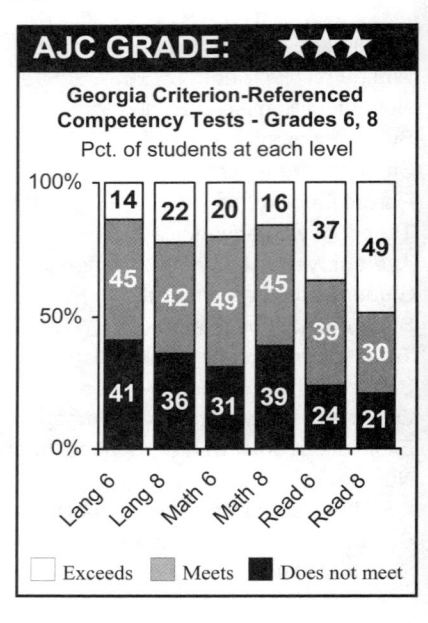

AJC GRADE: ★★★

Georgia Criterion-Referenced Competency Tests - Grades 6, 8
Pct. of students at each level

	Lang 6	Lang 8	Math 6	Math 8	Read 6	Read 8
Exceeds	14	22	20	16	37	49
Meets	45	42	49	45	39	30
Does not meet	41	36	31	39	24	21

West Hall Middle School

5470 McEver Rd, Oakwood, GA 30566
770-967-4871 · Grades 6 - 8

Enrollment:	835
White / black / other:	73.3% / 4.4% / 22.3%
Not native English-speaking:	67 / 8.0%
Student absenteeism:	5.1%
Students per teacher:	16.4
Parent friendliness:	① ❷ ❸ ④ ⑤ ❻
Teachers with advanced degrees:	62.7%
Average years' teaching experience:	12.7
Students in gifted program:	113 / 13.5%
Students held back a grade:	0.5%
Total suspensions and expulsions:	107
Suspensions only, pct. in-school:	107 / 82.2%
Offenses: violence: 70, drugs: 8, other: 32	
Eligible students, free or reduced lunch:	30.9%
Number of dropouts:	*
Pct. 8th-graders w/ basic computer skills: 100.0%	
Students at this school generally go on to:	
West Hall High	

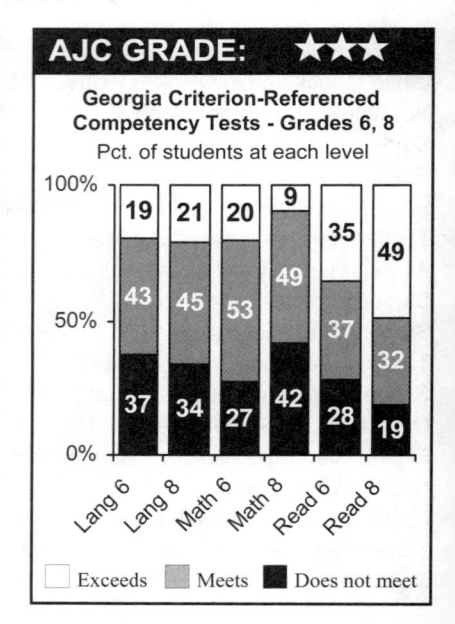

AJC GRADE: ★★★

Georgia Criterion-Referenced Competency Tests - Grades 6, 8
Pct. of students at each level

	Lang 6	Lang 8	Math 6	Math 8	Read 6	Read 8
Exceeds	19	21	20	9	35	49
Meets	43	45	53	49	37	32
Does not meet	37	34	27	42	28	19

Hall County Middle Schools

East Hall High School

3534 E Hall Rd, Gainesville, GA 30507
770-536-9921 · Grades 9 - 12

Enrollment:	923
White / black / other:	67.4% / 17.7% / 15.0%
Not native English-speaking:	36 / 3.9%
Limited English proficiency:	161 / 17.4%
Student absenteeism:	7.6%
Students per teacher:	15.6
Parent friendliness:	① ❷ ❸ ④ ⑤ ❻
Students in gifted program:	*
Students in remedial education:	*
High school completion rate:	70.0%
Students held back a grade:	9.5%
Number of dropouts:	74 / 7.0%
Students in alternative programs:	7 / 0.8%
Students in special education:	111 / 12.0%
Eligible students, free or reduced lunch:	32.2%
Total suspensions and expulsions:	114
Suspensions only, pct. in-school:	114 / 23.7%
Drugs/alcohol-related offenses:	8
Violence-related offenses:	46
Firearms-related offenses:	*
Vandalism-related offenses:	11
Theft-related offenses:	10
All other disciplinary offenses:	39
Teachers with advanced degrees:	62.5%
Average years' teaching experience:	13.0

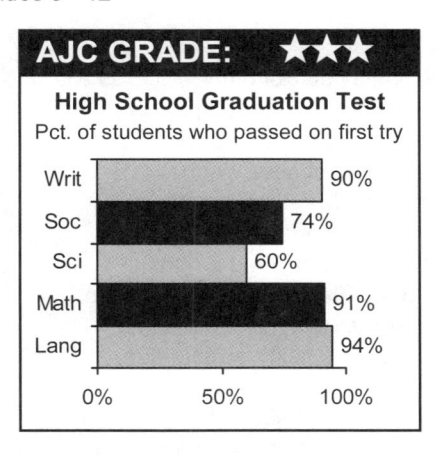

AJC GRADE: ★★★

High School Graduation Test
Pct. of students who passed on first try

- Writ: 90%
- Soc: 74%
- Sci: 60%
- Math: 91%
- Lang: 94%

GHSA classification:	7-AAA

Interscholastic sports offered:
BB, BS, CC, CL, FB, GO, RI, SB, SO, TE, TF, WR

Advanced Placement (AP) Exams
Students tested:	*
Tests taken:	*
Pct. of test scores 3 or higher (1 - 5 scale):	*

Languages other than English taught:
French, Spanish

2000-2001 high school graduates: 133

College prep/vocational diplomas:	20.3%
College prep endorsement diplomas:	29.3%
Vocational endorsement diplomas:	37.6%
General high school diplomas:	0.0%
Special education diplomas:	2.3%
Certificates of attendance (no diploma):	10.5%

Of the 2000-2001 graduates, 45.1% were eligible for the HOPE scholarship.

Of the 1999-2000 graduates, 27 attended a Georgia public college or university. Of those, 55% met the school's minimum academic requirements.

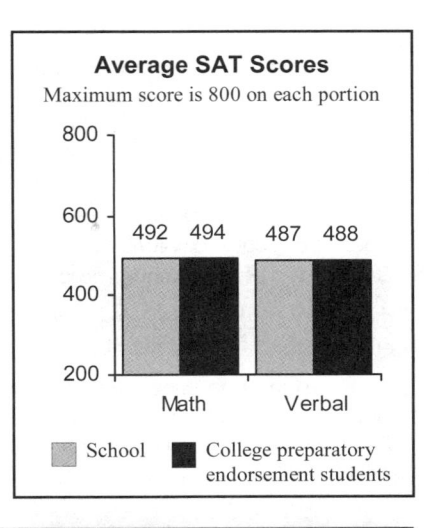

Average SAT Scores
Maximum score is 800 on each portion

- Math: School 492, College preparatory endorsement students 494
- Verbal: School 487, College preparatory endorsement students 488

The Atlanta Journal-Constitution / Page 431

Hall County High Schools

Johnson High School

3305 Poplar Springs Rd, Gainesville, GA 30507
770-536-2394 · Grades 9 - 12

Enrollment:	1,178
White / black / other:	59.8% / 6.6% / 33.5%
Not native English-speaking:	191 / 16.2%
Limited English proficiency:	467 / 39.6%
Student absenteeism:	5.8%
Students per teacher:	17.5
Parent friendliness:	① ❷ ❸ ❹ ❺ ❻
Students in gifted program:	50 / 4.2%
Students in remedial education:	*
High school completion rate:	81.3%
Students held back a grade:	7.3%
Number of dropouts:	49 / 3.8%
Students in alternative programs:	2 / 0.2%
Students in special education:	132 / 11.2%
Eligible students, free or reduced lunch:	35.8%
Total suspensions and expulsions:	158
Suspensions only, pct. in-school:	158 / 39.2%
Drugs/alcohol-related offenses:	16
Violence-related offenses:	61
Firearms-related offenses:	2
Vandalism-related offenses:	14
Theft-related offenses:	2
All other disciplinary offenses:	63
Teachers with advanced degrees:	69.8%
Average years' teaching experience:	14.3

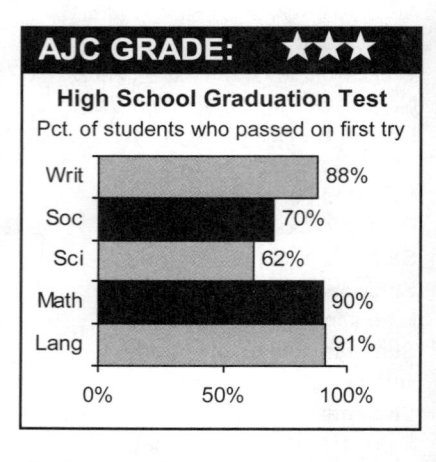

AJC GRADE: ★★★

High School Graduation Test
Pct. of students who passed on first try

- Writ: 88%
- Soc: 70%
- Sci: 62%
- Math: 90%
- Lang: 91%

GHSA classification: 7-AAA
Interscholastic sports offered:
BB, BS, CC, CL, FB, GO, SB, SO, TE, TF, VB, WR

Advanced Placement (AP) Exams
- Students tested: 6
- Tests taken: 6
- Pct. of test scores 3 or higher (1 - 5 scale): 66.7%

Languages other than English taught:
French, German, Spanish

2000-2001 high school graduates: 157

College prep/vocational diplomas:	5.7%
College prep endorsement diplomas:	22.3%
Vocational endorsement diplomas:	51.0%
General high school diplomas:	0.0%
Special education diplomas:	2.5%
Certificates of attendance (no diploma):	18.5%

Of the 2000-2001 graduates, 36.3% were eligible for the HOPE scholarship.

Of the 1999-2000 graduates, 58 attended a Georgia public college or university. Of those, 79% met the school's minimum academic requirements.

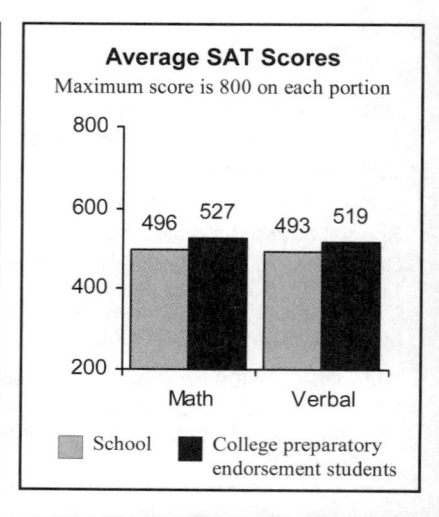

Average SAT Scores
Maximum score is 800 on each portion

- Math — School: 496, College preparatory endorsement students: 527
- Verbal — School: 493, College preparatory endorsement students: 519

The Atlanta Journal-Constitution / Page 432

Hall County High Schools

North Hall High School

4885 Mount Vernon Rd, Gainesville, GA 30506
770-983-7331 · Grades 9 - 12

Enrollment:	1,557
White / black / other:	94.2% / 0.5% / 5.3%
Not native English-speaking:	23 / 1.5%
Limited English proficiency:	90 / 5.8%
Student absenteeism:	5.9%
Students per teacher:	17.0
Parent friendliness:	❶❷❸④❺❻
Students in gifted program:	83 / 5.3%
Students in remedial education:	*
High school completion rate:	82.9%
Students held back a grade:	8.1%
Number of dropouts:	59 / 3.5%
Students in alternative programs:	2 / 0.1%
Students in special education:	144 / 9.2%
Eligible students, free or reduced lunch:	11.4%
Total suspensions and expulsions:	144
Suspensions only, pct. in-school:	144 / 38.2%
Drugs/alcohol-related offenses:	15
Violence-related offenses:	58
Firearms-related offenses:	4
Vandalism-related offenses:	6
Theft-related offenses:	10
All other disciplinary offenses:	51
Teachers with advanced degrees:	69.0%
Average years' teaching experience:	14.8

AJC GRADE: ★★★

High School Graduation Test
Pct. of students who passed on first try

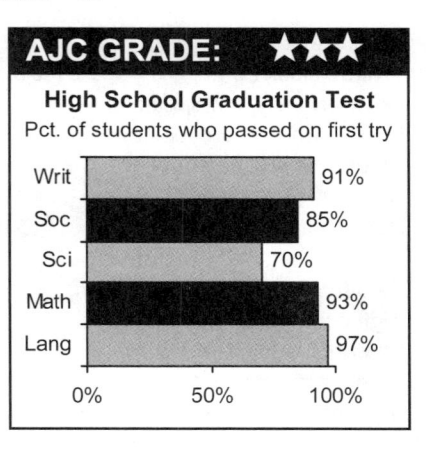

- Writ: 91%
- Soc: 85%
- Sci: 70%
- Math: 93%
- Lang: 97%

GHSA classification: 7-AAA
Interscholastic sports offered:
BB, BS, CC, CL, FB, GO, SB, SO, SW, TE, TF, VB, WR

Advanced Placement (AP) Exams
Students tested:	36
Tests taken:	52
Pct. of test scores 3 or higher (1 - 5 scale):	40.4%

Languages other than English taught:
French, Spanish

2000-2001 high school graduates: 266

College prep/vocational diplomas:	13.9%
College prep endorsement diplomas:	50.4%
Vocational endorsement diplomas:	33.5%
General high school diplomas:	0.0%
Special education diplomas:	2.3%
Certificates of attendance (no diploma):	0.0%

Of the 2000-2001 graduates, 65.0% were eligible for the HOPE scholarship.

Of the 1999-2000 graduates, 121 attended a Georgia public college or university. Of those, 85% met the school's minimum academic requirements.

Average SAT Scores
Maximum score is 800 on each portion

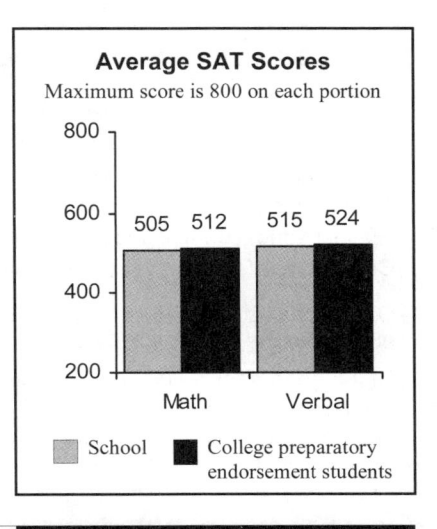

	Math	Verbal
School	505	515
College preparatory endorsement students	512	524

Hall County High Schools

West Hall High School

5500 McEver Rd, Oakwood, GA 30566
770-967-9826 · Grades 9 - 12

Enrollment:	1,543
White / black / other:	82.8% / 5.5% / 11.7%
Not native English-speaking:	48 / 3.1%
Limited English proficiency:	99 / 6.4%
Student absenteeism:	6.5%
Students per teacher:	17.9
Parent friendliness:	❶❷❸④❺❻
Students in gifted program:	29 / 1.9%
Students in remedial education:	*
High school completion rate:	88.0%
Students held back a grade:	6.9%
Number of dropouts:	47 / 2.8%
Students in alternative programs:	5 / 0.3%
Students in special education:	142 / 9.2%
Eligible students, free or reduced lunch:	13.0%
Total suspensions and expulsions:	252
Suspensions only, pct. in-school:	252 / 55.6%
Drugs/alcohol-related offenses:	23
Violence-related offenses:	52
Firearms-related offenses:	1
Vandalism-related offenses:	9
Theft-related offenses:	5
All other disciplinary offenses:	164
Teachers with advanced degrees:	64.6%
Average years' teaching experience:	14.0

AJC GRADE: ★★★

High School Graduation Test
Pct. of students who passed on first try

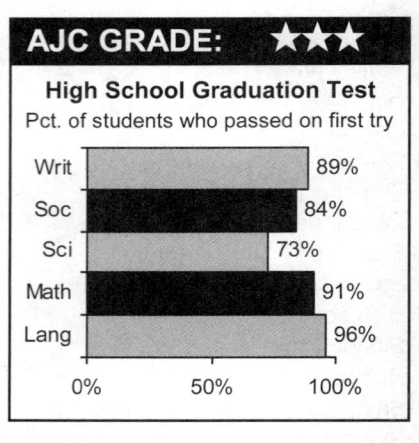

- Writ: 89%
- Soc: 84%
- Sci: 73%
- Math: 91%
- Lang: 96%

GHSA classification:	7-AAA
Interscholastic sports offered:	
BB, BS, CC, CL, FB, GO, SB, SO, TE, TF, VB, WR	

Advanced Placement (AP) Exams

Students tested:	38
Tests taken:	49
Pct. of test scores 3 or higher (1 - 5 scale):	57.1%

Languages other than English taught:
French, German, Spanish

2000-2001 high school graduates: 228

College prep/vocational diplomas:	14.5%
College prep endorsement diplomas:	57.0%
Vocational endorsement diplomas:	24.1%
General high school diplomas:	0.0%
Special education diplomas:	2.6%
Certificates of attendance (no diploma):	1.8%

Of the 2000-2001 graduates, 68.4% were eligible for the HOPE scholarship.

Of the 1999-2000 graduates, 108 attended a Georgia public college or university. Of those, 77% met the school's minimum academic requirements.

Average SAT Scores
Maximum score is 800 on each portion

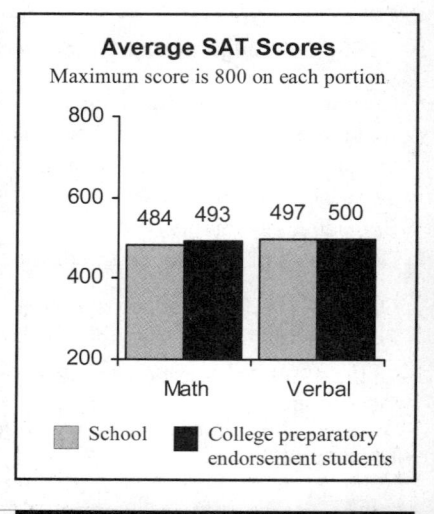

- Math: School 484, College preparatory endorsement students 493
- Verbal: School 497, College preparatory endorsement students 500

Hall County High Schools

AJC ranking of Hall County Schools

ELEMENTARY SCHOOLS

AJC Star Grade: ★★★★

McEver Elementary

AJC Star Grade: ★★★

Flowery Branch Elementary
Friendship Elementary
Mount Vernon Elementary
Myers Elementary
Oakwood Elementary
Riverbend Elementary
Spout Springs Elementary
Tadmore Elementary
Wauka Mountain Elementary
White Sulphur Elementary

AJC Star Grade: ★★

Chestnut Mountain Elementary
Jones Elementary
Lanier Elementary
Lula Elementary
Martin Elementary
Sardis Elementary

AJC Star Grade: ★

Lyman Hall Elementary

MIDDLE SCHOOLS

AJC Star Grade: ★★★

Chestatee Middle
Davis Middle
East Hall Middle
North Hall Middle
South Hall Middle
West Hall Middle

HIGH SCHOOLS

AJC Star Grade: ★★★

East Hall High
Johnson High
North Hall High
West Hall High

The Atlanta Journal-Constitution / Page 435

Hall County Public Schools

Henry County Public Schools

396 E Tomlinson St, McDonough, GA 30253
Phone: 770-957-6601 · Fax: 770-957-7971
http://www.henry.k12.ga.us

The following pages provide detailed information on every school in the Henry County school district. An asterisk (*) means the value of the data was zero or was not reported by the school district. A complete list of schools ranked by The Atlanta Journal-Constitution's star rating system follows the detailed school reports.

District enrollment:	23,551
White / black / other:	75.7% / 19.6% / 4.7%
Not native English-speaking:	126 / 0.5%
Expenditure per student (general fund):	$5,534
Students per teacher:	16.8
Teachers with advanced degrees:	46.4%
Average years, teaching experience:	10.7
Average teacher salary:	$41,758.91
Students in gifted program:	2,030 / 8.6%
Students held back a grade:	460 / 2.0%
Eligible students, free or reduced lunch:	4,420 / 18.7%
Number of dropouts (grades 9-12):	301 / 4.2%
High school completion rate:	81.7%
Graduates, pct. eligible for HOPE scholarships:	1,180 / 60.8%
Average combined SAT score (maximum 1,600):	1,002
Pct. of 11th-graders passing the Georgia High School Graduation Tests on first try:	71%
Percent of children 5 to 17 years of age living in poverty (2000 Census estimate):	5.3%

Austin Road Elementary School

50 Austin Rd, Stockbridge, GA 30281
770-389-6556 · Grades K - 5

Enrollment:	613
White / black / other:	56.0% / 41.9% / 2.1%
Not native English-speaking:	*
Limited English proficiency:	2 / 0.3%
Student absenteeism:	3.7%
Students per teacher:	16.6
Parent friendliness:	① ❷ ❸ ④ ⑤ ❻
Teachers with advanced degrees:	59.5%
Average years' teaching experience:	11.4
Students in gifted program:	33 / 5.4%
Students in remedial education:	*
Students held back a grade:	*
Total suspensions, pct. in-school:	23 / 0.0%
Offenses: violence: 28, drugs: *, other: 26	
Eligible students, free or reduced lunch:	15.6%
Before / after school program:	No / Yes
Students at this school generally go on to:	
Austin Road Middle	

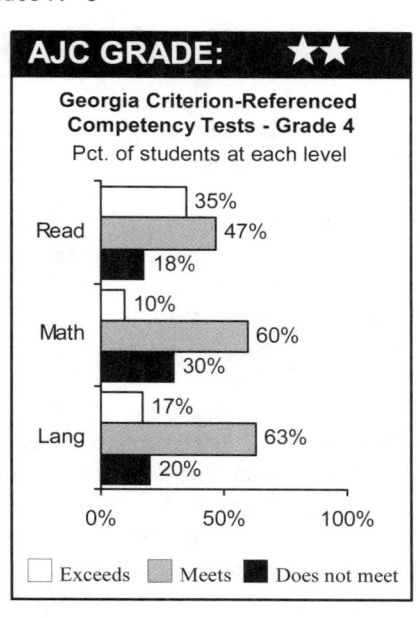

AJC GRADE: ★★

Georgia Criterion-Referenced Competency Tests - Grade 4
Pct. of students at each level

Read: Exceeds 35%, Meets 47%, Does not meet 18%
Math: Exceeds 10%, Meets 60%, Does not meet 30%
Lang: Exceeds 17%, Meets 63%, Does not meet 20%

Cotton Indian Elementary School

1201 Old Conyers Rd, Stockbridge, GA 30281
770-474-9983 · Grades K - 5

Enrollment:	556
White / black / other:	92.4% / 5.0% / 2.5%
Not native English-speaking:	4 / 0.7%
Limited English proficiency:	6 / 1.1%
Student absenteeism:	4.6%
Students per teacher:	15.8
Parent friendliness:	① ❷ ❸ ④ ⑤ ❻
Teachers with advanced degrees:	36.1%
Average years' teaching experience:	11.8
Students in gifted program:	33 / 5.9%
Students in remedial education:	*
Students held back a grade:	3.4%
Total suspensions, pct. in-school:	8 / 0.0%
Offenses: violence: 8, drugs: *, other: *	
Eligible students, free or reduced lunch:	11.2%
Before / after school program:	No / Yes
Students at this school generally go on to:	
Stockbridge Middle	

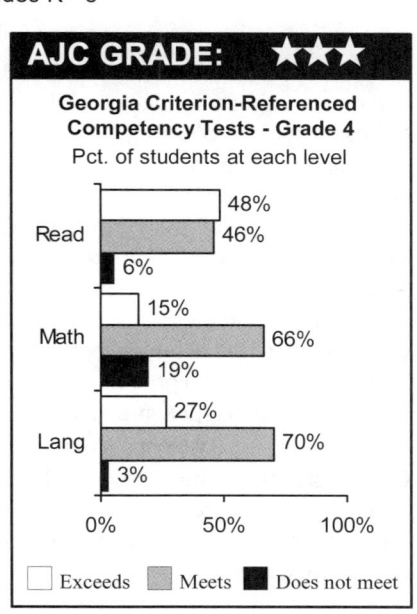

AJC GRADE: ★★★

Georgia Criterion-Referenced Competency Tests - Grade 4
Pct. of students at each level

Read: Exceeds 48%, Meets 46%, Does not meet 6%
Math: Exceeds 15%, Meets 66%, Does not meet 19%
Lang: Exceeds 27%, Meets 70%, Does not meet 3%

The Atlanta Journal-Constitution / Page 437

Henry County Elementary Schools

East Lake Elementary School

199 E Lake Rd, McDonough, GA 30252
678-583-8947 · Grades K - 5

Enrollment:	914
White / black / other:	92.5% / 5.0% / 2.5%
Not native English-speaking:	1 / 0.1%
Limited English proficiency:	8 / 0.9%
Student absenteeism:	4.0%
Students per teacher:	18.2
Parent friendliness:	①❷③④⑤❻
Teachers with advanced degrees:	82.4%
Average years' teaching experience:	13.8
Students in gifted program:	53 / 5.8%
Students in remedial education:	*
Students held back a grade:	0.7%
Total suspensions, pct. in-school:	8 / 0.0%
Offenses:	violence: 16, drugs: *, other: 3
Eligible students, free or reduced lunch:	15.0%
Before / after school program:	No / Yes

Students at this school generally go on to:
Union Grove Middle

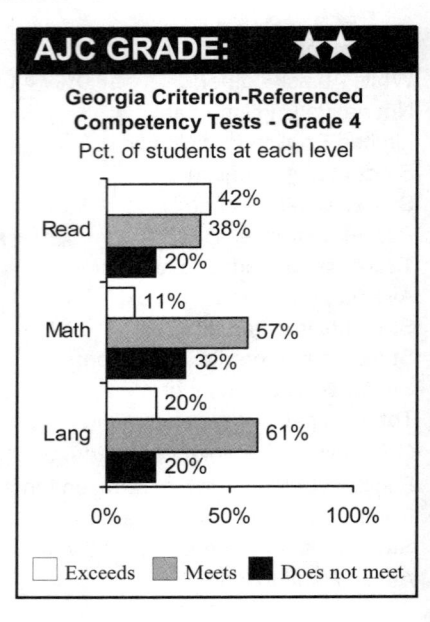

AJC GRADE: ★★

Georgia Criterion-Referenced Competency Tests - Grade 4
Pct. of students at each level

Read: 42% Exceeds / 38% Meets / 20% Does not meet
Math: 11% Exceeds / 57% Meets / 32% Does not meet
Lang: 20% Exceeds / 61% Meets / 20% Does not meet

Fairview Elementary School

458 Fairview Rd, Stockbridge, GA 30281
770-474-8265 · Grades K - 5

Enrollment:	696
White / black / other:	52.6% / 43.7% / 3.7%
Not native English-speaking:	*
Limited English proficiency:	3 / 0.4%
Student absenteeism:	4.0%
Students per teacher:	17.8
Parent friendliness:	①❷❸④⑤⑥
Teachers with advanced degrees:	43.6%
Average years' teaching experience:	8.9
Students in gifted program:	32 / 4.6%
Students in remedial education:	*
Students held back a grade:	1.0%
Total suspensions, pct. in-school:	7 / 0.0%
Offenses:	violence: 3, drugs: *, other: 6
Eligible students, free or reduced lunch:	26.0%
Before / after school program:	No / Yes

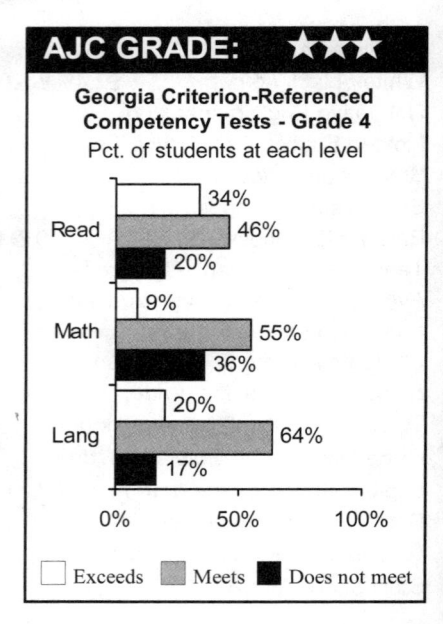

Students at this school generally go on to:
Austin Road Middle

AJC GRADE: ★★★

Georgia Criterion-Referenced Competency Tests - Grade 4
Pct. of students at each level

Read: 34% Exceeds / 46% Meets / 20% Does not meet
Math: 9% Exceeds / 55% Meets / 36% Does not meet
Lang: 20% Exceeds / 64% Meets / 17% Does not meet

Henry County Elementary Schools

Hampton Elementary School

10 Central Ave, Hampton, GA 30228
770-946-4345 · Grades K - 5

Enrollment:	711
White / black / other:	84.1% / 13.6% / 2.3%
Not native English-speaking:	4 / 0.6%
Limited English proficiency:	5 / 0.7%
Student absenteeism:	5.4%
Students per teacher:	16.1
Parent friendliness:	① ❷ ❸ ❹ ❺ ❻
Teachers with advanced degrees:	46.7%
Average years' teaching experience:	11.6
Students in gifted program:	15 / 2.1%
Students in remedial education:	*
Students held back a grade:	*
Total suspensions, pct. in-school:	8 / 0.0%
Offenses:	violence: 7, drugs: *, other: 1
Eligible students, free or reduced lunch:	38.7%
Before / after school program:	Yes / Yes

Students at this school generally go on to:
Luella Middle

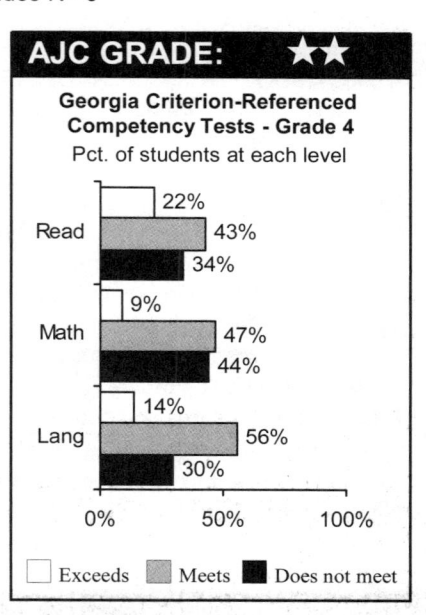

AJC GRADE: ★★

Georgia Criterion-Referenced Competency Tests - Grade 4
Pct. of students at each level

Read: Exceeds 22%, Meets 43%, Does not meet 34%
Math: Exceeds 9%, Meets 47%, Does not meet 44%
Lang: Exceeds 14%, Meets 56%, Does not meet 30%

Hickory Flat Elementary School

841 Brannan Rd, McDonough, GA 30253
770-898-0107 · Grades K - 5

Enrollment:	894
White / black / other:	67.9% / 22.1% / 10.0%
Not native English-speaking:	9 / 1.0%
Limited English proficiency:	28 / 3.1%
Student absenteeism:	4.8%
Students per teacher:	16.2
Parent friendliness:	❶ ❷ ❸ ④ ⑤ ❻
Teachers with advanced degrees:	39.3%
Average years' teaching experience:	8.1
Students in gifted program:	51 / 5.7%
Students in remedial education:	*
Students held back a grade:	0.9%
Total suspensions, pct. in-school:	20 / 0.0%
Offenses:	violence: 31, drugs: *, other: 109
Eligible students, free or reduced lunch:	19.1%
Before / after school program:	No / Yes

Students at this school generally go on to:
Eagle's Landing, Union Grove Middle

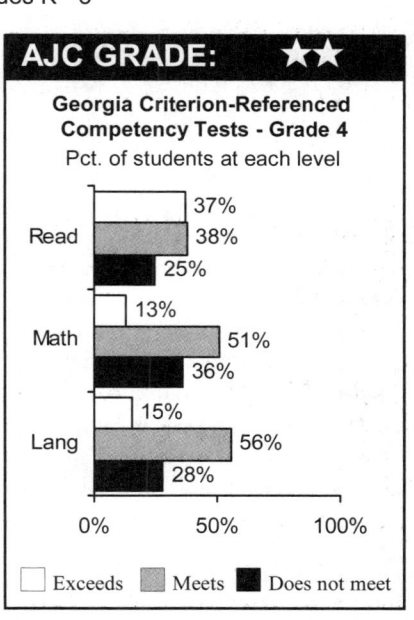

AJC GRADE: ★★

Georgia Criterion-Referenced Competency Tests - Grade 4
Pct. of students at each level

Read: Exceeds 37%, Meets 38%, Does not meet 25%
Math: Exceeds 13%, Meets 51%, Does not meet 36%
Lang: Exceeds 15%, Meets 56%, Does not meet 28%

Henry County Elementary Schools

Locust Grove Elementary School

95 L G Griffin Rd, Locust Grove, GA 30248
770-957-5416 · Grades K - 5

Enrollment:	772
White / black / other:	84.5% / 12.6% / 3.0%
Not native English-speaking:	*
Limited English proficiency:	8 / 1.0%
Student absenteeism:	5.1%
Students per teacher:	16.1
Parent friendliness:	① ❷ ❸ ④ ❺ ❻
Teachers with advanced degrees:	38.8%
Average years' teaching experience:	10.6
Students in gifted program:	62 / 8.0%
Students in remedial education:	*
Students held back a grade:	0.5%
Total suspensions, pct. in-school:	8 / 0.0%
Offenses: violence: 2, drugs: * , other: 98	
Eligible students, free or reduced lunch:	30.4%
Before / after school program:	Yes / Yes
Students at this school generally go on to:	
Luella Middle	

AJC GRADE: ★★★

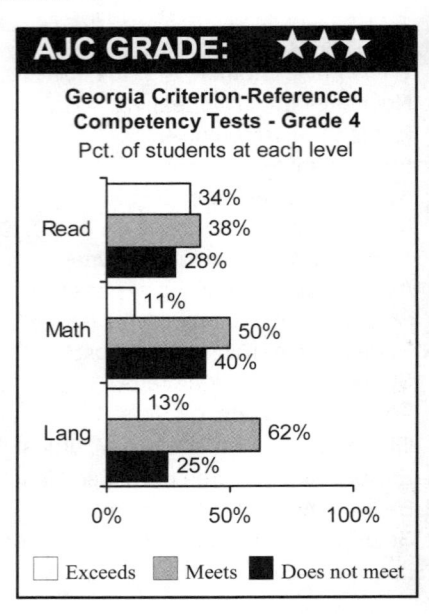

Georgia Criterion-Referenced Competency Tests - Grade 4
Pct. of students at each level

- Read: Exceeds 34%, Meets 38%, Does not meet 28%
- Math: Exceeds 11%, Meets 50%, Does not meet 40%
- Lang: Exceeds 13%, Meets 62%, Does not meet 25%

☐ Exceeds ▨ Meets ■ Does not meet

Mount Carmel Elementary School

2450 Mount Carmel Rd, Hampton, GA 30228
770-897-9799 · Grades K - 5

Enrollment:	580
White / black / other:	89.1% / 9.1% / 1.7%
Not native English-speaking:	*
Limited English proficiency:	5 / 0.9%
Student absenteeism:	4.8%
Students per teacher:	15.3
Parent friendliness:	① ❷ ❸ ④ ⑤ ❻
Teachers with advanced degrees:	55.3%
Average years' teaching experience:	11.2
Students in gifted program:	34 / 5.9%
Students in remedial education:	*
Students held back a grade:	1.4%
Total suspensions, pct. in-school:	1 / 0.0%
Offenses: violence: * , drugs: * , other: 6	
Eligible students, free or reduced lunch:	17.2%
Before / after school program:	No / Yes
Students at this school generally go on to:	
Eagle's Landing, Luella Middle	

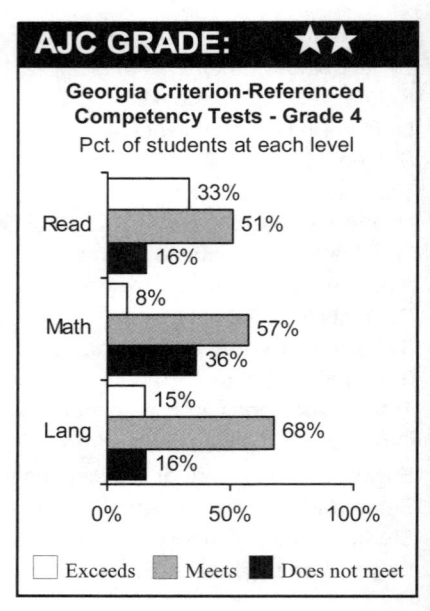

AJC GRADE: ★★

Georgia Criterion-Referenced Competency Tests - Grade 4
Pct. of students at each level

- Read: Exceeds 33%, Meets 51%, Does not meet 16%
- Math: Exceeds 8%, Meets 57%, Does not meet 36%
- Lang: Exceeds 15%, Meets 68%, Does not meet 16%

☐ Exceeds ▨ Meets ■ Does not meet

Henry County Elementary Schools

Oakland Elementary School

551 Highway 81 W, McDonough, GA 30253
770-954-1901 · Grades K - 5

Enrollment:	719
White / black / other:	67.3% / 27.5% / 5.1%
Not native English-speaking:	3 / 0.4%
Limited English proficiency:	18 / 2.5%
Student absenteeism:	4.7%
Students per teacher:	15.9
Parent friendliness:	①②❸④❺❻
Teachers with advanced degrees:	28.3%
Average years' teaching experience:	9.0
Students in gifted program:	15 / 2.1%
Students in remedial education:	*
Students held back a grade:	0.4%
Total suspensions, pct. in-school:	9 / 0.0%
Offenses: violence: 5, drugs: *, other: 14	
Eligible students, free or reduced lunch:	36.8%
Before / after school program:	No / Yes

Students at this school generally go on to:
Henry County, Luella Middle

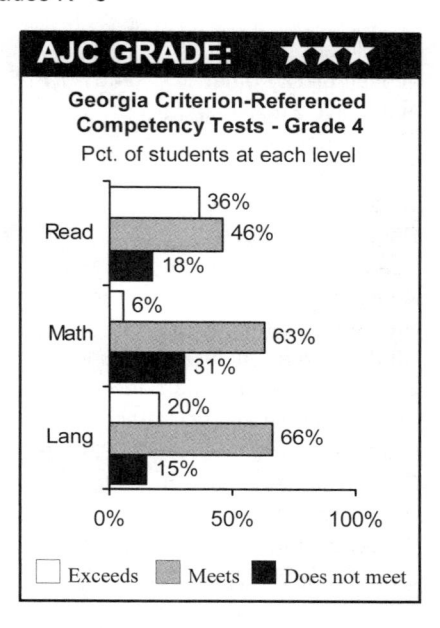

AJC GRADE: ★★★

Georgia Criterion-Referenced Competency Tests - Grade 4
Pct. of students at each level

Read: Exceeds 36%, Meets 46%, Does not meet 18%
Math: Exceeds 6%, Meets 63%, Does not meet 31%
Lang: Exceeds 20%, Meets 66%, Does not meet 15%

Ola Elementary School

278 N Ola Rd, McDonough, GA 30252
770-957-5777 · Grades K - 5

Enrollment:	934
White / black / other:	92.0% / 5.7% / 2.4%
Not native English-speaking:	4 / 0.4%
Limited English proficiency:	9 / 1.0%
Student absenteeism:	5.0%
Students per teacher:	19.0
Parent friendliness:	①②❸④⑤❻
Teachers with advanced degrees:	46.0%
Average years' teaching experience:	9.9
Students in gifted program:	41 / 4.4%
Students in remedial education:	*
Students held back a grade:	0.1%
Total suspensions, pct. in-school:	14 / 0.0%
Offenses: violence: 12, drugs: *, other: 8	
Eligible students, free or reduced lunch:	13.8%
Before / after school program:	No / Yes

Students at this school generally go on to:
Henry, Luella, Union Grove Middle

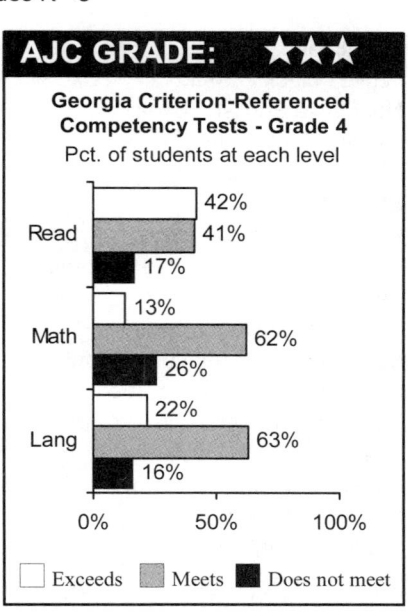

AJC GRADE: ★★★

Georgia Criterion-Referenced Competency Tests - Grade 4
Pct. of students at each level

Read: Exceeds 42%, Meets 41%, Does not meet 17%
Math: Exceeds 13%, Meets 62%, Does not meet 26%
Lang: Exceeds 22%, Meets 63%, Does not meet 16%

The Atlanta Journal-Constitution / Page 441

Henry County Elementary Schools

Pate's Creek Elementary School

1309 Jodeco Rd, Stockbridge, GA 30281
770-389-8819 · Grades K - 5

Enrollment:	767
White / black / other:	64.8% / 24.0% / 11.2%
Not native English-speaking:	7 / 0.9%
Limited English proficiency:	26 / 3.4%
Student absenteeism:	3.9%
Students per teacher:	16.8
Parent friendliness:	①❷❸④⑤❻
Teachers with advanced degrees:	42.6%
Average years' teaching experience:	7.9
Students in gifted program:	61 / 8.0%
Students in remedial education:	*
Students held back a grade:	0.1%
Total suspensions, pct. in-school:	11 / 0.0%
Offenses:	violence: 9, drugs: *, other: 4
Eligible students, free or reduced lunch:	13.8%
Before / after school program:	No / Yes

Students at this school generally go on to:
Eagle's Landing Middle

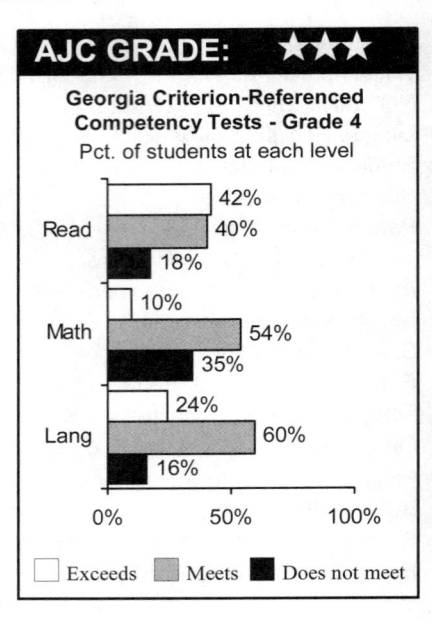

AJC GRADE: ★★★

Georgia Criterion-Referenced
Competency Tests - Grade 4
Pct. of students at each level

Read: Exceeds 42%, Meets 40%, Does not meet 18%
Math: Exceeds 10%, Meets 54%, Does not meet 35%
Lang: Exceeds 24%, Meets 60%, Does not meet 16%

Pleasant Grove Elementary School

150 Reagan Rd, Stockbridge, GA 30281
770-898-0176 · Grades K - 5

Enrollment:	606
White / black / other:	87.3% / 9.4% / 3.3%
Not native English-speaking:	3 / 0.5%
Limited English proficiency:	3 / 0.5%
Student absenteeism:	4.2%
Students per teacher:	15.8
Parent friendliness:	①❷❸④❺❻
Teachers with advanced degrees:	47.5%
Average years' teaching experience:	14.8
Students in gifted program:	34 / 5.6%
Students in remedial education:	*
Students held back a grade:	0.2%
Total suspensions, pct. in-school:	*
Offenses:	violence: *, drugs: *, other: *
Eligible students, free or reduced lunch:	11.9%
Before / after school program:	Yes / Yes

Students at this school generally go on to:
Union Grove Middle

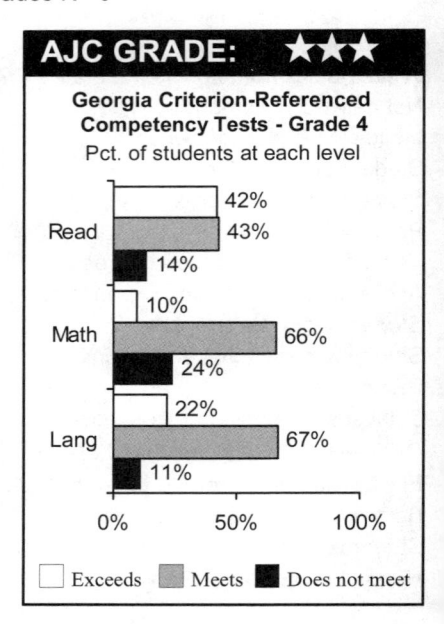

AJC GRADE: ★★★

Georgia Criterion-Referenced
Competency Tests - Grade 4
Pct. of students at each level

Read: Exceeds 42%, Meets 43%, Does not meet 14%
Math: Exceeds 10%, Meets 66%, Does not meet 24%
Lang: Exceeds 22%, Meets 67%, Does not meet 11%

The Atlanta Journal-Constitution / Page 442

Henry County Elementary Schools

Smith-Barnes Elementary School

147 Tye St, Stockbridge, GA 30281
770-474-4066 · Grades 4 - 5

Enrollment:	428
White / black / other:	70.3% / 22.4% / 7.2%
Not native English-speaking:	11 / 2.6%
Limited English proficiency:	18 / 4.2%
Student absenteeism:	4.7%
Students per teacher:	14.6
Parent friendliness:	① ❷ ❸ ④ ⑤ ❻
Teachers with advanced degrees:	46.7%
Average years' teaching experience:	9.1
Students in gifted program:	15 / 3.5%
Students in remedial education:	*
Students held back a grade:	*
Total suspensions, pct. in-school:	28 / 0.0%
Offenses: violence: 35, drugs: *, other: 70	
Eligible students, free or reduced lunch:	51.2%
Before / after school program:	Yes / Yes

Students at this school generally go on to:
Austin Road, Eagle's Landing, Stockbridge Middle

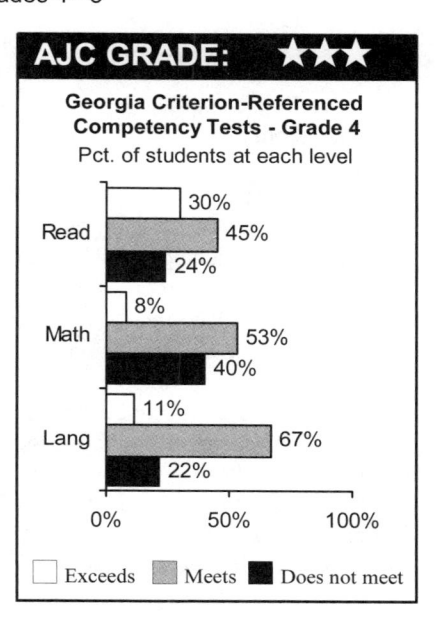

AJC GRADE: ★★★

Georgia Criterion-Referenced Competency Tests - Grade 4
Pct. of students at each level

Read: Exceeds 30%, Meets 45%, Does not meet 24%
Math: Exceeds 8%, Meets 53%, Does not meet 40%
Lang: Exceeds 11%, Meets 67%, Does not meet 22%

Wesley Lakes Elementary School

2200 McDonough Pkwy, McDonough, GA 30253
770-914-1889 · Grades K - 5

Enrollment:	794
White / black / other:	69.8% / 24.7% / 5.5%
Not native English-speaking:	6 / 0.8%
Limited English proficiency:	11 / 1.4%
Student absenteeism:	4.7%
Students per teacher:	16.5
Parent friendliness:	❶ ❷ ❸ ④ ❺ ❻
Teachers with advanced degrees:	57.1%
Average years' teaching experience:	12.6
Students in gifted program:	31 / 3.9%
Students in remedial education:	*
Students held back a grade:	0.5%
Total suspensions, pct. in-school:	*
Offenses: violence: 7, drugs: *, other: 6	
Eligible students, free or reduced lunch:	24.4%
Before / after school program:	No / Yes

Students at this school generally go on to:
Eagle's Landing, Henry County Middle

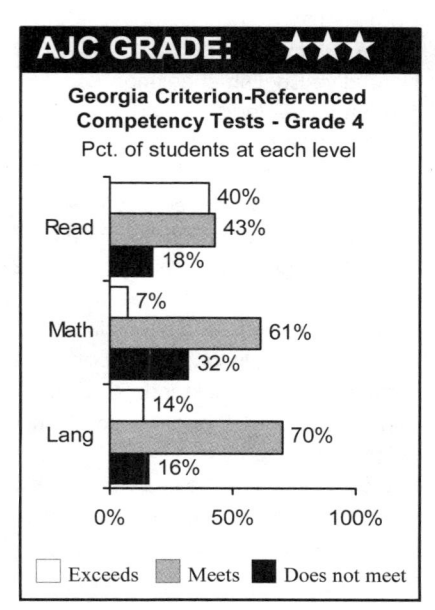

AJC GRADE: ★★★

Georgia Criterion-Referenced Competency Tests - Grade 4
Pct. of students at each level

Read: Exceeds 40%, Meets 43%, Does not meet 18%
Math: Exceeds 7%, Meets 61%, Does not meet 32%
Lang: Exceeds 14%, Meets 70%, Does not meet 16%

Henry County Elementary Schools

Austin Road Middle School

100 Austin Rd, Stockbridge, GA 30281
770-507-5407 · Grades 6 - 8

Enrollment:	796
White / black / other:	59.4% / 37.8% / 2.8%
Not native English-speaking:	5 / 0.6%
Student absenteeism:	4.4%
Students per teacher:	16.2
Parent friendliness:	①❷❸④⑤❻
Teachers with advanced degrees:	48.0%
Average years' teaching experience:	11.4
Students in gifted program:	135 / 17.0%
Students held back a grade:	4.3%
Total suspensions and expulsions:	58
Suspensions only, pct. in-school:	58 / 62.1%
Offenses:	violence: 30, drugs: 4, other: 55
Eligible students, free or reduced lunch:	18.7%
Number of dropouts:	*
Pct. 8th-graders w/ basic computer skills:	100.0%

Students at this school generally go on to:
Stockbridge High

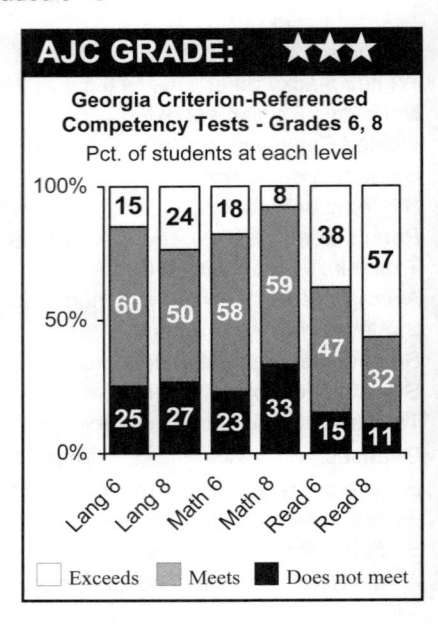

AJC GRADE: ★★★

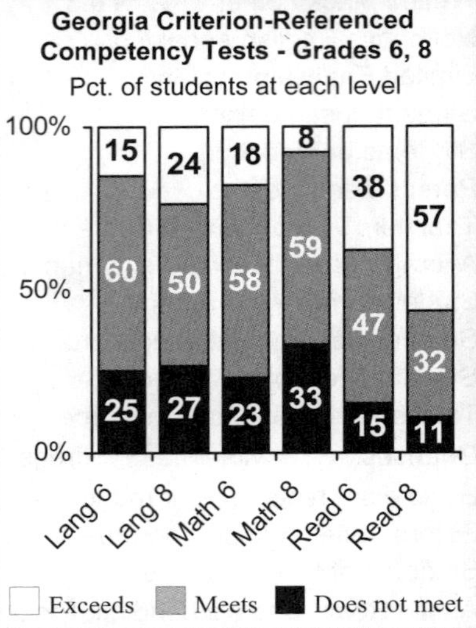
Georgia Criterion-Referenced Competency Tests - Grades 6, 8
Pct. of students at each level
100%
50%
0%
15
24
18
8
38
57
60
50
58
59
47
32
25
27
23
33
15
11
Lang 6
Lang 8
Math 6
Math 8
Read 6
Read 8
Exceeds
Meets
Does not meet

Eagle's Landing Middle School

295 Tunis Rd, McDonough, GA 30253
770-914-8189 · Grades 6 - 8

Enrollment:	1,222
White / black / other:	71.3% / 19.9% / 8.8%
Not native English-speaking:	3 / 0.2%
Student absenteeism:	5.1%
Students per teacher:	17.4
Parent friendliness:	❶❷❸④❺❻
Teachers with advanced degrees:	45.1%
Average years' teaching experience:	11.3
Students in gifted program:	279 / 22.8%
Students held back a grade:	0.3%
Total suspensions and expulsions:	91
Suspensions only, pct. in-school:	91 / 78.0%
Offenses:	violence: 54, drugs: 1, other: 88
Eligible students, free or reduced lunch:	14.4%
Number of dropouts:	*
Pct. 8th-graders w/ basic computer skills:	80.0%

Students at this school generally go on to:
Eagle's Landing High

AJC GRADE: ★★★

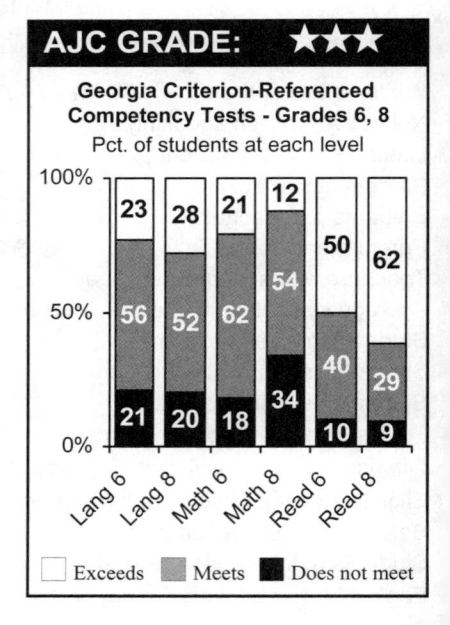

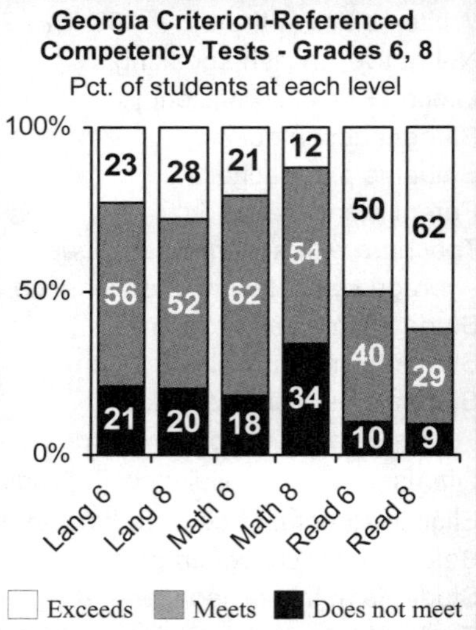
Georgia Criterion-Referenced Competency Tests - Grades 6, 8
Pct. of students at each level
100%
50%
0%
23
28
21
12
50
62
56
52
62
54
40
29
21
20
18
34
10
9
Lang 6
Lang 8
Math 6
Math 8
Read 6
Read 8
Exceeds
Meets
Does not meet

Henry County Middle School

166 Holly Smith Dr, McDonough, GA 30253
770-957-3945 · Grades 6 - 8

Enrollment:	996
White / black / other:	67.1% / 28.2% / 4.7%
Not native English-speaking:	7 / 0.7%
Student absenteeism:	6.0%
Students per teacher:	17.7
Parent friendliness:	❶❷❸④❺❻
Teachers with advanced degrees:	36.8%
Average years' teaching experience:	12.6
Students in gifted program:	135 / 13.6%
Students held back a grade:	1.3%
Total suspensions and expulsions:	108
Suspensions only, pct. in-school:	105 / 24.8%
Offenses: violence: 76, drugs: *, other: 115	
Eligible students, free or reduced lunch:	30.6%
Number of dropouts:	1 / 0.1%
Pct. 8th-graders w/ basic computer skills:	98.0%
Students at this school generally go on to:	
Eagle's Landing, Henry County High	

AJC GRADE: ★★★

Georgia Criterion-Referenced Competency Tests - Grades 6, 8
Pct. of students at each level

	Lang 6	Lang 8	Math 6	Math 8	Read 6	Read 8
Exceeds	11	20	10	6	34	50
Meets	53	49	58	45	46	35
Does not meet	36	31	31	48	20	15

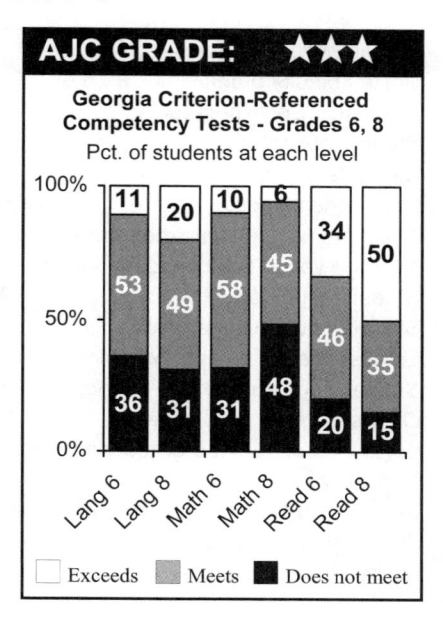

Luella Middle School

2075 Hampton Locust Grove Rd, Locust Grove, GA 30248
678-583-8919 · Grades 6 - 8

Enrollment:	982
White / black / other:	85.2% / 12.3% / 2.4%
Not native English-speaking:	6 / 0.6%
Student absenteeism:	5.9%
Students per teacher:	18.1
Parent friendliness:	①❷❸④❺❻
Teachers with advanced degrees:	32.7%
Average years' teaching experience:	8.0
Students in gifted program:	144 / 14.7%
Students held back a grade:	1.5%
Total suspensions and expulsions:	208
Suspensions only, pct. in-school:	208 / 48.6%
Offenses: violence: 122, drugs: 12, other: 185	
Eligible students, free or reduced lunch:	25.2%
Number of dropouts:	*
Pct. 8th-graders w/ basic computer skills:	96.0%
Students at this school generally go on to:	
Henry County High	

AJC GRADE: ★★★

Georgia Criterion-Referenced Competency Tests - Grades 6, 8
Pct. of students at each level

	Lang 6	Lang 8	Math 6	Math 8	Read 6	Read 8
Exceeds	17	17	12	6	35	52
Meets	49	52	55	51	44	33
Does not meet	34	31	33	43	21	15

Henry County Middle Schools

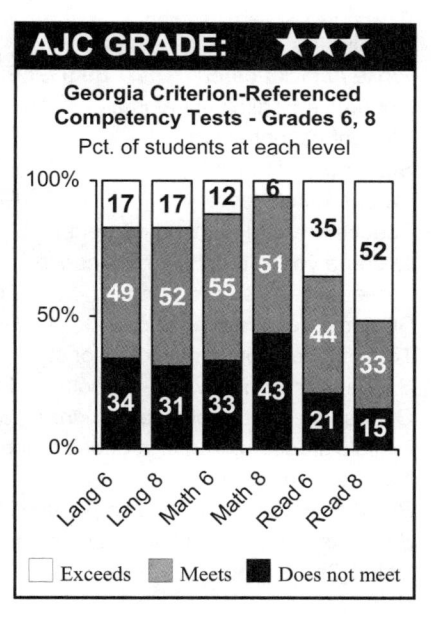

Stockbridge Middle School

533 Old Conyers Rd, Stockbridge, GA 30281
770-474-5710 · Grades 6 - 8

Enrollment:	668
White / black / other:	80.5% / 15.4% / 4.0%
Not native English-speaking:	3 / 0.4%
Student absenteeism:	6.0%
Students per teacher:	17.0
Parent friendliness:	① ❷ ❸ ④ ❺ ❻
Teachers with advanced degrees:	37.5%
Average years' teaching experience:	9.6
Students in gifted program:	92 / 13.8%
Students held back a grade:	3.7%
Total suspensions and expulsions:	43
Suspensions only, pct. in-school:	37 / 21.6%
Offenses:	violence: 38, drugs: 3, other: 46
Eligible students, free or reduced lunch:	20.7%
Number of dropouts:	*
Pct. 8th-graders w/ basic computer skills:	100.0%

Students at this school generally go on to:
Eagle's Landing, Stockbridge High

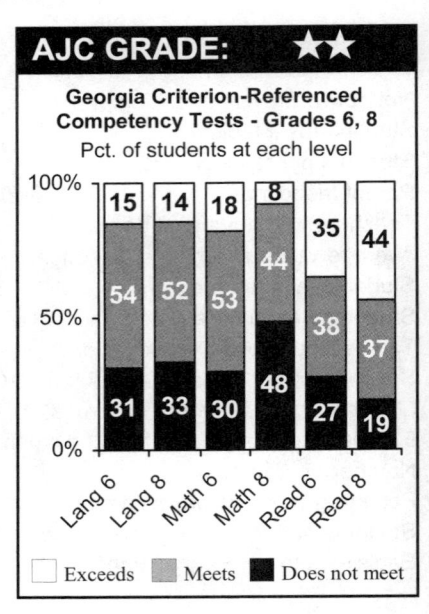

AJC GRADE: ★★

Georgia Criterion-Referenced Competency Tests - Grades 6, 8
Pct. of students at each level

	Lang 6	Lang 8	Math 6	Math 8	Read 6	Read 8
Exceeds	15	14	18	8	35	44
Meets	54	52	53	44	38	37
Does not meet	31	33	30	48	27	19

Union Grove Middle School

210 E Lake Rd, McDonough, GA 30252
678-583-8978 · Grades 6 - 8

Enrollment:	1,042
White / black / other:	89.9% / 6.7% / 3.4%
Not native English-speaking:	3 / 0.3%
Student absenteeism:	4.9%
Students per teacher:	17.4
Parent friendliness:	① ❷ ❸ ④ ❺ ❻
Teachers with advanced degrees:	54.1%
Average years' teaching experience:	9.8
Students in gifted program:	268 / 25.7%
Students held back a grade:	0.8%
Total suspensions and expulsions:	147
Suspensions only, pct. in-school:	147 / 86.4%
Offenses:	violence: 87, drugs: 5, other: 79
Eligible students, free or reduced lunch:	10.7%
Number of dropouts:	*
Pct. 8th-graders w/ basic computer skills:	100.0%

Students at this school generally go on to:
Union Grove High

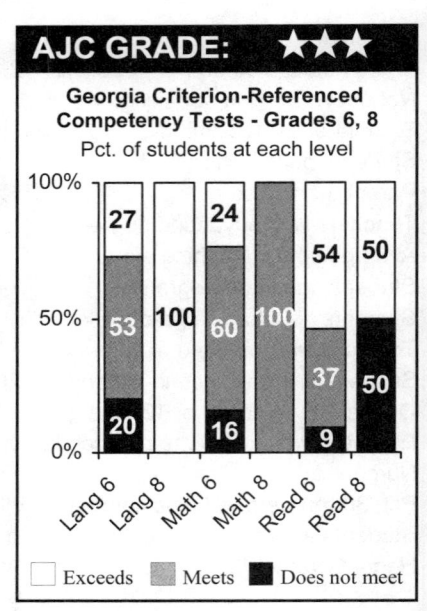

AJC GRADE: ★★★

Georgia Criterion-Referenced Competency Tests - Grades 6, 8
Pct. of students at each level

	Lang 6	Lang 8	Math 6	Math 8	Read 6	Read 8
Exceeds	27		24		54	50
Meets	53	100	60	100	37	50
Does not meet	20		16		9	

Henry County Middle Schools

Eagle's Landing High School

301 Tunis Rd, McDonough, GA 30253
770-954-9515 · Grades 9 - 12

Enrollment:	1,864
White / black / other:	69.9% / 20.9% / 9.2%
Not native English-speaking:	7 / 0.4%
Limited English proficiency:	51 / 2.7%
Student absenteeism:	8.4%
Students per teacher:	17.4
Parent friendliness:	① ❷ ❸ ④ ⑤ ❻
Students in gifted program:	134 / 7.2%
Students in remedial education:	7.3%
High school completion rate:	86.4%
Students held back a grade:	3.4%
Number of dropouts:	65 / 3.1%
Students in alternative programs:	24 / 1.3%
Students in special education:	163 / 8.7%
Eligible students, free or reduced lunch:	9.4%
Total suspensions and expulsions:	158
Suspensions only, pct. in-school:	158 / 57.0%
Drugs/alcohol-related offenses:	3
Violence-related offenses:	42
Firearms-related offenses:	9
Vandalism-related offenses:	1
Theft-related offenses:	2
All other disciplinary offenses:	166
Teachers with advanced degrees:	43.1%
Average years' teaching experience:	10.3

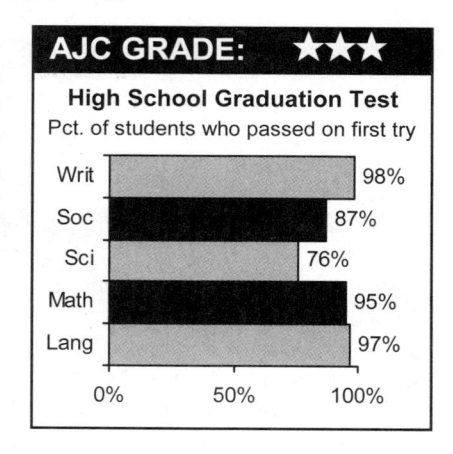

AJC GRADE: ★★★

High School Graduation Test
Pct. of students who passed on first try

- Writ: 98%
- Soc: 87%
- Sci: 76%
- Math: 95%
- Lang: 97%

GHSA classification: 2-AAAAA
Interscholastic sports offered:
BB, BS, CC, CL, FB, GO, RI, SB, SO, TE, TF, VB, WR

Advanced Placement (AP) Exams
Students tested:	109
Tests taken:	184
Pct. of test scores 3 or higher (1 - 5 scale):	44.6%

Languages other than English taught:
French, Spanish

2000-2001 high school graduates: 401

College prep/vocational diplomas:	20.2%
College prep endorsement diplomas:	55.6%
Vocational endorsement diplomas:	17.2%
General high school diplomas:	0.0%
Special education diplomas:	2.2%
Certificates of attendance (no diploma):	4.7%

Of the 2000-2001 graduates, 66.1% were eligible for the HOPE scholarship.

Of the 1999-2000 graduates, 178 attended a Georgia public college or university. Of those, 84% met the school's minimum academic requirements.

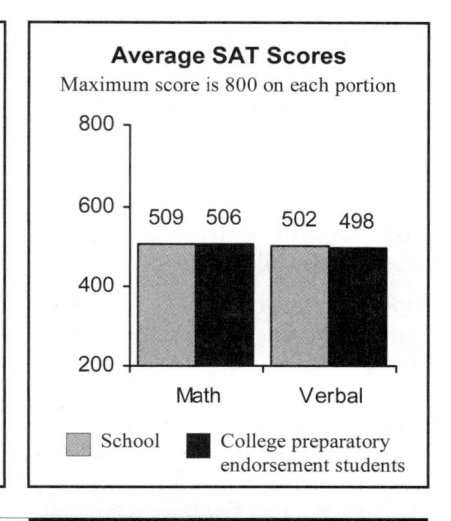

Average SAT Scores
Maximum score is 800 on each portion

- Math: School 509, College preparatory endorsement students 506
- Verbal: School 502, College preparatory endorsement students 498

Henry County High Schools

Henry County High School

401 E Tomlinson St, McDonough, GA 30253
770-957-3943 · Grades 9 - 12

Enrollment:	1,824
White / black / other:	77.1% / 20.5% / 2.4%
Not native English-speaking:	6 / 0.3%
Limited English proficiency:	20 / 1.1%
Student absenteeism:	10.2%
Students per teacher:	18.8
Parent friendliness:	❶❷❸④⑤❻
Students in gifted program:	112 / 6.1%
Students in remedial education:	8.7%
High school completion rate:	83.2%
Students held back a grade:	4.9%
Number of dropouts:	100 / 4.9%
Students in alternative programs:	*
Students in special education:	212 / 11.6%
Eligible students, free or reduced lunch:	15.6%
Total suspensions and expulsions:	230
Suspensions only, pct. in-school:	230 / 34.8%
Drugs/alcohol-related offenses:	23
Violence-related offenses:	81
Firearms-related offenses:	6
Vandalism-related offenses:	*
Theft-related offenses:	4
All other disciplinary offenses:	199
Teachers with advanced degrees:	44.9%
Average years' teaching experience:	10.2

AJC GRADE: ★★★

High School Graduation Test
Pct. of students who passed on first try

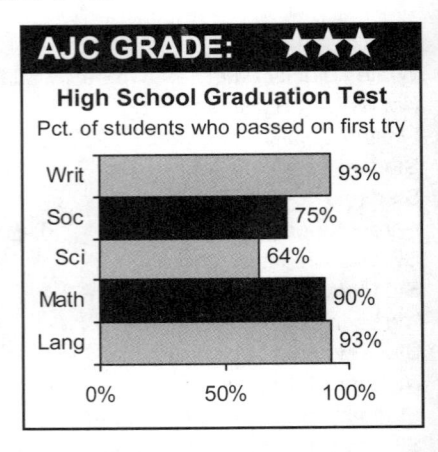

- Writ: 93%
- Soc: 75%
- Sci: 64%
- Math: 90%
- Lang: 93%

GHSA classification:	2-AAAAA

Interscholastic sports offered:
BB, BS, CC, CL, FB, GO, SB, SO, TE, TF, VB, WR

Advanced Placement (AP) Exams
Students tested:	121
Tests taken:	197
Pct. of test scores 3 or higher (1 - 5 scale):	37.1%

Languages other than English taught:
French, Spanish

2000-2001 high school graduates: 372

College prep/vocational diplomas:	22.0%
College prep endorsement diplomas:	38.7%
Vocational endorsement diplomas:	27.4%
General high school diplomas:	0.0%
Special education diplomas:	4.3%
Certificates of attendance (no diploma):	7.5%

Of the 2000-2001 graduates, 58.3% were eligible for the HOPE scholarship.

Of the 1999-2000 graduates, 109 attended a Georgia public college or university. Of those, 76% met the school's minimum academic requirements.

Average SAT Scores
Maximum score is 800 on each portion

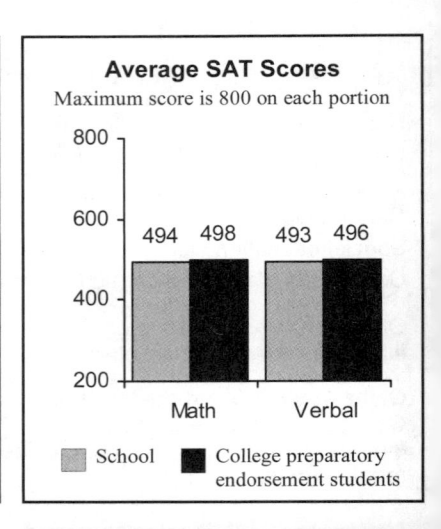

- Math — School: 494, College preparatory endorsement students: 498
- Verbal — School: 493, College preparatory endorsement students: 496

The Atlanta Journal-Constitution / Page 448

Henry County High Schools

Stockbridge High School

1151 Old Conyers Rd, Stockbridge, GA 30281
770-474-8747 · Grades 9 - 12

Enrollment:	1,750
White / black / other:	73.7% / 23.0% / 3.3%
Not native English-speaking:	3 / 0.2%
Limited English proficiency:	20 / 1.1%
Student absenteeism:	7.7%
Students per teacher:	17.1
Parent friendliness:	❶❷❸④⑤❻
Students in gifted program:	128 / 7.3%
Students in remedial education:	6.1%
High school completion rate:	85.0%
Students held back a grade:	4.9%
Number of dropouts:	44 / 2.3%
Students in alternative programs:	5 / 0.3%
Students in special education:	134 / 7.7%
Eligible students, free or reduced lunch:	6.8%

Total suspensions and expulsions:	192
Suspensions only, pct. in-school:	158 / 46.2%
Drugs/alcohol-related offenses:	23
Violence-related offenses:	23
Firearms-related offenses:	3
Vandalism-related offenses:	*
Theft-related offenses:	1
All other disciplinary offenses:	190

Teachers with advanced degrees:	49.5%
Average years' teaching experience:	10.6

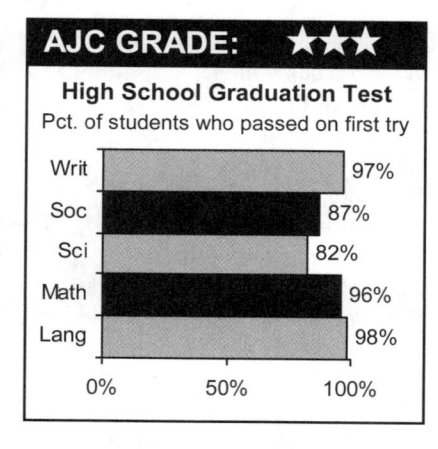

AJC GRADE: ★★★

High School Graduation Test

Pct. of students who passed on first try

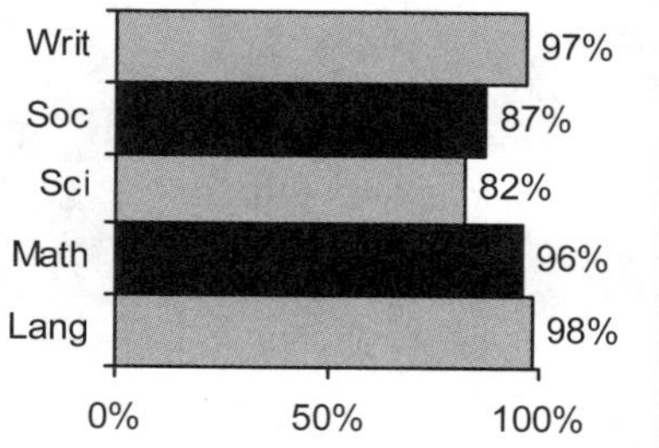
Writ
97%
Soc
87%
Sci
82%
Math
96%
Lang
98%
0%
50%
100%

GHSA classification:	2-AAAAA

Interscholastic sports offered:
BB, BS, CC, CL, FB, GO, RI, SB, SO, TE, TF, VB, WR

Advanced Placement (AP) Exams

Students tested:	122
Tests taken:	205
Pct. of test scores 3 or higher (1 - 5 scale):	54.1%

Languages other than English taught:
French, German, Spanish

2000-2001 high school graduates: 375

College prep/vocational diplomas:	17.3%
College prep endorsement diplomas:	54.9%
Vocational endorsement diplomas:	20.5%
General high school diplomas:	0.8%
Special education diplomas:	2.4%
Certificates of attendance (no diploma):	4.0%

Of the 2000-2001 graduates, 62.7% were eligible for the HOPE scholarship.

Of the 1999-2000 graduates, 150 attended a Georgia public college or university. Of those, 86% met the school's minimum academic requirements.

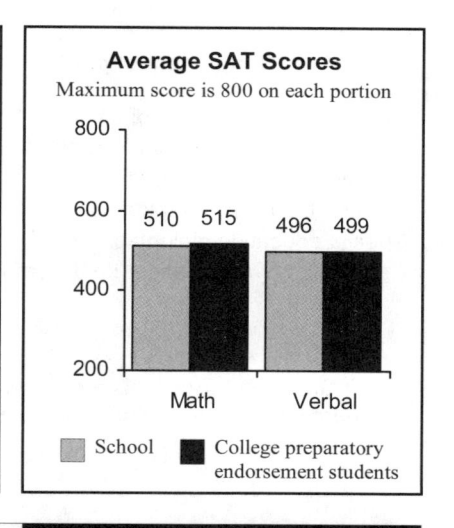

Average SAT Scores

Maximum score is 800 on each portion

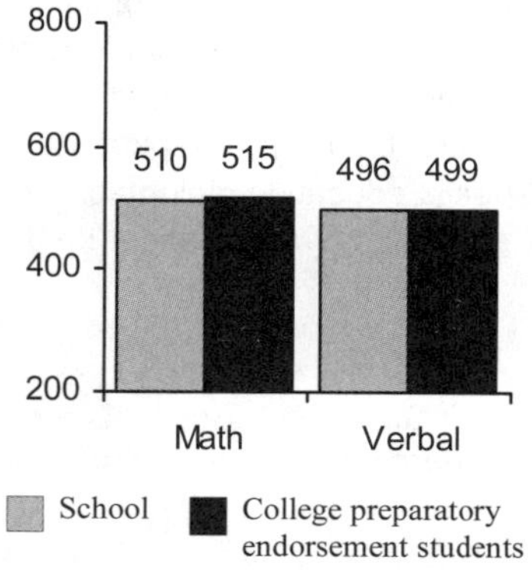
800
600
400
200
510
515
496
499
Math
Verbal
School
College preparatory endorsement students

Union Grove High School

120 E Lake Rd, McDonough, GA 30252
678-583-8502 · Grades 9 - 12

Enrollment:	801
White / black / other:	88.9% / 8.0% / 3.1%
Not native English-speaking:	5 / 0.6%
Limited English proficiency:	6 / 0.7%
Student absenteeism:	6.8%
Students per teacher:	17.0
Parent friendliness:	① ❷ ❸ ④ ⑤ ❻
Students in gifted program:	62 / 7.7%
Students in remedial education:	9.7%
High school completion rate:	*
Students held back a grade:	2.4%
Number of dropouts:	40 / 4.3%
Students in alternative programs:	*
Students in special education:	55 / 6.9%
Eligible students, free or reduced lunch:	6.0%

Total suspensions and expulsions:	103
Suspensions only, pct. in-school:	101 / 61.4%
Drugs/alcohol-related offenses:	2
Violence-related offenses:	27
Firearms-related offenses:	3
Vandalism-related offenses:	*
Theft-related offenses:	4
All other disciplinary offenses:	86

Teachers with advanced degrees:	51.0%
Average years' teaching experience:	11.7

AJC GRADE: ★★★

High School Graduation Test
Pct. of students who passed on first try

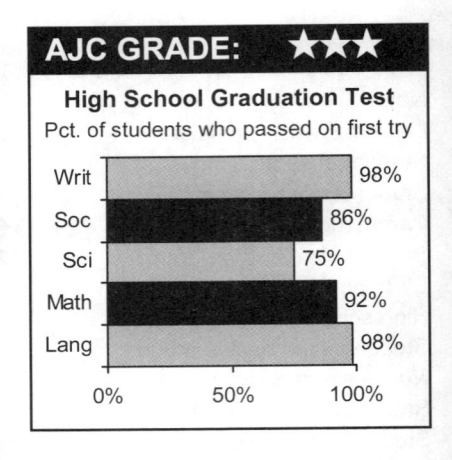

- Writ: 98%
- Soc: 86%
- Sci: 75%
- Math: 92%
- Lang: 98%

GHSA classification:	5-AA

Interscholastic sports offered:
BB, BS, CC, CL, FB, GO, RI, SB, SO, TE, TF, VB, WR

Advanced Placement (AP) Exams
Students tested:	14
Tests taken:	17
Pct. of test scores 3 or higher (1 - 5 scale):	17.6%

Languages other than English taught:
French, German, Spanish

2000-2001 high school graduates: 1

College prep/vocational diplomas:	0.0%
College prep endorsement diplomas:	0.0%
Vocational endorsement diplomas:	0.0%
General high school diplomas:	100.0%
Special education diplomas:	0.0%
Certificates of attendance (no diploma):	0.0%

Union Grove High School is a new school and therefore some data was not available for this report.

Average SAT Scores
Maximum score is 800 on each portion

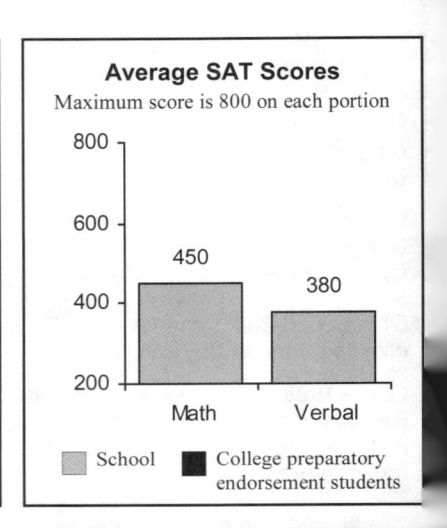

- Math: 450
- Verbal: 380

School / College preparatory endorsement students

The Atlanta Journal-Constitution / Page 450

Henry County High Schools

AJC ranking of Henry County Schools

ELEMENTARY SCHOOLS

AJC Star Grade: ★★★

Cotton Indian Elementary
Fairview Elementary
Locust Grove Elementary
Oakland Elementary
Ola Elementary
Pate's Creek Elementary
Pleasant Grove Elementary
Smith-Barnes Elementary
Wesley Lakes Elementary

AJC Star Grade: ★★

Austin Road Elementary
East Lake Elementary
Hampton Elementary
Hickory Flat Elementary
Mount Carmel Elementary

MIDDLE SCHOOLS

AJC Star Grade: ★★★

Austin Road Middle
Eagle's Landing Middle
Henry County Middle
Luella Middle
Union Grove Middle

AJC Star Grade: ★★

Stockbridge Middle

HIGH SCHOOLS

AJC Star Grade: ★★★

Eagle's Landing High
Henry County High
Stockbridge High
Union Grove High

Henry County Public Schools

Marietta City Public Schools

250 Howard St NE, Marietta, GA 30060
Phone: 770-422-3500 · Fax: 770-425-4095
http://www.marietta-city.k12.ga.us

The following pages provide detailed information on every school in the Marietta City school district. An asterisk (*) means the value of the data was zero or was not reported by the school district. A complete list of schools ranked by The Atlanta Journal-Constitution's star rating system follows the detailed school reports.

District enrollment:	7,331
White / black / other:	28.4% / 48.1% / 23.4%
Not native English-speaking:	899 / 12.3%
Expenditure per student (general fund):	$7,273
Students per teacher:	12.7
Teachers with advanced degrees:	54.5%
Average years, teaching experience:	9.5
Average teacher salary:	$44,456.62
Students in gifted program:	463 / 6.3%
Students held back a grade:	259 / 3.5%
Eligible students, free or reduced lunch:	2,988 / 40.6%
Number of dropouts (grades 9-12):	189 / 9.6%
High school completion rate:	63.9%
Graduates, pct. eligible for HOPE scholarships:	239 / 65.3%
Average combined SAT score (maximum 1,600):	1,036
Pct. of 11th-graders passing the Georgia High School Graduation Tests on first try:	65%
Percent of children 5 to 17 years of age living in poverty (2000 Census estimate):	20.3%

Burruss Elementary School

325 Manning Rd SW, Marietta, GA 30064
770-429-3144 · Grades K - 5

Enrollment:	614
White / black / other:	51.8% / 39.7% / 8.5%
Not native English-speaking:	7 / 1.1%
Limited English proficiency:	13 / 2.1%
Student absenteeism:	4.2%
Students per teacher:	14.0
Parent friendliness:	① ❷ ❸ ④ ❺ ❻
Teachers with advanced degrees:	56.3%
Average years' teaching experience:	11.4
Students in gifted program:	49 / 8.0%
Students in remedial education:	*
Students held back a grade:	2.1%
Total suspensions, pct. in-school:	27 / 77.8%
Offenses:	violence: 17, drugs: *, other: 14
Eligible students, free or reduced lunch:	30.0%
Before / after school program:	Yes / Yes
Students at this school generally go on to:	
Marietta Middle	

AJC GRADE: ★★★

Georgia Criterion-Referenced Competency Tests - Grade 4
Pct. of students at each level

Read: Exceeds 54%, Meets 28%, Does not meet 18%
Math: Exceeds 27%, Meets 51%, Does not meet 22%
Lang: Exceeds 23%, Meets 60%, Does not meet 17%

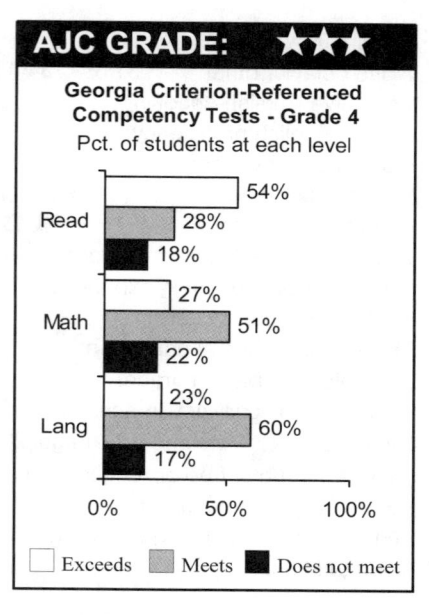

Dunleith Elementary School

120 Saine Dr SW, Marietta, GA 30008
770-429-3190 · Grades K - 5

Enrollment:	776
White / black / other:	11.7% / 59.5% / 28.7%
Not native English-speaking:	145 / 18.7%
Limited English proficiency:	254 / 32.7%
Student absenteeism:	5.1%
Students per teacher:	13.2
Parent friendliness:	① ❷ ❸ ④ ⑤ ❻
Teachers with advanced degrees:	35.5%
Average years' teaching experience:	7.2
Students in gifted program:	9 / 1.2%
Students in remedial education:	12.9%
Students held back a grade:	2.1%
Total suspensions, pct. in-school:	125 / 52.0%
Offenses:	violence: 60, drugs: *, other: 65
Eligible students, free or reduced lunch:	53.7%
Before / after school program:	Yes / Yes
Students at this school generally go on to:	
Marietta Middle	

AJC GRADE: ★★★

Georgia Criterion-Referenced Competency Tests - Grade 4
Pct. of students at each level

Read: Exceeds 30%, Meets 38%, Does not meet 32%
Math: Exceeds 8%, Meets 55%, Does not meet 37%
Lang: Exceeds 14%, Meets 54%, Does not meet 32%

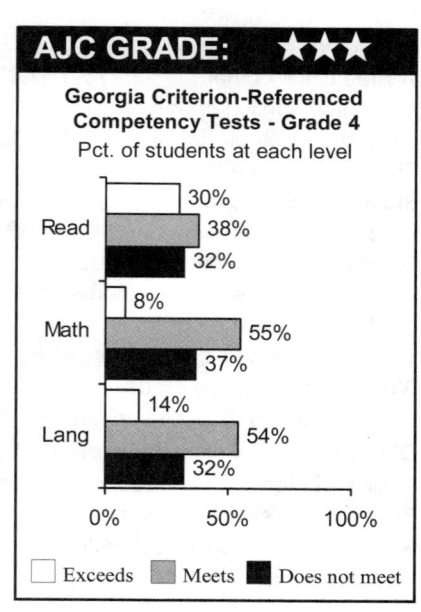

Hickory Hills Elementary School

500 Redwood Dr SW, Marietta, GA 30064
770-429-3125 · Grades K - 5

Enrollment:	393
White / black / other:	31.3% / 34.1% / 34.6%
Not native English-speaking:	88 / 22.4%
Limited English proficiency:	130 / 33.1%
Student absenteeism:	5.2%
Students per teacher:	10.6
Parent friendliness:	①❷❸④❺❻
Teachers with advanced degrees:	71.8%
Average years' teaching experience:	13.2
Students in gifted program:	16 / 4.1%
Students in remedial education:	17.7%
Students held back a grade:	1.8%
Total suspensions, pct. in-school:	12 / 8.3%
Offenses:	violence: 7, drugs: *, other: 11
Eligible students, free or reduced lunch:	53.7%
Before / after school program:	Yes / Yes
Students at this school generally go on to:	
Marietta Middle	

AJC GRADE: ★★★

Georgia Criterion-Referenced Competency Tests - Grade 4
Pct. of students at each level

Read: 39% / 37% / 25%
Math: 30% / 42% / 28%
Lang: 32% / 44% / 25%

☐ Exceeds ▒ Meets ■ Does not meet

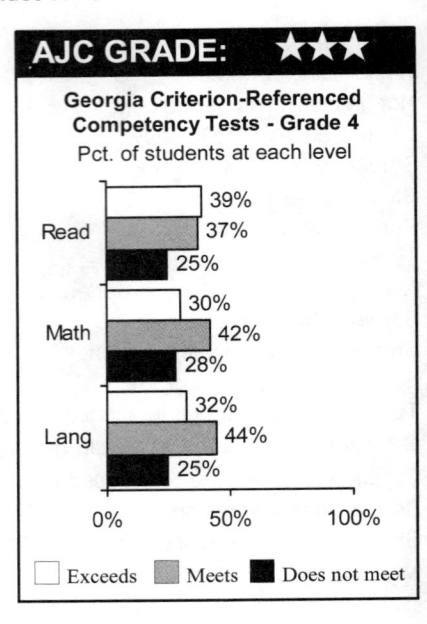

Lockheed Elementary School

1205 Merritt Rd, Marietta, GA 30062
770-429-3196 · Grades K - 5

Enrollment:	1,015
White / black / other:	19.7% / 51.8% / 28.5%
Not native English-speaking:	131 / 12.9%
Limited English proficiency:	320 / 31.5%
Student absenteeism:	5.5%
Students per teacher:	12.3
Parent friendliness:	①❷❸❹❺❻
Teachers with advanced degrees:	45.9%
Average years' teaching experience:	6.1
Students in gifted program:	20 / 2.0%
Students in remedial education:	32.9%
Students held back a grade:	2.0%
Total suspensions, pct. in-school:	104 / 0.0%
Offenses:	violence: 59, drugs: *, other: 46
Eligible students, free or reduced lunch:	69.3%
Before / after school program:	No / Yes
Students at this school generally go on to:	
Marietta Middle	

AJC GRADE: ★★★

Georgia Criterion-Referenced Competency Tests - Grade 4
Pct. of students at each level

Read: 31% / 38% / 31%
Math: 12% / 52% / 37%
Lang: 9% / 63% / 28%

☐ Exceeds ▒ Meets ■ Does not meet

Marietta City Elementary Schools

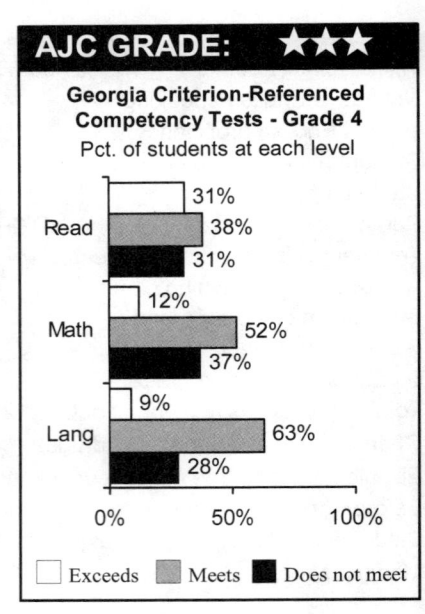

Park Street Elementary School

105 Park St SE, Marietta, GA 30060
770-429-3180 · Grades K - 5

Enrollment:	838
White / black / other:	5.3% / 48.1% / 46.7%
Not native English-speaking:	273 / 32.6%
Limited English proficiency:	310 / 37.0%
Student absenteeism:	5.9%
Students per teacher:	12.1
Parent friendliness:	① **❷❸❹❺❻**
Teachers with advanced degrees:	52.1%
Average years' teaching experience:	6.5
Students in gifted program:	8 / 1.0%
Students in remedial education:	22.4%
Students held back a grade:	1.2%
Total suspensions, pct. in-school:	58 / 25.9%
Offenses:	violence: 36, drugs: *, other: 22
Eligible students, free or reduced lunch:	63.1%
Before / after school program:	Yes / Yes

Students at this school generally go on to:
Marietta Middle

AJC GRADE: ★★★

Georgia Criterion-Referenced Competency Tests - Grade 4
Pct. of students at each level

- Read: Exceeds 27%, Meets 41%, Does not meet 31%
- Math: Exceeds 8%, Meets 53%, Does not meet 39%
- Lang: Exceeds 7%, Meets 57%, Does not meet 36%

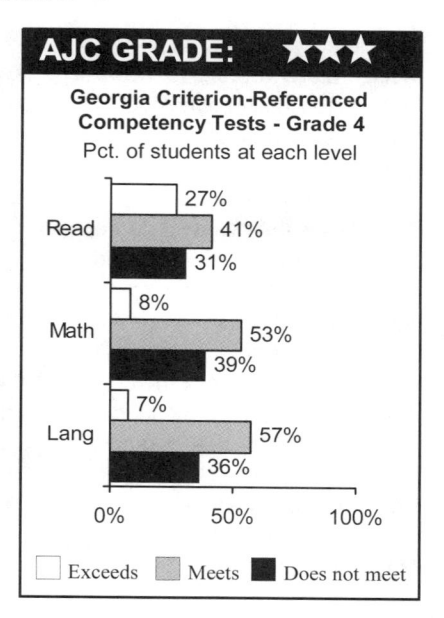

West Side Elementary School

344 Polk St NW, Marietta, GA 30064
770-429-3172 · Grades K - 5

Enrollment:	430
White / black / other:	46.5% / 44.4% / 9.1%
Not native English-speaking:	3 / 0.7%
Limited English proficiency:	8 / 1.9%
Student absenteeism:	4.3%
Students per teacher:	11.6
Parent friendliness:	① **❷❸**④**❺❻**
Teachers with advanced degrees:	52.6%
Average years' teaching experience:	9.4
Students in gifted program:	38 / 8.8%
Students in remedial education:	22.6%
Students held back a grade:	5.6%
Total suspensions, pct. in-school:	32 / 71.9%
Offenses:	violence: 10, drugs: *, other: 25
Eligible students, free or reduced lunch:	34.7%
Before / after school program:	No / Yes

Students at this school generally go on to:
Marietta Middle

AJC GRADE: ★★★

Georgia Criterion-Referenced Competency Tests - Grade 4
Pct. of students at each level

- Read: Exceeds 50%, Meets 34%, Does not meet 16%
- Math: Exceeds 24%, Meets 48%, Does not meet 28%
- Lang: Exceeds 28%, Meets 55%, Does not meet 16%

Marietta City Elementary Schools

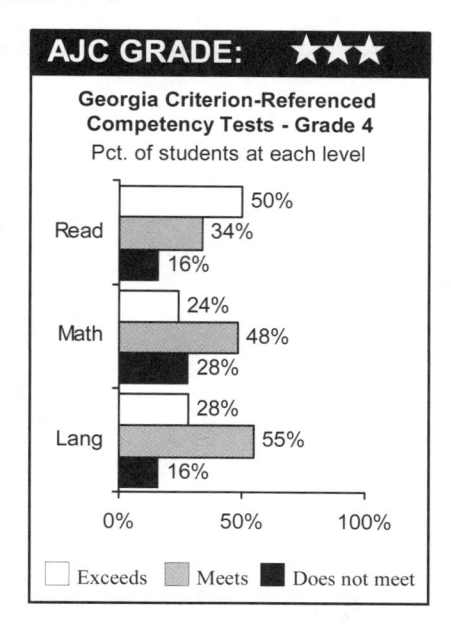

Marietta Middle School

121 Winn St NW, Marietta, GA 30064
770-422-0311 · Grades 7 - 8

Enrollment:	1,555
White / black / other:	28.9% / 50.0% / 21.2%
Not native English-speaking:	137 / 8.8%
Student absenteeism:	7.3%
Students per teacher:	12.8
Parent friendliness:	❶❷❸④❺❻
Teachers with advanced degrees:	50.4%
Average years' teaching experience:	10.0
Students in gifted program:	174 / 11.2%
Students held back a grade:	1.9%
Total suspensions and expulsions:	1,649
Suspensions only, pct. in-school:	1,646 / 56.6%
Offenses: violence: 488, drugs: 9, other: 1,363	
Eligible students, free or reduced lunch:	27.3%
Number of dropouts:	7 / 0.4%
Pct. 8th-graders w/ basic computer skills:	81.0%

Students at this school generally go on to:
Marietta High

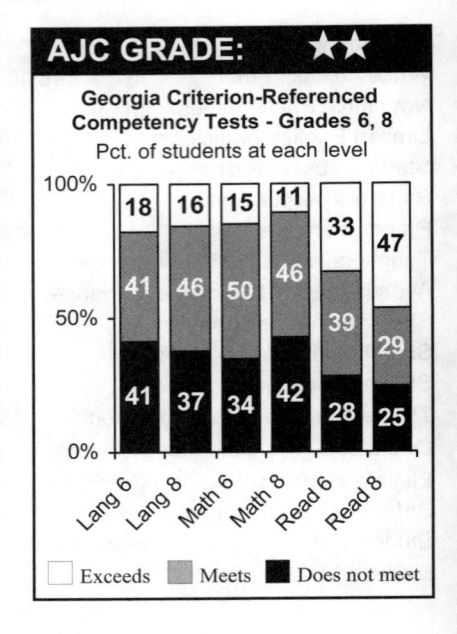

AJC GRADE: ★★

Georgia Criterion-Referenced Competency Tests - Grades 6, 8
Pct. of students at each level

	Lang 6	Lang 8	Math 6	Math 8	Read 6	Read 8
Exceeds	18	16	15	11	33	47
Meets	41	46	50	46	39	29
Does not meet	41	37	34	42	28	25

Marietta City Middle Schools

Marietta High School

1171 Whitlock Ave SW, Marietta, GA 30064
770-428-2631 · Grades 9 - 12

Enrollment:	1,710
White / black / other:	38.5% / 46.3% / 15.2%
Not native English-speaking:	115 / 6.7%
Limited English proficiency:	155 / 9.1%
Student absenteeism:	7.6%
Students per teacher:	14.7
Parent friendliness:	❶❷❸④❺❻
Students in gifted program:	149 / 8.7%
Students in remedial education:	1.5%
High school completion rate:	63.9%
Students held back a grade:	8.1%
Number of dropouts:	189 / 9.6%
Students in alternative programs:	84 / 4.9%
Students in special education:	214 / 12.5%
Eligible students, free or reduced lunch:	20.9%

Total suspensions and expulsions:	1,180
Suspensions only, pct. in-school:	1,180 / 71.1%
Drugs/alcohol-related offenses:	23
Violence-related offenses:	108
Firearms-related offenses:	12
Vandalism-related offenses:	3
Theft-related offenses:	9
All other disciplinary offenses:	1,102
Teachers with advanced degrees:	68.6%
Average years' teaching experience:	12.0

AJC GRADE: ★★★

High School Graduation Test
Pct. of students who passed on first try

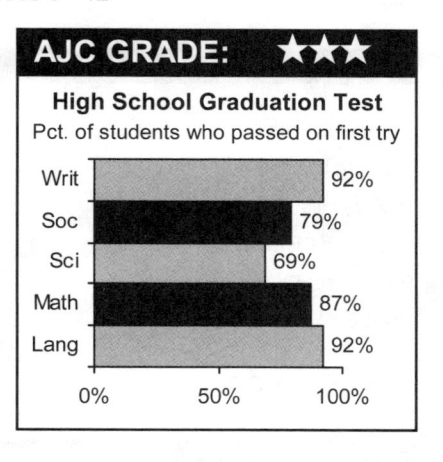

- Writ: 92%
- Soc: 79%
- Sci: 69%
- Math: 87%
- Lang: 92%

GHSA classification: 5-AAAAA
Interscholastic sports offered:
BS, CC, CL, FB, GO, SB, SO, SW, TE, TF, VB, WR

Advanced Placement (AP) Exams
Students tested:	84
Tests taken:	115
Pct. of test scores 3 or higher (1 - 5 scale):	59.1%

Languages other than English taught:
French, German, Latin, Spanish

2000-2001 high school graduates: 239

College prep/vocational diplomas:	33.1%
College prep endorsement diplomas:	42.7%
Vocational endorsement diplomas:	20.1%
General high school diplomas:	0.0%
Special education diplomas:	4.2%
Certificates of attendance (no diploma):	0.0%

Of the 2000-2001 graduates, 65.3% were eligible for the HOPE scholarship.

Of the 1999-2000 graduates, 103 attended a Georgia public college or university. Of those, 86% met the school's minimum academic requirements.

Average SAT Scores
Maximum score is 800 on each portion

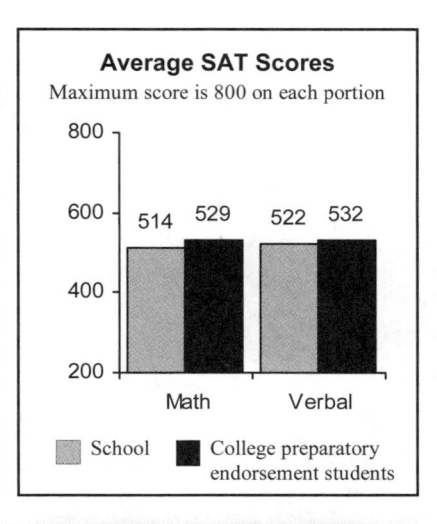

- Math — School: 514, College preparatory endorsement students: 529
- Verbal — School: 522, College preparatory endorsement students: 532

Marietta City High Schools

AJC ranking of Marietta City Schools

ELEMENTARY SCHOOLS

AJC Star Grade: ★★★

- Burruss Elementary
- Dunleith Elementary
- Hickory Hills Elementary
- Lockheed Elementary
- Park Street Elementary
- West Side Elementary

MIDDLE SCHOOLS

AJC Star Grade: ★★

- Marietta Middle

HIGH SCHOOLS

AJC Star Grade: ★★★

- Marietta High

Newton County Public Schools

3187 Newton Dr NE, Covington, GA 30014
Phone: 770-787-1330 · Fax: 770-784-2950
http://www.newtoncountyschools.org

The following pages provide detailed information on every school in the Newton County school district. An asterisk (*) means the value of the data was zero or was not reported by the school district. A complete list of schools ranked by The Atlanta Journal-Constitution's star rating system follows the detailed school reports.

District enrollment:	11,316
White / black / other:	64.7% / 30.9% / 4.3%
Not native English-speaking:	111 / 1.0%
Expenditure per student (general fund):	$5,674
Students per teacher:	15.4
Teachers with advanced degrees:	45.0%
Average years, teaching experience:	11.7
Average teacher salary:	$40,526.18
Students in gifted program:	887 / 7.8%
Students held back a grade:	534 / 4.7%
Eligible students, free or reduced lunch:	4,761 / 40.6%
Number of dropouts (grades 9-12):	164 / 5.3%
High school completion rate:	69.0%
Graduates, pct. eligible for HOPE scholarships:	387 / 66.1%
Average combined SAT score (maximum 1,600):	1,029
Pct. of 11th-graders passing the Georgia High School Graduation Tests on first try:	66%
Percent of children 5 to 17 years of age living in poverty (2000 Census estimate):	15.1%

The Atlanta Journal-Constitution / Page 459

East Newton Elementary School

2286 Dixie Rd, Covington, GA 30014
770-784-2973 · Grades K - 5

Enrollment:	532
White / black / other:	78.6% / 19.2% / 2.3%
Not native English-speaking:	*
Limited English proficiency:	1 / 0.2%
Student absenteeism:	3.8%
Students per teacher:	14.8
Parent friendliness:	①❷❸④⑤❻
Teachers with advanced degrees:	47.4%
Average years' teaching experience:	11.4
Students in gifted program:	34 / 6.4%
Students in remedial education:	22.8%
Students held back a grade:	1.1%
Total suspensions, pct. in-school:	16 / 0.0%
Offenses:	violence: 7, drugs: * , other: 9
Eligible students, free or reduced lunch:	36.7%
Before / after school program:	No / No

Students at this school generally go on to:
Indian Creek Middle

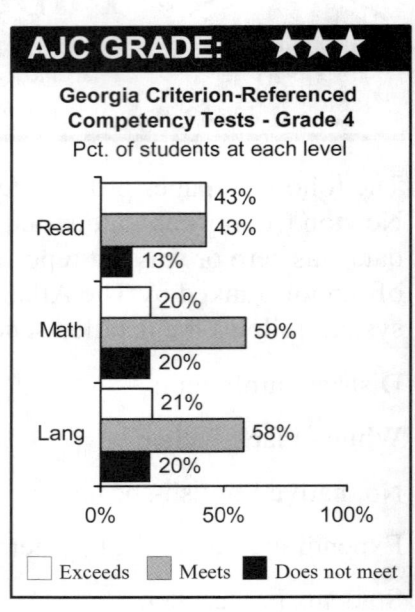

AJC GRADE: ★★★

Georgia Criterion-Referenced Competency Tests - Grade 4
Pct. of students at each level

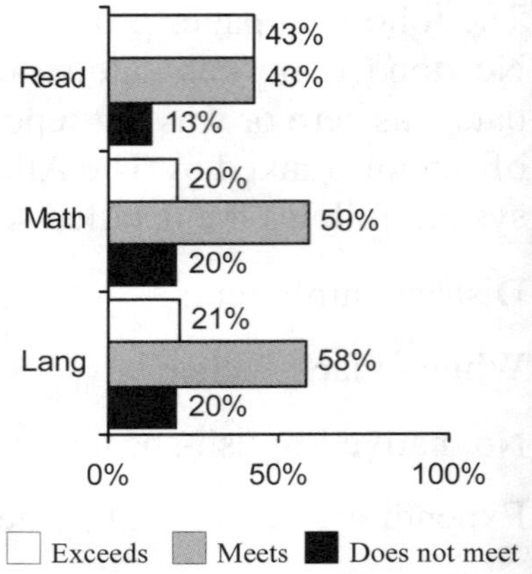
Read
43%
43%
13%
Math
20%
59%
20%
Lang
21%
58%
20%
0%
50%
100%
Exceeds
Meets
Does not meet

Fairview Elementary School

3325 Fairview Rd, Covington, GA 30016
770-784-2959 · Grades K - 5

Enrollment:	682
White / black / other:	59.8% / 33.9% / 6.3%
Not native English-speaking:	*
Limited English proficiency:	1 / 0.1%
Student absenteeism:	3.8%
Students per teacher:	16.1
Parent friendliness:	①❷❸❹❺❻
Teachers with advanced degrees:	39.5%
Average years' teaching experience:	10.6
Students in gifted program:	47 / 6.9%
Students in remedial education:	14.8%
Students held back a grade:	0.7%
Total suspensions, pct. in-school:	20 / 5.0%
Offenses:	violence: 7, drugs: * , other: 13
Eligible students, free or reduced lunch:	38.0%
Before / after school program:	No / No

Students at this school generally go on to:
Clements, Cousins Middle

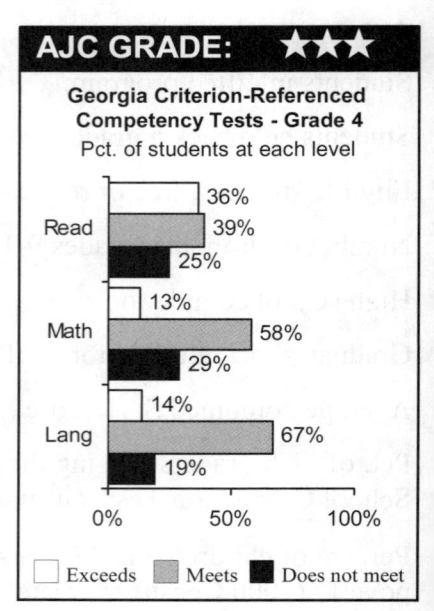

AJC GRADE: ★★★

Georgia Criterion-Referenced Competency Tests - Grade 4
Pct. of students at each level

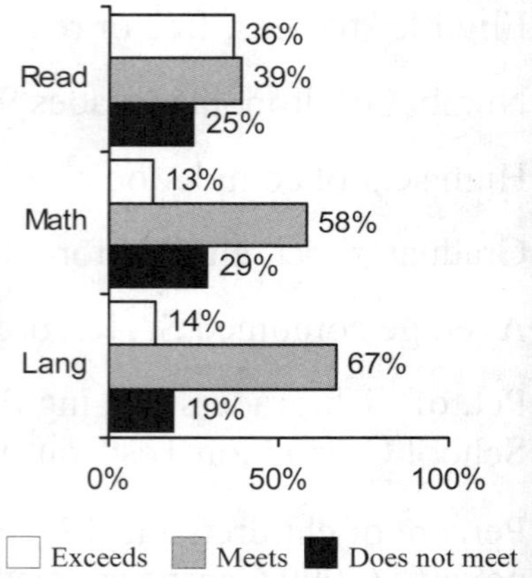
Read
36%
39%
25%
Math
13%
58%
29%
Lang
14%
67%
19%
0%
50%
100%
Exceeds
Meets
Does not meet

Ficquett Elementary School

2207 Williams St NE, Covington, GA 30014
770-786-2636 · Grades K - 5

Enrollment:	639
White / black / other:	51.0% / 35.7% / 13.3%
Not native English-speaking:	69 / 10.8%
Limited English proficiency:	111 / 17.4%
Student absenteeism:	3.4%
Students per teacher:	12.5
Parent friendliness:	❶❷❸❹❺❻
Teachers with advanced degrees:	32.1%
Average years' teaching experience:	10.3
Students in gifted program:	17 / 2.7%
Students in remedial education:	21.2%
Students held back a grade:	2.3%
Total suspensions, pct. in-school:	95 / 70.5%
Offenses:	violence: 60, drugs: *, other: 46
Eligible students, free or reduced lunch:	65.5%
Before / after school program:	Yes / No

Students at this school generally go on to:
Clements, Cousins, Indian Creek Middle

AJC GRADE: ★★★★★

Georgia Criterion-Referenced Competency Tests - Grade 4
Pct. of students at each level

Read: Exceeds 44%, Meets 35%, Does not meet 21%
Math: Exceeds 16%, Meets 65%, Does not meet 19%
Lang: Exceeds 21%, Meets 59%, Does not meet 20%

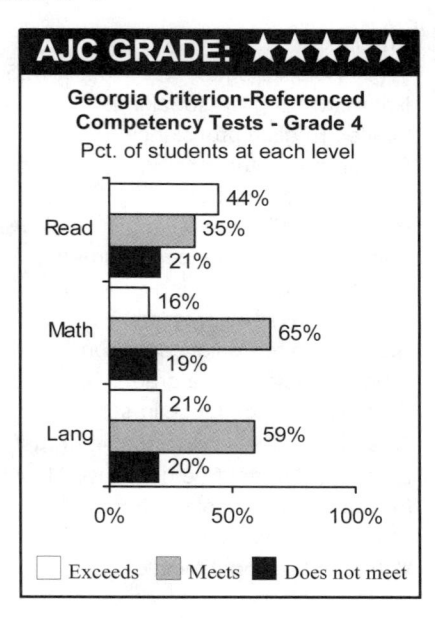

Heard-Mixon Elementary School

14110 Highway 36, Covington, GA 30014
770-784-2980 · Grades K - 5

Enrollment:	460
White / black / other:	68.5% / 30.7% / 0.9%
Not native English-speaking:	*
Limited English proficiency:	2 / 0.4%
Student absenteeism:	3.6%
Students per teacher:	15.0
Parent friendliness:	①❷❸④❺❻
Teachers with advanced degrees:	42.4%
Average years' teaching experience:	12.0
Students in gifted program:	17 / 3.7%
Students in remedial education:	23.0%
Students held back a grade:	3.9%
Total suspensions, pct. in-school:	1 / 0.0%
Offenses:	violence: *, drugs: 1, other: *
Eligible students, free or reduced lunch:	59.4%
Before / after school program:	No / No

Students at this school generally go on to:
Indian Creek Middle

AJC GRADE: ★★★

Georgia Criterion-Referenced Competency Tests - Grade 4
Pct. of students at each level

Read: Exceeds 24%, Meets 49%, Does not meet 27%
Math: Exceeds 7%, Meets 56%, Does not meet 38%
Lang: Exceeds 6%, Meets 68%, Does not meet 26%

Newton County Elementary Schools

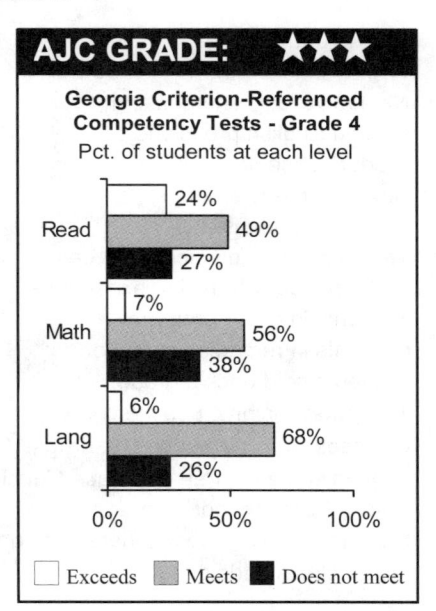

Livingston Elementary School

3657 Highway 81, Covington, GA 30016
770-784-2930 · Grades K - 5

Enrollment:	660
White / black / other:	67.7% / 25.5% / 6.8%
Not native English-speaking:	*
Limited English proficiency:	15 / 2.3%
Student absenteeism:	1.8%
Students per teacher:	16.8
Parent friendliness:	①❷❸④⑤❻
Teachers with advanced degrees:	27.9%
Average years' teaching experience:	11.1
Students in gifted program:	33 / 5.0%
Students in remedial education:	15.8%
Students held back a grade:	0.6%
Total suspensions, pct. in-school:	1 / 100.0%
Offenses:	violence: 4, drugs: *, other: 1
Eligible students, free or reduced lunch:	31.7%
Before / after school program:	Yes / Yes
Students at this school generally go on to:	
Veterans Memorial Middle	

AJC GRADE: ★★

Georgia Criterion-Referenced Competency Tests - Grade 4
Pct. of students at each level

- Read: Exceeds 28%, Meets 48%, Does not meet 23%
- Math: Exceeds 9%, Meets 62%, Does not meet 29%
- Lang: Exceeds 9%, Meets 63%, Does not meet 28%

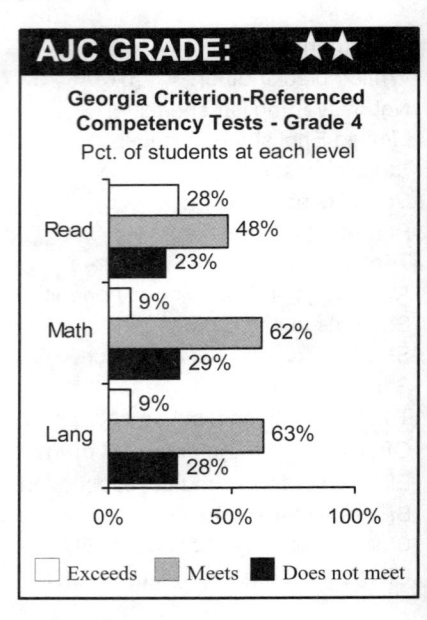

Mansfield Elementary School

45 E Third Ave, Mansfield, GA 30055
770-784-2948 · Grades K - 5

Enrollment:	370
White / black / other:	85.7% / 11.6% / 2.7%
Not native English-speaking:	*
Limited English proficiency:	*
Student absenteeism:	1.6%
Students per teacher:	15.9
Parent friendliness:	①❷❸④❺❻
Teachers with advanced degrees:	44.0%
Average years' teaching experience:	11.1
Students in gifted program:	34 / 9.2%
Students in remedial education:	7.6%
Students held back a grade:	0.8%
Total suspensions, pct. in-school:	79 / 88.6%
Offenses:	violence: 19, drugs: *, other: 66
Eligible students, free or reduced lunch:	32.6%
Before / after school program:	Yes / No
Students at this school generally go on to:	
Indian Creek Middle	

AJC GRADE: ★★★

Georgia Criterion-Referenced Competency Tests - Grade 4
Pct. of students at each level

- Read: Exceeds 37%, Meets 34%, Does not meet 29%
- Math: Exceeds 11%, Meets 62%, Does not meet 28%
- Lang: Exceeds 20%, Meets 49%, Does not meet 31%

The Atlanta Journal-Constitution / Page 462

Newton County Elementary Schools

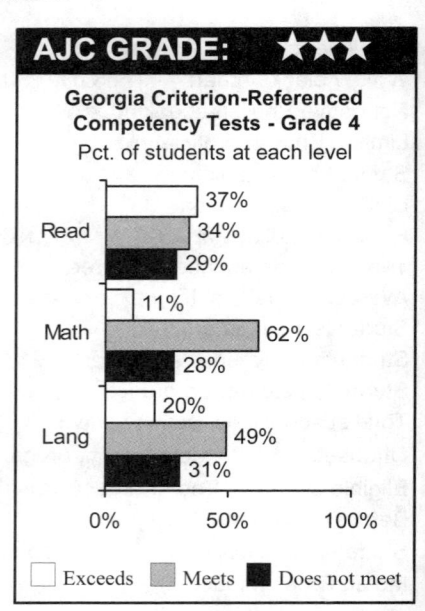

Middle Ridge Elementary School

11649 By Pass Rd, Covington, GA 30014
770-385-6463 · Grades K - 5

Enrollment:	637
White / black / other:	53.4% / 41.8% / 4.9%
Not native English-speaking:	*
Limited English proficiency:	4 / 0.6%
Student absenteeism:	4.1%
Students per teacher:	16.0
Parent friendliness:	①❷❸④❺❻
Teachers with advanced degrees:	48.8%
Average years' teaching experience:	8.0
Students in gifted program:	17 / 2.7%
Students in remedial education:	14.4%
Students held back a grade:	4.4%
Total suspensions, pct. in-school:	12 / 0.0%
Offenses:	violence: 5, drugs: *, other: 7
Eligible students, free or reduced lunch:	60.6%
Before / after school program:	Yes / No

Students at this school generally go on to:
Clements, Cousins, Indian Creek, Veterans Memorial Middle

AJC GRADE: ★★★

Georgia Criterion-Referenced Competency Tests - Grade 4
Pct. of students at each level

Read: Exceeds 28%, Meets 35%, Does not meet 37%
Math: Exceeds 12%, Meets 44%, Does not meet 43%
Lang: Exceeds 14%, Meets 47%, Does not meet 39%

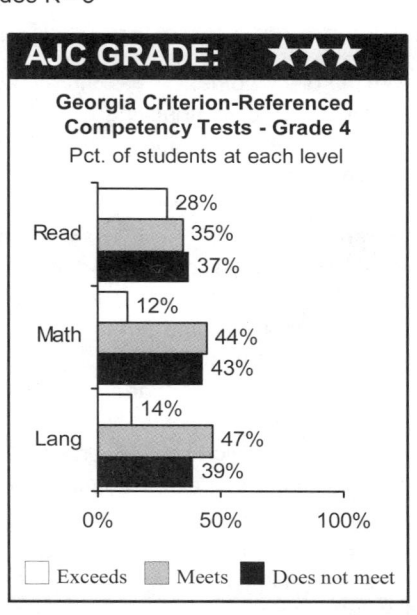

Palmer Stone Elementary School

1110 Emory St, Oxford, GA 30054
770-784-2969 · Grades K - 5

Enrollment:	481
White / black / other:	64.7% / 33.3% / 2.1%
Not native English-speaking:	*
Limited English proficiency:	1 / 0.2%
Student absenteeism:	3.5%
Students per teacher:	13.4
Parent friendliness:	①❷❸④⑤❻
Teachers with advanced degrees:	39.5%
Average years' teaching experience:	15.3
Students in gifted program:	7 / 1.5%
Students in remedial education:	15.4%
Students held back a grade:	2.5%
Total suspensions, pct. in-school:	45 / 13.3%
Offenses:	violence: 23, drugs: 1, other: 67
Eligible students, free or reduced lunch:	48.2%
Before / after school program:	No / No

Students at this school generally go on to:
Cousins Middle

AJC GRADE: ★★★

Georgia Criterion-Referenced Competency Tests - Grade 4
Pct. of students at each level

Read: Exceeds 26%, Meets 56%, Does not meet 18%
Math: Exceeds 13%, Meets 55%, Does not meet 32%
Lang: Exceeds 13%, Meets 60%, Does not meet 26%

The Atlanta Journal-Constitution / Page 463

Newton County Elementary Schools

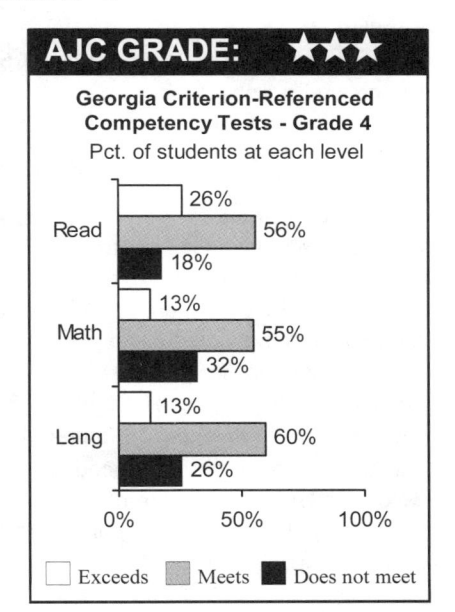

Porterdale Elementary School

45 Ram Dr, Covington, GA 30014
770-784-2928 · Grades K - 5

Enrollment:	592
White / black / other:	59.6% / 32.4% / 7.9%
Not native English-speaking:	*
Limited English proficiency:	4 / 0.7%
Student absenteeism:	2.5%
Students per teacher:	14.7
Parent friendliness:	①❷❸④❺❻
Teachers with advanced degrees:	32.6%
Average years' teaching experience:	13.1
Students in gifted program:	11 / 1.9%
Students in remedial education:	16.2%
Students held back a grade:	2.0%
Total suspensions, pct. in-school:	152 / 73.0%
Offenses: violence: 56, drugs: *, other: 114	
Eligible students, free or reduced lunch:	42.2%
Before / after school program:	No / No
Students at this school generally go on to: Clements Middle	

AJC GRADE: ★★

Georgia Criterion-Referenced Competency Tests - Grade 4
Pct. of students at each level

- Read: Exceeds 27%, Meets 41%, Does not meet 32%
- Math: Exceeds 4%, Meets 55%, Does not meet 41%
- Lang: Exceeds 10%, Meets 51%, Does not meet 39%

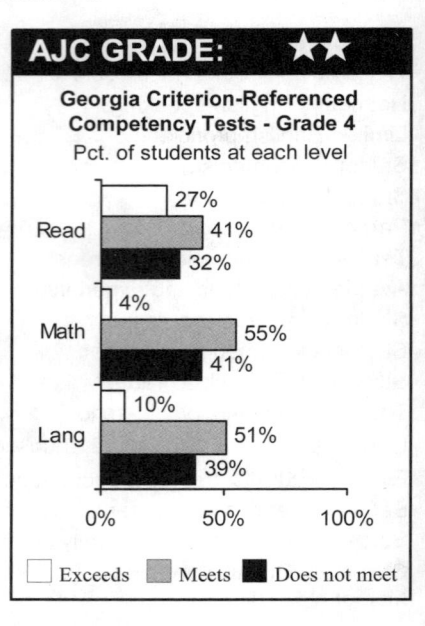

West Newton Elementary School

13387 Brown Bridge Rd, Covington, GA 30016
770-385-6472 · Grades K - 5

Enrollment:	688
White / black / other:	68.3% / 27.5% / 4.2%
Not native English-speaking:	*
Limited English proficiency:	1 / 0.1%
Student absenteeism:	3.9%
Students per teacher:	15.9
Parent friendliness:	①❷❸④❺❻
Teachers with advanced degrees:	53.3%
Average years' teaching experience:	12.8
Students in gifted program:	35 / 5.1%
Students in remedial education:	9.1%
Students held back a grade:	1.5%
Total suspensions, pct. in-school:	86 / 70.9%
Offenses: violence: 36, drugs: *, other: 52	
Eligible students, free or reduced lunch:	34.6%
Before / after school program:	Yes / No
Students at this school generally go on to: Clements Middle	

AJC GRADE: ★★

Georgia Criterion-Referenced Competency Tests - Grade 4
Pct. of students at each level

- Read: Exceeds 27%, Meets 41%, Does not meet 32%
- Math: Exceeds 9%, Meets 60%, Does not meet 31%
- Lang: Exceeds 9%, Meets 65%, Does not meet 25%

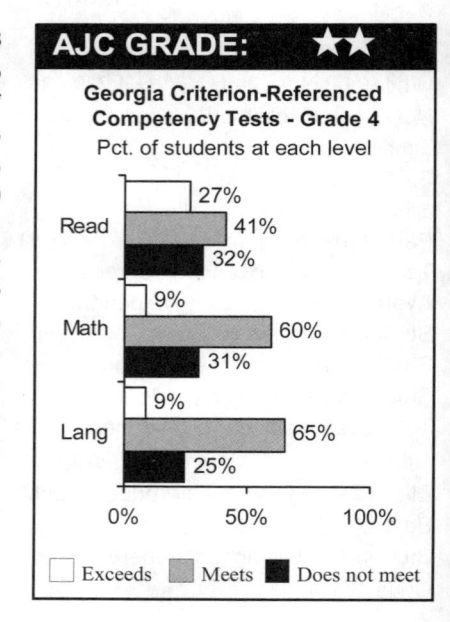

Clements Middle School

66 Jack Neely Rd, Covington, GA 30016
770-784-2934 · Grades 6 - 8

Enrollment:	1,036
White / black / other:	63.1% / 32.6% / 4.2%
Not native English-speaking:	*
Student absenteeism:	6.5%
Students per teacher:	15.9
Parent friendliness:	①❷❸④⑤❻
Teachers with advanced degrees:	53.0%
Average years' teaching experience:	13.4
Students in gifted program:	136 / 13.1%
Students held back a grade:	0.6%
Total suspensions and expulsions:	352
Suspensions only, pct. in-school:	352 / 58.5%
Offenses:	violence: 101, drugs: 6, other: 245
Eligible students, free or reduced lunch:	37.1%
Number of dropouts:	*
Pct. 8th-graders w/ basic computer skills:	90.0%
Students at this school generally go on to:	
Eastside, Newton High	

AJC GRADE: ★★★

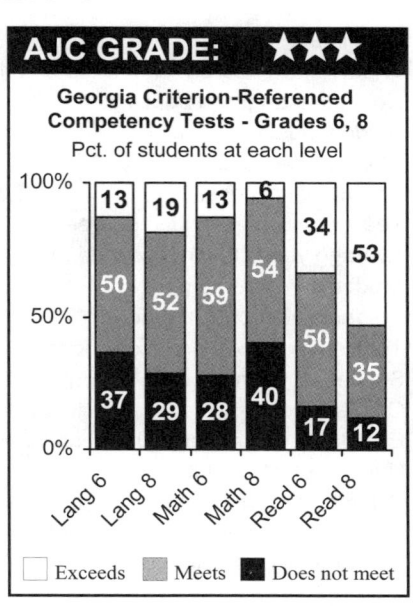

Georgia Criterion-Referenced Competency Tests - Grades 6, 8
Pct. of students at each level

	Lang 6	Lang 8	Math 6	Math 8	Read 6	Read 8
Exceeds	13	19	13	6	34	53
Meets	50	52	59	54	50	35
Does not meet	37	29	28	40	17	12

Cousins Middle School

8187 Carlton Trl NW, Covington, GA 30014
770-786-7311 · Grades 6 - 8

Enrollment:	778
White / black / other:	60.8% / 34.7% / 4.5%
Not native English-speaking:	22 / 2.8%
Student absenteeism:	8.4%
Students per teacher:	14.7
Parent friendliness:	①❷❸④❺❻
Teachers with advanced degrees:	45.3%
Average years' teaching experience:	12.8
Students in gifted program:	61 / 7.8%
Students held back a grade:	6.0%
Total suspensions and expulsions:	609
Suspensions only, pct. in-school:	609 / 76.8%
Offenses:	violence: 87, drugs: 4, other: 519
Eligible students, free or reduced lunch:	53.2%
Number of dropouts:	*
Pct. 8th-graders w/ basic computer skills:	98.9%
Students at this school generally go on to:	
Eastside, Newton High	

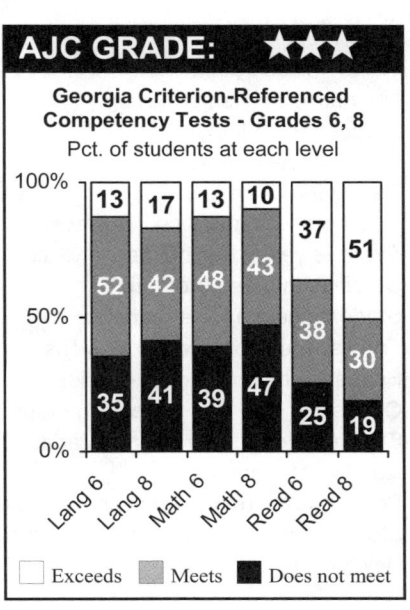

AJC GRADE: ★★★

Georgia Criterion-Referenced Competency Tests - Grades 6, 8
Pct. of students at each level

	Lang 6	Lang 8	Math 6	Math 8	Read 6	Read 8
Exceeds	13	17	13	10	37	51
Meets	52	42	48	43	38	30
Does not meet	35	41	39	47	25	19

Newton County Middle Schools

Indian Creek Middle School

11051 By Pass Rd, Covington, GA 30014
770-385-6453 · Grades 6 - 8

Enrollment:	902
White / black / other:	73.2% / 24.9% / 1.9%
Not native English-speaking:	*
Student absenteeism:	11.6%
Students per teacher:	15.3
Parent friendliness:	① ❷ ❸ ④ ❺ ❻
Teachers with advanced degrees:	44.1%
Average years' teaching experience:	9.5
Students in gifted program:	133 / 14.7%
Students held back a grade:	0.3%
Total suspensions and expulsions:	640
Suspensions only, pct. in-school:	640 / 70.0%
Offenses: violence: 80, drugs: 1, other: 562	
Eligible students, free or reduced lunch:	42.1%
Number of dropouts:	*
Pct. 8th-graders w/ basic computer skills:	87.2%
Students at this school generally go on to: Eastside, Newton High	

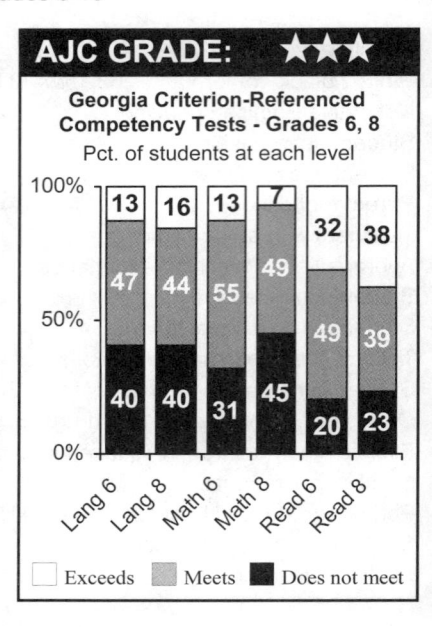

AJC GRADE: ★★★

Georgia Criterion-Referenced Competency Tests - Grades 6, 8
Pct. of students at each level

	Lang 6	Lang 8	Math 6	Math 8	Read 6	Read 8
Exceeds	13	16	13	7	32	38
Meets	47	44	55	49	49	39
Does not meet	40	40	31	45	20	23

Veterans Memorial Middle School

13357 Brown Bridge Rd, Covington, GA 30016
770-385-6893 · Grades 6 - 8

Enrollment:	76
White / black / other:	73.7% / 22.4% / 3.9%
Not native English-speaking:	*
Student absenteeism:	2.4%
Students per teacher:	15.8
Parent friendliness:	① ❷ ❸ ④ ❺ ❻
Teachers with advanced degrees:	42.9%
Average years' teaching experience:	13.6
Students in gifted program:	15 / 19.7%
Students held back a grade:	*
Total suspensions and expulsions:	1
Suspensions only, pct. in-school:	1 / 100.0%
Offenses: violence: *, drugs: *, other: 2	
Eligible students, free or reduced lunch:	32.9%
Number of dropouts:	*
Pct. 8th-graders w/ basic computer skills:	100.0%
Students at this school generally go on to: Newton High	

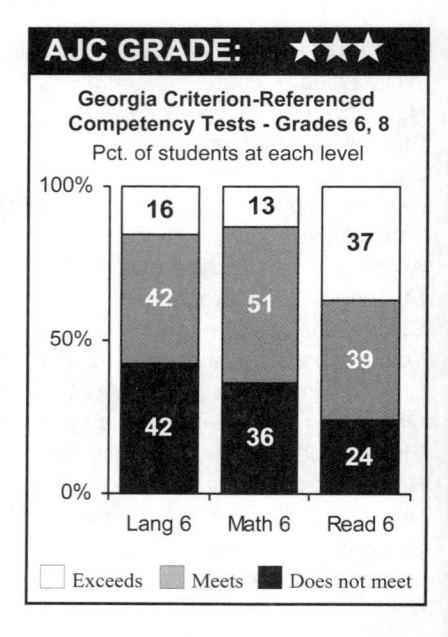

AJC GRADE: ★★★

Georgia Criterion-Referenced Competency Tests - Grades 6, 8
Pct. of students at each level

	Lang 6	Math 6	Read 6
Exceeds	16	13	37
Meets	42	51	39
Does not meet	42	36	24

Newton County Middle Schools

Eastside High School

10245 By Pass Rd, Covington, GA 30014
770-784-2920 · Grades 9 - 12

Enrollment:	1,170
White / black / other:	67.9% / 30.3% / 1.9%
Not native English-speaking:	5 / 0.4%
Limited English proficiency:	16 / 1.4%
Student absenteeism:	11.9%
Students per teacher:	15.8
Parent friendliness:	① ❷ ❸ ④ ⑤ ❻
Students in gifted program:	128 / 10.9%
Students in remedial education:	4.4%
High school completion rate:	68.8%
Students held back a grade:	11.0%
Number of dropouts:	53 / 4.1%
Students in alternative programs:	9 / 0.8%
Students in special education:	127 / 10.9%
Eligible students, free or reduced lunch:	27.9%
Total suspensions and expulsions:	608
Suspensions only, pct. in-school:	608 / 67.1%
Drugs/alcohol-related offenses:	14
Violence-related offenses:	71
Firearms-related offenses:	2
Vandalism-related offenses:	3
Theft-related offenses:	8
All other disciplinary offenses:	516
Teachers with advanced degrees:	45.9%
Average years' teaching experience:	11.0

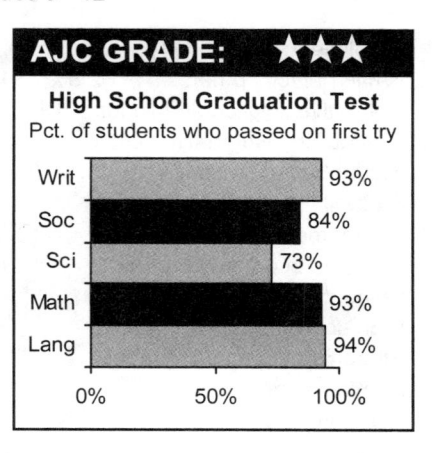

AJC GRADE: ★★★

High School Graduation Test
Pct. of students who passed on first try

- Writ: 93%
- Soc: 84%
- Sci: 73%
- Math: 93%
- Lang: 94%

GHSA classification: 8-AAAA
Interscholastic sports offered:
BB, BS, CC, CL, FB, GO, SB, SO, TE, TF, WR

Advanced Placement (AP) Exams
Students tested: 82
Tests taken: 126
Pct. of test scores 3 or higher (1 - 5 scale): 9.5%

Languages other than English taught:
French, Latin, Spanish

2000-2001 high school graduates: 183

College prep/vocational diplomas:	51.4%
College prep endorsement diplomas:	14.8%
Vocational endorsement diplomas:	29.0%
General high school diplomas:	0.0%
Special education diplomas:	4.9%
Certificates of attendance (no diploma):	0.0%

Of the 2000-2001 graduates, 69.4% were eligible for the HOPE scholarship.

Of the 1999-2000 graduates, 62 attended a Georgia public college or university. Of those, 75% met the school's minimum academic requirements.

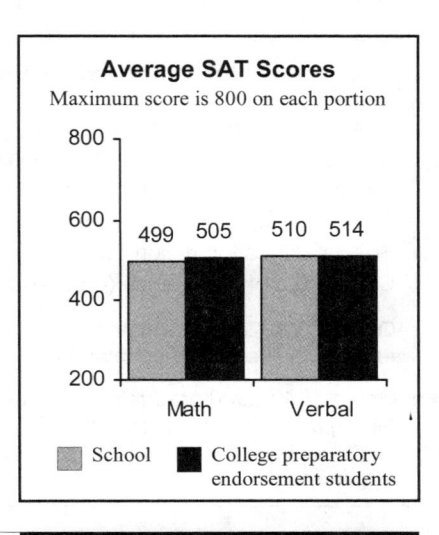

Average SAT Scores
Maximum score is 800 on each portion

- Math: School 499, College preparatory endorsement students 505
- Verbal: School 510, College preparatory endorsement students 514

Newton County High Schools

Newton High School

140 Ram Dr, Covington, GA 30014
770-787-2250 · Grades 9 - 12

Enrollment:	1,529
White / black / other:	62.3% / 34.1% / 3.5%
Not native English-speaking:	15 / 1.0%
Limited English proficiency:	38 / 2.5%
Student absenteeism:	0.2%
Students per teacher:	18.2
Parent friendliness:	①❷❸④⑤❻
Students in gifted program:	162 / 10.6%
Students in remedial education:	5.2%
High school completion rate:	74.2%
Students held back a grade:	12.9%
Number of dropouts:	76 / 4.4%
Students in alternative programs:	18 / 1.2%
Students in special education:	206 / 13.5%
Eligible students, free or reduced lunch:	26.0%
Total suspensions and expulsions:	563
Suspensions only, pct. in-school:	563 / 67.3%
Drugs/alcohol-related offenses:	7
Violence-related offenses:	90
Firearms-related offenses:	11
Vandalism-related offenses:	1
Theft-related offenses:	8
All other disciplinary offenses:	476
Teachers with advanced degrees:	56.0%
Average years' teaching experience:	13.3

AJC GRADE: ★★★

High School Graduation Test
Pct. of students who passed on first try

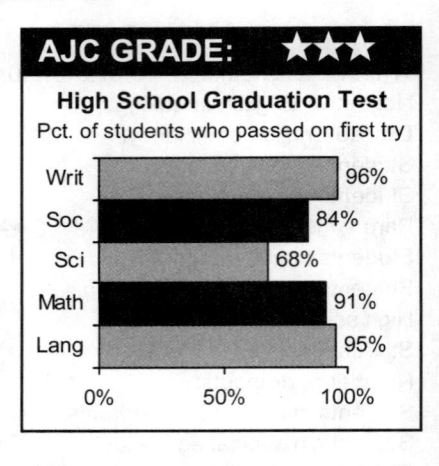

- Writ: 96%
- Soc: 84%
- Sci: 68%
- Math: 91%
- Lang: 95%

GHSA classification: 8-AAAA
Interscholastic sports offered:
BB, BS, FB, GO, SB, SO, TE, TF, WR

Advanced Placement (AP) Exams
Students tested:	45
Tests taken:	75
Pct. of test scores 3 or higher (1 - 5 scale):	44.0%

Languages other than English taught:
French, Latin, Spanish

2000-2001 high school graduates: 204

College prep/vocational diplomas:	1.5%
College prep endorsement diplomas:	49.0%
Vocational endorsement diplomas:	21.1%
General high school diplomas:	0.0%
Special education diplomas:	2.5%
Certificates of attendance (no diploma):	26.0%

Of the 2000-2001 graduates, 63.2% were eligible for the HOPE scholarship.

Of the 1999-2000 graduates, 66 attended a Georgia public college or university. Of those, 77% met the school's minimum academic requirements.

Average SAT Scores
Maximum score is 800 on each portion

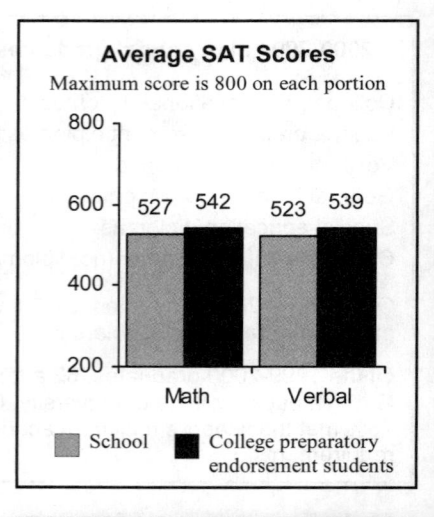

- Math — School: 527, College preparatory endorsement students: 542
- Verbal — School: 523, College preparatory endorsement students: 539

Newton County High Schools

AJC ranking of Newton County Schools

ELEMENTARY SCHOOLS

AJC Star Grade: ★★★★★

Ficquett Elementary

AJC Star Grade: ★★★

East Newton Elementary
Fairview Elementary
Heard-Mixon Elementary
Mansfield Elementary
Middle Ridge Elementary
Palmer Stone Elementary

AJC Star Grade: ★★

Livingston Elementary
Porterdale Elementary
West Newton Elementary

MIDDLE SCHOOLS

AJC Star Grade: ★★★

Clements Middle
Cousins Middle
Indian Creek Middle
Veterans Memorial Middle

HIGH SCHOOLS

AJC Star Grade: ★★★

Eastside High
Newton High

Newton County Public Schools

Paulding County Public Schools

522 Hardee St, Dallas, GA 30132
Phone: 770-443-8000 · Fax: 770-443-8089
http://www.paulding.k12.ga.us

The following pages provide detailed information on every school in the Paulding County school district. An asterisk (*) means the value of the data was zero or was not reported by the school district. A complete list of schools ranked by The Atlanta Journal-Constitution's star rating system follows the detailed school reports.

District enrollment:	16,417
White / black / other:	88.8% / 8.8% / 2.4%
Not native English-speaking:	12 / 0.1%
Expenditure per student (general fund):	$5,463
Students per teacher:	15.6
Teachers with advanced degrees:	41.3%
Average years, teaching experience:	9.0
Average teacher salary:	$39,751.92
Students in gifted program:	493 / 3.0%
Students held back a grade:	1,160 / 7.1%
Eligible students, free or reduced lunch:	3,324 / 20.0%
Number of dropouts (grades 9-12):	291 / 6.9%
High school completion rate:	71.0%
Graduates, pct. eligible for HOPE scholarships:	606 / 52.3%
Average combined SAT score (maximum 1,600):	967
Pct. of 11th-graders passing the Georgia High School Graduation Tests on first try:	65%
Percent of children 5 to 17 years of age living in poverty (2000 Census estimate):	5.6%

Abney Elementary School

4555 Dallas Acworth Hwy, Dallas, GA 30132
770-445-2656 · Grades K - 5

Enrollment:	502
White / black / other:	95.8% / 2.8% / 1.4%
Not native English-speaking:	*
Limited English proficiency:	2 / 0.4%
Student absenteeism:	4.8%
Students per teacher:	16.8
Parent friendliness:	① ❷ ❸ ④ ❺ ❻
Teachers with advanced degrees:	48.4%
Average years' teaching experience:	11.0
Students in gifted program:	10 / 2.0%
Students in remedial education:	29.0%
Students held back a grade:	3.4%
Total suspensions, pct. in-school:	5 / 0.0%
Offenses:	violence: 36, drugs: *, other: 12
Eligible students, free or reduced lunch:	19.6%
Before / after school program:	No / Yes

Students at this school generally go on to:
Moses Middle

AJC GRADE: ★★★

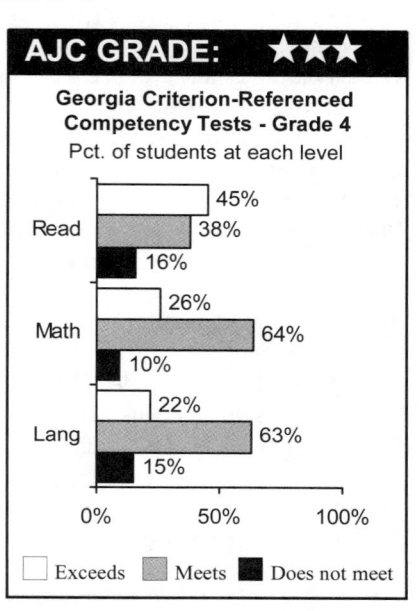

Georgia Criterion-Referenced Competency Tests - Grade 4
Pct. of students at each level

Read: Exceeds 45%, Meets 38%, Does not meet 16%
Math: Exceeds 26%, Meets 64%, Does not meet 10%
Lang: Exceeds 22%, Meets 63%, Does not meet 15%

Allgood Elementary School

312 Hart Rd, Dallas, GA 30157
770-443-8070 · Grades K - 5

Enrollment:	667
White / black / other:	93.3% / 5.8% / 0.9%
Not native English-speaking:	*
Limited English proficiency:	4 / 0.6%
Student absenteeism:	5.5%
Students per teacher:	15.7
Parent friendliness:	① ❷ ❸ ❹ ❺ ❻
Teachers with advanced degrees:	32.6%
Average years' teaching experience:	6.6
Students in gifted program:	*
Students in remedial education:	16.6%
Students held back a grade:	2.5%
Total suspensions, pct. in-school:	55 / 65.5%
Offenses:	violence: 25, drugs: *, other: 58
Eligible students, free or reduced lunch:	24.4%
Before / after school program:	No / Yes

Students at this school generally go on to:
Herschel Jones, South Paulding Middle

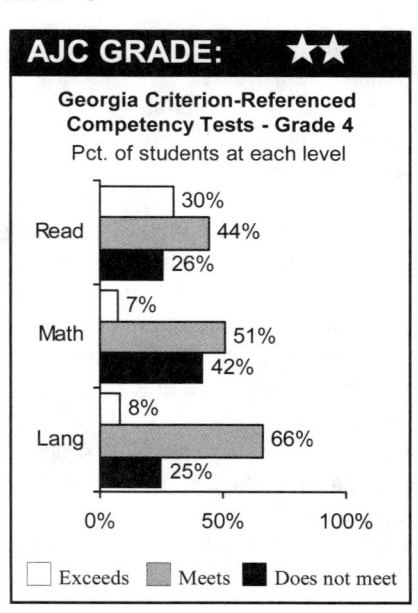

AJC GRADE: ★★

Georgia Criterion-Referenced Competency Tests - Grade 4
Pct. of students at each level

Read: Exceeds 30%, Meets 44%, Does not meet 26%
Math: Exceeds 7%, Meets 51%, Does not meet 42%
Lang: Exceeds 8%, Meets 66%, Does not meet 25%

Paulding County Elementary Schools

Dallas Elementary School

520 Hardee St, Dallas, GA 30132
770-443-8018 · Grades K - 5

Enrollment:	685
White / black / other:	79.4% / 13.9% / 6.7%
Not native English-speaking:	*
Limited English proficiency:	10 / 1.5%
Student absenteeism:	6.0%
Students per teacher:	15.1
Parent friendliness:	❶❷❸④❺❻
Teachers with advanced degrees:	52.2%
Average years' teaching experience:	10.8
Students in gifted program:	*
Students in remedial education:	27.3%
Students held back a grade:	6.7%
Total suspensions, pct. in-school:	138 / 75.4%
Offenses: violence: 33, drugs: *, other: 151	
Eligible students, free or reduced lunch:	46.5%
Before / after school program:	Yes / Yes
Students at this school generally go on to: Herschel Jones Middle	

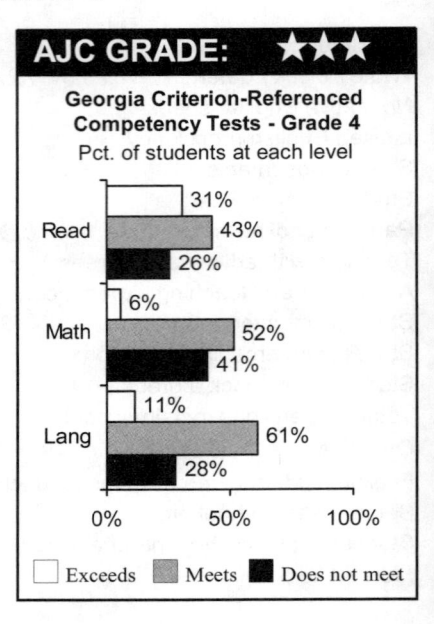

AJC GRADE: ★★★

Georgia Criterion-Referenced Competency Tests - Grade 4
Pct. of students at each level

Read: Exceeds 31%, Meets 43%, Does not meet 26%
Math: Exceeds 6%, Meets 52%, Does not meet 41%
Lang: Exceeds 11%, Meets 61%, Does not meet 28%

Floyd Shelton Elementary School

1531 Cedarcrest Rd, Dallas, GA 30132
770-443-4244 · Grades K - 5

Enrollment:	657
White / black / other:	95.9% / 2.1% / 2.0%
Not native English-speaking:	*
Limited English proficiency:	4 / 0.6%
Student absenteeism:	4.8%
Students per teacher:	16.4
Parent friendliness:	①❷❸④⑤❻
Teachers with advanced degrees:	37.5%
Average years' teaching experience:	9.8
Students in gifted program:	6 / 0.9%
Students in remedial education:	21.1%
Students held back a grade:	2.6%
Total suspensions, pct. in-school:	9 / 33.3%
Offenses: violence: 7, drugs: *, other: 16	
Eligible students, free or reduced lunch:	10.2%
Before / after school program:	No / Yes
Students at this school generally go on to: East Paulding, Moses Middle	

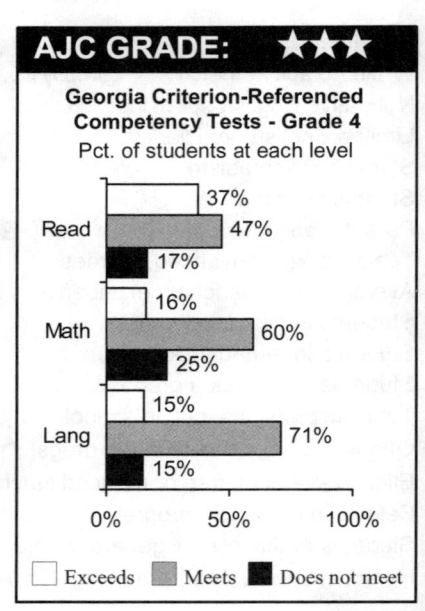

AJC GRADE: ★★★

Georgia Criterion-Referenced Competency Tests - Grade 4
Pct. of students at each level

Read: Exceeds 37%, Meets 47%, Does not meet 17%
Math: Exceeds 16%, Meets 60%, Does not meet 25%
Lang: Exceeds 15%, Meets 71%, Does not meet 15%

Paulding County Elementary Schools

Hiram Elementary School

200 Seaboard Ave, Hiram, GA 30141
770-943-5263 · Grades K - 5

Enrollment:	599
White / black / other:	90.2% / 7.8% / 2.0%
Not native English-speaking:	*
Limited English proficiency:	5 / 0.8%
Student absenteeism:	5.9%
Students per teacher:	14.8
Parent friendliness:	① ❷ ❸ ④ ⑤ ❻
Teachers with advanced degrees:	46.3%
Average years' teaching experience:	10.2
Students in gifted program:	15 / 2.5%
Students in remedial education:	21.6%
Students held back a grade:	2.0%
Total suspensions, pct. in-school:	31 / 29.0%
Offenses:	violence: 34, drugs: *, other: 24
Eligible students, free or reduced lunch:	30.6%
Before / after school program:	No / Yes

Students at this school generally go on to:
J.A. Dobbins, South Paulding Middle

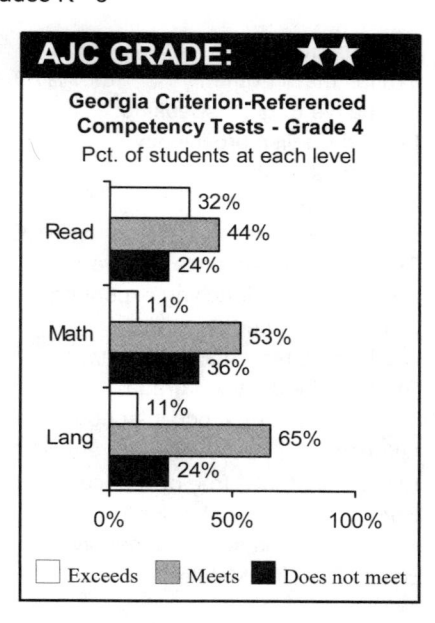

AJC GRADE: ★★

Georgia Criterion-Referenced Competency Tests - Grade 4
Pct. of students at each level

Read: 32% Exceeds, 44% Meets, 24% Does not meet
Math: 11% Exceeds, 53% Meets, 36% Does not meet
Lang: 11% Exceeds, 65% Meets, 24% Does not meet

McGarity Elementary School

262 Rakestraw Mill Rd, Hiram, GA 30141
770-445-9007 · Grades K - 5

Enrollment:	613
White / black / other:	90.4% / 6.9% / 2.8%
Not native English-speaking:	*
Limited English proficiency:	9 / 1.5%
Student absenteeism:	4.4%
Students per teacher:	16.0
Parent friendliness:	① ❷ ❸ ④ ❺ ❻
Teachers with advanced degrees:	51.3%
Average years' teaching experience:	11.6
Students in gifted program:	6 / 1.0%
Students in remedial education:	23.7%
Students held back a grade:	1.5%
Total suspensions, pct. in-school:	2 / 0.0%
Offenses:	violence: 2, drugs: *, other: 6
Eligible students, free or reduced lunch:	14.5%
Before / after school program:	No / Yes

Students at this school generally go on to:
East Paulding Middle

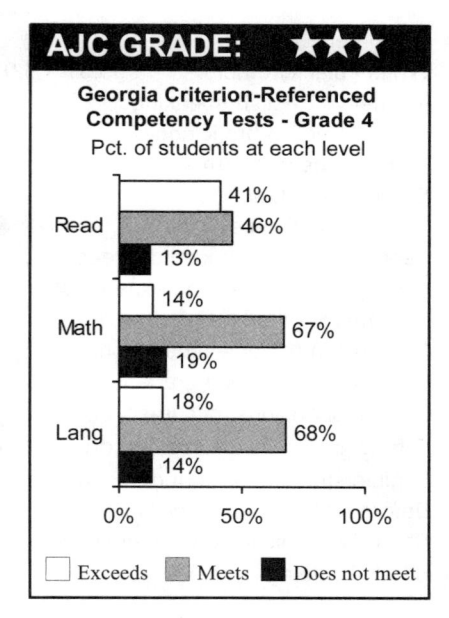

AJC GRADE: ★★★

Georgia Criterion-Referenced Competency Tests - Grade 4
Pct. of students at each level

Read: 41% Exceeds, 46% Meets, 13% Does not meet
Math: 14% Exceeds, 67% Meets, 19% Does not meet
Lang: 18% Exceeds, 68% Meets, 14% Does not meet

Paulding County Elementary Schools

Nebo Elementary School

2843 Nebo Rd, Dallas, GA 30157
770-443-8777 · Grades K - 5

Enrollment:	772
White / black / other:	87.7% / 9.1% / 3.2%
Not native English-speaking:	*
Limited English proficiency:	2 / 0.3%
Student absenteeism:	5.4%
Students per teacher:	14.5
Parent friendliness:	① ❷ ❸ ❹ ❺ ❻
Teachers with advanced degrees:	23.6%
Average years' teaching experience:	5.5
Students in gifted program:	32 / 4.1%
Students in remedial education:	15.1%
Students held back a grade:	2.7%
Total suspensions, pct. in-school:	2 / 50.0%
Offenses:	violence: 35, drugs: *, other: 18
Eligible students, free or reduced lunch:	23.1%
Before / after school program:	No / Yes
Students at this school generally go on to:	
South Paulding Middle	

AJC GRADE: ★★★

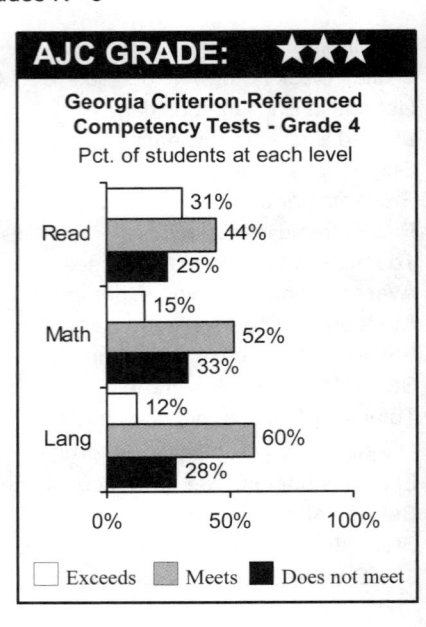

Georgia Criterion-Referenced Competency Tests - Grade 4
Pct. of students at each level

- Read: 31% Exceeds, 44% Meets, 25% Does not meet
- Math: 15% Exceeds, 52% Meets, 33% Does not meet
- Lang: 12% Exceeds, 60% Meets, 28% Does not meet

New Georgia Elementary School

5800 Mulberry Rock Rd, Villa Rica, GA 30180
770-445-3597 · Grades K - 5

Enrollment:	476
White / black / other:	93.3% / 5.0% / 1.7%
Not native English-speaking:	*
Limited English proficiency:	2 / 0.4%
Student absenteeism:	5.7%
Students per teacher:	14.3
Parent friendliness:	① ② ❸ ④ ⑤ ❻
Teachers with advanced degrees:	52.9%
Average years' teaching experience:	12.3
Students in gifted program:	*
Students in remedial education:	17.4%
Students held back a grade:	4.4%
Total suspensions, pct. in-school:	1 / 0.0%
Offenses:	violence: 91, drugs: *, other: 29
Eligible students, free or reduced lunch:	22.6%
Before / after school program:	No / Yes
Students at this school generally go on to:	
South Paulding Middle	

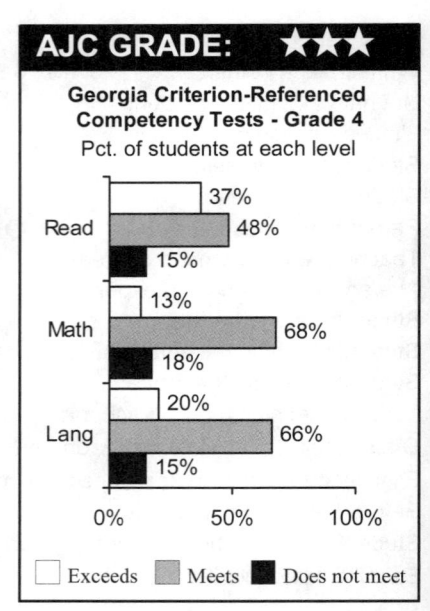

AJC GRADE: ★★★

Georgia Criterion-Referenced Competency Tests - Grade 4
Pct. of students at each level

- Read: 37% Exceeds, 48% Meets, 15% Does not meet
- Math: 13% Exceeds, 68% Meets, 18% Does not meet
- Lang: 20% Exceeds, 66% Meets, 15% Does not meet

Paulding County Elementary Schools

Northside Elementary School

2223 Cartersville Hwy, Dallas, GA 30132
770-443-7008 · Grades K - 5

Enrollment:	665
White / black / other:	94.3% / 3.5% / 2.3%
Not native English-speaking:	*
Limited English proficiency:	3 / 0.5%
Student absenteeism:	5.2%
Students per teacher:	14.0
Parent friendliness:	①❷❸❹❺❻
Teachers with advanced degrees:	41.7%
Average years' teaching experience:	10.1
Students in gifted program:	*
Students in remedial education:	19.8%
Students held back a grade:	3.9%
Total suspensions, pct. in-school:	54 / 68.5%
Offenses: violence: 25, drugs: * , other: 38	
Eligible students, free or reduced lunch:	23.5%
Before / after school program:	No / Yes

Students at this school generally go on to:
Herschel Jones, South Paulding Middle

AJC GRADE: ★★★

Georgia Criterion-Referenced Competency Tests - Grade 4
Pct. of students at each level

Read: 34% / 53% / 14%
Math: 9% / 65% / 27%
Lang: 16% / 68% / 16%

☐ Exceeds ▨ Meets ■ Does not meet

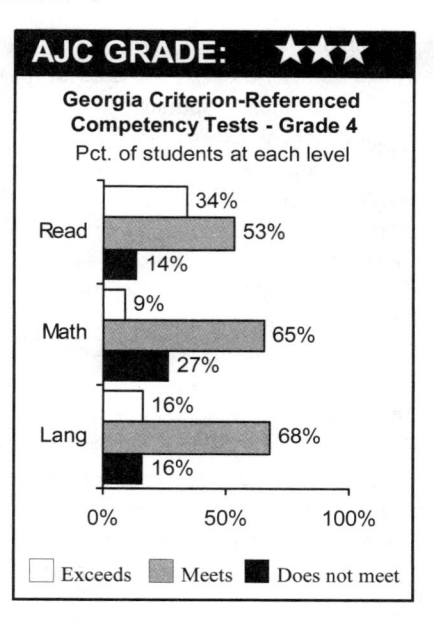

Panter Elementary School

190 Panter School Rd, Hiram, GA 30141
770-443-4303 · Grades K - 5

Enrollment:	930
White / black / other:	79.0% / 18.2% / 2.8%
Not native English-speaking:	7 / 0.8%
Limited English proficiency:	17 / 1.8%
Student absenteeism:	4.4%
Students per teacher:	17.3
Parent friendliness:	①❷❸❹❺❻
Teachers with advanced degrees:	38.2%
Average years' teaching experience:	6.7
Students in gifted program:	25 / 2.7%
Students in remedial education:	18.3%
Students held back a grade:	1.9%
Total suspensions, pct. in-school:	22 / 0.0%
Offenses: violence: 18, drugs: * , other: 30	
Eligible students, free or reduced lunch:	20.6%
Before / after school program:	No / Yes

Students at this school generally go on to:
J.A. Dobbins Middle

AJC GRADE: ★★★

Georgia Criterion-Referenced Competency Tests - Grade 4
Pct. of students at each level

Read: 36% / 51% / 13%
Math: 8% / 61% / 31%
Lang: 18% / 65% / 16%

☐ Exceeds ▨ Meets ■ Does not meet

Paulding County Elementary Schools

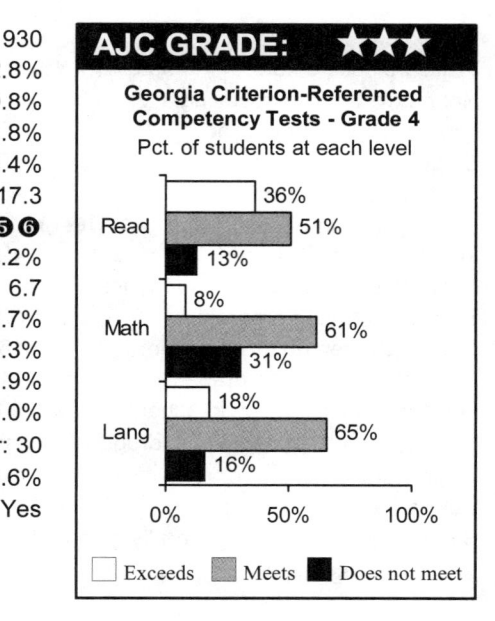

Ritch Elementary School

140 Bethel Church Rd, Hiram, GA 30141
770-443-4269 · Grades K - 5

Enrollment:	904
White / black / other:	85.8% / 11.6% / 2.5%
Not native English-speaking:	*
Limited English proficiency:	6 / 0.7%
Student absenteeism:	4.6%
Students per teacher:	16.2
Parent friendliness:	①❷❸④❺❻
Teachers with advanced degrees:	42.1%
Average years' teaching experience:	9.9
Students in gifted program:	42 / 4.6%
Students in remedial education:	20.2%
Students held back a grade:	2.8%
Total suspensions, pct. in-school:	31 / 0.0%
Offenses:	violence: 23, drugs: *, other: 104
Eligible students, free or reduced lunch:	11.6%
Before / after school program:	Yes / Yes

Students at this school generally go on to:
J.A. Dobbins, South Paulding Middle

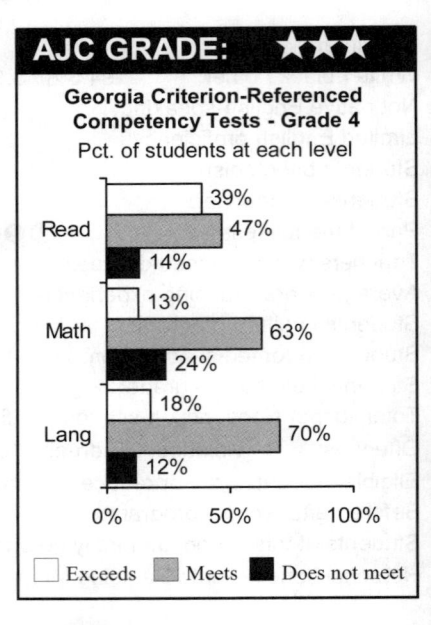

AJC GRADE: ★★★

Georgia Criterion-Referenced Competency Tests - Grade 4
Pct. of students at each level

- Read: Exceeds 39%, Meets 47%, Does not meet 14%
- Math: Exceeds 13%, Meets 63%, Does not meet 24%
- Lang: Exceeds 18%, Meets 70%, Does not meet 12%

Roberts Elementary School

1833 Mount Tabor Church Rd, Dallas, GA 30157
770-443-8060 · Grades K - 5

Enrollment:	682
White / black / other:	95.3% / 4.4% / 0.3%
Not native English-speaking:	*
Limited English proficiency:	*
Student absenteeism:	5.3%
Students per teacher:	13.9
Parent friendliness:	①❷❸④❺❻
Teachers with advanced degrees:	42.0%
Average years' teaching experience:	9.5
Students in gifted program:	17 / 2.5%
Students in remedial education:	18.7%
Students held back a grade:	4.4%
Total suspensions, pct. in-school:	62 / 87.1%
Offenses:	violence: 39, drugs: *, other: 79
Eligible students, free or reduced lunch:	17.4%
Before / after school program:	No / Yes

Students at this school generally go on to:
East Paulding Middle

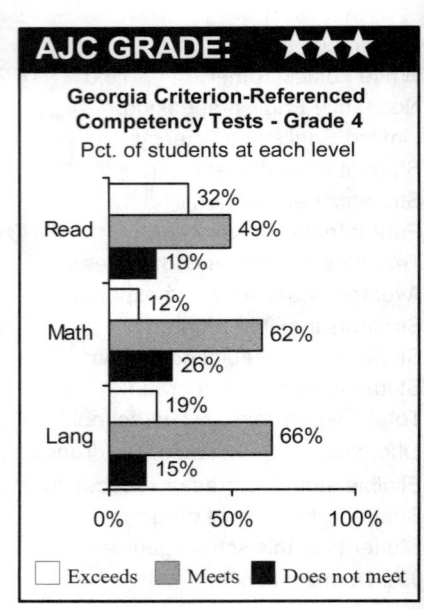

AJC GRADE: ★★★

Georgia Criterion-Referenced Competency Tests - Grade 4
Pct. of students at each level

- Read: Exceeds 32%, Meets 49%, Does not meet 19%
- Math: Exceeds 12%, Meets 62%, Does not meet 26%
- Lang: Exceeds 19%, Meets 66%, Does not meet 15%

Paulding County Elementary Schools

Union Elementary School

206 Highway 101 S, Temple, GA 30179
770-443-4191 · Grades K - 5

Enrollment:	471
White / black / other:	85.6% / 10.2% / 4.2%
Not native English-speaking:	*
Limited English proficiency:	3 / 0.6%
Student absenteeism:	5.4%
Students per teacher:	16.5
Parent friendliness:	① ❷ ❸ ④ ⑤ ❻
Teachers with advanced degrees:	46.7%
Average years' teaching experience:	8.9
Students in gifted program:	*
Students in remedial education:	17.8%
Students held back a grade:	2.3%
Total suspensions, pct. in-school:	10 / 0.0%
Offenses: violence: 26, drugs: *, other: 115	
Eligible students, free or reduced lunch:	34.0%
Before / after school program:	No / Yes

Students at this school generally go on to:
Herschel Jones, South Paulding Middle

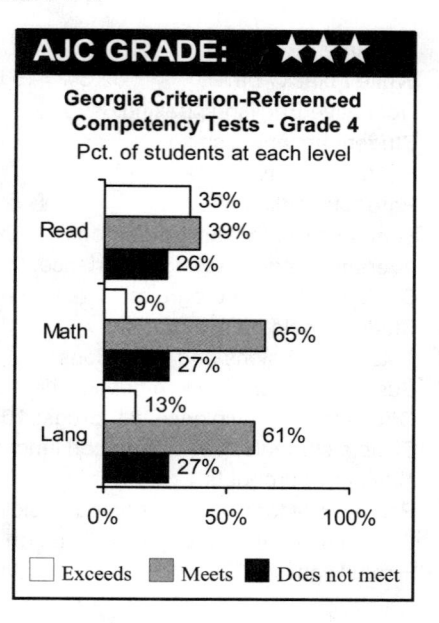

AJC GRADE: ★★★

Georgia Criterion-Referenced Competency Tests - Grade 4
Pct. of students at each level

Read: Exceeds 35%, Meets 39%, Does not meet 26%
Math: Exceeds 9%, Meets 65%, Does not meet 27%
Lang: Exceeds 13%, Meets 61%, Does not meet 27%

Paulding County Elementary Schools

Dobbins Middle School

637 Williams Lake Rd, Powder Springs, GA 30127
770-443-4835 · Grades 6 - 8

Enrollment:	1,061
White / black / other:	82.3% / 15.6% / 2.2%
Not native English-speaking:	*
Student absenteeism:	6.0%
Students per teacher:	16.9
Parent friendliness:	❶❷❸❹❺❻
Teachers with advanced degrees:	31.7%
Average years' teaching experience:	7.4
Students in gifted program:	63 / 5.9%
Students held back a grade:	2.5%
Total suspensions and expulsions:	113
Suspensions only, pct. in-school:	110 / 76.4%
Offenses:	violence: 81, drugs: 10, other: 96
Eligible students, free or reduced lunch:	21.5%
Number of dropouts:	4 / 0.3%
Pct. 8th-graders w/ basic computer skills:	94.6%
Students at this school generally go on to:	
Hiram High	

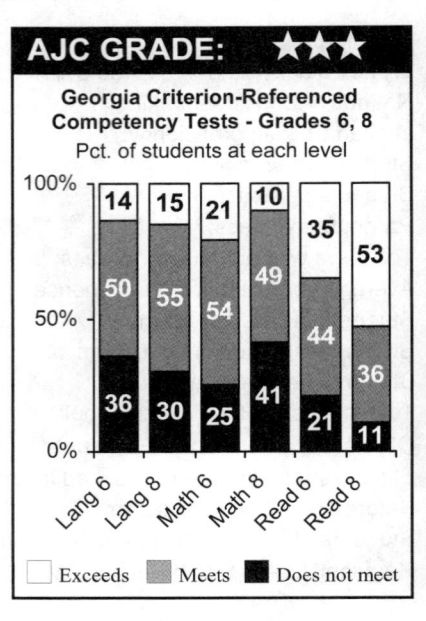

AJC GRADE: ★★★

Georgia Criterion-Referenced Competency Tests - Grades 6, 8
Pct. of students at each level

	Lang 6	Lang 8	Math 6	Math 8	Read 6	Read 8
Exceeds	14	15	21	10	35	53
Meets	50	55	54	49	44	36
Does not meet	36	30	25	41	21	11

East Paulding Middle School

2945 Hiram Acworth Hwy, Dallas, GA 30157
770-443-7000 · Grades 6 - 8

Enrollment:	1,198
White / black / other:	93.2% / 5.0% / 1.8%
Not native English-speaking:	*
Student absenteeism:	5.2%
Students per teacher:	17.4
Parent friendliness:	❶❷❸④⑤❻
Teachers with advanced degrees:	37.7%
Average years' teaching experience:	8.5
Students in gifted program:	105 / 8.8%
Students held back a grade:	4.3%
Total suspensions and expulsions:	58
Suspensions only, pct. in-school:	56 / 66.1%
Offenses:	violence: 54, drugs: 2, other: 43
Eligible students, free or reduced lunch:	13.8%
Number of dropouts:	2 / 0.2%
Pct. 8th-graders w/ basic computer skills:	55.0%
Students at this school generally go on to:	
East Paulding High	

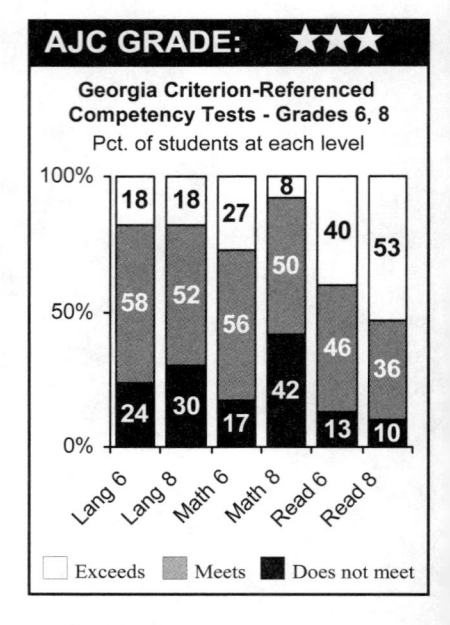

AJC GRADE: ★★★

Georgia Criterion-Referenced Competency Tests - Grades 6, 8
Pct. of students at each level

	Lang 6	Lang 8	Math 6	Math 8	Read 6	Read 8
Exceeds	18	18	27	8	40	53
Meets	58	52	56	50	46	36
Does not meet	24	30	17	42	13	10

Paulding County Middle Schools

Herschel Jones Middle School

100 Stadium Dr, Dallas, GA 30132
770-443-8024 · Grades 6 - 8

Enrollment:	844
White / black / other:	86.8% / 10.3% / 2.8%
Not native English-speaking:	*
Student absenteeism:	5.9%
Students per teacher:	15.1
Parent friendliness:	① ❷ ❸ ④ ⑤ ❻
Teachers with advanced degrees:	50.0%
Average years' teaching experience:	9.8
Students in gifted program:	24 / 2.8%
Students held back a grade:	7.0%
Total suspensions and expulsions:	104
Suspensions only, pct. in-school:	103 / 75.7%
Offenses: violence: 71, drugs: 3, other: 107	
Eligible students, free or reduced lunch:	32.6%
Number of dropouts:	1 / 0.1%
Pct. 8th-graders w/ basic computer skills:	100.0%

Students at this school generally go on to:
Paulding High

AJC GRADE: ★★★

Georgia Criterion-Referenced Competency Tests - Grades 6, 8
Pct. of students at each level

	Lang 6	Lang 8	Math 6	Math 8	Read 6	Read 8
Exceeds	11	28	16	6	35	57
Meets	50	48	51	54	39	30
Does not meet	39	24	34	39	26	13

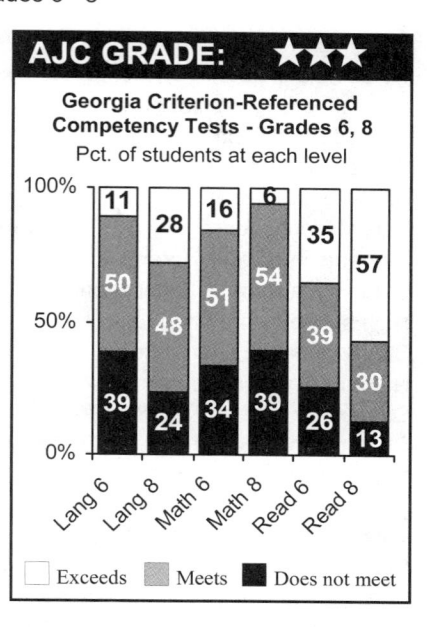

South Paulding Middle School

592 Nebo Rd, Dallas, GA 30157
770-445-8500 · Grades 6 - 8

Enrollment:	873
White / black / other:	90.4% / 6.5% / 3.1%
Not native English-speaking:	*
Student absenteeism:	6.7%
Students per teacher:	15.5
Parent friendliness:	❶ ❷ ❸ ④ ❺ ❻
Teachers with advanced degrees:	45.6%
Average years' teaching experience:	8.2
Students in gifted program:	59 / 6.8%
Students held back a grade:	3.7%
Total suspensions and expulsions:	94
Suspensions only, pct. in-school:	94 / 18.1%
Offenses: violence: 71, drugs: *, other: 104	
Eligible students, free or reduced lunch:	20.0%
Number of dropouts:	1 / 0.1%
Pct. 8th-graders w/ basic computer skills:	70.0%

Students at this school generally go on to:
Hiram, Paulding High

AJC GRADE: ★★★

Georgia Criterion-Referenced Competency Tests - Grades 6, 8
Pct. of students at each level

	Lang 6	Lang 8	Math 6	Math 8	Read 6	Read 8
Exceeds	11	21	15	8	33	55
Meets	45	54	52	53	40	31
Does not meet	44	25	33	39	27	14

Paulding County Middle Schools

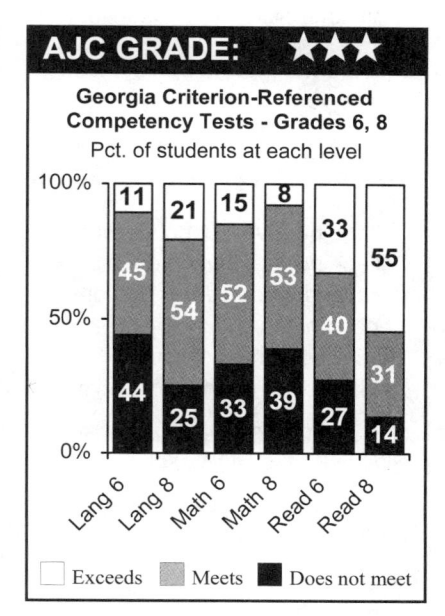

East Paulding High School

3320 E Paulding Dr, Dallas, GA 30157
770-445-5100 · Grades 9 - 12

Enrollment:	1,180
White / black / other:	93.1% / 4.9% / 1.9%
Not native English-speaking:	*
Limited English proficiency:	4 / 0.3%
Student absenteeism:	6.6%
Students per teacher:	16.3
Parent friendliness:	❶❷❸④⑤❻
Students in gifted program:	52 / 4.4%
Students in remedial education:	4.6%
High school completion rate:	78.5%
Students held back a grade:	14.4%
Number of dropouts:	91 / 7.1%
Students in alternative programs:	10 / 0.8%
Students in special education:	108 / 9.2%
Eligible students, free or reduced lunch:	8.1%
Total suspensions and expulsions:	80
Suspensions only, pct. in-school:	70 / 58.6%
Drugs/alcohol-related offenses:	7
Violence-related offenses:	34
Firearms-related offenses:	3
Vandalism-related offenses:	8
Theft-related offenses:	*
All other disciplinary offenses:	64
Teachers with advanced degrees:	41.7%
Average years' teaching experience:	10.0

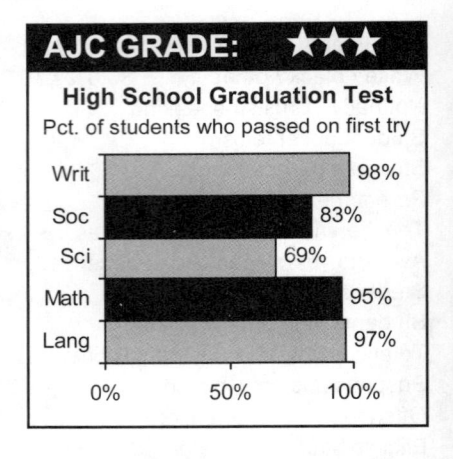

AJC GRADE: ★★★

High School Graduation Test
Pct. of students who passed on first try

- Writ: 98%
- Soc: 83%
- Sci: 69%
- Math: 95%
- Lang: 97%

GHSA classification:	7-AAAA

Interscholastic sports offered:
BB, CC, CL, FB, GO, SB, SO, TE, TF, VB, WR

Advanced Placement (AP) Exams
Students tested:	71
Tests taken:	111
Pct. of test scores 3 or higher (1 - 5 scale):	45.0%

Languages other than English taught:
French, Latin, Spanish

2000-2001 high school graduates:	**230**
College prep/vocational diplomas:	0.0%
College prep endorsement diplomas:	70.0%
Vocational endorsement diplomas:	24.8%
General high school diplomas:	0.0%
Special education diplomas:	2.2%
Certificates of attendance (no diploma):	3.0%

Of the 2000-2001 graduates, 56.5% were eligible for the HOPE scholarship.

Of the 1999-2000 graduates, 70 attended a Georgia public college or university. Of those, 91% met the school's minimum academic requirements.

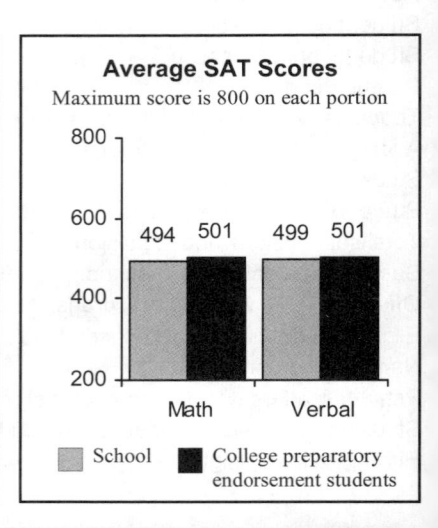

Average SAT Scores
Maximum score is 800 on each portion

- Math: School 494, College preparatory endorsement students 501
- Verbal: School 499, College preparatory endorsement students 501

The Atlanta Journal-Constitution / Page 480

Paulding County High Schools

Hiram High School

702 Ballentine Dr, Hiram, GA 30141
770-443-1182 · Grades 9 - 12

Enrollment:	1,228
White / black / other:	83.1% / 14.3% / 2.7%
Not native English-speaking:	5 / 0.4%
Limited English proficiency:	21 / 1.7%
Student absenteeism:	7.5%
Students per teacher:	18.0
Parent friendliness:	① ❷ ❸ ④ ⑤ ❻
Students in gifted program:	12 / 1.0%
Students in remedial education:	2.9%
High school completion rate:	*
Students held back a grade:	19.3%
Number of dropouts:	91 / 6.5%
Students in alternative programs:	30 / 2.4%
Students in special education:	127 / 10.3%
Eligible students, free or reduced lunch:	12.5%
Total suspensions and expulsions:	170
Suspensions only, pct. in-school:	165 / 38.2%
Drugs/alcohol-related offenses:	8
Violence-related offenses:	93
Firearms-related offenses:	3
Vandalism-related offenses:	2
Theft-related offenses:	*
All other disciplinary offenses:	102
Teachers with advanced degrees:	41.2%
Average years' teaching experience:	6.9

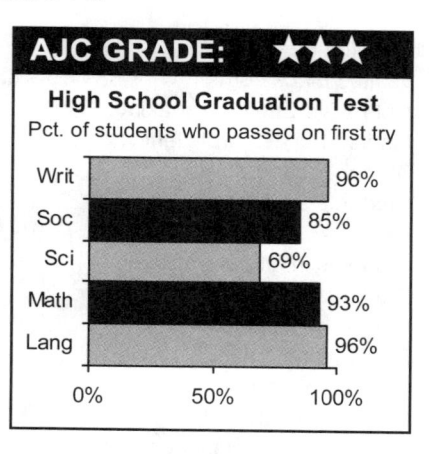

AJC GRADE: ★★★

High School Graduation Test
Pct. of students who passed on first try

- Writ: 96%
- Soc: 85%
- Sci: 69%
- Math: 93%
- Lang: 96%

GHSA classification: 7-AAAA
Interscholastic sports offered:
BB, BS, CC, CL, FB, GO, RI, SB, SO, TE, TF, VB, WR

Advanced Placement (AP) Exams
Students tested: 35
Tests taken: 60
Pct. of test scores 3 or higher (1 - 5 scale): 28.3%

Languages other than English taught:
French, Spanish

2000-2001 high school graduates: 149

College prep/vocational diplomas:	4.7%
College prep endorsement diplomas:	53.0%
Vocational endorsement diplomas:	40.9%
General high school diplomas:	0.0%
Special education diplomas:	1.3%
Certificates of attendance (no diploma):	0.0%

Of the 2000-2001 graduates, 43.6% were eligible for the HOPE scholarship.

Hiram High School is a new school and therefore some data was not available for this report.

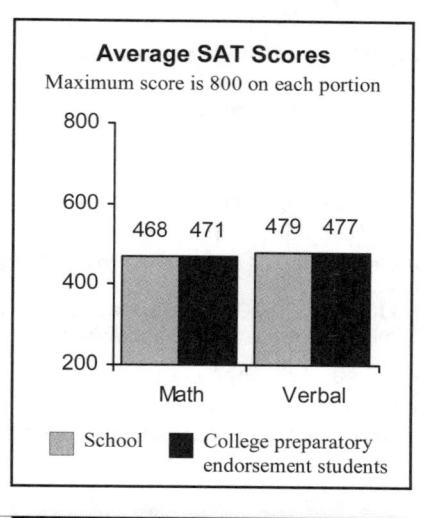

Average SAT Scores
Maximum score is 800 on each portion

Math: School 468, College preparatory endorsement students 471
Verbal: School 479, College preparatory endorsement students 477

Paulding County High Schools

Paulding County High School

1297 Villa Rica Hwy, Dallas, GA 30157
770-443-8008 · Grades 9 - 12

Enrollment:	1,410
White / black / other:	89.6% / 8.9% / 1.6%
Not native English-speaking:	*
Limited English proficiency:	9 / 0.6%
Student absenteeism:	7.8%
Students per teacher:	14.2
Parent friendliness:	① ❷ ❸ ④ ⑤ ❻
Students in gifted program:	25 / 1.8%
Students in remedial education:	2.8%
High school completion rate:	63.8%
Students held back a grade:	22.2%
Number of dropouts:	109 / 7.1%
Students in alternative programs:	29 / 2.1%
Students in special education:	192 / 13.6%
Eligible students, free or reduced lunch:	18.1%
Total suspensions and expulsions:	116
Suspensions only, pct. in-school:	109 / 39.4%
Drugs/alcohol-related offenses:	16
Violence-related offenses:	38
Firearms-related offenses:	3
Vandalism-related offenses:	6
Theft-related offenses:	*
All other disciplinary offenses:	91
Teachers with advanced degrees:	38.8%
Average years' teaching experience:	10.0

AJC GRADE: ★★★

High School Graduation Test
Pct. of students who passed on first try

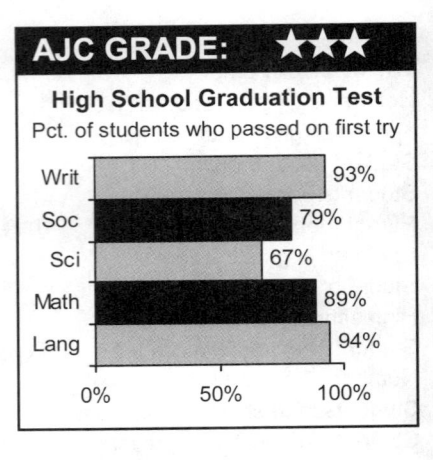

- Writ: 93%
- Soc: 79%
- Sci: 67%
- Math: 89%
- Lang: 94%

GHSA classification: 7-AAAA
Interscholastic sports offered:
BB, BS, CC, CL, FB, GO, SB, SO, TE, TF, VB, WR

Advanced Placement (AP) Exams
Students tested:	70
Tests taken:	96
Pct. of test scores 3 or higher (1 - 5 scale):	33.3%

Languages other than English taught:
French, German, Spanish

2000-2001 high school graduates: 227

College prep/vocational diplomas:	16.3%
College prep endorsement diplomas:	50.7%
Vocational endorsement diplomas:	28.2%
General high school diplomas:	0.0%
Special education diplomas:	4.8%
Certificates of attendance (no diploma):	0.0%

Of the 2000-2001 graduates, 53.7% were eligible for the HOPE scholarship.

Of the 1999-2000 graduates, 87 attended a Georgia public college or university. Of those, 86% met the school's minimum academic requirements.

Average SAT Scores
Maximum score is 800 on each portion

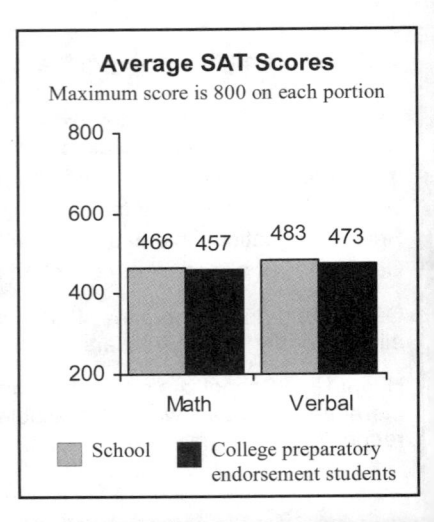

- Math: School 466, College preparatory endorsement students 457
- Verbal: School 483, College preparatory endorsement students 473

The Atlanta Journal-Constitution / Page 482

Paulding County High Schools

AJC ranking of Paulding County Schools

ELEMENTARY SCHOOLS

AJC Star Grade: ★★★

Abney Elementary
Dallas Elementary
Floyd Shelton Elementary
McGarity Elementary
Nebo Elementary
New Georgia Elementary
Northside Elementary
Panter Elementary
Ritch Elementary
Roberts Elementary
Union Elementary

AJC Star Grade: ★★

Allgood Elementary
Hiram Elementary

MIDDLE SCHOOLS

AJC Star Grade: ★★★

Dobbins Middle
East Paulding Middle
Herschel Jones Middle
South Paulding Middle

HIGH SCHOOLS

AJC Star Grade: ★★★

East Paulding High
Hiram High
Paulding County High

Paulding County Public Schools

Rockdale County Public Schools

954 N Main St NW, Conyers, GA 30012
Phone: 770-483-4713 · Fax: 770-860-4285
http://www.rockdale.k12.ga.us

The following pages provide detailed information on every school in the Rockdale County school district. An asterisk (*) means the value of the data was zero or was not reported by the school district. A complete list of schools ranked by The Atlanta Journal-Constitution's star rating system follows the detailed school reports.

District enrollment:	13,398
White / black / other:	67.9% / 23.9% / 8.2%
Not native English-speaking:	295 / 2.2%
Expenditure per student (general fund):	$6,099
Students per teacher:	15.5
Teachers with advanced degrees:	49.1%
Average years, teaching experience:	13.7
Average teacher salary:	$43,575.37
Students in gifted program:	1,017 / 7.6%
Students held back a grade:	335 / 2.5%
Eligible students, free or reduced lunch:	3,690 / 27.3%
Number of dropouts (grades 9-12):	152 / 3.5%
High school completion rate:	91.9%
Graduates, pct. eligible for HOPE scholarships:	726 / 64.9%
Average combined SAT score (maximum 1,600):	1,008
Pct. of 11th-graders passing the Georgia High School Graduation Tests on first try:	69%
Percent of children 5 to 17 years of age living in poverty (2000 Census estimate):	9.9%

Barksdale Elementary School

596 Oglesby Bridge Rd SE, Conyers, GA 30094
770-483-9514 · Grades K - 5

Enrollment:	670
White / black / other:	85.1% / 9.6% / 5.4%
Not native English-speaking:	*
Limited English proficiency:	1 / 0.1%
Student absenteeism:	3.6%
Students per teacher:	17.4
Parent friendliness:	❶❷❸④⑤❻
Teachers with advanced degrees:	48.7%
Average years' teaching experience:	16.4
Students in gifted program:	16 / 2.4%
Students in remedial education:	11.7%
Students held back a grade:	1.3%
Total suspensions, pct. in-school:	15 / 60.0%
Offenses:	violence: 10, drugs: * , other: 27
Eligible students, free or reduced lunch:	14.3%
Before / after school program:	No / Yes

Students at this school generally go on to:
Edwards, Memorial Middle

AJC GRADE: ★★★

Georgia Criterion-Referenced Competency Tests - Grade 4
Pct. of students at each level

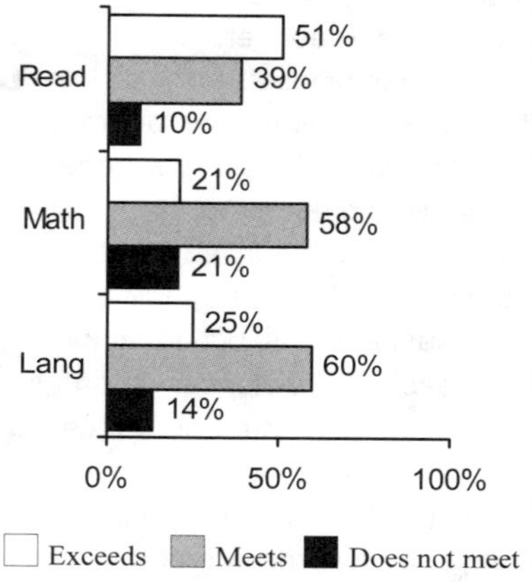
Read
51%
39%
10%
Math
21%
58%
21%
Lang
25%
60%
14%
0%
50%
100%
Exceeds
Meets
Does not meet

Flat Shoals Elementary School

1455 Flat Shoals Rd SE, Conyers, GA 30013
770-483-5136 · Grades K - 5

Enrollment:	804
White / black / other:	51.9% / 39.9% / 8.2%
Not native English-speaking:	1 / 0.1%
Limited English proficiency:	9 / 1.1%
Student absenteeism:	3.9%
Students per teacher:	16.8
Parent friendliness:	①❷❸④⑤❻
Teachers with advanced degrees:	43.8%
Average years' teaching experience:	12.2
Students in gifted program:	30 / 3.7%
Students in remedial education:	1.0%
Students held back a grade:	3.0%
Total suspensions, pct. in-school:	110 / 73.6%
Offenses:	violence: 68, drugs: * , other: 218
Eligible students, free or reduced lunch:	31.0%
Before / after school program:	No / Yes

Students at this school generally go on to:
Conyers, Memorial Middle

AJC GRADE: ★★★

Georgia Criterion-Referenced Competency Tests - Grade 4
Pct. of students at each level

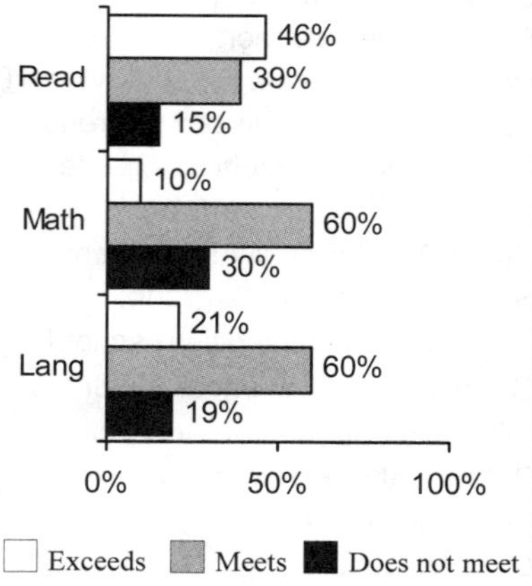
Read
46%
39%
15%
Math
10%
60%
30%
Lang
21%
60%
19%
0%
50%
100%
Exceeds
Meets
Does not meet

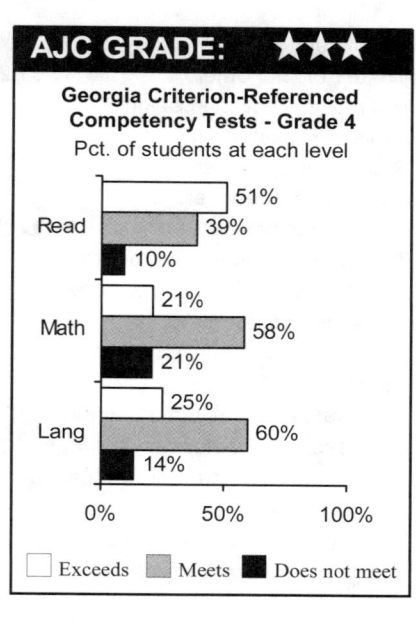

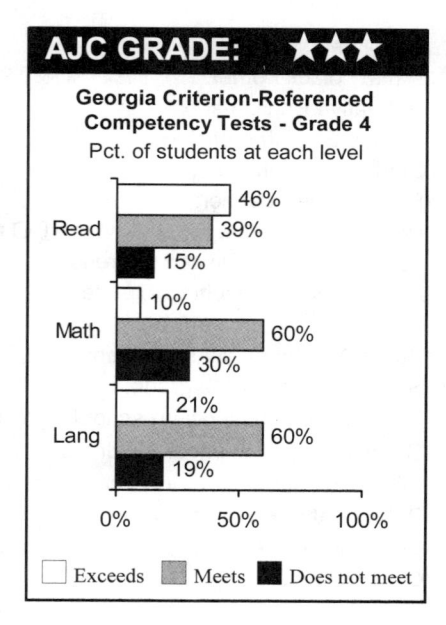

Hicks Elementary School

930 Rowland Rd NE, Conyers, GA 30012
770-483-4410 · Grades K - 5

Enrollment:	461
White / black / other:	35.8% / 51.2% / 13.0%
Not native English-speaking:	*
Limited English proficiency:	11 / 2.4%
Student absenteeism:	4.5%
Students per teacher:	15.1
Parent friendliness:	❶❷❸④❺❻
Teachers with advanced degrees:	41.9%
Average years' teaching experience:	11.1
Students in gifted program:	6 / 1.3%
Students in remedial education:	20.0%
Students held back a grade:	3.0%
Total suspensions, pct. in-school:	118 / 98.3%
Offenses: violence: *, drugs: *, other:	203
Eligible students, free or reduced lunch:	57.6%
Before / after school program:	No / Yes

Students at this school generally go on to:
Conyers, Edwards, Memorial Middle

AJC GRADE: ★★★

Georgia Criterion-Referenced Competency Tests - Grade 4
Pct. of students at each level

Read: Exceeds 20%, Meets 56%, Does not meet 24%
Math: Exceeds 10%, Meets 40%, Does not meet 50%
Lang: Exceeds 16%, Meets 57%, Does not meet 27%

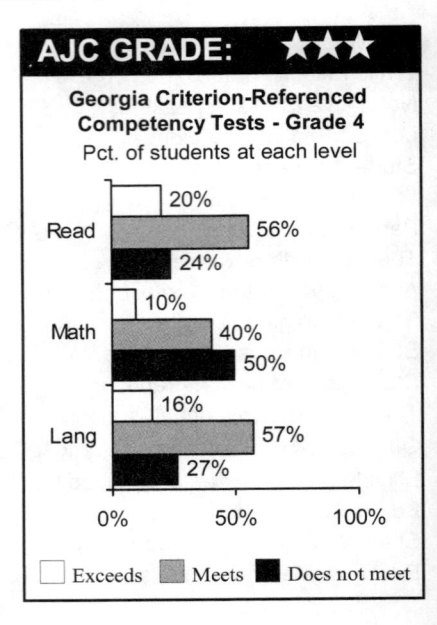

Hightower Trail Elementary School

2510 Highway 138 NE, Conyers, GA 30013
770-388-0751 · Grades K - 5

Enrollment:	573
White / black / other:	76.1% / 20.9% / 3.0%
Not native English-speaking:	*
Limited English proficiency:	5 / 0.9%
Student absenteeism:	4.7%
Students per teacher:	15.3
Parent friendliness:	①❷❸❹❺❻
Teachers with advanced degrees:	34.2%
Average years' teaching experience:	11.0
Students in gifted program:	10 / 1.7%
Students in remedial education:	16.5%
Students held back a grade:	1.7%
Total suspensions, pct. in-school:	55 / 25.5%
Offenses: violence: 29, drugs: *, other:	131
Eligible students, free or reduced lunch:	40.0%
Before / after school program:	Yes / Yes

Students at this school generally go on to:
Conyers Middle

AJC GRADE: ★★★

Georgia Criterion-Referenced Competency Tests - Grade 4
Pct. of students at each level

Read: Exceeds 26%, Meets 50%, Does not meet 24%
Math: Exceeds 14%, Meets 48%, Does not meet 38%
Lang: Exceeds 15%, Meets 58%, Does not meet 27%

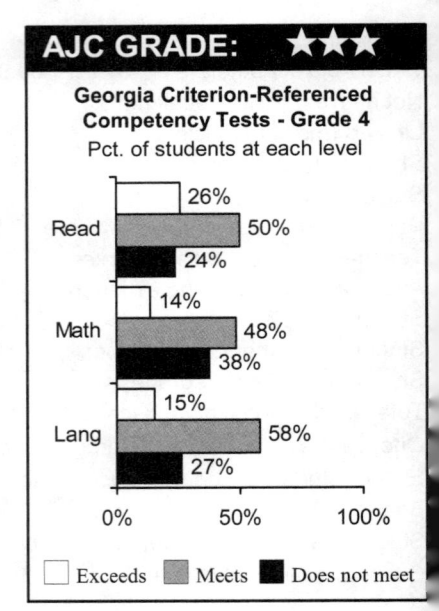

Honey Creek Elementary School

700 Honey Creek Rd SE, Conyers, GA 30094
770-483-5706 · Grades K - 5

Enrollment:	583
White / black / other:	80.3% / 14.6% / 5.1%
Not native English-speaking:	*
Limited English proficiency:	7 / 1.2%
Student absenteeism:	3.6%
Students per teacher:	12.7
Parent friendliness:	① ❷ ❸ ④ ⑤ ❻
Teachers with advanced degrees:	55.3%
Average years' teaching experience:	17.8
Students in gifted program:	28 / 4.8%
Students in remedial education:	11.7%
Students held back a grade:	1.5%
Total suspensions, pct. in-school:	7 / 0.0%
Offenses:	violence: *, drugs: *, other: 7
Eligible students, free or reduced lunch:	20.4%
Before / after school program:	No / Yes
Students at this school generally go on to:	Edwards, Memorial Middle

AJC GRADE: ★★★★

Georgia Criterion-Referenced Competency Tests - Grade 4
Pct. of students at each level

- Read: Exceeds 55%, Meets 33%, Does not meet 12%
- Math: Exceeds 24%, Meets 61%, Does not meet 15%
- Lang: Exceeds 30%, Meets 65%, Does not meet 5%

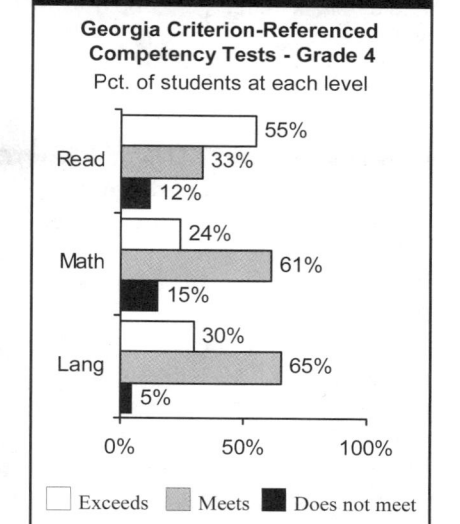

House Elementary School

2930 Highway 20 NE, Conyers, GA 30012
770-483-9504 · Grades K - 5

Enrollment:	570
White / black / other:	44.4% / 13.7% / 41.9%
Not native English-speaking:	129 / 22.6%
Limited English proficiency:	197 / 34.6%
Student absenteeism:	4.7%
Students per teacher:	15.0
Parent friendliness:	① ❷ ❸ ④ ⑤ ❻
Teachers with advanced degrees:	46.2%
Average years' teaching experience:	12.1
Students in gifted program:	1 / 0.2%
Students in remedial education:	*
Students held back a grade:	8.1%
Total suspensions, pct. in-school:	88 / 18.2%
Offenses:	violence: 11, drugs: *, other: 288
Eligible students, free or reduced lunch:	61.5%
Before / after school program:	Yes / No
Students at this school generally go on to:	Conyers, Edwards Middle

AJC GRADE: ★★★★

Georgia Criterion-Referenced Competency Tests - Grade 4
Pct. of students at each level

- Read: Exceeds 44%, Meets 46%, Does not meet 10%
- Math: Exceeds 14%, Meets 59%, Does not meet 27%
- Lang: Exceeds 15%, Meets 68%, Does not meet 17%

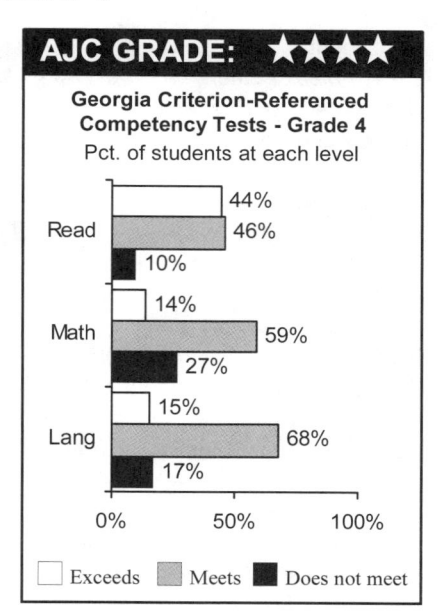

Lorraine Elementary School

3343 E Fairview Rd SW, Stockbridge, GA 30281
770-483-0657 · Grades K - 5

Enrollment:	640
White / black / other:	83.8% / 12.0% / 4.2%
Not native English-speaking:	*
Limited English proficiency:	5 / 0.8%
Student absenteeism:	3.2%
Students per teacher:	15.7
Parent friendliness:	①❷❸❹❺❻
Teachers with advanced degrees:	54.8%
Average years' teaching experience:	14.0
Students in gifted program:	10 / 1.6%
Students in remedial education:	13.6%
Students held back a grade:	0.5%
Total suspensions, pct. in-school:	26 / 30.8%
Offenses:	violence: 5, drugs: *, other: 112
Eligible students, free or reduced lunch:	8.4%
Before / after school program:	Yes / Yes

Students at this school generally go on to:
Edwards, Memorial Middle

AJC GRADE: ★★★

Georgia Criterion-Referenced Competency Tests - Grade 4
Pct. of students at each level

- Read: Exceeds 60%, Meets 31%, Does not meet 10%
- Math: Exceeds 17%, Meets 70%, Does not meet 12%
- Lang: Exceeds 27%, Meets 66%, Does not meet 7%

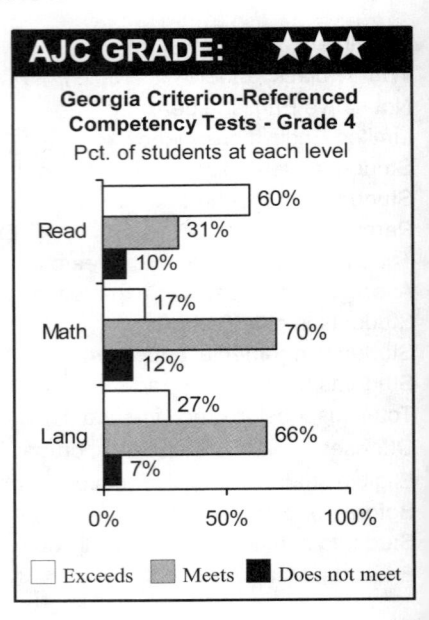

Pine Street Elementary School

960 Pine St NE, Conyers, GA 30012
770-483-8713 · Grades K - 5

Enrollment:	421
White / black / other:	49.4% / 44.2% / 6.4%
Not native English-speaking:	*
Limited English proficiency:	10 / 2.4%
Student absenteeism:	4.6%
Students per teacher:	12.8
Parent friendliness:	①❷❸④❺❻
Teachers with advanced degrees:	32.4%
Average years' teaching experience:	13.7
Students in gifted program:	3 / 0.7%
Students in remedial education:	19.0%
Students held back a grade:	2.6%
Total suspensions, pct. in-school:	66 / 34.8%
Offenses:	violence: 12, drugs: *, other: 81
Eligible students, free or reduced lunch:	61.0%
Before / after school program:	No / Yes

Students at this school generally go on to:
Conyers Middle

AJC GRADE: ★★★

Georgia Criterion-Referenced Competency Tests - Grade 4
Pct. of students at each level

- Read: Exceeds 22%, Meets 48%, Does not meet 31%
- Math: Exceeds 2%, Meets 49%, Does not meet 49%
- Lang: Exceeds 12%, Meets 55%, Does not meet 32%

Rockdale County Elementary Schools

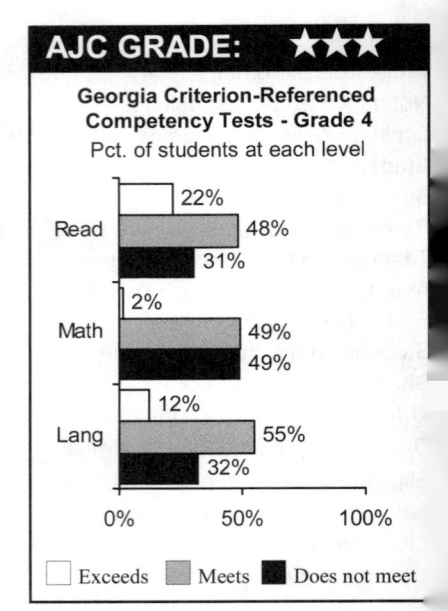

Shoal Creek Elementary School

1300 McWilliams Rd SW, Conyers, GA 30094
770-929-1430 · Grades K - 5

Enrollment:	706
White / black / other:	59.6% / 35.7% / 4.7%
Not native English-speaking:	*
Limited English proficiency:	3 / 0.4%
Student absenteeism:	4.0%
Students per teacher:	16.0
Parent friendliness:	①❷❸❹❺❻
Teachers with advanced degrees:	31.8%
Average years' teaching experience:	12.4
Students in gifted program:	23 / 3.3%
Students in remedial education:	15.7%
Students held back a grade:	2.7%
Total suspensions, pct. in-school:	96 / 72.9%
Offenses: violence: 37, drugs: *, other: 131	
Eligible students, free or reduced lunch:	34.6%
Before / after school program:	Yes / Yes

Students at this school generally go on to:
Conyers, Edwards, Memorial Middle

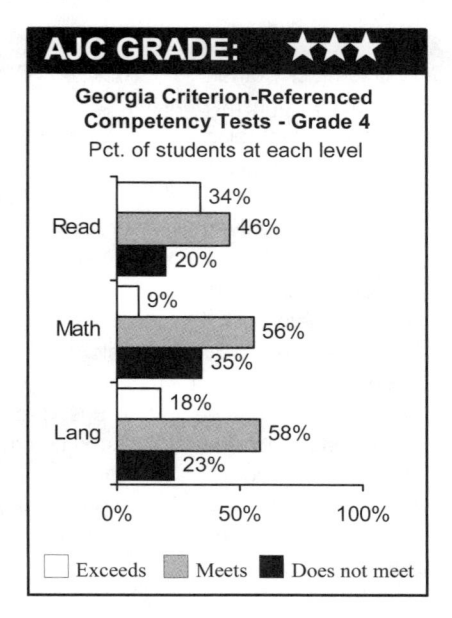

AJC GRADE: ★★★

Georgia Criterion-Referenced Competency Tests - Grade 4
Pct. of students at each level

- Read: Exceeds 34%, Meets 46%, Does not meet 20%
- Math: Exceeds 9%, Meets 56%, Does not meet 35%
- Lang: Exceeds 18%, Meets 58%, Does not meet 23%

Sims Elementary School

1821 Walker Rd SW, Conyers, GA 30094
770-922-0666 · Grades K - 5

Enrollment:	636
White / black / other:	61.3% / 23.7% / 14.9%
Not native English-speaking:	68 / 10.7%
Limited English proficiency:	112 / 17.6%
Student absenteeism:	3.9%
Students per teacher:	16.1
Parent friendliness:	①❷❸④⑤❻
Teachers with advanced degrees:	62.5%
Average years' teaching experience:	15.8
Students in gifted program:	4 / 0.6%
Students in remedial education:	10.2%
Students held back a grade:	2.7%
Total suspensions, pct. in-school:	45 / 46.7%
Offenses: violence: 16, drugs: *, other: 66	
Eligible students, free or reduced lunch:	34.0%
Before / after school program:	Yes / Yes

Students at this school generally go on to:
Edwards Middle

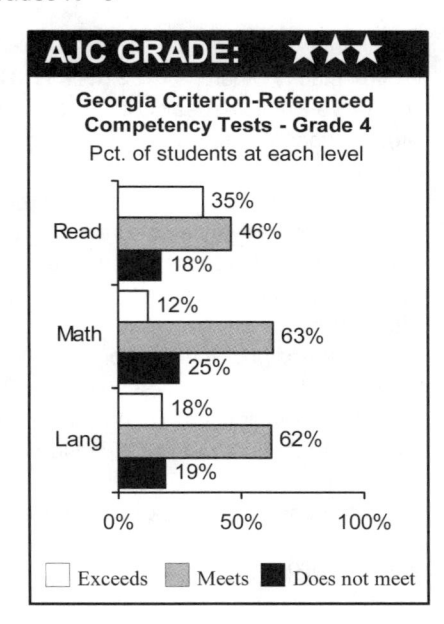

AJC GRADE: ★★★

Georgia Criterion-Referenced Competency Tests - Grade 4
Pct. of students at each level

- Read: Exceeds 35%, Meets 46%, Does not meet 18%
- Math: Exceeds 12%, Meets 63%, Does not meet 25%
- Lang: Exceeds 18%, Meets 62%, Does not meet 19%

Rockdale County Elementary Schools

Conyers Middle School

400 Sigman Rd NW, Conyers, GA 30012
770-483-3371 · Grades 6 - 8

Enrollment:	1,061
White / black / other:	63.2% / 32.1% / 4.6%
Not native English-speaking:	*
Student absenteeism:	5.8%
Students per teacher:	14.7
Parent friendliness:	①❷❸④⑤❻
Teachers with advanced degrees:	51.4%
Average years' teaching experience:	13.3
Students in gifted program:	102 / 9.6%
Students held back a grade:	1.0%
Total suspensions and expulsions:	1,661
Suspensions only, pct. in-school:	1,661 / 57.0%
Offenses:	violence: 471, drugs: 3, other: 1,365
Eligible students, free or reduced lunch:	44.5%
Number of dropouts:	1 / 0.1%
Pct. 8th-graders w/ basic computer skills:	95.1%

Students at this school generally go on to:
Rockdale High

AJC GRADE: ★★★

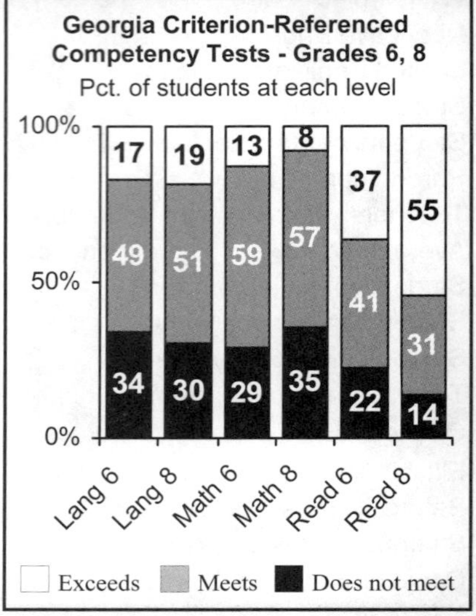
Georgia Criterion-Referenced Competency Tests - Grades 6, 8
Pct. of students at each level
100%
50%
0%
17 49 34
19 51 30
13 59 29
8 57 35
37 41 22
55 31 14
Lang 6
Lang 8
Math 6
Math 8
Read 6
Read 8
Exceeds
Meets
Does not meet

Edwards Middle School

2633 Stanton Rd SE, Conyers, GA 30094
770-483-3255 · Grades 6 - 8

Enrollment:	1,152
White / black / other:	72.6% / 17.0% / 10.4%
Not native English-speaking:	67 / 5.8%
Student absenteeism:	5.0%
Students per teacher:	15.6
Parent friendliness:	①❷❸④❺❻
Teachers with advanced degrees:	54.1%
Average years' teaching experience:	14.6
Students in gifted program:	181 / 15.7%
Students held back a grade:	2.5%
Total suspensions and expulsions:	923
Suspensions only, pct. in-school:	923 / 79.5%
Offenses:	violence: 170, drugs: 6, other: 1,502
Eligible students, free or reduced lunch:	25.3%
Number of dropouts:	3 / 0.2%
Pct. 8th-graders w/ basic computer skills:	42.9%

Students at this school generally go on to:
Heritage High

AJC GRADE: ★★★

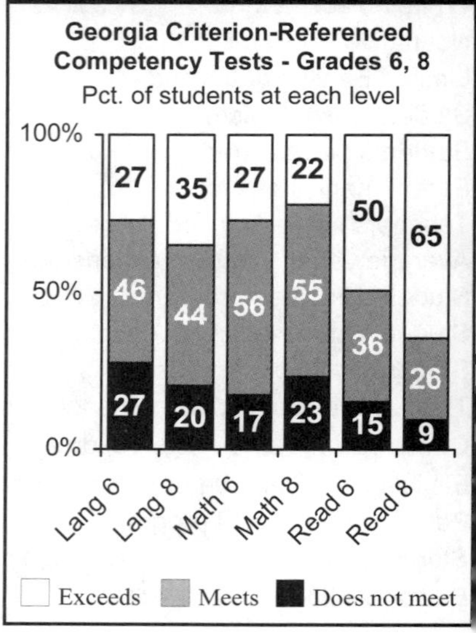
Georgia Criterion-Referenced Competency Tests - Grades 6, 8
Pct. of students at each level
100%
50%
0%
27 46 27
35 44 20
27 56 17
22 55 23
50 36 15
65 26 9
Lang 6
Lang 8
Math 6
Math 8
Read 6
Read 8
Exceeds
Meets
Does not meet

Memorial Middle School

3205 Underwood Rd SE, Conyers, GA 30013
770-922-0139 · Grades 6 - 8

Enrollment:	1,100
White / black / other:	70.6% / 24.3% / 5.1%
Not native English-speaking:	*
Student absenteeism:	4.5%
Students per teacher:	15.7
Parent friendliness:	① ❷ ❸ ④ ⑤ ❻
Teachers with advanced degrees:	51.4%
Average years' teaching experience:	12.3
Students in gifted program:	198 / 18.0%
Students held back a grade:	1.1%
Total suspensions and expulsions:	1,059
Suspensions only, pct. in-school:	1,059 / 84.9%
Offenses: violence: 171, drugs: 15, other: 1,134	
Eligible students, free or reduced lunch:	21.3%
Number of dropouts:	*
Pct. 8th-graders w/ basic computer skills:	95.0%
Students at this school generally go on to: Salem High	

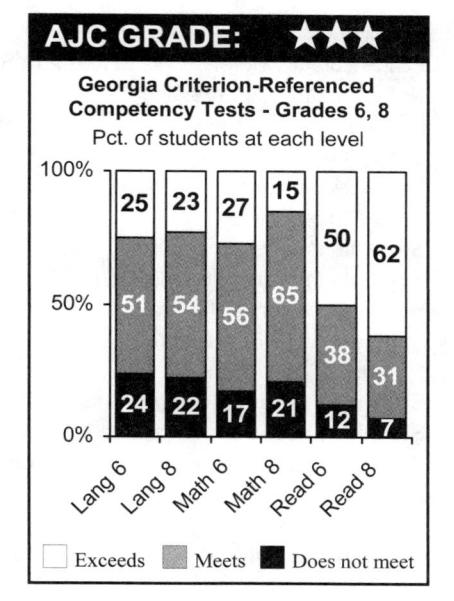

AJC GRADE: ★★★

Georgia Criterion-Referenced Competency Tests - Grades 6, 8
Pct. of students at each level

	Lang 6	Lang 8	Math 6	Math 8	Read 6	Read 8
Exceeds	25	23	27	15	50	62
Meets	51	54	56	65	38	31
Does not meet	24	22	17	21	12	7

Rockdale County Middle Schools

Heritage High School

2400 Granade Rd SW, Conyers, GA 30094
770-483-5428 · Grades 9 - 12

Enrollment:	1,407
White / black / other:	82.0% / 14.8% / 3.2%
Not native English-speaking:	*
Limited English proficiency:	13 / 0.9%
Student absenteeism:	6.0%
Students per teacher:	17.4
Parent friendliness:	① ❷ ❸ ④ ⑤ ❻
Students in gifted program:	171 / 12.2%
Students in remedial education:	5.2%
High school completion rate:	93.9%
Students held back a grade:	4.6%
Number of dropouts:	38 / 2.5%
Students in alternative programs:	*
Students in special education:	122 / 8.7%
Eligible students, free or reduced lunch:	8.3%
Total suspensions and expulsions:	751
Suspensions only, pct. in-school:	751 / 60.9%
Drugs/alcohol-related offenses:	6
Violence-related offenses:	58
Firearms-related offenses:	4
Vandalism-related offenses:	13
Theft-related offenses:	14
All other disciplinary offenses:	799
Teachers with advanced degrees:	50.0%
Average years' teaching experience:	16.4

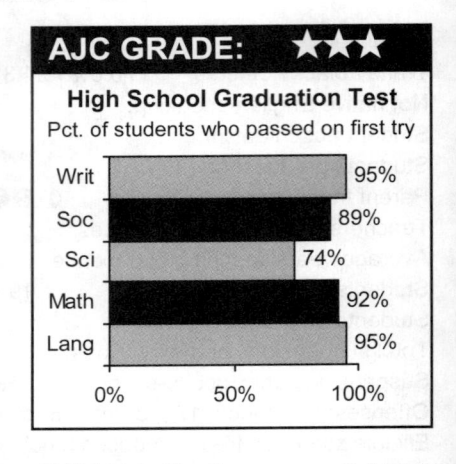

AJC GRADE: ★★★

High School Graduation Test
Pct. of students who passed on first try

- Writ: 95%
- Soc: 89%
- Sci: 74%
- Math: 92%
- Lang: 95%

GHSA classification: 8-AAAA
Interscholastic sports offered:
BB, BS, FB, GO, SB, SO, SW, TE, TF, VB, WR

Advanced Placement (AP) Exams
Students tested:	139
Tests taken:	264
Pct. of test scores 3 or higher (1 - 5 scale):	64.8%

Languages other than English taught:
French, German, Japanese, Latin, Spanish

2000-2001 high school graduates: 262

College prep/vocational diplomas:	44.7%
College prep endorsement diplomas:	34.0%
Vocational endorsement diplomas:	18.3%
General high school diplomas:	0.0%
Special education diplomas:	0.8%
Certificates of attendance (no diploma):	2.3%

Of the 2000-2001 graduates, 69.1% were eligible for the HOPE scholarship.

Of the 1999-2000 graduates, 126 attended a Georgia public college or university. Of those, 89% met the school's minimum academic requirements.

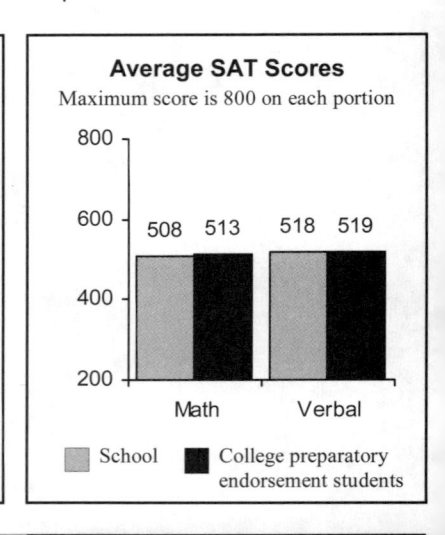

Average SAT Scores
Maximum score is 800 on each portion

- Math — School: 508, College preparatory endorsement students: 513
- Verbal — School: 518, College preparatory endorsement students: 519

Rockdale County High Schools

Rockdale County High School

1174 Bulldog Cir NE, Conyers, GA 30012
770-483-8754 · Grades 9 - 12

Enrollment:	1,271
White / black / other:	66.0% / 29.4% / 4.6%
Not native English-speaking:	*
Limited English proficiency:	*
Student absenteeism:	9.1%
Students per teacher:	16.4
Parent friendliness:	① ❷ ❸ ④ ⑤ ❻
Students in gifted program:	123 / 9.7%
Students in remedial education:	3.1%
High school completion rate:	91.2%
Students held back a grade:	4.4%
Number of dropouts:	70 / 5.1%
Students in alternative programs:	14 / 1.1%
Students in special education:	134 / 10.5%
Eligible students, free or reduced lunch:	24.3%

Total suspensions and expulsions:	1,407
Suspensions only, pct. in-school:	1,407 / 62.3%
Drugs/alcohol-related offenses:	14
Violence-related offenses:	96
Firearms-related offenses:	7
Vandalism-related offenses:	3
Theft-related offenses:	13
All other disciplinary offenses:	1,369
Teachers with advanced degrees:	53.2%
Average years' teaching experience:	11.6

AJC GRADE: ★★★

High School Graduation Test
Pct. of students who passed on first try

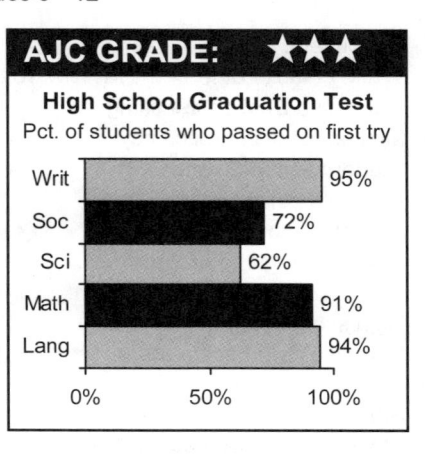

- Writ: 95%
- Soc: 72%
- Sci: 62%
- Math: 91%
- Lang: 94%

GHSA classification: 8-AAAA
Interscholastic sports offered:
BB, BS, CC, CL, FB, GO, GY, LC, SB, SO, TF, VB, WR

Advanced Placement (AP) Exams
- Students tested: 73
- Tests taken: 113
- Pct. of test scores 3 or higher (1 - 5 scale): 37.2%

Languages other than English taught:
French, Latin, Spanish

2000-2001 high school graduates: 217

College prep/vocational diplomas:	18.4%
College prep endorsement diplomas:	46.5%
Vocational endorsement diplomas:	28.1%
General high school diplomas:	0.0%
Special education diplomas:	1.4%
Certificates of attendance (no diploma):	5.5%

Of the 2000-2001 graduates, 59.4% were eligible for the HOPE scholarship.

Of the 1999-2000 graduates, 87 attended a Georgia public college or university. Of those, 80% met the school's minimum academic requirements.

Average SAT Scores
Maximum score is 800 on each portion

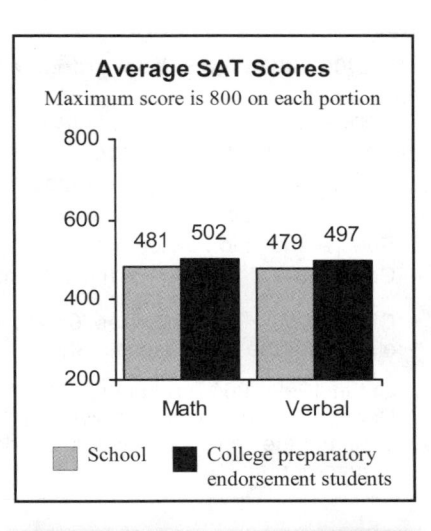

- Math: School 481, College preparatory endorsement students 502
- Verbal: School 479, College preparatory endorsement students 497

Salem High School

3351 Underwood Rd SE, Conyers, GA 30013
770-929-0176 · Grades 9 - 12

Enrollment:	1,343
White / black / other:	71.1% / 18.8% / 10.1%
Not native English-speaking:	30 / 2.2%
Limited English proficiency:	78 / 5.8%
Student absenteeism:	6.2%
Students per teacher:	16.3
Parent friendliness:	❶❷❸④❺❻
Students in gifted program:	111 / 8.3%
Students in remedial education:	6.1%
High school completion rate:	90.5%
Students held back a grade:	*
Number of dropouts:	44 / 3.1%
Students in alternative programs:	4 / 0.3%
Students in special education:	105 / 7.8%
Eligible students, free or reduced lunch:	10.9%

Total suspensions and expulsions:	795
Suspensions only, pct. in-school:	794 / 80.7%
Drugs/alcohol-related offenses:	14
Violence-related offenses:	52
Firearms-related offenses:	1
Vandalism-related offenses:	5
Theft-related offenses:	37
All other disciplinary offenses:	864
Teachers with advanced degrees:	54.2%
Average years' teaching experience:	13.1

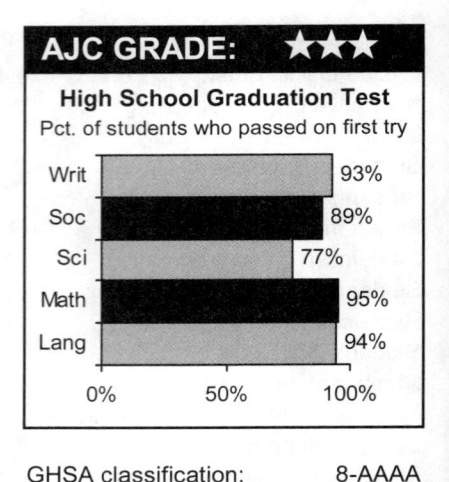

AJC GRADE: ★★★

High School Graduation Test
Pct. of students who passed on first try

- Writ: 93%
- Soc: 89%
- Sci: 77%
- Math: 95%
- Lang: 94%

GHSA classification:	8-AAAA

Interscholastic sports offered:
BB, BS, CC, FB, GO, GY, SO, TE, TF, VB, WR

Advanced Placement (AP) Exams
Students tested:	135
Tests taken:	207
Pct. of test scores 3 or higher (1 - 5 scale):	66.2%

Languages other than English taught:
French, German, Latin, Spanish

2000-2001 high school graduates: 247

College prep/vocational diplomas:	12.6%
College prep endorsement diplomas:	67.6%
Vocational endorsement diplomas:	11.3%
General high school diplomas:	0.0%
Special education diplomas:	4.0%
Certificates of attendance (no diploma):	4.5%

Of the 2000-2001 graduates, 65.2% were eligible for the HOPE scholarship.

Of the 1999-2000 graduates, 132 attended a Georgia public college or university. Of those, 81% met the school's minimum academic requirements.

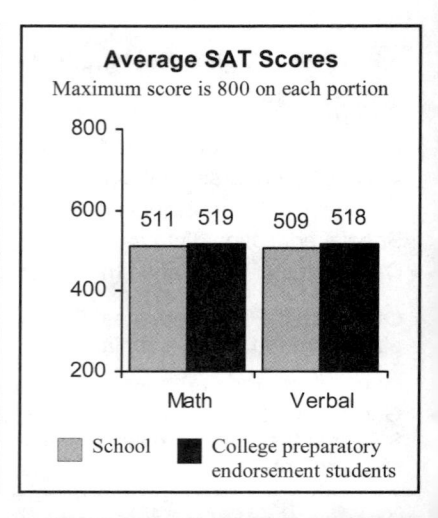

Average SAT Scores
Maximum score is 800 on each portion

- Math: School 511, College preparatory endorsement students 519
- Verbal: School 509, College preparatory endorsement students 518

Rockdale County High Schools

AJC ranking of Rockdale County Schools

ELEMENTARY SCHOOLS

AJC Star Grade: ★★★★

Honey Creek Elementary
House Elementary

AJC Star Grade: ★★★

Barksdale Elementary
Flat Shoals Elementary
Hicks Elementary
Hightower Trail Elementary
Lorraine Elementary
Pine Street Elementary
Shoal Creek Elementary
Sims Elementary

MIDDLE SCHOOLS

AJC Star Grade: ★★★

Conyers Middle
Edwards Middle
Memorial Middle

HIGH SCHOOLS

AJC Star Grade: ★★★

Heritage High
Rockdale County High
Salem High

Georgia Criterion-Referenced Competency Tests (CRCT)

The Georgia Criterion-Referenced Competency Tests are administered each spring to fourth-, sixth- and eighth-grade students. The CRCT's content coverage is based on the Georgia Quality Core Curriculum, the material that every student is supposed to be taught, so it is a good test to use for looking at school accountability. However, the CRCT was not fully implemented in 2001, so the only scores we have are reading, English/language arts and mathematics. These are important subjects, no doubt, but we also know that science and social studies are important as well. Still, the CRCT provides a good basis for comparing schools.

Using scale scores, The Atlanta Journal-Constitution ranked the Top 50 schools by grade and content area to show how metro Atlanta schools stack up locally and statewide. The test scores reflect the 2000-01 school year.

About the tests

- The reading portion measures reading and vocabulary improvement, reading for locating and recalling information, reading for meaning, and reading for critical analysis.

- The English/language arts portion measures sentence construction and revision, paragraph content and organization, grammar and mechanics, and research process.

- The mathematics portion measures number sense and numeration, geometry and measurement, patterns and relationships/Algebra, statistics and probability, computation and estimation, and problem solving.

Reading the scores

As a score-reporting technique, scale scores provide a standard range for test takers and permits direct comparisons of results from one administration of the test to another. The scale score used with the 2001 CRCT ranged from 150 to 450 and was derived from the number correct on each test. The scale score for those who exceeded the standards set by Georgia educators scored between 350 and 450; those who simply met the standards scored between 300 and 349; and those who did not meet the standards scored between 150 and 299.

FOURTH-GRADE READING

The reading portion of the Georgia Criterion-Referenced Competency Tests measures reading and vocabulary improvement, reading for locating and recalling information, reading for meaning, and reading for critical analysis. The Atlanta Journal-Constitution ranked the Top 50 schools by their 2000-2001 scale scores to show how metro Atlanta schools stack up locally and statewide. The average scale score for metro Atlanta was 333 and 329 statewide.

Top 50 Ranking of Metro Atlanta Elementary Schools

School, district and scale score (see page 496 for more on the CRCT and scale scores)

School	Score
Kittredge Magnet School (DeKalb)	398
Brandon (Atlanta City)	391
Oak Grove (DeKalb)	385
Jackson (Atlanta City)	383
Morningside (Atlanta City)	380
Crabapple Crossing (Fulton)	377
Peeples (Fayette)	377
Vanderlyn (DeKalb)	377
Tritt (Cobb)	375
Livsey (DeKalb)	372
Smith (Atlanta City)	372
Lake Windward (Fulton)	371
Sope Creek (Cobb)	371
Austin (DeKalb)	370
Braelinn (Fayette)	370
Findley Oaks (Fulton)	370
Mount Bethel (Cobb)	370
Mountain Park (Fulton)	369
Settles Bridge (Forsyth)	369
Timber Ridge (Cobb)	368
Dolvin (Fulton)	367
East Side (Cobb)	367
New Prospect (Fulton)	367
Ocee (Fulton)	367
Shakerag (Fulton)	367
Shallowford Falls (Cobb)	367
Summit Hill (Fulton)	367
Westchester (Decatur City)	367
Davis (Cobb)	366
Ford (Cobb)	366
Winnona Park (Decatur City)	365
Abbotts Hill (Fulton)	364
Heards Ferry (Fulton)	363
Murdock (Cobb)	363
Bascomb (Cherokee)	362
Big Creek (Forsyth)	362
Clairemont (Decatur City)	362
Garrison Mill (Cobb)	362
Kedron (Fayette)	362
Keheley (Cobb)	362
Fernbank (DeKalb)	361
Rocky Mount (Cobb)	361
Barnwell (Fulton)	360
Mountain View (Cobb)	360
Eastvalley (Cobb)	359
Northwood (Fulton)	359
Alpharetta (Fulton)	358
Due West (Cobb)	358
Manning Oaks (Fulton)	358
Mashburn (Forsyth)	358
Medlock Bridge (Fulton)	358
Sweet Apple (Fulton)	358

(Number of schools may exceed 50 because of schools with identical scores)

Georgia Criterion-Referenced Competency Tests

FOURTH-GRADE MATHEMATICS

The mathematics portion of the Georgia Criterion-Referenced Competency Tests measures number sense and numeration, geometry and measurement, patterns and relationships/Algebra, statistics and probability, computation and estimation, and problem solving. The Atlanta Journal-Constitution ranked the Top 50 schools by their 2000-2001 scale scores to show how metro Atlanta schools stack up locally and statewide. The average scale score for metro Atlanta was 315 and 311 statewide.

Top 50 Ranking of Metro Atlanta Elementary Schools
School, district and scale score (see page 496 for more on the CRCT and scale scores)

School	Score
Kittredge Magnet School (DeKalb)	363
Jackson (Atlanta City)	356
Vanderlyn (DeKalb)	355
Brandon (Atlanta City)	354
Crabapple Crossing (Fulton)	354
Oak Grove (DeKalb)	351
Smith (Atlanta City)	351
Braelinn (Fayette)	350
Mountain Park (Fulton)	350
Kedron (Fayette)	349
Peeples (Fayette)	349
New Prospect (Fulton)	347
Findley Oaks (Fulton)	346
Settles Bridge (Forsyth)	346
Sope Creek (Cobb)	346
Tritt (Cobb)	346
Dolvin (Fulton)	345
Morningside (Atlanta City)	344
Shakerag (Fulton)	344
Summit Hill (Fulton)	344
Barnwell (Fulton)	343
Austin (DeKalb)	342
Lake Windward (Fulton)	342
Murdock (Cobb)	342
Ocee (Fulton)	341
Shallowford Falls (Cobb)	341
Winnona Park (Decatur City)	341
Abbotts Hill (Fulton)	340
East Side (Cobb)	340
Ford (Cobb)	340
Livsey (DeKalb)	340
Mount Bethel (Cobb)	340
Garrison Mill (Cobb)	339
Manning Oaks (Fulton)	339
Medlock Bridge (Fulton)	339
State Bridge Crossing (Fulton)	338
Abney (Paulding)	337
Davis (Cobb)	337
Heards Ferry (Fulton)	337
Rocky Mount (Cobb)	337
Mountain View (Cobb)	336
Sweet Apple (Fulton)	336
Alpharetta (Fulton)	335
Keheley (Cobb)	335
Peyton Forest (Atlanta City)	335
Timber Ridge (Cobb)	335
Bascomb (Cherokee)	334
McEver (Hall)	334
Montgomery (DeKalb)	334
Northwood (Fulton)	334
South Douglas (Douglas)	334
Spring Hill (Fayette)	334

(Number of schools may exceed 50 because of schools with identical scores)

Georgia Criterion-Referenced Competency Tests

FOURTH-GRADE ENGLISH/LANGUAGE ARTS

The English/language arts portion of the Georgia Criterion-Referenced Competency Tests measures sentence construction and revision, paragraph content and organization, grammar and mechanics, and research process. The Atlanta Journal-Constitution ranked the Top 50 schools by their 2000-2001 scale scores to show how metro Atlanta schools stack up locally and statewide. The average scale score for metro Atlanta was 322 and 320 statewide.

Top 50 Ranking of Metro Atlanta Elementary Schools
School, district and scale score (see page 496 for more on the CRCT and scale scores)

Kittredge Magnet School (DeKalb) 366
Brandon (Atlanta City) 361
Jackson (Atlanta City) 358
Morningside (Atlanta City) 353
Sope Creek (Cobb) 353
Livsey (DeKalb) 352
Crabapple Crossing (Fulton) 350
Peeples (Fayette) 350
Settles Bridge (Forsyth) 350
Findley Oaks (Fulton) 349
Oak Grove (DeKalb) 349
Smith (Atlanta City) 349
Vanderlyn (DeKalb) 349
Summit Hill (Fulton) 348
Dolvin (Fulton) 347
Mount Bethel (Cobb) 347
Shakerag (Fulton) 347
Mountain Park (Fulton) 346
Ocee (Fulton) 346
Tritt (Cobb) 346
Big Creek (Forsyth) 345
Lake Windward (Fulton) 345
New Prospect (Fulton) 345
Shallowford Falls (Cobb) 345
Austin (DeKalb) 344
Braelinn (Fayette) 344
Davis (Cobb) 344
Peyton Forest (Atlanta City) 344
Ford (Cobb) 343
Abbotts Hill (Fulton) 342

Barnwell (Fulton) 342
Kedron (Fayette) 342
Mashburn (Forsyth) 342
East Side (Cobb) 341
Timber Ridge (Cobb) 341
Bascomb (Cherokee) 340
Garrison Mill (Cobb) 340
Heards Ferry (Fulton) 340
Manning Oaks (Fulton) 340
Medlock Bridge (Fulton) 340
Murdock (Cobb) 340
State Bridge Crossing (Fulton) 340
Alpharetta (Fulton) 339
Bethune (Atlanta City) 339
Huntley Hills (DeKalb) 339
Keheley (Cobb) 339
Mountain View (Cobb) 339
Rocky Mount (Cobb) 339
Buffington (Cherokee) 338
Eastvalley (Cobb) 338
Fernbank (DeKalb) 338
Honey Creek (Rockdale) 338
Vickery Creek (Forsyth) 338
Winnona Park (Decatur City) 338

(Number of schools may exceed 50 because of schools with identical scores)

Georgia Criterion-Referenced Competency Tests

SIXTH-GRADE READING

The reading portion of the Georgia Criterion-Referenced Competency Tests measures reading and vocabulary improvement, reading for locating and recalling information, reading for meaning, and reading for critical analysis. The Atlanta Journal-Constitution ranked the Top 50 schools by their 2000-2001 scale scores to show how metro Atlanta schools stack up locally and statewide. The average scale score for metro Atlanta was 336 and 327 statewide.

Top 50 Ranking of Metro Atlanta Middle Schools
School, district and scale score (see page 496 for more on the CRCT and scale scores)

School	Score
Hightower Trail (Cobb)	371
Dodgen (Cobb)	369
Webb Bridge (Fulton)	368
Crews (Gwinnett)	367
Dickerson (Cobb)	367
Inman (Atlanta City)	364
Simpson (Cobb)	364
Trickum (Gwinnett)	364
Northwestern (Fulton)	363
Mabry (Cobb)	362
Rising Starr (Fayette)	362
Taylor Road (Fulton)	360
Lanier (Gwinnett)	359
Durham (Cobb)	358
McConnell (Gwinnett)	358
Booth (Fayette)	357
Crabapple (Fulton)	357
Five Forks (Gwinnett)	357
Haynes Bridge (Fulton)	357
Lost Mountain (Cobb)	357
Shiloh (Gwinnett)	356
Whitewater (Fayette)	355
Creekland (Gwinnett)	352
Dacula (Gwinnett)	352
Pine Mountain (Cobb)	352
Union Grove (Henry)	352
Duluth (Gwinnett)	351
Hull (Gwinnett)	351
Otwell (Forsyth)	351
Snellville (Gwinnett)	351
South Forsyth (Forsyth)	351
Pinckneyville (Gwinnett)	350
Chapel Hill (Douglas)	349
Daniell (Cobb)	349
Flat Rock (Fayette)	348
Holcomb Bridge (Fulton)	348
Madras (Coweta)	348
Memorial (Rockdale)	348
Eagle's Landing (Henry)	347
Edwards (Rockdale)	347
McCleskey (Cobb)	347
North Hall (Hall)	347
Sutton (Atlanta City)	347
Renfroe (Decatur City)	346
Awtrey (Cobb)	345
Chapman Intermediate (Cherokee)	345
Fayette (Fayette)	345
Arnall (Coweta)	344
Fairplay (Douglas)	343
North Forsyth (Forsyth)	343

(Number of schools may exceed 50 because of schools with identical scores)

Georgia Criterion-Referenced Competency Tests

SIXTH-GRADE MATHEMATICS

The mathematics portion of the Georgia Criterion-Referenced Competency Tests measures number sense and numeration, geometry and measurement, patterns and relationships/Algebra, statistics and probability, computation and estimation, and problem solving. The Atlanta Journal-Constitution ranked the Top 50 schools by their 2000-2001 scale scores to show how metro Atlanta schools stack up locally and statewide. The average scale score for metro Atlanta was 320 and 314 statewide.

Top 50 Ranking of Metro Atlanta Middle Schools
School, district and scale score (see page 496 for more on the CRCT and scale scores)

School	Score
Hightower Trail (Cobb)	353
Simpson (Cobb)	353
Dodgen (Cobb)	352
Crews (Gwinnett)	351
Dickerson (Cobb)	351
Mabry (Cobb)	350
Rising Starr (Fayette)	348
Webb Bridge (Fulton)	348
Lanier (Gwinnett)	343
Shiloh (Gwinnett)	343
Taylor Road (Fulton)	343
Trickum (Gwinnett)	343
Booth (Fayette)	342
McConnell (Gwinnett)	341
Northwestern (Fulton)	341
Inman (Atlanta City)	339
Haynes Bridge (Fulton)	338
Hull (Gwinnett)	338
Creekland (Gwinnett)	337
Dacula (Gwinnett)	337
Five Forks (Gwinnett)	337
Whitewater (Fayette)	337
Crabapple (Fulton)	336
Duluth (Gwinnett)	336
McCleskey (Cobb)	335
South Forsyth (Forsyth)	335
Fayette (Fayette)	334
Lost Mountain (Cobb)	334
Pinckneyville (Gwinnett)	334
Sutton (Atlanta City)	333
Durham (Cobb)	332
Pine Mountain (Cobb)	331
Snellville (Gwinnett)	331
Daniell (Cobb)	330
Edwards (Rockdale)	330
Holcomb Bridge (Fulton)	330
Memorial (Rockdale)	330
North Hall (Hall)	330
Union Grove (Henry)	330
Chapel Hill (Douglas)	329
Chapman Intermediate (Cherokee)	329
East Paulding (Paulding)	329
Flat Rock (Fayette)	329
Madras (Coweta)	328
Richards (Gwinnett)	328
Eagle's Landing (Henry)	327
North Forsyth (Forsyth)	327
Otwell (Forsyth)	327
Vickery Creek (Forsyth)	327
Awtrey (Cobb)	326
Peachtree Charter (DeKalb)	326

(Number of schools may exceed 50 because of schools with identical scores)

Georgia Criterion-Referenced Competency Tests

SIXTH-GRADE ENGLISH/LANGUAGE ARTS

The English/language arts portion of the Georgia Criterion-Referenced Competency Tests measures sentence construction and revision, paragraph content and organization, grammar and mechanics, and research process. The Atlanta Journal-Constitution ranked the Top 50 schools by their 2000-2001 scale scores to show how metro Atlanta schools stack up locally and statewide. The average scale score for metro Atlanta was 318 and 311 statewide.

Top 50 Ranking of Metro Atlanta Middle Schools
School, district and scale score (see page 496 for more on the CRCT and scale scores)

School	Score
Dickerson (Cobb)	352
Dodgen (Cobb)	350
Hightower Trail (Cobb)	350
Webb Bridge (Fulton)	346
Crews (Gwinnett)	345
Mabry (Cobb)	344
Trickum (Gwinnett)	343
Rising Starr (Fayette)	342
Taylor Road (Fulton)	341
Inman (Atlanta City)	340
Simpson (Cobb)	340
Northwestern (Fulton)	338
Haynes Bridge (Fulton)	337
Lanier (Gwinnett)	337
Durham (Cobb)	336
Lost Mountain (Cobb)	336
Booth (Fayette)	335
Crabapple (Fulton)	335
Hull (Gwinnett)	335
McConnell (Gwinnett)	335
Pinckneyville (Gwinnett)	334
Five Forks (Gwinnett)	333
Shiloh (Gwinnett)	333
South Forsyth (Forsyth)	333
Creekland (Gwinnett)	332
Duluth (Gwinnett)	332
Otwell (Forsyth)	332
Snellville (Gwinnett)	332
Dacula (Gwinnett)	331
Sutton (Atlanta City)	330
Madras (Coweta)	329
McCleskey (Cobb)	329
Whitewater (Fayette)	329
Arnall (Coweta)	328
Chapman Intermediate (Cherokee)	328
Holcomb Bridge (Fulton)	328
Peachtree Charter (DeKalb)	328
Pine Mountain (Cobb)	328
Union Grove (Henry)	328
Daniell (Cobb)	327
Renfroe (Decatur City)	327
Awtrey (Cobb)	326
Eagle's Landing (Henry)	326
Edwards (Rockdale)	326
Memorial (Rockdale)	326
Roberts (Clayton)	326
Sandy Springs (Fulton)	326
Chapel Hill (Douglas)	325
Flat Rock (Fayette)	325
Fayette (Fayette)	324
North Hall (Hall)	324
Vickery Creek (Forsyth)	324

(Number of schools may exceed 50 because of schools with identical scores)

Georgia Criterion-Referenced Competency Tests

EIGHTH-GRADE READING

The reading portion of the Georgia Criterion-Referenced Competency Tests measures reading and vocabulary improvement, reading for locating and recalling information, reading for meaning, and reading for critical analysis. The Atlanta Journal-Constitution ranked the Top 50 schools by their 2000-2001 scale scores to show how metro Atlanta schools stack up locally and statewide. The average scale score for metro Atlanta was 353 and 343 statewide.

Top 50 Ranking of Metro Atlanta Middle Schools

School, district and scale score (see page 496 for more on the CRCT and scale scores)

Dickerson (Cobb) 397
Hightower Trail (Cobb) 388
Webb Bridge (Fulton) 388
Dodgen (Cobb) 387
Crews (Gwinnett) 386
Mabry (Cobb) 386
Northwestern (Fulton) 386
Inman (Atlanta City) 385
Taylor Road (Fulton) 382
Simpson (Cobb) 381
South Forsyth (Forsyth) 381
Durham (Cobb) 380
Chamblee (Dekalb) 379
Haynes Bridge (Fulton) 378
Lost Mountain (Cobb) 378
McCleskey (Cobb) 377
McConnell (Gwinnett) 377
Rising Starr (Fayette) 377
Booth (Fayette) 376
Five Forks (Gwinnett) 376
Trickum (Gwinnett) 376
Whitewater (Fayette) 376
Dacula (Gwinnett) 374
Lanier (Gwinnett) 372
Chapel Hill (Douglas) 371
Creekland (Gwinnett) 371
Fayette (Fayette) 371
Holcomb Bridge (Fulton) 371
Pine Mountain (Cobb) 371
Crabapple (Fulton) 370

Dean Rusk (Cherokee) 370
Roberts (Clayton) 370
Duluth (Gwinnett) 369
Awtrey (Cobb) 368
Hull (Gwinnett) 368
Daniell (Cobb) 367
Pinckneyville (Gwinnett) 367
Union Grove (Henry) 367
Edwards (Rockdale) 366
Snellville (Gwinnett) 366
Memorial (Rockdale) 365
Shiloh (Gwinnett) 365
Eagle's Landing (Henry) 364
Otwell (Forsyth) 364
Peachtree Charter (DeKalb) 364
Booth (Cherokee) 363
North Hall (Hall) 363
Shamrock (DeKalb) 362
Woodstock (Cherokee) 362
Flat Rock (Fayette) 361
Renfroe (Decatur City) 361
Sutton (Atlanta City) 361

(Number of schools may exceed 50 because of schools with identical scores)

Georgia Criterion-Referenced Competency Tests

EIGHTH-GRADE MATHEMATICS

The mathematics portion of the Georgia Criterion-Referenced Competency Tests measures number sense and numeration, geometry and measurement, patterns and relationships/Algebra, statistics and probability, computation and estimation, and problem solving. The Atlanta Journal-Constitution ranked the Top 50 schools by their 2000-2001 scale scores to show how metro Atlanta schools stack up locally and statewide. The average scale score for metro Atlanta was 310 and 304 statewide.

Top 50 Ranking of Metro Atlanta Middle Schools
School, district and scale score (see page 496 for more on the CRCT and scale scores)

School (District)	Score
Crews (Gwinnett)	342
Webb Bridge (Fulton)	342
Dickerson (Cobb)	340
Inman (Atlanta City)	336
Rising Starr (Fayette)	336
Hightower Trail (Cobb)	335
Mabry (Cobb)	333
Taylor Road (Fulton)	333
Booth (Fayette)	332
Simpson (Cobb)	332
Haynes Bridge (Fulton)	331
Northwestern (Fulton)	331
Trickum (Gwinnett)	330
Chamblee (Dekalb)	329
Dodgen (Cobb)	329
Duluth (Gwinnett)	329
Fayette (Fayette)	329
Five Forks (Gwinnett)	328
McConnell (Gwinnett)	328
Crabapple (Fulton)	327
Durham (Cobb)	326
South Forsyth (Forsyth)	325
Holcomb Bridge (Fulton)	324
Hull (Gwinnett)	324
Lost Mountain (Cobb)	324
McCleskey (Cobb)	324
Pinckneyville (Gwinnett)	324
Dacula (Gwinnett)	323
Dean Rusk (Cherokee)	323
Edwards (Rockdale)	323
Roberts (Clayton)	323
Creekland (Gwinnett)	322
Whitewater (Fayette)	322
Chapel Hill (Douglas)	321
Flat Rock (Fayette)	321
Peachtree Charter (DeKalb)	321
Lanier (Gwinnett)	320
Memorial (Rockdale)	320
Renfroe (Decatur City)	320
Sandy Springs (Fulton)	320
Pine Mountain (Cobb)	319
Union Grove (Henry)	319
Daniell (Cobb)	318
Snellville (Gwinnett)	317
Booth (Cherokee)	315
Turner (Douglas)	315
Fairplay (Douglas)	314
Lovejoy (Clayton)	314
Shiloh (Gwinnett)	314
Sutton (Atlanta City)	314
Woodstock (Cherokee)	314

(Number of schools may exceed 50 because of schools with identical scores)

Georgia Criterion-Referenced Competency Tests

EIGHTH-GRADE ENGLISH/LANGUAGE ARTS

The English/language arts portion of the Georgia Criterion-Referenced Competency Tests measures sentence construction and revision, paragraph content and organization, grammar and mechanics, and research process. The Atlanta Journal-Constitution ranked the Top 50 schools by their 2000-2001 scale scores to show how metro Atlanta schools stack up locally and statewide. The average scale score for metro Atlanta was 322 and 316 statewide.

Top 50 Ranking of Metro Atlanta Middle Schools
School, district and scale score (see page 496 for more on the CRCT and scale scores)

School	Score
Union Grove (Henry)	368
Mabry (Cobb)	357
Dickerson (Cobb)	355
Hightower Trail (Cobb)	354
Inman (Atlanta City)	353
Crews (Gwinnett)	350
Chamblee (Dekalb)	349
Webb Bridge (Fulton)	348
Dodgen (Cobb)	347
Haynes Bridge (Fulton)	346
Booth (Fayette)	345
Lost Mountain (Cobb)	345
South Forsyth (Forsyth)	345
Durham (Cobb)	344
McCleskey (Cobb)	342
Trickum (Gwinnett)	342
Whitewater (Fayette)	342
Rising Starr (Fayette)	341
Simpson (Cobb)	341
Taylor Road (Fulton)	341
Dean Rusk (Cherokee)	339
Fayette (Fayette)	339
Five Forks (Gwinnett)	338
Northwestern (Fulton)	338
Woodstock (Cherokee)	338
Duluth (Gwinnett)	337
Edwards (Rockdale)	336
Peachtree Charter (DeKalb)	336
McConnell (Gwinnett)	335
Pine Mountain (Cobb)	335
Chapel Hill (Douglas)	334
Dacula (Gwinnett)	334
Madras (Coweta)	333
Roberts (Clayton)	333
Crabapple (Fulton)	332
Creekland (Gwinnett)	332
Daniell (Cobb)	332
Holcomb Bridge (Fulton)	331
Lanier (Gwinnett)	331
Awtrey (Cobb)	330
Booth (Cherokee)	330
Eagle's Landing (Henry)	330
Otwell (Forsyth)	330
Pinckneyville (Gwinnett)	330
Renfroe (Decatur City)	329
Sandy Springs (Fulton)	329
Shiloh (Gwinnett)	329
East Cobb (Cobb)	328
Evans (Coweta)	328
Hull (Gwinnett)	328
Shamrock (DeKalb)	328
Snellville (Gwinnett)	328
Vickery Creek (Forsyth)	328

(Number of schools may exceed 50 because of schools with identical scores)

Georgia High School Graduation Tests

Students must pass the Georgia High School Graduation Tests (GHSGT) as part of the requirements to obtain a high school diploma. Students who do not pass all portions of the test but who have met all other graduation requirements are instead awarded a Certificate of Performance or Special Education Diploma.

The Atlanta Journal-Constitution ranked the Top 50 schools by content area to show how metro Atlanta schools stack up locally and statewide. The test scores reflect the 2000-01 school year.

About the tests

- The writing portion of the test consists of a written essay on an assigned topic. The persuasive essay is graded for content/organization, style, conventions of written language and sentence formation.

- The English/language arts portion measures reading/literature, critical thinking and writing/usage/grammar.

- The mathematics portion measures numbers and computation, data analysis, measurement and geometry, and Algebra.

- The social studies portion measures world studies, United States history to 1865, United States history since 1865, civics/citizenship, map and globe skills, and information process skills.

- The science portion measures process/research skills, physical science and biology.

Reading the scores

Students take the graduation tests for the first time in their junior year. The writing test is given in the fall and the four content area tests — English/language arts, mathematics, social studies and science — in the spring. Students have five opportunities to pass each portion of the test before the end of the 12th grade. The scores reflect the percent of 11th graders who passed each portion of the test on first administration.

Georgia High School Graduation Tests

ELEVENTH-GRADE ENGLISH/LANGUAGE ARTS

Students must pass the Georgia High School Graduation Tests (GHSGT) as part of the requirements to obtain a high school diploma. The Atlanta Journal-Constitution ranked the Top 50 schools to show how metro Atlanta schools stack up locally and statewide. The test scores reflect the 2000-2001 school year. The state and metro Atlanta average of students who passed the English/language arts portion of the test on the first try was 94%.

Top 50 Ranking of Metro Atlanta High Schools

School, district and pct. of students who passed on first try (see page 506 for more on the GHSGT)

School	%	School	%
Chattahoochee (Fulton)	100 %	East Paulding (Paulding)	97 %
DeKalb of the Arts (DeKalb)	100 %	Etowah (Cherokee)	97 %
Fayette County (Fayette)	99 %	Forsyth Central (Forsyth)	97 %
McIntosh (Fayette)	99 %	Grayson (Gwinnett)	97 %
Northgate (Coweta)	99 %	Kennesaw Mountain (Cobb)	97 %
Parkview (Gwinnett)	99 %	McEachern (Cobb)	97 %
Pope (Cobb)	99 %	North Hall (Hall)	97 %
Roswell (Fulton)	99 %	Sandy Creek (Fayette)	97 %
South Gwinnett (Gwinnett)	99 %	Sequoyah (Cherokee)	97 %
Brookwood (Gwinnett)	98 %	Alexander (Douglas)	96 %
Centennial (Fulton)	98 %	Buford (Buford City)	96 %
Collins Hill (Gwinnett)	98 %	Cedar Grove (DeKalb)	96 %
Dacula (Gwinnett)	98 %	Chapel Hill (Douglas)	96 %
Grady (Atlanta City)	98 %	Cherokee (Cherokee)	96 %
Harrison (Cobb)	98 %	Dunwoody (DeKalb)	96 %
Lakeside (DeKalb)	98 %	East Coweta (Coweta)	96 %
Lassiter (Cobb)	98 %	Hiram (Paulding)	96 %
Mays (Atlanta City)	98 %	South Forsyth (Forsyth)	96 %
Milton (Fulton)	98 %	Stephenson (DeKalb)	96 %
North Forsyth (Forsyth)	98 %	West Hall (Hall)	96 %
North Gwinnett (Gwinnett)	98 %	Woodstock (Cherokee)	96 %
North Springs (Fulton)	98 %		
Redan (DeKalb)	98 %		
Shiloh (Gwinnett)	98 %		
Sprayberry (Cobb)	98 %		
Starr's Mill (Fayette)	98 %		
Stockbridge (Henry)	98 %		
Union Grove (Henry)	98 %		
Walton (Cobb)	98 %		
Eagle's Landing (Henry)	97 %		

(Number of schools may exceed 50 because of schools with identical scores)

Georgia High School Graduation Tests

ELEVENTH-GRADE MATHEMATICS

Students must pass the Georgia High School Graduation Tests (GHSGT) as part of the requirements to obtain a high school diploma. The Atlanta Journal-Constitution ranked the Top 50 schools to show how metro Atlanta schools stack up locally and statewide. The test scores reflect the 2000-2001 school year. The state average of students who passed the mathematics portion of the test on the first try was 91%, and for metro Atlanta the average was 92%.

Top 50 Ranking of Metro Atlanta High Schools

School, district and pct. of students who passed on first try (see page 506 for more on the GHSGT)

School	%
DeKalb of the Arts (DeKalb)	100 %
Brookwood (Gwinnett)	99 %
Centennial (Fulton)	99 %
Chattahoochee (Fulton)	99 %
Parkview (Gwinnett)	99 %
Forsyth Central (Forsyth)	98 %
Grayson (Gwinnett)	98 %
Lakeside (DeKalb)	98 %
McIntosh (Fayette)	98 %
North Gwinnett (Gwinnett)	98 %
Northgate (Coweta)	98 %
Pope (Cobb)	98 %
Roswell (Fulton)	98 %
South Gwinnett (Gwinnett)	98 %
Starr's Mill (Fayette)	98 %
Walton (Cobb)	98 %
Collins Hill (Gwinnett)	97 %
Dacula (Gwinnett)	97 %
Fayette County (Fayette)	97 %
Harrison (Cobb)	97 %
Lassiter (Cobb)	97 %
Sequoyah (Cherokee)	97 %
Buford (Buford City)	96 %
Duluth (Gwinnett)	96 %
Mays (Atlanta City)	96 %
Milton (Fulton)	96 %
Shiloh (Gwinnett)	96 %
South Forsyth (Forsyth)	96 %
Stockbridge (Henry)	96 %
Woodstock (Cherokee)	96 %
Cherokee (Cherokee)	95 %
Eagle's Landing (Henry)	95 %
East Paulding (Paulding)	95 %
Etowah (Cherokee)	95 %
Jonesboro (Clayton)	95 %
Kennesaw Mountain (Cobb)	95 %
McEachern (Cobb)	95 %
North Forsyth (Forsyth)	95 %
Redan (DeKalb)	95 %
Salem (Rockdale)	95 %
Sandy Creek (Fayette)	95 %
Sprayberry (Cobb)	95 %
Alexander (Douglas)	94 %
Central Gwinnett (Gwinnett)	94 %
Chamblee Charter (DeKalb)	94 %
Norcross (Gwinnett)	94 %
Decatur (Decatur City)	93 %
Dunwoody (DeKalb)	93 %
Eastside (Newton)	93 %
Hiram (Paulding)	93 %
Lovejoy (Clayton)	93 %
Mount Zion (Clayton)	93 %
North Atlanta (Atlanta City)	93 %
North Cobb (Cobb)	93 %
North Hall (Hall)	93 %
North Springs (Fulton)	93 %
Riverwood (Fulton)	93 %
Stephenson (DeKalb)	93 %
Tucker (DeKalb)	93 %

(Number of schools may exceed 50 because of schools with identical scores)

Georgia High School Graduation Tests

ELEVENTH-GRADE SCIENCE

Students must pass the Georgia High School Graduation Tests (GHSGT) as part of the requirements to obtain a high school diploma. The Atlanta Journal-Constitution ranked the Top 50 schools to show how metro Atlanta schools stack up locally and statewide. The test scores reflect the 2000-2001 school year. The state average of students who passed the science portion of the test on the first try was 68%, and for metro Atlanta the average was 70%.

Top 50 Ranking of Metro Atlanta High Schools

School, district and pct. of students who passed on first try (see page 506 for more on the GHSGT)

School	%
Walton (Cobb)	92 %
Chattahoochee (Fulton)	91 %
Lassiter (Cobb)	90 %
McIntosh (Fayette)	90 %
Brookwood (Gwinnett)	89 %
Lakeside (DeKalb)	89 %
Centennial (Fulton)	88 %
Milton (Fulton)	88 %
Parkview (Gwinnett)	88 %
Roswell (Fulton)	88 %
Harrison (Cobb)	87 %
Pope (Cobb)	87 %
DeKalb of the Arts (DeKalb)	86 %
Fayette County (Fayette)	86 %
Sandy Creek (Fayette)	86 %
Sprayberry (Cobb)	85 %
Starr's Mill (Fayette)	85 %
Sequoyah (Cherokee)	83 %
Stockbridge (Henry)	82 %
Mays (Atlanta City)	81 %
North Springs (Fulton)	81 %
South Gwinnett (Gwinnett)	81 %
Woodstock (Cherokee)	81 %
Buford (Buford City)	80 %
Redan (DeKalb)	80 %
Collins Hill (Gwinnett)	79 %
Dunwoody (DeKalb)	79 %
Northgate (Coweta)	79 %
Shiloh (Gwinnett)	79 %
South Forsyth (Forsyth)	79 %
Chamblee Charter (DeKalb)	78 %
Etowah (Cherokee)	78 %
McEachern (Cobb)	78 %
North Cobb (Cobb)	78 %
North Forsyth (Forsyth)	78 %
North Gwinnett (Gwinnett)	78 %
Wheeler (Cobb)	78 %
Salem (Rockdale)	77 %
Chapel Hill (Douglas)	76 %
Eagle's Landing (Henry)	76 %
Central Gwinnett (Gwinnett)	75 %
Druid Hills Charter (DeKalb)	75 %
Duluth (Gwinnett)	75 %
Kennesaw Mountain (Cobb)	75 %
Union Grove (Henry)	75 %
Alexander (Douglas)	74 %
Cherokee (Cherokee)	74 %
Dacula (Gwinnett)	74 %
Grady (Atlanta City)	74 %
Heritage (Rockdale)	74 %
North Atlanta (Atlanta City)	74 %

(Number of schools may exceed 50 because of schools with identical scores)

ELEVENTH-GRADE SOCIAL STUDIES

Students must pass the Georgia High School Graduation Tests (GHSGT) as part of the requirements to obtain a high school diploma. The Atlanta Journal-Constitution ranked the Top 50 schools to show how metro Atlanta schools stack up locally and statewide. The test scores reflect the 2000-2001 school year. The state average of students who passed the social studies portion of the test on the first try was 80%, and for metro Atlanta the average was 82%.

Top 50 Ranking of Metro Atlanta High Schools

School, district and pct. of students who passed on first try (see page 506 for more on the GHSGT)

School (District)	%
DeKalb of the Arts (DeKalb)	98 %
Chattahoochee (Fulton)	97 %
Centennial (Fulton)	96 %
Lassiter (Cobb)	96 %
Roswell (Fulton)	96 %
Walton (Cobb)	96 %
Brookwood (Gwinnett)	95 %
Milton (Fulton)	95 %
Parkview (Gwinnett)	95 %
Lakeside (DeKalb)	94 %
Mays (Atlanta City)	94 %
McIntosh (Fayette)	94 %
Harrison (Cobb)	93 %
Starr's Mill (Fayette)	93 %
Fayette County (Fayette)	92 %
North Springs (Fulton)	92 %
Northgate (Coweta)	92 %
Redan (DeKalb)	92 %
Woodstock (Cherokee)	92 %
North Forsyth (Forsyth)	91 %
Pope (Cobb)	91 %
Collins Hill (Gwinnett)	90 %
Sandy Creek (Fayette)	90 %
Sprayberry (Cobb)	90 %
Wheeler (Cobb)	90 %
Heritage (Rockdale)	89 %
McEachern (Cobb)	89 %
Salem (Rockdale)	89 %
Chamblee Charter (DeKalb)	88 %
North Gwinnett (Gwinnett)	88 %
Sequoyah (Cherokee)	88 %
South Forsyth (Forsyth)	88 %
South Gwinnett (Gwinnett)	88 %
Chapel Hill (Douglas)	87 %
Dacula (Gwinnett)	87 %
Dunwoody (DeKalb)	87 %
Eagle's Landing (Henry)	87 %
Etowah (Cherokee)	87 %
Forsyth Central (Forsyth)	87 %
Grayson (Gwinnett)	87 %
Kennesaw Mountain (Cobb)	87 %
Shiloh (Gwinnett)	87 %
Stockbridge (Henry)	87 %
Buford (Buford City)	86 %
Grady (Atlanta City)	86 %
Jonesboro (Clayton)	86 %
Union Grove (Henry)	86 %
Duluth (Gwinnett)	85 %
Hiram (Paulding)	85 %
North Atlanta (Atlanta City)	85 %
North Cobb (Cobb)	85 %
North Hall (Hall)	85 %

(Number of schools may exceed 50 because of schools with identical scores)

Georgia High School Graduation Tests

ELEVENTH-GRADE WRITING

Students must pass the Georgia High School Graduation Tests (GHSGT) as part of the requirements to obtain a high school diploma. The Atlanta Journal-Constitution ranked the Top 50 schools to show how metro Atlanta schools stack up locally and statewide. The test scores reflect the 2000-2001 school year. The state and metro Atlanta average of students who passed the writing portion of the test on the first try was 92%.

Top 50 Ranking of Metro Atlanta High Schools
School, district and pct. of students who passed on first try (see page 506 for more on the GHSGT)

DeKalb of the Arts (DeKalb) .... 100 %
Milton (Fulton) .... 99 %
Pope (Cobb) .... 99 %
Walton (Cobb) .... 99 %
Brookwood (Gwinnett) .... 98 %
Chattahoochee (Fulton) .... 98 %
Eagle's Landing (Henry) .... 98 %
East Paulding (Paulding) .... 98 %
Fayette County (Fayette) .... 98 %
Lassiter (Cobb) .... 98 %
McIntosh (Fayette) .... 98 %
North Springs (Fulton) .... 98 %
Sprayberry (Cobb) .... 98 %
Union Grove (Henry) .... 98 %
Centennial (Fulton) .... 97 %
Chapel Hill (Douglas) .... 97 %
Collins Hill (Gwinnett) .... 97 %
Grayson (Gwinnett) .... 97 %
Harrison (Cobb) .... 97 %
McEachern (Cobb) .... 97 %
Northgate (Coweta) .... 97 %
Parkview (Gwinnett) .... 97 %
Roswell (Fulton) .... 97 %
Sandy Creek (Fayette) .... 97 %
Sequoyah (Cherokee) .... 97 %
Starr's Mill (Fayette) .... 97 %
Stockbridge (Henry) .... 97 %
Dacula (Gwinnett) .... 96 %

Etowah (Cherokee) .... 96 %
Forsyth Central (Forsyth) .... 96 %
Hiram (Paulding) .... 96 %
Newton (Newton) .... 96 %
North Gwinnett (Gwinnett) .... 96 %
Shiloh (Gwinnett) .... 96 %
South Forsyth (Forsyth) .... 96 %
South Gwinnett (Gwinnett) .... 96 %
Chamblee Charter (DeKalb) .... 95 %
Cherokee (Cherokee) .... 95 %
Heritage (Rockdale) .... 95 %
Lakeside (DeKalb) .... 95 %
North Cobb (Cobb) .... 95 %
North Forsyth (Forsyth) .... 95 %
Rockdale County (Rockdale) .... 95 %
Woodstock (Cherokee) .... 95 %
Alexander (Douglas) .... 94 %
Buford (Buford City) .... 94 %
Dunwoody (DeKalb) .... 94 %
East Coweta (Coweta) .... 94 %
Jonesboro (Clayton) .... 94 %
Kennesaw Mountain (Cobb) .... 94 %
Mount Zion (Clayton) .... 94 %
Newnan (Coweta) .... 94 %
Southwest DeKalb (DeKalb) .... 94 %
Stephenson (DeKalb) .... 94 %
Westlake (Fulton) .... 94 %

(Number of schools may exceed 50 because of schools with identical scores)

SAT College Entrance Exam

The SAT, formerly known as the Scholastic Assessment Test, is a three-hour, primarily multiple-choice test developed by The College Board. The SAT is designed to test a student's verbal and mathematics skills.

The Atlanta Journal-Constitution ranked the Top 50 schools by their average verbal, mathematics and composite score to show how metro Atlanta schools stack up locally and nationwide. The test scores reflect the 2000-01 school year.

About the tests

- The verbal portion of the exam measures a student's ability to grasp concepts presented in words, sentences and paragraphs.

- The mathematics portion of the exam measures problem solving and critical thinking.

Changes forthcoming

Starting in March 2005, the 76-year-old college entrance exam will include a writing test, more reading and tougher arithmetic. The changes include:

- Adding a writing portion to the test that will include a 25-minute essay and multiple-choice grammar usage questions. The new section will be scored on a 200-800 point scale, boosting the top cumulative SAT score to 2,400.

- Renaming the verbal section of the test "critical reading," and adding more passages to test reading ability. Analogies — such as, a car is to a road what a train is to a rail — will be eliminated from the test.

- Incorporating questions from third-year high school math classes, specifically Algebra II.

Reading the scores

The existing verbal and mathematics portions of the SAT are each scored on a 200-800 point scale, for a top cumulative SAT of 1,600. In 2001, only 587 perfect scores were recorded nationwide — including 16 in Georgia — out of more than 2 million exams.

SAT Verbal Scores

The verbal portion of the SAT college entrance exam measures a student's ability to grasp concepts presented in words, sentences and paragraphs. Students often take the SAT multiple times and colleges often use the students' highest scores in determining admission. The Atlanta Journal-Constitution ranked the Top 50 schools by their highest 2000-2001 verbal, math and composite scores to show how metro Atlanta schools stack up locally and statewide. The average verbal score for metro Atlanta was 528 and 524 statewide.

Top 50 Ranking of Metro Atlanta High Schools
School, district and score (see page 512 for more on the SAT and scoring system)

School	Score
Chapel Hill (Douglas)	590
Chamblee Charter (DeKalb)	579
Walton (Cobb)	564
Grady (Atlanta City)	562
Roswell (Fulton)	561
DeKalb School of the Arts (DeKalb)	560
Chattahoochee (Fulton)	549
Decatur (Decatur City)	548
Centennial (Fulton)	547
Lassiter (Cobb)	546
Milton (Fulton)	545
Pope (Cobb)	545
North Springs (Fulton)	544
McIntosh (Fayette)	541
Etowah (Cherokee)	540
Lakeside (DeKalb)	535
Harrison (Cobb)	534
Starr's Mill (Fayette)	534
Parkview (Gwinnett)	533
Brookwood (Gwinnett)	532
Duluth (Gwinnett)	530
Sequoyah (Cherokee)	530
Sprayberry (Cobb)	525
Kennesaw Mountain (Cobb)	524
Newton (Newton)	523
Sandy Creek (Fayette)	523
Collins Hill (Gwinnett)	522
Marietta (Marietta City)	522
Wheeler (Cobb)	522
Dunwoody (DeKalb)	521
Cherokee (Cherokee)	520
Campbell (Cobb)	519
South Forsyth (Forsyth)	519
Heritage (Rockdale)	518
Fayette County (Fayette)	515
North Gwinnett (Gwinnett)	515
North Hall (Hall)	515
Shiloh (Gwinnett)	513
South Gwinnett (Gwinnett)	513
Woodstock (Cherokee)	511
Eastside (Newton)	510
Jonesboro (Clayton)	510
McEachern (Cobb)	510
North Cobb (Cobb)	509
Salem (Rockdale)	509
Newnan (Coweta)	507
Norcross (Gwinnett)	507
East Coweta (Coweta)	505
Douglas County (Douglas)	504
Tucker (DeKalb)	504

(Number of schools may exceed 50 because of schools with identical scores)

SAT College Entrance Examination

SAT Mathematics Scores

The mathematics portion of the SAT college entrance exam measures problem solving and critical thinking. Students often take the SAT multiple times and colleges often use the students' highest scores in determining admission. The Atlanta Journal-Constitution ranked the Top 50 schools by their highest 2000-2001 verbal, math and composite scores to show how metro Atlanta schools stack up locally and statewide. The average mathematics score for metro Atlanta was 533 and 521 statewide.

Top 50 Ranking of Metro Atlanta High Schools
School, district and score (see page 512 for more on the SAT and scoring system)

School	Score
Chapel Hill (Douglas)	630
Chamblee Charter (DeKalb)	576
Chattahoochee (Fulton)	576
Walton (Cobb)	575
Roswell (Fulton)	567
McIntosh (Fayette)	559
Pope (Cobb)	559
Duluth (Gwinnett)	557
Lassiter (Cobb)	556
Centennial (Fulton)	555
Parkview (Gwinnett)	554
Brookwood (Gwinnett)	553
Milton (Fulton)	553
North Springs (Fulton)	552
Starr's Mill (Fayette)	550
Grady (Atlanta City)	540
Riverwood (Fulton)	540
Etowah (Cherokee)	539
Norcross (Gwinnett)	539
Lakeside (DeKalb)	535
Collins Hill (Gwinnett)	534
Sandy Creek (Fayette)	530
Sequoyah (Cherokee)	530
Shiloh (Gwinnett)	530
Wheeler (Cobb)	529
Newton (Newton)	527
North Gwinnett (Gwinnett)	526
South Gwinnett (Gwinnett)	526
Decatur (Decatur City)	524
Jonesboro (Clayton)	523
Woodstock (Cherokee)	522
Fayette County (Fayette)	521
Kennesaw Mountain (Cobb)	521
Berkmar (Gwinnett)	517
Dunwoody (DeKalb)	517
Campbell (Cobb)	516
Harrison (Cobb)	516
South Forsyth (Forsyth)	515
Marietta (Marietta City)	514
Druid Hills Charter (DeKalb)	512
Sprayberry (Cobb)	512
DeKalb School of the Arts (DeKalb)	511
Salem (Rockdale)	511
Newnan (Coweta)	510
Stockbridge (Henry)	510
Tucker (DeKalb)	510
Central Gwinnett (Gwinnett)	509
Eagle's Landing (Henry)	509
Heritage (Rockdale)	508
Cherokee (Cherokee)	506
Dacula (Gwinnett)	50

(Number of schools may exceed 50 because of schools with identical scores)

SAT Composite Scores

The SAT is designed to test a student's verbal and mathematics skills. Students often take the SAT multiple times and colleges often use the students' highest scores in determining admission. The Atlanta Journal-Constitution ranked the Top 50 schools by their highest 2000-2001 verbal, math and composite scores to show how metro Atlanta schools stack up locally and statewide. The average composite score for metro Atlanta was 1,062 and 1,045 statewide.

Top 50 Ranking of Metro Atlanta High Schools

School, district and score (see page 512 for more on the SAT and scoring system)

School	Score
Chapel Hill (Douglas)	1,220
Chamblee Charter (DeKalb)	1,155
Walton (Cobb)	1,139
Roswell (Fulton)	1,128
Chattahoochee (Fulton)	1,125
Pope (Cobb)	1,104
Centennial (Fulton)	1,102
Grady (Atlanta City)	1,102
Lassiter (Cobb)	1,102
McIntosh (Fayette)	1,100
Milton (Fulton)	1,098
North Springs (Fulton)	1,096
Duluth (Gwinnett)	1,087
Parkview (Gwinnett)	1,087
Brookwood (Gwinnett)	1,085
Starr's Mill (Fayette)	1,084
Etowah (Cherokee)	1,079
Decatur (Decatur City)	1,072
DeKalb School of the Arts (DeKalb)	1,071
Lakeside (DeKalb)	1,070
Sequoyah (Cherokee)	1,060
Collins Hill (Gwinnett)	1,056
Sandy Creek (Fayette)	1,053
Wheeler (Cobb)	1,051
Harrison (Cobb)	1,050
Newton (Newton)	1,050
Norcross (Gwinnett)	1,046
Kennesaw Mountain (Cobb)	1,045
Shiloh (Gwinnett)	1,043
North Gwinnett (Gwinnett)	1,041
Riverwood (Fulton)	1,039
South Gwinnett (Gwinnett)	1,039
Dunwoody (DeKalb)	1,038
Sprayberry (Cobb)	1,037
Fayette County (Fayette)	1,036
Marietta (Marietta City)	1,036
Campbell (Cobb)	1,035
South Forsyth (Forsyth)	1,034
Jonesboro (Clayton)	1,033
Woodstock (Cherokee)	1,033
Cherokee (Cherokee)	1,026
Heritage (Rockdale)	1,026
North Hall (Hall)	1,020
Salem (Rockdale)	1,020
Newnan (Coweta)	1,017
Berkmar (Gwinnett)	1,014
Tucker (DeKalb)	1,014
Druid Hills Charter (DeKalb)	1,011
Eagle's Landing (Henry)	1,011
Eastside (Newton)	1,009
North Cobb (Cobb)	1,009

(Number of schools may exceed 50 because of schools with identical scores)

Metro Atlanta Private Schools

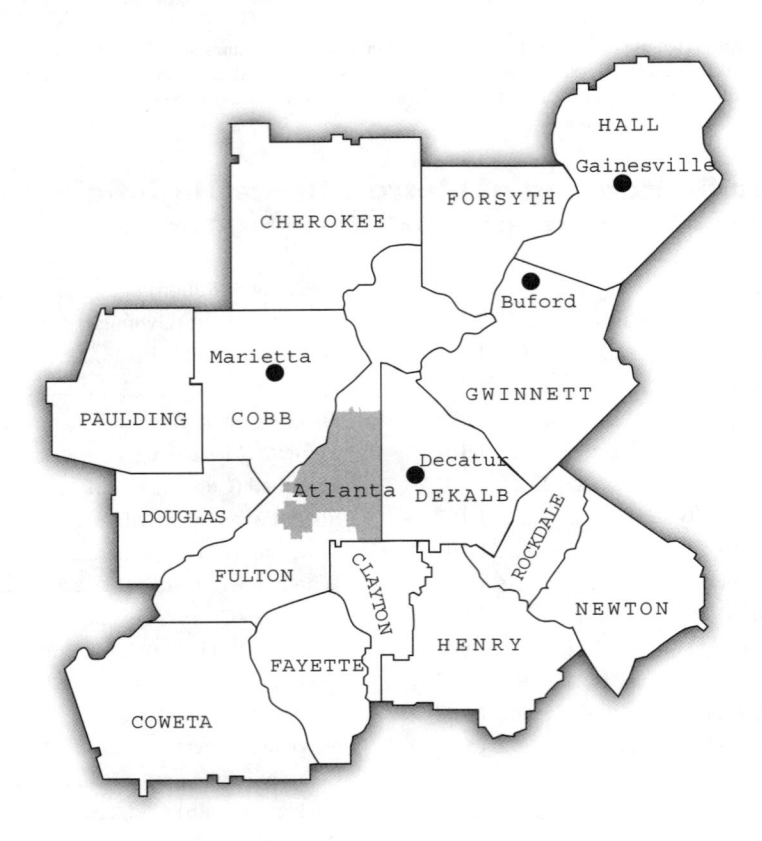

For this guide, we surveyed private schools across the metro Atlanta area. We've included all the schools — a total of 182 from 16 counties — that provided a response. An asterisk in any field indicates zero, not applicable or no response from the school. It is important to understand that all of the following information has been self-reported by these schools, many of which are reluctant to release standardized test scores or tuition costs. Various private schools in metro Atlanta offer scholarships or partial scholarships to needy students, so it would be prudent to check before ruling out a school based on cost.

Private School Index ▪ Pages 569 - 575

Ultimate Atlanta School Guide

Cherokee County Private Schools

CHEROKEE CHRISTIAN SCHOOL
3075 Trickum Rd, Woodstock, GA 30188 (o) 678-494-5464 (f) 770-592-4881
Principal: Michael Lee   E-mail: michael.lee@cherokeechristian.org
Annual tuition: $3,250 - $4,990   Internet: www.cherokeechristian.org
Grades: K - 9th   Enrollment: 280
Computers w/ Internet access: 26
Religion/affiliation: Christian (no specific denomination)
Curriculum: Private elementary and/or secondary
Total teachers, pct. w/ advanced degree: 21.5 / 22%
Serving Cherokee, Cobb, Fulton

CROSSROADS CHRISTIAN ACADEMY
2861 Ball Ground Hwy, Canton, GA 30114 (o) 770-479-7638 (f) 770-479-7638
Principal: Randy Collett   E-mail: No e-mail
Annual tuition: $2,000   Internet: No Web site
Grades: K - 12th   Enrollment: 57
Computers w/ Internet access: 1   Avg. score: ACT: * SAT: *
Religion/affiliation: Baptist
Curriculum: Private elementary and/or secondary
Total teachers, pct. w/ advanced degree: 7.0 / 12%
Total 2000-2001 graduates, pct. who went on to a four-year college: 2 / 100%
Top colleges graduates go on to: Pensacola Christian College (Fla.)
Serving Cherokee, Cobb, Forsyth, Pickens

Clayton County Private Schools

COMMUNITY CHRISTIAN ACADEMY
5900 Reynolds Rd, Morrow, GA 30260 (o) 770-961-9300 (f) 770-960-1875
Principal: Len McWilliams   E-mail: marylee@ccacademy.org
Annual tuition: $1,990 - $3,800   Internet: www.ccacademy.org
Grades: Pre-K - 8th   Enrollment: 303
Computers w/ Internet access: 25
Religion/affiliation: Christian (no specific denomination)
Curriculum: Private elementary and/or secondary
Total teachers, pct. w/ advanced degree: 20.0 / 25%
Serving Clayton, Coweta, Fayette, Fulton, Henry

Ultimate Atlanta School Guide

EVANGEL TEMPLE CHRISTIAN ACADEMY
2230 Rex Rd, Morrow, GA 30260 (o) 404-361-8046 (f) 404-366-9715
Principal:	Forrest Fraley	E-mail:	forrestfraley@hotmail.com
Annual tuition:	$2,500 - $3,600	Internet:	No Web site
Grades:	Pre-K - 12th	Enrollment:	68
Computers w/ Internet access: 8		Avg. score:	ACT: 14 SAT: 873

Religion/affiliation: Pentecostal
Curriculum: College preparatory
Total teachers, pct. w/ advanced degree: 9.0 / *
Total 2000-2001 graduates, pct. who went on to a four-year college: 3 / 100%
Top colleges graduates go on to: Clayton College & State Univ. (Ga.), State Univ. of West Georgia, Toccoa Falls College (Ga.)
Serving the greater metro Atlanta area

MT. ZION CHRISTIAN ACADEMY
7102 Mount Zion Blvd, Jonesboro, GA 30236 (o) 770-478-9842 (f) 770-478-4817
Principal:	Andrea Smith	E-mail:	No e-mail
Annual tuition:	$2,850 - $4,275	Internet:	www.mzca.org
Grades:	Pre-K - 12th	Enrollment:	719
Computers w/ Internet access: 5		Avg. score:	ACT: 19.4 SAT: 1170

Religion/affiliation: Baptist
Curriculum: Private elementary and/or secondary
Total teachers, pct. w/ advanced degree: 54.0 / 13%
Total 2000-2001 graduates, pct. who went on to a four-year college: 14 / 71%
Top colleges graduates go on to: Clayton College & State Univ. (Ga.), Georgia Military College, Toccoa Falls College (Ga.)
Serving Clayton, Fayette, Fulton, Henry, Spalding

WOODWARD ACADEMY - BUSEY CAMPUS
8009 Carlton Rd, Riverdale, GA 30296 (o) 404-765-4480 (f) 404-765-4489
Principal:	Andy Phillips	E-mail:	admissions@woodward.edu
Annual tuition:	$7,350 - $11,600	Internet:	www.woodward.edu
Grades:	Pre-K - 6th	Enrollment:	244

Computers w/ Internet access: 70
Religion/affiliation: None
Curriculum: College preparatory
Total teachers, pct. w/ advanced degree: 36.0 / 44%
Serving the greater metro Atlanta area

Ultimate Atlanta School Guide

Cobb County Private Schools

CARMAN ADVENTIST SCHOOL
1330 Cobb Pkwy N, Marietta, GA 30062 (o) 770-424-0606 (f) 770-420-9145
Principal: Verla Becker E-mail: caschool@bellsouth.net
Annual tuition: $2,700 - $4,800 Internet: www.tagnet.org/carman/
Grades: K - 8th Enrollment: 111
Computers w/ Internet access: 35
Religion/affiliation: Seventh-day Adventist
Curriculum: Private elementary and/or secondary
Total teachers, pct. w/ advanced degree: 9.0 / 30%
Serving Cobb

COBB COUNTY CHRISTIAN SCHOOL
545 Lorene Dr SW, Marietta, GA 30060 (o) 770-434-1320 (f) 770-434-1442
Principal: Brian Pitman E-mail: cccsoffice@aol.com
Annual tuition: $400 - $3,465 Internet: www.openbibletabernacle.com
Grades: Pre-K - 12th Enrollment: 75
Computers w/ Internet access: 2 Avg. score: ACT: * SAT: *
Religion/affiliation: Christian (no specific denomination)
Curriculum: Private elementary and/or secondary
Total teachers, pct. w/ advanced degree: 11.5 / *
Serving the greater metro Atlanta area

COVENANT CHRISTIAN MINISTRIES ACADEMY
268 N Fairground St NE, Marietta, GA 30060 (o) 770-426-4267 (f) 770-919-2098
Principal: Vanessa Anderson E-mail: apromise@bellsouth.net
Annual tuition: $2,670 - $3,250 Internet: No Web site
Grades: Pre-K - 12th Enrollment: 170
Computers w/ Internet access: * Avg. score: ACT: * SAT: 900
Religion/affiliation: Christian (no specific denomination)
Curriculum: College preparatory
Total teachers, pct. w/ advanced degree: 15.0 / 29%
Serving the greater metro Atlanta area

CRÈME DE LA CRÈME - MARIETTA
726 Woodlawn Dr NE, Marietta, GA 30068 (o) 770-971-2205 (f) 770-971-6240
Principal: Elisa Ezor E-mail: eezor@cremechildcare.com
Annual tuition: $4,815 - $8,055 Internet: www.cremechildcare.com
Grades: Kindergarten Enrollment: 20
Computers w/ Internet access: 3
Religion/affiliation: None
Curriculum: Early childhood program/day care center
Total teachers, pct. w/ advanced degree: 2.0 / 50%
Serving Cobb

Ultimate Atlanta School Guide

CUMBERLAND CHRISTIAN ACADEMY
2356 Clay Rd, Austell, GA 30106 (o) 770-819-6443 (f) 678-945-0224
Principal:	Larry Kendrick	E-mail:	cca01@bellsouth.net
Annual tuition:	$2,618 - $4,565	Internet:	www.cumberlandchristian.org
Grades:	K - 12th	Enrollment:	475
Computers w/ Internet access:	3	Avg. score:	ACT: 24 SAT: 1081

Religion/affiliation: Christian (no specific denomination)
Curriculum: Private elementary and/or secondary
Total teachers, pct. w/ advanced degree: 43.0 / 30%
Total 2000-2001 graduates, pct. who went on to a four-year college: 18 / 98%
Top colleges graduates go on to: Berry College (Ga.), Embry-Riddle Aeronautical Univ. (Fla.), Louisiana State Univ., North Georgia College & State Univ., Vanderbilt Univ. (Tenn.)
Serving Cherokee, Cobb, DeKalb, Douglas, Fulton, Paulding

DOMINION CHRISTIAN HIGH SCHOOL
4607 Burnt Hickory Rd NW, Marietta, GA 30064 (o) 770-420-2153 (f) 770-420-2510
Principal:	Rod Kirby	E-mail:	rkirby@dominionchristian.org
Annual tuition:	$6,450	Internet:	www.dominionchristian.org
Grades:	9th - 12th	Enrollment:	187
Computers w/ Internet access:	49	Avg. score:	ACT: * SAT: 1130

Religion/affiliation: Christian (no specific denomination)
Curriculum: Private elementary and/or secondary
Total teachers, pct. w/ advanced degree: 15.5 / 40%
Total 2000-2001 graduates, pct. who went on to a four-year college: 45 / 100%
Top colleges graduates go on to: Bryan College (Tenn.), Covenant College (Ga.), Kennesaw State Univ. (Ga.), Oglethorpe Univ. (Ga.), Toccoa Falls College (Ga.)
Serving Cherokee, Cobb, Douglas, Paulding

EASTSIDE CHRISTIAN SCHOOL
2450 Lower Roswell Rd, Marietta, GA 30068 (o) 770-971-2332 (f) 770-578-7967
Principal:	Beverly Smyly	E-mail:	admissions@ebcnet.org
Annual tuition:	$4,500	Internet:	www.eastsidechristianschool.com
Grades:	Pre-K - 8th	Enrollment:	590
Computers w/ Internet access:	*		

Religion/affiliation: Baptist
Curriculum: College preparatory
Total teachers, pct. w/ advanced degree: 40.0 / 40%
Serving the greater metro Atlanta area

Ultimate Atlanta School Guide

FAITH LUTHERAN SCHOOL
2111 Lower Roswell Rd, Marietta, GA 30068 (o) 770-973-8921 (f) 770-971-7796
Principal: Jon Wareham   E-mail: faithls@bellsouth.net
Annual tuition: $2,910 - $4,893   Internet: www.faithlcms.org
Grades: Pre-K - 8th   Enrollment: 175
Computers w/ Internet access: 10
Religion/affiliation: Lutheran Church - Missouri Synod
Curriculum: Private elementary and/or secondary
Total teachers, pct. w/ advanced degree: 15.5 / 33%
Serving Cherokee, Cobb

FIRST BAPTIST CHRISTIAN SCHOOL
2958 N Main St NW, Kennesaw, GA 30144 (o) 770-422-3254 (f) 770-427-2332
Principal: Nancy Thompson   E-mail: No e-mail
Annual tuition: $700 - $3,700   Internet: No Web site
Grades: Pre-K - 5th   Enrollment: 330
Computers w/ Internet access: 12
Religion/affiliation: Baptist
Curriculum: Private elementary and/or secondary
Total teachers, pct. w/ advanced degree: 12.0 / 30%
Serving Bartow, Cherokee, Cobb, Paulding

LAFAYETTE ACADEMY
2417 Canton Hwy, Marietta, GA 30066 (o) 770-429-9136 (f) 770-429-9174
Principal: Maria Delgado   E-mail: info@lafayetteacademy.com
Annual tuition: $3,375 - $8,665   Internet: www.lafayetteacademy.com
Grades: Pre-K - 10th   Enrollment: 77
Computers w/ Internet access: 2
Religion/affiliation: None
Curriculum: Private elementary and/or secondary with tailor-made program emphasis
Total teachers, pct. w/ advanced degree: 6.0 / 50%
Serving Cherokee, Cobb, Fulton, Pickens

MABLETON CHRISTIAN ACADEMY
6485 Factory Shoals Rd SW, Mableton, GA 30126 (o) 770-948-7971 (f) No fax
Principal: David Martin   E-mail: No e-mail
Annual tuition: $2,550 - $3,050   Internet: No Web site
Grades: K - 12th   Enrollment: 74
Computers w/ Internet access: *   Avg. score: ACT: * SAT: 1170
Religion/affiliation: Christian (no specific denomination)
Curriculum: Other
Total teachers, pct. w/ advanced degree: 9.0 / 20%
Total 2000-2001 graduates, pct. who went on to a four-year college: 2 / 0%
Top colleges graduates go on to: None specified
Serving Cobb, Douglas, Fulton

Greater Metro Atlanta Private School Listings

Ultimate Atlanta School Guide

MONTESSORI AMI CHILDREN'S HOUSE OF KENNESAW
3238 Cherokee St NW, Kennesaw, GA 30144 (o) 770-423-1044 (f) No fax
Principal:	Karen Driscoll	E-mail:	No e-mail
Annual tuition:	$3,000 - $6,500	Internet:	No Web site
Grades:	Ages 2 1/2 - 10 yrs	Enrollment:	49

Computers w/ Internet access: *
Religion/affiliation: None
Curriculum: Montessori
Total teachers, pct. w/ advanced degree: 6.5 / *
Serving Bartow, Cherokee, Cobb, Paulding

NOONDAY ACADEMY
4121 Canton Hwy, Marietta, GA 30066 (o) 770-926-8891 (f) 770-926-6092
Principal:	Luanne Trehern	E-mail:	lktrehern@hotmail.com
Annual tuition:	$2,750 - $3,500	Internet:	www.noondayacademy.org
Grades:	K - 3rd	Enrollment:	76

Computers w/ Internet access: 16
Religion/affiliation: Baptist
Curriculum: Private elementary and/or secondary pre-school
Total teachers, pct. w/ advanced degree: 11.0 / 27%
Serving Cherokee, Cobb

NORTH COBB CHRISTIAN SCHOOL
4500 Lakeview Dr NW, Kennesaw, GA 30144 (o) 770-975-0252 (f) 770-975-9051
Principal:	Byron Greene	E-mail:	bgreene@ncchristian.org
Annual tuition:	$3,050 - $6,600	Internet:	www.ncchristian.org
Grades:	Pre-K - 12th	Enrollment:	1,010
Computers w/ Internet access: 140		Avg. score: ACT: 22 SAT: 1072	

Religion/affiliation: Christian (no specific denomination)
Curriculum: Private elementary and/or secondary
Total teachers, pct. w/ advanced degree: 74.0 / 32%
Total 2000-2001 graduates, pct. who went on to a four-year college: 20 / 80%
Top colleges graduates go on to: Covenant College (Ga.), Georgia Institute of Technology, Kennesaw State Univ. (Ga.), Lee Univ. (Tenn.), Samford Univ. (Ala.)
Serving Bartow, Cherokee, Cobb, Fulton, Paulding

PATHWAYS ACADEMY
2147 Post Oak Tritt Rd, Marietta, GA 30062 (o) 770-973-5588 (f) 770-973-6997
Principal:	Jane Kyburz	E-mail:	pathwaysacademy@mindspring.com
Annual tuition:	$11,900	Internet:	www.pathwaysacademy.org
Grades:	1st - 5th	Enrollment:	50

Computers w/ Internet access: *
Religion/affiliation: None
Curriculum: Reading, writing & spelling problems
Total teachers, pct. w/ advanced degree: 11.5 / 70%
Serving the greater metro Atlanta area

Ultimate Atlanta School Guide

ROSWELL STREET BAPTIST CHRISTIAN SCHOOL
774 Roswell St SE, Marietta, GA 30060 (o) 770-424-9824 (f) 770-424-9823
Principal: Ralph Williams E-mail: rsbcschool@roswellstreet.com
Annual tuition: $4,060 Internet: www.roswellstreet.com
Grades: K - 7th Enrollment: 185
Computers w/ Internet access: 20
Religion affiliation: Christian (no specific denomination)
Curriculum: Private elementary and/or secondary
Total teachers, pct. w/ advanced degree: 21.0 / 15%
Serving the greater metro Atlanta area

SEEDS OF FAITH CHRISTIAN ACADEMY
1255 Veterans Memorial Hwy SW Ste 24, Mableton, GA 30126 (o) 770-944-1306 (f) 678-945-6041
Principal: David Kimbrough E-mail: sofacademy@aol.com
Annual tuition: $3,500 Internet: www.seedsoffaith.org
Grades: K - 6th Enrollment: 100
Computers w/ Internet access: 10
Religion affiliation: Christian (no specific denomination)
Curriculum: Private elementary and/or secondary
Total teachers, pct. w/ advanced degree: 9.5 / 100%
Serving Cobb, Douglas, Fulton

SHILOH HILLS CHRISTIAN SCHOOL
260 Hawkins Store Rd NW, Kennesaw, GA 30144 (o) 770-926-7729 (f) 770-926-3762
Principa : John Ward E-mail: school@shilohhills.com
Annual tuition: $2,105 - $4,470 Internet: www.shilohhills.com
Grades: Pre-K - 12th Enrollment: 525
Computers w/ Internet access: * Avg. score: ACT: 22 SAT: 1044
Religion affiliation: Baptist
Curriculum: Private elementary and/or secondary
Total teachers, pct. w/ advanced degree: 30.5 / 30%
Total 2000-2001 graduates, pct. who went on to a four-year college: 18 / 83%
Top colleges graduates go on to: Georgia Baptist College of Nursing of Mercer Univ., Kennesaw State Univ. (Ga.), North Georgia College & State Univ., Reinhardt College (Ga.), Young Harris College (Ga.)
Serving Bartow, Cherokee, Cobb, Fulton, Paulding

SHREINER ACADEMY
1340 Terrell Mill Rd SE, Marietta, GA 30067 (o) 770-953-1340 (f) 770-953-1340
Principa : David Shreiner E-mail: shreiner@shreiner.com
Annual tuition: $6,744 - $7,557 Internet: www.shreiner.com
Grades: Pre-K - 8th Enrollment: 270
Computers w/ Internet access: 22
Religion affiliation: None
Curriculum: Private elementary and/or secondary
Total teachers, pct. w/ advanced degree: 26.0 / 12%
Serving Cherokee, Cobb, Douglas, Fulton

ST. JOSEPH CATHOLIC SCHOOL
81 Lacy St NW, Marietta, GA 30060 (o) 770-428-3328 (f) 770-424-2960
Principal: Charles Kraft   E-mail: questions@stjosephschool.org
Annual tuition: $3,850   Internet: www.stjosephschool.org
Grades: K - 8th   Enrollment: 473
Computers w/ Internet access: 70
Religion/affiliation: Roman Catholic
Curriculum: Private elementary and/or secondary
Total teachers, pct. w/ advanced degree: 28.0 / 25%
Serving the greater metro Atlanta area

SWIFT SCHOOL (THE)
2663 Johnson Ferry Rd, Marietta, GA 30062 (o) 770-579-6377 (f) 770-579-6378
Principal: Gail Swift   E-mail: swiftsch@bellsouth.net
Annual tuition: $10,500   Internet: No Web site
Grades: 1st - 5th   Enrollment: 36
Computers w/ Internet access: 7
Religion/affiliation: None
Curriculum: Special education
Total teachers, pct. w/ advanced degree: 7.5 / 30%
Serving Cherokee, Cobb, DeKalb, Forsyth, Fulton, Gwinnett

TOTAL LEARNING CENTER CHRISTIAN SCHOOLS PRAISE ACADEMY
4052 Hiram Lithia Springs Rd, Powder Springs, GA 30127 (o) 770-943-2484 (f) 770-222-2279
Principal: Georgia White   E-mail: No e-mail
Annual tuition: $1,380 - $3,140   Internet: No Web site
Grades: Pre-K - 12th   Enrollment: 175
Computers w/ Internet access: 3   Avg. score: ACT: * SAT: 975
Religion/affiliation: Christian (no specific denomination)
Curriculum: Private elementary and/or secondary
Total teachers, pct. w/ advanced degree: 17.5 / 20%
Total 2000-2001 graduates, pct. who went on to a four-year college: 10 / 70%
Top colleges graduates go on to: Kennesaw State Univ. (Ga.), State Univ. of West Georgia, Wesley College (Miss.)
Serving Cobb, Douglas, Paulding

WALKER SCHOOL (THE)

700 Cobb Pkwy N, Marietta, GA 30062 (o) 770-427-2689 (f) 770-514-8122

Principal:	Don Robertson	E-mail:	No e-mail
Annual tuition:	$6,580 - $11,780	Internet:	www.thewalkerschool.org
Grades:	Pre-K - 12th	Enrollment:	1,014
Computers w/ Internet access:	380	Avg. score:	ACT: 26 SAT: 1248
Religion/affiliation:	None		
Curriculum:	College preparatory		

Total teachers, pct. w/ advanced degree: 110.0 / 80%

Total 2000-2001 graduates, pct. who went on to a four-year college: 72 / 100%

Top colleges graduates go on to: Georgia Institute of Technology, Univ. of Georgia, Univ. of Virginia, Vanderbilt Univ. (Tenn.), Wake Forest Univ. (N.C.)

Serving the greater metro Atlanta area

WHITEFIELD ACADEMY

1 Whitefield Dr SE, Mableton, GA 30126 (o) 678-305-3000 (f) 678-305-3010

Principal	George Lawrence	E-mail:	No e-mail
Annual tuition:	$7,900 - $11,745	Internet:	www.whitefieldacademy.com
Grades:	K - 12th	Enrollment:	400
Computers w/ Internet access:	37	Avg. score:	ACT: * SAT: 1203
Religion/affiliation:	Christian (no specific denomination)		
Curriculum:	Private elementary and/or secondary		

Total teachers, pct. w/ advanced degree: 46.5 / 40%

Total 2000-2001 graduates, pct. who went on to a four-year college: 19 / 100%

Top colleges graduates go on to: Auburn Univ. (Ala.), Duke Univ. (N.C.), Furman Univ. (S.C.), Univ. of Georgia, Vanderbilt Univ. (Tenn.)

Serving Cobb, DeKalb, Douglas, Fulton, Paulding

YOUTH CHRISTIAN SCHOOL

4967 Brownsville Rd, Powder Springs, GA 30127 (o) 770-943-1394 (f) 770-943-0756

Principal:	Moses Florence	E-mail:	No e-mail
Annual tuition:	$2,350 - $2,620	Internet:	No Web site
Grades:	K - 12th	Enrollment:	260
Computers w/ Internet access:	*	Avg. score:	ACT: * SAT: 1030
Religion/affiliation:	Baptist		
Curriculum:	College preparatory		

Total teachers, pct. w/ advanced degree: 21.5 / 40%

Total 2000-2001 graduates, pct. who went on to a four-year college: 12 / 70%

Top colleges graduates go on to: None specified

Serving Cobb, Paulding

Coweta County Private Schools

CAROLYN BARRON MONTESSORI
195 Jackson St, Newnan, GA 30263 (o) 770-253-2135 (f) 770-253-3444
Principal: Kevin O'Loughlin   E-mail: office@cbms.net
Annual tuition: $4,250 - $6,000   Internet: www.cbms.net
Grades: K - 5th   Enrollment: 84
Computers w/ Internet access: 2
Religion/affiliation: None
Curriculum: Montessori
Total teachers, pct. w/ advanced degree: 6.5 / 80%
Serving Carroll, Coweta, Fayette, Fulton

HERITAGE SCHOOL (THE)
2093 Ga. Highway 29 N, Newnan, GA 30263 (o) 770-253-9898 (f) 770-253-4850
Principal: Thomas Hudgins Jr.   E-mail: mcollier@heritagehawks.org
Annual tuition: $4,860 - $9,245   Internet: www.heritagehawks.org
Grades: Pre-K - 12th   Enrollment: 334
Computers w/ Internet access: 75   Avg. score: ACT: * SAT: 1124
Religion/affiliation: None
Curriculum: Private elementary and/or secondary
Total teachers, pct. w/ advanced degree: 37.5 / 53%
Total 2000-2001 graduates, pct. who went on to a four-year college: 20 / 100%
Top colleges graduates go on to: Auburn Univ. (Ala.), College of Charleston (S.C.), Georgia Southern Univ., Mercer Univ. (Ga.), Saint Louis Univ. (Mo.)
Serving Coweta, Douglas, Fayette, Fulton

NEWNAN CHRISTIAN SCHOOL
1608 Ga. Highway 29 N, Newnan, GA 30263 (o) 770-253-7175 (f) 770-253-4776
Principal: Paul Rowe   E-mail: No e-mail
Annual tuition: $1,945   Internet: No Web site
Grades: K - 12th   Enrollment: 203
Computers w/ Internet access: *   Avg. score: ACT: * SAT: 875
Religion/affiliation: Independent Baptist
Curriculum: College preparatory
Total teachers, pct. w/ advanced degree: 14.0 / 20%
Total 2000-2001 graduates, pct. who went on to a four-year college: 5 / 60%
Top colleges graduates go on to: Crown College (Tenn.), Univ. of West Georgia
Serving the greater metro Atlanta area

Ultimate Atlanta School Guide

NEWNAN CLASSICAL SCHOOL
195 Fischer Rd, Sharpsburg, GA 30277 (o) 678-423-9976 (f) 770-254-0890
Principal: Angie Gruner E-mail: neclsc@bellsouth.net
Annual tuition: $3,200 - $4,600 Internet: No Web site
Grades: K - 7th Enrollment: 50
Computers w/ Internet access: 3
Religion/affiliation: Christian (no specific denomination)
Curriculum: Other
Total teachers, pct. w/ advanced degree: 10.0 / 20%
Serving Clayton, Coweta, Fayette, Fulton, Henry

PEACHTREE BAPTIST ACADEMY
6675 Ga. Highway 16, Senoia, GA 30276 (o) 770-599-6888 (f) 770-599-2100
Principal: J. Alan Gaddy E-mail: agaddy1@juno.com
Annual tuition: $1,300 - $2,550 Internet: www.peachtreebaptist.org
Grades: Pre-K - 3rd Enrollment: 45
Computers w/ Internet access: *
Religion/affiliation: Baptist
Curriculum: Private elementary and/or secondary
Total teachers, pct. w/ advanced degree: 6.5 / 15%
Serving Coweta, Fayette, Meriwether, Troup

DeKalb County Private Schools

ALL STAR KIDS ACADEMY
4518 Covington Hwy, Decatur, GA 30035 (o) 404-284-2327 (f) 404-286-9140
Principal: Barbara Brown E-mail: bbboldt@msn.com
Annual tuition: $3,000 - $5,500 Internet: www.allstarkidsacademy.com
Grades: K - 3rd Enrollment: 45
Computers w/ Internet access: 2
Religion/affiliation: Christian (no specific denomination)
Curriculum: Private elementary and/or secondary
Total teachers, pct. w/ advanced degree: 3.0 / *
Serving DeKalb, Gwinnett

ARBOR MONTESSORI SCHOOL
2998 LaVista Rd, Decatur, GA 30033 (o) 404-321-9304 (f) 404-636-2700
Principal: Dianne Sherrill E-mail: info@arbormontessori.com
Annual tuition: $4,020 - $9,860 Internet: www.arbormontessori.org
Grades: Pre-K - 8th Enrollment: 310
Computers w/ Internet access: 6
Religion/affiliation: None
Curriculum: Montessori
Total teachers, pct. w/ advanced degree: 28.5 / 58%
Serving Clayton, Cobb, DeKalb, Fayette, Fulton, Gwinnett, Rockdale

BECKER ADVENTIST SCHOOL

3561 Covington hwy, Decatur, GA 30032 (o) 404-299-1131 (f) 404-299-1883
Principal: Harry J. Pappas E-mail: beckerschool@juno.com
Annual tuition: $2,200 - $3,900 Internet: www.beckerschool.com
Grades: K - 8th Enrollment: 70
Computers w/ Internet access: 4
Religion/affiliation: Seventh-day Adventist
Curriculum: Private elementary and/or secondary
Total teachers, pct. w/ advanced degree: 6.5 / 20%
Serving DeKalb, Gwinnett, Newton, Rockdale

BEN FRANKLIN ACADEMY

1585 Clifton Rd NE, Atlanta, GA 30329 (o) 404-633-7404 (f) 404-321-0610
Principal: Wood Smethurst E-mail: bfa@benfranklinacademy.org
Annual tuition: $19,400 Internet: www.benfranklinacademy.org
Grades: 10th - 12th Enrollment: 153
Computers w/ Internet access: 30 Avg. score: ACT: 22 SAT: 1015
Religion/affiliation: None
Curriculum: Alternative
Total teachers, pct. w/ advanced degree: 21.0 / 62%
Total 2000-2001 graduates, pct. who went on to a four-year college: 57 / 70%
Top colleges graduates go on to: Auburn Univ. (Ala.), Georgia State Univ., Savannah College of Art and Design (Ga.), Univ. of Georgia, Univ. of Mississippi
Serving the greater metro Atlanta area

CAMBRIDGE ACADEMY

2780 Flat Shoals Rd, Decatur, GA 30034 (o) 404-241-1321 (f) 404-241-3102
Principal: Judy Pruitt E-mail: rkinc2000@aol.com
Annual tuition: $4,200 - $5,800 Internet: www.yp.bellsouth.com/cambridge/
Grades: Pre-K - 7th Enrollment: 180
Computers w/ Internet access: 1
Religion/affiliation: Christian (no specific denomination)
Curriculum: Private elementary and/or secondary
Total teachers, pct. w/ advanced degree: 17.5 / 20%
Serving Clayton, Cobb, DeKalb, Fulton, Gwinnett, Henry

Ultimate Atlanta School Guide

CATHEDRAL ACADEMY
4650 Flat Shoals Pkwy, Decatur, GA 30034 (o) 404-243-3656 (f) 404-241-4234
Principal: Gregory Maxwell E-mail: cathedralacademy@mindspring.com
Annual tuition: $4,620 - $4,840 Internet: www.mindspring.com/~cathedralacademy/
Grades: Pre-K - 12th Enrollment: 285
Computers w/ Internet access: 25 Avg. score: ACT: * SAT: 1080
Religion/affiliation: Christian (no specific denomination)
Curriculum: Private elementary and/or secondary
Total teachers, pct. w/ advanced degree: 18.0 / 10%
Total 2000-2001 graduates, pct. who went on to a four-year college: 18 / 89%
Top colleges graduates go on to: Georgia Institute of Technology, Georgia State Univ., State Univ. of West Georgia, Tennessee Technological Univ., Univ. of Georgia
Serving the greater metro Atlanta area

CREATIVE BEGINNINGS ACADEMY
2982 Flat Shoals Rd, Decatur, GA 30034 (o) 404-241-0163 (f) 404-243-1351
Principal: Myron Daye E-mail: myrondaye@cs.com
Annual tuition: $4,680 - $5,720 Internet: No Web site
Grades: K - 2nd Enrollment: 18
Computers w/ Internet access: 6
Religion/affiliation: Baptist
Curriculum: Private elementary and/or secondary
Total teachers, pct. w/ advanced degree: 1.5 / 100%
Serving DeKalb

CROSS AND CROWN DAY SCHOOL
4276 Chamblee Dunwoody Rd Ste A, Atlanta, GA 30341 (o) 770-458-5274 (f) 770-458-5274
Principal: Pat McKibben E-mail: No e-mail
Annual tuition: $2,610 - $4,770 Internet: No Web site
Grades: Pre-K - 4th Enrollment: 52
Computers w/ Internet access: 2
Religion/affiliation: Evangelical Lutheran Church in America
Curriculum: Private elementary and/or secondary
Total teachers, pct. w/ advanced degree: 8.0 / 25%
Serving Cherokee, Cobb, DeKalb, Fulton, Gwinnett

DECATUR FIRST METHODIST WEEKDAY CHILDREN'S MINISTRIES
300 E Ponce de Leon Ave, Decatur, GA 30030 (o) 404-377-5784 (f) No fax
Principal: Joanne Hauserman E-mail: No e-mail
Annual tuition: $1,215 - $2,025 Internet: No Web site
Grades: Ages 2 1/2 - 5 yrs Enrollment: 138
Computers w/ Internet access: *
Religion/affiliation: Methodist
Curriculum: Early childhood program/day care center
Total teachers, pct. w/ advanced degree: 24.0 / *
Serving DeKalb, Fulton, Gwinnett, Henry

Ultimate Atlanta School Guide

DECATUR MONTESSORI
1429 Church St, Decatur, GA 30030 (o) 404-370-0620 (f) No fax
- Principal: Mariam Gilmer
- E-mail: mgilmer@decaturmontessori.org
- Annual tuition: $5,832 - $10,025
- Internet: www.decaturmontessori.org
- Grades: Ages 6 wks - 6 yrs
- Enrollment: 90
- Computers w/ Internet access: *
- Religion/affiliation: None
- Curriculum: Montessori
- Total teachers, pct. w/ advanced degree: 12.0 / *
- Serving the greater metro Atlanta area

DECATUR PRESBYTERIAN CHILDREN'S COMMUNITY SCHOOL
205 Sycamore St, Decatur, GA 30030 (o) 404-378-1770 (f) 404-636-5340
- Principal: Ellen McClure
- E-mail: No e-mail
- Annual tuition: $1,125 - $1,800
- Internet: www.dpchurch.org
- Grades: Ages 3 mths - 5 yrs
- Enrollment: 170
- Computers w/ Internet access: *
- Religion/affiliation: Presbyterian
- Curriculum: Early childhood program/day care center
- Total teachers, pct. w/ advanced degree: 13.0 / 20%
- Serving DeKalb, Fulton, Gwinnett

DISCOVERY ACADEMY
3174 Miller Rd, Lithonia, GA 30038 (o) 770-981-4522 (f) 770-981-6092
- Principal: Lorraine Ross
- E-mail: discacad@bellsouth.net
- Annual tuition: $4,400 - $6,850
- Internet: www.discovery-academy.com
- Grades: Pre-K - 6th
- Enrollment: 70
- Computers w/ Internet access: 4
- Religion/affiliation: None
- Curriculum: Private elementary and/or secondary
- Total teachers, pct. w/ advanced degree: 10.0 / 10%
- Serving DeKalb, Gwinnett, Rockdale

FIRST STEPS CHRISTIAN ACADEMY
1863 Brannen Rd SE, Atlanta, GA 30316 (o) 404-241-7862 (f) 404-241-0256
- Principal: Ron Williams
- E-mail: 1step2@bellsouth.net
- Annual tuition: $4,120
- Internet: No Web site
- Grades: Ages 3 mths - 12 yrs
- Enrollment: 130
- Computers w/ Internet access: 5
- Religion/affiliation: Christian (no specific denomination)
- Curriculum: Private elementary and/or secondary
- Total teachers, pct. w/ advanced degree: 12.0 / *
- Serving Clayton, DeKalb, Fulton, Gwinnett, Henry, Rockdale

FORREST HILLS CHRISTIAN

6826 James B Rivers Dr, Stone Mountain, GA 30083 (o) 770-469-3422 (f) 770-469-6219

Principal:	Rock Dearfield	E-mail:	dearfields@aol.com
Annual tuition:	$3,750	Internet:	No Web site
Grades:	K - 12th	Enrollment:	151
Computers w/ Internet access: 17		Avg. score:	ACT: 23 SAT: 1460
Religion/affiliation:	Baptist		
Curriculum:	Private elementary and/or secondary		

Total teachers, pct. w/ advanced degree: 21.5 / 31%

Total 2000-2001 graduates, pct. who went on to a four-year college: 30 / 33%

Top colleges graduates go on to: Crown College (Tenn.), Georgia Institute of Technology, Georgia State Univ., Heartland Baptist Bible College (Okla.), Univ. of Georgia

Serving DeKalb, Fulton, Gwinnett

FRIENDS SCHOOL OF ATLANTA

121 Sams St, Decatur, GA 30030 (o) 404-373-8746 (f) 678-990-1318

Principal:	James Withers	E-mail:	friends.school@friendsschoolatlanta.org
Annual tuition:	$8,800 - $9,540	Internet:	www.friendsschoolatlanta.org
Grades:	Pre-K - 8th	Enrollment:	172
Computers w/ Internet access: 13			
Religion/affiliation:	None		
Curriculum:	Private elementary and/or secondary		

Total teachers, pct. w/ advanced degree: 35.0 / 60%

Serving Cobb, DeKalb, Fulton, Gwinnett, Rockdale

GREENFOREST CHRISTIAN ACADEMIC CENTER

3250 Rainbow Dr, Decatur, GA 30034 (o) 404-286-0479 (f) 404-286-0052

Principal:	Albert Walker	E-mail:	al.walker@greenforest.org
Annual tuition:	$4,000 - $5,600	Internet:	www.gfca.net
Grades:	Pre-K - 12th	Enrollment:	900
Computers w/ Internet access: 28		Avg. score:	ACT: * SAT: 1020
Religion/affiliation:	Protestant Baptist		
Curriculum:	College preparatory		

Total teachers, pct. w/ advanced degree: 68.0 / 10%

Total 2000-2001 graduates, pct. who went on to a four-year college: 21 / 95%

Top colleges graduates go on to: Georgia Southern Univ., Morehouse College (Ga.), Morris Brown College (Ga.), Savannah State Univ. (Ga.), Tennessee State Univ.

Serving the greater metro Atlanta area

HORIZONS SCHOOL

1900 DeKalb Ave NE, Atlanta, GA 30307   (o) 404-378-2219   (f) 404-378-8946
Principal: Lorraine Wilson   E-mail: horizonsschool@mindspring.com
Annual tuition: $5,500 - $6,300   Internet: www.horizonsschool.com
Grades: K - 12th   Enrollment: 130
Computers w/ Internet access: 20   Avg. score: ACT: *   SAT: 1140
Religion/affiliation: None
Curriculum: College preparatory
Total teachers, pct. w/ advanced degree: 13.5 / 38%
Total 2000-2001 graduates, pct. who went on to a four-year college: 20 / 95%
Top colleges graduates go on to: Fisk Univ. (Tenn.), George Washington Univ. (D.C.), Georgia State Univ., Univ. of Georgia, Univ. of North Carolina
Serving the greater metro Atlanta area

IMMACULATE HEART OF MARY SCHOOL

2855 Briarcliff Rd NE, Atlanta, GA 30329   (o) 404-636-4488   (f) 404-636-1853
Principal: Patricia DeWitt   E-mail: tdewitt@ihmschool.org
Annual tuition: $4,160   Internet: www.ihmschool.org
Grades: K - 8th   Enrollment: 490
Computers w/ Internet access: 60
Religion/affiliation: Roman Catholic
Curriculum: Private elementary and/or secondary
Total teachers, pct. w/ advanced degree: 31.0 / 44%
Serving the greater metro Atlanta area

INTOWN COMMUNITY SCHOOL

2059 LaVista Rd NE, Atlanta, GA 30329   (o) 404-633-8081   (f) 404-329-7144
Principal: Kevin Bracher   E-mail: nicolec@intown.org
Annual tuition: $3,000 - $4,500   Internet: www.intownschool.org
Grades: 1st - 8th   Enrollment: 175
Computers w/ Internet access: 16
Religion/affiliation: Presbyterian
Curriculum: Alternative
Total teachers, pct. w/ advanced degree: 18.0 / 33%
Serving DeKalb

LIGHT OF THE WORLD CHRISTIAN SCHOOL

2135 Shamrock Dr, Decatur, GA 30032   (o) 404-286-4727   (f) 404-286-4153
Principal: Takiyah Smith   E-mail: No e-mail
Annual tuition: $2,700 - $4,500   Internet: www.the-lightoftheworld.org
Grades: Pre-K - 12th   Enrollment: 100
Computers w/ Internet access: 10   Avg. score: ACT: *   SAT: *
Religion/affiliation: Christian (no specific denomination)
Curriculum: Private elementary and/or secondary
Total teachers, pct. w/ advanced degree: 8.0 / *
Serving DeKalb, Fulton, Henry, Rockdale

LOVE & GRACE CHRISTIAN ACADEMY
1125 S Hariston Rd, Stone Mountain, GA 30088 (o) 404-296-7881 (f) 404-296-7881
Principal: Cleotha Griffith   E-mail: No e-mail
Annual tuition: $3,800 - $4,300   Internet: No Web site
Grades: Pre-K - 2nd   Enrollment: 47
Computers w/ Internet access: 3
Religion affiliation: Christian (no specific denomination)
Curriculum: Private elementary and/or secondary
Total teachers, pct. w/ advanced degree: 3.0 / 33%
Serving DeKalb, Rockdale

LOVE THY CHILDREN CHRISTIAN LEARNING CENTER
4164 Rainbow Dr, Decatur, GA 30034 (o) 404-288-2350 (f) 404-284-3779
Principal: Cleotha Griffith   E-mail: No e-mail
Annual tuition: $3,800 - $4,300   Internet: No Web site
Grades: Pre-K - 2nd   Enrollment: 20
Computers w/ Internet access: 2
Religion/affiliation: Christian (no specific denomination)
Curriculum: Private elementary and/or secondary
Total teachers, pct. w/ advanced degree: 2.0 / *
Serving DeKalb, Fulton, Rockdale

LULLWATER SCHOOL
705 S Candler St, Decatur, GA 30030 (o) 404-378-6643 (f) 404-377-0879
Principal: Joan Teach   E-mail: No e-mail
Annual tuition: $8,800 - $9,200   Internet: www.lullwaterschool.org
Grades: K - 8th   Enrollment: 61
Computers w/ Internet access: 13
Religion/affiliation: None
Curriculum: Alternative with focus serving students with attention deficits
Total teachers, pct. w/ advanced degree: 11.0 / 25%
Serving the greater metro Atlanta area

MARIST SCHOOL
3790 Ashford Dunwoody Rd NE, Atlanta, GA 30319 (o) 770-457-7201 (f) 770-457-8402
Principal: Joel Konzen   E-mail: admissions@marist.com
Annual tuition: $10,400   Internet: www.marist.com
Grades: 7th - 12th   Enrollment: 1,032
Computers w/ Internet access: 300   Avg. score: ACT: * SAT: 1228
Religion/affiliation: Roman Catholic
Curriculum: College preparatory
Total teachers, pct. w/ advanced degree: 82.0 / 88%
Total 2000-2001 graduates, pct. who went on to a four-year college: 193 / 100%
Top colleges graduates go on to: Duke Univ. (N.C.), Georgia Institute of Technology, Univ. of Georgia, Univ. of Notre Dame (Ind.), Vanderbilt Univ. (Tenn.)
Serving Cobb, DeKalb, Forsyth, Fulton, Gwinnett

Ultimate Atlanta School Guide

MEMORIAL DRIVE PRESBYTERIAN COMMUNITY CHILDREN'S PROGRAM
5140 Memorial Dr, Stone Mountain, GA 30083 (o) 404-296-1783 (f) 404-296-3770
Principal: Tonie Sanders E-mail: No e-mail
Annual tuition: $1,620 - $2,750 Internet: No Web site
Grades: Pre-K - 3rd Enrollment: 112
Computers w/ Internet access: 1
Religion/affiliation: Presbyterian
Curriculum: Early childhood program/day care center
Total teachers, pct. w/ advanced degree: 5.0 / 20%
Serving DeKalb, Gwinnett

MOHAMMED SCHOOLS OF ATLANTA
735 Fayetteville Rd SE, Atlanta, GA 30316 (o) 404-378-4219 (f) 404-378-4600
Principal: Sandra El-Amin E-mail: info@mohammedschoolsofatlanta.org
Annual tuition: $3,680 - $4,800 Internet: www.mohammedschoolsofatlanta.org
Grades: Pre-K - 12th Enrollment: 280
Computers w/ Internet access: 2 Avg. score: ACT: 21 SAT: 920
Religion/affiliation: Al-Islam
Curriculum: College preparatory
Total teachers, pct. w/ advanced degree: 24.5 / 27%
Total 2000-2001 graduates, pct. who went on to a four-year college: 15 / 87%
Top colleges graduates go on to: Agnes Scott College (Ga.), Clark Atlanta Univ. (Ga.), Georgia State Univ., Spelman College (Ga.), State Univ. of West Georgia
Serving the greater metro Atlanta area

MONTESSORI SCHOOL AT EMORY
1677 Scott Blvd, Decatur, GA 30033 (o) 404-634-5777 (f) 404-633-5373
Principal: Barbara Ann Doan E-mail: No e-mail
Annual tuition: $4,455 - $7,605 Internet: www.montessorischoolatemory.com
Grades: K - 6th Enrollment: 115
Computers w/ Internet access: 2
Religion/affiliation: None
Curriculum: Montessori
Total teachers, pct. w/ advanced degree: 7.0 / *
Serving DeKalb

MT. CARMEL CHRISTIAN SCHOOL
6015 Old Stone Mountain Rd, Stone Mountain, GA 30087 (o) 770-279-8443 (f) 770-935-8620
Principal: Gregg Wright E-mail: mccs@mindspring.com
Annual tuition: $1,600 - $7,500 Internet: www.mtcarmelchristiansch.org
Grades: Pre-K - 8th Enrollment: 410
Computers w/ Internet access: 30
Religion/affiliation: Christian (no specific denomination)
Curriculum: Private elementary and/or secondary
Total teachers, pct. w/ advanced degree: 31.0 / 30%
Serving the greater metro Atlanta area

Ultimate Atlanta School Guide

NEW ATLANTA JEWISH COMMUNITY HIGH SCHOOL
2012 Womack Rd, Atlanta, GA 30338 (o) 770-352-0018 (f) 770-352-0352

Principal:	Simcha Pearl	E-mail:	najchs@najchs.org
Annual tuition:	$12,250	Internet:	www.najchs.org
Grades:	9th - 12th	Enrollment:	102
Computers w/ Internet access: 34		Avg. score: ACT: * SAT: 1210	

Religion/affiliation: Jewish
Curriculum: Independent, college preparatory, coeducational Jewish day school
Total teachers, pct. w/ advanced degree: 26.0 / 50%
Total 2000-2001 graduates, pct. who went on to a four-year college: 10 / 100%
Top colleges graduates go on to: Georgia Institute of Technology, Harvard Univ. (Mass.), Indiana Univ., Univ. of Georgia, Washington Univ. (Mo.)
Serving the greater metro Atlanta area

NORTHWOODS MONTESSORI, INC.
3340 Chestnut Dr, Atlanta, GA 30340 (o) 770-457-7261 (f) 770-455-9211

Principal:	Beth Samples	E-mail:	No e-mail
Annual tuition:	$4,015 - $7,425	Internet:	No Web site
Grades:	K - 6th	Enrollment:	230

Computers w/ Internet access: 2
Religion/affiliation: None
Curriculum: Montessori
Total teachers, pct. w/ advanced degree: 9.5 / 44%
Serving DeKalb, Fulton, Gwinnett

OUR LADY OF THE ASSUMPTION SCHOOL
1320 Hearst Dr NE, Atlanta, GA 30319 (o) 404-364-1902 (f) 404-364-1914

Principal:	Joan Tiernan	E-mail:	ktravers@ola.cathsch.org
Annual tuition:	$4,000	Internet:	www.olaschoolga.org
Grades:	Pre-K - 8th	Enrollment:	496

Computers w/ Internet access: 140
Religion/affiliation: Catholic
Curriculum: Pre-preparatory
Total teachers, pct. w/ advanced degree: 28.5 / 30%
Serving the greater metro Atlanta area

Ultimate Atlanta School Guide

PAIDEIA SCHOOL (THE)
1509 Ponce de Leon Ave NE, Atlanta, GA 30307 (o) 404-377-3491 (f) 404-377-0032
Principal: Paul Bianchi E-mail: admissions@paideiaschool.org
Annual tuition: $11,406 - $12,789 Internet: www.paideiaschool.org
Grades: Pre-K - 12th Enrollment: 865
Computers w/ Internet access: 350 Avg. score: ACT: * SAT: *
Religion/affiliation: Non-sectarian
Curriculum: College preparatory
Total teachers, pct. w/ advanced degree: 113.0 / 64%
Total 2000-2001 graduates, pct. who went on to a four-year college: 85 / 100%
Top colleges graduates go on to: Brown Univ. (R.I.), George Washington Univ. (D.C.), New York Univ., Savannah College of Art and Design (Ga.), Univ. of Georgia
Serving Cobb, DeKalb, Fulton, Gwinnett, Henry, Rockdale

SEIGAKUIN ATLANTA INTERNATIONAL SCHOOL
3007 Hermance Dr NE, Atlanta, GA 30319 (o) 404-231-9699 (f) 404-231-9799
Principal: Sumiko Tomizawa E-mail: seigakuin@aol.com
Annual tuition: $5,530 - $6,890 Internet: www.seig.ac.jp/english/atlanta/
Grades: Pre-K - 6th Enrollment: 52
Computers w/ Internet access: 12
Religion/affiliation: Disciples of Christ
Curriculum: Bilingual (Japanese/English)
Total teachers, pct. w/ advanced degree: 13.5 / 22%
Serving Cherokee, Cobb, DeKalb, Forsyth, Fulton, Gwinnett

SHEPHERD'S TRAINING ACADEMY
4120 Presidential Pkwy, Atlanta, GA 30340 (o) 770-455-4781 (f) 770-455-3794
Principal: Althea Penn E-mail: 5shepard@bellsouth.net
Annual tuition: $3,530 - $4,900 Internet: www.acsi.org
Grades: Pre-K - 9th Enrollment: 99
Computers w/ Internet access: 43
Religion/affiliation: Christian (no specific denomination)
Curriculum: Private elementary and/or secondary with a special program emphasis
Total teachers, pct. w/ advanced degree: 8.5 / 30%
Serving DeKalb, Fulton, Gwinnett

SOLA SCRIPTURA LUTHERAN SCHOOL
2999 Flat Shoals Rd, Decatur, GA 30034 (o) 404-241-6093 (f) 404-241-6093
Principal: Mark Haefner E-mail: No e-mail
Annual tuition: $4,000 Internet: No Web site
Grades: K - 8th Enrollment: 22
Computers w/ Internet access: 1
Religion/affiliation: Lutheran
Curriculum: Private elementary and/or secondary
Total teachers, pct. w/ advanced degree: 2.0 / *
Serving DeKalb, Douglas, Fulton

Ultimate Atlanta School Guide

SPARKS CHRISTIAN ACADEMY OF EARLY CHILDHOOD EDUCATION
1901 Bodwin Pl, Decatur, GA 30035 (o) 404-286-2873 (f) 770-808-6648
Principal: Dannetta Sparks   E-mail: drsparks@aol.com
Annual tuition: $2,500 - $4,300   Internet: No Web site
Grades: Pre-K - kindergarten   Enrollment: 108
Computers w/ Internet access: 5
Religion/affiliation: Christian (no specific denomination)
Curriculum: Private pre-school and kindergarten
Total teachers, pct. w/ advanced degree: 12.0 / 10%
Serving the greater metro Atlanta area

SPARKS CHRISTIAN ACADEMY PREPARATORY SCHOOL FOR GIRLS
5949 Fairington Rd, Lithonia, GA 30038 (o) 770-808-0301 (f) 770-808-6648
Principal: Dannetta Sparks   E-mail: drsparks@aol.com
Annual tuition: $3,500 - $4,500   Internet: No Web site
Grades: Pre-K - 11th   Enrollment: 100
Computers w/ Internet access: 10
Religion/affiliation: Christian (no specific denomination)
Curriculum: Private pre-school, elementary and secondary school for girls
Total teachers, pct. w/ advanced degree: 8.0 / 25%
Serving the greater metro Atlanta area

ST. MARTIN'S EPISCOPAL SCHOOL
3110 Ashford Dunwoody Rd NE Ste A, Atlanta, GA 30319 (o) 404-237-4260 (f) 404-237-9311
Principal: James Hamner   E-mail: jswoope@stmartinschool.org
Annual tuition: $6,320 - $9,840   Internet: www.stmartinschool.org
Grades: Pre-K - 8th   Enrollment: 600
Computers w/ Internet access: 100
Religion/affiliation: Episcopal
Curriculum: Private elementary and/or secondary
Total teachers, pct. w/ advanced degree: 67.0 / 41%
Serving the greater metro Atlanta area

ST. PIUS X CATHOLIC HIGH SCHOOL
2674 Johnson Rd NE, Atlanta, GA 30345 (o) 404-636-3023 (f) 404-633-8387
Principal: Steve Spellman   E-mail: spellman@spx.org
Annual tuition: $7,300   Internet: www.spx.org
Grades: 9th - 12th   Enrollment: 999
Computers w/ Internet access: 184   Avg. score: ACT: * SAT: 1180
Religion/affiliation: Roman Catholic
Curriculum: Private secondary
Total teachers, pct. w/ advanced degree: 70.0 / 65%
Total 2000-2001 graduates, pct. who went on to a four-year college: 237 / 98%
Top colleges graduates go on to: Auburn Univ. (Ala.), College of Charleston (S.C.), Furman Univ. (S.C.), Georgia Institute of Technology, Univ. of Georgia
Serving Cherokee, Clayton, Cobb, DeKalb, Douglas, Fayette, Forsyth, Fulton, Gwinnett, Rockdale

ST. THOMAS MORE SCHOOL

630 W Ponce de Leon Ave, Decatur, GA 30030 (o) 404-373-8456 (f) 404-377-8554

Principal:	Gail Msezane	E-mail:	more@mindspring.com
Annual tuition:	$3,915 - $5,415	Internet:	www.catholicedga.org/stm/
Grades:	K - 8th	Enrollment:	456

Computers w/ Internet access: 135
Religion/affiliation: Roman Catholic
Curriculum: Private elementary and/or secondary
Total teachers, pct. w/ advanced degree: 30.0 / 60%
Serving Cobb, DeKalb, Fulton

TEMIMA HIGH SCHOOL

1839 LaVista Rd NE, Atlanta, GA 30329 (o) 404-315-0507 (f) 404-634-2111

Principal:	Miriam Feldman	E-mail:	admin@temima.org
Annual tuition:	$10,000 - $10,500	Internet:	www.temima.org
Grades:	9th - 12th	Enrollment:	40
Computers w/ Internet access:	12	Avg. score:	ACT: * SAT: 1140

Religion/affiliation: Jewish
Curriculum: Private elementary and/or secondary with a special program emphasis
Total teachers, pct. w/ advanced degree: 9.0 / 78%
Total 2000-2001 graduates, pct. who went on to a four-year college: 4 / 100%
Top colleges graduates go on to: Georgia State Univ., Maalot Baltimore (Md.), Touro College (N.Y.)
Serving DeKalb, Fulton

TORAH DAY SCHOOL OF ATLANTA

1959 LaVista Rd NE, Atlanta, GA 30329 (o) 404-982-0800 (f) 404-248-1039

Principal:	Kalmen Rosenbaum	E-mail:	No e-mail
Annual tuition:	$6,500 - $8,400	Internet:	No Web site
Grades:	K - 8th	Enrollment:	309

Computers w/ Internet access: 20
Religion/affiliation: Jewish
Curriculum: Private elementary and/or secondary with a special program emphasis
Total teachers, pct. w/ advanced degree: 23.5 / *
Serving Cobb, DeKalb, Fulton, Gwinnett

WALDORF SCHOOL OF ATLANTA

711 S Columbia Dr, Decatur, GA 30030 (o) 404-377-1315 (f) 404-377-5013

Principal:	Patricia Muesse	E-mail:	office@waldorfatlanta.org
Annual tuition:	$4,000 - $8,100	Internet:	www.waldorfatlanta.org
Grades:	Pre-K - 8th	Enrollment:	200

Computers w/ Internet access: *
Religion/affiliation: None
Curriculum: Private elementary and/or secondary with a special program emphasis
Total teachers, pct. w/ advanced degree: 23.0 / 21%
Serving the greater metro Atlanta area

Ultimate Atlanta School Guide

YESHIVA ATLANTA
3130 Raymond Dr, Atlanta, GA 30340 (o) 770-451-5299 (f) 770-451-5571
Principal: Dewey Holbrook E-mail: dholbrook.ya@atlchai.org
Annual tuition: $12,300 Internet: www.yeshivaatlanta.org
Grades: 9th - 12th Enrollment: 121
Computers w/ Internet access: 40 Avg. score: ACT: * SAT: 1200
Religion/affiliation: Jewish
Curriculum: Private elementary and/or secondary with a special program emphasis
Total teachers, pct. w/ advanced degree: 20.0 / 42%
Total 2000-2001 graduates, pct. who went on to a four-year college: 21 / 90%
Top colleges graduates go on to: Cornell Univ. (N.Y.), Georgia State Univ., Univ. of Georgia, Univ. of Pennsylvania, Yeshiva Univ. (N.Y.)
Serving Cobb, DeKalb, Fulton

Douglas County Private Schools

COLONIAL HILLS CHRISTIAN SCHOOL
7131 Mount Vernon Rd, Lithia Springs, GA 30122 (o) 770-941-6342 (f) 770-941-2090
Principal: Westley Smith E-mail: chbc@bellsouth.net
Annual tuition: $3,180 - $4,315 Internet: www.chrams.org
Grades: K - 12th Enrollment: 420
Computers w/ Internet access: 30 Avg. score: ACT: * SAT: 1070
Religion/affiliation: Baptist
Curriculum: Private elementary and/or secondary
Total teachers, pct. w/ advanced degree: 28.0 / 18%
Total 2000-2001 graduates, pct. who went on to a four-year college: 13 / 75%
Top colleges graduates go on to: Georgia Baptist College of Nursing of Mercer Univ., Georgia Institute of Technology, Georgia State Univ., North Georgia College & State Univ., State Univ. of West Georgia
Serving Carroll, Cobb, Douglas, Fulton, Paulding

DOUGLASVILLE SEVENTH-DAY ADVENTIST SCHOOL
2836 Bright Star Rd, Douglasville, GA 30134 (o) 770-949-6734 (f) 770-949-2954
Principal: Melinda Boyson E-mail: No e-mail
Annual tuition: $2,300 - $2,700 Internet: No Web site
Grades: K - 8th Enrollment: 28
Computers w/ Internet access: *
Religion/affiliation: Seventh-day Adventist
Curriculum: Private elementary and/or secondary
Total teachers, pct. w/ advanced degree: 2.0 / 100%
Serving Carroll, Cobb, Douglas, Paulding

HARVESTER CHRISTIAN ACADEMY

4241 Central Church Rd, Douglasville, GA 30135 (o) 770-942-1583 (f) 770-942-9332
Principal: Jack North E-mail: jackdnorth@earthlink.net
Annual tuition: $2,036 - $5,147 Internet: No Web site
Grades: Pre-K - 12th Enrollment: 262
Computers w/ Internet access: 36 Avg. score: ACT: * SAT: *
Religion/affiliation: Presbyterian
Curriculum: Private elementary and/or secondary
Total teachers, pct. w/ advanced degree: 35.0 / 20%
Total 2000-2001 graduates, pct. who went on to a four-year college: 7 / 100%
Top colleges graduates go on to: Auburn Univ. (Ala.), Berry College (Ga.), Kennesaw State Univ. (Ga.), Mercer Univ. (Ga.), State Univ. of West Georgia
Serving Carroll, Cobb, Douglas, Paulding

HEIRWAY CHRISTIAN ACADEMY

6758 Spring St, Douglasville, GA 30134 (o) 770-489-4392 (f) 770-489-4318
Principal: Phyllis Campbell E-mail: heirwaychristian@yahoo.com
Annual tuition: $2,998 - $3,998 Internet: No Web site
Grades: K - 12th Enrollment: 150
Computers w/ Internet access: * Avg. score: ACT: * SAT: 1100
Religion/affiliation: Christian (no specific denomination)
Curriculum: Private elementary and/or secondary
Total teachers, pct. w/ advanced degree: 16.0 / *
Total 2000-2001 graduates, pct. who went on to a four-year college: 12 / 40%
Top colleges graduates go on to: Georgia Institute of Technology, Lee Univ. (Tenn.), North Georgia College & State Univ., State Univ. of West Georgia, Young Harris College (Ga.)
Serving Carroll, Douglas, Paulding

KINGS WAY CHRISTIAN

6456 The Kings Way, Douglasville, GA 30135 (o) 770-949-0812 (f) 770-949-1045
Principal: Ray Conway E-mail: No e-mail
Annual tuition: $1,600 - $2,850 Internet: www.kings-highway.net
Grades: K - 12th Enrollment: 285
Computers w/ Internet access: * Avg. score: ACT: * SAT: *
Religion/affiliation: Baptist
Curriculum: Private elementary and/or secondary with a special program emphasis
Total teachers, pct. w/ advanced degree: 23.0 / 20%
Total 2000-2001 graduates, pct. who went on to a four-year college: 16 / 75%
Top colleges graduates go on to: None specified
Serving Coweta, Douglas, Fayette, Haralson, Paulding

Ultimate Atlanta School Guide

Fayette County Private Schools

CRESTWOOD CHRISTIAN ACADEMY
734 Senoia Rd, Tyrone, GA 30290 (o) 770-487-4852 (f) 770-487-4852

Principal:	Ferrell Dowdey	E-mail:	No e-mail
Annual tuition:	$1,000 - $1,600	Internet:	No Web site
Grades:	K - 12th	Enrollment:	23
Computers w/ Internet access:	2	Avg. score:	ACT: 22 SAT: *

Religion/affiliation: Baptist
Curriculum: Private elementary and/or secondary
Total teachers, pct. w/ advanced degree: 4.0 / *
Total 2000-2001 graduates, pct. who went on to a four-year college: 2 / 100%
Top colleges graduates go on to: Hyles-Anderson College (Ind.), Pensacola Christian College (Fla.), State Univ. of West Georgia
Serving Coweta, Fayette, Fulton

FAYETTE CHRISTIAN SCHOOL
152 Longview Rd, Fayetteville, GA 30214 (o) 770-461-3538 (f) 770-460-6013

Principal:	N. Phillip Woods	E-mail:	fayettechrsch@juno.com
Annual tuition:	$2,575 - $3,400	Internet:	www.fayetteministries.org
Grades:	K - 12th	Enrollment:	300
Computers w/ Internet access:	*	Avg. score:	ACT: * SAT: 950

Religion/affiliation: Baptist
Curriculum: College preparatory
Total teachers, pct. w/ advanced degree: 24.0 / 12%
Total 2000-2001 graduates, pct. who went on to a four-year college: 22 / 75%
Top colleges graduates go on to: Clayton College & State Univ. (Ga.), Georgia Institute of Technology, Georgia State Univ., Gordon College (Ga.), Pensacola Christian College (Fla.)
Serving Clayton, Fayette, Fulton, Henry

FAYETTE MONTESSORI SCHOOL
190 Weatherly Dr, Fayetteville, GA 30214 (o) 770-460-6790 (f) No fax

Principal:	Margaret Sisson	E-mail:	fayettems@cs.com
Annual tuition:	$1,800 - $5,700	Internet:	www.fayettemontessori.com
Grades:	Pre-K - kindergarten	Enrollment:	100
Computers w/ Internet access:	*		

Religion/affiliation: None
Curriculum: Montessori
Total teachers, pct. w/ advanced degree: 7.5 / *
Serving Clayton, Coweta, Fayette, Henry

GRACE CHRISTIAN ACADEMY
355 McDonough Rd, Fayetteville, GA 30214 (o) 770-461-0137 (f) 770-461-1190
Principal: Brian Fourman E-mail: No e-mail
Annual tuition: $2,400 - $3,000 Internet: www.gracechristian.info
Grades: K - 8th Enrollment: 195
Computers w/ Internet access: 15
Religion/affiliation: Christian (no specific denomination)
Curriculum: Private elementary and/or secondary
Total teachers, pct. w/ advanced degree: 14.5 / *
Serving Clayton, Coweta, Fayette, Henry

OUR LADY OF MERCY CATHOLIC HIGH SCHOOL
861 Ga. Highway 279, Fairburn, GA 30213 (o) 770-461-2202 (f) 770-461-9353
Principal: John Cobis E-mail: jcobis@om.cathsch.org
Annual tuition: $7,100 - $7,620 Internet: www.olmbobcats.com
Grades: 9th - 12th Enrollment: 260
Computers w/ Internet access: 250
Religion/affiliation: Roman Catholic
Curriculum: Private elementary and/or secondary
Total teachers, pct. w/ advanced degree: 22.0 / 55%
Serving Carroll, Clayton, Coweta, Fayette, Fulton, Henry, Spalding

PACE CHRISTIAN SCHOOL
193 Johnson Ave, Fayetteville, GA 30214 (o) 770-719-1633 (f) 770-716-1460
Principal: Evelyn Sellers E-mail: mhall@pacechristianschool.org
Annual tuition: $590 - $4,185 Internet: www.pacechristianschool.org
Grades: K - 12th Enrollment: 180
Computers w/ Internet access: 20 Avg. score: ACT: * SAT: 1010
Religion/affiliation: Christian (no specific denomination)
Curriculum: College preparatory
Total teachers, pct. w/ advanced degree: 18.0 / 50%
Total 2000-2001 graduates, pct. who went on to a four-year college: 11 / 85%
Top colleges graduates go on to: Atlanta Christian College (Ga.), Clayton College & State Univ. (Ga.), Georgia State Univ., LaGrange College (Ga.)
Serving the greater metro Atlanta area

SOLID ROCK ACADEMY
106 Commerce St, Riverdale, GA 30296 (o) 770-997-9744 (f) 770-997-0061
Principal: Sherry Moore-Wright E-mail: srajl@aol.com
Annual tuition: $5,000 Internet: www.solidrockacademy.com
Grades: Pre-K - 10th Enrollment: 150
Computers w/ Internet access: 15
Religion/affiliation: Christian (no specific denomination)
Curriculum: Private elementary and/or secondary
Total teachers, pct. w/ advanced degree: 13.0 / 20%
Serving Clayton, Fayette, Fulton

Ultimate Atlanta School Guide

ST. PAUL LUTHERAN SCHOOL
700 Ardenlee Pkwy, Peachtree City, GA 30269 (o) 770-486-3545 (f) 770-486-3545
Principal: Dan Palisch   E-mail: stpaulls@bellsouth.net
Annual tuition: $4,900 - $5,400   Internet: www.stpaulptc.com
Grades: Pre-K - 8th   Enrollment: 240
Computers w/ Internet access: 14
Religion/affiliation: Lutheran
Curriculum: Other
Total teachers, pct. w/ advanced degree: 14.0 / 40%
Serving Coweta, Fayette

Forsyth County Private Schools

ATLANTA COUNTRY DAY SCHOOL
5895 Shiloh Rd Ste 104, Alpharetta, GA 30005 (o) 678-455-1929 (f) 678-455-1969
Principal: Mary Ellen Nicol   E-mail: admin@atlantacountryday.org
Annual tuition: $13,950 - $30,150   Internet: www.atlantacountryday.org
Grades: 7th - 12th   Enrollment: 85
Computers w/ Internet access: 12   Avg. score: ACT: * SAT: 1100
Religion/affiliation: None
Curriculum: Private elementary and/or secondary
Total teachers, pct. w/ advanced degree: 10.0 / 20%
Total 2000-2001 graduates, pct. who went on to a four-year college: 16 / 100%
Top colleges graduates go on to: College of Charleston (S.C.), Georgia College & State Univ., Georgia State Univ., State Univ. of West Georgia, Univ. of North Carolina
Serving Cherokee, Cobb, DeKalb, Forsyth, Fulton

COVENANT CHRISTIAN ACADEMY
6905 Post Rd, Cumming, GA 30040 (o) 770-674-2990 (f) 770-674-2989
Principal: Johnathan Arnold   E-mail: jarnold@covenantrams.org
Annual tuition: $4,700 - $6,300   Internet: www.covenantrams.org
Grades: K - 12th   Enrollment: 182
Computers w/ Internet access: 15   Avg. score: ACT: * SAT: 1325
Religion/affiliation: Christian (no specific denomination)
Curriculum: Private elementary and/or secondary
Total teachers, pct. w/ advanced degree: 24.0 / 40%
Total 2000-2001 graduates, pct. who went on to a four-year college: 15 / 100%
Top colleges graduates go on to: Berry College (Ga.), Covenant College (Ga.), Georgia Institute of Technology, Georgia State Univ., Shorter College (Ga.)
Serving Forsyth, Fulton, Gwinnett, Hall

Ultimate Atlanta School Guide

PINECREST ACADEMY
955 Peachtree Pkwy, Cumming, GA 30041 (o) 770-888-4477 (f) 770-888-0404
Principal: Margaret Richardson E-mail: mrichardson@pinecrestacademy.org
Annual tuition: $7,603 Internet: www.pinecrestacademy.org
Grades: Pre-K - 8th Enrollment: 720
Computers w/ Internet access: 125
Religion/affiliation: Catholic
Curriculum: Pre-preparatory
Total teachers, pct. w/ advanced degree: 50.0 / 40%
Serving the greater metro Atlanta area

Fulton County Private Schools

ALFRED AND ADELE DAVIS ACADEMY (THE)
8105 Roberts Dr, Atlanta, GA 30350 (o) 770-671-0085 (f) 770-671-8838
Principal: Steven Ballaban E-mail: davis@davisacademy.org
Annual tuition: $9,600 - $10,500 Internet: www.davisacademy.org
Grades: K - 8th Enrollment: 550
Computers w/ Internet access: 100
Religion/affiliation: Jewish
Curriculum: General academic with integrated Judaic curriculum
Total teachers, pct. w/ advanced degree: 61.5 / 30%
Serving the greater metro Atlanta area

ALPHARETTA INTERNATIONAL ACADEMY
4772 Webb Bridge Rd, Alpharetta, GA 30005 (o) 678-475-0558 (f) No fax
Principal: Dixie Oliver E-mail: No e-mail
Annual tuition: $1,800 - $5,500 Internet: No Web site
Grades: Pre-K - 3rd Enrollment: 150
Computers w/ Internet access: 3
Religion/affiliation: None
Curriculum: Montessori
Total teachers, pct. w/ advanced degree: 6.0 / 20%
Serving Cobb, Forsyth, Fulton, Gwinnett

ALPHARETTA METHODIST CHRISTIAN ACADEMY
89 Cumming St, Alpharetta, GA 30004 (o) 770-518-1652 (f) 770-569-5548
Principal: Mary Dean Townsend E-mail: amcaone@bellsouth.net
Annual tuition: $3,250 - $4,830 Internet: www.alpharettamca.com
Grades: K - 4th Enrollment: 60
Computers w/ Internet access: 5
Religion/affiliation: Methodist
Curriculum: Private elementary and/or secondary
Total teachers, pct. w/ advanced degree: 14.0 / 15%
Serving Cobb, Forsyth, Fulton

Ultimate Atlanta School Guide

ATLANTA GIRLS' SCHOOL
4100 Roswell Rd NE, Atlanta, GA 30342 (o) 404-845-0900 (f) 404-845-0190
Principal   Susan Thompson   E-mail: inquiries@atlantagirlsschool.org
Annual tuition: $12,800   Internet: www.atlantagirlsschool.org
Grades: 6th - 11th   Enrollment: 165
Computers w/ Internet access: 175
Religion/affiliation: None
Curriculum: College preparatory
Total teachers, pct. w/ advanced degree: 19.0 / 42%
Serving the greater metro Atlanta area

ATLANTA NEW CENTURY SCHOOL
300 Luck e St NW, Atlanta, GA 30313 (o) 404-525-1909 (f) 404-586-9926
Principal: Cole Walker   E-mail: colew@atlantancs.com
Annual tuition: $8,000   Internet: www.atlantancs.com
Grades: Pre-K - 8th   Enrollment: 104
Computers w/ Internet access: 30
Religion/affiliation: None
Curriculum: Private elementary and/or secondary
Total teachers, pct. w/ advanced degree: 10.0 / 20%
Serving the greater metro Atlanta area

ATLANTA SCHOOL, INC. (THE)
1015 Edgewood Ave NE, Atlanta, GA 30307 (o) 404-688-9550 (f) No fax
Principal: Joy Ward   E-mail: tas@theatlantaschool.com
Annual tuition: $8,250   Internet: www.theatlantaschool.com
Grades: K - 8th   Enrollment: 62
Computers w/ Internet access: 3
Religion/affiliation: None
Curriculum: Private elementary and/or secondary
Total teachers, pct. w/ advanced degree: 18.0 / 50%
Serving the greater metro Atlanta area

ATLANTA SPEECH SCHOOL
3160 Northside Pkwy NW, Atlanta, GA 30327 (o) 404-233-5332 (f) 404-266-2175
Principal: Jane Blalock   E-mail: jblalock@atlantaspeechschool.org
Annual tuition: $15,464   Internet: www.atlantaspeechschool.org
Grades: K - 6th   Enrollment: 211
Computers w/ Internet access: 107
Religion/affiliation: None
Curriculum: Special education
Total teachers, pct. w/ advanced degree: 42.0 / 100%
Serving Clayton, Cobb, DeKalb, Fulton, Gwinnett, Hall

ATLANTA YOUTH ACADEMY
2500 Hosea L Williams Dr NE, Atlanta, GA 30317 (o) 404-370-1960 (f) 404-370-1210
Principal: Lynette Dandridge E-mail: lynetted@atlantayouthacademy.com
Annual tuition: $330 - $3,630 Internet: www.atlantayouthacademy.com
Grades: K - 7th Enrollment: 110
Computers w/ Internet access: 16
Religion/affiliation: Christian (no specific denomination)
Curriculum: Private elementary and/or secondary
Total teachers, pct. w/ advanced degree: 9.0 / 20%
Serving the greater metro Atlanta area

BEDFORD SCHOOL AND SQUIRREL HOLLOW CAMP (THE)
5665 Milam Rd, Fairburn, GA 30213 (o) 770-774-8001 (f) 770-774-8005
Principal: Betsy Box E-mail: bbox@thebedfordschool.org
Annual tuition: $11,300 - $11,700 Internet: www.thebedfordschool.org
Grades: 1st - 9th Enrollment: 112
Computers w/ Internet access: 24
Religion/affiliation: None
Curriculum: Special education
Total teachers, pct. w/ advanced degree: 14.0 / 40%
Serving Carroll, Clayton, Cobb, Coweta, DeKalb, Fayette, Fulton, Henry, Paulding

BELIEVERS BIBLE CHRISTIAN ACADEMY
3689 Campbellton Rd SW, Atlanta, GA 30331 (o) 404-344-7203 (f) 404-346-6564
Principal: Sam West E-mail: swest@believersbible.org
Annual tuition: $4,500 Internet: www.believersbible.org
Grades: Pre-K - 7th Enrollment: 127
Computers w/ Internet access: *
Religion/affiliation: Christian (no specific denomination)
Curriculum: Private elementary and/or secondary
Total teachers, pct. w/ advanced degree: 10.0 / *
Serving Clayton, DeKalb, Douglas, Fulton, Henry

BLESSED TRINITY CATHOLIC HIGH SCHOOL
11320 Woodstock Rd, Roswell, GA 30075 (o) 678-277-9083 (f) 678-277-9756
Principal: Frank Moore E-mail: No e-mail
Annual tuition: $7,580 Internet: www.bttitans.org
Grades: 9th - 12th Enrollment: 669
Computers w/ Internet access: 300
Religion/affiliation: Roman Catholic
Curriculum: Private elementary and/or secondary
Total teachers, pct. w/ advanced degree: 52.0 / 54%
Serving Cherokee, Cobb, DeKalb, Fayette, Forsyth, Fulton, Gwinnett

Ultimate Atlanta School Guide

BRANDON HALL SCHOOL
1701 Brandon Hall Dr, Atlanta, GA 30350 (o) 770-394-8177 (f) 770-804-8821
Principal: Paul Stockhammer E-mail: sboyce@brandonhall.org
Annual tuition: $18,500 - $24,000 Internet: www.brandonhall.org
Grades: 4th - 12th Enrollment: 190
Computers w/ Internet access: 70 Avg. score: ACT: * SAT: 1011
Religion/affiliation: None
Curriculum: College preparatory
Total teachers, pct. w/ advanced degree: 53.0 / 60%
Total 2000-2001 graduates, pct. who went on to a four-year college: 24 / 100%
Top colleges graduates go on to: Duke Univ. (N.C.), Georgia State Univ., North Georgia College, Univ. of Virginia, Washington and Lee Univ. (Va.)
Serving the greater metro Atlanta area

BRIMARSH ACADEMY
1565 Holcomb Bridge Rd, Roswell, GA 30076 (o) 770-992-0416 (f) 770-998-2369
Principal: Micki McGuire E-mail: No e-mail
Annual tuition: $5,000 - $7,200 Internet: www.brimarsh.com
Grades: K - 8th Enrollment: 65
Computers w/ Internet access: 27
Religion/affiliation: None
Curriculum: Private elementary and/or secondary
Total teachers, pct. w/ advanced degree: 10.0 / 30%
Serving Cobb, Fulton, Gwinnett

CHILDREN'S SCHOOL (THE)
345 10th St NE, Atlanta, GA 30309 (o) 404-873-6985 (f) 404-607-8565
Principal: Marcia Spiller E-mail: info@thechildrensschool.com
Annual tuition: $10,590 Internet: www.thechildrensschool.com
Grades: Pre-K - 6th Enrollment: 380
Computers w/ Internet access: 76
Religion/affiliation: None
Curriculum: Private elementary and/or secondary
Total teachers, pct. w/ advanced degree: 47.0 / 10%
Serving the greater metro Atlanta area

CHRIST LUTHERAN SCHOOL
2719 Delowe Dr, East Point, GA 30344 (o) 404-767-2892 (f) 404-767-0516
Principal: Ellinor White E-mail: clsprinebw1@aol.com
Annual tuition: $4,000 Internet: www.aliveatchrist.org
Grades: Pre-K - 5th Enrollment: 58
Computers w/ Internet access: 47
Religion/affiliation: Lutheran Church - Missouri Synod
Curriculum: Private elementary and/or secondary
Total teachers, pct. w/ advanced degree: 8.0 / 60%
Serving the greater metro Atlanta area

CHRIST THE KING ELEMENTARY SCHOOL
46 Peachtree Way NE, Atlanta, GA 30305 (o) 404-233-0383 (f) 404-266-0704
Principal: Peggy Warner E-mail: information@christking.org
Annual tuition: $5,300 - $8,100 Internet: www.christking.org
Grades: K - 8th Enrollment: 524
Computers w/ Internet access: 125
Religion/affiliation: Roman Catholic
Curriculum: Private elementary and/or secondary
Total teachers, pct. w/ advanced degree: 41.0 / 35%
Serving Cobb, DeKalb, Fulton, Gwinnett

COTTAGE SCHOOL (THE)
700 Grimes Bridge Rd, Roswell, GA 30075 (o) 770-641-8688 (f) 770-641-9026
Principal: Joe Digieso E-mail: tcs@cottageschool.org
Annual tuition: $13,000 - $15,000 Internet: www.cottageschool.org
Grades: 6th - 12th Enrollment: 200
Computers w/ Internet access: 20 Avg. score: ACT: * SAT: *
Religion/affiliation: None
Curriculum: Other
Total teachers, pct. w/ advanced degree: 24.0 / 70%
Total 2000-2001 graduates, pct. who went on to a four-year college: 28 / 46%
Top colleges graduates go on to: Andrew College (Ga.), Chattahoochee Technical College (Ga.), Georgia State Univ., Reinhardt College (Ga.), Savannah College of Art and Design (Ga.)
Serving Fulton

CRÈME DE LA CRÈME - ALPHARETTA
11675 Haynes Bridge Rd, Alpharetta, GA 30004 (o) 770-777-2960 (f) 770-777-5960
Principal: Elisa Ezor E-mail: eezor@cremechildcare.com
Annual tuition: $4,950 - $8,235 Internet: www.cremechildcare.com
Grades: Kindergarten Enrollment: 35
Computers w/ Internet access: 5
Religion/affiliation: None
Curriculum: Early childhood program/day care center
Total teachers, pct. w/ advanced degree: 2.0 / *
Serving Fulton

CRÈME DE LA CRÈME - ATLANTA
4669 Roswell Rd NE, Atlanta, GA 30342 (o) 404-256-4488 (f) 404-256-2808
Principal: Elisa Ezor E-mail: eezor@cremechildcare.com
Annual tuition: $4,950 - $8,235 Internet: www.cremechildcare.com
Grades: Kindergarten Enrollment: 30
Computers w/ Internet access: 3
Religion/affiliation: None
Curriculum: Early childhood program/day care center
Total teachers, pct. w/ advanced degree: 3.0 / *
Serving Fulton

Ultimate Atlanta School Guide

CRÈME DE LA CRÈME - ROSWELL
8730 Nesbit Ferry Rd, Alpharetta, GA 30022 (o) 770-998-1844 (f) 770-998-2808
Principal: Elisa Ezor
E-mail: eezor@cremechildcare.com
Annual tuition: $4,680 - $7,785
Internet: www.cremechildcare.com
Grades: Kindergarten
Enrollment: 14
Computers w/ Internet access: 3
Religion/affiliation: None
Curriculum: Early childhood program/day care center
Total teachers, pct. w/ advanced degree: 1.0 / *
Serving Fulton

DAR UN-NOOR SCHOOL
434 14th St NW, Atlanta, GA 30318 (o) 404-876-5051 (f) 404-874-8997
Principal: Nabilia Hawasli
E-mail: alnoor@negia.net
Annual tuition: $2,500 - $3,500
Internet: www.darunnoor.org
Grades: Pre-K - 8th
Enrollment: 180
Computers w/ Internet access: 12
Religion/affiliation: Islamic
Curriculum: Private elementary and/or secondary with a special program emphasis
Total teachers, pct. w/ advanced degree: 18.5 / 20%
Serving Clayton, Cobb, DeKalb, Fulton, Gwinnett

DONNELLAN SCHOOL (THE)
4820 Long Island Dr NE, Atlanta, GA 30342 (o) 404-255-0900 (f) 404-255-0914
Principal: Gary Delneo
E-mail: gdelneo@donnellan.org
Annual tuition: $2,500 - $9,975
Internet: www.donnellan.org
Grades: Pre-K - 9th
Enrollment: 230
Computers w/ Internet access: 128
Religion/affiliation: Roman Catholic
Curriculum: Private elementary and/or secondary
Total teachers, pct. w/ advanced degree: 32.0 / 43%
Serving Cobb, DeKalb, Fulton

EATON ACADEMY
800 Old Roswell Lakes Pkwy Ste 210, Roswell, GA 30076 (o) 770-645-2673 (f) 770-645-2711
Principal: Brigit Eaton-Partalis
E-mail: No e-mail
Annual tuition: $5,000 - $15,400
Internet: www.eatonacademy.org
Grades: K - 12th
Enrollment: 80
Computers w/ Internet access: 40
Avg. score: ACT: * SAT: 950
Religion/affiliation: None
Curriculum: Private elementary and/or secondary with a special program emphasis
Total teachers, pct. w/ advanced degree: 16.0 / 44%
Total 2000-2001 graduates, pct. who went on to a four-year college: 7 / 100%
Top colleges graduates go on to: Brevard College (N.C.), Reinhardt College (Ga.), Univ. of Colorado, Univ. of Georgia, Univ. of Mississippi
Serving Cobb, DeKalb, Forsyth, Fulton, Gwinnett

EPSTEIN SCHOOL (THE), SOLOMON SCHECHTER SCHOOL OF ATLANTA
335 Colewood Way NW, Atlanta, GA 30328 (o) 404-843-0111 (f) 404-843-0743
Principal: Stan Beiner E-mail: admissionoffice@epsteinatlanta.org
Annual tuition: $9,510 - $11,130 Internet: www.epsteinatlanta.org
Grades: Pre-K - 8th Enrollment: 680
Computers w/ Internet access: 250
Religion/affiliation: Conservative Judaism
Curriculum: Bilingual
Total teachers, pct. w/ advanced degree: 81.0 / 85%
Serving the greater metro Atlanta area

FELLOWSHIP CHRISTIAN ACADEMY
480 W Crossville Rd, Roswell, GA 30075 (o) 770-992-4975 (f) 770-641-5825
Principal: David Kinsey E-mail: paladins@fbcministries.org
Annual tuition: $6,540 - $6,732 Internet: www.fbcministries.org
Grades: K - 8th Enrollment: 440
Computers w/ Internet access: 65
Religion/affiliation: Christian (no specific denomination)
Curriculum: Private elementary and/or secondary
Total teachers, pct. w/ advanced degree: 35.0 / 11%
Serving Cherokee, Cobb, Fulton

FELLOWSHIP CHRISTIAN HIGH SCHOOL
480 W Crossville Rd, Roswell, GA 30075 (o) 770-993-1650 (f) 770-993-9262
Principal: David Kinsey E-mail: terri_boyle@fbcministries.org
Annual tuition: $7,956 - $8,352 Internet: www.fbcministries.org
Grades: 9th - 12th Enrollment: 210
Computers w/ Internet access: 8 Avg. score: ACT: 22.3 SAT: 1144
Religion/affiliation: Christian (no specific denomination)
Curriculum: College preparatory
Total teachers, pct. w/ advanced degree: 18.0 / 25%
Total 2000-2001 graduates, pct. who went on to a four-year college: 28 / 96%
Top colleges graduates go on to: Carson-Newman College (Tenn.), Georgia Southern Univ., Kennesaw State Univ. (Ga.), Samford Univ. (Ala.), Univ. of Georgia
Serving Cherokee, Cobb, Forsyth, Fulton, Gwinnett

FIRST MONTESSORI SCHOOL OF ATLANTA
5750 Long Island Dr NW, Atlanta, GA 30327 (o) 404-252-3910 (f) 404-843-9815
Principal: Vacant E-mail: jseidel@firstmontessori.org
Annual tuition: $6,690 - $11,450 Internet: www.firstmontessori.org
Grades: Pre-K - 8th Enrollment: 207
Computers w/ Internet access: 8
Religion/affiliation: None
Curriculum: Montessori
Total teachers, pct. w/ advanced degree: 12.0 / 16%
Serving Cobb, DeKalb, Fulton, Gwinnett

Ultimate Atlanta School Guide

GALLOWAY SCHOOL (THE)
215 W Wieuca Rd NW, Atlanta, GA 30342 (o) 404-252-8389 (f) 404-252-7770
Principal: Linda Martinson E-mail: info@gallowayschool.org
Annual tuition: $10,100 - $11,750 Internet: www.gallowayschool.org
Grades: Pre-K - 12th Enrollment: 738
Computers w/ Internet access: 300 Avg. score: ACT: * SAT: *
Religion/affiliation: None
Curriculum: College preparatory
Total teachers, pct. w/ advanced degree: 96.0 / 65%
Total 2000-2001 graduates, pct. who went on to a four-year college: 52 / 100%
Top colleges graduates go on to: None specified
Serving the greater metro Atlanta area

GREENFIELD HEBREW ACADEMY
5200 Northland Dr NE, Atlanta, GA 30342 (o) 404-843-9900 (f) 404-252-0934
Principal: Richard Wagner E-mail: ghalab@ghacademy.org
Annual tuition: $7,725 - $10,325 Internet: www.ghacademy.org
Grades: Pre-K - 8th Enrollment: 580
Computers w/ Internet access: 60
Religion/affiliation: Jewish
Curriculum: Pre-preparatory
Total teachers, pct. w/ advanced degree: 60.0 / 39%
Serving the greater metro Atlanta area

HEISKELL SCHOOL
3260 Northside Dr NW, Atlanta, GA 30305 (o) 404-262-2233 (f) 404-262-2575
Principal: Cyndie Heiskell E-mail: writeus@heiskell.net
Annual tuition: $2,775 - $8,790 Internet: www.heiskell.net
Grades: Pre-K - 8th Enrollment: 360
Computers w/ Internet access: *
Religion/affiliation: Christian (no specific denomination)
Curriculum: Private elementary and/or secondary
Total teachers, pct. w/ advanced degree: 25.0 / *
Serving the greater metro Atlanta area

HERITAGE PREPARATORY SCHOOL OF GEORGIA
1700 Piedmont Ave NE, Atlanta, GA 30324 (o) 404-679-9066 (f) 404-679-9068
Principal: Mitchell Ridgeway E-mail: administration@heritageprep.org
Annual tuition: $1,485 - $6,875 Internet: www.heritageprep.org
Grades: Pre-K - 5th Enrollment: 50
Computers w/ Internet access: *
Religion/affiliation: Christian (no specific denomination)
Curriculum: Private elementary and/or secondary with a special program emphasis
Total teachers, pct. w/ advanced degree: 11.0 / 45%
Serving Cobb, DeKalb, Fulton, Gwinnett

Ultimate Atlanta School Guide

HIGH MEADOWS SCHOOL
1055 Willeo Rd, Roswell, GA 30075 (o) 770-993-2940 (f) 770-993-8331
Principal: Paule Ebrahimi   E-mail: info@highmeadows.org
Annual tuition: $7,000 - $9,000   Internet: www.highmeadows.org
Grades: Pre-K - 8th   Enrollment: 370
Computers w/ Internet access: *
Religion/affiliation: Secular
Curriculum: General academic/integrated curriculum/project-based approach
Total teachers, pct. w/ advanced degree: 50.0 / 40%
Serving Cobb, Fulton, Gwinnett, Paulding

HOLCOMB BRIDGE SCHOOL
2675 Holcomb Bridge Rd, Alpharetta, GA 30022 (o) 770-998-2027 (f) No fax
Principal: Lou Vanek   E-mail: No e-mail
Annual tuition: $2,700 - $7,400   Internet: No Web site
Grades: Pre-K - 1st   Enrollment: 85
Computers w/ Internet access: *
Religion/affiliation: None
Curriculum: Early childhood program/day care center
Total teachers, pct. w/ advanced degree: 7.0 / *
Serving Cobb, DeKalb, Forsyth, Fulton, Gwinnett

HOLY INNOCENTS' EPISCOPAL SCHOOL
805 Mount Vernon Hwy NW, Atlanta, GA 30327 (o) 404-255-4026 (f) 404-303-2158
Principal: Susan Groesbeck   E-mail: andrew.payne@hies.org
Annual tuition: $6,908 - $13,219   Internet: www.hies.org
Grades: Pre-K - 12th   Enrollment: 1,300
Computers w/ Internet access: 350   Avg. score: ACT: 24   SAT: 1147
Religion/affiliation: Episcopal
Curriculum: College preparatory
Total teachers, pct. w/ advanced degree: 128.0 / 55%
Total 2000-2001 graduates, pct. who went on to a four-year college: 85 / 100%
Top colleges graduates go on to: Auburn Univ. (Ala.), Emory Univ. (Ga.), Univ. of Colorado, Univ. of Georgia, Vanderbilt Univ. (Tenn.)
Serving the greater metro Atlanta area

HOLY REDEEMER CATHOLIC SCHOOL
3380 Old Alabama Rd, Alpharetta, GA 30022 (o) 770-410-4056 (f) 770-410-1454
Principal: Mary Reiling   E-mail: No e-mail
Annual tuition: $5,100   Internet: No Web site
Grades: K - 8th   Enrollment: 519
Computers w/ Internet access: 198
Religion/affiliation: Catholic
Curriculum: Private elementary and/or secondary
Total teachers, pct. w/ advanced degree: 1.0 / 70%
Serving the greater metro Atlanta area

Ultimate Atlanta School Guide

HOWARD SCHOOL
1246 Ponce de Leon Ave NE, Atlanta, GA 30306 (o) 404-377-7436 (f) 404-377-0884
Principal: Sandra Kleinman E-mail: kerens@howardschool.org
Annual tuition: $11,000 - $15,300 Internet: www.howardschool.org
Grades: K - 12th Enrollment: 146
Computers w/ Internet access: 68 Avg. score: ACT: * SAT: *
Religion/affiliation: None
Curriculum: Private elementary and/or secondary with a special program emphasis
Total teachers, pct. w/ advanced degree: 46.0 / 55%
Total 2000-2001 graduates, pct. who went on to a four-year college: 10 / 90%
Top colleges graduates go on to: Elon Univ. (N.C.), Georgia Perimeter College, Middle Georgia College, Reinhardt College (Ga.)
Serving Cherokee, Cobb, DeKalb, Forsyth, Fulton, Gwinnett, Rockdale

HOWARD SCHOOL - NORTH CAMPUS
9415 Willeo Rd, Roswell, GA 30075 (o) 770-642-9644 (f) 770-998-1398
Principal: Virginia Carnes E-mail: virginiac@howardschool.org
Annual tuition: $11,000 - $15,300 Internet: www.howardschool.org
Grades: K - 8th Enrollment: 139
Computers w/ Internet access: 38
Religion/affiliation: None
Curriculum: Private elementary and/or secondary with a special program emphasis
Total teachers, pct. w/ advanced degree: 28.0 / 54%
Serving Cherokee, Cobb, DeKalb, Forsyth, Fulton, Gwinnett

IMHOTEP CENTER OF EDUCATION
541 Harwell Rd NW, Atlanta, GA 30318 (o) 404-696-8777 (f) 404-691-5636
Principal: Yvette Jackson E-mail: imhotep7@bellsouth.net
Annual tuition: $4,500 - $4,685 Internet: www.imhotepcenterofeducation.com
Grades: Pre-K - 8th Enrollment: 180
Computers w/ Internet access: 10
Religion/affiliation: None
Curriculum: Pre-preparatory
Total teachers, pct. w/ advanced degree: 17.0 / 11%
Serving the greater metro Atlanta area

INTERNATIONAL PREPARATORY INSTITUTE
1100 Cascade Rd SW, Atlanta, GA 30311 (o) 404-758-6691 (f) 404-758-6691
Principal: Vivien Davenport E-mail: ipi@mindspring.com
Annual tuition: $4,560 - $4,800 Internet: www.mindspring.com/~ipi/
Grades: K - 5th Enrollment: 130
Computers w/ Internet access: 12
Religion/affiliation: None
Curriculum: Private elementary
Total teachers, pct. w/ advanced degree: 12.0 / 45%
Serving Clayton, Cobb, DeKalb, Douglas, Fayette, Fulton, Henry, Newton, Paulding

Ultimate Atlanta School Guide

LOVETT SCHOOL (THE)
4075 Paces Ferry Rd NW, Atlanta, GA 30327   (o) 404-262-3032   (f) 404-261-1967
Principal: James Hendrix Jr.   E-mail: admissions@lovett.org
Annual tuition: $7,350 - $13,940   Internet: www.lovett.org
Grades: Pre-K - 12th   Enrollment: 1,512
Computers w/ Internet access: 450   Avg. score: ACT: *   SAT: 1225
Religion/affiliation: Judeo-Christian
Curriculum: Private elementary and/or secondary
Total teachers, pct. w/ advanced degree: 156.0 / 62%
Total 2000-2001 graduates, pct. who went on to a four-year college: 144 / 100%
Top colleges graduates go on to: Boston Univ. (Mass.), Southern Methodist Univ. (Texas), Univ. of Colorado, Univ. of Georgia, Univ. of Mississippi
Serving Cherokee, Clayton, Cobb, DeKalb, Douglas, Forsyth, Fulton, Gwinnett, Hall

MILL SPRINGS ACADEMY
13660 New Providence Rd, Alpharetta, GA 30004   (o) 770-360-1336   (f) 770-360-1341
Principal: Robert Moore   E-mail: rmoore@millsprings.org
Annual tuition: $15,450   Internet: www.millsprings.org
Grades: 1st - 12th   Enrollment: 240
Computers w/ Internet access: 280   Avg. score: ACT: 18   SAT: 1050
Religion/affiliation: None
Curriculum: College preparatory
Total teachers, pct. w/ advanced degree: 49.0 / 40%
Total 2000-2001 graduates, pct. who went on to a four-year college: 7 / 50%
Top colleges graduates go on to: LaGrange College (Ga.), Loyola Univ. (La.), Reinhardt College (Ga.), Southern Polytechnic State Univ. (Ga.), Valdosta State Univ. (Ga.)
Serving the greater metro Atlanta area

MT. PISGAH CHRISTIAN SCHOOL
9820 Nesbit Ferry Rd, Alpharetta, GA 30022   (o) 678-475-4989   (f) 678-336-3349
Principal: Chris Alexander   E-mail: calexander@mtpisgahschool.org
Annual tuition: $6,733 - $9,256   Internet: www.mtpisgahschool.org
Grades: Pre-K - 12th   Enrollment: 837
Computers w/ Internet access: 78   Avg. score: ACT: *   SAT: *
Religion/affiliation: Methodist
Curriculum: Private elementary and/or secondary
Total teachers, pct. w/ advanced degree: 42.0 / 34%
Serving Cherokee, Cobb, DeKalb, Forsyth, Fulton, Gwinnett, Hall

Ultimate Atlanta School Guide

MT. VERNON PRESBYTERIAN SCHOOL
471 Mount Vernon Hwy NE, Atlanta, GA 30328   (o) 404-252-3448   (f) 404-252-6777

Principal:	Jeff Jackson	E-mail:	j_jackson@mvpschool.com
Annual tuition:	$4,900 - $9,300	Internet:	www.mvpschool.com
Grades:	Pre-K - 8th	Enrollment:	650

Computers w/ Internet access: 40
Religion/affiliation: Christian (no specific denomination)
Curriculum: Private elementary and/or secondary
Total teachers, pct. w/ advanced degree: 87.0 / 42%
Serving Ccbb, DeKalb, Fulton, Gwinnett

PACE ACADEMY
966 W Paces Ferry Rd NW, Atlanta, GA 30327   (o) 404-262-1345   (f) 404-240-9124

Principal:	Michael Murphy	E-mail:	mmurphy@paceacademy.org
Annual tuit on:	$10,400 - $14,220	Internet:	www.paceacademy.org
Grades:	K - 12th	Enrollment:	824
Computers w/ Internet access:	350	Avg. score:	ACT: * SAT: 1296

Religion/affiliation: None
Curriculum: Private elementary and/or secondary
Total teachers, pct. w/ advanced degree: 90.0 / 69%
Total 2000-2001 graduates, pct. who went on to a four-year college: 83 / 100%
Top colleges graduates go on to: Denison Univ. (Ohio), Emory Univ. (Ga.), Univ. of Colorado, Univ. of Georgia, Wake Forest Univ. (N.C.)
Serving Clayton, Cobb, DeKalb, Douglas, Fayette, Fulton, Gwinnett

PATHWAY CHRISTIAN SCHOOL
1706 Washington Ave, Atlanta, GA 30344   (o) 404-763-3216   (f) 404-478-0444

Principal:	Barbara Miller	E-mail:	bmiller@pathwayc.org
Annual tuition:	$3,800	Internet:	www.pathwayc.org
Grades:	1st - 8th	Enrollment:	148

Computers w/ Internet access: 20
Religion/affiliation: Christian (no specific denomination)
Curriculum: Private elementary and/or secondary
Total teachers, pct. w/ advanced degree: 13.5 / 40%
Serving the greater metro Atlanta area

PERIMETER CHRISTIAN SCHOOL
9500 Medlock Bridge Rd, Duluth, GA 30097   (o) 678-405-2300   (f) 770-582-6685

Principal:	Robert Scott	E-mail:	klemon@perimeter.org
Annual tuition:	$3,252 - $4,440	Internet:	www.perimeter.org/school/
Grades:	1st - 8th	Enrollment:	480

Computers w/ Internet access: 16
Religion/affiliation: Presbyterian
Curriculum: Private elementary and/or secondary
Total teachers, pct. w/ advanced degree: 41.0 / 25%
Serving DeKalb, Forsyth, Fulton, Gwinnett

PORTER SCHOOL, INC.
200 Cox Rd, Roswell, GA 30075 (o) 770-509-1292 (f) 770-509-1292
Principal:	Claudia Porter	E-mail:	porterschool@yahoo.com
Annual tuition:	$11,500	Internet:	www.porterschool.com
Grades:	1st - 5th	Enrollment:	40

Computers w/ Internet access: 6
Religion/affiliation: None
Curriculum: Private elementary and/or secondary with a special program emphasis
Total teachers, pct. w/ advanced degree: 6.0 / 60%
Serving Cobb, DeKalb, Forsyth, Fulton, Gwinnett

RENAISSANCE MONTESSORI
2407 Cascade Rd SW, Atlanta, GA 30311 (o) 404-755-1915 (f) 404-755-1915
Principal:	Rita Merk	E-mail:	rita.merk@rmontessori.com
Annual tuition:	$3,320 - $4,620	Internet:	www.rmontessori.com
Grades:	Ages 2 1/2 - 12 yrs	Enrollment:	97

Computers w/ Internet access: 3
Religion/affiliation: None
Curriculum: Montessori
Total teachers, pct. w/ advanced degree: 7.0 / 20%
Serving Clayton, Douglas, Fayette, Fulton

SCHENCK SCHOOL (THE)
282 Mount Paran Rd NW, Atlanta, GA 30327 (o) 404-252-2591 (f) 404-252-7615
Principal:	Gena Calloway	E-mail:	office@schenck.org
Annual tuition:	$14,900 - $15,900	Internet:	www.schenck.org
Grades:	1st - 8th	Enrollment:	150

Computers w/ Internet access: 42
Religion/affiliation: None
Curriculum: Special education for dyslexic students
Total teachers, pct. w/ advanced degree: 34.0 / 58%
Serving the greater metro Atlanta area

SOPHIA ACADEMY
1199 Bellaire Dr NE, Atlanta, GA 30319 (o) 404-303-8722 (f) 404-303-8722
Principal:	Charlotte Hart	E-mail:	No e-mail
Annual tuition:	$10,500	Internet:	No Web site
Grades:	1st - 8th	Enrollment:	50

Computers w/ Internet access: 8
Religion/affiliation: Christian (no specific denomination)
Curriculum: Special education, learning disabilities
Total teachers, pct. w/ advanced degree: 7.5 / 75%
Serving Cobb, DeKalb, Fulton, Gwinnett

Ultimate Atlanta School Guide

SPELMAN COLLEGE CHILD DEVELOPMENT CENTER
350 Spelman Ln SW, Atlanta, GA 30314 (o) 404-223-1495 (f) 404-215-2776
Principal: Gracie Hutcherson E-mail: No e-mail
Annual tuition: $4,550 Internet: www.spelman.edu/mwec/
Grades: Pre-Kindergarten Enrollment: 56
Computers w/ Internet access: 8
Religion/affiliation: Christian (no specific denomination)
Curriculum: Early childhood program/day care center
Total teachers, pct. w/ advanced degree: 6.0 / 100%
Serving Clayton, Coweta, DeKalb, Fulton

ST. FRANCIS DAY SCHOOL - HIGH SCHOOL
13440 Cogburn Rd, Alpharetta, GA 30004 (o) 678-339-9989 (f) 678-339-0473
Principal: Drew Buccellato E-mail: No e-mail
Annual tuition: $12,900 Internet: www.stfranschool.com
Grades: 9th - 12th Enrollment: 300
Computers w/ Internet access: 70 Avg. score: ACT: * SAT: 1050
Religion/affiliation: None
Curriculum: College preparatory, learning disabilities
Total teachers, pct. w/ advanced degree: 60.0 / 65%
Total 2000-2001 graduates, pct. who went on to a four-year college: 70 / 95%
Top colleges graduates go on to: Auburn Univ. (Ala.), Clemson Univ. (S.C.), Elon Univ. (N.C.), Univ. of Alabama, Univ. of Tennessee
Serving Cherokee, Cobb, DeKalb, Forsyth, Fulton, Gwinnett

ST. FRANCIS DAY SCHOOL - LOWER SCHOOL
9375 Willeo Rd, Roswell, GA 30075 (o) 770-641-8257 (f) 770-641-0283
Principal: Drew Buccellato E-mail: No e-mail
Annual tuition: $12,300 Internet: www.stfranschool.com
Grades: K - 8th Enrollment: 600
Computers w/ Internet access: 50
Religion/affiliation: None
Curriculum: College preparatory, learning disabilities
Total teachers, pct. w/ advanced degree: 75.0 / 60%
Serving Cherokee, Cobb, DeKalb, Forsyth, Fulton, Gwinnett

ST. JOHN THE EVANGELIST CATHOLIC SCHOOL
240 Arnold St, Atlanta, GA 30354 (o) 404-767-4312 (f) 404-767-0359
Principal: Karen Vogtner E-mail: No e-mail
Annual tuition: $3,685 - $4,110 Internet: www.sjecs.org
Grades: Pre-K - 8th Enrollment: 258
Computers w/ Internet access: 75
Religion/affiliation: Roman Catholic
Curriculum: Private elementary and/or secondary
Total teachers, pct. w/ advanced degree: 19.0 / 90%
Serving Clayton, Fayette, Fulton, Henry

Ultimate Atlanta School Guide

TRINITY SCHOOL
4301 Northside Dr NW, Atlanta, GA 30327   (o) 404-231-8100   (f) 404-231-8111
Principal: Stephen Kennedy   E-mail: info@trinityatl.org
Annual tuition: $5,450 - $11,750   Internet: www.trinityatl.org
Grades: Pre-K - 6th   Enrollment: 477
Computers w/ Internet access: *
Religion/affiliation: None
Curriculum: Private elementary and/or secondary
Total teachers, pct. w/ advanced degree: 49.0 / 25%
Serving the greater metro Atlanta area

WESTMINSTER SCHOOL (THE)
1424 W Paces Ferry Rd NW, Atlanta, GA 30327   (o) 404-355-8673   (f) 404-355-6606
Principal: William Clarkson IV   E-mail: mainoffice@westminster.net
Annual tuition: $11,775 - $13,852   Internet: www.westminster.net
Grades: Pre-1st - 12th   Enrollment: 1,739
Computers w/ Internet access: 850   Avg. score: ACT: * SAT: 1358
Religion/affiliation: Christian (no specific denomination)
Curriculum: College preparatory
Total teachers, pct. w/ advanced degree: 222.0 / 70%
Total 2000-2001 graduates, pct. who went on to a four-year college: 192 / 100%
Top colleges graduates go on to: Duke Univ. (N.C.), Univ. of Georgia, Univ. of Virginia, Vanderbilt Univ. (Tenn.), Washington and Lee Univ. (Va.)
Serving the greater metro Atlanta area

WOODWARD ACADEMY
1662 Rugby Ave, College Park, GA 30337   (o) 404-765-4000   (f) 404-765-8259
Principal: David McCollum   E-mail: admissions@woodward.edu
Annual tuition: $9,000 - $13,300   Internet: www.woodward.edu
Grades: K - 12th   Enrollment: 2,850
Computers w/ Internet access: 300   Avg. score: ACT: * SAT: 1200
Religion/affiliation: None
Curriculum: College preparatory
Total teachers, pct. w/ advanced degree: 302.0 / 60%
Total 2000-2001 graduates, pct. who went on to a four-year college: 238 / 100%
Top colleges graduates go on to: Boston Univ. (Mass.), Furman Univ. (S.C.), Georgia Institute of Technology, Univ. of Georgia, Univ. of Michigan
Serving the greater metro Atlanta area

Ultimate Atlanta School Guide

WOODWARD ACADEMY - NORTH CAMPUS
6565 Boles Rd, Duluth, GA 30097 (o) 404-765-4490 (f) 404-765-4499
Principal: W. Lee Vincent E-mail: admissions@woodward.edu
Annual tuition: $7,350 - $12,000 Internet: www.woodward.edu
Grades: Pre-K - 6th Enrollment: 408
Computers w/ Internet access: 115
Religion/affiliation: None
Curriculum: College preparatory
Total teachers, pct. w/ advanced degree: 63.0 / 41%
Serving the greater metro Atlanta area

Gwinnett County Private Schools

CRÈME DE LA CRÈME - NORCROSS
4785 Peachtree Corners Cir, Norcross, GA 30092 (o) 770-409-0000 (f) 770-416-8665
Principal: Elisa Ezor E-mail: eezor@cremechildcare.com
Annual tuition: $4,770 - $7,965 Internet: www.cremechildcare.com
Grades: Kindergarten Enrollment: 33
Computers w/ Internet access: 3
Religion/affiliation: None
Curriculum: Early childhood program/day care center
Total teachers, pct. w/ advanced degree: 2.0 / 50%
Serving Gwinnett

DULUTH JUNIOR ACADEMY
2959 Duluth Highway 120, Duluth, GA 30096 (o) 770-497-8607 (f) 770-476-2133
Principal: Sharon Garner E-mail: sgarner@gccsda.com
Annual tuition: $3,650 Internet: www.duluthsda.org
Grades: K - 8th Enrollment: 115
Computers w/ Internet access: *
Religion/affiliation: Seventh-day Adventist
Curriculum: Private elementary and/or secondary
Total teachers, pct. w/ advanced degree: 7.0 / 28%
Serving the greater metro Atlanta area

GREATER ATLANTA CHRISTIAN SCHOOL

1575 Indian Trail Lilburn Rd, Norcross, GA 30093 (o) 770-243-2000 (f) 770-243-2259
Principal: David Fincher   E-mail: dfincher@gacs.pvt.k12.ga.us
Annual tuition: $7,545 - $8,900   Internet: www.greateratlantachristian.org
Grades: Pre-K - 12th   Enrollment: 1,615
Computers w/ Internet access: 450   Avg. score: ACT: * SAT: 1151
Religion/affiliation: Church of Christ
Curriculum: College preparatory
Total teachers, pct. w/ advanced degree: 129.0 / 60%
Total 2000-2001 graduates, pct. who went on to a four-year college: 146 / 100%
Top colleges graduates go on to: Auburn Univ. (Ala.), David Lipscomb Univ. (Tenn.), Georgia Institute of Technology, Samford Univ. (Ala.), Univ. of Georgia
Serving the greater metro Atlanta area

HARBOUR OAKS MONTESSORI SCHOOL

1741 Athens Hwy, Grayson, GA 30017 (o) 770-979-8900 (f) 770-979-8900
Principal: Anna Robichaux   E-mail: harbouroak@aol.com
Annual tuition: $4,250 - $6,000   Internet: No Web site
Grades: Pre-K - 4th   Enrollment: 150
Computers w/ Internet access: 5
Religion/affiliation: None
Curriculum: Montessori
Total teachers, pct. w/ advanced degree: 10.0 / 20%
Serving DeKalb, Gwinnett, Walton

JESUS-N-ME CHRISTIAN ACADEMY

2740 Five Forks Trickum Rd, Lawrenceville, GA 30044 (o) 770-979-3850 (f) 770-979-3851
Principal: Styleen Green   E-mail: jesus-n-me@mindspring.com
Annual tuition: $3,200 - $3,500   Internet: No Web site
Grades: K - 8th   Enrollment: 48
Computers w/ Internet access: 6
Religion/affiliation: Christian (no specific denomination)
Curriculum: Abeka
Total teachers, pct. w/ advanced degree: 5.0 / 100%
Serving the greater metro Atlanta area

KILLIAN HILL CHRISTIAN SCHOOL
151 Arcado Rd SW, Lilburn, GA 30047 (o) 770-921-3224 (f) 770-921-9395
Principal: Paul Williams E-mail: pwilliam@khcs.org
Annual tuition: $4,300 - $5,000 Internet: www.khcs.org
Grades: Pre-K - 12th Enrollment: 525
Computers w/ Internet access: 60 Avg. score: ACT: * SAT: 1126
Religion/affiliation: Baptist
Curriculum: College preparatory
Total teachers, pct. w/ advanced degree: 32.0 / 50%
Total 2000-2001 graduates, pct. who went on to a four-year college: 24 / 97%
Top colleges graduates go on to: Bob Jones Univ. (S.C.), Cedarville Univ. (Ohio), Georgia Southern Univ., North Georgia College
Serving Gwinnett

LANDMARK CHRISTIAN SCHOOL OF PEACHTREE CORNERS
3737 Holcomb Bridge Rd, Norcross, GA 30092 (o) 770-449-3493 (f) No fax
Principal Cindy Nesbit Kalfahs E-mail: No e-mail
Annual tuition: $3,200 - $4,000 Internet: No Web site
Grades: Kindergarten - 5th Enrollment: 60
Computers w/ Internet access: *
Religion/affiliation: Christian (no specific denomination)
Curriculum: Private elementary and/or secondary
Total teachers, pct. w/ advanced degree: 7.0 / 50%
Serving DeKalb, Fulton, Gwinnett

OAK MEADOW MONTESSORI SCHOOL
2145 Collins Hill Rd, Lawrenceville, GA 30043 (o) 770-963-8303 (f) 770-963-8422
Principal: Jody Sills E-mail: omms@charter.net
Annual tuition: $5,130 - $5,365 Internet: www.oakmeadowmontessori.com
Grades: K - 5th Enrollment: 52
Computers w/ Internet access: 6
Religion/affiliation: None
Curriculum: Montessori
Total teachers, pct. w/ advanced degree: 8.0 / *
Serving Barrow, Forsyth, Gwinnett, Hall

Ultimate Atlanta School Guide

OLD SUWANEE CHRISTIAN SCHOOL

4118 Old Suwanee Rd, Buford, GA 30518   (o) 770-945-5451   (f) No fax

Principal:	Tim Campbell	E-mail:	oldsuwanee@juno.com
Annual tuition:	$1,920 - $2,589	Internet:	www.oldsuwaneebaptist.org
Grades:	K - 12th	Enrollment:	230
Computers w/ Internet access:	15	Avg. score:	ACT: * SAT: 1000

Religion/affiliation: Baptist
Curriculum: Private elementary and/or secondary
Total teachers, pct. w/ advanced degree: 16.0 / 25%
Total 2000-2001 graduates, pct. who went on to a four-year college: 11 / 90%
Top colleges graduates go on to: Gainesville College (Ga.), Pensacola Christian College (Fla.), Shorter College (Ga.), Tabernacle Baptist Bible College (S.C.)
Serving Barrow, Forsyth, Gwinnett, Hall, Jackson

PROVIDENCE CHRISTIAN ACADEMY

4575 Lawrenceville Hwy NW, Lilburn, GA 30047   (o) 770-279-7200   (f) 770-279-7269

Principal:	James Vaught Jr.	E-mail:	pcastars@providencechristianacademy.org
Annual tuition:	$5,400 - $8,520	Internet:	www.providencechristian.net
Grades:	K - 12th	Enrollment:	916
Computers w/ Internet access:	210	Avg. score:	ACT: 23.5 SAT: 1103

Religion/affiliation: Christian (no specific denomination)
Curriculum: Private elementary and/or secondary
Total teachers, pct. w/ advanced degree: 84.5 / 32%
Total 2000-2001 graduates, pct. who went on to a four-year college: 71 / 93%
Top colleges graduates go on to: Auburn Univ. (Ala.), Georgia Institute of Technology, Georgia State Univ., Samford Univ. (Ala.), Univ. of Georgia
Serving Barrow, DeKalb, Forsyth, Fulton, Gwinnett, Hall

REDEEMER CHRISTIAN ACADEMY

641 Eva Kennedy Rd, Suwanee, GA 30024   (o) 770-271-7721   (f) 770-241-4552

Principal:	Sharon Bryant	E-mail:	redeemerchristian@msn.com
Annual tuition:	$4,200 - $5,500	Internet:	www.redeemerchristian.org
Grades:	Pre-K - 10th	Enrollment:	65
Computers w/ Internet access:	*		

Religion/affiliation: Christian (no specific denomination)
Curriculum: Private elementary and/or secondary with a special program emphasis
Total teachers, pct. w/ advanced degree: 10.0 / 50%
Serving Forsyth, Fulton, Gwinnett

Ultimate Atlanta School Guide

ST. JOHN NEUMANN CATHOLIC SCHOOL
791 Tom Smith Rd SW, Lilburn, GA 30047   (o) 770-381-0557   (f) 770-381-0276
- Principal: James Anderson
- E-mail: No e-mail
- Annual tuition: $4,150 - $7,350
- Internet: www.sjnrcs.org
- Grades: K - 8th
- Enrollment: 545
- Computers w/ Internet access: 69
- Religion/affiliation: Roman Catholic
- Curriculum: Private elementary and/or secondary
- Total teachers, pct. w/ advanced degree: 31.0 / 33%
- Serving DeKalb, Gwinnett, Rockdale, Walton

SUGAR HILL CHRISTIAN ACADEMY
4600 Nelson Brogdon Blvd, Buford, GA 30518   (o) 770-945-2845   (f) 770-945-7799
- Principal: Beth Compton
- E-mail: academy@sugarhillumc.org
- Annual tuition: $3,715
- Internet: www.myschoolonline.com/ga/shca/
- Grades: K - 3rd
- Enrollment: 90
- Computers w/ Internet access: 1
- Religion/affiliation: Methodist
- Curriculum: Private elementary and/or secondary
- Total teachers, pct. w/ advanced degree: 6.0 / 25%
- Serving Forsyth, Gwinnett, Hall

WESLEYAN SCHOOL
5405 Spalding Dr, Norcross, GA 30092   (o) 770-448-7640   (f) 770-448-3699
- Principal: Zach Young
- E-mail: zyoung@wesleyanschool.org
- Annual tuition: $9,860 - $12,280
- Internet: www.wesleyanschool.org
- Grades: K - 12th
- Enrollment: 1,040
- Computers w/ Internet access: 350
- Avg. score: ACT: *   SAT: 1166
- Religion/affiliation: Independent Christian
- Curriculum: College preparatory
- Total teachers, pct. w/ advanced degree: 118.0 / 41%
- Total 2000-2001 graduates, pct. who went on to a four-year college: 80 / 100%
- Top colleges graduates go on to: Florida State Univ., Georgia Institute of Technology, Presbyterian College (S.C.), Univ. of Georgia, Vanderbilt Univ. (Tenn.)
- Serving the greater metro Atlanta area

Ultimate Atlanta School Guide

Hall County Private Schools

BRENAU ACADEMY
1 Centennial Cir, Gainesville, GA 30501 (o) 770-534-6140 (f) 770-534-6298
- Principal: Frank Booth
- E-mail: enroll@lib.brenau.edu
- Annual tuition: $18,730
- Internet: www.brenauacademy.org
- Grades: 9th - 12th
- Enrollment: 80
- Computers w/ Internet access: *
- Avg. score: ACT: * SAT: *
- Religion/affiliation: Christian (no specific denomination)
- Curriculum: College preparatory, all girls boarding school
- Total teachers, pct. w/ advanced degree: 10.0 / 80%
- Total 2000-2001 graduates, pct. who went on to a four-year college: 20 / 100%
- Top colleges graduates go on to: College of Charleston (S.C.), Georgia Institute of Technology, Purdue Univ. (Ind.), Univ. of the South (Tenn.), Univ. of Wisconsin
- Serving the greater metro Atlanta area

JUBILEE CHRISTIAN ACADEMY
1221 Harmony Hall St, Gainesville, GA 30501 (o) 770-531-7576 (f) 770-534-8370
- Principal: Randall Roys
- E-mail: jubileeca@mindspring.com
- Annual tuition: $2,400 - $2,750
- Internet: No Web site
- Grades: K - 12th
- Enrollment: 56
- Computers w/ Internet access: 2
- Avg. score: ACT: * SAT: 950
- Religion/affiliation: Baptist
- Curriculum: Private elementary and/or secondary
- Total teachers, pct. w/ advanced degree: 5.5 / *
- Total 2000-2001 graduates, pct. who went on to a four-year college: 4 / 0%
- Top colleges graduates go on to: Crown College (Tenn.), Gainesville College (Ga.)
- Serving Banks, Forsyth, Habersham, Hall, Jackson, Lumpkin, White

LAKEVIEW ACADEMY
796 Lakeview Dr, Gainesville, GA 30501 (o) 770-532-4383 (f) 770-536-6142
- Principal: H. Ferrell Singleton
- E-mail: admissions@lakeview academy.com
- Annual tuition: $5,805 - $10,988
- Internet: www.lakeviewacademy.com
- Grades: Pre-K - 12th
- Enrollment: 551
- Computers w/ Internet access: 200
- Avg. score: ACT: 27 SAT: 1293
- Religion/affiliation: Non-sectarian
- Curriculum: College preparatory
- Total teachers, pct. w/ advanced degree: 72.0 / 52%
- Total 2000-2001 graduates, pct. who went on to a four-year college: 19 / 100%
- Top colleges graduates go on to: Davidson College (N.C.), Emory Univ. (Ga.), Georgia Institute of Technology, North Georgia College, Univ. of Georgia
- Serving Dawson, Forsyth, Fulton, Gwinnett, Habersham, Hall, Lumpkin, White

Ultimate Atlanta School Guide

RIVERSIDE MILITARY ACADEMY
2001 Riverside Dr, Gainesville, GA 30501 (o) 770-532-6251 (f) 678-291-3364
Principal: Michael Hughes E-mail: admissions@cadet.com
Annual tuition: $21,300 - $25,300 Internet: www.cadet.com
Grades: 7th - 12th Enrollment: 477
Computers w/ Internet access: 75 Avg. score: ACT: 23 SAT: 1068
Religion/affiliation: None
Curriculum: Private elementary and/or secondary
Total teachers, pct. w/ advanced degree: 65.0 / 75%
Total 2000-2001 graduates, pct. who went on to a four-year college: 70 / 100%
Top colleges graduates go on to: Auburn Univ. (Ala.), Emory Univ. (Ga.), Florida State Univ., United States Military Academy (N.Y.), Univ. of Georgia
Serving the greater metro Atlanta area

WESTMINSTER CHRISTIAN SCHOOL
1397 Thompson Bridge Rd, Gainesville, GA 30501 (o) 770-534-1081 (f) 770-534-1025
Principal: Samuel Smith E-mail: wcs1397@bellsouth.net
Annual tuition: $3,037 - $4,463 Internet: www.gainesvillewcs.org
Grades: Pre-K - 9th Enrollment: 304
Computers w/ Internet access: 24
Religion/affiliation: Presbyterian
Curriculum: Private elementary and/or secondary
Total teachers, pct. w/ advanced degree: 22.0 / 35%
Serving Dawson, Gwinnett, Habersham, Hall, Lumpkin, White

Henry County Private Schools

BIBLE BAPTIST CHRISTIAN SCHOOL
2780 Mount Carmel Rd, Hampton, GA 30228 (o) 770-946-4700 (f) 770-946-4715
Principal: Timothy Lee E-mail: info@biblebaptistministries.com
Annual tuition: $2,930 - $3,140 Internet: www.biblebaptistministries.com
Grades: K - 12th Enrollment: 263
Computers w/ Internet access: 50 Avg. score: ACT: * SAT: 922
Religion/affiliation: Baptist
Curriculum: College preparatory
Total teachers, pct. w/ advanced degree: 26.0 / 22%
Total 2000-2001 graduates, pct. who went on to a four-year college: 19 / 90%
Top colleges graduates go on to: Bob Jones Univ. (S.C.), Bob Jones Univ. (S.C.), Gordon College (Ga.), Northland College (Wisc.), Pensacola Christian College (Fla.)
Serving the greater metro Atlanta area

Ultimate Atlanta School Guide

EAGLES LANDING CHRISTIAN ACADEMY

2400 Ga. Highway 42 N, McDonough, GA 30253 (o) 770-957-2927 (f) 770-957-2290
Principal: Marshall Chambers   E-mail: chambers@eagleslanding.org
Annual tuition: $3,971 - $5,170   Internet: www.elcaonline.org
Grades: Pre-K - 12th   Enrollment: 1,050
Computers w/ Internet access: 75   Avg. score: ACT: 24 SAT: 1047
Religion/affiliation: Baptist
Curriculum: Private elementary and/or secondary
Total teachers, pct. w/ advanced degree: 65.0 / 25%
Total 2000-2001 graduates, pct. who went on to a four-year college: 30 / 98%
Top colleges graduates go on to: Georgia College & State Univ., Georgia Southern Univ., Gordon College (Ga.), Mercer Univ. (Ga.), Univ. of Georgia
Serving Butts, Clayton, DeKalb, Henry, Newton, Rockdale, Spalding

Lumpkin County Private Schools

BAY CREEK CHRISTIAN ACADEMY

385 Lumpkin County Pkwy Ste F, Dahlonega, GA 30533 (o) 706-864-0502 (f) No fax
Principal: Ann Chadwick   E-mail: No e-mail
Annual tuition: $3,000 - $3,500   Internet: No Web site
Grades: 1st - 12th   Enrollment: 4
Computers w/ Internet access: 4   Avg. score: ACT: * SAT: *
Religion/affiliation: Christian (no specific denomination)
Curriculum: Private elementary and/or secondary with a special program emphasis
Total teachers, pct. w/ advanced degree: 2.0 / 100%
Total 2000-2001 graduates, pct. who went on to a four-year college: 1 / 0%
Top colleges graduates go on to: None specified
Serving Forsyth, Hall, Lumpkin

Newton County Private Schools

TABERNACLE CHRISTIAN SCHOOL

10119 Access Rd, Covington, GA 30014 (o) 770-786-7920 (f) 770-786-7981
Principal: R. Hudson Moody   E-mail: btstudentministries@yahoo.com
Annual tuition: $2,200 - $2,400   Internet: No Web site
Grades: Pre-K - 12th   Enrollment: 125
Computers w/ Internet access: 9   Avg. score: ACT: * SAT: 1220
Religion/affiliation: Baptist
Curriculum: Private elementary and/or secondary
Total teachers, pct. w/ advanced degree: 12.0 / 17%
Total 2000-2001 graduates, pct. who went on to a four-year college: 2 / 100%
Top colleges graduates go on to: Temple Univ. (Penn.), Univ. of Tennessee
Serving the greater metro Atlanta area

Rockdale County Private Schools

PHILADELPHIA CHRISTIAN SCHOOL
2360 Old Covington Hwy SW, Conyers, GA 30012 (o) 770-483-7789 (f) 770-483-4391
Principal: R. Keith Scott   E-mail: pcsatl@bellsouth.net
Annual tuition: $3,000   Internet: www.pbcchurch.org
Grades: Pre-K - 12th   Enrollment: 355
Computers w/ Internet access: *   Avg. score: ACT: * SAT: 1000
Religion/affiliation: Baptist
Curriculum: College preparatory
Total teachers, pct. w/ advanced degree: 23.0 / 21%
Total 2000-2001 graduates, pct. who went on to a four-year college: 19 / 95%
Top colleges graduates go on to: Berry College (Ga.), Bob Jones Univ. (S.C.), Mercer Univ. (Ga.)
Serving DeKalb, Newton, Rockdale, Walton

SPRINGS ACADEMY
1240 Ga. Highway 138 SE, Conyers, GA 30013 (o) 770-483-4139 (f) 770-483-8606
Principal: Scott Frerking   E-mail: springsacademy@aol.com
Annual tuition: $4,000   Internet: No Web site
Grades: 7th - 12th   Enrollment: 31
Computers w/ Internet access: 6   Avg. score: ACT: * SAT: 1080
Religion/affiliation: Christian (no specific denomination)
Curriculum: Private elementary and/or secondary
Total teachers, pct. w/ advanced degree: 6.0 / 33%
Serving DeKalb, Gwinnett, Newton, Rockdale

VICTORY CHRISTIAN SCHOOL
1151 Flat Shoals Rd SE, Conyers, GA 30013 (o) 770-929-3758 (f) 770-929-8848
Principal: Deshuan Mills   E-mail: vcs@victorychristianschool.com
Annual tuition: $2,750 - $3,135   Internet: www.victorychristianschool.com
Grades: Pre-K - 12th   Enrollment: 400
Computers w/ Internet access: 12   Avg. score: ACT: * SAT: 1100
Religion/affiliation: Christian (no specific denomination)
Curriculum: Private elementary and/or secondary
Total teachers, pct. w/ advanced degree: 29.0 / *
Total 2000-2001 graduates, pct. who went on to a four-year college: 11 / 80%
Top colleges graduates go on to: Georgia Institute of Technology, Georgia Perimeter College, Georgia State Univ., Mercer Univ. (Ga.), Middle Georgia College
Serving DeKalb, Gwinnett, Henry, Newton, Rockdale

WOODLEE'S CHRISTIAN ADADEMY

2125 Old Salem Rd SE, Conyers, GA 30013 (o) 770-483-1448 (f) 770-760-8057
Principal: Terri Knight E-mail: woodlee1@bellsouth.com
Annual tuition: $2,500 Internet: No Web site
Grades: K - 7th Enrollment: 108
Computers w/ Internet access: * Avg. score: ACT: * SAT: *
Religion/affiliation: Christian (no specific denomination)
Curriculum: Private elementary and/or secondary
Total teachers, pct. w/ advanced degree: 9.0 / *
Serving Butts, DeKalb, Henry, Madison, Newton, Rockdale

Walton County Private Schools

LOGANVILLE CHRISTIAN ACADEMY

680 Tom Brewer Rd, Loganville, GA 30052 (o) 770-554-9888 (f) 770-554-9881
Principal: Christy Monda E-mail: christymonda@yahoo.com
Annual tuition: $3,200 - $4,950 Internet: www.loganvillechristianacademy.com
Grades: Pre-K - 10th Enrollment: 250
Computers w/ Internet access: 16
Religion/affiliation: Christian (no specific denomination)
Curriculum: Private elementary and/or secondary
Total teachers, pct. w/ advanced degree: 22.0 / 70%
Serving the greater metro Atlanta area

Metro Atlanta Private Schools

Alfred and Adele Davis Academy (The) (Atlanta)	544
All Star Kids Academy (Decatur)	527
Alpharetta International Academy (Alpharetta)	544
Alpharetta Methodist Christian Academy (Alpharetta)	544
Arbor Montessori School (Decatur)	527
Atlanta Country Day School (Alpharetta)	543
Atlanta Girls' School (Atlanta)	545
Atlanta New Century School (Atlanta)	545
Atlanta School, Inc. (The) (Atlanta)	545
Atlanta Speech School (Atlanta)	545
Atlanta Youth Academy (Atlanta)	546
Bay Creek Christian Academy (Dahlonega)	566
Becker Adventist School (Decatur)	528
Bedford School and Squirrel Hollow Camp (The) (Fairburn)	546
Believers Bible Christian Academy (Atlanta)	546
Ben Franklin Academy (Atlanta)	528
Bible Baptist Christian School (Hampton)	565
Blessed Trinity Catholic High School (Roswell)	546
Brandon Hall School (Atlanta)	547
Brenau Academy (Gainesville)	564
Brimarsh Academy (Roswell)	547
Cambridge Academy (Decatur)	528
Carman Adventist School (Marietta)	519
Carolyn Barron Montessori (Newnan)	526
Cathedral Academy (Decatur)	529
Cherokee Christian School (Woodstock)	517

The Ultimate Atlanta School Guide

Metro Atlanta Private Schools

Children's School (The) (Atlanta) 547

Christ Lutheran School (East Point) 547

Christ the King Elementary School (Atlanta) 548

Cobb County Christian School (Marietta) 519

Colonial Hills Christian School (Lithia Springs) 539

Community Christian Academy (Morrow) 517

Cottage School (The) (Roswell) 548

Covenant Christian Academy (Cumming) 543

Covenant Christian Ministries Academy (Marietta) 519

Creative Beginnings Academy (Decatur) 529

Crème de la Crème - Alpharetta (Alpharetta) 548

Crème de la Crème - Atlanta (Atlanta) 548

Crème de la Crème - Marietta (Marietta) 519

Crème de la Crème - Norcross (Norcross) 559

Crème de la Crème - Roswell (Alpharetta) 549

Crestwood Christian Academy (Tyrone) 541

Cross and Crown Day School (Atlanta) 529

Crossroads Christian Academy (Canton) 517

Cumberland Christian Academy (Austell) 520

Dar Un-Noor School (Atlanta) 549

Decatur First Methodist Weekday Children's Ministries (Decatur) 529

Decatur Montessori (Decatur) 530

Decatur Presbyterian Children's Community School (Decatur) 530

Discovery Academy (Lithonia) 530

Dominion Christian High School (Marietta) 520

Donnellan School (The) (Atlanta) 549

Metro Atlanta Private Schools

Douglasville Seventh-day Adventist School (Douglasville) 539

Duluth Junior Academy (Duluth) 559

Eagles Landing Christian Academy (McDonough) 566

Eastside Christian School (Marietta) 520

Eaton Academy (Roswell) 549

Epstein School (The), Solomon Schechter School of Atlanta (Atlanta) 550

Evangel Temple Christian Academy (Morrow) 518

Faith Lutheran School (Marietta) 521

Fayette Christian School (Fayetteville) 541

Fayette Montessori School (Fayetteville) 541

Fellowship Christian Academy (Roswell) 550

Fellowship Christian High School (Roswell) 550

First Baptist Christian School (Kennesaw) 521

First Montessori School of Atlanta (Atlanta) 550

First Steps Christian Academy (Atlanta) 530

Forrest Hills Christian (Stone Mountain) 531

Friends School of Atlanta (Decatur) 531

Galloway School (The) (Atlanta) 551

Grace Christian Academy (Fayetteville) 542

Greater Atlanta Christian School (Norcross) 560

Greenfield Hebrew Academy (Atlanta) 551

Greenforest Christian Academic Center (Decatur) 531

Harbour Oaks Montessori School (Grayson) 560

Harvester Christian Academy (Douglasville) 540

Heirway Christian Academy (Douglasville) 540

Heiskell School (Atlanta) 551

Metro Atlanta Private Schools

Heritage Preparatory School of Georgia (Atlanta) 551

Heritage School (The) (Newnan) 526

High Meadows School (Roswell) 552

Holcomb Bridge School (Alpharetta) 552

Holy Innocents' Episcopal School (Atlanta) 552

Holy Redeemer Catholic School (Alpharetta) 552

Horizons School (Atlanta) 532

Howard School (Atlanta) 553

Howard School - North Campus (Roswell) 553

Imhotep Center of Education (Atlanta) 553

Immaculate Heart of Mary School (Atlanta) 532

International Preparatory Institute (Atlanta) 553

Intown Community School (Atlanta) 532

Jesus-N-Me Christian Academy (Lawrenceville) 560

Jubilee Christian Academy (Gainesville) 564

Killian Hill Christian School (Lilburn) 561

Kings Way Christian (Douglasville) 540

Lafayette Academy (Marietta) 521

Lakeview Academy (Gainesville) 564

Landmark Christian School of Peachtree Corners (Norcross) 561

Light of The World Christian School (Decatur) 532

Loganville Christian Academy (Loganville) 568

Love & Grace Christian Academy (Stone Mountain) 533

Love Thy Children Christian Learning Center (Decatur) 533

Lovett School (The) (Atlanta) 554

Lullwater School (Decatur) 533

Metro Atlanta Private Schools

Mableton Christian Academy (Mableton) 521

Marist School (Atlanta) 533

Memorial Drive Presbyterian Community Children's Program (Stone Mountain) 534

Mill Springs Academy (Alpharetta) 554

Mohammed Schools of Atlanta (Atlanta) 534

Montessori AMI Children's House of Kennesaw (Kennesaw) 522

Montessori School at Emory (Decatur) 534

Mt. Carmel Christian School (Stone Mountain) 534

Mt. Pisgah Christian School (Alpharetta) 554

Mt. Vernon Presbyterian School (Atlanta) 555

Mt. Zion Christian Academy (Jonesboro) 518

New Atlanta Jewish Community High School (Atlanta) 535

Newnan Christian School (Newnan) 526

Newnan Classical School (Sharpsburg) 527

Noonday Academy (Marietta) 522

North Cobb Christian School (Kennesaw) 522

Northwoods Montessori, Inc. (Atlanta) 535

Oak Meadow Montessori School (Lawrenceville) 561

Old Suwanee Christian School (Buford) 562

Our Lady of Mercy Catholic High School (Fairburn) 542

Our Lady of the Assumption School (Atlanta) 535

Pace Academy (Atlanta) 555

Pace Christian School (Fayetteville) 542

Paideia School (The) (Atlanta) 536

Pathway Christian School (Atlanta) 555

Pathways Academy (Marietta) 522

Metro Atlanta Private Schools

School	Page
Peachtree Baptist Academy (Senoia)	527
Perimeter Christian School (Duluth)	555
Philadelphia Christian School (Conyers)	567
Pinecrest Academy (Cumming)	544
Porter School, Inc. (Roswell)	556
Providence Christian Academy (Lilburn)	562
Redeemer Christian Academy (Suwanee)	562
Renaissance Montessori (Atlanta)	556
Riverside Military Academy (Gainesville)	565
Roswell Street Baptist Christian School (Marietta)	523
Schenck School (The) (Atlanta)	556
Seeds of Faith Christian Academy (Mableton)	523
Seigakuin Atlanta International School (Atlanta)	536
Shepherd's Training Academy (Atlanta)	536
Shiloh Hills Christian School (Kennesaw)	523
Shreiner Academy (Marietta)	523
Sola Scriptura Lutheran School (Decatur)	536
Solid Rock Academy (Riverdale)	542
Sophia Academy (Atlanta)	556
Sparks Christian Academy of Early Childhood Education (Decatur)	537
Sparks Christian Academy Preparatory School for Girls (Lithonia)	537
Spelman College Child Development Center (Atlanta)	557
Springs Academy (Conyers)	567
St. Francis Day School - High School (Alpharetta)	557
St. Francis Day School - Lower School (Roswell)	557
St. John Neumann Catholic School (Lilburn)	563

Metro Atlanta Private Schools

St. John the Evangelist Catholic School (Atlanta) 557

St. Joseph Catholic School (Marietta) 524

St. Martin's Episcopal School (Atlanta) 537

St. Paul Lutheran School (Peachtree City) 543

St. Pius X Catholic High School (Atlanta) 537

St. Thomas More School (Decatur) 538

Sugar Hill Christian Academy (Buford) 563

Swift School (The) (Marietta) 524

Tabernacle Christian School (Covington) 566

Temima High School (Atlanta) 538

Torah Day School of Atlanta (Atlanta) 538

Total Learning Center Christian Schools Praise Academy (Powder Springs) 524

Trinity School (Atlanta) 558

Victory Christian School (Conyers) 567

Waldorf School of Atlanta (Decatur) 538

Walker School (The) (Marietta) 525

Wesleyan School (Norcross) 563

Westminster Christian School (Gainesville) 565

Westminster School (The) (Atlanta) 558

Whitefield Academy (Mableton) 525

Woodlee's Christian Adademy (Conyers) 568

Woodward Academy (College Park) 558

Woodward Academy - Busey Campus (Riverdale) 518

Woodward Academy - North Campus (Duluth) 559

Yeshiva Atlanta (Atlanta) 539

Youth Christian School (Powder Springs) 525

The Ultimate Atlanta School Guide

About the Author

David A. Milliron is at the forefront of an emerging field – computer-assisted reporting. In this field, journalists are not simply accepting government claims about what data shows, they are turning the tools of government around – they are asking for the data and crunching it themselves.

As The Atlanta Journal-Constitution's director of computer-assisted reporting and analysis since March 1998, Milliron routinely acquires and analyzes public databases in conjunction with newsworthy investigative projects. He also uses his analytical and programming skills to deploy searchable databases on ajc.com for the newspaper's readers, and to develop information resources for the public including *The Ultimate Atlanta School Guide*.

Milliron began his journalism career as a crime reporter at the Fort Myers (Fla.) News-Press. He also has worked for the Tampa Tribune and Gannett News Service in Washington, D.C. He is a graduate of the University of Florida's College of Journalism and Communications and also teaches computer-assisted reporting at Emory University in Atlanta.

Acknowledgements

Nobody writes and publishes a book without the help of other people, and *The Ultimate Atlanta School Guide* is no exception. Many people have contributed to help improve the quality and content of the fourth edition of the book. I would especially like to thank Carol L. Folsom, Nicole M. DeWitt, Myra L. Evans and Carmen M. Dixon for handling the bulk of the thousands of survey forms it took to compile data for the book. And to Brenda Carson who managed the facsimile machines in addition to her regular duties as the schools sent back their survey forms and proof sheets in droves.

And much thanks to Jim Greene who spent countless hours copy-editing the book; to Dale Dodson and Chuck Blevins for their graphics help; to Kevin Austin for the cover design; to Ben Gray for the cover photograph; and to Paul F. Kraach (Clayton County Public Schools) and Valya S. Lee (Edwin S. Kemp Elementary School) for providing the bus and students who appear on the cover.

And finally I save the biggest thanks of all for my wife, Barbara Fishburne Milliron, who supported me all the way as I worked many late nights conducting data analysis and handling the layout and design of the book.

Keepsake pages from the AJC!

Commemorate that special day – a birthday, anniversary, graduation or other special event – with color reprints of AJC front pages. And we've also saved other distinctive pages – like a "Whole Lotta Luckovich" – just for you.

Great prices!
Easy online shopping!
Buy yours today.

SHOWCASE
PHOTO • VIDEO • DIGITAL EQUIPMENT & SUPPLIES

The Atlanta Journal-Constitution
ajc.com

Order online anytime at ajc.com/photos@ajc
or call 1-888-511-9947.

ajc.com/photos@ajc

Metro Atlanta Public Schools

School	Page
Abbotts Hill Elementary	321
Abney Elementary	471
Acworth Elementary	125
Adamson Middle	110
Adamsville Elementary	17
Addison Elementary	126
Alexander High	286
Allgood Elementary (DeKalb)	205
Allgood Elementary (Paulding)	472
Alpharetta Elementary	322
Anderson Elementary	95
Anderson Park	18
Annistown Elementary	369
Arbor Springs Elementary	182
Arbor Station Elementary	275
Arcado Elementary	370
Argyle Elementary	126
Arkwright Elementary	18
Arnall Middle	190
Arnco-Sargent Elementary	182
Arnold Elementary	96
Arnold Mill Elementary	76
Ashford Park Elementary	206
Atherton Elementary	206
Atkinson Elementary	183
Austell Elementary	126
Austin Elementary	206
Austin Road Elementary	437
Austin Road Middle	444
Avondale Elementary	207
Avondale High	254
Avondale Middle	246
Awtrey Middle	156
Babb Middle	110
Baker Elementary	127
Ball Ground Elementary	76
Banneker High	351
Barksdale Elementary	485
Barnwell Elementary	322
Bascomb Elementary	77
Bear Creek Middle	344
Beaver Ridge Elementary	370
Beecher Hills Elementary	18
Bells Ferry Elementary	128
Belmont Hills Elementary	128
Benefield Elementary	370
Benteen Elementary	19
Berkeley Lake Elementary	371
Berkmar High	403
Bethesda Elementary	372
Bethune Elementary (Atlanta)	20
Bethune Elementary (Fulton)	322
Beulah Elementary	276
Big Creek Elementary	308
Big Shanty Elementary	128
Bill Arp Elementary	276
Birney Elementary	129
Blackwell Elementary	130
Blalock Elementary	20
Bob Mathis Elementary	208

The Atlanta Journal-Constitution / Page 578

The Ultimate Atlanta School Guide

Metro Atlanta Public Schools

Booth Middle (Cherokee)	86	Camp Creek Elementary	373
Booth Middle (Fayette)	299	Camp Creek Middle	344
Bouie Elementary	208	Campbell Elementary	324
Boyd Elementary	20	Campbell High	166
Braelinn Elementary	292	Campbell Middle	156
Brandon Elementary	21	Canby Lane Elementary	210
Briar Vista Elementary	208	Canongate Elementary	184
Briarlake Elementary	209	Canton Elementary	78
Bright Star Elementary	276	Capitol View Elementary	22
Britt Elementary	372	Carmel Elementary	78
Brockett Elementary	210	Carver High	58
Brooks Elementary	292	Cary Reynolds Elementary	211
Brookview Elementary	323	Cascade Elementary	22
Brookwood Elementary	372	Cedar Grove Elementary	212
Brookwood High	404	Cedar Grove High	255
Brown Elementary (Clayton)	96	Cedar Grove Middle	246
Brown Elementary (Cobb)	130	Cedar Hill Elementary	374
Brown Middle	50	Centennial High	352
Browns Mill Elementary	210	Centennial Place Elementary	23
Brumby Elementary	130	Centerville Elementary	374
Bryant Elementary	131	Central Gwinnett High	405
Buffington Elementary	78	Chalker Elementary	132
Buford Academy	71	Chamblee Charter High	256
Buford High	73	Chamblee Middle	247
Buford Middle	72	Chapel Hill Elementary (DeKalb)	212
Bunche Middle	50	Chapel Hill Elementary (Douglas)	278
Burch Elementary	293	Chapel Hill High	287
Burgess Elementary	22	Chapel Hill Middle (DeKalb)	248
Burnett Elementary	277	Chapel Hill Middle (Douglas)	283
Burruss Elementary	453	Chapman Intermediate	86

Metro Atlanta Public Schools

School	Page
Charles R. Drew Charter	24
Chattahoochee Elementary (Forsyth)	308
Chattahoochee Elementary (Gwinnett)	374
Chattahoochee High	353
Cheatham Hill Elementary	132
Cherokee High	89
Chesnut Charter Elementary	212
Chestatee Elementary	309
Chestatee Middle	428
Chestnut Log Middle	284
Chestnut Mountain Elementary	419
Church Street Elementary	96
Clairemont Elementary	198
Clarkdale Elementary	132
Clarkston High	257
Clay Elementary	133
Clayton Elementary	79
Clements Middle	465
Cleveland Avenue Elementary	24
Clifton Elementary	213
Coal Mountain Elementary	310
Coan Middle	51
College Heights Elementary	198
College Park Elementary	324
Collier Heights Elementary	24
Collins Hill High	406
Columbia Elementary	214
Columbia High	258
Compton Elementary	134
Conley Hills Elementary	324
Connally Elementary	25
Continental Colony Elementary	26
Conyers Middle	490
Cook Elementary	26
Cotton Indian Elementary	438
Cousins Middle	466
Crabapple Crossing Elementary	325
Crabapple Middle	345
Craig Elementary	375
Creekland Middle	395
Creekside High	354
Crews Middle	396
Crim High	59
Cross Keys High	259
Cumming Elementary	310
D.H. Stanton Elementary	26
Dacula Elementary	376
Dacula High	407
Dacula Middle	396
Dallas Elementary	472
Daniell Middle	157
Daves Creek Elementary	310
Davis Elementary	134
Davis Middle	428
Dean Rusk Middle	87
Decatur High	202
DeKalb of the Arts	260
Dickerson Middle	158
Dobbins Middle	478
Dobbs Elementary	27

Metro Atlanta Public Schools

School	Page
Dodgen Middle	158
Dolvin Elementary	326
Dorsett Shoals Elementary	278
Douglas County High	288
Douglass High	60
Dowell Elementary	134
Dresden Elementary	214
Druid Hills Charter High	261
Due West Elementary	135
Duluth High	408
Duluth Middle	396
Dunaire Elementary	214
Dunbar Elementary	28
Dunleith Elementary	454
Dunwoody High	262
Dunwoody Springs Elementary	326
Durham Middle	158
Dyer Elementary	376
Eagle's Landing High	447
Eagle's Landing Middle	444
East Clayton Elementary	97
East Cobb Middle	159
East Coweta High	193
East Coweta Middle	190
East Fayette Elementary	294
East Hall High	431
East Hall Middle	429
East Lake Elementary (Atlanta)	28
East Lake Elementary (Henry)	438
East Newton Elementary	460
East Paulding High	480
East Paulding Middle	478
East Side Elementary	136
Eastside Elementary (Coweta)	184
Eastside Elementary (Douglas)	278
Eastside High	467
Eastvalley Elementary	136
Edmonds Elementary	98
Edwards Middle	490
Eldridge Miller Elementary	215
Elm Street Elementary	184
Etowah High	90
Evans Middle	191
Evansdale Elementary	216
F.L. Stanton Elementary	28
Factory Shoals Elementary	279
Fain Elementary	29
Fair Oaks Elementary	136
Fair Street Elementary	364
Fairington Elementary	216
Fairplay Middle	284
Fairview Elementary (Henry)	438
Fairview Elementary (Newton)	460
Fayette County High	302
Fayette Middle	300
Fayetteville Intermediate	294
Fernbank Elementary	216
Fickett Elementary	30
Ficquett Elementary	461
Findley Oaks Elementary	327

Metro Atlanta Public Schools

Five Forks Middle	397
Flat Rock Middle	300
Flat Shoals Elementary (DeKalb)	217
Flat Shoals Elementary (Rockdale)	486
Florine Dial Johnston Elementary	80
Flowery Branch Elementary	420
Floyd Middle	160
Floyd Shelton Elementary	472
Ford Elementary	137
Forest Park High	116
Forest Park Middle	111
Forrest Hills Elementary	218
Forsyth Central High	316
Fort Daniel Elementary	376
Fountain Elementary	98
Free Home Elementary	80
Freedom Middle	248
Freeman's Mill Elementary	377
Frey Elementary	138
Friendship Elementary	420
Gainesville High	366
Gainesville Middle	365
Garden Hills Elementary	30
Garrett Middle	160
Garrison Mill Elementary	138
Gideons Elementary	30
Glen Haven Elementary	218
Glennwood Elementary	199
Grady High	61
Grayson Elementary	378
Grayson High	409
Green Acres Elementary	138
Gresham Park Elementary	218
Griffin Middle	160
Grove Park Elementary	31
Gullatt Elementary	328
Gwin Oaks Elementary	378
Hambrick Elementary	219
Hampton Elementary	439
Hapeville Elementary	328
Harbins Elementary	378
Harmony Elementary	379
Harmony Leland Elementary	139
Harriet Tubman Elementary	328
Harris Elementary	380
Harrison High	167
Hawthorne Elementary (Clayton)	98
Hawthorne Elementary (DeKalb)	220
Hayes Elementary	140
Haynes Bridge Middle	346
Haynie Elementary	99
Head Elementary	380
Heard-Mixon Elementary	462
Heards Ferry Elementary	329
Henderson Middle	248
Henderson Mill Elementary	220
Hendrix Drive Elementary	100
Henry County High	448
Henry County Middle	445
Heritage Academy	32

The Ultimate Atlanta School Guide

Metro Atlanta Public Schools

School	Page
Heritage Elementary	330
Heritage High	492
Herndon Elementary	32
Herschel Jones Middle	479
Hickory Flat Elementary (Cherokee)	80
Hickory Flat Elementary (Henry)	440
Hickory Hills Elementary	454
Hicks Elementary	486
Highpoint Elementary	330
Hightower Elementary	220
Hightower Trail Elementary	486
Hightower Trail Middle	161
Hill Elementary	32
Hiram Elementary	473
Hiram High	481
Holcomb Bridge Middle	346
Holly Springs Elementary (Cherokee)	81
Holly Springs Elementary (Douglas)	280
Hollydale Elementary	140
Honey Creek Elementary	487
Hooper Alexander Elementary	221
Hope Elementary	33
Hopkins Elementary	380
House Elementary	488
Huddleston Elementary	294
Huie Elementary	100
Hull Middle	398
Humphries Elementary	34
Huntley Hills Elementary	222
Hutchinson Elementary	34
Idlewood Elementary	222
Indian Creek Elementary	222
Indian Creek Middle	466
Inman Middle	52
Jackson Elementary (Atlanta)	34
Jackson Elementary (Fulton)	326
Jackson Elementary (Gwinnett)	381
Jefferson Parkway Elementary	185
Johnson High	432
Jolly Elementary	223
Jones Elementary (Atlanta)	35
Jones Elementary (Hall)	420
Jonesboro High	117
Jonesboro Middle	112
Kanoheda Elementary	382
Kedron Elementary	295
Keheley Elementary	140
Kelley Lake Elementary	224
Kemp Elementary	100
Kendrick Middle	112
Kennedy Middle	52
Kennesaw Elementary	141
Kennesaw Mountain High	168
Kilpatrick Elementary	101
Kimberly Elementary	36
Kincaid Elementary	142
King Springs Elementary	142
Kingsley Charter Elementary	224
Kittredge Magnet for High Achievers	224
Kleven Boston Elementary	82

The Ultimate Atlanta School Guide

Metro Atlanta Public Schools

School	Page
Knight Elementary	382
Knollwood Elementary	225
LaBelle Elementary	142
Lake City Elementary	102
Lake Ridge Elementary	102
Lake Windward Elementary	330
Lakeside High	263
Lakewood Elementary	36
Lanier Elementary	421
Lanier Middle	398
Lassiter High	169
Laurel Ridge Elementary	226
Lawrenceville Elementary	382
Lee Street Elementary	102
Lewis Elementary (Cobb)	143
Lewis Elementary (Fulton)	331
Lilburn Elementary	383
Lilburn Middle	398
Lin Elementary	36
Lindley Middle	162
Lithia Springs Elementary	280
Lithia Springs High	289
Lithonia High	264
Little River Elementary	82
Livingston Elementary	462
Livsey Elementary	226
Lockheed Elementary	454
Locust Grove Elementary	440
Long Middle	52
Lorraine Elementary	488
Lost Mountain Middle	162
Lovejoy High	118
Lovejoy Middle	112
Luella Middle	446
Lula Elementary	422
Lyman Hall Elementary	422
Mableton Elementary	144
Mabry Middle	162
Macedonia Elementary	82
Madras Middle	192
Magill Elementary	384
Manning Oaks Elementary	332
Mansfield Elementary	462
Marbut Elementary	226
Marie Archer Teasley Middle	88
Marietta High	457
Marietta Middle	456
Martin Elementary	422
Martin Luther King Jr. Middle	53
Mashburn Elementary	311
Mason Elementary	384
Mays High	62
McCleskey Middle	163
McConnell Middle	399
McEachern High	170
McEver Elementary	423
McGarity Elementary	474
McGarrah Elementary	103
McGill Elementary	37
McIntosh High	303

Metro Atlanta Public Schools

McKendree Elementary 384	Mount Olive Elementary 333
McLendon Elementary 227	Mount Vernon Elementary 424
McNair Middle 346	Mount Zion Elementary 104
Meadowcreek Elementary 385	Mount Zion High 120
Meadowcreek High 410	Mountain Park Elementary (Fulton) 334
Meadowview Elementary 228	Mountain Park Elementary (Gwinnett) 386
Medlock Bridge Elementary 332	Mountain Road Elementary 84
Medlock Elementary 228	Mountain View Elementary 145
Memorial Middle 491	Mundy's Mill Middle 114
Middle Ridge Elementary 463	Murdock Elementary 146
Midvale Elementary 228	Murphey Candler Elementary 230
Midway Elementary 312	Myers Elementary 424
Miles Elementary 38	Nancy Creek Elementary 230
Milford Elementary 144	Narvie Harris Elementary 231
Miller Grove Middle 249	Nebo Elementary 474
Milton High 355	Nesbit Elementary 386
Mimosa Elementary 332	New Georgia Elementary 474
Minor Elementary 386	New Prospect Elementary 334
Mitchell Elementary 38	Newnan Crossing Elementary 186
Montclair Elementary 229	Newnan High 194
Montgomery Elementary 230	Newton High 468
Moore Elementary 83	Nicholson Elementary 146
Moreland Elementary 186	Nickajack Elementary 146
Morningside Elementary 38	Nolan Elementary 334
Morrow Elementary 104	Norcross Elementary 387
Morrow High 119	Norcross High 411
Morrow Middle 113	North Atlanta High 63
Mount Bethel Elementary 144	North Clayton High 121
Mount Carmel Elementary (Douglas) ... 280	North Clayton Middle 114
Mount Carmel Elementary (Henry) 440	North Cobb High 171

Metro Atlanta Public Schools

School	Page
North Fayette Elementary	296
North Forsyth High	317
North Forsyth Middle	314
North Gwinnett High	412
North Hall High	433
North Hall Middle	430
North Springs High	356
Northcutt Elementary	104
Northgate High	195
Northside Elementary (Coweta)	186
Northside Elementary (Paulding)	475
Northwestern Middle	347
Northwood Elementary	335
Norton Elementary	388
Norton Park Elementary	147
Oak Grove Elementary (Cherokee)	84
Oak Grove Elementary (DeKalb)	232
Oak Grove Elementary (Fayette)	296
Oak Knoll Elementary	336
Oakcliff Traditional Theme	232
Oakhurst Elementary	200
Oakland Elementary	441
Oakwood Elementary	424
Ocee Elementary	336
Oglethorpe Elementary	39
Ola Elementary	442
Oliver Elementary	105
Osborne High	172
Otwell Middle	314
Palmer Stone Elementary	464
Palmetto Elementary	336
Panola Way Elementary	232
Panter Elementary	476
Park Street Elementary	455
Parklane Elementary	337
Parks Middle	54
Parkview High	413
Partee Elementary	388
Pate's Creek Elementary	442
Paulding County High	482
Peachcrest Elementary	233
Peachtree Charter Middle	250
Peachtree City Elementary	296
Peachtree Elementary	388
Pebblebrook High	173
Peeples Elementary	297
Perkerson Elementary	40
Peterson Elementary	40
Peyton Forest Elementary	40
Pharr Elementary	389
Pinckneyville Middle	400
Pine Mountain Middle	164
Pine Ridge Elementary	234
Pine Street Elementary	488
Pitts Elementary	41
Pleasant Grove Elementary	442
Pleasantdale Elementary	234
Pointe South Elementary	106
Pointe South Middle	114
Pope High	174

The Ultimate Atlanta School Guide

Metro Atlanta Public Schools

Poplar Road Elementary 187	Rockbridge Elementary (DeKalb) 236
Porterdale Elementary 464	Rockbridge Elementary (Gwinnett) 390
Powder Springs Elementary 148	Rockdale County High 493
Powers Ferry Elementary 148	Rocky Mount Elementary 149
Price Middle 54	Ronald McNair Middle 250
Ragsdale Elementary 42	Ronald McNair Senior High 266
Rainbow Charter Elementary 234	Roswell High 358
Randolph Elementary 338	Roswell North Elementary 338
Redan Elementary 235	Rowland Elementary 237
Redan High 265	Rusk Elementary 42
Renfroe Middle 201	Russell Elementary 150
Richards Middle 400	Ruth Hill Elementary 188
Ridgeview Middle 348	Sagamore Hills Elementary 238
Rising Starr Middle 300	Salem High 494
Ritch Elementary 476	Salem Middle 250
River Eves Elementary 338	Sanders Elementary 150
Riverbend Elementary 425	Sandy Creek High 304
Riverdale Elementary 106	Sandy Springs Middle 348
Riverdale High 122	Sardis Elementary 426
Riverdale Middle 115	Sawnee Elementary 312
River's Edge Elementary 106	Scott Elementary 43
Rivers Elementary 42	Seaborn Lee Elementary 339
Riverside Elementary (Cobb) 148	Sedalia Park Elementary 150
Riverside Elementary (Gwinnett) 390	Sequoyah High 91
Riverwood High 357	Sequoyah Middle 251
Robert Shaw Elementary 236	Settles Bridge Elementary 312
Roberts Elementary 476	Shadow Rock Elementary 238
Roberts Middle 116	Shakerag Elementary 340
Rock Chapel Elementary 236	Shallowford Falls Elementary 151
Rock Springs Elementary 390	Shamrock Middle 252

The Atlanta Journal-Constitution / Page 587

The Ultimate Atlanta School Guide

Metro Atlanta Public Schools

School	Page
Shiloh Elementary	391
Shiloh High	414
Shiloh Middle	400
Shoal Creek Elementary	489
Simonton Elementary	392
Simpson Elementary	392
Simpson Middle	164
Sims Elementary	490
Sixes Elementary	84
Sky Haven Elementary	238
Sky View Elementary	152
Slater Elementary	44
Smith Elementary (Atlanta)	44
Smith Elementary (Clayton)	107
Smitha Middle	164
Smith-Barnes Elementary	443
Smoke Rise Elementary	239
Smokey Road Middle	192
Snapfinger Elementary	240
Snellville Middle	401
Sope Creek Elementary	152
South Atlanta High	64
South Cobb High	175
South Douglas Elementary	281
South Forsyth High	318
South Forsyth Middle	315
South Gwinnett High	415
South Hall Middle	430
South Paulding Middle	480
Southside High	65
Southwest DeKalb High	267
Spalding Drive Elementary	340
Spout Springs Elementary	426
Sprayberry High	176
Spring Hill Elementary	298
Starr's Mill High	305
State Bridge Crossing Elementary	340
Steele Elementary	240
Stephenson High	268
Stephenson Middle	252
Stewart Middle	284
Still Elementary	152
Stockbridge High	449
Stockbridge Middle	446
Stone Mill Elementary	240
Stone Mountain Charter	252
Stone Mountain Elementary	241
Stone Mountain High	269
Stone Mountain Middle	253
Stoneview Elementary	242
Stonewall Tell Elementary	341
Stripling Elementary	392
Suder Elementary	108
Sugar Hill Elementary	393
Summerour Middle	402
Summit Hill Elementary	342
Sutton Middle	54
Suwanee Elementary	394
Sweet Apple Elementary	342
Sweetwater Elementary	282

Metro Atlanta Public Schools

School	Page	School	Page
Sweetwater Middle	402	Usher Middle	56
Swint Elementary	108	Vanderlyn Elementary	244
Sylvan Hills Middle	55	Varner Elementary	154
Tadmore Elementary	426	Vaughan Elementary	155
Tapp Middle	165	Venetian Hills Elementary	46
Tara Elementary	108	Veterans Memorial Middle	466
Taylor Elementary	394	Vickery Creek Elementary	313
Taylor Road Middle	348	Vickery Creek Middle	316
Teasley Elementary	153	Victory Charter	342
Terry Mill Elementary	242	Wadsworth Elementary	244
Therrell High	66	Walden Middle	56
Thomas Crossroads Elementary	188	Walnut Grove Elementary	394
Thomasville Heights Elementary	44	Walton High	177
Tilson Elementary	242	Washington High	67
Timber Ridge Elementary	154	Waters Elementary	46
Tippens Elementary	85	Wauka Mountain Elementary	427
Toney Elementary	243	Webb Bridge Middle	349
Toomer Elementary	45	Wesley Lakes Elementary	444
Towers High	270	West Clayton Elementary	109
Towns Elementary	46	West Elementary	343
Tri-Cities High	359	West Fulton Middle	57
Trickum Middle	402	West Hall High	434
Tritt Elementary	154	West Hall Middle	430
Tucker High	271	West Manor Elementary	47
Turner Middle (Atlanta)	56	West Middle	350
Turner Middle (Douglas)	285	West Newton Elementary	464
Tyrone Elementary	298	West Side Elementary	456
Union Elementary	477	Westchester Elementary	200
Union Grove High	450	Western Elementary	188
Union Grove Middle	446	Westlake High	360

The Atlanta Journal-Constitution / Page 589

The Ultimate Atlanta School Guide

Metro Atlanta Public Schools

Wheeler High	178
White Elementary	48
White Oak Elementary	189
White Sulphur Elementary	428
Whitefoord Elementary	48
Whitewater Middle	301
Williams Elementary	48
Winn Elementary	282
Winnona Park Elementary	200
Winston Elementary	282
Woodland Charter Elementary	344
Woodland Middle	350
Woodridge Elementary	244
Woodson Elementary	49
Woodstock Elementary	86
Woodstock High	92
Woodstock Middle	88
Woodward Elementary	245
Young Middle	58

SEARCH OUR WEB ARCHIVE AT **stacks.ajc.com**

Get the story on schools and neighborhoods

Search The Stacks archive

We've put the news archives of The Atlanta Journal-Constitution at your fingertips – including more than a million staff-written stories from 1985 to today.

SEARCHING IS ALWAYS FREE.
Pay only to view the full text of articles in your results list.

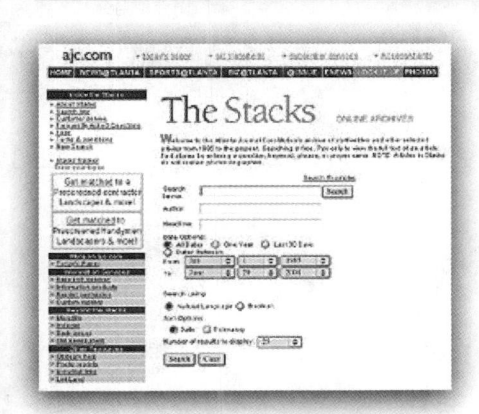

stacks.ajc.com

The Atlanta Journal-Constitution
ajc.com

**Satisfy your curiosity.
Search us today.**

● **The Stacks**
The AJC's Information Store

The Atlanta Journal-Constitution
ajc.com

How to Contact Us

The Atlanta Journal-Constitution is your community newspaper and has news bureaus throughout the metro area. We invite you to contact us with news tips and information about your community.

NEWS BUREAU	PHONE	FAX
Cherokee	770-373-8700	770-373-8704
City Life (Atlanta)	404-526-5342	404-526-7256
Clayton/Henry	770-282-8300	770-282-8311
Cobb	770-509-4080	770-509-4170
DeKalb/Rockdale	404-479-8600	404-370-7293
Fayette/Coweta	770-716-8500	770-716-8520
Gwinnett	770-263-3653	770-263-3011
North Fulton	404-526-5342	404-526-7256
South Fulton	404-526-5342	404-526-7256

The Ultimate Atlanta School Guide